THE OXFORD ENCYCLOPEDIA OF
QUEER STUDIES AND COMMUNICATION

EDITORIAL BOARD

Editor in Chief
Isaac West
VANDERBILT UNIVERSITY

Associate Editors
E Cram
UNIVERSITY OF IOWA

Frederik Dhaenens
GHENT UNIVERSITY

Pamela J. Lannutti
WIDENER UNIVERSITY

Gust A. Yep
SAN FRANCISCO STATE UNIVERSITY

THE OXFORD ENCYCLOPEDIA OF
QUEER STUDIES AND COMMUNICATION

Isaac West

EDITOR IN CHIEF

VOLUME 1

OXFORD
UNIVERSITY PRESS

Oxford University Press is a department of the University of Oxford.
It furthers the University's objective of excellence in research, scholarship,
and education by publishing worldwide. Oxford is a registered trade mark of
Oxford University Press in the UK and in certain other countries.

Published in the United States of America by Oxford University Press
198 Madison Avenue, New York, NY 10016, United States of America.

© Oxford University Press 2024

All rights reserved. No part of this publication may be reproduced, stored in a retrieval system,
or transmitted, in any form or by any means, without the prior permission in writing of Oxford
University Press, or as expressly permitted by law, by license or under terms agreed with the
appropriate reprographics rights organization. Inquiries concerning reproduction outside the scope
of the above should be sent to the Rights Department, Oxford University Press, at the address above.

You must not circulate this work in any other form and you must impose this same condition on any acquirer

Library of Congress Cataloging-in-Publication Data
Names: West, Isaac, editor.
Title: The Oxford encyclopedia of queer studies and communication /
Isaac West, editor in chief.
Description: New York, NY : Oxford University Press, [2023] |
Series: Oxford research encyclopedia of communication |
Includes bibliographical references and index.
Identifiers: LCCN 2023026346 (print) | LCCN 2023026347 (ebook) |
ISBN 9780190099671 (2 vol. set; hardback) | ISBN 9780190099695 (vol. 1 ; hardback) |
ISBN 9780190099701 (vol. 2 ; hardback) | ISBN 9780190099688 (ebk)
Subjects: LCSH: Gay and lesbian studies. | Queer theory. |
Mass media and gays. | Communication—Study and teaching.
Classification: LCC HQ75.I15 O94 2023 (print) | LCC HQ75.I15 (ebook) |
DDC 306.7601—dc23/eng/20230830
LC record available at https://lccn.loc.gov/2023026346
LC ebook record available at https://lccn.loc.gov/2023026347

Integrated Books International, United States of America

About the *Oxford Research Encyclopedia of Communication*

The *Oxford Encyclopedia of Queer Studies and Communication* is published as part of the *Oxford Research Encyclopedia of Communication*, a dynamic and scholarly digital resource. This online collection of overview articles provides in-depth, foundational essays on both core and emerging topics in communication. All articles are commissioned under the editorial leadership of international experts of the highest caliber and are vetted through rigorous peer review. A living reference work, the online publication is updatable and enriched with crosslinking and multimedia features. The essays are intended for scholars, practitioners, and university-level readers, including advanced undergraduates, graduate students, and researchers.

Oxford Research Encyclopedia of Communication
Editor in Chief: Matthew Powers

Selected print titles from the *Oxford Research Encyclopedia of Communication*:

The Oxford Encyclopedia of Health and Risk Message Design and Processing
Edited by Roxanne L. Parrott

The Oxford Encyclopedia of Intergroup Communication
Edited by Howard Giles and Jake Harwood

The Oxford Encyclopedia of Journalism Studies
Edited by Henrik Örnebring

The Oxford Encyclopedia of Communication and Critical Cultural Studies
Edited by Dana L. Cloud

Contents

List of Articles   ix

Preface   xv

Acknowledgments   xix

THE OXFORD ENCYCLOPEDIA OF
QUEER STUDIES AND COMMUNICATION

Directory of Contributors (vol. 2)   1263

Index (vol. 2)   1269

List of Articles

VOLUME 1

GLOBAL QUEER STUDIES

1. Brazilian Queer Cinema — 3
   JOÃO NEMI NETO
2. Chinese Pink Markets — 25
   TERRIE SIANG-TING WONG
3. Cultural Productions of Queer Asia — 44
   SHINSUKE EGUCHI
4. Queer Migration and Digital Media — 64
   ANDREW DJ SHIELD
5. Queer Sexualities in Latin America — 76
   HÉCTOR DOMÍNGUEZ-RUVALCABA
6. Spanish Queer Cinema — 91
   SANTIAGO FOUZ HERNÁNDEZ
7. Transnational and Queer Diasporic Sexualities — 105
   FATIMA ZAHRAE CHRIFI ALAOUI
8. Transnational Queer Translations — 117
   AHMET ATAY

KEY TERMS

9. Disidentification — 135
   MEGAN ELIZABETH MORRISSEY
10. Homonormativity — 152
    DAWN MARIE D. MCINTOSH
11. Queer Memory — 168
    THOMAS R. DUNN
12. Queer Perspectives in Communication Studies — 187
    ISAAC WEST
13. Queer Temporalities — 209
    DUSTIN GOLTZ

QUEER HEALTH

14. Crip Theory — 229
    JEFFREY BENNETT
15. HIV/AIDS: The Queer Communication of HIV in the LGBTQ Community — 243
    ANDREW R. SPIELDENNER AND BOLIVAR X. NIETO
16. Queer Healthcare Communication — 259
    NICOLE HUDAK
17. Queer Safer Sex Communication — 276
    KAMI KOSENKO
18. Sexual Orientation and Gender Identity Disclosure in the Medical Context — 295
    L. BROOKE FRILEY AND MARIA K. VENETIS
19. Stress and Coping in Sexual and Gender Minority Relationships — 321
    STEVEN SAMROCK, KAI KLINE, AND ASHLEY K. RANDALL

QUEER IDENTITIES

20. Alternatives to Coming-Out Discourses — 341
    SHUZHEN HUANG
21. Coming Out in Interpersonal and Relational Perspectives — 353
    YACHAO LI
22. Coming Out Narratives in Audiovisual Culture — 366
    PARIS S. CAMERON-GARDOS
23. Gay Aging and Discourses of Future — 385
    DUSTIN GOLTZ
24. Jotería Studies and/in Communication — 400
    LUIS M. ANDRADE
25. Kuaer Theory — 417
    RYAN M. LESCURE
26. LGBTQ+ Workers — 424
    ELIZABETH K. EGER, MORGAN L. LITRENTA, SIERRA R. KANE, AND LACE D. SENEGAL

27. Performance of Brown Sexualities 457
    SHANE MOREMAN
28. Queer Intercultural Communication: Sexuality and Intercultural Communication 471
    TAISHA MCMICKENS, MIRANDA DOTTIE OLZMAN, AND BERNADETTE MARIE CALAFELL
29. Queer Men's Bodies and Digital Media 483
    JAMIE HAKIM
30. Transfeminisms 496
    DANIEL COLEMAN

QUEER INTIMACIES

31. LGBTQ+ Marriage: Relational Communication Perspectives 521
    PAMELA J. LANNUTTI AND HILARY WERMERS
32. Molecular Images, Leaky Masculinities: Pain, Photography, and Queer Desire 534
    KATRIN KÖPPERT
33. Relational Communication and Consensual Non-Monogamy 552
    VALERIE RUBINSKY AND LUCY C. NIESS
34. Sex Work, Queer Economic Justice, and Communicative Ethics 568
    CARLY LEILANI FABIAN
35. Sexual Pleasure in Queer Communication Studies 582
    MICHAELA FRISCHHERZ

VOLUME 2

QUEER KINSHIP

36. Divorce and Relational Termination 599
    MADELEINE REDLICK HOLLAND AND PAMELA J. LANNUTTI
37. Minority Stress and Relationships 613
    ROBERT CARROLL
38. Parenting of Queer Offspring 627
    PAMELA J. LANNUTTI AND MARIA BUTAUSKI
39. Queer African Studies 637
    GODFRIED ASANTE
40. Queer People's Communication with Families of Origin 656
    CIMMIARON ALVAREZ AND KRISTINA M. SCHARP
41. Queer Safe Spaces and Communication 674
    LITAL PASCAR, YOSSI DAVID, GILLY HARTAL, AND BRANDON WILLIAM EPSTEIN
42. Queer Worldmaking 686
    HAILEY N. OTIS AND THOMAS R. DUNN
43. Queer(ing) Reproductive Justice 705
    NATALIE FIXMER-ORAIZ AND SHUI-YIN SHARON YAM

44. Queering the Study of U.S. Military Family Communication — 723
ERIN SAHLSTEIN PARCELL AND DANIELLE C. ROMO
45. Same-Sex Couple Relationship Maintenance — 734
STEPHEN M. HAAS
46. Sexual Communication Between Queer Partners — 750
BRANDON T. PARRILLO AND RANDAL D. BROWN
47. Sexual Satisfaction in LGB Relationships — 756
MADELEINE REDLICK HOLLAND
48. Social Support and LGBTQ+ Individuals and Communities — 767
ÁINE M. HUMBLE

QUEER MEDIA

49. African American Queer Cinema — 791
VICTOR EVANS
50. Agonistic Queer TV Studies for Western Europe — 810
FLORIAN VANLEE
51. Black Gay Men in Television Comedy — 831
CAMERON LYNN BROWN AND ALFRED L. MARTIN
52. Gay Pornography — 847
JOSEPH BRENNAN
53. Homonationalism and Media — 874
ALEXANDER DHOEST
54. Homonationalism's Viral Travels — 889
HANA MASRI
55. LGBTQ Youth Cultures and Social Media — 906
OLU JENZEN
56. LGBTQ+ Epistolary Rhetoric/Letter Writing — 934
PAMELA VANHAITSMA
57. Media Depictions of Sexual Attitudes — 952
KEREN EYAL
58. Queer Chinese Media and Pop Culture — 969
JAMIE J. ZHAO
59. Queer Comics — 991
KC COUNCILOR
60. Queer Melodrama — 1011
CORA BUTCHER-SPELLMAN
61. Queer Memory and Film — 1027
ANAMARIJA HORVAT
62. Queer Music Practices in the Digital Realm — 1042
BEN DE SMET
63. Queer Production Studies — 1062
EVE NG

64. Queer(ing) Popular Music Culture — 1075
    DORIS LEIBETSEDER
65. Representations of Drag Culture — 1089
    NIALL BRENNAN
66. Speculative Fiction and Queer Theory — 1112
    WENDY GAY PEARSON

QUEER METHODS

67. Arts-based Queer Communication Studies — 1145
    SANDRA L. FAULKNER AND MADISON A. POLLINO
68. Methodological and Statistical Considerations in Studying Sexual Minority and Gender Diverse Relationships — 1162
    GABRIEL A. LEÓN AND ASHLEY K. RANDALL
69. Queer Communication Pedagogy — 1185
    LORE/TTA LEMASTER
70. Queer Studies and Organizational Communication — 1207
    JAMIE MCDONALD AND SEAN C. KENNEY
71. Queer/ing Archives — 1224
    MORGAN DICESARE AND CHARLES E. MORRIS
72. Queering Colonialisms and Empire — 1242
    ROBERTA CHEVRETTE

Preface

Why Communication Studies and Queer Studies?

Now, more than ever, we need queer communication studies. By custom and by law, queer lives and ideas continue to be threatened by violence, censure, and erasure. This hatred is not innate in people. It is taught and perpetuated through language and images. What symbols have created, symbols can change.

Whatever else it might be, communication studies is concerned with how we organize and live our lives together through the use of symbols. We can choose flexible or inflexible grammars in this endeavor. Unfortunately, discourse communities often choose the latter to ease their own minds and keep strangers from unsettling the norms of their rhetorical cultures. For instance, gender binaries are categories of cultural convenience rather than stable and innate experiences of one's sense of self. Over time, participants in these publics naturalize these comforting ideas into truths, forgetting their role in creating them as truths. In practice, sexual desires, gender identity and expression, and forms of family and kinship rarely conform to these rigid cultural scripts, and deviations from these norms can produce new grammars of cultural legibility. Communication studies enables us to trace how and why people enable and resist revisions to their cultural scripts. When combined with queer topics and perspectives, queer communication studies exposes discourses of gender and sexuality as cultural fictions and explores how we might organize ourselves otherwise. Additionally, queer communication studies reveals how gender, sexuality, and their intersections with other forms of identity matter for everyone, not just sexual and gender minorities.

Queer communication studies is not a new field of study, although the uneven and hesitant embrace of queer topics and perspectives across the subfields of communication studies is evident to anyone who browses a book series or our journals. Gathering the world's expertise on these topics in one volume allows readers to appreciate the work of the scholars who have persevered at this intellectual intersection to demonstrate how the central questions of these two seemingly disparate disciplines share common concerns about bodies, modes of relationality, representation, and cultural norms.

Queer communication studies draws upon those who engaged queer theory and topics before this rubric existed as a coherent field of study (Yep, Lovaas, & Elia, 2003). Much of this research demanded the inclusion of gay and lesbian subjects into the canons of communication studies (Chesebro, 1981; Gross, 1991; Ringer, 1994; Morris, 1996; 1998). The rhetorical dimensions of HIV/AIDS produced valuable scholarship about how communities imagine and experience risk, fear, and disease (Erni, 1994; Patton, 1985; 1990; Treichler, 1999). As queer theory developed more coherent frames for cultural analysis, communication scholars employed them to study activism (Slagle, 1995) and increasingly popular media representations of queer life (Erni, 1998; Fejes & Petrich, 1993). And when queer theories needed revision, especially to account for the whiteness encoded in their figurations of queer life, communication scholars have proposed alternative categories such as quare (Johnson, 2001) and kuaer (Lee, 2003) to capture what had been obscured by theorizing from social locations of privilege.

Together and separately, communication studies and queer studies are troubling disciplines. They are relatively new disciplines, if judged by the markers of free-standing departments and publication outlets (Peters, 1986; de Lauretis, 1991). They lack proper objects of study uniquely their own when compared to history or literature (Butler, 1994; Shepherd, St. John, & Striphas, 2013). They are inherently interdisciplinary, adapting approaches from other disciplines when needed in the process of forming theories and interpretive strategies. And, they often probe what is taken for granted as normative and normal in the course of their inquiries. In their own ways and taken together, communication studies and queer studies can make the familiar unfamiliar and unsettle common sense. The following chapters accept this charge across a range of topics, mapping out existing scholarship and suggesting future directions for research.

Several chapters address the international flows of queer identities, practices, and representation. Each valuable on its own, together these essays call our attention to the importance of understanding queerness as a contextualized set of communicative relations informed by localized conditions. Communication studies and queer studies rightfully have been critiqued for their Western biases. Far too often, scholarship about communicative practices assumes a universal subject removed from the specific circumstances of their communities, thus necessitating corrective action to account for a fuller array of how communication matters differently to those outside of Euro-American contexts (Atay & Chen, 2020). Similarly, queer studies faces challenges regarding the mobility and legibility of queerness as a category of identity (Eguchi, 2021). With these problematics in mind, then, our authors interrogate whether and how queerness matters on five continents. Appropriately enough, no one conclusion can be drawn from their work, but separately they contribute to our understanding of what queer communication studies can illuminate in these varied contexts. Moreover, they demonstrate how specific locations speak back to queer communication studies.

The chapters centered on trans identities and representations also highlight the productive pressures of probing the boundaries of queerness as an analytic. Over the last three decades, the explosion of gender expansive terminology and identities (e.g., transsexual, genderqueer, gender nonconforming, nonbinary) demonstrates the creative capacity of persons to mark the limits of language as well as its plasticity (Valentine, 2007). Communication scholars are beginning to account for these developments and revisit the violence imposed by gender binaries (Spencer & Capuzza, 2015). Even those efforts to undo the gender binary, such as the popularization of cisgender, which is a recognition that all persons have gender identities, may contribute to the stabilization to gender binaries (Enke, 2012). Greater attention has been paid to the racialized histories of these categories (Snorton, 2017) but much remains to be done. And, some question whether or not queer epistemologies can accommodate trans topics and identities (Stryker 2004), hence the development of trans studies as a form of inquiry that sometimes is compatible with and sometimes combative with queer studies. Our chapters present several ways of thinking through these concerns to contribute to this ongoing conversation.

The chapters rooted in interpersonal and intergroup communication research display the importance of questioning the norms of research protocols and the need to qualify our generalizations about human communication practices. Often in the name of expediency, communication researchers have tended to focus on cisgender heterosexuals due to their relative numbers in a community and the ability to then generalize from these data sets. In romantic relational communication research, the problems with this approach are most glaring but also it extends to the workplace, health care settings, and families. The contributors in this volume reassess communication theory through a queer lens to make visible the creative capacities of individuals and groups to redefine default assumptions about relationships and communities.

And, finally, among the subfields of communication studies, media studies may be the most hospitable to queer studies. Mediated representations of queerness are everywhere, and, for many, their connection to queer lives and worldmaking practices is made possible by screens, what some have termed parasocial relationships (Schiappa, Gregg, & Hewes, 2005; 2006). As a result, the importance of mediated forms of queerness is a topic of chief concern for communication scholars. Several contributors explore how sounds and images subvert genres, expected tropes, and attempts to suppress them. From film to television to music, the representational landscape is populated with examples of nascent and established forms of queerness, much of which is covered in the following pages.

Queer communication studies evidences the wisdom in the adage "the only constant is change." It is a dynamic, ever-evolving field of study as it refracts back to us cultural changes in identity, representations, and relationships. We hope the following chapters will continue this transformation of the discipline of communication studies to more account for all the ways queerness makes us human.

Isaac West

REFERENCES

Atay, A., & Chen, Y. (Eds.). (2020). *Postcolonial turn and geopolitical uncertainty: Transnational critical intercultural communication pedagogy*. Lexington Books.

Butler, J. (1994). Against proper objects. *Differences, 6*(2–3), 1–26.

Chesebro, J. (Ed.). (1981). *Gayspeak: Gay male & lesbian communication*. Pilgrim Press.

de Lauretis, T. (1991). Queer theory: Lesbian and gay sexualities, an introduction. *Differences, 3*(2), iii–xviii.

Eguchi, S. (2021). On the horizon: Desiring global queer and trans* studies in international and intercultural communication. *Journal of International and Intercultural Communication, 14*(4), 275–283.

Enke, F. (2012). The education of little cis: Cisgender and the discipline of opposing bodies. In F. Enke (Ed.), *Transfeminist perspectives: In and beyond transgender and gender studies* (pp. 60–71). Temple University Press.

Erni, J. N. (1994). *Unstable Frontiers: Technomedicine and the Cultural Politics of "Curing" AIDS*. University of Minnesota Press.

Erni, J. N. (1998). Queer figurations in the media: Critical reflections on the Michael Jackson sex scandal. *Critical Studies in Mass Communication, 15*, 158–180. doi: 10.1080/15295039809367040.

Fejes, F., & Petrich, K. (1993). Invisibility, homophobia, and heterosexism: Lesbians, gays, and the media. *Critical Studies in Mass Communication, 10*(4), 396–422.

Gross, L. (2002). *Up from invisibility: Lesbians, gays, and the media in America*. Columbia University Press.

Johnson, E. P. (2001). "Quare" studies, or (almost) everything I know about queer studies I learned from my grandmother. *Text and Performance Quarterly, 21*(1), 1–25.

Lee, W. (2003). *Kuaering* queer theory: My autocritography and a race-conscious, womanist, transnational turn. In G. Yep, K. Lovaas, & J. Elia (Eds.), *Queer theory and communication: From disciplining queers to queering the discipline(s)* (pp. 147–170). Harrington Park.

Morris III, C. (1996). Contextual twilight/critical liminality: J. M. Barrie's *Courage* at St. Andrews, 1922. *Quarterly Journal of Speech, 82*, 207–227. doi: 10.1080/00335639609384153.

Morris III, C. (1998). "The responsibilities of the critic": F.O. Matthiessen's homosexual palimpsest. *Quarterly Journal of Speech, 84*, 261–282. doi: 10.1080/00335639809384219.

Patton, C. (1985). *Sex and germs: The politics of AIDS*. South End Press.

Patton, C. (1990). *Inventing AIDS*. Routledge.

Peters, J. D. (1986). Institutional sources of intellectual poverty in communication research. *Communication Research, 13*(4), 527–559.

Ringer, J. (Ed.). (1994). *Queer words, queer images: Communication and the construction of homosexuality*. New York University Press.

Schiappa, E., Gregg, P., & Hewes, D. (2005). The parasocial contact hypothesis. *Communication Monographs, 72*, 92–115.

Schiappa, E., Gregg, P., & Hewes, D. (2006). Can one TV show make a difference? *Will & Grace* and the parasocial contact hypothesis. *Journal of Homosexuality, 51*(4), 15–37.

Shepherd, G., St. John, J., & Striphas, T. (Eds.). (2013). *Communication as . . .: Perspectives on theory*. Sage Publications.

Slagle, R. A. (1995). In defense of Queer Nation: From *identity politics* to a *politics of difference*. *Western Journal of Communication, 59*, 85–102.

Snorton, C. R. (2017). *Black on both sides: A racial history of trans identity*. University of Minnesota Press.

Spencer, L., & Capuzza, J. (Eds.). (2015). *Transgender communication studies: Histories, trends, and trajectories*. Lexington Books.

Stryker, S. (2004). Transgender studies: Queer theory's evil twin. *GLQ, 10*(2), 212–215.

Treichler, P. (1999). *How to have theory in an epidemic: Cultural chronicles of AIDS*. Duke University Press.

Valentine, D. (2007). *Imagining transgender: An ethnography of a category*. Duke University Press.

Yep, G., Lovaas, K., & Elia, J. (Eds.). (2003). *Queer theory and communication: From disciplining queers to queering the discipline(s)*. Harrington Park.

Acknowledgments

This volume would not have crossed the finish line without the expertise and labor of two teams. At Oxford University Press, Toby Wahl championed this project from its inception and kept it afloat during a global pandemic, which was no small task if you ask anyone in the publishing world. Brianne Alphonso, Sam Green, and Andrew Jung's behind-the-scenes support alleviated much of the organizational labor related to the volume so that my editorial team could focus on other tasks. The volume's Associate Editors, E Cram, Frederik Dhaenens, Pamela Lannutti, and Gust Yep, transformed an idea into a reality. At every step in the process, from the soliciting of the entries on through to their reviews of the chapters, they provided valuable counsel to me and the authors. In the service of elevating the arguments of others, they selflessly sacrificed time that could have been used to further their own research projects. Words cannot repay them this debt, but I trust the circulation of the chapters they edited will have been worth it.

Isaac West

January 2023

Global Queer Studies

BRAZILIAN QUEER CINEMA

INTRODUCTION

In Brazil, the turn of the 20th century marks a self-conscious will toward modernization: The rapidly changing cities, the unparalleled urbanization, and the economic growth (that eventually led to the 1929 crash which deeply affected the mainly coffee monoculture in Brazil) incited a strong desire to modernize the country, especially in rapidly growing urban centers such as São Paulo and Rio de Janeiro. Pereira Passos, mayor of the city of Rio de Janeiro between 1902 and 1906, tellingly created the slogan "O Rio Civiliza-se" [Rio civilizes itself]. This article argues that in particular, cinema, a technological novelty, embodied this yearning for modernity. As in the United States, the new technological art brought an ideal of modernization along with the appearance and novel applications of electricity, trolleys, skyscrapers, and other innovations. As Mario de Andrade, one of the nation's most prominent modernist artists, wrote in 1922, "Cinema is the most representative art form of modern times. We must observe it and learn from it" (Conde, 2018, p. 1).

Brazilian cinema came into being at the end of the 19th century; the first historical research dates its emergence in 1905 (Araújo, 1976) when Antonio Leal filmed an avenue at the then capital, Rio de Janeiro. Vicente de Paula Araújo (1976), in his detailed account of the birth of

National Cinema in *A Bela Época do Cinema Brasileiro* [The Belle Epoque of Brazilian Cinema], cites João do Rio—famed writer who is now associated with LGBTQ+ identities (see "Queer Identities in Brazil and National Cinema")—for noting that cinema was one of the seven pleasures of Rio de Janeiro in the first decade of the 20th century (p. 18). As the country started to modernize, cinema became privileged as a tool for both documenting and fictionalizing different perspectives of a fast-growing country eager for cultural transformation and large-scale urbanization.

QUEER IDENTITIES IN BRAZIL AND NATIONAL CINEMA

From the times of the original peoples, among them the Tupinambás, to the first Portuguese explorers who set foot in the 1500s, homosexual practices were present in these lands beneath the equator.[1] Luiz Mott points out that "in the Brazilian case, as is well known, the hegemonic matrix was strongly disrupted, especially by contacts with the indigenous sexual culture, notably the indigenous people of the Tupinambá tribe" (Mott, 2003, p. 168).[2]

Thus, the idea of a sinless land became a common point for most European travelers throughout the first centuries of colonization. Later in the 20th century, local artists incorporated such a claim and made it their own, using it as a sense of liberation. Brazilian cinema, for instance, incorporated that idea in films such as *Como era gostoso meu francês* (1971) [How tasty was my little Frenchman], by Nelson Pereira dos Santos, *Macunaíma* (1969), by Joaquim Pedro de Andrade, and *Orgia ou o Homem que deu cria* (1970) [Orgy or the man who gave birth], by João Silvério Trevisan.

Mary Del Priore (2012), in her comprehensive work on the history of sexuality in Brazil, sheds important light on representations of sexuality in Brazil since its first years of colonization into the early decades of the 20th century. In her analysis of the magazine *Rio Nu* (p. 133), for instance, she presents a collection of erotica in texts and images that presented narratives, anecdotes, and comics interlaced with images of nudity. In 1914, this magazine published a short story called *O menino do Gouveia* [The boy from Gouveia] by Capadócio Maluco, probably a pseudonym. The narrative deals with the sexual experience of a younger boy and an older man, making it one of the first recognizably queer narratives in 20th-century Brazil. This is significant; homosexual identity in literary and cultural discourse became visible in cinema as well. Cinema came to existence at the turn of the 20th century more or less simultaneously with the development of visible homosexual identities. João do Rio (1881–1921) said in 1910, "the whole city wants to see the cinematographers. In every corner, there are ads gathering thousands of people" (quoted in Araújo, 1976, p. 18).

The search for identity and representation is part of the construction of a possible queer historiography. As Alexander Doty (2000) explains in *Flaming Classics: Queering the Film Canon*, queer identity, in order to be identified, must be marked, made visible on the screen. Doty briefly discusses that even queer-identified people fall into this notion of a clear visibility in order to be acknowledged. He mentions *The Blair Witch Project* and the fact that one of the characters references his girlfriend as clear indication of his heterosexuality. However, the other two characters are silent about their partners. Doty explains he had just assumed "that all characters in a film are straight unless labeled, coded, or otherwise obviously proven to be queer" (p. 18).

Homosexual identity was initially constructed as "sexual deviance" and "sexual inversion," thus, as something that could be treated, reversed, or fixed. If homosexuality as a fixed category came to light at the same time that cinema evolved, it is plausible to say that queer cinema was born with cinema itself. The need to portray queer lives, or rather queer desire, was born with cinema. Early on, one can find images of sexual dissidence as depictions of queer identities. It is the case, for instance, in *The Dickson Experimental Sound Film* in which, in 1895–1896, two men are seen dancing together.[3]

By delineating the topic as Brazilian queer cinema, it seems important to delineate the understanding of queer in Brazil as well. Unlike the United States, where certain gay and lesbian activists in the 1980s and early 1990s defiantly started calling themselves queer, in Brazil, the concept of queer appeared only in the 2000s and almost exclusively in academic contexts. According to Richard Miskolci (2012), "the benchmark of our creative incorporation of queer can be established in 2001 when Guacira Lopes Louro published the article 'Teoria Queer: uma política pós-identitária para a educação' in the Revista de Estudos Feministas" (p. 38). Since then, a great number of books and articles have been published on the topic and the incorporation of the term queer seems to be mostly accepted by academics and a new generation of queer identified people who have been using the Anglophone term as a form of identity.[4] However, one could question the choice of terminology in Brazil. Other words to describe same-sex desire in Portuguese—*bicha, veado, sapatão*—have a long, if complicated and often vexed existence and are still used by the general population alongside the English term "gay." The occurrence of various terminologies from the start has created tension between those who identify with the local vernacular, on one side, and a group that not only identifies with the English word gay, but also considers the Portuguese terms extremely negative, on the other.

This dissension regarding the appropriate use of local and international vernaculars continues a similar debate at the heart of the history of Brazilian cinema. Since the first cinematic soirées, the preoccupation between local and foreign was a center for discussion among artists, critics, and society at large. Cinema was at the center of such discussion. As early as the 1920s, critics worried that the influence of American cinema was no less than a pervasive invasion. Galvão and Bernardet (1983, p. 40) show how local critics discussed the issue in their analysis of the *Revista Cinearte*, the first journal devoted to cinema in Brazil, which, in 1926, published articles worried about the invasion of North American cinema and the erasure of Brazilian production.

So too, Brazilian scholars of sexuality have observed the contentious nature of imported sexual terminology. If one thinks in terms of a globalized same-sex experience, it seems reasonable to use words such as "gay" or "queer," since most of the Western world recognizes same-sex experience through those vernacular terms. As Dennis Altman (2002) observes about English names for commercial stores in different countries, "the name reminds us that to be 'American' is in many places to be 'modern'" (p. 29). Similarly, cinema—perhaps queer cinema in particular—gave Brazil a vessel to feel modern. Identifying with the American ideal of society, be it through cinema or sexual identities, words like "gay" or "queer" could mean being modern, or at least acknowledge acceptance by another place other than your own country. In that regard, Altman argues that "members of particular groups have more in common across national and continental boundaries than they do with others in their own geographically defined societies" (p. 87). Similarly, Lina Meruane (2012), in her book *Viajes*

Virales, mentions that words like "gay" or "gay culture" were incorporated in Latin America during democratic transitions, but argues that these terms were problematized due to their colonial connotations (p. 27).

It is worth noting that in spite of the fact that "homosexual rights progressed much further in the countries of northern Europe" (Altman, 2002, p. 87), and even other countries such as Spain and Portugal in which equal marriage laws have been approved in 2005 and 2010, respectively, the United States still seems to serve as a model of a possible gay life free of prejudice.[5] Néstor Perlongher (2008), once again foreseeing this Americanized trend, wrote back in the early 1980s:

> It is interesting to note the adoption of the term gay after the beginning of the homosexual movement. The English language provides the word that gives more visibility to the gay man. Distancing himself from the *bichas, travestis*.... The adoption of the word in English is fundamental in a society that sees a factor of social and cultural mobility in the American culture. (p. 126)

This notion of a globalized gay man who shares taste, life activities, and even some sort of history may represent what Meruane (2012) calls *orden neoimperial* (p. 32); that is, the maintenance of imperialism, since the "sharing" aspect of this globalized gay man ends up being the dissemination of the American way of life, or, in this case, the Gay American way of life. This globalized notion is seen, for example, in the use of the English word "pride" in most LGBT celebrations around the world (Madrid Pride, Brussels Pride, among many others). Shangay Lily (2016), a Spanish drag queen, has named this phenomenon "gaycapitalism," following John D'Emilio's idea that gay identity follows capitalism.

In a mass media-oriented and spectacularized society, the search for role models that hold some fame or visibility in the media became, since the beginning of the gay movement in the United States in the late 1960s, a way to give positive reinforcement for the struggling queer youth. Once the market began to accept and understand queer people as consumers, more people have come out without damaging their "public" persona, as had happened in the early days of cinema.

If one takes into consideration cinema, it seems odd to absorb the term "queer," such a local and unique term to the United States, with its own historical perspective relevant to the American experience, in order to translate local needs. By absorbing "queer," Brazilian queer cinema studies risks ignoring the nation's own social reality and praxis. One is reminded here again of Altman, who remarked that "reading work by young queer scholars in Australia I am struck by how often they will invoke Butler and Foucault, while ignoring the particular his/her stories of the Australian movements" (p. 159). Notwithstanding some necessary caution, the notion of queer arguably has made a productive entry into Brazilian culture; the term has enabled Brazilian filmmakers to reach a broader audience, since the adoption of the word put Brazil into the midst of the international discussion. As Viteri et al. (2013) write in their *Latin American Dossier*, when discussing the use of queer in Brazil, the fact that this term is not institutionalized in the local academia does not "imply that there is not a variety of studies about sexualities or the articulations between race, class or gender since past decades. Such studies also evoked categories or approaches similar to *queer*" (p. 54). Many scholars find that Brazilian queer cinema has learned its lessons, and without losing track of its own national identities; it has opened space for a mesh of possibilities in regard to representation and visibility.

Therefore, for this article, queer works in the article as a traveling theory (in Edward Said's terms) and as an omnibus term. The author, then, refers to queer as first, "a form of understanding the politics of the body" (Ruvalcaba, 2016, p. 2), and second, as Eve Sedgwick has famously said, "the open mesh of possibilities, gaps, overlaps, dissonances and resonances, lapses and excesses of meaning when the constituent elements of anyone's gender, of anyone's sexuality aren't made (or *can't be* made) to signify monolithically" (*Tendencies*, p. 7). Brazilian queer cinema, consequently, is a national cinema aware of its local vicissitudes without losing sight of an international perspective that has formed a possible global queer cinema.

BRAZILIAN CINEMA AT LARGE

The history of Brazilian cinema is well documented. Fernão Pessoa Ramos and Sheila Schvarzman (2018) organized a comprehensive two-volume collection of essays discussing Brazilian cinema from its inception until the second decade of the 21st century. Lucia Nagib, Robert Stam, Randal Johnson, Maite Conde, and Jean-Claude Bernardet are among many who have published extensively on Brazilian cinema in English. Nonetheless, work on queer sexualities and cinema still lags behind. Many recent scholarly works briefly mention gender and sexuality but do not deal explicitly with questions regarding identities that do not conform to a heteronormative view. With regard to representations of gender identity and sexual orientation, the first comprehensive study on homosexuality in Brazilian cinema was published in 2001 by Antonio Moreno. *O Personagem Homossexual do Cinema* [The homosexual character in cinema] presents a detailed and important account of the presence of LGBTQI+ visibility in Brazilian cinema throughout the 20th century. Moreno presents an extensive and comprehensive list of films that deal with homosexuality and his work is clearly representative of its times. In his view, none of the films present a "positive" perspective of homosexuality. He herein follows Vito Russo's classic, *The Celluloid Closet*'s (1987), activist tone.

However fundamental this line of research, Moreno's perspective inevitably tends to problematize, criticize, or even erase those queer identities who do not conform to his preferred ideal of homosexual visibility, revealing a sense of what Lisa Duggan (2002) calls homonormativity. Normative ideas tend to indirectly present an idea that there should be a "correct" way to be represented as gay. This normative way should, then, be the one represented on television and cinema (e.g., in the manner of Will Truman, the main character of the popular American TV show *Will & Grace*, or Kevin Kline in *In and Out* (1997), who, in a classic scene, attempts to not dance too flamboyantly to disco music). Therefore, normativity still plays an important role in visual media. Representations that tend to crystalize homosexual identities into a heteronormative model erase other identities that do not conform to the anxieties of mainstream media.[6]

There is also a large body of scholarship on specific films and their connections with sexuality (Rich, 2013; Shaw, 2007; Subero, 2014, among others). In 2015, Stevan Letisch published *Cine arco-íris: 100 anos de cinema LGBT nas telas brasileiras* [Rainbow cinema: 100 years of LGBT cinema on Brazilian screens], presenting a list of films in several languages that present "rainbow" (arco-íris in Portuguese) identities. Although this overview is not primarily concerned with academic analysis, Letisch is a great source of research for titles and filmmakers and those interested in production and reception, since the book presents the release dates of every film in Brazil. In the same year, Luiz Francisco Buarque de Lacerda Júnior (2015) defended his dissertation "Cinema Gay Brasileiro: Políticas de representação e além." His work attempts to revisit Moreno's work, presenting a new scenario of less solidified sexualities (p. 23). Lacerda Júnior extends Moreno's list, reaching the first decade of the 21st century, and discusses some films in light of more recent theory readings.

All these works complement each other, for there cannot be a definite work for all terms: Brazilian, queer, and cinema are always in constant (r)evolution. As much as one's understandings of sexual orientation and gender identity evolves, work on queer cinema must also be (re)defined as new concepts are explored.

THE FIRST DECADES, MODERNISM AND AVANT-GARDE

In 1922, a group of artists, mostly from São Paulo, developed, curated, and presented the *Semana de Arte Moderna* [Modern art week]. The 4-day event became the most influential artistic event of the century in Brazil, leaving its repercussions up the present. However, as informed as these artists were regarding modern art and innovations, cinema was not present in the week. Film informed their desire toward modernity, however, as Conde (2012) explains in discussing Ismail Xavier's work; the Brazilian author "examines how novel ideas regarding 'film language' came to shape and influence the theoretical and critical ideas present in the modernist group's publication, encompassing texts produced from 1922 to 1930" (p. 7). Xavier's study clearly illustrates how much of the avant-garde aesthetics elaborated by Brazilian modernism from 1922 onward pertained to foreign theories regarding the movies' "modernist" techniques and qualities (p. 183).

While Brazilian artists were eager to appropriate the language of cinema, they did not make films but limited themselves to writing cinematic novels (a famous example is Alcantara Machado's 1925 novel *Pathé Baby*). However, it is known from the travel journal of French poet Blaise Cendrars that these modernist writers also were interested in making films but lacked access to the necessary technical and material means. Filmmaking in the early decades of the 20th century was overall a limited enterprise. The period is not well documented: Less than 10% of the archive of the first decades remain today. From that time, two films mark an avant-garde language in cinema: *Ganga Bruta* (1933), by Humberto Mauro, and *Limite* (1931) [Margin], by Mario Peixoto. Especially *Limite* has recently attracted a great deal of scholarly attention as a case study for early queer representations.[7] A number of scholars have tried to reclaim Peixoto's only film—considered by most critics as the best Brazilian film ever made—as having a part in a history of queer filmmaking.[8]

Limite had an unsuccessful screening at the time of its release, prompting the filmmaker to withdraw the movie from public viewing. More than 30 years later, the film was rediscovered, restored, and ever since has been part of the Brazilian canon. A lot has been said about Mario Peixoto's sexual orientation despite the fact that he was clearly reluctant to disclose anything on the matter. Nonetheless, biographers have discussed it relentlessly. Denilson Lopes (2019) has been working with the diaries Peixoto wrote in his youth. Lopes is more concerned with the affects and sensations than with outing Peixoto, however. To Lopes, this archive of feelings could lead to a queer reading of the film and Peixoto's work generally. Peixoto's journal, according to Lopes, indicates an adolescent queer experience that could have informed his film *Limite*. Besides *Limite*, it is also important to mention Luiz de Barros. He was one of the most prolific filmmakers in Brazil. Barros directed more than 80 films in a career that spanned over seven decades. Among his many films, he directed in 1924 *Augusto Aníbal quer casar* [Augusto Aníbal wants to get married], a comedy about a man, Augusto Aníbal, who wants to get married. Vera, one of his conquests, tires of Augusto's flirts and hires Darwin, a known female impersonator performing in the clubs and theaters of Rio's night life, in order to marry Augusto. After their marriage, Augusto finds out his wife is a man and flees in a hydroplane. Unfortunately, there is no copy left of the film, so the reconstruction of Barros's film was made through journalist and archival research. Luciana Corrêa de Araújo (2015) presented her archival research that allowed the reconstruction of some of the film based on images and specialized journals of the time. Barros, in his autobiography, said that the film was a big hit at the time. According to the filmmaker, it was *Augusto Aníbal quer casar*'s success that made him turn his career toward comedy. It is important to note that Barros returned to the topic later in his career. One of his last films was *Ele, Ela Quem* (1978) [He, she, who?], also dealing with questions of sexuality. In his prolific career, Barros seemed very interested in playfully transgressive representations of gender. Barros, in the 1930s and 1940s, became one of the biggest producers and directors of *chanchadas*, the famed popular Brazilian musical comedies.

CHANCHADA AND QUEER REPRESENTATION

The 1930s saw the rise of a very popular genre in Brazilian cinemas. The *chanchada*, according to the *Oxford Dictionary of Film Studies* (2020), is a "distinctively Brazilian take on the musical, with roots in the nation's traditions of comic theatre, popular music and dance, and carnival, and typically featuring vibrant song-and-dance numbers."[9] Carmen Miranda, who would later become a Hollywood sensation in the following decades, filmed her first hits during this cycle of Brazilian cinema. Between the 1930s and the 1950s, hundreds of *chanchadas* were made, and these films are still regarded as inextricably bound with Brazilian identity. This genre produced the first Brazilian movie stars: Oscarito, Grande Otelo, Carmen Miranda, Emilinha, Eliana, and several singers who transitioned from radio to the big screen, singing in the musical comedies at the time. Lisa Shaw (2003) explains that some of the common motifs of *chanchadas* were "gender bending, the subversion of racial stereotypes and prejudices, and the elevation of the status of the popular at the expense of the pillars of erudite or hegemonic culture characterized much of Atlântidas's production in the era" (p. 74).

Several films portray men dressing up as women in what Shaw calls gender bending. The author resist identifying these characters as queer, for they represent a *clownesque* version of women, with the sole intent of ridicule or to make the audience laugh. Carnival has included this tradition of gender bending since its beginning. The popular appeal of a man being ridiculed and demoralized by acting as a woman even today proves a recipe for easy laughs in Brazilian culture. Its play on gender bending seems revealing of misogyny rather than illuminating an interest in or affinity with queer representation. *Chanchada*'s misogynistic gender stereotyping is also relevant for discussing the dynamics of denial and erasure queer culture.

This casts a different light on films that have been treated as exceedingly critical by scholarship to the history of queer cinema in Brazil; the effeminate characters in films like *Alô Alô Carnaval* (1936), *A Dupla do Barulho* (Carlos Manga, 1953), *Carnaval no Fogo* (Watson Macedo, 1949), *Garotas e Samba* (Carlos Manga, 1957), and *Dois Ladrões* (Carlos Manga, 1960) can be seen as reductive characters, as Lacerda Júnior (2015) points out in his work. However, they are also more than merely embarrassing or negative representations of homosexuality; they reveal cinema's engagement with a national past that is still worthwhile to study. More pertinently, while stereotypical to contemporary sensibilities, these characters reveal subjectivities that are too easily cast aside in today's pull toward a homonormative center. Effeminacy exists and deserves visibility as well. In the Brazilian *chanchadas*, one cannot dissociate character development and the genre itself. After all, most characters—protagonists and supporting roles—were flat characters at the service of an easy laugh for a popular audience.

One example, however, seems to stand out from the hundreds of musical comedies of the time: *Poeira de Estrelas* (1948) [Star dust], by Moacyr Fenelon, deals with a subliminal love story between two women. Nagime (2016) has analyzed this story about two singers who break up so one of them can get married to her fiancé. Critics at the time were divided about the film. On one hand, it presented the classic elements of the *chanchada*, such as the musical numbers. On the other hand, the dramatic element of the relationship between the two friends did not please the critics.

1950s and 1960s. It seems plausible then, that the acceptance of the gay man by modern and contemporary society is carried out through a series of mechanisms of power and control in which the gay man has to be "depathologized"; that is, he will perform as a stereotypical heterosexual. If they are not well adjusted yet (with family and all), they are at least visibly "normalized," that is, they adhere to a masculine fashion, as in most of the movies of the 1950s and 1960s.

What seems perverse here is that in order to become socially visible, this man will have to erase and deny other queer bodies that may threaten this depathologized life; hence the criticism of Vito Russo and Antonio Moreno, for instance. As Warner (1999) notes, "people whose gender identity differs from the norm are despised, often violently, whether they desire those of their own sex or not .... In the same contexts, homosexuals whose gender conforms more to the norm can often be silently accepted" (p. 37). And later on in his book he writes: "can it be very surprising if those who are most concerned with winning respect might find themselves wishing that their peers in shame would be a little less queer, a little more decent?" (p. 50).

It is in this context that in the 1950s, Luiz de Barros filmed *Aí vem os cadetes!* (1959) [Here come the cadets], whose conflict lies in the subtextual homoerotic relationships between young, often shirtless cadets. This is the first film in which the flamboyant effeminate character gives space to a postwar new man.

The following decade marks a growth in cinematic productions in Brazil as a whole. Moreno counts 13 films in the 1960s. The visibility of a new urban homosexual, now identified as gay in the United States and Brazil as well, came at the same time as the new man proposed by fashion houses and style magazines. Paul Preciado (2010) provides a detailed account of the ideal of the American dream and the beginnings of *Playboy* magazine. This image of a cosmopolitan urban man also influenced homosexual identity. The dandy of the turn of the century is replaced by a cosmopolitan groomed man. These images began to appear in cinema. Hitchcock in 1948 already saw that trend when he filmed *Rope* with two young cosmopolitan men in New York City. The ideal of happiness was still a couple of decades away, however, but the change in their visual depiction is striking in most cinematic production.

The effeminate man from the *chanchadas* tended to disappear completely and a new urban, heteronormative man appeared in Brazilian screens. The attempt to erase the effeminate character in the 1950s is part of a visibility project aiming at "normalizing" queer bodies. This perspective of visibility is accepted only if it reproduces dominant—masculine—social roles. Paradoxically, since it reproduces the standards of heteronormativity, such a strategy ends up erasing other queer bodies that are not rendered such visibility. Queer theory needs to question and challenge these dominant roles and power relations within same-sex communities, making visible not only White gay men (who in terms of gender expression oftentimes occupies a similar position of privilege with the straight White man), but also other queer identities who are often erased by normative expectations.

For instance, queer critics in Brazil and throughout the Anglophone world have argued that even in the gay movement, prejudices against effeminate gay men or "non-heteronormative queer people" thrive; effeminacy in gay men by some is shunned and a normative concept of "normality" espoused, as Giancarlo Cornejo (2013) has made explicit in his article "La Guerra declarada contra el niño afeminado: Una autoetnografía 'queer'" [The declared war against the effeminate boy: A queer autoethnography].

Therefore, by denying the "gayness" of a group of self-identified gay men, the author sees a conformity with or adaptation to a stereotypical straight identity as a model to be followed. The question is evidently crucial for approaching the question of representation in Brazilian cinema. We ought to take to heart Butler's (1993) question: "Which version of lesbian or gay men ought to be rendered visible, and which internal exclusions will that rendering visible institute?" (p. 308).

From the 1960s, it is worth mentioning three films: *Bahia de todos os santos* (1960) [Bay of all saints], by Trigueira Neto, *O Beijo* (1964) [The kiss], by Flavio Tambellini, and *O menino e o vento* (1967) [The boy and the wind], by Carlos Hugo Christenssen. Each film has its own new ideal homosexual present in its story. *Bahia de todos os Santos* focuses on a biracial love story in the northern state of Bahia between a Black man and a White woman. One of the main character's best friend is an artist who decides to move to São Paulo to live with another man. *O Beijo* deals with homosexual panic when a man, at the request of a dying stranger, kisses him on the lips as a last favor.[10] *O menino e o vento* tells the story of a man accused of murdering a boy in a remote village in Brazil. As in the short story upon which the film is based a subtle homoerotic tone is dealt with.

The representation of these gay men is what brings these films together. They are all depicted as a new urban man. They are all in suits and live or come from big urban centers. They are polite, well-educated, and are artists. As mentioned, the birth of Brazilian cinema in the 1910s and 1920s cannot be understood separately from a national urge to modernize the country: Cinema, a recent technology associated with a U.S. style of modernity, became the fetishized medium par excellence to project an ideal wish image of a Brazilian modernity within reach. The 1950s, if anything, continued this close association between cinema, modernity, and—more covertly, and often contradictorily—desire: In a postwar world, cinema became a tool (a technology of gender, in Teresa de Lauretis's famous phrase) to imagine a new cosmopolitan man—be he straight or gay—who, in spite of his sexual orientation, is an urbanite. However, identities are not fully named yet. We understand, as the audience, their "inclinations." Gay, trans, or lesbian as fixed named identities will only appear in the next decade.

THE BIRTH OF QUEER CINEMA AS AN IDENTITY

Since the 1960s and early 1970s, Brazil has witnessed great changes in same-sex desire activism and cinematic work. A large number of Brazilian films at international festivals deal with queer and dissident sexualities. (These films are discussed in "Retomada [1995] and after.") Since the early years of the 1970s, or what has been conventionally called the birth of LGBTQAI+ rights in many centers all over the world, cities like São Paulo, Rio de Janeiro, and other major urban centers have produced a great deal of work both intellectually and politically that deals with queer liberation. Activism and social awareness also brought to light the country's high level of hate crimes, vicious trans-bi-lesbian-homophobe attacks in major cities that have become frequent in the news along with the difficulties in passing laws criminalizing homophobia. This awareness has also brought same-sex desire to the center of newspapers and magazines and shown that homosexuality has reached higher levels of acceptance, equivalent to its levels of hate.[11]

It is now a common idea among Brazilian scholars that an LGBT cinema developed in the late 1960s and early 1970s in parallel with the organization of political groups rallying against dictatorship (Green, Trevisan, Mott, Simões, and Louro, among others). The scholar, writer, filmmaker, and activist João Silvério Trevisan (2018), for instance, provides a detailed account of this era, often in a personal manner, in his important book *Devassos no paraíso*.[12] Trevisan states: "I know I am immersed in the facts narrated here, and I do not intend to be 'scientific' in this narrative. On the contrary, I intend to give some sort of testimony, as the protagonist I was" (p. 336). Arguably, Trevisan's only film, *Orgia ou o homem que deu cria* [Orgy, or the man who gave birth], in 1970 inaugurates a queer filmmaking in Brazil. While the 1960s was an important and dynamic period for filmmaking in Brazil, *Orgia* as a queer film marks a new tone and style: The film not only illustrates the pitfalls and paragons of the then influential and dominant movement of "Cinema Novo," but also inscribes itself in the short-lived underground style in filmmaking that critics often refer to as "Cinema Marginal."

Cinema Novo has been widely studied throughout the past decades.[13] Some consider Cinema Novo to be the birth of modern cinema in Brazil, and it is arguably one of the most recognized Latin American film movements of the 20th century. As David William Foster (1999) stated, Cinema Novo "became probably the only truly international movement in Latin American filmmaking" (p. 2). The filmmakers themselves have theorized their aims and aesthetics in well-known manifestos and testimonials. In that regard, director Glauber Rocha's text, *The Aesthetics of Hunger*, is arguably the most important, but other significant statement are Paulo Emílio Sales Gomes' critical essays from the 1960s and 1970s, Estève Michel's study *Le Cinema Novo brésilien*, Robert Stam's *Tropical Multiculturalism: A Comparative History of Race in Brazilian Cinema and Culture*, Ismail Xavier's *Allegories of Underdevelopment: Aesthetics and Politics in Brazilian Cinema*, and Lucia Nagib's recent *Brazil on Screen: Cinema Novo, New*

Cinema, Utopia. Randal Johnson calls Cinema Novo the start of modern cinema in Brazil (in the *Encyclopedia of Latin American History and Culture*), and in his study *Cinema Novo x5: Masters of Contemporary Brazilian Film* (1984), Johnson details the careers of five filmmakers associated with the movement: Joaquim Pedro Andrade, Carlos Diegues, Ruy Guerra, Glauber Rocha, and Nelson Pereira dos Santos. The movement, according to Glauber Rocha, aimed at raising consciousness among the Brazilian population of their own misery; his tellingly titled *Aesthetics of Hunger* details the rationale behind the movement, clarifying in which ways "[t]he time when Cinema Novo had to explain itself in order to exist has passed" (MacKenzie, 2014, p. 219). Cinema Novo was, however, a movement made by man. The only woman associated with the 1960s was Helena Solberg with her 1966 documentary, *A Entrevista* [The interview]. As the only woman in her generation, she points to the gender issue in a unique form. Fernão Ramos (2018) calls her a lone star in the Cinema Novo boy's club (p. 63).

Nevertheless, and simultaneously with the heyday of Cinema Novo, another current in filmmaking developed: Cinema Marginal was created out of a necessity to explore themes left uncovered by Cinema Novo. Cinema Marginal or Cinema de Invenção' [Invention cinema] registered a break or rupture in tone and style, distancing itself from Glauber Rocha's Cinema Novo.[14] Rogério Sganzerla, one of the founders of the Cinema Marginal movement, called Cinema Novo right-wing conservative, paternalizing, and anti-avant-garde (quoted in Ramos, 2018, p. 178). Glauber Rocha ungenerously responded to such provocations in a later interview, saying that Cinema Marginal is a restorative abortion of decadent formalism (Ramos, 2018, p. 178). Trevisan, however, recognized in the predominantly masculinist perspective of Cinema Novo a disturbing depiction of manhood. In reaction, he turned toward developing a new style in cinema, intending to present a revolution in gender identities and placing himself as a filmmaker between the two major movements of the time: Cinema Novo and Cinema Marginal. Trevisan mentioned in an interview that as much as he couldn't place himself as a homosexual man either in the left or the right political movements, he couldn't place himself in any film movement either.[15] At the time of *Orgia e o homem que deu cria*'s re-lease, Trevisan wrote a manifesto accompanying the film. Trevisan's manifesto delineates some of the criticism toward Cinema Novo and the debauchery he presents in his film. In fact, *Manifesto Entendido* might as well be translated as Queer Manifesto. "Entendido" is an adjective in Portuguese derived from the verb "entender" (to understand), which, before the introduction of the English term "gay," was used by the lesbian and gay communities in Brazil in either masculine (entendido) or feminine form (entendida) to disclose one's sexual identity. To ask "você é entendida/o?" (do you understand/are you knowledgeable?) was a way to declare their "understanding" as a dissident group.[16] Hence, Trevisan self-consciously finishes his manifesto with a provocative question: "by the way, do you understand too?"

Guiomar Ramos (2014), in *Um Cinema Brasileiro Antropofágico 1970–1974*, argues that *Orgia ou o homem que deu cria* is one of several "anthropophagic films" that combines elements of Cinema Novo and Cinema Marginal, including references to Rogério Sganzerla's *O Bandido da Luz Vermelha* (considered by many critics to be one of the best Brazilian films ever made), which was foundational to Cinema Marginal.[17] Yet, Trevisan's pioneering effort in queer filmmaking, in the author's estimation, is mostly overlooked. Trevisan inaugurates a queer filmmaking because, for the first time, the director made it clear he had made a film for those "who understood." Therefore, he paved the way for other filmmakers to create more space in cinema. After *Orgia ou o homem que deu cria*, therefore, a whole new tradition in queer filmmaking began. In the 1980s, a surge in productions took place from independent and marginal filmmaking to internationally acclaimed films. Such a perspective leads to a fecund and diverse production in the 21st century: the 1970s and 1980s.

1970s and 1980s. During the 1970s and 1980s, four Brazilian film genres prevailed in the box office: children's movies, such as *Os Trapalhões* and *Xuxa*; pornographic films that since 1982 had been a viable commercial genre; erotic dramas and serious films originating from Cinema Marginal and Cinema Novo, which were well-received by critics but not always per se translated into commercial success; and finally, the genre of Pornochanchada, which originated in the 1970s and continued to draw large crowds to movie theaters.[18] From these four genres, the latter three are relevant for a queer historiography of Brazilian cinema.

In Brazil, many erotic comedies—politically inoffensive and culturally conservative—were produced with the support of the government, a trend that would culminate in the 1980s, a decade wherein downright pornography became a state-sanctioned genre. Alongside these movies, other films were produced that tried to distance themselves from the popular comedies or pornographic genre. These films gained international recognition and at times, popular acclaim as well. At about the same time, new and more explicit notions of sexual orientation and gender identity began to permeate film narratives. Moreno notes that Brazilian cinema went from 13 LGBTQAI+ films in the 1960s to 71 films the following decade. Apart from the films in which crossdressing is simply used for comedic relief, with no intention of adding anything to the story besides physical comedy (in the style of 1940s genre comedies), these films do represent a wide diversity of characters and gender identities. *Rainha Diaba* (1974) [The devil queen] by Antonio Carlos da Fontoura is an important representative of this decade for telling the story of a flamboyant person of color who transitions between gender identities. The story is loosely based on the life of João Francisco dos Santos—Madame Satã, a famed homosexual rogue from Rio de Janeiro (whose biopic is presented in "Retomada [1995] and After").

The 1980s is a crucial decade in the history of Brazil: The dictatorship ended in 1984 and in the following year José Sarney was appointed as the first civil president. The first democratically elected president, however, was Fernando Collor de Mello in 1989. By that time, the country's economic state was disastrous, hitting a yearly inflation rate of 5000% by the early 1990s. During Fernando Collor's presidency, Embrafilme closed down, leading to an almost complete halt in cinema production in Brazil in 1992. José Mario Ortiz and Arthur Autran (2018) explain that in 1992, only three Brazilian films were released, and local production corresponded to 0.05% of the market in the same year. In the onslaught of economic disaster throughout the 1980s, one cinema genre that survived and even flourished was pornography. In fact, more generally, the era saw a rise of interest in sex as a topic that was easy to sell to a wide audience. Between 1985 and 1991, the majority of films in Brazil were pornographic releases. A brief look at the 1988 box office chart further reveals that some of the successful movies, with the exception of six children's films, have explicitly sexualized titles, and many among them are indeed pornographic films (e.g., *Eles comem cu* [They eat/fuck ass], 1988).

The 1980s was marked by the end of the 1964–1984 military dictatorship in Brazil. These topics appear in cinema in different ways. Dictatorship and its aftermath are the topics of *O torturador* (1981) [The torturer], by Antonio Calmon. This film, for unknown reasons, has been overlooked by most critics dealing with queer and gay cinema. It is not mentioned in the comprehensive work by Antonio Moreno nor in Lacerda Júnior's most recent research. However, it is a film that fits a recognizable narrative template: that of the homosexual protagonist with a tormented soul whose life meets a tragic end (as in the films described from the 1960s, *O menino e o vento* and *O beijo*). Worth mentioning, the film was advertised in the only gay publication at the time, *Lampião da Esquina* (created by João Silvério Trevisan and other gay activists). In the advertisement for the film, the editors of *Lampião da Esquina* make sure that it is a movie for *entendidos* (a gay movie).

The most important queer films of the decade are *Vera* (1986) by Sérgio Toledo and *Amor Maldito* (1984) [Condemned love] by Adélia Sampio.[19] The former tells the story of Vera-Anderson, a transman (even though the term is not used in the film) who struggles to be identified as a man. The film is groundbreaking (Ana Beatriz Nogueira won the Silver Bear in Berlin for her work) for telling a story that even these days is rarely told. The latter is the first film ever directed by a woman of color in Brazil. Adélia Sampaio tells the story of a lesbian relationship and the outcomes of race, class, and identity in Brazil postdictatorship.

The AIDS epidemic also marks the 1980s and its film production. In Brazil, three films deal with the topic in different ways. Sergio Bianchi, director of *Romance* (1988), presents a tormented homosexual character dealing with the outcomes of his possible infection. Fauzi Mansur (under the pseudonym of Victor Triunfo), director of *AIDS, furor do sexo* (1986) [AIDS, furor of sex], presents a moralistic but rather pornographic tale in which the main character contracts HIV through reckless sexual behavior with transwomen and other men.[20] Finally, David Cardoso directs *Estou com AIDS* (1985) [I have AIDS], a documentary about the epidemic and its effects in Brazil. *Via Appia*, a German-Brazilian production, also depicts the outcomes of the AIDS epidemic in the 1980s. Filmed in 1989 by Jochen Hick, the movie explores the documentary and fiction genres following the life of a fictitious German flight attendant who goes back to Brazil in order to find the male prostitute who allegedly infected him.

A final film to end the 1980s is a Swiss-Brazilian production by the Swiss filmmakers Pierre-Alain Meier and Matthias Kälin: *Douleur d'amour* (1988) [Love hurts]. The film documents the lives of a group of transgender women in São Paulo, showing their daily lives through interviews and conversations among them.

RETOMADA (1995) AND AFTER

After the dictatorship ended and the country entered a period of *redemocratização* (re-democratization), Brazilian cinema had another boost in the period commonly known as the *retomada* [resurgence] of local cinema production. According to Lucia Nagib (2003), this *retomada* was enabled by the Audio-Visual Law promulgated in 1993 "prompting a boom in film production" (p. xvii). In terms of audience, the *retomada* has thus far successfully created new markets and found new publics. Among recent productions, some movies obtained both critical and commercial success. For instance, *Cidade de Deus* (2002) [City of God] by Fernando Meirelles, *Central do Brasil* (1998) [Central station] by Walter Salles, *O Quatrilho* (1995) by Fábio Barreto, *Tropa de Elite I and II* (2007, 2010) [Elite squad] by José Padilha, and *Carandiru* (2003) by Hector Babenco won both local and international awards. The 1990s ended with a film that was rarely considered queer due to the nature of the relationship presented: *Eu, Tu,*

Eles (1999) [Me, you, them] (Honorable Mention at *Un certain regard* in Cannes) by Andrucha Washington. It tells the story of a woman with three husbands, each with his specialty, as she explains in the film. The scenes of cordiality among the men, as when one is shaving the other, may not necessarily show same-sex desire but can definitely be read as queer affection or as a way of queering straight culture and one's perceptions about normativity and friendship.

The 1990s also mark the first iteration of the *Festival Mix Brasil de Cultura da Diversidade* (1993). The festival, organized by André Fisher, is the first film festival in Brazil oriented for LGBTQ production and, even today, focuses on films dealing with the diversity of gender identities and sexual orientation from all over the world.

Most recently, Globo Films (a sister company from the giant media and entertainment company Globo) has produced, with tremendous commercial success, films for a mass audience eager to watch local movies, mainly comedies and TV-related movies (movies that derive from *telenovelas* and TV series aired on TV Globo). The current list of the most watched movies in the country besides American productions consists mostly of Globo Filmes movies, most of them drawn from the pornochanchada and *chanchada* traditions. Popular comedies such as *Minha mãe é uma peça* (2013, 2016, 2019) [My mother is a character] and the two sequels are among these record-breaking films.[21] In that sense, Luis de Barros (1978) was certainly right when, in the 1920s, he observed a fondness in Brazilian audiences for comedies. The most recent success of *Minha mãe é uma peça*'s trilogy [My mother is a character] proves that men in drag and *chanchadas* that exploit sexual innuendo jokes (*De Pernas pro ar*) (2010, 2012, 2019) [Head over heels] as well as family comedies (*Se eu fosse você*) (2006, 2009) [If I were you] by Daniel Filho are safe bets for Brazilian audiences.[22] The trilogy *Minha mãe é uma peça* is an interesting case for study. Paulo Gustavo, an openly gay man, created the character at first for the theater and then for the cinema. In all three films, he plays a mother struggling to adapt to her new life after her divorce. A quick look may tempt one to see the movie in the ranks of *Mrs. Doubtfire* (1993) or *Tootsie* (1982); however, neither of these comparisons are viable. Paulo Gustavo plays a mother. He is in drag but he is not a man in drag in the movie. He plays a woman, as John Travolta did in the musical version of John Waters's *Hairspray* (2007).[23]

Alongside the great commercial successes promoted by Globo Films and other major international production companies, the first decades of this century have seen a great number of independent and queer-oriented productions in Brazil. Queer cinema continues to evolve as the understandings of gender identities change. New films in Brazil will not only discuss alternate views of homosexuality, but also alternate regional views outside the major urban centers of São Paulo and Rio de Janeiro. These films represent multiple identities and also reframe queer identities.

Listing all the films produced would be exhaustive. Instead, a discussion of some of the different types of genres, identities, and regions depicted in contemporary Brazilian cinema is presented. During these past years, a common genre is the coming-of-age narrative, films narrating the questions and sensibilities of young people around their sexuality. *Hoje eu quero voltar sozinho* (2015) [The way he looks] is probably the most famous of the type. It tells the story of a gay blind teenager falling in love with his best friend. *Mãe só há uma* (2016) [Don't call me son] and *Beira-mar* (2015) [Sea shore], and *Sócrates* (2019), by Alexandre Moratto are also films that fit into the coming-of-age narrative. *Sócrates*, however, places the teenage narrative out of the White middle-class life depicted in the previous films. Sócrates is a young Black teenager dealing with his sexuality in a poor neighborhood of Santos, a port city in the state of São Paulo. While most films have the option of ignoring questions of race and class, films like *Sócrates* remind the audience that the Brazilian population is mostly Black (54%, according to the last census) but is nonetheless still underrepresented in Brazilian cinema and television at large.

Another genre that seems to be thriving relates to films that revisit a queer past, that is, films based on real-life characters. *Madame Satã* (2002) [Madame Satan] is by far one of the most studied recent Brazilian films (B. Ruby Rich, Subero, Rodrigues, and Nemi Neto, among others). *Flores Raras* (2013) [Reaching for the moon] fictionalizes the story of the American poet Elisabeth Bishop and her relationship with Brazilian architect Lota de Macedo Soares. *Tatuagem* (2016) [Tattoo] also belongs here, since it is loosely based on the diaries of Tulio Carella, an Argentinian theater director who lived in Recife in the 1970s.

Love stories and more traditional dramas have also been visible. *Praia do Futuro* (2014) [Futuro beach], by Karim Aïnouz, *Como esquecer* (2010) [So hard to forget], by Malu di Martino, and *Paraísos Artificiais* (2013) [Artificial paradises], by Marcos Prado are three examples of the genre. *Simone* (2013), by Juan Zapata, is also important for bringing to the front lesbian desire and female sexuality, usually overlooked in cinematic productions, as Viviane Ferreira explains.[24]

Auteur films are represented with pictures such as *Tinta Bruta* (2018) [Hard paint], directed by Filipe Matzembacher and Marcio Reolon, and *Corpo Elétrico* (2018) [Body electric], by Marcelo Caetano. Films that portray queer familial representations have made their way onto the big screen. *Paraíso Perdido* (2018) [Lost paradise], by Monique Gardenberg, is one of the few films recently directed by women.[25] Her film is an example of the depiction of nonnormative families and lesbian romance. Eroticism is also present in queer contemporary cinema. These films present a queer view in the traditional Brazilian genre, portraying different bodies and sexualities, such as the films *O porteiro do dia* (2016) [The daytime doorman] and *Tinta Bruta* (2018) [Hard paint]. Finally, *As Boas Maneiras* (2018) [Good manner] is an interesting take on the horror genre, playing with traditional Brazilian folklore and urban life. It is also important to mention *Ilha* (2018) [Island], by Glenda Nicácio and Ary Rosa, and *Um dia com Jerusa* (2019) [A day with Jerusa], by Viviane Ferreira. Glenda Nicácio and Viviane Ferreira both represent a young generation of Black women (and queer, in Ferreira's case) directors opening spaces for more diversity in Brazilian cinema.

Short film has enriched LGBTQ visibility in Brazilian cinema, for example, *Negrum3* (2018) by Diego Paulino. *Eu não quero voltar sozinho* (2014) [The way he looks], by Daniel Ribeiro, and *O dia de Jerusa* (2014) [Jerusa's day], by Viviane Ferreira are two short films that, after finding a good response from the critics and audiences, were later shot as long feature films, the former in 2015 and the latter in 2019. Viviane Ferreira's film marks an important landmark in Brazilian cinema for being the first film made by a queer Black woman after more than 30 years from the release of *Amor Maldito* in 1984.[26]

These films are mainly representative of the current situation of Brazilian queer cinema since 2000. The list of queer-oriented films in the current decades is arguably longer than any other decade before. The films also portray a large variety of directors, including more women than ever before in Brazilian film production.[27]

THE DOCUMENTARY TRADITION IN BRAZIL

Amir Labaki (2003) explains that Brazil "boasts a rigorous tradition of documentary filmmaking, proof of which can be seen in the excursions made into this medium by every great Brazilian filmmaker" (p. 97). The country has a long tradition of documentary filmmaking that explores, and sometimes blurs the relation between documentary and fiction. In 1929, the city documentary *São Paulo, Symphony of a Metropolis* combined the procedures of realist documentary with fictional frames. Another example is the work of Helena Solberg, the only female director to be recognized as part of the Cinema Novo movement. Her 1966 documentary, *A Entrevista* [The interview], offers a feminist take on documentary, for instance, by commenting in voice-over with the then new Nagra technology, still used in 2020. In *A Entrevista*, the voice-over often creates a striking juxtaposition: The interviews made with 27 women from Rio de Janeiro do not always match the images. The critical distancing effect of this technique afterward became a major influence in documentary. Solberg also made the film *Banana Is My Business* (1999), an awarded documentary about the life of Carmen Miranda, perhaps the most famous Brazilian personality in Hollywood. Miranda became a myth in Brazil and a queer symbol for future generations (an analogy to Judy Garland—*The Wizard of Oz*—can be made here). In the documentary on her life, Solberg alternates historical footage of Carmen Miranda with images of drag queen Erick Barreto, who became famous in Brazil as a Miranda impersonator.

Blending the languages of video art and cinema, Rita Moreira's work is important to the understanding of queer documentary in Brazil. Her videos (published on her YouTube page) deal with questions of repression, sexuality, and violence. Rita Moreira, along with Norma Bahia Pontes, is a pioneer in discussing LGBTQ visibility in art in Brazil. Moreira and Pontes made a series of short videos while in New York in the 1970s. Their video *Lesbian Mothers* (1972) documents the lives of a lesbian couple and their custody battle to raise their kid. In 1974, they won a Guggenheim Foundation Award for their video *Lesbianismo-Feminismo*. In 1988, Rita Moreira directed the video *Hunting Season*, which discusses the murder of the theater director Luiz Antonio Martinez Correa in São Paulo. *Hunting Season* is the artist's most recognized and awarded video, which—in a way—may shed light on the misogyny and visibility that she has attempted to discuss throughout her career. Her most recent work, *Caminhada Lésbica por Marielle* [Lesbian march for Marielle], was filmed in 2018 in São Paulo.

Not only Rita Ribeiro's work but documentary at large has been a great source for Brazilian filmmakers to reframe queer identities in the country and to the world. Several films have been produced dealing with topics from historical queer representation to contemporary issues on homophobia. The 2010 documentary *Dzi Croquetes*, for instance, inaugurates a perspective on queer documenting that will lead to several other films produced later. The film presents a theater troupe in the 1970s in Brazil that, despite all adversities—dictatorship, lack of sponsorship, and conservatism—gained national and international success. At a time when dissident sexuality was meant to be hidden from public view, *Dzi Croquetes* reclaimed queer bodies for performance, redefining a genealogy in Brazilian queer images. Documentary makers Tatiana Issa and Rafael Alvarez in turn found in this icon of queer performance a national archive to engulf a burgeoning tradition in national documentary.

Following suit, *Bixa Travesti* (2018) [Tranny queen] is arguably one of the most creative documentaries made in Brazil. The filmmakers were recognized in Berlin with a Teddy Award for their depiction of the life of Linn da Quebrada, a Brazilian artist who identifies as trans. The film at first resembles the traditional musical numbers of the *chanchadas*; however, the lyrics and the performance reclaim a position erased in classic Brazilian films. *Chanchadas* presented White artists in blackface, singing and appropriating Black culture. In *Bixa Travesti*, a Black trans woman takes the stage to sing "strange, crazy, Black tranny/when she walks by everybody laughs at her/Pay attention, though, macho/Sit down and observe your destruction."

Bichas, o documentário (2016) [Faggots, the documentary], directed by Marlon Parente, also brings visibility and voice to nonnormative bodies. This documentary discusses precisely what scholars have said is a "negative view of homosexuality": effeminacy and masculinity. Through a series of testimonies, the documentary debates homophobia, effeminophobia, and other forms of oppression that nonconforming and nonbinary bodies suffer daily in Brazil.

Laerte-se (2017), by Lygia Barbosa and Eliane Brum, is the first full-length documentary produced by Netflix in Brazil, bringing to the fore the new form of production and the disruption Netflix has been causing in the market. The documentary portrays the life of Laerte Coutinho, a famous cartoonist who, in her late 50s, came out as transgender. Her coming out made it possible for people to discuss issues related to class, race, and visibility. As a White middle-class person, her story opened a space for old fractures in Brazilian society pertaining to racism, misogyny, and classicism.

Other documentaries that have portrayed once invisible lives is *Divinas Divas* (2016) [Divine divas], by Leandra Leal. *Divinas Divas* is the story of seven important trans women and performers with careers spanning over five decades. *Carta para além dos muros* (2019) [Letter for beyond the walls], by André Canto, discusses the AIDS epidemic in Brazil with testimony from survivors and doctors and archive footage from the past four decades. Finally, *Meu corpo é político* (2018) [My body is political], by Alice Riff, presents the lives of several trans men and trans women and discusses how intersectional aspects such as gender, race, and class influence the lives of different people in Brazil.

The documentary short subject category has also been a way to depict queer lives. A series of films has been produced recently and received recognition in different festivals. Among many of them, it is important to mention *Filme para poeta cego* (2012) [Film for blind poet], by Gustavo Vinagre. The awarded short documentary follows Glauco Matoso, a famed Brazilian poet who identifies as a gay man. Finally, *Carne* (2019) [Flash], by Camila Katter is not a documentary per se; it is an animated movie. However, the animations are juxtaposed with the voices of five women narrating their experiences. The interviews can be seen in direct relationship with Helena Solberg's 1966 *A Entrevista*. Both films depict important aspects of Brazilian society and the changes cinematic production has experienced.

2019 AND BEYOND

Unfortunately, 2020 has seen a halt in film production and release. Due to the Covid-19 pandemic, most films set to release this year have been delayed and film festivals are in limbo. Nonetheless, one last film from 2019 needs to be mentioned: *Bacurau*, by Kléber Mendonça and Juliano Dornelles (Jury Priz at Cannes). Drawing on the trope of both Brazilian and American cinema, their film tells the story of a queer community in the north of Brazil.

Of particular interest here is one of the main characters, Lindu, who seems to fluently transition in between genders. They (the neutral "they" singular is used here to describe the main character) are a violent character who is crucial to the survival of a local community besieged by corrupted politicians, foreign invaders, and the destruction of natural resources. Unsure whether there is a happy end to this movie, it seems more productive to consider its conclusion from the point of view of queer failure: as an unconventional mode of living that helps a marginalized community to survive.

FINAL REMARKS

In the third decade of the 21st century, one can talk about queer(s) perspectives. The urban gay man from the 1960s, the flamboyant comic relief character from the 1970s, and the tormented souls from the 1980s are multiplied in a wide range of characters from different regions of the country. Urban cities like Recife and Fortaleza are also part of the cinematic landscape. Travestis, trans men, trans women, effeminate men, drag queens, and nonbinary individuals have found a voice in different films, both in fiction and documentary.

In 1993, during the first years of the last decade of the millennium, a fashion brand in São Paulo created a tee shirt with three letters, GLS: G for gay, L for lesbians, and S for *simpatizantes* (allies). Almost 30 years later, it seems farfetched to believe that a brand concerned with queer lives would so blatantly overlook trans identities. Yet, it was a hit among the clubber kids of the early 1990s (*Party Monster*, the film with Macaulay Culkin, accurately describes that era) who were for the first time coming out of the closet outside marginal regions of the city.

Also in the 1990s, Caio Fernando Abreu, a well-known gay writer, in a letter to a friend wrote about his inability to understand a "woman who wanted to be a man but also desired sex with men." He could not grasp how a trans man (an expression not widely used at the time) could also be a homosexual. In the same decade, Vito Russo, in *Celluloid Closet*, criticized Mae West for her understanding of homosexuality in the 1920s when she said that "a homosexual is a female soul in a male body" (p. 55).

These examples serve to understand that as much as cinema as a technological apparatus has evolved, our understanding of gender identities and sexual orientation has changed through time as society changes. By observing the history of cinema and its connections to gender identity and sexual orientation, one can see how societal aspirations are also visible on the screen.

ACKNOWLEDGMENTS

The author would like to acknowledge the support received from the Institute of Latin American Studies at Columbia University during the 2019–2020 school year.

DIGITAL RESOURCES

Cinema Sapatão: an online community devoted to promoting lesbian visibility through cinema and video (https://www.youtube.com/channel/UCRV8N27z6e4emNRPA9E9lzA).
Cinemateca Brasileira: the largest cinematic film archive in Latin America.

Festival Mix Brasil de Cultura da Diversidade (https://www.mixbrasil.org.br/): the largest queer film festival in Brazil; also, their website is a rich archive for short films, posters, and information about LGBTQ cinema both in Brazil and in the world.

Hunting Season (https://www.youtube.com/watch?v=rjan_Yd0C5g), by Rita Moreira, available at: Interview with Viviane Ferreira for Cinema Sapatão (https://www.youtube.com/watch?v=MFqQyy7d428).

FURTHER READING

Caulfield, S., & Schettini, C. (2017). Gender and sexuality in Brazil since independence. In W. Beezley (Ed.), *Oxford research encyclopedia of Latin American history*. Advance online publication. https://doi.org/10.1093/acrefore/9780199366439.013.296

Gerstner, D. A. (2006). *Manly arts: Masculinity and nation in early American cinema*. Duke University Press.

Johnson, R., & Stam, R. (1995). *Brazilian cinema*. Columbia University Press.

Marsh, L. L. (2012). *Brazilian women's filmmaking: From dictatorship to democracy*. University of Illinois Press.

Rosa, M. L. (2018). Disidencias sexuales y video documental feminista en los años 70: Las cineastas brasileñas Rita Morena y Norma Bahia Pontes pioneras en las denuncias sobre la opresión de las mujeres y la invisibilidad lésbica. *Arte Y Políticas De Identidad*, 16(16), 37. https://doi.org/10.6018/317031

Santos, É. R. S. dos, & Tedesco, M. C. (2017). Feminist initiatives and actions in contemporary Brazilian audiovisual. *Revista Estudos Feministas*, 25(3), 1373–1391. https://doi.org/10.1590/1806-9584.2017v25n3p1373

Shaw, L., & Dennison, S. (2014). *Brazilian national cinema*. Routledge.

Souza, E. P. de. (2013). *Cinema na panela de barro: Mulheres Negras, narrativas de amor, afeto e identidade* [Unpublished doctoral dissertation]. Universidade de Brasília.

REFERENCES

Altman, D. (2002). *Global sex*. University of Chicago Press.

Andrade, O. (2008). Marco Zero I. *A revolução melancólica*. Editora Globo.

Araújo, L. C. de. (2015). Teatro popular e cinema hollywoodiano em Augusto Annibal quer casar! (1923). *Revista Alceu*, 16(31), 62–73. http://revistaalceu-acervo.com.puc-rio.br/cgi/cgilua.exe/sys/start.htm?infoid=564&sid=43

Araújo, V. de P. (1976). *A bela época do cinema brasileiro*. Editora Perspectiva.

Barros, L. (1978). *Minhas memórias de cineasta*. Editora Artenova.

Butler, J. (1993). Imitation and gender insubordination. In H. Abelove, M. A. Barale, & D. M. Halperin (Eds.), *The lesbian and gay studies reader* (pp. 307–320). Routledge.

Conde, M. (2012). *Consuming visions: Cinema, writing, and modernity in Rio de Janeiro*. University of Virginia Press.

Conde, M. (2018). *Foundational films: Early cinema and modernity in Brazil* (pp. 21–38). California Scholarship Online. https://doi.org/10.1525/california/9780520290983.003.0002

Cornejo, G. (2013). La guerra declarada contra el niño afeminado: Una autoetnografía "queer." *Íconos—Revista De Ciencias Sociales*, 39, 79. https://doi.org/10.17141/iconos.39.2011.747

Dominguez Ruvalcaba, H. (2016). *Translating the queer: Body politics and transnational conversations*. Zed Books.

Doty, A. (2000). *Flaming classics: Queering the film canon*. Routledge.

Duggan, L. (2002). The new homonormativity: The sexual politics of neoliberalism. In R. Castronovo & D. D. Nelson (Eds.), *Materializing democracy: Toward a revitalized cultural politics* (pp. 175–194). Duke University Press.

Foster, D. W. (1999). *Gender & society in contemporary Brazilian cinema*. University of Texas Press.
Galvão, M. R., & Bernardet, J. (1983). *Cinema: Repercussões em caixa de eco ideológica (as ideias de "nacional" e "popular" no pensamento cinematográfico brasileiro)*. Editora Brasiliense.
Goes, T. (1984). Vitórias nos EUA mostram que maré mudou para os gays. *Revista H Magazine, 6*.
Johnson, R. (1984). *Cinema novo x 5: Masters of contemporary Brazilian film*. University of Texas Press.
Kuhn, A., & Westwell, G. (2020). *A dictionary of film studies*. Oxford University Press.
Labaki, A. (2003). It's all Brazil. In L. Nagib (Ed.), *New Brazilian cinema* (pp. 97–104). I.B. Tauris.
Lacerda Jr., L. F. B. (2015). *Cinema gay Brasileiro: Políticas de representação e além*. [Unpublished doctoral dissertation]. Universidade Federal do Pernambuco, Repositório Digital da UFPE.
Lekitsch, S. (2011). *Cine arco-íris 100 anos de cinema LGBT nas telas brasileiras*. Edições GLS.
Lily, S. (2016). *Adiós, Chueca: Memorias del gaypitalismo: La creación de la "marca gay."* Foca.
Lopes, D. (2019). Um calafrio anda pelo meu corpo. *Significação: Revista De Cultura Audiovisual, 46*(52). https://doi.org/10.11606/issn.2316-7114.sig.2019.152046
Macedo, W. (1949). *Carnaval no Fogo*. Atlântida Empresa Cinematográfica do Brasil S.A.
MacKenzie, S. (2014). *Film manifestos and global cinema cultures: A critical anthology*. University of California Press.
Manga, C. (1953). *A dupla do barulho*. Atlântida Empresa Cinematográfica do Brasil S.A.
Manga, C. (1957). *Garotas e Samba*. Atlântida Empresa Cinematográfica do Brasil S.A.
Manga, C. (1960). *Dois ladrões*. Atlântida Empresa Cinematográfica do Brasil S.A.
Meruane, L. (2012). *Viajes virales: La crisis del contagio global en la escritura del sida*. Fondo de Cultura Económica.
Miskolci, R. (2012). *Teoria Queer: Um aprendizado pelas diferenças*. Autêntica Editora.
Moreno, A. (2014). *O personagem homossexual no cinema brasileiro*. Caixa Cultural.
Mott, L. (2003). Crypto-sodomites in colonial Brazil. In P. H. Sigal (Ed.), *Infamous desire: Male homosexuality in colonial Latin America* (pp. 168–189). University of Chicago Press.
Nagib, L. (2003). *The new Brazilian cinema*. I.B. Tauris in association with the Centre for Brazilian Studies, University of Oxford.
Nagime, M. (2016). *Em busca das origens de um cinema queer no Brasil* [Unpublished doctoral dissertation]. Universidade Federal de São Carlos, Repositório Digital da UFSCar.
Nemi Neto, J. (2021). *Anthropophagic queer: Contemporary Brazilian cinema*. Wayne State University Press.
Ortiz, J. M., & Autran, A. (2018). O cinema brasileiro das décadas de 1970 e 1980. In F. P. Ramos & S. Schvarzman (Eds.), *Nova história do cinema brasileiro* (Vol. 2). Edições Sesc.
Perlongher, N. O. (2008). *O negócio do michê: Prostituição viril em São Paulo*. Editora Fundação Perseu Abramo.
Preciado, P. (2010). *Pornotopía: Arquitectura y sexualidad en "Playboy" durante la guerra fría*. Anagrama.
Priore, M. D. (2012). *Histórias íntimas: Sexualidade e erotismo na história do Brasil*. Planeta.
Ramos, F. (2018). Cinema Novo, Cinema Marginal e Depois (1955–1980). In F. Ramos & S. Schvarzman. *Nova história do cinema brasileiro* (Vol. 1, pp. 16–201). Edições SESC.
Ramos, F., & Schvarzman, S. (2018). *Nova história do cinema brasileiro* (Vol. 1). Edições SESC.
Ramos, G. (2008). *Um cinema brasileiro antropofágico? (1970–1974)*. Annablume.
Rich, R. (2013). *New queer cinema: Director's cut*. Duke University Press.
Russo, V. (1987). *The celluloid closet: Homosexuality in the movies*. Harper & Row.
Sadoul, G., & Morris, P. (1972). *Dictionary of filmmakers*. University of California Press.
Santos, E., & Tedesco, M. (2017). Feminist initiatives and actions in contemporary Brazilian Audiovisual. *Revista Estudos Feministas, 25*(3). https://doi.org/10.1590/1806-9584.2017v25n3p1373
Sedgwick, E. K. (1993). *Tendencies*. Duke University Press.
Shaw, L. (2003). The Brazilian chanchada and Hollywood paradigms (1930–1959). *Framework: The Journal of Cinema and Media, 44*(1), 70–83. http://www.jstor.org/stable/41552353

Shaw, L. (2007). Afro-Brazilian identity. Malandragem and homosexuality in Madame Satã. In D. Shaw (Ed.), *Contemporary Latin American cinema: Breaking into the global market* (pp. 87–104). Rowman & Littlefield Publishers, Inc.

Sigal, P. H. (2003). *Infamous desire: Male homosexuality in colonial Latin America*. University of Chicago Press.

Stam, R. (2004). *Tropical multiculturalism: A comparative history of race in Brazilian cinema and culture*. Duke University Press.

Subero, G. (2014). *Queer masculinities in Latin American cinema. Male bodies and narrative representations*. I.B. Tauris.

Trevisan, J. S. (1986). *Perverts in paradise*. GMP.

Trevisan, J. S. (2018). *Devassos no Paraíso. A homosexualidade no Brasil da colônia até a atualidade*. Objetiva

Viteri, M. A., Serrano J. A., & Vidal-Ortiz, S. (2013). ¿Cómo se piensa lo "queer" en América Latina? (Presentación Dossier). *Íconos—Revista De Ciencias Sociales*, 39, 47. https://doi.org/10.17141/iconos.39.2011.742

Warner, M. (1999). *The trouble with normal: Sex, politics, and the ethics of queer life*. Harvard University Press.

NOTES

1. "Lands beneath the Equator" refers to the Dutch historian who, in 1660, wrote in *Travel Journeys in Brazil*: "Beneath the equator, sin does not exist." His comment referred to the non-Christian sexual practices among the original peoples; among these practices were sodomy and multiple partners.
2. Luiz Mott considers as the hegemonic matrix the Portuguese customs and traditions. To the author, the encounters between the Portuguese and the indigenous populations changed their own understanding of sexuality.
3. Early representations in cinema also deal with that idea. For instance, *Anders als die Andern* (1919) [Different from others], the classic German movie by Richard Oswald, is a case in point. The film has been described by many as the first movie with a proper notion of a homosexual identity, as proposed by Magnus Hirshfeld, a cowriter for the screenplay. Even though Hirshfeld was an active member and proponent of the homosexual liberation movement, still, as a sign of its times, the main character commits suicide, as if confirming an impossibility of a guiltless homosexual identity.
4. Both in academia and in the arts, one can see the use of the term "queer." For instance, different centers of research focusing on sexuality and identity, such as NuQueer at Universidade Federal Rural do Pernambuco, have been recently created.
5. Tony Goes, a Brazilian journalist, wrote a short article in the gay-oriented *H magazine* in which he states that the United States is the "pátria do movimento gay" ("nation for the gay movement"). Commenting on the recent votes for marriage equality in Washington, Maryland, and Maine, he argues that Brazil is behind the United States. Nonetheless, the author would like to point out that in 2011, the Brazilian Supreme Court recognized same-sex civil union at a national level and that since then, five states have already changed such civil unions into marriages. See Justiça autoriza servidor homossexual a alterar estado civil para Casado (http://www1.folha.uol.com.br/cotidiano/1224972-justica-autoriza-servidor-homossexual-a-alterar-estado-civil-para-casado.shtml).
6. Russel Tovey, an American actor and openly gay man, said in an interview in 2015 that he is "glad that he is not one of those effeminate men." Also, Luiz Mott, an important LGBT Brazilian scholar, also said in 2018 that most gay men look masculine. These two examples, both in the United States and in Brazil, confirm the problematic notion of an ideal gay man. This representation, in the end, answers to the anxieties of effeminophobia in the gay community.
7. Denilson Lopes (2019) has recently published an article about Peixoto's queer sensibility. According to Lopes, Peixoto's diary could be reconsidered as a queer experience.

8. Abraccine, the Brazilian Association of Cinema critics, released their list with the best 100 Brazilian films of all time in 2016.
9. *Oxford Dictionary of Film Studies.*
10. *O Beijo no Asfalto*, a 1961 play by Nelson Rodrigues, deserves more detailed attention in future research. The play has had three different film adaptations, the second in 1981 and the most recent in 2018. The story of a man who kisses another man on his deathbed and creates havoc in society still resonates with the public. All three adaptations deal with homosexual panic in different ways, which also shows the signs of the times in which they were produced.
11. Most recent data show that Brazil has the highest numbers in regard to hate crimes, especially against the trans community. Trans-identified individuals are disproportionately murdered in Brazil. More on the topic can be found at Brasil é o país que mais procura por transexuais no RedTube—e o que mais comete crimes transfóbicos nas ruas.
12. An abbreviated version, titled *Perverts in paradise*, was published by GMP in 1986.
13. Cinema Novo is a Brazilian movement normally associated with Third Cinema in Latin America. Glauber Rocha coined the movement's motto: "a camera in your hand and an idea in your head." Through allegorical representations of contemporary Brazil, the movement aimed at critical representations of the country. Important films are *Black God, White Devil* (1964) by Glauber Rocha and *The Guns* (1965) by Ruy Guerra, among many others.
14. Glauber Rocha is arguably the most recognized name associated with Cinema Novo. He wrote the manifesto *Aesthetics of Hunger* and helped delineate the movement from its inception to its end. So far, Rocha is the only Brazilian director to ever have been recognized with a major award at Cannes Film Festival (1969).
15. This interview is going to be published by Wayne State University Press as part of the series "Queer Screens" in late 2021.
16. A similar understanding also happens in Spanish. ¿Entiendes? (Do you understand?) also refers to a hidden question with the same subtle meaning as in Portuguese. In 1995, Duke University Press published a collection of articles called *¿Entiendes? Queer Reading. Hispanic Writings* (edited by Paul Julian Smith and Emilie L. Bergmann), mapping out same-sex desire and gender identities across the Hispanic world.
17. In 1992, Sganzerla produced and directed *Perigo Negro*, a film based on Oswald de Andrade's book *Marco Zero*. The persistence of Antropofagia into the final decades of the 20th century is seen in other works produced in Brazil. Besides Sganzerla's film, for instance, one can mention *O homem do pau-Brasil* by Joaquim Pedro Andrade Macunaíma in 1982.
18. A quick note must be made about one of the major successes of the decades of 1970–1990: Os Trapalhões. The group of four comedians was responsible for 16 of the top 25 box office hits in Brazilian history between 1970 and 1990. The group had a TV show that ran for decades on national television, and every year (sometimes twice a year), they released a film for children that drew millions of spectators to the cinema. Following their tradition, Xuxa, known as the "queen of the children," also produced extremely popular films in Brazil during the decades of the 1980s and 1990s.
19. It was more than 30 years later that another queer Black woman directed their own movie, *Um dia com Jerusa* (2019), by Viviane Ferreira. Glenda Nicácio broke the hiatus a couple of years before. However, Nicácio directed alongside Ary Rosa.
20. The film has also appeared with the titles *Furor do sexo explícito* [Furor of explicit sex], *AIDS, a fúria do sexo* [AIDS, the fury of sex], and *AIDS, o furor do sexo* [AIDS, the furor of sex]. Nonetheless, the author has opted to keep the title on the original poster when the film was released in 1985.
21. It is relevant for this article to mention that for the third installment of the franchise, Paulo Gustavo, the creator and main actor (he plays the mother in the main title), decided not to add a kiss between two men in the film. According to him, the audience would not accept it.
22. Each installment of the trilogy was directed by a different person: the first by André Pellens, the second by César Rodrigues, and the third by Susana Garcia. The direction by a woman in the third film possibly

(and hopefully) indicates the opening of the market for women in Brazil. The *De pernas para o ar* trilogy also indicates a similar trend, as in *Minha mãe é uma peça*. The third installment is also directed by a woman, Julia Rezende.
23. The producer's decision was possibly linked to the original *Hairspray* (1988) in which Divine played the role of the mother. In the later Broadway production that originated the 2007 film, Harvey Fierstein (*Torch Song Trilogy*) played the role of the mother.
24. Interview for *Cinema Sapatão* in 2020 (see "Digital Resources").
25. Santos and Tedesco (2017), in their article "Feminist Initiatives and Actions in Contemporary Brazilian Audiovisual," explains that "it can be noticed that between 2005 and 2015 there was a significant increase in the total number of Brazilian films released, but the number of productions directed by women who managed to debut did not grow in the same proportion. In fact, since 2007 we were in a period where underrepresentation was declining, very slowly, and short of women's expectations and needs (p. 1387)."
26. Viviane Ferreira points out in 2020 in an interview for Cinema Sapatão that the landmark refers to a film directed by a Black woman. Other women of color have also codirected films with men. She references *Até o fim* (2020) and *Café com canela* (2017) by Glenda Nicácio with Ari Rosa, and *Vamos fazer um brinde* (2011) by Sabrina Rosa and Cavi Borges.
27. Some important pictures from the 1980s and 1990s were made by women but are not mentioned here because the core of this article is about queer productions. However, the importance of women filmmakers for recent Brazilian productions is clear. The "retomada" in the 1990s was led by Carla Camurati and her film *Carlota Joaquina*, which inaugurated cinema in Brazil after the disastrous presidency of Collor de Melo. Also, in 1985 Susana Amaral directed *The Hour of the Star*, an internationally recognized film (Marcela Cartaxo won the Grand Prix at Cannes). Tata Amaral, Ana Carolina, and Tizuka Iamazaki are among other filmmakers who have made an important contribution to gender equality, feminism, and visibility in Brazil.

João Nemi Neto

CHINESE PINK MARKETS

INTRODUCTION

In contemporary Chinese societies, queer needs and desires are perceived as cash cows by corporations and marketers. Starting from the late 20th century, businesses have been increasingly targeting Chinese *tongzhi* as a niche market. This interest in the Chinese pink market is fueled by the stereotype of the double-income, no-kids "rich gay" as well as market research predictions of a large but closeted Chinese *tongzhi* consumer population. For example, marketers estimate that the LGBTQ population in China is the largest in the world—with an estimated 60–70 million people—which is bigger than the entire population size of many countries (Doland, 2014). Further, the market research industry estimates that the value of LGBT-linked spending in China is between $300 billion and $500 billion dollars (Wakefield, 2020). Corporations and marketers regard these statistical estimates as evidence of a hidden, wealthy consumer market waiting to be mined for profit (see, e.g., Juan, 2016). In the following paragraphs, the definitions and terminologies most frequently encountered in research on the Chinese pink market are first clarified. This is followed by an overview of the historical accounting of the relationship between market economy and *tongzhi* subject formation. The article concludes with a discussion of the commonalities and divergences in research writings on China, Hong Kong, and Taiwan pink markets as well as future research directions and methodological considerations.

DEFINITIONS AND TERMINOLOGY

The term "Chinese" in *Chinese pink market* is delicate. Research on "Chinese pink market" uses the term "Chinese" to mean either ethnicity, geography, or both. With regard to ethnicity, research on the Chinese pink market includes all for-profit activities in the Chinese vernacular targeting the LGBTQ community living in Chinese-majority societies. Geographically, research on the Chinese pink market is located in the PRC, Hong Kong, or Taiwan—Sinophone locales where the Han Chinese form the ethnic majority. That said, although all three geographical locales are Chinese-ethnic-majority societies, LGBTQ communities in the PRC, Hong Kong, and Taiwan experience different challenges and affordances due to the different regulations and restrictions on LGBTQ individuals and LGBTQ activism in each geographical locale. Further, the different economic and political histories of the PRC vis-à-vis Hong Kong and Taiwan are reflected in the unique manifestations and politics of their local Chinese pink markets. Given this context, it may thus be argued that there is not one but multiple Chinese pink markets.

Literature on the Chinese pink markets discusses the commodification and consumerization of LGBTQ needs, desires, and spaces that are specific to China, or Hong Kong, or Taiwan, rather than addressing "the Chinese" as one generalized ethnic group. When more than one Chinese *tongzhi* community is discussed, such as in Travis Kong's (2011) oral history study of Chinese gay men or in Chou Wah-shan's (2000) analysis of *tongzhi* politics, geographical specification and cross-cultural comparisons are made. To reflect the complexity of the term "Chinese" in this discussion of the Chinese pink markets, this article will employ the phrase "Chinese pink market" when the focus is on ethnicity and pink economy endeavors in the Mandarin vernacular. The phrase "Chinese pink markets" will be used in instances where the focus is on geographical location with the terms China/PRC, Taiwan, and/or Hong Kong used to additionally specify and qualify the geographic region that is being discussed.

Further to the aforementioned dual-meaning of Chinese as ethnicity and geography, the unwieldiness of current literature on the Chinese pink market is compounded by the wide variety of terms used to reference the Chinese pink economy in different texts. Specifically, there are variances in terminology used by mass-market literature, such as newspapers and magazines, versus academic literature. There are also variances in terminology between Chinese-language and English-language publications. The term *pink market* is favored by English-language media reports, while the terms *pink economy* and *pink market* are used interchangeably in English-language academic publications. In Chinese-language newsprint and academic literature, the pink market is referred to using a variety of terms, the most frequently used terms being pink economy (*fenhong jingji*), rainbow economy (*caihong jingji*), homosexual economy (*tongxinglian jingji*), and *tongzhi* economy (*tongzhi jingji*).

The term *tongzhi* bears explaining here. *Tongzhi* is a popular contemporary term commonly used by Chinese LGBTQ subjects in the PRC, Hong Kong, as well as Taiwan for self-identification. For example, in the first Hong Kong pride parade, the declaration of the parade began with the phrase: "We are *tongzhi*" (Kong, 2011, p. 1). The phrase and hashtag *wo shi tongzhi* (I am *tongzhi*) are also frequently used in Chinese popular culture and online. In terms of etymology, *tongzhi* is an appropriation of the communist revolutionary term *comrade*. Like the term *queer*, *tongzhi* is likewise a nonbinary term. However, *tongzhi* is not replaceable by *queer*, as *tongzhi* is a particular consciousness and subjectivity: one is considered a homosexual and not *tongzhi* if one is homophobic and does not support LGBTQ rights (Wong & Zhang, 2000, p. 266). Further, the direct linguistic translation for *queer* in the Chinese language is *ku'er*. The term *ku'er* is also popular amongst Taiwan LGBTQ for self-identification. The connotative meaning of *ku'er* in vernacular usage is to emphasize coolness (Wong & Zhang, 2000, p. 257).

Wah-shan Chou's (2000) discussion of *tongzhi* politics in Taiwan, Hong Kong, and China serves as an excellent starting resource for a historical account of the adoption of the term *tongzhi* for self-identification by Chinese LGBTQ communities in China, Hong Kong, and Taiwan. Andrew Wong and Qing Zhang's (2000) linguistic analysis of the Taiwanese gay and lesbian publication *G&L Magazine* complements Chou's (2000) account of how the term *tongzhi* came to be the preferred term for self-identification in Taiwan. Further to the above, Travis Kong (2011) and Ya-chen Chen (2016) discuss other self-identification terms used by local *tongzhi* in Hong Kong and Taiwan respectively, such as *memba*, *lazi*, and *ku'er*.

In consideration of the aforementioned terminology variances in both the Chinese language and the English language, this entry employs the terms *pink market* and *pink economy* interchangeably to reflect the prevalence of both terms in English-language literature. The ubiquitously adopted and understood term of self-reference by Chinese LGBTQ—*tongzhi*—will be used when referencing Chinese LGBTQ peoples, spaces, issues, and concerns in the PRC, Hong Kong, and Taiwan such as in the concepts of *tongzhi* subjectivity, *tongzhi* politics, and *tongzhi* consciousness. The term *queer* will be used when discussing contributions of Chinese pink market research to current literature, such as in the discussions on queer consumption, queer space, and queer visibility.

TRACING THE GENEALOGY OF THEORIZATION ON THE CHINESE PINK MARKET

Early scholarship on the Chinese pink market predominantly focused on articulating the relationship between market economy and *tongzhi* subject formation. In the following sections, the article discusses why there was such a strong focus in early Chinese pink market research on theorizing *tongzhi* subject formation as mediated by market economy. It then discusses the different accounts and weighing of the influence of the pink economy on *tongzhi* subject formation in each geographic location. Literature focusing on the PRC will be summarized, followed by that on Hong Kong and, finally, Taiwan.

A Political Economy Perspective on Early Chinese Pink Market Research.

Literature on North American gay movements argue that gay identities, social networks, and group consciousness are first developed in commercial sites (see, e.g., D'Emilio, 1998; Hennessy, 1995; Jackson, 2009). The neoliberal market economy is an important force in North American gay subject formation as it affords individual agency in terms of the pursuit of goods and services to fulfill one's needs and desires. The pink market satisfies the need for a safe queer space by offering the option to socialize and to go public in discos, clubs, and bars. Turning to queer subject formation in Asia, the scholarship then argues that not only is the neoliberal market economy also crucial for queer subject formation in Asia, but that the global flows of culture and capital encourage the development of a "global gayness" in Asian countries. In response to this line of theorizing, research on Chinese pink markets adopted a political economy approach to theorize against the Western-centric teleological assumptions about *tongzhi* subjectivity and subject formation.

A political economy of sexuality "recognizes the interrelationship of political, economic, and cultural structures" (Altman, 2001, p. 157) by relating the market "to both the localizing and the transnational dimensions of cultural globalization, and explain(ing) how capitalism produces both modern forms of sex-cultural differentiation in some domains alongside convergence in others" (Jackson, 2009, p. 361). The political economy of sexuality regards capitalism as the engine of cultural globalization, and the analytic task of such an approach is to explain "how the market produces both new local forms of sexual difference and transnational commonalities" (Jackson, 2009, p. 361). Research on *tongzhi* subjectivity and subject formation from the political economy perspective contributes to scholarship on sexual citizenship by investigating queer subjectivity as mediated by global capitalism and the market economy. The concept of sexual citizenship branches off from a broader theorizing on citizenship. The broad conception of *citizenship* from which the concept of *sexual citizenship* emerged is focused on the definition of citizenship as the rights, entitlements, duties, and responsibilities of membership in a society. Scholars and activists define the concept of *sexual citizenship* as that which has vital material consequence to sexual minorities including but not limited to issues such as "access to government welfare benefits, taxation requirements, healthcare entitlements, immigration matters, and whether one can visit or make decisions regarding an ill partner in hospital" (Johnson & Mackie, 2020, p. 340). Theorizations on sexual citizenship entail discussions on the decriminalization of male homosexuality, recognition of same-sex relationships, fighting for same-sex marriage, same-sex family rights, access to adoption, surrogacy, and reproduction (Johnson & Mackie, 2020, p. 340). Using a political economy approach, research on PRC, Hong Kong, and Taiwan pink markets describe different accounts and weighings on the influence of the pink economy on local *tongzhi* subject formation and issues of sexual citizenship.

Tongzhi *Subject Formation in an Emerging PRC Market Economy.* Scholarship on the PRC pink market theorizes local *tongzhi* subject formation as being intimately related to the evolution of the market economy in China. Specifically, scholars who adopt a political economy approach in order to investigate the construction of *tongzhi* subjectivity in China frequently trace the history of PRC *tongzhi* consciousness to the reform era post 1978. While it is beyond the scope of this entry to provide a full account of the evolution of the market economy in China, it is necessary to provide some historical background as context for understanding how PRC *tongzhi* subjectivity is theorized as being intimately related to the emergence of the PRC market economy in current literature.

The PRC began as a planned economy following communist principles set by Mao Zedong. In December 1978, the general secretary of the Communist Party of China at the time, Deng Xiaoping, initiated the *Open Door Policy*. This policy manifested widespread societal reforms such as the creation of a market economy, internationalization, the enhancement of social mobility, and agricultural decollectivization. The discourse of "reform and opening up" is known locally as *gaige kaifang*, and the impetus of *gaige kaifang* is to "combine socialism with global capitalism in order to elevate China into an economic superpower on the world stage" (Ho, 2010, p. 1). *Kaifang* was considered an important sociopolitical-economic strategy as it is thought that "it is only by opening up that China can develop its economy and society, and thereby ensure its sovereignty and independence" (Ho, 2010, p. 7). In the reform period, it is thus observed that "the mode of citizenship changed from 'socialist' citizenship to 'market citizenship,' in which economic discourses...have all been emphasized" (Kong, 2011, p. 169).

The emergence of contemporary local urban *tongzhi* subjectivity and the PRC pink market is related to the reform era in several ways. First, the reform era saw a reduced significance of the *danwei* in everyday life. Second, the reform era provided opportunities for large-scale migration from rural to urban areas, thereby freeing many *tongzhi* from the scrutiny of family and kinship networks in their personal lives. Third, public discussions of sexuality were invigorated during this historical time due to the advancement of technologies such as the mobile phone, phone-in radio shows, telephone hotlines, Internet chat rooms, and online dating apps (Kong, 2011, p. 154), as well as a resurgence of gay-friendly Chinese-language literature (Ho, 2010, p. 4). In this sense, *gaige kaifang* "created a new social environment for young people in general, and gay men in particular, to engage in sexual and romantic interactions" (Kong, 2011, p. 6). In short, the reform era post 1978 not only introduced the market economy as the new economic structure but also resulted in new affordances for personal space and the exploration of sexuality. This change in the economic structure of society also led to observations of PRC gay identity becoming increasingly associated with consumption and material privileges since the 1980s (Chiang, 2019, p. 194).

Upon analyzing media reports on the PRC pink market, Huang and Wong (2019) trace a spike in corporate interest in that market to 2014. In August 2014, the first China Pink Market Conference was held in Shanghai. Jointly organized by market research company Community Marketing & Insights (CMI), local *tongzhi* organization and gay dating app Dan Lan/Blued, lesbian dating app the L (later renamed Rela), and 20 local LGBTQ corporate partners, the event was the first large-scale, highly visible effort by local and multinational corporations to target PRC *tongzhi* for profit. Prior to 2014, there was a dearth of statistics on LGBTQ population demographics and psychographics in China; there were no official estimates on how large the local LGBTQ population might be and what their consumption habits might be. It was thus significant that CMI unveiled the first-ever LGBTQ Consumer Lifestyle Survey during the 2014 China Pink Market Conference. During the conference, large-scale survey data on local *tongzhi* demographics, coming out percentages, and consumer habits were made freely available to the business community and the public. The market research data promised a large closeted consumer base that was cash-rich. With these financial projections in hand, businesses became more explicit and aggressive in their effort to encourage local *tongzhi* to come out as intelligible and identifiable queer consumers. In short, the phrase "more coming out, bigger market" (Yicai Net, 2015) epitomizes the profiteer perspective on the relationship between *tongzhi* subjectivity and the PRC pink market.

For-profit corporations are not the only institutions interested in the development of local *tongzhi* consciousness through pink market activities; local LGBTQ nongovernmental organizations (NGOs) joined the profit bandwagon and began encouraging individuals to come out as *tongzhi* and to participate as consumers in the vibrant pink market as well. A key reason for PRC LGBTQ NGO interest in the pink market is the reduction in foreign funding avenues for LGBTQ activism in recent years. During this same time period when large amounts of corporate funding were being directed to the PRC pink market, many *tongzhi* activists and local LGBTQ NGOs were, unfortunately, struggling to secure funding for everyday operations, in part due to increased scrutiny from the state with regards to Western funding sources (Bielinski, 2014). Witnessing the rise of a profitable pink market in China, LGBTQ activists and NGOs began to wade into the pink market to explore ways to translate their network and influence amongst local *tongzhi* and on social media platforms into economic capital. Commercial entities and LGBTQ NGOs are thus both major players in the PRC pink market and even cooperate with each other to monetize and profit from local *tongzhi* in various ways. The section "Self-Censorship in the PRC Pink Market" provides a discussion of some of the ways that local LGBTQ NGOs and pink businesses cooperate in the pink market in China and the issues that arise in the process.

Given the large geographical land mass that China occupies, it is important to highlight that the PRC pink market is concentrated only in specific locations and that the pink market is unevenly developed across China. *Tongzhi*-friendly/focused businesses and activities tend to be more concentrated in urban cities such as Beijing, Shanghai, Chengdu, and Guangzhou. There are also regional differences between the pink markets in each of these urban cities. Operators of gay and lesbian establishments in second-tier cities with large LGBT populations such as Chengdu, Chongqing, and Hangzhou report feeling "largely ignored by big companies," whom they perceive as being primarily focused on investing in the pink markets in Beijing and Shanghai (see e.g., Chen et al., 2019).

Conflicting Accounts of the Importance of the Pink Economy for Hong Kong Tongzhi Subject Formation. In contrast to China, where the market economy is a fairly recent structural change in society, the capitalist economic structure was instituted in Hong Kong and Taiwan at a much earlier time. At the time when China was rolling out *gaige kaifang* policies, Hong Kong and Taiwan already had highly developed capitalist market economies. In fact, both Hong Kong and Taiwan were known in the 1990s as part of the "Four Asian Tigers" because of their exceptionally high economic growth rates and urban industrialization.

While all observations of the Hong Kong pink market agree that the local pink economy is mature, vibrant, and well-developed, there are differing accounts as to when the Hong Kong pink market first bloomed. For example, Chou (2000) traces the uptick of the Hong Kong pink economy to the 1970s, where there was "an unprecedented opening" of gay venues such as discos, bars, steam baths, and karaoke clubs (p. 87). Chou (2000) argues that a new social class was emerging in Hong Kong in the 1970s. This new social class was a dual product of: (1) an expanding market economy where a rising middle class emerged and was eager to establish a "Westernized middle-class lifestyle"; and (2) an emerging identity consciousness, where Hong Kong individuals wished to distinguish themselves from the mainland Chinese (p. 85). The Hong Kong pink market began to blossom at this time in Hong Kong's economic history.

By Chou's (2000) account, the Hong Kong pink market was well-developed before the formation of a distinct *tongzhi* identity and consciousness. Chou (2000) traces Hong Kong *tongzhi* consciousness and activism to a critical incident in 1980, when a 29-year-old Scottish police inspector committed suicide in the territory when faced with impending homosexual charges. Also known as the MacLennan Incident of 1980, this incident triggered a discussion in Hong Kong about whether or not the territory should continue enforcing a law adopted from the British colonizers that criminalized private homosexual activity between consenting male adults. The recommendation to decriminalize male homosexuality stirred vigorous public debate about homosexuality and homosexual identity in Hong Kong. Key voices in the debate included public figures of the medical profession, the Hong Kong Chinese Christian churches, as well as prominent members of the public from the education, social services, manufacturing, and commerce sectors of society. During this time, a ground-up, *tongzhi* identity and consciousness began to spring forth: "It was the first time they (*tongzhi*) entered into the public area to define and construct their own subjectivity and identity. Groups were formed, and new identities, languages and alliances were generated" (Chou, 2000, p. 74).

In contrast, Kong (2011) traces the boom in *tongzhi* consumption venues and commercial entities in Hong Kong to a later time period, after 1991, when homosexuality was decriminalized in Hong Kong. Kong (2011) argues that strict political control by both the colonial and postcolonial administration led Hong Kong *tongzhi* to gradually divert their energies from political activism into the creation of a "substantial queer infrastructure of consumption venues" (p. 11). He describes *tongzhi* identities in Hong Kong as being constituted "more by conspicuous consumption rather than political activism" (p. 3). Kong's (2011) research on the Hong Kong pink market focuses on articulating the manners in which Hong Kong *tongzhi* subjectivity is classed and highly consumerist. The research problematizes the Hong Kong pink economy in terms of how the pink market provides a safe space for the construction of an indigenous Hong Kong *tongzhi* identity, yet, at the same time, encourages an exclusionary *tongzhi* subjectivity in a continually evolving, making and remaking of sexual citizenship.

Arguing Against the Centrality of the Pink Economy for Taiwan* Tongzhi *Subject Formation. As was the case with the literature on the Hong Kong pink market, there are differing accounts in the literature regarding when the Taiwan pink market bloomed as well. Some scholars trace the Taiwan pink market to the 1990s, while other accounts describe a vibrant pink market in Taiwan as early as the 1970s. Wong and Zhang (2000), for example, observe an increase in queer consumption venues and commodity options for the *tongzhi* community in Taiwan in the 1990s. *G&L Magazine* was launched in 1996, the first women-, feminist-, and lesbian-oriented bookstore Fembook established in 1994, and GinGin (the first LGBT "culture shop" in Taipei) was established in 1999. *G&L Magazine* is particularly significant for Taiwan *tongzhi* and is repeatedly featured in Taiwan pink market research by several different scholars. This was the first magazine published in the Chinese language to cater specifically to gay and lesbian Chinese in Hong Kong and Taiwan (Wong & Zhang, 2000). The mission of the magazine is to "give support and encouragement to gay and lesbian people and to promote the movement for equality in Hong Kong and Taiwan" (Wong & Zhang, 2000, p. 250). Following the success of emerging businesses in the pink market, established businesses such as Elite Bookstores, Books.com.tw and ETmall.com.tw jumped on the pink economy bandwagon quickly to promote themselves as being "gay-friendly" (Hsieh & Wu, 2011).

In contrast to Wong and Zhang's (2000) account, Chou (2000) traces the blossoming of the Taiwan pink market to an earlier time, the 1970s. In Chou's (2000) account, in the 1970s there were already multiple commercial queer spaces such as bars and coffeeshops where Taiwan *tongzhi* could network and socialize. Novels that featured *tongzhi* prominently were also widely sold at that time. Based on Chou's (2000) account, a vibrant pink market was already developing in Taiwan prior to the development of a distinct Taiwan *tongzhi* identity and voice.

Some scholarship on the Taiwan pink market argues that capitalism and queer consumption are not central drivers in the initial articulation of a distinct, identifiable *tongzhi* subjectivity amongst Taiwan LGBTQ. Rather, Taiwan *tongzhi* subjectivity and subject formation are described as contemporary developments that emerged from the political changes in Taiwan in the 1990s. While it is beyond the scope of this article to provide an in-depth account of the political history of Taiwan, a brief account is necessary for context.

Taiwan experienced martial rule under the Kuomintang administration. It was not until 1987 that martial law was waived. The lifting of martial law saw many changes in Taiwanese society, notably a "deep-rooted anger, discontent and tension" (Chou, 2000, p. 143) about what constituted unique Taiwanese identity and cultural heritage. It was during this time that Taiwan *tongzhi* emerged as a visible, identifiable identity and voice in the form of *tongzhi* activism:

> The emergence of Taiwan's *tongzhi* movement was effected and sheltered by the social outcry for human rights and social justice, hallmarked by the political movement of aboriginals, Taiwan independence activists, labor unions, environmentalists, the Hakka, political pluralists, and most important, the women's movement. (Chou, 2000, p. 143)

In addition to political change in society during that time period, *tongzhi* activism on college campuses, the wide availability of LGBTQ literature, and robust discussions about homosexuality in the media and online also contributed to the development of an indigenous Taiwan *tongzhi* identity in the 1990s (see, e.g., Erni & Spires, 2001, for a discussion).

Comparing the *tongzhi* communities across the three geographic locales—China, Hong Kong, and Taiwan—Chou (2000) stresses that *tongzhi* culture is different in Taiwan compared to Hong Kong and China. Specifically, unlike in China and Hong Kong where confrontational politics is generally eschewed by local *tongzhi* communities, Taiwan *tongzhi* subject formation is characterized by processes of "active intellectual theorization... aggressive political activism, strategic media manipulation, strong women's voices, prolific university activism and... an explosion and diversification of strategies of resistance" (Chou, 2000, p. 141). In this sense, unlike scholars writing about the Chinese pink economies in Hong Kong and the PRC, those writing about the Taiwan pink market do not give as much credit to the pink economy for developing a distinct local *tongzhi* consciousness and subjectivity.

To summarize, in contrast to the evolution of the market economy in the PRC, the market economy in Hong Kong and Taiwan matured much earlier. The different economic trajectories between the three geographic locales are reflected in the differing accounting and weighing of the centrality of the market economy for the formation of local *tongzhi* subjectivities. The section "Common Trajectories in Research on the Chinese Pink Markets" will discuss the commonalities and divergences in research on the PRC, Hong Kong and Taiwan pink markets.

COMMON TRAJECTORIES IN RESEARCH ON THE CHINESE PINK MARKETS

Chinese pink market research on the political economy of sexuality converges on the following issues. First, research on the PRC, Hong Kong, and Taiwan pink markets all argue against the global queering thesis. Second, Chinese pink market research explains the local cultural norms in terms of use of space and describes how the pink market exploits *tongzhi*'s need for safe queer space. Third, Chinese pink market research critiques *tongzhi* visibility in the pink market as exclusionary and marginalizing in terms of class, age, gender, and racial performance. Finally, Chinese pink market research on the political economy of sexuality critiques the monetization of queer affect, particularly in virtual platforms.

Against the Global Queering Thesis. Western scholarship that links capitalism to queer subject formation argues that globalization encourages the development of a "global gayness" in Asian countries. Studies on the Chinese pink markets collectively argue against adopting the global gay thesis to make sense of Chinese *tongzhi* subjectivity and subject formation. Specifically, studies on Chinese pink markets argue that Chinese *tongzhi* subjectivity is not evidence of global gayness but rather a unique hybrid of the local and the global (see, e.g., Rofel, 2007). Here, the global gayness/global queering thesis is first summarized, before arguments against the global queering thesis in Chinese pink market research are discussed.

Simply put, the "global gayness" thesis, or global queering thesis, argues that Asian gay subjectivity is a copy of Western gay subjectivity, a product of cultural assimilation in the global flow of capital and cultural products. The global gayness thesis argues that the world is seeing the development of a distinct global gay identity. For example, Altman (1997) argues that despite the variety of constructions of homosexuality in any one society/nation, "there has emerged (since the 1970s) a definable group of self-identified homosexuals...who see themselves as part of a global community whose commonalities override but do not deny those of race and nationality" (Altman, 1997, p. 424). He argues that with globalization, the flow of cultural products across borders from the West to the East sees much assimilation of Asian cultures to Western influence: "In a world where more and more cultural styles are imported and assimilated there seems no reason why a western-style gayness should not prove as attractive as other western identities" (Altman, 1997, p. 420). Therefore, Altman (1997) argues, "clearly, Asians who adopt les, bi and gay identities are conscious of and in part molded by these western examples" (p. 428). Along a similar vein of thought, Adam and colleagues (1999) argue that gay movements "follow more or less comparable paths, pass through the same phases, and draw names from other social and political movements with which there is some resemblance of ideology, goals, or methods of resistance" (pp. 369–370).

Contributions to the literature on the Chinese pink markets resoundingly reject the global queering thesis through their theorizations of local *tongzhi* subjectivity and subject formation. For example, drawing on the work of Lisa Rofel (2007), scholars such as Kong (2011), Wang (2019), and Wei (2006) argue that gay identity in China is "neither another exemplar of a global gay identity nor mere local particularity" (Rofel, 2007, p. 89). Eschewing a global queering perspective, research on the PRC pink market follows Rofel (2007) to argue that PRC *tongzhi* subject formation is a "search for postsocialist cosmopolitan humanity" (Rofel, 2007, p. 20) and that research on China *tongzhi* subjectivity is an investigation into *tongzhi* identities, communities, and consciousness-raising as new forms of neoliberal subjectification. For example, Wang (2019) argues that China gay identity "demonstrates dynamic processes of transcultural practices in which sex, desire, and sexual identities combine in the search for cultural belonging" (p. 7). Using an oral history approach to research on Chinese gay men, Kong (2011) articulates how contemporary Chinese gay male subjectivity in the PRC should be read as a process of transformation into a kind of a "new humanity" (Rofel, 2007, p. 1) in the 21st century, where China gay male subjects "tap into individuality, difference, sophistication, liberation and modernity" (Kong, 2011, p. 7). In short, capitalist market forces are theorized as important to the understanding of PRC *tongzhi* subject formation as "a social process of transcultural practices" (Rofel, 2007, p. 93).

In their articulation of the linguistic construction of *tongzhi* community in Taiwan and Hong Kong, Wong and Zhang (2000) also eschew the global queering thesis, stating that "narratives of 'global gayness' disregard the agency of gay and lesbian Asians in the development of sexuality-based social movements as well as the cultural production of different forms of 'gayness' in their respective countries" (p. 252). A primary objective of their essay is thus to challenge the global queering thesis by showing how *G&L Magazine* "adopts and reworks linguistic strategies associated with gay and lesbian cultures in the West, the feminist movement, Chinese revolutionist discourse, and the Chinese kinship system to create a space and a language of its own" (Wong & Zhang, 2000, p. 252). In short, a key argument that has been explored in Chinese pink market literature is the (ir)relevance of the global queering thesis for understanding *tongzhi* subjectivity in Hong Kong, Taiwan, and China.

Pink Market Exploitation of Tongzhi's Need for Safe Space. In Taiwan, Hong Kong, and the PRC, housing is in short supply and/or is prohibitively priced for young, adult *tongzhi*. Further, there is a cultural expectation that one would continue to live with one's family until marriage. Consequently, unmarried Chinese *tongzhi* find themselves living with their families. These cultural norms mean that Chinese *tongzhi* are surrounded by kin and neighbors in daily life. The lack of personal space and privacy to explore queer desires and friendships translates into a demand for safe queer space in the pink market, especially for Chinese *tongzhi* who are not out to their family in daily life. In short, Chinese *tongzhi* look to commercial offerings in the marketplace, outside of biogenetic family and kinship networks, in search of safe queer space, queer community, and access to queer imagination/imagery.

Places and events form the material bases of queer community. Commercial queer spaces afford opportunities to meet other queer people and be open in public as queer. For example, Chou (2000) highlights the importance of Lan Kwai Fong (LKF) for Hong Kong *tongzhi* subject formation, socialization, and belonging. LKF is a commercial area in the Central district in Hong Kong where establishments of nightlife such as bars and clubs are concentrated:

> A trip to LKF represented an escape to a "free world of gay paradise"... an imaginary space of otherness, a safe home for the sexual minority who may not be able to become gay without such a space. (Chou, 2000, p. 89)

In his historical account of commercial queer spaces, Chou (2000) traces the emergence of *tongzhi*-exclusive bars and discos in the PRC to the late 1990s. Chou (2000) observes a "very obvious trend" of new bars in urban PRC cities like Beijing, Shanghai, and Guangdong that were "started by *tongzhi* for *tongzhi*" in the late 1990s. Similar to how gay bars in LKF in Hong Kong were set up, many *tongzhi*-friendly bars in the PRC in the 1990s were centralized in areas of the city where there were many Caucasian customers. The PRC *tongzhi* bars, like that of the LKF gay bars, also often played English music and catered to an English-speaking, middle-class clientele that consisted predominantly of male *tongzhi*.

In contrast to these descriptions of gay nightlife in Hong Kong and Taiwan, Antonia Chao's (2001) description of Taiwan T bars (lesbian bars) is that the majority of them "retained (a) strong Japanese flavor" such as by "providing hostesses, encouraging heavy drinking, and, over the past two decades, singing karaoke" (p. 192). Using participant observation and in-depth interviews, Chao (2001) describes how T bars afford a safe space for the exploration and creation of T identity amongst Taiwan lesbians. In the process, Chao (2001) articulates the differences between T identity prior to the creation of T bars versus contemporary T identity after T bars became widely popular in Taiwan.

That *tongzhi*-friendly, *tongzhi*-exclusive, and/or *tongzhi*-targeting commercial nightspots are safe spaces for *tongzhi* subject formation must be qualified with the caveat that becoming an identifiably *tongzhi*-friendly space comes at a cost to business operators. For example, Wei's (2006) study of gay culture in Chengdu suggests that in the PRC, homophobic policing of urban queer spaces is not an infrequent occurrence:

> Although there has never been any law against homosexuality or homosexual behaviors in the legal codes of communist China, gay men were often harassed and detained, and sometimes arrested and jailed, albeit usually briefly, under the charge of hooliganism by participants in mass, Party-mobilized campaigns, by the police, or by the relevant work unit. Harassment did not always affect the daily lives of those targeted, but some gay men lost jobs and had to worry (about a) record of detention. (Wei, 2006, p. 100)

One of the ways that PRC *tongzhi* businesses survive homophobic policing and state interference is by negotiating and collaborating with the state on LGBTQ events and activities. For example, Variation, a gay bar in Chengdu, participated in the China U.K. AIDS Prevention and Care Project that was managed by the Sichuan provincial government so as to free their bar from police harassment (Wei, 2006, p. 107). The pressure on *tongzhi* businesses to collaborate with the state to ensure interference-free pink market engagements brings its own problems and research questions. These problems and research questions are explored in the section "Self Censorship in the PRC Pink Market."

The search for safe queer space in the pink market opens the *tongzhi* community to monetary exploitation. For example, Variation is known to charge drinks at a rate of 5 to 10 times the retail price, thereby exploiting the need amongst gay *tongzhi* to have their own social space protected from official and unofficial interference (Wei, 2006). The provision of queer space by the pink market thus functions as a double-edged sword, offering both unique opportunities and unique challenges for *tongzhi*. What started as serving the basic needs of the *tongzhi* community for safety, security, and privacy, sometimes morphs into discriminatory pricing. The section "Critiquing Class-Based *Tongzhi* Visibility in the Chinese Pink Market" further elaborates on how the commodification of queer space in the pink market functions as a double-edged sword, namely in the affordances that it provides for enhancing *tongzhi* visibility while at the same time encouraging exclusionary practices that promote a particular class-based *tongzhi* identity.

Critiquing Class-Based* Tongzhi *Visibility in the Chinese Pink Market. Social visibility is important for LGBTQ communities. Visibility is important for LGBTQ identity affirmation and serves as the foundation for the fight for LGBTQ rights. Amongst PRC *tongzhi*, visibility is about "going public" (*gongkai*) in public spaces. *Going public* is not the same as what is understood in the West as coming out. The notion of "going public" amongst PRC *tongzhi* is focused on "participating in public gay scenes, developing gay social networks, and committing to a gay lifestyle" (Wei, 2006, p. 17). In other words, going public is about being visible in public spaces as *tongzhi*. In that sense, consumption venues specifically targeted at Chinese gays, such as teahouses, bathhouses, bars, and health clubs, are important for the development of local gay identity and consciousness, as these are relatively safe locations for going public.

A critique of queer consumption is that capitalism is "a double-edged sword where queer subjects are 'welcome to be visible as consumer subjects but not as social subjects'" (Hennessy, 2000, p. 192). In the PRC, the dominant marketeer narrative of the pink market is that market economy is a path of progress for local *tongzhi* politics as it offers "basic visibility" (Erni & Spires, 2001, p. 31) for local *tongzhi*. For example, in 2015, during the Rainbow Love online wedding competition in the PRC, Geng Le, one of the primary organizers of the Rainbow Love wedding competition, suggests that the gains from queer coming out in Rainbow Love would outweigh any potential economic exploitation:

> There have been arguments about whether companies use LGBT marketing as a gimmick...but whatever their purposes are, they're making LGBT people more visible. It's a good thing, and the impact of the economy as the force of social progress is beyond our imagination. (Fullerton, 2017)

Huang and Wong (2019) critique this dominant narrative that the PRC pink market is *the* path for political progress for PRC *tongzhi*. Employing critical rhetorical analysis to analyze the marketing materials used in the Rainbow Love online wedding competition, Huang and Wong (2019) argue that the Chinese pink market encourages a display of particular types of queer subjectivity for mass consumption—one that is associated with visibility, mobility, and luxury consumption:

> If Rainbow Love is a marketing campaign, then the product or commodity being marketed is this particular version of queerness—Chinese queer bodies living a classed, consumerist lifestyle, enjoying political freedom elsewhere as a sign of one's "social progress." In this case, the commodity that is being sold to the masses is not an object or a body but a *narrative commodity*—a particular queer imaginary... Queer subjectivity is a commodity that is produced *for* Chinese queers through creating a desirable subjectivity *in* Chinese queers. (Huang & Wong, 2019, pp. 293, 296, emphasis in original)

Another critique of queer visibility in the Chinese pink market has to do with its overwhelming focus on catering to the needs of the gay population to the exclusion of other sexual minorities from being welcomed and included in the booming pink economy. For example, there have been observations that the PRC pink market leans heavily gay-centric (Wang, 2020a, 2020b) and some scholars have wondered where the lesbians are in the pink market. Chou (2000) observed the invisibility of lesbian groups and lesbian *tongzhi* in the Hong Kong *tongzhi* scene as well. Chou (2000) writes that most Hong Kong *tongzhi* groups have very few lesbians, and many *tongzhi* gatherings focus on male-specific issues such as the decriminalization of anal penetration, cruising, and sauna culture. Further, Chou (2000) presents interview data from female *tongzhi* who described her experience of being rejected from entering a *tongzhi* bar because she was not a man: "Gay power only means gay male power" (p. 93). Similarly, in their study of Taiwan gay male identity development, Hsieh and Wu (2011) also observe that prior research on Asian homosexuality have typically focused on gay men, while research on lesbians, particularly as consumers, is relatively scarce. They identify some key obstacles in collecting data about Taiwanese lesbians:

> Taiwanese lesbians...struggle with gender repositioning and traditional social orders such as male dominance, gender roles, and family values...Although traces of their voices and activities can be found on various publications, conferences, and street demonstrations (parades) from time to time, these activities and outlets remain dominated by the interests and needs of gay men. Second, the sexual orientation and homoerotic feelings of Taiwanese lesbians tend to be either suppressed under a patriarchal ideology or overshadowed by a legitimating sense of sisterhood...Moreover, lesbians in Taiwan are subjected to multiple social taboos that prohibit them from asserting their self-identity. Consequently, the lack of a self-identity makes it especially challenging to identify and recruit informants. (Hsieh & Wu, 2011, p. 397)

Given the context just described, locating Chinese lesbians in the pink market will be a fruitful area of future research and exploration.

A Classed and Raced* Tongzhi *Subjectivity in the Pink Market. The argument that the Chinese pink market affords safe space and is welcoming for *tongzhi* subject formation and networking is countered by observations in Hong Kong that commercial queer spaces are partial to individuals of a particular class and particular racial performance. For example, writing on Hong Kong *tongzhi* subjectivity and subject formation, Chou (2000) observes that *tongzhi* culture in Hong Kong is classed and raced. In terms of racial performance, English is a crucial cultural marker for local *tongzhi* in Hong Kong (Chou, 2000, p. 91). Hong Kong *tongzhi* gay venues tend to have only English names, with no Chinese names. In addition, most local *tongzhi* organizations use only their English names even if they had Chinese names, and very few local Chinese male *tongzhi* would use their Chinese names when socializing in *tongzhi* circles (Chou, 2000, p. 85). Chou (2000) interprets these racial performances in Hong Kong *tongzhi* culture as a result of the long history of British colonization of Hong Kong:

> Western names and images stand for high-class culture, taste, modernity, sexual liberality and trendiness... what is consumed in these *tongzhi* venues is not just a space for same-sex pleasure but appeals to a very specific racial, class and cultural imagery—to be white, Westernized, modern, classy, stylish and young is what the Hong Kong gay image is about. (Chou, 2000, p. 87)

The reinforcement of such raced *tongzhi* subjectivity in the pink market results in the marginalization of working-class and older *tongzhi* in Hong Kong who either do not speak English and/or have limited use of the English language. Working-class and older *tongzhi* report feeling out of place and excluded from the English-centric *tongzhi* commercial scene. Their feelings of marginalization are compounded by class-based exclusion in the pink market:

> There is a strong "we versus they dichotomy" in LKF: to be in, you must wear the right clothes, have the right look, acquire cosmopolitan knowledge, speak a certain level of English and have a minimal sensitivity to cultural and sexual diversity. (Chou, 2000, p. 92)

In addition to race and class, age is also a factor of discrimination in the Hong Kong pink market. Chou (2000) compares his analysis of Hong Kong *tongzhi* culture to that of Taiwan *tongzhi* culture: "Unlike the Taiwan *tongzhi* scene, which at least has several *tongzhi* bars for middle-aged people, the Hong Kong *tongzhi* scene seems to exhibit a strong fetishism for youth and beauty" (p. 94). Given the above cross-geographic observations, it may thus be argued that the pink markets in Hong Kong, Taiwan, and China each have a unique *tongzhi* culture and flavor even though they share many similarities. It thus follows that there are not only multiple Chinese pink markets but also multiple *tongzhi* cultures.

Different *tongzhi* cultures across the Chinese pink markets lead to different arguments on the centrality of class-based queer consumption in *tongzhi* subject formation. Some scholars writing on the Taiwan pink market, for instance, do not agree that a class-based analysis of queer consumption is an important research trajectory. They argue instead that family challenges faced by Taiwan *tongzhi* are more important for understanding queer consumption. Erni and Spires (2001), for example, resist a class-based analysis of queer consumption culture in Taiwan. They argue that "queer consumerism in G&L (and other similar cultural products) must be seen as something that is situated between the market and the national imagination of traditional family morality" (p. 40). In particular, they argue that:

> Analyses of queer consumerism assume interdependence between queer identity and class experience or consciousness, thus contributing to an underestimation of other forms of social and ideological positioning for queers... We shall suggest that G&L evinces not a class politics, but family politics, that underwrites queer consumption of popular culture in Taiwan. (p. 27)

The Monetization of Queer Affect in Digital Platforms. Queer affect is an important aspect of research at the intersection of consumerism and queer desire. For example, Erni and Spires (2001) report that queer consumer products such as the Taiwan-published *G&L Magazine* promote "a strong collective social desire for affirmation through the promotion of what can be called Chinese 'queer affect' (*tongzhi de qinggan*)" (p. 31). They argue that queer consumption products, spaces, and services build "communities of desire" (Erni & Spires, 2001) through shared emotional experiences.

With the increasing popularity of social media and dating apps, literature on the monetization of queer affect has recently moved beyond a focus on traditional media to include research on digital platforms. For example, in his analysis of the China-founded gay dating app Blued, Wang (2019) examines the circulation of affective signs and affective capacities in Blued live streaming. Using participant observation of publicly available live streamlining events and in-depth interviews with gay streamers, and viewers, Wang (2019) examines "how same-sex affective encounters are experienced, circulated and monetized on Blued live streaming... (so as to articulate) how affective encounters and economic factors combine to shape sexual normativity in China" (p. 87). Further, in a separate essay, Wang (2020a) describes how sexually affective data flows in Blued (e.g., virtual gifting, following, liking, commenting, and sharing produced by gay live streamers) are used as corporate assets by the company to attract venture capital. Wang's (2020a) analysis reveals Blued's exploitation of its *tongzhi* users by transforming users into performative laborers and transforming their activities into tradeable data flows. Wang (2020b) thus argues that "the monetization of gay dating apps has... expanded into a large spectrum of affective needs... (and) the monetization of affective needs requires further critical attention, for it produces subtle tensions related to different forms of sexual normativity" (p. 15). In his dissertation study, Zhou (2020) conducts interviews and digital ethnography to investigate same-sex desires and perceptions of ideal gayness in China as mediated by the interrelationship between transnational queer media, queer businesses, and activism. The project reveals how queer transnationalism has created new sexual norms and how new divisions and sexual hierarchies are created amongst queer men in China based on modes of identification, body types, sexual labels and embodied masculinities, race and ethnicity, and class. Given the importance of digital queer spaces for contemporary *tongzhi* communities, the digital Chinese pink market will continue to be a productive site for future research on *tongzhi* subjectivity and subject formation.

SELF-CENSORSHIP IN THE PRC PINK MARKET

A unique question debated only in PRC pink market research and not Hong Kong or Taiwan pink market research is to what degree LGBTQ NGOs operating in the pink market should cooperate with the state. As discussed earlier, a unique situation in the PRC pink market is that LGBTQ NGOs have entered into the market as profiteers so as to fund the activities and programs that serve local *tongzhi* communities. The cooperation between *tongzhi* activists and pink business in the pink market is further complicated by the phenomena where *tongzhi* businesses themselves get organized and start LGBTQ NGOs in order to protect their business interest. For example, the owners of the Chengdu gay bar Variation, discussed earlier, founded a local NGO called the Chengdu Gay Care Organization (CGCO) as part of their collaboration with the state to help the state address HIV prevention among the urban gay population. Assisting the state's effort for HIV prevention was Variation's way of overcoming homophobic policing and interference in their everyday business. In fact, most of the first founders of CGCO were either owners of local gay bars or working for the local gay bars (Wei, 2006, p. 188). From the perspective of these gay business owners, they were interested in developing a cooperative relationship with the government in the form of setting up an LGBTQ NGO, as they expected that such a relationship with the state would not only facilitate their quest for legitimacy but also likely benefit their business interests (Chiang, 2019, p. 189).

However, the intertwining of business financial stakes and *tongzhi* activism has led to unhappiness and questions as to whether such close collaboration between commercial enterprise, *tongzhi* activism, and the state is helping or exploiting *tongzhi* communities. For example, Miao and Chan (2020) critique that such close relationships between the PRC state and pink businesses that are also LGBTQ organizations lead to self-censorship and depoliticization of LGBTQ events. In their case study of Blued, the largest gay social dating app in China, Miao and Chan (2020) describe its evolution from an organization that actively promoted gay rights to a business organization that banned the word *tongzhi* from appearing in its promotional materials. In recent years, Blued has also begun deliberately keeping a distance from the more vocal activist organizations that champion for LGBTQ rights. Geng Le, the founder of Blued and Danlan, explains the mellowing of his advocacy for PRC *tongzhi* rights in recent years in this manner:

> We need an angle from which the government notices our existence and supports us. If you talk about equality and rights for homosexual people, the government won't be happy; if you tell the government that you can help with HIV/AIDS prevention, the government will be very happy. (Zuo, 2016, as cited in Miao & Chan, 2020, p. 4)

This is in contrast to an interview that Geng gave in June 2015 to *Gay Star News* on his advocacy for gay marriage and *tongzhi* rights in China in his capacity as the founder of Blued and Danlan:

> There are three aspects to this... Number one, to present to the audience back in China—straight people, gay people, whatever—to show them what it's like in other places in the world: This is what is allowed in America; there's nothing wrong with it; and we should start making steps (towards) this level of freedom ourselves... The second aspect would be directly to the gay community in China, to give them hope for the future and say: this is what can happen when you really love someone; don't give up hope, don't be sad—keep on fighting for it. (Hudson, 2015)

In their analysis of the marketing materials of the Rainbow Love online wedding competition, Huang and Wong (2019) articulate the rhetorical mechanisms used in the depoliticization of queerness in PRC pink marketing. In their essay, Huang and Wong (2019) argue that the progress narrative touted by profiteers of the PRC pink market functions by conceptually conflating the *politics of visibility* with the *economies of visibility*. The politics of visibility refers to practices of queer visibility that work to promote political change, while the economies of visibility focuses on the visibility of queer identities as ends unto themselves (Banet-Weiser, 2015). In their analysis of the Rainbow Love marketing materials, Huang and Wong (2019) argue that the PRC pink market manifests an economy of visibility by appropriating discourses that promote a politics of visibility while depoliticizing Rainbow Love's queerness. Research that continues to interrogate the exploitation versus benefits for the *tongzhi* community resulting from close cooperation between pink businesses, LGBTQ activism, and the state will be a fruitful area of study.

FUTURE DIRECTIONS AND METHODOLOGICAL CONSIDERATIONS

This article describes the genealogy of theorizing as well as the commonalities and divergences in literature on the Chinese pink market. The article also demonstrates how, by adopting the political economy approach, Chinese pink market research articulated the ways in which the interrelationship between political, economic, and cultural structures afforded opportunities for the development of unique *tongzhi* consciousness. At the same time, adopting a political economy perspective in research design reveals the Chinese pink markets as exploitative, exclusionary, and marginalizing sites of overarching consumption. In short, extant research reveals the neoliberal capitalist techniques of homonormativity in the pink economies of China, Taiwan, and Hong Kong, especially that which targets urban Chinese middle-class queers. This section offers some directions for future research and the concomitant methodological considerations.

In the introduction to her essay on the HIV/AIDS economy in China, Ye (2021) astutely observes that Chinese/Sinophone queer studies that interrogate the "political economy of homonormativity" has "predominantly focused on marketized subjectivity and identity… [and] on middle-class consumerist queer space such as queer clubs, queer media and online culture" (p. 4). Ye (2021) argues that "the asymmetrical emphasis on the exceptional urban middle-class practices overlooks how homonormativity is reproduced through lived experiences of the ordinary everyday life and labour under uneven and spatially specific condition of neoliberalism" (pp. 3–4).

Thinking with Ye (2021), a productive direction for future research on the Chinese pink markets is to (re)conceptualize the pink economy as a site of both production and consumption that sees *tongzhi*/queer subjects not merely as consumers but also as labor in the pink economy. An example of such research is Tian's (2020) essay that employs a queer Marxist intervention to analyze discourse (1) in the hiring of queer subjects at the China LGBT Talent Job Fair and (2) of the online group "Queer Workers" to highlight how working-class and migrant queers conceive of the impact of transnational capital on their lives. Another example is Miao and Chan's (2021) study that takes a "production-side approach" to examine the politics of sexuality and professionalism in Blued. Queer subjects should not be limited/reduced to consumers; rather, they are also producers/labors in the Chinese pink markets. Therefore, more research is needed to investigate and reveal the complex roles of queer subjects and their articulation into the Chinese pink markets.

Finally, as discussed throughout the article, the focus of extant scholarship on the Chinese pink market is overwhelmingly on the urban upper/middle-class Chinese male gay consumer. A key methodological consideration for future research is to take an intersectional approach in research design and analysis to investigate PRC, Hong Kong, and Taiwan queers at the intersection of age, race, class, gender, and ability. Specifically, it is important to highlight that there are many minoritized populations in Chinese-majority socieities. For example, there are 56 non-Han ethnic groups in China and 16 non-Han ethnic groups in Taiwan. There is also a significant South Asian and Southeast Asian population in Hong Kong. In contrast, current research predominantly centers on the Han Chinese, making other ethnic populations in Sinophone societies invisible. Therefore, in pursuing research on queer subjects in the Chinese pink markets, an intersectional approach towards investigating the political economy of sexuality is critical.

FURTHER READING

Chan, L. S. (2021). *The politics of dating apps: Gender, sexuality, and emergent publics in urban China*. MIT Press.
Chen, Y.-C. (2016). Queering women in Taiwan. *American Journal of Chinese Studies, 23*(2), 239–256. https://www.jstor.org/stable/44289157
Chou, W.-S. (2000). *Tongzhi: Politics of same-sex eroticism in Chinese societies*. Haworth Press.
D'Emilio, J. (1983). Capitalism and gay identity. In A. B. Snitow, C. Stansell, & S. Thompson (Eds.), *Powers of desire: The politics of sexuality* (pp. 100–113). Monthly Review Press.
Engebretsen, E. L., & Schroeder, W. F. (Eds). (2015). *Queer/tongzhi China: New perspectives on research, activism and media cultures*. NIAS Press.
Hennessy, R. (1995). Queer visibility in commodity culture. In L. Nicholson & S. Seidman (Eds.), *Social postmodernism: Beyond identity politics* (pp. 142–183). Cambridge University Press.
Hennessy, R. (2000). *Profit and pleasure: Sexual identities in late capitalism*. Routledge.
Jackson, P. (2009). Capitalism and global queering: National markets, parallels among sexual cultures and multiple queer modernities. *GLQ: A Journal of Lesbian and Gay Studies, 15*(3), 357–395. https://doi.org/10.1215/10642684-2008-029
Kong, T. S. K. (2011). *Chinese male homosexualities: Memba, tongzhi and golden boy*. Routledge.
Rofel, L. (2007). *Desiring China: Experiments in neoliberalism, sexuality, and public culture*. Duke University Press.
Wang, S. (2020a). Chinese affective platform economies: Dating, live streaming, and performative labor on Blued. *Media, Culture & Society, 42*(4), 502–520. https://doi.org/10.1177/0163443719867283
Wang, S. (2020b). Live streaming, intimate situations, and the circulation of same-sex affect: Monetizing affective encounters on Blued. *Sexualities, 23*(5–6), 934–950. https://doi.org/10.1177/1363460719872724
Wong, A., & Zhang, Q. (2000). The linguistic construction of the Tóngzhì community. *Journal of Linguistic Anthropology, 10*(2), 248–278. https://doi.org/10.1525/jlin.2000.10.2.248
Yue, A. (2016). Queer migration: Going south from China to Australia. In G. Brown & K. Browne (Eds.), *The Routledge research companion to geographies of sex and sexualities* (pp. 213–220). Routledge.

REFERENCES

Adam, B. D., Duyvendak, J. W., & Krouwel, A. (1999). *The global emergence of gay and lesbian politics: National imprints of a worldwide movement*. Temple University Press.
Altman, D. (1997). Global gaze/global gays. *GLQ: A Journal of Lesbian & Gay Studies, 3*(4), 417–436. https://doi.org/10.1215/10642684-3-4-417

Altman, D. (2001). *Global sex*. University of Chicago Press.
Banet-Weiser, S. (2015). Keynote address: Media, markets, gender: Economies of visibility in a neoliberal moment. *The Communication Review*, 18(1), 53–70. https://doi.org/10.1080/10714421.2015.996398
Bielinski, S. P. (2014, October 7). A rising tide: Pink social responsibility means business. *WorkforLGBT*.
Chao, A. (2001). Drink, stories, penis, and Breasts: Lesbian tomboys in Taiwan from the 1960s to the 1990s. *Journal of Homosexuality*, 40(3–4), 185–209. https://doi.org/10.1300/J082v40n03_10
Chen, S., Miao, H., Huang, Z., & Li, D. (2019, June 18). A $300 billion rainbow economy is booming in the middle of China. *Bloomberg News*. https://www.bloomberg.com/news/articles/2019-06-18/chengdu-is-tapping-into-china-s-300-billion-rainbow-economy
Chen, Y.-C. (2016). Queering women in Taiwan. *American Journal of Chinese Studies*, 23(2), 239–256. https://www.jstor.org/stable/44289157
Chiang, H. (2019). Gay and lesbian communities in urban China. In R. Yep, J. Wang, & T. Johnson (Eds.), *Handbook on urban development in China* (pp. 187–201). Edward Elgar Publishing.
Chou, W.-S. (2000). *Tongzhi: Politics of same-sex eroticism in Chinese societies*. Haworth Press.
D'Emilio, J. (1998). *Sexual politics, sexual communities: The making of a homosexual minority in the United States, 1940–1970* (2nd ed.). University of Chicago Press.
Doland, A. (2014, August 22). LGBT marketing comes to China. *AdAge*. https://adage.com/article/global-news/lgbt-marketing-china-starting/294645
Erni, J. N., & Spires, A. J. (2001). Glossy subjects: *G&L* magazine and "tongzhi" cultural visibility in Taiwan. *Sexualities*, 4(1), 25–49. https://doi.org/10.1177/136346001004001002
Fullerton, J. (2017, January 4). The pink yuan: How Chinese business is embracing the LGBT market. *The Guardian*. https://www.theguardian.com/sustainable-business/2017/jan/05/the-pink-yuan-how-chinese-business-is-embracing-the-lgbt-market
Hennessy, R. (1995). Queer visibility in commodity culture. In L. Nicholson & S. Seidman (Eds.), *Social postmodernism: Beyond identity politics* (pp. 142–183). Cambridge University Press.
Hennessy, R. (2000). *Profit and pleasure: Sexual identities in late capitalism*. Routledge.
Ho, L. W. W. (2010). *Gay and lesbian subculture in urban China*. Routledge Contemporary China Series.
Hsieh, M. H., & Wu, S. L. (2011). Gay men's identity attempt pathway and its implication on consumption. *Psychology & Marketing*, 28(4), 388–416. https://doi.org/10.1002/mar.20394
Huang, S., & Wong, T. S.-T. (2019). "More coming out, bigger market": Queer visibility and queer subjectivity in the Chinese pink market. *Queer Studies in Media & Popular Culture*, 4(3), 287–302. https://doi.org/10.1386/qsmpc_00013_1
Hudson, D. (2015, June 9). Meet the businessman flying Chinese gay couples to the US to get married. *Gay Star News*. https://www.gaystarnews.com/article/meet-businessman-flying-chinese-gay-couples-us-get-married-today090615/
Jackson, P. (2009). Capitalism and global queering: National markets, parallels among sexual cultures and mutiple queer modernities. *GLQ: A Journal of Lesbian and Gay Studies*, 15(3), 357–395. https://doi.org/10.1215/10642684-2008-029
Johnson, C., & Mackie, V. (2020). Sexual citizenship in comparative perspective. In N. A. Naples (Ed.), *Companion to sexuality studies* (pp. 337–356). Wiley Blackwell.
Juan, S. (2016, December 1). LGBT market grows. *China Daily Global Edition (USA)*. https://www.pressreader.com/usa/china-dailyusa/20161201/281706909295024
Kong, T. S. K. (2011). *Chinese male homosexualities: Memba, tongzhi and golden boy*. Routledge.
Miao, W., & Chan, L. S. (2020). Social constructivist account of the world's largest gay social app: Case study of Blued in China. *The Information Society*, 36(4), 214–225. https://doi.org/10.1080/01972243.2020.1762271

Miao, W., & Chan, L. S. (2021). Between sexuality and professionalism: Experiences of gay workers at Blued, a Chinese gay social app company. *New Media & Society*, 23(7), 1882–1898. https://doi.org/10.1177/1461444820920876

Rofel, L. (2007). *Desiring China: Experiments in neoliberalism, sexuality, and public culture*. Duke University Press.

Tian, I. L. (2020). Perverse politics, postsocialist radicality: Queer Marxism in China. *QED: A Journal in GLBTQ Worldmaking*, 7(2), 48–68. https://www.muse.jhu.edu/article/773399

Wakefield, L. (2020, February 21). China now has the biggest LGBT economy in the world, but still no same-sex marriage. *PinkNews*. https://www.pinknews.co.uk/2020/02/21/lgbt-economy-world-china-same-sex-marriage-rights-conversion-therapy-alibaba-pink-yuan/

Wang, H. (2015, February 1). Zhongguo tongxinglian jingji quan: Yifen chugui, yifen shichang (Homosexual economy in China: more coming out, bigger market). *Yicai Net*. https://www.yicai.com/news/4570620.html

Wang, S. (2019). *Living with censorship: The political economy and cultural politics of Chinese gay dating apps* [Doctoral dissertation, University of Amsterdam]. University of Amsterdam, Digital Academic Repository. https://hdl.handle.net/11245.1/553a17f6-7c90-48ac-b3be-a7fd82d6670a

Wang, S. (2020a). Chinese affective platform economies: Dating, live streaming, and performative labor on Blued. *Media, Culture & Society*, 42(4), 502–520. https://doi.org/10.1177/0163443719867283

Wang, S. (2020b). Live streaming, intimate situations, and the circulation of same-sex affect: Monetizing affective encounters on Blued. *Sexualities*, 23(5–6), 934–950. https://doi.org/10.1177/1363460719872724

Wei, W. (2006). *Going public: The production and transformation of queer spaces in postsocialist Chengdu, China* [Doctoral dissertation, Loyola University, Chicago]. Publication No. 3229807. ProQuest Dissertations.

Wong, A., & Zhang, Q. (2000). The linguistic construction of the tóngzhì community. *Journal of Linguistic Anthropology*, 10(2), 248–278. https://doi.org/10.1525/jlin.2000.10.2.248

Ye, S. (2021). "Paris" and "scar": Queer social reproduction, homonormative division of labour and HIV/AIDS economy in postsocialist China. *Gender, Place & Culture*, 28(22). https://doi.org/10.1080/0966369X.2021.1873742

Yicai Net. (2015, February 1). Zhongguo tongxinglian jingji quan: Yifen chugui, yifen shichang (Homosexual economy in China: more coming out, bigger market). Retrieved from Yicai, https://www.yicai.com/news/4570620.html

Zhou, Z. B. (2020). *Homonormative desires: Identities, masculinities, and sexual hierarchies in urban China* [Doctoral dissertation, Northwestern University]. Publication No. 28148925. ProQuest Dissertations.

Zuo, H. (2016). Geng Le: Zhitong, daohe (Geng Le: Congruence in spirit, congruence in path). Retrieved from ifanr, https://www.ifanr.com/707055

Terrie Siang-Ting Wong

CULTURAL PRODUCTIONS OF QUEER ASIA

INTRODUCTION

The term *Queer Asia* is a nonnormative border-crossing geopolitical label, strategically representing multiple axes of differences (i.e., sexuality, gender, race, ethnicity, class, nationality, language, coloniality, and the body; see Eguchi, 2021; Luther & Ung Loh, 2019; Martin et al.,

2008). Queer Asia responds to how the contemporary logic of capitalism enables global and transcultural formations of queer identities, discourses, and politics originating from Western national cultures, such as Australia, the United Kingdom, and the United States (see Chiang & Wong, 2016; Suganuma, 2012; Yu, 2020; Yue, 2012). The contemporary realities of globalization that normalize the Western political economy of liberal capitalism enable a paradoxically contested space of temporality where the cultural productions of Queer Asia are performed, represented, and materialized in and across Asia and Asian diasporas (Yue & Leung, 2017).

Accordingly, Queer Asia introduces alternative possibilities that trouble, remix, and remap how the logic of Whiteness that operates as a colonial, imperial, and capitalist power homogenizes culturally heterogenous paradigms of minoritized sexualities and genders through LGBTQIA+ identities, discourses, and politics (Eguchi, 2021). Hence, Queer Asia, which questions and critiques the multidimensional flows of power (e.g., globalization, market capitalism, state capitalism, and/or Western queer formation), is a process of reimagining historically specific and culturally saturated nuances of minoritized sexualities and genders (see Chiang & Wong, 2016, 2017; Yu, 2020). Still, Queer Asia is a fluid, multiple, and dynamic concept in and across social, political, economic, and historical contexts (Chiang & Wong, 2017). There is no unified, stable, and singular notion of knowing, being, and acting that regulates the cultural productions of Queer Asia. In the words of Yue (2017), Queer Asia not only challenges the settler-colonialist logics of Whiteness as an imperial and capitalist power, but also serves as an alternative reference point for reimagining geopolitical modernities of minoritized sexualities and genders.

Ongoing discussions of Queer Asia are happening in interdisciplinary venues, such as *Inter-Asia Cultural Studies* (see Mitsuhashi, 2006; Yue, 2017), *Gender, Place and Culture: A Journal of Feminist Geography* (see Chiang & Wong, 2016), and *Culture, Theory, & Critique* (see Chiang & Wong, 2017). However, Queer Asia is a great interest of communication scholars who work on queer studies. By presenting quantitative data on publication and citation rates and editorial positions, Chakravartty et al. (2018) called out how non-White scholars are underrepresented in communication in the prominent journal, *Journal of Communication*. Ng et al. (2020) edited a special issue of #Communicationsowhite, published from *Communication, Culture, and Critique*, that provided further evidence of this unfortunate situation. Scholars like Calvente et al. (2020), Chakravartty and Jackson (2020), Flores and Gomez (2020), and McCann et al. (2020), who were featured in Nakayama's (2020) special forum on Whiteness and communication in *Communication and Critical/Cultural Studies*, also showcased everyday operations of Whiteness in and across communication. However, this criticism is not unique to queer studies in communication. Originating from White, Western intellectualism, the paradigm of queer studies is undeniably White and Western. Hence, scholars like Alexander (2008), Boylorn and Adam (2016), Chávez (2013a), Eguchi and Asante (2016), Eguchi and Calafell (2020), Johnson (2001), Lee (2003), Nakayama (1994), and Yep (2013) argue that queer studies in communication must attend to historically nuanced issues and concerns of non-White, non-Western minoritized sexualities and genders. Because of these interventions, transnational/global queer-of-color studies are gaining visibility. On this basis, the cultural productions of Queer Asia that examine new geopolitical modernities provide alternative possibilities in expanding the circumferences of queer studies in communication (Eguchi, 2021).

Hence, this article focuses on the possibilities of Queer Asia. To do so, the article first contextualizes the contemporary realities of globalization that circulate the White, Western, and U.S.-American queer paradigm as the transnational/global standard. Then, the article examines an idea that scholars like Yu (2020), Yue (2017), and Yue and Leung (2017) have proposed: the cultural productions of Queer Asia are disjunctive modernities. By this means, contemporary global capitalism enables a paradoxically contested space of temporality through which new geopolitical imaginaries of minoritized sexualities and genders can emerge. This reexamination of Queer Asia as disjunctive modernities is organized into three sections: "Identifications and Affinities," "Relationalities and Spatialities," and "Media and Popular Culture." Here, it is noteworthy to mention that scholars who argue for the cultural productions of Queer Asia as disjunctive modernities are inspired by inter-Asia cultural studies scholars Yoshimi (2005) and Chen (2010)'s proposal for Asia as method. Their intellectual and political proposal is to centralize Asia in order to engage in the reconceptualization of Asia by decolonizing and deimperializing the Western(ized) consequences of Asia. At the same time, the article draws on the work of scholars like Yu (2020), Yue (2017), and Yue and Leung (2017), who argue for both *queer* and *Asia*. The article highlights how *queer* is a verb or practice that offers alternative moments of minoritized sexual and gender transgression against the localized logics of cis-heterosexism in and across Asia. In so doing, the article aims to offer an additional reference point for promote the historically specific and culturally saturated developments of transnational/global queer-of-color studies in communication.

Before exemplifying possibilities of Queer Asia, it is important to acknowledge the limitation of this article's geographic assumptions and representations up front. Asia is a massive region that includes large numbers of different nations, cultures, ethnicities, genders, and religions from East, Southeast, South, Central, and West Asia. The vaguely otherized region of Asia is indeed a White, Western colonial cartography that reifies ongoing histories of racial formation. At the same time, the cultural productions of Queer Asia point to possible emergences, developments, and negotiations of new geopolitical modernities of minoritized sexualities and genders cutting into and across the five regions of Asia. As Yue (2017) observed, "to 'queer' Asia is to de-essentialize Asia as 'area' and [to] use alternative methodologies that do not privilege 'area'" (p. 21). However, examining all regions of Asia is impossible for this article. Thus, the article pays attention to possibilities of Queer Asia that may be relevant to specific geographic areas. Therefore, the article is not a comprehensive overview of all geographic areas in Asia; it should be read as a point of intervention to showcase how Queer Asia requires further attention in the field of communication.

QUEER GLOBALIZATION AND HUMAN RIGHTS

The cultural productions of Queer Asia cannot ignore the material conditions and communication processes of the contemporary globalization that promote the Western queer formations of identities, discourses, and politics. Recognizing such contextual influence, Queer Asia not only pays attention to ongoing histories of minoritized sexualities and genders in and across Asia and Asian diasporas, but also seeks to retrieve the indigenous forms of minoritized sexualities and genders that remain undiscovered (see Gopinath, 2018; Lim, 2014; Suganuma, 2012; Welker, 2017; Wu, 2018; Yue, 2012). In so doing, Queer Asia remixes ongoing interplays of historical tensions between the local and the global to reimagine geopolitical modernities of minoritized sexualities and genders. Hence, Queer Asia points to the complex conditions of existence that both resist and reify a normative architecture of place(s) and space(s) that one is oriented to (Chiang & Wong, 2017; Yue & Leung, 2017).

During the 1860s and 1870s, British colonial administrators began to record and criminalize localized people of color who exemplified Indigenous sexualities and genders in Northern India (Hinchy, 2017). The transgender Hijras, who expressed their third gender, were targeted under the British colonial rule. Their localized gender nonconformity was framed to disrupt the cis-normative construct of a male–female binary and to trouble the heteronormative assumptions and systems of a biological family and kinship. The Hijras, "to whom connotations of criminality [were] cemented in colonial discourse" (Rao, 2020, p. 7), went against the current queer globalization that transnationally advances the Whiteness of sexual and gender modernities as the power. Capitalizing on the cis-normative male–female binary, the logic of Whiteness disadvantages the Indigenous forms of gender nonconformities and transgressions as signs of backwardness (Puar, 2007). In the case of the Hijras, backwardness implied a lower class status in India's caste system, which categorizes low-caste Hindis and people outside the caste into the untouchables, known as *Dalit*. As Rao (2020) observed, "Gender and caste are co-constitutive, in the sense that caste is constituted and reproduced through the regulation of gender and vice versa" (p. 177). Here, the geopolitical backwardness of gender signals the localized slowness of economic growth in the contemporary realities of globalization that privileges Whiteness of sexual and gender modernities. Given that the colonized imagination of the Indian nation had been effeminate, a martial and masculine Hindu nationalism was forged to develop India's economic growth (Rao, 2020). In this context, the Hijras represent the historically specific and culturally saturated production of the minoritized gender marked as primitive in post-colonial India (see Hinchy, 2017; Rao, 2020).

This example reinforces the finding that the Western queer formations circulated by the logic of liberal capitalism ignore, erase, and/or marginalize localized, Indigenous nuances of minoritized sexualities and genders in and across Asia and Asian diasporas (Gopinath, 2018). The transnational/global promotion of the human rights campaign (HRC) movement normalizes the LGBTQIA+ identities, discourses, and politics as a White settler-colonialist and imperialist project (see Chávez, 2013a; Puar, 2007). It repeats the idea of the backwardness of Indigenous sexualities and genders performed by people of color. To further exemplify the strategic workings of Whiteness, this article turns its attention to the cultural conditions of minoritized sexualities and genders in two nations: Singapore and Japan.

When it comes to the issues and concerns of minoritized sexual and gender subjects, Singapore remains one of the highly contested nations in Asia. The social institutions of Singapore still maintain the nominal criminalization of (male) homosexuality, although people are rarely punished for male-to-male sex (Yue, 2012). This paradoxical architecture of Singapore points to the historical legacy of British colonialism that generated the backwardness of (local) people of color. The British colonial law that criminalizes sodomy, section 377A of the penal code, was introduced in Singapore in late 1930s (Leong, 1997). Even after Singapore became an independent nation in 1960s, the criminalization of homosexuality was still institutionally in effect. Simultaneously, because of the government's creative economy that promotes infrastructure development, global queer sexual cultures that emerged from the

West have also been present (Yue & Leung, 2017). Media, theater, entertainment, and nightlife activities materialize global queer sexual cultures available for consumption in Singapore (see Lim, 2014; Yue, 2012). Singapore takes advantage of global queer sexual cultures to boost its current political economy while (male) homosexuality is still illegal. At the same time, Singapore recognized sex-reassignment surgery in early 1970s and has been tolerant of transgender issues and concerns, including sex registry change and marriage (Yue, 2012). Still, this institutional policy medicalizes transgender people as having disorders, which reinserts the logic of healthism that normalizes cisgender people. Therefore, Singapore's current system ignores, erases, and marginalizes Indigenous traditions and forms of transgender people that do not conform to the Western medical paradigm of sex-reassignment surgery (Yue & Leung, 2017). Thus, discourses and performances around minoritized sexualies and genders in Singapore sustain the historical tensions between the local and global.

Similarly, in Japan, the current Western queer formation shapes and reshapes the material realities of minoritized sexualities and genders. However, the displays of Whiteness that maneuver Japan's politics of culture, history, and economy look different from those in Singapore. Prior to Westernization and modernization in the mid-1800s, Japan had a tradition of male same-sex desire called *nanshoku* (男色; male eros; Leupp, 1997). In the Tokugawa period (1603–1868), *nanshoku* "contained a wide variety of terms for describing the partners involved in homosexual acts depending upon such factors as age (their junior or senior role), status, and the context in which the acts took place" (McLelland, 2000, p. 7). When the modernization, industrialization, and Westernization of Japan's social institutions took place in the mid to late 1800s, Japan institutionally adopted Western cis-heteronormative family values and highly stigmatized its Indigenous forms of homoerotic traditions (Pflugfelder, 2007). This stigmatization continues via the normative Japanese cultural communication processes in which nonverbal codes and cues, including silence, maintain the historical marginalization of minoritized sexualities and genders (Eguchi, 2017). Still, culturally saturated and locally creative paradigms of minoritized sexual and gender identities, performances, and politics remain (see Mitsuhashi, 2006; Suganuma, 2012; Welker, 2010). As McLelland (2000) showcased, Japan has historically gendered the embodied performances of same-sex desires. By this means, "The idea that same-sex attraction necessarily involves some kind of transgenderism or desire to be like or even become the opposite of one's biological sex is constantly reinforced by Japanese media, which discuss homosexuality and transgenderism in the same context" (p. 9). This phenomenon highlights ongoing histories of Japan's social institutions that conceptualize sexualities as private forms of entertainment. Because sexuality is not a public matter, sexuality is not supposed to be a communal way of life (see Eguchi, 2019a; McLelland, 2000). Hence, for discussion of sexuality in public, the Japanese cultural expectation of communication conflates sexuality with gender. The regulations of sexuality are gendered. However, contemporary globalization promotes the Westernization and U.S.-Americanization of Japan's minoritized sexual and gender cultures in the post-World War II context where the United States and its allied forces have directly reformed Japan's social institutions (Suganuma, 2012). Thus, following the West, the structural incorporation of same-sex marriage serves as a measure of Japan's progress toward sexual and gender liberalism. While same-sex marriage has not been nationally recognized yet, several local governments, such as municipalities and prefectures, have expanded the (nominal) recognition of same-sex partnerships since 2015 (Maree, 2017).

Therefore, Japanese cultural discourses around minoritized sexualities and genders are constantly shifting.

These two examples point out the paradox between the local and the global surrounding the cultural productions of Queer Asia. On the one hand, ongoing histories of globalization normalize the Whiteness of queer identities, discourses, and politics in and across various "Asian" localities. To be exact, the White, Western, and U.S.-American queer paradigm of minoritized sexualities and genders signals the logic of exceptionalism that maintains the backwardness of people of color (see Chávez, 2013b; Eng, 2010; Ferguson, 2019). The minoritized sexualities and genders found among people of color are constructed as primitive, unprogressive, and less advanced (see Gopinath, 2018; Puar, 2007; Suganuma, 2012; Yep et al., 2020). On the other hand, social institutions in and across Asia negotiate their local logics of cis-heterosexism in responding to Western queer formations. In the case of Singapore, British colonial law is an institutional legacy that sustains the nominal criminalization of (male) homosexuality (Yue & Leung, 2017), yet, as discussed, Singapore capitalizes on global queer sexual cultures to boost its economy. Still, the contemporary globalization that normalizes U.S.-based HRC advocacy actively pressures Singapore to amend its British colonial legacy (Chávez, 2013a). In the case of Japan, Westernization is one of the major historical roots for both reifying and rejecting the logic of cis-heterosexism. The industrialization of Japan that adapted Westernization perpetuated the stigmatizations of homoerotic traditions. However, Western queer formations have prompted several of Japan's local governments to establish (nominal) recognition of same-sex partnerships. Thus, Queer Asia cannot ignore the material conditions and communication processes of contemporary globalization that point to ongoing interplays of historical tensions between the local and the global.

QUEER ASIA AS DISJUNCTIVE MODERNITIES

The cultural productions of Queer Asia that unavoidably identify and disidentify with the multidirectional operations of power (e.g., globalization, market capitalism, state capitalism, and Western queer formations) should be understood as disjunctive modernities (see Yue, 2017; Yue & Leung, 2017). Queer Asia is a strategically eclectic (re)configuration of temporality that represents new geopolitical imaginaries of minoritized sexualities and genders shaped by the messiness of power (Yu, 2020). Having originally used the term *disjunctive modernities* in conceptualizing Queer Asia, Yue (2017) asserts the following:

> Disjunctive queer modernity accounts for the presencing of queer through a process that does not conform to the teleological rights-and-recognition model of the West. It reveals how recognition is attributed without rights, and how such an ontology is non-Western and non-teleological. (p. 21)

Possibile processes and productions of Queer Asia decenter, denaturalize, and transgress the Western-centric, patriarchal, cis-heteronomative, and capitalist modes of knowing, being, and acting ingrained in "queer" and "Asia" first. Then, the cultural productions of Queer Asia that self-fashion new geopolitical imaginaries in/across/from Asia point to the (re)configurations of disjunctive modernities, assembling bits and pieces of differences as alternative paradigms of "queer" and "Asia." As Yue and Leung (2017) observed, "Queer spaces proliferate, provide solidarity for marginalized communities, and challenge the status quo of the nation-state" (p. 749). Yue and Leung's (2017) proposal of "queer Asia as disjunctive modernities offers a relatively up-to-date framework that effectively highlights how market capitalism has enabled the recent proliferation of queer Asia" (Yu, 2020, p. 864). Hence, the alternative paradigms of Queer Asia as disjunctive modernities are paradoxical by nature in the material realities of globalization and local governments and politics that foster new geopolitical discourses around "queer" and "Asia."

To exemplify the (re)configuring processes of Queer Asia as disjunctive modernities, this article organizes the demonstration into three sections: "Identifications and Affinities," "Relationalities and Spatialities," and "Media and Popular Culture." The section "Identifications and Affiliations" investigates the way identifications and affiliations with a particular minoritized sexual and gender group represent the historically specific and culturally nuanced productions of Queer Asia. The section "Relationalities and Spatialities" demonstrates how the geopolitical hierarchies of differences, as historicized and contextualized in and across Asia and Asian diasporas, complicate the cultural productions of Queer Asia. "Media and Popular Culture" explicates how the logic of capitalism enables media and popular cultural platforms where the productions of Queer Asia are materialized for consumption. These three sections are not comprehensive overviews of all anchoring points to Queer Asia; they provide examples for contemplation of the possibilities of Queer Asia as disjunctive modernities. With this limitation in mind, it is appropriate to begin by reviewing identifications and affiliations.

Identifications and Affiliations. How minoritized sexual and gender subjects develop and negotiate their identifications and affiliations reveals contested sites of struggle in and across Asia and Asian diasporas (see Gopinath, 2018; Han, 2015; Lim, 2014; Nguyen, 2014; Wu, 2018; Yue, 2012). The Western queer formations of identities, discourses, and politics shape the geopolitical complexities of Queer Asia (Chiang & Wong, 2016). At the same time, local cultures, economies, politics, and histories reshape the cultural productions of Queer Asia as disjunctive modernities. To showcase the multidirectional flows of power defining Queer Asia, both Cho (2017) and Yu (2020) oriented the localized concepts of class and economic status to unpack how gay men develop and negotiate their desires, intimacies, and relations.

By focusing on South Korean gay men in their 40s and 50s, Cho (2017) analyzed how the national social system of retirement that privileges the cis-heteropatriarchal family system creates socioeconomically insecure lives. To contextualize their lived experiences, Cho paid attention to the way middle-aged local gay men went through the early 1990s social movements when Western queer formations were first introduced to South Korea. This was a time when cisgender male same-sex lovers begun to label themselves as *gay* to appropriate the Western sexual liberations. Still, having originated from the ancient Chinese philosophy of Confucianism, South Korean cis-heteronormative family values emphasize strong and close connections to parents (Seo, 2001). Because of this ideology, most gays did not come out, in order to maintain strong and close relationships with parents who wished them to be heterosexual. Most of the men remained part-time, weekend gays who went out to queer parties. Cho (2017) suggested, "Korean gay men imagined their closet as a temporary holding pad from which they would emerge as fulltime gays once their parents passed away" (p. 252). Hence, they privileged their heteronormative ties to their parents over their queer sexualities.

However, because of the Asian financial catastrophe of 1997/1998 (also known as the IMF crisis), President Dae-Jung promoted three intertwined policies, neofamilism, neoliberalism, and informatization, which disrupted the lived experiences of gay men (Cho, 2017). The policies reified the significance of the cis-heteropatriarchal family and nation, pushed the restructuring of political economies and employment conditions, and increased the advancement of technologies. While technological advancement provided an online space where gay men could meet other gay men, the policies also forced them to renegotiate what it means to gay in the South Korea's political economy. Hence, in response to the structural changes, some middle-aged gay men whom Cho (2017) interviewed articulated how gay identities gradually become less significant than before. When they were younger, the men had opportunities for queer sex, romance, and dating. However, such opportunities decreased as they aged. So, some gay male participants of the study continued to remain single and/or to maintain their sexual discretion. Some stated that they might marry a woman in order to avoid dying alone in post-retirement (Cho, 2017). These circumstances reinforced the cis-heteropatriarchal family system as a major social and cultural capital that organizes life in South Korea. Thus, the political economic system disadvantages middle-aged gay men, who are not married cis-heterosexual men. For example, gay men in South Korea remain economically isolated from the material realities of privilege, such as insurance plans and retirement benefits given to heterosexually married couples (Cho, 2017). Still, some economically privileged local gay men dream of, and plan for, retirement in the countryside or in foreign countries (Cho, 2017). Hence, social institutional issues of retirement, family, and cultural economics represent the culturally nuanced way South Korean gay men negotiate and renegotiate their sexualities to intersect with class and economic status as the multidirectional flows of power constrain their material realities.

To further locate the issues and concerns of class and economic status in Queer Asia, Yu (2020) examined the lived experiences of middle-aged, working-class, gay men residing in Hong Kong. Yu's ethnographic study contextualized Hong Kong as a highly contested space of struggle. For example, since the 1970s, the political economy of Hong Kong has transformed from a disadvantaged migrant society to Asia's financial tiger (Carroll, 2007). Hence, in Hong Kong, the disparity between the rich and the poor is widening, and housing prices are some of the worst in the world. At the same time, Hong Kong, which transferred from Britain to the People's Republic of China (PRC) in 1997, is a highly complex borderland in which Western and Chinese ideologies, values, and beliefs collide (Yue & Leung, 2017). Hong Kong's gay men are known to have actively used the Westernized entertainment industry and commercialized global gay sexual culture to resist cultural changes after Hong Kong became a part of the PRC (Shiu-Ki, 2004). Thus, the multidirectional flows of power constrain the material realities of Hong Kong's middle-aged, working-class gay men. Still, these men may not have had an opportunity to articulate how class inequalities shape and reshape their lived experiences. For this reason, Yu (2020) sampled middle-aged, working-class gay participants from a local NGO that works to improve the health and well-being of gay men.

In the study, the participants expressed their class consciousness without naming their class profiles. This is different from the Western identity politics, where individuals are socialized to easily name their class profiles. The middle-aged, working-class gay men in Hong Kong focused on their dissatisfaction and loss of hope for finding love because they are aging. Specifically, aging is a major aspect of their sexual identity, and the men feel very anxious about their well-being and preparation for retirement. They feel stuck, unable not only to find love but also to pursue upward career mobility. The feeling of social immobility reinforces how the recent proliferation of Hong Kong-based, middle-class-oriented, queer sexual cultures has excluded middle-aged working-class gay men, who didn't experience such cultures when they were younger. In addition, these men do not have access to the capital needed to consume such cultures. Therefore, the men participated in the NGO in hope of finding new friends, and they ignored class differences among other NGO participants because they wanted to cultivate queer social networks. Hence, the men subtly expressed their class inequalities by suggesting that they were "'old gay men' or 'gay men of the older generation'" (Yu, 2020, p. 880). Clearly, generational differences matter to them. The recent proliferation of Hong Kong-based middle-class-oriented queer sexual cultures excludes them because of their age.

In addition to class consciousness and economic status, the concept of romantic love produces the nuances of Queer Asia(nness). For example, Huang (2017) examined Chinese local cultures of lala, a woman desiring another woman, in order to argue against the dominant LGBTQIA+ activism that privileges a same-sex marriage as its goal. A powerful feeling of romantic love drives lala-identified local women to engage in female same-sex relationships. The women are not interested in the Western queer formations of sexual identity politics. Therefore, they do not identify with the sexualized label *lesbian*. The LGBTQIA+ identities, discourses, and politics that embrace the logics of individualism and sexual and gender freedom do not fully capture the culturally nuanced way the powerful feeling of romantic love is a major root of lala desires. As Huang (2017) argued, "Lalas expect that sexual partners should be lovers, and lovers should be life partners, to the exclusion of others" (p. 231). However, this concept of romantic love conflicts with the cis-heteropatriarchal realities of family and kinship structure (Kam, 2013). Solely rooted in romantic love, lala attachments are materially separated from privileges (i.e., institutional benefits, career mobilities, and public status) given to heterosexually married couples in today's neoliberal China. Consequently, some lala women often end up marrying men to survive the social institutional system (Huang, 2017). Some of them engage in a convenient marriage with a queer man (Huang & Brouwer, 2018). Therefore, Huang (2017) suggested the concept of *precariousness* to understand the nuances of lala culture in China. The future of lala's relational attachement and progression is supposed to be vague, uncertain, and queer. Still, precariousness points to the way the Chinese collectivist system of cis-heteronormative family and kinship emphasizes that the lives of elderly people depend on their children and descendants taking care of them. The imperative of heterosexual marriage makes it impossible to imagine a family based on a woman's desiring another woman. The social institutions of China strictly institutionalize heterosexual marriage as a communal life beyond the married couple. Extended family matters. Thus, lala cultures point to how women negotiate and renegotiate temporalties of their same-sex desires and intimacies under the multidirectional effects of power.

In Japan, it is relatively a recent phenomenon that the sexualized label *lesbian* has gained popularity. For example, Welker (2017) traced the written record of Japanese lesbian history.

Discourses around lesbianism increasingly appeared in the literature after the end of World War II in 1945. The United States and its allied occupation of Japan (1945–1952) changed (or Westernized) the structures of Japan's social institutions in a way that created an alternative space for imagining lesbianism. However, lesbian visibility associated with the Western queer formation of identities, discourses, and politics did not resonate well with the local females who identified as same-sex lovers called *dōseiaisha* (Welker, 2017). Thse women did not invest in the Western conception of lesbianism as mostly rooted in sexual desire. Hence, the increased focus on lesbianism in the literature did not initiate a proliferation of the Japanese lesbian community between the 1950s and 1980s. However, the 1990s gay boom that appropriated the Western queer formations of identities, discourse, and politics circulated in the mass media (Welker, 2017), set the stage for the current "lesbian and gay" community. Welker (2017) said that it was the 1990s when "the lesbian community began to take its contemporary shape, including LGBT film festivals and pride parades, and large-scale women-only nightclubs" (p. 156). Since then, the term *lesbian* has gained media, popular cultural, and academic attention. The 1990s gay boom also set the stage for the current LGBTQIA+ activism that has same-sex marriage as its goal in Japan (Maree, 2017).

The discussion in this section exemplifies the Western queer formations of identities, discourses, and politics that cannot capture the cultural ambiguities of queer Asia(nness). The multidirectional flows of power that work with local cultures, economies, politics, and histories complicate the way minoritized individuals perform their desires and intimacies in and across Queer Asia. The next section advances the discussion by focusing on the conditions of relationship and space that expose complex and paradoxical performances of queer desires and intimacies.

Relationalities and Spatialities. The states or conditions of queer relationships and spaces expose often-invisible and hierarchal power relations of differences (i.e., sexuality, gender, race, ethnicity, class, nationality, language, coloniality, and the body; see Han 2015; Nguyen, 2014; Wu, 2018). How minoritized individuals develop and navigate around queer relationships points to the reproduction and reconstitution of spatial power, differences, and inequalities. Queer relationships are never apolitical and ahistorical (see Eguchi, 2020; Lim, 2014; Suganuma, 2012).

For example, Kang (2017) interrogated the historically specific and culturally saturated modes of middle-class Thai gay male preferences for same-sex sexual and romantic relationships. Middle-class gay men who navigate between the poor and the rich have a complicated relationship with their queer lives. Because Thailand is known as a major global destination for sex tourism, some middle-class gay men are concerned with the social stigma of being sex workers. While sex workers should not be stigmatized, the multidirectional flows of power complicate discourses around sex workers in Thailand (Bourdieu, 1987). The context of the socially constructed stigma around sex workers was described by Kang (2017):

> As the "Thai economic miracle" was built on sex (rest and recuperation) sold to the U.S. military during the American War in Southeast Asia and, subsequently, to tourists, sexual commerce continues to shape national ideologies of gender, sexuality and individual agency. (p. 186)

Historical globalization via U.S. military imperialism racializes the representation of Thailand as a major sex tourists' destination where local people of color serve visitors and tourists from economically privileged nations. In this context, sex work signals the lower political economic status of Thailand. The stigma of sex work shapes how some Thais reject and resist the disadvantaged status of Thailand in the context of global capitalism. A Thai–*farang* male same-sex intercultural coupling represents a prototypical sex-work relationship, but under the power dynamic at play, middle-class gay men in Thailand often avoid hanging out with and dating *farang* (White people) who are older and larger than they are (Kang, 2017).

Hence, middle-class Thai gay men are known to prefer relationships with "White" Asians (Kang, 2017). White Asians include South Korean nationals, Japanese nationals, and members of the Chinese diaspora from Taiwan, Hong Kong, Singapore, and other parts of Asia. As Kang (2017) clarified, "'White Asian' here encapsulates a cluster of associations including skin color, advanced economic development (as a nation or as a minority), cultural proximity and Thai imaginings of what 'Asia' and cosmopolitan 'Asians' look like" (p. 189). Because White Asians signal the modernities and economic status that some middle-class Thais aspire to, middle-class gay men see relationships with White Asians as advancing their social capital and upward mobility while resisting the stigma attached to sex work. According to Kang (2017), middle-class gay men have found that a queer coupling of a Thai with an Asian does not invite negative reactions in public. This is not to say that Asians do not engage sex workers. However, a Thai–Asian couple can pass as friends or acquaintances in and across public places and spaces. A Thai–Asian couple do not stand out as much as a Thai–White couple because the physical attributes and characteristics of Asians can be similar to those of Thai people. Still, most participants in Kang's study maintained that they end up dating Thais because of cultural differences with White Asians. Thus, Kang's study (2017), which examined the temporal spaces of middle-class Thai gay men, showed how queer desires are not apolitical and ahistorical.

The intraregional flows of power that shape the states or conditions of same-sex sexual and romantic relationships can be seen in Japan as well (Suganuma, 2012). However, the rhetorical framings of such relationships mirror Japan's historical ethnocentrisms that positioned the nation as an Asian financial tiger aspiring to be Western. To interrogate racialized same-sex desire in Japan, Baudinette (2016) conducted an ethnographic study of Tokyo's major queer district, Shinjuku Ni-chome. While the cultural architecture of Shinjuku Ni-chome is known to welcome all different kinds of queer people (McLelland, 2000), it privileges youthful masculine-presenting cismales. Baudinette (2016) focused on two different kinds of queer male bars in Shinjuku Ni-chome. One type is mainly for Japanese patrons, while the other, called *gaisen* (literally, "mainly foreign"), is for both Japanese and foreign patrons. Japanese patrons have the unearned privilege of going back and forth between the two kinds of bars. However, it is important to note that foreign patrons mainly mean White men (see Eguchi, 2015; Mackintosh, 2010; Suganuma, 2012). The privileging of racialized desire for Whiteness in *gaisen* bars marginalizes, ignores, and erases people of color in general, and Asians (such as Chinese and Korean) in particular (Baudinette, 2016). Hence, Baudinette (2016) interviewed some Chinese, Korean, and Japanese queer male individuals in Shinjuku Ni-chome.

Baudinette's Chinese and South Korean informants who were frequent travelers to Japan expressed their hopes of developing relationships with Japanese men. Because they saw Japan as more modern and progressive than their countries, they desired Japanese men (Baudinette, 2016). The consumption of Japanese literature, popular culture, and gay pornography also drove their desire (Baudinette, 2016). However, they expressed their dislike for Western, U.S.-American gay sexual cultures rooted in capitalism through which sex is overly sold. Hence, the Chinese and South Korean informants were not interested in developing relationships with White men (Baudinette, 2016). Simultaneously, both Chinese and South Korean informants felt excluded from *gaisen* bars, and this exclusion reinforced how the Japanese informants rarely thought of Chinese and South Korean men when they went to *gaisen* bars. Instead, some of them saw Shinjuku Ni-chome as a space for Japanese and White men (Suganuma, 2012). Also, some Japanese subjects saw South Korean men as threats, who "steal" White men via the current sensational consumption of Korean popular culture (Baudinette, 2016). Because Japan's ethnocentrism operates with anti-Koreanness, some Japanese men are unable to understand that South Korean men may be interested in Japanese men. However, some Japanese are much more concerned about the Chinese than the South Koreans. Their xenophobic anxiety hints at the view of Chinese travelers as "backward hooligans" (Baudinette, 2016, p. 481). Still, these perceptions reinforce the homogenized notion of Japaneseness that ignores the historical presence of Korean Japanese and Chinese Japanese (Toyosaki & Eguchi, 2017). Hence, the states or conditions of same-sex sexual and romantic relationships that take place in Shinjuku Ni-chome can never be separate from Japan's spatial politics and xenophobia (Suganuma, 2012).

Because specific architectures of space govern states or conditions of sexual and romantic relationships, discourses around same-sex marriage alter, shape, and reinforce relationalities and spatialities of Queer Asia as disjunctive modernities. Western queer formations influence the LGBTQIA+ activism that aims for the institutionalization of same-sex marriage (see Huang, 2017; Maree, 2017; Welker, 2017; Yue & Leung, 2017). For example, Tang et al. (2020) examined the nuanced ways sexually minoritized females and males make sense of marriage, family, and citizenship in three "Asian" localities: Hong Kong, Japan, and Taiwan. It is important to note that Taiwan is currently the only Asian country that nationally recognizes the institution of same-sex marriage, which it legalized in 2019. This achievement was very significant for LGBTQIA+ activism. No other Asian country has legalized same-sex marriage. This is significant because interview participants from all three locations expressed the perspective that views Western queer discourses of same-sex marriage as either an assimilation or a betrayal of queer politics (Tang et al., 2020). Instead, they maintained that the institution of same-sex marriage opens an alternative space where minoritized sexual groups can ideally maintain their strong ties to their families and kin as a way of communal life (Tang et al., 2020). In Hong Kong and Taiwan, the historical influence of Confucianism sustains the cultural significance of strong extended family and kinship ties. A similar practice is seen in Japan, where the *ie* ("house") ideology rooted in the patriarchal family system organizes everyday social life. Hence, according to Tang et al. (2020), interview participants from all three locations believed: recognition of same-sex marriage allows minoritized sexual groups to be publicly integrated into every major aspect of extended familial and communal life, the performance of a wedding as a public ritual or the act of registering a marriage license endorses the value of same-sex lovers to extended family and community members, and legal recognition of same-sex couples fosters social change in and across communities. Therefore, the discourses around same-sex marriage alter, shape, and reinforce how minoritized sexual groups negotiate and renegotiate their relationships and spaces in and across Queer Asia.

In summary, the multidirectional flows of power (e.g., globalization, market capitalism, state capitalism, and Western queer formation) that work with local politics, economies, and cultures shape temporal spaces in which minoritized sexual individuals engage in relationships. The next section turns to the roles of media and popular culture as paradoxical spaces of temporality through which new geopolitical imaginaries of Queer Asia are produced and constituted.

Media and Popular Culture. Contemporary globalization normalizes the rapid flow of ideas, beliefs, and values via information technology. In this landscape, media and popular culture promote the intraregional cultural flows of sexuality, gender, and geopolitics (see Lim, 2014; Yue, 2012). As already alluded to, the consumption of media and popular culture informs how minoritized sexual and gender individuals from various "Asian" localities learn about differences that organize Asia as heterogeneously queer. For example, the consumption of Japanese literature, popular culture, and gay pornography shapes Chinese and South Korean men's aspirations to develop relationships with Japanese men (Baudinette, 2016). Also, in Hong Kong, gay men and lesbian women use information technology to measure the state's progress toward same-sex marriage by comparing their institutional conditions to Taiwan's legal recognition of same-sex marriage (Tang et al., 2020). Hence, the intraregional flow of ideas, beliefs, and values promoted by media and popular culture shapes and reshapes the cultural productions of Queer Asia as disjunctive modernities (see Chiang & Wong, 2017; Suganuma, 2012; Yue, 2012; Yue & Leung, 2017).

For example, in Singapore, the tomboy band scene emerged from Singapore's annual lesbian event called the Butch hunt competition, which began in 2001. Yue (2017) said, "Inspired by the competition, young butches (contestants and patrons) [came] together to form modeling, singing and dancing groups" (p. 18). Some of the tomboy bands are invited to perform at major lesbian events, and they also travel to nightclubs in other cities, such as Bangkok, Taipei, and Manila. Yue (2017) wrote about a Singapore-based band called SMZ Tomboy Crew, which consisted of 13 members age 18 to 25. The band members, who were either college students or retail workers, were 11 Chinese Singaporeans and two Malay Singaporeans. The aesthetics of SMZ resemble those of K-pop boybands. Consequently, SMZ engages in trans performances that imply intraregional cross-border flows. Yue (2017) maintained, "SMZ's inter-Asian influences are evident not only from their borrowing of K-pop music and fashion, but also their self-fashioning of an Asian butch style dominant of the tom or 't' cultures in Thailand and Taiwan" (p. 18). By remixing fragmentations in and across borders, the SMZ collectively performs disjunctive modernities.

Cinema is another major site that represents new geopolitical imaginaries of Queer Asia. The rise of queer film festivals reinforces the significance of cinema in shaping the politics of LGBTQIA+ activism in and across Asia and Asian diasporas (Yue, 2014). There are many cinematic productions that have centralized the Asian queerscape "as a new spatial culture across Asia and its Asian diasporas that have emerged as a result of the multidirectional flows of queer globalization" (Yue, 2014, p. 149). Here, the notion of "scape" defines cultural flows of power. For example, *The Wedding Banquet* (1993), co-produced by Taiwan and the United

States, has become a major text that represents the culturally nuanced issues of a New York-based Taiwanese gay male coming out to his Taiwanese family (Yep & Lescure, 2014). The circulation of *The Wedding Banquet* in the early 1990s coincided with the time that Western queer formations of identities, discourses, and politics rooted in the paradigm of coming out began to shape LGBTQIA+ activism in and across Asia (Yue, 2014). In addition, the international filmmaker Ray Yeung directed the U.K./Hong Kong-produced 26-minute short film *Yellow Fever* (1998), which focused on the Western gay vernacular of "sticky rice." Sticky rice means an "Asian" man who is interested in relationships with other "Asian" men (Eguchi, 2020). Later, *Yellow Fever* was remade into the 87-minute film *Front Cover* (2015), produced in the United States. Both *Yellow Fever* and *Front Cover* showed how a Chinese male immigrant struggled with falling in and out of love with a Chinese/Mandarin-speaking foreign male. By portraying a sticky rice couple, Yeung resisted the Whiteness of global gay sexual culture that marginalizes Asian men as undesirable and unattractive (Eguchi, 2020). An additional important cinematic site is India's Bollywood, formally known as Bombay Cinema. Bollywood increasingly represents multiple queer forms of desire and pleasure, including the paradoxical roles of India's third gender Hijras (Gopinath, 2000). Saria (2021) asserted that "the mythic role of Hijras is baked into contemporary understandings of 'transgenders,' as revealed in the films, and this seamless transition is made possible by the resounding encouragement that Hijras receive from Hindu religious groups" (p. 98). At the same time, the focus on the Hijras marginalizes heterogeneous forms of transgenders, especially transmasculine identities and performances (Rao, 2020). Yet, these examples of cinema suggest how the Western queer globalization that promotes intraregional cultural flows creates a space of paradox to materialize disjunctive queer modernities in and across Asia.

It is noteworthy to mention that the Japanese comic and animation genre Boys' Love (BL) builds on disjunctive queer modernities. Welker (2006) suggested, "What set Boys' Love narratives apart was their presentation of androgynous beautiful boys who love other beautiful boys rather than girl characters" (pp. 841–842). However, the genre's representation of homoeroticism emerged as a subgenre of girls' comics called *shôjo* manga, wherein *shôjo* manga readers fantasized about two beautiful boys falling in love. As Welker (2006) added, the "beautiful boy is visually and psychically neither male nor female; his romantic and erotic interests are directed at other beautiful boys, but his tastes are not exclusively homosexual; he lives and loves outside the heteropatriarchal world" (p. 842). Because the BL genre, which started in the 1970s, has been sensationally consumed, Japan's legacy networks have remade some BL comics as TV drama series (Eguchi & Kimura, 2021). At the same time, the genre has been exported for transnational consumption outside of Japan, including in various Asian localities. For example, Ng and Li (2020) examined the Chinese web series *Guardian*, which represents queer forms of desire and pleasure appropriated from a BL novel. Given that the PRC regulates media practices and contents like queer representations and readings, the significance of the web series is "how deliberate fans were in seeking to ensure that their activities stayed in line with what the state would allow" (Ng & Li, 2020, p. 489). Because *Guardian* represents pure love between two boys that is not really male homosexuality, it offers an ambiguous space to envision and re-envision queer forms of desire and pleasure. Hence, the transnational influence of BL media texts that develop disjunctive queer modernities cannot be ignored.

Simultaneously, pornography is an additional industry that adds to the cinematic phenomenon that produces new geopolitical imaginaries of Queer Asia (see Fung, 2005; Han, 2015; Lim, 2014; Nguyen, 2014). Western gay media that represent Asian men as soft, feminine, and submissive are well circulated transnationally (Ayres, 1999). This racialized gender image permeates the pornographic representation of Asian men that is commodified and consumed across the world. Fung (2005) contextualized how the political economic rankings of some Asian nations in requiring financial assistance from the Global North enabled the stereotype of youthful, feminine, and submissive Asian men seeking older, masculine, and dominant White men. This prototypical homoeroticism of an Asian–White coupling added to the image of Asian men as sexual bottoms who receive anal penetration (see Han, 2015; Lim, 2014). Nguyen (2014) unpacked the way U.S.-based productions of gay pornography perpetuate the "lower" position of Asian bottoms through their unassimilated, foreign performances. The industry rarely assigns the roles of sexual tops who are anal sex penetrators to Asian and Asian American men. Accordingly, the California-born and raised Vietnamese American model and gay porn entertainer and producer Peter Le described a glass ceiling for Asian and Asian American men in the U.S.-based gay pornographic industry (Eguchi, 2019b). This career struggle exemplifies how Asian and Asian American men are historically racialized as having failed to attain (White) manhood in the Western imagination (see Eng, 2001; Han, 2015; Shimizu, 2012). Accordingly, the pornographic image of an Asian man having sex with another Asian man is constructed as sisterly or improperly gay (Nguyen, 2014). Despite the fact that some ethnic markers are occasionally used to construct Filipino men as sexually available and Japanese men as kinky, the feminized stereotype of Asian men is globally pervasive (Fung, 2005). Hence, the gay male performances in the groundbreaking Singapore-based theatrical production of *Asian Boys Vol. 1* (2000) appropriated the pornographic femininization of Asian men (Lim, 2014).

In addition to music, cinema, animation, and pornography, social media and digital platforms offer alternative spaces of possibilities where minoritized sexual and gender individuals connect in and across Queer Asia. For example, Queer Azaadi Mumbai (QAM), also known as Mumbai Pride March, has used social media to promote its social engagements and political goals since 2008. As Sharma (2021) observed, "As much of the publicity for QAM takes place through social media, they use catchy hashtags, based on popular phrases, to represent the annual theme of the March" (p. 163). Hence, while access to media technology is still limited to certain economic groups, social media offer an alternative space for developing social and political connectivities in and across Queer India. In addition, queer social networking websites, such as fridae.asia, privilege intraregional Asian connectivities (Kang, 2017), and fridae mostly targets gay male users who are interested in meeting gay male users in and across Queer Asia. Such online spaces are supposed to counter the logic of Whiteness that sustains the historical subordination of Asians. As Nguyen (2014) observed, while hiding their faces, some Asian men strategically emphasize their light skin and well-toned bodies to gain social capital in and across online global gay sex cruising spaces. They reject the way Asian men have been historically disadvantaged as having failed to meet the White masculine ideal. Still, although these examples suggest how social media and digital platforms offer indefinite and uncertain spaces of possibilities in and across Queer Asia, media and popular culture play an essential role in the production and constitution of disjunctive queer modernities.

CONCLUSION

This article examines Queer Asia. Specifically, the article first addresses Western queer formations of identities, discourses, and politics that shape and reshape the cultural productions of Queer Asia. Then, the article showcases three topics that represent Queer Asia as disjunctive modernities. Identification and affiliation point to the historically specific and culturally nuanced productions of Queer Asia. Next, the discussion turns to how the relationalities and spatialities of Queer Asia alter, shape, and/or reinforce geopolitical hierarchies of differences uniquely produced by the multidirectional flows of power. Moreover, the logic of capitalism requires media and popular cultural platforms where productions of Queer Asia as disjunctive modernities are materialized and commodified for consumption. Overall, the article serves as a reference point for transnational/global queer-of-color studies in communication.

Before closing, it is important to reiterate that the article is not a comprehensive overview of Queer Asia as disjunctive modernities. The article is limited to particular geographic assumptions and representations that can re-establish the hierarchical relations of nations and cultures in Asia, yet cultural productions of Queer Asia are rapidly taking place within and beyond East, Southeast, South, Central, and West Asia. In addition to its geographic limitation, the article largely depends on the examples that draw upon non-trans queer Asianness. As LeMaster and Stephenson (2021) observed, queer studies in communication marginalize transness in theorizing queerness. Hence, the possibilities of Queer Asia suggested by this article are intellectually and politically meant to push communication scholars, teachers, and practitioners to begin questioning, criticizing, and practicing the productions of Queer Asia as disjunctive modernities. With further examination of Queer Asia, queer studies in communication can advance more historically specific and culturally saturated developments of the field than are now available.

FURTHER READING

Chambers-Letson, J. (2018). *After the party: A manifesto for queer of color life*. New York University Press.

Chen, J. N. (2019). *Trans exploits: Trans of color cultures & technologies in movement*. Duke University Press.

Crusz-Malave, A., & Manalansan, M. F. (Eds.). (2002). *Queer globalizations: Citizenship and the afterlife of colonialism*. New York University Press.

Eguchi, S. (2011). Negotiating sissyphobia: A critical/interpretive analysis of one "femme" gay Asian body in the heteronormative world. *Journal of Men's Studies*, *19*(1), 37–56. https://doi.org/10.3149/jms.1901.37

Eguchi, S. (2015). Queer intercultural relationality: An autoethnography of Asian-Black (dis)connections in White gay America. *Journal of International and Intercultural Communication*, *8*(1), 27–43. https://doi.org/10.1080/17513057.2015.991077

Fung, R. (2017). Re: Orienting Queer/Asian/Canadian. *TOPIA: Canadian Journal of Cultural Studies*, *38*, 81–86. https://doi.org/10.3138/topia.38.81

Gopinath, G. (2005). *Impossible desires: Queer diasporas and South Asian public cultures*. Duke University Press.

Khubchandani, K. (2020). *Ishtyle: Accenting gay Indian nightlife*. University of Michigan Press.

Kojima, D. (2017). Bootstraps, sugar daddies, silence and civility: A queer reflection on Japanese endurance. *TOPIA: Canadian Journal of Cultural Studies*, *38*, 115–122. https://doi.org/10.3138/topia.38.115

Kojima, D., Catungal, J. P., & Diaz, R. (2017). Introduction: Feeling queer, feeling Asian, feeling Canadian. *TOPIA: Canadian Journal of Cultural Studies, 38*, 69–80. https://doi.org/10.3138/topia.38.69

Lee, W. (2003). Kuaering queer theory: My autocritography and a race-conscious, womanist, and transnational Turn. In G. A. Yep, K. E. Lovaas, & J. P. Elia (Eds.), *Queer theory and communication: From disciplining queers to queering the discipline(s)* (pp. 147–170). The Haworth Press.

Leung, H. H-S. (2017). Multiple Queer Asias: An intimate reflection from Vancouver. *TOPIA: Canadian Journal of Cultural Studies, 38*, 87–92. https://doi.org/10.3138/topia.38.87

Martin, F., Jackson, P. A., McLelland, M., & Yue, A. (Eds.). (2008). *AsiaPacifiQueer: Rethinking genders and sexualities*. University of Illinois Press.

Manalansan, M. F. (2003). *Global divas: Filipino gay men in the diaspora*. Duke University Press.

Otalvaro-Hormillosa, S. (1999). The homeless diaspora of queer Asian Americans. *Social Justice, 26*(3), 103–122.

Pérez, H. (2015). *A taste for brown bodies: Gay modernity and cosmopolitan desire*. New York University Press.

Takemoto, T. (2014). Looking for Jiro Onuma: A queer meditation on the incarceration of Japanese Americans during World War II. *GLQ: A Journal of Lesbian and Gay Studies, 20*(3), 241–275. https://doi.org/10.1215/10642684-2422665

Velasco, G. K. (2019). *Queering the global Filipina body: Contested nationalisms in the Filipina/o diaspora*. University of Illinois Press.

Yep, G. A., Lovaas, K. E., & Ho, P. C. (2001). Communication in "Asian American" families with queer members: A relational dialectics perspective. In M. Bernstein & R. Reimann (Eds.), *Queer families, queer politics: Challenging culture and the state* (pp. 152–172). Columbia University Press.

Yue, A. (2008). Same-sex migration in Australia: From interdependency to intimacy. *GLQ: A Journal of Lesbian and Gay Studies, 14*(2–3), 239–262. https://doi.org/10.1215/10642684-2007-032

Yue, A. (2011). Critical regionalities in Inter-Asia and the Queer diaspora. *Feminist Media Studies, 11*(1), 131–138. https://doi.org/10.1080/14680777.2011.537042

REFERENCES

Alexander, B. K. (2008). Queer(y)ing the postcolonial through the Western. In N. K. Denzin, Y. S. Lincoln, & L. T. Smith (Eds.), *Handbook of critical and indigenous methodologies* (pp. 101–133). SAGE.

Ayres, T. (1999). China doll—The experience of being a gay Chinese Australian. In P. A. Jackson & G. Sullivan (Eds.), *Multicultural queer: Australian narratives* (pp. 87–97). Harrington Park Press.

Baudinette, T. (2016). Ethnosexual frontiers in queer Tokyo: The production of racialised desire in Japan. *Japan Forum, 28*(4), 465–483. https://doi.org/10.1080/09555803.2016.1165723

Bourdieu, P. (1987). *Distinctions: A social critique of the judgement of taste*. Harvard University Press

Boylorn, R., & Adams, T. (2016). Queer and quare autoethnography. In N. K. Denzin & M. D. Giardina (Eds.), *Qualitative inquiry through a critical lens* (pp. 85–98). Routledge.

Carroll, J. M. (2007). *A concise history of Hong Kong*. Rowman & Littlefield.

Calvente, L. B. Y., Calafell, B. M., & Chávez, K. R. (2020). Here is something you can't understand: The suffocating Whiteness of communication studies. *Communication and Critical/Cultural Studies, 17*(2), 202–209. https://doi.org/10.1080/14791420.2020.1770823

Chakravartty, P., & Jackson, S. J. (2020). The disavowal of race in communication theory. *Communication and Critical/Cultural Studies, 17*(2), 210–219. https://doi.org/10.1080/14791420.2020.1771743

Chakravartty, P., Kuo, R., Grubbs, V., & McIlwain, C. (2018). #CommunicationSoWhite. *Journal of Communication, 68*(2), 254–266. https://doi.org/10.1093/joc/jqy003

Chávez, K. R. (2013a). Pushing boundaries: Queer intercultural communication. *Journal of International and Intercultural Communication, 6*(2), 83–95. https://doi.org/10.1080/17513057.2013.777506

Chávez, K. R. (2013b). *Queer migration politics: Activist rhetoric and coalitional possibilities*. University of Illinois Press.

Chen, K.-H. (2010). *Asia as method: Toward deimperialization*. Duke University Press.

Chiang, H., & Wong, A. K. (2016). Queering the transnational turn: Regionalism and Queer Asias. *Gender, Place and Culture: A Journal of Feminist Geography, 23*(11), 1643–1656. https://doi.org/10.1080/0966369X.2015.1136811

Chiang, H., & Wong, A. K. (2017). Asia is burning: Queer Asia as critique. *Culture, Theory and Critique, 58*(2), 121–126. https://doi.org/10.1080/14735784.2017.1294839

Cho, J. (2017). "Deferred futures": The diverse imaginaries of gay retirement in post-IMF South Korea. *Culture, Theory and Critique, 58*(2), 243–259. https://doi.org/10.1080/14735784.2016.1278558

Eguchi, S. (2017). Japanese male-queer femininity: An autoethnographic reflection on *Matsuko Deluxe* as an *onē-kei* talent. In S. Toyosaki & S. Eguchi (Eds.), *Intercultural communication in Japan: Theorizing homogenized discourse* (pp. 73–85). Routledge.

Eguchi, S. (2019a). Transnational LGBTQ pride: Whiteness, health, and wellbeing in VICELAND's *Gaycation*. *China Media Research, 15*(3), 83–92.

Eguchi, S. (2019b). Queerness as strategic whiteness: A queer Asian American critique of Peter Le. In D. M. D. McIntosh, D. G. Moon, & T. K. Nakayama (Eds.), *Interrogating communicative power of Whiteness* (pp. 29–44). Routledge.

Eguchi, S. (2020). Sticky rice politics: Impossible possibilities of queerness in and across *Yellow Fever* and *Front Cover*. *Women's Studies in Communication, 43*(1), 67–84. https://doi.org/10.1080/07491409.2019.1696435

Eguchi, S. (2021). What is "Queer Asia?": A struggling pathway to globalizing queer studies in communication. *Communication and Critical/Cultural Studies, 18*(2), 196–203. https://doi.org/10.1080/14791420.2021.1907848

Eguchi, S., & Asante, G. (2016). Disidentifications revisited: Queer(y)ing intercultural communication theory. *Communication Theory, 26*(2), 171–189. https://doi.org/10.1111/comt.12086

Eguchi, S., & Calafell, B. M. (2020). Introduction: Reorienting queer intercultural communication. In S. Eguchi & B. M. Calafell (Eds.), *Queer intercultural communication: The intersectional politics of belonging in and across differences* (pp. 1–16). Rowman & Littlefield.

Eguchi, S., & Kimura, K. (2021). Racialized im/possibilities: Intersectional queer-of-color critique on Japaneseness in Netflix's *Queer Eye: We're in Japan! Journal of International and Intercultural Communication, 14*(3), 221–239. https://doi.org/10.1080/17513057.2020.1829675

Eng, D. L. (2001). *Racial castration: Managing masculinity in Asian America*. Duke University Press.

Eng, D. L. (2010). *The feeling of kinship: Queer liberalism and the racialization of intimacy*. Duke University Press.

Ferguson, R. A. (2019). *One-dimensional queer*. Polity.

Flores, L. A., & Gomez, L. A. (2020). Disciplinary containment: Whiteness and the academic scarcity narrative. *Communication and Critical/Cultural Studies, 17*(2), 236–242. https://doi.org/10.1080/14791420.2020.1770818

Fung, R. (2005). Looking for my penis: The eroticized Asian in gay video porn. In R. Guins & O. Z. Cruz (Eds.), *Popular culture: A reader* (pp. 338–348). SAGE.

Gopinath, G. (2000). Queering Bollywood: Alternative sexualities in popular Indian cinema. *Journal of Homosexuality, 39*(3/4), 283–297. https://doi.org/10.1300/J082v39n03_13

Gopinath, G. (2018). *Unruly visions: The aesthetic practices of queer diaspora*. Duke University Press.

Han, C. W. (2015). *Geisha of a different kind: Race and sexuality in gaysian America*. New York University Press.

Hinchy, J. (2017). The eunuch archive: Colonial records of nonnormative gender and sexuality in India. *Culture, Theory and Critique, 58*(2), 127–146. https://doi.org/10.1080/14735784.2017.1279555

Huang, A. (2017). Precariousness and the queer politics of imagination in China. *Culture, Theory and Critique, 58*(2), 226–242. https://doi.org/10.1080/14735784.2017.1287580

Huang, S., & Brouwer, D. C. (2018). Negotiating performances of "real" marriage in Chinese queer *xinghun*. *Women's Studies in Communication, 41*(2), 140–158. https://doi.org/10.1080/07491409.2018.1463581

Johnson, E. P. (2001). "Quare" studies or (almost) everything I know about queer studies I learned from my grandmother. *Text and Performance Quarterly, 21*(1), 1–25. https://doi.org/10.1080/10462930128119

Kam, L. (2013). *Shanghai lalas: Female Tongzhi communities and politics in urban China*. Hong Kong University Press.

Kang, D. B. (2017). Eastern orientations: Thai middle-class gay desire for "White Asians." *Culture, Theory and Critique, 58*(2), 182–208. https://doi.org/10.1080/14735784.2017.1288580

LeMaster, B., & Stephenson, M. (2021). Trans (gender) trouble. *Communication and Critical/Cultural Studies, 18*(2), 190–195. https://doi.org/10.1080/14791420.2021.1907851

Leupp, G. (1997). *Male colors: The construction of homosexuality in Tokugawa Japan*. University of California Press.

Leong, L.-T. (1997). Singapore. In D. J. West & R. Green (Eds.), *Sociolegal control of homosexuality: A multi-nation comparison* (pp. 127–144). Plenum Press.

Lim, E.-B. (2014). *Brown boys and rice queens: Spellbinding performances in the Asias*. New York University Press.

Luther, J. D., & Ung Loh, J. (2019). *"Queer" Asia: Decolonising and reimagining sexuality and gender*. Zed Books.

Mackintosh, J. D. (2010). *Homosexuality and manliness in postwar Japan*. Routledge.

Maree, C. (2017). Weddings and white dresses: Media and sexual citizenship in Japan. *Sexualities, 20*(1/2), 212–233. https://doi.org/10.1177/1363460716645790

Martin, F., Jackson, P. A., McLelland, M., & Yue, A. (2008). Introduction. In F. Martin, P. A. Jackson, M. McLelland, & A. Yue (Eds.), *AsiaPacifiQueer: Rethinking genders and sexualities* (pp. 1–28). University of Illinois Press.

McCann, B., Mack, A. N., & Self, R. (2020). Communication's quest for Whiteness: The racial politics of disciplinary legitimacy. *Communication and Critical/Cultural Studies, 17*(2), 243–252. https://doi.org/10.1080/14791420.2020.1770822

McLelland, M. (2000). *Male homosexuality in modern Japan: Cultural myths and social realities*. Routledge.

Mitsuhashi, J. (2006). The transgender world in contemporary Japan: The male to female cross-dressers' community in Shinjuku. *Inter-Asia Cultural Studies, 7*(2), 202–227. https://doi.org/10.1080/14649370600673847

Nakayama, T. K. (1994). Show/down time: "Race," gender, sexuality, and popular culture. *Critical Studies in Media Communication, 11*(2), 162–179. https://doi.org/10.1080/15295039409366893

Nakayama, T. K. (2020). Whiteness is not contained. *Communication and Critical/Cultural Studies, 17*(2), 199–201. https://doi.org/10.1080/14791420.2020.1770821

Nguyen, H. T. (2014). *A view from the bottom: Asian American masculinity and sexual representation*. Duke University Press.

Ng, E., & Li, X. (2020). A queer "socialist brotherhood": The *Guardian* web series, boys' love fandom, and the Chinese state. *Feminist Media Studies, 20*(4), 479–495. https://doi.org/10.1080/14680777.2020.1754627

Ng, E., White, K. C., & Saha, A. (2020). #CommunicationSoWhite: Race and power in the academy and beyond. *Communication, Culture and Critique, 13*(2), 143–151. https://doi.org/10.1093/ccc/tcaa011

Pflugfelder, G. M. (2007). *Cartographies of desire: Male-male sexuality in Japanese discourse, 1600–1950*. University of California Press.

Puar, J. K. (2007). *Terrorist assemblages: Homonationalism in queer times*. Duke University Press.

Rao, R. (2020). *Out of time: The queer politics of postcoloniality*. Oxford University Press.

Saria, V. (2021). The queer narrator: Violence, ethics, and sexuality. *GLQ: A Journal of Lesbian and Gay Studies, 27*(1), 85–102. https://doi.org/10.1215/10642684-8776876

Seo, D.-J. (2001). Mapping the vicissitudes of homosexual identities in South Korea. *Journal of Homosexuality*, 40(3/4), 65–79. https://doi.org/10.1300/J082v40n03_04

Sharma, D. (2021). Representing pride through hashtags. *Feminist Media Studies*, 21(1), 162–164. https://doi.org/10.1080/14680777.2021.1864878

Shimizu, C. P. (2012). *Straight sexualities: Unbinding Asian American manhoods in the movies*. Stanford University Press.

Shiu-Ki, T. K. (2004). Queer at your own risk: Marginality, community and Hong Kong gay male bodies. *Sexualities*, 7(1), 5–30. https://doi.org/10.1177/1363460704040136

Suganuma, K. (2012). *Contact moments: The politics of intercultural desire in Japanese male-queer cultures*. Hong Kong University Press.

Tang, D. T.-S., Knor, D., & Chen, Y.-C. (2020). Legal recognition of same-sex partnerships: A comparative study of Hong Kong, Taiwan and Japan. *The Sociological Review*, 68(1), 192–208. https://doi.org/10.1177/0038026119858222

Toyosaki, S., & Eguchi, S. (2017). Powerful uncertainty for the future of Japan's cultural diversity: Theorizing Japanese homogenizing discourses. In S. Toyosaki & S. Eguchi (Eds.), *Intercultural communication in Japan: Theorizing homogenized discourse* (pp. 1–23). Routledge.

Welker, J. (2006). Beautiful, borrowed, and bent: "Boys' Love" as girls' love in *shôjo manga*. *Signs: Journal of Women in Culture and Society*, 31(3), 841–870. https://doi.org/10.1086/498987

Welker, J. (2010). Telling her story: Narrating a Japanese lesbian community. *Journal of Lesbian Studies*, 14(4), 359–380. https://doi.org/10.1080/10894161003677265

Welker, J. (2017). Toward a history of "lesbian history" in Japan. *Culture, Theory and Critique*, 58(2), 147–165. https://doi.org/10.1080/14735784.2017.1282830

Wu, C. (2018). *Sticky rice: A politics of intraracial desire*. Temple University Press.

Yep, G. A. (2013). Queering/quaring/kauering/crippin'/transing "other bodies" in intercultural communication. *Journal of International and Intercultural Communication*, 6(2), 118–126. https://doi.org/10.1080/17513057.2013.777087

Yep, G. A., & Lescure, R. M. (2014). Kuareing "home" in Ang Lee's *The Wedding Banquet*. In E. Patton & M. Choi (Eds.), *Home sweet home: Perspectives on housework and modern relationships* (pp. 167–182). Rowman & Littlefield.

Yep, G. A., Alaoui, F. Z. C., & Lescure, R. M. (2020). Relationalities in/through difference: Explorations in queer intercultural communication. In S. Eguchi & B. M. Calafell (Eds.), *Queer intercultural communication: The intersectional politics of belonging in and across differences* (pp. 19–45). Rowman & Littlefield.

Yoshimi, T. (2005). Asia as method. In R. F. Calichman (Ed., Trans.), *What is modernity? Writings of Takeuchi Yoshimi* (pp. 149–166). Columbia University Press.

Yu, T.-F. (2020). Reconfiguring Queer Asia as disjunctive modernities: Notes on the subjective production of working-class gay men in Hong Kong. *Journal of Homosexuality*, 67(6), 863–884. https://doi.org/10.1080/00918369.2018.1560126

Yue, A. (2012). Queer Singapore: A critical introduction. In A. Yue & J. Zubillaga-Pow (Eds.), *Queer Singapore* (pp. 1–25). Hong Kong University Press.

Yue, A. (2014). Queer Asian cinema and media studies: From hybrid to critical regionality. *Cinema Journal*, 53(2), 145–151. https://doi.org/10.1353/cj.2014.0001

Yue, A. (2017). Trans-Singapore: Some notes towards Queer Asia as method. *Inter-Asian Cultural Studies*, 18(1), 10–24. https://doi.org/10.1080/14649373.2017.1273911

Yue, A., & Leung, H. H.-S. (2017). Notes towards the queer Asian city: Singapore and Hong Kong. *Urban Studies*, 54(3), 747–764. https://doi.org/10.1177/0042098015602996

Shinsuke Eguchi

QUEER MIGRATION AND DIGITAL MEDIA

INTRODUCTION

The global movement of queer people could be studied through various lenses, such as comparative law, political culture, organizational activism, or—as this article overviews—the various ways queer migration relates to digital media. Each of the three main sections in this article overviews new research related to queer transnational networks, migrations, and diasporas. The first section, "Transnational Queer Networks and Media: A Brief History," shows that media have shaped transnational queer networks and mobility for over a century and that developments in online communication accelerated these movements of information and people. The second section, "Decisions and Paths to Migration," looks at how queer migrants use digital media before and during the migration process, and thus expands on the argument that online networks bolster queer identities and mobilities. The third section, "Settling In," focuses on the role of digital media for recent queer migrants, including both the positive experiences finding friends or jobs and the negative occasions confronting xenophobia and racism.

This article uses "queer" as both an umbrella term for LGBT identities as well as a term that encompasses other identities outside of the heterosexual–cisgender norm (such as pansexual, nonbinary, agender, terms that exist outside of the English language or Western cultural norm, and terms that do not yet exist). That being said, many of the citations in this article refer to studies of cisgender people who seek same-sex contact and who have knowledge of global LGBT movements. Next, this article understands "digital media" to include a range of outputs, including text, audio, and visual platforms, from podcasts to gaming platforms to Instagram stories; that being said, many of the citations in this article focus on social media, including hook-up apps like Grindr as well as mainstream platforms like Facebook. Finally, while this article applies to internal migration—such as rural-to-urban movements, which are central to many queer people's narratives—the focus of this article is on those who have crossed international borders for any reason. This article also pays specific attention to race, but rejects the usage of "migrant" to apply to racial minorities who are the children of migrants. Migration can be a privilege, and for many queer people, international migration is never possible due to economic position, family situation, migration laws and restrictions, or other personal constraints.

Queer studies, migration studies, and communication studies are relatively new scholarly fields when compared to those disciplines from which they emerged (sociology, history, anthropology, literature, theater arts, etc.). This article represents a portion—but certainly not all—of literature on the topic of queer migration and digital media, and the literature published thus far represents just a sliver of the possibilities for future research within this field. New communication technologies will broaden the range of online communication methods, which in turn will accelerate global movements as well as broaden the range of queer identities.

TRANSNATIONAL QUEER NETWORKS AND MEDIA: A BRIEF HISTORY

Digital media enable the transnational flows of words, images, and related people, but while the ability to chat and share information online facilitates new types of networks and media for queer people, these online communities emerged from and built upon predigital queer cultures.

Predigital Media and Transnational Flows. In the first decades of the 20th century, printed publications enabled early advocates for homosexual rights across Europe to build transnational connections. During these years, Berlin was renowned for its diverse homosexual subcultures and cutting-edge scientific research on sexuality, such as those related to Magnus Hirschfeld's Scientific-Humanitarian Committee (founded 1897) (Beachy, 2014). During these decades, scientific publications on homosexuality inspired international visitors to travel to Berlin, some of whom returned to their countries of origin with new ideas about homosexuality, sexual rights, and subcultures (Herzog, 2011, pp. 77–81; von Rosen, 2007). Though the Nazis destroyed key institutions and networks in Germany, homosexual groups and activists survived underground in various countries. Due partly to these early transnational networks, scientific writings on homosexuality survived across borders and empowered individuals to rethink laws and norms about sexuality across Europe in the first decade after World War II, namely, in Belgium, Denmark, France, the Netherlands, Norway, Sweden, Switzerland, West Germany, and the United States.

Postwar "homophile" publications (roughly 1945–1969) focused on domestic issues, but their content always included key international developments, mainly in Western Europe and North America (Jackson, 2015; sometimes writers included observations about queerness in the histories or cultural practices of other geographies, such as North Africa and East Asia). Readers learned about nascent homosexual organizations, which encouraged new patterns of international tourism, such as to Amsterdam (Schrover & Kampman, 2020), as well as internal migrations, such as to Washington, DC (Johnson, 2004). These movements even sparked the attention of government officials concerned with curbing homosexual migrants and tourists (Johnson, 2004; Schrover & Kampman, 2020; Sommerville, 2005).

The radicalization of "gay and lesbian" activism in the 1970s increased the number and visibility of printed periodicals aimed at the emancipation of queer people and loosening pornography laws enabled the production of sexually explicit visual media that translated across borders. Whereas in the 1970s many queer publications sought to raise "consciousness" about gay or lesbian identity in order to foster activist networks, periodicals in the 1980s had the additional task of disseminating reliable information on HIV and AIDS.

Predigital periodicals were already "social media" in that readers actively engaged with the media, not only by placing and responding to "contact advertisements" or writing letters to the editor, but also by sharing the media with likeminded people from other cultural backgrounds. Those who got their hands on a printed publication could interact with other readers, thus the media linked locals with potential tourists or migrants from other parts of the world (Shield, 2014, 2017, pp. 177–218). For example, in Poland in the 1980s, local publications were heavily dependent on cross-border exchanges. One key bulletin was produced in Vienna and mailed from Budapest in order to remain under the radar of Polish authorities (Szulc, 2017, pp. 139–141), whereas another publication was produced in the coastal area around Gdańsk, where the publisher had "regular contacts with homosexual sailors, mainly Poles but also foreigners, who were bringing him gay magazines from the West" (Szulc, 2017,

p. 143). Early queer media facilitated new transnational networks, and in turn, these networks enabled media aimed at new queer audiences.

Transition Online. In the 1990s and early 2000s, news media aimed at LGBT people gradually transitioned online, whether in the form of online versions of legacy periodicals (e.g., the *Bay Area Reporter*, founded 1971), or as new, online-only platforms (e.g., PlanetOut, Inc. 1994–2009; or *Queerty*, founded 2005). Online content facilitated sharing across borders without the cost and labor of printing and transferring physical material. Thus, online infrastructures accelerated communication between readers ("users") of a platform. Discussion forums and instant messaging led to new cross-cultural and cross-border exchanges, and LGBT dating sites emerged as a popular space for online communication and offline network-building (Mowlabocus, 2010).

As individuals around the globe accessed these platforms, the Western and often Anglo–U.S.-centric LGBTQ vocabularies globalized (Provencher, 2004; Szulc, 2020a). For example, drop-down menus reified binary notions about "butch" versus "femme," and erotic imagery favored White models adhering to Western aesthetic trends. Anamarija Horvat has argued that depictions of LGBTQ populations in U.S. and U.K. television continued to focus on White, middle-class characters until recently (Horvat, 2020). Yet, in the meantime, diverse users of queer online media adapted the platforms to new local and cultural contexts, such as among the Beirut-based users of PlanetRomeo (Gagné, 2012), the Turkish-speaking users of CamQueer (Atay, 2015), or the queer users who forged online subcultures in Hong Kong (Nip, 2004), Taiwan (Lin, 2006), and Tunis (Collins, 2012).

Around the turn of the millennium, internet-carrier advertisements and journalists propagated the "cyberutopia" myth: On the internet, ideas supposedly superseded bodies, and race, gender, sexual orientation, ability, and age were fluid or irrelevant. Critical race scholarship challenged this myth by noting that the default assumption online was that a user was White, male, heterosexual, and able-bodied (Kolko et al., 2000). While it is true that some online gamers experimented with other racial or gender identities, their chosen avatars tended to reinforce (rather than deconstruct) stereotypes, such as non-Japanese people "masquerading as exotic samurais or horny geishas" in chat rooms and online gaming spaces (Nakamura, 2002). Within queer subcultures and dating platforms, sexualized stereotypes negatively affected the experiences of many racial minorities (see the section "Racism in Queer Digital Cultures"). Scholars working with LGBTQ digital cultures also debunked the myth that online cultures were bodiless: Many users swapped digital photos and sought face-to-face meetings (Mowlabocus, 2010; Shaw, 2002). Queer people were using the internet to forge new connections with strangers and neighbors, also offline.

Around 2004–2006, highly visual network-building and information-sharing platforms grabbed widespread attention, such as Facebook, YouTube, and Twitter. Some writers use the phrase "Web 2.0" to differentiate between earlier text-heavy internet cultures and the social media cultures that proliferated after 2004. Yet media scholars underscore that earlier internet cultures were also user-generated and social (Baym, 2015); thus, the major development since 2004 is the change in cultural attitudes toward online participation that accompanied the boom in content creation and sharing via social media (Ellison & boyd, 2013). With the advent of smartphone technologies in the 2010s, new app platforms brought about further changes in the ways many queer people and migrants used media technologies.

The Geolocative Turn. With the proliferation of mobile smartphones in the 2010s, individuals could connect more casually to the online world—also outside the home—and geolocative technologies allowed for apps that connected people by physical proximity. For example, Grindr launched in 2009 almost immediately after the first iPhone, and gay men deployed the technology in a variety of new ways and settings, such as while waiting for a bus or while out with heterosexual friends at a bar in order to connect with other gay men at other heterosexual bars; thus media scholars observed the revolutionary potential of geolocative apps (Mowlabocus, 2010, pp. 183–206) as a type of queer space that could be "layered on top of a range of physical places" (Blackwell et al., 2015, p. 1126).

Alongside the boom in social media platforms, queer people with smartphones read and shared content in new ways—via news feeds, video "stories," visual memes, etc.—and were always connected to a source of new information. Tailored ads and algorithms could facilitate some users' exposure to new queer content, though these same technologies could have the opposite effect of narrowing one's range of media products.

Geolocative platforms like Grindr facilitate interactions between users in close proximity; compared to the websites of the 1990s and early 2000s, geolocative apps were initially less useful for those interested in international correspondence, such as potential migrants. After several years, these apps created new features to allow for "exploration," such as Tinder Passport, which encourages users to meet singles outside of one's usual radius. Further, geolocative apps remain important for recent migrants looking to interact with others in a new city or country, as they enable newcomers to connect to people with more knowledge of local information. As the rest of this article shows, online media can facilitate all aspects of the queer migration process, including by connecting queer migrants to political and activist networks in a host country, which could ultimately improve the living situation for themselves and future queer migrants (Chavez, 2013).

DECISIONS AND PATHS TO MIGRATION

Having established that queer individuals have long utilized various media to build transnational networks, the remainder of this article shows how these media and networks facilitate migration and settling in a new land. For many, the first "step" into a queer space occurs online, where a longing to participate in LGBTQ subcultures might eventually become a decision to migrate. Digital platforms inspire not only new aspirations, but also practical information to assist with migration before and sometimes during the migration process.

Gathering Long-Distance Information. "…I got to know that if I can prove my homosexuality and that my life and future was at risk in Iran, I would [be] eligible to apply for asylum and leave Iran…when I left in 2009 there were weblogs about this, and they were writing about their experiences, so I contacted one of the bloggers.…I am not sure if I would still be alive if it were not for this asylum option." (Interviewee cited in Karimi, 2020, p. 77)

Aryan Karimi's recent interviews with gay refugees in Canada, like the man just cited, demonstrate not only how queer sexuality relates to decisions to migrate internationally, but also how digital media and transnational networks assist with the migration process.

To begin with an overview of queer migration: Sexual orientation and gender identity play a role in some individuals' decisions to migrate, and their paths of migration (Luibhéid & Cantu, 2005). Yet even in queer asylum cases (i.e., when an asylum seeker applies for protection based on "membership in a particular social group" due to LGBT or intersex identity), the queer migrant does not always migrate from "oppression" to "liberation": Sexual minorities and gender nonconforming people have historically carved out positions in societies worldwide, and by immigrating, many migrants face new discriminations (Manalasan, 2003, 2005). Nevertheless, queer people have taken large risks in immigrating internationally, often based on knowledge of the host country's more liberal laws or social attitudes about sexual orientation or gender identity. Gathering long-distance information is necessary for selecting the destination country and for gaining insight into how best to enter and remain in that country.

Without an internet connection, people living in areas with limited queer visibility could still gain information about LGBTQ subcultures through printed media, films, or word of mouth. With the internet, information exchange becomes significantly easier. Separately, the boom in scholarly attention to queer actors and to global migrations since the 1990s means more empirical documentation and analysis of queer migrations exists in the digital age than of historic queer migrations.

Potential migrants can use digital platforms to explore new cities and countries. Nicholas Boston used the term "speculators" in his research with Polish individuals who utilized queer social media in Poland to "travel" to London in order to chat with local queer people there and to weigh the benefits of a possible move to the city (Boston, 2015, p. 305); similar behaviors have been documented in other cases, such as with Middle Eastern asylum seekers who eventually fled to San Francisco (Rodrigues, 2017).

Information about LGBTQ hotspots also encourages rural-to-urban migrations within a country. In many of these instances, the speculator shares a common language and culture with the urban residents and faces fewer legal obstacles in moving. Queer online platforms have mediated internal migrations in diverse areas, for example, to Delhi, India (Katyal, 2011); however, some scholars argue that the rise in internet technologies—in tandem with increased tolerance for LGBTQ people—has made rural-to-urban movements less necessary, such as in Sweden (Wimark, 2014, p. 149).

Other Practicalities of Migrating. In addition to using the internet to gain general knowledge about LGBTQ subcultures or tolerance in a distant location, prospective migrants might use digital media to help with migration logistics. For example, prospective Chinese migrants to Australia have used online forums to ask for tips on the best airlines for travel (Cassidy & Wang, 2018, p. 9). Some in developing countries contact queers in Western Europe to request money for visas and travel to Europe, though there is a lack of empirical data on whether these requests came from real queer people or bots and whether anyone actually benefited from these online communications (Shield, 2018, pp. 98–101).

Refugees and asylum seekers have used digital media platforms to expose homophobic and transphobic violence in their countries of birth in order to bolster cases for LGBTI asylum, such as with the case of a transgender woman from Malaysia in the United Kingdom (Yue, 2012) or gay Iranians in Canada (Karimi, 2018).

Identity-Building and Belonging. Digital media can connect a prospective migrant with logistical information about another country or city, but one should not disregard another more abstract effect of digital media: Representations of LGBTQ identities and relationships online can foster identification with and feelings of belonging to an LGBTQ community. The internationalization of queer media has privileged Western and Anglo–U.S.-centric representations of LGBTQ relationships and identities, but there are also countless examples of people "not simply adopting but adapting, hybridizing, or creolizing Western concepts of queerness" (Szulc, 2020b, p. 5). Nevertheless, a feeling of connectedness to LGBTQ people in other parts of the world could be a precondition for a potential migrant's decision to emigrate.

Feelings of belonging to a global LGBTQ community might encourage international migration, but the opposite is also true. For example, interactions between Western foreign aid workers and locals in Tacloban, Philippines after the 2013 typhoon might have fostered a spirit of "resilience and human rights" at the first Tacloban Pride 2016 parade and week, which was "not dissimilar from advocacies circulated by foreign aid workers and their various projects at the height of their operations" after the typhoon (Ong, 2017, p. 671). In any case, cross-cultural interactions via digital platforms can empower local queers to build subcultures, and knowledge of LGBTQ subcultures can indeed encourage global movement, if not migration.

During the Move. Digital media technologies can assist during the move from one country to another, such as in the case of queer refugees temporarily living in Turkey while in transit from the Arab Middle East to the European Union (Bayramoğlu & Lünenborg, 2018) or while in transit from Iran to Canada (Karimi, 2020). The information gathered in transit might affect the final destination of the migrant (Lennes, 2020). Practical information can be sent back to queer contacts in one's country of origin, thus sparking new migrations along the same (or a different) trajectory (Karimi, 2020). In sum, digital media facilitate interpersonal networks that assist with information-gathering and other practical logistics of migration while simultaneously fostering a sense of belonging to a larger LGBTQ community.

"NEW IN TOWN": SETTLING IN

Queer individuals' access to digital media and transnational networks not only aids with migration, but also with an individual's ability to settle into a new society. Recent migrants might turn to online platforms for making new friends or for finding an apartment or job, and in doing so, these online platforms might engender the migrant's feeling of belonging to a local LGBTQ community. Yet online cultures often mirror the sociopolitical context of the geography in which they are deployed (Shield, 2019, p. 180), and foreigners and ethnic minorities face xenophobia and racism online.

Logistics and Networks in a Host Country. Upon arrival in a new country or city, LGBTQ-identified newcomers—whether immigrants, refugees, tourists, or students—are often optimistic that local LGBTQs will help them with some of the practicalities of settling in.

Thus, newcomers turn to social media to build networks that can assist with finding housing or jobs, finding local information, or practicing the language (Shield, 2019, pp. 111–142). That being said, not all immigrants benefit equally from this online networking; those with more socioeconomic capital might have better luck harnessing queer networks to their advantage (McPhail & Fisher, 2015).

Indeed, immigrants often have more success connecting with other migrants—such as those from their country of origin—than they do linking with locals (Shield, 2019, pp. 137–138). Many turn to diasporic networks merely to find friends or to communicate in one's native tongue (Cassidy & Wang, 2018; see also the section "Queer Diasporic Communities").

Queer Identities and Coming Out. Media aimed at LGBTQ people can foster feelings of belonging to a larger community, as established in the aforementioned section about prospective migrants living in areas with little or no LGBTQ visibility; the same can be said for recent migrants who continue to live in areas with low LGBTQ visibility, whether they are living in refugee camps, in smaller towns, or with family. In connecting recent migrants to those with more knowledge of local LGBTQ information, digital media can bolster the newcomer's identification with the LGBTQ community (Patterson & Leurs, 2019).

In some cases, those forging connections with LGBTQ individuals take pains to ensure that their new (queer) network does not overlap with their older network of family or friends from their country of origin or with (non-LGBTQ) members of their diasporic community in the host country; this relates to the digital media theory of "context collapse" wherein one's multiple identities collide in an online environment (something that, offline, usually only happens when one hosts large parties). Thus, some queer migrants create parallel online profiles, such as on Facebook, in order to keep their LGBTQ and non-LGBTQ worlds separate (Dhoest, 2016).

Yet others take advantage of context collapse and post about LGBTQ rights in order to provoke conversations with older contacts in their network (Rodriguez, 2017) or even use these platforms to "come out" about their sexuality or gender identity to all the disparate members of their social network (Dhoest & Szulc, 2016).

Racism in Queer Digital Cultures. Literature about online LGBTQ racism has historically been written by racial minorities—though not necessarily immigrants—in White majority countries; thus, this section focuses on the experience of queer people of color. Especially recently, scholars have also considered race-based prejudice and queer racial hierarchies in non-White majority geographies, such as Singapore (Ang et al., 2021). Further, not all immigrants experience racism: White immigrants in White majority countries might feel excluded from LGBTQ networks on grounds related to cultural differences, but a blond refugee in Sweden, for example, does not experience the same prejudices that foreign and Swedish-born racial minorities face on apps like Grindr (Shield, 2019, pp. 135–137).

Patterns of racist speech in queer digital cultures can be theorized in several ways. There are speech acts that relate to "everyday racism" (Essed, 1990, 1991), such as when locals repeatedly ask questions about the origins of people of color (e.g., "Where are you *really* from?"). There are at least two types of "sexual racism" (Callander et al., 2015): exclusions (e.g., "Sorry, no Asians") and fetishes (e.g., "Into submissive Asian guys"). And there are incidents of "entitlement racism" when the perpetrator justifies disparaging comments as "freedom of speech" (Essed, 2013), even when spewing insults directly related to race, migration status, or religion. Not all immigrants categorize their experiences with race-based prejudice as racism, partly because of the impersonal nature of online correspondences. Stephanie Ortiz shows that even in extreme cases of entitlement racism, a person of color might excuse the behavior because it happened online, a phenomenon she refers to as "racists without racism" (Ortiz, 2020).

While popular media lament a supposed proliferation of overtly racist texts on gay male platforms, the evidence is not always obvious; thus, Jesus Smith has theorized a "two-faced racism" in which users perform as nonracist in the "front stage," but still act with racist behaviors "back stage" (Smith, 2018). Indeed, many people of color sense that they are ignored and excluded for race-based reasons, and investigate by creating secondary White profiles in order to observe how they are treated differently: In various experiments on various gay male platforms, White profiles received more invitations to chat than non-White profiles (e.g., Gosine, 2007; Robinson, 2008; Shield, 2019, p. 160; Tsang, 1994). Shaka McGlotten argues this "state of heightened awareness" about race produces anxiety and paranoia among queer people of color online (McGlotten, 2014, pp. 66, 76).

But a digital media platform can also promote race-related thinking and communications. On many LGBTQ dating platforms, users are encouraged to identify by "ethnicity" or "origin," and these platforms allow users to search and filter out people of particular races. Drop-down menu options reflect the dominant understandings of racial difference in the context in which the app is developed; for example, "whiteness" is bounded differently on the U.S. American platforms Grindr and Scruff, the German platform GayRomeo, and the Swedish platform Qruiser (Shield, 2019, pp. 198–205).

Queer Diasporic Communities. Because online platforms are not tethered to national borders, speakers of a common language or members of a shared ethnic group can communicate easily online. These transnational communities can develop in the "homeland" and then spread to contacts abroad, or they can form abroad and empower people in the "homeland," such as with Khush List, the first global community for LGBTQ South Asians, founded in the United States in 1993 (Roy, 2003). Queer people living in areas with less LGBTQ visibility rely on these diasporic networks for information about LGBTQ subcultures, laws, or organizations.

Online diasporic communities assist both potential and recent migrants, such as by enabling international chats about logistical information, but many diasporic communities are more explicitly political. One such example is the UndocuQueer movement, which has given visibility to undocumented queer young people in the United States through art and personal narratives shared via YouTube videos, personal blogs, and a range of hashtagged media on various other platforms (Serrano, 2017).

CONCLUSION

In reflecting on the queer networks of the past, one notices a feedback loop between niche media and transnational communication. Individuals communicated across borders and connected with fellow readers through the pages of printed media, which sometimes resulted in international tourism or migration. In turn, mobile individuals propagated existing media in new settings (both when traveling and upon returning home), which inspired more individuals to produce fresh publications in different languages aimed at new, queer populations.

Just before the turn of the 21st century, this feedback loop between networks of mobile queer individuals and the media they consumed and produced accelerated tremendously with the advent of online communication technologies and personal computers. Transnational networks did not need to rely as heavily on material objects, like limited-run magazines or postage stamps. Information became available to seemingly unlimited audiences. With the "turn" toward social media and subsequent "turn" in smartphone technologies, LGBTQ individuals had even fewer obstacles to producing their own content. Via TikTok or Blued, queer people continue to harness new technologies to build networks, and these networks might ultimately connect potential migrants to diasporic communities, speculators to locals, people in transit to tourists, and more.

The relatively recent visibility of queer migration is not wholly related to online technologies. Legal developments are fundamental to this history, including the broadening of marriage laws to include same-sex, binational couples or the formalization of asylum procedures to protect LGBT and intersex people following the declaration of the Yogyakarta Principles. Other developments relate to changes in political cultures: LGBTQ activism has increased in almost every country, yet anti-LGBTQ crusades simultaneously grow fiercer and more visible. The availability of cheap airfare or the effects of chain migration must also be taken into consideration. There are endless reasons that more and more migrants identify as LGBTQ or migrate directly or partly due to personal circumstances related to sexual orientation and gender identity. A comprehensive look at queer migration must seriously consider the role of digital media in enabling transnational networks, border crossings, and prospects for new futures.

FURTHER READING

Akin, D. (2016). Queer asylum seekers: Translating sexuality in Norway. *Journal of Ethnic and Migration Studies, 42*, 15.

Alencar, A. (2020). Mobile communication and refugees: An analytical review of academic literature. *Sociology Compass, 14*(8), e12802.

Alinejad, D., & Ponzanesi, S. (2020). Migrancy and digital mediations of emotion. *International Journal of Cultural Studies, 23*(5), 621–638.

Chen, X. (2020). *Dating, digital media, and diaspora: Contextualising the cultural uses of Tinder and Tantan among Australian Chinese diasporas* [Unpublished doctoral dissertation]. Queensland University of Technology.

Dhoest, A. (2020). Digital (dis)connectivity in fraught contexts: The case of gay refugees in Belgium. *European Journal of Cultural Studies, 23*(5), 784–800. https://doi.org/10.1177/1367549419869348

Dhoest, A., & Szulc, L. (2019). Queer migration and digital media. *Oxford bibliographies.* https://doi.org/10.1093/obo/9780199756841-0228

Giametta, C. (2017). *The sexual politics of asylum: Sexual orientation and gender in the UK asylum system.* Routledge.

Guðmundsdóttir, L. S., & Skaptadóttir, U. D. (2017). LGBQ migrations: Racialization and (un)belonging in Iceland. *Lambda Nordica, 22*(4), 40–65.

James, D., Condie, J., & Lean, G. (2019). Travel, Tinder and gender in digitally mediated tourism encounters. In C. J. Nash & A. Gorman-Murray (Eds.), *The geographies of digital sexuality* (pp. 49–68). Palgrave Macmillan.

Koçak, M. (2020, November 5). Legally unrecognized but bureaucratically tolerated: Queer Iranian refugees living in Turkey. *Network for Migration Matters*. https://www.networkformigrationmatters.com/post/legally-unrecognized-but-bureaucratically-tolerated-queer-iranian-refugees-living-in-turkey

Kuntsman, A. (2008). Genealogies of hate, metonymies of violence: Immigration, homophobia, homopatriotism. In A. Kuntsman & E. Miyake (Eds.), *Out of place: Interrogating silences in queerness/raciality* (pp. 97–118). Raw Nerve.

Lee, J. (2019). *Talking about race and gender with Tinder: Raced and gendered visibility of non-white women* [Unpublished doctoral dissertation]. Southern Illinois University at Carbondale.

Li, H. (2020). Transnational togetherness through Rela: Chinese queer women's practices for maintaining ties with the homeland. *International Journal of Cultural Studies, 23*(5), 692–708.

Lim, X. Q. (2019). *Gay Asian migrants and the problem of desirability: Racism and sexuality on gay mobile dating apps*. Media, Film and Television, University of Auckland.

Luibhéid, E. (2008). Queer/migration: An unruly body of scholarship. *GLQ: A Journal of Lesbian and Gay Studies, 14*(2–3), 169–190.

Martin, F. (2009). That global feeling: Sexual subjectivities and imagined geographies in Chinese-language lesbian cyberspaces. In G. Goggin & M. McLelland (Eds.), *Internationalizing internet studies: Beyond anglophone paradigms* (pp. 285–301). Routledge.

Mitra, R. (2010). Resisting the spectacle of pride: Queer Indian bloggers as interpretative communities. *Journal of Broadcasting & Electronic Media, 54*(1), 163–178.

Noel, U. (2019). The queer migrant poemics of #Latinx instagram. *New Literary History, 50*(4), 531–557.

Peumans, W. (2014). "No Asians, please": Same-sex sexualities and ethnic minorities in Europe. In J. Boulton (Ed.), *Hand picked: Stimulus respond* (pp. 128–139). Pavement Books.

Porter, G. (2012). Mobile phones, livelihoods and the poor in sub-Saharan Africa: Review and prospect. *Geography Compass, 6*(5), 241–259.

Rahbari, L. (2020). Duffs and puffs: Queer fashion in Iranian cyberspace. *Middle East Critique, 29*(1), 69–86.

Rodriguez, N. S. (2016). Communicating global inequalities: How LGBTI asylum-specific NGOs use social media as public relations. *Public Relations Review, 42*(2), 322–332.

Ruez, D. (2016). "I never felt targeted as an Asian...until I went to a gay pub": Sexual racism and the aesthetic geographies of the bad encounter. *Environment and Planning A: Economy and Space, 49*(4), 893–910.

Szulc, L. (2020). Queer migrants and digital culture. In K. Smets, K. Leurs, M. Georgiou, S. Witteborn, & R. Gajjala (Eds.), *The SAGE handbook of media and migration* (Chapter 24, pp. 220–232). SAGE.

Wu, S., & Ward, J. (2018). The mediation of gay men's lives: A review of gay dating app studies. *Sociology Compass, 12*(2), 1–10.

Yue, A. (2003). Paging "new Asia": Sambal is a feedback loop, coconut is a code, rice is a system. In C. Berry, F. Martin, & A. Yue (Eds.), *Mobile cultures: New media in queer Asia* (pp. 245–265). Duke University Press.

REFERENCES

Ang, M. W., Tan, J. C. K., & Lou, C. (2021). Navigating sexual racism in the sexual field: Compensation for and disavowal of marginality by racial minority Grinder users in Singapore. *Journal of Computer-Mediated Communication, 26*(3), 129–147. https://doi.org/10.1093/jcmc/zmab003

Atay, A. (2015). *Globalization's impact on cultural identity formation: Queer diasporic males in cyberspace.* Lexington Books.

Baym, N. K. (2015). *Personal connections in the digital age* (2nd ed.). Polity Press.

Bayramoglu, Y., & Lunenborg, M. (2018). Queer migration and digital affects: Refugees navigating from the Middle East via Turkey to Germany. *Sexuality & Culture, 22*(4), 1019–1036.

Beachy, R. (2014). *Gay Berlin: Birthplace of a modern identity.* Vintage Books.

Blackwell, C., Birnholtz, J., & Abbott, C. (2015). Seeing and being seen: Co-situation and impression formation using Grindr, a location-aware gay dating app. *New Media & Society, 17,* 1117–1136.

Boston, N. (2015). Libidinal cosmopolitanism: The case of digital sexual encounters in post-enlargement Europe. In S. Ponzanesi & G. Colpani (Eds.), *Postcolonial transitions in Europe: Contexts, practices and politics* (pp. 291–312). Rowman & Littlefield.

Callander, D., Newman, C. E., & Holt, M. (2015). Is sexual racism really racism? Distinguishing attitudes toward sexual racism and generic racism among gay and bisexual men. *Archives of Sexual Behavior, 44,* 1991–2000.

Cassidy, E., & Wang, W. (2018). Gay men's digital cultures beyond Gaydar and Grindr: LINE use in the gay Chinese diaspora of Australia. *Information, Communication & Society, 21*(6), 851–865.

Chávez, K. R. (2013). *Queer migration politics: Activist rhetoric and coalitional possibilities.* University of Illinois Press.

Collins, R. (2012). Efféminés, gigolos, and MSMs in the cyber-networks, coffeehouses, and 'secret gardens' of contemporary Tunis. *Journal of Middle East Women's Studies, 8*(3), 89–112.

Dhoest, A. (2016). Media, visibility and sexual identity among gay men with a migration background. *Sexualities, 19*(4), 412–431.

Dhoest, A., & Szulc, L. (2016). Navigating online selves: Social, cultural and material contexts of social media use by diasporic gay men. *Social Media + Society, 2*(4), 1–10.

Ellison, N. B., & boyd, d. (2013). Sociality through social network sites. In W. H. Dutton (Ed.), *The Oxford handbook of internet studies* (pp. 151–172). Oxford University Press.

Essed, P. (1990). *Everyday racism. Reports from women of two cultures.* Hunter House.

Essed, P. (1991). *Understanding everyday racism: An interdisciplinary theory.* SAGE.

Essed, P. (2013). Entitlement racism: License to humiliate. In European Network Against Racism (ENAR) (Ed.), *Recycling hatred: Racism(s) in Europe today* (pp. 62–77). ENAR.

Gagné, M. (2012). Queer Beirut online: The participation of men in Gayromeo.com. *Journal of Middle East Women's Studies, 8*(3), 113–137.

Gosine, A. (2007). Brown to blonde at gay.com: Passing white in queer cyberspace. In K. O'Riordan & D. J. Phillips (Eds.), *Queer online: Media technology and sexuality* (pp. 139–154). Peter Lang.

Herzog, D. (2011). *Sexuality in Europe: A twentieth-century history.* Cambridge University Press.

Horvat, A. (2020). Crossing the borders of queer TV: Depictions of migration and (im)mobility in contemporary LGBTQ television. *Critical Studies in Television: The International Journal of Television Studies, 15*(3), 280–301.

Jackson, J. (2015). The homophile movement. In D. Paternotte & M. Tremblay (Eds.), *The Ashgate research companion to lesbian and gay activism* (pp. 31–44). Routledge.

Johnson, D. K. (2004). *The lavender scare: the Cold War persecution of gays and lesbians in the federal government.* University of Chicago Press.

Karimi, A. (2018). Sexuality and integration: A case of gay Iranian refugees' collective memories and integration practices in Canada. *Ethnic and Racial Studies.* Advance online publication. https://doi.org/10.1080/01419870.2018.1550207

Karimi, A. (2020). Refugees' transnational practices: Gay Iranian men navigating refugee status and cross-border ties in Canada. *Social Currents, 7*(1), 71–86.

Katyal, A. (2011). Playing a double game: Idioms of same sex desire in India [Unpublished doctoral dissertation]. University of London.

Kolko, B., Nakamura, L., & Rodman, G. (2000). Introduction. In B. Kolko, L. Nakamura, & G. Rodman (Eds.), *Race in cyberspace* (pp. 1–14). Routledge.

Lennes, K. (2020). Queer (post-)migration experiences: Mexican men's use of gay dating apps in the USA. *Sexualities*. Advance online publication. https://doi.org/10.1177/1363460720944591

Lin, D. C. (2006). Sissies online: Taiwanese male queers performing sissinesses in cyberspaces. *Inter-Asia Cultural Studies*, 7(2), 270–288.

Luibhéid, E., & Cantú, L. (2005). *Queer migrations: Sexuality, U.S. citizenship, and border crossings*. University of Minnesota Press.

Manalansan, M. F. (2005). Migrancy, modernity, mobility: Quotidian struggles and queer diasporic intimacy. In E. Luibhéid & L. Cantú, Jr. (Eds.), *Queer migrations: Sexuality, U.S. citizenship, and border crossings* (pp. 146–160). University of Minnesota Press.

Manalansan, M. F. IV. (2003). *Global divas: Filipino gay men in the diaspora*. Duke University Press.

McGlotten, S. (2014). *Virtual intimacies: Media, affect, and queer sociality*. State University of New York Press.

McPhail, R., & Fisher, R. (2015). Lesbian and gay expatriates use of social media to aid acculturation. *International Journal of Intercultural Relations*, 49, 294–307.

Mowlabocus, S. (2010). *Gaydar culture: Gay men, technology and embodiment*. Ashgate.

Nakamura, L. (2002). *Cybertypes: Race, ethnicity, and identity on the internet*. Routledge.

Nip, J. Y. M. (2004). The queer sisters and its electronic bulletin board: A study of the internet for social movement mobilization. *Information, Communication and Society*, 7(1), 23–49.

Ong, J. C. (2017). Queer cosmopolitanism in the disaster zone: "My Grindr became the United Nations." *International Communication Gazette*, 79(6–7), 656–673.

Ortiz, S. M. (2020). Racists without racism? From colourblind to entitlement racism online. *Ethnic and Racial Studies*. Advance online publication. https://doi.org/10.1080/01419870.2020.1825758

Patterson, J., & Leurs, K. (2019). "We live here, and we are queer!" Young adult gay connected migrants' transnational ties and integration in the Netherlands. *Media and Communication*, 7(1), 90–101.

Provencher, D. M. (2004). Vague English creole: (Gay English) cooperative discourse in the French gay press. In W. L. Leap & T. Boellstorff (Eds.), *Speaking in queer tongues: Globalization and gay language* (pp. 23–45). University of Illinois Press.

Robinson, R. (2008). Structural dimensions of romantic preferences. *Fordham Law Review*, 76, 2786–2820.

Rodriguez, N. S. (2017). San Francisco's queer diaspora and the gay Middle Eastern refugee/asylee. *JOMEC Journal*, 11, 111–126.

Roy, S. (2003). From khush list to gay Bombay: Virtual webs of real people. In C. Berry, F. Martin, & A. Yue (Eds.), *Mobile cultures: New media in queer Asia* (pp. 180–197). Duke University Press.

Schrover, M., & Kampman, F. (2020). Charter flights full of homosexuals: The changing rights of homosexual immigrants in the Netherlands, 1945–1992. *TSEG: The Low Countries Journal of Social and Economic History*, 16(3/4), 5–36.

Serrano, X. K. (2017). Dreaming a radical citizenship: How undocumented queers in the United States configure sites of belonging and being through art and media technologies. *European Journal of American Studies*, 11(3), 1–14.

Shaw, D. (2002). Gay men and computer communication: A discourse of sex and identity in cyberspace. In S. Jones (Ed.), *Virtual culture: Identity and communication in cybersociety* (pp. 133–146). SAGE.

Shield, A. D. J. (2014). "Suriname—Seeking a lonely, lesbian friend for correspondence": Immigration and homo-emancipation in the Netherlands, 1965–79. *History Workshop Journal*, 78(1), 246–264.

Shield, A. D. J. (2018). Grindr culture: Intersectional and socio-sexual. *Ephemera: Theory & Politics in Organization*, 18(1), 149–161.

Shield, A. D. J. (2017). *Immigrants in the sexual revolution: Perceptions and participation in Northwest Europe.* Palgrave Macmillan.
Shield, A. D. J. (2019). *Immigrants on Grindr: Race, sexuality and belonging online.* Palgrave Macmillan.
Smith, J. G. (2018). Two-faced racism in gay online sex: Preference in the frontstage or racism in the backstage? In P. Nixon & I. Düsterhöft (Eds.), *Sex in the digital age* (pp. 134–145). Routledge.
Somerville, S. B. (2005). Sexual aliens and the racialized state: A queer reading of the 1952 U.S. Immigration and Nationality Act. In E. Luibhéid & L. Cantú (Eds.), *Queer migrations* (pp. 75–91). University of Minnesota Press.
Szulc, L. (2017). *Transnational homosexuals in communist Poland: Cross-border flows in gay and lesbian magazines.* Palgrave Macmillan.
Szulc, L. (2020a). Pink press. In K. Ross, I. Bachmann, V. Cardo, S. Moorti, & M. Scarcelli (Eds.), *The international encyclopedia of gender, media, and communication* (Vol. 2). Wiley.
Szulc, L. (2020b). Queer globalization and the media. In K. Ross, I. Bachmann, V. Cardo, S. Moorti, & M. Scarcelli (Eds.), *The international encyclopedia of gender, media, and communication* (Vol. 3). Wiley.
Tsang, D. (1994). Notes on queer 'n Asian virtual sex. *Amerasia Journal, 20*(1), 117–128.
Von Rosen, W. (2007). Denmark 1866–1976: From sodomy to modernity. In J. Rydström & K. Mustola (Eds.), *Criminally queer: Homosexuality and criminal law in Scandinavia, 1842–1999* (pp. 61–90). Aksant.
Wimark, T. (2014). *Beyond bright city lights: The migration patterns of gay men and lesbians.* Stockholm University Press.
Wu, S., & Trottier, D. (2021). Constructing sexual fields: Chinese gay men's dating practices among pluralized dating apps. *Social Media + Society.* Advance online publication. https://doi.org/10.1177/20563051211009014
Yue, A. (2012). Queer Asian mobility and homonational modernity: Marriage equality, Indian students in Australia and Malaysian transgender refugees in the media. *Global Media and Communication, 8*(3), 269–287.

Andrew DJ Shield

QUEER SEXUALITIES IN LATIN AMERICA

QUEER COLONIALITY AND MORAL INSUBORDINATION

Representations of what we now call Latin American queer sexuality have been present throughout Latin American history, most often taking the form of condemnation or censure. In fact, it is exclusion itself that defines queer bodies: a body outside the norm, where sexuality and diverse gender expressions are grounds for rejection. The Latin American queer studies research that is dedicated to analyzing the colonial period allows us to understand that the exclusion of these bodies and, therefore, the establishment of sexual dissidence, begins with the dislocation of the pre-Columbian cultural orders, a product of European colonization. To punish the bodies of the non-heterosexual population and to refer to them only through insult and slander is an essential part of the process of colonization. Beyond this punishment and slander, any public reference to this sector of society has been eliminated from much of the region's history. It is since colonial times that different sexualities have been banned from the public arena and condemned to silence. However, the exercise of such forms of denial and exclusion cannot suppress the emergence—and permanence—of the subversive behaviors that appear at every point on the map of the sexuality of the Latin American hemisphere.

Because of these strategies of invisibilization, scholars of colonial sexuality have had to turn to the judicial archives to find traces of dissident sexualities. Here in these archives, they have discovered that it is not the case that because those representations have been banned, proscribed sexualities are no longer practiced. Instead, it is clear that this prohibition leads to the emergence of new ways of challenging such norms. Latin American queerness must be interpreted as a consequence of the colonizing prohibition of sexuality, whereby a series of practices are repudiated as a result of their determination as sin. The texts that Zeb Tortorici has published on marginal sexualities in the Spanish colony stand out among the research that deals with the constitution of the queer in the judicial archives of the Spanish colony. For Tortorici, the notion of visceral archives, which provides the definition of sin with its repulsive and abject aspect, is of central importance. Tortorici's work allows us to understand that the queer is a discursive field in dispute where all references to nefarious acts are already loaded with severe denigration. It is precisely in those expressions of hatred that, according to Tortorici, the queer body has been archived. In this language of sin, the queer body is rendered undesirable by the simple fact of performing forbidden actions (Tortorici, 2018). However, one effect of prohibition is the emergence of the desire for the forbidden: It is from resistance to prohibition that the forbidden spaces of colonial societies are opened up. Hence, the queer is understood as disobedience to the rules of desire.

Pete Sigal, for his part, studies the way in which the discourse of slander and insult is established, which functions through the reduction of the pre-Columbian Mesoamerican gender system to European norms of the body, thereby disrupting a cultural system where homoeroticism was not proscribed. In his analysis of the 16th-century Florentine Codex—drawn by a group of noble-born Nahua converts under the direction of Fray Bernardino de Sahagún—Sigal demonstrates that translation is itself a method of colonization. The reference to the case of *xochihua* exemplifies this process: In the pictograms and explanatory texts of the *tlacuilos*, or scribes, we find the description of an effeminate man as "*el que lleva flores* (the one who carries flowers),*"* a description that could conceivably be applied to the god Xochipilli, whose iconography presents him as covered with flowers. However, the Spanish translation does not describe; instead, it insults: "*puto*" (Sigal, 2007, p. 13). By bringing into relation two incommensurate gender systems, the way is opened to a process of translation that subjects meaning itself to the order of the colonizer: that is, ecclesiastical interpretations of bodily practices enact violence upon those who are anomalous to their system of behavioral norms. In this sense, insult is itself a moral instrument that pronounces exclusion and establishes the barriers of hatred that protect the colonial regime from sodomite contamination. Sigal's book *The Flower and the Scorpion* (2011) traces these misrepresentations of different symbols of the Nahua script when subjected to the colonizer's interpretation-translation.

The order to silence practices considered offensive to the colonial gender system has only encouraged the production of forms of resistance that will eventually nurture what we will call the field of queer representation. Faced with prohibition, several discursive and performative strategies are put into play that implicitly question the effectiveness of the Western patriarchal discourse's ordering of bodies. In his *Decolonizing the Sodomite* (2005), Michael Horswell illustrates how through the distortion and encryption of Quechua history itself, the converted indigenous chroniclers maintain a queer attitude. They do not declare their rejection of the new Spanish sexual culture, nor do they clearly communicate the contents of their own culture, thus hindering colonial indoctrination. Quechua chroniclers distort the stories that other indigenous people have previously told (or at least offer a different version), thereby producing a state of symbolic instability, a deliberate misunderstanding (Horswell, 2005, p. 140).

In various cultural manifestations of colonized populations, a dispute can be observed between Christian hegemony over the knowledge and ordering of bodies, and the symbolic dispersion produced as clandestine response in various popular representations, where each colonizing order finds its underside, its negation, its distortion, and its contradiction. Such is the case of Tinkuy, a cross-dressing character who has been assimilated to the ritual dances of Catholic festivals, which alludes to pre-Columbian bisexual deities that, although having been reduced in transculturation to a kind of third-sex imprint of Andean cultures, are nevertheless an archive that testifies to the nonbinary gender system of the pre-Columbian world and the ways in which the colonized exercised their symbolic resistance (Horswell, 2005, p. 4). This representational struggle is a primary aspect of the academic conversation regarding the queer both in the field of the histories of sexuality of the colony, and the anthropological research and cultural studies identified with the theoretical current of decoloniality. One of the most plausible works that delve into indigenous homoerotic practices that resist hegemonic gay culture is that of Marinella Miano Borruso, *Men, Women and Muxe' in the Isthmus of Tehuantepec* (2003), which studies the *muxe* culture in Oaxaca, Mexico, referring to the identity that is closer to the idea of the third sex of some Native American cultures than to modern gay culture.

Given the contentious situation of its enunciation, the representation of the queer itself necessarily brings into play a dispute over the significance of bodies. The disciplining of sexual practices is essential to the colonizing process of the territory we call Latin America: This is how there exists the distinction between correct bodies and deviant bodies. Colonization means the installation of a new gender system. The body is colonized with the establishment of the notion of the sin of the flesh: a list of prohibited practices whose purpose is to restrict and punish pleasure. In Christian ideology, the body is the battlefield of the war between good and evil. Non-heterosexual, polygamous, interspecies, fetishistic, and incestuous practices pass into the plane of evil as nefarious (the repudiable and unmentionable) sin. Among the texts that address this contentious condition of the Latin American queer in the colonial context, and in addition to those of Tortorici, Sigal, and Horswell, mention must be made of Oswaldo Bazán's *Historia de la homosexualidad en Argentina* (2004), which reviews the chronicles of the conquest in order to underscore homophobia as one of the reasons for genocidal actions; and also Federico Garza Carvajal's *Butterflies Will Burn* (2003), that, rather than focusing on the indigenous sector, reviews transgressions of the Spanish heteronorm by the colonizers themselves, especially the soldiers who serve the crown. Garza Carvajal focuses on the case of the trans soldier, Alonso Díaz, who ultimately gains recognition of his male identity by the Pope himself. For Garza Carvajal, Hispanic masculinity is made more legible by the construction of manliness that the nun Catalina de Erauso performs. In this way, Garza Carvajal demonstrates how the queer perspective is an effective methodological instrument in the deconstructive knowledge of heterosexualities.

MODERN ADVERSITIES OF THE QUEER

History monographs on sexual diversity in Cuba (Bejel, 2001; Lumsden, 1996; Sierra Madero, 2006), Brazil (Figari, 2009; Green, 1999), Argentina (Bazán, 2004; Salessi, 1995), Uruguay

(Sempol, 2013), Chile (Sutherland, 2009), and Mexico (Domínguez Ruvalcaba, 2007; Irwin, 2003) can also be read as narratives of official and social homophobia. More specifically, they are a narrative of how homophobic discourse has taken various forms of representation: from the judicial document punishing the sodomite by considering him a sinner, to the political caricature that uses the notion of the effeminate as a tool to denigrate ideological enemies, there is a continuity where dissident sexuality is made worthy of social condemnation.

The relationship between sexual diversity and the construction of modern Latin American states takes place on a symbolic battlefield where the voice of sexual dissidence breaks through between heteronormative conventions that impose the invisibilization of non-heterosexual sexual practices. Nevertheless, the presence of sexual dissidence is indelible, despite the concerted efforts to deny its existence. Already in *El Periquillo Sarniento* by Joaquín Fernández de Lizardi—written in the last decade of the colony in Mexico, at a time when writing and reading novels was strictly monitored by the authorities—we find male characters who experience intimacy with other men, a narrative rich in descriptions of affections and bodily proximity. Ambiguous characters are visible, although reduced to secondary roles and, most of the time, as circumstantial vignettes where the transgression of dominant heteronormative models is hinted at (Irwin, 2003, pp. 4–5).

Although the colonial norms for which nefarious sin was a judicial matter had been abrogated in much of the continent after the establishment of the independent republics, policies against sexual dissent remained. As Jorge Salessi argues for the Argentine case, hygiene and criminology replaced the semantic field of sin with that of disease, vice, and crime. The disciplinary apparatuses of modernity, according to Foucauldian thought, are put into operation to produce desirable citizens (Salessi, 1995, p. 222). Scientific discourse, in alliance with nationalist doctrines, constitutes borders of exclusion, punishment, seclusion, and the restriction of sexuality. Through a censorious gaze, denigrating representations are constructed that present diverse sexualities as crimes and psycho-biological defects. Examples abound in literature, cinema, television comedies, press cartoons, and theatrical and musical performances. A classic example is Relumbrón, a secondary character in *Los bandidos de Río Frío* by Manuel Payno (1982), one of the most canonical novels in Mexican literature, who is depicted as an extravagant, corrupt, and unscrupulous character.

Homosexuality is considered a vice or a disease of the modern world. In the context of the Mexican revolution, the novel by Salvador Quevedo y Zubieta, *Mexico marimacho* (1933), suggests that lesbianism is a disease that is eliminated through the relationship with men, such that at the end of the plot, the protagonist "recovers" her heterosexual condition. This same idea that homosexuality is a pathology that is acquired by contagion due to the social environment where one lives can be read in the Cuban novel *Hombres sin mujer* by Carlos Montenegro (1938). Even in literature that offers no homophobic intentionality, homosexuality is carried as a penalty, a burden to live with, a suffering that is exquisite and tragic at the same time, which destines homoerotic desires to be conceived of as the misfortune of fate, one of the most frequently used motives among the authors of the end of the 19th century and the first half of the 20th century (Adolfo Caminha, Xavier Villaurrutia, José Lezama Lima, Ofelia Rodríguez Acosta, etc.).

In this way, the discourses of comedy, medicine, vices, and disease contribute to keeping sexual dissidents in a place external to the community, to the nation, to the dominant gender system—in short, to the different sources of normativity. The symbolic acts of exclusion range from the discriminatory and dehumanizing laughter of homophobic television comedies (Domínguez Ruvalcaba, 2016) to violent acts of repression as a measure of social "sanitation." In the field of literary representations, as well as in official and social action, modernity means the rendering visible of diverse sexualities, albeit through a strategy whose logic is that of the sanitization of society: to point out vices for the purpose of eradicating them. Modernity brings with it the scrutiny of difference and its disciplining. The institutional strategies for addressing sexuality make homophobia one of the axes of education, the design of public policies, and the set of stigmatizing representations produced in the media and culture industries.

If representations of sexual diversity occupy the press and television as a prolific source of scandal, the vindication of sexual dissidents will have to pass through the discourses of human rights and civil claims. Juan Pablo Sutherland describes how Chilean media experience a convulsion that he calls "guerrilla mediática (mediatic guerilla warfare)": TV and radio presenters freely offer up a series of fallacious arguments to justify and spread their hatred of sexual differences (Sutherland, 2009). The fear of the contagion of homosexuality circulates as a homophobic joke in television sketches. The most conservative sectors of Latin American societies have resorted to biologist discourse to explain their homophobia, now no longer in terms of sin but pathology. These societies understand that sexual diversity is an evil to be exterminated, and the state, through its police force, undertakes punitive policies. It is precisely this kind of police abuse that sets off the first protests of the LGBT (lesbian, gay, bisexual, and transgender) movement, a struggle for the civil right to use public space.

POLITICAL USES OF THE HOMOPHOBIC INSULT

Puto and *sodomita* are terms that inaugurate a long list of words whose use has had throughout Latin American history and geography the sense of perpetuating the line of the exclusion of "incorrect" bodies maintained since the establishment of Christianity within the logics of life of the region. Public derision is encouraged by the civil and ecclesiastical authorities as a form of pedagogy of the bodies that the colonial power promotes. *Maricón, joto, pájaro, tortillera, lencha, garzona, pato, cochón, hueco, viado, puto*... all are denigrating words and aggressions that nourish much of the comedic narratives since the appearance of the political cartoon in the newspapers of the 19th century: They are the very image of the abject, the contempt with which one attacks one's enemies. The rendering effeminate, thus, serves a defamatory function. In the compilation by Robert M. Irwin, Edward J. McCaughan, and Michelle Rocío Nasser, *The Famous 41: Sexuality and Social Control in Mexico* (2003)—the scandal of a cross-dressing male dance that was propagated in the Mexico City press in November 1901—serves as a starting point for revising representations of sexual diversity in the press at the time. The theme of social homophobia and its implications in politics and the arts runs through many of the collaborations in this volume. The use of effeminacy in political caricature to denigrate adversaries characterizes the political altercations of the early 20th century. For Robert Buffington (2003, p. 221), the popular press (penny press) adds a class aspect to this homophobic expression: The working class sees in the bourgeois complacency of the *Porfiriato* (1876–1910) a reason to denigrate it through cross-dressing representation.

Another form of the political use of effeminacy is that which links it to foreign influence, where homophobia and xenophobia shake hands. In his book *Del otro lado del espejo*, Abel Sierra Madero analyzes press cartoons of the prerevolutionary era in Cuba and finds that the effeminate expressions of men or masculinized expressions of women are portrayed as symptoms of North American cultural colonization (Sierra Madero, 2006, pp. 81–102). Similarly, the Mexican press of the 1920s and 1930s is the scene of heated polemics where expressions of sexual dissent are judged as counter-revolutionary, imperialist, and corrupting of the fatherland (Balderston, 1998b). In the Mexican political cartoon, this perception of homosexuality has also been observed as a foreign contamination. Such is the case of the work of one of the most important cartoonists of the Mexican press of the 20th century, Abel Quesada. If in the 19th century gallicization was associated with effeminacy, in the 20th century it is Americanization. Antiimperialist politics raises suspicions against behavior that deviates from gender norms.

The representations of the male members of the elite social class of the prerevolutionary period in Mexico can help us to explain this association of effeminacy with modern colonization. In his text on male consumption of fashion in the *Porfiriato* era, Víctor Macías-González observes that the modernization of aspects of everyday culture, for example dress, represents a relaxation of heteronormative models. In his analysis of the advertising of the time, Macías-González suggests that the dandyism of the men of the ruling classes, with their effeminate and frivolous features, defines modernity itself. To be modern is to compulsively consume the sumptuous articles of the metropolitan centers: Paris, London, New York, and so on (Macías-González, 2003).

Just as in the colonial period where sodomites were considered enemies of religion and therefore deserving of punishment, in the modern history of Latin America, it is possible to observe a tendency to consider homosexuals as counter-revolutionary and antinationalist. In the same way that the postrevolutionary Mexican press suspects that homosexuals are enemies of the fatherland, the triumph of the Cuban revolution and the proposal of the "new man" as the masculinity that the revolution would build, according to Ernesto Guevara, provokes an airing of expressions of the rejection of sexual diversity (Bejel, 2001, pp. 113–156; Quiroga, 2000, pp. 101–144; Sierra Madero, 2006, pp. 196–205).

The works that analyze the political processes of sexual diversity draw attention to the development of a liberationist discourse in the first LGBT organizations: to liberate this group of people defined by their expressions of sexuality and gender that dissent from the norm that oppress them. That is to say: to repeal a series of normative cultural provisions that begin by identifying certain bodies as defective and harmful in order to justify punitive action against these very bodies. The first two LGBT associations in Latin America (formed in Argentina and Mexico) have the name Frente de Liberación Homosexual (FLH). In his chronicles on the Argentine FLH, Néstor Perlongher, one of the central figures for the study of sexual diversity in the Southern Cone, speaks of state persecution manifested by groups of police officers and hate crimes perpetrated by the citizenry (Perlongher, 1997). *Sueños de exterminio*, authored by Gabriel Giorgi (2004), offers us an analysis of Argentine literature that traces the common thread of homophobia as state politics, and in this way echoes the work of Jorge Salessi (1995) on the medicalization and criminalization of homophobia in that country.

Two authors staging political analyses of the LGBT movements in Latin America are Rafael de la Dehesa and Jordi Díez. In his *Queering the Public Sphere in Mexico and Brazil* (2010), de la Dehesa offers a broad review that describes the emergence of the LGBT movement and how it positions itself in the public sphere. In his research, this political scientist draws on the archives of sexual diversity organizations, as well as legal and parliamentary legislative archives, and the ones of political parties and religious institutions, while also conducting interviews with key personalities. In this way, this research offers us a vision of how the political agendas of sexual dissidence have been formed and advanced: the struggle against discrimination, public policies to address the HIV/AIDS pandemic, egalitarian marriage, the right to adoption, and the recognition of transgender identity. De la Dehesa's work demonstrates that the politics of sexual diversity evolves from a liberationist discourse starting point toward a discourse of citizens' rights. It is not only about liberating sexual diversity but also about opening up institutional spaces in order to address LGBT rights.

The Politics of Gay Marriage in Latin America, by Jordi Díez (2015), is a comparative study on the advancement of the agenda of egalitarian marriage in Argentina, Mexico, and Chile that highlights two thematic axes: networks of political alliances developed by sexual diversity organizations, and conceptual frameworks disseminated in the media to advance this agenda. The pro–same-sex marriage movement in Argentina has been more successful than in Chile and Mexico because of the networks formed with political parties and the penetration of the official bureaucracy by sexual diversity activists in that country. However, it is the conceptual framework of human rights with which the media campaign achieved popular support for this initiative that is the key aspect of this legal conquest.

The political transformations that de la Dehesa and Díez analyze result in new forms of socialization that gradually abandon clandestine spaces and begin to rethink the possibility of turning sexual diversity into a politically, economically, and socially influential sector. Ernesto Meccia's book, *Los últimos homosexuales* (2011), testifies to this transformation of identity.

QUEER ETHNOGRAPHIES

Based on stories of daily life in the 16th century, the novel *Crónica de las destrucciones* by Olivier Debroise (1998) reconstructs the clandestine spaces of dissipation in indigenous neighborhoods of Mexico City, such as Tepito and San Juan. It speaks of relationships that, to this day, are recognizable within the peripheral homosexuality of Mesoamerica. The case of Cotita de la Encarnación and the network of more than a hundred practitioners of sodomy in 1657–1658 is perhaps the most remembered of the stories of homosexuality in New Spain. The process that this network followed reveals to us that homoerotic practices are transversal to all social classes and races, and that they are organized as clandestine trade that is exercised on public roads and within brothels. The public execution of Cotita and 13 other men (Indians, mestizos, and mulattos, because the Creole sodomites enjoyed impunity) is accompanied by insults launched by the plebian population who in turn see the executions as a spectacle of exemplary punishment (Novo, 1979, pp. 11–16). Just as the only sanctioned words to speak of proscribed sexual practices have been insults, the spaces in which diverse sexualities unfold must be considered places of sin, vice, and crime.

The late-20th-century developments in the field of the anthropology of sexual identities contribute sexuality conversations with nuances in the significations of bodies and their economic, aesthetic, religious, and social implications. Drawing from this rich library of queer ethnography, we can pinpoint cultural traits that distinguish the universe of sexuality in Latin America from that of the hegemonic Western cultures. A foundational work in this sense is the research of Néstor Perlongher, *O negócio do michê: A prostituição viril em São Paulo* (1987). Already in this early work, Perlongher poses one of the contemporary problematics of academic discussion surrounding sexual diversity: Homoerotic practices do not necessarily correspond to identities articulated from sexual orientation. The ethnographic work of Joseph Carrier *De los otros* (1995), undertaken in cities in western and northwestern Mexico, reveals that bisexuality, practiced within a system of double morality, has reserved for itself spaces of homosocial entertainment that allow for the escape from social and official surveillance.

One of the most significant works regarding the ways to avoid repression against clandestine homoerotic practices is that of the Argentine Flavio Rapisardi and Alejandro Modarelli, *Fiestas, baños y exilios: Los gays porteños en la última dictadura* (2001), which describes the uses of spaces, stealthy sexual practices, and language in an atmosphere of repression against sexual dissidence. As far as clandestine spaces are concerned, the ethnography produced by Annick Prieur, *Mema's House, Mexico City: On Transvestites, Queens, and Machos* (1998), allows one to delve into the specific ways of organizing and defining homoerotic relations in the context of the working class of Mexico City. Although the texts of Rapisardi and Modarelli and that of Prieur refer to very different contexts, we can observe an element common to both works: the constitution of a space to escape from heteropatriarchal surveillance. These are spaces of exception, where the doors are opened to proscribed practices; drawing on the language of Michel Foucault, they are speaking of heterotopias, "other places" at the very edge of the social norm and dominant ideas about bodies.

Beyond the delimitation of spaces where forbidden desire is liberated, the great ethnographic production around dissident sexuality leads to destabilize the dividing line between heterosexuality and homosexuality. From these ethnographic works a contrast between the construction of LGBT identities in the central countries, that is, North America and Europe, and the practices and significations articulated in Latin America can be established. The ethnography of diverse sexuality in the region reveals that sexual practices do not necessarily conform to the identity pronouncements of the LGBT movement. It is common among intellectuals, artists, and academics of sexual diversity in Latin America to refer to the terms gay and queer as North American imports that can only be applied to the upper-middle-class sector of the sexually diverse population. The need to create new categories that reflect the specificity of local sexuality has occupied much of the conversation in various academic and activist forums in the subcontinent. Canonical intellectuals of sexual dissidence such as Carlos Monsiváis, Pedro Lemebel, and José Joaquín Blanco all agree in flagging the term gay as a reductive and normative imposition that finds its coherence in the capitalist culture of consumption. Diego Falconí Trávez has pointed out that the concept gay is reductionist, since only one sector of Latin American sexual dissidence identifies with this term (Falconí Trávez, 2018, p. 25). For Pedro Lemebel, the gay person is white, consumerist, and neoliberal (Lemebel, pp. 70–71). For Carlos Monsiváis, the gay person is upper-middle class, cosmopolitan, and bourgeois (Monsiváis, 2001, p. 9). For José Joaquín Blanco, the gay person enjoys the privileges of the middle class, while the *puto* suffers from social homophobia (Blanco, 1981, p. 83).

With the growth of HIV infections among the population not identified as LGBT, the category "men who have sex with men" was created, which, on the one hand, dissolves the stigmatizing association between homosexuality and HIV; and on the other, allows for the particularization of the sexual practices developed within a macho culture, where the institution of the closet harbors the homoerotic experiences rejected by social homophobia. Guillermo Núñez Noriega's book, *Sexo entre varones* (1999), is an ethnographic text focused on exploring the ways in which men who have sex with men negotiate their sexual practices within and against the mandates of hegemonic gender codes. Above all, however, this ethnography describes how these subjects resignify these mandates in order to exercise their desire. In *Just Between Us*, Núñez Noriega (2014) studies homoerotic and homosocial affections in rural areas of northern Mexico. In an ethnography rich in evocations, gestures and ambiguous expressions are privileged in constant resistance to definitions that could expose to homophobia the intimacy between men.

SEXILE OR QUEER MIGRATION

Research on Latin American sexual diversity in the context of migration has allowed us to underscore the contrast between different cultures of sexuality, which in turn requires a continuous review of the categories that allow us to understand how homoerotic practices, like all sexualities, are constructed and deconstructed to infinity.

Carlos Decena's book *Tacit Subjects: Belonging and Same-Sex Desire Among Dominican Immigrant Men* (2011), is an ethnography of masculinity and homoeroticism among Dominican migrants in the United States. He proposes the concept of "tacit subject" to refer to the evasive and ambiguous forms of male sexuality that resist being contained under established identities. Decena focuses on the strategies created by these diasporic subjects to navigate between cultures and circumvent forms of exclusion within the Dominican migrant population. In 1997, Puerto Rican sociologist Manolo Guzmán (now known as Manolo Estavillo) coined the concept of *sexile*, which applies to people who have had to leave their country because of their sexual orientation (Guzmán, 1997, p. 227). This idea has been at the core of several papers that discuss Latin American migration. Among the authors who have developed their discussions of queer migration around this concept are Yolanda Martínez-San Miguel (2011), Lawrence La Fountain-Stokes (2004), and Norma Mogrovejo (2016). From the study of the factors that force sexual dissidents to leave their places of origin (Guzmán), to the decolonizing features of this migration (Martínez-San Miguel), and even the ways in which these exiles have influenced queer culture and politics in the countries of destination (La Fountain-Stokes), sexiled migration brings about a series of transformations for these people, both of their own culture of origin and of the societies where they will settle (Decena).

These processes of sexile are most often tense and contradictory. Queer Latin American migration in the United States generates forms of resignification of sexuality that arise in the subalternity of the sexiliados in and against the categories centrally established by the North American LGBT movement. María Amelia Viteri's (2014) work highlights the lack of identification between the sexually diverse migrant population and mainstream LGBT groups in the city of Washington, DC. The intersection of various factors of oppression function to distance the hegemonic LGBT organizations from these migrant communities.

From a sociological framework, Héctor Carrillo has studied closely sexual dissidence in Mexican migration. His book *Pathways of Desire* (2017) points toward various nuances of the way in which migrants' homosexuality is conceived, nuances that distinguish both generational and social and cultural differences between sexual exiles. In the same way, he observes a broad fluidity and adaptability to the different sexual cultures with which these individuals relate themselves. The various ways of conceiving and practicing homoerotic relationships that are formed in the migratory experience allow these migrants to assume different identities that can be taken up and abandoned as practical need requires. The fluidity that living in the liminal space between two cultures provides prevents these migrants from fully assimilating to the forms of American sexual culture and leads them to create their own notions of sexuality.

The issue of sexual migration acquires relevance insofar as it is a field of cultural dispute that takes place at the level of bodies. In addition to the disagreements and nonconformity before the politics and culture of sexual diversity in destination countries that María Amelia Viteri observes, the experience of sexile is a breeding ground for political ideas and novel bodily identities and practices that have contributed not only to the advancement of sexuality studies, but have also offered conceptualizations and modes of expression located beyond national boundaries in a kind of counter-globalization or decoloniality of bodies. Beyond the concept of liberation from traditional homophobic cultures or the conflicts between assimilating or resisting the cultures to which sexually diverse Latin Americans migrate, there have been processes of transnationalization and disidentification. It is toward this sense that the works of Lawrence La Fountain-Stokes (2021) and José Esteban Muñoz (1999, 2009)—which we will review in the section dedicated to performance—are articulated.

QUEER LATIN AMERICAN CINEMA

In the 1970s, both on television and in the cinema, and amid a myriad of derisive performances, there begin to appear homosexual and trans characters from a non-homophobic perspective. Without a doubt, the author who has made the biggest review so far of queer cinema in Latin America is David William Foster. His books *Gender and Society in Contemporary Brazilian Cinema* (1999), *Mexico City in Contemporary Mexican Cinema* (2002), and *Queer Issues in Contemporary Latin American Cinema* (2003) constitute a critical corpus where themes such as the closet, homophobia, and even the corporalities whose differences transcend the field of sexuality are the axis of public discussions in which the agendas of the demand for sexual diversity are addressed. It can be said that film representations of the queer population are a relevant part of the political effort of LGBT organizations to install the agenda of sexual dissidence within the public arena. Foster's extensive review of what we can consider the canon of queer Latin American cinematography allows us to delve into the debates on the issues of sexual diversity that cinema itself has fostered.

Among the films that received the most critical attention are *El lugar sin límites* (Arturo Ripstein, 1978), *Doña Herlinda y su hijo* (Jaime Humberto Hermosillo, 1985), *Yo la peor de todas* (María Luisa Bemberg, 1990), and *Fresa y chocolate* (Tomás Gutiérrez Alea, 1993). The contradictions between the homophobia and the homoerotic desire of the *macho* that frames the tragedy of Ripstein's film (de la Mora, 2006); the strategies to maintain the institution of the closet as a way to enable homoerotic love and at the same time escape from social heteronormative models and codes in the film by Hermosillo (Balderston, 1998a); the review of historical characters in order to rewrite history by making the queer visible, in the film by Bemberg (Bergmann, 1998); and the dispute over the inclusion of sexual dissidents in the discourse of the Cuban revolutionary state in the film by Gutiérrez Alea (Bejel, 2001; Quiroga, 2000) are all issues relevant to the understanding of how the queer breaks through the moral, social, and political constraints of the region.

Vinodh Venkatesh's book *New Maricón Cinema: Outing Latin American Film* (2016) continues this conversation by defining two modes of representation-reception in cinema from the perspective of the theory of affect. To do this, he analyzes a series of films highlighting this perceptive distinction: On the one hand, the films that emphasize the visual aspect (scopic), where the queer subjects are seen with the rational cognitive distance that objectifies them; on the other hand, the tactile or palpable aspect (haptic), where the queer subject is not only observed but "sensed," in an operation of perception whereby the viewer not only vindicates but also empathizes with said subject, responding to the demand to understand the queer from within the framework of emotions. In a similar theoretical framework, Denilson Lopes reviews a group of Brazilian films that appeared between 2009 and 2016 in his *Afetos, relações e encontros com filmes brasileiros contemporáneos* (2016). This text focuses on the ways in which cinema relates directly to viewers through emotions that are loaded with signification. Both Venkatesh and Lopes find in the cinema an affective complex that constitutes a corporal knowledge that is at one and the same time ethical, aesthetic, and political.

QUEER AS PERFORMANCE

One of the most prolific fields of queer studies in Latin America is that which is dedicated to the study of performance. Among the outstanding scholars in this conversation are Laura G. Gutiérrez, José Esteban Muñoz, Antonio Prieto, Licia Fiol-Matta, and Ramón H. Rivera-Servera.

One of the most relevant works with respect to Mexican lesbian performance is the book *Performing Mexicanidad* by Laura G. Gutiérrez (2010), that offers an analysis of the performance art produced by Mexican and Mexican-American queer women. The artists of the Mexican queer cabaret recover emblematic figures of national femininity, such as the Virgin of Guadalupe or La China Poblana, in order to reinvent them through queering. From this characterization, which enacts a symbolic appropriation of the nation from their queer transgression, the performers that Gutiérrez analyzes become critical voices of the national reality: political conflicts, environmental issues, corruption, violence, and so on. The second part of the book is dedicated to two avant-garde video artists: Nao Bustamante and Ximena Cuevas. Gutiérrez analyzes the works of these video performers emphasizing how, from the queer body, they intervene in the power of media companies such as Televisión Azteca and Cinépolis, or how they shame transnational companies like McDonald's. The sexual dissidence of contemporary queer women performance artists assaults the emblematic spaces of migrant globalization, as Gutiérrez's work allows us to see.

José Esteban Muñoz studied Latino migrant performance in the United States from a transnational perspective. This author proposed two concepts that have marked the conversations about diasporic queer: *disidentification* and *queer utopia* (Muñoz, 1999, 2009). Disidentification consists of escaping from a stigmatizing identity through the resources of aesthetic performance such as parody, rhapsody, hybridization, and appropriation. The queer migrant performance is a symbolic battlefield where the body sets out from its marginalization in an intersection of sexuality, race, language, nationality, and class, to deconstruct the hegemonic assumptions that produce its exclusion. With the idea of queer utopia, Muñoz's book *Cruising Utopia* opens up a field of discussion regarding the future in the making, which is in the route of being, or the historical direction that the processes of queer subjectivation follow. In this way, Muñoz led the readers to conceive of the queer as an infinite process of the construction of subjectivities, and where the categories of gender and sexuality are infinitely malleable.

Also positioning himself within a transnational perspective, Lawrence La Fountain-Stokes, in his book *Translocas* (2021), embarks on a tour of the stages of Puerto Rico and the United States with his concept of *transloca*, by which he means to refer to a constant state of transformation that generates and develops the diaspora of queer characters from the Caribbean. His work covers various aesthetic expressions such as drag performance, cinema, and queer television celebrities. The themes of hybridity, colonialism, bilingualism, prejudice, displacement, and violence are intertwined to transmit to us a liminal place that escapes the constant homophobic, xenophobic, and racist harassment through aesthetic strategies. Also located on the Caribbean-American circuit, Licia Fiol-Matta's book *The Great Woman Singer: Gender and Voice in Puerto Rican Music* (2017) studies the trajectory, political position, and transgressive acts of four celebrities of the Puerto Rican popular music of the first half of the 20th century. In an extensive archival review, Fiol-Matta carries out a psychoanalysis of the mediatic performance of the bolero divas to find links between feminist postures, nationalism, and transgression of heteronormative models and conventions of the period.

Employing an ethnographic methodology, *Performing Queer Latinidad: Dance, Sexuality, Politics*, by Ramón H. Rivera-Servera (2014), reviews cases of performance practiced as part of queer activism and in spaces of the socialization of sexual diversity in some cities in North America. Social protest realized through performative resources allows us to revise the concepts of minority racial identity in order to insist as much on the intersectional character of Latin American diasporic subjects as on the globalization of Latin American forms of aesthetic expression.

The book by Giuseppe Campuzano, *Saturday Night Thriller* (2013), unfolds a series of artistic interventions that range from performance to the formation of an itinerant museum—El Museo Travesti del Perú—which is in itself a performance that tries to render visible the history of the trans population in the Andean country. Also located within the trans from daily performance is *Queen for a Day*, by Marcia Ochoa (2014). In this text, Ochoa draws a parallel between the construction of the femininity to be exhibited on the catwalks of beauty contests (an industry in which Venezuela has had a great presence) and that of the trans sex workers of downtown Caracas. It is research that combines ethnography, urban studies, and media studies, to demonstrate how the queer body is built on aesthetic and gender bases that identify the national body that has been promoted from and by the media.

CONCLUSION AND FUTURE DIRECTIONS

Representations of queer bodies have been present in Latin America since the colonial period as political strategies that have been central for the circulation and propagation of homophobic ideas for centuries: From nefarious sin to disease and crime, the representation of sexual difference has been the axis for the policies that kept sex and gender dissidence in the margin of citizenship for centuries. Literature, journalism, film, and television have been the main tools to propagate and consolidate modern Latin America homophobia.

A counterpart of this homophobic apparatus comes from multidisciplinary expressions from scholarship to alternative media, where the representation and analysis of dissident erotic and social practices show that Latin American sexual culture has specific features that distance themselves from Western conceptualizations. We can observe a process of decolonization of public arena regarding queer representations in performance, migration studies, and intellectual and activist interventions. Thus, current debates on sexualities in Latin America develop intersectional analyses of queerness that ultimately overcome the hegemonic LGBT representations.

Current developments of queer studies in Latin America are oriented to explore cyberspace, where discussions on emerging forms of sexuality, legal protection, commercial sex, and so forth also imply novel methodologies such as cyberethnography. Other research routes include sex trafficking, chem-sex, sex tourism, and topics involving issues on transgender, intersex, and nonbinary populations.

FURTHER READING

Balderston, D., & Castro Matute, A. (Eds.). (2014). *Cartografías queer: Sexualidades y activismo LGBT en América Latina*. Instituto Internacional de Literatura Iberoamericana.

Corrales, J., & Pecheny, M. (Eds.). (2010). *The politics of sexuality in Latin America: A reader on lesbian, gay, bisexual, and transgender rights*. University of Pittsburgh Press.

Dominguez-Ruvalcaba, H. (2016). *Translating the queer: Body politics and transnational conversations*. Zed Books.

Falconí Trávez, D., Castellanos, S., & Viteri, M. A. (Eds.). (2014). *Resentir lo queer en América Latina: diálogos desde/con el sur*. Egales.

Foster, D. W. (2003). *Queer issues in contemporary Latin American cinema*. University of Texas Press.

Molloy, S., & Irwin, R. M. (Eds.). (1998). *Hispanisms and homosexualities*. Duke University Press.

Muñoz, J. E. (1999). *Disidentifications: Queer of color and the performance of politics*. University of Minnesota Press.

Muñoz, J. E. (2009). *Cruising Utopia: The then and there of queer futurity*. New York University Press.

Quiroga, J. (2000). *Tropics of desire: Interventions from queer Latino America*. New York University Press.

Viteri, M. A., & Lavinas Picq, M. (Eds.). (2016). *Queering paradigms V: Queering narratives of modernity*. Peter Lang.

REFERENCES

Balderston, D. (1998a). ¿El tercero incluido? La bisexualidad en Doña Herlinda y su hijo. In D. Balderston & D. J. Guy (Eds.), *Sexo y sexualidades en América Latina* (pp. 277–290). Paidós.

Balderston, D. (1998b). Poetry, revolution, homophobia: Polemics from the Mexican revolution. In S. Molloy & R. M. Irwin (Eds.), *Hispanisms and homosexualities* (pp. 57–75). Duke University Press.

Bazán, O. (2004). *Historia de la homosexualidad en Argentina: De la conquista de América al siglo XXI*. Marea.

Bejel, E. (2001). *Gay Cuban nation*. University of Chicago Press.

Bemberg, María Luisa, director. *Yo, la peor de todas*. GEA cinematográfica, 1990.

Bergmann, E. (1998). Abjection and ambiguity: Lesbian desire in Bemberg's *Yo la peor de todas*. In S. Molloy & R. M. Irwin (Eds.), *Hispanisms and homosexualities* (pp. 229–247). Duke University Press.

Blanco, J. J. (1981). *Función de medianoche*. Era.

Buffington, R. (2003). Homophobia and the Mexican working class, 1900–1910. In R. M. Irwin, E. J. McCaughan, & M. R. Nasser (Eds.), *The famous 41: Sexuality and social control in Mexico, c. 1901* (pp. 193–225). Palgrave Macmillan.

Campuzano, G. (2013). *Saturday night thriller y otros escritos, 1998–2013*. Estruendomudo.

Carrier, J. (1995). *De los otros: Intimacy and homosexuality among Mexican men*. Columbia University Press.

Carrillo, H. (2017). *Pathways of desire: The sexual migration of Mexican gay men*. University of Chicago Press.

De la Mora, S. (2006). *Cinemachismo: Masculinity and sexuality in Mexican film*. University of Texas Press.

Debroise, O. (1998). *Crónica de las destrucciones*. Era.

Decena, C. U. (2011). *Tacit subjects: Belonging and same-sex desire among Dominican immigrant men*. Duke University Press.

Díez, J. (2015). *The politics of gay marriage in Latin America: Argentina, Chile and Mexico*. Cambridge University Press.

Domínguez Ruvalcaba, H. (2007). *Modernity and the nation in Mexican representations of masculinity: From sensuality to bloodshed*. Palgrave Macmillan.

Domínguez Ruvalcaba, H. (2016). Los mecanismos cómicos de la homofobia en algunos programas de Televisa. In H. Domínguez Ruvalcaba (Ed.), *La cuestión del odio: la violencia homofóbica en México* (pp. 117–138). Universidad Veracruzana.

Falconí Trávez, D. (2018). Introducción. In D. Falconí Trávez (Ed.), *Inflexión marica: Escrituras del descalabro gay en América Latina*. Egales (Kindle version).

Figari, C. (2009). *Eróticas de la disidencia en América Latina: Brasil, siglos XVII al XX*. Fundación Centro de Integración, Comunicación, Cultura y Sociedad–CICCUS-CLACSO.

Fiol-Matta, L. (2017). *The great woman singer: Gender and voice in Puerto Rican music*. Duke University Press.

Foster, D. W. (1999). *Gender and society in contemporary Brazilian cinema*. University of Texas Press.

Foster, D. W. (2002). *Mexico City in contemporary Mexican cinema*. University of Texas Press.

Foster, D. W. (2003). *Queer issues in contemporary Latin American cinema*. University of Texas Press.

Garza Carvajal, F. (2003). *Butterflies will burn: Prosecuting sodomites in early modern Spain and Mexico*. University of Texas Press.

Giorgi, G. (2004). *Sueños de exterminio: Homosexualidad y representación en la literatura argentina contemporánea*. Beatriz Viterbo.

Green, J. N. (1999). *Beyond carnival: Male homosexuality in twentieth-century Brazil*. University of Chicago Press.

Gutiérrez Alea, T. (Director). (1993). *Fresa y chocolate*. ICAIC, IMCINE, Telemadrid.

Gutiérrez, L. G. (2010). *Performing Mexicanidad. Vendidas y Cabareteras on the Transnational Stage*. Austin: The University of Texas Press.

Guzmán, M. (1997). "Pa la escuelita con mucho cuida'o y por la Orillita": A journey through the contested terrains of the nation and sexual orientation. In F. Negrón-Muntaner & R. Grosfogel (Eds.), *Puerto Rican jam: Essays on culture and politics* (pp. 209–228). University of Minnesota Press.

Hermosillo, Jaime Humberto, director. *Doña Herlinda y su hijo*. Clasa films, 1985.

Horswell, M. J. (2005). *Decolonizing the sodomite: Queer tropes of sexuality in colonial Andean culture*. University of Texas Press.

Irwin, R. M. (2003). *Mexican masculinities*. University of Minnesota Press.

La Fountain-Stokes, L. (2004, April). De sexilio(s) y diáspora(s) homosexual(es) latina(s): Cultura puertorriqueña y lo nuyorican queer. *Debate Feminista*, 138–157.

La Fountain-Stokes, L. (2021). *Translocas: The politics of Puerto Rican drag and trans performance*. University of Michigan Press.

Lopes, D. (2016). *Afetos, relações e encontros com filmes brasileiros contemporáneos*. Hucitec.

Lumsden, I. (1996). *Machos, maricones & gays: Cuba and homosexuality*. Temple University Press.
Macías-González, V. (2003). The *Lagartijo* at *The High Life*: Masculine consumption, race, nation, and homosexuality in Porfirian Mexico. In R. M. Irwin, E. J. McCaughan, & M. R. Nasser (Eds.), *The famous 41: Sexuality and social control in Mexico, 1901* (pp. 227–249). Palgrave Macmillan.
Martínez-San Miguel, Y. (2011). "Sexilios": Hacia una nueva poética de la erótica caribeña. *América Latina Hoy, 58*, 15–30.
Meccia, E. (2011). *Los últimos homosexuales: Sociología de la homosexualidad y la gaycidad*. Gran Aldea Editores.
Miano Borruso, M. (2003). *Hombres, mujeres y muxe' en el Istmo de Tehuantepec*. Conaculta/INAH-Plaza y Valdés.
Mogrovejo, N. (2016). Sexilio político. In H. Domínguez Ruvalcaba (Ed.), *La cuestión del odio: la violencia homofóbica en México*. Universidad Veracruzana.
Monsiváis, C. (2001). Una exposición, varias exposiciones, un tiempo de inauguraciones. In Círculo Cultural Gay (Ed.), *Una exposición, varias exposiciones, un tiempo de inauguraciones* (pp. 9–11). Difusión Cultural UNAM–Museo Universitario del Chopo.
Montenegro, C. (1938). *Hombres sin mujer*. Letras Cubanas.
Muñoz, J. E. (2009). *Cruising Utopia: The then and there of queer futurity* New York-London: Nuew York University Press, 2009.
Munoz, J. E. (1999). *Disidentifications. Queer of color and the performance of politics*. Minneapolis: University of Minnesota Press.
Novo, S. (1979). *Las locas, el sexo y los burdeles*. Editorial Diana.
Núñez Noriega, G. (1999). *Sexo entre varones: Poder y resistencia en el campo sexual*. Programa Universitario de Estudios de Género–Universidad Nacional Autónoma de México; Miguel Ángel Porrúa; El Colegio de Sonora.
Núñez Noriega, G. (2014). *Just between us: An ethnography of male identity and intimacy in rural communities of northern Mexico*. University of Arizona Press.
Ochoa, M. (2014). *Queen for a day: Transformistas, beauty queens and the performance of femininity in Venezuela*. Duke University Press.
Payno, M. (1982). *Los bandidos de Río Frío*. Porrúa.
Perlongher, N. (1987). *O negócio do michê: A prostituçäo viril em São Paulo*. Editora Brasiliense.
Perlongher, N. (1997). *Prosa plebeya*. Ediciones Colihue.
Prieur, A. (1998). *Mema's house, Mexico City: On transvestites, queens, and machos*. University of Chicago Press.
Quevedo y Zubieta, S. (1933). *México marimacho: Novela histórica revolucionaria*. Ediciones Botas.
Rapisardi, F., & Modarelli, A. (2001). *Fiestas, baños y exilios: los gays porteños en la última dictadura*. Editorial Sudamericana.
Ripstein, A. (Director). (1979) *El lugar sin límites*. Conacite, 110 min.
Rivera-Servera, R. H. (2014). *Performing queer latinidad: Dance, sexuality, politics*. University of Michigan Press.
Salessi, J. (1995). *Médicos maleantes y maricas: Higiene, criminología y homosexualidad en la construcción de la nación argentina (Buenos Aires, 1871–1914)*. Viterbo.
Sempol, D. (2013). *De los baños a la calle: Historia del movimiento lésbico, gay, trans uruguayo (1984–2013)*. Random House Mondadori.
Sierra Madero, A. (2006). *Del otro lado del espejo: La sexualidad en la construcción de la nación cubana*. Casa de la Américas.
Sigal, P. (2007, Winter). Queer Nahuatl: Sahagún's faggots and sodomites, lesbians and hermaphrodites. *Ethnohistory, 54*(1), 10–34.

Sigal, P. (2011). *The flower and the scorpion: Sexuality and ritual in early Nahua culture*. Duke University Press.
Sutherland, J. P. (2009). *Nación marica: Prácticas culturales y crítica activista*. Ripio Ediciones.
Tortorici, Z. (2014). Visceral archives of the body: Consuming the dead, digesting the divine. *GLQ: A Journal of Lesbian and Gay Studies, 20*(4), 407–437.
Tortorici, Z. (2018). *Sins against nature: Sex and archive in colonial New Spain*. Duke University Press.
Venkatesh, V. (2016). *New maricón cinema: Outing Latin American film*. University of Texas Press.
Viteri, M. A. (2014). *Desbordes: Translating racial, ethnic, sexual, and gender identities across the Americas*. State University of New York.

Héctor Domínguez-Ruvalcaba

SPANISH QUEER CINEMA

LGBTQ+ HISTORIES IN SPAIN: LAWS, ACTIVISM, MEMORY

It may come as a surprise for those unfamiliar with contemporary Spain, that despite a four-decade dictatorship and heavy influence of the Catholic Church on Spanish society for much of the 20th century, more recently Spain has emerged as one of the most forward-thinking countries in the world in terms of legal recognition of equal rights, visibility, and acceptance of LGBTQ+ people. The "Stonewall Global Workplace Briefings" paper in 2018 sums up some of these legal rights and protections, which include equal marriage (approved in 2005), equal conditions for the adoption of children, residency rights for foreign spouses, criminalization of hate crimes and discrimination at the workplace or the legal right for trans people to change their gender in official documentation subject to some requirements (Stonewall, 2018). The introduction of all these legal advances throughout the 2000s under the left-wing Partido Socialista Obrero Español (PSOE) government of Rodríguez Zapatero faced considerable resistance from the main opposition party, the conservative Partido Popular (PP), and has intensified in recent years with the unexpected reemergence of the farright. The main far-right party, Vox, founded in 2013, has gained traction in more recent regional and general elections, entering the Spanish parliament after the 2019 elections with 52 seats in the Congreso de los Diputados and a regional government for the first time (in coalition with the PP in Castilla y León) in April 2022. Despite rejecting accusations of homophobia, Vox opposes equal marriage and promotes active policing/banning of what they regard as feminist, gender, and queer ideology in schools.

One of the most notable controversies of the 2020s is the so-called "Ley Trans" (Trans Law), proposed by the left coalition government in 2021 (the draft was approved in June 2022) with the aim of advancing rights of trans people to legally change their gender without the current requirements which, as of 2022, include compulsory evidence such as medical reports and a history of hormone therapy. The new law seeks to remove those requirements for anyone over 16 (and with parental consent from age 14) and, among other things, proposes a blanket ban of conversion therapies. These proposals have found considerable opposition not just from right-wing and far-right parties, but also from some sectors of the left and of the Spanish feminist movement, leading to a split perhaps best illustrated by the organization of two separate feminist marches on International Women's Day 2022 in Madrid. A separate law, the so-called "Ley Zerolo," named after the late LGBTQ+ activist and politician Pedro Zerolo who instigated it years ago, was passed in June 2022. It strengthens previous (2011 and 2013) anti-LGBTQ+ discrimination laws.

During the Franco dictatorship (1939–1975), homosexuality was a taboo topic prevalently associated with criminality. "Homosexuals" were officially classed as offenders from 1954 and were added to the 1933 "Ley de Vagos y Maleantes" (Vagrancy Law). As Fernández Galeano (2016) notes, the revision of the law was meant to stigmatize homosexuals, "relying on and encouraging the already prevalent social intolerance toward sexual deviance" (p. 27). As Huard (2014) has explained, implementation often depended on class and other social hierarchies and it could lead to harsh penalties, including long prison sentences. The law was replaced (in 1970) with the "Ley sobre peligrosidad y rehabilitación social" (Law of dangerousness and social and rehabilitation) but was rarely applied after the death of the dictator. It was fully abolished surprisingly late, in 1995. Just 10 years later, in 2005, Spain would become the fourth country in the world to legalize equal marriage, a milestone that symbolizes the culmination of a decade of increasing visibility on the screen and in the streets, and growing social acceptance of LGBTQ+ people.

Around the same time, the publication of a series of books about LGBTQ+ histories would mark if not the start, an important momentum in the making of queer histories of Spain (Arnalte, 2003; de Fluvià, 2003; Mira, 2004; Olmeda, 2004; Petit, 2003, 2004). In his book, Arturo Arnalte argued that the lack of publications of this kind until then was partly due to the 50-year legal protection of those arrested under the aforementioned laws, delaying the possibility of a full account of their consequences until at least 2028 (Arnalte, 2003, p. 22). Thus, those important books published in the early 2000s (and Spanish LGBTQ+ history) relied in part on oral histories, newspaper cuttings, public legal documents and, in some cases, speculation.

Activists Armand de Fluvià and Jordi Petit contributed very considerably to this momentum; de Fluvià (2003) with a book focused on the emergence of the "gay movement" in Catalonia in the last five years of the dictatorship, Petit with two volumes that look back at the years of the democratic transition and the emergence of open and proud LGBTQ+ communities since then. Importantly, in their books both authors collate key archival materials that document queer history during all those years. De Fluvià includes interviews and written correspondence with key players of the emerging *moviment gai* and a selection of his own letters to newspaper editors and various authorities denouncing homophobic practices—and their responses. In 25 *años más* ("25 More Years," 2003) Petit offers a selection of his writings on LGBTQ+ issues in the Spanish printed media between 1980 and 2004, alongside a fascinating selection of relevant news items and notes from a wide range of publications that cover roughly the same period. Petit's follow-up book (Petit, 2004) includes a selection of "agony uncle" type letters and other personals that appeared in then cagy "gay" magazines from the late 1970s (*Party, Mensual*). Combined, these are precious archival materials that help rebuild and draw attention to LGBTQ+ memories in Spain during those crucial decades.

A key contributor in this rewriting of Spanish history from LGBTQ+ perspectives is Alberto Mira, whose acclaimed study, brilliantly titled *De Sodoma a Chueca* ("From Sodom to Chueca") was also published in this period (Mira, 2004). This important book, complemented with his equally pioneering encyclopedic guide to LGBTQ+ culture (Mira, 1999), traces milestones in the history of same-sex desire in and beyond Spain, quite literally from the Bible until the emergence of so-called gay villages in major Spanish cities, best symbolized by Madrid's globally famous Chueca. This work is an indispensable source for the study of Spanish LGBTQ+ history, as proven by the inclusion of *De Sodoma a Chueca* in the Instituto Cervantes "Letters" Vault to mark Pride celebrations in June 2022.

These trailblazing volumes were in fact preceded by Martínez Expósito's groundbreaking queering of the Spanish literary canon (Martínez Expósito, 1998), and followed by many more, with more specific concerns, queering Franco and the culture of the transition (Pérez-Sánchez, 2007), the history of lesbian activism (Trujillo Barbadillo, 2009), hermaphroditism and medical discourses in the 19th and 20th centuries (Cleminson & Vázquez García, 2007), male homosexuality (Cleminson & Vázquez García, 2009), and even an elegy to Chueca written by the late drag queen Shangay Lily (2016) which denounces the "gaypitalism" that arguably permeates Spain's most iconic gayborhood and *Orgullo* (Pride) celebrations.

Madrid's extraordinarily successful hosting of record-setting Europride in 2007 and World Pride 10 years later, in 2017, would seem to evidence the widespread social acceptance of LGBTQ+ communities in Spain. People from every age bracket, sexual orientation, class, origin, and most political backgrounds, now join the celebrated parades, perhaps out of curiosity, but in most cases genuine solidarity. Attendance to the Madrid World Pride march in 2017 reached a then world record, with an estimate of 3.5 million. In contrast, the brutal homophobic murder of 24-year-old Samuel Luiz on July 3rd, 2021, in A Coruña, in northwestern Spain was a tragic reality check and a reminder that Spain is by no means immune from new global waves of homophobia and that LGBTQ+ communities around the world must remain vigilant and never take progress and rights for granted. This entry is dedicated to the memory of Samuel.

LGBTQ+ CINEMA IN SPAIN: FROM THE 1940S UNTIL NOW

Paul Julian Smith's pioneering book *Laws of Desire: Questions of Homosexuality in Spanish Writing and Film 1960–1990*, published in 1992 (and in Spanish in 1998) was a considerable landmark in the study of Spanish LGBTQ+ cinema in Spain. Countless journal articles, PhD dissertations, edited collections, and monographs about the subject have been published since then. In addition to the works by Mira already cited, and his later study of "gays and lesbians on film" (2008) that covers key works in world cinema (not just Spain), very important overviews in monographs by Melero Salvador (2010, 2017), Perriam (2013), and Berzosa (2014), a recent teaching guide authored by Zurián and García Ramos (2021), and more specific studies, such as Gutiérrez-Albilla's queer reading of Buñuel (Gutiérrez-Albilla, 2008) are significant building blocks for the study and understanding of queer desire in the history of Spanish cinema.

It would be impossible to include here anything close to a representative list of films featuring LGBTQ+ characters in the history of Spanish cinema. What follows is a review of some notable case studies that illustrate various milestones and that are frequently discussed in the secondary literature. It is fair to say that, although explicit representations of same-sex and queer desire did not exist until the abolition of censorship in 1978, there were some significant "veiled representations," to use Alfeo Álvarez's (2000) term, that must be mentioned.

Dictatorship and Censorship. Ironically, the obsession with war narratives and military contexts meant to bolster nationalist ideals and exalt a certain understanding of (straight) masculinities in early Francoist cinema, gave rise to the popularity of the crusade film, which, in turn, inevitably created memorable scenes in homosocial scenarios with the potential to be read as some of the first examples of same-sex desire in the history of Spanish cinema. Carlos Arévalo's film ¡Harka! (1941) is often cited as an example of this. Set in the 1920s during a military conflict in the Spanish Protectorate of Morocco, the film celebrates the loyal friendship between Captain Santiago Valcázar, played by early Francoist cinema star Alfredo Mayo, and younger officer Carlos Herrera (Luis Peña). It is possible to read the parallel conflict that the film establishes between the real battles and the drama that ensues between the two male friends following Valcázar's decision to leave for Madrid to follow a (female) love interest and get married. Inevitably, Herrera will die in service, prompting Valcázar to return and continue his friend's mission in an allegoric (and melodramatic) rectification of his mistake. The all-male contexts and implicit love triangles of this and other films of the genre encourage queer readings inspired by Sedgwick's (1985) work on homosocial desire (see Epps, 2017; Melero Salvador, 2017, pp. 29–49).

Luis María Delgado's *Diferente/Different* (1961) is another classic case study (Alfeo Álvarez, 2000; Melero Salvador, 2017; Zurián & García Ramos, 2021), not only due to the hypothetical "homosexual" identity and lifestyle of its "artistic" protagonist Alfredo (played by Argentinian actor Alfredo Alaria) but also because the film includes what is believed to be the first explicit example of the queer gaze in a lengthy POV shot of Alfredo staring at the flexed bicep of a workman who, amusingly, is drilling a hole in the ground with a very large and obviously phallic drill (see Fouz-Hernández & Martínez-Expósito, 2007). Alfredo's sense of isolation from his bourgeois family (just for being "different"), his narcissism, and the tragic plot twists (including the death of the patriarch, which Alfredo feels partly responsible for) anticipate some of the recurring motifs that would characterize some LGBTQ+ narratives in the Spanish cinema of the transition years.

In *Violetas de España* (Melero Salvador, 2017), a prequel to his acclaimed study on lesbian and gay representation in the transition years, *Placeres Ocultos* ("Hidden Pleasures," 2010), Alejandro Melero uncovers a wealth of Spanish films featuring coded representations of gay and lesbian characters or that at least had clear queer-reading potential. His examples include gay men in films including the already mentioned *Diferente, ¡Harka!* (and other crusade films), spaghetti-westerns shot in Spain or peplum films, but also cult horror cinema (and its parodies) that often featured easily recognizable lesbian characters under the guise of oversexed vamps. His fascinating examples include two by mainstream filmmaker Vicente Aranda (*Las crueles/The Exquisite Cadaver* [1961] and *La novia ensangrentada/The Blood Spattered Bride* [1972]) as clear illustrations of threatening/murderous lesbian characters. This model, as Melero explains, was exploited by cult filmmaker Jess Franco (active and very prolific from the 1950s until his death in 2013), who worked mostly in international productions (initially to avoid censorship). Although arguably contributing to visibility of lesbians and (less often) gay men, queer characters in these films were depicted as destabilizing and dark/dangerous forces. Jess Franco made over 200 films (many of which were released only on video and only in some markets). *Vampyros Lesbos/Lesbian Vampires* (1971) is a good example both for the sexploitation aesthetics and for the depiction of leading lady Countess Nadine Carody

(Soledad Miranda) as an insatiable, predatory vixen vampire who will stop at nothing to quench her bloodthirst—and her lesbian desires.

Surprisingly, transvestism and transgender issues are also central to the narrative of two important films of the Francoist period. Even more remarkably, these were not underground or obscure movies, but major feature films directed by commercially successful mainstream filmmakers and starring major stars at the time playing recognizable queer roles. In Fernando Fernán Gómez's *El extraño viaje/The Strange Journey* (1964) the male protagonist, played by Carlos Larrañaga, is an attractive man who occasionally dresses up in women's clothes for the erotic enjoyment of his wealthy female lover but who will later become a key suspect in the investigation of her murder. The film had little commercial impact at the time of its original release (it was rereleased in 1970), but it is now considered a classic and an allegory of Spanish society at the time (see Pavloviç, 2003). In *Mi querida señorita/My Dearest Lady* (dir. Jaime de Armiñán, 1972) middle-aged small-town spinster Adela, played by José Luis López Vázquez, an iconic male star in Spanish cinema of this period, struggles with certain aspects of her body and gender identity, only to be told by a doctor that (s)he is, in fact, a man. This finding precipitates a move to Madrid where the character will now have a new life as a man with a new identity and a new male name, Juan.

It is in ambiguous examples such as these where LGBTQ+ visibility must and can be found in late Francoist cinema. A more problematic and most oft discussed example is *No desearás al vecino del quinto/Thou Shalt not Covet Thy Fifth Floor Neighbour* (dir. Ramón Fernández, 1970), a film that includes a memorable (but, for many, infamous) performance by another major star at the time, Alfredo Landa, who would later become known for his "stereotypically Spanish" roles in the *destape* "sexy Iberian comedies" of the transition. The film was the most commercially successful Spanish production domestically for decades, thus reaching very large sectors of the public and many queer men of that generation would see in this character the first ever representation of what society would expect a gay man to look and act like. Landa plays a very camp dressmaker whose effeminate persona is eventually revealed as an act to seduce women, who are drawn to him for his unthreatening façade. As Mira (2008, p. 388) suggests, the film is not only homophobic but also misogynistic. It is also an example where the ambiguous narrative frustrates any hopes of identification or desire for the queer spectator, who instead would see himself quite literally erased from the screen and used as a buffoon at the service of male heterosexual desire. Unfortunately, the film anticipated the fate of gay male characters in the "sexy Iberian comedies" that followed during the democratic transition. Gay male roles in comedies of that period were not only secondary, but as argued by Melero Salvador (2010, pp. 129–180), seemed planted there to reinforce stereotypes, portraying those characters as lonely, pathetic, sick, predatory and above all, the object of laughter. The popular comedies of Mariano Ozores, studied by Melero, are a significant example of this.

The Transition. Yet the transition would bring some progress at least in terms of greater visibility and openness with which topics such as transsexuality were depicted, just as post-Franco society would gradually became more sexually liberated and audiences more openly curious. Another Vicente Aranda film released in the year when censorship was abolished, 1978, *Cambio de sexo/Forbidden Love* (the literal translation of the title would be "Sex Change") stars Spain's first out transgender performer Bibiana Fernández (then known as Bibi Andersen), remarkably, playing herself. She would later become a regular in LGBTQ+ films in the 1980s and 1990s, including Pedro Almodóvar classics *Matador* (1986), *La ley del deseo/Law of Desire* (1987), *Tacones lejanos/High Heels* (1991) and *Kika* (1993). In *Cambio de sexo*, Fernández (again, as herself) plays the mentor of the central, adolescent trans character played by another iconic *"chica Almodóvar,"* Victoria Abril. In the same year, queer filmmaker Ventura Pons released the documentary *Ocaña, retrat intermittent/Ocaña, an Intermittent Portrait* (1978; figure 1), a fundamental and groundbreaking must-see film to understand the history of LGBTQ+ cinema in Catalonia and Spain. The film alternates street performances of Ocaña in drag (which pointedly often include an element of full-frontal nudity or other performative strategies that reveal his male genitals) with dialogue (often headshots) where Ocaña reflects on memories of his risky sexual encounters with other boys while growing up in Andalucía in Francoist times and then as a sexually liberated adult in liberal and cosmopolitan 1970s Barcelona (all these and other relevant films are discussed in detail in Fouz-Hernández & Martínez Expósito, 2007, pp. 140–160).

Trailblazers: Ventura Pons, Eloy de la Iglesia, Pedro Almodóvar. *Ocaña* is one of the films studied by Berzosa (2014) in his essential-reading volume about subversive homosexual cinema in the Spanish transition. Berzosa's vital research draws attention to some experimental and underground activist film and video, but also some mainstream works by key gay male filmmakers including Eloy de la Iglesia and Almodóvar. Indeed, no overview of

Figure 1. José Pérez Ocaña.
Source: Ocaña, retrat intermitent/Ocaña, An Intermittent Portrait dir. Ventura Pons, 1978. Prozesa and Teide PC.

Spanish LGBTQ+ cinema would be complete without a discussion of acclaimed films by these filmmakers who, with Pons, are essential viewing for anyone interested in the history of Spanish LGBTQ+ film.

De la Iglesia (b. 1944–d. 2006) is widely regarded as the first Spanish filmmaker to have dealt consistently with male homosexual narratives throughout his career, with a certain preference for young delinquents of the urban underclass, often protagonists of what in the late 1970s and early 1980s would become a genre of its own, *quinqui* cinema. His best-known gay-themed films, *Los placeres ocultos/Hidden Pleasures* (1977, figure 2), *El diputado/The Deputy* (1978) and the much later *Los novios búlgaros/Bulgarian Lovers* (2003) seemed to follow a Greek model of homosexual relationships, where the young delinquent would become involved in a physical but also mentoring relationship with a much older man of certain social/political status. This class and power imbalance encourages heightened drama caused by breaches of confidence, secretiveness, and jealousy, but it also activates a homoerotic visual economy that produced milestone scenes of erotic tension between men in Spanish film history where desirable young male bodies are shot adoringly from the older men's perspective—meant to match that of the then most likely repressed homosexual male spectator, thus opening a door for both queer identification and desire (Berzosa, 2014, pp. 184–202; Melero Salvador, 2010, pp. 219–264; or Smith, 1992, pp. 129–162; Tropiano, 1997 are key references to study these films from a queer perspective).

Although there seems to be a consensus among Spanish cinema critics that the films of Pedro Almodóvar have decreased in subversive content at the same speed with which budget and stylization increased over the years, his early work—but also, arguably, his most recent including the semi-autobiographical *Dolor y Gloria/Pain and Glory* (2019) and *Madres paralelas/Parallel Mothers* (2021)—must be acknowledged for bringing attention to nonnormative gender and sexual identities. *La ley del deseo/Law of Desire* (1987) is perhaps the most significant example, attracting considerable critical attention from queer cinema scholars around the world (Alfeo Álvarez, 2000; Fouz-Hernández & Perriam, 2000, Jackson, 1995; Levy, 2015;

Figure 2. Simón Andreu and Ángel Pardo.
Source: Los placeres ocultos/Hidden Pleasures dir. Eloy de la Iglesia, 1977. Alborada PC.

Smith, 1992, 1997; or Zurián & García Ramos, 2021 are just some examples). Early Spanish queer scholarship also praised the film (Aliaga & Cortés, 1997) for the casual and respectful way in which same-sex couples and LGBTQ+ lives are presented. Importantly the film, released at a time when Almodóvar was becoming increasingly popular with domestic and international audiences, features the then leading *chica Almodóvar* Carmen Maura as a trans woman as well as the soon-to-become Hollywood star Antonio Banderas in what was already his third gay male role in an Almodóvar film, but here in a much more sexually explicit performance. Although the queer aspects of the narrative and the characters are perhaps not developed fully (see Fouz-Hernández & Perriam, 2000) and the famous sex scenes are not as subversive as they may seem (see Fouz-Hernández, 2017), the film deserves a special place in the history of not just Spanish but LGBTQ+ cinema more generally. The well-deserved prominence of this film, however, should not obscure Almodóvar's earlier work. Both *Laberinto de pasiones/Labyrinths of Passion* (1982, figure 3) and *Matador* (1986), both also starring Banderas, were pioneering in the representation of same-sex male desire, just like *Entre tinieblas/Dark Habits* (1983) was for lesbian desire and like the much later film *La mala educación/Bad Education* (2004) was for trans narratives and narratives of queer memory in Spanish cinema. Almodóvar's 1980s films were key in normalizing same-sex relationships on the Spanish screen by presenting them in a casual way. These characters are surrounded by drama, but their sexuality itself is not presented as taboo or as drama-inducing (e.g., unlike in the films of Eloy de la Iglesia).

Increasing Visibility in the 1990s. Bolstered by the success of Almodóvar and reflecting new levels of social acceptance, new generations of LGBTQ+ filmmakers released numerous LGBTQ+ themed films in the 1990s, especially comedies, in what became known as a mini-boom of the genre (see Collins & Perriam, 2000; Fouz-Hernández & Perriam, 2000). Films such as *Perdona Bonita, pero Lucas me quería a mí/Excuse Me Darling, but Lucas Loved Me* (Félix Sabroso and Dunia Ayaso, 1996), *Más que amor, frenesí?/Not Love…Just Frenzy* (Miguel Bardem, Alfonso Albacete and David Menkes, 1996) or *Amor de hombre/The Love of a Man* (Yolanda García Serrano and Juan Luis Iborra, 1997) exemplify this trend. Often codirected

Figure 3. Antonio Banderas and Imanol Arias.
Source: *Laberinto de pasiones/Labyrinth of Passion* dir. Pedro Almodóvar, 1982. Alphaville.

and set in the then emerging global gay village of Chueca in Madrid, these films had an important role not only in normalizing LGBTQ+ communities, but in giving visibility to queer friendships, same-sex romantic and sexual relationships, drag culture, and the LGBTQ+ scene (especially, but not exclusively, the nightlife). Although in the 1990s people in large urban centers would have become used to seeing same-sex couples holding hands in the street, small-scale Pride marches and would have at least some awareness of LGBTQ+ people and lifestyles, these fairly mainstream films did a good job in showing these urban realities to those living elsewhere in the country (and beyond), at a time where LGBTQ+ characters were only emerging on primetime television. One of the most popular series in the history of Spanish Television, *Farmacia de Guardia/24-Hour Pharmacy* (Antena 3 TV, 1991–1996) featured a trans character in its first season in 1991 and a recurring gay male character since 1995, but LGBTQ+ people were often featured in the news, invited to live audience shows and included in "reality" television shows such as *Gran Hermano* (*Big Brother*). This group of films, however, also arguably recycles some of the stereotypes of the "sexy Iberian comedy" and, like the later *Chuecatown/Boystown* (Flahn, 2007), still connect LGBTQ+ stories to murder and violent plot twist. In contrast, and although still much less frequent than gay men or drag queens, lesbian characters make some progress during this time in films directed by women and that provide a radically different vision of lesbian women than what had been seen before. The most significant example is Marta Balletbó-Coll's *Costa Brava/A Family Album* (1995), where the couple formed by Anna (played by the director herself) and Montserrat (Desi del Valle) is given time and space for development (figure 4). The film replaces the old oppressive stereotypes and sexual objectification with a relationship based on mutual love and respect and a story motivated by a shared curiosity for discovery and adventure (see Gómez Beltrán, 2017; Pelayo, 2009).

Diverse Representation in the 2000s. Throughout the 2000s LGBTQ+ narratives became much more diverse and reflected almost in real time various developments within the community. *Cachorro/Bear Cub* (Albaladejo, 2004) is a milestone in the depiction of

Figure 4. Marta Balletbò-Coll and Desi del Valle.
Source: Costa Brava/A Family Album dir. Marta Balletbò-Coll, 1995. Costa Brava Films.

non-normative queer bodies on the Spanish screen. The film opens, unapologetically, with a very explicit sexual scene that includes frontal nudity and penetrative sex between "bear" men. Importantly, the very active sexual lifestyle of protagonist Pedro (José Luis García Pérez), who frequently visits outdoor cruising areas, gay saunas, and sex clubs, is presented as an exemplary father figure to his little nephew Bernardo (David Castillo), who ends up living with him for an extended period of time while the boy's parents are away. The increasing visibility of LGBTQ+ people and, in turn, the creation of diverse families and the relationships between LGBTQ+ characters and their extended families are also reflected in comedies of this period. *A mi madre le gustan las mujeres/My Mother Likes Women* (Fejeman and París, 2002) or *Reinas/Queens* (Gómez Pereira, 2005) focus on same-sex marriage, while the melodrama *Segunda Piel/Second Skin* (Gerardo Vera, 2000) and the comedy *Fuera de carta/Chef's Special* (García Velilla, 2008) center around coming-out stories of characters who were previously involved in heterosexual relationships. *Spinnin* (Pastrana, 2007) develops more fully the issue of same-sex parenthood. All these films star major actors arguably at the height of their popularity in leading queer roles. The late Rosa María Sardà (a frequent leading lady in Pons' films) and Leonor Watling (another "chica Almodóvar") are the leading couple in *A mi madre le gustan las mujeres* (Fejeman & París, 2002) the by-then more mature "chicas Almodóvar" Marisa Paredes and Carmen Maura are two of the mothers in *Reinas*; while Javier Bardem and Jordi Mollà play leading roles as lovers in *Segunda Piel* and Javier Cámara is the protagonist of *Fuera de carta* (see Ellis, 2010; Fouz-Hernández, 2010, 2017; Pérez, 2017).

The prolific 2000s also saw the release of the first LGBTQ+ musical, *20 centímetros/20 centimetres* (Salazar, 2005), whose protagonist is a preop transgender woman Marieta (Mónica Cervera) who suffers from narcolepsy and fantasizes about having a sex change. She falls in love with the local market's shelf-stacker, an apparently stereotypically, muscular "alpha male" but who is obsessed with Marieta's large penis. Marieta uses song to release her frustration, creating spectacular performances of Spanish cinema and pop classics that could make this film appear the Spanish response to the then hugely popular Abba musical, *Mamma Mia*, although despite a happy ending, the underlying dark narrative sets it closer to Lars von Trier's *Dancer in the Dark* (2000) (see Biddle & Fouz-Hernández, 2012).

Explicit Representation in the 2020s. LGBTQ+ films have continued to engage with evolving attitudes and to reflect social change more widely. *Clandestinos/In Hiding* (Hens, 2007) broke new taboos by featuring sex between a retired Civil Guard (a member of the national law enforcement agency) and an aspiring member of the Basque terrorist group Euskadi Ta Askatasuna (ETA) who is preparing an attack in Madrid in collaboration with an ETA member and two immigrants from Mexico and Morocco. Predictably, the film caused considerable social uproar and (unsuccessful) attempts to force the organizers of Spain's most established LGBTQ+ film festival, LesGaiCineMad (founded in 1996), to pull it from their program. Films like the Basque *Ander* (Roberto Castón, 2009) or *A escondidas/Hidden Away* (Mikel Rueda, 2014) deal with romantic relationships between Spanish and immigrant men (from Perú and Morocco, respectively), a subject already embraced by Eloy de la Iglesia in his 2003 film *Los novios búlgaros* (on this topic see Martínez-Expósito & Fouz-Hernández, 2020). In the documentary *Ignasi M* (2013) Ventura Pons implicitly updates the subversive portrait of Spanish queer men of his 1978 *Ocaña, retrat intermitent*, this time focusing on Ignasi Millet, a respected Catalan museologist who used to be married to a woman and has two children. The film focuses on Ignasi's real-life family relations with his two kids (one of whom is quite religious and struggles to accept his dad's new life), his former wife (who is now disabled and has come out as a lesbian), and his divorced and elderly parents. A major part of the film deals with his medical routine (he is HIV+), but this is combined with frequent scenes of his unapologetically active sex life, which reflects a more sophisticated and open approach to sex between men in Barcelona than the risky public-space cruising scenes recounted by Ocaña 35 years earlier. Ignasi uses modern technology to treat the side effects of his HIV medication, but also to organize his sex life through smartphone apps, and sophisticated sex toys and other pleasure-enhancing complements. Like Eloy de la Iglesia and Pedro Almodóvar, Pons is a key filmmaker who has consistently introduced LGBTQ+ characters and plots in his many films to date. In addition to *Ocaña* and *Ignasi M*, his films *Amic/Amat/Beloved/Friend* (1999) and the English-language *Food of Love* (2002), an adaptation of Leavitt's *The Page Turner* (1998), are popular LGTBQ+ world cinema titles, beyond Catalonia and Spain (see Fouz-Hernández, 2009, 2015, 2021; Perriam, 2013, pp. 48–51, 73–79).

The proliferation of LGBTQ+ characters in many mainstream Spanish films continues to increase, although perhaps with less focus on LGBTQ+ stories, which instead are usually subplots in films about other things and still focusing disproportionately on gay men over lesbian, bisexual, or trans characters—as has been the case historically. Younger generations of queer filmmakers such as Eduardo Casanova or Los Javis, the professional duo and also couple formed by Javier Ambrossi and Javier Calvo, are known internationally not just for their films but also as "content creators" and red-carpet celebrities. Casanova, who is also an actor, premiered his esthetically and narratively queer film *Pieles/Skins* (2017) on Netflix and has since directed a series on Spanish porn actor Nacho Vidal. Los Javis created the domestic box-office hit *La llamada/Holy Camp!* (2017) with a lesbian subplot, but are best-known for the internationally successful comedy series *Paquita Salas* (2016–2019) featuring actor Brays Efe (Brays Fernández Vidal) in the role of a (female) struggling has-been talent agent, and, especially, their limited-series *Veneno* (2020), an adaptation of the memoir of real-life trans celebrity La Veneno, who became a frequent guest on Spanish television late-night shows in the 1990s after she was discovered by a crew preparing a report on prostitution in Madrid. Los Javis are also regular judges in the Spanish version of *Ru Paul Drag Race* (*Drag Race España*, ATRESMedia 2021; on Los Javis see Smith, 2021, pp. 9–28).

More independent queer film Spanish productions also continue to proliferate. Juanma Carrillo made a series of impactful queer shorts between 2009 and 2013, the best-known being *Fuckbuddies* (2011), where two men attempt to have full penetrative sex in a car but see their efforts interrupted by awkward situations (taking a long time to put on a condom) and conversations about anal sex with their female partners (Fouz-Hernández, 2017, pp. 230–232; Perriam, 2013, pp. 15–16, 108–111). Adrián Silvestre's *Sedimentos/Sediments* (2021), a documentary about a group of six trans women set in the provincial Spanish town of León, was selected and nominated for awards in major mainstream domestic festivals such as San Sebastián (Sebastiane Award nominee), SEMINCI Valladolid (Rainbow Spike winner), and Feroz Awards (Arrebato Award winner). It won several awards at the LesGaiCineMad festival 2021 (Audience and Jury Award for Best Documentary, Jury Award for Best Documentary

Director) and it was also showcased internationally at festivals including New Fest in New York and LA's Outfest.

Queer stories have also builtup momentum on streaming services, with series such as *Élite/Elite* (five seasons since 2018) on Netflix (figure 5), the 2021 limited series *Maricón Perdido/Queer We Are* on TNT (in Spain, HBO Max internationally), or the mentioned *Veneno* (limited series, 2020), *Luimellia* (four seasons since 2020) and *La edad de la ira/The Age of Anger* (limited series, 2020) on Spanish streaming service ATRESPlayer Premium. Set in an American-style private high school for rich kids and featuring very explicit sex scenes between handsome young men and a sexually and gender diverse group of characters, *Élite* is as transgressive as it is problematic in terms of LGBTQ+ representation, with the main plot lines circling around crime, unsolved murders, and drug addiction that seem to disproportionately affect queer characters and yet it contributes to normalizing and giving visibility to a much wider range of queer stories than we are used to on major releases. In addition to some diversity in terms of race, ethnicity, and nationality (Las Encinas is, after all, an international school), gay, lesbian, bisexual, and to a lesser extent trans and nonbinary, characters are given plenty of screen time. Far from omitting sex scenes, the camera does not shy away from showing passionate scenes covering a wide range of sexual positions and practices, including some group sex, to an extent that would be very rare on public television. This also has the risk of hypersexualizing queer lives and the casting is also problematic, since it contributes to glamorizing a very specific type: the mostly normative, very young, extremely fit, attractive bodies of rich kids who clearly have the time and money to invest in their appearance. Based on a popular novel by Nando López, also set in a secondary school at the center of a murder investigation, the mini-series *La edad de la ira* does not reach the same levels of sexual explicitness as *Élite*, but arguably takes advantage of its popularity by exploiting some familiar scenarios and esthetic preoccupation with young male bodies. *Luimellia* is another important series for two reasons: first because it is a spin-off of one of the most successful and longest-running series in the history of Spanish television, the Antena 3 TV historical drama *Amar es para siempre* ("Love is Forever," since 2013 and previously with different title in RTVE since 2005), and second because it is the first Spanish television series to focus on two principal lesbian characters from the main series, the couple formed by Luisita Gómez (Paula Usero) and

Figure 5. Arón Piper and Manu Ríos.
Source: *Élite/Elite*, Season 4, Episode 1 dir. Eduardo Chapero-Jackson, 2021. Zeta Studios, Netflix.

Amelia Ledesma (Carla Rovira). The title is made up of their names combined: Lui(sita)(A)Melia. Finally, *Maricón Perdido*, directed by Alejandro Marín is a semi-autobiographical account of writer Roberto Enríquez's (author and media personality also known as Bob Pop) life experiences with homophobia and the escapism provided by musicals and popular culture. It won a Spanish "Ondas" Award for Best Comedy Series in 2021 and a GLAAD Media Award for "Outstanding Spanish-Language Scripted Television Series" in 2022.

This selection of successful streaming productions, featuring gay men, a real-life trans icon, and a lesbian couple that made their way from the margins of an enormously popular story to the center of the narrative seems an ideal way to close this overview of the history of LGBTQ+ characters in Spanish cinema. Importantly, while it would not be good news if LGBTQ+ stories and productions were somewhat relegated to highly volatile and commercially driven streaming services as opposed to cinema (where more independent productions still thrive, supported by specialist festivals), the domestic and international popularity of these series is a good stepforward in terms of distribution and reach, and therefore visibility. LGBTQ+ creators have historically relied on alternative forms of distribution such as home video, festivals, and other specialized events anyway, but this also meant that those stories did not always reach those audiences who may have needed them the most (on Spanish LGBTQ+ festivals see Perriam, 2013, pp. 112–121). Premium streaming services are not accessible to everyone, but once aired, these series usually find their way into homes much more easily than feature films do. Most importantly, younger generations of Spaniards are no longer forced to read against the grain or to endure destructive stereotypes or fake images to see themselves represented on the screen.

FURTHER READING

Lema-Hincapié, A., & Conxita, D. (Eds.). (2020). *Indiscreet fantasies: Iberian queer cinema*. Rutgers University Press.

Melero, A. (2022). *25 años de cine y series LGTB en España (1981-2005)*. Vía láctea editorial.

REFERENCES

Aliaga, J. V., & García Cortés, J. M. (1997). *Identidad y diferencia: Sobre la cultura gay en España*. Egales.

Álvarez, A. (2000). El enigma de la culpa: La homosexualidad y el cine español 1962–2000. *International Journal of Iberian Studies*, 13(3), 136–147.

Arnalte, A. (2003). *Redada de violetas: La represión de los homosexuales durante el franquismo*. La Esfera de Los Libros.

Berzosa, A. (2014). *Homoherejías fílmicas: Cine homosexual subversivo en España en los años setenta y ochenta*. Brumaria.

Biddle, I., & Fouz-Hernández, S. (2012). Voicing gender: Performativity, nostalgia and the National Imaginary in Spanish cinema of the democratic era. In L. Shaw & R. Stone (Eds.), *Screening songs in Hispanic and Lusophone cinema* (pp. 30–50). Manchester University Press.

Cleminson, R., & Vázquez García, F. (2007). *"Los invisibles": A history of male homosexuality in Spain, 1850–1940*. University of Wales Press.

Cleminson, R., & Vázquez García, F. (2009). *Hermaphroditism, medical science and sexual identity in Spain, 1850–1960*. Pickering & Chatto.

Collins, J., & Perriam, C. (2000). Representation of alternative sexualities in contemporary Spanish writing and film. In B. Jordan & R. Morgan-Tamosunas (Eds.), *Contemporary Spanish cultural studies* (pp. 214–222). Arnold.

Ellis, R. R. (2010). Spanish constitutional democracy and cinematic representations of queer sexuality, or, saving the family: *Los novios búlgaros*, *Reinas* and *Fuera de carta*. *Revista Canadiense de Estudios Hispánicos*, 35(1), 67–80.

Epps, B. (2017). Impressions of Africa: Desire, sublimation and looking "otherwise" in three Spanish colonial films. In S. Fouz-Hernández (Ed.), *Spanish erotic cinema* (pp. 37–54). Edinburgh University Press.

Fernández Galeano, J. (2016). Is he a "social danger"? The Franco regime's judicial prosecution of homosexuality in Málaga under the ley de Vagos y Maleantes. *Journal of the History of Sexuality*, 25(1), 1–31.

de Fluvià, A. (2003). *El moviment gai a la clandestinitat del franquisme (1970–1975)*. Egales.

Fouz-Hernández, S. (2009). Caresses: The male body in the films of Ventura Pons. In S. Fouz-Hernández (Ed.), *Mysterious skin: Male bodies in contemporary cinema* (pp. 143–157). I. B. Tauris.

Fouz-Hernández, S. (2010). Assimilation and its discontents: Representations of gay men in Spanish cinema of the 2000s. *Revista Canadiense de Estudios Hispánicos*, 35(1), 81–104.

Fouz-Hernández, S. (2015). La mirada homoerótica en el cine de Ventura Pons. De *Ocaña* a *Ignasi M*. In A. Lema-Hincapié & C. Domènech (Eds.), *Ventura Pons: Una mirada excepcional desde el cine catalán* (pp. 304–327). Vervuert/Iberoamericana.

Fouz-Hernández, S. (2017). Boys interrupted: Sex between men in post-Franco Spanish cinema. In S. Fouz-Hernandez (Ed.), *Spanish erotic cinema* (pp. 219–238). Edinburgh University Press.

Fouz-Hernández, S. (2021). Tablas, memoria, deseo: La vejez en el cine de Ventura Pons. In B. Zecchi, R. Medina Bañón, C. Moreiras-Menor, & M. P. Rodríguez Pérez (Eds.), *Envejecimientos y cines ibéricos* (pp. 141–168). Tirant Lo Blanch.

Fouz-Hernández, S., & Martínez-Expósito, A. (2007). *Live flesh: The male body in contemporary Spanish cinema*. I. B. Tauris.

Fouz-Hernández, S., & Perriam, C. (2000). Beyond Almodóvar: "Homosexuality" in Spanish cinema of the 1990s. In D. Alderson & L. Anderson (Eds.), *Territories of desire in queer culture: Refiguring contemporary boundaries* (pp. 96–111). Manchester University Press.

Gómez Beltrán, I. (2017). Lesbian subject in Spanish cinema directed by women: The example of Marta Balletbó-Coll: *Costa Brava* (1995) and *Sévigné* (2004). *Asparkía*, 31(2), 29–46.

Gutiérrez-Albilla, J. D. (2008). *Queering Buñuel: Sexual dissidence and psychoanalysis in his Mexican and Spanish cinema*. Tauris Academic Studies.

Huard, G. (2014). *Los antisociales: Historia de la homosexualidad en Barcelona y 1945–1975*. Marcial Pons.

Jackson, E. (1995). *Studies in gay male representation*. Indiana University Press.

Levy, E. (2015). *Gay directors, gay films? Pedro Almodóvar, Terence Davis, Todd Haynes, Gus Van Sant, John Waters*. Columbia University Press.

Martínez Expósito, A. (1998). *Los escribas furiosos: Configuraciones homoeróticas en la narrativa española*. University Press of the South.

Martínez-Expósito, A., & Fouz-Hernández, S. (2020). Transnational and migrant queer affects in two Basque films. In J. Williams (Ed.), *Queering the migrant in contemporary European cinema* (pp. 59–71). Routledge.

Melero Salvador, A. (2010). *Placeres ocultos: Gays y lesbianas en el cine español de la transición*. Notorious.

Melero Salvador, A. (2017). *Violetas de España, gays y lesbianas en el cine de Franco*. Notorious.

Mira, A. (1999). *Para entendernos: Diccionario de cultura homosexual, gay y lésbica*. Ediciones de la Tempestad.

Mira, A. (2004). *De Sodoma a Chueca: Una historia cultural de la homosexualidad en España en el siglo XX*. Egales.

Mira, A. (2008). *Miradas insumisas: Gays y lesbianas en el cine*. Egales.

Olmeda, F. (2004). *El látigo y la pluma: Homosexuales en la España de Franco*. Oberón.
Pavlovič, T. (2003). *Despotic bodies and transgressive bodies: Spanish culture from Francisco Franco to Jess Franco*. State University of New York Press.
Pelayo, I. (2009). *Imagen fílmica del lesbianismo a través de los personajes protagonistas en el cine español* [Tesis doctoral, Universidad Complutense de Madrid].
Pérez, J. (2017). Who's your daddy? Queer masculinities and parenthood in recent Spanish cinema. In L. Ryan & A. Corbalán (Eds.), *The dynamics of masculinity in contemporary Spanish culture* (pp. 99–112). Routledge.
Pérez-Sánchez, G. (2007). *Queer transitions in contemporary Spanish culture: From Franco to la Movida*. State University of New York Press.
Perriam, C. (2013). *Spanish queer cinema*. Edinburgh University Press.
Petit, J. (2003). *25 años más: Una perspectiva sobre el pasado, el presente y futuro del movimiento de gays, lesbianas, bisexuales y transexuales*. Icaria.
Petit, J. (2004). *Vidas del arco iris: Historias del ambiente*. De Bolsillo.
Sedgwick, E. K. (1985). *Between men. English literature and male homosocial desire*. Columbia University Press.
Shangay, L. (2016). *Adiós, Chueca: Memorias del gaypitalismo: la creación de la marca gay*. Foca.
Smith, P. J. (1992). *Laws of desire: Questions of homosexuality in Spanish writing and film 1960–1990*. Clarendon Press.
Smith, P. J. (1997). Pornography, masculinity, homosexuality: Almodovar's *matador* and *La ley del Deseo*. In M. Kinder (Ed.), *Refiguring Spain: Cinema/media/representation* (pp. 178–195). Duke University Press.
Smith, P. J. (2021). *Reimagining history in contemporary Spanish media: Theater, cinema, television, streaming*. Legenda.
Stonewall. (2018). *Global workplace briefings: Spain: Stonewall global workplace equality index*. https://www.stonewall.org.uk/system/files/spain_global_workplace_briefing_2018.pdf
Tropiano, S. (1997). Out of the cinematic closet: Homosexuality in the films of Eloy de la Iglesia. In M. Kinder (Ed.), *Refiguring Spain: Cinema/media/representation* (pp. 157–177). Duke University Press.
Trujillo Barbadillo, G. (2009). Del sujeto político la Mujer a la agencia de las (otras) mujeres: El impacto de la crítica queer en el feminismo del Estado español. *Política y Sociedad, 46*(1), 161–172.
Zurián, F. A., & García Ramos, F. J. (2021). *Una mirada queer del cine español del siglo XX. Guía didáctica*. Fundamentos.

Santiago Fouz Hernández

TRANSNATIONAL AND QUEER DIASPORIC SEXUALITIES

QUEER BEGINNINGS

Studies focusing on sexualities in academia have been present since the emergence of social constructionism and have defined sexuality as "the individual capacity to respond to physical experiences which are capable of producing body-centered genital excitation, that only subsequently becomes associated with cognitive constructs" (Goettsch, 1989, p. 250). Although there is no singular definition, sexuality is generally understood to be socially constructed across cultures, and hegemonic perceptions of sexuality have long revolved around "the stimulation of bodies, desires, and pleasures through direct genital contact between 'opposing genders'—a penis entering a vagina—has been normalized and hegemonic in current conceptualizations of sexuality in a number of cultural systems" (Yep et al., 2020, p. 24). Similarly, queer and the conceptualization of queerness work as a resistive framework against standard or conventional ways of thinking about binary sexuality (e.g., gay and lesbian). Credited with coining queer theory, de Lauretis (1991) underscores this point, noting that terms such as "gay" and "lesbian" further project the idea of a politically fixed identification, whereas queer works to "recast or reinvent the terms of our sexualities, to construct another discursive horizon, another way of thinking the sexual" (p. iv). In other words, queer resists fixed definitions and moves against the idea that identities are stable and unmalleable, pushing back against the social and political homogeneity of hetero/homonormativity. To resist heteronormativity and binary labeling and acknowledging its own problematics, this article utilizes "queer" to refer to "a range of dissident and non-heteronormative practices and desires that may very well be incommensurate with the identity categories of 'gay' and 'lesbian'" (Gopinath, 2005, p. 11).

Considering the multiple vectors that make up queer perceptions and lived experiences, cultural constructs about sexuality differ between belief and value systems, and scholars must recognize that hegemonic social scripts reify "appropriate sexual partners, contexts, and activities," but do not construct people's sexualities (Goettsch, 1989, p. 251). Sender (2017) implores scholars to consider the liminality of borders, culture, sex, and sexualities by inquiring, "What role do sex and sexuality have in increasingly vigorous circuits of transnational mobility?" (p. 73). Although there has been an uptick in research that imbues itself in the intersectional reach of transnational and diasporic queer belonging, much has been yet to be written.

The impact that transnationalism and diasporic migration have had on identities is based on the realizations of both long-standing and emerging ways of understanding sexualities and should remain at the forefront of consideration for researchers. As Cantú (2009) explains, works related to migration are typically "framed by heteronormative assumptions that not only deny the existence of non-heterosexual subjects but also cloak the ways in which sexuality itself influences migratory processes" (p. 21). This is especially significant because transnational and diasporic communities are increasing and "large numbers of people now live in social worlds that are stretched between, or dually located in, physical places and communities in two or more nation-states" (Vertovec, 2001, p. 578). *Transnationalism* broadly refers to "persons who live dual lives: speaking two languages, having homes in two countries, and making a living through continuous regular contact across national borders" (Portes et al., 1999, p. 217). Furthermore, transnational and diasporic connections offer more nuance into the intersections of identities as they inhabit "considerable economic, socio-cultural and political impacts on migrants, their families and collective groups, and the dual (or more!) localities in which they variably dwell" (Vertovec, 2001, p. 575).

Levitt and Glick Schiller (2004) ask scholars to examine the ways that individuals maintain connections to their home countries, recognizing "that some migrants and their descendants remain strongly influenced by their continuing ties to their home country or by social networks that stretch across national borders" (p. 1002). Specifically, their call suggests that social study must be understood outside of national borders, noting, "Our analytical lens, must necessarily broaden and deepen because migrants are often embedded in multi-layered, multi-sited transnational social fields, encompassing those who move and those who stay behind" (Levitt & Glick Schiller, 2004, p. 1003). The sheer multiplicity and duality of those occupying transnational and queer diasporic sexualities provide an avenue to explore queerness from myriad perspectives. Therefore, to better understand sexualities holistically, transnational and queer diasporic interventions must be made within research concerning social migration, race, and sexualities.

Thus, this article offers an overview of transnational and queer diasporic sexualities by first discussing lesbian, gay, bisexual, transgender, and queer (LGBTQ) politics and queer theory, followed by transnational and diasporic sexualities. Three specific themes emerge from transnational and queer diasporic sexualities: heteronormativity and Western hegemony, transnational and diasporic queer families, and blurring the First/Third World binary. Finally, this article offers thoughts on the future of transnational and queer diasporic sexualities as well as a list of readings that scholars may find useful in their own academic journeys. It is hoped that this article provides an outline that can emphasize the need for more research dedicated to the nuances of transnational and queer diasporic sexualities.

LGBTQ POLITICS AND QUEER THEORY

The materialization of lesbian, gay, bisexual, transgender, and queer (LGBTQ) politics of identity in the United States and the West has led to queer studies centering "sexual nonnormativities and representations" and has since focused largely on Western, White, male, classed, cisgender notions of binary (gay/straight) sexuality (Binnie, 2004; Cruz-Malavé & Manalansan, 2002; Grewal & Kaplan, 2001; Yep et al., 2014; Yep et al., 2020, p. 39). Considering binary conceptualizations of "gay" and "lesbian" as the only legitimate forms of queer identity, the hegemonic reinforcement of "LGBTQ" identity from a Western perspective as the only valid form of identification is problematic. Concentrating largely on national boundaries, queer theory emerged during the post-structuralist shift in sexuality studies, giving scholars the tools to deconstruct binaries, although not in relation to racial and colonial biases (Chiang & Wong, 2016; Cohen, 2005; de Lauretis, 1991; see also Butler, 1990; Foucault, 1978; Sedgwick, 1990). Queer theory is often critiqued for its homonormative and inadequate examination of race, nation, and materiality, in turn (un)consciously reinforcing non-Western ways of experiencing sexualities as illegitimate.

In addition to labels, the Western LGBTQ movement also produces authenticating symbols to signify gay pride, such as the rainbow flag, which can be identified globally, "officially transgress[ing] borders, as it can be sent to all corners of the world" (Klapeer & Laskar, 2018, p. 524). Symbols hold immense power, but the universality of the rainbow flag does a disservice to the ways in which sexualities are understood and embodied across borders because it reconstitutes the idea of Western hegemony and reinforces the West as morally superior. The reinforcement of nationalistic Western sexual normativity describes what Puar (2007) coins *homonationalism*, or the "deep critique of lesbian and gay liberal rights discourses and how those rights discourses produce narratives of progress and modernity" (Puar, 2013, p. 337). In other words, queer theory's inherent homonationalism fosters the persistent delegitimization of non-Western queer identities, marking them as the antithesis of Western modernity.

To offset these critiques, critical sexuality scholars have begun defining queer studies more inclusively. For instance, Eng et al. (2005) describe queer studies as ever vigilant to the fact that sexuality is intersectional, not extraneous to other modes of difference, and calibrated to a firm understanding of queer as a political metaphor without a fixed referent. A renewed queer studies, moreover, insists on the broadened consideration of the late-20th-century global crises that have configured historical relations among political economies, the geopolitics of war and terror, and national manifestations of sexual, racial, and gendered hierarchies. (p. 1)

Further addressing the omissions in queer theory is the introduction of E. Patrick Johnson's (2001) *quare* theory. Advancing "theories of the flesh" (Moraga & Anzaldúa, 2015), quare theory was derived as a critique of queer theory's hegemonic limitations and omissions by providing an analytical framework for queers of color to "critique stable notions of identity and, at the same time, to locate racialized and class knowledges" (p. 3). Going further, Lee (2003) joins and extends Johnson's quare to include layered transnational sexualities, *Kuaer*, "a transnational study of sexuality with related dimensions of inequality (race, gender, class, and educational background) firmly in mind" (p. 165). In line with these critical departures, Yep et al. (2020) ask scholars to consider and recognize sexuality as "socially constructed by power, geopolitics, and history" (p. 23).

By examining intersecting identity vectors in relation to sexualities, scholars can begin to see where transnational and queer diasporic sexualities can be negotiated to include the experiences outside of Western confinement. Despite the acknowledgments that cultural specificity in relation to queer sexualities is paramount to offering a holistic view of myriad nonnormative sexualities, little research in communication studies has explored the ways in which transnationalism affects the study of sexualities all together.

TRANSNATIONAL AND DIASPORIC SEXUALITIES

Ghosh (2020) describes transnationalism in relation to sexuality as a move that "challenges local–global binaries in sexuality, viewing it rather as constructed as a simultaneous outcome of localization and globalization" (p. 550). Connecting geography, space, location, gender, ethnicity, and nationalism is crucial when discussing global sexualities and is one way scholars have pushed back against hegemonic understandings of sex and sexuality, which in turn shines a light on "the movements of people, capital, and images across national boundaries; follow the desires, aspirations, and desperations that prompted these movements; and chronicle the effects of these movements on sexual subjectivities, identifications, and intimate practices" (Povinelli & Chauncey, 1999, p. 446).

Accordingly, to map and contextualize transnational and queer diasporic sexualities, particular attention must be given to the tensions between the interconnectivity of local and global discourses about sexualities and queer subjectivities. This move necessitates scholars to unpack sexualities across cultures and borders and must be met with a respect to how dominant Western discourses of binary sexualities (heterosexual/homosexual) are categorically re/enforced through power and hegemony. Furthermore, scholars must attend to the influential ways Western hegemony has influenced how sexuality is understood globally, imposing and inscribing binary positions that mark sexualized bodies as either "authentic" or "inauthentic."

Accordingly, the shift toward a transnational and diasporic context for transdisciplinary queer studies gives space to resist long-standing narratives and delve into the nuances and specificities of *other* sexualities that exist beyond Western ideality.

To grasp the inherent connectivity and linkages between transnationalism and identity, these must be thought of as juxtaposing concepts because "many peoples' transnational networks are grounded upon the perception that they share some form of common identity, often based upon a place of origin and the cultural and linguistic traits associated with it" and typically span more than one place (Vertovec, 2001, p. 573). Considering transnational and diasporic subjectivities, therefore, inherently offers restorative potentialities to understanding and dismantling nationalist ideologies related to identities, particularly sex and sexuality (Gopinath, 2005). As Sinnott (2010) argues, "The turn to issues of transnationalism, diaspora, and border crossings works toward interrogating and deconstructing assumptions of steamrolling Westernization or stable identity categories that fall along binaries such as traditional/modern or local/global" (p. 17).

Similarly, as globalization, migration, and global media continue to shift the geopolitical landscape, Ghabra and Alaoui (2020) call for scholars to center intersectional "voices from a transnational perspective" (p. 1). This call is more urgent than ever, particularly as an increased focus on transnational sexualities permeates across the humanities and social sciences.

Often utilized as a synonym for transnational, *diaspora* (describing the migration and dispersal of people across borders) is one way to understand the amalgamation of cultural identities that defy borders and resist nation-states (Grewal & Kaplan, 2001). As Clifford (1994) argues, "Diasporic discourses reflect the sense of being part of an ongoing transnational work that includes the homeland, not as something simply left behind, place of attachment in a contrapuntal" (p. 311). Accordingly, Clifford (1994) highlights the ways in which, "diaspora cultures...mediate, in tension, the experiences of separation and entanglement, of living here bering/desiring another place" (p. 311). Gopinath (2005) describes queer diaspora as a move to both locally and transnationally decenter Whiteness and the colonial Western narrative of modernity in relation to sexuality. Thus, the notion of a queer diaspora makes space for multiple ways of knowing/learning/performing/engaging with sexualities through entangled knowledges and histories. In contrast to traditional diasporic understandings that "mobilizes questions of the past, memory, and nostalgia," queer diaspora places desire and body alongside reflections of a "past time and place riven with contradictions and the violences of multiple uprootings, displacements, and exiles" (Gopinath, 2005, p. 4).

THEMES IN TRANSNATIONAL AND QUEER DIASPORIC SEXUALITIES

Although the study of transnational and queer diasporic sexualities is still in its relative infancy, it has become a burgeoning topic of transdisciplinary study, bridging sexuality and gender studies, communication studies, postcolonial studies, critical race studies, among other humanities and social science disciplines. Exemplars of this work in their particularity span across global contexts and include authors focused on myriad transnational diasporic sexualities. Scholars such as Asante (2020), Epprecht (2004), Matebeni (2014), Nyanzi (2014), and Osinubi (2018) critically integrate queerness within myriad African contexts, specifically centering the conversation around queer African identity, which in and of itself remains fragmented across African nations. Authors dedicated to telling the stories of transnational Asian and Southwest Asian/North African diasporic sexualities, including Abdi (2014, 2020), Blackwood (2005), Boellstorff (2005), Chiang and Wong (2016), Chuang (2020), Eguchi (2014), Eng (2001), Gopinath (2005), Huang and Brouwer (2018), Islam (1993), Loos (2009), Manalansan (1995, 2003), Massad (2007), Puar (1998, 2001, 2005, 2007, 2013), Sinnott (2010), and Yep et al. (2020), redefine what it means to be transnational and diasporic queer subjects as they navigate the terrains of culture, religion, Western imperialism, and the family. Furthermore, there are those invested in the transnational and diasporic Latinx experiences centering issues of gender, religion, family, mestizaje, and sexile (Alvarez, 2018; Anzaldúa, 1999; Calafell, 2017; Carrillo, 2017; Falconí, 2014; Guzmán, 1997; La Fountain-Stokes, 2008, 2009; Moraga & Anzaldúa, 2015; Muñoz, 1991, 1995, 1997; Ochoa, 2008; Ruvalcaba, 2016; Viteri, 2017). Each of these authors offers foundational perspectives on transnational and queer diasporic sexualities by highlighting the contextual and culturally nuanced understanding of identities outside rigid definitional boxes.

Aligned with Puar's (2005) assessment of transnational sexuality research, the previously mentioned authors consider "whether globalization produces queerness (queer identities) as part of Western imperialism or whether queerness is produced as an identity of liberation from and resistance to dominant narratives" (p. 399). Blackwood (2005) suggests that transnational sexualities are "shaped by a large number of processes implicated in globalization, including capitalism, diasporic movements, political economies of state, and the disjunctive flow of meanings produced across these sites" (p. 221). This is particularly noteworthy in that critical scholarship examining transnational sexualities can push back against the notion that borders and nation-states are what impact identities, instead considering the impact cultures have on identities. Thus, rather than pitting the local and global against each other, scholars must consider their inseparability while examining the omnipresent influence of heteronormativity and Western hegemony.

Heteronormativity and Western Hegemony. Hegemony and power are defined as "social, cultural, political, structural, and institutional resources and dominance of one identity, practice, or conceptualization over others" (Yep et al., 2020, p. 31). Power determines much of what perpetuates dominant discourses that consequently become unquestionable truths about sexualities. Heteronormativity describes the sexual system derived from Western (White, middle class, male) hegemony, which has "marginalized, erased, and made different cultural understandings of sexual practices, eroticism, and sexuality unintelligible—making these conceptions into transnational weapons of colonialism and imperialism" (Yep et al., 2020, p. 31). In other words, hegemony and power reinforce the binary that deems all modes of sexuality beyond the purview of Western cultural systems as backward or archaic. In reality, many sexual subjectivities are unaccounted for and are dismissed on the basis of not fitting into Western modes of identity articulation, and transnational and queer diasporic sexualities are contextually consistently redefined.

Making space for transnational sexualities means considering sexualities in relation to their contextual vernacular and localizations and how they are interconnected—a task that has been made increasingly difficult to do without recentering and privileging Western language and experiences of sexuality. Heteronormativity describes "the numerous ways in which heterosexual privilege is woven into the fabric of social life, pervasively and insidiously ordering everyday existence" (Weeks, 1985, p. 108). Yep (2003) explains heteronormativity as the moment that heterosexuality becomes omnipresent and the standard way to understand sexuality: "When the view is that institutionalized heterosexuality constitutes the standard for legitimate, authentic, prescriptive, and ruling social, cultural, and sexual arrangements, it becomes heteronormativity" (p. 13). Seidman (2005) explains, "normative heterosexuality 'not only establishes a heterosexual/homosexual hierarchy but also creates hierarchies among heterosexualities,' resulting in 'hegemonic and subordinate forms of heterosexuality'" (p. 40).

It is this standard that leads to transnational and queer diasporic sexualities remaining largely invisible or abject, thus resulting in what Yep (2003) describes as the "symbolic, discursive, psychological, and material violence of heteronormativity" (p. 14). Furthermore, as Jackson (2006) posits, "heterosexuality, while depending on the exclusion or marginalization of other sexualities for its legitimacy, is not precisely coterminous with heterosexual sexuality. Heteronormativity defines not only a normative sexual practice but also a normal way of life" (p. 107). Scholars wanting to delve into transnational and queer diasporic sexualities must also underscore the pervasiveness with which heteronormativity continues its role across cultural contexts, challenging our understanding of the specificities of myriad sexual identities and often recentering Western norms (Yep, 2003, 2017).

The danger that lies in the maintenance of heteronormativity is its ability to replicate and create "a range of subaltern groups, including lesbians, gay men, trans people, poor and racialized parents, interracial couples, sex workers, migrant and colonized sexual subjects, and others" (Luibhéid, 2018, p. 305). This is exemplified when speaking about queer sexualities utilizing terms such as "gay" and "lesbian," reinforcing the Western binary that suggests non-heteronormativity requires specific labeling in order to reach "authenticity." However, as Abdi (2020) contends, there is no such thing as an authentically queer story because "authenticity is language used to make others who have historically been absent in the master narrative feel inferior" (p. 57). Stella (2011) articulates the omnipresence and imbalance of Western notions of sexuality versus everyone else, noting that "the development of Western-style sexual identity politics, and achievements in the fields of gay rights and sexual citizenship are often uncritically taken to be a measure of a nation's development and successful modernization" (p. 215).

Transnational and queer diasporic sexualities as an area of study "enables a simultaneous critique of heterosexuality and the nation form while exploding the binary oppositions between nation and diaspora, heterosexuality and homosexuality, original and copy" (Gopinath, 2005, p. 11). In this way, three major themes come to the fore as scholars throughout the world write about, interrogate, and resist long-standing suppositions and impositions about sexuality as always already measured against Western hegemonic idealities. When researching queer diasporic South Asian populations, Puar (1998) actively disrupts master narratives of sex and sexuality, noting "diasporic queers have not only various relationships to different states but indeed different relationships to common states, determined by highly diverse histories of ethnicity, migration, class, generation, gender, and religious identity" (pp. 409–410). Puar asks scholars to consider questions such as the following:

> How could/should one "queer" the diaspora(s) or "diasporicize" the queer? How does inclusion/exclusion from diasporas affect queers of color who have relationships to

nations other than the United States? How do diasporic subjects construct queer selves through experiences of displacement? (p. 406)

To answer these questions, Puar (1998) makes clear that each diasporic context is unique and therefore contextualizing diasporic experiences must be purposeful and explicit.

Transnational and Diasporic Queer Families. Documenting the use of a queer diasporic framework gives space for a more holistic exploration of "messy" sexualities that do not fit neatly in any nationalistic conversation about sexuality. Abdi (2014), for instance, writes an unconventional "coming out" narrative documenting the diasporic tensions of being a queer Iranian American while navigating her identities with her immediate and extended family both in the United States and in Iran, in conversation with divergent transnational sexual norms. Through a critical autoethnographic account, Abdi (2014) walks readers through different stages of negotiating her own queer identity, her disparate cultural identities as a U.S. American-born Iranian, as well as the dueling familial and cultural norms that complicated the way she came to understand and ultimately articulate her sexuality to her mother and sister. Resisting and reifying norms from both cultural influences highlight the complex nature of making sense of sexuality as not a stand-alone identity but, rather, one that is directly linked to family, class, nationality, gender, religion, and communal expectations. Abdi's (2014) story accounts for a queer diasporic narrative that challenges Western notions of coming out while also negotiating with the Western script about queer sexuality, making space for a diasporic borderless liminality of queerness, noting "juxtaposing the Iranian narrative with my own challenges the narrative fidelity of both, creating a paradox within myself" (p. 17). Like many diasporic queer scholars in the United States, Abdi's (2014, 2020) intersectional narrative gives space to hear a version of a story often untold that is necessary to combating hegemonic Western norms: "It is imperative to transgress heteronormativity and homonormativity so that we can make space for other nuanced conversations about the realities of embodied simultaneity" (Abdi, 2020, p. 48). This is particularly true as these narratives function to shed light on the intricate ways diasporic queers experience "unique and important daily issues: racism, exile, immigration and deportation threats, cultural isolation, and Western hybridization" (Islam, 1993, p. 45).

La Fountain-Stokes (2008) underscores the political identification of Latinx sexuality by placing focus on the Puerto Rican queer diasporic experience of queer exile, or the "exile of those who have had to leave their nations of origin on account of their sexual orientation" (Guzmán, 1997, p. 277). By placing focus on the embodied experiences of queer Puerto Ricans, La Fountain-Stokes (2008) emphasizes the notion of feeling queer and yet being compelled to leave their places of origin—both by personal choice and by expulsion—due to familial, religious, and political abuses that lead to persecution and bigotry based on sexuality and gender.

Blurring the First/Third World Binary. Although there certainly are many benefits to telling stories from the margin, Puar (1998) cautions against utilizing narratives as the only means of "authenticating" diasporic queerness because if visibility equates authenticity, then coming out would be "understood as a conclusion to the linear teleology of a modernist, rational subject emerging unrepressed and therefore as empowered as any white queer" reinforcing the "West as a place of sexual freedom and liberation" (p. 414)—thus re-establishing the binary of First World/Third World while attempting to subvert those very same binaries. Furthermore, scholars must be attuned to the fact that narratives about sexuality as a primary identity in relation to locality and diaspora have the potential to become the only story of a global community. As such, Puar (1998) asks scholars engaging in narrative work to consider "when and how the diasporic becomes the globalizing discourse" (p. 413). This is of particular importance as diasporic narrators discuss their intersectional identities as the

> privileging of being out sets forth sexual identity as separate from other identities, or at least as primary and uninflected by other subject positionings... posit[ing] a domestic perspective as a diasporic perspective that becomes a globalizing tendency. (p. 415)

Similarly, Gopinath (2005) asks, "How do we allow for the fact that same-sex eroticism exists and signifies very differently in different diasporic contexts, while simultaneously recognizing the common forms of violence that we face everyday because of our sexuality?" (p. 122).

CONCLUSION: TRANSNATIONAL FUTURES

Emerging research critically engaging transnational and queer diasporic sexualities is quickly becoming an area of inquiry for myriad sexuality scholars examining how "constructions of diaspora may suggest new formations for queer politics" (Puar, 1998, p. 418). Ultimately, the contextualization of the trajectory of transnational sexualities, queer studies, sexual identities, hegemony and power, queer theory, and queer diasporas provides a road map for scholars interested in pursuing research in these subfields.

Transnational and queer diaspora sexuality studies will continue to evolve as our understandings of sexualities and genders shift, but it is also crucial to recognize how multiple cultural codes impact and influence individuals' relationship to sexuality. By ensuring a more holistic overview of transnational sexuality, researchers can begin to create and sustain a more culturally competent and holistic understanding of sexualities beyond the binary. That is the hope, anyway.

FURTHER READING

Alvarez, S. E. (2018). Afterword: Maneuvering the "U-turn". In E. J. Freedman (Ed.), *Seeking rights from the left* (pp. 305–312). Duke University Press. https://doi.org/10.1515/9781478002604-011

Falconí, D. (2014). De lo queer/cuir/cuy(r) en América Latina: Accidentes y malosentendidos en la narrativa de Ena Lucía Portela. *Mitologías Hoy, 10,* 95–113. https://doi.org/10.5565/rev/mitologias.191

Guzmán, M. (1997). Pa' la escuelita con muchocuida'o y por la orillita [Going to school with caution and without making waves]: A journey through the contested terrains of the nation and sexual orientation. In F. Negrón-Nuntaner & R. Grosfoguel (Eds.), *Puerto Rican jam: Rethinking colonialism and nationalism* (pp. 209–228). University of Minnesota Press.

Huang, S., & Brouwer, D. C. (2018). Coming out, coming home, coming with: Models of queer sexuality in contemporary China. *Journal of International and Intercultural Communication, 11*(2), 97–116. https://doi.org/10.1080/17513057.2017.1414867

La Fountain-Stokes, L. (2008). Queer diasporas, Boricua lives: A meditation on sexile. *Review: Literature and Arts of the Americas, 41*(2), 294–301. https://doi.org/10.1080/08905760802404259

La Fountain-Stokes, L. (2009). *Queer Ricans: Cultures and sexualities in the diaspora.* University of Minnesota Press.

Massad, J. A. (2007). *Desiring Arabs.* University of Chicago Press.

Ochoa, M. (2008). Perverse citizenship: Divas, marginality, and participation in "localization". *WSQ: Women's Studies Quarterly, 36*(3–4), 146–169. https://doi.org/10.1353/wsq.0.0102

Patton, C., & Sánchez-Eppler, B. (2000). *Queer diasporas.* Duke University Press.

Puar, J. K. (2007). *Terrorist assemblages: Homonationalism in queer times.* Duke University Press.

Ruvalcaba, H. D. (2016). *Translating the queer: Body politics and transnational conversations.* Zed Books.

Viteri, M. A. (2017). Intensiones: Tensions in queer agency and activism in Latino América. *Feminist Studies, 43*(2), 405–417. https://doi.org/10.1353/fem.2017.0028

Yep, G. A., Alaoui, F. Z. C, & Lescure, R. M. (2020). Relationalities in/through difference: Explorations in queer intercultural communication. In S. Eguchi & B. M. Calafell (Eds.), *Queer intercultural communication: The intersectional politics of belonging in and across differences* (pp. 19–45). Rowman & Littlefield.

REFERENCES

Abdi, S. (2014). Staying I(ra)n: Narrating queer identity from within the Persian closet. *Liminalities, 10*(2), 1–20. http://liminalities.net/10-2/staying.pdf

Abdi, S. (2020). Revisiting a letter for someday: Writing toward a queer Iranian diasporic potentiality. In S. Eguchi & B. M. Calafell (Eds.), *Queer intercultural communication: The intersectional politics of belonging in and across differences* (pp. 47–62). Rowman & Littlefield.

Alvarez, S. E. (2018). Afterword: Maneuvering the "U-turn". In E. J. Freedman (Ed.), *Seeking rights from the left* (pp. 305–312). Duke University Press. https://doi.org/10.1515/9781478002604-011

Anzaldúa, G. (1999). *Borderlands/la Frontera: The new mestiza.* Aunt Lute Books.

Asante, G. (2020). Decolonizing the erotic: Building alliances of (queer) African Eros. *Women's Studies in Communication, 43*(2), 113–118. http://doi.org/10.1080/07491409.2020.1745588

Binnie, J. (2004). *The globalization of sexuality.* SAGE.

Blackwood, E. (2005). Transnational sexualities in one place: Indonesian readings. *Gender & Society, 19*(2), 221–242. https://www.jstor.org/stable/30044584

Boellstorff, T. (2005). *The gay archipelago: Sexuality and nation in Indonesia.* Princeton University Press. http://dx.doi.org/10.1177/0891243204272862

Butler, J. (1990). *Gender trouble: Feminism and the subversion of identity.* Routledge.

Calafell, B. M. (2017). Brown queer bodies. *Qualitative Inquiry, 23*(7), 511–512. https://doi.org/10.1177/1077800417718290

Cantú, L. (2009). *The sexuality of migration: Border crossings and Mexican immigrant men.* New York University Press.

Carrillo, H. (2017). *Pathways of desire: The sexual migration of Mexican gay men.* University of Chicago Press.

Chiang, H., & Wong, A. (2016). Queering the transnational turn: Regionalism and queer Asias. *Gender, Place & Culture, 23*(11), 1643–1656. http://doi.org/10.1080/0966369X.2015.1136811

Chuang, A. K. (2020). A local gay man/tongzhi or a transnational queer/qu-er/kuer: (Re)organizing my queerness and Asianness through personal reflection. In S. Eguchi, B. M. Calafell, & S. Abdi (Eds.), *Dewhitening intersectionality: Race, intercultural communication, and politics* (pp. 101–118). Lexington Books.

Clifford, J. (1994). Diasporas. *Cultural Anthropology, 9*(3), 302–338. http://doi.org/10.1525/can.1994.9.3.02a00040

Cohen, C. J. (2005). Punks, bulldaggers, and welfare queens: The radical potential of queer politics? In M. Henderson & E. P. Johnson (Eds.), *Black queer studies: A critical anthology* (pp. 21–51). Duke University Press.

Cruz-Malavé, A., & Manalansan, M. F. (2002). *Queer globalizations: Citizenship and the afterlife of colonialism*. New York University Press.

de Jong, S., & Dannecker, P. (2018). Connecting and confronting transnationalism: Bridging concepts and moving critique. *Identities, 25*(5), 493–506. https://doi.org/10.1080/1070289x.2018.1507962

de Lauretis, T. (1991). Habit changes. *differences, 6*(2–3), 296–313. https://doi.org/10.1215/10407391-6-2-3-296

Eguchi, S. (2014). Ongoing cross-national identity transformation: Living on the queer Japan–U.S. transnational borderland. *Sexuality & Culture, 18*(4), 977–993. http://dx.doi.org/10.1007/s12119-014-9234-5

Eng, D. L. (2001). *Racial castration: Managing masculinity in Asian America*. Duke University Press.

Eng, D. L., Halberstam, J., & Muñoz, J. E. (2005). Introduction: What's queer about queer studies now? *Social Text, 23*(3–4), 1–17. https://doi.org/10.1215/01642472-23-3-4_84-85-1

Epprecht, M. (2004). *Hungochani: The history of a dissident sexuality in southern Africa*. McGill–Queen's University Press.

Falconí, D. (2014). De lo queer/cuir/cuy(r) en América Latina: Accidentes y malos entendidos en la narrativa de Ena Lucía Portela. *Mitologías Hoy, 10*, 95–113. https://doi.org/10.5565/rev/mitologias.191

Foucault, M. (1978). *The history of sexuality, Volume 1: An introduction*. Vintage Books.

Ghabra, H., & Alaoui, F. Z. (2020). Introduction. In H. Ghabra, F. Z. C. Alaoui, S. Abdi, & B. M. Calafell (Eds.), *Negotiating identity and transnationalism: Middle Eastern and North African communication and critical cultural studies* (pp. 1–14). Lang.

Ghosh, A. (2020). From moral ambivalence to differential congruence: Understanding transnational sexuality using cultural schemas. *Sexualities, 23*(4), 549–573. http://doi.org/10.1177/1363460719850022

Goettsch, S. L. (1989). Clarifying basic concepts: Conceptualizing sexuality. *Journal of Sex Research, 26*(2), 249–255. https://doi.org/10.1080/00224498909551509

Gopinath, G. (2005). *Impossible desires: Queer diasporas and South Asian public cultures*. Duke University Press.

Grewal, I., & Kaplan, C. (2001). Global identities: Theorizing transnational studies of sexuality. *GLQ, 7*(4), 663–679. http://dx.doi.org/10.1215/10642684-7-4-663

Guzmán, M. (1997). Pa' la escuelita con muchocuida'o y por la orillita [Going to school with caution and without making waves]: A journey through the contested terrains of the nation and sexual orientation. In F. Negrón-Nuntaner & R. Grosfoguel (Eds.), *Puerto Rican jam: Rethinking colonialism and nationalism* (pp. 209–228). University of Minnesota Press.

Huang, S., & Brouwer, D. C. (2018). Coming out, coming home, coming with: Models of queer sexuality in contemporary China. *Journal of International and Intercultural Communication, 11*(2), 97–116. https://doi.org/10.1080/17513057.2017.1414867

Islam, S. (1993). Toward a global network of Asian lesbians. In R. Ratti (Ed.), *A lotus of another color: An unfolding of the South Asian gay and lesbian experience* (pp. 405–424). Alyson Books.

Jackson, S. (2006). Gender, sexuality and heterosexuality: The complexity (and limits) of heteronormativity. *Feminist Theory, 7*(1), 105–121. https://doi.org/10.1177/1464700106061462

Johnson, E. P. (2001). "Quare" studies, or (almost) everything I know about queer studies I learned from my grandmother. *Text and Performance Quarterly, 21*(1), 1–25. http://doi.org/10.1215/9780822387220-008

Klapeer, C. M., & Laskar, P. (2018). Transnational ways of belonging and queer ways of being: Exploring transnationalism through the trajectories of the rainbow flag. *Identities, 25*(5), 524–541. https://doi.org/10.1080/1070289x.2018.1507958

La Fountain-Stokes, L. (2008). Queer diasporas, Boricua lives: A meditation on sexile. *Review: Literature and Arts of the Americas, 41*(2), 294–301. https://doi.org/10.1080/08905760802404259

La Fountain-Stokes, L. (2009). *Queer Ricans: Cultures and sexualities in the diaspora*. University of Minnesota Press.

Lee, W. (2003). Kuaering queer theory. *Journal of Homosexuality, 45*(2–4), 147–170. http://dx.doi.org/10.1300/J082v45n02_07

Levitt, P., & Glick Schiller, N. (2004). Conceptualizing simultaneity: A transnational social field perspective on society. *International Migration Review, 38*(3), 1002–1039. https://doi.org/10.1111/j.1747-7379.2004.tb00227.x

Loos, T. (2009). Transnational histories of sexualities in Asia. *American Historical Review, 114*(5), 1309–1324. http://doi.org/10.1086/ahr.114.5.1309

Luibhéid, E. (2018). Heteronormativity: A bridge between queer migration and critical trafficking studies. *Women's Studies in Communication, 41*(4), 305–309. http://doi.org/10.1080/07491409.2018.1544001

Manalansan, M. (1995). In the shadows of Stonewall: Examining gay transnational politics and the diasporic dilemma. *GLQ, 2*(4), 425–438. http://doi.org/10.1215/10642684-2-4-425

Manalansan, M. (2003). *Global divas: Filipino gay men in the diaspora*. Duke University Press.

Massad, J. A. (2007). *Desiring Arabs*. University of Chicago Press.

Matebeni, Z. (2014). *Reclaiming Afrikan: Queer perspectives on sexual and gender identities*. Modjaji Books.

Moraga, C. (2000). *Loving in the war years: Lo que nunca pasó por sus labios*. South End Press.

Moraga, C., & Anzaldúa, G. (2015). *This bridge called my back: Writings by radical women of color* (4th ed.). State University of New York Press.

Morrissey, M. E. (2013). A DREAM disrupted: Undocumented migrant youth disidentifications with U.S. citizenship. *Journal of International & Intercultural Communication, 6*(2), 145–162. http://doi.org/10.1080/17513057.2013.774041

Muñoz, J. E. (1991). *Disidentifications: Queers of color and the performance of politics*. University of Minnesota Press.

Muñoz, J. E. (1995). The autoethnographic performance: Reading Richard Fung's queer hybridity. *Screen, 21*(1/2), 83–99. http://dx.doi.org/10.1093/screen/36.2.83

Muñoz, J. E. (1997). "The white to be angry": Vaginal Davis' terrorist drag. *Social Text, 52*(3), 90–103. http://doi.org/10.2307/466735

Nyanzi, S. (2014). Queering queer Africa. In Z. Matebeni (Ed.), *Reclaiming Afrikan: Queer perspectives on sexual and gender identities* (pp. 61–66). Modjaji Books.

Ochoa, M. (2008). Perverse citizenship: Divas, marginality, and participation in "localization". *WSQ: Women's Studies Quarterly, 36*(3–4), 146–169. https://doi.org/10.1353/wsq.0.0102

Osinubi, T. A. (2018). Introduction: Denormativizing imperatives in African queer scholarship. *College Literature, 45*(4), 596–612. https://doi.org/10.1353/lit.2018.0034

Patton, C., & Sánchez-Eppler, B. (2000). *Queer diasporas*. Duke University Press.

Portes, A., Guarnizo, L. E., & Landolt, P. (1999). The study of transnationalism: Pitfalls and promise of an emergent research field. *Ethnic and Racial Studies, 22*(2), 217–237. https://doi.org/10.1080/014198799329468

Povinelli, E. A., & Chauncey, G. (1999). Thinking sexuality transnationally: An introduction. *GLQ, 5*(4), 439–449. http://doi.org/10.1215/10642684-5-4-439

Puar, J. K. (1998). Transnational sexualities: South Asian (trans)nation(alism)s and queer diasporas. In D. L. Eng & A. Y. Hom (Eds.), *Q & A: Queer in Asian America* (pp. 405–424). Temple University Press.

Puar, J. K. (2001). Global circuits: Transnational sexualities and Trinidad. *Signs, 26*(4), 1039–1065. http://doi.org/10.1086/495647

Puar, J. K. (2005). Transversal circuits: Transnational sexualities and Trinidad. In L. Nelson & J. Seager (Eds.), *A companion to feminist geography* (pp. 398–416). Blackwell.

Puar, J. K. (2007). *Terrorist assemblages: Homonationalism in queer times*. Duke University Press.

Puar, J. K. (2013). Rethinking homonationalism. *International Journal of Middle East Studies, 45*(2), 336–339. http://doi.org/10.1017/S002074381300007X
Ruvalcaba, H. D. (2016). *Translating the queer: Body politics and transnational conversations*. Zed Books.
Sedgwick, E. K. (1990). *Epistemology of the closet*. University of California Press.
Seidman, S. (2005). From polluted homosexual to the normal gay: Changing patterns of sexual regulation in America. In C. Ingraham (Ed.), *Thinking straight: New work in critical heterosexuality studies* (pp. 39–62). Routledge.
Sender, K. (2017). Expanding media and sexuality studies: A transnational study of sex museums. *Critical Studies in Media Communication, 34*(1), 73–79. https://doi.org/10.1080/15295036.2016.1266685
Sinnott, M. (2010). Borders, diaspora, and regional connections: Trends in Asian "queer" studies. *Journal of Asian Studies, 69*(1), 17–31. http://doi.org/10.1017/S0021911809991586
Stella, F. (2011). The language of intersectionality: Researching "lesbian" identity in urban Russia. In Y. Taylor, S. Hines, & M. E. Casey (Eds.), *Theorizing intersectionality and sexuality* (pp. 212–234). Palgrave Macmillan.
Vertovec, S. (2001). Transnationalism and identity. *Journal of Ethnic and Migration Studies, 27*(4), 573–582. https://doi.org/10.1080/13691830120090386
Viteri, M. A. (2017). Intensiones: Tensions in queer agency and activism in Latino América. *Feminist Studies, 43*(2), 405–417. https://doi.org/10.1353/fem.2017.0028
Weeks, J. (1985). *Sexuality and its discontents: Meanings, myths, and modern sexualities*. Taylor & Francis.
Yep, G. A. (2003). The violence of heteronormativity in communication studies. *Journal of Homosexuality, 45*(2), 11–59. http://doi.org/10.1300/J082v45n02_02
Yep, G. A. (2017). Further notes on healing from "the violence of heteronormativity in communication studies". *QED, 4*(2), 115–122. http://doi.org/10.14321/qed.4.2.0115
Yep, G. A., Alaoui, F. Z. C., & Lescure, R. M. (2020). Relationalities in/through difference: Explorations in queer intercultural communication. In S. Eguchi & B. M. Calafell (Eds.), *Queer intercultural communication: The intersectional politics of belonging in and across differences* (pp. 19–45). Rowman & Littlefield.
Yep, G. A., Lovaas, K., & Elia, J. P. (2014). *Queer theory and communication: From disciplining queers to queering the discipline(s)*. Routledge.

Fatima Zahrae Chrifi Alaoui

TRANSNATIONAL QUEER TRANSLATIONS

The applications of queer theory and queer methodological approaches within communication studies do not have a long history. While the links were developed during the 1990s, as compared to the other humanities disciplines (such as literary studies, film studies, comparative literature, ethnic studies, and others), communication studies scholars who worked within humanistic paradigms and perspectives were slow to adopt and embrace queer theory and its agenda. Hence, the early presence of queer theory in the discipline did not make the intended wider impact despite the work produced by Chesboro (1981), Ringer (1994), Slagle (1995), and others. However, Corey and Nakayama's (1997) "Sextext" became one of the pioneering essays to chart new territories for queer studies within communication studies. As the queer communication studies scholarship further developed and gained some momentum within rhetorical studies and performance studies, other subdisciplines struggled to embrace queer studies' frameworks or flat-out rejected its critical and political agenda. Because of the subdisciplines in which these scholars were working, most of the early queer communication scholarship was produced by mainstream white U.S.-based scholars. Historically, some of the subdisciplines were not welcoming scholarly communities for transnational scholars and domestic minority scholars. However, the works of E. Patrick Johnson (2001), Gust Yep (2003), Bryant Keith Alexander (2003), and some of the other early pioneers brought a much-needed diversity of approach to queer communication studies in the early 2000s.

As Karma Chávez (2013) and Gust Yep (2013) articulate, the absence of diverse queer voices within the queer communication studies subdiscipline was striking. First Chávez and, later, others such as Atay (2015, 2020, 2021), Eguchi and Calafell (2020), and Gutierrez-Perez and Andrade (2020) articulate that even subdisciplines that focus on culture and communication, such as intercultural communication, struggled to incorporate queer theory and queer scholarship. Even though there is more visibility in some of these fields, the absence of queer issues and worldmaking is strikingly apparent and visible. As queer communication studies began gaining momentum through the work of scholars in the field throughout the early and mid-2000s and more scholars of color or scholars who represent domestic diversity joined the scholarly discussion, with very few exceptions, most of them heavily reflected queer lives and experiences in the United States. The absence of transnational queer scholarship within the discipline is not only striking but also alarming. Although queer communication studies promises a critical lens through which to approach and make sense of queer realities and lives, these realities and stories are still limited to certain diverse bodies. Moreover, the lack of transnational queer voices in the discipline often hinders the very agenda that queer theorizing aims to do in communication studies. On one hand, it queers the discipline and offers limited diverse queer experiences via a queer-of-color critique. On the other hand, most of this scholarship is produced by domestic diverse scholars or transnational queer scholars within U.S. academia.

This particular historical contextualization and scholarly critique are important for this article. The intention behind this chapter is to highlight the experiences of transnational queer bodies. To achieve this goal, in this article, the author focus on the idea of transnational queer slippages. This particular framework is built on Atay's previous work (2020, 2021). Before I present the idea of transnational queer slippages and translations, the relevant literature must be reviewed that helped to develop this idea. Therefore, in this article, first, I will briefly examine Chávez's critique of intercultural communication scholarship and the lack of queer frameworks and visibility. Second, I focus on Gust Yep's (2016) idea of thick intersectionalities, particularly the notion of nation or nationality. Third, I will review the relevant literature on identity formations and transnationality. Next, I will explore the agenda of transnational queer communication. Finally, after reviewing three essential concepts for the development of transnational queer slippages and translations as a framework, that is, home, belonging, and transnational, I will present an autoethnographic account to illustrate transnational queer slippages and translations from my own lived experiences.

THE LACK OF DIVERSE QUEER VISIBILITY

Since the early 2010s the growing number of queer communication studies scholars, particularly in critical/cultural studies and critical intercultural communication, have articulated the lack of queer scholarship in general, as well as a lack of queer scholarship that focuses on non-white experiences in communication studies journals. In "Pushing Boundaries: Queer Intercultural Communication," published in the *Journal of International and Intercultural Communication*, Karma Chávez (2013) articulates that "no journal of the National Communication Association has previously hosted a special issue or forum dedicated to queer studies" (p. 83). This particular critique triggers other important critiques about the whiteness of our field and the absence of certain voices and scholarship that features those voices in our journals. While her critique helped her to conceptualize the special issue in the *Journal of International and Intercultural Communication* and carved out a much-needed scholarly space for the articulation of various queer critiques, the arguments and recommendations that emerged from this special journal issue faced some resistance in terms of the further inclusion of different voices in queer communication studies research. Chávez wrote, "A significant body of queer scholarship still emphasizes the United States and other western countries, continuing to produce theory that can make life more livable for queer and trans people in those locales" (p. 84). Chávez, along with other queer scholars, such as Atay (2015, 2020, 2021), Eguchi (2021), Eguchi and Calafell (2020), and Yep (2013), demanded revisions and new pathways for queer studies in our discipline.

Although scholars such as Asante (2018, 2020), Atay (2020), Eguchi (2021), Huang (2021), and others published their work on transnational queer lives and lived experiences in various journals and edited books, it was not until 2021 that the *Journal of International and Intercultural Communication* dedicated a special issue on Global Queer/Trans Studies (edited by Shinsuke Eguchi) and a forum in *Communication and Critical/Cultural Studies* on New Directions for Queer Communication Studies (edited by Ahmet Atay). These works, along with others, began filling the academic void that Chávez articulated in her 2013 essay. It is important to highlight that, although transnational queer communication scholarship appeared in several publication outlets and edited books, it was not easy to publish this research in traditional communication journals. As a concept or a framework, when I developed transnational queer slippages and translations, I wanted to capture some of these cultural and academic resistances to transnational queer academic voices.

Intersectionality, as a theoretical framework and social justice-oriented practice developed by Black feminist scholar Kimberlé Williams Crenshaw (1991), articulates how our cultural identities have differing yet intersecting properties. Hence, she particularly focused on Black women's experience within the U.S. legal system to spotlight how Black women's experiences are different from those of their white counterparts and rather distinct in the Black community because of their gender. Crenshaw's work on intersectionality builds on that of other Black feminist and Chicana or Latinx theorists, such as Audre Lorde, bell hooks, Patricia Hill Collins, Gloria Anzaldua, and Angela Davis, who focused on the intersection of race, gender, and sexuality. As Crenshaw's theory gained more visibility in Black or Africana studies, gender and sexuality studies, queer studies, and communication studies, scholars began articulating other dimensions of our identities to discuss how not only race and gender, but these other properties are also intersecting with one another. Hence, they maintained that we must take a broader perspective on the dimensions of our identities to understand people's unique experiences. Although these new extensions moved away from the original intent, which was the examination of the Black women's experiences, they are also helpful lenses with which to explain how our identity markers influence our experience of the world around us, as well as our individualized experiences may be slightly or even radically different from those the others. In addition to intersections of race and gender, Black queer scholars, such as E. Patrick Johnson and Mae G. Henderson (2005) and E. Patrick Johnson (2016) formulated Black queer theory to highlight queerness in Black culture and Black experiences in queer culture. Similarly, Wenshu Lee's (2003) work, Kuaring Queer Theory, articulated the intersections between race and queerness. In this discussion, Lee called attention to Asian queer experiences.

"Thick(er) intersectionalities," a concept developed by Gust Yep (2010, 2016), spotlight certain identity markers that are often disregarded within the discourse on intersectionality. Yep (2016) argues that "The race/class/gender/sexuality manta produces a flat, formulaic, superficial, and 'roster like approach' to intersectionality by simply listing such categories as components of an individual's identity" (p. 87). Yep offers a valid criticism because this process, as Yep explains, "homogenize[s] people inhabiting similar intersections" (p. 87). Moreover, as Yep maintains, "The mantra leaves out certain significant aspects of identity—nation and the body, for example—in the current global neoliberal social world" (p. 88). While the idea of nationality often remains under examined when, for example, we talk about queer experiences in the United States, most existing scholarship, as explained above, adopts white- and U.S.-centric perspective to examine queer issues and disregards the nationality of the subjects under examination. Needless to say, there are drastic differences between a U.S.-citizen white queer individual and a non–U.S. citizen queer individual because of their nationalities and citizenship statuses. Their experiences are different, their oppressions are different, and there are also differences (legal and cultural) regarding who can speak out, in what capacity, and to what end. Finally, the punishments are different if the individuals are challenged or questioned about their subject positions and their articulation and critiques of the dominant oppressive structures. At the end of the day, one's nationality and citizenship status represent certain privileges or the lack of them. The status of queer individuals also determines their access to certain benefits, and it provides certain types of queer experiences and realities. In this essay, I further these arguments by spotlighting key issues and also offering transnational queer slippages and translations as a framework via which to examine some of these under examined issues that both Yep and I articulate regarding queer experiences and worldmaking.

CULTURAL IDENTITY FORMATIONS

To closely examine the idea of transnational queer slippages and translations, first, I must discuss the notion of cultural identity. Theories of identity will help to explain how certain bodies embody and perform intersectional identities and how these performances may be radically different based on subject position. Moreover, these identity performances may look different for immigrants, diasporic individuals, and transnational bodies (both queer and nonqueer) because they cross physical, emotional, linguistic, and cultural borders and maneuver between and among nation-states and cultural experiences as queer and nonqueer bodies.

Because our communication and lived experience are influenced by everyday situations and cultural, economic, and political happenings, these forces shape our cultural identities. As Yep (2004) argues, "our cultural identities are always formed, produced, reproduced, and challenged in symbolic, historical, socioeconomic and political contexts" (p. 77). This is particularly relevant to diasporic and transnational bodies (particularly queer bodies) because history (the history of the former homeland and new homelands) is always present and often influences how our identity makers are understood and performed. This is particularly relevant for diasporic and transnational queer bodies because they have to negotiate various queer, gendered, and sexualized histories and translate between them.

As Woodward (1997) maintains, identity is relational and marked by differences. Hence, we make sense of who we are in terms of others, that is, who we are not. For example, to be an immigrant means that we were born in another nation-state and moved to the United States permanently. Similarly, being a U.S. citizen means that one would have legal rights to perform certain acts (such as voting) and participate in a legal and civic culture, while noncitizens are "othered" by being provided with certain legal papers allowing them to live in the country but not participate in certain acts or have certain powers and freedoms. Communication and cultural studies scholars such as Hall (1990), Minh-ha (1994), Langellier (2004), Weedon (2004), and Yep (2004, 2016) extensively theorize regarding the relationship between the self and the other. The idea of difference plays the paramount role in how we negotiate this relationship. As Hall (1996) puts it, our identities are contested "through, not outside, difference" (p. 4). Moreover, Hall maintains the following:

> This entails the radically disturbing recognition that it is only through the relation to Other, the relation to what is not, to precisely what it lacks, to what has been called its constitutive outside that the "positive" meaning of may term—and this its "identity"—can be constructed. (pp. 4–5)

For example, diasporic identities are constructed through difference, that is, diasporic individuals, or immigrants, are outsiders who are not completely part of the host or home culture. The other example would be of the category of citizen. A citizen within the nation-state makes sense only in relation to noncitizens. The similar idea can also be observed regarding queerness. This concept makes sense only in relation to nonqueers, or mainstream, heteronormative individuals. Hence, the idea of difference is crucial to the context of transnational queer identities because, like the other identity binaries, they will be defined in terms of what they are not.

Both Woodward (1997) and Yep (2004) remind us that we have to understand our cultural identities in relation to social and cultural happenings because our identities are created, performed, and understood through social and cultural conditions. For example, carrying a particular nation-state's passport or being a citizen of a country, in which one resides provides certain powers to individuals that others may not have. Individuals can move around and among nation-states freely, perhaps without needing a visa. At the same time, diasporic or transnational bodies who belong to more than one nation-states, cultural group, or identity marker would negotiate these experiences, such as border crossing, defining home, or belonging somewhere, differently depending on their status. As they navigate these experiences and make sense of their identities and belonging, they translate. Moreover, diasporic or transnational queer bodies not only translate between nation-states but also translate between the dominant queer culture and the periphery or between the queer cultures in the host countries and the homeland. Hence, citizenship, or holding a particular nation-state's passport, radically differentiate these experiences for transnational and diasporic bodies. Their experiences are not generic or homogeneous. These experiences are all shaped by or impacted differently by divergent political, cultural, and political histories. Thus, the way they translate and what to make of these experiences vastly differ.

Cultural identities are never complete and always in process (Hall, 1990). Hall postulates that cultural identity is "always constructed through memory, fantasy, narrative, and myth. Cultural identities are points of identification, the unstable points of identification or suture which are made, within the discourses of history and culture" (p. 26). This particular way of envisioning identity is important for the purpose of this essay because transnational or diasporic queer identities are always shaped or informed by history and, more importantly, by personal and collective memory and narratives. These narratives construct, govern, maintain, challenge our local, national, and transnational identities; how we understand and perform them; and how we use these narratives or memories to translate between experiences and contexts.

Last, it is important to address the fact that our identities are always open to change, never fixed, and always in flux. Weedon (2004) reminds us that our identities are temporarily fixed. That means they are never static. Hence, when we negotiate aspects of our identities and translate between them, we change. Weedon maintains, "Identity is perhaps best understood as a limited and temporary fixing for the individual of a particular mode of subjectivity as apparent what one *is*" (p. 27). This temporary fixing influences subjectivity in many ways, until a new formation is formed, embodied, and performed. Weedon continues, "One of the key ideological roles of identity is to curtail the plural possibilities of subjectivity inherent in the wider discursive field and to give individuals a singular sense of who they are and where they belong" (p. 19). While I recognize that plurality of subjectivity is the key because we all occupy different subject positions, I also argue that these subject positions are interlocked and constantly evolve and change. Hence, as individuals, we experience the world around us very differently than the person next to us, who may or may not have similar lived experiences. Because of our intersectional identities, we experience events and everyday encounters differently. This remains true even for members of the diasporic communities and transnational queer bodies because of the different subject positions that such people occupy and the identities they perform. For example, I previously (Atay, 2015) noted that "Diasporic queer bodies are examples of these positions because they are often maneuvering among different cultural groups, such as diaspora, mainstream culture, and queer culture, to consistently renegotiate their identity positions" (p. 28). This constant maneuvering is what I want to further focus on because, when transnational or diasporic queer bodies maneuver, they also translate their experiences. Not everything can be translated, and not every translation accurately captures the meaning or the emotions behind the original or intended message.

TRANSNATIONAL COMMUNICATION AND TRANSNATIONAL (QUEER) IDENTITIES

In this section, I will present the working definitions of transnational identity and transnational communication. Historically, the subfields of cross-cultural communication and intercultural communication have focused on the examination of a particular experience, issue, concept, or cultural practice within a cultural context or by a cultural group and comparing it to another via a comparative analysis. Typically, a cultural practice within another culture or nation-state was compared to the cultural practice in the United States, making the United States the norm or center. When this comparative analysis was performed within the U.S. context, a historically marginalized community was compared to the mainstream white and heterosexual U.S. society. For example, Kim (2002) comparatively examined the nonverbal communication expressions by Korean and U.S.-American advertising. Similarly, Smith (2002) compared the cross-cultural adaption and reentry of U.S. subjects with subjects from other nation-states. This type of comparative analysis is built on the idea of the homogeneity of the subjects, erasing their intersectional identity positions. It also disregards the fact that certain individuals, such as immigrants and diasporic bodies, will occupy two nationalities (or more) and constantly maneuver among them; hence, they are not easily categorized and compared.

Instead of focusing on a cross-cultural analysis or comparing cultural practices within one nation-state to another, transnational communication, as an approach, adopts a broader perspective and examines the communication processes, lived experiences, and identity constructions that occur across international borders. It recognizes that due to political, cultural, and economic globalization, people, ideas, and goods are moving around, and people constantly cross national borders (immigrants, diasporic bodies, cosmopolitans, and tourists). These constant border crossings are also influencing one's cultural identity formations (particularly the cultural identity formations and performances of queer and trans bodies).

People leave their homelands for several reasons, and these reasons, along with the passports that these people have, determine their journeys and trajectories. First, while some people leave their homelands because of political reasons, others leave due to war or disasters. Hence, they may become asylum seekers or refugees living in various nation-states, with little to no hope of returning to their homeland. Second, others leave their homelands to seek better financial opportunities; therefore, they immigrate to new locations and form diasporic communities or join to existing diasporic communities in large urban areas. While some of these movements occur due to the colonial pasts, individuals moving from the former colonies to the urban centers of the colonizers (the Indian diaspora in Bradford, United Kingdom, or the Moroccan diaspora in Paris), others move as part of the economic globalization (Kenyans living in China or Turks living in Germany).

Third, a significant number of international students decide to leave their homelands and seek higher education in various parts of the world. The United States still hosts the largest number of the international students in the world. While some of these movements are voluntary, not all international students enjoy affluent financial lifestyles. Some of them are on scholarships (such as Fulbright or domestic scholarships), and they are sent to receive higher education and return to their homelands to contribute to the development of the nation or participate in a growing economy. The experiences of these students are also very diverse, even though they are often categorized as "international students" and their intersectional identities are erased or reduce to "the other" or "the outsider." Their experiences are also shaped by the passports of their home nation-states. While certain segments of these international students enjoy freer movements between nation-states and fewer visa restrictions, others face significant hurdles and challenges (such as limited visas, long waiting periods, and other strict regulations). Finally, people who belong to particular nation-states and have higher income status move between and among nation-states very differently. They are the cosmopolitans. Their movements are voluntary, and they cross borders much as they cross streets in their hometowns. For example, Brits easily fly to New York, and the educated and affluent Indian elite can travel to London or Singapore. Although the aforementioned groups of people move around, they move around differently, for different reasons, and they experience very different realities.

Because people move around for different reasons, depending on their intersectional identities, the passports they hold, their homelands, and their destinations, they take very different cultural, political, economic, and emotional journeys. Hence, they translate differently as they cross borders, move between nation-states, and maneuver between cultures. At the same time, these journeys produce very different types of transnational identities. While some settle into a diasporic community and move between the homeland and the host culture, others consistently cross the boundaries of nation-states and move around differently. For example, members of the EU move around different nation-states freely. They also have certain privileges which grant them easier movement between other nation-states. Hence, their transnational identities are differently constructed (legally and cultural), embodied, and performed. As we peel back the layers of cultural identities, we realize that, even within these different groups of people and communities, some people experience fewer privileges because of their race, socioeconomic status, religion, and ability/disability. One of these groups is transnational queer individuals who experience the world around them and their transnational journeys inversely.

TRANSNATIONAL QUEER

Since its emergence, queer communication studies have remained reluctant to include transnational perspectives and voices. This reality also mirrors the whiteness- and U.S.–American centric nature of communication studies as a field. As Chakravartty et al. (2018) argued, like some of other disciplines, communication studies has largely failed to diversity itself and its theoretical perspectives and carve out a space for non-white and non-U.S. scholars to break into the mainstream conceptualization of the discipline. Similar arguments were also made by several transnational queer scholars, such as Asante and Hanchey (2021), Eguchi and Calafell (2020) Eguchi (2021), Huang (2021), and Atay (2020, 2021), regarding queer communication studies. Although queer studies promise inclusivity and different ways of examining bodies and their lived experiences, these opportunities have often remained limited to U.S.-American scholars.

Why do transnational queer scholars offer critiques and challenge the ethnocentric conceptions of queer communication studies? The answer to this question is both easy and very complicated. The lack of publishing opportunities for transnational queer scholars in mainstream communication journals (both National Communication Association and International Communication Association journals) was among the main reasons for such intersectional and transnational critiques. The question is why even certain journals whose focus is on critical and cultural work remained distant to such voices. The reviewers, editors, and other gatekeepers play a major role in deciding whose work can be published and heard. Often, the work of transnational queer scholars is featured in interdisciplinary journals or less mainstream journals.

In addition to these issues, perhaps the idea of transnational queer as an identity category and performance is not well understood; hence, they are largely unexamined due to heteronormativity, U.S.-American homonormativity, and pushback from scholars within certain segments of the communication field, including intercultural communication, who did not see queer work as part of their main discourse or focus of inquiry. Therefore, in the remainder of this section, I define the notion of a transnational queer body.

As I pointed out above, we must adopt an intersectional perspective to make sense of transnational and diasporic bodies and their experiences. If scholars would adopt an essentialist perspective in examining diasporic and transnational bodies and their experiences, they would homogenize them and erase their differences by reducing them to their immigration status or the diasporic community that they might belong to. Hence, scholars often disregard the gendered and sexualized nature of transnational or diasporic bodies. Historically, scholars who examined diasporic communities (Anthias, 2001; Hall, 1996; Safran, 1991) did not articulate the experiences of queer bodies. This trend was also very visible in diaspora studies in the field of communication studies, as well as queer communication studies, as I articulated above. While the works of Manalansan (2006), Yep (2002), and Gopinath (2002) charted new disciplinary territories, they also articulated the intersectional and fluid nature of cultural identities. Hence, particularly Manalansan (2006), Gopinath (2002), and Rahman (2010), and, later, the collective scholarship by myself, Abdi (2021), Asante and Hanchey (2021), Eguchi (2021), Huang (2021), and Pindi (2018) began pointing out that our transnational and diasporic bodies are intersectional; thus, our gender and sexualities set us apart from other diasporic and transnational bodies. Similarly, as transnational and diasporic bodies, we are also different from our domestic counterparts because of our transnational experiences, accented lives, nationalities, and legal situations (such as possessing certain visas, green card, or citizenships). For example, Rahman (2010) maintains that gay Muslims in the United States, Canada, or in other Western societies must negotiate their queerness and being Muslim within the predominant mainstream culture, as well as their queerness within Islamic cultures and societies, despite the denial of queerness on the part of the dominant culture of these societies. Therefore, transnational and diasporic queer bodies often experience the world rather differently than the other members of the cultural groups they belong to. Hence, they maneuver between cultures and nation-states differently; they produce and engage with different levels of cultural and linguistic translations; and, finally, they negotiate their identities, sense of home, and belonging differently.

As transnational and diasporic queer individuals move between and among nation-states and maneuver between the cultures and cultural groups that they belong to, they translate. On one hand, some nation-states have progressed with regard to their politics on lesbian, gay, bisexual, transgender, queer, asexual, and intersex (LGBTQAI+) rights, homosexuality and queerness are criminalized in some others, and queer and trans individuals are surveilled, jailed, and killed there. On the other hand, some nation-states, including the United States, perform complicated politics regarding queer lives. Although there are federal laws that protect certain LGBTQAI+ rights, some states have passed very discriminatory laws to limit and punish of queer bodies. Hence, transnational and diasporic bodies who travel between nation-states and maneuver between cultures and cultural groups (within and outside of the United States) must negotiate their identities, particularly queerness. Certain segments of this particular group surveille and police their own queerness depending on their locations to protect their lives and also perform certain gendered and sexual identities to survive.

Moreover, as some diaspora studies scholars have previously argued, diasporic communities that resides in the urban centers of the Western nations can also be very conservative in nature.

Hence, they often reject or punish queer individuals. Similarly, transnational and queer individuals must also negotiate their racially or ethnically accented queerness within the majority queer cultures in the United States and other major queer cultures in other parts of the Western societies. As they negotiate their identities between the diasporic community and the queer culture in their host counties or between different nation-states as they circulate and maneuver between them, as well as between the queer cultures of their homeland and host country, they negotiate and translate. For example, every time I move between my two home nation-states, the United States and Cyprus, I must negotiate my identity. As an openly queer person in the United States, when I travel back home, I have to leave my queer identity behind. While I leave certain parts of my identity behind, I also readopt identity parts that are not salient and visible in the U.S. context. While I translate between languages, I also translate between parts of my identity. This type of a labor, however, is often unnoticed by the mainstream LGBTQAI+ in the United States since they may not have to do this type of translation. Moreover, since queerness is banned or criminalized in certain parts of the world, luckily I do not have to experience that, diasporic queer bodies also must navigate the legal systems between and among nation-states.

In each such translation, there are queer slippages that are only understood or embodied by transnational and diasporic queer individuals. Hence, it is important to acknowledge that queerness is understood, embodied, and performed differently by different people in different parts of the world. When they step into and out of romantic and familial relationships or perform their identities in a workplace, in a classroom, or at a gathering, they negotiate their queerness. As they negotiate, they pick and choose their identity markers. In this process, they negotiate and translate. Some meanings are understood, unspoken, or felt but never mirrored in proper words. These slippages are where transnational and diasporic queerness resides. When the accented bodies embody U.S.-American queerness, their transnational queerness morphs. It is negotiated and presented differently so as to be understood or accepted. When their accented bodies articulate words that cannot match their experiences or their experiences are not mirrored in those words, they struggle to translate their transnational or diasporic queerness. As their bodies feel and perform their queerness, the words that they use to describe them in English may fail them. Words are slippery; hence, in these slippages, transnational queer individuals experience struggle. In some cases, queerness cannot be translated, leaving the transnational and diasporic queer bodies' queerness to be understood, embodied, and sensed in one reality but properly and accurately articulated in the other. Although these slippages can be seen as failures, on the contrary, they are possibilities to create and, hopefully, express new transnational queerness. They are also spaces of resistance in which transnational and diasporic bodies may resist the conventional and often commercialized U.S.-American queer culture. Hence, these slippages are accented, emulating and embodying the struggles of transnational and diasporic queer experiences. They are glimpses of empowerment for transnational queer possibilities.

I translate. I embody these slippages. Hence, my transnational accented queer lived experiences sets me apart from the queers at home and queers at "the home." My queerness shape-shifts as move and translate. It loses certain meanings, but it gains others that I cannot translate, only feel and sense. In the next section, through autoethnographic writing, I illustrate some of these transnational queer translations and slippages as I experienced them. Mine are only some of the many translations and slippages.

QUEER TRANSLATIONS, QUEER TRANSLATORS

I story my life to make sense of it. Hence, I use narrative-based research or autoethnographic methods (critical, decolonizing, and digital) to articulate my transnational queer patched-together and in-between experiences. These methods help me to make sense of own lived experiences as I translate or, as sometimes I do, fail to translate. I am an accented body; hence, I translate. Sometimes, I translate for the reader to read my writing and have an entry point into transnational queer experiences. Other times, I translate for myself, to make sense, to perform, to live, and keep on going as an immigrant and transnational queer body. I translate simply to exist. This story is one of those moments. Like so many other stories, I translate as I story it.

I always dreaded packing. Maybe, it's because I don't like saying goodbyes. Maybe, I produce anxieties about travel, crossing borders, and stepping in and out of familiar and new cultures and contexts. Even though I used to travel more often, this has been interrupted by the COVID-19 global pandemic. The idea of packing always made me uncomfortable, a bit uneasy. Maybe, this is because I don't know what to pack. Before packing, I typically make a long list of what I need to be carrying on my transnational and even trans-Atlantic journeys. Sometimes, I start packing the night before of my trip, and sometimes, I begin the process of packing in my head and in heart. How can a simple act be anxiety inducing? Even though I dread packing and I am often uneasy about it, I also enjoy traveling. On one hand, I dread traveling, and on the other, I love it so much that I often want to stay at those places that I travel to rather than come back to my small town in Ohio. Contradictions are where translation starts for some of us. I will return to this idea shortly. I have already moved away from the idea of packing. Perhaps, I am anxious as I write these lines. This is also how I have learned to tell stories, not in a linear way. We take detours and return to the main story. Hence, when people listen to my stories or read them on paper, I have to translate. Translation is a cultural and emotional work that some of us endure and others never have to engage with.

When I make my long lists to figure out what to pack, I start with easy things, such as my gadgets and cables. Then, I move to toiletries. I often add "books" to my long list, so I have companions when I am bored or lonely or trying to find something to connect with. Then, I put "clothes and shoes" on the list. Packing those is hard. I often debate with myself about what to take. What would I wear at "home" or at my next destination that I would not wear in my small town, and *vice versa*? I pick and choose. I leave certain garments in the closet, and I carefully fold the others. I pay attention to their color, fabrics, and textures. Some must stay behind; I don't have space for them in my suitcase or in my "other" life. Then, I write "documents" on the list. Those are important. I worry about those the most. Like every other international student or scholar, immigrant, or free-floating transnational body, I worry about my documents. Every time I pack them, I check them again and again, making sure that I don't leave anything behind. I guess this is part of the fear of border crossing. I cannot translate this fear, but my body knows I am afraid.

I always add one more type of item to my list: words, "Queer" in particular. While I pack, I make conscious choices about what to pack and what to bring. Some things are more important than others, such as my passport and other documents. Some things can be left behind and repurchased at the next destination. Some things are essential, such as my novels and snacks. The hardest thing to pack and carry is my identity. Like so many other transnational queer bodies who may or may not be publicly out to their families and people outside of the U.S. context, the aspects of ourselves we choose to pack matter. Some aspects of who we are must come with us, and some are better left behind. Like our identities, we also negotiate what words we pack and what words could be left behind, never to be uttered. We take some words, even though we know they will be hard to negotiate and translate.

The word "queer" was not among the things I packed in my suitcase two decades ago when I moved from Cyprus to the United States for higher education purpose. I do remember packing two suitcases for my very first transnational and trans-Atlantic journey. Nicely folded shirts, t-shirts, trousers, shorts, and sweaters took up most of the space, leaving only a little room to pack books or other personal items. Although I was an English speaker, speaking English every day, for academic purposes and to carry on my life, was not my part of my language portfolio. I had words to define my experiences and broadly understand the world around me through another language. Some words were foreign, and others were not even translatable. I struggled with the words that I could not mirror in my mother tongue, and I struggled to find words to mirror how I felt as an international student. When I fail to translate or mirror feelings with the right words, I realize that my body struggles. "Queer" became one of those words. First, the word appeared in my course readings; then, it was uttered by my friends, and it was embodied by people I knew (Atay, 2021). Queer became the symbol of personal struggle to understand my own sexuality and patched-together intersectional identity. First, I was scared of the word, and then, I failed to translate it. When I negotiated its meaning, I feared it. I fear words that slip. I fear the words that I don't know how to translate. I fear some words because they make sense in one reality but their meanings dissolve or vanish in another. Our bodies feel the words differently. Some words are caught in the middle, making our bodies feel or hurt, without being translated. Queer is one of these words.

I went through my list again and again to make sure I packed everything I needed and also left some things behind. I finished packing. Once again, I decided not to take the word "queer" and thus, a part of myself, on this journey. As I go home to visit, like most transnational and diasporic bodies do, I leave parts of myself behind. Like me, others around the world leave the words "queer," "gay," "trans," or asexual behind. Sometimes, this is because we fear the words. Other times, we can't translate them. Sometimes, we don't take them with us on our transnational journeys because we don't want to utter them. We translate some words, we perform and embody the others, and we only whisper certain words to ourselves as we maneuver between cultures, cross borders, or go home to visit.

CONCLUSION

Translation is a work. It is a cultural and linguistic work that immigrants, transnational bodies who move between nation-states for different reasons, and diasporic bodies who occupy different cultural spaces often perform. It is a work that not many observe or understand. Some transnational or diasporic bodies translate differently because they must translate between here and there, host and home nations, and various minoritized cultural groups. Transnational queer bodies negotiate words and worlds. Sometimes, they translate, and other times, they reside in queer slippages, in which words do not mirror how they feel or their experiences. They translate their queerness between host and home nation-states, as well as between their accented queerness and the mainstream queer culture. Because of their nationality-accented bodies, their bodies and experiences are or can be consistently otherized by the members of queer cultures (both at home and in the host nations), the diasporic community, and normative mainstream cultures (both home and in the host nations). As they are otherized, they translate to make sense of and negotiate their experiences, cultural differences, and identity categories. Hence, transnational queer bodies translate, and when they cannot, they reside in queer slippages. These hybrid queer spaces can be both empowering and overwhelming, liberating and a source of struggle. They are also ontological and epistemological because they represent and embody our constant state of being, but they are also our ways of knowing, sensing, and feeling.

Of course, not everybody can translate all the time. Sometimes the translation might not or cannot happen, and people might be stuck in a liminal space. Gains would be limited since diasporic queer bodies would only be able to understand their queerness or that queer moment in one language and culture. Their experience would be static and perhaps caught in the domination of English and English-driven queer discourse. This situation would induce anxiety and cause real challenges for people's identities, and sometimes their situations. Last, it will reduce the diasporic queer experience into one culture and does not allow the fluidity that "queer" promises. Hence, the negatives of not being able to translate are plentiful. On the other hand, there are also queer possibilities when one is stuck in transnational queer slippages because in that space, they can negotiate their identities and explore new possibilities.

I developed the idea of transnational queer translations and slippages because I was struggling to make sense of my own transnational queer identities. We experience translations and slippages differently because of who we are in the world. This is an intersectional approach that recognizes that our privileges, struggles, and disempowerments shape and influence these transnational translations and slippages differently. We translate differently because we occupy different identity layers, and we experience these layers differently in different contexts through different languages. Therefore, our bodies feel pains, joys, limitations, shortcomings, and opportunities differently.

FURTHER READING

Asante, G. (2018). "Where is home?" Negotiating comm(unity) and un/belonging among queer African migrants on Facebook. *Borderlands, 17*(1), 1–22.

Asante, G. (2020). Decolonizing the erotic: Building alliances of African (queer) eros. Forum on African feminist and queer African possibilities. *Women's Studies in Communication Journal, 43*(2), 113–118.

Asante, G., & Hanchey, J. N. (2021). Decolonizing queer modernities: The case for queer (post)colonial studies in critical/cultural communication. *Communication and Critical/Cultural Studies, 18*(2), 212–220. https://doi.org/10.1080/14791420.2021.1907849

Atay, A. (2021a). Digital transnational queer isolations and connections. *Journal of International and Intercultural Communication, 14*(4), 351–365. https://doi.org/10.1080/17513057.2021.1939404

Atay, A. (2021b). Charting the future of queer studies in communication and critical/cultural studies: New directions and pathways. *Communication and Critical/Cultural Studies, 18*(2), vii–xi. https://doi.org/10.1080/14791420.2021.1907847

Atay, A. (2021c). Transnational and decolonizing queer digital/quick media and cyberculture studies. *Communication and Critical/Cultural Studies*, 18(2), 183–189. https://doi.org/10.1080/14791420.2021.1913284

Atay, A. (2022). Transnational queer screen mobilities: Quick media application, home, love, and sex online. In R. Trandafoiu (Ed.), *Border crossings and mobilities on screen* (pp. 61–72). Routledge.

Atay, A., & Pensoneau-Conway, S. (Eds.). (2020). *Queer communication pedagogy*. Routledge.

Eguchi, S. (2021a). On the horizon: Desiring global queer and trans* studies in international and intercultural communication. *Journal of International and Intercultural Communication*, 14(4), 275–283. https://doi.org/10.1080/17513057.2021.1967684

Eguchi, S. (2021b). What is "queer Asia?": A struggling pathway to globalizing queer studies in communication. *Communication and Critical/Cultural Studies*, 18(2), 196–203.

Eguchi, S., & Calafell, B. M. (Eds.). (2020). *Queer intercultural communication: The intersectional politics of belonging in and across differences*. Rowman & Littlefield.

REFERENCES

Abdi, S. (2021). Stating I(ra)n: Negotiating queer identity through narrative trespass from within the Iranian American closet. In T. A. Adams, S. H. Jones, & C. Ellis (Eds.), *Handbook of autoethnography* (pp. 421–430). Routledge.

Alexander, B. K. (2003). Querying queer theory again (or queer theory as drag performance). *Journal of Homosexuality*, 45(2–4), 349–352.

Anthias, F. (2001). New hybridities, old concepts: The limits of "culture." *Ethnic and Racial Studies*, 24(4), 619–641.

Asante, G., & Hanchey, J. H. (2021). Decolonizing queer modernities: The case for queer (post)colonial studies in critical/cultural communication. *Communication and Critical/Cultural Studies*, 18(2), 212–220. https://doi.org/10.1080/14791420.2021.1907849

Atay, A. (2015). *Globalization's impact on cultural identity formation: Queer diasporic males on cyberspace*. Lexington Books.

Atay, A. (2020). Intercultural queer slippages and translations. In S. Eguchi & B. M. Calafell (Eds.), *Queer intercultural communication: The intersectional politics of belonging in and across differences* (pp. 141–156). Rowman and Littlefield.

Atay, A. (2021). Charting the future of queer studies in communication and critical/cultural studies: New directions and pathways. *Communication and Critical/Cultural Studies*, 18(2), vii–xi. https://doi.org/10.1080/14791420.2021.1907847

Chakravartty, P., Kuo, R., Grubbs, V., & McIlwain, C. (2018). #CommunicationSoWhite. *Journal of Communication*, 68(2), 254–266.

Chávez, K. R. (2013). Pushing boundaries: Queer intercultural communication. *Journal of International and Intercultural Communication*, 6(2), 83–95.

Chesboro, J. W. (1981). *Gayspeak: Gay male and lesbian communication*. The Pilgrim Press.

Corey, C. F., & Nakayama, T. K. (1997). Sextext. *Text and Performance Quarterly*, 17(1), 58–68. https://doi.org/10.1080/10462939709366169

Crenshaw, K. (1991). Mapping the margins: Intersectionality, identity politics, and violence against women of color. *Stanford Law Review*, 43(6), 1241–1299. https://doi.org/10.2307/1229039

Eguchi, S. (2021). What is "queer Asia?": A struggling pathway to globalizing queer studies in communication. *Communication and Critical/Cultural Studies*, 18(2), 196–203. https://doi.org/10.1080/14791420.2021.1907848

Eguchi, S., & Calafell, B. M. (2020). Introduction: Reorienting queer intercultural communication. In S. Eguchi & B. M. Calafell (Eds.), *Queer intercultural communication: The intersectional politics of belonging in and across differences* (pp. 1–16). Rowman and Littlefield.

Gopinath, G. (2002). The transnational trajectories of Deepa Mehta's fire'. In A. Cruz-Malave & M. F. Manalansan IV (Eds.), *Queer globalizations: Citizenship and the afterlife of colonialism* (pp. 146–161). New York University Press.

Gutierrez-Perez, R., & Andrade, L. M. (2020). How queer (of color) is intercultural communication? Then and there, Joteria the game as a praxis of queerness, advocacy and utopian aesthetic. In S. Eguchi & B. M. Calafell (Eds.), *Queer intercultural communication: The intersectional politics of belonging in and across differences* (pp. 179–193). Rowman and Littlefield.

Hall, S. (1990). Cultural identity and diaspora. In J. Rutherford (Ed.), *Identity: Community, culture, difference* (pp. 222–237). Lawrence & Wishart.

Hall, S. (1996). Introduction: Who needs "identity"? In S. Hall & P. du Gay (Eds.), *Questions of cultural identity* (pp. 1–17). SAGE.

Huang, S. (2021). Why does communication need transnational queer studies? *Communication and Critical/Cultural Studies*, *18*(2), 204–211. https://doi.org/10.1080/14791420.2021.1907850

Johnson, E. P. (2001). 'Quare' studies or (almost) everything I know about queer studies I learned from my grandmother. *Text and Performance Quarterly*, *21*(1), 1–25.

Johnson, E. P. (2016). *No tea, no shades: New writings in black queer studies*. Duke University Press.

Johnson, E. P., & Henderson, M. G. (2005). *Black queer studies: A critical anthology*. Duke University Press.

Kim, M.-S. (2002). A comparative analysis of nonverbal expressions as portrayed by Korean and American print-media advertising. In J. N. Martin, T. K. Nakayama, & L. A. Flores (Eds.), *Readings in intercultural communication: Experiences and contexts* (pp. 181–192). McGraw Hill.

Langellier, K. M. (2004). "Where I come from is where I want to be": Communicating Franco American ethnicity. In M. Fong & R. Chuang (Eds.), *Communicating ethnic & cultural identity* (pp. 297–312). Rowman and Littlefied.

Lee, W. (2003). Kuaring queer theory. *Journal of Homosexuality*, *45*(2–4), 147–170. https://doi.org/10.1300/J082v45n02_07

Manalansan, M. F. (2006). *Global divas: Filipino gay men in the diaspora*. Duke University Press.

Minh-ha, T. T. (1994). Other than myself/my other self. In G. Robertson, M. Mash, L. Tickner, J. Bird, B. Curtis, & T. Putman (Eds.), *Travelers' tale: Narratives of home and displacement* (pp. 9–26). Routledge.

Pindi, G. (2018). Hybridity and identity performance in diasporic context: An autoethnographic journey of the self across culture. *Cultural Studies<=> Critical Methodologies*, *18*(1), 23–31.

Rahman, M. (2010). Queer as intersectionality: Theorizing gay Muslim identities. *Sociology*, *44*(5), 944–961. https://doi.org/10.1177/0038038510375733

Ringer, R. J. (1994). *Queer words, queer images: Communication and the construction of homosexuality*. New York University Press.

Safran, W. (1991). Diasporas in modern societies: Myths of homeland and return. *Diaspora*, *1*(1), 83–99.

Slagle, R. A. (1995). In defense of queer nation: From identity politics to a politics of difference. *Western Journal of Communication*, *59*, 85–102.

Smith, S. L. (2002). The cycle of cross-cultural adaptation and reentry. In J. N. Martin, T. K. Nakayama, & L. A. Flores (Eds.), *Readings in intercultural communication: Experiences and contexts* (pp. 246–259). McGraw Hill.

Weedon, C. (2004). *Culture and identity: Narratives of difference and belonging*. Open University Press.

Woodward, K. (1997). *Identity and difference*. SAGE.

Yep, G. A. (2002). My three cultures: Navigating the multicultural identity landscape. In J. N. Martin, T. K. Nakayama, & L. A. Flores (Eds.), *Readings in intercultural communication: Experiences and contexts* (pp. 60–66). McGraw Hill.

Yep, G. A. (2003). The violence of heteronormativity in communication studies: Notes on injury, healing and queer world-making. *Journal of Homosexuality, 45*(2/3), 11–59.

Yep, G. A. (2004). Approaches to cultural identity: Personal notes from an autoethnographical journey. In M. Fong & R. Chuang (Eds.), *Communicating ethnic & cultural identity* (pp. 69–81). Rowman & Littlefield.

Yep, G. A. (2010). Toward the de-subjugation of racially marked knowledges in communication. *Southern Communication Journal, 75*(2), 171–175.

Yep, G. A. (2013). Queering/Quaring/Kauering/Crippin'/Transing "other bodies" in intercultural communication. *Journal of International and Intercultural Communication, 6*(2), 118–126. https://doi.org/10.1080/17513057.2013.777087

Yep, G. A. (2016). Toward thick(er) intersectionalities: Theorizing, researching, and activating the complexities of communication and identities. In K. Sorrells & S. Sekimoto (Eds.), *Globalizing intercultural communication: A reader* (pp. 86–94). SAGE.

Ahmet Atay

Key Terms

Key Terms

DISIDENTIFICATION

INTRODUCTION

Disidentification is a theory of subject formation that draws from interdisciplinary roots to theorize the experiences, modes of resistance, and practices of worldmaking in which multiply marginalized individuals engage. Despite its interdisciplinary trajectory, communication studies has extended disidentification in important ways, most notably in terms of imagining its persuasive capacity—that is, its ability to revise, reimagine, and restructure the ideological and structural mechanisms that organize people's lives. This article will detail how Muñoz's theory of disidentification has been taken up within communication studies and will proceed by discussing what disidentification is, outlining the theoretical traditions that inform this orientation, and then moving into a discussion that thematically organizes its extensions within communication studies.

WHAT IS DISIDENTIFICATION?

Disidentification is a heuristic that provides critical scholars with a framework for theorizing the relationships between subject formation, ideology, politics, and power while also offering a way to see how people from marginalized communities navigate intersecting forms of oppression and enact agency. Described as a mode of resistance, a survival strategy, and a performance of worldmaking (Muñoz, 1999), disidentification is a theoretical lens and a political strategy. As both a theoretical framework and a performative practice, disidentification is an antiracist, decolonial, queer tool that can be utilized to theorize, respond to, and undermine normative power structures. As Muñoz (1999) describes,

> disidentification is meant to be descriptive of the survival strategies the minority subject practices in order to negate the phobic majoritarian public sphere that continuously elides or punishes the existence of subjects who do not conform to the phantasm of normative citizenship. (p. 4)

In this way, Muñoz's theory of disidentification offers disidentification as a way to address how minority subjects construct their identity in, through, and despite the normative discourses that interpellate them.

THE INTELLECTUAL TRADITIONS THAT INFORM MUÑOZ'S THEORY OF DISIDENTIFICATION

As a primarily U.S.-centric frame, disidentification borrows heavily from women of color feminists, psychoanalysis, and queer theory. Muñoz's theory of disidentification attempts to account for the utopian, political, and pragmatic ways that marginalized individuals work within and against the systems and discourses that organize their lives. Notably, disidentification emerges from difference, which is to say, the experiences of people at/along the margins. Theorizing how identity and subject formation develop in these spaces of marginality situates Muñoz's theory of disidentification within intellectual traditions that see the personal as political.

Women of color feminists, especially Chicana theorists, establish some of Muñoz's primary orientations toward difference. Cherríe Moraga, Gloria Anzaldúa, Chela Sandoval, and Linda Alarcón reconfigured existing theories of identity to reimagine how the process of identity formation could be leveraged for progressive political purposes, pushing forward a radicalized and expanded understanding of identity that assumed its coalition-building potential. Of particular interest to Muñoz are the sites of emergence that inspire the differential consciousness or the "not yet/that's not it" position that these scholars negotiate (Alarcón, 1996, p. 129). As Muñoz (1999) explains, "these identities-in-difference emerge from a failed interpellation within the dominant public sphere. Their emergence is predicated on their ability to disidentify with the mass public and instead, through this disidentification, contribute to the function of a counterpublic sphere" (p. 7). The marginality that pushes minority subjects to the borders of nations, communities, and identity categories is also the site from which resistance and political action emerge.

The process of identification, and how individuals come to understand themselves in relation to their world and to other people, is a primary consideration for Muñoz as he theorizes the eventual ways such identifications lead to disidentification. Psychoanalysts suggest that it is through a series of identifications that one's sense of self develops, but Muñoz is interested not in the experiences and moments when an individual's sense of self aligns with(in) normative structures, but rather in the moments of disjunction. He asks, "can a self or a personality be crafted without proper identifications?" (Muñoz, 1999, p. 7). Indeed, it is more interesting to Muñoz what happens when such alignments do not occur and how these tensions are negotiated by those who often lack the social and institutional influence to produce change.

Drawing on portions of psychoanalytic theory that intersect with queer theory, Muñoz extrapolates elements of this work that resist the false dichotomy of desire and identification, instead focusing on how the two mutually inform one another. Quickly moving past Sigmund Freud to Diana Fuss and Teresa de Lauretis, who take a revisionary approach to the former's theory of identification, Muñoz (1999) extends their discussion on desire and identification to argue that disidentification works by putting "pressure on the distinction between wanting the other and wanting to be other" (p. 14). Through this lens, the way one comes to form one's sense of self is both an act of love and a political action to center that which may be most different or loathsome about oneself according to normative standards. As Muñoz (1999) explains, "to disidentify is to read oneself and one's own life narrative in a moment, object or subject that is not culturally coded to 'connect' with the disidentifying subject" (p. 12). Such actions are productively informed by queer theory generally, and queer of color scholarship in particular, which Muñoz asserts must account for the multiple and intersecting identifications of race, class, gender, sexuality, social class, and so forth. Disidentification demands an intersectional approach, both in theory and in practice, and in this way is well positioned to be a productive heuristic and performative practice for advancing social justice efforts.

Although relying on intersectionality is an essential commitment of disidentification, Muñoz draws on the scholarship and experience of queer people of color, adopting the language of *hybridity* as a more particular description of disidentifying subjects' experiences. The people from marginalized communities that are centered by Muñoz's theory are hybridized insofar as their subject formation and performance of identity are the result of their precarious participation in and resistance to the sociocultural surrounds that structure their lives. As he explains, "hybridity in this study, like the term disidentification, is meant to have an indexical use in that it captures, collects, and brings into play various theories of fragmentation in relation to minority identity practices" (Muñoz, 1999, p. 31). In this way, disidentification begins with the assumption that subject formation and resistance are not neat and linear, but rather fragmentary and disjunct. He further articulates that the different components of identity that compose the experience of queers of color "occupy adjacent spaces and are not comfortably situated in any one discourse of minority subjectivity. These hybridized identificatory positions are always in transit shuttling between different identity vectors" (Muñoz, 1999, p. 31). Thus, the experience of disidentifying subjects is born from their conflicting and fragmentary efforts to negotiate social, cultural, and national spaces that have always excluded them—that have always marked their difference.

Disidentifying subjects' public emergence "is predicated on their ability to disidentify with the mass public and instead, through this disidentification contribute to the function of a counterpublic sphere" (Muñoz, 1999, p. 7). Within rhetorical studies, counterpublics are theorized as discursive communities that form based on social actors' efforts to resist and/or oppose inequality and exclusion (see Brouwer, 2006; Fraser, 1992). As Asen (2015) notes, "reacting against the legitimating discourses of the bourgeois public sphere, which advanced a universality claim to represent the interests of society as a whole, counterpublic analysis emphasizes the multiple character of contemporary public sphere" (p. 139). Subjects participating in this counterpublic sphere depend on their hybridity and the ongoing negotiations in which they must participate to survive the discursive and material violences of normativity. The pressures to conform render marginalized subjects especially vulnerable as this often requires risking their material safety and their symbolic inclusion. Scholars who have taken up Muñoz's theory of disidentification discuss how the threat of violence haunts these hybridized subjects' identity formation and informs their resistance strategies.

The violence that always already threatens the marginalized subjects about whom Muñoz writes stems from the ideological apparatuses that dictate what can and should be a livable life. Tracing Marxist theorist Louis Althusser's (1971) influences on his theory of disidentification, Muñoz explains that ideology is inescapable and is a primary component in the process of subject formation. Drawing on both French linguist Michel Pêcheux (1982) and queer theorist Judith Butler (1993), Muñoz explains that disidentifying subjects who come to their sense of self in and through these sites of discursive and material violence reckon not only with the ways to build a livable life, but also with the cultural logics of heteronormativity and white supremacy that undergird the state's authority.

Scholars in the communication studies subdisciplines of performance studies, critical race theory, queer theory, and intercultural communication have advanced the most substantive disciplinary scholarship to extend Muñoz's theory. Work in these areas has utilized disidentification to analyze, for example, social justice efforts, popular culture, gender norms, dating websites, and trademark law. The section that follows outlines how disidentification has been discussed and developed in communication studies and highlights the scholarship producing these extensions.

DISIDENTIFICATION IN COMMUNICATION STUDIES

An investment in understanding how communication produces, scaffolds, organizes, and potentially revises our world coheres critical rhetorical inquiry. Regardless of methods or assumptions, scholars in this discipline share a commitment to language—to theorize the symbolic systems of communication that make life meaningful. In this way, disidentification offers scholars in the discipline a way to consider how communication can be used by people to resist, survive, and thrive. Through these efforts, disidentification has the potential to revise the canon of communication studies, incorporating marginalized voices, experiences, and methodologies into the very epistemological commitments of the discipline.

Some of the primary ways that scholars in communication studies, specifically those in the subdisciplines previously mentioned, have used disidentification as a heuristic and/or theorized disidentification as a performative practice are outlined here. These extensions are organized to begin with work that theorizes disidentification (1) as a mode of *survival*, (2) as a mode of *resistance and/or subversion*, (3) as a mode of *queer (of color) worldmaking*, and (4) as a way to address the *hybridity* of identity. These first four sections directly expand on the contributions articulated by Muñoz in his foundational text and are taken up in communication studies in myriad ways that to decenter the disciplinary canon. The sections that follow are extensions and applications that engage the less explored considerations that disidentification can provoke, including thinking about disidentification as (5) a mode of *reinforcing normative influences*, (6) as a way to theorize *space*, and finally (7) as a way to *extend, critique, and broaden existing theory*. The map of usages that the remainder of the article develops should demonstrate the relatively small U.S.-centric footprint that disidentification has so far made and compel readers to consider new directions for scholarship that foregrounds the lives, experiences, and scholarship of those on our cultural, national, and institutional margins.

DISIDENTIFICATION AS A MODE OF SURVIVAL

Minority individuals utilize disidentification as a way to survive the violences of normative culture that regularly diminish or erase one's experience and one's subjectivity. As Muñoz (1999) notes, "disidentification is about cultural, material, and psychic survival. It is a response to state global power apparatuses that employ systems of racial, sexual, and national subjugation" (p. 161). Some of the earliest work in communication studies that uses disidentification theorizes it as a survival strategy. These scholars draw conclusions about the ways marginalized subjects tactically disidentify as a way to maintain their status and/or safety.

The symbolic and material violence that marginalized subjects encounter increases exponentially with each normative identity category that is crossed. In this way, a queer person of color, for example, risks their safety both because of the way they are raced, as well as their sexual orientation and/or gender performance. After regularly attending the gay nightclub Reincarnation for its "Latin Night" drag show, Moreman and McIntosh (2010) developed a critical performance ethnography to examine the disidentificatory practices of Latina drag queens who performed there. Almost 10 years after the publication of Muñoz's formative text, and in one of the earliest Communication pieces to utilize this theory, these scholars extended disidentification into the discipline to theorize how the marginalized subjects at the heart of these drag performances survived. They noted that minority subjects are constantly pulled toward the sociocultural norms of heteronormativity, white supremacy, and misogyny: "they are compelled to seek outside of the fiction created as one's identity to negotiate, in Muñoz's terms 'counterpublic spheres.' This seeking is necessary in order to survive foreclosed, overdetermined constructions that privilege normative groups" (Moreman & McIntosh, 2010, p. 120). As we learn, Latina drag performers revise the race and gender of their diva, replacing binary understandings of identity with something much more fluid—an act that insists on critiquing those normative structures while also manipulating their bodies to survive the oppressive norms and regulations that confine difference.

Disidentification is a rhetorical and performative act that allows marginalized and vulnerable individuals to align with normative value systems in the present moment in an effort to deflect hostility, but also to work toward securing their future safety by undermining the narratives of exclusion that mark their difference in the first place. Eguchi et al. (2018) engage in an insightful intersectional analysis that examines how disidentification is used as a way for Black male performances of queerness to survive in the hip-hop industry. The authors analyze VH1's show *Love and Hip Hop*, arguing that the coming out narrative of one Black cast member (Miles) makes certain versions of Black masculinity and queerness commodifiable in U.S. culture. Specifically, they argue that Miles's coming out story is a means for him and other audience members to survive the ongoing erasure and exclusion of members of those categories. The authors note that in order to survive in this inhospitable context, Black men who have and practice same-sex desire must make themselves palatable (which is to say *marketable*) in order to survive the normative pressures to assimilate into a White, heteronormative, patriarchal, capitalist system (Eguchi et al., 2018). Indeed, neoliberal and capitalist value structures inform a person's ability to successfully survive in an inhospitable social, cultural, and/or national landscape such that if one is able to make oneself and one's subjectivity desirable in this way, one may be able to gain some level of cultural capital—enough to secure one's safety, and potentially enough to resist and subvert those same systems.

DISIDENTIFICATION AS A MODE OF SUBVERSION/RESISTANCE

Diverse scholarship across the discipline explores what resistance can look like, and what normative modes of power can be disrupted using disidentification. This scholarship extends from Muñoz's claims that disidentification is a performative practice that allows minoritarian subjects to work within and against normative logics in order to subvert them. As Muñoz (1999) explains,

> disidentification is about recycling and rethinking encoded meaning. The process of disidentification scrambles and reconstructs the encoded messages of a cultural text in a fashion that both exposes the encoded message's universalizing and exclusionary machinations and recircuits its workings to account for, include, and empower minority identities and identifications. Thus, disidentification is a step further than cracking open the code of the majority; it proceeds to use this code as raw material for representing a disempowered politics or positionality that has been rendered unthinkable by the dominant culture. (p. 31)

Importantly, disidentification foregrounds a brand of resistance that is subversive. This article proceeds by detailing some of the normative sites of power that disidentification has been used to disrupt and that scholars in the discipline have analyzed including heteronormativity, whiteness, capitalism, and U.S. citizenship. While these discourses are isolated for the sake of discussion, it is worth noting that these normative commitments depend on one another to retain authority and influence; thus, separating each from the other is not as coherent a task as the article may suggest. It is also the case that throughout communication studies scholarship these categories of influence are intertwined in the discussion and analysis of the authors whose work is reviewed here. In all cases, disidentification is understood as both a performative practice that minority subjects engage in, as well as a theoretical tool that scholars and critics can use to make sense of the communicative processes of marginalized populations.

Resisting and Subverting Heteronormativity. The ways in which marginalized subjects can both use and unsettle normative structures that determine appropriate performances of race, gender, sexuality, and beauty set disidentification apart from other grammars of resistance. In particular, heteronormativity speaks to normative pressures (and institutionalized protections) for those who embody "beauty" in mainstream ways, and those who practice monogamous, heterosexual, cisgender desire. As Yep (2003) articulates, "heteronormativity, as the invisible center and the presumed bedrock of society, is the quintessential force creating, sustaining, and perpetuating the erasure, marginalization, disempowerment, and oppression of sexual others" (p. 18). Some minoritarian subjects and critical scholars disidentify with these expectations to reframe what counts as desirable, and then use this revised standard to undermine the integrity of heteronormativity in creative ways. In their virtual ethnography about FatClub.com, Adams and Berry (2013) utilize disidentification to make sense of how participants on the website use proweight language and performances to subvert normative gay male health and beauty standards. In this essay the authors trace two different ways that members of the group disidentify. First, they note that participants "reframe weight gains and bigger bodies as desirable and erotic" (p. 321), and second, "many of these gay men use bigger bodies to work against the thin and fit, Twink norms of beauty associated with some gay male contexts" (p. 321). As Adams and Berry reveal, disidentification can be a theoretical heuristic for making sense of what the authors describe as "counterintuitive cultural scenes" (p. 308) that may otherwise be dismissed. As they describe, disidentification can be a way to investigate the performances of identity that occur on the website that insist upon a diversity of embodiments and desires that decenter heteronormativity.

Normative expectations for the embodiment and performance of gender regulate people's lives and restrict cultural understandings of gender diversity and fluidity. These rigid formulations for sex and gender are effectively decentered by performative practices of disidentification and critical interventions that utilize this heuristic. As mentioned earlier, Eguchi et al. (2018), in their analysis of *Love and Hip Hop*, use disidentification as a way to critique the coming out narrative and how it works to regulate and inform Black gay masculinity. Tabarez (2012) traces the influences of heteronormative masculinity in his discussion of *narcocorridos* or "narrative songs glorifying the underworld of drug trafficking" (p. 228), noting the effects such lyrics had on his (queer) and his brother's (heterosexual) performance of masculinity. Hartzell (2016) extends disidentification to explore how White mothers who participated in the "We are not Trayvon Martin" blog worked within and against standards of normative motherhood that characterize White femininity as passive and/or as protectors of whiteness. Gutierrez-Perez and Andrade (2018) interrogate the function of marriage for the LGBTQIA+ community, describing the disruptive ways they participate in their respective marriages to undermine the cultural, religious, and state-sponsored credibility it is supposed to preserve. In each of these examples, the heteronormative expectations for performing gender and sexuality are a primary lens through which subjects see themselves, as well as the very thing that undermines their enactments of coming out, of marriage, or their pronouncements of antiracism. Extending the work of Muñoz, then, these scholars offer diverse ways that disidentification can be taken up to critically investigate the communication practices and subject formations that occur at and along the margins of heteronormativity.

Resisting and Subverting the Logics of Capitalism. Embedded within critiques of normativity is a challenge to the ideologies that assign value—both symbolically and materially—to different bodies, relationships, and subject formations. Although marginalized people can garner cultural capital by aligning with(in) heteronormative standards, this is not the same thing as benefiting from the structural and institutional systems that generate, distribute, and protect wealth and property. Indeed, these systems, supported by a neoliberal and capitalist ideology, powerfully constrain the possibilities many minority subjects have to build in a livable life. As Vats (2016) demonstrates, one of the most powerful modes of resistance that disidentification affords is its ability to deconstruct and subvert how value is culturally assigned and materially distributed. By analyzing trademark laws, Vats argues that communities of difference can symbolically and materially benefit from using the systems that assign and protect property. Tracing Marshawn Lynch's Beast Mode trademark, and the clothing it brands with slogans such as "I'm just here so I won't get fined," Vats argues that "Lynch's refusal to act in 'respectable' ways depropertizes his body" and creates "commodity value in his moments of resistive agency" (2016, p. 245), as opposed to in his Black laboring body. Significantly, Vats demonstrates that disidentification can meaningfully be used to redistribute material resources using the very systems that once rendered Black bodies the property of White slave owners. Ideologies of capitalism, neoliberalism, and intersectionality are tied to discourses of whiteness and citizenship that preserve these logics—each bracing the others in an intricately engineered effort to preserve the interests of the privileged. Despite the interstitial ways that these dominant logics cohere, resisting one mode of oppression is not necessarily indicative of resisting all modes of oppression. In spite of this, as Vats illustrates, disidentification can offer a strategy for marginalized individuals to use that allows for a multifaceted subversion of the mechanisms of power and domination that organize social life.

Resisting and Subverting Whiteness and U.S. Citizenship. Whiteness and U.S. citizenship work in tandem with other interlocking systems of oppression to protect the interests and the investments of a narrow few. In the same ways that institutions of power are propped up by these interlocking systems, disidentification is an essential part of antiracist practice and scholarship that can work in multifaceted ways to subvert complex positions of privilege. In one important example of this, we see how White-identifying people can disidentify with the privileged category from which they benefit. This presents an important extension for the ways this heuristic is frequently theorized, demonstrating how disidentification may be a performative practice that majority subjects can use to participate in antiracist, queer, or decolonial efforts. Hartzell (2016), who has already been briefly referenced, studied White women's contribution to the thread "We are not Trayvon Martin," noting that "unpacking performative disidentifications with dominant racial subjectivities can therefore reveal how racially privileged subjects can work within and against the norms of the racial identities into which they have been interpellated" (p. 68). As Hartzell discusses, the subversive potential of disidentification is not limited to communities who must scrap for social and cultural recognition but can instead be a tool that people with privilege utilize to critique the systems from which they benefit. Thus, unlike *divestment*, which calls for people with a vested interest in something to rid themselves of the privileges and benefits that come with such relationships, White people can *disidentify* with whiteness by both disrupting *and* using the structures of racial privilege that elevate and protect their status.

Muñoz allows for the possibility that majoritarian subjects may practice disidentification, noting that even individuals in positions of power likely negotiate intersectional and sometimes conflicting sites of identification. As Martínez Guillem (2017) explores, precarious privilege may be a way to think about what the practice of disidentification can actually accomplish. Exploring the movement/community of *indignados* that formed around political resistance to the government in Spain, Martínez Guillem argues that disidentification can cohere groups based on a shared emotion rather than a political ideology or political identity. As she argues, this sets *indignados* apart from traditional social movements and extends the applications of disidentification to demonstrate that affect may be an additional site of disidentification with the potential to disrupt and subvert institutional power. Martínez Guillem, citing Pêcheux, points out that disidentification develops from within dominant/normative ideological structures, reminding us that those with varying levels of privilege are uniquely positioned to use that status in the service of disrupting the status quo.

Fischer (2019), who explores the performance artist Cassils's exhibition "Monumental," offers another important extension for the ways disidentification can be used and theorized as a subversive mechanism to undermine the categories of whiteness and citizenship. Fischer (2019) describes *PISSED* as an "immense Plexiglass cube filled with 200 gallons of Cassils's urine and [was] framed by the hundreds of orange cartons used to collect, store, and disinfect the artist's waste" (p. 397). Fischer goes on to note that "the minimalist sculpture was overlaid with surround-sound audio from the testimonial in *G.G. v. Gloucester County School Board*, a case that considered the right of transgender students to use bathrooms of their choice" (p. 397). Further, "at the opening of 'Monumental' Cassils performed *Fountain* (2017), where, "standing on a simple white platform elevated above the heads of audience members, Cassils, dressed in all black, continuously drank water and, when necessary urinated in a container identical to the orange receptacles that lined the wall behind them" (p. 398). As Fischer argues, the exhibition, *PISSED*, and the corresponding performance, *Fountain*, captured the influential ways that U.S. citizenship discourses produce categories of people and how those categories can be disrupted from within. As she explains, "in deploying the state's own conceptualization for 'deviant' bodies and their 'toxic' excretions as potential weapons that can terrorize the state, *PISSED/Fountain* challenge viewers to rethink the commonly accepted differentiation between male and female, health and disease, citizens and aliens and/or terrorists" (p. 409). Importantly, Fischer's critique, and the careful ways in which the author thinks through the communicative productions and effects of art, extend how those with social, cultural, and institutional status can organize intentional and pointed criticisms of institutional and state power.

While many acts of resistance are organized, intentional, and overtly disruptive, this is not always the case. Indeed, disidentification is a practice that requires working within and against normative ideologies and institutions; thus, by its very definition, disidentification can be insidious, ordinary, and vernacular. Muñoz indicates that disidentification occurs in everyday spaces and interactions—those that don't draw robust attention or audiences, but rather those that scaffold the day-to-day choices a person makes that enable them to have a livable life. Hartzell (2016), in her exploration of White mothers' posts on the "We are not Trayvon Martin" blog, notes that everyday life experiences can be disidentificatory. She explains that a specific focus on performativity within disidentification "reveals how everyday acts of transgression can rework dominant subjectivities by exploiting imperfections in identity (re)citation" (p. 68). By tracing how White mothers declared "I am not Trayvon Martin," Hartzell suggests that they enacted a performative disidentification with normative racial discourses of colorblindness via the call to proclaim "We are [all] Trayvon." Relatedly, Hatfield (2017) introduces the term *quare disidentification* to address yet another style of disidentification that is unintentional. He explores the 1989 funeral of the famous choreographer Alvin Ailey, Jr. in which selections from his ballet *Revelations* were performed, exploring how disidentification may be used to describe the "racialized performances by minority populations that may not have been intended as political or resistant but nevertheless have subversive effects upon their actualizing" (p. 52). Drawing critical attention to the way that disidentification functions unintentionally, Hatfield's *quare disidentification* produces nuanced critiques of social movement organizing and protest. In this way, while disidentification is always resistive and capable of revising lived experience, it is not always intentional (Hatfield, 2017) nor out of the ordinary (Hartzell, 2016).

DISIDENTIFICATION AS A PROCESS OF QUEER OF COLOR WORLDMAKING

As much as disidentification is about negotiating the violence of normative culture and undermining the institutions that afford it, it is also about imagining new futures, new modes of relation, and new worlds. In this way, one of the utopian prospects of disidentification is queer worldmaking and the future it imagines. Muñoz (1999) notes that

> disidentificatory performances and readings require an active kernel of utopian possibility. Although utopianism has become the bad object of much contemporary political thinking, we nonetheless need to hold on to and even *risk* utopianism if we are to engage in the labor of making a queer world. (p. 25)

The risk and the promise of utopianism and the queer world that it helps marginalized people imagine is essential to disidentification—indeed, it is the worldmaking possibility of disidentification that makes it a compelling heuristic from which to theorize and organize. For example, Forst (2016), in his analysis of Denasia Lawrence's decision to kneel while singing the national anthem at an NBA game in 2016, notes that part of disidentification's potential is in producing a third space "between civil assimilation, and outright separation" (p. 13) that, if sustained, can produce alternative futures. The possibility for a third space—one that has not yet been actualized but that remains the utopian promise of radical and imaginative thinking and action—is a theoretical and material promise with the potential to propel antiracist, queer, and decolonial initiatives. As Gutierrez-Perez and Andrade (2018) explain, "queer of color worldmaking refers to the ways queers of color create ephemeral spatiotemporal resistance strategies in the face of heteronormative and intersectional oppressive conditions" (p. 4). Queer of color individuals and scholars deserve particular recognition for the ways worldmaking has been theorized in communication studies literature and for the ways the utopian future it imagines can be realized through disidentification. Gutierrez-Perez and Andrade (2018), writing about their own participation in "gay marriages," explain that it is short-sighted to think about LGBTQIA+ people's participation in marriage as assimilationist. Instead, they argue that their participation in this institution is an embodied ideograph that produces new worlds and new modes of relation. Specifically, Gutierrez-Perez explains that he and his partner actively practice polyamory in their marriage, while Andrade describes how his decision to take his male partner's *appellido* (last name) defied patriarchal and heteronormative expectations. As they suggest, the ways each man embodies marriage creates alternate way of being (married)—produces a third space—that is enabled by the alternate mode of relations these men practice.

When an individual disidentifies, they must do so with the hope they will be able to craft a different way of being in the world—one that leaves behind the exclusions and disenfranchisement that normative systems and institutions regularly impose on minority subjects. Andrade (2019) argues that disidentification is the process that enables queer worldmaking, noting that "queer world-making tactics destabilize notions of identity, the nation, and normativity, and queer of color world-making attends to the cultural heteronormativity and violence that occurs in communities of color" (p. 206). Although violence and the threat of exclusion cohere those on the margins, it is a person's hope for a different future that motivates many on the margins to continue surviving, fighting, and/or dreaming.

Disidentification, as an act of queer of color worldmaking, forces a reconsideration of our temporal environments, blurring the lines between past, present, and future. Imagining a future beyond the logics of the present and that defies the violences of the past (Sandoval, 2018) characterizes the practice of worldmaking and affords acts of disidentification a particularly powerful role in materializing that future. The way that disidentification collapses and expands time enables those in the cultural fray to break free from restrictive normative institutions and to instead participate in "a world-making project that traverses and transgresses the limits of the here and now" (Fischer, 2019, p. 410), oftentimes in the service of creatively imagining a not-yet-realizable future. Exploring the opioid epidemic in Philadelphia and the official and public discourse it produced, Ferrell (2019) suggests that revising the past is in fact a primary way in which people can disidentify and build new futures. Specifically, the author suggests that community members disrupted the city's public health discourse when they disidentified with the narrative past of the city. She argues that this exigency

> involved a recovery of sorts, as narratives wove collective past experiences of racial injustices into the present and articulated the histories of the crack epidemic in connection to CUES [supervised injection sites otherwise known as Comprehensive User Engagement Sites] to mark the city's substantially different engagements across time and remedy their accompanying silences. (p. 536)

As Ferrell's analysis demonstrates, disidentification traverses expansive temporal contexts, providing tools and modes of thinking that can adjust the normative and exclusionary discourses of the *past* to manage the *present* pressures of marginalization that daily keep minority populations on the fringe, and nevertheless anticipate a more inclusive alternate *future*. As Ferrell illustrates, disidentification is regularly theorized as a way for hybrid subjects to negotiate complex and contradictory interpellations across time and space.

DISIDENTIFICATION IS ABOUT NEGOTIATING HYBRIDITY

As scholars in communication studies have demonstrated, disidentification is a theoretical construct that requires sitting with contradictions and foregrounding the both/and, as opposed to the either/or, of identity. Indeed, border identities and border performances have been some of the first and most productive sites where the discipline has extended Muñoz's theory of disidentification. In 2009, Chávez used disidentification to explore the tensions of being Latina in Nebraska—a geographic location not typically aligned with the urban or border regions associated with Latina/o/xs. Since this early application of disidentification within communication studies, scholars have used disidentification as a lens to explore the hybrid subject formation of Latina drag queens (Moreman & McIntosh, 2010), Black protesters (Forst, 2016), social movement groups (Martínez Guillem, 2017), DREAMers (Morrissey, 2013), and Black gay men living on the "down low" (Eguchi et al., 2018). In each of these iterations, disidentification has emerged as a heuristic well suited to examine the contradiction, hybridity, and fluidity of identity categories. Minority groups often must construct border performances (strategic self-representations) in order to survive; however, such efforts also serve to critique "hegemonic identity scripts that are placed on and read through their body" (Moreman & McIntosh, 2010, p. 120). In this way, scholars who have theorized disidentification assert that minoritarian subjects are both outside and inside cultural spaces and that it is an oversimplification to read their subject formation and performance of identity as simply assimilationist or resistant. As Eguchi and Asante (2016) explain, "disidentifications offer a symbolic prism to show varying, complex, and multiple levels of identity border performances, which sometimes work within/against the normative constructions of race/gender/sexuality" (p. 175).

Indeed, disidentification provides an important heuristic for theorizing the both/and of subject formation, as well as the complexities of this work. As an example of these messy contestations, Andrea Smith, a White scholar who has been accused of misrepresenting her ethnic background as Cherokee in her work in Native Studies, offers an ironic critique of disidentification's utility. According to Smith (2011), the hybridity that disidentification and queer of color critique foregrounds may be harmful, insofar as it could dilute the experiences and politics of some communities, in particular Native communities. She explains that while disidentification may be a useful tool for the project of decolonization, it is also at once the admission that a population has been "inevitably marked by processes of colonization" (Smith, 2011, p. 56)—a characterization that could be especially troubling for Native communities. As a phenotypically White woman falsely claiming her own Cherokee background, the irony of such a comment is significant. Smith explains that the reality that Native populations are hybridized at once suggests that these populations no longer "have to carry the burden of political or cultural purity" and can be more "flexible and creative in engaging multiple strategies and creating a plethora of alliances" (Smith, 2011, p. 56), but she notes that "while political organizing is enabled by disidentification, sometimes it is also enabled by counteridentification that clearly identifies the United States as a settler colonial state" (p. 56). In this way, Smith both asserts the value of disidentification and cautions scholars to recognize that in certain situations, counteridentification (not disidentification) may be more appropriate as a theoretical lens or as an organizing strategy. Appearing to offer Native communities the particular cultural moment with which to counteridentify, Smith's performance of identity forces a careful consideration of hybridity. In particular, Smith's performance and critique indicate that identity is less about finding one's way to a singular, authentic sense of self, and more about living in the myriad, complex, and intersecting ways that identity is always already experienced and sourcing those for the purpose of survival, resistance, and/or worldmaking. Smith herself, though offering an important caution for the ways disidentification may be uncritically embraced as a liberatory mode of engagement for marginalized communities, embodies that which she argues is at stake for Native communities who embrace a hybrid identity.

As the previous sections have illustrated, communication studies scholars have theorized disidentification as a mode of survival, resistance, worldmaking, and hybrid identity. This work captures the breadth of scholarship being done on and around disidentification; however, as the next portion of the article will demonstrate, there are some less familiar offshoots of disidentification that deserve attention. These include thinking about disidentification as (5) a mode of reinforcing normative influences, (6) a way to theorize space, and (7) a way to extend, critique, and broaden existing theory.

DISIDENTIFICATION CAN REINFORCE NORMATIVE IDEOLOGY

As scholarship in the field has indicated, disidentification, while radical in its potential to revise, undermine, and challenge normative culture, can also reinforce the authority of those institutions and narratives as well. Muñoz and others have pointed out that subjects on the cultural margins walk a fine line when they disidentify as they must work both within and against the system. This kind of negotiation likely leads one to take steps over the line into assimilation or radical resistance at different points in one's subject formation.

As some scholars have noted, a person or a group's move into assimilationist practices and policies is often part of a larger strategy to revise systemic inequalities and exclusions. Julian Carter (2009), writing about the protagonist of Ann Bannon's lesbian cult fiction novels, notes that the main character's decision to marry her gay male friend is one such example of disidentification that leads people to "cling to convention" (p. 589). Carter suggests that "while disidentification provides minority subjects with the possibility of shaping their worlds, instead of simply being done in by them, it does not therefore guarantee or even imply that the worlds they will make will be progressive ones" (2009, p. 604). Echoing these limitations for disidentification, Morrissey (2013) notes that DREAMers appealing for U.S. citizenship and inclusion by using queer strategies, metaphors, and subjectivities aligned them with ideologies that scaffold the American Dream, ultimately reinforcing normative citizenship standards that continue to exclude their own immigrant parents. Corrigan (2017) explores how hip-hop, as a language, was adopted by the Bernie Sanders campaign to win over more voters, and concludes that even though the candidate was able to harness Black rage to disidentify with White liberal ideology, Sanders's efforts ultimately reinforced the value of whiteness. Corrigan draws on Vats (2016) to argue that "at best, disidentification is an incomplete curative for harmful racial formations" (p. 336) and produces a cautionary critique of the ways disidentification can work. As these scholars note, participation within the institutions that exclude them becomes a pivotal way for minoritarian subjects to subvert their authority; however, there are slippages that come with walking such a narrow line that, as we see demonstrated, can also strengthen the value of normative ideologies.

DISIDENTIFICATION ENABLES AND CONSTRAINS CULTURAL UNDERSTANDINGS OF SPACE

In addition to considering how disidentification may produce more normative ends, some of the recent scholarship that utilizes disidentification as a framework considers how space and place may be theorized. Specifically, this work indicates that disidentification enables and constrains our cultural understanding of space and informs how we are able to move in, around, and through the world. Chávez (2009), crafting what she refers to as a performance cartography, reflects on Latina/o/x identity formation in Nebraska, explaining that Nebraska (as a space) is both what she seeks to disidentify with and yet also the thing that enables her disidentification. As she explains, "because space is always a process, where new relationships and juxtapositions are possible, the disidentificatory practices enabled by one space can in fact become part of another" (Chávez, 2009, p. 179). Sandoval (2018), writing in/from the field of Human Geography, takes up these questions in his analysis of *UndocuQueers*, a term used by "undocumented queer migrants to claim that their multiple positionalities should be understood as intersecting" (p. 1760). Sandoval (2018) explains that *UndocuQueers* disidentify to transform present-day spaces and imagine more inviting future worlds. In particular, Sandoval (2018) notes that these individuals use disidentification as a performative practice to repurpose the norms of various spaces (clubs, agricultural fields, and airports). In both of these examples, space is a quality that affects and is affected by performances of disidentification, opening up future considerations for the ways disidentification may be theorized. In particular, this line of inquiry provokes questions such as: how might borderlands, airports, or protest zones of major cities emblazoned with phrases such as "Black Lives Matter" produce different disidentificatory possibilities? How are identities and performances of identity constrained in those spaces? How does the experience of rurality or urbanity inform the possibilities for disidentification? Answering these kinds of questions would certainly push our disciplinary understanding of disidentification into insightful new territories.

DISIDENTIFICATION IS A WAY TO BROADEN EXISTING THEORY

Using disidentification as a way to remap the normative ideological constructs that organize social life is an important aspect of the theory of disidentification; however, it is important to highlight how disidentification has been used to theorize and deconstruct the practices of knowledge production in academic disciples as well. In two particular examples (one from communication studies and one from Sociology), disidentification has been discussed as a way to build theory, decenter whiteness, and foreground minoritarian voices to revise disciplinary knowledge production. Roderick Ferguson (2003), a sociologist writing about queer of color scholarship, argues for using disidentification as a mode of self-reflexive disciplinary critique. He notes that scholars producing queer of color analysis could not practice this work (based in historical materialism) without disidentifying with it, claiming that "since historical materialism has traditionally privileged class over other social relations, queer of color critique cannot take it up without revision, must not employ it without disidentification" (Ferguson, 2003, p. 172). Similarly, Eguchi and Asante (2016), writing about communication studies (generally) and intercultural communication (specifically), note that much of the literature considered mainstream intercultural communication scholarship has failed to sufficiently address questions of gender and sexual fluidity. The authors argue that disidentification can be a way to "rearticulate and reimagine possibilities for queer(y)ing intercultural communication" (Eguchi & Asante, 2016, p. 172), opening the possibility for scholars in the field to become similarly reflexive about their own areas of research and positioning disidentification as a mechanism for revising disciplinary canons (knowledge produced, knowledge production, knowledge producers). Though to date disidentification has been taken up almost exclusively in U.S. contexts, applying and utilizing it in intercultural and/or transnational contexts is an essential way to enrich the field of communication studies and to promote a necessary practice of critical self-reflexivity in the discipline.

Using disidentification as a heuristic for unsettling disciplinary knowledge production seems an especially important area of future inquiry, especially in a discursive moment in which the field of communication studies has been called to attend to the discipline's investments in whiteness (see e.g., Báez & Ore, 2018; Baugh-Harris & Wanzer-Serrano, 2018; Chakravartty et al., 2018; Colpean & Dingo, 2018; Flores, 2016, 2018; Hester & Squires, 2018; Houdek, 2018; Law & Corrigan, 2018; McGee & Cisneros, 2018; Towns, 2015; Vega & Chávez, 2018; Yousuf & Calafell, 2018). Considering how disidentification can dismantle and revise exclusionary practices of knowledge production not only has the potential to expand the theory and practice produced therein, but is also an ethical project that insists on centering different voices and experiences. While marginalized scholars have long advocated for the discipline to acknowledge its investments in whiteness, masculinity, heteronormativity, Christianity, and its U.S.-centric orientations, there remains inconsistent progress made across these areas. Despite shifts in the discipline's management and conferral of awards (such as the Distinguished Scholar Awards), its selection of more diverse editors and reviewers for the discipline's flagship journals and editorial boards, and its efforts to expand the work being published in the discipline to be more critically self-reflexive, there is still much work to be done. To this end, disidentification may be a way for those advocating for epistemological and cultural changes to imagine their next steps. Certainly, a more robust effort on the part of disciplinary gatekeepers to utilize their status within the discipline to centralize marginalized voices and concerns is an important step for revising the scaffolding of the discipline, but so too is the ongoing disidentificatory effort of marginalized scholars to use the grammars and logics of the discipline to insist on the inclusion and visibility of difference.

CONCLUSION

As a performative practice and as a heuristic, disidentification is a valuable tool for reconsidering and revising normative and exclusionary ideologies. This article should signal to researchers in communication studies the robust contributions that scholars and activists whose identities are situated on the cultural, social, and disciplinary margins can contribute to the field. Muñoz's work, and the scholarship that has since taken it up, center the voices, the practices, the performances, and the methodologies of those on the margins and offer a way for those contributions to be integrated in our disciplinary inquiries. In particular, work that is published in communication studies demonstrates how disidentification can be persuasive—indeed, the ways it can compel shifts in these structures and mechanisms that disenfranchise so many voices and experiences. Utilizing this heuristic in our scholarship works in manifold ways to decenter the canon of communication studies, center voices from the margin, enact a politics of resistance and critical self-reflection, and invest energy and attention to institutionally and systemically marginalized populations. In spite of the relatively small U.S.-centric footprint this mode of inquiry has so far had on the discipline of communication studies, this article should command scholars in the field to do more to center the work of those on the margins—to disidentify with the traditional theories and methods that structure the field.

Language and the action it inspires is a tool by and through which systems of power can be dismantled, knowledge can be produced, and justice can be sought. The scholarship outlined in this article should serve as a starting point for scholars seeking to do critical, intersectional, decolonial, and antiracist work. Taking up this lens and foregrounding the marginalized voices cited here is an important way that activists and scholars can work within and against the discipline's epistemological, ontological, and axiological commitments to demand better from the discipline and to extend the important mode of inquiry and performative practice that disidentification offers.

FURTHER READING

Alarcón, N. (1990). The theoretical subject(s) of *This bridge called my back* and Anglo-American feminism. In G. Anzaldúa (Ed.), *Making face, making soul/hacienda caras: Creative and critical perspectives by feminists of color* (pp. 356–369). Aunt Lute Books.

Crenshaw, K. W. (1990). Beyond racism and misogyny: Black feminism and 2 live crew. In M. Matsuda, C. R. Lawrence, R. Delgado, & K. W. Crenshaw (Eds.), *Words that wound: Critical race theory, assaultive speech, and the First Amendment* (pp. 111–132). Westview Press.

Moraga, C., & G. Anzaldúa, G. (Eds.). (2015). *This bridge called my back: Writings by radical women of color* (4th ed.). State University of New York Press.

Sedgwick, E. K. (1990). *Epistemology of the closet*. University of California Press.

Yarbro-Bejarano, Y. (1995). Expanding the categories of race and sexuality in lesbian gay studies. In G. E. Haggerty & B. Zimmerman (Eds.), *Professions of desire: Lesbian and gay studies in literature* (pp. 124–135). Verso Press.

REFERENCES

Adams, T. E., & Berry, K. (2013). Size matters: Performing (il)logical male bodies on *Fatclub.com*. *Text and Performance Quarterly*, 33(4), 308–325. http://dx.doi.org/10.1080/10462937.2013.818704

Alarcón, N. (1996). Conjugating subjects in the age of multiculturalism. In A. F. Gordon & C. Newfield (Eds.), *Mapping multiculturalism* (pp. 127–148). University of Minnesota Press.

Althusser, L. (1971). *Lenin, Marxism and other essays* (Ben Brewster, Trans.). St. Martin's Press.

Andrade, L. M. (2019). CAUTION: On the many, unpredictable iterations of a yellow border sign ideograph and migrant/queer world-making. *Text and Performance Quarterly*, 39(3), 203–228. http://dx.doi.org/10.1080/10462937.2019.1595123

Asen, R. (2015). Critical engagement through public sphere scholarship. *Quarterly Journal of Speech*, 101(1), 132–144. http://dx.doi.org/10.1080/00335630.2015.999983

Báez, K. L., & Ore, E. (2018). The moral imperative of race for rhetorical studies: On civility and walking-in-white in academe. *Communication and Critical/Cultural Studies*, 15(4), 331–336. http://dx.doi.org/10.1080/14791420.2018.1533989

Baugh-Harris, S., & Wanzer-Serrano, D. (2018). Against canon: Engaging the imperative of race in rhetoric. *Communication and Critical/Cultural Studies*, 15(4), 337–342. http://dx.doi.org/10.1080/14791420.2018.1526386

Brouwer, D. C. (2006). Communication as counterpublic. In G. J. Shepherd, J. St. John, & T. Striphas (Eds.), *Communication as…: Perspectives on theory* (pp. 195–208). SAGE.

Butler, J. (1993). *Bodies that matter: On the discursive limits of "sex"*. Routledge.

Carter, J. (2009). Gay marriage and pulp fiction: Homonormativity, disidentification, and affect in Ann Bannon's lesbian novels. *GLQ: A Journal of Lesbian and Gay Studies, 15*(4), 583–609. http://dx.doi.org/10.1215/10642684-2009-003

Chakravartty, P., Kuo, R., Grubbs, V., & McIlwain, C. (2018). #CommunicationSoWhite. *Journal of Communication, 68*, 254–266. http://dx.doi.org/10.1093/joc/jqy003

Chávez, K. R. (2009). Remapping *Latinidad*: A performance cartography of Latina/o identity in rural Nebraska. *Text and Performance Quarterly, 29*(2), 165–182. http://dx.doi.org/10.1080/10462930902774866

Colpean, M., & Dingo, R. (2018). Beyond drive-by race scholarship: The importance of engaging geopolitical contexts. *Communication and Critical/Cultural Studies, 15*(4), 306–311. http://dx.doi.org/10.1080/14791420.2018.1533988

Corrigan, L. (2017). The unlikely prophets of rage: Bernie Sanders and Killer Mike. Symposium: Rhetoric, race, and resentment. *Rhetoric Review, 36*, 331–341.

Eguchi, S., & Asante, G. (2016). Disidentifications revisited: Queer(y)ing intercultural communication theory. *Communication Theory, 26*, 171–189. https://doi.org/10.1111/comt.12086

Eguchi, S., Files-Thompson, N., & Calafell, B. (2018). Queer (of color) aesthetics: Fleeting moments of transgression in VH2's *Love & Hip-Hop: Hollywood Season 2*. *Critical Studies in Media Communication, 35*(2), 180–193. http://dx.doi.org/10.1080/15295036.2017.1385822

Ferguson, R. (2003). *Aberrations in black: Toward a queer of color critique*. University of Minnesota Press.

Ferrell, A. P. (2019). "Righting past wrongs": Rhetorical disidentification and historical reference in response to the opioid epidemic. *Rhetoric & Public Affairs, 22*(4), 533–568.

Fischer, M. (2019). Piss(ed): The biopolitics of the bathroom. *Communication, Culture, & Critique, 12*, 397–415. http://dx.doi.org/10.1093/ccc/tcz024

Flores, L. (2016). Between abundance and marginalization: The imperative of racial rhetorical criticism. *Review of Communication, 16*, 4–24. http://dx.doi.org/10.1080/15358593.2016.1183871

Flores, L. A. (2018). Towards an insistent and transformative racial rhetorical criticism. *Communication and Critical/Cultural Studies, 15*(4), 349–357. http://dx.doi.org/10.1080/14791420.2018.1526387

Forst, M. L. (2016). Kneeling but still singing: Threshold identity, disidentification, and invitation in U.S. American National Anthem protest. *Kaleidoscope: A Graduate Journal of Qualitative Research, 15*, 1–18.

Fraser, N. (1992). Rethinking the public sphere: A contribution to the critique of actually existing democracy. In C. Calhoun (Ed.), *Habermas and the public sphere* (pp. 109–142). MIT Press.

Freud, S. (1959). *Group psychology and the analysis of the ego* (James Stranchey, Trans.). W. W. Norton.

Gutierrez-Perez, R., & Andrade, L. (2018). Queer of color worldmaking: <marriage> in the rhetorical archive and the embodied repertoire. *Text and Performance Quarterly, 38*(1–2), 1–18. http://dx.doi.org/10.1080/10462937.2018.1435130

Hartzell, S. (2016). An (in)visible universe of grief: Performative disidentifications with white motherhood in the We are not Trayvon Martin blog. *Journal of International and Intercultural Communication, 10*(1), 62–79. http://dx.doi.org/10.1080/17513057.2016.1177106

Hatfield, J. E. (2017). Dancing southern diaspora: Alvin Ailey's blood and the backwardness of quare disidentification. *Text and Performance Quarterly, 37*(1), 51–67. https://doi.org/10.1080/10462937.2017.1307441

Hester, S. L., & Squires, C. R. (2018). Who are we working for? Recentering Black feminism. *Communication and Critical/Cultural Studies, 15*(4), 343–348. http://dx.doi.org/10.1080/14791420.2018.1533987

Houdek, M. (2018). The imperative of race for rhetorical studies: Toward divesting from disciplinary and institutionalized whiteness. *Communication and Critical/Cultural Studies, 15*(4), 292–299. http://dx.doi.org/10.1080/14791420.2018.1534253

Law, M., & Corrigan, L. M. (2018). On white-speak and gatekeeping: Or, what good are the Greeks? *Communication and Critical/Cultural Studies, 15*(4), 326–330. http://dx.doi.org/10.1080/14791420.2018.1533640

Martínez Guillem, S. (2017). Precarious privilege: Indignad@s, daily disidentifications, and cultural (re)production. *Communication and Critical/Cultural Studies, 14*(3), 238–253. http://dx.doi.org/10.1080/14791420.2017.1310387

McGee, A., & Cisneros, J. D. (2018). Looking back, looking forward: A dialogue on "the imperative of racial rhetorical criticism". *Communication and Critical/Cultural Studies, 15*(4), 300–305. http://dx.doi.org/10.1080/14791420.2018.1533643

Moreman, S. T., & McIntosh, D. M. (2010). Brown scriptings and rescriptings: A critical performance ethnography of Latina drag queens. *Communication & Critical Cultural Studies, 7*(2), 115–135. http://dx.doi.org/10.1080/14791421003767912

Morrissey, M. E. (2013). A DREAM disrupted: Undocumented migrant youth disidentifications with U.S. citizenship. *Journal of International and Intercultural Communication, 6*(2), 145–162. http://dx.doi.org/10.1080/17513057.2013.774041

Muñoz, J. E. (1999). *Disidentifications: Queers of color and the performance of politics*. University of Minnesota Press.

Pêcheux, M. (1982). *Language, semantics and ideology*. St. Martin's Press.

Sandoval, E. (2018). More than violence: UndocuQueers' narratives of disidentification and world-making in Seattle, Washington, USA. *Gender, Place & Culture, 25*(2), 1759–1780. http://dx.doi.org/10.1080/0966369x.2018.1558179

Smith, A. (2011). Queer theory and native studies: The heteronormativity of settler colonialism. In Q. Driskill, C. Finley, B. J. Gilley, & S. L. Morgenson (Eds.), *Queer Indigenous studies: Critical interventions in theory, politics, and literature* (pp. 43–65). University of Arizona Press.

Tabarez, U. M. (2012). Trafficking across dangerous borders (shores): An open letter to a brother. *Text & Performance Quarterly, 32*(3), 227–243. http://dx.doi.org/10.1080/10462937.2012.691331

Towns, A. (2015). The (racial) biases of communication: Rethinking media and Blackness. *Social Identities: Journal for the Study of Race, Nation and Culture, 21*(5), 474–488. http://dx.doi.org/10.1080/13504630.2015.1093469

Vats, A. (2016). Marking disidentification: Race, corporeality, and resistance in trademark law. *Southern Communication Journal, 81*(4), 237–251. https://doi.org/10.1080/1041794X.2016.1200128

Vega, K. S., & Chávez, K. R. (2018). Latinx rhetoric and intersectionality in racial rhetorical criticism. *Communication and Critical/Cultural Studies, 15*(4), 319–325. http://dx.doi.org/10.1080/14791420.2018.1533642

Yep, G. (2003). The violence of heteronormativity in Communication Studies. *Journal of Homosexuality, 45*(2–4), 11–59. http://dx.doi.org/10.1300/J082v45n02_02

Yousuf, S., & Calafell, B. (2018). The imperative for examining anti-Muslim racism in rhetorical studies. *Communication and Critical/Cultural Studies, 15*(4), 312–318. http://dx.doi.org/10.1080/14791420.2018.1533641

Megan Elizabeth Morrissey

HOMONORMATIVITY

INTRODUCTION

Our sexuality is always present, and always influential in the decisions that we make about our lives in general, and our communication in particular.
(Slagle, 2003, p. 134)

In service to sexual normativity, sexuality remains a hushed topic at the normative dinner table. Despite its disciplined silence, secretive mannerisms, and hidden attributes, sexuality is a primary aspect of individual identities and, as Slagle (2003) pointedly notes, serves as a central influence in how people live their lives (p. 134). Not surprisingly, the importance of studying sexuality is indisputable yet continues to remain a developing field in communication studies (Yep & Lescure, 2019; Yep et al., 2019). Strides in queer theory and communication continue to build sexuality studies, but certainly more work must be done. Sexual normativity forms the cultural building block of queer theory development. As such, theoretical tracings of hegemony and sexuality led to the coined theory of heteronormativity. On a primary level, the hegemonic backlash to normalized heterosexuality is the root violence of heteronormativity. Normalized sexuality, however, is not isolated to heterosexual contexts. The normalization of homosexuality, including gay and lesbian lifestyles, relationships, and spaces, specific to White and Western contexts, is the birthplace of homonormativity. Through an interdisciplinary theory of sexual hegemony, homonormativity traces the normalization of homosexuality and the hegemonic violence that ripples from queer politics and embodiments that become assimilated into normalization. The primary plight of homonormativity scholarship is problematizing the normalization of queer, gay, and lesbian politics, identities, and performatives. This article explores the definitive complexity of homonormativity from an interdisciplinary perspective and maps four trajectories of homonormativity specific to communication studies.

DEFINING HOMONORMATIVITY

To grasp the definitive properties of homonormativity, one must take a step back and explore theoretical and political articulations of heteronormativity. In her foundational piece, Rich (1980) lays bare the power laden in compulsory heterosexuality, denoting the harms of normalizing sexual desires from heterosexual constructions. Rich demonstrates that heterosexism removes the possibilities and realities of lesbian desires. Warner (1991, 1993) coined the term "heteronormativity" to denote the normalization of heterosexual desires and sexual practices for purposes of marginalizing any sexuality outside the heterosexual construct, which furthermore necessitates a binary gender foundation to orchestrate heterosexuality (e.g., cisgender man sexually desires cisgender woman). Robinson's (2016) definition of heteronormativity is particularly succinct and clear. He states, "Heteronormativity is a hegemonic system of norms, discourses, and practices that constructs heterosexuality as natural and superior to all expressions of sexuality" (p. 1). Hegemonic systems function strategically here, both overtly and covertly, to ensure that heterosexuality and heterosexism remains at the center. Heteronormativity laid the groundwork for homophobia, the justification of overt violence against non-normative sexualities and gender performances, and the illusive cultural binds of internal and social compulsory heterosexual desires. These violent cultural assumptions are constructed through an ideology that normalizes heterosexism in all its intricate capacities.

Heteronormativity quickly became a popular theory for scholars to articulate the cultural workings of power inflicted by heterosexism. Arguably, the most fundamental piece on the academic landscape of heteronormativity is Gust Yep's (2003) article "The Violence of Heteronormativity." Yep's foundational essay on heteronormativity powerfully outlined the matrix of power that heteronormativity functions within and through. Yep's article moves heteronormativity from a liner trajectory of heteronormative power toward an intersectional mapping of heteronormativity. He articulates multiple locations of heteronormative violence in a multiplex power system across different identities. Over two decades later, the importance of this piece remains. Yep (2017) challenges individuals and scholars alike to continue to unpack the multiple normatives, specifically noting "cisnormativity, homonormativity, body normativity, transnormativity, and Western cultural normativity that are directly and less directly derived from heteronormativity" (p. 116). Yep encourages scholarship to engage heteronormativity in important new directions and calls attention to the interconnections of heteronormativity and homonormativity.

Like heteronormativity, homonormativity functions through the normalization of homosexuality, gay and lesbian, transgender and transpolitics, and queer politics, movements, and communities. To further empower heteronormativity, queer politics and movements become absorbed and accepted into mainstream dominant cultural norms. Popularized acceptance of LGBT communities, movements, and spaces functions to normalize queer visibility. Yep and Elia (2012) clarify, "As such, GLQ images in commercial media create the appearance of political progress, cultural acceptance, and social equality for sexual minorities" (p. 895). Homonormative constructions work through a saturation of normative representations of LGBT identities as tokenized, unremarkable, and assumed. However, the increased presence of queer visibility has not removed heteronormative or anti-queer violence. As such, homonormativity is less about the acceptance of homosexuality and more about a power move of heteronormativity to culturally control marginalized sexuality.

Whereas heteronormativity originates from the center (Slagle, 2003, pp. 135–136), homonormativity pulls *from* the center to gain power (Rosenfeld, 2009). Since heteronormativity defines the cultural norms of power, homonormativity actually depends on heteronormativity to access power. Rosenfeld (2009) demonstrates how LGBT individuals utilize heteronormative premises. Rosenfeld also claims that these heteronormative practices not only provide access to power but are intentionally enacted by the queer community for survival. One cannot fully grasp the workings of homonormativity without concurrently locating heteropatriarchal authority. However, like a zeppelin bend heteronormativity and homonormativity are two primary lines of power, where one construct does not make the other tighter or more powerful but the two work together to maintain rigidity. Now that the codependent relationship of heteronormativity and homonormativity is defined, the next step is to define homonormativity.

Homonormativity began as a political term referring to the popularization of sexual minorities that assimilate into, acquire normative practices from, and serve heteronormative constructs of binary gender, sexuality, and homo or hetero definitions. The grounds for homonormativity trace back to trans scholars and activists in the early 1990s. Trans scholars critiqued queer and LGBT communities' binary constructions of gender and their relationship to sexuality in service to heteronormativity (Stryker, 2008). Stryker states, "A decade before homonormative became a critically chic term elsewhere, I thus suggest, transgender praxis and critique required an articulation of the concept of homonormativity" (p. 194). In their provocative book, Halberstam (1998) points to the problematic nature of confining gays and lesbians to hetero-gender relational performances. Halberstam challenges the common conversation on labels such as lesbian and gay and rather promotes de-essentializing these frameworks through conversations about sexual practices and erotic desires which, as they note, "destabilizes other hierarchical structures of difference sustained by the homosexual/heterosexual binary system" (p. 114). Transgender activists/scholars in the early 1990s sought to locate terminology for the violence they experience within and through the cis-gender-conforming lesbian and gay community and furthermore the privilege experienced by queer people who adhered to heterosexual gender relations within the queer community (e.g., butch with femme).

From that time, trans and gender-nonconforming activists and scholars played an integral role in advancing the articulations of homonormativity in the LGBT community (e.g., Denny, 2006; Johnson, 2013; Minter, 2006; Stryker, 2008). Inaugural in the communication field, West (2013) correlated the normalization of citizenship in the LGBT community with transgender performativities. West directs scholars to resist settling for a simplistic reading of normative constructs by exploring transgender-mediated depictions as trans lives are assimilated into mainstream popularity. Admittedly, the capacity to slip into homonormative consequences is ever present. Nevertheless, West challenges theorists in their applications of homonormativity to be careful not to "undersell the queer potential and *queering* critiques present in the modes of trans depictions" (p. 177). In the early 21st century, trans scholars connected workings of homonormativity with cisheteronormativity, denoting the ways in which mainstream lesbian/gay political agendas and discursive constructs advance cisgenderism and cisheteronormativity (Chevrette & Eguchi, 2020; Eguchi & Kimura, 2021; LeMaster, 2015, 2017, 2020; LeMaster & Stephenson, 2021; Vitulli, 2010). Through their challenging relationship with homonormativity in the LGBT community, transgender activists/scholars laid the groundwork for challenging the heteronormative, racist, and hegemonic politics enacted and empowered by the cisgender and transphobic LGBQ community. Homonormativity grew its theoretical roots here.

Defining homonormativity, while necessary for academic endeavors and understandings, is problematic in nature. Defining the practices of sexual identities lays the groundwork for power structures within sexuality, sexual acts, and sexual practices. Thus, defining homonormativity, like defining homosexuality, lesbian, gay, transgender, bisexual, straight, or any other sexual identity, serves as a binary sounding board for power constructs. Historian Regina Kunzel (2018) articulates, "It was not until well into the twentieth century that people regularly identified themselves using the vocabularies of LGBT's component parts" (p. 1564). Through her brilliant work on LGBT activism coinciding with prison culture and prison sexual politics, Kunzel (2002, 2008) explains that what is and is not quintessentially homosexual was defined not necessarily by prisoners' sexual acts but more so through the regulation of prisoners' sexual identities. Her instrumental work on mapping sexuality and sexual practices within prisons is monumental in orientating homonormativity. Kunzel (2008) charts the relationship between gay activists and prisoner sexuality, demonstrating the need for clarifying who is "really gay," denoting that homosexuality or same-sex desire/sexual practice is more a rhetorical practice than a sexual truism. Stated in Kunzel's (2008) own words here,

> Sexual practices observed in prison unsettled the public's convictions about "true" homosexuality; inevitably, and potentially more catastrophically, they called true

heterosexuality into question as well. Revealing that the border between homosexuality and heterosexuality was slippery and permeable, prison sexuality suggested that desire and even sexual subject positions were fleeting and unstable, produced at particular moments, in particular circumstances, rather than inherent in the psyche or the body. (p. 265)

Through her work on the instability of sexuality, Kunzel demonstrates a cultural demand for definitive lines of sexual identities. Furthermore, the orientation of homonormativity is realized by defining sexual identity in order to control what is and is not homosexuality and thus heterosexuality. These normative rhetorical practices formulate the hegemonic relationship to sexuality. The origins of homonormativity are tracked through the thick terrain of binary gender definitions, performances in relationship to sexuality/sexual identities, and the co-creation, with other cultural isms, of normative restraints to sexuality that manufacture binary lines defining what was and was not "purely gay." Overall, Kunzel (2002) clarifies that homonormativity is more a discursive maneuver manufactured for social control than really dependent on sexual acts and sexual desires.

Coined by Duggan (2002), "new homonormativity" grew in scholastic popularity and is predominately the homonormativity widely discussed in the early 21st century. Duggan (2002) expanded homonormativity into a theoretical construct by laying claim that "neoliberalism in fact *has* sexual politics" which locates sexuality and sexual politics in a cultural spectrum of consumerism, privatization, and consumption (p. 177). In doing so, Duggan's new homonormativity demonstrates a means by which LGBT and gender-marginalized people access power by neutralizing their difference. Duggan (2002) clarifies, the new homonormativity

> is a politics that does not contest dominant heteronormative assumptions and institutions but upholds and sustains them while promising the possibility of a demobilized gay constituency and a privatized, depoliticized gay culture anchored in domesticity and consumption. (p. 179)

Said differently, Robinson (2016) states, "Sexually marginalized individuals can stake a claim for their rights through asserting that gay and lesbian individuals are just like their heterosexual counterparts, except for their same-sex attractions and partnerships" (p. 1). Duggan's new homonormativity provided a theoretical landscape for scholars to locate the workings of heteronormativity enacted within the LGBTQ community.

From here, homonormativity expanded into multiple fields of study and grew into a theoretical cornerstone in sexuality research. Ng (2013) took homonormativity into the communication field through a discursive analysis of mediated queer aesthetics, termed "gaystreaming." Andersson (2019) brought homonormativity from "not just politics, but also an aesthetic" (p. 2). He asserts, "Homonormativity does not necessarily mean desexualisation or assimilation into heterosexual kinship structures, but instead refers to the abandonment of progressive alliance in favor of… gentrified practices" (p. 4). Like West's (2013) nudge, Brown (2009, 2012; Browne et al., 2021) critiques the all-encompassing theoretical application of homonormativity to homogenize lesbian and gay people. While this premise is debatable, the logic in which Brown constructs his claim lays a foundation to move new homonormativity toward an aesthetic of homonormativity that expands articulations of homonormativity from political agendas to performative embodiments.

In sum, homonormativity is a discursive and embodied practice, or set of practices, by sexual minorities and aligns with and reinforces power constructs. The transitions from macro-orientations (political strategies/movements) to microstructures (aesthetics/embodied performances) of homonormativity are arguably best located within the communication studies field. The remainder of this article details four trajectories homonormativity through the contributions of communication studies and the directions these academic ideas take homonormativity. The four trajectories are as follows: intersectional homonormativity, homonormative whiteness, transnational homonormativity, and homonormative possibilities. Certainly, these four trajectories are not mutually exclusive, but they uniquely equip homonormativity and therefore must be detailed individually.

EMBODIED HOMONORMATIVITY AND INTERSECTIONAL HOMONORMATIVITY

Homonormativity cannot be understood outside the politics of the body. However, the research on homonormativity did not begin here. Moving homonormativity toward the body and discursive realms challenges linear compositions of homonormative analysis and binary articulations of homo/hetero. While the roots for homonormativity did not originate from an enfleshed politic, homonormative scholarship to date moves toward an incorporation of embodied politics. Yep (2017) claims, "The current version of homonormativity—with its accompanying and mutually constituting raced, classed, gendered, and bodily assumptions—continues to reify the structures of heteronormativity in sexual minority communities" (p. 117). Correlating the body with homonormativity contextualized the intersectional relationship(s) that LGBT people manage/maintain with their cultural normalization, and enactment(s) of racism, classism, xenophobia, cisnormativity, and body normativity.

Integration of the body requires that queer scholarship take an intersectional approach to homonormativity. The feminists of color theory, intersectionality, is certainly a foundational aspect to all cultural research in the early 21st century. (For more on intersectionality, see Calafell et al., 2020; Collins & Bilge, 2020; Combahee River Collective, 1983; Crenshaw, 1991; Moraga & Anzaldúa, 2015; Yep, 2010, 2016; Yep & Lescure, 2019). However, past research on homonormativity did not incorporate intersectionality, resulting in linear findings of homonormativity, whitening homonormativity, and essentializing U.S. queer politics. The research of the 21st century has made homonormativity inseparable from an intersectional approach. If, in fact, homonormativity locates itself on and through queer bodies, then theoretical applications must come from an intersectional homonormative perspective. These queer bodies include multiplex skin colors/races/ethnicities, diverse national origins/citizenships, various shapes/sizes, multiple gender orientations, and different classes, which all compound to produce different principles of homonormativity. Approaching homonormativity from any starting point except embodied intersectionality removes the full spectrum of its functions.

Queer communication scholars push homonormativity toward intersections of immigration politics (Chávez, 2017), cissexism and gender normativities (Eguchi, 2009; Johnson, 2013; LeMaster, 2015; Yep & Elia, 2012), transgender politics (LeMaster & Stephenson, 2021;

Moreira, 2020), racial politics and racism (Eguchi, 2019a, 2019b; McIntosh, 2020; Yep & Elia, 2012), body normativities (LeMaster et al., 2020), sexuality and bisexuality (Johnson & Calafell, 2019), ability politics and ableism (Moreman & Briones, 2018), and transnational politics (Chuang, 2020; Eguchi, 2014, 2019b; Moreira, 2020). While certainly this intersectional list is not exhaustive, it can and should be more robust. Unearthing the matrix of homonormative power principles demands an examination of enfleshed, performative natures. Homonormativity grounds itself within and through queer bodies. The exhaustive and empowering process of locating intersectional intricacies unlocks the power to dismantle sexual normatives.

RACE, RACISM, AND HOMONORMATIVE WHITENESS

Ferguson's (2005) "Race-ing Homonormativity" first correlated race and racism to homonormativity. For Ferguson, the privatization of homo-erotic practices and desires is a heteronormative move that centers on racist and classist agendas. He states, "Regulating homosexual difference in order to claim coherence as a public citizen is part of the homonormative subject's entrance into racial privilege" (p. 61). A key connection that Ferguson (2005) makes is

> that regulation is part of the racialized regimes of American citizenship. In other words, the appeal to gender and sexual normativity by gays and lesbian in this moment, inevitably, operates as a mode to state identification that promotes racial exclusion. (p. 61)

Ferguson augments these claims of racial privilege and exclusion through discourses on gay rights movements for rights to marriage, hate crime protection, and military inclusion (pp. 61–65). Homonormativity, here, is defined less by political agendas and more by *how* these gay rights are accomplished through a discourse of erasure and assimilation into White middle-class heteronormative identities (Cervulle, 2008). Cervulle's (2008) framing of "universal homosexuality" explicates racist discursive motivations and implicates the erasure of difference as an acquisition of power. Cervulle (2008) defines universal homosexuality as the following:

> This universal homosexuality rests obviously on Enlightenment rhetoric, a kind of normalization project in and of itself inasmuch as it erases the differences among homosexuals, therefore assuming all homosexuals to be equal in conditions, oppressions, and struggle. This minority version of the abstract French universal Republican model tends, as it still so relentlessly does, to wipe out race, class, and gender power differentials to the advantage of a normalized white male middleclass model of homosexuality. (p. 174)

While trans scholars make substantial ground complicating the binary understandings of gender and sexuality within LGBT communities, Cervulle and Ferguson simultaneously articulate the discursive workings of normalizing the universal homosexual and the ripple effects of removing difference on intersectional identities within sexually marginalized groups. Imperative here is the relationship to homonormativity and erasure of difference as a means "to wipe out race, class and gender power differentials to the advantage of a normalized white male middleclass model of homosexuality" (p. 174). The erasure of difference is critical to how sexually marginalized individuals as a community acquired power through racism, sexism, and classism. Homonormativity, then, is dependent on workings of whiteness to acquire power. While much work in communication studies examines the intersection of race, sexuality, and class (Abdi & Calafell, 2017; Abdi & Van Gilder, 2016; Eguchi & Roberts, 2015; Eguchi & Washington, 2016; Eguchi et al., 2014; McCune, 2015; Yep & Elia, 2012), the relationship between homonormativity and race remains a less examined area in this field. More than a decade later, Yep and Elia's (2012) work remains an inaugural piece to unpack the relationship between homonormativity and the intersectional workings of racism.

The normalization of a "universal white gay" propelled sexually marginalized people to acquire power by propitiating racism, sexism, and classism. Similar to the relationship that Jews have to the acquisition of whiteness, normalizing White gay men into whiteness perpetuates White elitism and strengthens whiteness. For example, in the 1920–1930s, the need to expand the White majority became necessary (see Brodkin, 2012). In response, the Jews and other Euroethnics became accepted into the White working class in the United States (pp. 50–52). In the process, this more inclusive version of whiteness expanded the number of individuals who access economic power and in turn expanded the White majority and strengthened whiteness. Similarly, whites and whiteness gain power through normalizing the "white gay man." Cervulle's (2008) "universal homosexuality" is the groundwork for homonormative whiteness. Calling scholars and activists to locate the intersectional workings of race, racism, and other identity constructs empowered through the normalization of White bourgeois gay men. Ferguson (2005) suggested that one way to understand homonormative formations "is to explore the ways in which the formation of homonormative subjectivities and social relations names homosexuality's entrance into white supremacy" (p. 65). Thus, homonormative whiteness is perhaps the key direction that scholarship must go to unearth the power formations of homonormativity.

The research correlating whiteness and homonormativity is growing but remains bleak. Some key pieces worth noting here are King (2009), Eguchi (2019a), Hinkson (2021), and McIntosh (2019). First, King (2009) examines the intersectional workings of race, class, and sexuality. King outlines the workings of whiteness to remove the racial acknowledgement of Swoop's coming-out interview. King denotes the dynamic relationship that homonormativity plays in constructing White individualism and consumer culture. Furthermore, Black lesbianism is neutralized as a means to centralize White queer bodies rather than destabilize queerness through racial critiques. Building from here, Eguchi's scholarship exposes the intersections of whiteness, race, and sexuality (see Eguchi, 2019a, 2019b, 2020a; 2020b; Eguchi et al., 2018). In regard to homonormativity and whiteness in particular, Eguchi's (2019a) piece details how the queer Asian American man Peter Le is performatively framed as "almost White," acquiring homonormative power through the framings of an idealized gay jock persona and the acquisition of whiteness while subsequently projecting his muscular gay Asian body as forever foreign to the White homonormative gaze (pp. 35–39). Eguchi demonstrates the strategic functions of whiteness to performatively position homonormative desire as intrinsically White.

Through a quantitative analysis, Hinkson (2021) details an investment of whiteness within the LGBT community to access U.S. political gains for the gay rights movement. Here,

Hinkson assumes homonormativity's direct correlation to whiteness rather than detailing that relationship. Finally, McIntosh's (2019) article coins the term homonormative whiteness, claiming that "homonormativity is always driven by ideologies of whiteness, but I find using this theoretical coupling of White homonormativity reminds readers, and myself, of the specific workings of whiteness in and through homonormativity" (p. 119). Her piece outlines the functions of White homonormativity enacted and embodied by White gay cowboys and White lesbian cowgirls to authenticate and qualify the queer rodeo community. McIntosh's work extends the research on homonormativity by connecting international/national landscapes to the lived experiences of bodies. Responding to Brown's (2012) critique of homonormativity scholarship only examining visible representations on grand scales, McIntosh's critical performance ethnographically delves into micro-heteronormative embodied moments and the enfleshed violence experienced from these performances. Despite McIntosh's piece, Brown's critique continues to stand true. There remains a lack of scholarship on everyday, lived, embodied norms of homonormativity, unveiling how the embodied intricacies of White homonormativity beg to be rendered.

HOMO-COLONIALISM AND TRANSNATIONAL HOMONORMATIVITY

In response to the September 11th attacks, Puar (2018) articulates a realm of U.S. exceptionalism in relationship to sexual exceptionalism, which she terms *homonationalism* (p. 2). Puar claims, "This brand of homosexuality operates as a regulatory script not only of normative gayness, queerness, or homosexuality, but also of the racial and national norms that reinforce these sexual subjects" (p. 2). Important to her project, Puar lays bare the intersectional identity constructs of race, class, and nationality in relationship to queer/homosexual frameworks. Puar then connects these identities with a U.S. imperial political agenda. In her later work, Puar (2013) clarifies that homonationalism is "neither identity or political position" (p. 337), a provocative claim that challenged the connections between homonationalism, identity, and political agendas from her earlier work. Puar claims that homonationalism is "instead the historical convergence of state practices, transnational circuits of queer commodity culture and human rights paradigms, and broader global phenomena such as the increasing entrenchment of Islamophobia" (p. 337). Like homonormativity, homonationalism does not identify "good" gays and "bad" gays but rather constructs a map of how homonormativity and U.S. elitism conflate to exhibit the marginalizing effects of hegemonic power. Puar's homonationalism manifests an extensive area of scholarship, but this piece notes homonationalism as a historical tail of homonormativity's correlation to national imagery, nationalism, and transnationality.

At its very foundation, homonormativity is rooted in a macro spatial relationship to power and nationality. For example, Duggan's (2002) work looks at the landscape of U.S. LGBT political organizations, whereas Puar's (2018) piece examines the orientalism and terrorist discursive framings of non-Western queer embodiments. Homonormativity is vastly grounded in the understanding of queer bodies in relationship to nationalism, transnationalism, and xenophobia. Colonial/settler practices in relationship to sexuality certainly maintain power through whiteness and Western nations' normatives that assume both sexual elitism and hetero and homo enlightenment. Thus, homonormativity in connection to national and transnational politics centers on U.S. exceptionalism. The correlation between race, racism, and homonormativity is intricately tied to White national elitism. This correlation between homonormativity and colonizing nation/states perhaps is best understood as homo-colonialism (see Kehl, 2020; Rahman, 2014), in which research extrapolates the intersectional workings of colonialism and the neoliberal politics of sexual minorities. Not surprisingly, the landscape of homo-colonialism grounds itself in White nation/states (e.g., South Africa, European countries, Canada, and the USA; McIntosh, 2019).

U.S. conversations on immigration politics and global economic concerns prove that transnational homonormativity remains a pertinent and demanding topic of exploration for queer scholarship. Chávez is certainly one of the most prominent scholars in the area of homonationalism (see Aiello et al., 2013; Chávez, 2013, 2015, 2017, 2010). Chávez (2015) exposes the violence of homonationalism and the importance of investigating the intersections of nationalism, Western normativity, and transnational politics. Morrissey's (2013) work on DREAMers rhetoric provides a beautiful example of queer citizenship tactics and survival techniques against White U.S. heterosexual citizenship. For Chávez (2017), mainstream movements for gay and lesbian rights must highlight the role that citizenship and immigration play in LGBTQ people's lives. In her own words, "Anything else is nothing less than homonormative violence" (p. 134).

Eguchi leads the field in transnational homonormative scholarship, in which they critique centralized notions of Western, White, cisgender, queer masculinity (see Eguchi, 2019a, 2014, 2015, 2016, 2020b). Calafell (2017a, 2017b) exposes the violence of U.S. imperialism on queerness. Other leading scholarship in queer intercultural communication in transnational homonormativity is Asante's (2019) research that details the dichotomous embodiments of queer African being and belonging, accomplished through the totalization of queer African experiences as perpetual victims because of the homonationalist discourse of U.S. exceptionalism. Moreira's (2020) scholarship on transfeminismo explores the intersectional workings of Western, whitened, feminist theories, denoting the importance in transnational queer theory development to move queer scholarship beyond the boundaries of queer Western academic binary modes. Additionally, Atay (2021) exposes the dismantling possibilities of homonormativity when taking a queer transnational focus. Finally, Chuang's (2020) personal transnational queer/qu-er/kuer reflective essay beautifully exposes the fluidity of transnational queer bodies and the deconstructive, disidentificatory possibilities they occupy.

While scholarship on transnational homonormativity spans across disciplines and continues to grow, it remains sparse. Queer transnational scholars challenge the Western centrality to queer intercultural scholarship (Chávez, 2013; Eguchi, 2015; Eguchi & Asante, 2016), calling for queer intercultural scholars "to show the profound ways through which those with non-Western racialized, gendered, and sexual identities challenge, resist, and enact their identities within/across the boundaries of the nation" (Asante, 2019, p. 159). Atay (2021) adds,

> even though some progress has been made in terms of queering our discipline, queer studies has unfortunately not made a meaningful impact on our field, at least not as much as critical cultural, transnational, postcolonial, and decolonial scholars want to see. (p. 1)

Atay's critique echoes the resounding lack of transnational homonormative research present in the field. Transnational homonormativity demonstrates the way that queer politics, global gay elitist performatives, and U.S. queer exceptionalism must be addressed when doing work on homonormativity. Yep and colleagues (2020) claim that "heteronormativity, nationalism, and orientalism constitute the bedrocks of hegemonic sexuality as grounding the understanding and meaning in which sexualities are considered to be 'deviant' or 'normal'" (p. 31). Thus, I conclude here by claiming that new work on homonormativity must move toward transnational homonormativity, or, quite frankly, it is simply homonormative at its core.

DECONSTRUCTING HOMONORMATIVITY AND HOMONORMATIVE POSSIBILITIES

In many respects, homonormativity is a dismal mark on queer world-making. Homonormativity transposes gay and lesbian communities and movements into spaces of intersecting racism, classism, cissexism, transphobia, and xenophobia. While the areas of research previously noted locate the workings of homonormativity, another direction for homonormative research and application is deconstructing it. While much of the previous research may be deconstructive in nature, this article calls specific attention to the research that seeks active deconstruction of homonormativity by exposing something more, something dawning, something queering. Duggan and Muñoz (2009) remind us that "these bad sentiments can signal the capacity to transcend hopelessness" (p. 176). Muñoz (2019) denotes that queer failure is the antithesis of normative or straight time. His gesture toward failure here is more about intentional failure rather than homonormative flops, but the sentiment remains. McIntosh and Hobson (2013) inform scholars and activists of the exponential possibilities hidden within reflexive failures. Deconstructing homonormativity begins to unveil these potentials.

Muñoz's (1999) work on disidentification and queer utopia remains one of the foundational theoretical tools for deconstructing homonormativity. Deconstructing homonormativity is not about locating it and articulating the hegemonic workings. Rather, deconstruction is the actual process of locating spaces, bodies, discourses, performances, and texts that tear into homonormativity and expose the slight glimmer of light that shines through queer futurities or homonormative possibilities. Some early examples of work that deconstructs homonormativity and envisioning queer potentialities are Holmes (2009), Carter (2009), and Riggs and Due (2013). Each of these pieces deconstructs homonormativity in literature, legal rulings, and pedagogy. Eguchi (2014) performatively deconstructs White gay normativity through an autoethnographic exploration of their queer transnational realms of desire. Overall, early scholarship in deconstructing homonormativity demonstrates that deconstruction must not only outline the strategies of homonormativity but furthermore expose texts, discourses, performatives, or embodiments that challenge homonormative binds.

The communication field brings the deconstruction of homonormativity one step further into queer homonormative possibilities or queer futurities. Moreman and Briones (2018) detail the queer world-making and homonormative deconstructions embodied by Deaf Queer possibilities. The authors articulate the embodiments of Deaf Queers, demonstrating how

Deaf Queers reject homonormativity and conclude with how Deaf Queer world-making gesture to something outside of heteronormative, homonormative, and hearing normatives. Eguchi and colleagues (2018) offer a rhetorical analysis of a reality TV show that not only offers a deconstruction of homonormative dominant projections of Black queer masculinity but also moves beyond deconstruction toward "some fleeting moments of transgression from dominant scripts of queerness" where Black masculinity's hegemonic narratives are challenged (p. 181). Building here, Moreman (2019) offers a deconstruction of homonormativity from both methodological practice and content. Moreman performatively scripts on the page a Latinx contextual embodied complexity that denotes a yearning for an example of sexuality outside of White homonormative explanations. Additionally, Moreman (2020) provides an account of methodological practices that deconstruct homonormativity through queer Latinx memory and queer youth literature. Finally, McIntosh's (2019) critical performance ethnography of the International Gay Rodeo Association (IGRA) deconstructs homonormativity at the intersections of neocolonialism, racism, cissexism, and transphobia. McIntosh concludes by decolonizing Western White queer cowboys through an examination of a Black gay cowboy, Dannie. McIntosh details the quare aesthetics that deconstruct the White neocolonial, cisnormative, homonormative space. She claims, "Daniella's participation in the IGRA nudges a thinking of *Otherwise*, all the while usurping the center by providing a racialized sexual performance unbound by U.S. White, lesbian homonormative constraints" (p. 133). McIntosh demonstrates the communication field's investment not to simply deconstruct but to demonstrate the presence of queer futurities that exist outside of homonormativity and to detail the possibilities that these embodiments provide.

CONCLUSION

Homonormativity is a complex and ever-evolving theory of sexual normativity. This article began by defining homonormativity. It then provided four trajectories of homonormativity broadly and the contributions that communication studies specifically has made to homonormativity. Robinson (2016) stakes the claim that homonormativity is a practice solely connected to those within the LGBT communities. This article challenges this position by noting the need for a more complex intersectional, whiteness, and transnational reading of homonormativity. Intersectional homonormativity demands more from scholars on homonormativity, shedding light on the plethora of intersectional aspects of homonormativity that remain unexamined. Homonormative whiteness sheds light on the powerful role that racism plays in projecting sexuality and sexual marginalization. Queer intercultural communication scholars must unveil the coupled power entities of homonormativity and whiteness. Additionally, the piece clarifies that homonormativity must move toward transnational homonormative examinations or else it will remain homonormative at its core. Perhaps the most momentous contribution that communication studies can offer homonormativity is the scholarship foci of deconstructing homonormativity and homonormative possibilities.

Undeniably, the era of new homonormativity has arrived. In this era, "the process of assimilating and blending into the U.S. heteronormative mainstream produces docile and depoliticized gay-bodies and identities that are more interested in consumption and domesticity than politics" (Yep & Elia, 2012, p. 849). The scholarship detailed here serves as a starting point for homonormativity. Each trajectory of homonormativity detailed here concludes with more questions than answers, but that is the nature of academic exploration. Thus, this piece concludes by challenging scholars and activists to action. Homonormativity dawns each day into something greater. Scholars must locate the workings of homonormative power, deconstruct its intersectional transnational embodiments of whiteness, and unveil the possibilities in those lived experiences deconstructing it.

FURTHER READING

Atay, A. (2019). Defining transnational queer media and popular culture. *Queer Studies in Media & Popular Culture, 4*(3), 233–239.

Eguchi, S., & Calafell, B. (Eds.). (2019). *Queer intercultural communication: The intersectional politics of belonging in and across differences*. Rowman & Littlefield.

Johnson, E. P., Henderson, M. G., Holland, S. P., & Cohen, C. J. (2005). *Black queer studies: A critical anthology*. Duke University Press.

Kunzel, R. (2022). *Criminal intimacy*. University of Chicago Press.

Nakayama, T. K., & Krizek, R. L. (1995). Whiteness: A strategic rhetoric. *Quarterly Journal of Speech, 81*(3), 291–309.

Yep, G. A. (2010). Toward the de-subjugation of racially marked knowledges in communication. *Southern Communication Journal, 75*(2), 171–175.

REFERENCES

Abdi, S., & Calafell, B. M. (2017). Queer utopias and a (feminist) Iranian vampire: A critical analysis of resistive monstrosity in *A Girl Walks Home Alone at Night*. *Critical Studies in Media Communication, 34*(4), 358–370.

Abdi, S., & Van Gilder, B. (2016). Cultural (in) visibility and identity dissonance: Queer Iranian-American women and their negotiation of existence. *Journal of International and Intercultural Communication, 9*(1), 69–86.

Aiello, G., Bakshi, S., Bilge, S., Hall, L. K., Johnston, L., Pérez, K., & Chávez, K. (2013). Here, and not yet here: A dialogue at the intersection of queer, trans, and culture. *Journal of International and Intercultural Communication, 6*(2), 96–117.

Andersson, J. (2019). Homonormative aesthetics: AIDS and 'de-generational unremembering'in 1990s London. *Urban Studies, 56*(14), 2993–3010.

Asante, G. (2019). "Queerly ambivalent": Navigating global and local normativities in postcolonial Ghana. In S. Eguchi & B. M. Calafell (Eds.), *Queer intercultural communication: The intersectional politics of belonging in and across difference* (pp. 157–176). Rowman & Littlefield.

Atay, A. (2021). Charting the future of queer studies in communication and critical/cultural studies: New directions and pathways. *Communication and Critical/Cultural Studies*, 1–5.

Brodkin, K. (2012). How Jews became white folks. In P. S. Rothenberg (Ed). *White privilege: Essential reading on the other side of racism* (pp. 45–57). Worth Publishers.

Brown, G. (2009). Thinking beyond homonormativity: Performative explorations of diverse gay economies. *Environment and Planning A, 41*(6), 1496–1510.

Brown, G. (2012). Homonormativity: A metropolitan concept that denigrates "ordinary" gay lives. *Journal of Homosexuality, 59*(7), 1065–1072.

Browne, K., Brown, G., & Catherine, J. N. (2021). Geography and sexuality II: Homonormativity and heteroactivism. *Progress in Human Geography*.

Calafell, B. M. (2017a). Brown queer bodies. *Qualitative Inquiry, 23*(7), 511–512.

Calafell, B. M. (2017b). Brownness, kissing, and US imperialism: Contextualizing the Orlando massacre. *Communication and Critical/Cultural Studies, 14*(2), 198–202.

Calafell, B. M., Eguchi, S., & Abdi, S. (2020). De-whitening intersectionality in intercultural communication. In S. Eguchi, B. M. Calafell, & S. Abdi (Eds.), *De-whitening intersectionality: Race, intercultural communication, and politics* (pp. xvii–xxvii).

Carter, J. (2009). Gay marriage and pulp fiction: Homonormativity, disidentification, and affect in Ann Bannon's lesbian novels. *GLQ: A Journal of Lesbian and Gay Studies, 15*(4), 583–609.

Cervulle, M. (2008). French homonormativity and the commodification of the Arab body. *Radical History Review, 2008*(100), 171–179.

Chávez, K. R. (2010). Border (in) securities: Normative and differential belonging in LGBTQ and immigrant rights discourse. *Communication and Critical/Cultural Studies, 7*(2), 136–155.

Chávez, K. R. (2013). Pushing boundaries: Queer intercultural communication. *Journal of International and Intercultural Communication, 6*(2), 83–95.

Chávez, K. R. (2015). The precariousness of homonationalism: The queer agency of terrorism in post-9/11 rhetoric. *QED: A Journal in LGBTQ Worldmaking, 2*(3), 32–58.

Chávez, K. R. (2017). Homonormativity and violence against immigrants. *QED: A Journal in LGBTQ Worldmaking, 4*(2), 131–136.

Chevrette, R., & Eguchi, S. (2020). "We don't see LGBTQ differences": Cisheteronormativity and concealing phobias and irrational fears behind rhetorics of acceptance. *QED: A Journal in LGBTQ Worldmaking, 7*(1), 55–59.

Chuang, A. K. (2020). A local gay man/Tongzhi or a transnational queer/qu-er/kuer: (Re)organizing my queerness and Asianness through personal reflection. In S. Eguchi, B. M. Calafell, & S. Abdi (Eds.), *De-whitening intersectionality: Race, intercultural communication and politics* (pp. 101–118). Lexington Books.

Collins, P. H., & Bilge, S. (2020). *Intersectionality*. John Wiley & Sons.

Combahee River Collective. (1983). The Combahee River Collective statement. *Home Girls: A Black Feminist Anthology, 1*, 264–274.

Crenshaw, K. (1991). Mapping the margins: Intersectionality, identity politics, and violence against women of color. *Stanford Law Review, 43*, 1241.

Riggs, D. W., & Due, C. (2013). Moving beyond homonormativity in teacher training: Experiences from South Australia. *Sex Education, 13*(Suppl. 1), S99–S112.

Denny, D. (2006). Transgender communities of the United States in the late twentieth century. In P. Currah, R. M. Juang, & S. P. Minter (Eds.), *Transgender rights* (pp. 171–191). University of Minnesota Press.

Duggan, L. (2002). The new homonormativity: The sexual politics of neoliberalism. In R. Castronovo & D. D. Nelson (Eds.), *Materializing democracy: Towards revitalized racial politics* (pp. 175–194). Duke University Press.

Duggan, L., & Muñoz, J. E. (2009). Hope and hopelessness: A dialogue. *Women & Performance, 19*(2), 275–283. https://www.tandfonline.com/doi/full/10.1080/07407700903064946

Eguchi, S. (2009). Negotiating hegemonic masculinity: The rhetorical strategy of "straight-acting" among gay men. *Journal of Intercultural Communication Research, 38*(3), 193–209.

Eguchi, S. (2014). Ongoing cross-national identity transformation: Living on the queer Japan-US transnational borderland. *Sexuality & Culture, 18*(4), 977–993.

Eguchi, S. (2015). Queer intercultural relationality: An autoethnography of Asian–Black (dis) connections in white gay America. *Journal of International and Intercultural Communication, 8*(1), 27–43.

Eguchi, S. (2016). The Orlando Pulse massacre: A transnational Japanese queer response. *QED: A Journal in LGBTQ Worldmaking, 3*(3), 164–167.

Eguchi, S. (2019a). Queerness as strategic whiteness: A queer Asian American critique of Peter Le. In *Interrogating the communicative power of whiteness* (pp. 29–45). Routledge.

Eguchi, S. (2019b). Transnational LGBTQ pride: Whiteness, health, and welling in Viceland's Gaycation. *China Media Research*, 15(3).

Eguchi, S. (2020a). A transnational queer of color vision: Toward the "future" of autoethnography. *Journal of Autoethnography*, 1(3), 309–314.

Eguchi, S. (2020b). Sticky rice politics: Impossible possibilities of queerness in and across *Yellow Fever* and *Front Cover*. *Women's Studies in Communication*, 43(1), 67–84.

Eguchi, S., & Asante, G. (2016). Disidentifications revisited: Queer(y)ing intercultural communication theory. *Communication Theory*, 26(2), 171–189.

Eguchi, S., Calafell, B. M., & Files-Thompson, N. (2014). Intersectionality and quare theory: Fantasizing African American male same-sex relationships in *Noah's Arc: Jumping the broom*. *Communication, Culture & Critique*, 7(3), 371–389.

Eguchi, S., Files-Thompson, N., & Calafell, B. M. (2018). Queer (of color) aesthetics: Fleeting moments of transgression in VH1's *Love & Hip-Hop: Hollywood* Season 2. *Critical Studies in Media Communication*, 35(2), 180–193.

Eguchi, S., & Kimura, K. (2021). Racialized im/possibilities: Intersectional queer-of-color critique on Japaneseness in Netflix's *Queer Eye: We're in Japan! Journal of International and Intercultural Communication*, 14(3), 221–239.

Eguchi, S., & Roberts, M. N. (2015). Gay rapping and possibilities: A quare reading of "Throw that Boy P***y". *Text and Performance Quarterly*, 35(2–3), 142–157.

Eguchi, S., & Washington, M. S. (2016). Race-ing queerness: Normative intimacies in LOGO's *DTLA*. *Journal of Communication Inquiry*, 40(4), 408–423.

Ferguson, R. A. (2005). Race-ing homonormativity: Citizenship, sociology, and gay identity. In *Black queer studies* (pp. 52–67). Duke University Press.

Halberstam, J. (1998). *Female masculinity*. Duke University Press.

Hinkson, K. (2021). The colorblind rainbow: Whiteness in the gay rights movement. *Journal of Homosexuality*, 68(9), 1393–1416.

Holmes, C. (2009). Destabilizing homonormativity and the public/private dichotomy in North American lesbian domestic violence discourses. *Gender, Place & Culture*, 16(1), 77–95.

Johnson, J. A., & Calafell, B. M. (2019). Disrupting public pedagogies of bisexuality. In A. Atay, & S. L. Pensoneau-Conway (Eds.), *Queer communication pedagogy* (pp. 62–72). Routledge.

Johnson, J. R. (2013). Cisgender privilege, intersectionality, and the criminalization of CeCe McDonald: Why intercultural communication needs transgender studies. *Journal of International and Intercultural Communication*, 6(2), 135–144.

Kehl, K. (2020). Homonationalism revisited. *lambda nordica*, 25(2), 17–38.

King, S. (2009). Homonormativity and the politics of race: Reading Sheryl Swoopes. *Journal of Lesbian Studies*, 13(3), 272–290.

Kunzel, R. (2002). Situating sex. *GLQ*, 8(3), 253–270.

Kunzel, R. (2008). Lessons in being gay: Queer encounters in gay and lesbian prison activism. *Radical History Review*, 2008(100), 11–37.

Kunzel, R. (2018). The power of queer history. *The American Historical Review*, 123(5), 1560–1582.

LeMaster, L. (2015). Discontents of being and becoming fabulous on *RuPaul's Drag U* Queer criticism in neoliberal times. *Women's Studies in Communication*, 38(2), 167–186.

LeMaster, L. (2017). Notes on trans relationality. *QED: A Journal in LGBTQ Worldmaking*, 4(2), 84–92.

LeMaster, L. (2020). Notes on some especially (not so) subtle dissatisfactions. *QED: A Journal in LGBTQ Worldmaking*, 7(1), 75–82.

LeMaster, L., Johnson, A., & Olzman, M. (2020). What are you? In S. Eguchi, B. M. Calafell & S. Abdi (Eds.), *De-whitening intersectionality: Race, intercultural communication, and politics* (p. 119). Lexington Books.

LeMaster, L., & Stephenson, M. (2021). Trans (gender) trouble. *Communication and Critical/Cultural Studies, 18*(2), 190–195.

McCune, J. Q., Jr. (2015). The queerness of blackness. *QED: A Journal in LGBTQ Worldmaking, 2*(2), 173–176.

McIntosh, D. M. D. (2019). Ain't my first rodeo in homonormative whiteness. In S. Eguchi & B. M. Calafell (Eds.), *Queer intercultural communication: The intersectional politics of belonging in and across differences* (p. 117). Rowman & Littlefield.

McIntosh, D. M. D. (2020). Intersectional assemblages of whiteness. In S. Eguchi, B.M. Calafell & S. Abdi (Eds.), *De-whitening intersectionality: Race, intercultural communication, and politics* (p. 59). Lexington Books.

Minter, S. P. (2006). Do transsexuals dream of gay rights? Getting real about transgender inclusion. In P. Currah, R. M. Juang, & S. P. Minter (Eds.), *Transgender rights* (pp. 141–170). University of Minnesota Press.

McIntosh, D. M. D., & Hobson, K. (2013). Reflexive engagement: A white (queer) women's performance of failures and alliance possibilities. *Liminalities: A Journal of Performance Studies, 9*(4), 1–23.

Moraga, C., & Anzaldúa, G. (Eds.). (2015). *This bridge called my back: Writings by radical women of color.* SUNY Press.

Moreira, R. (2020). De-whitening intersectionality through *Transfeminismo.* In S. Eguchi, B. M. Calafell, & S. Abdi (Eds.), *De-whitening intersectionality: Race, intercultural communication and politics* (pp. 203–222). Lexington Books.

Moreman, S. T. (2019). A queer futurity autofantasía: Contouring discourses of Latinx through memory and queer youth literature. *Text and Performance Quarterly, 39*(3), 185–202.

Moreman, S. T. (2020). Narrative embodiment of Latinx queer futurity: Pause for dramatic affect. In Al Johnson & L. LeMaster (Eds.), *Gender futurity, intersectional autoethnography* (pp. 223–236). Routledge.

Moreman, S. T., & Briones, S. R. (2018). Deaf Queer world-making: A thick intersectional analysis of the mediated cultural body. *Journal of International and Intercultural Communication, 11*(3), 216–232.

Morrissey, M. E. (2013). A DREAM disrupted: Undocumented migrant youth disidentifications with US citizenship. *Journal of International and Intercultural Communication, 6*(2), 145–162.

Muñoz, J. E. (1999). *Disidentifications: Queers of color and the performance of politics* (Vol. 2). University of Minnesota Press.

Muñoz, J. E. (2019). *Cruising utopia.* New York University Press.

Ng, E. (2013). A "post-gay" era? Media gaystreaming, homonormativity, and the politics of LGBT integration. *Communication, Culture & Critique, 6*(2), 258–283.

Puar, J. (2013). Rethinking homonationalism. *International Journal of Middle East Studies, 45*(2), 336–339.

Puar, J. K. (2018). *Terrorist assemblages.* Duke University Press.

Rich, A. (1980). Compulsory heterosexuality and lesbian existence. *Signs: Journal of Women in Culture and Society, 5*(4), 631–660.

Robinson, B. A. (2016). Heteronormativity and homonormativity. In N. Naples, R. Hoogland, C. Wickramasinghe, W. Maithree, & W. C. Angela (Eds.), *The Wiley Blackwell encyclopedia of gender and sexuality studies* (pp. 1–3). https://doi.org/10.1002/9781118663219.WBEGSS013

Rahman, M. (2014). Queer rights and the triangulation of Western exceptionalism. *Journal of Human Rights, 13*(3), 274-289.

Rosenfeld, D. (2009). Heteronormativity and homonormativity as practical and moral resources: The case of lesbian and gay elders. *Gender & Society, 23*(5), 617–638.

Slagle, R. A. (2003). Queer criticism and sexual normativity: The case of Pee-wee Herman. *Journal of Homosexuality*, 45(2–4), 129–146.

Stryker, S. (2008). Transgender history, homonormativity, and disciplinarity. *Radical History Review, 100*, 144–157.

Vitulli, E. (2010). A defining moment in civil rights history? The Employment Non-Discrimination Act, trans-inclusion, and homonormativity. *Sexuality Research and Social Policy*, 7(3), 155–167.

Warner, M. (1991). Introduction: Fear of a queer planet. *Social Text, 29*, 3–17.

Warner, M. (Ed.). (1993). *Fear of a queer planet: Queer politics and social theory* (Vol. 6). University of Minnesota Press.

West, I. (2013). *Transforming citizenships*. New York University Press.

Yep, G. A. (2003). The violence of heteronormativity in communication studies: Notes on injury, healing, and queer world-making. *Journal of Homosexuality*, 45(2–4), 11–59.

Yep, G. A. (2010). Toward the de-subjugation of racially marked knowledges in communication. *Southern Communication Journal*, 75(2), 171–175.

Yep, G. A. (2016). Toward thick(er) intersectionalities: Theorizing, researching, and activating the complexities of communication and identities. In K. Sorrells & S. Skeimoto (Eds.), *Globalizing intercultural communication: A reader* (pp. 86–94). SAGE.

Yep, G. A. (2017). Further notes on healing from "the violence of heteronormativity in communication studies". *QED: A Journal in LGBTQ Worldmaking*, 4(2), 115–122.

Yep, G. A., Alaoui, F. Z. C., & Lescure, R. (2020). Relationalities in/through difference: Explorations in queer intercultural communication. In S. Eguchi & B. M. Calafell (Eds.), *Queer intercultural communication: The intersectional politics of belonging in and across differences* (pp 19–45). Roman & Littlefield.

Yep, G. A., & Elia, J. P. (2012). Racialized masculinities and the new homonormativity in LOGO's *Noah's Arc. Journal of Homosexuality*, 59(7), 890–911.

Yep, G. A., & Lescure, R. (2019). A thick intersectional approach to microaggressions. *Southern Communication Journal*, 84(2), 113–126.

Yep, G. A., Lescure, R. M., & Russo, S. E. (2019). *Queer intercultural communication*. Oxford Research Encyclopedia of Communication.

Dawn Marie D. McIntosh

QUEER MEMORY

QUEER MEMORIES, NOW AND THEN

Prior to 1980, a scholarly search for the term "queer memory" would have revealed only stray expressions detailing the sometimes curious ways memory works. For example, the phrase "queer memory phenomenon" appears in G. E. Anscombe's 1953 translation of Ludwig Wittgenstein's celebrated monograph *Philosophical Investigations* (Wittgenstein, 1953, passage 342). Therein, Wittgenstein uses the phrase to describe the recollections of a deaf and mute man on his prelinguistic struggle to articulate his thoughts without language, a memory exercise Wittgenstein finds, well, *queer* (p. 342). That Wittgenstein had several male lovers throughout his life might prompt speculation there was some secret meaning to the phrase (Bartley, 1982–1983, pp. 166–167). But on cursory review, it seems that Wittgenstein meant only a memory or remembering process that is "'odd,' 'strange,' or 'curious'" (Wittgenstein, 2009, p. xiii).

Today, by contrast, the phrase "queer memory" describes a burgeoning subfield within queer communication studies that also draws from and references numerous other academic disciplines. Though the words "queer" and "memory" are themselves used with different emphases and meanings that sometimes make murky what we mean by "queer memory," queer memory today can largely be understood as the work to recover, preserve, circulate, and, in some cases, invent the pasts of often intentionally forgotten lesbian, gay, bisexual, transgender, and queer people, institutions, and moments. In doing so, queer memory asks us to consider what the unique opportunities and challenges of remembering by, for, and with queers requires. Or, more simply, in the words of Charles E. Morris, III (2004), queer memory is the "revolution of memory... initiated when public memory and (homo)sexuality collide... in a symbolic contest for the communal meaning of historical identity" (p. 91).

Although the study of queer memory is not exclusive to Communication, its uptake in the field is rich and draws greater attention than in many other disciplines. More specifically, work on queer memory in Communication is found in performance studies and rhetoric, owing in part to performance as an avenue for investigating memory, memory's long-standing relationship to speech-making, and the emergence of public memory studies. Indeed, invocations of queer memory appear prominently in protests, movements, agitation, oratory, archives, and artistic expressions, the very "stuff" that occupies rhetoric and performance studies scholars. In addition, queer memory studies have been conversant with other scholars just outside the discipline in English, composition, writing, women and gender studies, feminism, lesbian and gay studies, and queer theory, each having strong connections to the rhetoric and performance parts of the field.

The intradisciplinary home spaces of queer memory, however, also bring pressing challenges. Most pressing among them: Scholarship in queer memory within Communication is not immune from valid critiques of the oppressive Whiteness of Communication more generally (Chakravarty et al., 2018). Indeed, as we will see, extant queer memory scholarship reveals a disbalanced attention to the memories of White, male, cisgender queers—even as that work actively marks and questions this disbalance itself. Further, with only a few notable exceptions, queer memory scholarship has grappled with issues of geography, nation, and colonialism (among others) in only limited ways. These are challenges the subfield will need to wrestle with urgently in the years to come and may drive major growth in queer memory studies moving forward.

Rhetoric and performance studies' devotion to queer memory is also driven by a real-world exigency—the HIV/AIDS crisis. The crisis's magnitude and political and public health leaders' dispassionate, counterproductive responses amplified the emergence of queer politics, theory, and activism, including among leading Communication scholars. This impetus can be seen in the work of Daniel C. Brouwer (2009, 2011), who asks scholars of Communication not just to remember HIV/AIDS but to consider "how might we animate it, use it, participate in it" (Brouwer, 2012, p. 116). Likewise, Karma Chávez highlights how memory and HIV/AIDS collide at the intersection of border, race, nation, and migration—returning to memory a "modern-day concentration camp" run by the U.S. government for HIV+ Haitian migrants that was "essentially forgotten" (Chávez, 2012, p. 63). These are just two examples of how HIV/AIDS is explored in queer memory in the field.

At the same time, other Communication researchers have shown how HIV/AIDS did not inaugurate queers' reliance on memory. For example, Thomas R. Dunn points to the uses of queer memory as a resource for judicial rhetoric in the trials of Oscar Wilde (Dunn, 2016b, p. 13) and E. Cram considers queer memory as an object of academic inquiry and ambient sentimentality produced in traces of Grace Hebard and Agnes Wergeland's queer material culture (Cram, 2016a, p. 112). In both cases, the memories at hand predate HIV/AIDS by decades, suggesting that while HIV/AIDS was a major accelerant in queer memory's emergence, it was only one of several factors at work in the development of this topic in Communication, factors that still shape its theorization and practice today.

THE EMERGENCE OF QUEER MEMORY

Like all queer subjects, queer memory has a long history of practice that can be traced to individuals and collective acts of remembrance, commemoration, and heritage-building well before academics coined the phrase (Dunn, 2016b, pp. 13–20). As an academic subject, however, the study of queer memory in Communication chiefly represents the confluence of two significant interdisciplinary projects: the study of memory and the emergence of queer theory.

The first of these phenomena is commonly referred to as the "memory boom," an era of cultural and individual interest in the consideration, preservation, and retention of memory, dating from the late 1960s onward. While memory booms are multiple and recurrent in history, appearing after major events like the end of the U.S. Civil War or World War I (Hass, 2009, p. 268), the current memory boom is considered the most sweeping and impactful to date, driven in large part by the need to confront the Holocaust (Winter, 2001). As a result, the determination to preserve and share memories has become a hallmark of recent decades.

Within this wider memory boom emerged memory studies—an interdisciplinary project on memory's various forms, enactments, and responsibilities. Traced to scholars like Maurice Halbwachs (1992) and Pierre Nora (1989), an intermittent interest in memory soon became a phenomenon. Central to memory studies is the belief that memory, rather than history, reflects an innate human need for the past that is lived, usable, and responsive to the times (Nora, 1989). Similarly, memory studies locates memories in people's communal experiences—collectives, nations, cultures, or publics—rather than individuals (Halbwachs, 1992).

Memory studies' celebration of situatedness, usability, and intersubjectivity appealed strongly to Communication scholars, particularly in rhetoric, starting in the 1990s. Early investigations examining memory's role in communication, politics, and culture quickly grew into an expansive subfield with hundreds of articles and dozens of monographs. Together, these studies examine intersections between collective or public memory and subjects as varied as gender, race, (trans-)nationalism, place/space, and science. Hence, memory has again become central to the modern discipline. Queer memory scholarship relied heavily on these investments from the outset and contributed substantially to the elaboration of memory studies in the field.

The second phenomenon is the inauguration of queer theory, often dated to the 1990s. But memory was critical to queer theory and practice years before it was named an academic subject. Michel Foucault (1978), for instance, relied on memory to study the exercise of power in his genealogy of sexuality. And memories appear meaningfully in the writings of queer women of color in the 1980s. For example, *La Prieta* by Gloria Anzaldúa (1981, pp. 198–209) relies on personal reminiscences to confront and foment queer, feminist, Chicana, and indigenous pasts and both Cherríe Moraga and Audre Lorde point to the need for what Moraga later calls "political memory" (Moraga, 2015, p. xix) to craft queer-affirming, intersectional futures. Each of these thinkers deeply influenced José Esteban Muñoz (1996, p. 11) who elaborates on "the necessity of... strategies of self-enactment"—like memory and ephemera—for queer, "minoritarian subject[s]" years later. Many accounts of the lineage of queer memory via queer theory bypass these queer thinkers of color, reinscribing the Whiteness that continues to permeate queer memory scholarship today.

Instead, these accounts often point to "Sex in Public" by Berlant and Warner (1998) as the origin that informs dual roles for memory in queer theory. In defining heteronormativity, the authors illuminate, on one hand, how the "structural relation" between property ownership and the bourgeois family disciplined queers by "prevent[ing] the recognition, memory, elaboration, or institutionalization of all the nonstandard intimacies that people have in everyday life" (p. 560). On the other hand, Berlant and Warner see memory as a powerful force for disrupting heteronormativity via queer world-making, particularly to "support forms of affective, erotic, and personal living that are public in the sense of accessible, available to memory, and sustained through collective activity" (Berlant & Warner, 1998, p. 562). Building queer-affirmative worlds and resisting those who would discipline them therefore requires attention to memory. Ultimately, the collision of memory studies and queer theory leads to the emergence of queer memory studies.

By the late 1990s, the concept of queer memory can be seen emerging sporadically within published scholarship outside Communication. One of the earliest is "Sexual Trauma/Queer Memory" by Ann Cvetkovich (1995), quickly followed by consideration of queer memory's ephemerality by Muñoz (1996), a subject he returns to several more times (Muñoz, 1999, 2009). A few years later, Christopher Capozzola (2002) engages the politics of memory as it relates to the AIDS Memorial Quilt while Christopher Castiglia and Christopher Reed (2004) make queer issues of memory central to their analysis of "Will & Grace." And the search for "new models of queer memory and history" by J. Jack Halberstam (2005, p. 161) does much to incite an explosion of interest in queer memory across the academy. At the same time, queer memory also makes tentative but incomplete appearances in Communication, including in "Sextext" by Frederick Corey and Thomas Nakayama (1997), an essay on public representations of Brandon Teena by John Sloop (2000), the investigation of media framings of Matthew Shepard by Brian Ott and Eric Aoki (2002), groundbreaking "quare studies" by E. Patrick Johnson, and *Memory's Caretaker* by Paul Bonin-Rodriguez and Steve Bailey (2004). Clearly, the early aughts presaged a queer memory moment soon to arrive.

A fully formed concept of queer memory first appears in Communication in "My Old Kentucky Homo: Lincoln and the Politics of Queer Public Memory" by Charles E. Morris, III (2004). In this chapter, Morris investigates for the first time a subject he returns to frequently: the rhetorical force of a "queer Lincoln" expressed in a speech by infamous HIV/AIDS polemicist, Larry Kramer. The memory of Lincoln as queer exemplifies the rhetorical potential in rendering a memory of the past anew in a queer light. The chapter by Morris also affords one of the first definitions of queer memory in the discipline (2004, p. 91), one that can be adapted for wider application beyond Kramer's speech. A revised and extended version of the essay was later republished in an edited volume, *Queering Public Address*, by Morris (2007b).

In the nearly two decades since Morris's publication, the subject of queer memory has grown in attention and importance in Communication at a cascading rate. It has been the subject of numerous conference papers, preconferences, symposiums, journal articles, special issues, and several notable monographs, including *Remembering the AIDS Quilt* (Morris, 2011) and *Queerly Remembered* (Dunn, 2016b). Engaging that scholarship is the focus of the balance of this article.

FRAMING QUEER MEMORY IN COMMUNICATION

The emergence of queer memory in Communication can be explained numerous ways. Meanwhile, scholarship in queer memory by Communication researchers has principally fallen into three primary frames: the recovery and circulation of the memories of queer persons, movements, and institutions; the (re)theorizing of memory from queer perspectives; and connections between queer memories and the archive.

Memories of Queers. A significant aspect of queer memory scholarship in Communication is the recovery and circulation of historical homosexuals, lesbians, gay men, transgender people, and queers and their communicative discourses (other members of the LGBTQ+ community remain woefully underrepresented in this work). By recovery, I mean the restoration to memory of individuals, entities, and events that (1) have been previously remembered in the public sphere, but detached from their sexuality and gender identity or (2) have been ignored, subjugated, or forgotten due to homo/transphobia, hetero/cisnormativity, mnemonicide, or similar abuses. By circulation, I mean the injection of queer memories into wider public discourses to shape current and future debates.

Exemplary of this work in Communication are Morris's already noted efforts to queer Lincoln's memory (Morris, 2004, 2006, 2007b, 2013, 2015a, 2015b). Inaugurated by Morris's analysis of Kramer's 1999 speech, Morris's oeuvre amplifies Kramer's aim to remember Lincoln queerly and to "mandate that gays and lesbians, in order to survive, must learn to remember" (2004, p. 106). Simultaneously, Morris shows the rhetorical capacity of memory to advance queer concerns or, in Morris' words, to: "deplo[y] the usable symbolic resources of the past as an organizing principle in the present and moral vision for a sustainable queer future" (p. 107). Morris's fascination by queer Lincoln—as symbolic and inventional resource, queer inspiration, and pedagogical tool—explains, in part, why Lincoln is the most significant historical figure to appear in queer memory scholarship in Communication.

Following queer Lincoln, Communication scholars have often worked to recover the sexuality of other public figures who are typically remembered as heterosexual to investigate how queering these individuals may produce rhetorical consequentiality. Both early work by Morris (2002) on J. Edgar Hoover and the "pink herring" and the more recent return to Hoover's queer "after life" by Dunn (2016b) qualifies in this area. So, too, might the skeptical study by Dana Cloud (2007) of the merits of this work as it relates to the memory of Eleanor Roosevelt's sexuality. A similar undertaking appears in a study of Willa Cather's framing as a lesbian at the Nebraska History Museum in an essay by Carly Woods et al. (2013). In each case, scholars show how recalling distinguished figures as queer can engage contemporary questions of public concern.

This recovery work is in line with other strains of memory scholarship that turn to the past to advance a more LGBTQ+ inclusive present, but it is not without its flaws. In particular, due to Communication's deep ties to Western and U.S.-American traditions, values, beliefs, and structures of power (Whiteness, masculinity, and cisnormativity), attempts to restore famous, noted, or historical LGBTQ+ people to memory often does not sufficiently disentangle the field from these problematic commitments. Indeed, the list of recovered queer figures described in the previous paragraph are overwhelmingly White, and Whiteness permeates much of this work to date.

Scholars writing about queer memory in the field have made this point directly. For instance, Alexandra Juhasz (2012) critiques the privileged memories of the overwhelmingly White male membership of ACT UP and the forgotten contributions of "the rag-tag group of feminists, lesbians, drug addicts, people of color, homeless people, poor people, immigrants, mothers, and Haitians who were also engaged in activism at this time" both "across the broader AIDS activist community, and within ACT UP itself" (p. 72). Likewise, Sara Mourad (2013) relies on memories extensively to point out how the field's Anglophone tendencies limit considerations of same-sex sexuality in Arabic and other non-English languages. And Karma Chávez (2012, 2021) has illustrated the rich potential of queer memory—particularly surrounding HIV/AIDS—when race, nation, and migration are considered intersectionally and placed at the forefront of theses analyses rather than sidelined.

There are ample explanations for the problematic tendency to privilege White (and male and cis) figures in this recovery work, including a largely White field of scholars trained in an academic tradition that is always a priori infused with Whiteness, slow-to-change publication processes that can make non-White and non-cis scholars feel unwelcome and unvalued, and a homonormativity (often yoked to Whiteness) that limits how we imagine whose lives and what acts can produce meaningful social change (typically defined as legislation, judicial rulings, and public pronouncements). It is also the case that rich archives of people like Lincoln, Hoover, Roosevelt, and Cather exist to be consulted, each highly amendable to time-tested communicative methods—despite the need for archival queerness (Morris, 2006, p. 145). Meanwhile, historical queers of color have found their places in the past more robustly erased, more actively forgotten, more alienated from the traditional "archive," and more deeply constrained by insidious double binds, leading to what Matt Richardson (2013, p. 3) calls the "queer limit of Black memory." Beyond these structural issues, scholars of queer public memory must also simply make the choice to confront this Whiteness going forward. However, none of these issues should be deemed insurmountable and a richer, more inclusive, and more reflective queer memory archive is possible. Indeed, as Chávez (2012, p. 64) argues as it relates to activism, when largely "White and more affluent" folks who tend to occupy a privileged place in queer memory politics work in "an AIDS and queer coalition building" with poor people, people of color, and other queers and trans folks who are often "recalled only secondarily," meaningful reckonings with the past are possible—as is the potential for a better present and future.

Another subset in this area is the amplification and reinvigoration of the communication of/about established queer figures. Herein, the focus is less on queering a person's memory than answering if and how these folks have been made memorable and the consequences thereof.

A significant category in this area focuses on victims of anti-gay, anti-trans, and anti-queer violence and/or homo/transphobia, particularly victims whose suffering garnered public attention. Matthew Shepard, a 21-year-old Wyoming college student murdered in 1998, is exemplary of this kind of figure, and the complex dimensions of remembering Shepard have been a prominent area of scholarly investigation. As previously noted, Shepard's memory is first addressed by Ott and Aoki (2002) but is soon followed by others. For instance, Balter-Reitz and Stewart examine Shepard's memory as a facet of his depiction in visual arguments drawn from the Western mythos (2006) and John Lynch (2007) shows how the connection between journalism and television drama constrains audience's capacity to imagine Shepard—and other LGBTQ+ people—in two television movies. Dunn (2010, pp. 628–631) draws attention to tensions over Shepard's memory in the wider public but also within the LGBTQ+ community itself. Cram (2016c) also considers Shepard's memory, with a particular focus on returning imaginings of rurality to his life and death. In his book-length treatment of queer memory, Dunn (2016b) adds that Shepard's memory within the gay and lesbian counterpublic is exemplary of the "monumental quality of epideictic rhetoric" that emerges regularly in queer memory writ large (p. 30).

Highly publicized transgender victims in public memory are also prominent subjects of investigations. Brandon Teena, a transgender man murdered in 1993, and Angie Zapata, a transgender woman murdered in 2008, are particularly noteworthy. Although the essay by John Sloop (2000) does not focus on memory, its careful reconstruction of "doxastic understandings of gender/sexuality" (p. 183) in Teena's public representations are exemplary of how broader understandings of LGBTQ+ lives are found and remade within discourses surrounding trans victims. Meanwhile, the essay by Cram (2012) on the rhetorical circulation of photography in the wake of Zapata's murder offers clues for "how we might respond to bias crimes within the emotionality of the category of 'citizenship'" (p. 414).

Balancing the tendency of queers to be remembered in the wider public only as criminals or victims, queer memory research has also concentrated on notable historical individuals' roles in LGBTQ+ activism. The problematic hero-ification of certain kinds of queers (read: White, male, cis) is a regular concern expressed by Communication scholars, even as the overt Whiteness of those selected as reputable "heroes" remains hard to ignore—if marginally better than in some other subareas of queer memory. Nonetheless, this strain of queer memory scholarship takes seriously building an affirmative queer archive that can empower queers to act as subjects in their own narratives.

Assorted figures are highlighted in this undertaking, representing a broader swath of the actually existing LGBTQ+ past. Among them, Lisbeth Lipari (2007) works to recover Lorraine Hansberry as a Black and queer rhetorical persona who "evades easy identification" (p. 220), Julie Thompson (2007) attends to Marlon Riggs's empowerment of queer Black men, and Lester Olson highlights the powerful voice of the Black lesbian feminist icon, Audre Lorde (Olson, 2007). But the greatest attention has been devoted to figures most well-known by the general public. Harvey Milk is perhaps the most studied figure in this vein (Foss, 2007; Morris, 2015c), particularly the notable collection of Milk's speeches and writings, by Morris and Jason Edward Black (2013), which advances memories of Milk and attends to how his rich rhetorical works animate some key moments in gay and lesbian activism. Oscar Wilde, too, is a popular subject of memory work in communication, both as an epigram for wider ideas about queer rhetoric (Morris, 2010) and as a figure who resonates with today's queer values (Dunn, 2014). Other studied queer heroes and heroines of note include the bohemian writer, Richard Halliburton (Morris, 2009); the scandalous 19th-century Toronto merchant, Alexander Wood (Dunn, 2011); transgender political figure, Chelsea Manning (Morris & Nakayama, 2014); and gay military veteran Sgt. Leonard Matlovich (Dunn, 2016b).

Notable groups and social movements are also the focus of this memory work. One of the most emphasized subjects in this area is the NAMES Project AIDS Memorial Quilt. Addressed first in a special issue of *Rhetoric & Public Affairs* (Morris, 2007a) and then in the edited monograph *Remembering the AIDS Quilt* (Morris, 2011), a diverse array of scholars in communication consider the intersection of queer memory and this powerful symbol, covering topics as varied as the politics of loss (Yep, 2011), public emotionality (Bennett, 2011), mobility and notions of home (Brouwer, 2011), and critical ethnointerpretive methodology and "the voices of Black men living with HIV/AIDS" (Alexander, 2011, p. 192). Similarly, a 2012 forum issue of the *Quarterly Journal of Speech* offered scholars from across the discipline and outside the opportunity to engage questions of remembrance related to the AIDS activist organization, ACT UP. Significant topics in this special issue include racism (Gould, 2012); alternative memories, the migrant experience, and coalition-building (Chavez, 2012); "pride" and affect (Rand, 2012); and the archive (Brouwer, 2012). Elsewhere, Alyssa Samek (2015, 2016) has focused on the memory and rhetoric of lesbian feminism in the 1970s.

More recently, the locus of recovery work has bypassed noted historical figures for less known subjects whose memories have animated modern queer audiences. For instance, the reclamation by Pamela VanHaitsma (2019b) of the epistolary exchanges between Addie Brown and Rebecca Primus draws attention to the rhetorical invention of women-loving-women of previous eras. Similarly, Cram (2016a) turns to the "intimate" archive of two female 19th-century Wyoming professors, to highlight the potential for a queer sensibility in the U.S.-American West. And the investigation by Dunn (2016b) of Patricia Cronin's *Memorial to a Marriage* burial installation shows how monumentality can enshrine memories counter to normative avenues for commemoration.

While remembering queer historical figures is clearly an important strain in Communication, not all scholars have found this exercise compelling. Cloud (2007), in particular, investigates the memory of Eleanor Roosevelt to question the material value of such recovery projects. For Cloud: "it matters less what someone is than what they and the texts that represent them do; queering public address must do more than affirm queer existence" (p. 40). In a slightly different way, Cram argues for a queer memory that exceeds recovery by emphasizing "theories of invention distant from modern 'discovery.'" In particular, Cram argues for valuing queer memories beyond their "content," suggesting such a turn portends greater opportunities to "unsettle the past and generate memories refashioned for the urgencies of the present" (Cram, 2016a, p. 124). This scholarship questions the very idea of what queer memory means and is discussed in greater detail in the next section.

The Queering of Memory. A second significant strain of scholarship in Communication and queer memory has focused on the queering of memory itself. Memory's role as the tool of the rhetor has deep roots in the field; but Communication's traditional concern with memory changed with the emergence of memory studies in the 1990s. This scholarship straddled disciplinary boundaries to retheorize memory and its utility in collective, social, and public contexts. The emergence of queer memory in the early aughts was part of this retheorization, raising questions about what queer theory might require of us in thinking about the term "memory" in Communication. The answers to these questions demonstrate that thinking queerly about memory is new, different, and ripe with future discovery.

First, Communication scholars have added robust insights into how memory has been denied to queer people. Some of the earliest gay and lesbian historical work attributed the dearth of existing histories of lesbians and gays to either the absence of past queers, the lack of evidence, or an inability to imagine tools or resources that would make such investigations possible (Escoffier et al., 1995). Queer memory, by contrast, attributes this absence to ongoing, sustained, and well-resourced efforts to erase LGBTQ+ people from a wider hetero/cisnormative and homo/transphobic society. Morris (2007b, p. 103) coins the phrase "mnemonicide"—"the assassination of memory"—to describe this process. Dunn (2016b, pp. 3–4) elaborates on practices akin to mnemonicide that have disconnected queer generations, "including heteronormativity, misrepresentation, the subjugation of knowledge, destruction of records, disqualification of evidence," as well as the tendency of queer memories to be inadequately or equitably resourced (Dunn, 2017b). Such recognition of queers' denial of memory is a precursor to considering queer memory scholarship political work.

Second, queer memory scholarship in Communication asserts that memory need not be conservative but rather possesses a radically progressive and liberatory potential (Dunn, 2010, p. 638). Said otherwise, Communication scholars have argued memory can be an inventional resource for LGBTQ+ people who seek to make change in the world (Morris, 2004, p. 107). If heteronormativity, for example, actively works to discipline and erase gay, lesbian, and bisexual people through the denial of their memories, then the recuperation and recreation of queer memories can be considered a highly rhetorical act of resistance. What's more, these memories can serve other interests, including building individual and collective identities, sharing tools for survival and self-creation, and generating queer worlds that can nurture future communities.

This potential, however, does not mean that queer memories cannot also be conservative (e.g., homonormative or reiterative of Whiteness) or, perhaps more precisely, oppressive. In fact, many trans people, whose experience are often collapsed under the "queer" or "LGBT+" moniker can have different relationships to memory, so much so that lesbian, gay, and bisexual turns to memory may question, minimize, or territorialize the transgender experience. Work building on the existing studies in the discipline (e.g., Cram, 2019a; Cram & Cassils, 2019; Horvat, 2020; VanHaitsma, 2019a) of the unique needs of memory and the past within the transgender community are necessary and may suggest queer memories—at least as often invoked in cisgender and/or gay, lesbian, or bisexual contexts—may be of limited value for all facets of the LGBTQ+ community. Nonetheless, emphasizing the progressive potential of the queer memories will likely remain common in queer memory scholarship.

Queer memory scholarship in Communication has also dramatically questioned the role of "discovery" in past-oriented work. As already noted, Cram has advocated for rethinking queer memory to deemphasize the traditional role of identification in favor of a phenomenological and affective approach to memory that shifts the locus to invention. In particular, Cram argues for disrupting actor-oriented notions of agency in favor of a focus on the "affectability of bodies, sexualities, and built environments." In doing so, Cram challenges scholars to consider how, for example, "material cultures enable the generation of intimate relationalities and kinships that transgress historically contextualized understandings of heteronormative sociality" (Cram, 2016a, p. 112). Said otherwise: rather than align queer memory with discovering queers in the archive, Cram asks Communication scholars to consider how past figures can be rendered queer in situ. Doing so requires co-construction between the materiality of the past, the audience's embodiment and affectivities, and the archives own ambivalences. Thus, Cram charts a provocative course for queer memory, placing it closely in line with other recent turns toward affect, the sensorium, and decoloniality.

Spanning the discovery/invention debate in queer memory is a shared interest in form. Given that Communication's historic concerns have been language and symbols, it is not surprising that scholars have gravitated to the appearance of queer memories in these familiar forms. For instance, Morris's inaugural discussion focuses on the deployment of queer Lincoln in public address, a form he directs wider attention to in his edited monograph *Queering Public Address* (2007b). Other scholars have pursued queer memory in forms of public address as well, including in the polemic (Rand, 2008), letters (Lipari, 2007; VanHaitsma, 2019b), and literature (Morris, 2009). How queer memories appear and are shaped in newspapers and public dialogue has also been a common site of investigation (Cram, 2012; Dunn, 2010, 2016b; Morris, 2005).

But, beyond the most traditional forms and genres, scholars have also highlighted more material and visual forms in which queer memories reside. In this way, the study of queer memory has pushed Communication scholars to think deeper about what qualifies as communication. Hardscape monuments and memorials—particularly their place-making abilities, use of unexpected materials, and impact on audiences—have been a significant focus (Dunn, 2011, 2014, 2016b, 2017b, 2019; Reyes et al., 2018), with Dunn particularly interested in the potential to render memories of the queer past in more durable forms, what he calls "queer monumentality" (Dunn, 2016b; p. 21). At the same time, the AIDS quilt's capacity to convey powerful emotional and cultural meanings via cozy materials is foregrounded by numerous other scholars (Morris, 2011). Meanwhile, more visual and imagistic texts have played an important role. Landscapes, geographies, and cartographies, for example, have been prominent sites in which Communication scholars read queer memories at work (Balter-Reitz & Stewart, 2006; Cram, 2016b, 2016c, 2019b; Dunn, 2016b). Made-for-television movies (Lynch, 2007), award-winning films (Dunn, 2015; Morris, 2015a, 2015b; Sloop, 2000), and fictional television series (Horvat, 2020) matter here as well. Similarly, photography has been emphasized as a primary driver of queer memory rhetorics, including the use of victim photography (Cram, 2012); portraiture (Morris, 2007b, 2010); music videos (Dunn, 2016a, p. 277); and profile photos on gay hookup apps (Dunn, 2019). Different viewing practices, too, have been emphasized as important to queer memory (Cram, 2012; Dunn, 2011, 2014).

Across each of these forms, ephemerality matters. Memory's ephemerality is, of course, well known—and yet is regarded almost wholly as a limitation within most non-queer scholarship. To be sure, rendering queer memories in ephemeral forms can be problematic, making them prime targets for mnemonicide; however, within queer memory, ephemerality is often regarded as a feature rather than a bug. Muñoz (1996) makes this point expressly: "queerness has...existed as innuendo, gossip, fleeting moments, and performances that are meant to be interacted with by those within its epistemological spheres—while evaporating at the touch of those who would eliminate queer possibility" (pp. 5–7). Morris (2002, p. 230) emphasizes this claim with his theory of the "fourth persona" or a "collusive audience constituted by the textual wink." Dunn (2016b, pp. 14–15) also makes this connection to ephemerality in his discussion of tactical and ephemeral queer memory rhetorics prior to the 1980s, "pasts preserved on the fly, enacted in the moment, and derived from the 'stuff' that constitutes heterosexual history." As a result, queer memory scholarship has offered new ways to consider ephemerality as a strength rather than weakness.

Another issue at work in theorizing queer memory is its capacity—and often failure—to represent the diversity of the queer community. As indicated at the start of this article, Whiteness in particular is a significant challenge embedded in queer memory scholarship. But concerns about diversity go beyond race. The queer community includes people of all genders and no genders, different classes, ages, nationalities, abilities, and so forth—and yet, queer memory itself is often slow to center and elevate women, trans folks, rural queers, poor people, and others, as well as queer people of color. Scholars have pointed out that the most prominent and efficacious ways of theorizing queer memory often leave out significant portions of the community. Eric King Watts (2007) engages this point in his analysis of queer Harlem. Dunn (2010) makes this point in explaining how LGBTQ+ people of color and trans people often did not find themselves represented in Matthew Shepard's memory, while an analysis by Cram (2012) of Angie Zapata's murder shows how a transgender woman of color has been forgotten by the traditional levers of commemoration despite the pyrrhic victory of her murderer's conviction. The intersecting politics of memory surrounding sexuality and gender also illuminate this concern, prompting consideration of alternative ways of commemorating lesbians in queer memory (Dunn, 2017b; Samek, 2015, 2016) and the relationships between some transgender people and memory writ large (Dunn, 2015). It is important to reiterate here that the public memories of other queer people, like bisexual, pansexuals, and asexuals have gone relatively unaddressed in the field to date (Dunn, 2017b, p. 214, n. 14).

Queer memory scholarship has also touched on the different emotional and affective dimensions of some queer commemorations. Within non-queer arenas of collective/public memory, affective notes tend to oscillate between epideictic feelings of pride, sadness, and respect. Queer memories, by virtue of their deep connection to suffering and marginalization and the biting tonality of queer critique, often resonate elsewhere—to productive rhetorical consequence. Cram (2016a) makes this point powerfully in the appeal to "archival ambient and sensory memory" in the archive, but queer memory's diverse emotional and affective registers also extend to expressions of secrecy and silence (Morris, 2002, 2005), alienation (Rand, 2008), accusation (Dunn, 2019; Rand, 2008), fear (Dunn, 2010), mourning (Morris, 2011), panic (Gingrich-Philbrook, 2012), grotesquery and ridicule (Dunn, 2011), rage (West, 2012), failure and shame (Dunn, 2019; Rand, 2012), and sentimentality (Dunn, 2014; Reyes et al., 2018). That is not to say that queer memories do not also rely on affective appeals common of marginalized groups seeking wider acceptance, like "pride" and "contribution" (Dunn, 2016b; Rand, 2012). But, queer memories often do their work by engaging in emotional and affective remembrances atypical of heteronormative society.

A more recent focus of queer memory is its pedagogical potential in service of emerging queer and transgender generations. Such connections seem inevitable given education has been an important front in the struggle for LGBTQ+ rights, since at least the Briggs Initiative (Darsey, 1981, pp. 243–244). Morris (2013) advances this concern most directly in what he refers to as a "queer rhetorical pedagogy." Thereunder, Morris sees the entry of queer Lincoln into the K–12 classroom not only as the opportunity to give students tools and skills to participate in the life of the community, but also to "facilitate[e] incipient and emergent queer futures" (p. 398). Morris's idea is reemphasized in Dunn's analyses of efforts to remember the "contributions" of LGBTQ+ people in California's K–12 curriculum in the early aughts (Dunn, 2016b) and attempts to shift the memory of Oscar Wilde with a "proto-queer sensibility" to render him "a more resonant figure for contemporary queer audiences" (Dunn, 2014, p. 213). Other Communication scholars have focused on how to incorporate queer memory more fully into the teaching of historical and archival methods in the classroom, something elaborated upon later in this article.

Finally, temporality is a key topic connected to the study of queer memory. As a means of engaging time that privileges the backward glance, anachronisms, and reminiscences, queer memories make certain assertions about time that scholars use to propose queer world-making possibilities. These include the past as a site of "queer temporal camp" (Gholz, 2012, p. 101), memory performance (Hatfield, 2017), and anachronistic inspiration (Dunn, 2014). Not all scholars, however, see the past as a generative site for queer world-making. Rather than look backward, many scholars follow Muñoz (2009) in the call for a "queer futurity" in the search for more livable queer lives—even while Muñoz himself connects "queer utopian memory" to his sense of futurity (p. 35). Regardless: Queer memory clearly has situated itself meaningfully in Communication scholarship and its capacity for reimagining the past—and how we come to the past—makes it a rich resource that is unlikely to be rescinded anytime soon.

Archives of Queer Memory. A final frame from which to consider queer memory in Communication is its connection to the archive, a concept that bridges the need to remember queers and the requirement to rethink the consequences of/for queering memory.

On Communication's humanistic side, scholars often rely on archives to do their work. Whether reading historic speeches or letters, rediscovering meaningful maps or pamphlets, or analyzing discourses in newspaper databases, archives are old friends to many Communication scholars. However, a recent "archival turn" has driven researchers to reconsider the role of the archive in their work, particularly the fact of "archives as a rhetorical construction" (Morris, 2006, p. 113). Queer memory has been an important part of that turn from the start.

Queer memory scholars' role informing the archival turn makes sense because queers have often seen archives as homophobic and heteronormative institutions. Multiple scholars have recounted their incidents and concerns with how some archives and archivists do the business of keeping the past (Cram, 2016a; Dunn, 2016b; Morris, 2006; Morris & Rawson, 2013) and how they can injure queer subjects and scholars alike. Still, queers often need archives to do some of the work of queer memory, an irony that explains the founding of LGBTQ+ archives in the 1970s, 1980s, and 1990s. Yet, more is needed, including "queer ephemeral archives" and the like that can hold the radicality of queer life (Muñoz, 1996, p. 116). Thus, the (re)turn to the archive in Communication in new ways resonates with specific concerns for queer memory.

At least two prominent calls from scholars of queer memory are of note here.

On the one hand, the study of queer memory requires scholars to ask themselves how they engage and construct the archive in their work. Despite the great accomplishments of LGBTQ+ archives, Morris (2006) notes much of what needs to be studied about the queer past resides in "straight archives," obliging queer scholars to "queer the archive" as the "deftest of…archival queers" (p. 147). Doing so both requires "tireless cruising in vexed pursuit of the elusive artifacts" (Morris, 2006, p. 148) and the engagement and explanation of these texts so that they can be "recuperated and extracted, that is, analyzed and theorized" (Morris, 2006, p. 148). To this end, we are asked to make the memory of queers the very stuff of rhetorical culture while each of us, regardless of our sexuality or gender-identity, is called upon to queer the archive.

Queer memory scholars have answered this call with vigor. K. J. Rawson, E. Cram, and Pamela VanHaitsma's work is particularly notable here. Rawson, a scholar of the transgender past and founder of the Digital Transgender Archive (DTA), all too well understands the impediments to working with archives and the innovations needed. Rawson delivers in a series of articles that push scholars to consider queer/trans logics in the archives (2009), the queering of archival practice (2012), the terminological power of the term "transgender" (Rawson & Williams, 2014), and archival descriptions of "gender transgression images" (Rawson, 2018). As already noted, Cram (2016a) draws researchers' attention to memory and its relationship to bodies, sensation, and feeling in the cultivation of "archival ambience" and VanHaitsma (2016) articulates numerous tactics for queering the archive, including valuing gossip and doing digital curation (VanHaitsma & Book, 2019). Being an archival queer also extends to the classroom, as represented in the work of scholar-teachers pushing themselves and their students to engage with the queer past meaningfully (Enoch & VanHaitsma, 2015; Samek & Donofrio, 2013).

On the other hand, the archival turn has prompted scholars not only to write about queer memory but to archive those memories as well. While this archival imperative includes contributing research materials to extant institutional archives, it also includes creating and/or collaborating with archives in various ways.

A profoundly important contribution to the queer archive is Black and Morris's already-mentioned volume of Harvey Milk's speeches and writings entitled *An Archive of Hope* (2013). This volume is the very first collection of Milk's rhetorical documents, including his speeches, newspaper columns, editorials, press releases, and other notable messaging. As the description suggests, this project is not a criticism of Milk's rhetoric but a preservation of it by two leading scholars. This project follows a similar if more general effort by Robert B. Ridinger (2004) to collect important historical speeches in gay and lesbian rights.

But not all archival creations must take the shape of scholarly monographs. Some efforts can be found within institutions, such as ongoing efforts to gather and publish founding documents related to the National Communication Association's Caucus on LGBTQ Concerns. More can be found in interviews and oral histories conducted by scholars as part of larger projects (Chávez, 2012, 2021; Cram & Cassils, 2019; Dunn, 2016b). Still others can be found in classes, symposiums, and digital humanities projects scattered across the departments, conferences, and associations that make up the queer Communication community.

Archive-building has also taken place online. The most notable digital project to appear in this vein is Rawson's DTA, described as "an online hub for digitized historical materials, born-digital materials, and information on archival holdings throughout the world." As an "international collaboration among more than fifty colleges, universities, nonprofit organizations, and private collections," the project is sweeping, expanding "access to trans history for academics and independent researchers alike in order to foster education and dialog" (Rawson, 2020). In setting a high standard, the DTA invites growing digital humanities projects of this kind to further expand the notion of queer and trans memories in the archive.

CONCLUSION

Despite significant growth in the study of queer memory in Communication, the potential and need for future work in this area is more noteworthy. Future directions in queer memory vary widely, but some key areas moving forward are clear.

One of the most pressing future directions of queer memory scholarship is continuing to grapple with the excessive Whiteness already noted earlier and deploying new pathways to decenter the White LGBTQ+ experience. Such work has already been begun (Chávez, 2012, 2021; Juhasz, 2012; Richardson, 2013) but the pervasive Whiteness within queer memory's subjects, tools, and methods will require committed efforts to rebalance the scales. Essential to this work will be the continued expectation that intersectional perspectives be at the heart of any work on the queer past.

Similarly, inter/transnationalizing queer memory scholarship is another promising area for future work. Much as existing work privileges the past experiences of White, cisgender gay men, scholarship in queer memory is also predominantly U.S.-centric and shows a significant English-speaking bias toward other Anglophone nations. Chávez's forthcoming volume, *The Borders of AIDS* (2021), promises to disrupt some of these tendencies and makes a compelling demand for queer memory work to engage the politics of race, nation, and migration more fully. But more will be needed, including significant attention to the indigenous queer past in the United States and elsewhere and further efforts to decolonize queer memory.

Within U.S. borders, future queer memory work will also need to further break free from the confines of coasts and metropolises to engage the queer pasts of the nation's middle, its suburbs, and its countryside. Or, as E. Cram asks us to consider: "what forms of desire are generated in landscapes beyond the already legible and metropolitan archive" (2016a, p. 113)? This work has already begun in earnest and more is forthcoming, including Cram's monograph *Violent Inheritance* (in press). Significant opportunities exist to do this work in Communication as most graduate programs and major research institutions in the field are located in the nation's interior. Such opportunities mark not only the potential that lies beyond the urban and coastal but also the prospects of the local in doing the queer past.

If form has already shifted the terrain of queer memory scholarship in the last decade, it is likely to become an even more central occupation of queer memory researchers in the years ahead on two counts. First, although we should expect to see more work on already-established queer commemorative forms (especially social media), the transition to yet more diverse forms of queer memory expression (in next-generation apps, AI-infused software, and cyborgic constructions) also seems certain. Second, questions of form will also extend to the types of labor scholars interested in queer memory will (or should) produce. With increasing interest in rhetorical production, rhetorical field methods, and digital humanities—as well as mounting demands for more public-facing scholarship—we should expect to see queer memory scholars *producing* past-oriented queer rhetorics (archives, exhibits, monuments, etc.), not just studying them.

Finally, as notions of identity continue to shift within intergenerational LGBTQ+ communities, so too will queer memory scholarship have to grapple with the question of who counts as "queer" (now) and, as such, whose memories mattered in this work (then)? A recent Gallup survey (Jones, 2021) is illustrative here, revealing one in six Generation Z respondents as LGBTQ+, a full percentage increase from a decade earlier. This expansion prompts questions about the durability of once firm categories like "gay" and "lesbian," terms which may soon sound as anachronistic to future queer memory scholars as "invert" or "urning" do today. From this limited vantage point, it seems likely the alphabet soup of queerness will not congeal in the years ahead but only become more malleable still. And yet, this indulgent undefinability remains the radical potential of "queer," largely by choice. It will then be for queer scholars of the future to continually adjust, making the study of queer memory—whatever that might mean then—meaningful, relevant, and engaging.

Born from the collision of two interdisciplinary projects and the practical needs of a people in search of a past, queer memory represents an exciting topic in the study of Queer communication. Since the early 2000s, communication scholarship in this area has expanded swiftly and its reach has grown by the year. What seems likely at this time, however, is that while much queer past is yet to be unearthed, the capacity and ambition to do this work in the field of communication are unbounded.

DIGITAL MATERIALS

ACT UP Oral History Project. http://www.actuporalhistory.org/
Digital Transgender Archive. https://www.digitaltransgenderarchive.net/
GLBT Historical Society Museum and Archives. San Francisco, CA. https://www.glbthistory.org/
Leather Archives and Museum. Chicago, IL. https://leatherarchives.org/
Lesbian Herstory Archives. New York, NY. https://lesbianherstoryarchives.org/
ONE/International Gay and Lesbian Archives. Los Angeles, CA. https://one.usc.edu/
Stonewall National Monument. New York, NY. https://www.nps.gov/ston/index.htm
Transgender Archives. Victoria, British Columbia. https://www.uvic.ca/transgenderarchives

FURTHER READING

Black, J. E., & Morris, C. E., III. (2013). *An archive of hope: Harvey Milk's speeches and writings.* University of California Press.
Chávez, K. R. (2021). *The borders of AIDS: Race, quarantine, and resistance.* University of Washington Press.
Cram, E. (2016). Archival ambience and sensory memory: Generating queer intimacies in the settler colonial archive. *Communication and Critical/Cultural Studies, 13*(2), 109–129.
Dunn, T. R. (2016). *Queerly remembered: Rhetorics for representing the GLBTQ past.* University of South Carolina Press.

Morris, C. E., III. (2004). My old Kentucky homo: Lincoln and the politics of queer public memory. In K. R. Phillips (Ed.), *Framing public memory* (pp. 89–114). University of Alabama Press.

Morris, C. E., III. (Ed.). (2007). *Queering public address: Sexualities in American historical discourse*. University of South Carolina Press.

Morris, C. E., III. (Ed.). (2011). *Remembering the AIDS quilt*. Michigan State University Press.

REFERENCES

Alexander, B. K. (2011). Rhetorics of loss and living. In C. E. Morris, III (Ed.), *Remembering the AIDS quilt* (pp. 189–228). Michigan State University Press.

Anzaldúa, G. (1981). La prieta. In C. Moraga & G. Anzaldúa (Eds.), *This bridge called my back* (pp. 198–209). State University of New York Press.

Balter-Reitz, S. J., & Stewart, K. A. (2006). Looking for Matthew Shepard: A study in visual argument field. In D. S. Hope (Ed.), *Visual communication and social change: Rhetorics and technologies* (pp. 111–126). Hampton Press.

Bartley, W. W., III. (1982–1983). Wittgenstein and homosexuality. *Salmagundi, 58–59*(4/1), 166–196. http://www.jstor.org/stable/40547569

Bennett, J. A. (2011). A stitch in time: Public emotionality and the repertoire of citizenship. In C. E. Morris, III (Ed.), *Remembering the AIDS quilt* (pp. 133–160). Michigan State University Press.

Berlant, L., & Warner, M. (1998). Sex in public. *Critical Inquiry, 24*(2), 547–566. http://www.jstor.org/stable/1344178

Black, J. E., & Morris, C. E., III. (2013). *An archive of hope: Harvey Milk's speeches and writings*. University of California Press.

Bonin-Rodriguez, P., & Bailey, S. (2004). Memory's caretaker. *Text & Performance Quarterly, 24*(2), 161–181. https://doi.org/10.1080/1046293042000288371

Brouwer, D. C. (2009). The precarious visibility politics of self-stigmatization: The case of HIV/AIDS tattoos. *Text and Performance Quarterly, 18*(2), 114–136. https://doi.org/10.1080/10462939809366216

Brouwer, D. C. (2011). From San Francisco to Atlanta and back again. In C. E. Morris, III (Ed.), *Remembering the AIDS quilt* (pp. 161–188). Michigan State University Press.

Brouwer, D. C. (2012). Activating the AIDS archive. *Quarterly Journal of Speech, 98*(1), 109–117. https://doi.org/10.1080/00335630.2011.639385

Capozzola, C. (2002). A very American epidemic: Memory politics and identity politics in the AIDS memorial quilt, 1985–1993. *Radical History Review, 82*, 91–109. https://www.muse.jhu.edu/article/30227

Castiglia, C., & Reed, C. (2004). "Ah, yes, I remember it well": Memory and queer culture in Will and Grace. *Cultural Critique, 56*, 158–188. https://www.jstor.org/stable/1354720

Chakravarty, P., Kuo, R., Grubbs, V., & McIlwain, C. (2018). #CommunicationSoWhite. *Journal of Communication, 68*(2), 254–266. https://doi.org/10.1093/joc/jqy003

Chávez, K. R. (2012). ACT UP, Haitian migrants, and alternative memories of HIV/AIDS. *Quarterly Journal of Speech, 98*(1), 63–68. https://doi.org/10.1080/00335630.2011.638659

Chávez, K. R. (2021). *The borders of AIDS: Race, quarantine, and resistance*. University of Washington Press.

Cloud, D. (2007). The first lady's privates: Queering Eleanor Roosevelt for public address studies. In C. E. Morris, III (Ed.), *Queering public address: Sexualities in American historical discourse* (pp. 23–44). University of South Carolina Press.

Corey, F., & Nakayama, T. K. (1997). Sextext. *Text & Performance Quarterly, 17*(1), 58–68. https://doi.org/10.1080/10462939709366169

Cram, E. (2012). "Angie was our sister:" Witnessing the trans-formation of disgust in the citizenry of photography. *Quarterly Journal of Speech, 98*(4), 411–438. https://doi.org/10.1080/00335630.2012.714899

Cram, E. (2016a). Archival ambience and sensory memory: Generating queer intimacies in the settler colonial archive. *Communication and Critical/Cultural Studies, 13*(2), 109–129. https://doi.org/10.1080/14791420.2015.1119290

Cram, E. (2016b). Feeling cartography. *Women's Studies in Communication, 39*(2), 141–146. https://doi.org/10.1080/07491409.2016.1176814

Cram, E. (2016c). (Dis)locating queer citizenship: Imagining rurality in Matthew Shepard's memory. In M. L. Gray, C. R. Johnson, & B. J. Gilley (Eds.), *Queering the countryside: New frontiers in queer studies* (pp. 267–289). New York University Press.

Cram, E. (2019a). Feeling a monumental Midwest: Reflections from monument push. *QED: A Journal in GLBTQ Worldmaking, 6*(1), 79–86. https://www.muse.jhu.edu/article/729605

Cram, E. (2019b). Queer geographies and the rhetoric of orientation. *Quarterly Journal of Speech, 105*(1), 98–115. https://doi.org/10.1080/00335630.2019.1553587

Cram, E. (in press). *Violent inheritance: Sexuality, land, and the making of the North American west*. University of California Press.

Cram, E., & Cassils. (2019). Cassils: On violence, witnessing, and the making of trans worlds. *QED: A Journal of GLBTQ Worldmaking, 6*(1), 117–130. https://www.muse.jhu.edu/article/729605

Cvetkovich, A. (1995). Sexual trauma/queer memory: Incest, lesbianism, and therapeutic culture. *GLQ: A Journal of Lesbian and Gay Studies, 2*(4), 351–377. https://doi.org/10.1215/10642684-2-4-351

Darsey, J. (1981). From "Commies" and "Queers" to "Gay is Good". In J. W. Chesebro (Ed.), *Gayspeak: Gay male and lesbian communication* (pp. 224–247). Pilgrim Press.

Dunn, T. R. (2010). Remembering Matthew Shepard: Violence, identity, and queer counterpublic memories. *Rhetoric and Public Affairs, 13*(4), 611–651. https://www.jstor.org/stable/41940504

Dunn, T. R. (2011). Remembering 'a great fag': Visualizing public memory and the construction of queer space. *Quarterly Journal of Speech, 97*(4), 435–460. https://doi.org/10.1080/00335630.2011.585168

Dunn, T. R. (2014). "The quare in the square": Queer memory, sensibilities, and Oscar Wilde. *Quarterly Journal of Speech, 100*(2), 213–240. https://doi.org/10.1080/00335630.2014.959987

Dunn, T. R. (2015). Public memory: Historical trans-cription: Struggling with memory in *Paris Is Burning*. In L. G. Spencer & J. C. Capuzza (Eds.), *Transgender communication studies: Histories, trends, and trajectories* (pp. 217–232). Lexington Books.

Dunn, T. R. (2016a). Playing neoliberal politics: Post-racial and post-racist strategies in "Same Love". *Communication and Critical/Cultural Studies, 13*(3), 269–286. https://doi.org/10.1080/14791420.2016.1149201

Dunn, T. R. (2016b). *Queerly remembered: Rhetorics for representing the GLBTQ past*. University of South Carolina Press.

Dunn, T. R. (2017a). Dr. H[omosexual] Anonymous, gay liberation activism, and the American Psychiatric Association, 1963–1973. In R. J. Jensen (Ed.), *Social controversy and public address in the 1960s and early 1970s* (pp. 181–220). Michigan State University Press.

Dunn, T. R. (2017b). Whence the lesbian in queer monumentality? Intersections of gender and sexuality in public memory. *Southern Communication Journal, 82*(4), 203–215. https://doi.org/10.1080/1041794X.2017.1332090

Dunn, T. R. (2019). Grinding against genocide: Rhetorics of shame, sex, and memory at the *Memorial to the Murdered Jews of Europe*. *Rhetoric Society Quarterly, 49*(4), 365–386. https://doi.org/10.1080/02773945.2019.1645347

Enoch, J., & VanHaitsma, P. (2015). Archival literacy: Reading the rhetoric of digital archives in the undergraduate classroom. *College Composition and Communication, 67*(2), 216–242. https://www.jstor.org/stable/24633856

Escoffier, J., Kunzel, R., & McGarry, M. (1995). The queer issue: New visions of America's lesbian and gay past. *Radical History Review, 62*, 1–5. https://doi.org/10.1215/01636545-1995-62-1

Foss, K. A. (2007). Harvey Milk and the queer rhetorical situation: A rhetoric of contradiction. In C. E. Morris, III (Ed.), *Queering public address: Sexualities in American historical discourse* (pp. 74–92). University of South Carolina Press.

Foucault, M. (1978). *History of sexuality: Volume 1: An introduction* (R. Hurley, Trans.). Random House.

Gholz, D. B. (2012). Love(sick) aliens in the wasteland: Queer temporal camp in Araki's teen apocalyptic trilogy. *Critical Studies in Media Communication, 29*(2), 97–112. https://doi.org/10.1080/15295036.2010.514935

Gingrich-Philbrook, C. (2012). ACT UP as a structure of feeling. *Quarterly Journal of Speech, 98*(1), 81–88. https://doi.org/10.1080/00335630.2011.638660

Gould, D. B. (2012). ACT UP, racism, and the question of how to use history. *Quarterly Journal of Speech, 98*(1), 54–62. https://doi.org/10.1080/00335630.2011.638661

Halberstam, J. J. (2005). *In a queer time and place: Transgender bodies, subcultural lives*. New York University Press.

Halbwachs, M. (1992). *On collective memory* (L. A. Coser, Trans.). University of Chicago Press.

Hass, K. (2009). Remembering the "forgotten war" and containing the "remembered war." In U. J. Hebel (Ed.), *Transnational American memories* (pp. 267–284). Walter de Gruyter.

Hatfield, J. E. (2017). Dancing southern diaspora: Alvin Ailey's blood and the backwardness of quare disidentification. *Text & Performance Quarterly, 37*(1), 51–67. https://doi.org/10.1080/10462937.2017.1307441

Horvat, A. (2020). Haunting and queer histories: Representing memory in Jill Soloway's *Transparent*. *Feminist Media Studies, 20*(3), 398–413. https://doi.org/10.1080/14680777.2019.1609060

Jones, J. M. (2021, February 24). LGBT identification rises to 5.6% in latest U.S. estimate. *Gallup*. https://news.gallup.com/poll/329708/lgbt-identification-rises-latest-estimate.aspx

Juhasz, A. (2012). Forgetting ACT UP. *Quarterly Journal of Speech, 98*(1), 69–74. https://doi.org/10.1080/00335630.2011.638662

Lipari, L. (2007). The rhetoric of intersectionality: Lorraine Hansberry's 1957 letters to the *Ladder*. In C. E. Morris, III (Ed.), *Queering public address: Sexualities in American historical discourse* (pp. 220–248). University of South Carolina Press.

Lynch, J. (2007). Memory and Matthew Shepard: Opposing expressions of public memory in television movies. *Journal of Communication Inquiry, 31*(3), 222–238. https://doi.org/10.1177/0196859907300948

Moraga, C. (2015). Catching fire. In C. Moraga & G. Anzaldúa (Eds.), *This bridge called my back* (pp. xv–xxvi). State University of New York Press.

Morris, C. E., III. (2002). Pink herring and the fourth persona: J. Edgar Hoover's sex crime panic. *Quarterly Journal of Speech, 88*(2), 228–244. https://doi.org/10.1080/00335630209384372

Morris, C. E., III. (2004). My old Kentucky homo: Lincoln and the politics of queer public memory. In K. R. Phillips (Ed.), *Framing public memory* (pp. 89–114). University of Alabama Press.

Morris, C. E., III. (2005). Passing by proxy: Collusive and convulsive silence in the trial of Leopold and Loeb. *Quarterly Journal of Speech, 91*(3), 264–290. https://doi.org/10.1080/00335630500350350

Morris, C. E., III. (2006). Archival queer. *Rhetoric & Public Affairs, 9*(1), 145–151. https://www.jstor.org/stable/41940042

Morris, C. E., III. (Ed.). (2007a). The AIDS memorial quilt at 20: Commemoration and critique of the epidemic text [Special issue]. *Rhetoric & Public Affairs, 10*(4), 557–721. https://www.jstor.org/stable/i40090332

Morris, C. E., III. (Ed.). (2007b). *Queering public address: Sexualities in American historical discourse*. University of South Carolina Press.

Morris, C. E., III. (2009). Richard Halliburton's bearded tales. *Quarterly Journal of Speech, 95*(2), 123–147. https://doi.org/10.1080/00335630902842061

Morris, C. E., III. (2010). (Self-)Portrait of Prof. R.C.: A retrospective. *Western Journal of Communication, 74*(1), 4–42.

Morris, C. E., III. (Ed.). (2011). *Remembering the AIDS quilt*. Michigan State University Press.

Morris, C. E., III. (Ed.). (2012). Forum: Remembering AIDS Coalition to Unleash Power (ACT UP) 1987–2012 and beyond. *Quarterly Journal of Speech, 98*(1), 49–108. https://doi.org/10.1080/00335630.2011.638658

Morris, C. E., III. (2013). Sunder the Children: Abraham Lincoln's queer rhetorical pedagogy. *Quarterly Journal of Speech, 99*(4), 395–422.

Morris, C. E., III. (2015a). Introduction: Abraham Lincoln's Hollywood Rebirth of Freedom. *Rhetoric & Public Affairs, 18*(1), 113–116.

Morris, C. E., III. (2015b). Lincoln's queer hands. *Rhetoric & Public Affairs, 18*(1), 135–140.

Morris, C. E., III. (2015c). Milk memory's queer rhetorical futurity. In J. Alexander & J. Rhodes (Eds.), *Sexual rhetorics: Methods, identities, publics* (pp. 79–92). Routledge.

Morris, C. E., III., & Nakayama, T. (2014). Leaking Chelsea Manning. *QED: A Journal in GLBTQ Worldmaking, 1*(1), vi–vii. https://www.muse.jhu.edu/article/537878

Morris, C. E., III., & Rawson, K. J. (2013). Queer archives/archival queers. In M. Baliff (Ed.), *Theorizing histories of rhetoric* (pp. 74–89). Southern Illinois University Press.

Mourad, S. (2013). Queering the mother tongue. *International Journal of Communication, 7*, 2533–2546.

Muñoz, J. E. (1996). Ephemera as evidence: Introductory notes to queer acts. *Women & Performance: A Journal of Feminist Theory, 8*(2), 5–16. https://doi.org/10.1080/07407709608571228

Muñoz, J. E. (1999). *Queers of color and the performance of politics*. University of Minnesota Press.

Muñoz, J. E. (2009). *Cruising utopia: The then and there of queer futurity*. New York University Press.

Nora, P. (1989). Between memory and history: Las lieux de mémoire. *Representations, 26*, 7–24. https://doi.org/10.2307/2928520

Olson, L. (2007). Traumatic styles in public address: Audre Lorde's discourse as exemplar. In C. E. Morris, III (Ed.), *Queering public address: Sexualities in American historical discourse* (pp. 249–282). University of South Carolina Press.

Ott, B. L., & Aoki, E. (2002). The politics of negotiating public tragedy: Media framing of the Matthew Shepard murder. *Rhetoric & Public Affairs, 5*(3), 483–505. https://www.jstor.org/stable/41939768

Rand, E. J. (2008). An inflammatory fag and a queer form: Larry Kramer, polemics, and rhetorical agency. *Quarterly Journal of Speech, 94*(3), 297–319. https://doi.org/10.1080/00335630802210377

Rand, E. J. (2012). Gay pride and its queer discontents: ACT UP and the political deployment of affect. *Quarterly Journal of Speech, 98*(1), 75–80. https://doi.org/10.1080/00335630.2011.638665

Rawson, K. J. (2009). Accessing transgender//desiring queer(er?) archival logics. *Archivaria, 68*, 123–140. https://archivaria.ca/index.php/archivaria/article/view/13234

Rawson, K. J. (2012). Archive this! Queer(ing) archival practices. In K. Powell & P. Takayoshi (Eds.), *Practicing research in writing studies: Reflections on ethically responsible research* (pp. 237–250). Hampton Press.

Rawson, K. J. (2018). The rhetorical power of archival description: Classifying images of gender transgression. *Rhetoric Society Quarterly, 48*(4), 327–351. https://doi.org/10.1080/02773945.2017.1347951

Rawson, K. J. (2020). About me. kjrawson.net. http://kjrawson.net

Rawson, K. J., & Williams, C. (2014). Transgender*: The rhetorical landscape of a term. *Present Tense, 3*(2), 1–9. https://www.presenttensejournal.org/volume-3/transgender-the-rhetorical-landscape-of-a-term/

Reyes, G. M., Schulz, D. P., & Hovland, Z. (2018). When memory and sexuality collide: The homosentimental style of gay liberation. *Rhetoric & Public Affairs, 21*(1), 39–74. https://doi.org/10.14321/rhetpublaffa.21.1.0039

Richardson, M. (2013). *The queer limit of Black memory*. Ohio State University Press.

Ridinger, R. P. (Ed.). (2004). *Speaking for our lives: Historic speeches and rhetoric for gay and lesbian rights*. Harrington Park Press.

Samek, A. A. (2015). Pivoting between identity politics and coalitional relationships: Lesbian-feminist resistance to the woman-identified woman. *Women's Studies in Communication, 38*(4), 393–420. https://doi.org/10.1080/07491409.2015.1085938

Samek, A. A. (2016). Violence and identity politics: 1970s lesbian-feminist discourse and Robin Morgan's 1973 West Coast Lesbian Conference keynote address. *Communication Critical/Cultural Studies, 13*(3), 232–249. https://doi.org/10.1080/14791420.2015.1127400

Samek, A. A., & Donofrio, T. A. (2013). "Academic drag" and the performance of the critical personae: An exchange of sexuality, politics, and identity in the academy. *Women's Studies in Communication, 36*(1), 28–55. https://doi.org/10.1080/07491409.2012.754388

Sloop, J. M. (2000). Disciplining the transgendered: Brandon Teena, public representation, and normativity. *Western Journal of Communication, 64*(2), 165–189. https://doi.org/10.1080/10570310009374670

Thompson, J. M. (2007). On the development of counter-racist quare public address studies. In C. E. Morris, III (Ed.), *Queering public address: Sexualities in American historical discourse* (pp. 121–148). University of South Carolina Press.

VanHaitsma, P. (2016). Gossip as rhetorical methodology for queer and feminist historiography. *Rhetoric Review, 35*(2), 135–147. https://doi.org/10.1080/07350198.2016.1142845

VanHaitsma, P. (2019a). Digital LGBTQ archives as sites of public memory and pedagogy. *Rhetoric & Public Affairs, 22*(2), 253–280. https://doi.org/10.14321/rhetpublaffa.22.2.0253

VanHaitsma, P. (2019b). *Queering romantic engagement in the postal age: A rhetorical education.* University of South Carolina Press.

VanHaitsma, P., & Book, C. (2019). Digital curation as collaborative archival method in feminist rhetorics. *Peitho: Journal of the Coalition of Feminist Scholars in the History of Rhetoric and Composition, 21*(2), 505–531.

Watts, E. K. (2007). Queer Harlem: Exploring the rhetorical limits of a Black "gay" utopia. In C. E. Morris, III (Ed.), *Queering public address: Sexualities in American historical discourse* (pp. 174–194). University of South Carolina Press.

West, I. (2012). Reviving rage. *Quarterly Journal of Speech, 98*(1), 97–102. https://doi.org/10.1080/00335630.2011.638666

Winter, J. (2001). The generation of memory: Reflections on the "memory boom" in contemporary historical studies. *Canadian Military History, 10*(3), 57–66.

Wittgenstein, L. (1953). *Philosophical investigations* (G. E. Anscombe, Trans.). Basil Blackwell.

Wittgenstein, L. (2009). *Philosophical investigations* (G. E. Anscombe, P. M. S. Hacker, & J. Schulte, Trans.). Wiley-Blackwell.

Woods, C. S., Ewalt, J. P., & Baker, S. J. (2013). A matter of regionalism: Remembering Brandon Teena and Willa Cather at the Nebraska History Museum. *Quarterly Journal of Speech, 99*(3), 341–363. https://doi.org/10.1080/00335630.2013.806818

Yep, G. A. (2011). The politics of loss and its remains in *Common Threads*. In C. E. Morris, III (Ed.), *Remembering the AIDS quilt* (pp. 43–68). Michigan State University Press.

Thomas R. Dunn

QUEER PERSPECTIVES IN COMMUNICATION STUDIES

QUEER ORIGIN STORIES

Attempts to summarize or define queer theory invariably begin with qualifying remarks regarding the enigmatic qualities of queerness. Although conceptualizations of queerness vary greatly, even from author to author, they typically rely upon some sense of resistance, including the refusal to afford legitimacy to discrete classificatory schema or essentialized elements of identities. In this way, as Sara Salih (2002) explains, the slipperiness of the term "queer" confounds the cataloguing of queerness because a queer perspective "is not concerned with definition, fixity or stasis, but is transitive, multiple, and anti-assimilationist" (p. 9). As a thoroughly anti-essentialist enterprise, then, queer theory may not yield itself to the easy capture of generalizations, but even so, its theoretical lineages may be traced and usages mapped, both inside and outside of the disciplines of communication studies.

In many histories of queer studies, Teresa de Lauretis (1991) is credited with coining the term "queer theory" at a conference at the University of California, Santa Cruz, in 1990. "The term 'queer,' juxtaposed to 'lesbian and gay,'" de Lauretis argued, was "intended to mark a certain critical distance from the latter, by now established and often convenient formula" (p. iv) of presenting lesbians and gay men as a homogenous whole with fixed identities, predictable politics, and similar styles. Expounding further, de Lauretis stressed how "queer theory" provided a name for a loosely tethered set of perspective that would, in reference to stable notions of identity and politics, "transgress and transcend them—or at the very least problematize them" (p. v).[1] In concrete terms, de Lauretis named what previously had been a loose assemblage of critical practices concerned with challenging naturalized assumptions about genders, bodies, sexualities, and desires.

Of course, like all histories, this origin story is an incomplete accounting of the multiple sites of queer theory's emergence inside and outside of the academy. A more expansive history would recount: communication studies scholars Paula Treichler (1999) and Cindy Patton's (1985, 1990, 1993, 2002) contributions to our understanding of HIV/AIDS; Esther Newton (1972, 2000) and Gayle Rubin's (1984) anthropological challenge to the cultural construction of naturalized and deviant genders and sexualities in American life; the convergence of queer readings in literature and art in the work of Lauren Berlant and Elizabeth Freeman (1993), Leo Bersani (1987, 1995), D. A. Miller (1992), Adrienne Rich (1980), Eve Kosofsky Sedgwick (1985, 1990), and Michael Warner (1993, 1999); Judith Butler's (1990, 1993, 1997) queering of the stable subjectivities in feminist philosophy and politics and similar moves by Sandy Stone (1991) and Donna Haraway (1991) in feminist science studies; the excavation of queer lives by historians John D'Emilio (1983), Estelle Freedman (1988), Jonathan Ned Katz (1995), George Chauncey (1995), and Leslie Feinberg (1996); and racialized readings of gender and sexuality from Gloria Anzaldúa (1987), Cathy Cohen (1997, 1999), and Audre Lorde (1984).[2] More often than not, political and cultural developments outside academia informed these scholars and intellectuals. As Michael Warner (2012) reminds us, when we try to locate an origin story for queer theory, "What is often forgotten about that moment is that the term came from grass-roots politics before it became theory" (p. B7). The direct action protests of various incarnations of AIDS Coalition to Unleash Power (ACT UP), Queer Nation, Transgender Nation, and Transexual Menace infused academic queer theory with urgency and righteousness about the need to decenter the hegemonic matrixes that privileged White, heteronormative[3] masculinities and femininities. Likewise, the flows between academia and the arts, such as film critic B. Ruby Rich's attention to new queer cinema, Kate Bornstein's performance art, and the poetry and documentaries of Essex Hemphill and Marlon Riggs, produced productive pathways for rethinking well-established and accepted critical theories.

Finally, narrowing the focus back to communication studies, no retelling of queer theory's early trajectories would be complete without also charting a parallel, internal history of the research rejected by those invested in conscious and unconscious forms of heteronormativity and queer erasure, including scholars who preferred LGBT studies to queer studies (Morris & Palczewski, 2014). In practice, LGBT and queer studies have never been discrete lines of inquiry or linearly sequential as their adherents might portray them to be, yet, nevertheless, schisms between LGBT and queer studies have flared up, owing some of their genesis to real or perceived generational differences, political priorities, and personal conflicts (Gross, 2005). Also, in some articulations of queer theory, scholars deployed it as a corrective to LGBT studies, condemning the recuperation of LGBT speakers or the identification of sexuality as a variable as irreparably intertwined with essentialized sexual identities. Although now we may read these projects as more complementary than antagonistic to one another, the hard-fought struggle of LGBT studies in communication studies should be acknowledged as part of queer theory's intellectual lineage.[4] All of this is to say, in reviewing the development of queer theory in communication studies, readers must keep in mind that researchers have had to negotiate multiple forms of gatekeeping along the way.

DEFINING THE QUEER IN QUEER THEORY

Without any one authoritative or germinal definition from which to work, say an explicitly defined concept more typically found in social science research, scholars have operationalized "queer" in various ways. For example, some have stressed queer theory's emphasis on sexualities and desires as a way to distinguish it from feminist theory's primary interest in gender. Annamarie Jagose (1996) proposed the following definition of the term queer:

> Broadly speaking, queer describes those gestures or analytical models which dramatize incoherencies in the allegedly stable relations between chromosomal sex, gender, and sexual desire. Resisting that model of stability—which claims heterosexuality as its origin, when it is more properly its effect—queer focuses on mismatches between sex, gender, and desire. (p. 3)[5]

Although there has been and continues to be significant disagreement about whether or not queer has a necessary correspondence to sexuality, many of the earliest formulations of queer as a category of analysis included some consideration of non-normative sexualities as a constitutive component of queerness.

In addition to queerness as a mode of individual expression, queer can be defined as a mode of analysis that toggles between individuals and cultures to give presence to instruments of heteronormativity and the resistances practiced against these forces. Michael Warner (1991) explained this critical enterprise in the following terms:

> The insistence on "queer"—a term defined against "normal" and generated precisely in the context of terror—has the effect of pointing out a wide field of normalization, rather than simple intolerance, as a site of violence. Its brilliance as a naming strategy lies in combining resistance on the broad social terrain of the normal with more specific resistance on the terrains of phobia and queer-bashing, on one hand, or of pleasure on the other. (p. 16)

By directing attention to cultural inducements to heteronormative conformity as well as exposing potential cracks in these networks, Warner's definition highlights the twin impulses of queer theory: critical analysis and praxis for changing these conditions of possibility.

More recently, the category of queerness has taken on a more ecumenical tone as it has been defined as an umbrella term that exceeds differentiation based on sexuality alone to imagine queerness in more capacious terms to include the shared concerns of trans folk, single persons, people of color, and transnational alliances of oppressed persons. Moreover, a more explicit emphasis on activism and collective action against a broader range of normativities than heteronormativity alone is increasingly prevalent. Cathy Cohen (1997) asked queer theorists and political actors to think of queerness more broadly to expand, rather than limit, its coalitional possibilities by reconsidering the shared conditions of multiple, even overlapping and intersectional, groups, such as racial minorities and economically disadvantaged persons. For similar reasons, José Esteban Muñoz (2009) emphasized the creative capacities of queer thought and movement when he described queerness as "that thing that lets us feel that this world is not enough, that indeed something is missing," and in its goading for something else, queerness is a "rejection of a here and now and an insistence on potentiality or concrete possibility for another world" (p. 1).

As stated earlier, part of the difficulty in mapping out queer's queer career is rooted in the academic appropriations of this theory from activists and activism outside of the academy, including the ever-changing terminologies of queerness as well as the cultural productions of queerness (e.g., protests, art, political formations, the proliferation of filial bonds, and so on). Judith Butler (1999) identifies this academic interchange as "necessarily impure, where it emerges in and as the very event of cultural translation" (p. ix). In addition, rather than lament queer's indeterminacy, its protean qualities afford communication studies significant latitude as a perspective for research. In Butler's (1993) estimation,

> If the term "queer" is to be the site of collective contestation, the point of departure for a set of historical reflections and futural imaginings, it will have to remain that which is, in the present, never fully owned, but always and only redeployed, twisted, queered from a prior usage and in the direction of urgent and expanding political purposes. (p. 228)

Consequently, queer as a critical category is deconstructive in the most productive sense of the term, leaving itself open for revision and challenge from what has been excluded and occluded in its definition (Rand, 2004; Sewell, 2014). For those interested in practicing queer criticism in communication studies, however, the varied aims and objects of queer theory have frustrated attempts to develop a consensus about its conventions (Alexander & Rhodes, 2015; Rand, 2013; Spencer, 2014; West, 2013).

This short genealogy of the term "queer" evidences the difficulty in trying to pin down a word that can function as a noun, adjective, and verb (Jakobsen, 1998). Of course, these different forms are interrelated and inform one another. To tease out some of the differences, subsequent sections will review communication studies scholarship related to identities (noun), representations (adjectives), and politics (verb). Although it is an imprecise and incomplete grafting of different parts of speech onto complex scholarly conversations, what it allows is an opportunity to trace some emergent themes across the subfields of communication studies without any necessary assumptions about how a particular subfield does or does not employ queer studies in their work. Before that, however, two figures loom large enough in this work that it requires a pause to explore further their corpus: first, Michel Foucault, then Butler, are taken up in turn.

MICHEL FOUCAULT: DISCOURSE, KNOWLEDGE, POWER

The nexus between discourse, knowledge, and power motivated Michel Foucault's inquiries into topics as varied as the penal system, psychiatry, and academic disciplines. As someone suspicious of the desires behind discrete classifications, Foucault (1969, 1971/1972) never defined or delimited the term "discourse," opting instead to "[treat] it sometimes as the general domain of all statements, sometimes as an individualizable group of statements, and sometimes as a regulated practice that accounts for a certain number of statements" (p. 80). In his studies of discursive formations, Foucault performed genealogical investigations into how experts and lay people alike employed discourses to create knowledges that would then be recirculated through discourses as truths, thereby concealing their status as merely one way of understanding the world against all other possibilities. In this way, Foucault challenged the prevailing trends in critical theory whereby communication had been treated as an epiphenomenal consideration in critical theory, meaning communication often served an instrumental role in the service of securing and perpetuating dominant ideologies.

Rather than accept this nihilistic rendering of power, wherein human agency could be found only in the elimination of ideologies, Foucault sought out to demonstrate how discourses participate in the formation of knowledges and exercises of power that are productive. In Foucault's (1980) estimation, ideology, as a critical category of analysis, fails us because it relies on at least three problematic assumptions: (1) most theories of ideology involve some form of obfuscation vis-à-vis an external and transcendent truth, which Foucault refused to ratify; (2) many theories of ideology rely on the recuperation of a sovereign subject who can somehow transcend existing power relations and step outside of them into a field devoid of power; and (3) the process of demystifying ideologies repeats the epiphenomenal error that grants undue agency to external forces acting on us as opposed to power operating in and through us. In short, ideological analysis, for Foucault, makes the mistake of presuming that ideologies can be overcome, once and for all, in the final instance, by a shift in consciousness. Yet, Foucault understood that cultures are dependent upon shared and naturalized assumptions for the living of our lives together. As a result, rooting out all ideologies is a quixotic task because even in the event of an overthrowing of one ideological regime, we would be immersed into another set of ideological regimes. All is not lost, according to Foucault, because not all ideologies or norms operate equally or harmfully, as he demonstrated in his writings on human sexuality.

When Foucault set his sights on sexuality, he sought out to draw a diachronic map of the knowledges of sexuality, including the regulation of sexuality and desires as well as its practices.[6] Foucault would die before he finished the complete series, but the first volume, *La volonté de savoir* (*The Will to Knowledge*; 1976/1978), served as one of the foundational texts for queer theorists due to its subject matter and its attention to resistance as a political project.

For communication studies scholars, four moves in this volume are valuable touchstones for theorizing communication, identity, and politics.

First, Foucault rejected the repressive hypothesis. In brief, the repressive hypothesis suggested that people felt and described themselves as sexually repressed by multiple sources of prohibition, such as churches and the state. Foucault documented that a very different state of affairs persisted despite these supposed prohibitions. Less a case of prohibition, people enjoyed recirculating the idea of the repressive hypothesis so they could experience the pleasure of violating it through talk about sex, if not participating in prohibited sex acts themselves. This critique of the repressive hypothesis laid the groundwork to challenge psychological cures for nonnormative personalities, which often depended upon the excavation of a sovereign subject from a traumatic event. In the same stroke, Foucault's critique of the repressive hypothesis refused to acknowledge it as an ideology capable of creating one and only one kind of subject. In this way, Foucault valued communication as a subjective experience capable of producing pleasure and pain.

Second, Foucault traced how desires are translated in power-knowledge through discourse, from religious practices like confession to psychiatric discourses of proper sexualities. The slow codification of *scientia sexualis* over *ars erotica*, or the intensification of truths about sex over and against a culture concerned with maximizing pleasures (multiplying discourses instead of multiplying pleasures), demanded that desires be translated into discourses about the self that could be classified, placed within hierarchies, and valued and devalued. As truths about sex cohered into overarching theories of personage, what might have been previously understood as a sexual act performed by a person transformed into a reflection of their true identity. Thus, when Foucault (1976/1978) states, "The sodomite had been a temporary aberration; the homosexual was now a species" (p. 43), he is not saying that same-sex sexual acts or attractions did not exist prior to 1870, only that the consolidation of medical discourses settled upon homosexuality as an identity category characterized by same-sex sexual practices as expressions of an inner, true self.[7] Part and parcel with the repressive hypothesis, Foucault wanted to use these examples to demonstrate how identities are an effect of discourse, rather than discourse reflecting one's core identity.

Third, identities allow for resistance, as demonstrated through multiple examples of persons using categories of identity to resist their oppression. In spite of some of the more horrific experiences suffered by those with deviant sexualities, Foucault read against the grain to expose how these identities afforded subjects avenues for resistance. At the nexus of power-knowledge is an opportunity to be recognized and work the weaknesses of the hegemonic logics operative in a particular context, thus providing communication as a necessary site of agency and politics.

Fourth, if power is not possessed but is instead exercised through the joining of power-knowledge in specific exercises of power, a different kind of politics is in order—not the demystifying agenda of many critical theorists, but instead, a politics of resistance that works within existing power relations. For Foucault, there is nothing outside of the network of power relations operative in our cultural webs. Instead of trying to seize power away from someone else, a logic of revolution proves to be liable to the ideological trappings noted above. Yet, opportunities for resistance are created by exercises of power. Thus, identities and recognition create chances to shift, but not escape, power relations.

Taken together, these four principles from Foucault have informed communication studies scholarship in important ways, especially with regard to the interconnectedness of discourses, power, identities, and resistance. Foucault's work also forms some of the primary foci for Butler.

JUDITH BUTLER, SPEECH ACTS, AND PERFORMATIVITY

Judith Butler's conception of performativity circulates widely in communication studies due to its emphasis on the communicative flows of identities in specific contexts, thus allowing for a theory of agency located in the negotiation of symbols between persons and institutions. In an extension of Foucault's thoughts on the communicative dimensions of identities, agency, and politics, Butler presents a compelling case for reevaluating multiple foundational logics operative in communication studies, particularly speakers, identities, and effects.

For Butler, performativity is different from performance. On Butler's reading, performance relies on a sovereign subject imbued with intentions, such as someone who is performing a role or putting on a performance.[8] In contrast, performativity questions the concept of the speaking and thinking subject from the outset. Indebted to Friedrich Nietzsche's metaphysical challenge to the idea of the subject, Butler asks us to rethink the subject: "there is no 'being' behind doing, effecting, becoming; the 'doer' is merely a fiction added to the deed—the deed is everything" (as cited in Butler, 1999, p. 33). Along with Nietzsche, Butler is not denying the existence of persons who speak and move, but Butler questions the temporalities associated with common conceptions of subjectivity, meaning, in the case of communication studies, foregoing fundamental assumptions such as the premise that the speaker precedes the act of speaking. Why? In brief, belief in the sovereign subject imbued with discernable intents and self-mastery inhibits the possibility to question how those subjects came into being through discourses. Echoing Foucault, what happens if we approach subjects not as sources of discourse, but as effects of discourse?

With this in mind, Butler negotiates different understandings of speech acts and their effects, especially J. L. Austin's (1962) speech act theories and Louis Althusser's (1970/1971) earlier theorizations of interpellation to explain how subjects share space and time with one another through intersubjective experiences with one another.

For Austin, among the various types of speech acts are constative statements and performative utterances. Even for Austin himself, the distinctions between these were difficult to uphold, but the general idea is that some statements convey information (constative utterances) and some utterances do something as they are announced (performative utterances). When a layperson says, "I hope that criminal is put to death," it is a constative claim in Austin's formulation, while a criminal judge's performative utterance, "I sentence you to death," is both informative but also carries with it the force of the law behind it. More than an instrumental act of communication, such a performative utterance sets into motion the machinery of the death penalty. Butler rejects this bifurcation and its underlying temporalities. For Butler, this distinction collapses under the weight of its logic because the constative claim is also performative, although not always in the grand ways associated with performative utterances such as a death sentence. To name something is to performatively reproduce a set of assumptions and norms as subjects negotiate the meanings of such statements. Owing something to Jacques

Derrida's work on citationality, subjects exist in chains of signification—today, we may think of these as networks of meaning—that precede and exceed any one person's intentions.

What Butler wants to preserve is the notion that language (symbols) participates in intersubjective relations, meaning, language (speech acts) and establishes relationalities based on contexts and prior knowledges as well as the historicity of those symbols. Also, then, speech acts help to situate interlocutors in signifying chains that precede and exceed them—we are not sovereign subjects outside of the reach of the subjectivizing radiances of power-knowledges. The signifying chain is not determinative in the final instance because symbols are porous and polysemous, which requires revisiting Althusser and interpellation if a statement is never self-contained or self-executing in line with the speaker's intentions.

On Althusser's accountings of ideology and subjectivity, interpellation explains how ideologies constitute subjects and solidify certain kinds of consciousness. In contrast to Foucault, for Althusser, subjects are placed into ideological positions by an institution or one of its agents through the hailing of the subject. As the subject accepts this recognition, they are interpellated or constrained by the ideological conditions of the hail. What Butler wants to recuperate is a sense of recognition with a looser ideological grasp, hence the interjection of Foucault to help explain how discourses constitute multiple subjectivities rather than a singular, ideologically-secured position. That is, for Butler, this is recognition without ideological capture, which does not deny that ideology acts, but that its capture is not complete or determining (recalling Foucault's notion, where there is power, there is resistance). For Butler, agency is found in the resistances negotiated by subjectivities and institutions and each other in a complex web where nothing is guaranteed in advance as negotiations and renegotiations of these ever-shifting power relations continually do and undo each other. Undoubtedly, some relations of power are more sticky and recalcitrant than others, but agency is not found in the reversal of power—it is temporally situated in its disruption at more localized levels.

Together, Foucault and Butler have assisted communication scholars to highlight the communicative dimensions of identities, representations, and politics as worthwhile sites of analysis.

QUEER PEOPLE

The term "queer" can operate as a noun naming a person and/or their identity (e.g., queers), a collective noun (e.g., queers of color), or as an adjective to modify an individual or a class of persons (e.g., queer students). As a result, some scholars employ "queer" in imprecise ways, sometimes as a synonym for LGBT persons, sometimes as an umbrella term that is meant to convey something more inclusive and capacious than LGBT, or as something divorced completely from sexual orientation and gender identity altogether.

In some ways, reflecting the tension in Foucault, the identity category of queer is one open to patrol and discipline by those who may identify as queer and those who do not (Brookey, 2002; Cram, 2012; Brouwer, 2004; Fox & Warber, 2015; Grindstaff, 2006; Poirot, 2009). Alternatively, others anchor their analysis in the performativities of queer identities wherein the fluidity of queer categories of identity is unstable and unpredictable (Bennett, 2003; Brookey, 1998; Faulkner & Hecht, 2011; Fox, 2007, 2010; Morris, 1996, 1998, 2010; Wight, 2011). For example, historical inquiry into the communicative patterns and choices of those we may classify as queer have demonstrated the variety of subject positions available to individuals that complicate our understanding of what it means to be marked or not by queerness in those times and spaces (Cram, 2016; Dunn, 2016; Morris, 1996, 1998). Many of the earlier incarnations centered cisgender, White gay men, but, more recently, challenges to this academic norms are making communication studies accountable to these blindspots, including research emphasizing ethnic and racialized identities (Abdi & Van Gilder, 2016; Lee, 2003; McCune, 2008, 2014; Moreman & McIntosh, 2010; Pelle, 2010; Snorton, 2014; Van Gilder & Abdi, 2014) as well as trans identities (Cavalcante, 2016; Nuru, 2014; Wagner, Kunkel, & Compton, 2016). More direct challenges to queer articulations of performativity, derived from the experiences of people of color, have destabilized the mythic status of White, gay, cisgender men as the norm for communication studies scholarship (Howard, 2014). Most notably, E. Patrick Johnson's (2001) coining of "quare studies" as a perspective that makes scholars accountable to the embodiedness of racialized sexualities has spawned others to model this decentering of dominant norms and assumptions in queer studies.

In relative terms, scholars working in intercultural, interpersonal, organizational, relational, and family communication have adopted and employed queer perspectives at a slower pace than their counterparts in rhetorical, media, and performance studies. In line with other social sciences, these subfields have tended to treat non-normative sexual relationships and gender identities as outliers when crafting calls for participation, collecting data, and interpreting results (Chevrette, 2013; Goins & Pye, 2013; Heinz, 2002; Wood & Duck, 1995). Scholars have called for their colleagues to recognize and resist the myriad ways that heteronormativity is implicitly and explicitly privileged in these subfields (Elia, 2003; Foster, 2008; Lovaas, 2003; McDonald, 2015; Rich, Schutten, & Rogers, 2012). More than just additive measures of including self-identified queers in research questions, scholars have requested a fuller accounting of how heteronormativity operates in the conventions of communication research, including: disproportionate focus on dyads and dyadic communication, an overreliance on conventional family structures as the sources of knowledge instead of kinship networks, measures of family structures that tend to incorporate and strengthen naturalized assumptions about normative genders and sexualities, and how language choices such as alternative families or conclusions that stress similarities between LGBT and non-LGBT families can reinforce heterosexual norms as normative. These concerns are not the provenance of these subfields alone, but they do help to explain why queer theory has been explored less in these lines of research.

That said, there are some notable exceptions in these subfields, particularly in family communication. More recent work emphasizing the discursive challenges associated with lesbian motherhood (Bergen, Suter, & Daas, 2006; Breshears, 2010, 2011; Suter, Seurer, Webb, Grewe, & Koenig Kellas, 2015), the communicative potential of non-hetero-nuclear families to subvert prevailing understandings of families and relational norms (Bacon, 2012; Baxter, 2014; Bevan & Lannutti, 2002; Breshears & Braithwaite, 2014; Suter & Strasser, 2014), how families can redeploy symbols such as rings and homes in a non-heteronormative key (Suter & Daas, 2007), and how transgender individuals introduce new modes of identification for their families (Norwood, 2012, 2013a, 2013b, 2014).

Likewise, a nascent interest in queer topics is blossoming in intercultural communication as well (Chávez, 2013b; Eguchi, 2015; Eguchi & Asante, 2016). At the heart of this work is scholarly pressure upon national, regional, and racialized assumptions about genders, sexualities, bodies, and desires. In turn, queer intercultural communication studies is queering the field through studies on how bodies are made legible to each other (McKinnon, 2016), how transnational flows of bodies and discourses inform legal regimes (Erni, 2017), and the need for critical self-reflexivity in analyzing the discourses of persons in and out of their immediate cultural contexts (Goltz, Zingsheim, Mastin, & Murphy, 2016).

QUEER REPRESENTATIONS

One of the most robust sites of queer communication studies has been and continues to be critiques of mediated representations of queerness. Some of the earliest work functioned more in the mode of consciousness-raising in its focus on heterosexism across various media (Erni, 1998; Fejes & Petrich, 1993; Gamson, 1998; Gross, 2002; Thompson, 2002). As LGBT characters gained greater visibility, examinations of predictable patterns of stereotypical representations dominated this vein of critical practice. With more frequent and visible representations on television, particular programs or characters elicited significant academic attention, including Ellen DeGeneres (Dow, 2001; Skerski, 2007), *Queer Eye for the Straight Guy* (Booth, 2011; Clarkson, 2005; Papacharissi & Fernback, 2008; Pearson & Lozano-Reich, 2009; Ramsey & Santiago, 2004; Sender, 2006; Shugart, 2008; Weiss, 2005; Westerfelhaus & Lacroix, 2006), and *Will & Grace* (Battles & Hilton-Morrow, 2002; Schiappa, Gregg, & Hewes, 2005; Wolf, 2013). Likewise, movies attracted similar lines of critique, such as *Philadelphia* (Brookey, 1996) and *Brokeback Mountain* (Cooper & Pease, 2008; Grindstaff, 2008), multiple filmic treatments of Matthew Shepard (Ott & Aoki, 2002; Lynch, 2007), and filmic representations of trans lives (Booth, 2011; Cooper, 2002; Sloop, 2004).

At the heart of much of this work is what kinds of visibilities are afforded prominence and to what effect for the audiences interacting with them. In general, this branch of queer critique retains as its deconstructive mission the demystification of seemingly queer texts to demonstrate their complicity in hegemonic and normative constructs (Cherney & Lindemann, 2014; Dunn, 2015; Enck & Morrisey, 2015; Goltz, 2010; Gray, 2009b; Landau, 2009; LeMaster, 2015; Sender, 2004). One of the vexing questions with all media criticism, of which queer critique is not immune, is how the critic imagines the relationship between texts, contexts, and audiences. That is, what are the operative assumptions in the critic's reading strategy regarding the textual agency of the text and how audiences are implicated or not in those textual agencies? So, for example, if a critic claims a text reinforces heteronormativity more than it challenges it, is this an ontological judgment about the text or is it one interpretive possibility that exists alongside other possible judgments? In spite of queer theory's anti-essentialist assumptions, much of the critique of mediated representations tends toward the former over the latter (Brookey & Westerfelhaus, 2001; Draper, 2010). Greater attention to circulation and audience interpretations has challenged this prevailing practice.

Within communication studies, Edward Schiappa has developed the most extensive critique of the assumed relationship between critical readings of texts and audience uptakes of these messages. Through extensive empirical research, Schiappa (2008) developed the parasocial contact hypothesis, which argues that audiences may not always decode messages in ways predicted by queer critiques of media texts. As an example, Schiappa, Gregg, and Hewes (2006) argues that viewers of *Will & Grace* changed their beliefs about gay men after watching the program, and not always in ways that align with accepted stereotypes about gay men. Although not directly related to Schiappa's theories, others have started to think through the implications of more agentic takes on audiences and discourses, wherein audiences may be processing and articulating textual interpretations that differ from expected readings of queer representations (Bennett, 2014; Dhaenens, 2014; LeMaster, 2011; Marwick, Gray, & Ananny, 2014; Sender, 2015). Additionally, some scholars are working through reading strategies that embrace the multiplicities in text whereby either-or choices about complicity with dominant cultures are an insufficient interpretation of representations (Bennett, 2010; Cavalcante, 2015; Ciszek, 2014; Goltz, 2013; King, 2010, 2016; King & West, 2013; West, Frischherz, Panther, & Brophy, 2013). In sum, then, this area of research remains a fertile ground for engaging queer cultural productions.

POLITICS

One of the earliest uses of and elaborations on queer in communication studies focused on queer social movements, such as Queer Nation (Slagle, 1995). What was already latent in other works, especially considerations of HIV/AIDS representations and activism, found a different articulation when framed within academic forms of queer theory (Gilder, 1989; Dow, 1994; Christiansen & Hanson, 1996; DeLuca, 1999; Smith & Windes, 2000; Scott, 2003; Brouwer, 2005; Morris, 2011). Like other political formations, queer political formations questioned their own organizing logics, including the centrality of a fixed identity as a precursor for political action and the ability of political groups to accomplish goals without strict organizational structures or hierarchies (Fejes, 2008; Gross, 2005; Rand, 2014). In many cases, queer political actions questioned the very foundations of publics and their norms of decorum and propriety allowing for expanded notions of politics and publics (Brouwer, 1998, 2005; DeLuca, 1999; Morris & Sloop, 2006). More recently, greater attention has been focused on the rhetorics of rights and citizenship, yet no clear consensus has developed about the queer (im)possibilities of queer citizenships (Bennett, 2009; Campbell, 2012; Chávez, 2010; Lipari, 2002; Moscowitz, 2013; West 2014, 2015).

Of course, the articulation of identities and politics is usually fraught with difficulties as disparate groups attempt to identify with one another in common cause. Differences can impede political action if political actors are not able to overcome these divides (Chávez, 2004).

The communicative dimensions of queer coalitional politics is a burgeoning area of research in its attempt to unite communication theories with political action (Awwad, 2010; Chávez, 2013a; Kearl, 2015; Perez & Goltz, 2010; Samek, 2015; Tate, 2005).

CONCLUSIONS

Although in many ways the uptake of queer studies has been frustrated by the norms of communication studies research protocols and ideologies, a substantial body of research exists across the subfields of communication studies to challenge naturalized assumptions about our bodies, genders, relationships, and desires. The communicative dimensions of queer identities are now open for critique regarding their fixity and permanence. What may have once been understood as a medical, legal, or cultural fact may now be thought of as one discursive possibility among others that may fluctuate across one's lifespan, different contexts, and evolving sense of one's self. In a similar manner, queer critiques of representations have demonstrated the limits and possibilities of queer words, images, and affects to transform our symbolic landscapes. And investigations of queer political formations remind us of how people navigate more and less hospitable terrains together in and through their similarities and differences. As this work proliferates across communication studies, it will continue to undo the norms and conventions of cultural categories and research practices.

PRIMARY SOURCES

The Digital Transgender Archive. https://www.digitaltransgenderarchive.net/.
The Kinsey Institute for Research in Sex, Gender, and Reproduction. Indiana University. (https://www.kinseyinstitute.org/).
ONE/International Gay and Lesbian Archives, University of Southern California, Los Angeles. https://one.usc.edu/.

FURTHER READING

Berlant, L., & Warner, M. (1995). What does queer theory teach us about X? *PMLA, 110*, 343–349.
Bronski, M. (2011). *A queer history of the United States*. Beacon Press.
Chesebro, J. (Ed.). (1981). *Gayspeak: Gay male and lesbian communication*. Pilgrim Press.
Currah, P., & Stryker, S. (Eds.). (2014). Postposttranssexual: Key concepts for a twenty-first-century transgender studies [Special issue]. *Transgender Studies Quarterly, 1*(1–2), 1–272.
Henderson, L. (2000). Queer communication studies. In W. Gudykunst (Ed.), *Communication yearbook* (pp. 465–484). SAGE.
Jagose, A. (1996). *Queer theory: An introduction*. New York University Press.
Johnson, E. P., & Henderson, M. (Eds.). (2005). *Black queer studies: A critical anthology*. Duke University Press.
Morris, C., III. (Ed.). (2007). *Queering public address: Sexualities in American historical discourse*. University of South Carolina Press.
Morris, C., III. (Ed.). (2009). Queering the South [Special issue]. *Southern Communication Journal, 74*(3), 233–337.
Ringer, J. (Ed.). (1994). *Queer words, queer images: Communication and the construction of homosexuality*. New York University Press.
Spencer, L., & Capuzza, J. (Eds.). (2015). *Transgender communication studies: Histories, trends, and trajectories*. Lexington.
Stryker, S. (2008). *Transgender history*. Seal Press.
Sullivan, N. (2003). *A critical introduction to queer theory*. New York University Press.
Turner, W. (2000). *A genealogy of queer theory*. Temple University Press.
Valentine, D. (2007). *Imagining transgender: An ethnography of a category*. Duke University Press.
Wilchins, R. (2004). *Queer theory, gender theory: An instant primer*. Alyson Books.
Yep, G., Lovaas, K., & Elia, J. (Eds.). (2003). *Queer theory and communication: From disciplining queers to queering the disciplines*. Hawthorn.

REFERENCES

Abdi, S., & Van Gilder, B. (2016). Cultural (in)visibility and identity dissonance: Queer Iranian-American women and their negotiation of existence. *Journal of International & Intercultural Communication, 9*(1), 69–86. http://dx.doi.org/10.1080/17513057.2016.1120850

Alexander, J., & Rhodes, J. (Eds.). (2015). *Sexual rhetorics: Methods, identities, publics.* Routledge.

Althusser, L. (1971). *Lenin and philosophy and other essays* (B. Brewster, Trans.). Monthly Review Press. (Original work published in 1970.)

Anzaldúa, G. (1987). *Broderlands/la frontera: The new mestizo.* Aunt Lute.

Austin, J. L. (1962). *How to do things with words* (2nd ed.). (Eds. J. O. Urmson & M. Sbisá). Harvard University Press.

Awwad, J. (2010). The postcolonial predicament of gay rights in the *Queen Boat* affair. *Communication and Critical/Cultural Studies, 7,* 318–336. http://dx.doi.org/10.1080/14791420.2010.504598

Bacon, J. (2012). Until death do us part: Lesbian rhetorics of relational divorce. *Women's Studies in Communication, 35,* 158–177. http://dx.doi.org/10.1080/07491409.2012.724523

Battles, K., & Hilton-Morrow, W. (2002). Gay characters in conventional spaces: *Will and Grace* and the situation comedy genre. *Critical Studies in Media Communication, 19,* 87–105. http://dx.doi.org/10.1080/07393180216553

Baxter, L. (Ed.). (2014). *Remaking "family" communicatively.* Peter Lang.

Bennett, J. (2003). Love me gender: Normative homosexuality and "ex-gay" performativity in reparative therapy narratives. *Text and Performance Quarterly, 23,* 331–352. http://dx.doi.org/10.1080/1046293042000190603

Bennett, J. (2009). *Banning queer blood: Rhetorics of citizenship, contagion, and resistance.* University of Alabama Press.

Bennett, J. (2010). Queer teenagers and the mediation of utopian catastrophe. *Critical Studies in Media Communication, 27,* 455–476. http://dx.doi.org/10.1080/15295030903583580

Bennett, J. (2014). "Born This Way:" Queer vernacular and the politics of origin. *Communication and Critical/Cultural Studies, 11,* 211–230. http://dx.doi.org/10.1080/14791420.2014.924153

Bergen, K. M., Suter, E. A., & Daas, K. L. (2006). "About as solid as a fish net": Symbolic construction of a legitimate parental identity for nonbiological lesbian mothers. *Journal of Family Communication, 6*(3), 201–220. http://dx.doi.org/10.1207/s15327698jfc0603_3

Berlant, L., & Freeman, E. (1993). Queer nationality. In M. Warner (Ed.), *Fear of a queer planet: Queer politics and social theory* (pp. 193–229). University of Minnesota Press.

Berlant, L., & Warner, M. (1998). Sex in public. *Critical Inquiry, 24,* 547–566.

Bersani, L. (1987). Is the rectum a grave? *October, 43,* 197–222.

Bersani, L. (1995). *Homos.* Harvard University Press.

Bevan, J. L., & Lannutti, P. J. (2002). The experience and expression of romantic jealousy in same-sex and opposite-sex romantic relationships. *Communication Research Reports, 19,* 258–268. http://dx.doi.org/10.1080/08824090209384854

Booth, E. T. (2011). Queering *Queer Eye*: The stability of gay identity confronts the liminality of trans embodiment. *Western Journal of Communication, 75,* 185–204. http://dx.doi.org/10.1080/10570314.2011.553876

Breshears, D. (2010). Coming out with our children: Turning points facilitating lesbian parent discourse with their children about family identity. *Communication Reports, 23*(2), 79–90. http://dx.doi.org/10.1080/08934215.2010.511398

Breshears, D. (2011). Understanding communication between lesbian parents and their children regarding outsider discourse about family identity. *Journal of GLBT Family Studies, 7,* 264–284. http://dx.doi.org/10.1080/1550428X.2011.564946

Breshears, D., & Braithwaite, D. (2014). Discursive struggles animating individuals' talk about their parents' coming out as lesbian or gay. *Journal of Family Communication, 14*, 189–207. http://dx.doi.org/10.1080/15267431.2014.908197

Brookey, R. A. (1996). A community like *Philadelphia*. *Western Journal of Communication, 60*(1), 40–56. http://dx.doi.org/10.1080/10570319609374532

Brookey, R. (1998). Keeping a good wo/man down: Normalizing Deborah Sampson Gannett. *Communication Studies, 49*, 73–85. http://dx.doi.org/10.1080/10510979809368519

Brookey, R., & Westerfelhaus, R. (2001). Pistols and petticoats, piety and purity: *To Wong Foo*, the queering of the American monomyth, and the marginalizing discourse of deification. *Critical Studies in Media Communication, 18*, 141–156. http://dx.doi.org/10.1080/07393180128080

Brookey, R. A. (2002). *Reinventing the male homosexual: The rhetoric and power of the gay gene*. Indiana University Press.

Brouwer, D. (1998). The precarious visibility politics of self-stigmatization: The case of HIV/AIDS tattoos. *Text and Performance Quarterly, 18*, 114–136. http://dx.doi.org/10.1080/10462939809366216

Brouwer, D. (2004). Corps/corpse: The U.S. military and homosexuality. *Western Journal of Communication, 68*, 411–430. http://dx.doi.org/10.1080/10570310409374811

Brouwer, D. (2005). Counterpublicity and corporeality in HIV/AIDS zines. *Critical Studies in Media Communication, 22*, 351–371. http://dx.doi.org/10.1080/07393180500342860

Butler, J. (1990). *Gender trouble: Feminism and the subversion of identity*. Routledge.

Butler, J. (1993). *Bodies that matter: On the discursive limits of "sex."* Routledge.

Butler, J. (1997). *Excitable speech: A politics of the performative*. Routledge.

Butler, J. (1999). *Gender trouble: Feminism and the subversion of identity* (10th anniversary ed.). Routledge.

Campbell, P. (2012). The procedural queer: Substantive due process, *Lawrence v. Texas*, and queer rhetorical futures. *Quarterly Journal of Speech, 98*, 203–229. http://dx.doi.org/10.1080/00335630.2012.663923

Cavalcante, A. (2015). Anxious displacements: The representation of gay parenting on *Modern Family* and *The New Normal* and the management of cultural anxiety. *Television & New Media, 16*(5), 454–471. http://dx.doi.org/10.1177/1527476414538525

Cavalcante, A. (2016). "I did it all online": Transgender identity and the management of everyday life. *Critical Studies in Media Communication, 33*(1), 109–122. http://dx.doi.org/10.1080/15295036.2015.1129065

Chauncey, G. (1995). *Gay New York: Gender, urban culture, and the making of the gay male world, 1890–1940*. Basic Books.

Chávez, K. (2004). Beyond complicity: Coherence, queer theory, and the rhetoric of the "Gay Christian Movement". *Text and Performance Quarterly, 24*, 255–275. http://dx.doi.org/10.1080/1046293042000312760

Chávez, K. (2010). Border (in)securities: Normative and differential belonging in LGBTQ and immigrant rights discourse. *Communication & Critical/Cultural Studies, 7*, 136–155. http://dx.doi.org/10.1080/14791421003763291

Chávez, K. (2013a). *Queer migration politics: Activist rhetorics and coalitional possibilities*. University of Illinois Press.

Chávez, K. (Ed.). (2013b). Out of bounds? Queer intercultural communication [Special issue]. *Journal of International and Intercultural Communication, 6*(2). http://dx.doi.org/10.1080/17513057.2013.777506

Cherney, J., & Lindemann, K. (2014). Queering Street: Homosociality, masculinity, and disability in *Friday Night Lights*. *Western Journal of Communication, 78*(1), 1–21. http://dx.doi.org/10.1080/10570314.2013.792388

Chesebro, J. (Ed.). (1981). *Gayspeak: Gay male & lesbian communication*. Pilgrim Press.

Chevrette, R. (2013). Outing heteronormativity in interpersonal and family communication: Feminist applications of queer theory "beyond the sexy streets". *Communication Theory, 23,* 170–190. http://dx.doi.org/10.1111/comt.12009

Christiansen, A., & Hanson, J. (1996). Comedy as cure for tragedy: ACT UP and the rhetoric of AIDS. *Quarterly Journal of Speech, 82,* 157–170. http://dx.doi.org/10.1080/00335639609384148

Clarkson, J. (2005). Contesting masculinity's makeover: *Queer Eye,* consumer masculinity, and "straight-acting" gays. *Journal of Communication Inquiry, 29,* 235–255. http://dx.doi.org/10.1177/0196859905275234

Ciszek, E. (2014). Cracks in the glass slipper. Does it really "Get Better" for LGBTQ youth, or is it just another Cinderella story? *Journal of Communication Inquiry, 38,* 325–340. http://dx.doi.org/10.1177/0196859914551607

Coates, J. (2013). The discursive production of everyday heterosexualities. *Discourse & Society, 24,* 536–552. http://dx.doi.org/10.1177/0957926513486070

Cohen, C. (1997). Punks, bulldaggers, and welfare queens: The radical potential of queer politics? *GLQ, 3,* 437–465. http://dx.doi.org/10.1215/10642684-3-4-437

Cohen, C. (1999). *The boundaries of blackness: AIDS and the breakdown of black politics.* University of Chicago Press.

Cooper, B. (2002). *Boys Don't Cry* and female masculinity: Reclaiming a life and dismantling the politics of normative heterosexuality. *Critical Studies in Media Communication, 19,* 44–63. http://dx.doi.org/10.1080/07393180216552

Cooper, B., & Pease, E. (2008). Framing *Brokeback Mountain:* How the popular press corralled the "gay cowboy movie". *Critical Studies in Media Communication, 25,* 249–273. http://dx.doi.org/10.1080/15295030802192020

Cram, E. (2012). "Angie was our sister": Witnessing the trans-formation of disgust in the citizenry of photography. *Quarterly Journal of Speech, 98,* 411–438. http://dx.doi.org/10.1080/00335630.2012.714899

Cram, E. (2016). Archival ambivalence and sensory memory: Generating queer intimacies in the settler colonial archive. *Critical Communication/Cultural Studies, 13,* 109–129. http://dx.doi.org/10.1080/14791420.2015.1119290

D'Emilio, J. (1983). *Sexual politics, sexual communities: The making of a homosexual minority in the United States, 1940–1970.* University of Chicago Press.

de Lauretis, T. (1991). Queer theory: Lesbian and gay sexualities, an introduction. *differences, 3*(2), iii–xviii.

de Lauretis, T. (1994). Habit changes. *differences, 6*(2–3), 296–313.

DeLuca, K. (1999). Unruly arguments: The body rhetoric of Earth First!, ACT UP, and Queer Nation. *Argumentation & Advocacy, 36,* 9–21.

Dhaenens, F. (2014). Articulations of queer resistance on the small screen. *Continuum, 28*(4), 520–531. http://dx.doi.org/10.1080/10304312.2014.907869

Dow, B. (1994). AIDS, perspective by incongruity, and gay identity in Larry Kramer's "1,112 and Counting". *Communication Studies, 45*(3–4), 225–240. http://dx.doi.org/10.1080/10510979409368426

Dow, B. (2001). *Ellen,* television, and the politics of gay and lesbian visibility. *Critical Studies in Media Communciation, 18,* 123–140. http://dx.doi.org/10.1080/07393180128077

Draper, J. (2010). "Gay or not?!": Gay men, straight masculinities, and the construction of the *Details* audience. *Critical Studies in Media Communication, 27,* 357–375. http://dx.doi.org/10.1080/15295030903583630

Dunn, T. (2015). Family time: *Brothers & Sisters* and managing temporal anxieties. *Western Journal of Communication, 79*(2), 133–150. http://dx.doi.org/10.1080/10570314.2014.943420

Dunn, T. (2016). *Queerly remembered: Rhetorics for representing the GLBTQ past.* University of South Carolina Press.

Eguchi, S. (2015). Queer intercultural relationality: An autoethnography of Asian-Black (dis)connections in White gay America. *Journal of International & Intercultural Communication*, 8(1), 27–43. http://dx.doi.org/10.1080/17513057.2015.991077

Eguchi, S., & Asante, G. (2016). Disidentifications revisited: Queer(y)ing intercultural communication theory. *Communication Theory*, 26(2), 171–189. http://dx.doi.org/10.1111/comt.12086

Eguchi, S., Calafell, B., & Files-Thompson, N. (2014). Intersectionality and quare theory: Fantasizing African American male same-sex relationships in *Noah's Arc: Jumping the Broom*. *Communication, Culture & Critique*, 7(3), 371–389. http://dx.doi.org/10.1111/cccr.12054

Elia, J. P. (2003). Queering relationships: Toward a paradigmatic shift. *Journal of Homosexuality*, 45(2), 61–86. http://dx.doi.org/10.1300/J082v45n02_03

Enck, S., & Morrisey, M. (2015). If *Orange is the New Black*, I must be color blind: Comic framings of post-racism in the prison-industrial complex. *Critical Studies in Media Communication*, 32(5), 303–317. http://dx.doi.org/10.1080/15295036.2015.1086489

Eng, D., Halberstam, J., & Muñoz, J. E. (Eds.). (2005). What's queer about queer studies now? [Special issue]. *Social Text*, 23(3–4), 1–308. http://dx.doi.org/10.1215/01642472-23-3-4_84-85-1

Eribon, D. (2004). *Insult and the making of the gay self*. (Michael Lucey, Trans.). Duke University Press.

Erni, J. N. (1998). Queer figurations in the media: Critical reflections on the Michael Jackson sex scandal. *Critical Studies in Mass Communication*, 15, 158–180. http://dx.doi.org/10.1080/15295039809367040

Erni, J. N. (2017). *Cultural studies, human rights, and the legal imagination: Reframing critical justice*. Routledge.

Faulkner, S., & Hecht, M. (2011). The negotiation of closetable identities: A narrative analysis of lesbian, gay, bisexual, transgendered queer Jewish identity. *Journal of Social & Personal Relationships*, 28, 829–847. http://dx.doi.org/10.1177/0265407510391338

Feinberg, L. (1996). *Transgender warriors: Making history from Joan of Arc to Dennis Rodman*. Beacon Press.

Fejes, F., & Petrich, K. (1993). Invisibility, homophobia, and heterosexism: Lesbians, gays, and the media. *Critical Studies in Mass Communication*, 10(4), 396–422. http://dx.doi.org/10.1080/15295039309366878

Fejes, F. (2008). *Gay rights and moral panic: The origins of America's debate on homosexuality*. Palgrave Macmillan.

Foster, E. (2008). Commitment, communication, and contending with heteronormativity: An invitation to greater reflexivity in interpersonal research. *Southern Communication Journal*, 7, 84–101. http://dx.doi.org/10.1080/10417940701815683

Foucault, M. (1972). *The archaeology of knowledge & the discourse on language* (A. M. S. Smith, Trans.). Pantheon. (Original work published in 1969 and 1971.)

Foucault, M. (1978). *The history of sexuality, an introduction*. (Vol. 1; R. Hurley, Trans.). Random House. (Original work published in 1976.)

Foucault, M. (1980). *Power/knowledge: Selected interviews & other writings, 1972–1977* (C. Gordon, L. Marshall, J. Mepham, & K. Soper, Trans.). C. Gordon (Ed.). Pantheon.

Fox, J., & Warber, K. (2015). Queer identity management and political self-expression on social networking sites: A co-cultural approach to the spiral of silence. *Journal of Communication*, 65(1), 79–100. http://dx.doi.org/10.1111/jcom.12137

Fox, R. (2007). Skinny Bones #126-774-835-29: Thin gay bodies signifying a modern plague. *Text & Performance Quarterly*, 27, 3–19. http://dx.doi.org/10.1080/10462930601045956

Fox, R. (2010). Tales of a fighting bobcat: An "auto-archaeology" of gay identity formation and maintenance. *Text & Performance Quarterly*, 30, 122–142. http://dx.doi.org/10.1080/10462931003650153

Fox, R. (2013). "Homo"-work: Queering academic communication and communicating queer in academia. *Text and Performance Quarterly, 33,* 58–76. http://dx.doi.org/10.1080/10462937.2012.744462

Freedman, E., & D'Emilio, J. (1988). *Intimate matters: A history of sexuality in America.* Harper & Row.

Gamson, J. (1998). *Freaks talk back: Tabloid talk shows and sexual nonconformity.* University of Chicago Press.

Gilder, E. (1989). The process of political *praxis*: Efforts of the gay community to transform the social significance of AIDS. *Communication Quarterly, 37,* 27–38. http://dx.doi.org/10.1080/01463378909385523

Goins, E., & Pye, D. (2013). Check the box that best describes you: Reflexively managing theory and praxis in LGBTQ health communication research. *Health Communication, 28,* 397–407. http://dx.doi.org/10.1080/10410236.2012.690505

Goltz, D. B. (2010). *Queer temporalities in gay male representation.* New York: Routledge.

Goltz, D. B. (2013). It gets better: Queer futures, critical frustrations, and radical potentials. *Critical Studies in Media Communication, 30,* 135–151. http://dx.doi.org/10.1080/15295036.2012.701012

Goltz, D. B., Zingsheim, J., Masint, T., & Murphy, A. G. (2016). Discursive negotiations of Kenyan LGBTI identities: Cautions in critical humility. *Journal of International & Intercultural Communication, 9*(2), 104–121. http://dx.doi.org/10.1080/17513057.2016.1154182

Gray, M. (2009a). *Out in the country: Youth, media, and queer visibility in rural America.* New York University Press.

Gray, M. (2009b). "Queer Nation is dead/long live Queer Nation": The politics and poetics of social movement and media representation. *Critical Studies in Media Communication, 26,* 212–236. http://dx.doi.org/10.1080/15295030903015062

Grindstaff, D. (2006). *Rhetorical secrets: Mapping gay identity and queer resistance in contemporary America.* University of Alabama Press.

Grindstaff, D. (2008). The fist and the corpse: Taming the queer sublime in *Brokeback Mountain. Communication & Critical/Cultural Studies, 5,* 223–244. http://dx.doi.org/10.1080/14791420802206817

Gross, L. (2002). *Up from invisibility: Lesbians, gays, and the media in America.* Columbia University Press.

Gross, L. (2005). The past and the future of gay, lesbian, bisexual, and transgender studies. *Journal of Communciation, 55,* 508–528. http://dx.doi.org/10.1111/j.1460-2466.2005.tb02683.x

Halley, J., & Parker, A. (Eds.). (2011). *After sex? On writing since queer theory.* Duke University Press.

Haraway, D. (1991). *Simians, cyborgs and women: The reinvention of nature.* Routledge.

Heinz, B. (2002). Enga(y)ging the discipline: Sexual minorities and communication studies. *Communication Education, 51,* 95–104. http://dx.doi.org/10.1080/03634520216503

Howard, S. (2014). *Black queer identity matrix: Towards an integrated queer of color framework.* Peter Lang.

Jagose, A. (1996). *Queer theory: An introduction.* New York University Press.

Jakobsen, J. (1998). Queer is? Queer does? Normativity and the problem of resistance. *GLQ, 4*(4), 511–536. http://dx.doi.org/10.1215/10642684-4-4-511

Johnson, E. P. (2001). "Quare" studies, or (almost) everything I know about queer studies I learned from my grandmother. *Text and Performance Quarterly, 21*(1), 1–25. http://dx.doi.org/10.1080/10462930128119

Katz, J. N. (1995). *The invention of heterosexuality.* New York: Dutton Books.

Kearl, M. K. (2015). "Is Gay the New Black?": An intersectional perspective on social movement rhetoric in California's Proposition 8 debate. *Communication & Critical/Cultural Studies, 12*(1), 63.82. http://dx.doi.org/10.1080/14791420.2014.995684

King, C. S. (2010). Un-queering horror: *Hellbent* and the policing of the "gay slasher". *Western Journal of Communication, 74*, 249–268. http://dx.doi.org/10.1080/10570311003767159

King, C. S. (2016). American queerer: Norman Rockwell and the art of queer feminist critique. *Women's Studies in Communication, 39*(2), 157–176. http://dx.doi.org/10.1080/07491409.2016.1165778

King, C. S., & West, I. (2014). This could be the place: Queer acceptance in *Lars and the Real Girl*. *QED, 1*(3), 59–84. http://dx.doi.org/10.14321/qed.1.3.0059

Landau, J. (2009). Straightening out (the politics of) same-sex parenting: Representing gay families in U.S. print news stories and photographs. *Critical Studies in Media Communication, 26*, 80–100. http://dx.doi.org/10.1080/15295030802684018

Lee, W. (2003). Speaking to silence: Toward queering nonverbal communication. *Journal of Homosexuality, 45*(2), 147–170. http://dx.doi.org/10.1300/J082v45n02_07

LeMaster, B. (2011). Queer imag(in)ing: Liminality as resistance in Lindquist's *Let the Right One In*. *Communication & Critical/Cultural Studies, 8*, 103–123. https://dx.doi.org/10.1080/14791420.2011.566277

LeMaster, B. (2015). Discontents of being and becoming fabulous on *RuPaul's Drag U*: Queer criticism in neoliberal times. *Women's Studies in Communication, 38*(2), 167–186. http://dx.doi.org/10.1080/07491409.2014.988776

Lipari, L. (2002). Queering the public sphere: Liberalism and the rhetoric of rights. *Argumentation & Advocacy, 38*, 169–175.

Lorde, A. (1984). *Sister outsider: Essays and speeches*. Crossing Press.

Lovaas, K. E. (2003). Speaking to silence: Toward queering nonverbal communication. *Journal of Homosexuality, 45*(2), 87–107. http://dx.doi.org/10.1300/J082v45n02_04

Lynch, J. (2007). Memory and Matthew Shepard: Opposing expressions of public memory in television movies. *Journal of Communication Inquiry, 31*, 222–238. http://dx.doi.org/10.1177/0196859907300948

McCune, J. (2008). "Out" in the club: The down low, hip-hop, and the architecture of black masculinity. *Text & Performance Quarterly, 28*, 298–314. http://dx.doi.org/10.1080/10462930802107415

McCune, J. (2014). *Sexual discretion: Black masculinity and the politics of passing*. Chicago: University of Chicago Press.

McDonald, J. (2015). Organizational communication meets queer theory: Theorizing relations of "difference" differently. *Communication Theory, 25*(3), 310–329. http://dx.doi.org/10.1111/comt.12060

McGrath, K. (2014). Teaching sex, gender, transsexual, and transgender concepts. *Communication Teacher, 28*(2), 96–101. http://dx.doi.org/10.1080/17404622.2013.865764

McKenna-Buchanan, T., Munz, S., & Rudnick, J. (2015). To be or not to be out in the classroom: Exploring Communication Privacy Management strategies of lesbian, gay, and queer college teachers. *Communication Education, 64*(3), 280–300. http://dx.doi.org/10.1080/03634523.2015.1014385

McKinnon, S. (2016). *Gendered asylum: Race and violence in U.S. law and politics*. University of Illinois Press.

Manning, J. (2015). Paradoxes of (im)purity: Affirming heteronormativity and queering heterosexuality in family discourses of purity pledges. *Women's Studies in Communication, 38*, 99–117. http://dx.doi.org/10.1080/07491409.2014.954687

Marwick, A., Gray, M., & Ananny, M. (2014). "Dolphins are just gay sharks": *Glee* and the queer case of transmedia as text and object. *Television & New Media, 15*(7), 627–647. http://dx.doi.org/10.1177/1527476413478493

Meyerowitz, J. (2002). *How sex changed: A history of transsexuality in the United States*. Harvard University Press.

Miller, D. A. (1992). *Bringing out Roland Barthes*. University of California Press.

Moreman, S., & McIntosh, D. (2010). Brown scriptings and rescriptings: A critical performance ethnography of Latina drag queens. *Communication & Cultural Studies, 7*, 115–135. http://dx.doi.org/10.1080/14791421003767912

Morris, C., III. (1996). Contextual twilight/critical liminality: J.M. Barrie's *Courage* at St. Andrews, 1922. *Quarterly Journal of Speech, 82*, 207–227. http://dx.doi.org/10.1080/00335639609384153

Morris, C., III. (1998). "The responsibilities of the critic": F. O. Matthiessen's homosexual palimpsest. *Quarterly Journal of Speech, 84*, 261–282. http://dx.doi.org/10.1080/00335639609384153

Morris, C., III. (Ed.). (2007). *Queering public address: Sexualities in American historical discourse*. University of South Carolina Press.

Morris, C., III. (2010). Sexuality and public address: Rhetorical pasts, queer theory, and Abraham Lincoln. In S. Parry-Giles & J. M. Hogan (Eds.), *The handbook of rhetoric and public address* (pp. 398–421). Blackwell.

Morris, C., III. (Ed.). (2011). *Remembering the AIDS quilt*. Michigan State University Press.

Morris, C., III. (2013). Sunder the children: Abraham Lincoln's queer rhetorical pedagogy. *Quarterly Journal of Speech, 99*, 395–422. http://dx.doi.org/10.1080/00335630.2013.836281

Morris, C., III., & Palczewski, C. (2014). Sexing communication: Hearing, feeling, remembering sex/gender and sexuality in the NCA. In P. Gehrke & W. Keith (Eds.), *A century of communication studies: The unfinished conversation* (pp. 128–165). Routledge.

Morris, C., III., & Sloop, J. (2006). "What these lips have kissed": Refiguring the politics of queer public kissing. *Communication and Critical/Cultural Studies, 3*, 1–26. http://dx.doi.org/10.1080/14791420500505585

Moscowitz, L. (2013). *The battle over marriage: Gay rights activism through the media*. University of Illinois Press.

Muñoz, J. E. (2009). *Cruising utopia: The then and there of queer futurity*. Duke University Press.

Newton, E. (1972). *Mother camp: Female impersonators in America*. Prentice-Hall.

Newton, E. (2000). *Margaret Mead made me gay: Personal essay, public ideas*. Duke University Press.

Ng, E. (2013). A "post-gay" era? Media gaystreaming, homonormativity, and the politics of LGBT integration. *Communication, Culture & Critique, 6*, 258–283. http://dx.doi.org/10.1111/cccr.12013

Norwood, K. (2012). Transitioning meanings? Family members' communicative struggles surrounding transgender identity. *Journal of Family Communication, 12*, 75–92. http://dx.doi.org/10.1080/15267431.2010.509283

Norwood, K. (2013a). Meaning matters: Framing trans identity in the context of family relationships. *Journal of GLBT Family Studies, 9*, 152–178. http://dx.doi.org/10.1080/1550428X.2013.765262

Norwood, K. (2013b). Grieving gender: Trans-identities, transition, and ambiguous loss. *Communication Monographs, 80*, 24–45. http://dx.doi.org/10.1080/03637751.2012.739705

Norwood, K. (2014). When a daughter becomes a son. In D. Braithwaite & J. T. Wood (Eds.), *Casing interpersonal communication: Case studies in personal and social relationships* (2d ed., pp. 33–39). Kendall Hunt Publishing.

Nuru, A. (2014). Between layers: Understanding the communicative negotiation of conflicting identities by transgender individuals. *Communication Studies, 65*(3), 281–297. http://dx.doi.org/10.1080/10510974.2013.833527

Ott, B., & Aoki, E. (2002). The politics of negotiating public tragedy: Media framing of the Matthew Shepard murder. *Rhetoric & Public Affairs, 5*, 483–505. http://dx.doi.org/10.1353/rap.2002.0060

Papacharissi, Z., & Fernback, J. (2008). The aesthetic power of the Fab 5: Discursive themes of homonormativity in *Queer Eye for the Straight Guy*. *Journal of Communication Inquiry, 32*, 348–367. http://dx.doi.org/10.1177/0196859908320301

Patton, C. (1985). *Sex and germs: The politics of AIDS*. South End Press.
Patton, C. (1990). *Inventing AIDS*. Routledge.
Patton, C. (1993). Tremble, hetero swine! In M. Warner (Ed.), *Fear of a queer planet: Queer politics and social theory* (pp. 143–177). University of Minnesota Press.
Patton, C. (2002). *Globalizing AIDS*. University of Minnesota Press.
Pearson, K., & Lozano-Reich, N. M. (2009). Cultivating queer publics with an uncivil tongue: *Queer Eye's* critical performance of desire. *Text and Performance Quarterly, 29*, 383–402. http://dx.doi.org/10.1080/10462930903242848
Pelle, S. (2010). The "grotesque" pussy: "Transformational shame" in Margaret Cho's stand-up performances. *Text & Performance Quarterly, 30*, 21–37. http://dx.doi.org/10.1080/10462930903366977
Perez, K., & Goltz, D. (2010). Treading across lines in the sand: Performing bodies in coalitional subjectivity. *Text & Performance Quarterly, 30*, 247–268. http://dx.doi.org/10.1080/10462937.2010.481797
Poirot, K. (2009). Domesticating the liberated woman: Containment rhetorics of second wave radical /lesbian feminism. *Women's Studies in Communication, 32*, 263–292. http://dx.doi.org/10.1080/07491409.2009.10162391
Ramsey, E. M., & Santiago, G. (2004). The conflation of male homosexuality and femininity in *Queer Eye for the Straight Guy*. *Feminist Media Studies, 4*, 353–355. http://dx.doi.org/10.1080/1468077042000309973
Rand, E. (2004). A disunited nation and a legacy of contradiction: Queer Nation's construction of identity. *Journal of Communication Inquiry, 28*, 288–306. http://dx.doi.org/10.1177/0196859904267232
Rand, E. (2013). Queer critical rhetoric bites back. *Western Journal of Communication, 77*, 533–537. http://dx.doi.org/10.1080/10570314.2013.799285
Rand, E. (2014). *Reclaiming queer: Activist and academic rhetorics of resistance*. University of Alabama Press.
Rich, A. (1980). Compulsory heterosexuality and lesbian existence. *Signs, 5*(4), 631–660.
Rich, C., Schutten, J., & Rogers, R. (2012). "Don't Drop the Soap": Organizing sexualities in the repeal of the U.S. military's "Don't Ask, Don't Tell" policy. *Communication Monographs, 79*, 269–291. http://dx.doi.org/10.1080/03637751.2012.697633
Ringer, J. (Ed.). (1994). *Queer words, queer images: Communication and the construction of homosexuality*. New York University Press.
Rubin, G. (1984). Thinking sex: Notes for a radical theory of the politics of sexuality. In C. Vance (Ed.), *Pleasure and danger: Exploring female sexuality* (pp. 267–319). Routledge.
Salih, S. (2002). *Judith Butler*. Routledge.
Samek, A. (2015). Pivoting between identity politics and coalitional relationships: Lesbian-feminist resistance to the woman-identified woman. *Women's Studies in Communication, 38*(4), 393–420. http://dx.doi.org/10.1080/07491409.2015.1085938
Samek, A., & Donofrio, T. (2013). "Academic drag" and the performance of the critical personae: An exchange of sexuality, politics, and identity in the academy. *Women's Studies in Communication, 36*, 28–55. http://dx.doi.org/10.1080/07491409.2015.1085938
Schiappa, E. (2008). *Beyond representational correctness: Rethinking criticism of popular media*. Albany, NY: SUNY Press.
Schiappa, E., Gregg, P., & Hewes, D. (2005). The parasocial contact hypothesis. *Communication Monographs, 72*, 92–115. http://dx.doi.org/10.1080/0363775052000342544
Schiappa, E., Gregg, P., & Hewes, D. (2006). Can one show make a difference? *Will & Grace* and the parasocial contact hypothesis. *Journal of Homosexuality, 51*(4), 15–37. http://dx.doi.org/10.1300/J082v51n04_02
Scott, B. (2003). *Risky rhetoric: AIDS and the cultural practices of HIV testing*. Southern Illinois University Press.

Sedgwick, E. K. (1985). *Between men: English literature and male homosocial desire.* Columbia University Press.
Sedgwick, E. K. (1990). *Epistemology of the closet.* University of California Press.
Sender, K. (2004). *Business, not politics: The making of the gay market.* New York: Columbia University Press.
Sender, K. (2006). Queens for a day: *Queer Eye for the Straight Guy* and the neoliberal project. *Critical Studies in Media Communication, 23,* 131–151. http://dx.doi.org/10.1080/07393180600714505
Sender, K. (2015). Reconsidering reflexivity: Audience research and reality television. *Communication Review, 18*(1), 37–52. http://dx.doi.org/10.1080/10714421.2015.996414
Sewell, J. (2014). "Becoming rather than being:" Queer's double-edged discourse as deconstructive practice. *Journal of Communication Inquiry, 38,* 291–307. http://dx.doi.org/10.1177/0022002714553900
Shugart, H. (2008). Managing masculinities: The metrosexual moment. *Communication and Critical/Cultural Studies, 5,* 280–300. http://dx.doi.org/10.1080/14791420802206833
Sinfield, A. (1994). *The Wilde century: Effeminacy, Oscar Wilde, and the queer moment.* Columbia University Press.
Skerski, J. (2007). From prime-time to daytime: The domestication of Ellen DeGeneres. *Communication and Critical/Cultural Studies, 4,* 363–381. http://dx.doi.org/10.1080/14791420701632964
Slagle, R. A. (1995). In defense of queer nation: From *identity politics* to a *politics of difference. Western Journal of Communication, 59,* 85–102. http://dx.doi.org/10.1080/10570319509374510
Sloop, J. (2004). *Disciplining gender: Rhetorics of sex identity in contemporary U.S. culture.* University of Massachusetts Press.
Sloop, J. (2012). "This is not natural": Caster Semenya's gender threats. *Critical Studies in Media Communication, 29,* 81–96. http://dx.doi.org/10.1080/15295036.2012.670876
Smith, R., & Windes, R. (2000). *Progay/antigay: The rhetorical war over sexuality.* SAGE.
Snorton, C. R. (2014). *Nobody is supposed to know: Black sexuality on the down low.* University of Minnesota Press.
Spencer, L. (2014). Performing transgender identity in *The Little Mermaid*: From Anderson to Disney. *Communication Studies, 65,* 112–127. http://dx.doi.org/10.1080/10510974.2013.832691
Stern, D. (2011). You had me at Foucault: Living pedagogically in the digital age. *Text & Performance Quarterly, 31,* 249–266. http://dx.doi.org/10.1080/10462937.2011.573191
Stone, S. (1991). The *Empire* strikes back: A posttranssexual manifesto. In J. Epstein & K. Straub (Eds.), *Body guards: The cultural politics of gender ambiguity* (pp. 280–304). New York: Routledge.
Suter, E., & Strasser, D. (2014). Lesbian and gay families. In K. Floyd & M. Morman (Eds.), *Widening the family circle: New research on family communication* (pp. 133–150). Thousand Oaks, CA: SAGE.
Suter, E., Seurer, L., Webb, S., Grewe, B., & Koenig Kellas, J. (2015). Motherhood as contested ideological terrain: Essentialist and queer discourses of motherhood at play in female-female co-mothers' talk. *Communication Monographs, 82,* 458–483. http://dx.doi.org/10.1080/03637751.2015.1024702
Suter, E. A., & Daas, K. (2007). Negotiating heteronormativity dialectically: Lesbian couples' display of symbols in culture. *Western Journal of Communication, 71,* 177–195. http://dx.doi.org/10.1080/10570310701518443
Tate, H. (2005). The ideological effects of a failed constitutive rhetoric: The co-option of the rhetoric of white lesbian feminism. *Women's Studies in Communication, 28,* 1–31. http://dx.doi.org/10.1080/07491409.2005.10162482
Thompson, J. (2002). *Mommy dearest: Contemporary rhetorics of lesbian maternal identity.* University of Massachusetts Press.
Treichler, P. (1999). *How to have theory in an epidemic: Cultural chronicles of AIDS.* Duke University Press.
Van Gilder, B., & Abdi, S. (2014). Identity management and the fostering of network ignorance: Accounts of queer Iranian women in the United States. *Journal of Intercultural Communication Research, 43*(2), 151–170. http://dx.doi.org/10.1080/17475759.2014.892895

Wagner, P., Kunkel, A., & Compton, B. (2016). (Trans)lating identity: Exploring discursive strategies for navigating the tensions of identity gaps. *Communication Quarterly, 64*(3), 251–272. http://dx.doi.org/10.1080/01463373.2015.1103286

Warner, M. (1991). Introduction: Fear of queer planet [Special issue]. *Social Text, 29,* 3–17.

Warner, M. (Ed.). (1993). *Fear of a queer planet: Queer politics and social theory.* University of Minnesota Press.

Warner, M. (1999). *The trouble with normal: Sex, politics, and the ethics of queer life.* Free Press.

Warner, M. (2012, January 6). Queer and then? *The Chronicle of Higher Education.* B6–B9.

Weiss, D. (2005). Constructing the queer "I": Performativity, citationality, and desire in *Queer Eye for the Straight Guy. Popular Communication, 3,* 73–95. http://dx.doi.org/10.1207/s15405710pc0302_1

West, I. (2013). Queer generosities. *Western Journal of Communication, 77,* 538–541. http://dx.doi.org/10.1080/10570314.2013.784351

West, I. (2014). *Transforming citizenships: Transgender articulations of the law.* New York University Press.

West, I. (2015). Racial analogies and same-sex civil marriage advocacy. *Philosophy and Rhetoric, 48,* 561–582. http://dx.doi.org/10.5325/philrhet.48.4.0561

West, I., Frischherz, M., Panther, A., & Brophy, R. (2013). Queer world-making in the "It Gets Better" campaign. *QED, 49,* 85. http://dx.doi.org/10.1353/qed.2013.0003

Westerfelhaus, R., & Lacroix, C. (2006). Seeing "straight" through *Queer Eye*: Exposing the strategic rhetoric of heteronormativity in a mediated ritual of gay rebellion. *Critical Studies in Media Communication, 23,* 426–444. http://dx.doi.org/10.1080/07393180601046196

Whitney, E. (2006). Capitalizing on camp: Greed and the queer marketplace. *Text & Performance Quarterly, 26,* 36–46. http://dx.doi.org/10.1080/10462930500382401

Wight, J. (2011). Facing gender performativity: How transgender performances and performativity trouble facework research. *Kaleidoscope: A Graduate Journal of Qualitative Communication Research, 10,* 73–90.

Wolf, J. (2013). Resurrecting camp: Rethinking the queer sensibility. *Communication, Culture & Critique, 6,* 284–297.

Wood, J., & Duck, S. (1995). Off the beaten-track: New shores for relationship research. In J. Wood & S. Duck (Eds.), *Under-studied relationships: Off the beaten track* (pp. 1–21). SAGE.

Yep, G., Lovaas, K., & Elia, J. (Eds.). (2003). *Queer theory and communication: From disciplining queers to queering the discipline(s).* Harrington Park Press.

NOTES

1. De Lauretis (1994) dismissed the utility and vibrancy of queer theory a short while later due to its institutional currency, characterizing it as a "conceptually vacuous creature of the publishing industry" (p. 297). More recently, responding to the sense that queer theory "if not already passé, was rapidly approaching its expiration date" (Halley & Parker, 2011, p.1), numerous conferences and forums have addressed the health of queer studies (Eng, Halberstam, & Muñoz, 2005).
2. Erin Rand's (2014) genealogy of queer theory in academia and its relationship to external articulations of queerness outside academe is an accessible and wide-ranging introduction to this topic.
3. Lauren Berlant and Michael Warner (1998) define heteronormativity in the following manner:

> By heteronormativity we mean the institutions, structures of understanding, and practical orientations that make heterosexuality seem not only coherent—that is, organized as a sexuality—but also privileged. Its coherence is always provisional, and its privilege can take several (sometimes

contradictory) forms: unmarked, as the basic idiom of the personal and the social; or marked as a natural state; or projected as an ideal or moral accomplishment. It consists less of norms that could be summarized as a body of doctrine than of a sense of rightness produced in contradictory manifestations—often unconscious, immanent to practice or to institutions. (p. 548n2)

4. The struggle for academic legitimacy and the contested terrain of LGBT studies are chronicled in implicit and explicit ways in Chesebro (1981), Ringer (1994), Yep, Lovaas, and Elia (2003), and Morris (2007).
5. More recently, scholars are using queer theory to name and interrogate queer heterosexualities (Coates, 2013; Manning, 2015).
6. It should be noted that Foucault's own myopia limited this study to European contexts, except for passing references to other cultural practices.
7. Didier Eribon (2004) challenges the idea of counter-discourse as Foucault describes the temporalities of identities and medical discourses. Eribon flips the script to demonstrate how medical professionals borrowed these discourses of identity from gay subcultures, not vice versa. Also, Sinfield (1994) challenges Foucault's primacy on medical and legal discourses as a necessary precursor for a more stable sense of gay personage. A parallel case for trans identities can be found in Joanne Meyerowitz's (2002) history of transsexual medical and psychological care.
8. Performance studies scholars have objected to these characterizations of performance because Butler generalizes a theory of performance to a more varied field of ideas about performance and performativity.

Isaac West

QUEER TEMPORALITIES

INTRODUCTION: QUEERNESS AND THE POLITICS OF TIME

Queer work emerges in reactionary tension and response to the oppressive workings of normativity. Queerness—as an identity, as a mode of resistance, or as a process or performance in culture and media—is framed in discourse as a deviation or "a certain unsettling" (Freccero, 2007, p. 485) from and, at times, in outright opposition with social norms constructed as correct and assumed to be natural. In recent years, queer tensions with, if not outright resistance to, normativity have examined the cultural implications of the governing logics of time. The term "time," itself, carries with it a certitude, a durability, and an assumed naturalness that appears fixed and correct. As much as society works to tame the unruliness of time, time is—as queercore poet and author Dennis Cooper states—"a false finite. A blasphemy on forever." Time is political, cultural, and hegemonic. Thus, the notion of "temporality" becomes useful as a term that speaks to questions that interrogate the functions and logics of time, opening time up for reflection, examination, and analysis. Foundational to queer theorizing, Foucault's *History of Sexuality Vol. 1* (alongside Katz, Sedgwick, and multiple others) traced the temporal and contextual discourses of sexual identity. Disrupting universalizing progay claims that "we have always been here," queer theorists assert "the past was different from the present and that presentist categories for past sexualities did not apply" (Freccero, 2007, p. 487). Homosexuality, heterosexuality, and all forms of sexual identity are not merely a question of a "who" or a "what," but just as significantly a matter of "when"—marking shifting meanings, possibilities, and understandings across time. From the outset, queer theory has been a temporal interrogation.

How does one feel in synch or out of step with time? Out of pace, rhythm, or sequence with cultural patterns? What norms and values are assigned to time? How do the moment-by-moment, daily, and long-term ways we engage time reflect competing ideologies? In other words, how does time work to shape and constrain our lives, and how life might be experienced? How do norms of time impact trauma, mourning, or illness? What is construed as being "on time" in one's life, one's maturation, one's professional, personal, or romantic development (and even how we are taught to understand what constitutes "development") all draw attention to a broad range of normative investments. These investments are culturally produced, and discursively constrained, to shape what we can describe as a normative temporality. Time is a tool of power and discipline. Take, for example, romantic relational formation. Assuming this is a relationship directed toward monogamy (as the culture will often do), what is the proper amount of time for two people to date (if we are to assume monogamous courtship) before exclusive commitment? To date before having sex (which assumes sex comes after dating, as well as a discussion on what constitutes "sex")? Before saying "I love you" (assuming this is the relational destination)? Before meeting one's parents (assuming biological parents are alive, connected, and important to the individuals)? There is a tacit heteronormative cultural understanding that saying "I love you" on the first date is a "red flag," is a little "off," and, we could even say, is a bit queer. It deviates from relational/temporal norms. The culture also has norms established for where in life a person "should be" in their twenties (first "adult" job, doing the "single thing"), their thirties ("settling down," in a serious relationship, own property, start a "family"), and so on. The default understanding of where one "should be" in time is often constructed in terms of family, career, procreation, and home. Temporality places understandings of time under scrutiny, calling into question certitudes and patterns that frame one's life through ideological systems of meaning, such as the Child (Edelman, 2004) fairytale narrative closures of "happily ever after" and a wealth of stories that work to symbolize and concretize what happiness and success should look like. Time normalizes and time disciplines queer modes of aging, maturation, forming relationships, and how one is to live in one's world and one's body. Freeman (2010) interrogates this in relationship to capitalism through the concept of "chrononormativity," tracing the regulations of temporality and "the use of time to organize individual human bodies toward maximum productivity" (p. 3). Queer temporality opens a space of intervention to challenge these fixed meanings and regulatory structures, to question relationships to pasts and presents and the values and logics we place upon time. Additionally, queer temporality also marks a process of creation and queer world-making, an opening of potentiality, considering new ways to think, feel, and engage pasts, the present, and potential futures. It's a creative imagining of what living, being, maturation, age, and future might be when we glimpse outside and beyond the trappings of discourse. So, queer temporality encapsulates a project of critique and creation, skepticism and hope, analysis and play. The scholarly areas of queer theory and queer communication studies have no clear or necessary boundary. The detailing of queer temporal work in communication will begin with many of the writers and thinkers who came to define and build this area of queer theory. Within this discussion, this overview will move through various works within the field of communication that work to push, extend, ground, and examine the contours and potentials of queering time.

THE TEMPORAL IMPACT OF THE AIDS CRISIS

Queer temporal theorizing has been significantly shaped and framed by the impact of the AIDS pandemic on queer lives and queer communities. Time, age, and maturation were forced to be radically reconfigured in the face of so many lives lost, the assumed fatality of contracting HIV, and the broader cultural narrative of death that came to define queer communities in the 1980s and 1990s. By the end of 2004, in the United States alone, over half a million AIDS-connected deaths had been reported, of which a disproportionate number of deaths and infections were, and continue to be, gay and bisexual men. The AIDS pandemic forced queer communities to wrestle with queered approaches to thinking and experiencing time. However, "Queer time, even as it emerges from the AIDS crisis, is not only about compression and annihilation; it is also about the potentiality of a life unscripted by the conventions of family, inheritance, and child rearing" (Halberstam, 2005, p. 2). Thus, the AIDS crisis greatly impacted how gay men experienced a queer relationship to time—the experience of "living in/out of time" (Dunn, 2015). Forced out of step with mainstream narratives of time, queer communities were faced with temporal realities that included countless losses, inhumane inaction from the federal government, and a homophobic culture that perpetuated the discursive equation of queerness with death, threat, and illness. Time weighed differently on queer lives: "How long?" and "Who is next?" This "cultural logic of inevitability" (Román, 1997, p. 164) drew strong associations between queerness and AIDS, where the two were framed and produced as symmetrical, inherently tied, and fused in the cultural mindset. The queer life was an abbreviated life. And, for those who survived the plague in the earliest years, temporal understandings were often shaped by the experience of survivors' guilt in the face of so much loss.

With the development of antiretroviral cocktails in the mid-1990s, the "inevitable death sentence" (Dean, 2011, p. 75) of HIV/AIDS shifted, mutated (p. 77), as those contracting HIV were no longer facing certain fatality. Dean looks to the queer temporal impact of antiretroviral medical advancements through the lens of bareback culture. "The altered tempo of HIV disease has generated new uncertainties, new anxieties, new contingencies" (p. 76), suggesting that the exposure to HIV is also the new exposure to time itself. This "double temporality" exposes one to the once-death sentence that is now deferred (but not eliminated entirely) and the newfound time that emerges through these medical advancements. In working through a temporal reflection on bareback culture, Dean argues that we are all "inhabited by asynchronous temporalities" (p. 92), marking "the timelessness of unconscious mental processes" (p. 84) as a way of understanding how "sexual life may appear out of sequence" (p. 84). While we may move through time chronologically, as living organisms, "the psyche follows a different temporal path" (p. 84).

THE SACRED CHILD AND FUTURITY: EDELMAN AND QUEER TEMPORALITY

The theoretical discussion framed as queer temporalities emerges to directly question the histories, assumptions, and narratives that normalize the temporal commitments of heteronormativity and deconstruct its operations. Berlant's *The Queen of America Goes to Washington City* (1997) sets forth the argument that "In the process of collapsing the political and the personal into a world of public intimacy, a nation made for adult citizens has been replaced by one imagined for fetuses and children" (p. 1). Interrogating the "iconicity of the current modal citizen, the child or youth on whose behalf national struggle is being waged" (p. 21), Berlant's work lays the groundwork for queer interventions into how the image of the Child came to determine and define political discourse and how liberty is being sacrificed in the name of the collective investment of the child's protection. The publication of Lee Edelman's fiery and playful polemic *No Future: Queer Theory and the Death Drive* (2004) built from the work of Berlant (as well as many other queer thinkers, including Crimp and Sedgwick), ushering in a generative moment of theorizing examining the relationship between queers and discourses of the future. Asserting the concept of "reproductive futurism," Edelman details how historically, queers have been written as antifuture, anti-Child, and in opposition to innocence, future, and social order. The queer is constructed as the end to order, the threat to the Sacred Child. This Child is not real. It is not yet born. It is an ideal, "entitled to claim full rights to its future share in the nation's good, though always at the cost of limiting the rights 'real' citizens are allowed" (p. 11). Edelman argues that the future has been highjacked in the name of the Sacred Child, calling for the defiant embracing of queer negativity. The future does not belong to the queer, and thus it should be dismissed, suggesting queers ought to embrace their exclusion, and explore pleasures and possibilities when freed from the confines of normativity.

Perhaps the most notable and influential critical engagement with Edelman's polemic was in the work of Jose Esteban Muñoz, who questioned the raced and classed assumptions and limitations of Edelman's outright rejection of futurity. Muñoz (2009) questioned the stakes and inherent privileges to be able to "hand over futurity to normative white reproductive futurity" (p. 365), in an abandonment of all hope and a "forward-dawning futurity" (p. 357). Rather than Edelman's call for queers to "fuck the future" and lean into queer negativity and antirelationality, Muñoz's temporal project is grounded in a politics of hope, approaching queerness outside the here and now, as an "ideality" and potential, and "a mode of desiring that allows us to see beyond the quagmire of the present" (p. 1), which is bankrupt, stifling. Queerness is present but not yet here, unintelligible, "that thing that lets us feel that this world is not enough" (p. 1). Herein, Muñoz's conception draws conceptual parallels to Butler's theorization of "fantasy" in *Undoing Gender* (2004) and De Lauretis's "space-off" in *Technologies of Gender* (1987). It marks queerness and queer time as existing, relating, and connecting in a mode (Freeman, 2007) that is not yet here, not yet present, and never will be—always lingering outside the here and now.

Queer temporal theorists trouble the framings and connections of "history," as something now removed, in the past. Freeman's (2010) *Time Binds: Queer Temporalities and Queer Histories* troubles the logics of the seamless, forward-driving time of the temporal order, looking to historical moments and movements to "propose other possibilities for living in relation to indeterminately past, present, and future others; that is, of living historically" (p. xxii). Her method of "autohistoriography" seeks to trouble how bodily engagement, the bodily experience of encountering historical materials, is not merely a "restoration of bygone times" (p. 95). Rather, these encounters carry distinct knowledges that are not just about the past being reintroduced into the present, but are a rich, affective, bodily, sensuous encounter in the present, "treating the present itself as hybrid" (95). Freccero narrates her relationship to time in her work, reflecting "I often work on the dead, and as time goes by I have begun to think of myself as a future dead person writing myself out of my time while time is running out" (in Dinshaw et al., 2007, p. 184). As a medievalist, Dinshaw sees her work as building cross-temporal communities, "touching across time, collapsing time through affective contact between marginalized people now and then" (Dinshaw et al., 2007, p. 178).

Additionally, queer temporality reorients the past with the lingering anticipation of the perpetual not-yet and the potentiality of anticipation. For example, Muñoz looks to a collection of works by photographer Kevin McCarthy (Muñoz, 2005), depicting queer and punk club spaces and stages that are not-yet occupied, anticipatory of what is, what might occur. Who might inhabit these spaces and what forms of relationships and identities might emerge? Herein, the antirelational thesis is rescripted in search for queer modes of collectivity and imagination. Muñoz theorizes that these images linger in "potentiality." Forward-driving and hopeful, potentiality is tied to futurity, a not-yet that remains at the margins of intelligibility, the discursive horizon (Butler, 1993). The future, in all its limitations and confinements, marks all that we can see, imagine, anticipate—what is possible. But futurity is located beyond the possible, into potentiality, exceeding the constraints and limitations of futures imaginable in the present (Muñoz, 2006). "In its most ideal formation, queer temporality enlarges our life possibilities by allowing us to imagine connections to other times and other bodies; it expands our ideas of what it means to be a body in time" (Dinshaw, 2015, p. 43).

Halberstam's (2005) work in queer temporality offers a grounded and applicable investigation of heteronormative temporal modes, or what they refer to as "straight time." Extending beyond the disciplinary workings of reproductive futurism, Halberstam maps out a range of systems and heteronormative investments that work to erect straight time's dominion. Yes, in this sense, it is literally straight, marking a series of plot points on a timeline that one ought to aspire to, and once achieved, is awarded with cultural recognition and validation. It is an orientation tied to goal attainment and neoliberal productivity. Thus, the name "straight time" is a play on heterosexuality and time, but also identifies the rigid, one-directional linearity that frames dominant conceptions of proper living, aging, development, and maturation. There is, according to straight time, a correct path, a proper pace, and series of milestones that have become entrenched in the cultural imagination as desirable and accomplished. While marriage and procreation, the bedrocks of heteronormativity, are core tenants of straight time, Halberstam also examines intersecting logics of maturation and inheritance. Inheritance refers to systems of financial inheritance, but also speaks to governing and pervasive logics where values and morals are passed down and preserved through procreative family systems. The very notion of a previous generation passing on, paying forward, and forming the next generation is tethered to the logics of straight time. Halberstam also draws attention to the construction and careful monitoring of adult/youth binary formations, how the culture constructs correct and proper understandings of maturation, and the "conventional emphasis on longevity and futurity" (p. 2). Halberstam discusses the "perverse turn away from the narrative coherence of adolescence" (in Dinshaw et al., 2007, p. 182), and the sequence of development it insists upon, theorizing "the embrace of late childhood in place of early adulthood or immaturity in place of responsibility" (p. 182). The very communicative symbols we use to mark maturation, such as "old" and "young" and how they produce meaning within our culture, become significations of heteronormative temporal ordering, indexes to the logics and assumptions of straight time. Halberstam's engagement and theorizing of queer time looks to extended and elongated (if not circular) periods of queer adolescence, questioning the dominance of linear "phase" or "stage" logics, while reconsidering how queer subcultural involvement can stretch across one's whole life (p. 174).

EXPANSIVE SCOPE OF QUEER TEMPORALITIES

Discussions of straight time and queer temporality interanimate broad intersections of temporal commitments that underlie the workings of multiple systems, including modernity, capitalism, Whiteness, masculinity, cisgenderism, and ableism. In *Revisitation: A Trans Phenomenology of the Media Image*, Keegan argues, "I never fully leave behind the dysphoric child, never fully arrive as the hegemonic ideal" (cited in King, 2022). King (2022) argues that, when looking at the foundational text and structures that teach narrative and screenwriting, all of the governing models are tethered to limited conventions of struggle, transformation, and change that replicate White, straight, and masculine notions of time. Keegan's experience as a trans man challenges the temporal script of cis-White-maleness, wherein stories narrate linear trajectories of adversity, struggle, and triumph, yet never troubling notions of a coherent self. Keegan argues trans experiences, as well as the experiences of many who live in spaces of marginalization, more commonly understand their own lives through narratives of fragmentation and multiplicity.

Aizura (2012) interrogates the temporal implication in transexual travel narratives that repeat a story structure of a journey out and then a return to home, transformed. The narrative is both spatialized (a leaving to elsewhere and then a return) but also framed in temporal terms that work to obscure the liminal dimensions of gender transition—the very inbetweenness and indeterminacy that works to problematize binary logics. Aizura argues these travel narratives effect the "containment of the temporal moment of gendered indeterminacy within a spatialized elsewhere" (p. 153), working to shore up and preserve an "idealized temporal template" (p. 146) of transition as happening all at once—a binary switch rather than a more complex, nonlinear, and queer process. He further argues that the temporary absence from one's workplace that is needed for the transitional journey, the leaving and return from their place of employment, works to reinforce gender binary intelligibility for coworkers, allowing time for their adjustment from one fixed sexed identity to another.

The norms of academia reveal a broad range of temporal commitments, privileging productivity and output, and sedimented norms of progress and development. The implications of these logics are many, yet to provide a few concrete examples, such an approach charts the development of ideas, of research, of one's understanding in a direct sequence from A to Z. Likened to Google Maps, it efficiently, but with great consequence and investment, charts every course in the most immediate route, concretizing one mode or trajectory as idealized, correct, and efficient. It automates and standardizes time in terms of production, economy, and progress. Normative temporality also works to place trauma and grief on a linear plotline, where one experiences, moves through and then "gets past" the pains of loss—to get beyond it.

Cast as a failure of proper (a.k.a. normative) scripts of aging and maturation, the queer and the work of queering poses a threat to the existing social order of temporality and future.

Queer temporality is the disruption and intervention into this hegemonic system of efficiency, progress, and reproduction in the service of straight time. Within this threat, this perpetual disturbance or disruption, there enters a potential for both examining the limits of straight time and its foreclosures, and perhaps, imagining time, temporality, and futurity otherwise.

While the discussion so far has focused upon the critical interrogations of straight temporality, revealing its violences and foreclosures, much of the contemporary work on queer temporality focuses on creation and imagination—the project of queer world-making. Working from queer articulations as a horizon at the margins of discourse (Butler, 1993) or a potentiality that is present but does not exist in present things (Muñoz, 2009), queer world-making is a project, a hope, a self-reflexive mandate and a commitment that "seeks an elsewhere, a disruption, and a rejection of the legitimized and routinized conventions of normativity" (Goltz et al., 2015, p. 12). As this area of inquiry began to be taken up across queer circles, a broad range of temporal projects investigated, questioned, troubled, and reimagined how we might step outside the limits of straight time and imagine a temporal orientation that is more queer, more hopeful, and less disciplinary. For example, Luciano's (2007) analysis of Todd Hayne's *Far From Heaven* argues the film enlists interrogations of temporal progress, displacement, a disruption to the assumed naturalness of time, and a criticism of "the time patterns of the straight world" (p. 259) that shifts from an investigating the past "to the speculative time of the not-yet" (p. 253). A disparate constellation of projects emerged that saw potential in temporality as an optic of creative investigation. Keeling (2009) interrogates the limits of racial imaginaries in representation, while opening up the speculative possibilities in creative work to launch new modes of Black futures and freedom. Specifically, in looking at the 2005 documentary *The Aggressives*, Keeling attends to what the film "escapes attempts to contain" (p. 567) yet "exceed its expression" (p. 566) through a surplus of sensation, of affect, that resists being seen or fully understood. While rooted within the violences present, Keeling argues the film may "feel, even without recognition, the rhythms from a poetry of a future" (p. 579). In the field of communication, the world-making project has been taken up in a broad range of approaches, most specifically in the fields of rhetoric and performance studies.

RHETORICAL STUDIES OF QUEER TEMPORALITY

In the area of rhetorical criticism, queer communication scholars have made significant contributions to the temporal project of queer world-making. A major portion of this work is invested in examining, troubling, and developing new and liberatory ways of seeing, feeling, and making meaning of both mainstream and more fringe mediated texts. This work stems from a long history of queer writings that coach, enact, and theorize the power and possibility of queer audiencing practices. Compulsory heterosexuality works to frame texts in popular culture as fixed, normative, and confined to a predictable set of meanings. Queering a text, as a practice, works to unearth and reclaim nonstraight audiencing positions. The notion of queer space opens up the ever-existent multitude of possible positions in the creation and receiving of pop cultural texts. Not misreading or merely wishful, queer audiencing is the "recognition and articulation of the complex range of queerness that has been in popular culture texts and their audiences all along" (Storey, 2001, p. 144). Texts like Alexander Doty's reading of *The*

Wizard of Oz as lesbian fantasia or Mary Rogers's analysis of Barbie as a drag queen in "Hetero Barbie" exemplify the power of reclamation and queer possibilities in this work.

Additionally, this work is conceptually and historically tied to the ever-slippery discussion of camp, and specifically camp reading practices. Embracing the inherent queerness and politicism of camp, pulling from the work of Meyer (1994) and Cleto (1999), camp is less a fixed text, style, or object (that *is* camp) than a way of seeing, negotiating, and responding to a text (I can see this *as* camp). In this political space of possibility, this negotiated relationship between text and viewer, camp emerges as a strategy of survival (Halperin, 2012) for queer audiences. Mainstream texts have a long-established pattern to position queers in damning and degrading narratives, often facing violent ends that work to concretize and restate the naturalness and rightness of heterosexuality and straight temporal formations. "Happily ever after," as a narrative convention and heteronormative promise, remains tethered to scripts of marriage, monogamy, and procreation. Queerness, in turn, is positioned in perpetual tension and opposition with "happily ever after," the wicked witch, the evil stepmother, and the sinister—slightly effeminate—villain, twirling their mustache. A camp engagement with damning narratives permits an audience strategy for shifting allegiances and discipline, resisting the normative thrust to identify with queer punishment and normative correctness. Taking a cue from queer audiences and camp practices, queer filmmakers (e.g., New Queer Cinema's gregg araki) have taken stories of queer punishment to affective and aesthetic extremes to cue audiences into camp readings. In a style of "queer temporal camp" (Goltz, 2012), a broad range of alienating and excessive directorial and acting strategies are used to hold the audience at a distance, resisting passive consumption, and coaching a critical reception of queer temporal violence.

When looking at popular media, a queer temporal read might seek to explore how narratives of marriage, childrearing, and "proper" maturation are encoded and reinforced within a text. A queer temporal analysis may also explore how notions of progress and future are erected through hegemonic systems. For example, the highly contentious and much debated *It Gets Better* video campaign, initiated by Dan Savage and Terry Miller, encouraged older queer participants to upload videos to YouTube to combat elevated rates of queer teen suicide with messages of hope. Almost as quickly as the campaign was initiated, a handful of notable queer critics (i.e., Jack Halberstam, Jaspir Puar, Eng-Ben Lim) sought to complicate a range of perceived assumptions at the heart of the campaign, including its centralizing of the bodies and experiences of White, cis, able-bodied, upper-middle-class, urban gay male culture. The very notion of "it gets better" was criticized for its privileged foundations, and its disconnect from the experiences and struggles of many queers who face—every day—broad intersections of disenfranchisement. In the field of communication, two studies (Goltz, 2013; West et al., 2013) sought to examine the broader *It Gets Better* archive beyond a singular reading of Savage. These projects located a far more expansive body of meanings for how the message *It Gets Better* was being discussed and enacted through a growing collection of tens of thousands of videos. West et al. (2013) detail how the project rejects a monolithic reading, locating a broad range of queer worldbuilding resources in the project. Asking the power of focusing on a vernacular video by an individual responding to the campaign, rather than Savage's and Miller's, they closely consider the three-and-a-half minute video uploaded by dykeumentary1. While not suggesting there will not be struggles, the video offers a playfully sexual, hopeful message where she claims to not have much money, but asserts, "Be a butch dyke, be hot, you're gonna love it" (p. 73). Thus, while it can surely be argued Savage's and Miller's initial video reflected a privileged perspective that could be read for its many simplifications and blind spots, Goltz (2013) argues that the project is most productively understood through a historical context. The project, on the level of discourse, offers an important counternarrative to the enduring promise of queer temporal misery, offering a multiracial, multigendered, diverse archive of testimonials of queer lives surviving, finding unimagined and unexpected joys and relations that, they wish, their younger selves could have seen, known, and heard. Employing a queer youthist criticism, wherein value and meaning in queer culture is singularly preoccupied with serving the next generation and the queer children, Goltz (2021a, 2021b) questions why the sole value of *It Gets Better* must reside in its effective service to LGBT youth. Rather, challenging straight temporal modes of inheritance that suggest value is always tethered to serving the needs of the future generation—a preoccupation in our political imaginaries that builds upon the work of Berlant and Edelman—Goltz posits the queer value of a project that unapologetically celebrates and honors aging queers, queer survival, and queer slippages in time.

Thus, from a communication perspective, queer temporal work can contextualize and trouble how language and symbolicity (such as the word "better") can come to function, operate, and shift in important ways that facilitate queer negotiation and survival. For example, Bennet's analysis of the *Born This Way* website questions how this seemingly essentialist message—that queerness is ever-present and fixed from a young age—is negotiated by its contributors, who are encouraged to upload photos of their younger selves. Bennet shows that the very notion claiming one is "born this way" is actually broadened, rather than flattened, through the project to reflect a broad and expansive body of meanings, uniquely queer, and not firmly tethered to the assumed essentialist criticism. In these multiple posts, the very words "born this way" are destabilized and expanded to allow queer investment and reclamations. This is the work of world-making, when the confines and rigid discourses available become tools of disruption, bending, and making do, in order to crack open a new possibility, articulation or imaginary.

Furthermore, queer critics may engage cultural texts to help coach and identify where queer meanings are being hinted, anticipated, or suggested to audiences, as read through the queer eyes of the critic. Looking to mediated texts that performatively gesture forward—that enact alternative possibilities for imagining future—Abdi and Calafel (2017) analyze the 2014 Iranian Horror film *A Girl Walks Home Alone at Night*. The authors read this black and white vigilante vampire tale through the lens of Iranian feminisms, queer monstrosity, and queer temporality, wherein "the trope of the vampire becomes a resistive tool for (queer) Iranian and Iranian-American feminists" (p. 367). Situated in the borderland liminal space of the fictional Bad City, the film enlists the genre of the spaghetti western to tell the tale of a monstrous vampire who works to protect women against the oppression of violent masculinity. Within their analysis, the authors locate resistant moments in the text, wherein "glimmers of the past, present, and future" (pp. 367–368) blend, suggesting a queer temporality and queer relationality that anticipates new minoritarian possibilities for existing in a postcolonial diasporic global experience.

When looking at mainstream mediated texts, De Lauretis's (1987) concept of the "space-off" offers a generative tool for spatializing queer temporality, wherein the off space just to the margins of the filmic screen, the boundaries of representation, offers the domain where queer lives and queer possibilities exist. Akin to Muñoz's (2005) reflection on McCarthy's blank stages, De Lauretis (1987) calls attention to the lives, bodies, and stories at the periphery of the cultural screen, beyond the centralized represented space of the filmic lens. Goltz (2010) enlists De Lauretis's framework to theorize the ever-present lingering of queer temporalities in mainstream popular culture, looking to texts like *The History Boys*, *DeLovely*, and Omar Little from *The Wire* that rupture the filmic boundary that works to centralize (and thus normalize) straight narratives and conventions. Herein, the existence of queer lives, queer modes of being in and out of time, and queer relations are present, but obscured, lingering with potential at the margins of the cultural screen.

Extending the work of queer media criticism's interrogation of explicit and "progressive" queer representation in mainstream media, several communication scholars have explicitly used temporality as a central optic of investigation. In the essay, "'My whole life I've been dressing up like a man': Negotiations of queer aging and queer temporality in the TV series *Transparent*," Hess (2017) argues the television show *Transparent* provides a rare intersectional look at the processes of aging, sexuality, and gender identity. Offering the first aging trans protagonist on an American television program, Hess argues the important perspective afforded through the character of Maura, resisting linear life scripts and showcasing a trans woman who, in her seventies, is starting over. Queering both narratives that attempt to fix and define maturation and age, as well as interrupting the temporal narrative momentum through flashback and temporal breaks, Hess details how *Transparent* offers fresh and important complications to long reified scripts of LGBT temporal representation.

Examining the production of the character Kevin in the network television drama *Brothers and Sisters*, Dunn (2015) argues that queer figures are initially presented in a queer mode of time, yet this temporality is short-lived and intentional, for it is shifted and utilized to focus and serve the needs of the centralized heterosexual family. Dunn traces how the character of Kevin is introduced through a queerer relationship to time, but is reframed within a "'new' embodiment of family time" (p. 138). Kevin moves from a state of excess time (untethered by the demands of normal heterosexual time) and a stand-in with available time to assist all those "who lack temporal agency" (p. 145), to a form of temporal mastery, a resource for serving and preserving the institution of the heterosexual family (p. 147), while "drained of its radical potential" (p. 138).

In the edited volume *Queer Praxis: Questions for LGBTQ Worldmaking* (2015), an author team of six communication scholars and thirty-one contributing authors sought to explore the possibilities of examining queer theoretical work through a relational lens, framing queer world-making as a project of self-reflexivity, dialogue, and accountability. The queer praxis project explores time in relationship to queerness, asking "who has the privilege to age out of queerness" (p. 215) and exploring the liminality of queerness and queer relations. The project explores the temporal move in queerness from frameworks of the personal and individual, the "I," to queer models of relationality and accountability. In their chapter "Tomorrow Be-longs to Us," Bennett and West (2015) chart a course for this project by revisiting Edelman's antirelational thesis, and specifically his offhand reference to the song "Tomorrow Belongs to Me," the rise-of-fascism anthem from the film and stage play of *Cabaret*. Arguing the limits of the Edelman's antirelational individualism, they assert the inescapable relational dimensions of humanity and pleasure. Furthermore, they question the true danger and violence of futurity that may exist in a departure from collectivity—from systems of connectivity—calling forth models of queer futurity that are grounded in communal belonging. The authors trace a body of communication research, including Camillo-Rowe's work on the politics of location (p. 255), that pushes against Edelman's antirelational thrust for a collective model for approaching queer futurity. The work claims to move "the conversation in a much more productive discussion than anti-relationality, wherein communication plays more than an instrumental role in refiguring our futures together" (p. 258). In Russo and Roysters's contributed chapter "Stone soup: Building community, creating family," the authors reflect on the temporal queering of two women, in their forties and fifties, adopting their daughter, and forging a life path of queer mothering, queer community building, and cultivating networks of belonging. "Learning to embrace older motherhood without shame or apology" (p. 232), the authors explore the queer possibilities of what older age, older parenting, and queer aging can and might look like.

QUEER TEMPORALITY IN PERFORMANCE STUDIES

A second, and sometimes overlapping, area of study in communication that has examined queer temporality as a space of criticism and invention is the field of performance studies. The study of performance, the study of ritualized or patterns of behavior, at its core, examines the construction and potential disruption of repeated systems of meaning. Performance, as an artistic medium and mode of intervention, is always working with and playing with temporality. It is a time-based art, and a way of engaging culture that examines moment by moment, action by action negotiation of norms and patterns—how we move through the world, negotiate social and physical space, perform identity, and produce culture.

The stories we create and tell will always navigate and potentially intervene in hegemonic notions of temporality. Personal narrative, the crafting and presentation of one's story, from one's body and experience, is a performative act with critical temporal implications and potentials. Pérez (2019) suggests, "the ways personal narrative negotiate with what is—in discourse, space, temporality, relations—can reveal the spark of potentiality that initiates change" (p. 374). In Corey's (1998) discussion of the personal and the master narrative, he argues the personal narrative is a space of potential agency and action, wherein one can resist norms of temporal doom and punishment, and write, craft, and perform oneself otherwise. As Allison (1994) reminds us, we are story livers, not story tellers, and narration is the act of placing events into a temporal structure. Thus, when narrating, we mediate and manipulate time—how we and others experience time through our narrative creation. Gingrich-Philbrook (2014) suggests, when storying oneself and one's experiences, we can explore and seek to capture the very queer ways that memories will always layer upon the present, how the past is always returning and reworking. Dillard's (1997) performative essay "Breathing Darrell," exemplifies how the personal and the poetic can collapse and rupture time, making the past so deeply present, slowed down, suspended and inhabited. No longer history, it conjures immediacy, queering logics of then and now, and linear temporal modes of how we experience life, death, and breath. Personal narrative work extends beyond recreations of the past, as well as the present, but forges into the imagined, desired and anticipated future. Gutierrez-Perez and Andrade

(2018) argue, "Our personal narratives rooted in the experience of an embodied, complex repertoire offer a queer potentiality for silenced and/or not yet imagined queer of color worlds" (p. 2).

Performative writing as a mode of inquiry, engagement, and investigation offers a strategy to queer how we construct knowledge and reflect one's experience. It draws attention to the ways writing, narration, and the temporal dimensions of scholarship are not neutral, but rather carry and reflect hegemonic commitments to temporality that so often uphold and normalize the whiteness, masculinity and heteronormativity that are entrenched in the academy. All writing is performative, it *does* something, even when guised in the seeming neutrality of reason, logic, sequence, and objectivity. Corey and Nakayama's (1997) landmark and highly controversial performative essay "Sextext" sparked a discipline wide discussion about what voices, forms, and modes of appropriateness define and confine scholarship: "Sextext was reaching for a better future" (Corey & Nakayama, 2012). "Sextext" was a temporal intervention.

In his essay "A Journey to El Mundo Zurdo," Gutierrez-Perez (2017) uses performative writing and personal narrative to resist the linear, flattened, hegemonic temporality of academic writing, seeking to reflect and examine culture in a more circular and holistic approach. He argues queers of color experience time in unique and differing ways. He asserts, "until you touch and feel how 'fellow citizens' espoused hate from pulpits after the Pulse massacre; how 'allies' turned an ignorant eye to the NBA or NHL Finals instead of mobilizing for our community; or how 'family' and 'friends' went back to posting pictures of their children and pets as if nothing had even happened, then you do not understand how queer bodies of color exist in a different temporality" (p. 180). He enlists Anzaldúa's concept of "El Mundo Zurdo," or "The Lefthand World" to interrogate the ways that heteronormativity "is intimately connected to cultural orientations to time, race, class, nationality, gender, and ability" (p. 179).

In performance-based research, the personal narrative becomes a space of reflection, but also an assertion of agency and imagination to think through and imagine time and future in innovative ways. Goltz (2009) conducted creative focus group research with a group of college-aged participants who identified as gay, lesbian, and queer, wherein personal meanings and anxieties of aging and future were processed and explored through creative group projects. Core temporal systems and life stages were placed under a critical dialogic investigation, and the collective group sought to reflect, experiment with, and reimagine lives and futures that located success and happiness beyond the temporal mandates of straight time.

Calafell (2007) writes of queer temporality to mark temporal displacement, both nostalgia and memory or anticipation—"a space that longs for what never was and never will be" (p. 65). Her project explores shared feeling and shared experience, specifically "the feeling of being positioned outside of dominant narratives" (p. 65). Queer temporality, in this project, disrupts how power works to claim, define, and contain marginalized experiences and memory, opening up possibilities for counternarratives and communities—the possibility of queer diaspora—constructed through excess of feeling, longing, and experiences of marginalization. Wherein performance theory commonly works to examine the duality of the performative act, what Diamond (2000) has succinctly marked as the "doing and the thing done" (p. 66), Calafell (2007) connects the workings of queer temporality to the future-driving potentials of performance. Thus, she works alongside other scholars who look to performance to conjure unimaginable futures, to gesture and sketch new openings and imaginative styles that perhaps inspire or feel us forward. In this configuration, queer temporality is a performative strategy for building and connecting, a forward-driving projection of possibility for the future. "Thus, I offer my own narrative, my own rewriting of the space, and my own story of mourning to re-perform possibilities for recuperating colonial narratives" (pp. 66–67).

In the performative script "Once Upon a Time," Cosenza (2013) explicated this idea that *how* one tells one's story, how time is constructed and reflected in the telling, shapes the content and possibilities of what the story says, does, and can potentially speak to. Using Halberstam's call for considering how queer understandings of time might offer a space for reclaiming disqualified knowledges and experiences, Consenza unpacks the workings of time in the process of writing the performance script. Specifically, Consenza examines the notions of condensed time, suspended time and equivalent time and how they operate in the scripting and performance process. Moreman (2019) looks to queer temporality in performance as a space of creative intervention and imagination. Building from Muñoz, he writes, "the lived variance and mystery of queer temporality is actually a source for possibility. As queer individuals navigate a life outside of heteronormativity, we improvise a life in creative ways" (p. 189). He specifically looks to the discursive act of "Latinx" as an embodiment of "queer futurity via a latinidad framework of inclusivity," a performative act of collectivity, difference, and possibility (p. 189). As a queer temporal intervention, Moreman writes his personal history in relationship to contemporary queer youth literature—literatures that did not exist when he was a child—to "invoke magical realism to resist a linearity of time" (p. 190) through an autofantasia. What is constructed in these is "affective Latinx presentations in their aesthetic arrangement of a queer past that is performed for the benefit of projecting a queer future" (p. 191).

Outside of creative writing practices and personal narration, performance studies most immediately works in staged performance, the live-embodied action and audience engagement as a method for theorizing queer temporality and imagining/creating queer potentials. Although much queer performance work is not explicitly framed under the title or project of queer temporalities, queer performance *is* queer temporal theorizing in space, in relationship with audience, and in time. Traumas of queer pasts are reentered and reexamined in the works of queer performance artists.

In performance studies and communication, a long lineage of queer performers (i.e., but surely not limited to, Bryant Keith Alexander, Scott Dillard, Laila Farah, Ragan Fox, Terry Galloway, Craig Gingrich-Philbrook, Dustin Goltz, Robert Gutierrez-Perez, Jonny Gray, E. Patrick Johnson, Omi Osum Olomo, Kimberlee Pérez, Jackie Taylor, and Elizabeth Whitney) enlist performance as a tool to transport us outside of the here and now, and to feel and imagine our pasts and our futures beyond the limitations of heteronormative discourse. The aesthetic performance is a space of imaginary and potentiality. Performance has the power to open these temporal imaginaries, offering what D. Soyini Madison refers to as the performance of possibilities—the possibility of intersubjective traveling between performer and audience. Jill Dolan (2005) writes of the utopian performative to capture the hope and possibility she finds in audiencing theater. Never finished, fixed, or concrete, the utopian performative is a momentary lifting up, a suspension from the here and now, that traces or hints to a feeling of personas, relations, and social imaginaries outside the confines of the present. In many ways mirroring Muñoz's project, where the yet to be inhabited spaces of punk and queer bars linger in anticipation, of potentiality of who we might/could be, and what could/might happen—just resting beyond the discursive limitations of the imaginable.

Pérez and Goltz (2010) look to the power of collaborative performance and collaborative personal narrative to interrogate the how different bodies experience time in differing and hegemonic modes. Staging their temporal orientations in tension as "Brown Dyke Girl" and "White Gay Jew Guy," interrogations of colonialism and bordering discourses are embodied in conflict to the ahistorical temporal frameworks of whiteness and masculinity—those that work to disconnect, sever, and move past the lingering traumas of "the past." Through dialogue, love, agitation, and commitment, two bodies carrying very different experiences, work to find connection across their differing ways of living in time, living in history, and moving through the world. Pryor (2017) examines visual art and performance for its queering potential to enact what she calls "time slips," where time is deliberately queered in moments that challenge the idealized timelines of capital, inheritance, and normativity. She examines the temporality of trauma and of grief as spaces where discreet linear timelines of past, present, and future fail, bleed, and discipline. Pryor enlists the example of 9/11 and the rush to heal and move forward as representative of the competing investments of straight capitalist temporality and temporalities of trauma, wherein the ability to push forward, solider onward, and position the past as merely events now behind us, unravels. She challenges the national temporal project of letting go of the past and centralizes performance-based case studies that disrupt and interrogate the operations and violences of straight temporality. In her analysis, she marks moments of where pasts and presents collide, slipping into one another in a way that seeks to actively challenge the linearity of (and thus the tidy separations of) past, present, and future.

TEMPORALITY AND GENERATIONAL CONNECTIONS

Internationally recognized performance artists such as Holly Hughes, Peggy Shaw, and Tim Miller have spent years developing work that speaks with and alongside queer youth, forging new modes and possibilities for thinking about shared history and queered generation. Live performance events offer opportunities for forging dialogue and meetings of differing generational understandings of community, identity, and history. Morrison (2015) analyzes the annual La MaMa Squirts variety show to help bridge "the queer generation gap," wherein complex tensions and "untapped frustrations" (p. 231) of different generations can be exposed and engaged. For example, Morrison theorizes the performance of spoken word artist Penny Arcade, whose work unites generations across themes of struggle and self-acceptance, but then takes queer youth's "entrenched academic perspective...devoid of real-world experience" (p. 231). While at points, Morrison marks her critique as harsh, the work calls for queer youth "to re-examine their individual and collective principles" (p. 231). In this collective, intergenerational space, complex tensions of queer generation are laid bare and negotiated through aesthetic performance work.

Moments and projects are emerging in the literature, where notions of queer modes of intergenerational connection and possibility are being constructed. Gumbs and Wallace (2016) look to the Mobile Homecoming Experimental Archive, which is designed to highlight, honor, and share the work of Black writers, and the Black community, across generational divides, connecting younger Black youth with Black histories and elder Black thinkers. Emmer (2012) looks to ACT-UP Philadelphia through the lens of metageneration, for a unique mode of sharing and processing histories with and across differing age groups and generations. Rather than an inheritance model of history being something fixed into place, solidified, held onto, and then passed down, metageneration marks a process by which histories are brought into dialogue, contemplation, negotiation, and criticism. Herein the contextual blind spots, the privileged perspectives, and the minoritized viewpoints of history can be interrogated, reflected up, and discussed. This shifting landscape anticipates a broader discussion of what could and what may more queered forms of thinking about time, aging, and generativity look like for future generations. What is the relationship between the queer past and the emerging queer future?

As a relatively recent mode of inquiry, work in queer temporality has a broad range of questions and applications that are only beginning to take form. One area that is likely to garner future work is the ongoing question of how youth/adult logics function in the shifting LGBTQ cultural landscape. Halberstam (2018) begins tracing the recent emergence of discourse around the trans* child, a trend in trans youth wherein greater social acceptance of queerness—both in certain families as well as schools and the broader culture—is leading to a disconnect between queer kids and queer histories. Not unlike patterns in gay male communities, Halberstam reports a contradictory present of entitlement and fragility, wherein some, more privileged "young trans* activists simultaneously express an unquestioned sense of their own legitimacy and the need for safe space and trigger warnings" (p. 72). As an additional point of inquiry, the notion of inheritance—a core structure of queer time—poses a question for what queer modes of inheritance can and might look like. Building on the gerontological notion of generativity, which marks how meaning and value are constructed by aging populations by giving back or paying forward to younger generations, there is the work of tracing and imaging what queer modes of generativity can and might look. How might intergenerational meaning and value be constructed outside the logics of inheritance, ones that push past youthist commitments that centralize youth (even queer youth) in our political imaginaries (Goltz, 2021a, 2021b). Where and how might we push past moralizing timelines of "get a job, stop drugging" (Corey & Nakayama, 2012) and anticipate alterative legacies beyond the Sacred Child, youthism, and normalizing narratives of proper maturation and life meaning are not the locus of all meaning?

While the impulse of the work can be traced back decades ago, the body of work in communication under an umbrella of "queer temporalities" is still relatively new and ever expanding. Necessary directions for this work include the ongoing interrogation of how whiteness and masculinity shape temporal modes, not just for the future, but in the daily present—how these hegemonic structures work normalize ideals of productivity, efficiency, rationality, and pace. Furthermore, the cross-section of queer temporalities and mental health provides another rich avenue only beginning to be examined. The study of communication marks a necessary contribution to queer temporal work, examining how symbolic systems work to regulate and concretize the ways we see, know, experience, and navigate time, and then, in turn, how time works to discipline us. As part of the broader project of queer work, queer temporal investigations further our interrogations of institutionalized normativity. As Yep (2003) explains, systems of heteronormativity continue to construct "the equation 'heterosexual experience = human experience.'" While rendering "all other forms of human sexual expression pathological, deviant, invisible, unintelligible, or written out of existence" (cited in Yep, 2003, p. 48). Queer temporality seeks to disturb this equation that straight time is human time, and the foreclosing of queer ways of experiencing time, relating to history, and approaching future. This work, also, provides "analytical tools to create new openings and possibilities for change and transformation" (Yep, 2003, p. 48) in our knowledges, negotiations, and experiences in and of time.

FURTHER READING

Ahmed, S. (2011). Happy futures, perhaps. In E. L. McCallum & M. Tuhkanen (Eds.), *Queer times, queer becomings* (pp. 159–182). State University of New York.

Bennett, J. (2014). Born this way: Queer vernacular and the politics of origin. *Communication and Critical/Cultural Studies*, 11(3), 211–230.

Carter, J. (2013). Embracing transition, or dancing in the folds of time. In S. Stryker & A. Z. Azura (Eds.), *The transgender studies reader 2* (pp. 130–143). Routledge.

Corey, F. C., & Nakayama, T. K. (2012). DeathText. *Western Journal of Communication*, 76(1), 17–23.

Dolan, J. (2005). *Utopia in performative: Finding hope at the theater*. University of Michigan Press.

Edelman, L. (2004). *No future: Queer theory and the death drive*. Duke University Press.

Freeman, E. (2010). *Time binds: Queer temporalities, queer histories*. Duke University Press.

Goltz, D. B. (2010). *Queer temporalities in gay male representation: Tragedy, normativity, and futurity*. Routledge.

Goltz, D. B., Zingsheim, J., Pérez, K., Carrillo-Rowe, A., Tiffe, R., & Bagley, M. (2015). Queer love: Futurity and potentiality. In D. Goltz & J. Zingsheim (Eds.), *Queer praxis: Questions of LGBTQ worldmaking*. Peter Lang.

Gutierrez-Perez, R. (2017). A journey to El Mundo Zurdo: Queer temporality, queer of color temporal heritages. *Communication and Critical/Cultural Studies*, 14(2), 177–181.

Halberstam, J. (2005). *In a queer time and place: Transgender bodies, subcultural lives*. NYU Press.

Keeling, K. (2019). *Queer times, black futures*. NYU Press.

Muñoz, J. E. (2009). *Cruising utopia: The then and there of queer futurity*. NYU Press.

Pryor, J. I. (2017). *Time slips: Queer temporalities, contemporary performance, and the hole of history*. Northwestern University Press.

Russo, A., & Royster, F. (2015). Stone soup: Building community creating family—expansive possibilities of queer love. In D. Goltz & J. Zingsheim (Eds.), *Queer Praxis: Questions for LGBTQ Worldmaking* (pp. 231–238). Peter Lang.

REFERENCES

Abdi, S., & Calafell, B. M. (2017). Queer utopias and a (feminist) Iranian vampire: A critical analysis of resistive monstrosity in *A Girl Walks Home Alone at Night*. *Critical Studies in Media Communication*, 34(4), 358–370.

Aizura, A. Z. (2012). Persistence of transgender travel narratives. In T. T. Cotton (Ed.), *Transgender migrations: The bodies, borders and politics of transition* (pp. 139–156). Routledge.

Allison, J. M. (1994). Narrative and time: A phenomenological reconsideration. *Text & Performance Quarterly*, 14(2), 108–125.

Bennett, J., & West, I. (2015). Tomorrow be-longs to us. In D. Goltz & J. Zingsheim (Eds.), *Queer Praxis: Questions for LGBTQ Worldmaking* (pp. 249–259). Peter Lang.

Berlant, L. (1997). *The queen of America goes to Washington: Essays on sex and citizenship*. Duke.
Butler, J. (2004). *Undoing gender*. Routledge.
Butler, J. (1993). *Bodies that matter: On the discursive limits of "sex."* Routledge.
Calafell, B. M. (2007). *Latina/o communication studies: Theorizing performance*. Peter Lang.
Cleto, F. (1999). Introduction: Queering the camp. In F. Cleto (Ed.), *Camp: Queer aesthetics and the performing subject* (pp. 1–43). University of Michigan Press.
Corey, F. C. (1998). The personal: Against the master narrative. In S. J. Dailey (Ed.), *The future of performance studies: Visions and revisions* (pp. 249–253). National Communication Association.
Corey, F. C., & Nakayama, T. K. (1997). Sextext. *Text and Performance Quarterly, 17*(1), 58–88.
Corey, F. C., & Nakayama, T. K. (2012). DeathText. *Western Journal of Communication, 76*(1), 17–23.
Cosenza, J. (2013). Once upon a time: Looking to the ecstatic past for queer futurity. *Liminalities: A Journal of Performance Studies, 9*(2), 28–38. http://liminalities.net/9-2/cosenza.pdf
Dean, T. (2011). Bareback time. In E. L. McCallum & M. Tuhkanen (Eds.), *Queer times, queer becomings* (pp. 75–99). State University of New York.
De Lauretis, T. (1987). *Technologies of gender: Essays on theory, film and fiction*. Indiana University Press.
Diamond, E. (2000). Performance and cultural politics. In L. Goodman & J. de Gay (Eds.), *The Routledge reader in politics and performance* (pp. 66–69). Routledge.
Dillard, S. (1997). Breathing Darrell: Solo performance as a contribution to a useful queer mythology. *Text and Performance Quarterly, 20*(1), 74–83.
Dinshaw, C. (2015). Response time: Linear, nonlinear, queer. *Studies in Gender and Sexuality, 16*, 40–43.
Dinshaw, C., Edelman, L., Ferguson, R. A., Freccero, C., Freeman, E., Halberstam, J., Jagose, A., Nealon, C., & Hoang, N. T. (2007). Theorizing queer temporalities: A roundtable discussion. *GLQ, 13*(2–3), 177–195.
Dolan, J. (2005). *Utopia in performative: Finding hope at the theater*. University of Michigan Press.
Dunn, T. R. (2015). (Queer) family time: *Brothers & Sisters* and managing temporal anxieties. *Western Journal of Communication, 79*(2), 133–150.
Edelman, L. (2004). *No future: Queer theory and the death drive*. Duke University Press.
Emmer, P. (2012). Talkin' about meta-generation: ACT UP history and queer futurity. *Quarterly Journal of Speech, 98*(1), 89–96.
Freccero, C. (2007). Queer times. *South Atlantic Quarterly, 106*(3), 485–494.
Freeman, E. (2007). Queer belongings: Queer theory and kinship theory. In G. E. Haggerty & M. McGarry (Eds.), *A companion to lesbian, gay, bisexual, transgender, and queer studies* (pp. 295–314). Blackwell.
Freeman, E. (2010). *Time binds: Queer temporalities, queer histories*. Duke University Press.
Gingrich-Philbrook, C. (2014). On gratitude, for my father. In J. Wyatt & T. E. Adams (Eds.), *On writing families: Autoethnographies of presence and absence, love and loss* (pp. 23–30). Sense Publishers.
Goltz, D. B. (2009). Investigating queer future meanings: Destructive perceptions of "the harder path." *Qualitative Inquiry, 15*(3), 561–586.
Goltz, D. B. (2010). *Queer temporalities in gay male representation: Tragedy, normativity, and futurity*. Routledge.
Goltz, D. B. (2012). (Love)sick aliens in the wasteland: Queer temporal camp in Araki's teen apocalyptic trilogy. *Critical Studies in Media Communication, 29*(2), 97–112.
Goltz, D. B. (2013). It gets better: Queer futures, critical frustrations, and radical potentials. *Critical Studies in Media Communication, 30*(2), 135–151.
Goltz, D. B. (2021a). Queer generativity: Temporal collisions of *Fred Astaire's Dancing Lessons*. *Text and Performance Quarterly, 41*(1–2), 106–122.
Goltz, D. B. (2021b). Framing our story: Youthist and queer temporalities in Lopez's *The Inheritance*. *QED: A Journal for LGBTQ Worldmaking, 8*(1), 1–24.
Goltz, D. B., Zingsheim, J., Pérez, K., Carrillo-Rowe, A., Tiffe, R., & Bagley, M. (2015). Queer love: Futurity and Potentiality. In D. Goltz & J. Zingsheim (Eds.), *Queer praxis: Questions of LGBTQ worldmaking*. Peter Lang.

Gumbs, A. P., & Wallace, J. R. (2016). Something else to be. In E. P. Johnson (Ed.), *No tea, no shade: New writings on Black Queer Studies* (pp. 380–394). Duke University Press.

Gutierrez-Perez, R. (2017). A journey to El Mundo Zurdo: Queer temporality, queer of color temporal heritages. *Communication and Critical/Cultural Studies, 14*(2), 177–181.

Gutierrez-Perez, R., & Andrade, L. (2018). Queer of color worldmaking: <Marriage> in the archive and the embodied repertoire. *Text & Performance Quarterly, 38*(1–2), 1–18.

Halberstam, J. (2005). *In a queer time and place: Transgender bodies, subcultural lives.* NYU Press.

Halberstam, J. (2018). *Trans*: A quick and quirky account of gender variability.* University of California Press.

Halperin, D. M. (2012). *How to be Gay.* Belknap Press.

Hess, L. (2017). My whole life I've been dressing up like a man": Negotiations of queer aging and queer temporality in the TV series *Transparent. European Journal of American Studies, 11*(3), 1–19.

Keeling, K. (2009). Looking for m:___: Queer temporality, black political possibility, and poetry from the future. *GLQ, 15*(4), 565–582.

King, J. (2022). *Inclusive screenwriting for film and television.* Routledge.

Luciano, D. (2007). Coming around again: The queer momentum of *Far From Heaven. GLQ, 13*(2–3), 249–272.

Meyer, M. (Ed.). (1994). *The politics and poetics of camp.* Routledge.

Moreman, S. (2019). A queer futurity autofantasía: Contouring discourses in Latinx through memory and queer youth literature. *Text & Performance Quarterly, 39*(3), 185–202.

Morrison, J. A. (2015). La MaMa Squirts: Igniting queer intergenerational dialogue through performance. *Text & Performance Quarterly, 35*(2–3), 226–233.

Muñoz, J. E. (2005). Impossible spaces: Kevin McCarthy's Chameleon Club. *GLQ, 11*(3), 427–436.

Muñoz, J. E. (2006). Stages: Punks, queers, and the utopian performance. In D. S. Madison & J. Hamera (Eds.), *The SAGE handbook of performance studies* (pp. 9–20). SAGE.

Muñoz, J. E. (2009). *Cruising utopia: The then and there of queer futurity.* NYU Press.

Ott, B. L., & Aoki, E. (2002). The politics of negotiating public tragedy: Media framing of the Matthew Shepard murder. *Rhetoric & Public Affairs, 5*(3), 483–505.

Pérez, K. (2019). Staging the family unfamiliar: The queer intimacies *in Ramble-Ations: A One D'Lo Show. Text & Performance Quarterly, 39*(4), 371–387.

Pérez, K., & Goltz, D. B. (2010). Treading across our "Lines in the Sand": Performing bodies in coalitional subjectivity. *Text & Performance Quarterly, 30*(3), 247–268.

Pryor, J. I. (2017). *Time slips: Queer temporalities, contemporary performance, and the hole of history.* Northwestern University Press.

Román, D. (1997). Negative identifications: HIV-negative gay men in representation and performance." In M. Duberman (Ed.), *Queer representations: Reading lives, reading cultures* (pp. 162–176). NYU Press.

Storey, J. (2001). *Cultural theory and popular culture* (3rd ed.). Prentice Hall.

West, I., Frischherz, M., Panther, A., & Brophy, R. (2013). Queer worldmaking in the "It Gets Better" campaign. *QED: A Journal for LGBTQ Worldmaking, 0*(1), 49–86.

Yep, G. A. (2003). The violence of heteronormativity in communication studies: Notes on injury, healing and queer world-making. In G. A. Yep, K. E. Lovaas, & J. P. Elia (Eds.), *Queer theory and communication: From disciplining queers to queering the discipline(s)* (pp. 11–60). Harrington Park Press.

Dustin Goltz

Queer Health

Queer Health

CRIP THEORY

CRIPPING COMMUNICATION STUDIES

Josh Hepple is a gay man with cerebral palsy who lives in London and relies on Grindr to have sex. In an essay published in *The Guardian*, Hepple (2016) noted, "I use a wheelchair, I have jerky involuntary movements, I rely on assistants 24/7 and I have a speech impairment. At the same time I have a good sex life and really enjoy challenging men's conceptions of disability." When Hepple joined the popular hook-up app, he had never had a sexual encounter with a man. Within 18 months, he had met at least 60 men and found the experiences both rewarding and liberating. He reflected, "The health benefits have been enormous and there's no denying it's been a lot of fun. I don't forget how disabled I am and I often admire how open-minded these men are. It is a far cry from how I am often treated in public." Hepple subverts a number of ableist expectations in the space of a few words: Contrary to prudish conceptions of sexual activity, he situates his many sex partners as a health benefit; presuppositions of cruelty are not given prominence; the public ambivalence frequently directed at disabled people is replaced by the generative capacities of desire.

Melissa Blake is a writer, blogger, and activist with bylines in outlets that include CNN, *Cosmo*, and *Glamour*. She regularly takes to social media to discuss living with a disability and to unload about the malicious trappings of ableism. In a post to her 115,000 Twitter followers, she writes, "Fun fact: I literally never get asked why I'm not married yet, even though society loves to ask women that very question. It goes back to how society views disabled women. We're not seen as women or worthy romantic partners or even desirable. That's ableism and I hate it here" (Blake, 2021). Blake adopts a critical perspective that captures the extent to which disabled people are located outside normative social scripts (including the most notoriously unwelcome gestures) because of prejudices about who counts as desirable. Like Hepple, her response reflects the complicated interplay of public and private cultural performances. Both of the advocates' posts underscore how disabled people are cast as either asexual or aromantic, not as a matter of personal identification, but because of backward glancing stereotypes. Their observations also illustrate how social media provides access to sex and solidarity that would be more challenging in a world without these technologies. For all these reasons and more, Hepple's and Blake's experiences exhibit the import and vitality of "crip theory."

In its most basic rendering, crip theory "critiques systems of compulsory ablebodiedness" and challenges the "ongoing consolidation of heterosexual, ablebodied hegemony" (McRuer, 2006, p. 19). The resistive potential suggested in this definition points to crip's origins as a reclaimed derogatory term ("cripple") by disabled people, just as "queer" once was for LGBT folk. In a widely cited passage, Clare (1999) describes the pair as "cousins" and argues that these lexical kin are "words to shock, words to infuse with pride and self-love, words to resist internalized hatred, words to help forge a politics" (p. 70). True to Clare's observation, activists and scholars have taken up crip as a broad critical heuristic for assessing the normative features of everyday life that inhibit disabled people from accessing material and symbolic resources. Over the past two decades, crip theory has evolved into a vibrant field of study for generating new forms of knowledge that scrutinize dominant assumptions of the social world and strive to incorporate diffuse bodily experiences into otherwise restrictive structures. In doing so, thinkers indebted to crip theory have developed original categories of epistemological consideration, often referred to as "cripistemologies," and modes of critique, such as "cripping." The uptake of this project has been both long-standing and ongoing. Despite the fact that activists and academics have been utilizing crip as an interpretive tool for years, the idea remains as much an emergent perspective as it does an essentially contested concept.

Crip, as with queer, invites definitional uncertainty. Although they are inseparable, "crip" and disability are not inherently synonymous. Just as "queer" and LGBTQ studies assume divergent political investments, crip is explicitly committed to dissecting the nonnormative mechanisms of everyday life to chart paths of resistance and novel ways of being. Crip is frequently taken up in tandem with "queer" positionalities but, in some contexts, simply acts as the nonnormative accompaniment to disability studies, which has long been preoccupied with White male subjectivities. Such definitional qualities certainly hold implications for how we imagine the scope of crip theory. Are studies of HIV or transness necessarily tied to crip theory because of their historical relationships to medicalization, surveillance, and biopolitical renderings of disability? Is crip best situated as a universalized positionality that embraces all forms of debility and bodily function or a minoritized standpoint experienced by a sliver of the population (Sedgwick, 1990)? Can a crip sensibility be assumed even when the term is nowhere to be found in a specific scholarly analysis or movement? These are ongoing inquiries that academics and activists will grapple with for years to come. For the purposes of this article, I sometimes invoke literature that never uses the word "crip" because I believe particular works reflect a critical interpretive practice that is captured well by the heuristic. That is, I situate crip as both a methodology *and* a sensibility; it is both a tool *and* an attitude. Further, I tend to adopt identity-first language in this entry (i.e., disabled people) rather than person-first language (i.e., people with disabilities) because the former is currently the preferred terminology among numerous disability communities and because such an emphasis better reflects the critical impulses of crip theory. This essay probes three discernable qualities of crip theory as it relates to communication studies: normative understandings of the body, the contingent materialization of crip practices, and the political character of these approaches. I do not believe these three touchstones are the only ways that queer and crip may be convivial, but they provide a useful map for capturing the scope of this entry, which then turns to studies of media representation, public communication, and performance studies.

QUEER/CRIP STARTING POINTS

As interpretive lenses and modes of critique, both queer and crip suggest, and reside outside of, culturally sanctioned normativities. I use the term "normativities" to refer to the systems through which norms, normalization, and normative categories of being are naturalized and made to seem ideal. Normativities constitute and constrain processes of meaning-making and render certain cultural practices acceptable and morally endorsed, while others are conceived as taboo, impure, or unintelligible. Sex education, for example, is a frequently cited example of how the relay of a specific kind of knowledge and practice constitutes righteous behavior and model citizenship. The terms "queer" and "crip" denote the presence of a body or an identity that is not easily assimilable to prevailing notions of personhood. In their otherness, queer and crip are the constitutive outside of bodily normality, which could not be conceived without them. As Robert McRuer (2006) notes,

> Able-bodied identity and heterosexual identity are linked in their mutual impossibility and in their mutual incomprehensibility–they are incomprehensible in that each is an identity that is simultaneously the ground on which all identities supposedly rest and an impressive achievement that is always deferred and thus never really guaranteed. (p. 9)

In other words, both able-bodiedness and heterosexuality demand constant performative gestures to approximate the identities they represent, but always with a remainder because neither category is ontologically stable. Although LGBTQ+ people and disabled people are often regarded as "more embodied" than their normative counterparts, the intense focus given to them actually illustrates the illusory sleight of hand in materializing heterosexual and able-bodied identities.

These normativities become self-evident when we contemplate the ways that disabled people, as well as those who identify as queer, have been repeatedly abused by institutions such as the medical establishment. The cures and endless experimentation that have historically been thrust on queers and crips elucidates the ways vulnerable populations have been consistently harmed by disciplinary medical directives. The "ableist conflation" of disability "with pain and suffering" or the long-held belief that being queer constitutes a "hard life" illustrates the injurious legacies of these apparatuses (Reynolds, 2017, p. 150). Of course, norms are complicated and malleable. Makkawy and Moreman (2019) remind us that "crip can acknowledge how disability is pathologized from a medical perspective, but crip still honors longings for cure—if desired" by disabled people (p. 402). The blurry line between structure and agency in such assertions highlights the convoluted nature of normativities and the necessity of nuanced crip critique.

Second, both queer and crip are necessarily contingent terms (Meade & Serlin, 2006, p. 3). Generations of scholars have taught us that what is regarded as queer in one context may not necessarily be recognized as queer in another. Likewise, what is understood as a crip is never fixed or static. As with queer, crip will vary across spheres and change depending on the circumstances of the situation. The social model of disability, for example, hints at the contingent nature of bodily practices. Whereas much of society might hold that disabilities are self-evident, the social model gives deep focus to the built environment that, often consciously, excludes disabled people. Purposeful architecture or design that is crafted with the multifarious nature of the body in mind highlights the provisional dynamics of the environment and, in doing so, resists reductive notions of disability. Activist groups such as ADAPT have been especially consequential in spotlighting the limits of ableist perspectives and the ways contexts can be fundamentally altered with attention to accessibility. In this way, crip is potentially tactical and not transparently ontological (Lindemann, 2008, pp. 99–100). The adoption of crip perspectives can help to alter the conditions of space, time, and experience.

Third, like queer, crip is a notably politicized term (McRuer & Wilkerson, 2003). Critiques giving emphasis to crip theory might tackle everything from the production of bathroom spaces to the affective nature of protest to the cultural production of desire. Sandahl (2003) recognized the expansive nature of crip by envisioning it "as a body politic circulating among disabled people out of interruptive meanings generated through their interactions within normative discourses" (in Makkawy & Moreman, 2019, p. 402). The end goal of such a politic might include the development of new cripistemologies that seek to redefine ways of knowing from the perspective of those living with disabilities. Although such sensibilities have long been a defining feature of life for many disabled people, the constitution of crip politics has continued to expand its reach. People with diabetes, for example, are a relatively recent political coalition thanks in part to social media platforms such as Twitter. Those living with the condition have cripped social media exchanges about who should wear continuous glucose monitors (only people with diabetes or those who want to surveil their sugars for other health purposes); they have documented conversations with skeptical health care providers about the destructive nature of capitalism; they have engaged in terse exchanges with administrators and politicians who set the price of insulin without community input. People with diabetes have also increasingly debated the plasticity of signifiers such as "disabled."

These touchstones for contemplating disability guide the remainder of this entry, which gives close attention to three areas of communication studies: media representations, political rhetoric, and performance studies.

Media Representations of Disability. Representations of disabled people and representations of LGBTQ+ people are catnip for Hollywood's awards season. Over 60 actors have been nominated for Academy Awards for portraying people with disabilities and, of those, over two dozen have won. About the same number of heterosexual actors have been nominated for playing LGBTQ+ characters and, again, roughly the same number have received a trophy. Only three actors with disabilities—Troy Kotsur, Marlee Matlin, and Harold Russell—have ever taken a statue home. The conversation about identity and recognition becomes a bit more complicated for queer actors because several have won, but many were not "out" when they collected the prize, were merely rumored to be queer, or never went public with their sexuality. Statistics and confessionals aside, there is little denying that disabled and queer identities have been essential components of media history.

The relationship between disability and sexuality does not rest apart, especially when we consider their mutual constitution in media such as cinema or television. The visual markers that have tended to define both disabled people and LGBTQ+ people are essential elements of media narratives. Incorporating a crip sensibility might ask how these two features of identity are intertwined in both expected and often surprising ways. In his text *Crip Theory: Cultural Signs of Queerness and Disability*, McRuer (2006) probes how disabilities are depicted in relation to sexuality. In particular, he offers extended attention to the late 1990s romantic comedy *As Good As It Gets*, starring Jack Nicholson, Helen Hunt, and Greg Kinnear. McRuer finds that able-bodied status is achieved "in direct proportion to increasing need for heterosexual love." Drawing off of Emily Martin's notion of the flexible body, McRuer argues that heteronormative epiphanies of love are repeatedly, and often necessarily, able-bodied ones. These epiphanic moments require straight characters to materialize as flexible, where wholeness can be performed through crisis and the stability of heterosexuality can be confirmed (p. 17). Nicholson's character Melvin is able to overcome his obsessive–compulsive disorder only through an explicit performance of heterosexual courtship—as his need for love increases, his disability fades away. Importantly, however, these struggles are not carried out on the heterosexual body but are invariably projected onto the bodies of visibly queer and disabled folk. McRuer notes that it is Kinnear's queer character Simon who experiences the greatest amount of trauma and whose redemption ultimately benefits Melvin. Disability and queerness are markers of instability throughout the production, but heterosexuality's flexibility permits a reaffirmation of its prized normativity.

Barounis (2009) has complicated McRuer's arguments about the flexibility of queer/crip bodies by looking to texts that fortify notions of identity rather than position them as fluid. In her analysis of the films *Murderball* and *Brokeback Mountain*, Barounis focuses on the role of masculinity in the construction of queer/crip bodies, finding that each of them is not simply compatible with masculinity but "celebrated as the logical extension of masculinity's excess" (p. 55). Barounis situates masculinity as the "visual mechanism through which disability and homosexuality distance themselves from one another, each identity to some extent disciplining the other" (p. 55). She asserts,

> In *Brokeback Mountain* and *Murderball*, systems of heterosexuality and able-bodiedness do not combine in order to produce a stigmatized disabled/queer subjectivity. Instead, these two films set up a world where the mainstreaming of homosexuality stigmatizes disability and where claiming an in-your-face crip subjectivity relies on successful heterosexual conquest. (p. 56)

In this way, bodies are not flexible so much as they are "resolute and resistant to change" (Barounis, 2009, p. 56). Even as identities are performatively crafted, they are often imagined as ontologically grounded in markers such as masculinity to perpetuate cultural assumptions about gender, disability, and sexuality.

The relationship between masculinity and disability has been the foundation of numerous Hollywood productions, which have tended to focus specifically on the redemption narratives of White heterosexual cisgender men. The trope of transcending disability via masculinist heterosexuality is persistent in films that include *Coming Home, Born on the Fourth of July, Breaking the Waves, Forrest Gump*, and *The Sessions*, among many others. Scholars such as Cherney and Lindemann dissect this oft-conceived association by scrutinizing the relationship between masculinity, sport, and disability in productions such as *Murderball* and *Friday Night Lights* (Lindemann & Cherney, 2008). They argue that texts such as *Murderball*, a film that details the everyday lives of people participating in a wheelchair rugby league, can counter ableist assumptions about the vitality of people with quadriplegia (p. 108). However, they also relay that such representations can reinforce ableist and masculinist ideals, thereby working against the political goals of disability activists in the United States. For instance, they observe that *Murderball* "frames quadriplegia with a utilitarian view of the body and a daredevil masculinity, both of which accept rather than reject the dominant cultural definition of disability" (p. 121). The film's hegemonic tendencies inhibit more nuanced and variable understandings of identity and the body that might better serve disabled people.

Cherney and Lindemann (2014) produced one of the clearest examples of queer/crip critique in their analysis of the television series *Friday Night Lights*. Coupling Sedgwick's (1985) notion of the triangulation of desire, wherein homoerotic desire and homosocial relationships are closeted via a normatively rendered love triangle, the authors explore how disability and queer longing are carefully mediated by both medicalized contexts and particularly scripted relationships. Giving attention to specific "erotic triangles" of desire on the program, Cherney and Lindemann contemplate how disability obscures homosocial desire among two of the characters after one of them becomes quadriplegic. They write, "media depictions of disability that obscure displays of homosociality sustain and integrate compulsory systems of able-bodiedness and heterosexuality. This reinforces the appropriateness, utility, and oppressive potential of ableist and heterosexist strategies of viewing" (p. 14). For all of the progressive critiques forwarded on *Friday Night Lights*, including those of class and race, representations of masculinity and disability invariably fall short of more refined critiques of ableism and heteronormativity.

Communication studies scholars have also probed the generative potential of media texts that explore the relationship among queerness and disability. King and West (2014), for instance, turn to the film *Lars and the Real Girl* to engage how productions might reimagine approaches to trauma. *Lars* situates mental health crises as best treated through community efforts that understand trauma in culturally incisive ways rather than as a condition to be individually treated or managed. The main character Lars, played by Ryan Gosling, is not stigmatized or marginalized but "is accepted on his terms as a valuable community member" by those who embrace his fantastical and precarious relationship to the world. They read the film as offering a "utopian invocation of acceptance, rather than tolerance, as a communal norm" that playfully reproduces and "undoes normative understandings of identity, community, and relationality" (p. 60). Likewise, in their analysis of the postapocalyptic film *Mad Max: Fury Road*, Fletcher and Primack (2017) contend that depictions of disability are conceptualized generatively as adaptive conditions of human life and "not as a debilitating, life-ending, or marginalizing experience" (p. 344). These positive conceptions of disability, they argue, challenge "normative notions of able-bodiedness" (p. 345).

Studies of representation that emphasize normative conceptions of the visual are themselves artifacts that invite and demand crip critique. In the text *Trans**, Halberstam (2018) offers one path forward for displacing the overemphasis on the visual as a corporeal marker of transness, especially in regard to reductive practices such as passing that dominate trans representation. Halberstam focuses on the notion of the haptic to think through embodiment in productive ways divorced from visuality. Halberstam's emphasis on the haptic seeks to disrupt cultural scripts emphasizing a naturalness or taken-for-granted understanding of the body. For Halberstam, the haptic both "names the way the mind grasps for meanings that elude it while still holding on to the partial knowledge available" (p. 90). Halberstam's innovative and productive approach sparks countless questions for those invested in crip critique: How might we contemplate widespread representations free of visuality? Does the haptic present its own limitations for disabled people? Although more work needs to be done to answer these thought-provoking possibilities, the haptic is among the most generative and original approaches we might have for thinking anew crip critiques invested in trans representation.

Politics, Public Culture, and Critiques of the Productive Body. Crip suggests an explicit political positionality that is dedicated, in part, to resisting the exclusionary dynamics of ableism and expanding opportunities for access in a world not made for disabled people. According to Sandahl (2003), queer/crip standpoints "refuse to minimize their differences by passing as either straight or able-bodied. Instead, they appropriate and rearticulate labels that the mainstream once used to silence or humiliate them and that the liberal factions of their subcultures would like to suppress" (p. 36). She observes that people who identify as both queer and crip must embrace a radical relationship to normality, as they have probably encountered variable forms of oppression. For example, queers and crips have likely experienced ableism and homophobia not only from strangers in the polity but also within queer or disabled communities. As a political sensibility, crip must necessarily be malleable because it has to be utilized in variable situations and among different audiences. This plasticity can be felt in various crip critiques, which scrutinize everything from structural barriers to care to the suffocating allure of the "productive individual" prized in capitalistic cultures.

In communication studies, crip frequently acts as a movement signifier that enables novel identifications, meanings, and actions. Writing about this particular uptake of the term, Kuppers (2007) contends that naming "oneself part of a larger group, a social movement, or a subject position in modernity can help to focus energy, and to understand that solidarity can be found–precariously, in improvisation, and always on the verge of collapse" (p. 90). This melds well with McRuer and Wilkerson's (2003) argument that a "queercrip consciousness resists containment and imagines other, more inventive, expansive, and just communities" (p. 7). This was exactly what West (2010) found in his study of the coalitional politics practiced by the campus organization PISSAR, a queer/crip collective that advocated for safer and more accessible bathrooms. PISSAR's members found common cause in making a series of symbolic and material interventions in this banal site of cultural anxiety and, in doing so, imparted agency to those not typically imagined when restrooms are constructed. PISSAR's success stemmed, in part, from their carefully cultivated activist practices that allowed them to reduce the threat of violence or harassment while also advocating for queer/crip justice.

Disabled people have often had to develop their own norms of protest because typical renderings of activism regularly exclude them. As Vanessa Beasley has surmised, disabled people are often marginalized from common activist practices such as marching. Beasley (2020) suggests that people with visible disabilities are "subject to a double-bind: when they are seen (and thereby repudiate the historic norms of invisibility), they may not be viewed as having political agency" (p. 171). Given these historically oppressive forces, disabled people have pursued alternative venues for making their voices heard. Parsloe and Holton (2018) have examined the cyberactivist tactics of disabled people who sought to counter biomedical discourses employed by organizations such as Autism Speaks. Turning their attention to the #boycottautismspeaks hashtag on social media, they found that participants were able to forward a powerful "counternarrative of neurodiversity" by cultivating ingroup identification and creating bridges to outside communities (p. 1122). Mann (2018) has likewise explored the expanded possibilities for social movement communication in Twitter campaigns such as #CripTheVote. New forms of digital expression, he argues, can "uniquely address the concerns of disabled populations and challenge the compulsory able-bodiedness of movement necessitating embodiment" (p. 604). Even when the language of crip is not explicitly tied to notions of queerness, the influence of such theories is readily transparent with references to the normative pitfalls of "compulsory able-bodiedness" that Mann highlights.

The momentary points of identification initiated by movement politics can forge larger points of resistance against ideological frameworks, such as neoliberalism, that rarely work in the service of disabled people. Neoliberal economic models, which extol policies stressing privatization, deregulation, and austerity, generally function to harm both queers and people with disabilities. Neoliberal measures have repeatedly siphoned resources that would help to facilitate a better world for such folk by resituating public goods in the private sphere and enhancing the fictive role of "personal responsibility" onto individual bodies. This pilfering includes not only access to health care but also institutional endeavors that would expand education, housing, transportation, and environmental protections. In short, cultural "notions of privacy and economic relations of privatization...work together to facilitate heteronormativity" (McRuer & Wilkerson, 2003, p. 9). Far from an innocuous discourse, neoliberalism constructs reductively disempowering visions of disability and queerness "when it fails to accommodate those who fall outside the conception of able-bodiedness and heterosexuality" (D'Souza & Rauchberg, 2020, p. 184).

Relatedly, scholars such as Puar (2017) have engaged the relationship among geopolitical disparities and neoliberalism in the service of producing bodies that are disabled, sometimes through labor exploitation and at other times through state violence (p. 65). Access to health care and home services are among such concerns because these benefits may well become "the defining factor" in one's relationship to the prospects of a livable future (Puar, 2017, p. xvi). Here the creation and perpetuation of disability is a biopolitical end unto itself, "moving neither toward life nor death as the aim" (Puar, 2017, p. xviii). To claim disability justice, then, "is not to call for one's rights within existing social relations but to envision and demand a profoundly different set of social relations" (Crosby & Jakobsen, 2020, p. 78). De La Garza (2019) takes up Puar's notion of debility to eulogize Roxsana Hernández, a stateless transgender person living with HIV who died in the custody of U.S. Immigration and Customs Enforcement (ICE). The agency denied Hernández access to medical care and incarcerated her in one of their notoriously freezing holding cells, which are generally overcrowded and where people are denied adequate food and water. ICE officials cited "complications due to HIV" as the cause of Hernández's death, but De La Garza points out that her suffering actually stemmed from "systemic poverty, endemic violence, and institutional neglect" (p. 96).

In this vein, scholarship that forwards crip-inspired frameworks have focused on the production of disabled subjectivities in numerous public cultures. These works are often extensions of the critiques of neoliberalism mentioned above, and they scrutinize how disabled positionalities are effects of discourses that emanate from varied institutional and vernacular spheres (D'Souza & Rauchberg, 2020). For example, "super crip" narratives generally depict disabled folks as transcendent figures who "overcome" their disabilities through discipline, hard work, and individual triumph. Such tales frequently occlude criticisms of systematic exclusion or structural barriers to care by focusing on the fortunes of a single person who does not (and cannot) capture the varied ways disabilities might affect different people. Super crips are sometimes labeled "inspiration porn" because these depictions center the feelings and ideologies of audiences unfamiliar, or willfully ignorant, of the lives of disabled people.

Media industries, war, and the American judicial process have all garnered attention from communication studies scholars for the ways they facilitate the production of disability and its normative accompaniments. Kirkpatrick (2012), for instance, uses McRuer's notion of "compulsory able-bodiedness" to explore how technologies such as radio produced "differently abled bodies with differing degrees of citizenship for different applications and techniques of governance" (p. 167). Policy creation, he argued, can function as a "normalizing discourse that works to medicalize and regulate populations" (p. 168). These normative tendencies are also given attention by Gilbert (2014), who contends that a consequence of modern warfare is that the "wounded soldier body is a new norm of the body politic" (p. 146). Just as injured veterans often act as a stand-in for a wounded or conflicted polity in Hollywood, the figure of the disabled veteran is repeatedly manipulated by the state for the imagistic purposes of nationalism and patriotism. In this way, disabled people are carefully mediated by state actors for political purposes. During Sonia Sotomayor's judicial confirmation process, for example, the Obama administration forwarded her diabetes management to highlight what a deliberate and contemplative justice she would be on the bench. Bennett (2018) argued that this was no accident. Sotomayor was assailed constantly with racist and sexist accusations, including that she was temperamental and emotional, qualities that would have disallowed her from serving on the high court. The White House's decision to use her disability to discursively "contain" her race and gender illustrated the plasticity of intersectional politics and the dubious ways disabled subjectivities are articulated to cultural markers for political gain.

Performance, Narrative, Embodiment. Performance studies has been essential to the development of crip theory in communication studies. The persistent focus on queer/crip critique is not surprising when we consider how such lives are organized around the fields of visuality, embodiment, and relationality. Sandahl (2003) writes that queering and cripping are both "theatrical and everyday practices deployed to challenge oppressive norms, build community, and maintain the practitioners' self-worth" (p. 38). The extended attention paid to concepts such as narration and voice is given vitality in such works, which often confront the detractive normativities of daily life and offer affective experiences for altering audience expectations of disability and queerness. Henderson and Ostrander (2008) extend this line of thinking by contending that disability studies is always already performance studies and performance studies a form of disability studies. In their words:

> Performance studies, in its practices of oral interpretation of literature in the 20th century, has always been open to varieties of embodiment, psychology, and cognition, and prized a kind of egalitarian willingness to admit those individuals whose body conditions may not have matched in mimetic fashion with those of the texts they chose to perform. (p. 2)

Such an approach permits the investigation of previously "unexamined discourse and acts of difference" that might get lost, overlooked, or purposefully excluded in day-to-day exchanges (Henderson & Ostrander, 2008, p. 3). In doing so, such works strive to explore fissures and instabilities in the social fabric in order to foster resistance and possibility.

Performance scholars who have embraced crip interpretive practices to investigate the discursive parameters of disabilities often evince a conviviality with queer reading strategies. As a mode of scholarly engagement, performance studies can disrupt, disturb, and question the quotidian features of culture that give rise to particularly normative expressions of the body or disability. Kuppers (2008), for example, has used crip readings to consider how mental health acts as a metaphor that can "influence representational and performance practice" (p. 192). Turning to Mark Haddon's *The Curious Incident of the Dog in the Nighttime*, she probes the main character's "strange" voice, which she finds compelling in its otherness and deep familiarity (Kuppers, 2008, p. 193). Despite the otherwise queer narration structuring the show, she concludes that *Incident* is successful in part because of its startling simplicity (p. 193). Autism is "domesticated" in the production and can be made intelligible by nondisabled audiences in ways that are straightforward and without the communicative differences that often organize the lived experiences of people who actually live with autism.

Performance studies scholarship has also played a pivotal role in giving presence to the experiences of disabled people and thereby expanding the possibilities of thinking embodiment anew. Whereas a text such as *Curious Incident* was written by a nondisabled author and utilizes autism as a means of reaching nondisabled audiences, scholars in performance studies have spotlighted disabled performers and artists. Kuppers (2007), for example, has turned to the poems of Jim Ferris and Stephen Kuusisto to explore how "disability culture emerges as an impossible horizon of desire, and as the ground for contemporary performances of criticism and writing" (p. 89). In such work, she ponders the ways "literary lyrical disability culture poetry can perform the binding of community and the singularity of experience, sharing and isolation, stepping in and out of meaning" (Kuppers, 2007, p. 90). Scott (2012) likewise explores how a performer's atypical body "allowed them to narrate from a position of 'hyperembodiment,' illuminating the implications of mortal embodiment that those unmarked by difference potentially ignore" (p. 100). The attention given to atypical embodiment, she argued, allowed disabled people "to narrate from a place of hyperawareness of the body's role in the creation of personal and shared reality" when drawing on the past or imagining the future (p. 101). Ultimately, she finds that these understandings of embodiment hold implications not only for those with disabilities but also those with normative bodily privileges. Scott argues that some people are given permission to forget that we become who we are in relation to other bodies and encounters with difference. Such is not the case for queers, crips, and those who occupy the margins and whose identities are always already positioned as a digression from the norm.

The field of performance studies indicates not just the space of theatrical productions but also the everyday practices that bring identities into being. Lindemann (2008) suggests that most of the scholarly focus on disability in performance has turned to explicitly theatrical undertakings rather than the interchanges of everyday life (p. 101). In particular, Lindemann probes how members of a wheelchair rugby league engage in practices of "sandbagging," wherein men perform an enhanced version of their disabled selves, in order to receive more favorable classifications from physical therapists. He notes, "It behooves teams to get their players classified as more immobile than the players might actually be, as a team will then be able to use a greater number of mobile players–and, presumably, more skilled players–on the court at one time" (Lindemann, 2008, p. 99). As a result, he finds that these performances have potentially broad-ranging consequences for players and their teams. They both resist the medicalized gaze but also "foster a form of surveillance that imitates the ableist gaze and reifies traditional notions of ability" (Lindemann, 2008, p. 98).

CONCLUSION

Crip theory is an ever-expanding body of work, and its horizons of possibility are limitless. So long as there are normativities that forcibly marginalize disabled people and those who identify as LGBTQ+, we will require activism, research, and creative forms of critique that challenge exclusionary cultural norms. Communication scholarship, in particular, is well positioned to engage the many ways that crip theory might be articulated to a range of identities, practices, and bodies. Recent works on neurodiversity, the environment, mobility, mental health, and chronic conditions all hold the potential to expand and further complicate the meanings associated with disability, health, disease, and illness. Indeed, even the signifier "disability" is being slowly taken up by communities that have traditionally not identified as such. Younger people with diabetes, for example, are increasingly adopting the label when describing their experiences with the condition in ways that older folk may not. Crip still occupies a "minoritizing" position among people living with a range of disabilities, but the concept has the potential to evolve into an umbrella term that critically assesses various aspects of the social world (Sedgwick, 1990).

Studies that take up the mantle of crip would benefit from further engagement with theories of intersectionality that give attention to a broad range of identities and identifications. There remains a dearth of scholarship in communication studies that surveys the complicated relationships among race, class, age, nationality, disability, sexual orientation, gender, and gender identity, among others. Cognate fields in the humanities such as queer theory, English, and gender studies have more robustly engaged these fruitful intersections. This is not to adopt a paranoid approach that finds only absence and insufficient representation but to note that the field is well positioned to think about the reparative possibilities of crip and its expansive potential in the public sphere (Sedgwick, 2003). The emergence of a critical heuristic such as neuroqueer, for example, points to the exciting theoretical, political, and cultural possibilities that await communication studies. Although neuroqueer has no single definition, it forwards crip critiques by resisting cure narratives, challenging expectations of conformity, and extolling "queerness and neurodiversity as human variations not to be devalued" (Oswald et al., 2021). Despite this promising work, studies utilizing crip theory in the field tend to be centered in the United States and often focus on White people.

On that note, crip theory might be more robustly taken up in different parts of the discipline. Work on crip theory has tended to rest in rhetoric, media, and performance studies. What might it look like to take up crip sensibilities in organizational communication? In interpersonal or small group? I do not intend to single out any one area of the field, only to note that these specialties would enliven the idea of crip in novel and creative ways. Makkawy and Moreman's (2019) study of crip theory in *Communication Education* provides an excellent model for further investigating the concept's potential influence on the discipline. They focus on three widely employed communication theories and then reread them through "a crip inflection that converts impairment to debility and, therefore, changes incapacity to capacity" (p. 401). In doing so, they illustrate the ableism that undergirds many of our field's most foundational concepts and also chart compelling ways for moving forward. As a discipline, Communication Studies has brought much to crip theory's intellectual corpus, but much work remains to realize the concept's full potential, especially when thinking through the dynamics of keywords such as ableism and disability.

FURTHER READING

Agnew, L. (2020). Managing visibility: Emotion, mascots, and the birth of US cancer rhetorics. *Rhetoric Society Quarterly*, 50(3), 194–202.

Burnside, A. (2019). Growing up different than your family: Exploring the intersection of LGBTQ identity, disability, and family. *QED: A Journal in GLBTQ Worldmaking*, 6(3), 106–110.

Cedillo, C. (2020). Disabled and undocumented: In/visibility at the borders of presence, disclosure, and nation. *Rhetoric Society Quarterly*, 50(3), 203–211.

Cherney, J. (2020). *Ableist rhetoric: How we know, value, and see disability*. Penn State University Press.

Clare, E. (2017). *Brilliant imperfection: Grappling with cure*. Duke University Press.

deon, a. (2019). Between the worlds of the colonizer and the conjure woman. *QED: A Journal in GLBTQ Worldmaking*, 6(3), 143–148.

Dolmage, J. (2016a). *Academic ableism: Disability and higher education*. University of Michigan Press.

Dolmage, J. (2016b). *Disability rhetoric*. Syracuse University Press.

Egner, J. E. (2019). "The disability rights community was never mine": Neuroqueer disidentification. *Gender & Society*, 33(1), 123–147.

Eguchi, S. (2019). Intersections among queerness and disability: A case of *Out at the Olympics*. *QED: A Journal in GLBTQ Worldmaking*, 6(3), 127–135.

Escoffier, J. (2019). When love is blind: Critical ontology and queer desire. *QED: A Journal in GLBTQ Worldmaking*, 6(3), 119–126.

Hobson, K. (2019). Fibromyalgia: A queer-femme crip narrative essay. *QED: A Journal in GLBTQ Worldmaking*, 6(3), 100–105.

Hsu, S. (2019). Notes on a pedagogy of debility. *QED: A Journal in GLBTQ Worldmaking, 6*(3), 81–87.
Johnson, J. (2020). Breaking down: On publicity as capacity. *Rhetoric Society Quarterly, 50*(3), 175–183.
Johnson, J., & Kennedy, K. (2020). Introduction: Disability, in/visibility, and risk. *Rhetoric Society Quarterly, 50*(3), 161–165.
Kafer, A. (2013). *Feminist, queer, crip*. Indiana University Press.
Kattari, S. (2019). Troubling binaries, boxes, and spectrums: A galactic approach to queerness and crip-ness. *QED: A Journal in GLBTQ Worldmaking, 6*(3), 136–142.
Kennedy, K. (2020). "I forgot I'm deaf!": Passing, kairotic space, and the midcentury cyborg woman. *Rhetoric Society Quarterly, 50*(3), 184–193.
McRuer, R., & Johnson, M. (2014). Cripistemologies: Introduction. *Journal of Literary & Cultural Disability Studies, 8*(2), 127–147.
Moreman, S. (2019). Accommodating desires of disability: A multi-modal methodological approach to Terry Galloway and the Mickee Faust Club. *QED: A Journal in GLBTQ Worldmaking, 6*(3), 149–162.
Reeders, D. (2019). Disability and the queer politics of disclosure. *QED: A Journal in GLBTQ Worldmaking, 6*(3), 111–118.
Spieldenner, A. (2019). Considering the queer disabled/debilitated body: An introduction of queer cripping. *QED: A Journal in GLBTQ Worldmaking, 6*(3), 76–80.
Vazquez-Pacheco, R. (2019). Being poor is a full-time job: A narrative of applying to be disabled. *QED: A Journal in GLBTQ Worldmaking, 6*(3), 88–93.
Yep, G. (2013). Queering/quaring/kauering/crippin'/transing "other bodies" in intercultural communication. *Journal of International and Intercultural Communication, 6*(2), 118–126.
Yergeau, M. (2018). *Authoring autism: On rhetoric and neurological queerness*. Duke University Press.
Yergeau, M. (2020). Cassandra isn't doing the robot: On risky rhetorics and contagious autism. *Rhetoric Society Quarterly, 50*(3), 212–221.

REFERENCES

Barounis, C. (2009). Cripping heterosexuality, queering able-bodiedness: *Murderball, Brokeback Mountain* and the contested masculine body. *Journal of Visual Culture, 8*(1), 54–75.
Beasley, V. (2020). The trouble with marching: Ableism, visibility, and exclusion of people with disabilities. *Rhetoric Society Quarterly, 50*(3), 166–174.
Bennett, J. (2018). Containing Sotomayor: Rhetorics of personal restraint, judicial prudence, and diabetes management. *Quarterly Journal of Speech, 104*(3), 257–278.
Blake, M. (2021, May 17). Tweet. https://twitter.com/melissablake/status/1394515232123363328
Cherney, J. L., & Lindemann, K. (2014). Queering street: Homosociality, masculinity, and disability in *Friday Night Lights*. *Western Journal of Communication, 78*(1), 1–21.
Clare, E. (1999). *Exile and pride: Disability, queerness, and liberation*. South End Press.
Crosby, C., & Jakobsen, J. (2020). Disability, debility, and caring queerly. *Social Text, 38*(4), 77–103.
De La Garza, A. T. (2019). A eulogy for Roxsana Hernández: Tracing the relationship between border rhetoric and queer debility. *QED: A Journal in GLBTQ Worldmaking, 6*(3), 94–99.
D'Souza, R., & Rauchberg, J. (2020). Neoliberal values & queer/disability in *Margarita with a Straw*. *Journal of International and Intercultural Communication, 13*(2), 183–196.
Fletcher, B., & Primack, A. (2017). Driving toward disability rhetorics: Narrative, crip theory, and eco-ability in *Mad Max: Fury Road*. *Critical Studies in Media Communication, 34*(4), 344–357.
Gilbert, C. (2014). Standing up to combat trauma. *Text and Performance Quarterly, 34*(2), 144–163.

Halberstam, J. (2018). *Trans*: A quick and quirky account of gender variability*. University of California Press.

Henderson, B., & Ostrander, R. N. (2008). Introduction to special issue on disability studies/performance studies. *Text and Performance Quarterly, 28*(1–2), 1–5.

Hepple, J. (2016, December 1). If you're a disabled, gay twentysomething, Grindr is a godsend. *The Guardian*. https://www.theguardian.com/commentisfree/2016/dec/01/disabled-gay-twentysomething-grindr-cerebral-palsy

King, C. S., & West, I. (2014). This could be the place: Queer acceptance in *Lars and the Real Girl*. *QED: A Journal in GLBTQ Worldmaking, 1*(3), 59–84.

Kirkpatrick, B. (2012). "A blessed boon": Radio, disability, governmentality, and the discourse of the "shut-in," 1920–1930. *Critical Studies in Media Communication, 29*(3), 165–184.

Kuppers, P. (2007). Performing determinism: Disability culture poetry. *Text and Performance Quarterly, 27*(2), 89–106.

Kuppers, P. (2008). Dancing autism: The *Curious Incident of the Dog in the Nighttime* and Bedlam. *Text and Performance Quarterly, 28*(1–2), 192–205.

Lindemann, K. (2008). 'I can't be standing up out there': Communicative performances of (dis)ability in wheelchair rugby. *Text and Performance Quarterly, 28*(1–2), 98–115.

Lindemann, K., & Cherney, J. (2008). Communicating in and through *Murderball*: Masculinity and disability in wheelchair rugby. *Western Journal of Communication, 72*(2), 107–125.

Makkawy, A., & Moreman, S. (2019). Putting crip in the script: A critical communication pedagogical study of communication theory textbooks. *Communication Education, 68*(4), 401–416.

Mann, B. (2018). Rhetoric of online disability activism: #CripTheVote and civic participation. *Communication Culture and Critique, 11*(4), 604–621.

McRuer, R. (2006). *Crip theory: Cultural signs of queerness and disability*. New York University Press.

McRuer, R., & Wilkerson, A. (2003). Introduction: Cripping the (queer) nation. *GLQ, 9*(1–2), 1–23.

Meade, T., & Serlin, D. (2006). Disability and history: Editor's introduction. *Radical History Review, 94*, 1–8.

Oswald, A. G., Avory, S., & Fine, M. (2021). Intersectional expansiveness born at the neuroqueer nexus. *Psychology & Sexuality*, 1–12.

Parsloe, S., & Holton, A. (2018). #Boycottautismspeaks: Communicating a counternarrative through cyberactivism and connective action. *Information, Communication & Society, 21*(8), 1116–1133.

Puar, J. (2017). *The right to maim: Debility, capacity, disability*. Duke University Press.

Reynolds, J. (2017). "I'd rather be dead than disabled"—the ableist conflation and the meanings of disability. *Review of Communication, 17*(3), 149–163.

Sandahl, C. (2003). Queering the crip or cripping the queer? Intersections of queer and crip identities in solo autobiographical performance. *GLQ, 9*(1–2), 25–56.

Scott, J. (2012). Stories of hyperembodiment: An analysis of personal narratives of and through physically disabled bodies. *Text and Performance Quarterly, 32*(2), 100–120.

Sedgwick, E. K. (1985). *Between men: English literature and male homosocial desire*. Columbia University Press.

Sedgwick, E. K. (1990). *Epistemology of the closet*. University of California Press.

Sedgwick, E. K. (2003). *Touching feeling: Affect, pedagogy, performativity* (pp. 123–151). Duke University Press.

West, I. (2010). PISSAR's critically queer and disabled politics. *Communication and Critical/Cultural Studies, 7*(2), 156–175.

Jeffrey Bennett

HIV/AIDS: THE QUEER COMMUNICATION OF HIV IN THE LGBTQ COMMUNITY

INTRODUCTION

The HIV epidemic has had a far-reaching impact in queer life. HIV was noted in the early 1980s in Los Angeles, San Francisco, and New York City as a "gay cancer" (Brier, 2009). Emergency rooms and health care services in these cities became overwhelmed by the mystery malady destroying immune function in gay men. It was first labeled "gay-related immune disease" (GRID), even though similar symptoms were seen in other populations (Altman, 1982). The public health infrastructure was slow to respond to HIV because the most visible impact was disproportionately on populations that were already stigmatized and largely excluded from public life: gay and bisexual men, people of trans experience, people who use drugs, sex workers, people of color, and immigrants (Cohen, 1999; Treichler, 1999). People most impacted by HIV organized politically and socially in order to advance technologies, organizations, and community organizing to help meet the needs brought on by the epidemic. HIV has been studied extensively, and so have communities—leading to a greater understanding of personal, communal, and structural barriers and facilitators to health and health disparities (Chase, 2011; Jolivette, 2016; Ramirez-Valles, 2011; Strub, 2014; Watkins-Hayes, 2019).

Gay and bisexual men and trans people continue to bear a disproportionate burden of HIV in North America, Asia, Europe, and Latin America (UNAIDS, 2020). Even in places where the epidemic is more centered among the heterosexual population, gay and bisexual men and trans people face considerable challenges with HIV—from obtaining gender- and sexuality-inclusive health care to punitive laws and policies about gender and/or sexual identity (Ayala & Spieldenner, 2021). Public health agencies and governments have struggled with messaging around HIV and resourcing community groups amid the epidemic's stigma. The political push against those most impacted by conservative governments and lawmakers has slowed the HIV response considerably. This has been met by community activism, advocacy, and organizing, especially within the LGBTQ community.

The HIV epidemic disrupted understandings of marginalization at the community level, in academia, and with regard to public health. As a disease, it remained a mystery and untreatable for more than a decade. This uncertainty on the part of medical and government institutions left communities with an opening to produce something different, to find and educate and support each other, to understand how little their lives meant with regard to global capitalism, and to protest (Brier, 2009; Mumford, 2016; Spieldenner, Sprague, et al., 2019; Strub, 2014). Even with treatment, HIV is still incurable. This article examines how the HIV epidemic has affected communication in LGBTQ relationships, within communities, in organizations, and in academic discourses on the body, dying, and medical expertise.

IMPACT ON LGBTQ RELATIONSHIPS

HIV disrupted the ways that the LGBTQ community engaged in interpersonal relationships both organizationally and interpersonally. Contextually, LGBTQ persons had lived under homophobic laws and institutions that determined non-heterosexual normative sexuality as deviant, criminal, and pathological (Ferguson, 2019). People were forced into invisible sexual lives, without imagining the possibilities of same-sex and trans happiness in a relationship. When these images appeared in popular culture and magazines, they were depicted as scandalous or salacious, often leading to imprisonment or suicide. In large urban areas, gay neighborhoods began to develop, and LGBTQ persons traveled to those places in order to find community. The early gay and lesbian rights movement of the 1970s set the stage for a more radical vision of sexuality in a homophobic world (Ferguson, 2019). By the 1980s, the question of "coming out" was still a radical idea. Without more "out" LGBTQ persons, building LGBTQ institutions remained difficult, and gay and lesbian groups had sporadic support. Activism around HIV radicalized the LGBTQ movements further and helped develop LGBTQ institutions through the transformation of policies and social norms (Halcli, 1999). Sexually, HIV has affected relationships in multiple ways, resulting in a robust HIV prevention movement among gay men in particular. Finally, HIV-related stigma has permeated the LGBTQ community and wider society, leading to various community concerns.

Creating LGBTQ Centers. One impact of pathologizing LGBTQ sexuality was the focus on individual behaviors and the belief that the only connection between LGBTQ individuals was sexual. One of the early LGBTQ interventions was narrative—critiquing stereotypes in mainstream media and documenting LGBTQ lives through various art media (Russo, 1981). From a group of people who shared sexual preferences to a thriving network of interrelated persons, LGBTQ individuals began the ongoing work of building economic, political, and social institutions (Ferguson, 2019). Due to the disproportionate impact of HIV, individual sexual freedom and community altruism were both viewed as integral to the LGTBQ community (Schulman, 2012; Yep et al., 2002). Diversity has been a key concern because differences across race, class, gender, sexuality and disability continue to present challenges as the LGBTQ community grows (Mumford, 2016).

The development of LGBTQ communities in urban centers meant economic and political power for some. Gay and lesbian bars, bookstores, porn stores, coffee shops, restaurants, florists, and retailers all grew and flourished in these LGBTQ communities (Escoffier, 2018). Lesbians and gay men took up leadership roles in the early nonprofit LGBTQ community groups—which were largely White and cisgender endeavors (Ferguson, 2019). These community groups would become vital in dealing with the growing HIV epidemic.

As the HIV epidemic raged, government neglect and social discrimination radicalized groups of people that were experiencing high HIV incidence and mortality. The AIDS Coalition to Unleash Power (ACT UP) is the most recognized and memorialized of these efforts, but HIV activism occurred throughout the United States and the world (Chavez, 2012; Gamson, 1989). ACT UP was emblematic of the cross-movement work that occurred with regard to HIV. At the start of the HIV epidemic, the LGBTQ community was centered in a few major urban centers. HIV was associated with gay men in particular in the first cases, and in fact it was categorized as "gay cancer" or GRID. The massive loss of life in the LGBTQ community brought together lesbians, trans persons, and gay men to visibly organize against the government and research industries that did not prioritize HIV treatment (Schulman, 2021). ACT UP was a multiracial coalition that included gay men, lesbians, bisexual people, trans people, people who use drugs, sex workers, medical providers, researchers, people living with

HIV, and HIV-negative people. Although many of the documentaries and discourse about ACT UP focus on some key White cisgender gay leaders, in fact ACT UP had quite vocal lesbian, transgender, and people of color—especially gay men of color—leadership and membership (Schulman, 2021).

ACT UP and other advocacy groups transformed public health funding to include people living with HIV, people who use drugs, LGBTQ persons, people of color including immigrants, and sex workers. This funding served as a foundation to institutionalize some organizations and advance community-building efforts (Arno, 1986). For LGBTQ persons, this included the development of community centers, advocacy groups, and, in some places, medical clinics (Arno, 1986; Martos et al., 2017). These changes helped build LGBTQ communities beyond the first few urban enclaves. As more visible LGBTQ areas, neighborhoods, and businesses emerged, the LGBTQ community was able to more formally cultivate its cultural and sexual norms in the context of a global pandemic.

HIV Prevention as Communication. Preventing the spread of HIV became a central part of the sex lives of members of LGBTQ communities. Even before any government guidance on HIV prevention was issued, a group of gay men published the short comic guidebook *How to Have Sex in an Epidemic* (Berkowitz & Callen, 1983). Recommendations included condom use for anal and oral sex, and the book included instructions for how to use condoms. Stopping the spread of HIV became something gay men did for themselves and for the community, as the disproportionate death toll left its mark (Schulman, 2012). Gay men developed complex, unique languages and practices around HIV risk, protection, and vulnerability (Brouwer, 2005). These were idiosyncratic and varied between regions, ethnic groups, and individuals based on experiences, resources, and opportunities. In some areas, venue-based sex was more available than in other places due to the presence of bathhouses, erotic movie theaters, porn stores with booths, or similar businesses (Escoffier, 2018). For those living with HIV, several tactics emerged, including serosorting (choosing only other sex partners living with HIV), disclosure of serostatus, strategic positioning in sex so that HIV transmission was less likely, and reducing or eliminating anal sex from their sexual repertoires (Serovich et al., 2005). These prevention practices were embedded in public HIV prevention campaigns and other community-based efforts.

HIV prevention efforts entered into interpersonal and community discourses of the LGTBQ community, normalizing shifts in public policy and narratives about gay sex. Whereas the 1970s and early 1980s were about sexual liberation, HIV moved public health institutions to take more conservative actions, including banning businesses where sex was permitted on-site, such as bathhouses (Escoffier, 2018; Ferguson, 2019). The fear of HIV contagion was so powerful that some states developed laws that criminalized the potential transmission of HIV—penal codes that remain active in more than half of the U.S. states and much of the world (Hoppe, 2018). The mantra of "use a condom" was ubiquitous in gay life and overshadowed other prevention efforts (Crimp, 2002; Spieldenner, 2017). Where once multiple sex partners and various kinds of sex were embraced publicly in the gay community, HIV prevention initiatives imagined a world in which people only had anal sex, had one primary partner, and "knew their partner" as part of preventing HIV transmission. These early efforts assumed (1) that "knowing" was about HIV status, sexual history, and monogamy and (2) that the gay subject did not already have HIV. The model's capacity to intervene in HIV transmission was limited because people may not share the same priorities and meaning about "knowing," may not have a single partner, may prefer other kinds of sex than anal, and/or may already have HIV. Furthermore, the emphasis on individual behavior change ignored structural solutions, such as stigma-free, affordable, and effective health care; guaranteed housing; and accessible education.

Treichler's (1999) analysis of HIV as "an epidemic of signification" reveals how HIV prevention is a critical part of how communities discuss vulnerability, marginalization, sex, and the body. HIV prevention focused on risk and vulnerability solely in the context of sex (particularly anal sex) and individual behaviors. The community that rose up to respond to HIV was much larger, including lesbians, trans people, and other populations including sex workers, people who use drugs, and people of color. HIV risk was also associated with other behaviors, such as drug use, homelessness, lack of employment, and violence. HIV prevention has been resourced more heavily than other kinds of LGBTQ narrative making, leading to a narrowing of the community and its vulnerabilities.

HIV-Related Stigma as Queer Defamation. The role of HIV-related stigma also impacted the LGBTQ community broadly because most people were assumed to have HIV and treated accordingly if they were "out" about their sexuality. This assumption was pervasive in interactions with institutions, including health care and law enforcement. When an LGBTQ person visited the clinic setting or was involved in an altercation with police, the assumption was that the person had HIV. Law enforcement used gloves and were careful in approaching HIV activists during protests (Schulman, 2021); clinicians offered HIV tests automatically, no matter what, if any, sexual or drug-using risk had been revealed (Brier, 2009). Because LGBTQ individuals were often associated with HIV, LGBTQ sexuality carried with it a strong social stigma.

The stigma against queer sexuality and HIV has often been conflated. Both provoke responses in a heteronormative and homophobic world; each involves behaviors such as gay sex, sex without condoms, and/or drug use that sit outside of acceptable norms (Ferguson, 2019). By invoking these acts, queer sexuality and HIV are marked as deviant by the wider society. In addition, queer sexuality and HIV mark the body as different—as an unstable site (Yep, 2013). As the queer person marks themself (either through aesthetics or overt declaration), they claim a "wrongness" in society—a declaration that normative social expectations do not work. People's beliefs about HIV and queerness are often rooted in the fear of infection because both are deemed dangerous to those considered "innocent" (read: young, White, heterosexual, and often cisgender). Research on HIV-related stigma has surfaced many connections between queerness and other stigmatized conditions with the disease (Odets, 1995). These connections help facilitate an understanding of how processes of marginalization function, as well as the material expressions of intersectionality involved in multiple kinds of stigma.

Stigma on gender identity persists, even within the LGBTQ community. Although trans women were at the forefront of the queer movement, they are often excluded from gay and lesbian organizations in both implicit and explicit ways. Trans women are often identified as gay men in public health data, leading to inaccurate understanding of how various health conditions, including HIV, impact the trans community (Appenroth et al., 2021). Trans men continue to be largely ignored in public health data. The invisibility of trans people in the health data is also reflected in their lack of visibility in lesbian and gay organizations. In addition, trans women are more vulnerable to violence compared to other groups, and they are less likely to be protected by laws and policies (Spade, 2015). Trans health care differs from gay and lesbian health care, and there remains a dearth of gender-affirming health care (Appenroth et al., 2021).

These overlapping and connecting stigmas do not negate each other. Even in the LGBTQ community, HIV-related stigma remains persistent. Within the community, there remains a group of self-identified HIV-negative men who deny sexual and sometimes social access to people living with HIV (Spieldenner, 2017). In some cases, this is due to HIV status, whereas in other cases it involves the multifaceted dimensions that made the person vulnerable to HIV in the first place, such as mental health, substance use, homelessness, age, impact of racism, homophobia or transphobia, or ableism (Alexander, 1999; Chavez, 2012; Ferguson, 2019; Hoppe, 2018). This stigma can result in a denial of social, political, and clinical resources. Often, the ongoing HIV-related stigma is also associated with the new homonormativity, a term coined by Lisa Duggan (2002) to describe LGBTQ individuals who believe in neoliberal notions of normativity, insisting that sexual difference does not matter in their lives.

HIV impacted organizational and interpersonal relationships in the LGBTQ community, leading to new ways of interacting and the development of cultural norms and understandings. In the mid-1990s, HIV activists promoted the wearing of a red ribbon in public in order to signify HIV. Celebrities and politicians sported red ribbons, organizations put them in their logos and on their signage, and people wore them in public. The red ribbon would be the first of many ribbons to signify a specific concern or condition. The red ribbon would transform from an activist statement to a simple logo during the course of its life. The transition of HIV into the larger public consciousness has presented growth opportunities and challenges for community groups and institutions for more than four decades as HIV has politicized sexuality, health, and identity. As knowledge and science regarding HIV advanced, HIV technologies would also frame new industries.

IMPACT OF HIV ON ORGANIZATIONS AND TECHNOLOGIES

HIV prevention came about as a discrete set of practices meant to interrupt disease transmission. HIV prevention programs started as community-based solutions—such as using condoms for penetrative sex and cleaning hypodermic needles for drug use—and became institutionalized in funded research and government agencies. This section discusses how HIV prevention messages have promoted normative discourses around sex, substance use, and relationships, as well as how little they have changed in the context of advances in HIV science.

Health care and treatment were also transformed during the epidemic. Public health and medical science were confounded by the emergence of HIV/AIDS. Activism pushed the development of effective HIV treatment and also expanded the way that health care was provided. In the early years, people living with HIV were often the experts in their own care, and this sense of empowerment has remained in the HIV movement.

Community building was a core part of combating the HIV epidemic. Due to HIV, people came together for a variety of purposes: identity (ethnicity, race, sexual orientation, and gender expression) connectivity, support, advocacy, information-sharing, and healing. With the disproportionate impact of HIV on the African American community, particularly Black gay men, HIV resources were used to create organizations to ostensibly provide HIV services as well as to offer a community space for these populations (Cohen, 1999). These movements built off earlier organizing to develop community centers for LGBTQ groups and people of color.

During the epidemic, community centers and social- and identity-based LGBTQ grassroots groups became nonprofits—a check box to fill as an eligibility requirement to access, apply for, and receive government, foundation, and other HIV funding. In New York City, during the 1990s, many social LGBTQ groups formed on the basis of Latino ethnicity, such as Primer Movimiento Peruano (First Peruvian Movement), Latitud 0, Ecuadorian LGBT Movement, Gay and Lesbian Dominican Empowerment, Colectivo Mexicano (Mexican Collective), Colombian Lesbian and Gay Association, and others. These identity-associated social groups were established to provide support, healing, connectivity, and advocacy (Ramirez-Valles, 2011). In order to receive funding, these groups sought partnerships with larger AIDS service organizations or developed their own corporate nonprofit structure. By 2019, these organizations had ceased to exist for a variety of reasons, such as mission drift, rigid structures, and changes to the groups' original purpose as a result of funding expectations that becoming a nonprofit brought upon these groups.

Similarly, advances in HIV prevention and treatment have challenged community-based organizations' survival as they change the way these groups must operate (Vega, 2009). By the early 2000s, federal, state, and local health departments restricted prevention funding to a narrow group of interventions that had been proven effective through randomized control trials (Collins et al., 2006). In addition, the introduction of pre-exposure prophylaxis (PrEP) and treatment as prevention (TasP) as biomedical options in the 2010s changed how nonprofit HIV organizations were expected to operate (Cohen et al., 2012; Diffenbach & Fauci, 2011). These advances in the HIV field were a challenge because they required different mechanisms, funding, staffing, and guidelines. The new funding restrictions, monopolized by funders, provided few options for HIV nonprofit community groups to continue with their grassroots work. Rather, they were required to adapt to changing internal infrastructure, culture, and operations to comply with new funding guidelines and services. Some abandoned their grassroots nature to become—through their own process or through a merger or acquisition—a federally qualified health center—a clinic (Garcia et al., 2015). Many have had to cease operations due to their inability and lack of resources to adapt or transform to meet new requirements to compete for funding.

Leadership at the federal level determined the implementation at all levels of government, and the conservative Reagan administration was resistant to engage HIV and remained adversarial against LGBTQ communities throughout its time. The federal, state, and local governments were originally adversarial or restricted by politics around HIV (Brier, 2009; Strub, 2014). As people from the community entered government jobs—particularly in health departments and federal agencies—they were able to push the system to be more responsive to community needs. Their efforts resulted in community funding but often failed to address the structural issues behind HIV vulnerability: racism, classism, homophobia, and patriarchy. Employment or education programs, for instance, remain outside of mainstream HIV funding. Therefore, challenges to effectively respond to community needs may not only be the lack of community representation and understanding but also systems that function under a particular set of capitalist and conservative cultures and values. Organization culture change continues to be needed, but it is a long, difficult process to achieve in bureaucratic organizations that are pressured by national, regional, and local government, politics, policies, and legislature (Anderson, 2011).

Government agencies continue to be producers of social discourse on HIV, including social marketing campaigns, epidemiology reports, and policies. Organizational culture is inclusive of values, beliefs, attitudes, and perceptions, and these influence expectations at work, from departmental to individual worker, and approaches to work. The values, beliefs, attitudes, and perceptions of health departments toward and about LGBTQ people, HIV, sexuality, race, gender, etc. influence how populations are defined and described (e.g., transgender women categorized as men who have sex with men on forms, in epidemiology data reports, and for grants); how new advances are communicated (e.g., guidelines to emphasize condom use when talking about PrEP or TasP based on the idea of risk compensation, which research has refuted); and how technology is adopted, marketed, and funded, or not (e.g., the fear of promoting at-home HIV testing based on the perception that individuals at home are not capable of self-testing and processing the results).

As with community-based organizations, government entities dedicated to disease prevention and health promotion are also forced to adopt and adapt to changes in the environment. HIV queers even government organizations—which must transform to the shifts in the particular field of HIV, in communities (migrations and immigration), in policies, and in leadership. The United Nations (UN) formed UNAIDS in 1996 as a joint program to organize the multiple UN agency HIV programs, member state efforts in the area, and the global HIV response. The U.S. President's Emergency Plan for AIDS Relief (PEPFAR) began in 2003, and it resources the HIV response in more than 50 countries. PEPFAR also carries with it the policies of the U.S. government, which at different times have included specific rules to exclude sex workers, sexual and reproductive health and rights, and harm reduction initiatives such as syringe exchange. The U.S. Office of National Policy released the first National HIV/AIDS Strategy (NHAS) in 2010 and its update in 2015. Rather than a top-down process, NHAS had inputs from communities, as well as public health leaders, resulting in an additional focus on particular communities (e.g., Black gay and bisexual men) in the 2015 update. The NHAS provides guidelines for funding with regard to HIV, affecting federal, regional, and local initiatives. These resources produce particular discourses regarding risk (e.g., Who is at risk? What is risky?), vulnerability (e.g., What states need the most resources? Who is least likely to have health care?), and treatment (e.g., What kinds of treatment should be available? Are structural solutions such as housing part of treatment?) (Spieldenner, Robinson, et al., 2019).

The pharmaceutical industry has both been impacted by the epidemic and become an integral player in communication about HIV. In the early years, activism against pharmaceutical companies spurred the development of HIV medication (Brier, 2009; Epstein, 2008). The availability and accessibility of effective HIV treatment transformed HIV discourse from a "death sentence" to a manageable chronic disease (Spieldenner, 2017). HIV medications are a multibillion-dollar business, and pharmaceutical companies have clearly profited. In order to maintain good relationships with the HIV community, pharmaceutical companies have also invested back into community-based organizations, as well as partnerships with university researchers and government organizations. The corporate social responsibility frame in HIV does two things for pharmaceutical companies: It provides material good for communities that may not get support for certain initiatives due to the way that government public health funding is restricted (e.g., focusing on aging and HIV or on HIV criminalization), and it creates a cycle in which the company profits from the association of its products as public goods rather than as items that are for sale in capitalist markets. PrEP, for instance, is a clinical intervention that greatly reduces HIV disease acquisition, and yet in most social marketing, pharmaceutical advertisements, and community programs, PrEP is marketed as a public good (Spieldenner & Hawkins, 2020). This corporate responsibility has additional impacts on the HIV community. Funding organizations may limit or otherwise impact the ways that they advocate on issues, as they did in the early period of the epidemic (Strub, 2014). Finally, pharmaceutical companies recruit personnel directly from HIV organizations, which reduces the talent pool available for developing and implementing community solutions.

Pharmaceutical advertisements are interventions targeting specific communities. Much of the early HIV treatment campaigns feature athletic, attractive people engaging in activities such as mountain climbing. The sexuality of these individuals could be assumed by the audience because few were in couples. More recently—in the past decade—these ads have included a much larger range of people with different body types—explicit gay couples, Black gay men, and trans women—performing a much larger range of activities. In addition, pharmaceutical ads for HIV treatment and PrEP have been more narrative in their approach. This serves two purposes: to normalize the use of these technologies and to differentiate these ads from other kinds of pharmaceutical ads by being more "community-based" (Spieldenner & Hawkins, 2020).

HIV organizations—whether community-based or governmental—are produced by and producers of discourses in the epidemic. They are shaped by the voices in policy and advocacy—whether these organizations resist or adopt this communication. The organizations are proven to be changeable, reflecting how HIV continues to alter the ways people understand once-fixed categories such as a business, a nonprofit, a community, and even a body.

IMPACT OF HIV ON THINKING ABOUT THE BODY

HIV altered academic discourse, encouraging the turn in early gay and lesbian studies to queer studies. Gay and lesbian studies was a seminal approach to sexuality studies that centered gay and lesbian—and occasionally trans and bi—experiences. In the 1970s and 1980s, gay and lesbian studies scholars were often not tenure-track faculty due to institutional homophobia that minimized and excluded explicit LGBTQ involvement; rather, gay and lesbian studies grew from community sites—such as gay and lesbian political and social groups—and in places where academics forced institutional support, such as the City University of New York's seminal Center for Gay and Lesbian Studies (Duberman, 1999; Escoffier, 2018). Much of this work was about documenting, theorizing, and intervening in LGBTQ lives across a variety of fields, often using interdisciplinary methods. With the onset of the HIV epidemic, the massive loss in the LGBTQ communities spurred more radical approaches to sexuality and social discourse. Queer studies became central to making sense of the social discourses surrounding HIV. This section discusses the HIV epidemic and its impact on LGBT life as a catalyst toward the development of queer studies.

Queering the Body. As the HIV epidemic raged, LGBTQ community members had to cope with radical shifts in understanding the body. The pervasive normative idea of able-bodiedness had a complicated relationship to LGBTQ individuals, people who use drugs, sex workers, people of color, immigrants, and poor people—all groups disproportionately impacted by the HIV epidemic (Yep, 2013). These groups had histories of being marked as unclean and deviant, actively excluded from institutions such as health care and education, and considered criminal by law enforcement (Duberman, 1999; Ferguson, 2019). LGTBQ individuals were considered mentally ill in the *Diagnostic and Statistical Manual of Mental Disorders* until the early 1970s, and a federal ban on criminalization on the basis of sexuality did not occur until 2003 in the United States (Hoppe, 2018). People of color and immigrants have been characterized as criminal, unclean, and inhuman for centuries; these characterizations have justified such policies as slavery, land invasions, limits on mobility and family development, increased policing, and unfair and unsafe working and living conditions (Ferguson, 2019). The social protections enjoyed by other citizens were not extended to these groups. Sex workers, for instance, were historically excluded from privacy protections in public health investigations (Fairchild et al., 2007). Simply stated, those most impacted by the HIV epidemic were more likely to be socially marginalized on a variety of facets, and thus HIV-related stigma is situated in relation to multiple kinds of stigmatized identities.

Regardless of race, disability, gender, and socioeconomic class, the HIV epidemic claimed hundreds of thousands of LGBTQ community members. From mystery illnesses to rapid physical and mental deterioration, HIV disrupted the control people had over their own bodies. The body and health proved to be unfixed conditions—ones that could and would change. In a community in which sex and sexuality are primary organizing features, how one looks and interacts are key factors in successful engagement with other LGBTQ individuals (Escoffier, 2019). HIV complicated this scenario because the body as an object of desire and representation took on physical manifestations of HIV: the presence of rashes, lumps, discolorations, and other marks; rapid weight loss; the absence of people from gay bars, bathhouses, and other venues due to hospitalizations and deaths; and the loss of employment due to disability. Although these did not impact everyone equally, the combination of these events changed how LGBTQ individuals came to understand the body.

In one way, homonormative ideas of the body were a direct response to HIV. Duggan (2002) describes the new homonormativity as a way of being LGBTQ that is not so different from heterosexual norms—a need to fit successfully into normative behaviors, identities, and socioeconomics. Homonormativity allows for some LGBTQ individuals to imagine themselves "normal" and "fitting in" regardless of the repressive homophobic, transphobic, heterosexist, misogynist, racist, and ableist frames that prevent other LGBTQ individuals the opportunity to thrive, or sometimes even live. As HIV treatment became available in the mid-1990s in the United States and other developed countries, people were less likely to view the physical impact of HIV in social and interpersonal settings, and homonormative standards emerged in popular culture and in advocacy settings. Rather than focusing on human rights and health care, the LGBTQ organizations started advocating for marriage rights, a clear shift in tactics and goals (Ferguson, 2019). Whereas human rights and health care are needed for all members of the community, marriage licensing and events only affected a narrow portion of LGBTQ people. Homonormativity persists as a tempting narrative to LGBTQ life, one in which people can imagine homophobia over because "they have gay friends" rather than addressing the ongoing criminalization of LGBTQ individuals globally or the violence directed at people of trans experience, particularly trans women of color (Ahmed, 2016).

HIV also created identities. The strategy of "coming out" among LGBTQ individuals was made activist and widespread during the epidemic. HIV caused some people to be "outed" because their physical condition made visible their sexual orientation. For others, the activism in the epidemic spurred their political activism in having a political sexual identity (Brier, 2009; Strub, 2014). The presence or absence of HIV within a body would also become an identity. With the onset of HIV testing, community members went through the process of diagnosis, instantiating HIV-positive and HIV-negative identities (Odets, 1995; Spieldenner, 2014). The HIV-positive identity, or person living with HIV, has been a critical development in the HIV movement. People living with HIV became a community through diagnosis, sharing physical conditions, treatment options, rumors, support, and physical and emotional companionship (Adelman & Frey, 1997; Strub, 2014). Having HIV means something: It indicates some common needs around health care, housing, economics, criminalization, HIV-related stigma, and isolation (Alexander, 1999; Chase, 2011; Watkins-Hayes, 2019). By coming together as a community, people living with HIV have been and continue to be a critical part of advocacy efforts in the global HIV response.

HIV disrupted and continues to disrupt how organizations and communities come to understand the body and the various institutions and discourses that intersect or act on it. The epidemic "requires a critical rethinking of all of culture: of language and representation, of science and medicine, of health and illness, of sex and death, of the public and private realms" (Crimp, 1987, p. 15). Early in the epidemic, the LGBTQ community created interventions that were activist, public, and often artistic, whether in the art of Gran Fury or the various actions and protests led by ACT UP and others (Schulman, 2021). Examining how representation mattered—and how the presentation of HIV and LGBTQ persons was often in the context of suicide and deviancy—led to new understandings of how stigma operates. This stigma was present in the political, medical, and institutional responses to HIV, and it continues to permeate the HIV response globally for LGBTQ persons, sex workers, and people who use drugs, leaving these groups criminalized, underserved, and left behind. In the LGBTQ community, HIV became central to the ways people connect—or disconnect—through friendship, desire, intimate physical contact, and support.

The queering of the body is an important part of the HIV narrative. Even as homonormative narratives would posit that LGBTQ individuals are "not so different," those who are living with HIV have different understandings. Effective and accessible HIV treatment still places people living with HIV in a relationship to pharmaceutical and medical industries that others are not (Spieldenner, 2014). In addition, living with an incurable, chronic immunosuppressant condition means being identified by public health agencies with cautions about flu vaccinations or other diseases (e.g., the COVID-19 pandemic). Also, the use of high-impact medication on the body affects organ use over time, potentially leading to liver, kidney, or cognitive complications (Kalyesubula & Perazella, 2011). Although all bodies exist within a relationship to medical care and government institutions, people living with HIV are forced to be more aware of these relationships to successfully navigate living (Vazquez-Pacheco, 2019).

HIV's impact on understandings of the body parallels advances in thinking on disability. Whereas disability was once understood as the ways that non-normative conditions need access to society, disability studies has since come to include an analysis of the value of non-normative bodies, as well as questioned what accessibility means. Out of disability studies, crip studies provides a critical intervention in the normative body, interrogating how a narrow range of bodies are upheld as valuable and all others are determined to be damaged or "less than" in the distribution of power and access to resources (McRuer, 2006). Even the idea of "healthy" has been challenged as culturally coded and socially constructed, with material implications for policy and practices (Spieldenner & Anadolis, 2017). The HIV community has struggled with these social discourses for decades.

Queering Dying and Grief. The specter of HIV loomed large, especially before effective HIV treatment became accessible. The early decades of HIV connected an HIV diagnosis with dying, automatically forcing people to consider their lives and deaths. One popular narrative of HIV activism is that White gay cisgender men became politicized partially because they did not believe they would die and they felt betrayed by a government they expected to work for them (this narrative obfuscates the generation of LGBTQ people who had been politically organizing earlier) (Ferguson, 2019; Shahani, 2016). The death toll concentrated in some communities and regions produced public and personal reckonings around practices and policies about HIV. The mass deaths impacted communities in multiple ways, leading to different understandings and practices around death and grieving.

Within the LGBTQ communities in major urban centers, weekly funerals were commonplace in the 1980s and 1990s (Strub, 2014). People who did not appear in social settings in this context were often considered dead by others (e.g., "Oh, girl, I thought you died"). For some, the LGBTQ identity had estranged them from families who would not be aware of or present at the time of death. The "cemetery angel" Ruth Coker Burks earned her appellation by opening her family graveyard to the unclaimed people who had died from HIV in her home state of Arkansas; hundreds are estimated to lie there (Doane, 2019). Funerals were not centered on the biological family and its needs, and complicated policies prioritized the biological family in dying and death. Hospitals, for instance, often restricted visitation rights to legal relatives of patients, excluding friends and LGBTQ lovers. HIV caused a disruption in the understanding of "family" in the context of dying, expanding to include those who cared for and sometimes buried the person (Cohen, 1999; Strub, 2014; Watkins-Hayes, 2019; Yep, 2007). One part of HIV advocacy was changing policies about death and dying in terms of a more inclusive definition of family.

Along with dying came a different, more politicized understanding of grief. Freud's psychoanalytic frame about grief and mourning was influential, leading people to understand them as largely passive, time-fixed behaviors that were problematic if they went on for too long. HIV spurred different practices of mourning, including political activism and art (Brouwer, 2005). The art collective Gran Fury, for instance, produced a program insert that read "During this program at least 6 people with AIDS will die" in 1988 for the New York Dance and Performance Awards (a.k.a. the Bessies). In the insert, Gran Fury "cordially invites" the audience to do many things, including explicitly "turn grief into action" (Gran Fury, 1988). The piece both acknowledges the impact of HIV in the New York arts community and insists that action is possible from this grieving. The NAMES Project AIDS Memorial Quilt is the largest piece of community folk art in the world, consisting of more than 48,000 quilt panels commemorating more than 96,000 people who have died of HIV-related complications (Morris, 2012). Although the work of making each quilt panel comes from a sense of loss and mourning, the public presentation of these collectively marks the sheer impact of the HIV epidemic, provoking people to contemplate the magnitude of the loss and inspiring people to carry on advocacy efforts on behalf of those who have passed (Blair & Michel, 2007). These actions rearrange the relationships of the living to the dying: Rather than just passively grieving a loss, these acts recognize the loss as politically motivated and the result of negligence and discrimination (Crimp, 2002). They demand those still alive to work to change the systems that produce these grim results.

Queering Health Expertise. As in other ways of understanding the body, HIV challenged notions of expert power, particularly in the areas of health and medicine. Whereas for hundreds of years medical doctors were unquestioned experts in determining health care, HIV was a mystery illness that seemed to present differently in each person. Medical doctors struggled with providing advice to patients, and there were few treatments available for opportunistic infections deriving from a deteriorating immune system (Brier, 2009). Before diagnostic and treatment technologies, people living with HIV came together and shared knowledge, experiences, and advice (Strub, 2014). Prior to effective and accessible HIV treatment, people living with HIV were partners in clinical care, telling medical doctors options and deciding on treatment plans. People living with HIV were considered experts, and physicians seemed to welcome this partnership. These changes were the result of activism and empowerment of community groups, as well as the hesitance that the medical establishment exhibited in the face of an unknown and stigmatized disease.

Activism also changed who could be at tables to discuss standards of care and policies. This movement of community expertise impacted the HIV response locally, nationally, and even globally as the UN developed a new agency to manage a joint program between various UN agencies (World Health Organization [WHO] et al., 2011). UNAIDS had a mandate that included members of nongovernmental organizations at the table along with UN member states and other UN agencies. Although resources and knowledge about public health, development, and diplomacy were vital in addressing HIV globally, UNAIDS acknowledged that the experience of people from marginalized groups who understood HIV with embodied expertise was important. This was the result of more than a decade of HIV activism throughout the world, as communities most impacted by HIV had mobilized to hold governments and corporations accountable. The HIV movement was an early proponent of "nothing about us without us"—that is, that HIV responses had to be centered on the needs, goals, and priorities of those most impacted by the disease.

With this mantra as their foundation, activists were also responsible for changes in the federal drug development programs. Some people living with HIV had trained themselves in peer education groups on clinical best practices; treatment guidelines and side effects; and complex biomedical concepts about HIV, including immune responses, opportunistic infections, and neurology. After several protests and other actions, the U.S. Food and Drug Administration (FDA) changed policies to fast track some drugs through the pipeline and to allow people living with HIV access to experimental drugs at a much earlier time (Brier, 2009; Epstein, 1996). The FDA also permitted community activists, without graduate degrees in public health or biological sciences, to sit on review and policy boards as peers to doctors (Strub, 2014). Due to these changes, the protocols for medication development included the oversampling of people of color, people who use drugs, and women—populations that were often overlooked in earlier medical science (Epstein, 2008).

HIV as a disease, and the activism that it spurred in communities, changed academic discourse in multiple areas. Ideas about the body, dying, and medical expertise all became contested grounds during the HIV epidemic. HIV as a queer force in communication studies persists, leading society to question normative ideas of community, health, and stigma.

UNTIL THERE IS A CURE: CONCLUSIONS?

The HIV epidemic reshaped 20th-century thinking about health care, community, and sex. In the 21st century, HIV remains significant in the way that health disparities and pandemics have come to be understood. Lessons learned from the epidemic—including the value of public health and community partnerships, harm reduction messaging, community health education, fast tracking research, and the importance of policy—are part of the public health response locally (through health departments), federally (through agencies such as the Centers for Disease Control and Prevention), and internationally (through multilateral organizations such as UNAIDS). After more than four decades of the HIV epidemic and with effective and accessible HIV treatments available, many of these organizations have begun developing official plans to end the HIV epidemic by an arbitrary date (Fauci et al., 2019).

HIV increasingly seems to be two epidemics: one that is being analyzed as a historically important moment in activism, community building, public health, and global policy; and one that is experienced by the approximately 38 million people living with HIV as well as the approximately 2 million people who are diagnosed with HIV each year globally (UNAIDS, 2020). The vast majority of new diagnoses are in gay, bisexual, and other men who have sex with men; sex workers; people who use drugs; trans people; and people who have been in correctional settings (UNAIDS, 2020). This ongoing marginalization of certain groups demonstrates the myriad areas in which interventions are still necessary—in terms of policies, resources, research, and discourse (Bernard et al., 2020). The historicizing of HIV has been problematic in terms of depoliticizing and erasing marginalized groups' involvement for the sake of more normalized identities, such as White cisgender gay men (Ferguson, 2019; Schulman, 2021; Shahani, 2016).

As a disease, HIV highlights how some identities and communities are valued in society and some are not. After four decades of the HIV epidemic—including its art, community responses, technologies, research, resources, policies, and interventions—there remains a disproportionate impact on those without power in society. Academic interventions have worked to uplift marginalized voices (Chase, 2011; Cohen, 1999; Jolivette, 2016; Ramirez-Valles, 2011; Watkins-Hayes, 2019) and to resist easy historicization of the early years (Schulman, 2021; Shahani, 2016; Spieldenner, 2017; Strub, 2014).

FURTHER READING

Brier, J. (2009). *Infectious ideas: U.S. political responses to the AIDS crisis*. University of North Carolina Press.
Cohen, C. J. (1999). *The boundaries of Blackness: AIDS and the breakdown of Black politics*. University of Chicago Press.
Crimp, D. (2002). *Melancholia and moralism: Essays on AIDS and queer politics*. MIT Press.
Epstein, S. (1996). *Impure science: AIDS, activism and the politics of knowledge*. University of California Press.
Ferguson, R. A. (2019). *One-dimensional queer*. Polity.
Jolivette, A. J. (2016). *Indian blood: HIV and colonial trauma in San Francisco's two-spirit community*. University of Washington Press.
Ramirez-Valles, J. (2011). *Compañeros: Latino activists in the face of AIDS*. University of Illinois Press.
Schulman, S. (2021). *Let the record show: A political history of ACT UP New York, 1987–1993*. Farrar, Straus & Giroux.
Strub, S. (2014). *Body counts: A memoir of politics, sex, AIDS, and survival*. Scribner.
Treichler, P. A. (1999). *How to have theory in an epidemic: Cultural chronicles of AIDS*. Duke University Press.

REFERENCES

Adelman, M. B., & Frey, L. R. (1997). *The fragile community: Living together with AIDS*. Erlbaum.
Ahmed, S. (2016). An affinity of hammers. *Transgender Studies Quarterly*, 3(1–2), 22–34.
Alexander, B. K. (1999). Standing at the crossroads. *Callaloo*, 22(2), 343–345.
Altman, L. K. (1982, May 11). New homosexual disorder worries health officials. *The New York Times*. https://www.nytimes.com/1982/05/11/science/new-homosexual-disorder-worries-health-officials.html
Anderson, D. (2011). *Organization development: The process of leading organizational change*. SAGE.
Appenroth, M., Davids, J. D., Feuer, C., Kgositau, T. R., & Mugo, I. N. (2021). *No data no more: A manifesto to align HIV prevention research with trans and gender-diverse realities*. AVAC.
Arno, P. S. (1986). The nonprofit sector's response to the AIDS epidemic: Community-based services in San Francisco. *American Journal of Public Health*, 76(11), 1325–1330.
Ayala, G., & Spieldenner, A. R. (2021). HIV is a story first written on the bodies of gay and bisexual men. *American Journal of Public Health*, 111(7), 1240–1242. https://doi.org/10.2105/AJPH.2021.306348
Berkowitz, R., & Callen, M. (1983). *How to have sex during an epidemic*. Tower Press.
Bernard, E., McClelland, A., Cardell, B., Chung, C., Castro-Bojorquez, M., French, M., Hursey, D., Khanna, N., Minalga, B., Spieldenner, A., & Strub, S. (2020). We are people, not clusters! *American Journal of Bioethics*, 20(10), 1–4.
Blair, C., & Michel, N. (2007). The AIDS Memorial Quilt and the contemporary culture of public commemoration. *Rhetoric & Public Affairs*, 10(4), 595–626.
Brier, J. (2009). *Infectious ideas: U.S. political responses to the AIDS crisis*. University of North Carolina Press.
Brouwer, D. C. (2005). Counterpublicity and corporeality in HIV/AIDS zines. *Critical Studies in Media Communication*, 22(5), 351–371.
Chase, S. M. (2011). *Surviving HIV/AIDS in the inner city: How resourceful Latinas beat the odds*. Rutgers University Press.
Chavez, K. (2012). ACT UP, Haitian migrants, and the alternative memories of HIV/AIDS. *Quarterly Journal of Speech*, 98(1), 63–68.

Cohen, C. J. (1999). *The boundaries of Blackness: AIDS and the breakdown of Black politics*. University of Chicago Press.

Cohen, M., McCauley, M., & Gamble, T. (2012). HIV treatment as prevention and HPTN 052. *Current Opinion in HIV and AIDS, 7*(2), 99–105.

Collins, C., Harshbarger, C., Sawyer, R., & Hamdallah, M. (2006). The diffusion of effective behavioral interventions project: Development, implementation, and lessons learned. *AIDS Education and Prevention, 18*(Suppl.), 5–20.

Crimp, D. (1987). *AIDS: Cultural analysis/cultural activism*. MIT Press.

Crimp, D. (2002). *Melancholia and moralism: Essays on AIDS and queer politics*. MIT Press.

Diffenbach, C., & Fauci, A. (2011). Thirty years of HIV and AIDS: Future challenges and opportunities. *Annals of Internal Medicine, 154*(11), 768–770.

Doane, S. (2019). All her sons: Ruth Coker Burks, the "Cemetary Angel" [Video]. *CBS News*. https://www.cbsnews.com/news/all-her-sons-ruth-coker-burks-the-cemetery-angel

Duberman, M. B. (1999). *Left out: The politics of exclusion*. Basic Books.

Duggan, L. (2002). The new homonormativity: The sexual politics of neoliberalism. In R. Castronovo & D. D. Nelson (Eds.), *Materializing democracy: Toward a revitalized cultural politics* (pp. 175–194). Duke University Press.

Epstein, S. (1996). *Impure science: AIDS, activism and the politics of knowledge*. University of California Press.

Epstein, S. (2008). *Inclusion: The politics of difference in medical research*. University of Chicago Press.

Escoffier, J. (2018). *American homo: Community and perversity*. Verso.

Escoffier, J. (2019). When love is blind: Critical ontology and queer desire. *QED, 6*(3), 119–126.

Fairchild, A. L., Bayer, R., & Colgrove, J. (2007). *Searching eyes: Privacy, the state, and disease surveillance in America*. University of California Press.

Fauci, A. S., Redfield, R. R., Sigounas, G., Weahkee, M. D., & Giroir, B. P. (2019). Ending the HIV epidemic: A plan for the United States. *JAMA, 321*(9), 844–845.

Ferguson, R. A. (2019). *One-dimensional queer*. Polity.

Gamson, J. (1989). Silence, death, and the invisible enemy: AIDS activism and social movement "newness." *Social Problems, 36*(4), 351–367.

Garcia, J., Parker, C., Parker, R. G., Wilson, P. A., Philbin, M. M., & Hirsch, J. S. (2015). "You're really gonna kick us all out?" Sustaining safe spaces for community-based HIV prevention and control among Black men who have sex with men. *PLOS ONE, 10*(10), e0141326. https://doi.org/10.1371/journal.pone.0141326

Gran Fury. (1988). *During this program at least 6 people with AIDS will die* [Program insert]. New York Dance and Performance Awards. https://www.granfury.org/list-of-work

Halcli, A. (1999). AIDS, anger, and activism: ACT UP as social movement organization. In J. Freeman & V. Johnson (Eds.), *Waves of protests: Social movements since the sixties* (pp. 135–150). Rowman & Littlefield.

Hoppe, T. (2018). *Punishing disease: HIV and the criminalization of sickness*. University of California Press.

Jolivette, A. J. (2016). *Indian blood: HIV and colonial trauma in San Francisco's two-spirit community*. University of Washington Press.

Kalyesubula, R., & Perazella, M. A. (2011). Nephrotoxicity of HAART. *AIDS Research and Treatment, 2011*, 562790. https://doi.org/10.1155/2011/562790

Martos, A. J., Wilson, P. A., & Meyer, I. H. (2017). Lesbian, gay, bisexual, and transgender (LGBT) health services in the United States: Origins, evolution, and contemporary landscape. *PLOS ONE, 12*(7), 0180544. https://doi.org/10.1371/journal.pone.0180544

McRuer, R. (2006). *Crip theory: Cultural signs of queerness and disability*. New York University Press.

Morris, C. E., III. (2012). ACT UP 25: HIV/AIDS, archival queers, and mnemonic world making. *Quarterly Journal of Speech, 98*(1), 49–53.

Mumford, K. J. (2016). *Not straight, not White: Black gay men from the March on Washington to the AIDS crisis.* University of North Carolina Press.

Odets, W. (1995). *In the shadow of the epidemic: Being HIV-negative in the age of AIDS.* Duke University Press.

Ramirez-Valles, J. (2011). *Compañeros: Latino activists in the face of AIDS.* University of Illinois Press.

Russo, V. (1981). *The celluloid closet: Homosexuality in the movies.* Harper & Row.

Schulman, S. (2012). *The gentrification of the mind: Witness to a lost generation.* University of California Press.

Schulman, S. (2021). *Let the record show: A political history of ACT UP New York, 1987–1993.* Farrar, Straus & Giroux.

Serovich, J. M., Oliver, D. G., Smith, S. A., & Mason, T. L. (2005). Methods of HIV disclosure by men who have sex with men to casual sexual partners. *AIDS Patient Care and STDs, 19*(12), 823–832. https://doi.org/10.1089/apc.2005.19.823

Shahani, N. (2016). How to survive the whitewashing of AIDS: Global pasts, transnational futures. *QED, 3*(1), 1–33.

Spade, D. (2015). *Normal life: Administrative violence, critical trans politics, & the limits of law.* Duke University Press.

Spieldenner, A. R. (2014). Statement of ownership: An autoethnography of living with HIV. *Journal of Men's Studies, 22*(1), 12–27.

Spieldenner, A. R. (2017). Infectious sex? An autoethnographic exploration of HIV prevention. *QED, 4*(1), 121–129.

Spieldenner, A. R., & Anadolis, E. (2017). Bodies of dis-ease: Towards the re-conception of "health" in health communication. In M. S. Jeffress (Ed.), *Pedagogy, disability and communication: Applying disability studies in the classroom* (pp. 97–110). Routledge.

Spieldenner, A. R., & Hawkins, D. (2020). Queerying race, culture and sex: Examining HIV pre-exposure prophylaxis (PrEP) discourses for Black and Latino gay and bisexual men. In S. Eguchi & B. Calafell (Eds.), *Queer intercultural communication: The intersectional politics of belonging in and across differences* (pp. 195–215). Rowman & Littlefield.

Spieldenner, A. R., Robinson, T. M., & Woodruffe, A. (2019). The end of AIDS? A critical examination of the National HIV/AIDS Strategy. In H. Harris (Ed.), *Neorace realities in the Obama era* (pp. 93–105). State University of New York Press.

Spieldenner, A. R., Sprague, L., Hampton, A., Smith-Davis, M., Peavy, D., Bagchi, A., Cardell, B., Johnson, V., Brown, G., & Brewer, R. (2019). From consumer to community-based researcher: Lessons from the PLHIV Stigma Index. In P. Kellett (Ed.), *Narrating patienthood: Engaging diverse voices on health, communication, and the patient experience* (pp. 151–166). Lexington Books.

Strub, S. (2014). *Body counts: A memoir of politics, sex, AIDS, and survival.* Scribner.

Treichler, P. A. (1999). *How to have theory in an epidemic: Cultural chronicles of AIDS.* Duke University Press.

UNAIDS. (2020). *Global HIV & AIDS statistics–2020 fact sheet.* https://www.unaids.org/en/resources/fact-sheet

Vazquez-Pacheco, R. (2019). Being poor is a full-time job: A narrative of applying to be disabled. *QED, 6*(3), 88–93.

Vega, M. Y. (2009). The CHANGE approach to capacity-building assistance. *AIDS Education and Prevention, 21*(Suppl. B), 137–151.

Watkins-Hayes, C. (2019). *Remaking a life: How women living with HIV/AIDS confront inequality.* University of California Press.

World Health Organization, UNAIDS, and UNICEF. (2011). *Global HIV/AIDS response: Epidemic update and health sector progress towards universal access progress report.* World Health Organization.

Yep, G. A. (2007). The politics of loss and its remains in "Common Threads: Stories from the Quilt." *Rhetoric & Public Affairs, 10*(4), 681–699.

Yep, G. A. (2013). Queering/quaring/kauering/crippin'/transing "other bodies" in intercultural communication. *Journal of International and Intercultural Communication, 6*(2), 118–126.

Yep, G. A., Lovaas, K. E., & Pagonis, A. V. (2002). The case of "riding bareback": Sexual practices and the paradoxes of identity in the era of AIDS. *Journal of Homosexuality, 42*(4), 1–14.

Andrew R. Spieldenner and Bolivar X. Nieto

QUEER HEALTHCARE COMMUNICATION

MEDICALIZATION OF QUEER BODIES

The history of queer healthcare is an important beginning to the discussion. Queer healthcare has a troubling history that is still influential. Medicalization, as defined by Eckhert (2016), is the "process by which organisms, tangible objects, or social constructions are rendered into biomedical terms" (p. 239). Essentially, medicalization is when we decide that something or someone is considered a medical issue. For queer identity, medicalization occurred when medical providers labeled anyone who identified as anything other than heterosexual as diseased or deviant.[1] Until 1986, the *Diagnostic and Statistical Manual of Mental Disorders* (*DSM*) labeled "homosexuality" as a mental disorder (Herek, 2012). The *DSM* labeling homosexuality as a mental disorder meant that if a person declared a sexual interest in a person of the opposite sex, they were said to be mentally ill.

Through the labeling of homosexuality as a mental disorder, psychiatrists would then attempt to treat homosexuality through pharmacological and behavioral treatments (Carmack, 2014). Although the *DSM* has since removed homosexuality from its pages, health researchers have still tried to prove different health outcomes on the physiological level between "homosexual" and "heterosexual" bodies (Fish, 2006). Furthermore, queer patients are aware of this history and feel as though it is still embodied in practice. Rounds et al. (2013) found that queer patients believed that even though queer identity is no longer labeled a mental disorder, providers still categorize queer identity as abnormal. A participant in their study remarked that they felt queer identity was still treated as a mental illness by medical providers (Rounds et al., 2013). Therefore, even though there is an assumption of progression through how bodies are labeled, the history of medicine is still relevant to 21st-century practice (Fish, 2006).

HETEROSEXISM IN HEALTH EDUCATION

Before delving into discrimination within healthcare, it is necessary to cover the foundations for discrimination. Negative attitudes toward queer individuals are not solely based on homophobia. Heterosexism plays an essential role in how healthcare treats queer patients and heterosexism is prevalent in the U.S. healthcare system (Saulnier, 2002; Zuzelo, 2014). To elaborate on the healthcare structure, first there is a discussion on how medical education imposes heterosexism, and then how heterosexism is experienced in healthcare interactions.

Medical schools are the first site of heterosexism in healthcare for newly emerging healthcare providers. Medical schools perpetuate heterosexist perceptions through the use of their medical materials and training programs (Murphy, 2016; Zuzelo, 2014). Medical students are typically not aware of the potential of encountering queer patients because of the "curricular inattentiveness toward sexually marginalized groups that is experienced during formative years of professional education" (Zuzelo, 2014, p. 520). To counter the invisibility of queer patients, some medical schools have specific Lesbian, Gay, Bisexual, Transgender, Queer (LGBTQ) training programs. In their survey on LGBTQ specific curricula in North American medical schools, Obedin-Maliver et al. (2011) found only a median of five hours in a student's entire medical education discussed LGBTQ topics. Although some schools reported more than five hours on LGBTQ training, nine reported that they did not devote any time to it.

Overall, there has been limited effort spent on queer curriculum in medical schools. In Murphy's (2016) ethnographic study on medical curriculum, she talked to faculty at Buena Vista, a top 20 medical school in the United States, and the faculty stated that their sexuality-related curricula were "limited" and "haphazard" (p. 269). Although faculty could cover queer content in their classes, they were also not required to incorporate queer content. In Robertson's (2017) study on queer (in)visibility in medical education, he found that medical students expressed concern about the inadequate training they received about queer health issues and stated that they wanted more curricular attention on the topic. The only education medical students in this study received about queer health was limited to small pieces of information that were distributed across the curriculum. The longest amount of time spent on queer patients included a single lecture on sexuality in a behavioral class (Robertson, 2017).

Medical schools can disrupt heterosexism; however, they can also perpetuate heterosexist assumptions. One issue with medical school training is patients used in case studies are generally assumed to be heterosexual. Robertson's (2017) medical student participants stated that case study patients were assumed to be heterosexual and their sexual identity was never explicitly stated. One of his participants claimed that the assumption of heterosexuality was "at the core of our academics" (p. 164). Further, Robertson (2017) found that sexual identity was never a part of a patient's intake information and was considered irrelevant to their care.

However, there was one meaningful exception where sexual identity became relevant in medical training. The only time sexual identity was stated for a case study patient was when the patient was a gay man who had HIV (Robertson, 2017). In these instances, the attention was not explicitly on sexual identity, but rather on sexual behavior. Medical students have been taught to ask if patients have sex with men, women, or both (Murphy, 2016; Robertson, 2017). This question only concerns the assumed outcomes of sexual behavior, which then can be attached to sexually transmitted diseases or infections. Robertson (2017) explained, "when the medical gaze is turned to sexual behavior, it is often focused on maintaining heterosexual reproductive functionality or treating sexually transmitted infections rather than sexual subjectivity" (p. 164). When medical programs do focus on queer health issues, the focus is often on sexual dysfunction, sexual functioning in relation to illness or disability, sexually transmitted diseases, infertility, or sexual abuse (Solursh et al., 2003). Essentially, the queer health focus emphasizes sexual dysfunction or disease, which can then lead to further discrimination against the population by promoting heterosexuality as healthier.

The discussion of sex in medical education also has its limited boundaries. Murphy (2016) found that even when the boundaries of what is considered sexual activity is pushed, instructors could not move beyond a heterosexual understanding of sex. Instructors discounted what gender can look like on bodies, as well as how the relationship operates between gender identity, genitalia, sex toys, and surgical interventions. Queer students in a class on sex felt marginalized by the class discussion, but they could not express exactly why they felt that way. Although there were no derogatory remarks made in the class, the exclusion of sexual possibilities can create the feeling of marginalization. "Sex," defined within the boundary of heterosexuality, limits understandings of how individuals can engage in sexual acts, promoting misinformation about sexual health.

Language is a key component of heterosexism. Murphy's (2016) study attended to language use in medical courses. One instructor would use the word "partner" when discussing his marriage but would often refer to students as "guys" and "gals," thereby erasing the idea of gender neutrality and/or flexibility. Furthermore, when discussing a potential male patient's romantic partner, he would use the term "wife." When responding to female students' questions, he would use "he" to refer to their romantic partners. Finally, the instructor also discussed birth control in the framework of "marriage and sex and children don't have to be a package deal anymore" (Murphy, 2016, p. 277). Simply incorporating the gender-neutral term "partner" does not erase other aspects of heterosexist language. By using gendered language and constantly positioning opposite-sex partnerships, the instructor reinforced heterosexist paradigms. As Murphy (2016) stated, "their cumulative impact on students' understandings of sexual diversity was drowned out by the consistency and prevalence of heteronormative embedded messages" (p. 278).

Having special days devoted to queer curriculum can be a way to address discrimination within healthcare. In focusing on the specialty nature of queer-focused health programs, Murphy (2016) discussed a transgender panel that was hosted by the medical school. Even with their good intentions, Murphy (2016) argued, "the transgender panel raised as many questions as answers, and reified heteronormative conceptions of sexuality, gender, and personhood in addition to providing the medical students with at least a little sheer exposure to transgender persons" (p. 275). Although many of the students expressed interest in the panel, citing how they had never "seen" a transgender person before, they described their experience as seeing something "exotic" (Murphy, 2016, p. 276). Panels can be helpful, but transgender individuals were never included on other panels related to other medical experiences. Through not being included in other health-related panels and the students seeing transgender patients as something "exotic," transgender patients become positioned as the "other." For example, one panel addressed "families with young children," and only included heterosexual couples. Moreover, the panelists' comments referenced their biological relationships to their children, reinforcing heterosexist assumptions (Murphy, 2016).

Heterosexism in Healthcare. Moving from medical school, healthcare spaces then enact heterosexism. Providers in family practices often assume that their patients are part of opposite-sex parental pairs, are heterosexual themselves, and expect the patient to correct the provider if they are not heterosexual. Part of the reason providers may not ask about sexual identity is because they are concerned they may offend heterosexual patients (Westerstahk & Bjorkelund, 2003). However, this excuse is in and of itself heterosexist. By saying that a different sexual identity that is not heterosexual can be offensive, it states that being of a diverse sexual identity *is* offensive.

Another way that heterosexism is communicated within healthcare is through the assumption of promiscuity of queer patients. Although homophobia can play a part in this assumption, believing that queer individuals are promiscuous is an example of symptomatic heterosexism. In disclosing a queer identity, the patient breaks the heterosexist assumption. However, this then places the patient into an "other" category, or at least that is how many providers process them. In being an "other" from a heterosexual, the patient becomes a deviant individual. For this population, the deviant brand is in the assumption of sexual promiscuity. Although sexual liberty is not necessarily a bad thing, in this context it is considered a deviant act. Sexual liberty, in this population, is assumed to lead to sexual disease and infections. In a healthcare encounter, queer patients may seek healthcare for a health problem that is unrelated to their sexual identity (e.g., migraines). Once they disclose their sexual identity, however, the health problem can be assumed to be a sexual infection. For example, several participants in a study on heterosexism brought up similar stories of how their disclosure of their sexual identity caused their provider to focus on potential STIs (sexually transmitted infections) or HIV. Some participants mentioned that they were even treated or tested for STIs/HIV without their knowledge or consent (Hudak, 2016).

Perceptions of heterosexist attitudes from providers can impact queer individuals' decision to seek out certain healthcare providers. Saulnier's (2002) study of lesbian and bisexual women found that heterosexist attitudes from healthcare providers were one of five things that influenced women's healthcare decisions, including whether to seek out a healthcare provider. If they did choose to see a healthcare provider, some lesbian women believed that their providers' heterosexist attitudes impacted the care that they received. Heterosexism can negatively affect queer individuals by blocking access to healthcare, decreasing the quality of patient–provider interaction, and decreasing the overall quality of healthcare (DeHart, 2008).

PROVIDER KNOWLEDGE

The healthcare provider perspective is essential for exploring queer healthcare as providers have access to medical resources that are unavailable to patients without their assistance (Beisecker, 1990). One contention with healthcare providers is that there is not a unified response as to whether a person's sexual and gender identity matters. Some providers believe it does not make a difference, others believe it is relevant for providing holistic care, and others think it depends on individual circumstances (Beagan et al., 2015). When providers are uncertain about whether sexual and gender identity matters, they may not attempt to regularly discuss those identities with their patients (Kitts, 2010). Also, a lack of discussion can be attributed to providers believing that they do not have the skills required to address sexual and gender identity (Kitts, 2010; Stott, 2013).

The skill level is not the only contribution to providing queer healthcare; comfort in providing care also plays a role. In a study on nurse-practitioners' attitudes toward queer patients, the nurse-practitioners discussed having a baseline level of comfort in providing care for this population. The nurse-practitioners who were more comfortable either identified as queer themselves, had close relationships with queer individuals, or had watched role models provide exemplary care for queer patients (Dorsen & Devanter, 2016). If they could discuss sexual identity with patients, it was only under the discussion of sexual practices. The nurse participants were also unable to differentiate between the HIV/STI risk for gay/bisexual men and lesbian/bisexual women. Finally, the nurse practitioners in the study recognized that queer patients are considered under the diversity umbrella. Still, most did not know about specific cultural differences in this population and attempted to treat them just like heterosexual patients (Dorsen & Devanter, 2016). This study demonstrates that comfort cannot be the only way to understand how providers treat queer patients.

DISCRIMINATION WITHIN HEALTHCARE

Past research has focused on the ways in which queer individuals have experienced discrimination within healthcare. Rounds et al. (2013) argued that when queer people are in healthcare spaces "they face the fear and very real possibility of discrimination" (p. 99). The ways in which queer folk experience discrimination within healthcare can range from outward comments to more covert expressions of discomfort. Discrimination can occur on many levels, from preventing a partner from being in the hospital room to ignoring a queer patient's call light (Rounds et al., 2013).

One of the ways that queer people can experience discrimination is from spoken, offensive comments. For instance, a gay patient mentioned his sexual identity to his doctor during his appointment. His doctor "told him he had given more information" than "he needed to know" (Mimiaga et al., 2007, p. 117). In another incident, a lesbian woman explained that when she revealed her sexual identity to her doctor, her doctor started to talk about AIDS (Politi et al., 2009). A further example can be found in Rounds et al. (2013) when a queer patient went to see their healthcare provider because of low energy and chills and the provider's response was that she should get a boyfriend. Offensive comments range from basic discriminatory remarks to ones that communicate a lack of knowledge or discomfort. For example, a queer woman noted that when she disclosed her sexual identity, the healthcare provider wrote down in their notes that she did not engage in sex (Politi et al., 2009). The healthcare provider may have been stating that her identity was not real, or the healthcare provider mistakenly believed that sex is based on penetration between men and women. Hearing verbal comments that demonstrate discriminatory beliefs from their healthcare providers are not uncommon for queer patients.

Beyond commentary, healthcare providers also demonstrate discrimination of queer patients by their non-verbal behavior. In Mimiga et al.'s (2007) study, queer men experienced discrimination from their providers through various forms of communication. They cited clinicians who appeared to be judgmental based on body language and speaking style.

Rounds et al. (2013) found that queer patients often softened their responses about gender and sexual identity because providers would make faces, stare blankly, look confused, or blush when they provided an honest answer. Healthcare providers have also expressed shock to a queer patient disclosing their sexual identity (Mimiaga et al., 2007). And sometimes in these shocked moments, when healthcare providers continue the conversation, they may then emphasize sexual identity when it is not necessary. As Rounds et al. (2013) noted, "sometimes that cold is just a cold, not a gay cold" (p. 106). Discrimination from healthcare providers is not just about blatant discriminatory comments, but also how providers' bodily reactions signal to queer patients that they are uncomfortable with a non-heterosexual identity.

One of the reasons that healthcare providers can be discriminatory toward patients is because they have power over them. Healthcare providers have power because they provide a service that others cannot easily live without (Beisecker, 1990). A patient cannot make adequate medical decisions or obtain essential medical services without interacting with healthcare providers and, therefore, will have to interact with such a person at some point in his or her life. Additionally, queer patients must deal with another layer of power because healthcare providers have the ability to turn away patients because of the patients' sexual identity without repercussions. However, patients may not be able to receive the medical attention that they need if their provider is not aware of their sexuality. This might force queer patients into a bind because if they reveal their sexual identity, a healthcare provider may turn them away or create an uncomfortable or discriminatory situation (Fish, 2006). Due to this, healthcare providers have further power over queer patients because they inevitably decide what medical attention they receive and how they will receive it.

Queer Invisibility. An element of discrimination for queer individuals is the feeling of invisibility projected by healthcare providers. Lesbian and bisexual women noted that their feelings of invisibility stemmed from being assumed to be heterosexual (Hudak, 2016). The invisibility was connected to providers' not giving them space to state their sexual identity in their intake questions or forms. Many healthcare forms do not provide a space to state a person's sexual or gender identity (Goins & Pye, 2012). In a 2016 study on heterosexism, queer patients also were asked inappropriate questions related to their healthcare that left the patients feeling invisible. Inappropriateness was defined by the fact the questions were based on heterosexist assumptions (Hudak, 2016). Baker and Beagan's (2014) study participants recalled heterosexist questions that started with "Does your husband...?" (p. 588). This framing assumes that a woman is engaging in heterosexual relations, is monogamous, and is defined by her relationship status. Another typical healthcare script ascribes women's sexual identity to existing solely with men. When entering a healthcare appointment, it is typical of a healthcare provider to ask, "are you sexually active" (Silverman et al., 2012)? In a yes response, the provider then asks, "are you on any form of birth control or use a form of birth control?" When the woman responds no, the provider, confused, typically then promotes that the woman uses some form of birth control (Silverman et al., 2012), even if a cis-woman exclusively has sex with a partner who does not produce sperm. The healthcare provider rarely stops to think that a woman can have sexual relations without the potential of becoming pregnant (Hudak, 2016).

Queer individuals may also have to correct the providers constantly. In Hudak's (2016) study on heterosexism, several of the participants expressed frustration at how often they would have to correct a healthcare provider about their sexual identity and who their romantic partner was. When other women in medical appointments accompanied queer women, providers assumed they were just friends. However, whenever they were with men, it was automatically assumed that the man was a romantic partner (Hudak, 2016). Heterosexism exists in these interactions because women are consistently being placed into cross-sexed romantic relationships, erasing the potential for same-sex relationships. As Saulnier (2002) found, this can then prevent non-same-sex romantic partners from being involved in healthcare communication.

DISCLOSING QUEER IDENTITY IN HEALTHCARE

Disclosure, in the context of queer healthcare, occurs when a queer patient actively informs their provider of their sexual/gender identity. When it comes to sexual identity, disclosure is often necessary if the patient wants the provider to be aware of this, as there is no marker on their body that may indicate that identity.

Varying factors can influence the choice to disclose sexual identity to a healthcare provider. In a study on disclosure of lesbian identity, the research found that having resources, access to a queer community, and being "out" in the community impacted whether a woman was more or less likely to disclose to their providers (Austin, 2013). Identity also plays a role in disclosure as men are more likely to disclose their sexual identity compared to women. Specifically, White men tend to disclose to male doctors (Klitzman & Greenberg, 2008). Other factors that influence disclosure included experiences with families, fear of gossip from providers, providers' unawareness, religious signifiers, and a level of trust with providers (Hudak & Carmack, 2018). Many of these listed factors are not directly connected to providers or clinical communication. However, they do provide important information to consider when researching queer healthcare communication.

The ability to disclose sexuality or gender identity can be important for many patients. One study focused on the necessity of disclosure and found that lesbian women in Norway thought disclosure was medically relevant, explained medical circumstances, and created the feeling of being seen as a whole person by their medical provider (Bjorkman & Malterud, 2007). However, disclosure is not always that easy. Disclosure to a primary care physician can be just as complicated and challenging as coming out to family and friends (Law et al., 2015). Even with the challenge, providers have an opportunity to help facilitate disclosure. Research has indicated that disclosure happens during appointment introductions, small talk, and when collecting patient intake (Venetis et al., 2017). Providers can use these moments to have questions that allow for disclosure. For example, providers can ask about romantic partners in a gender-neutral way, ask about sexual history without assuming the gender of sexual partners, and generally provide openings for patients to talk about their home lives. Many queer patients want to be seen as "a whole person with a social context rather than an object with a certain disease" (Law et al., 2015, p. 4). Moreover, sexually diverse patients have expressed that in order for disclosure to occur, providers need to build trust (Hudak & Carmack, 2018; Law et al., 2015).

Although the literature has explored the disclosure of queer patients, there is a lack of detail as to how trust is established between providers and queer patients. Notably, research has yet to discuss how queer patients feel about disclosure with other members of the medical staff, including nurses, medical assistants, and receptionists. Furthermore, religious symbols often deterred disclosure, whether on the provider's body (e.g., cross necklace) or the walls of the exam room (Hudak & Carmack, 2018). While religious symbols can act as a deterrent to disclosure, some artifacts communicate the welcoming of queer disclosure. In a study on queer phenomenology, participants expressed that having allyship signs would provide comfort in disclosure as "such signs show that queer patients are expected in the space" (Heyes et al., 2016, p. 145). The use of signs and symbols can deter or facilitate disclosure (Heyes et al., 2016; Hudak & Carmack, 2018).

MEDICAL FORMS

Communication by healthcare providers has not been the only way in which discrimination has been documented by scholars. Medical forms can communicate exclusion of queer identities or even promote discriminatory beliefs. Goins and Pye (2012) described how, under the category of "risk factors" on a generic intake form, "same-sex partner" was listed alongside "unprotected sex." In addition, medical intake forms may not always have language that includes queer identities. When looking at queer pregnancy and parenthood in healthcare, several medical forms would present heterosexual parent names (i.e., mother and father) as the only option and were actively not inclusive (Larsson & Dykes, 2009). Some queer women felt that the standardized forms were offensive, conservative, and stereotypical (Röndahl et al., 2009). The language used in the medical setting, as well as the forms, presented as heterosexist as it did not include the co-mother. In addition, women felt that they did not have an avenue to issue complaints about heterosexist issues, such as not having lesbian representation in the literature passed out in the clinic or given away with free diapers and other baby products (Cherguit et al., 2013). Even when clinics would advertise for lesbian couples, their forms did not reflect having lesbian patients. Healthcare forms and materials need to be adjusted with creativity (Spidsberg & Sørlie, 2012) to include lesbian parents.

SEEKING QUEER-FRIENDLY CARE

One way that queer individuals have attempted to cope with discrimination within healthcare is to find queer-friendly healthcare providers. Queer individuals have wanted healthcare providers who are culturally competent when it comes to queer health issues (Rounds et al., 2013). In a study on queer patient experiences, Hudak and Bates (2019) found that queer individuals did seek out queer-friendly healthcare providers through interpersonal networks and online sources. However, there have been limitations on finding queer-friendly healthcare providers. Rounds et al. (2013) noted that just because a provider labels themselves as culturally competent this does not mean they possess that skill set. Hudak and Bates (2019) also found that there were barriers to seeking out queer-friendly healthcare providers. Insurance can dictate what providers are "in-network," which may not include queer-friendly providers.

Also, queer individuals may not be able to physically get to queer-friendly providers because they do not have the ability to travel. Participants in this study also echoed Rounds et al.'s (2013) study by saying that they did not always trust providers to adequately label themselves as queer friendly (Hudak & Bates, 2019).

Queer women have also considered how they choose their providers to support them in a pregnancy. Sometimes, the choice of care was not about finding queer-friendly support, but more of a generic assumption about the type of care provider and how they supported lesbian couples. Female gynecologists were perceived as more understanding of lesbians (Larsson & Dykes, 2009). Other women preferred midwives and doulas because they were helpful advocates with other healthcare providers (Ross et al., 2006). For some queer women, it was not about the type of provider, but how they were perceived. Lesbian couples identified the need to find medical professionals who were considered trustworthy and supportive (Chabot & Ames, 2004).

Choices may not have been consistent between multiple pregnancies. In a study in Sweden (Röndahl et al., 2009), women were asked what choice they made in deciding where to give birth. Several of the women chose a clinic that specialized in lesbian competency for the first pregnancy, but then opted for a hometown clinic for their second. They chose the culturally competent clinic initially because they were new to the experience and were less confident. In the second pregnancy, they gained confidence. They did not want their providers to focus on their sexual identity and instead emphasized the pregnancy and parenting.

PROVIDER RECOMMENDATIONS

In recognizing the need for queer-friendly healthcare, past studies have emphasized how healthcare providers can improve upon offering this type of care. In Law et al.'s (2015) study, participants explain that they want their primary care physicians to deliberately acknowledge that heteronormativity is a social norm in medicine. In addition, queer research participants have given recommendations about communicative practices. McNair and Hegarty (2010) found that provider attitudes should be expressed as nonjudgmental and affirming, and should call out negative attitudes in other providers. Language is an important aspect of providing care and it should be gender-neutral, culturally aware, and inclusive. Providers should also clarify patient's identity terms. Disclosure was another key point. Providers should be the ones who facilitate the disclosure process. They should be careful of their own reactions during moments of disclosure and respect the choice to not disclose.

In McNair and Hegarty's (2010) research, they conducted an analysis of existing literature on clinical recommendations for providing care for queer patients. In their article, they discussed the difficulty of searching for the literature across global databases and only found 11 sources where none of the sources fully met their criteria, and only two focused on primary care. However, they were still able to provide a chart of suggestions based on those materials. They found that their needs to be a culturally competent and social model of health that is person-centered and recognizes queer as a culture and lifestyle issues. Additionally, they need to be aware of the queer population, removing assumptions of heterosexuality, and be aware of multiple identities beyond sexuality. To have an inclusive clinic environment they can benefit from having overt signs of inclusivity such as rainbow stickers, posters, and brochures. The staff should be sensitive of their language, and inclusive and culturally appropriate forms should be available. Furthermore, there should be clear anti-discrimination policies that specifically mention queer individuals. Queer patients should also be included in service planning and have any opportunity to provide feedback (McNair & Hegarty, 2010).

SPECIAL TOPICS

In this section, three topics will be discussed that are extensions of queer healthcare communication. The first is an argument why transgender healthcare communication needs its own article. Second, a subsection on HIV is provided that demonstrates the topic's limitation within queer healthcare communication. Finally, the section ends with queer pregnancy as a subset of queer healthcare communication.

Transgender Healthcare. Transgender healthcare is an essential area of research. Previous research has demonstrated a need for improved care of the trans population (Poteat et al., 2013; Redfern & Sinclair, 2014; Ross & Castle Bell, 2017; Snelgrove et al., 2012). However, this article does not go into the depth necessary to cover trans health-related care as it is separate from diverse sexual identity care needs. Parkhill et al. (2014) noted a distinct difference between queer sexual identities and transgender identities concerning healthcare. They stated that queer individuals have the capacity to choose whether or not to disclose their sexual identity to their healthcare providers. In contrast, trans patients must disclose their gender identity to their providers. This forced choice could be due to legal versus chosen name, seeking out gender-specific medical treatment (i.e., hormonal therapy and surgeries), or being aware of how their gender medical treatments could impact other medical treatments and health outcomes. Because of this distinction, trans health must be separated. There cannot be a conflation of gender and sexual identities.

HIV Research. Research on HIV and healthcare communication can fall into several different categories. Past research has looked at patient racial differences in provider communication (Beach et al., 2010, 2011; Laws et al., 2014). Other research has explored communication preferences between HIV-positive patients and providers (Mulder et al., 2016). Outside of the United States, researchers have also looked at healthcare communication surrounding HIV. In western Kenya, researchers found that HIV providers preferred patients who adhered to their treatment plans, and they did not like when patients challenged their authority (Wachira et al., 2018). Another study looked at HIV patients in Mali who were in antiretroviral therapy programs and their perceptions of positive patient–provider communication. They found that establishing rapport was a key feature of positive interactions (Hurley et al., 2018). Finally, in China, where stigma against people living with HIV is common, researchers looked at Chinese village doctors' beliefs about HIV. They found that more information on HIV could increase a provider's self-efficacy in caring for HIV patients (Li et al., 2019). In looking at PrEP-related (pre-exposure prophylaxis) research, there have been studies on provider communication. For example, one study looked at barriers healthcare providers had with regard to discussing PrEP with their patients (Wilson et al., 2020). Finally, there has been research on the youth population. For example, Fisher et al. (2018) found that MSMs (men who have sex with men) aged 14–17 were fearful of discrimination from healthcare providers. They did not disclose their sexual identity to their provider and avoided getting HIV/STI testing. In Córdova et al.'s (2018) study, they focused on predominately African American adolescent women's perspective on discussing sexual health with their providers, emphasizing HIV/STI communication.

What is important to note about the mentioned studies is that only one of them focused specifically on a queer population. The rest did not differentiate between sexual identities. One of the issues of focusing on HIV research within queer healthcare communication is that queer populations are not the only ones at risk of contracting HIV. Further, overly emphasizing HIV can have negative implications. In Hudak's (2016) research, she found that healthcare providers would automatically assume that their queer patients had HIV and would test them without their knowledge or permission. Additionally Hudak (2016) also found that healthcare providers would assume that all identities within the LGBTQ acronym had equal risk factors because of the association between queer and HIV/STIs. This assumption is not accurate as lesbians have lower rates of HIV and STIs. Researchers need to be careful about how they discuss HIV within queer healthcare communication.

Finally, the limitation of queer healthcare communication literature is that it is just one subset of queer health communication. There is excellent research on HIV and sexuality, such as Spieldenner's (2016) work on PrEP and HIV prevention. Yet this research falls outside of this article's purview as it does not discuss healthcare communication but falls under the larger umbrella of health communication. The research on HIV and communication often focuses on macro and micro issues outside of a healthcare context, such as stigmatization and partner communication. As this section focuses just on healthcare communication, that research falls outside of this section's purview.

Queer Pregnancy. Queer healthcare communication includes how queer pregnancy is experienced within healthcare settings. In this subsection, literature on queer pregnancy will be discussed, presenting both negative and positive experiences. Extension of this literature will also provide an overarching focus on queer healthcare.

Negative Experiences. Many lesbian pregnancy couples have had negative experiences dealing with the healthcare system and healthcare providers. Spidsberg (2007) found that being a theme was how lesbian women described their sexual identity in relation to healthcare. The process of having a baby is meant to be private but being an *out* lesbian pregnant woman makes you a public person. There is no privacy. The act of being an out lesbian pregnant woman causes individuals to ask many questions about the process and the experience of being pregnant and a lesbian. Many lesbian pregnant women described how they felt insecure or nervous about how healthcare providers would react if they learned of their lesbian identity (Röndahl et al., 2009). Co-mothers also experienced vulnerability with healthcare providers and would approach them with fear and trepidation because they were worried that they would not be recognized as a parent (McKelvey, 2014). When attempting to assess potential discrimination, women would look for prejudice by reading body language and signals that occurred in their interactions. Once in the system, women grew tired of having to constantly explain their situation and family dynamics to the providers. They felt that there was a lack of communication between providers that led to confusion and constant explanations (Spidsberg, 2007). One of the reasons for the constant confusion was that healthcare providers seemed to be unprepared to have healthcare interactions with lesbian couples, making the lesbian women feel excluded or underrepresented (Wojnar & Katzenmeyer, 2014).

There were specific moments where lesbian parents had negative interactions. Co-mothers have found that the medical staff do not recognize them as new parents. When the co-mothers were not recognized, they felt invisible and drained from the interactions (or lack thereof) (Erlandsson et al., 2010). Further, pediatric services sometimes would not recognize the co-mother as an equal parent (Ross et al., 2006). In addition, "Co-mothers were subject to unexpressed opinions about co-motherhood and homosexuality by midwives assisting at the birth of their child, and experienced an attitude of non-cooperation" (Erlandsson et al., 2010, p. 102). Postpartum nurses were also described as providing poor care. Nurses would often ignore the co-mothers and did not recognize them as equal parents and partners (McKelvey, 2014).

Beyond failing to provide patient-centered care, healthcare providers can unintentionally cause discomfort in the interactions between patient and provider. Curiosity about a patient's sexual identity can take over the appointment, creating a situation where patients must educate the provider instead of the other way around. Singer (2012) explained, "healthcare providers do not ask their heterosexual patients to teach them about their sexual practice nor do they look confused or disgusted when a man and woman present to their office for a new obstetrical visit" (p. 38). Antenatal providers that overly inquired about the patients' lesbian identities were described as "on the verge" (Spidsberg, 2007, p. 481). In a similarly covert form of discrimination, midwives have been caught gossiping about patients' sexual identities (Spidsberg & Sørlie, 2012). There can be overfocus on a lesbian identity or this can became a reason to provide poor healthcare.

One reason for the overall negative experiences of both mothers is that medical staff can present as having negative attitudes toward lesbian families wherein which they do not recognize the possibility of lesbian parenthood. However, it is hard to identify if poor treatment comes from homophobia or just generic poor treatment (Cherguit et al., 2013). Some lesbian women felt that their negative experience was not related to their sexual identity but just "bad chemistry" between patient and provider (Röndahl et al., 2009). Some lesbian women may not believe that they are experiencing heterosexist attitudes from providers because these attitudes can be subtle or unintentional. In Lee et al.'s (2011) study, they found that some women did not want to admit there was homophobia and attributed the negative treatment to other causes. Lee et al. (2011) suggested that with the implementation of new laws, people were not being as overtly homophobic but tried to hide this for fear of a lawsuit.

Positive Experiences. Not all lesbian couples described having negative experiences with healthcare providers. In Cherguit et al.'s (2013) study, co-mothers identified having positive experiences, valuing staff and fertility services' intentional inclusion of lesbian families. They valued the ability to receive equal treatment. It was helpful when the maternity staff celebrated the two-mother families. If a couple had positive experiences, they expected less prejudice and discrimination. Yet positive experiences were still viewed as the exception (Cherguit et al.,

2013). In another study (McKelvey, 2014), women described their experiences with labor/delivery and the NICU as positive. In the NICU, the staff often relied on the co-mother to make decisions and provide information. Even with no legal rights, the co-mother was recognized as the parent. Several women stated that the NICU providers made no distinctions between the co- and birth mother, and one woman talked about how the nurse listed both mothers on the crib card. Some women felt that the questions asked by midwives about their identity and family were sweet and positive. They thought that the midwives were trying to obtain new knowledge (Spidsberg, 2007). Another positive experience stemmed from the obstetricians and nurses respecting co-mothers by including them in the care as equal partners (McKelvey, 2014).

Provider Recommendations. Specific recommendations have also been given for queer pregnant patients. One issue that lesbian couples found was that healthcare providers would not bring up their lesbian identity. While a lesbian identity should not be the sole focus of the visit, it is an important identity to openly recognize. When providers do not use the word "lesbian," lesbian women can assume that providers do not want them to bring up their lesbian identity, or that they had a lot of uncertainty surrounding a lesbian identity. These women said that it would be better if providers just admitted that they were uncertain instead of ignoring the topic (Spidsberg, 2007). Overall, healthcare providers should be open about sexual identities and ask questions to demonstrate their openness (Larsson & Dykes, 2009). One way to show openness would be by providing an opening for the patient, such as by saying "So tell me the story of how you became pregnant" (Singer, 2012, p. 38). This open statement allows for a background story that is inclusive of all people. Any language used by healthcare providers should also be inclusive.

One major area that healthcare providers need to work on is their heteronormative communication. Regardless of intent, language used in healthcare interactions can promote heterosexuality as the only possibility, thereby erasing queer people. Healthcare providers can try to communicate more neutrally and ask for the preferences of the parents in terms of language. Throughout the pregnancy, healthcare providers should evaluate how they are communicating and check their assumptions (Pharris et al., 2016). Healthcare providers should not assume that everyone can accidentally become pregnant because the assumption can ignore life situations (Singer, 2012). Further, healthcare providers and staff should also be aware of nonverbal communication and reject any use of heteronormative language (Erlandsson et al., 2010). They should also be inclusive of the co-mother from the very beginning and the inclusion should be in a conscientious and natural way (Röndahl et al., 2009).

Curiosity about lesbian couples can be nice, but most lesbian couples want healthcare providers to already have knowledge about lesbian families and how to work with lesbian patients (Erlandsson et al., 2010). Women suggested that midwives should be educated on lesbian issues to help ask questions and communicate in more neutral ways at the initial meeting. However, some women felt that this was not needed but that the midwives just needed to have an open mind and be sensitive to prospective parents' vulnerability. Some lesbian women felt that those who worked in postnatal care were more aware of different family makeups and demonstrated this through their actions. Regardless of how providers can show awareness or education, providers should not use lesbian parents as an educational resource (Röndahl et al., 2009).

Beyond education, medical staff can demonstrate helpfulness by allowing the co-mother to stay overnight and offer support with breastfeeding. In addition, gender neutral language can be used to acknowledge co-mothers (Erlandsson et al., 2010; Spidsberg & Sørlie, 2012). Going further than language use, healthcare systems can arrange themselves to automatically be designed for the inclusion of lesbian couples. They can label the healthcare system as lesbian friendly, assuming they are friendly, which would alleviate fears of discrimination and vulnerability. This way, lesbian couples know that their healthcare providers are already aware of same-sex parenthood (Erlandsson et al., 2010).

Medical forms also need to be evaluated and updated, along with other types of forms that are distributed in medical spaces. Medical forms should use terms such as "non-biological mother, co-parent, social mother, other mother and second female parent" (Pharris et al., 2016, p. 23). Another way to show inclusion would be to ask the parents how they want to be referred to by their unborn child and not to question their choices. Finally, lesbian couples may need help navigating different systems. Healthcare providers should know the legal system of their local area. Lesbian couples may need help navigating local legal systems and having knowledgeable contacts can help. Beyond the legal system, providers need to pay attention to unasked questions and to help identify support networks that are inclusive of sexually diverse parents (Pharris et al., 2016). Overall, women mostly just want respect (Spidsberg & Sørlie, 2012).

FURTHER READING

Dean, M. A., Victor, E., & Guidry-Grimes, L. (2016). Inhospitable healthcare spaces: Why diversity training on LGBTQIA issues is not enough. *Journal of Bioethical Inquiry, 13*(4), 557–570.

Manning, J. (2014). *Coming out conversations and gay/bisexual men's sexual health: A constitutive metamodel study*. Lexington Books.

Müller, A. (2018). Beyond "invisibility": Queer intelligibility and symbolic annihilation in healthcare. *Culture, Health & Sexuality, 20*(1), 14–27.

REFERENCES

Austin, E. L. (2013). Sexual orientation disclosure to health care providers among urban and non-urban southern lesbians. *Women & Health, 53*(1), 41–55. https://doi.org/10.1080/03630242.2012.743497

Baker, K., & Beagan, B. (2014). Making assumptions, making space: An anthropological critique of cultural competency and its relevance to queer patients. *Medical Anthropology Quarterly, 28*(4), 578–598.

Beach, M. C., Saha, S., Korthuis, P. T., Sharp, V., Cohn, J., Wilson, I. B., Eggly, S., Cooper, L. A., Roter, D., Sankar, A., & Moore, R. (2010). Differences in patient–provider communication for Hispanic compared to non-Hispanic White patients in HIV care. *Journal of General Internal Medicine, 25*(7), 682–687. https://doi.org/10.1007/s11606-010-1310-4

Beach, M. C., Saha, S., Korthuis, P. T., Sharp, V., Cohn, J., Wilson, I. B., Eggly, S., Cooper, L. A., Roter, D., Sankar, A., & Moore, R. (2011). Patient–provider communication differs for Black compared to White HIV-infected patients. *AIDS and Behavior, 15*(4), 805–811. https://doi.org/10.1007/s10461-009-9664-5

Beagan, B., Fredericks, E., & Bryson, M. (2015). Family physician perceptions of working with LGBTQ patients: Physician training needs. *Canadian Medical Education Journal, 6*(1), e14–e22.

Beisecker, A. E. (1990). Patient power in doctor–patient communication: What do we know? *Health Communication, 2*(2), 105–122.

Bjorkman, M., & Malterud, K. (2007). Being lesbian—does the doctor need to know? A qualitative study about the significance of disclosure in general practice. *Scandinavian Journal of Primary Health Care, 25*(1), 58–62. https://doi.org/10.1080/02813430601086178

Carmack, H. J. (2014). Medicalization. In T. Thompson (Ed.), *Encyclopedia of health communication* (pp. 845–846). SAGE.

Chabot, J. M., & Ames, B. D. (2004). "It wasn't 'let's get pregnant and go do it' ": Decision making in lesbian couples planning motherhood via donor insemination. *Family Relations, 53*(4), 348–356. https://doi.org/10.1111/j.0197-6664.2004.00041.x

Cherguit, J., Burns, J., Pettle, S., & Tasker, F. (2013). Lesbian co-mothers' experiences of maternity healthcare services. *Journal of Advanced Nursing, 69*(6), 1269–1278. https://doi.org/10.1111/j.1365-2648.2012.06115.x

Córdova, D., Lua, F. M., Ovadje, L., Fessler, K., Bauermeister, J. A., Salas-Wright, C. P., Vaughn, M. G., & Youth Leadership Council. (2018). Adolescent experiences of clinician–patient HIV/STI communication in primary care. *Health Communication, 33*(9), 1177–1183. https://doi.org/10.1080/10410236.2017.1339379

DeHart, D. (2008). Breast health behavior among lesbians: The role of health beliefs heterosexism and homophobia. *Women & Health, 48*(4), 409–427. https://doi.org/10.1080/03630240802575146

Dorsen, C., & Devanter, N. V. (2016). Open arms, conflicted hearts: Nurse-practitioner's attitudes towards working with lesbian, gay, and bisexual patients. *Journal of Clinical Nursing, 25*, 3716–3727. https://doi.org/10.1111/jocn.13464

Eckhert, E. (2016). A case for the demedicalization of queer bodies. *Yale Journal of Biology and Medicine, 89*(2), 239–246.

Erlandsson, K., Linder, H., & Häggström-Nordin, E. (2010). Experiences of gay women during their partner's pregnancy and childbirth. *British Journal of Midwifery, 18*(2), 99–103. https://doi.org/10.12968/bjom.2010.18.2.46407

Fish, J. (2006). *Heterosexism in health and social care*. Palgrave Macmillan.

Fisher, C. B., Fried, A. L., Macapagal, K., & Mustanski, B. (2018). Patient–provider communication barriers and facilitators to HIV and STI preventive services for adolescent MSM. *AIDS and Behavior, 22*(10), 3417–3428. https://doi.org/10.1007/s10461-018-2081-x

Goins, E. S., & Pye, D. (2012). Check the box that best describes you: Reflexivity managing theory and praxis in LGBTQ health communication research. *Health Communication, 28*, 397–407. https://doi.org/10.1080/10410236.2012.690505

Herek, G. M. (2007). Confronting sexual stigma and prejudice: Theory and practice. *Journal of Social Issues, 63*(4), 905–925. https://doi.org/10.1111/j.1540-4560.2007.00544.x

Herek, G. M. (2012). *Facts about homosexuality and mental health*. https://psychology.ucdavis.edu/rainbow/html/facts_mental_health.html

Heyes, C., Dean, M., & Goldberg, L. (2016). Queer phenomenology, sexual orientation, and health care spaces: Learning from the narratives of queer women and nurses in primary health care. *Journal of Homosexuality, 63*(2), 141–155. https://doi.org/10.1080/00918369.2015.1083775

Hudak, N. (2016, November). *"Do you have to ask me one more time?" Communicating heterosexism in healthcare*. National Communication Association, Philadelphia, PA.

Hudak, N., & Bates, B. R. (2019). In pursuit of "queer friendly" healthcare: An interview study of how queer individuals select care providers. *Health Communication, 34*(8), 818–824. https://doi.org/10.1080/10410236.2018.1437525

Hudak, N. C., & Carmack, H. J. (2018). Waiting for the doctor to ask: Influencers of lesbian, gay, and bisexual identity disclosure to healthcare providers. *Qualitative Research in Medicine & Healthcare, 2*, 20–29. https://doi.org/10.4081/qrmh.2018.7157

Hurley, E. A., Harvey, S. A., Winch, P. J., Keita, M., Roter, D. L., Doumbia, S., Diarra, N. H., & Kennedy, C. E. (2018). The role of patient-provider communication in engagement and re-engagement in HIV treatment in Bamako, Mali: A qualitative study. *Journal of Health Communication, 23*(2), 129–143. https://doi.org/10.1080/10810730.2017.1417513

Kitts, R. L. (2010). Barriers to optimal care between physicians and lesbian, gay, bisexual, transgender, and questioning adolescent patients. *Journal of Homosexuality, 57*(6), 730–747. https://doi.org/10.1080/00918369.2010.485872

Klitzman, R. L., & Greenberg, J. D. (2008). Patterns of communication between gay and lesbian patients and their health care providers. *Journal of Homosexuality, 42*(4), 65–75. https://doi.org/10.1300/J082v42n04_04

Larsson, A.-K., & Dykes, A.-K. (2009). Care during pregnancy and childbirth in Sweden: Perspectives of lesbian women. *Midwifery, 25,* 682–690. https://doi.org/10.1016/j.midw.2007.10.004

Law, M., Mathai, A., Veinot, P., Webster, F., & Mylopoulos, M. (2015). Exploring lesbian, gay, bisexual, and queer (LGBQ) people's experiences with disclosure of sexual identity to primary care physicians: A qualitative study. *BMC Family Practice, 16,* 1–8. https://doi.org/10.1186/s12875-015-0389-4

Laws, M. B., Lee, Y., Rogers, W. H., Beach, M. C., Saha, S., Korthuis, P. T., Sharp, V., Cohn, J., Moore, R., & Wilson, I. B. (2014). Provider–patient communication about adherence to anti-retroviral regimens differs by patient race and ethnicity. *AIDS and Behavior, 18*(7), 1279–1287. https://doi.org/10.1007/s10461-014-0697-z

Lee, E., Taylor, J., & Raitt, F. (2011). "It's not me, it's them": How lesbian women make sense of negative experiences of maternity care: A hermeneutic study. *Journal of Advanced Nursing, 67*(5), 982–990. https://doi.org/10.1111/j.1365-2648.2010.05548.x

Li, J.-Y., Harrison, S., Qiao, S., & Li, X. (2019). Utility of theory to explain village doctors' willingness to treat people living with HIV in rural China. *Journal of Health Communication, 24*(2), 174–182. https://doi.org/10.1080/10810730.2019.1587112

McKelvey, M. M. (2014). The other mother: A narrative analysis of the postpartum experiences of nonbirth lesbian mothers. *Advances in Nursing Science, 37*(2), 101–116. https://doi.org/10.1097/ANS.0000000000000022

McNair, R. P., & Hegarty, K. (2010). Guidelines for the primary care of lesbian, gay, and bisexual people: A systematic review. *Annals of Family Medicine, 8*(6), 533–541. https://doi.org/10.1370/afm.1173

Meyer, I. (2003). Prejudice, social stress, and mental health in the lesbian, gay, and bisexual populations: Conceptual issues and research evidence. *Psychological Bulletin, 129,* 674–697. https://doi.org/10.1037/0033-2909.129.5.674

Mimiaga, M. J., Goldhammer, H., Belanoff, C., Tetu, A. M., & Mayer, K. H. (2007). Men who have sex with men: Perceptions about sexual risk, HIV and sexually transmitted disease testing, and provider communication. *Sexually Transmitted Diseases, 34*(2), 113–119. https://doi.org/10.1097/01.olq.0000225327.13214.bf

Mulder, B. C., van Lelyveld, M. A. A., Vervoort, S. C. J. M., Lokhorst, A. M., van Woerkum, C. M. J., Prins, J. M., & de Bruin, M. (2016). Communication between HIV patients and their providers: A qualitative preference match analysis. *Health Communication, 31*(1), 35–46. https://doi.org/10.1080/10410236.2014.933017

Murphy, M. (2016). Hiding in plain sight: The production of heteronormativity in medical education. *Journal of Contemporary Ethnography, 45*(3), 256–289. https://doi.org/10.1177/0891241614556345

Obedin-Maliver, J., Goldsmith, E. S., Stewart, L., White, W., Tran, E., Brenman, S., Wells, M., Fetterman, D. M., Garcia, G., & Lunn, M. R. (2011). Lesbian, gay, bisexual, and transgender-related content in undergraduate medical education. *JAMA, 306*(9), 971–977. https://doi.org/10.1001/jama.2011.1255

Parkhill, A. L., Mathews, J. L., Fearing, S., & Gainsburg, J. (2014). A transgender health care panel discussion in a required diversity course. *American Journal of Pharmaceutical Education, 78*(4), 1–7.

Pharr, S. (1997). *Homophobia: A weapon of sexism.* Chardon Press.

Pharris, A., Bucchio, J., Dotson, C., & Davidson, W. (2016). Supporting lesbian couples during pregnancy. *International Journal of Childbirth Education, 31*(3), 23.

Politi, M. C., Clark, M. A., Armstrong, G., McGarry, K. A., & Sciamanna, C. N. (2009). Patient–provider communication about sexual health among unmarried middle-aged and older women. *Journal of General Internal Medicine, 24*(4), 511–516. https://doi.org/10.1007/s11606-009-0930-z

Poteat, T., German, D., & Kerrigan, D. (2013). Managing uncertainty: A grounded theory of stigma in transgender health care encounters. *Social Science & Medicine, 84*, 22–29. https://doi.org/10.1016/j.socscimed.2013.02.019

Redfern, J. S., & Sinclair, B. (2014). Improving health care encounters and communication with transgender patients. *Journal of Health Communication, 7*(1), 25–40. https://doi.org/10.1179/1753807614Y.0000000045

Robertson, W. J. (2017). The irrelevance narrative: Queer (in)visibility in medical education and practice. *Medical Anthropology Quarterly, 31*(2), 159–176. https://doi.org/10.1111/maq.12289

Röndahl, G., Bruhner, E., & Lindhe, J. (2009). Heteronormative communication with lesbian families in antenatal care, childbirth and postnatal care. *Journal of Advanced Nursing, 65*(11), 2337–2344. https://doi.org/10.1111/j.1365-2648.2009.05092.x

Ross, K. A., & Castle Bell, G. (2017). A culture-centered approach to improving healthy trans-patient–practitioner communication: Recommendations for practitioners communicating with trans individuals. *Health Communication, 32*(6), 730–740. https://doi.org/10.1080/10410236.2016.1172286

Ross, L. E., Steele, L. S., & Epstein, R. (2006). Service use and gaps in services for lesbian and bisexual women during donor insemination, pregnancy, and the postpartum period. *Journal of Obstetrics and Gynaecology Canada, 28*, 505–511. https://doi.org/10.1016/S1701-2163(16)32181-8

Rounds, K. E., Mcgrath, B. B., & Walsh, E. (2013). Perspectives on provider behaviors: A qualitative study of sexual and gender minorities regarding quality of care. *Contemporary Nurse: A Journal for the Australian Nursing Profession, 44*(1), 99–110. https://doi.org/10.5172/conu.2013.44.1.99

Saulnier, C. F. (2002). Deciding who to see: Lesbians discuss their preferences in health and mental health care providers. *Social Work, 47*(4), 355–365.

Silverman, R. E., Araujo, M., & Nicholson, A. (2012). Including gynecological teaching associates' perspectives in women's health exams: Lessons for improved communication practices. *Health Communication, 27*(7), 723. https://doi.org/10.1080/10410236.2012.666714

Singer, R. B. (2012). Improving prenatal care for pregnant lesbians. *International Journal of Childbirth Education, 27*(4), 37–40.

Snelgrove, J. W., Jasudavisius, A. M., Rowe, B. W., Head, E. M., & Bauer, G. R. (2012). "Completely out-at-sea" with "two-gender medicine": A qualitative analysis of physician-side barriers to providing healthcare for transgender patients. *BMC Health Services Research, 12*(1), 110. https://doi.org/10.1186/1472-6963-12-110

Solursh, D. S., Ernst, J. L., Lewis, R. W., Prisant, L. M., Mills, T. M., Solursh, L. P., Jarvis, R. G., & Salazar, W. H. (2003). The human sexuality education of physicians in North American medical schools. *International Journal of Impotence Research, 15*(Suppl. 5), S41–S45. https://doi.org/10.1038/sj.ijir.3901071

Spidsberg, B. D. (2007). Vulnerable and strong: Lesbian women encountering maternity care. *Journal of Advanced Nursing, 60*(5), 478–486. https://doi.org/10.1111/j.1365-2648.2007.04439.x

Spidsberg, B. D., & Sørlie, V. (2012). An expression of love: Midwives' experiences in the encounter with lesbian women and their partners. *Journal of Advanced Nursing, 68*(4), 796–805. https://doi.org/10.1111/j.1365-2648.2011.05780.x

Spieldenner, A. (2016). PrEP whores and HIV prevention: The queer communication of HIV pre-exposure prophylaxis (PrEP). *Journal of Homosexuality, 63*(12), 1685–1697. https://doi.org/10.1080/00918369.2016.1158012

Stott, D. B. (2013). The training needs of general practitioners in the exploration of sexual health matters and providing sexual healthcare to lesbian, gay and bisexual patients. *Medical Teacher, 35*(9), 752–759. https://doi.org/10.3109/0142159X.2013.801943

Venetis, M. K., Meyerson, B. E., Friley, L. B., Gillespie, A., Ohmit, A., & Shields, C. G. (2017). Characterizing sexual orientation disclosure to health care providers: Lesbian, gay, and bisexual perspectives. *Health Communication, 32*(5), 578–586. https://doi.org/10.1080/10410236.2016.1144147

Wachira, J., Genberg, B., Kafu, C., Koech, B., Akinyi, J., Owino, R. K., Laws, M. B., Wilson, I. B., & Braitstein, P. (2018). The perspective of HIV providers in western Kenya on provider–patient relationships. *Journal of Health Communication, 23*(6), 591–596. https://doi.org/10.1080/10810730.2018.1493061

Weinberg, G. (1972). *Society and the healthy homosexual.* St. Martin's Press.

Westerstahk, A., & Bjorkelund, C. (2003). Challenging heteronormativity in the consultation: A focus group among general practitioners. *Scandinavian Journal of Primary Health Care, 21*, 205–208.

Wilson, K., Bleasdale, J., & Przybyla, S. M. (2020). Provider–patient communication on pre-exposure prophylaxis (PrEP) for HIV prevention: An exploration of healthcare provider challenges. *Health Communication,* (advanced copy published online) 1–10. https://doi.org/10.1080/10410236.2020.1787927

Wojnar, D. M., & Katzenmeyer, A. (2014). Research: Experiences of preconception, pregnancy, and new motherhood for lesbian nonbiological mothers. *Journal of Obstetric, Gynecologic & Neonatal Nursing, 43*, 50–60. https://doi.org/10.1111/1552-6909.12270

Zuzelo, P. R. (2014). Improving nursing care for lesbian, bisexual, and transgender women. *Journal of Obstetric, Gynecological & Neonatal Nursing, 43*(4), 520–530. https://doi.org/10.1111/1552-6909.12477

NOTE

1. *Queer*: In this article, queer is used as an all-encompassing term to describe sexual identities that are outside of a heterosexual identity. This includes, but is not limited to gay, lesbian, bisexual, pansexual, and so on.

    Heterosexism: Heterosexism is a power structure that infiltrates all institutions. It is the belief that heterosexual identity is the primary or only identity (Pharr, 1997). This belief then positions queer identities as those that are different or even wrong (Meyer, 2003). Heterosexism is systemic and works to disadvantage queer people (Herek, 2007).

    Homophobia: Homophobia a negative reaction toward queer individuals or often the fear of those individuals (Weinberg, 1972).

    Co-mother: A co-mother describes a queer woman in a partnership who did not give birth to their child.

Nicole Hudak

QUEER SAFER SEX COMMUNICATION

INTRODUCTION

It was 1981, and Dr. Michael Gottlieb, an assistant professor of immunology, was looking for a good teaching case for his postdoctoral fellow at the University of California, Los Angeles (UCLA) Medical Center. He and his fellow received permission to meet with a patient, a gay man named Michael, who presented with thrush, weight loss, fevers, and pneumonia. T-cell testing revealed that Michael's immune system had been decimated, and Gottlieb suspected that a virus was to blame. Discussions with colleagues led to the identification of four other gay men with similar symptoms, and testing revealed that they, too, were immune compromised (Fee & Brown, 2006). Gottlieb and colleagues (1981) described this disease cluster in an article published in the Centers for Disease Control and Prevention's (CDC's) *Morbidity and Mortality Weekly Report*—a piece that is now known as the first official report on AIDS in America. Since the publication of that report, the AIDS pandemic has claimed the lives of over 700,000 Americans and over 35 million individuals around the world (CDC, 2020; Kaiser Family Foundation, 2019).

Nearly four decades later, in 2019, doctors encountered another unusual respiratory illness with a viral basis, and the world soon found itself in the middle of the COVID-19 pandemic (CDC, 2019a). Without a cure or a vaccine, preventing the spread of infectious diseases, such as COVID-19 and HIV/AIDS, hinges on behavioral change. However, unlike donning a mask in order to reduce the risk of contracting the novel coronavirus, engaging in safer sexual practices to prevent HIV and other sexually transmitted infections (STIs) is a dyadic (and, in some cases, group) process. For example, condom use, which is how most studies conceive of safer sexual behavior, requires a certain amount of cooperation and negotiation between sexual partners (Browne & Minichiello, 1994). Despite evidence that humans have been engaging in various practices to reduce sexual risks for thousands of years (Khan et al., 2013), the term *safe sex* did not enter the public lexicon until the AIDS crisis emerged (Alexander et al., 2011). Similarly, although studies exploring the links between interpersonal communication and sexual risk reduction date back to the 1960s (e.g., Angrist, 1966), it was not until the late 1980s that scholars started using terms such as *safe sex communication* or *safe sex talk* (e.g., Linn et al., 1989). To more accurately reflect the risks inherent in every sexual interaction, scholars and practitioners started referring to *safer sex*, but many still use the terms interchangeably (Kalichman, 2014).

Regardless of the terms used, scholars seem to agree on the protective potential of sexual communication with partners. In fact, in a widely cited meta-analysis comparing the different psychosocial factors associated with the use of prophylactics, interpersonal communication emerged as the strongest correlate of condom use (Sheeran et al., 1999). This study, along with the ones included in the meta-analytic review, signaled the importance of research, campaigns, and interventions focused on safer sex communication and sexual risk reduction. This article describes the conceptual and definitional issues associated with these efforts, the main findings from this literature, and some considerations for future research in this area. Although this piece will draw upon the broader sexual communication and safer sexual communication literatures, its chief concern is queer individuals, a group disproportionately affected by HIV/AIDS and other STIs (CDC, 2020). Moreover, given vast cultural, linguistic, and legal differences regarding sexual identities and behaviors around the world, this article will center on queer safer sex communication in the United States.

CONCEPTUAL AND DEFINITIONAL ISSUES

In a Supreme Court case from the 1960s, Justice Potter Stewart struggled to define pornography and obscenity: "I shall not today attempt further to define the kinds of material I understand to be embraced... but I know it when I see it" (Bybee, 2016, p. 149). Although Stewart was mocked and criticized for his non-definition, many have struggled to define *sex* and its related concepts. Various researchers have tried to determine what individuals "count" as sex, with most studies asking participants to reflect on a list of behaviors and to indicate which ones they consider to be sex (Peterson & Muehlenhard, 2007). However, the sampling approaches and the behavioral checklists used in these studies tend to focus on cisgender heterosexuals, leaving queer definitions of sex unilluminated (Sewell et al., 2017). For cisgender heterosexuals, the standard definition of "having sex" involves vaginal penetration. The few studies that have included lesbian, gay, bisexual, or transgender participants have found that queer individuals' definitions of sex also focus on penetrative acts. For example, in the study by Sewell et al. (2017), female-identified participants were more likely to count acts involving dildos as "having sex" than encounters involving frottage (colloquially known as "scissoring"). Given that individuals are less likely to use condoms during encounters that they do not consider to be "real sex" (Peterson & Muehlenhard, 2007), how people define sex has very real public health implications.

Discrepancies in definitions of sex complicate efforts to define related concepts, such as safer sex and safer sex communication. The notion of safer sex emerged during the AIDS crisis; not surprisingly, many definitions of safer sex focus on reducing the risk of HIV transmission. For example, Kalichman (2014) wrote that "safer sex is defined by activities that significantly reduce but do not eliminate risks for HIV infection, such as is the case of condom use during anal and vaginal intercourse" (p. 37). Emmers-Sommer and Allen (2004) offered a similar definition: "We define safer sex as a description of any action a person takes to diminish the level of risk for HIV infection. Most frequently, the term is used to describe the use of a condom..." (p. 3). Although some scholars and public health agencies, such as the World Health Organization (WHO), have adopted broader definitions of sexual health and safer sex, most continue to conceptualize and operationalize safer sex as condom use behavior (Albarracín et al., 2005). When used correctly and consistently, male condoms significantly reduce the risk of HIV infection (CDC, 2019b), but male condoms are not appropriate for all types of bodies and sex acts. For example, transmasculine individuals may have a surgically constructed or hormonally induced phallus, for which male condoms are a poor fit. In past studies, some transmasculine individuals reported that finger cots (i.e., a latex glove designed to cover a single finger) were a better fit for their bodies (Kosenko, 2010). For individuals who do not engage in penetrative sex acts, other barriers to the exchange of bodily fluids, such as dental dams and clothing, are more relevant than condoms. When we broaden the definition of safer sex to include more than just HIV prevention, the focus on condom use becomes even more problematic as a growing body of research indicates that condoms offer little protection against some other STIs, such as the human papillomavirus (HPV; Dizon & Krychman, 2010). Taken together, these findings point to a need for broader definitions of safer sex that recognize the various risks associated with sex as well as the range of risk mitigation strategies at people's disposal.

Given that safer sex is typically defined as condom use, it is not surprising that condoms are part of most conceptual and operational definitions of safer sex communication. For example, Li and Samp (2019) defined safer sex communication as "discussions about using a condom during sexual encounters" (p. 59). Xiao et al. (2013) offered a similar definition: "negotiation on use of condoms between couples or partners" (p. 481). Broader definitions of safer sex communication describe its various forms or dimensions. For example, Reynolds-Tylus et al. (2015) defined safer sex communication as "a type of substantive communication that may include topics such as (1) inquiring about a partner's sexual history, (2) revealing one's own sexual history, (3) probing about a partner's STI/HIV serostatus, or (4) asking about a partner's last date of testing" (p. 1214). Noar and Edgar's (2008) definition also outlined the various topics covered during safer sex conversations: "the discussions and negotiations that sexual partners have with one another about their sexual histories, AIDS and sexually transmitted diseases (STDs), and condom use" (p. 3). In their meta-analysis of the literature on safer sex communication, Noar et al. (2006) found that the topic of the conversation mattered, such that condom and sexual history discussions exhibited the strongest links with protective behavior.

Operationalizations of safer sex communication also focus on condom discussions, presumably because condom use is the behavioral outcome of interest in most HIV prevention studies. Most research on safer sex communication relies on retrospective reports of condom discussions with sexual partners (Peasant et al., 2015). For greater precision, these measures typically specify a time frame, such as the last three months or one's most recent sexual encounter. Researchers interested in the *incidence* of condom discussions and use tend to use single-item, dichotomous measures (Noar et al., 2006). For example, in a study exploring the links between condom discussions and sexual risk among Latino men who have sex with men (MSM),[1] Lo et al. (2011) asked participants to report if there had been "any verbal or nonverbal communication about the use of condoms" during their last sexual encounter (p. 615). Crosby et al. (2018) used a similar approach, asking participants if they had discussed condoms with any sexual partners that they had had in the last two months. Researchers interested in the *frequency* of safer sex conversations tend to use multi-item measures of the concept. One commonly used measure, the Partner Sexual Communication Scale developed by Milhausen et al. (2007), consists of five items designed to assess the frequency with which individuals have discussed safer sex issues with partners in the past six months. Although the scale has been validated and translated into other languages (e.g., Gubert et al., 2013), it has limited applicability in its current form to queer bodies and same-sex relationships. For example, one item, which asks about the frequency with which partners discuss pregnancy prevention (Milhausen et al., 2007), is only relevant if reproduction is a possibility, which, for partners who have the same reproductive parts, it is not. Another item asks about the frequency with which partners have discussed male condoms, which, as mentioned, is only pertinent to sexual encounters involving at least one penis. Researchers have adapted the scale for use with MSM samples by deleting the pregnancy prevention item (e.g., Crosby et al., 2016); however, further revisions are necessary to make the scale applicable to female-bodied individuals whose sexual partners are also female-bodied.

Researchers have studied the *content* of safer sex conversations in various ways, but qualitative data have proven particularly useful. Early research on condom negotiation relied on open-ended reports of the strategies that individuals might use or have used to insist on condom use during sexual activity. For example, in one of the first studies on condom negotiation strategies, Edgar et al. (1992) used free-response data to identify the influence strategies used by users and nonusers of condoms. De Bro et al. (1994) presented participants with a hypothetical situation in which they wanted to use a condom but were not sure about their partner's response. Participants were asked to describe how they would try to convince their partner that a condom should be used. De Bro et al. (1994) identified six different negotiation strategies described by participants: offering a reward for compliance, threatening punishment for noncompliance, presenting risk information, lying, using seduction, and withholding sex. Guided by these and other qualitative findings, Noar et al. (2002) created a condom influence strategy questionnaire for heterosexuals, with subscales addressing six different influence tactics: withholding sex, directly requesting condoms, expressing care or concern for one's partner or relationship, lying, discussing risk information, and being seductive. Although the now dated scale has been used in several studies of heterosexual, cisgender adults (e.g., Holland & French, 2012; Peasant et al., 2018), comparatively few focus on queer individuals, which limits our understanding of the scale's applicability outside of the context of heterosexual relationships.

The safer sex communication literature is also concerned with the incidence, frequency, and content of HIV status disclosures. HIV secondary prevention efforts stress the importance of status disclosure to past, present, and prospective partners as a means of reducing high-risk sexual behavior among serodiscordant individuals (O'Connell et al., 2015). Although medical and legal authorities contend that persons living with HIV have a responsibility to disclose their status to potential sexual partners (Stein et al., 1998), research suggests that many seropositive individuals fail to fully disclose. A survey of the relevant literature on HIV disclosure rates revealed figures as high as 97% (Shacham et al., 2012); however, other studies uncovered less promising disclosure rates, ranging from 52% (Cook et al., 2015) to 60% (Stein et al., 1998). Using data from a national probability sample of individuals infected with HIV, Ciccarone et al. (2003) estimated that over 45,000 gay or bisexual men and over 15,000 heterosexual men and women become intimate without disclosing their HIV status. Because nondisclosure reduces the ability of sexual partners of individuals with HIV to make informed decisions about the risks involved in sexual intimacy, researchers contend that "substantial numbers of new HIV infections could occur among partners of HIV-positive persons who do not disclose their status" (Ciccarone et al., 2003, p. 950).

Those who are currently infected represent the potential source of future infections, so prevention efforts involve providing individuals living with HIV with counseling on sexual communication, including skill-building exercises that emphasize the importance of disclosure to sexual partners (De Rosa & Marks, 1998). The primary assumption of these prevention efforts is that full disclosure will lead to protective behavior. However, research has failed to support this claim (Simoni & Pantalone, 2004). In fact, those who fail to disclose their seropositive status may engage in safer sex practices as a proxy for full disclosure, and those who do disclose may not engage in protective behaviors (Crepaz & Marks, 2003). Because of the mixed results of studies investigating the link between disclosure and safe sex practices, further investigation into the decisions involved in disclosing HIV status and its relationship to risk behaviors is necessary.

Studies of queer safer sex conversations have revealed additional ways in which individuals think and talk about sexual safety. Some of these studies have uncovered grassroot harm-reduction strategies specific to queer individuals. For example, in a study of the HIV prevention strategies used by gay men, Kippax et al. (1993) observed that some of the men were engaging in a practice that the authors called "negotiated safety." Individuals practicing negotiated safety stopped using barrier methods with their primary partner after HIV/STI testing but promised to use protection with other partners. Some transgender adults who participated in a study of safer sex communication described engaging in a similar practice, which they called *fluid bonding* (Kosenko, 2011b). Research involving MSM revealed additional grassroots harm-reduction strategies, including serosorting and strategic sexual positioning. Serosorting involves selecting sexual partners and safer sexual practices based on HIV status, often so that partners in seroconcordant relationships (i.e., one in which both partners have the same HIV status) can engage in barrier-free sex (Eaton et al., 2009). Individuals in serodiscordant relationships (i.e., one in which one partner is HIV-positive and the other is not) might choose to engage in strategic sexual positioning as a safer sexual practice. Strategic sexual positioning involves choosing one's role as the insertive or receptive partner in anal sex based on serostatus (van de Ven et al., 2002). Given evidence that the risk of HIV transmission is lower when seropositive individuals serve as the receptive partner during anal sex, strategic sexual positioning usually entails barrier-free sex in which the HIV-negative partner adopts the insertive role and the HIV-positive partner takes on the receptive role (Grov et al., 2015). Although these strategies might not be as effective as condom use at preventing HIV transmission (van den Boom et al., 2014), they underscore the importance of considering the range of ways in which individuals conceive of and practice safer sex.

Conceptual and operational definitions of safer sex talk and behavior also inform and are informed by theory. For instance, researchers interested in understanding and predicting safer sex behavior and behavioral intentions tend toward health behavior theories, such as the theory of planned behavior and social cognitive theory (Noar, 2007). How one defines safer sex talk also dictates and is dictated by one's theory of choice. Those who draw on principles and theories of social influence usually frame safer sex talk in terms of condom influence and resistance. For example, Edgar (1992) used Dillard's (1990) Goal-Driven Model of Interpersonal Influence to examine the role of compliance-gaining in safer sexual relationships, and Reynolds-Tylus et al. (2015) explored the use of Cialdini's (1984) six principles of influence in safer sex conversations. In fact, studying safer sex talk in terms of compliance gaining or social influence is so common that those doing meta-analytic reviews of the safer sexual communication literature use those terms in their literature search (e.g., Widman et al., 2014). Those who frame safer sex talk in terms of an informational exchange rely on a different set of theories, including uncertainty-related and information-management theories. Edgar et al. (1992) explored the information-seeking and uncertainty-reduction strategies employed by individuals in new sexual relationships, and Afifi and Weiner (2004) developed the theory of motivated information management to account for safer sex decision-making processes. Broad conceptualizations of safer sex talk result in (or are the result of) equally broad theoretical perspectives. A multiple goals approach, for example, helps explain goal conflict and pursuit in safer sex conversations. Buysse and Ickes (1999) examined laboratory-based discussions of safer sex and found that these conversations created goal conflicts for participants. Relational goals, such as closeness and intimacy, were deemed incompatible with the conversational goal of mutual honesty about sexual history. Kosenko's (2010) study of the safer sex conversations of transgender adults came to similar conclusions. Participants described conflicts between identity, relational, and instrumental goals in their safer sex conversations. In summary, studies of safer sex talk have referenced various theories, with one's theory of choice dictating (and being dictated by) one's conceptualization of safer sexual communication.

MAIN FINDINGS FROM THE QUEER SAFER SEX LITERATURE

Although much of the literature on safer sex talk and behavior is theory driven, it still suffers from a cisgender, heteronormative bias, which limits its applicability to queer individuals. Studies focused specifically on queer experiences with safer sex talk and behavior have revealed issues of particular relevance to gender non-conforming individuals and/or sexual minorities. These studies have highlighted demographic differences, contextual issues, and the impact of pre-exposure prophylaxis (PrEP).

Demographics

Age. For male-bodied individuals who have sex with other male-bodied individuals, "youth is one of the strongest and most consistent correlates of sexual risk-taking" (Molitor et al., 1999, p. 336). Yet there is growing evidence of a curvilinear relationship between chronological age and sexual risk-taking behaviors in this population, such that younger and older individuals are more likely to engage in unprotected sex than middle-aged adults (e.g., Chen et al., 2003; Hampton et al., 2013). Given that almost half of the individuals living with HIV in America are 50 or older (CDC, 2019c), unprotected sex at a later age is particularly concerning. Some studies suggest that older male-bodied individuals no longer see HIV as a threat and, thus, do not feel the need to engage in safer sexual practices (Jacobs et al., 2010). Others have found that erectile dysfunction, which is common at older ages, and the drugs used to treat it, make condom use more difficult (Jacobs et al., 2013). Jacobs et al. (2016) argued that the changes in appearance that come with older age make one feel less sexually desirable, which undermines one's efficacy to negotiate condom use or other safer sexual practices.

Issues related to developmental age have been identified in safer sex studies with transgender participants. For example, Kosenko (2011a) found that transgender adults experienced a second adolescence after coming to terms with their trans identity. For some, this was related to the initiation of hormone therapy, which participants likened to going through a second puberty. Others described coming out or coming to terms with their gender identity as a rebirth and the period that followed as reminiscent of their teenage years. Participants linked this second adolescence to sexual risk behavior and poor sexual decision-making. Other studies have focused on chronological age and its links to sexual risk behavior among transgender individuals. Cook-Daniels and Munson (2010) found that midlife and older trans adults lacked information about sexual risks and forms of protection as well as the communication skills necessary to achieve sexual safety. The authors also acknowledged the influence of developmental age on sexual risk behavior and safer sex communication. They expressed concern for those transitioning during middle age, arguing that these individuals have not had the opportunity to develop negotiation skills and that they might prioritize gender confirmation from sex partners over sexual safety. Studies have implicated both chronological and developmental age in the sex lives of queer individuals.

Race. Most sex research focuses on White, cisgender heterosexuals; however, samples in studies of sexual risk and safety among trans individuals or MSM tend to be more racially diverse. In fact, Becasen et al.'s (2019) meta-analysis of the literature on HIV and sexual risk behavior among transgender individuals reported that 77% of the studies included in their analysis "consisted of majority non-White participants" (p. 6). The literature on sexual risks among MSM is equally diverse, with numerous studies stratifying HIV risk behaviors by race (Millett et al., 2007). According to the CDC (2016), Black MSM and trans individuals are disproportionately impacted by HIV, such that, if 2016 rates persist, half of all Black MSM will be diagnosed as HIV-positive at some point in their lifetime. CDC surveillance reports also point to high HIV infection rates among Black and Hispanic trans individuals (CDC, 2020). Although these alarming statistics have prompted numerous studies of HIV and sexual risk behavior among Black and Hispanic queer individuals (e.g., Ramirez-Valles et al., 2008; Siembida et al., 2016), their safer sexual practices, including talking about safer sex, have been given relatively little attention. Diversifying the safer sexual communication literature in terms of gender identity, sexuality, and race/ethnicity is necessary for further insight into these risk disparities.

Contextual Issues

Intimate Partner Violence. High rates of HIV among justice-involved, cisgender women prompted researchers to examine the factors that put these women at risk. They found that one factor—intimate partner violence (IPV)—was linked to both one's risk of being incarcerated and contracting HIV (Swan & O'Connell, 2012). Further examination of the possible links between IPV and HIV transmission revealed both direct and indirect effects. Forced sex, one form of IPV, is a direct risk factor (El Bassel et al., 2005), but IPV's link to inconsistent condom use suggests indirect effects, as well. Cisgender women with abusive partners have described a reluctance to discuss sexual safety due to the fear of a violent response (Amaro, 1995). Swan and O'Connell (2012) found that IPV undermined cisgender women's confidence in their ability to negotiate condom use with partners. Given that cisgender men with a history of violence are more likely to forgo condoms than their nonviolent counterparts and that cisgender women in abusive relationships have low condom negotiation self-efficacy (Frye et al., 2011), IPV's link with HIV is not surprising.

Although rates of partner abuse in queer relationships are comparable to IPV rates in cisgender, heterosexual relationships (Tjaden et al., 1999), abusive queer relationships and their potential links to sexual risks have received less attention from researchers (Heintz & Melendez, 2006). This small but growing literature indicates that both childhood and adult experiences with IPV put queer individuals at increased risk of HIV infection. Childhood sexual abuse and IPV function as syndemic conditions that create a unique context of risk for transgender adults. Syndemics involve multiple, mutually reinforcing epidemics that increase disease susceptibility and severity (Singer, 1996). For example, Parsons et al. (2018) found that childhood sexual abuse and IPV were associated with HIV risk behavior among transgender adults and that those who had experienced both syndemics were more likely to engage in sexual risk-taking behavior, including transactional sex, than those who had experienced one or none. Transgender individuals who have participated in transactional sex, or survival sex, in which there is an exchange of sex for resources, such as money or housing, have described difficulties negotiating safer sexual practices with "paying" partners. These individuals feared losing resources that they desperately needed if they broached the topic of safer sex (Nemoto et al., 2004). Safer sex talk is also problematic for trans IPV survivors who fear being rejected or violently victimized if they insist on safer sexual practices (Kosenko, 2010). The links between IPV, sexual risk-taking, and safer sexual communication avoidance are all the more troubling in light of studies documenting IPV prevalence rates ranging from 31% to 50% of transgender adults (Garthe et al., 2018).

IPV also undermines sexual safety for MSM and female-bodied individuals who have sex with female-bodied individuals. Among MSM, those with a history of IPV are 50–60% more likely to be HIV-positive than those without a history of abuse (Stall et al., 2003), and studies of IPV among women who have sex with women (WSW)[2] have found high rates of sexual violence, which is a direct risk factor for STIs (West, 2002). In a study of IPV's effects on the safer sex negotiation practices of queer individuals, Heintz and Melendez (2006) found that those who had been forced to have sex with an abusive partner were 10 times more likely to report avoiding safer sex discussions out of fear of their partner's response than those who had not experienced forced sex. This is particularly concerning given that, in some studies, as many as 69% of transgender participants describe having been sexually assaulted (Stotzer, 2009). Moreover, in a systematic review of the literature on sexual violence perpetrated against queer individuals, Rothman et al. (2011) found that sexual assault prevalence rates ranged from "15.6–85% for lesbian and bisexual women, and 11.8–54% for gay and bisexual men" (p. 5). These high rates of interpersonal and sexual violence problematize condom and safer sex promotion efforts, which can pit a person's desire for sexual health against their need for physical safety. Campaigns and interventions designed to increase safer sex talk among queer individuals must acknowledge that, at least for some, these conversations "occur against a backdrop of violence or threats of violence" (Stephenson et al., 2016, p. 369).

Place. Researchers have explored the impact of place—both the places in which people find sex partners and the places in which they engage in sex acts—on sexual risk-taking behavior and safer sex talk. For MSM, this includes studies comparing the frequency of unprotected sexual encounters between partners found online versus those met offline. A growing body of research explores the impact of mobile dating apps on the sexual risk practices of MSM but with mixed results. For example, Lehmiller and Ioerger (2014) found no significant differences between rates of unprotected sex among MSM mobile dating app users and nonusers, but other studies have noted higher STI incidence rates among those whose most recent partner was someone they met online (e.g., Beymer et al., 2014; DeVost et al., 2018). A study by Goedel and Duncan (2016) offers one possible explanation for these discrepant findings. They found that the context of app use mattered, such that using dating apps while intoxicated or to arrange paid sexual encounters were linked to unprotected insertive and receptive anal sex. Findings regarding online safer sex talk and its link to safer sexual behavior are also mixed. Several studies have found that MSM and transgender individuals are more likely to discuss safer sexual practices online than in person and that online safer sex negotiation is associated with condom use (e.g., Carballo-Diéguez et al., 2006; Kosenko, 2010; Sevelius, 2009). Other studies indicate that deception is common in online sexual negotiation and that app users frequently misrepresent their serostatus in online interactions (e.g., Carballo-Diéguez et al., 2006; Ross et al., 2006). Despite these discrepant findings, researchers and public health practitioners have considered using these apps in HIV prevention efforts. Studies of the acceptability of app-based sexual health promotion efforts indicate that MSM are receptive to these kinds of interventions and that they want apps that help them negotiate safer sex (Aliabadi et al., 2015; Jenkins Hall et al., 2017). Researchers have developed internet-based (ehealth) and mobile app-based (mhealth) HIV prevention interventions targeting transgender individuals and MSM, but female-bodied individuals who have sex with female-bodied individuals have received little to no attention in the ehealth or mhealth literatures.

Since the publication of Humphreys' (1970) *Tearoom Trade* book, which was based on his ethically questionable dissertation study on sexual interactions between males in public restrooms, researchers have been interested in the impact of physical spaces, such as bathhouses, public sex venues, and private sex parties, on the sexual risk behavior and risk reduction practices of MSM. Private sex parties, otherwise known as group sex events (GSE), have been linked to high-risk sexual practices among MSM (Mimiaga et al., 2011). For example, some report attending bareback sex parties, where individuals gather with the express purpose of engaging in unprotected sex. Pollock and Halkitis (2009) found that the MSM in their sample who met partners at bareback sex parties reported frequenting bathhouses, as well. Also known as "gay saunas" or "gay steambaths," bathhouses are designated as "sex on-premise" venues where patrons pay to be able to use the site for sex acts (Prior, 2008). Although research involving convenience samples suggests that unprotected sex is uncommon in these venues, more recent studies based on probability samples found that as many as 14% of patrons reported engaging in unprotected sex at the bathhouse (e.g., Binson et al., 2010). In recognition of this unique context of risk, researchers and practitioners have implemented HIV prevention interventions, involving onsite, rapid HIV testing and free condoms, in bathhouses (e.g., Huebner et al., 2010; Woods et al., 2010); however, these prevention efforts must contend with communicative norms in these venues that undermine safer sex. Elwood et al. (2003) interviewed bathhouse patrons and found evidence of a norm of silence that facilitated anonymous sex but limited condom negotiation. Haig (2006) spoke of a similar norm of silence in bareback sex parties where communication of any sort, including serostatus disclosure, was seen as threatening the mood. Meunier (2013), in an ethnographic study of a private sex party for MSM in New York, found that party structure, such as the use of different rooms for different kinds of sex acts or the designation of certain spaces as social and others as sexual, affected communicative and sexual dynamics. For example, parties with some spaces designated for socializing and others specified for sex had norms of silence in the sexual spaces that precluded safer sex talk. Architectural elements, including the presence of "glory holes," or penis-sized holes cut in walls to facilitate anonymous, faceless sex acts, also encourage norms of silence in public sex venues, such as restrooms (Holmes et al., 2010). Identifying the spaces in which sexual risk-taking is most likely to occur allows for targeted prevention efforts and highlights the need for additional research on the communication environment and its impact on sexual behavior.

PrEP. PrEP has changed the landscape of HIV prevention by offering a biomedical (as opposed to completely behavioral) means of risk reduction. PrEP involves the use of antiretrovirals, commonly used to treat HIV infection, as a preventive measure among HIV-negative individuals. In 2012, the Food and Drug Administration (FDA) approved a once-daily pill called Truvada, and both the CDC and WHO have encouraged its use among MSM (Grov et al., 2015). Several studies have shown that Truvada significantly lowers the risk of HIV infection and transmission for adherent users but that it offers little to no protection for those who do not take it every day. Given that Truvada's efficacy is so intimately tied to adherence, it is not surprising that a growing body of work examines reasons for non-adherence (Sidebottom et al., 2018). Researchers have found that concurrent drug use (e.g., Grov et al., 2019), periods of abstinence (e.g., Kintu et al., 2015), negative side effects (e.g., Vaccher et al., 2018), and social stigma (e.g., Golub, 2018) are some of the contributing factors. Communication scholars, having developed multiple models and theories of stigma communication and management (e.g., Meisenbach, 2010; Smith, 2007), are uniquely and ideally positioned to add to the literature on PrEP stigma and its effects on uptake and adherence. In one such study, Schwartz and Grimm (2019) found that MSM had experienced stigmatizing responses to their PrEP use from healthcare providers and prospective partners. Studying how stigma undermines adherence and how PrEP users manage stigma are necessary next steps.

Even prior to its approval by the FDA, PrEP prompted concerns about risk compensation (Blumenthal & Haubrich, 2014). The concept of risk compensation is derived, at least in part, from risk homeostasis theory, which assumes that individuals are willing to accept a certain amount of risk associated with an activity, called their target level of risk. When individuals perceive a mismatch between the amount of risk associated with an activity and their target risk level, they adjust their behavior accordingly (Wilde, 1998). According to the theory, interventions and regulations that make an activity less risky can result in compensatory risk-taking behavior as individuals try to reconcile their perceived risk level with their target one. Historically, major biomedical advancements in pregnancy and STI prevention have been met with concerns about risk compensation. For example, some worried (and some still worry) that taking birth control pills will lead to promiscuity and sexual risk-taking behavior. Similar concerns were raised about needle exchange programs and the HPV vaccine (Castro et al., 2019). Perhaps not surprisingly, PrEP has engendered the same response, making some worry that it will give users a false sense of security in sexual encounters and encourage risk-taking behavior. Research findings regarding risk compensation among PrEP users are inconsistent, with some studies noting increases in condomless sex and STI diagnoses among PrEP users and others reporting that PrEP use is associated with a greater likelihood of using condoms (Hojilla et al., 2016). Researchers have argued that an understanding of the social dynamics of PrEP implementation and use is needed to contextualize and potentially reconcile these discrepant findings (e.g., Castro et al., 2019). Although few communication scholars have as yet answered this call, a handful of studies point to communication variables that might serve as moderators. For example, Ji (2020) found an association between PrEP-related information-seeking behaviors and risk compensation intentions, such that those whose PrEP information came from social media were most likely to report that they intended to "acquire more sexual partners" once on PrEP (p. 7). Huang et al. (2019) examined the roles of uncertainty management and problematic integration in the sexual decision-making practices of MSM who had used PrEP. They found that uncertainty about the effects of switching from a daily PrEP regimen to an on-demand one influenced participants' sexual decision-making and sexual communication with potential partners. Given PrEP's growing popularity and acceptability among MSM and transgender individuals (Finlayson et al., 2019; Restar et al., 2018), continued study of its potential link to queer individuals' sexual risk-taking and risk reduction practices, including safer sexual communication, is warranted.

CONSIDERATIONS FOR FUTURE RESEARCH

This article points to some gaps in our knowledge about queer safer sexual communication and suggests some avenues for future research. Any undertaking of this sort must also contend with some broader issues facing researchers interested in queer health and/or sex. First, there is a tendency to treat queer individuals as a monolith, as evidenced by repeated references to the "queer community" or "LGBT community" in research papers. Researchers do not refer to the "heterosexual community" because it makes no sense to lump such a large group of individuals together and dub them a "community." Referring to the LGBT (lesbian, gay, bisexual, and transgender) or queer community is equally problematic and fails to recognize the diversity and complexity of queer identities and experiences. Those who lump lesbian, gay, bisexual, and transgender individuals into a single group or community also risk conflating gender and sexual identity. Furthermore, despite being important subjects in their own right, gender and sexual identity should not be treated like proxies for sexual behavior. Knowing if an individual identifies as gay or part of the "LGBT community" tells us little about that person's sexual behavior, which should be the central concern of those involved in sexual risk reduction efforts.

These efforts would also benefit from a more sex-positive approach. Those who study and write about sex tend to justify its study by problematizing it. As a result, the focus tends to be on reducing the risks associated with sexual activity instead of promoting sexual health. Reframing and refocusing efforts on sexual health promotion should produce changes in the kinds of questions asked about safer sexual behavior and communication. For example, how individuals construct healthy sexual relationships or how people pursue sexual health goals in conversation could be considered. Rather than continuing to focus on the risks of sexual activity, there must be a pivot toward sexual health promotion.

Various organizations, including WHO and the United Nations, set lofty HIV prevention goals to be met by 2020; however, COVID-19 derailed those efforts. Countries have set a new goal of fully eradicating HIV by 2030, but achieving this goal will require a renewed commitment to biomedical and behavioral research and interventions. Communication scholars can contribute to these efforts by continuing to study safer sex communication, critically evaluating its conceptual and operational definitions, and considering the impact of demographic variables, the communication environment, and PrEP on queer safer sex communication. Along the way, communication researchers can shift the tone of the safer sex literature to a more sex-positive one focused on sexual health promotion as opposed to disease prevention.

FURTHER READING

Noar, S., Carlyle, K., & Cole, C. (2006). Why communication is crucial: Meta-analysis of the relationship between safer sexual communication and condom use. *Journal of Health Communication, 11*, 365–390. https://doi.org/10.1080/10810730600671862

REFERENCES

Afifi, W. A., & Weiner, J. L. (2004). Toward a theory of motivated information management. *Communication Theory, 14*, 167–190. https://doi.org/10.1111/j.1468-2885.2004.tb00310.x

Albarracín, D., Gillette, J. C., Earl, A. N., Glasman, L. R., Durantini, M. R., & Ho, M. (2005). A test of major assumptions about behavior change: A comprehensive look at the effects of passive and active HIV-prevention interventions since the beginning of the epidemic. *Psychological Bulletin, 131*, 856–897. https://doi.org/10.1037/0033-2909.131.6.856

Alexander, K., Coleman, C., Deatrick, J., & Jemmott, L. (2011). Moving beyond safe sex to women-controlled safe sex: A concept analysis. *Journal of Advanced Nursing, 68*, 1858–1869. https://doi.org/10.1111/j.1365-2648.2011.05881.x

Aliabadi, N., Carballo-Diéguez, A., Bakken, S., Rojas, M., Brown, W., Carry, M., Mosley, J. P., Gelaude, D., & Schnall, R. (2015). Using the information-motivation-behavioral skills model to guide the development of an HIV prevention smartphone application for high-risk MSM. *AIDS Education and Prevention, 27*, 522–537. https://doi.org/10.1521/aeap.2015.27.6.522

Amaro, H. (1995). Love, sex, and power: Considering women's realities in HIV prevention. *American Psychologist, 50*, 437–447. https://doi.org/10.1037/0003-066x.50.6.437

Angrist, S. S. (1966). Communication about birth control: An exploratory study of freshman girls' information and attitudes. *Journal of Marriage and the Family, 28*, 284–286. https://doi.org/10.2307/349876

Becasen, J., Denard, C., Mullins, M., Higa, D., & Sipe, T. (2019). Estimating the prevalence of HIV and sexual behaviors among the US transgender population: A systematic review and meta-analysis, 2006–2017. *American Journal of Public Health, 109*, e1–e8. https://doi.org/10.2105/AJPH.2018.304727

Beymer, M., Weiss, R., Bolan, R., Rudy, E., Bourque, L., Rodriguez, J., & Morisky, D. (2014). Sex on demand: Geosocial networking phone apps and risk of sexually transmitted infections among a cross-sectional sample of men who have sex with men in Los Angeles County. *Sexually Transmitted Infections, 90*, 567–572. https://doi.org/10.1136/sextrans-2013-051494

Binson, D., Pollack, L., Blair, J., & Woods, W. (2010). HIV transmission risk at a gay bathhouse. *Journal of Sex Research, 47*, 580–588. https://doi.org/10.1080/00224490903216755

Blumenthal, J., & Haubrich, R. (2014). Will risk compensation accompany pre-exposure prophylaxis for HIV? *Virtual Mentor, 16*, 909–915. https://doi.org/10.1001/virtualmentor.2014.16.11.stas1-1411

Browne, J., & Minichiello, V. (1994). The condom: Why more people don't put it on. *Sociology of Health & Illness, 16*, 229–251. https://doi.org/10.1111/1467-9566.ep11347391

Buysse, A., & Ickes, W. (1999). Communication patterns in laboratory discussions of safer sex between dating versus nondating partners. *Journal of Sex Research, 36*, 121–134. https://doi.org/10.1080/00224499909551977

Bybee, K. (2016). Potter Stewart meets the press. In H. Knowles & S. Lichtman (Eds.), *Judging free speech* (pp. 147–168). Palgrave Macmillan.

Calabrese, S. K., & Underhill, K. (2015). How stigma surrounding the use of HIV preexposure prophylaxis undermines prevention and pleasure: A call to destigmatize "Truvada whores." *American Journal of Public Health, 105*, 1960–1964. https://doi.org/10.2105/AJPH.2015.302816

Carballo-Diéguez, A., Miner, M., Dolezal, C., Rosser, B., & Jacoby, S. (2006). Sexual negotiation, HIV-status disclosure, and sexual risk behavior among Latino men who use the Internet to seek sex with other men. *Archives of Sexual Behavior, 35*, 473–481. https://doi.org/10.1007/s10508-006-9078-7

Castro, D., Delabre, R., & Molina, J. (2019). Give PrEP a chance: Moving on from the "risk compensation" concept. *Journal of the International AIDS Society, 22*, e25351. https://doi.org/10.1002/jia2.25351

CDC (Centers for Disease Control and Prevention). (2016). Lifetime risk of HIV diagnosis. Press release, February 23. https://www.cdc.gov/nchhstp/newsroom/2016/croi-press-release-risk.html

CDC (Centers for Disease Control and Prevention). (2019a). COVID-19 fact sheet. https://www.cdc.gov/coronavirus/2019-ncov/your-health/need-to-know.html

CDC (Centers for Disease Control and Prevention). (2019b). *Condoms*. https://www.cdc.gov/hiv/risk/condoms.html

CDC (Centers for Disease Control and Prevention). (2019c). HIV and older Americans [Fact sheet]. https://www.cdc.gov/hiv/group/age/olderamericans/index.html

CDC (Centers for Disease Control and Prevention). (2020). *HIV surveillance report*.

Chen, S., Weide, D., & McFarland, W. (2003). Are the recent increases in sexual risk behavior among older or younger men who have sex with men? Answer: Both. *AIDS, 17*, 942–943. https://doi.org/10.1097/00002030-200304110-00031

Cialdini, R. B. (1984). *Influence: How and why people agree to things*. William Morrow and Company, Inc.

Ciccarone, D., Kanouse, D., Collins, R., Miu, A., Chen, J., Morton, S., & Stall, R. (2003). Sex without disclosure of positive HIV serostatus in a US probability sample of persons receiving medical care for HIV infection. *American Journal of Public Health, 93,* 949–954. https://doi.org/10.2105/ajph.93.6.949

Cook, S., Valera, P., Wilson, P., & Adolescent Trials Network for HIV/AIDS Interventions. (2015). HIV status disclosure, depressive symptoms, and sexual risk behavior among HIV-positive young men who have sex with men. *Journal of Behavioral Medicine, 38,* 507–517. https://doi.org/10.1007/s10865-015-9624-7

Cook-Daniels, L., & Munson, M. (2010). Sexual violence, elder abuse, and sexuality of transgender adults, age 50+: Results of three surveys. *Journal of GLBT Family Studies, 6,* 142–177. https://doi.org/10.1080/15504281003705238

Crepaz, N., & Marks, G. (2003). Serostatus disclosure, sexual communication and safer sex in HIV-positive men. *AIDS Care, 15,* 379–387. https://doi.org/10.1080/0954012031000105432

Crosby, R. A., Graham, C. A., Yarber, W. L., Sanders, S. A., Milhausen, R. R., & Mena, L. (2016). Measures of attitudes toward and communication about condom use: Their relationships with sexual risk behavior among young Black men who have sex with men. *Sexually Transmitted Diseases, 43,* 94–98. https://doi.org/10.1097/OLQ.0000000000000392

Crosby, R. A., Skakoon-Sparling, S., Milhausen, R., Sanders, S., Graham, C., & Yarber, W. (2018). The protective value of discussing condom use: A study of young Black men attending STI clinics in the southern United States. *Health Education & Behavior, 45,* 706–713. https://doi.org/10.1177/1090198118775496

De Bro, S. C., Campbell, S. M., & Peplau, L. A. (1994). Influencing a partner to use a condom: A college student perspective. *Psychology of Women Quarterly, 18,* 165–182. https://doi.org/10.1111/j.1471-6402.1994.tb00449.x

De Rosa, C., & Marks, G. (1998). Preventive counseling of HIV-positive men and self-disclosure of serostatus to sex partners: New opportunities for prevention. *Health Psychology, 173,* 224–231. https://doi.org/10.1037/0278-6133.17.3.224

DeVost, M. A., Beymer, M. R., Weiss, R. E., Shover, C. L., & Bolan, R. K. (2018). App-based sexual partner seeking and sexually transmitted infection outcomes: A cross-sectional study of HIV-negative men who have sex with men attending a sexually transmitted infection clinic in Los Angeles, California. *Sexually Transmitted Diseases, 45,* 394–399. https://doi.org/10.1097/OLQ.0000000000000770

Dillard, J. (1990). A goal-driven model of interpersonal influence. In J. Dillard (Ed.), *Seeking compliance: The production of interpersonal influence messages* (pp. 41–56). Gorsuch.

Dizon, D., & Krychman, M. (2010). *Questions and answers about HPV.* Jones & Bartlett.

Eaton, L., Kalichman, S., O'Connell, D., & Karchner, W. (2009). A strategy for selecting sexual partners believed to pose little/no risks for HIV: Serosorting and its implications for HIV transmission. *AIDS Care, 21,* 1279–1288. https://doi.org/10.1080/09540120902803208

Edgar, T. (1992). A compliance-based approach to the study of condom use. In T. Edgar, M. A. Fitzpatrick, & V. Freimuth (Eds.), *AIDS: A communication perspective* (pp. 47–68). Lawrence Erlbaum.

Edgar, T., Freimuth, V., Hammond, S., McDonald, D., & Fink, E. (1992). Strategic sexual communication: Condom use resistance and response. *Health Communication, 4,* 83–104. https://doi.org/10.1207/s15327027hc0402_1

El-Bassel, N., Gilbert, L., Wu, E., Go, H., & Hill, J. (2005). Relationship between drug abuse and intimate partner violence: A longitudinal study among women receiving methadone. *American Journal of Public Health, 95,* 465–470. https://doi.org/10.2105/AJPH.2003.023200

Elwood, W., Greene, K., & Carter, K. (2003). Gentlemen don't speak: Communication norms and condom use in bathhouses. *Journal of Applied Communication Research, 31,* 277–297.

Emmers-Sommer, T., & Allen, M. (2004). *Safer sex in personal relationships: The role of sexual scripts in HIV infection and prevention.* Lawrence Erlbaum.

Fee, E., & Brown, T. M. (2006). Michael S. Gottlieb and the identification of AIDS. *American Journal of Public Health, 96*, 982–983. https://doi.org/10.2105/AJPH.2006.088435

Finlayson, T., Cha, S., Xia, M., Trujillo, L., Denson, D., Prejean, J., Kanny, D., Wejnert, C., & National HIV Behavioral Surveillance Study Group. (2019). Changes in HIV preexposure prophylaxis awareness and use among men who have sex with men: 20 urban areas, 2014 and 2017. *Morbidity and Mortality Weekly Report, 68*, 597–603. https://doi.org/10.15585/mmwr.mm6827a1

Frye, V., Ompad, D., Chan, C., Koblin, B., Galea, S., & Vlahov, D. (2011). Intimate partner violence perpetration and condom use-related factors: Associations with heterosexual men's consistent condom use. *AIDS and Behavior, 15*, 153–162. https://doi.org/10.1007/s10461-009-9659-2

Garthe, R. C., Hidalgo, M. A., Hereth, J., Garofalo, R., Reisner, S. L., Mimiaga, M. J., & Kuhns, L. (2018). Prevalence and risk correlates of intimate partner violence among a multisite cohort of young transgender women. *LGBT Health, 5*, 333–340. https://doi.org/10.1089/lgbt.2018.0034

Goedel, W., & Duncan, D. (2016). Contextual factors in geosocial-networking smartphone application use and engagement in condomless anal intercourse among gay, bisexual, and other men who have sex with men who use Grindr. *Sexual Health, 13*, 549–554. https://doi.org/10.1071/SH16008

Golub, S. (2018). PrEP stigma: Implicit and explicit drivers of disparity. *Current HIV/AIDS Reports, 15*, 190–197. https://doi.org/10.1007/s11904-018-0385-0

Gottlieb, M., Schanker, H., Fan, P., Saxon, A., Weisman, J., & Pozalski, I. (1981). Pneumocystis pneumonia: Los Angeles. *Morbidity and Mortality Weekly Report, 30*, 1–3.

Grov, C., Rendina, H., John, S., & Parsons, J. (2019). Determining the roles that club drugs, marijuana, and heavy drinking play in PrEP medication adherence among gay and bisexual men: Implications for treatment and research. *AIDS & Behavior, 23*, 1277–1286. https://doi.org/10.1007/s10461-018-2309-9

Grov, C., Rendina, H., Moody, R., Ventuneac, A., & Parsons, J. (2015). HIV serosorting, status disclosure, and strategic positioning among highly sexually active gay and bisexual men. *AIDS Patient Care & STDS, 29*, 559–568. https://doi.org/10.1089/apc.2015.0126

Grov, C., Whitfield, T., Rendina, H., Ventuneac, A., & Parsons, J. T. (2015). Willingness to take PrEP and potential for risk compensation among highly sexually active gay and bisexual men. *AIDS and Behavior, 19*, 2234–2244. https://doi.org/10.1007/s10461-015-1030-1

Gubert, F., Vieira, N., Francenely, C., Pinheiro, P., Oriá, M., Ferreira, A., & Arcanjo, G. (2013). Translation and validation of the partner communication scale: Brazilian version with female teenagers. *Revista da Escola de Enfermagem da USP, 47*, 822–829. https://doi.org/10.1590/S0080-623420130000400008

Haig, T. (2006). Bareback sex: Masculinity, silence, and the dilemmas of gay health. *Canadian Journal of Communication, 31*, 859–877. https://doi.org/10.22230/cjc.2006v31n4a1699

Hampton, M., Halkitis, P., Storholm, E., Kupprat, S., Siconolfi, D., Jones, D., Steen, J. T., Gillen, S., & McCree, D. (2013). Sexual risk taking in relation to sexual identification, age, and education in a diverse sample of African American men who have sex with men (MSM) in New York City. *AIDS and Behavior, 17*, 931–938. https://doi.org/10.1007/s10461-012-0139-8

Heintz, A., & Melendez, R. (2006). Intimate partner violence and HIV/STD risk among lesbian, gay, bisexual, and transgender individuals. *Journal of Interpersonal Violence, 21*, 193–208. https://doi.org/10.1177/0886260505282104

Hojilla, J., Koester, K., Cohen, S., Buchbinder, S., Ladzekpo, D., Matheson, T., & Liu, A. (2016). Sexual behavior, risk compensation, and HIV prevention strategies among participants in the San Francisco PrEP Demonstration Project: A qualitative analysis of counseling notes. *AIDS and Behavior, 20*, 1461–1469. https://doi.org/10.1007/s10461-015-1055-5

Holland, K., & French, S. (2012). Condom negotiation strategy use and effectiveness among college students. *Journal of Sex Research, 49*, 443–453. https://doi.org/10.1080/00224499.2011.568128

Holmes, D., O'Byrne, P., & Murray, S. (2010). Faceless sex: Glory holes and sexual assemblages. *Nursing Philosophy, 11,* 250–259. https://doi.org/10.1111/j.1466-769X.2010.00452.x

Huang, P., Wu, H., Strong, C., Jan, F., Mao, L., Ko, N., Li, C.-W., Cheng, C.-Y., & Ku, S. (2019). Unspeakable PrEP: A qualitative study of sexual communication, problematic integration, and uncertainty management among men who have sex with men in Taiwan. *Journal of Applied Communication Research, 47,* 611–627. https://doi.org/10.1080/00909882.2019.1693608

Huebner, D., Binson, D., Dilworth, S., Neilands, T., Grinstead, O., & Woods, W. (2010). Rapid vs. standard HIV testing in bathhouses: What is gained and lost? *AIDS and Behavior, 14,* 688–696. https://doi.org/10.1007/s10461-008-9442-9

Humphreys, L. (1970). *Tearoom trade: Impersonal sex in public places.* Aldine de Gruyter.

Jacobs, R., Fernandez, M., Ownby, R., Bowen, G., Hardigan, P., & Kane, M. (2010). Factors associated with risk for unprotected receptive and insertive anal intercourse in men aged 40 and older who have sex with men. *AIDS Care, 22,* 1204–1211. https://doi.org/10.1080/09540121003615137

Jacobs, R., Kane, M., & Ownby, R. (2013). Condom use, disclosure, and risk for unprotected sex in HIV-negative midlife and older men who have sex with men. *American Journal of Men's Health, 7,* 186–197. https://doi.org/10.1177/1557988312463417

Jacobs, R., Kane, M., & Sklar, E. (2016). Sexual communication and seroadaptation practices in HIV-negative midlife and older men who have sex with men. *Journal of Social Service Research, 43,* 1–12. https://doi.org/10.1080/01488376.2016.1248268

Jenkins Hall, W., Sun, C., Tanner, A., Mann, L., Stowers, J., & Rhodes, S. (2017). HIV prevention opportunities with GPS-based social and sexual networking applications for men who have sex with men. *AIDS Education and Prevention, 29,* 38–48. https://doi.org/10.1521/aeap.2017.29.1.38

Ji, Y. (2020). A study of seeking information about preexposure prophylaxis (PrEP) and risk compensation intention among men who have sex with men. *Communication Studies, 71*(5), 783–799. https://doi.org/10.1080/10510974.2020.1778053

Kaiser Family Foundation. (2019). The HIV/AIDS epidemic in the United States: The basics, March 25. https://www.kff.org/hivaids/fact-sheet/the-hivaids-epidemic-in-the-united-states-the-basics/

Kalichman, S. (2014). *Preventing AIDS: A sourcebook for behavioral interventions.* Taylor & Francis.

Khan, F., Mukhtar, S., Dickinson, I., & Sriprasad, S. (2013). The story of the condom. *Indian Journal of Urology, 29,* 12–15.

Kintu, A., Hankinson, S., Balasubramanian, R., Ertel, K., Tumwesigye, E., Bangsberg, D., Haberer, J., & Partners Ancillary Adherence Study Team. (2015). Sexual relationships outside primary partnerships and abstinence are associated with lower adherence and adherence gaps: Data from the partners PrEP ancillary adherence study. *Journal of Acquired Immune Deficiency Syndromes, 69,* 36–43. https://doi.org/10.1097/QAI.0000000000000538

Kippax, S., Crawford, J., Davis, M., Rodden, P., & Dowsett, G. (1993). Sustaining safe sex: A longitudinal study of a sample of homosexual men. *AIDS, 7,* 257–263. https://doi.org/10.1097/00002030-199302000-00015

Kosenko, K. (2010). Meanings and dilemmas of sexual safety and communication for transgender individuals. *Health Communication, 25,* 131–141. https://doi.org/10.1080/10410230903544928

Kosenko, K. (2011a). Contextual influences on sexual risk-taking in the transgender community. *Journal of Sex Research, 48,* 285–296. https://doi.org/10.1080/00224491003721686

Kosenko, K. (2011b). The safer sex communication of transgender adults: Processes and problems. *Journal of Communication, 61,* 476–495. https://doi.org/10.1111/j.1460-2466.2011.01556.x

Lehmiller, J., & Ioerger, M. (2014). Social networking smartphone applications and sexual health outcomes among men who have sex with men. *PLoS One, 9,* e86603. https://doi.org/10.1371/journal.pone.0086603

Li, Y., & Samp, J. (2019). Sexual relationship power, safer sexual communication, and condom use: A comparison of heterosexual young men and women. *Western Journal of Communication, 83*, 58–74. https://doi.org/10.1080/10570314.2017.1398835

Linn, L., Spiegel, J., & Mathews, W. (1989). Recent sexual behaviors among homosexual men seeking primary care. *Archives of Internal Medicine, 149*, 2685–2690. https://doi.org/10.1001/archinte.1989.00390120049010

Lo, S. C., Reisen, C. A., Poppen, P. J., Bianchi, F. T., & Zea, M. C. (2011). Cultural beliefs, partner characteristics, communication, and sexual risk among Latino MSM. *AIDS and Behavior, 15*, 613–620. https://doi.org/10.1007/s10461-010-9760-6

Meisenbach, R. J. (2010). Stigma management communication: A theory and agenda for applied research on how individuals manage moments of stigmatized identity. *Journal of Applied Communication Research, 38*, 268–292. https://doi.org/10.1080/00909882.2010.490841

Meunier, É. (2013). No attitude, no standing around: The organization of social and sexual interaction at a gay male private sex party in New York City. *Archives of Sexual Behavior, 43*, 685–695. https://doi.org/10.1007/s10508-013-0182-1

Milhausen, R., Sales, J., Wingood, G., Diclemente, R., Salazar, L., & Crosby, R. (2007). Validation of a partner sexual communication scale for use in HIV/AIDS prevention interventions. *Journal of HIV/AIDS Prevention in Children & Youth, 8*, 11–33. https://doi.org/10.1300/J499v08n01_02

Millett, G., Flores, S., Peterson, J., & Bakeman, R. (2007). Explaining disparities in HIV infection among Black and White men who have sex with men: A meta-analysis of HIV risk behaviors. *AIDS, 21*, 2083–2091. https://doi.org/10.1097/QAD.0b013e3282e9a64b

Mimiaga, M., Reisner, S., Bland, S., Driscoll, M., Cranston, K., Isenberg, D., VanDerwarker, R., & Mayer, K. (2011). Sex parties among urban MSM: An emerging culture and HIV risk environment. *AIDS and Behavior, 15*, 305–318. https://doi.org/10.1007/s10461-010-9809-6

Molitor, F., Facer, M., & Ruiz, J. (1999). Safer sex communication and unsafe sexual behavior among young men who have sex with men in California. *Archives of Sexual Behavior, 28*, 335–343. https://doi.org/10.1023/A:1018748729070

Nemoto, T., Operario, D., Keatley, J., & Villegas, D. (2004). Social context of HIV risk behaviours among male-to-female transgenders of colour. *AIDS Care, 16*, 724–735. https://doi.org/10.1080/09540120413331269567

Noar, S. (2007). An interventionist's guide to AIDS behavioral theories. *AIDS Care, 19*, 392–402. https://doi.org/10.1080/09540120600708469

Noar, S., Cole, C., & Carlyle, K. (2006). Condom use measurement in 56 studies of sexual risk behavior: Review and recommendations. *Archives of Sexual Behavior, 35*, 327–345. https://doi.org/10.1007/s10508-006-9028-4

Noar, S., & Edgar, T. (2008). The role of partner communication in safer sexual behavior: A theoretical and empirical review. In T. Edgar, S. M. Noar, & V. Freimuth (Eds.), *Communication perspectives on HIV/AIDS for the 21st century* (pp. 3–28). Lawrence Erlbaum.

Noar, S., Morokoff, P., & Harlow, L. (2002). Condom negotiation in heterosexually active men and women: Development and validation of a condom influence strategy questionnaire. *Psychology and Health, 17*, 711–735. https://doi.org/10.1080/0887044021000030580

O'Connell, A., Reed, S., & Serovich, J. (2015). The efficacy of serostatus disclosure for HIV transmission risk reduction. *AIDS and Behavior, 19*, 283–290. https://doi.org/10.1007/s10461-014-0848-2

Parsons, J., Antebi-Gruszka, N., Millar, B., Cain, D., & Gurung, S. (2018). Syndemic conditions, HIV transmission risk behavior, and transactional sex among transgender women. *AIDS and Behavior, 22*, 2056–2067. https://doi.org/10.1007/s10461-018-2100-y

Peasant, C., Parra, G., & Okwumabua, T. (2015). Condom negotiation: Findings and future directions. *Journal of Sex Research, 52*, 470–483. https://doi.org/10.1080/00224499.2013.868861

Peasant, C., Sullivan, T., Ritchwood, T., Parra, G., Weiss, N., Meyer, J., & Murphy, J. (2018). Words can hurt: The effects of physical and psychological partner violence on condom negotiation and condom use among young women. *Women & Health, 58*, 483–497. https://doi.org/10.1080/03630242.2017.1316345

Peterson, Z., & Muehlenhard, C. (2007). What is sex and why does it matter? A motivational approach to exploring individuals' definitions of sex. *Journal of Sex Research, 44*, 256–268. https://doi.org/10.1080/00224490701443932

Pollock, J., & Halkitis, P. (2009). Environmental factors in relation to unprotected sexual behavior among gay, bisexual, and other MSM. *AIDS Education and Prevention, 21*, 340–355. https://doi.org/10.1521/aeap.2009.21.4.340

Prior, J. (2008). Planning for sex in the city: Urban governance, planning, and the placement of sex industry premises in inner Sydney. *Australian Geographer, 39*, 339–352. https://doi.org/10.1080/00049180802270531

Ramirez-Valles, J., Garcia, D., Campbell, R. T., Diaz, R. M., & Heckathorn, D. D. (2008). HIV infection, sexual risk behavior, and substance use among Latino gay and bisexual men and transgender persons. *American Journal of Public Health, 98*, 1036–1042. https://doi.org/10.2105/AJPH.2006.102624

Restar, A., Kuhns, L., Reisner, S. L., Ogunbajo, A., Garofalo, R., & Mimiage, M. (2018). Acceptability of antiretroviral pre-exposure prophylaxis from a cohort of sexually experienced young transgender women in two US cities. *AIDS and Behavior, 22*, 3649–3657. https://doi.org/10.1007/s10461-018-2127-0

Reynolds-Tylus, T., Rinaldi-Miles, A., & Quick, B. (2015). Examining the principles of influence on safer sex communication during casual and committed sexual encounters. *Journal of Health Communication, 20*, 1214–1223. https://doi.org/10.1080/10810730.2015.1018631

Ross, M., Rosser, B., Coleman, E., & Mazin, R. (2006). Misrepresentation on the Internet and in real life about sex and HIV: A study of Latino men who have sex with men. *Culture, Health & Sexuality, 8*, 133–144. https://doi.org/10.1080/13691050500485604

Rothman, E., Exner, D., & Baughman, A. (2011). The prevalence of sexual assault against people who identify as gay, lesbian, or bisexual in the United States: A systematic review. *Trauma, Violence & Abuse, 12*, 55–66. https://doi.org/10.1177/1524838010390707

Schwartz, J., & Grimm, J. (2019). Stigma communication surrounding PrEP: The experiences of a sample of men who have sex with men. *Health Communication, 34*, 84–90. https://doi.org/10.1080/10410236.2017.1384430

Sevelius, J. (2009). "There's no pamphlet for the kind of sex I have": HIV-related risk factors and protective behaviors among transgender men who have sex with nontransgender men. *Journal of the Association of Nurses in AIDS Care, 20*, 398–410. https://doi.org/10.1016/j.jana.2009.06.001

Sewell, K., McGarrity, L., & Strassberg, D. (2017). Sexual behavior, definitions of sex, and the role of self-partner context among lesbian, gay, and bisexual adults. *Journal of Sex Research, 54*, 825–831. https://doi.org/10.1080/00224499.2016.1249331

Shacham, E., Small, E., Onen, N., Stamm, K., & Overton, E. (2012). Serostatus disclosure among adults with HIV in the era of HIV therapy. *AIDS Patient Care & STDS, 26*, 29–35. https://doi.org/10.1089/apc.2011.0183

Sheeran, P., Abraham, C., & Orbell, S. (1999). Psychosocial correlates of heterosexual condom use: A meta-analysis. *Psychological Bulletin, 125*, 90–132. https://doi.org/10.1037/0033-2909.125.1.90

Sidebottom, D., Ekström, A. M., & Strömdahl, S. (2018). A systematic review of adherence to oral pre-exposure prophylaxis for HIV: How can we improve uptake and adherence? *BMC Infectious Diseases, 18*, 581–595. https://doi.org/10.1186/s12879-018-3463-4

Siembida, E. J., Eaton, L. A., Maksut, J. L., Driffin, D. D., & Baldwin, R. (2016). A comparison of HIV-related risk factors between Black transgender women and Black men who have sex with men. *Transgender Health, 1*, 172–180. https://doi.org/10.1089/trgh.2016.0003

Simoni, J., & Pantalone, D. (2004). Secrets and safety in the age of AIDS: Does HIV disclosure lead to safer sex? *Topics in HIV Medicine, 12*, 109–118.

Singer, M. (1996). A dose of drugs, a touch of violence, a case of AIDS: Conceptualizing the SAVA syndemic. *Free Inquiry in Creative Sociology, 24*, 99–110.

Smith, R. A. (2007). Language of the lost: An explication of stigma communication. *Communication Theory, 17*, 462–485. https://doi.org/10.1111/j.1468-2885.2007.00307.x

Stall, R., Mills, T., Williamson, J., Hart, T., Greenwood, G., Paul, J., Pollack, L., Binson, D., Osmond, D., & Catania, J. (2003). Association of co-occurring psychosocial health problems and increased vulnerability to HIV/AIDS among urban men who have sex with men. *American Journal of Public Health, 93*, 939–942. https://doi.org/10.2105/ajph.93.6.939

Stein, M., Freedberg, K., Sullivan, L., Savetsky, J., Levenson, S., Hingson, R., & Samet, J. (1998). Sexual ethics: Disclosure of HIV-positive status to partners. *Archives of Internal Medicine, 158*, 253–257. https://doi.org/10.1001/archinte.158.3.253

Stephenson, R., Freeland, R., & Finneran, C. (2016). Intimate partner violence and condom negotiation efficacy among gay and bisexual men in Atlanta. *Sexual Health, 13*, 366–372. https://doi.org/10.1071/SH15212

Stotzer, R. L. (2009). Violence against transgender people: A review of United States data. *Aggression and Violent Behavior, 14*, 170–179. https://doi.org/10.1016/j.avb.2009.01.006

Swan, H., & O'Connell, D. (2012). The impact of intimate partner violence on women's condom negotiation efficacy. *Journal of Interpersonal Violence, 27*, 775–792. https://doi.org/10.1177/0886260511423240

Tjaden, P., Thoennes, N., & Allison, C. (1999). Comparing violence over the life span in samples of same-sex and opposite-sex cohabitants. *Violence and Victims, 14*, 413–425. https://doi.org/10.1891/0886-6708.14.4.413

Vaccher, S., Kaldor, J., Callander, D., Zablotska, I., & Haire, B. (2018). Qualitative insights into adherence to HIV pre-exposure prophylaxis (PrEP) among Australian gay and bisexual men. *AIDS Patient Care and STDs, 32*, 519–528. https://doi.org/10.1089/apc.2018.0106

Van den Boom, W., Konings, R., Davidovich, U., Sandfort, T., Prins, M., & Stolte, I. G. (2014). Is serosorting effective in reducing the risk of HIV infection among men who have sex with men with casual sex partners? *Journal of Acquired Immune Deficiency Syndromes, 65*, 375–379. https://doi.org/10.1097/QAI.0000000000000051

Van de Ven, P., Kippax, S., Crawford, J., Rawstorne, P., Prestage, G., Grulich, A., & Murphy, D. (2002). In a minority of gay men, sexual risk practice indicates strategic positioning for perceived risk reduction rather than unbridled sex. *AIDS Care, 14*, 471–480. https://doi.org/10.1080/09540120208629666

West, C. (2002). Lesbian intimate partner violence. *Journal of Lesbian Studies, 6*, 121–127. https://doi.org/10.1300/J155v06n01_11

Widman, L., Noar, S. M., Choukas-Bradley, S., & Francis, D. B. (2014). Adolescent sexual health communication and condom use: A meta-analysis. *Health Psychology, 33*, 1113–1124. https://doi.org/10.1037/hea0000112

Wilde, G. (1998). Risk homeostasis theory: An overview. *Injury Prevention, 4*, 89–91. https://doi.org/10.1136/ip.4.2.89

Woods, W. J., Euren, J., Pollack, L. M., & Binson, D. (2010). HIV prevention in gay bathhouses and sex clubs across the United States. *Journal of Acquired Immune Deficiency Syndromes, 55*, s88–s90. https://doi.org/10.1097/QAI.0b013e3181fbca1b

Xiao, Z., Li, X., Lin, D., Jiang, S., Liu, Y., & Li, S. (2013). Sexual communication, safer sex self-efficacy, and condom use among young Chinese migrants in Beijing, China. *AIDS Education and Prevention, 25*, 480–494. https://doi.org/10.1521/aeap.2013.25.6.480

NOTES

1. Noting that not all men who engage in sex acts with other men identify as gay, researchers started eschewing the term *gay men* in favor of MSM. Although they were trying to signal that they were more concerned with sexual behavior than sexual identity, researchers who latched on to the term did so without fully considering gender identity and the implications of the word *men*. To be more inclusive of all individuals with male body parts that they use during sexual encounters, I prefer terms such as male-bodied, but, throughout this article, I use MSM when referencing studies that used that terminology.
2. WSW presents similar problems as MSM. Although I prefer other terms, I use this terminology when referencing studies that have employed it.

Kami Kosenko

SEXUAL ORIENTATION AND GENDER IDENTITY DISCLOSURE IN THE MEDICAL CONTEXT

INTRODUCTION

For individuals who identify under the LGBTQ+ umbrella, disclosing their sexual orientation and/or gender identity can be a complex and, at times, risky conversation. However, in the medical context this conversation frequently becomes a central part of the communication between patient and provider. In many instances, this disclosure is necessary for a patient to receive appropriate and comprehensive care. In other instances, this disclosure becomes a brick in the foundation of a strong patient–provider relationship. Unfortunately, this conversation can also become a barrier that prevents patients from receiving or even accessing necessary medical care. "LGBTQ+ Background Information" presents an overview of disclosure, particularly of sexual orientation and gender identity, in the medical context. The discussion is situated in the context of Western cultures, particularly the United States, and discusses health issues that many LGBTQ+ individuals experience and the importance that disclosing this information can have to receiving quality care. "Patient–Provider Disclosure" also describes the experiences of LGBTQ+ individuals when managing this disclosure, as well as how providers' responses affect LGBTQ+ patients. Finally, the article reviews "Current Recommendations, Guidelines, and Programs" being implemented across the United States to improve the healthcare experiences of LGBTQ+ individuals and, in "Future Directions," thoughts for moving forward with these efforts, before presenting its "Conclusion."

LGBTQ+ BACKGROUND INFORMATION

The LGBTQ+ acronym is a shortened version of the full sexual orientation and gender identity acronym LGBTQQIPAA, which represents individuals who identify as lesbian, gay, bisexual, transgender, queer, questioning, intersex, pansexual, asexual, and ally. The majority of research conducted on communication regarding sexual orientation and gender identity uses either LGB or LGBTQ+ to represent study samples and reference groups.

The terms "lesbian" and "gay" refer to women and men who primarily engage in sexual and romantic relationships with individuals of the same gender. The term "bisexual" refers to individuals who engage in sexual and romantic relationships with individuals of both the same and other genders (UC Davis Health, n.d.). The term "Q+" refers to individuals who identify as queer and/or any other identity represented by the full acronym.

The term "transgender" refers to any individual whose gender identity and/or gender expression is different from their sex assigned at birth (Bockting et al., 2020; Spack, 2013). Gender identity encompasses an individual's internal sense of their gender, and this gender identity manifests outwardly as gender expression. Anderson (2020, p. 324) defines gender expression as "the ways in which one's gendered understanding of self is embodied and communicated to others." We also use the term "cisgender," which is representative of individuals whose assigned sex at birth is concordant with their gender identity and/or gender expression (Oxford Lexico Dictionary, 2015).

According to reports of a collaborative data collection effort in 2018 between Gallup and the Williams Institute on Sexual Orientation and Gender Identity Law and Public Policy at UCLA (Williams Institute, 2019), approximately 4.5%, or just under 14.9 million, adults in the United States identify as LGBT. In a separate 2016 report published by the Williams Institute, it was estimated that approximately 0.6% of the population, or 1.4 million adults, in the United States identify as transgender (Flores et al., 2016). Despite the fact that the LGBTQ+ population represents a sizeable portion of the United States' population, these individuals continue to be affected negatively as a result of how others view their sexual orientation and/or gender identity.

LGBTQ+ Discrimination. According to results from the Generations Study (Meyer, 2019), in a sample of 1,131 LGB adults, participants reported discrimination based on sexual orientation. Specifically, 60% of participants reported being fired from or denied a job; 48% reported being denied a promotion or having a negative employment evaluation; 15% reported being denied rental or purchase of a home or apartment; and 41% reported being bullied before the age of 18. Similarly, according to results from the 2015 United States Transgender Survey (USTS), in a sample of 27,715 transgender adults, participants reported discrimination based on gender identity. Thirty percent had been fired, denied a promotion, or verbally or physically harassed or assaulted in the workplace; 30% reported having been homeless in their lifetime; 54% reported being verbally harassed in school; and 24% reported being physically attacked in school (James et al., 2016). These experiences of discrimination extend into LGBTQ+ individuals' experiences with healthcare.

Lambda Legal's (2010) national survey, When Health Isn't Caring, exploring discrimination against LGBTQ+ individuals, reported that nearly 56% of LGB respondents indicated experiencing at least one category of healthcare discrimination. Categories of healthcare discrimination include refusal of care, refusal of provider to touch them, provider verbal and/or physical abuse, or being blamed for their own health problems. Additionally, nearly 8% of respondents reported denial of care because of sexual orientation. Similarly, in the 2015 USTS, 23% of respondents reported delaying seeking necessary care because of fear that providers would mistreat them (James et al., 2016). Further, 33% of respondents reported that in the past year they experienced at least one negative healthcare experience including verbal harassment, refusal to treat, or having a provider who was not educated in appropriate practices to care for transgender patients (James et al., 2016). These reports from LGBTQ+ individuals that they are postponing necessary medical care are particularly alarming as it is well documented in research that LGBTQ+ individuals experience significant health disparities as compared to heterosexual and/or cisgender individuals (U.S. Department of Health and Human Services, 2016).

LGBTQ+ Health Issues. LGBQ individuals, as compared to the heterosexual population, present with higher rates of serious health risks, such as increased risk of stroke and heart disease, as well as higher rates of obesity, hypertension, and alcohol and tobacco consumption (Jackson et al., 2016). According to a metanalysis conducted by Lick et al. (2013), LGB individuals also report higher rates of early onset disabilities and asthma, as well as more headaches, chronic illnesses, allergies, and gastrointestinal issues as compared to heterosexual individuals.

Roller et al. (2015) found that transgender individuals have an HIV/AIDS infection rate that is approximately four times higher than the national average among cisgender individuals, as well as a higher rate of infection with other sexually transmitted infections (STIs). These STIs also result in higher rates of related cancer risks associated with both HIV infection and anal intercourse. Quinn et al. (2014) also found that transgender individuals experience higher rates of cancer risk. In addition to increased cancer risks associated with STIs, transgender individuals have increased risks of cancers associated with smoking, substance use, and dietary concerns (Quinn et al., 2014; Roller et al., 2015). Finally, Roller et al. (2015) also reported that transgender individuals experience significantly higher rates of mental health issues, including depression, self-harm, substance abuse, and suicide. Specifically, they found that about 41% of transgender individuals have attempted suicide compared to around 2% of cisgender individuals.

In a meta-analysis of LGBTQ+ health behaviors, King and colleagues (2008) found that in comparison to heterosexual individuals, LGBTQ+ individuals are more likely to suffer from increased anxiety and depression as well as alcohol and drug abuse. Additionally, gay men and bisexual individuals were more susceptible to suicidal ideation and intentional self-harm (King et al., 2008). Gay men also have increased susceptibility to gonorrhea, syphilis, and chlamydia (Makadon, 2006). Although beyond the scope of this article, sexual minority youth present with a higher prevalence of anxiety, depression, unmet health needs, suicide, and victimization, contributing to potentially lifelong health concerns (Williams & Chapman, 2011).

In addition to these health and disease risks, LBGTQ+ individuals are subject to further health issues related to lack of care from being uninsured. In 2019, the Williams Institute conducted an analysis of data from the 2014–2017 Behavioral Risk Factor Surveillance Survey to explore experiences of poverty among LGBTQ+ individuals in the United States. Results showed that 21.6% of LGBTQ+ individuals were living in poverty as compared to 15.7% of the cisgender, heterosexual population (Badgett et al., 2019). In an analysis from the same 2014–2017 Behavioral Risk Factor Surveillance System report, Gonzalez and Henning-Smith (2017) found that 15.7% of LGB adults lacked insurance coverage. The 2015 USTS found that 14% of transgender respondents lacked insurance coverage as compared to 11% of the overall

United States population. Kcomt et al. (2020) found that transgender individuals living in poverty and without health insurance showed greater tendencies to avoid healthcare than those not living in poverty and those with insurance coverage. Thus, it is to be expected that higher rates of uninsured individuals correlate with a greater likelihood of missed checkups, screenings, and exams among the LGBTQ+ population. Given the increased health risks faced by the LGBTQ+ population, this is of particular concern.

A comparison of lesbian and heterosexual women indicated that lesbians are less likely to have had a recent pelvic examination or mammogram and are more likely to incorrectly perceive that they do not need a pap smear (Aaron et al., 2001; Austin & Irwin, 2010; Cochran et al., 2001; King et al., 2008; Lehmann et al., 1998, Makadon, 2006). This perception often is tied to the belief that abstinence from vaginal intercourse precludes one's need for a pap smear. Disclosure of sexual orientation could help providers identify patients who may be unknowingly due for these exams and screenings. Devarajan et al. (2020) reported that for men who have sex with men (MSM) and who are visiting a PrEP (pre-exposure prophylactic) provider, open communication between the provider and themselves allowed for greater comfort discussing sexual behavior and, in turn, more appropriate recommendations from the provider regarding STI testing. As noted above, evidence highlights LBGTQ+ unique health needs particularly related to screening, diagnosis, and treatment for sexually transmitted infections (e.g., Benson & Hergendroeder, 2005). Patient disclosure of orientation may assist providers in targeting specific health needs and concerns while providing platforms to engage in more complete discussions of patient health and well-being.

LGBTQ+ Healthcare and Provider Education. Because the LGBTQ+ population experiences increased health disparities, providers may need to administer care that focuses on detecting, addressing, and reducing these disparities. Some research has been conducted to investigate providers' experience with and preparedness for treating LGBTQ+ patients. Shaver et al. (2019) surveyed 113 rural providers, assessing their experience caring for LGBTQ+ patients and their knowledge about specific needs of LGBTQ+ patients. A majority of these knowledge items focused on health risks and disease screening benefits for LGB individuals. Of the respondents, 96.5% reported having a patient disclose LGBTQ+ status to them, and 98.2% reported feeling comfortable providing care to LGBTQ+ patients. However, when responding to LGBTQ health knowledge items, participant responses varied widely, reflecting inconsistencies in provider knowledge of LGBTQ+ patient needs and care. For example, almost all participants knew that LGBTQ+ young people have a high risk of suicide, but only 6% of participants knew that among individuals under the LGBTQ+ umbrella, bisexual women have the highest rates of teen pregnancy. Additionally, fewer than 50% of participants knew about the existence of PrEP. Not surprisingly, only 54.9% of providers reported having received formal training related to LGBTQ+ care, but 88.5% of all participants stated that such training should be required.

Shetty et al. (2016) found similar results in a study of 108 oncology providers' experience with and comfort treating LGBTQ+ patients. Of these respondents, 94% indicated they are comfortable treating LGBTQ+ patients, and 87% indicated that they believe the LGBTQ+ population has health needs unique from the general population. Again, participant responses also indicated significant gaps in knowledge of LGBTQ+ patient care. On a cumulative knowledge score scale with a range of 0 to 13 correct responses, participants' mean score was 7.7 (SD = 1.9). Many items focused on cancer risks and screening benefits, but the survey also included several items related to mental health and social issues within the LGBTQ+ population. Only 28% of respondents felt they had adequate training, and only 36% of respondents stated that they should have mandatory education related to treating LGBTQ+ patients. Thus, a discrepancy is apparent between provider intent, knowledge, and commitment to education. Not surprisingly, it is difficult for patients to receive quality care when providers report a lack of knowledge and training on how to treat LGBTQ+ patients, and unfortunately, provider motivation to receive education related to this is low.

Barriers to LGBTQ+ Healthcare. There are many concerns for LGBTQ+ patients with respect to the quality of care they are able to receive from providers, and these concerns extend beyond providers' practical knowledge to their preparedness for engaging with patients in inclusive ways. Unfortunately, with the dearth of inclusivity training available to providers contributing to the issue of lower quality care, many LGBTQ+ patients experience major social and psychological barriers to accessing care. As noted above, more than 50% of LGB respondents reported they avoid accessing care because of general bias from people in their communities. Further, in a 2005 survey conducted by Harris Interactive and The National Lesbian Health Organization, researchers found that 74% of lesbians reported experiencing discrimination related to their sexual orientation while visiting a medical provider, and 16% of the respondents reported a delay in seeking care because of fear of discrimination (DeBold, 2007).

In a focus group study with 48 transgender individuals in the Southeast United States, Johnson et al. (2020) identified four major barriers to transgender individuals' ability to access healthcare: (1) patients' fear and mistrust of providers based on prior experiences of stigmatization and discrimination; (2) inconsistencies in treatment availability and access to care because of a limited number of trans-inclusive providers per area and overbooked schedules at trans-inclusive offices; (3) experiences of disrespect and insensitivity, such as misgendering, at medical offices; and (4) intersectional barriers where gender, race, socioeconomic status, and/or geographic location, combined with transgender identity, resulted in low-quality care or diminished access to care.

Meyer et al. (2020) interviewed 27 trans and gender-diverse individuals in the Great Plains region of the United States about their medical encounters. While the researchers did learn of positive experiences where patients reported receiving vocal support, validation of their transgender identity, and compassionate care, a majority of the experiences participants reported on were negative. These experiences included probing, or asking inappropriate questions, broaching irrelevant subjects, and making inappropriate requests to examine genitals; gatekeeping, or providers raising barriers to care, such as additional steps, requirements, or milestones leading to care; overt and covert stigmatization, such as laughing, teasing, or "othering"; and misgendering or deadnaming through the use of incorrect pronouns and/or the patient's previous name.

These social and psychological barriers to care that LGBTQ+ patients experience serve not only to limit actual receipt of care but also to complicate the relationship between patients and providers when care is accessed. Non-inclusive office practices can create intimidating environments for LGBTQ+ patients to navigate as they may feel uncomfortable or unsafe sharing their LGBTQ+ identity in those spaces. However, much research on disclosure in the medical context has highlighted the importance of information sharing between patient and providers with respect to quality of care and building the patient–provider relationship.

PATIENT–PROVIDER DISCLOSURE

Derlega et al. (1993, p. 1) define self-disclosure as information including "what individuals verbally reveal about themselves to others (including thoughts, feelings, and experiences)." Engaging in disclosure helps individuals improve their social interactions, express themselves, and further develop their own identities (Derlega et al., 1993). Self-disclosure often is described in terms of breadth, or the range of information one discloses, and depth, or how personal the information is that one discloses (Altman & Taylor, 1973).

In the healthcare context, patient self-disclosure to providers is a key component of successful patient–provider relationships (Chaudoir & Fisher, 2010; Duggan & Thompson, 2011). According to Ong et al. (1995), patient–provider communication can create a good interpersonal relationship, promote the exchange of medical information, and facilitate medical decision making.

Ong et al. (1995) posit that the exchange of information is essential as doctors need information from patients in order to establish diagnoses and offer treatments, and patients need information from providers in order to understand health conditions and associated treatment plans. In the medical interaction, information about personal and family health histories that pertains to the current visit constitutes a majority of disclosure. However, at times, the content of these conversations may become more personal when more private information becomes necessary (i.e., disclosure of information not requested on medical forms or in the routine patient interview, such as sexual orientation). When this happens, patients may experience increased vulnerability because of perceptions of risk associated with disclosing sensitive personal information (Petronio, 2002). Realistically, though, there are times when it may be absolutely necessary for an individual to disclose personal details about an identity that may be uncomfortable (e.g., when immediate medical care is needed, and disclosure of stigmatizing health information is essential to receiving proper treatment). In other situations where this is less necessary, the benefits to disclosing may not clearly outweigh the risks (e.g., when choosing to disclose sexual orientation or gender identity to a temporary provider or a provider administering completely unrelated care).

Across these varying situations, individuals must evaluate the benefits and consequences associated with disclosing sexual orientation or gender identity information before making a decision to disclose or not. Further complicating this matter is the fact that in most medical situations, patients are assumed to be heterosexual unless otherwise stated (Röndahl, 2011). This is reinforced by the heteronormative nature of paperwork, office environments, and history taking (Röndahl, 2011). While this may present difficulties, the benefits of self-disclosure are not limited solely to the provider's ability to accurately assess a patient's medical issue and provide appropriate treatment. Patient disclosure also helps the provider to better understand the patient's perspectives on healthcare so that more accommodating and feasible care plans may be established and adherence to these plans may be more likely. Therefore, sexual orientation and gender identity information can make up an important part of these disclosures.

Disclosure of sexual orientation and gender identity to providers can be vital for a variety of reasons. One such reason research has documented is that that those LGBTQ+ patients who have shared their orientation have received more appropriate screening and improved their relationship with their provider (e.g., White & Dull, 1998). Sharing orientation also assists with avoidance of unnecessary tests, such as for pregnancy, and unnecessary prescriptions, such as birth control (Lehmann et al., 1998). Disclosure may also reduce the burden of psychological stress on the individual who is attempting to conceal information, as they may receive positive support from others (Chaudoir & Fisher, 2010). Venetis et al. (2014)[1] asked participants who self-identified as LGBQ to discuss their experiences related to sharing their sexual orientation with providers. As one participant noted, "It's more to build a trust and to give them a complete picture, and it's always nice to just be able to tell the truth. Yeah. It's relieving to be able to open up." However, given the documentation of discrimination against LGBTQ+ patients, disclosure of sexual orientation and gender identity can be particularly difficult.

Disclosure and Stigma. Disclosure literature has long documented challenges of sharing information that could be negatively received and stigmatizing (Greene et al., 2006). An individual who identifies as LGBTQ+ may bear a concealable stigmatized identity (Chaudoir & Fisher, 2010). This means it may not be readily apparent that an individual identifies as a particular sexual orientation or gender identity. However, individuals may sometimes present with particular cues (e.g., vocal cues, body language, physical appearance, etc.) that could lead others to stereotype their sexual orientation or gender identity. Venetis et al. (2014) reported the following description from a participant that helps to further illuminate the concept, as one bisexual individual reported how she can conceal her bisexual identity:

> I don't think it's obvious at all. I'm just an ordinary girl. I look like one. I act like one. I'm always the female. I'm always the submissive partner. So that fits the stereotypical woman very well. So there would be no way you tell that I would go both ways.

In cases such as these, when individuals are not visibly different from others' expectations, they may choose whether to disclose this identity that could potentially be stigmatizing (Goffman, 1963). In writing about stigma, Goffman (1963) coined a term, "discreditable," which is an appropriate description for individuals bearing a concealable stigmatized identity. The risk associated with disclosure is that the discrediting factor (i.e., a particular stigmatizing identity) may lead the disclosure recipient to no longer have a positive impression of the individual. The possibility of concealment does transfer some communicative power back to the individual because they can choose to avoid the risk of potentially negative responses such as discrimination or verbal or physical abuse. However, researchers have found that concealing a stigmatized identity can lead to feelings of stress resulting from preoccupation with concealing it (Afifi & Caughlin, 2006; Smart & Wegner, 1999). Additionally, individuals may experience guilt as a result of hiding this information from others (Derlega et al., 1993). In medical situations specifically, individuals must consider how their healthcare could be affected by disclosure. And in many cases a patient may engage in impression management behaviors to avoid negative responses, which can include not disclosing their sexual orientation or gender identity to a provider. Because being LGBTQ+ is often a concealable stigmatized identity, each interaction an LGBTQ+ individual engages in presents a situation where the individual must consider whether the other person(s) knows or thinks they are LGBTQ+, whether it is essential to the interaction that their sexual orientation or gender identity be disclosed, and how the other(s) will respond to this information (Pachankis, 2007).

When individuals do not feel their stigmatized identity can be reasonably concealed within an interaction, they may avoid certain situations altogether to maintain secrecy. Along these lines, Kcomt et al. (2020) found that transgender individuals who wished to conceal their transgender identity but felt they presented with visual cues that would reveal this identity showed greater healthcare avoidance than those who felt their appearance aligned more with providers' expectations of social norms. In other words, if individuals felt their visual appearance resulted in a lower ability to conceal their transgender identity, they were more likely to avoid visiting providers.

When individuals are concerned about saving face in their interactions with providers and choose to withhold information that is essential to their healthcare, they are likely to experience poor quality of care and potentially negative health outcomes. In most cases, providers obtain information from patients through lab tests and medical procedures or through the medical history the patient provides. These modes of information gathering do not necessarily give the provider a comprehensive view of a patient's entire history or the litany of factors that could be related to a patient's overall health and well-being (Champion, 2007). Unfortunately, many patients may also choose to curate the information they share with the provider for the purpose of impression management. By limiting the personal information they share, individuals may feel they can reduce the risk of being stigmatized. Link et al. (2002) posited that individuals keep secrets as a way to conceal any personal characteristics that could lead to stigmatization. While preventing stigmatization may be ideal, keeping secrets in the medical setting could be detrimental to patients as the provider may be unable to identify medical needs and concerns or recommend appropriate and necessary treatment.

It is important to consider that, although a patient may feel they are able to successfully conceal information related to their sexual orientation and/or gender identity, there may be particular situations where the information the patient discusses with the provider leads the provider to question or make assumptions about the patient's sexual orientation and/or gender identity. Further, depending on the content of the interaction, the provider could also make assumptions about the patient's health and wellness behaviors, leading to further stigmatization.

The potential for stigmatization can complicate patients' decision-making processes in terms of what or when to disclose about their sexual orientation and/or gender identity. They may simultaneously desire to disclose to the provider in order to build a relationship and/or seek specific care, but they may fear the stigmatization they may experience if the provider makes these assumptions about them. Wells and Kline (1987) write about a "double bind" of disclosure and Gershman (1983) writes about a "Catch-22" of disclosure. Each of these terms describes the feelings one has associated with the conflict between desiring to disclose sexual orientation and the fear of stigmatization upon disclosure.

In the health context, Greene and Magsamen-Conrad (2014) write about a "double disclosure," or a situation where an individual discloses a diagnosis that could result in stigmatization (e.g., HIV/AIDS) and then by association directly (i.e., tells the recipient) or indirectly (i.e., the recipient assumes) shares another characteristic about themselves that could result in stigmatization (e.g., homosexuality). This can have additional implications in the context of sexual orientation. For example, if a patient identifying as a cisgender male visits a provider seeking PrEP medication, the provider may also question the patient's sexual orientation or simply assume the patient identifies as non-heterosexual. These assumptions could result in stigmatization. Along these lines, the provider may also make assumptions about the riskiness of a patient's sexual history or current practices (e.g., unprotected sex), which could result in further stigmatization. This compounding effect could result in an increasingly negative situation for the patient.

These situations may not be viewed as negative by all patients. Some may find relief in this type of conversation serving as the impetus for a disclosure of sexual orientation and/or gender identity information. Despite the possibility that for some patients this could inadvertently become an opportunity to disclose, for those who are actively trying to conceal these identities, this becomes a potentially risky scenario.

Disclosure of Sexual Orientation and Gender Identity. Although social norms are evolving, sexual orientation and gender identity continue to be topics of polarization and debate. In Venetis et al.'s (2014) study, one participant expressed the following thought related to the public attitude toward sexual orientation: "Sexual orientation is regarded as taboo, even though societal things have changed." Another participant reflected,

> I think that disclosing sexual orientation is such a bad subject right now and so many people are openly against it, against gays or against bisexuals, or asexuals or whatever, it is so likely that it will go against the moral fiber that it is a completely different kettle of fish, and I hate that. So, it's tough.

These reflections illustrate the experiences of members of the LGBTQ+ population who continually have to determine when and with whom they share information about their sexual orientation or gender identity, as "coming out" is an ongoing process (Denes & Afifi, 2014). In addition to loved ones, friends, and family, individuals consider if, when, and how much about their sexual lives and practices they want to share with medical providers. These disclosures can carry some risk related to the expected and/or unexpected responses of disclosure recipients. As discussed, the disclosure of personal information that could result in stigmatization (e.g., sexual orientation and gender identity) from the patient to the provider can be very difficult. Further complicating these disclosures is the consideration of how necessary disclosure of sexual orientation or gender identity is to the medical interaction, and this can also be dependent on how likely it is the provider will assume a patient's sexual orientation or gender identity falls into a category that is not heteronormative or cisnormative.

There are many factors at play when individuals are considering the disclosure of a concealable stigmatizing identity, and many of these factors can contribute to making this disclosure decision process psychologically uncomfortable for the discloser (Chaudoir & Fisher, 2010). Some factors that individuals must consider include the possibility that disclosure recipients will go on to reveal this stigmatizing information to others without the discloser's permission or involvement (a.k.a., being outed); an inability to seek out and receive support from others who share this stigmatizing identity, because many wish to continue concealing that information; and also the possibility that even though the stigmatizing identity has been disclosed, the individual must continue to conceal some information that could be further stigmatizing or result in more negative consequences in the long term (Pachankis, 2007). In addition to these difficulties associated with the general disclosure of a concealable stigmatizing identity, transgender individuals report specific concerns related to disclosure of that identity to providers. These concerns include not only stigmatization but also the possibility they will be unable to receive necessary care, that their transgender identity will be revealed to others, and that they may be subject to verbal or physical abuse (Poteat et al., 2013).

Venetis et al. (2014) also learned about ways participants have perceived they are stigmatized by providers. One participant, Lawrence, when commenting on provider perceptions stated, "Well, immediately they're gonna think you have more STIs, which you probably do, and they're probably gonna think you're more likely to get them." Similarly, Caitlyn said, "Well, I always think that they assume that I practice unsafe sex. It's just because I sleep with one or two girls, God I must be dirty. I must be taking risks. [I'm] treated a lot like I'm irresponsible." It is not surprising that experiences like these could lead to patients deciding against disclosure of their sexual orientation or gender identity to providers.

Concealment as Information Management. Disclosure literature has identified strategies for information management, including both approaches to disclosure and concealing information (Afifi & Weiner, 2004; Brashers, 2001). In the case of information that could be perceived as negative or information that is sensitive or risky, individuals may find more benefit from concealing that information in order to avoid negative consequences of sharing (Afifi & Caughlin, 2006). As such, concealing sexual orientation or gender identity information can be an act of information management in the same way disclosing that identity can be an act of information management. Much research has documented reasons for reluctance in sharing sexual orientation with medical providers. Klitzman and Greenberg (2002) reported that although gay men are more confident in sharing their orientation, and particularly to White male providers, lesbians hold more disclosure reservations. Specific to lesbian disclosure, Diamant et al. (2000) also found that 40% of lesbians actively selected to withhold sexual orientation from medical providers. And in a landmark study surveying asexual individuals, Flanagan and Peters (2020) found that only 28% of the 125 participants who had ever visited a medical provider had disclosed their sexual orientation.

Camacho et al. (2020) conducted a meta-analysis in which they found that active concealment rather than disclosure of concealable stigmatized identities may result in more positive psychological outcomes for individuals possessing such identities. These positive outcomes of active concealment were related to the likelihood the recipient of the information would respond in an unsupportive manner. In the case of LGBTQ+ disclosure, individuals may benefit most from selective disclosure, or sharing this identity with close others (e.g., friends and family) who they are confident will respond positively.

Feinstein et al. (2020) conducted a study with 345 individuals to examine motivations for bisexual, pansexual, queer, and fluid (bi+) individuals to conceal their sexual identity. Researchers found that 48.3% reported concealment and that younger participants, cisgender women, and bisexual participants reported the greatest likelihoods to conceal. The researchers also asked about intrapersonal motivations for concealment (i.e., being bi+ is not a central part of participant identity, and participant is not comfortable being bi+) and interpersonal motivations for concealment (i.e., participant is concerned about being judged, mistreated, or in danger) to explore specific motivations for concealment. They also asked participants about mental health diagnoses, including depression and generalized anxiety. The researchers found that interpersonal motivations for concealment were associated with increased levels of depression and generalized anxiety, indicating that the potential social risks related to disclosure may cause mental distress. The researchers also found that participants' interpersonal motivations more strongly influenced concealment than intrapersonal motivations. Here again is evidence illustrating the influence of potential stigmatization and the recipient's response when individuals are making decisions about the disclosure of risky information and concealable stigmatizing identities.

Austin and Irwin (2010) found similar results in a study they conducted to ask lesbian participants about disclosing their sexual orientation to providers. Their sample was focused particularly in the Southeastern United States. Like the participants in Feinstein et al.'s study, over 40% of Austin and Irwin's respondents also reported they had not disclosed their sexual orientation. Overall, Austin and Irwin attributed this lack of disclosure to the fact that many providers across the country, and particularly in the Southeast, are underequipped to treat patients who identify as a minority sexual orientation or gender identity. As such, they asserted that providers may not understand differences in sexual orientation or gender identity and likely assume most patients are heterosexual and cisgender. Although those assumptions could make it easier for patients who wish to conceal their sexual orientation or gender identity from a provider, in situations where information related to sexual orientation or gender identity is related to necessary medical care those assumptions could lead a provider to overlook that information or further discourage patient disclosure. As mentioned before, these heteronormative and cisnormative assumptions can also create a sense of exclusion for patients and limit the opportunity for beneficial disclosure.

Evidence of this is also reported in a study where Haas (2018) interviewed 61 males in long-term, same-sex relationships about their experiences sharing sexual orientation with providers. Participants reported intentionally behaving in manners they believed would convey a heterosexual identity to medical providers. Haas identified three primary reasons for this: fear of being stigmatized and receiving low quality of care, perceived irrelevance of their sexual orientation to the visit, and perceived provider discomfort with LGBTQ+ patients. Unfortunately, several participants reported prior experiences of bias, discrimination, and refusal of care. As a result, they felt it was safer to conceal their sexual orientation. Along similar lines, participants felt it was safer and more comfortable to avoid disclosing their sexual orientation when they felt the reason for the visit was not at all related to their sexual orientation, as the information was simply unnecessary. Similarly, if they perceived the provider was not comfortable with LGBTQ+ individuals, they deemed it to be more comfortable and less taxing to avoid having the conversation.

These findings that LGBTQ+ individuals actively and frequently conceal their sexual orientation and gender identity within patient–provider interactions serve to support both Goffman's (1963) and Garfinkel's (1967) assertions regarding the use of impression management strategies to reduce, avoid, or prevent stigmatization. By declining to reveal information related to their sexual orientation or gender identity, LGBTQ+ patients may be able to save face and avoid potential discrimination.

Disclosure Motivations. Despite evidence showing many LGBTQ+ individuals choose to conceal sexual orientation and gender identity information, there are also many instances where this information is disclosed, and various factors may motivate individuals differently to disclose.

In general, motivations to disclose information within relationships can serve several purposes, such as for relationship initiation and escalation (Derlega et al., 1993), to encourage reciprocal disclosure of information (Berger, 1979), and to receive social support or even for catharsis (Greene et al., 2003). Although it may indeed be the case that LGBTQ+ patients disclose to providers to establish and build relationships or to experience the relief of disclosing, in outlining the Disclosure Decision Model (DDM) Omarzu (2000) posits that people may also disclose to clarify their identity or, put simply, to provide accurate information about themselves. This seems particularly well aligned with the disclosure of sexual orientation and gender identity information. Omarzu (2000) also suggests that individuals evaluate subjective utility, or the benefits of disclosure, against subjective risk, or the potential risks of disclosure, when deciding whether to disclose. Once again, this also aligns well with the context of disclosing sexual orientation or gender identity information to medical providers as LGBTQ+ patients are weighing positive and negative health outcomes in considering their disclosure. Building on Omarzu's ideas, Afifi and Steuber's (2009) Risk Revelation Model (RRM) adds an individual's readiness to disclose, or their willingness to take on disclosure risks, to the list of factors motivating disclosure. In building the Disclosure Decision-Making Model (DD-MM), Greene (2009) explores other factors influencing disclosure, including the relevance of information to the interaction, the potential reaction of the disclosure recipient, and the individual's ability to share information. Greene (2009) posits that the more relevant the information, the more positive the potential reaction, and the more well-equipped the discloser is will all positively influence likelihood of disclosure (e.g., Pahwa et al., 2017). Once again, this research aligns particularly well with disclosure of sexual orientation and gender identity information, as many researchers have found evidence that, when considering disclosure to a medical provider, LGBTQ+ individuals indeed consider how relevant sexual orientation or gender identity information is to the situation, as well as how the provider might respond to the disclosure.

In support of Greene's assertions about relevance are findings from an interview-based study conducted by Bjorkman and Malterud (2007), in which lesbian participants were asked about disclosing their sexual orientation to providers. The participants reported concern about how providers would react if they disclosed their sexual orientation. Because of these concerns, they strongly considered how relevant their sexual orientation was to the visit and whether the relevance of that information superseded their concerns about how the provider might react.

Ultimately, participants who determined the information was essential did disclose, and those who determined it was not essential did not disclose. In further support of this finding, in their survey of asexual individuals, Flanagan and Peters (2020) found that 80% of respondents did not disclose their gender identity because they felt it was not relevant to their care.

Venetis et al. (2014) found relevance to be a factor with strong influence over patients' likelihood to disclose their sexual orientation to providers, and one participant explained that in situations where sexual orientation is definitely relevant to the interaction, it increases the efficiency of the visit to disclose. She described the following experience:

> I went in and I told her that I was having stomach issues, and she immediately asked me if I was pregnant. Then I told her, "No," and so without pause, she asked me if I changed up any birth control, to which I stated, "No," and before she could get another question out, I was so frustrated, I'm like "Look, okay, I'm gay, and so any pregnancy issues or anything of the like, would not apply here."

Finally, in further support of how the provider's potential reaction to the disclosure can influence disclosure decisions, Johnson and Nemeth (2014) found that among a sample of lesbian and bisexual women, those participants attempted to locate LGB-inclusive providers for their medical care based on the assumption that their reaction to disclosure of sexual orientation would be generally positive. However, this was not always possible because of time constraints, insurance-related issues, or emergency situations requiring immediate care. As such, participants more often than not attended medical visits where they were unsure how the provider would respond to information about their sexual orientation. Many participants unfortunately reported negative provider responses to their disclosure. As a result, participants reported that they limited future interactions with those providers, declined to take their partners to medical visits, and sought different providers.

Once again these experiences provide evidence that aligns with Goffman's (1963) and Garfinkel's (1967) work describing the strategies individuals will undertake in order to either continue to conceal a stigmatizing identity or to selectively reveal information related to that identity in ways that will help to reduce stigmatization and hopefully prevent negative outcomes, such as discrimination or harassment.

Disclosure Strategies. In addition to research examining motivations for individuals to disclose, other research has been conducted to explore the nature and content of conversations during which a patient reveals their sexual orientation or gender identity to a medical provider. Many of these disclosure conversations reflect disclosure strategies outlined in the extant disclosure literature and tie in directly to the primary motivations for disclosure discussed in "Disclosure Motivations."

In general, individuals who are preparing for disclosure of information must consider how they want to communicate that information. That is, they must consider exactly what they will share and how they will share it, not only in terms of breadth and depth but also in terms of the language they use and the conversational entry point they take. Early research on disclosure strategies focused primarily on direct disclosure versus indirect disclosure.

Derlega et al. (2000) explored strategies individuals use to disclose HIV-positive status to sexual partners and found that 56.3% of participants informed their partner directly, whereas 23.4% informed their partner indirectly. While knowing these participants more frequently shared their HIV status explicitly with their partner is informative with respect to the nature of this type of disclosure, further research has explored more detailed nuances of disclosure conversations.

Greene et al. (2003) identified three features of HIV disclosures: mode, context, and content. Mode encompasses face to face (i.e., a conversation), non-face to face (i.e., a mediated channel), and third-party disclosures (i.e., another person serving as the discloser). Context encompasses the disclosure setting (i.e., the physical environment), whether the discloser brought someone with them to the interaction, and the timing of the disclosure (i.e., when in the interaction the disclosure took place). Content encompasses practicing (i.e., planning, rehearsing, scripting) and incremental disclosure (i.e., revealing pieces of information gradually). Afifi and Steuber (2009) identified six strategies individuals use to disclose general secrets: preparation and rehearsal (i.e., planning and practicing disclosure), directness (i.e., overt and complete disclosure), third-party revelations (i.e., another person serving as the discloser), incremental disclosures (i.e., revealing pieces of information gradually), entrapment (i.e., forced disclosure), and indirect mediums (i.e., use of a mediated channel). Evidence of these disclosure features and strategies is present in research specifically exploring LGBTQ+ patients' disclosure of sexual orientation and gender identity to medical providers.

For example, similar to Derlega et al.'s (2000) findings showing direct disclosure as a more frequently used strategy than indirect disclosure, Eliason and Schope (2001) found that 37% of LGB individuals who reported on their disclosure of sexual orientation to providers had disclosed directly, and only 15% reported indirect disclosure. Direct disclosure was defined as using clear and non-abstract language to disclose, whereas an example of indirect disclosure included talking about a partner. Thirty-eight percent of participants stated that they avoided talking about sexuality altogether in order to avoid disclosing. These strategies also allude to later research where participants described discussing a partner or using other points of conversation to disclose.

In a survey of 220 women who have sex with women, Willes and Allen (2014) found that 30% of participants who had disclosed shared their sexual orientation to a provider during a conversation about sexual behaviors, and 24% of those who disclosed indicated they had brought their female partners with them to their appointment. These findings overlap with Greene et al.'s (2003) findings that showed individuals look for particular points within the conversation to disclose and that they sometimes bring a companion with them for both support and a starting point for the disclosure itself. This also aligns with Afifi and Steuber's (2009) strategies of preparation and directness, as it must be planned for a partner to attend a medical visit, and the presence and introduction of that individual serves as overt evidence of the patient's sexual orientation.

Further research on LGBTQ+ patients' experiences disclosing sexual orientation to medical providers has attempted to connect the literature on disclosure message features and strategies to the specific context of coming out. Manning (2014) examined gay and bisexual men's coming out and sexual health conversations with medical providers. Results of that study revealed three types of scenarios where sexual health and sexual orientation were discussed. The first involved routine questioning where the patient found it necessary to reveal their sexual orientation to the provider in order to respond appropriately to a question (e.g., do you have a girlfriend?). The second involved situations where providers seemed suspicious about the truthfulness of patients' descriptions of their sexual behaviors (e.g., accusing them of engaging in risky behaviors). The third entailed providers' inabilities to remain calm and demonstrate competence within the interaction (e.g., avoiding questions related to sexual behaviors). Each of these cases represents the complexity of and, at times, discriminatory nature of these disclosure conversations.

Complementing these findings are results from another study conducted by Manning (2015) to explore various types of coming out conversations. Through this study, Manning was able to identify seven categories of coming out conversations: preplanned, emergent, coaxed, confrontational, romantic or sexual, educational or activist, and mediated. Manning focused specifically on sexual orientation disclosure, but these descriptions may also extend to gender identity disclosure. In particular, Manning's descriptions of preplanned and emergent coming out conversation types seem to align closely with strategies LGBTQ+ patients report using to disclose to providers. Manning describes preplanned conversations as those where an individual has made a decision ahead of an interaction that they will reveal their sexual orientation, and emergent conversations as those where the disclosure becomes a relevant part of the conversation as it progresses. In both cases, Manning explains, the discloser is in control of initiating the disclosure. Reports from LGBTQ+ individuals about planning how or when they will disclose sexual orientation or gender identity and using typical conversational turning points within medical interactions (e.g., history taking) to disclose reflect both preplanning and emergent patterns.

In their exploration of asexual patients' experiences, Flanagan and Peters (2020) found that of those participants who did disclose their asexual orientation to a medical provider, 31.4% did so because they felt they had no other choice during the interaction. This aligns with Afifi and Steuber's (2009) description of entrapment, as well as Manning's (2015) forced coming out conversation type.

Venetis et al. (2014) learned some information about specific disclosure strategies participants used to reveal their sexual orientation to providers. One participant explained how she reveals her sexual orientation as well as how she manages the provider's response:

> I said, "I'm going to be honest. I am bi, and I have sex with both male and female, and so is it okay if I ask you questions about both?" So, I usually come out and just say that I do have relationships with both sexes. I'm bisexual... So I made a deal with myself that if I was going to reveal this, I would say that I am bisexual, which is the most commonly used term, and if I need to expand on it, I would say that I sleep with both men and women.

These descriptions of disclosure align with the research findings related to factors that influence an individuals' decision to disclose, as both the relevance of sexual orientation and provider responses were at the center of these conversations. This strategy also reflects direct disclosure (Afifi & Steuber, 2009; Greene et al. 2003) and preplanning of the conversation content (Afifi & Steuber, 2009; Manning, 2015).

In a similar study exploring patients' disclosure of their sexual orientation to providers, Venetis et al. (2017) examined how these disclosure conversations take place and the way patients choose to disclose this information. Results of that study revealed two opportunities for conversation initiation and three strategies for disclosure. Some individuals opt to disclose their sexual orientation upon introducing themselves to a provider during initial small talk or by introducing their entire family if a partner and/or child(ren) were present. Some participants described accomplishing the same goal by bringing up a relevant piece of information, such as the occupation of their partner who was not present. This strategy is a good example of prepared, preplanned, direct disclosure (Afifi & Steuber, 2009; Greene et al., 2003; Manning, 2015). Similar to Manning's (2014) findings, some participants reported sharing their sexual orientation during routine questioning (e.g., recording contraceptive use). In many of these cases, female participants who did not need birth control for contraception related to sex with a male described questions about birth control as situations where they felt they either had to disclose their sexual orientation or appear as though they practiced unsafe sex if they indicated they did not use birth control but were sexually active. Similar situations where providers had to be convinced the patient was not pregnant were also described. These conversations also show entrapment (Afifi & Steuber, 2009) in action, as the patients felt they had no other choice than to disclose in order to bring clarity to the interaction. Additionally, the patients ended up using disclosure as an impression management strategy in order to prevent providers from making negative assumptions about their sexual health (Garfinkel, 1967; Goffman, 1963).

Participants described various disclosure strategies of limiting the amount of information revealed, keeping the tone of the conversation calm, and using indirect cues (e.g., partner's pronouns). In terms of limiting the amount of information revealed, most participants explained that informing a provider about sexual orientation typically does not require a great deal of elaboration or justification, thus a simple and concise statement providing just the necessary information is sufficient (Manning, 2015). Participants also explained that using casual language to disclose helps to keep the tone of the conversation calm and to minimize the discomfort that might be associated with the disclosure. Finally, participants indicated that, often, indirect cues are helpful for facilitating the disclosure by further minimizing discomfort and drawing less attention to their sexual orientation through more subtle language (Greene et al., 2003).

CURRENT RECOMMENDATIONS, GUIDELINES, AND PROGRAMS

The body of research describing how LGBTQ+ individuals consider providers' potential reaction to learning about their sexual orientation or gender identity, as well as LGBTQ+ individuals' descriptions of conversational opportunities that encourage disclosure, shines a light on ways these patient–provider interactions can be improved. One starting point may be with providers' attitudes. As mentioned previously, Johnson and Nemeth (2014) learned from participants that they would attempt to seek out LGB-inclusive providers prior to medical visits. Poteat et al. (2013) found similar results in their interviews with transgender participants where they also reported attempting to seek out providers who were known to be transgender inclusive. As expected, when providers demonstrated inclusivity, patients felt more comfortable visiting with the provider and discussing information related to their sexual orientation or gender identity.

Venetis et al. (2014) also found support for the idea that a provider who is perceived as more open and inclusive toward LGBTQ+ patients is preferable, as one participant, Amanda, from their study suggested: "I definitely think that if they have LBGTQ relevant literature... [it] makes them definitely seem like they're open to such things. So yeah, just like the small cues—having the literature, not having everything be so very hetero-normative." This illustrates the possibility that small shifts in how providers present themselves could increase perceptions of LGBTQ+ inclusivity and encourage patient disclosure—assuming the provider themself is LGBTQ+ inclusive in practice.

Based on participant accounts of their experiences with providers and revealing information related to sexual orientation and gender identity, researchers have been able to compile rather extensive suggestions and recommendations for improving the healthcare experiences of sexual-and gender-minority patients. Given the barriers to disclosure outlined by the extant literature on disclosure of sexual orientation and gender identity, many of these recommendations are aimed at supporting more comfortable and safe disclosure by reducing stigmatization and discrimination and facilitating more inclusive and productive patient–provider interactions. Recently some groups of researchers have conducted meta-analyses to compile these guidelines and recommendations into single reference sources.

In a meta-analysis, Bolderston and Ralph (2016) reviewed a series of articles covering topics related to LGBTQ+ patients, healthcare professionals, and health systems. Through this review, the authors were able to identify three major areas of improvement for LGBTQ+ patients, including changes to the healthcare environment, updated intake and health history paperwork, and provider training. Similarly, in a meta-analysis, Bizub and Allen (2020) reviewed 24 articles discussing recommendations for improving transgender and gender non-conforming care. The primary areas for improvement they uncovered include the physical healthcare environment, office policies, methods for documenting sex and gender, confidentiality procedures, insurance coverage, interactions between patients and staff or providers, and training for health professionals.

These findings also show that provider presentations of LGBTQ+ inclusivity could encourage patient disclosure, not only by increasing patient comfort levels but also by making it tangibly easier for patients to disclose. If paperwork is modified to reflect a wider range of sexual orientations and gender identities, LGBTQ+ patients can simply select options that apply to them when completing this paperwork and the office staff and provider(s) will then be made aware of this information without a disclosure conversation even having to take place. The office staff and providers then also have the opportunity to ensure they are using accurate and inclusive language with all patients. Additionally, if the routine questioning process is modified to reflect more inclusive language that does not originate from a heteronormative and cisnormative perspective, LGBTQ+ patients can use the responses to those questions as an opportunity to provide sexual orientation or gender identity information in a normalized way. Training procedures, confidentiality protocols, and ensuring that healthcare will be financially manageable are also ways to increase LGBTQ+ patients' feelings of comfort and safety while also ensuring that they are treated equitably as compared to non-LGBTQ+ patients. Again, this can help promote safe and healthy disclosure through minimizing patients' perceptions of risk associated with disclosing.

Lastly, in a report, Radix (2020) outlined opportunities for medical facilities to employ guidelines from the American Academy of Family Physicians regarding effective and inclusive care for transgender patients. Although there are many recommendations specific to medical treatment and procedures, there are also recommendations for creating more positive experiences for transgender patients. Specifically, Radix discussed demonstrating respect for people's identities and experiences through increasing staff training, gathering information to ensure appropriate gendering and naming, and providing inclusive office environments. Radix also discussed the importance of avoiding assumptions concerning gender identity and gender conformity in clinical interactions by suggesting providers work to understand the specifics of gender-affirming procedures and care, acknowledge health disparities experienced by transgender patients, and take care to approach procedures that are cisgender-oriented with sensitivity. Again, these recommendations support LGBTQ+ comfort and safety. Training that specifically focuses on providers' language use and appropriate responses could not only encourage LGBTQ+ patients to disclose sexual orientation or gender identity information but also ensure that when they do disclose, the provider response is accepting and supportive.

The expanded research on patients' experiences disclosing sexual orientation and gender identity to providers has created a wealth of suggestions and recommendations for best medical practices. This has evolved into various educational projects and programs designed to improve medical professionals' knowledge and understanding of sexual orientation and gender identity, as well as to increase inclusivity in healthcare environments.

With respect to provider training, Kuzma et al. (2019) reported on an education program developed for nurse practitioners to provide them with opportunities to interact with LGBTQ+ patients and to gain cultural awareness about best care practices. This program included course readings on cultural humility and how to obtain a comprehensive sexual health history, a 1-hour lecture covering cultural humility and LGBTQ+ health, a 90-minute lecture on how to obtain a comprehensive sexual health history, role-playing exercises in taking sexual histories of LGBTQ+ standardized patients, a 15-minute patient visit with an LGBTQ+ standardized patient seeking care for abdominal pain, and a series of structured debriefing sessions. Overall, participants reported increased awareness about their lack of preparedness to interact with LGBTQ+ patients, a motivation to avoid assumptions and bias in interacting with LGBTQ+ patients to ensure patient comfort and safety, and an increase in confidence in their ability to interact with LGBTQ+ patients post-training.

Similarly, Jann et al. (2019) reported on the creation of an elective course in LGBT health for second- and third-year doctor of pharmacy students. This course focused on sexuality and sexual health; how to take a sexual history; LGBT health disparities and health issues; gender identity; legal and ethical issues related to LGBT health; interdisciplinary care; HIV and STD prevention, screening, and treatment; and mental health and substance abuse issues for LGBT individuals. Participants engaged in peer teaching exercises, self-reflection, journaling and discussion groups, guest-speaker presentations and meetings with LGBT community groups and transgender patients, and a capstone presentation project. Overall, students demonstrated a significant increase in their knowledge about LGBT patients and related healthcare needs, particularly with respect to medications. Students also demonstrated significant reflection on social issues related to LGBT individuals, such as discrimination and politicization of care, as well as reflections on their own sexuality.

In 2014, the University of Louisville in Kentucky launched an LGBT Health Certificate program for students in the schools of medicine, nursing, dentistry, and public health and information sciences (Sawning et al., 2017). This elective program covered topics such as LGBT health issues and working with LGBT patients; inclusivity in LGBT care; ethical, legal, and leadership issues in LGBT health; and LGBT mental health. Pre- and post-assessments were administered to measure effects of the program on students' LGBT health knowledge and attitudes. Overall, the results indicated that participants' knowledge increased significantly, as did favorable attitudes toward LGBT patients, and participants also indicated increased awareness of the challenges related to LGBT care.

Following the success of the health certificate program, the university established the eQuality curriculum, which was designed to function as an education model for improving the training of medical professionals with respect to providing equitable care for LGBTQ+ patients (Holthauser et al., 2017). The eQuality curriculum was designed to integrate into the 4-year medical school curriculum and aims to develop provider competencies across eight domains. These include patient care, provider knowledge, practice-based learning and improvement, interpersonal or communication skills, professionalism, practicing within systems of bias, interprofessional collaboration, and personal and professional development. Outcomes of this program are under evaluation.

The Vanderbilt University Medical Center (VUMC, n.d.) at Vanderbilt University in Nashville, Tennessee, has implemented a Program for LGBTQ Health that connects the university and medical school with the Vanderbilt health network. The comprehensive program includes training for medical professionals that leads to a certification in LGBTQ+ care as well as a research program with ongoing work related to LGBTQ+ health. The program also provides connections for LGBTQ+ patients to the certified practitioners. Finally, the program includes a subsidiary program called the Trans Buddy Program, which is designed to train individuals as peer advocates who assist transgender patients during their health care experiences by providing emotional support as they navigate medical visits and make health decisions (VUMC, n.d.). Their LGBTQ health program currently boasts a 100% rating on the national Healthcare Equality Index (Human Rights Campaign Foundation, 2019).

FUTURE OPPORTUNITIES

The select list of projects and programs discussed here represents several steps forward in the effort to increase health equity for LGBTQ+ patients, but there are always new avenues to be explored along the march toward progress. Many of these recommendations and programs seek to improve LGBTQ+ patient care and experiences through the adaptation of office environments and procedures as well as through increasing provider knowledge about LGBTQ+ people and related health. Several of the recommendations do address the connection between provider training and interactions with patients, but these recommendations often center on language use, such as terminology, names, and pronouns, as well as ways to avoid overt discrimination and stigmatization of LGBTQ+ patients. There is opportunity in research for further exploring specific communication mechanisms that can directly improve interactions between LGBTQ+ patients and providers.

For example, in the (2014) exploration of gay and bisexual men's coming out experiences, Manning was able to analyze the conversations about which participants reported to identify four positive receiver behaviors: open communication channels, affirming direct relational statements, laughter and joking, and nonverbal immediacy. Manning also identified five negative receiver behaviors: expressing denial; religious talk; inappropriate questions, comments, and concerns; shaming statements; and aggression. These receiver behaviors explicitly reference verbal and nonverbal cues that providers used in these conversations and identify how these cues influenced the conversational outcomes. Knowledge about these verbal and nonverbal cues can be integrated into provider training programs that focus specifically on how providers communicate with LGBTQ+ patients, in addition to what is being said.

Racial or ethnic minority groups continue to experience significantly worse health outcomes as compared to their majority race counterparts. This effect is compounded for individuals who identify across the intersections of race, sexual, and/or gender minorities. Although a number of LGBTQ+ health programs and facilities operate in areas more heavily populated by racial- or ethnic-minority individuals, it is important that research on best practices take into account how racial or ethnic differences might impact access to care and provider attitudes toward care. Although many current recommendations extend across all individuals who identify as LGBTQ+, additional recommendations may be needed to address further disparities.

Social media and new technologies present new opportunities for both provider education and training and patient access to information and resources. In a study on transgender coming out conversations on social media, Haimson and Veinot (2020) examined 240 blogs on the site Tumblr to explore how transgender individuals disclose to various audiences. Interestingly, they found that health professionals are generally the first individuals to whom transgender individuals disclose, and these professionals tend to include therapists or counselors as well as providers who can assist with transition-related needs. Similar to other research findings, bloggers posted about disclosure anxiety and instances of unplanned disclosures due to medical relevance and/or confusion on the part of the office staff. This innovative use of social media for data analysis could open the door for other opportunities for researchers and health professionals to connect with LGBTQ+ individuals on social media for both data collection and as a way to offer resources to those individuals.

CONCLUSION

This article has provided a broad overview of the issues related to patients' disclosure of sexual orientation and gender identity to medical providers. It is important to note that here, the discussion is situated within the context of Western cultures, specifically the United States. In many countries around the world, there are significant legal and social issues associated with identifying as LGBTQ+ and/or being known by others as LGBTQ+. Additionally, access to healthcare and the structure of and practices within healthcare organizations may vary widely. As a result, it is expected that the risks associated with disclosure of sexual and/or gender minority information may be vastly different from those in the United States. Along these lines, it is likely that any disclosure conversations wherein sexual and/or gender minority information is revealed are different as well.

Years of research has documented discrimination against sexual- and gender-minority individuals, particularly in the healthcare context. This article has highlighted that in the United States, LGBTQ+ individuals experience a high number of health disparities compared to the cisgender, heterosexual population, yet have significant difficulty accessing safe, quality healthcare. Research has also documented the positive impacts of patient disclosure of sexual orientation and gender identity, including not only increased quality of care but also improved patient–provider relationships. These benefits extend to more positive long-term health outcomes. There are also many barriers that make this disclosure difficult and, at times, impossible for LGBTQ+ individuals. Despite the risks of stigmatization and discrimination associated with disclosure, LBGTQ+ patients often find themselves having to weigh health necessity against these risks. Many individuals make use of particular opportunities in conversation with their providers to disclose, such as during medical history taking. Even though a great deal of research has documented the negative experiences LGBTQ+ individuals have endured post-disclosure, a great deal of research has also highlighted many opportunities for improvement to the LGBTQ+ patient experience and patient–provider relationship. Fortunately, that body of work has evolved into several innovative programs where scholars, health professionals, students, and many more involved parties are working to increase healthy equity for LGBTQ+ individuals. Despite these efforts, instances of discrimination and violence against LGBTQ+ individuals continue to be reported. As such, there is still much room for continued work toward developing and implementing programs that take advantage of advances in technology and continue to expand services to the most underserved individuals in the LGBTQ+ population.

FURTHER READING

Afifi, T., & Afifi, W. (Eds.). (2015). *Uncertainty, information management, and disclosure decisions: Theories and applications*. Routledge.

Bonvicini, K. A. (2017). LGBT healthcare disparities: What progress have we made? *Patient Education & Counseling, 100*(12), 2357–2361. http://doi.org/10.1016/j.pec.2017.06.003

Cahill, S., & Makadon, H. (2014). Sexual orientation and gender identity data collection in clinical settings and in electronic health records: A key to ending LGBT health disparities. *LGBT Health, 1*(1), 34–41. https://doi.org/10.1089/lgbt.2013.0001

Catona, D., & Greene, K. (2015). Self-disclosure. In C. R. Berger & M. E. Roloff (Eds.), *The international encyclopedia of interpersonal communication* (pp. 1–5). Wiley.

Centers for Disease Control and Prevention. (2018, March). *Lesbian, gay, bisexual, and transgender health*. https://www.cdc.gov/lgbthealth/

Harvey, V. L., & Housel, T. H. (Eds.). (2014). *Health care disparities and the LGBT population*. Lexington Books.

Hatzenbuehler, M. L., Flores, A. R., & Gates, G. J. (2017). Social attitudes regarding same-sex marriage and LGBT health disparities: Results from a national probability sample. *Journal of Social Issues, 73*(3), 443–681. http://doi.org/10.1111/josi.12229

Keuroghlian, A. S., Ard, K. L., & Makadon, H. J. (2017). Advancing health equity for lesbian, gay, bisexual and transgender (LGBT) people through sexual health education and LGBT-affirming health care environments. *Sexual Health, 14*(1), 119–122. http://doi.org/10.1071/SH16145

Lehman, J. R., Diaz, K., Ng, H., Petty, E. M., Thatikunta, M., & Eckstrand, K. (Eds.). (2020). *The equal curriculum: The students and educator guide to LGBTQ health.* Springer.

Masur, P. K. (2018). *Situational privacy and self-disclosure: Communication processes in online environments.* Springer International Publishing.

Streed, C. G., Jr., Grasso, C., Reisner, S. L., & Mayer, K. H. (2020). Sexual orientation and gender identity data collection: Clinical and public health importance. *American Journal of Public Health, 110,* 991–993. https://doi.org/10.2105/AJPH.2020.305722

U.S. Department of Health and Human Services. (2017, June). *Health & well-being for lesbian, gay, bisexual and transgender Americans.* https://www.hhs.gov/programs/topic-sites/lgbt/index.html

REFERENCES

Aaron, D. J., Markovic, N., Danielson, M. E., Honnold, J. A., Janosky, J. E., & Schmidt, N. J. (2001). Behavioral risk factors for disease and preventative health practices among lesbians. *American Journal of Public Health, 91,* 972–975. http://doi.org/10.2105/ajph.91.6.972

Afifi, T., & Steuber, K. (2009). The revelation risk model (RRM): Factors that predict the revelation of secrets and the strategies used to reveal them. *Communication Monographs, 76*(2), 144–176. http://doi.org/10.1080/03637750902828412

Afifi, W. A., & Caughlin, J. P. (2006). A close look at revealing secrets and some consequences that follow. *Communication Research, 33*(6), 467–488. http://doi.org/10.1177/0093650206293250

Afifi, W. A., & Weiner, J. L. (2004). Toward a theory of motivated information management. *Communication Theory, 14*(2), 167–190. http://doi.org/10.1111/j.1468-2885.2004.tb00310.x

Altman, I., & Taylor, D. A. (1973). *Social penetration: The development of interpersonal relationships.* Holt, Rinehart & Winston.

Anderson, S. M. (2020). Gender matters: The perceived role of gender expression in discrimination against cisgender and transgender LGBQ individuals. *Psychology of Women Quarterly, 44*(3), 323–341. https://doi.org/10.1177/0361684320929354

Austin, E. L., & Irwin, J. A. (2010). Health behaviors and health care utilization of Southern lesbians. *Women's Health Issues, 20*(3), 178–184. https://doi.org/10.1016/j.whi.2010.01.002

Badgett, M. V. L., Choi, S. K., & Wilson, B. D. M. (2019). *LGBT poverty in the United States: A study of differences between sexual orientation and gender identity groups.* https://williamsinstitute.law.ucla.edu/wp-content/uploads/National-LGBT-Poverty-Oct-2019.pdf

Benson, P. A. S., & Hergenroeder, A. C. (2005). Bacterial sexually transmitted infections in gay, lesbian, and bisexual adolescents: Medical and public health perspectives. *Seminars in Pediatric Infectious Diseases, 16*(3), 181–191. http://doi.org/10.1053/j.spid.2005.04.007

Berger, C. R. (1979). Beyond initial interaction: Uncertainty, understanding, and the development of interpersonal relationships. In H. Giles & R. Clair (Eds.), *Language and social psychology* (pp. 122–144). Blackwell.

Bizub, B., & Allen, B. (2020). A review of clinical guidelines for creating a gender-affirming primary care practice. *WMJ, 119*(1), 8–16. https://wmjonline.org/wp-content/uploads/2020/119/1/8.pdf

Bjorkman, M., & Malterud, K. (2007). Being lesbian—Does the doctor need to know? A qualitative study about the significance of disclosure in general practice. *Scandinavian Journal of Primary Health Care, 25*(1), 58–62. https://doi.org/10.1080/02813430601086178

Bockting, W. O., Miner, M. H., Swinburne Romine, R. E., Dolezal, C., Robinson, B. E., Simon Rosser, B. R., & Coleman, E. (2020). The Transgender Identity Survey: A measure of internalized transphobia. *LGBT Health, 7*(1), 15–27. https://doi.org/10.1089/lgbt.2018.0265

Bolderston A., & Ralph, S. (2016). Improving the healthcare experiences of lesbian, gay, bisexual and transgender patients. *Radiography, 22*(3), e207–e211. http://dx.doi.org/10.1016/j.radi.2016.04.011

Brashers, D. E. (2001). Communication and uncertainty management. *Journal of Communication, 51*(3), 477–497. https://doi.org/10.1111/j.1460-2466.2001.tb02892.x

Camacho, G., Reinka, M. A., & Quinn, D. M. (2020). Disclosure and concealment of stigmatized identities. *Current Opinion in Psychology, 31*, 28–32. https://doi.org/10.1016/j.copsyc.2019.07.031

Catona, D., Greene, K., & Magsamen-Conrad, K. (2015). Disclosure message choices: An analysis of strategies for disclosing HIV+ status. *Journal of Health Communication, 20*(11), 1294–1301. https://doi.org/10.1080/10810730.2015.1018640

Champion, C. D. (2007). *Effects of participant disclosure tendencies and physician verbal behavior on participant willingness to disclose facts: An analogue study.* (Unpublished doctoral dissertation). University of Notre Dame.

Chaudoir, S. R., & Fisher, J. D. (2010). The disclosure processes model: Understanding disclosure decision making and postdisclosure outcomes among people living with a concealable stigmatized identity. *Psychological Bulletin, 136*(2), 236–256. https://doi.org/10.1037/a0018193

Cochran, S. D., Mays, V. M., Bowen, D., Gage, S., Bybee, D., Roberts, S. J., Goldstein, R. S., Robison, A., Rankow, E. J., & White, J. (2001). Cancer-related risk indicators and preventative screening behaviors among lesbians and bisexual women. *American Journal of Public Health, 91*, 591–597. https://doi.org/10.2105/ajph.91.4.591

DeBold, K. (2007). Focus on lesbian health. *Women's Health Activist, 32*(2), 1–7.

Denes, A., & Afifi, T. D. (2014). Coming out again: Exploring GLBQ individuals' communication with their parents after the first coming out. *GLBT Family Studies, 10*(3), 298–325. https://doi.org/10.1080/1550428X.2013.838150

Derlega, V. J., Metts, S., Petronio, S., & Margulis S. T. (1993). *Self-disclosure.* SAGE.

Derlega, V. J., Winstead, B. A., & Folk-Barron, L. (2000). Reasons for and against disclosing HIV seropositive test results to an intimate partner: A functional perspective. In S. Petronio (Ed.), *Balancing the secrets of private disclosures* (pp. 53–70). Lawrence Erlbaum.

Devarajan, S., Sales, J. M., Hunt, M., & Comeau, D. L. (2020). PrEP and sexual well-being: A qualitative study on PrEP, sexuality of MSM, and patient-provider relationships. *AIDS Care, 32*(3), 386–393. https://www.tandfonline.com/doi/full/10.1080/09540121.2019.1695734

Diamant, A. L., Schuster, M. A., & Lever, J. (2000). Receipt of preventative health care service by lesbians. *American Journal of Preventative Medicine, 19*(3), 141–148. https://doi.org/10.1016/S0749-3797(00)00192-6

Duggan, A. P., & Thompson, T. L. (2011). Provider-patient interaction and related outcomes. In T. L. Thompson, R. Parrott, & J. F. Nussbaum (Eds.), *The Routledge handbook of health communication* (pp. 414–427). Routledge.

Eliason, M. J., & Schope, R. (2001). Does "don't ask don't tell" apply to health care? Lesbian, gay, and bisexual people's disclosure to health care providers. *Journal of the Gay and Lesbian Medical Association, 5*, 125–134. https://doi.org/10.1023/A:1014257910462

Feinstein, B. A., Xavier Hall, C. D., Dyar, C., & Davila, J. (2020). Motivations for sexual identity concealment and their associations with mental health among bisexual, pansexual, queer, and fluid (Bi+) individuals. *Journal of Bisexuality, 20*(3), 324–341. https://www.tandfonline.com/doi/full/10.1080/15299716.2020.1743402

Flanagan, S. K., & Peters, H. J. (2020). Asexual-identified adults: Interactions with health-care practitioners. *Archives of Sexual Behavior, 49,* 1631–1643. https://doi.org/10.1007/s10508-020-01670-6

Flores, A. R., Herman, J. L., Gates, G. J., & Brown, T. N. T. (2016). *How many adults identify as transgender in the United States?* The Williams Institute, UCLA School of Law. https://williamsinstitute.law.ucla.edu/wp-content/uploads/How-Many-Adults-Identify-as-Transgender-in-the-United-States.pdf

Gard, L. H. (1990). Patient disclosure of human immunodeficiency virus (HIV) status to parents: Clinical considerations. *Professional Psychology: Research and Practice, 21*(4), 252–256. https://doi.org/10.1037/0735-7028.21.4.252

Garfinkel, H. (1967). *Studies in ethnomethodology.* Prentice-Hall.

Gershman, H. (1983). The stress of coming out. *American Journal of Psychoanalysis, 43*(2), 129–138. https://doi.org/10.1007/BF01253472

Goffman, E. (1963). *Stigma.* Prentice-Hall.

Gonzales, G., & Henning-Smith, C. (2017). The Affordable Care Act and health insurance coverage for lesbian, gay, and bisexual adults: Analysis of the Behavioral Risk Factor Surveillance System. *LGBT Health, 4*(1), 62–67. https://doi.org/10.1089/lgbt.2016.0023

Greene, K. (2009). An integrated model of health disclosure decision-making. In T. D. Afifi & W. A. Afifi (Eds.), *Uncertainty and information regulation in interpersonal contexts: Theories and applications* (pp. 226–253). Routledge.

Greene, K., Derlega, V. J., & Mathews, A. (2006). Self-disclosure in personal relationships. In A. L. Vangelisti & D. Perlman (Eds.), *Cambridge handbook of personal relationships* (pp. 409–427). Cambridge University Press.

Greene, K., Derlega, V. J., Yep, G. A., & Petronio, S. (2003). *Privacy and disclosure of HIV in interpersonal relationships.* Lawrence.

Greene, K., & Magsamen-Conrad, K. (2014). Methodological challenges for health research with stigmatized populations. In B. B. Whaley (Ed.), *Research methods in health communication: Principles and application* (pp. 298–317). Routledge.

Haas, S. M. (2018). Stigma, heteronormative passing with health care providers, and partner health involvement in male same-sex couples. In J. A. Theiss & K. Greene (Eds.), *Contemporary studies on relationships, health, and wellness* (pp. 30–48). Cambridge University Press.

Haimson, O. L, & Veinot, T. C. (2020, September 2). Coming out to doctors, coming out to "everyone": Understanding the average sequence of transgender identity disclosures using social media data. *Transgender Health, 5*(2), 158–165. https://doi.org/10.1089/trgh.2019.0045

Holthauser, A., Sawning, S., Leslie, K. F., Jones, V. F., Steinbock, S., Noonan, E. J., Martin, L. J., Weingartner, L. A., Potter, J., Davis, J., Eckstrand, K. L., & Shaw, M. A. (2017). eQuality: A process model to develop an integrated, comprehensive medical education curriculum for LGBT, gender nonconforming, and DSD health. *Medical Science Educator, 27,* 371–383. https://doi.org/10.1007/s40670-017-0393-5

Human Rights Campaign Foundation. (2019). *Healthcare Equality Index.* https://hrc-prod-requests.s3-us-west-2.amazonaws.com/files/assets/resources/HEI-2019-FinalReport.pdf

Jackson, C. L., Agenor, M., Johnson, D. A., Austin, S. B., & Kawachi, I. (2016). Sexual orientation identity disparities in health behaviors, outcomes, and services use among men and women in the United States: A cross-sectional study. *BMC Public Health, 16*(1), 807. https://doi.org/10.1186/s12889-016-3467-1

James, S. E., Herman, J. L., Rankin, S., Keisling, M., Mottet, L., & Anafi, M. (2016). *The report of the 2015 U.S. Transgender Survey.* National Center for Transgender Equality. https://transequality.org/sites/default/files/docs/usts/USTS-Full-Report-Dec17.pdf

Jann, M. W., Penzak, S., White, A., & Tatachar, A. (2019). An elective course in lesbian, gay, bisexual, and transgender health and practice issues. *Journal of Pharmaceutical Education, 83*(8), 1723–1731. https://doi.org/10.5688/ajpe6967

Johnson, A. H., Hill, I., Beach-Ferrara, J., Rogers, B. A., & Bradford, A. (2020). Common barriers to healthcare for transgender people in the U.S. Southeast. *International Journal of Transgender Health*, 21(1), 70–78. http://doi.org/10.1080/15532739.2019.1700203

Johnson, M. J., & Nemeth, L. S. (2014). Addressing health disparities of lesbian and bisexual women: A grounded theory study. *Women's Health Issues*, 24(6), 635–640. https://doi.org/10.1016/j.whi.2014.08.003

Kcomt, L. Gorey, K. M., Barrett, B. J., & McCabe, S. E. (2020). Healthcare avoidance due to anticipated discrimination among transgender people: A call to create trans-affirmative environments. *SSM-Population Health*, 11, 1–8. https://doi.org/10.1016/j.ssmph.2020.100608

King, M., Semlyen, J., Tai, S. S, Killaspy, H., Osborn, D., Popelyuk, D., & Nazareth, I. (2008, August 18). A systematic review of mental disorder, suicide, and deliberate self-harm in lesbian, gay and bisexual people. *BMC Psychiatry*, 8(70). http://doi.org/10.1186/1471-244X-8-70

Klitzman, R. L., & Greenberg, J. D. (2002). Patterns of communication between gay and lesbian patients and their health care providers. *Journal of Homosexuality*, 42(4), 65–75. https://doi.org/10.1300/J082v42n04_04

Kuzma, E. K., Graziano, C., Shea, E., Schaller, F. V., Pardee, M., & Darling-Fisher, C. S. (2019). Improving lesbian, gay, bisexual, transgender, and queer/questioning health: Using a standardized patient experience to educate advanced practice nursing students. *Journal of the American Association of Nurse Practitioners*, 31(12), 714–722. http://doi.org/10.1097/JXX.0000000000000224

Lambda Legal. (2010). *When health care isn't caring: Lambda Legal's survey of discrimination against LGBT people and people with HIV*. https://www.lambdalegal.org/sites/default/files/publications/downloads/whcic-report_when-health-care-isnt-caring.pdf

Lehmann, J. B., Lehmann, C. U., & Kelly, P. J. (1998). Development and health care needs of lesbians. *Journal of Women's Health*, 7(3), 379–387. https://doi.org/10.1089/jwh.1998.7.379

Lick, D. J., Durso, L. E., & Johnson, K. L. (2013). Minority stress and physical health among sexual minorities. *Perspectives on Psychological Science*, 8(5), 521–548. http://doi.org/10.1177/1745691613497965

Link, B. G., Struening, E. L., Neese-Todd, S., Asmussen, S., & Phelan, J. C. (2002). On describing and seeking to change the experience of stigma. *Psychiatric Rehabilitation Skills*, 6(2), 201–231. https://doi.org/10.1080/10973430208408433

Makadon, H. J. (2006). Improving health care for the lesbian and gay communities. *New England Journal of Medicine*, 354, 895–897.

Manning, J. (2014). Coming out conversations and gay/bisexual men's sexual health: A constitutive model study. In V. L. Harvey & T. H. Housel (Eds.), *Health care disparities and the LGBT population* (pp. 27–54). Lexington Books.

Manning, J. (2015). Positive and negative communicative behaviors in coming-out conversations. *Journal of Homosexuality*, 62(1), 67–97. http://doi.org/10.1080/00918369.2014.957127

Meyer, H. M., Mocarski, R., Holt, N. R., Hope, D. A., King, R. E., & Woodruff, N. (2020). Unmet expectations in health care settings: Experiences of transgender and gender diverse adults in the Central Great Plains. *Qualitative Health Research*, 30(3), 409–422. http://doi.org/10.1177/1049732319860265

Meyer, I. (2019). *Experiences of discrimination among lesbian, gay, and bisexual people in the US*. The Williams Institute, UCLA School of Law. https://williamsinstitute.law.ucla.edu/publications/lgb-discrimination-experiences/

Omarzu, J. (2000). A disclosure decision model: Determining how and when individuals will self-disclose. *Personality and Social Psychology Review*, 4(2), 174–185. https://doi.org/10.1207/S15327957PSPR0402_05

Ong, L. M., De Haes, J. C., Hoos, A. M., & Lammes, F. B. (1995). Doctor-patient communication: A review of the literature. *Social Science & Medicine*, 40(7), 903–918. https://doi.org/10.1016/0277-9536(94)00155-M

Oxford Lexico dictionary online. (n.d.). Cisgender. http://www.oxforddictionaries.com/us/definition/american_english/cisgender

Oxford University Press. (2020). *Definition of cisgender* [online]. Lexico. https://www.lexico.com/en/definition/cisgender

Pachankis, J. E. (2007). The psychological implications of concealing a stigma: A cognitive-affective-behavioral model. *Psychological Bulletin, 133*(2), 328–345. http://doi.org/10.1037/0033-2909.133.2.328

Pahwa, R., Fulginiti, A., Brekke, J. S., & Rice, E. (2017). Mental illness disclosure decision making. *American Journal of Orthopsychiatry, 87*(S5), 575–584. https://doi.org/10.1037/ort0000250

Petronio, S. (2002). *Boundaries of privacy: Dialectics of disclosure.* State University of New York Press.

Poteat, T., German, D., & Kerrigan, D. (2013). Managing uncertainty: A grounded theory of stigma in transgender health care encounters. *Social Science & Medicine, 84*, 22–29. http://doi.org/10.1016/j.socscimed.2013.02.019

Quinn, G. P., Schabath, M. B., Sanchez, J. A., Sutton, S. K., & Green, B. L. (2014). The importance of disclosure: Lesbian, gay, bisexual, transgender/transsexual, queer/questioning, and intersex individuals and the cancer continuum. *Cancer, 121*(8), 1160–1163. http://doi.org/10.1002/cncr.29203

Radix, A. E. (2020). Addressing needs of transgender patients: The role of family physicians. *Journal of the American Board of Family Medicine, 33*(2), 314–321. https://doi.org/10.3122/jabfm.2020.02.180228

Roller, C. G., Sedlak, C., & Draucker, C. B. (2015). Navigating the system: How transgender individuals engage in health care services. *Journal of Nursing Scholarship, 47*(5), 417–424. https://doi.org/10.1111/jnu.12160

Röndahl, G. (2011). Heteronormativity in health care education programs. *Nurse Education Today, 31*(4), 345–349. https://doi.org/10.1016/j.nedt.2010.07.003

Sawning, S., Steinbock, S., Croley, R., Combs, R., Shaw, A., & Ganzel, T. (2017). A first step in addressing medical education curriculum gaps in lesbian, gay, bisexual, and transgender-related content: The University of Louisville lesbian, gay, bisexual, and transgender health certificate program. *Education for Health, 30*(2), 108–114. https://doi.org/10.4103/efh.EfH_78_16

Shaver, J., Sharma, A., & Stephenson, R. (2019). Rural primary care providers' experiences and knowledge regarding LGBTQ health in a midwestern state. *Journal of Rural Health, 35*(3), 362–373. https://doi.org/10.1111/jrh.12322

Shetty, G., Sanchez, J. A., Lancaster, J. M., Wilson, L. E., Quinn, G. P., & Schabath, M. B. (2016). Oncology healthcare providers' knowledge, attitudes, and practice behaviors regarding LGBT health. *Patient Education and Counseling, 99*(10), 1676–1684. https://dx.doi.org/10.1016/j.pec.2016.05.004

Smart, L., & Wegner, D. M. (1999). Covering up what can't be seen: Concealable stigma and mental control. *Journal of Personality and Social Psychology, 77*(3), 474–486.

Spack, N. P. (2013). Management of transgenderism. *Journal of the American Medical Association, 309*(5), 478–484. https://doi.org/10.1001/jama.2012.165234

The Williams Institute, UCLA School of Law. (2019, January). *LGBT demographic data interactive.* https://williamsinstitute.law.ucla.edu/visualization/lgbt-stats/?topic=LGBT#about-the-data

UC Davis Health, Office for Health Equity, Diversity and Inclusion. (n.d.). *LGBTQ+ glossary.* https://health.ucdavis.edu/diversity-inclusion/LGBTQI/LGBTQ-Plus.html

U.S. Department of Health and Human Services. (2016). *Advancing LGBT health and well-being 2016 report.* https://www.hhs.gov/sites/default/files/2016-report-with-cover.pdf

Vanderbilt University Medical Center. (n.d.). *Program for LGBTQ health.* https://www.vumc.org/lgbtq/welcome-co-founder

Venetis, M. K., Friley, L. B., Myerson, B., Gillespie, T., Roberson, C., Carter, G., & Shields, C. (2014, November). "I just don't want to be judged:" Application of the disclosure decision-making model when *sharing sexual orientation with medical providers* [Paper presentation]. National Communication Association, Chicago, Illinois.

Venetis, M. K., Meyerson, B. E., Friley, L. B., Gillespie, A., Ohmit, A., & Shields, C. G. (2017). Characterizing sexual orientation disclosure to health care providers: Lesbian, gay, and bisexual perspectives. *Health Communication*, 32(5), 578–586. http://doi.org/10.1080/10410236.2016.1144147

Wells, J. W., & Kline, W. B. (1987). Self-disclosure of homosexual orientation. *The Journal of Social Psychology*, 127(2), 191–197. http://dx.doi.org/10.1080/00224545.1987.9713679

White, J. C., & Dull, V. T. (1998). Room for improvement: Communication between lesbians and primary care providers. *Journal of Lesbian Studies*, 2(1), 95–110. http://doi.org/10.1300/J155v02n01_07

Willes, K., & Allen, M. (2014). The importance of sexual orientation disclosure to physicians for women who have sex with women. In V. L. Harvey & T. H. Housel (Eds.), *Health care disparities and the LGBT population* (pp. 16–29). Lexington Books.

Williams, K. A., & Chapman, M. V. (2011). Comparing health and mental health needs, service use, and barriers to services among sexual minority youths and their peers. *Health & Social Work*, 36(3), 197–206. https://doi.org/10.1093/hsw/36.3.197

The Williams Institute, UCLA School of Law. (2019, January). LGBT demographic data interactive. https://williamsinstitute.law.ucla.edu/visualization/lgbt-stats/?topic=LGBT#about-the-data

NOTE

1. Venetis et al. (2014), conducted by the authors and other researchers, included interviews with LGBQ individuals about disclosing sexual orientation to medical providers. Some results from this study are reported throughout this article. The authors would like to acknowledge their study sponsor, Indiana Minority Health Coalition.

L. Brooke Friley and Maria K. Venetis

STRESS AND COPING IN SEXUAL AND GENDER MINORITY RELATIONSHIPS

EMOTIONAL EXPERIENCES OF LGBTQ+ INDIVIDUALS IN A ROMANTIC RELATIONSHIP: EXPERIENCING AND COPING WITH MINORITY STRESS

LGBTQ+[1] is an inclusive term used to encompass sexual and gender minority (SGM) individuals in aspects of their diversity related to sexual and gender expression (American Psychological Association [APA], n.d.). Specifically, LGBTQ+ refers to individuals who may identify as lesbian (L), gay (G), bisexual (B), transgender (T), queer (Q), or other identities (+). Various identities exist within the LGBTQ+ community, including both diverse sexual and gender identities, also referred to as sexual and gender minority identities. Sexual minority refers to those who are sexually attracted to or have sex with people of the same gender who may identify as LGB. Gender minority refers to those whose gender identity (e.g., man, woman, nonbinary, trans man, trans woman, two spirit, etc.) or gender expression (e.g., masculine, feminine, fluid) differ from their sex assigned at birth (i.e., male, female, intersex; APA, 2021). Gender minority individuals may hold such identities as transgender, gender nonconforming, nonbinary, gender fluid, and agender. Sexual minority individuals' romantic attraction, affectual orientation, and/or sexual characteristics differ from heterosexual identified individuals (APA, 2021), whereas gender minority individuals' gender identity differs from cisgender.

Historically, the term LGBTQ+ has been referenced as a singular group of individuals who identify outside of being heterosexual and/or cisgender.[2] However, it is important to note that those who identify as members of the LGBTQ+ community are diverse. Each person's identity is linked to multiple social categories, which includes but is not limited to age, race, ethnicity, religion, socioeconomic status, ability status, geographical location, and so on (Centers for Disease Control and Prevention [CDC], n.d.-a, n.d.-b). Based on one's collective intersectional identities, each person navigates society with a certain positionality (i.e., alignment with power, disadvantage, and privileged status; Atewologun, 2018).

According to Crenshaw (1989), *intersectionality* is a critical framework drawing attention to how one's multiple identities and positionality impact their experience of interlocking oppressions (Collins, 1990), which in turn affects the way they navigate systems (e.g., family, workplace, and sociopolitical). For example, it centers experiences of transgender people of color, theorizing a working model to address the complex, multifaceted, nonbinary nature of institutional inequalities that affect people with multiple marginal positions. Keeping in mind the need to engage in reflective practices (Lazard & McAvoy, 2020), we, as authors, acknowledge our positionality in this work. The first author acknowledges his positionality as a White, gay, able-bodied, cisgender, doctoral student in counseling psychology, which informs his engagement with scholarship. The second author identifies as a White, queer, binary transgender man and recognizes the various positions of power that inform his understanding and relationship with the presented topics. The third author identifies as a White, lesbian, cisgender woman, who holds a PhD in Family Studies and Human Development. Collectively, the authors acknowledge their limitations of operating from a White, Global North (United States)–based perspective and acknowledge the need to expand researchers and clinicians' understanding of such topics (for a review, see Randall et al., in 2022).

Brief Historiography of LGBTQ+ Relationship Science Scholarship. Research on LGBTQ+ romantic relationships spans the fields of communication, law, family science, political science, psychology, sociology, and beyond. LGBTQ+ relationship science has political and legal significance that affects individual, familial, and societal well-being. For example, LGBTQ+ relationship research has informed debates over legalizing same-sex marriage (see Ogolsky et al., 2019; Umberson et al., 2015).

To date, empirical work has focused on research questions and topics including but not limited to (1) how stigma and prejudice impact LGBTQ+ relational experiences (Cao et al., 2017; Feinstein et al., 2018; LeBlanc et al., 2015); (2) how LGBTQ+ relationships protect against the impacts of stigma and prejudice (Biblarz & Savci, 2010; Randall & Messerschmitt-Coen, 2019); (3) factors contributing to stable and healthy LGBTQ+ relationships (Goldberg & Romero, 2018; Haas & Lannutti, 2021); (4) factors contributing to relationship instability and dissolution among LGBTQ+ people (Balsam et al., 2016; Cooper et al., 2019; Goldberg

& Garcia, 2015); (5) the psychosocial impacts of legal recognition on LGBTQ+ relationships (Drabble et al., 2021; Riggle et al., 2010); (6) effective intervention strategies and techniques for working with LGBTQ+ couples (Randall et al., 2022; Whitton et al., 2017); and (7) how social identity factors including gender, race/ethnicity, immigration status, and economic status intersect and affect LGBTQ+ relationship issues (Calabrese et al., 2015; Kornblith et al., 2016; Whitton et al., 2021).

Population-based survey studies have provided information on LGBTQ+ relationship frequency, stability, and dissolution (e.g., Rosenfeld, 2014; Walker & Taylor, 2021); however, based on the samples included in the research, this information is limited to individuals living in Europe and the United States (Manning & Joyner, 2018). Around the world, there remain significant methodological challenges to conducting LGBTQ+ relationship research with population-level data sets. For example, defining a singular study population is complex and researchers must determine the parameters of their target population, e.g., recruiting a sample of all LGBTQ+-identified individuals compared to recruiting only those who identify as bisexual. Once a study population is defined, people in LGBTQ+ relationships may not be identified via a direct question and rather by comparing the genders of both partners within a data set. As per Régnier-Loilier (2018), it is methodologically problematic and unreliable for researchers to identify and analyze LGBTQ+ relationships by indirect measures such as comparing both partners' gender (e.g., due to numerous coding errors). At the data collection level, future researchers are encouraged to include direct indicators of LGBTQ+ relationship status.[2]

Generating theoretical and empirical knowledge on LGBTQ+ relationships has historically been approached by examining individuals who are in a relationship (e.g., Haas & Lannutti, 2022) or obtaining both partner reports (i.e., collecting dyadic data; Randall et al., 2017a, 2017b). Most LGBTQ+ relationship science involves research with individuals who are in a relationship, especially nationally representative samples and those comparing queer relationships with heterosexual relationships (Umberson et al., 2015). As per Umberson and colleagues (2015), there remain opportunities to build upon the body of work with dyads by employing methodologies such as dyadic research designs, quasi-experimental designs, and a relationship biography approach. The relationship biography approach is an organizing research framework which focuses on the various changing components of relationship histories, e.g., temporal changes, status changes, etc. To this end, work by Randall et al. (2017a) examined dyadic coping behaviors in 95 same-sex couples. The researchers found that perceived emotion-focused support from one's partner weakened the positive association between experiences of discrimination and depressive symptoms. Beyond this one example, researchers interested in collecting dyadic data are encouraged to be mindful of addressing gendered contexts and inequities experienced by individuals with intersecting identities along spectrums of race, ethnicity, socioeconomic status, and other social factors (for a discussion on intersectionality, see Moradi & Gzranka, 2017). Notably, future researchers are encouraged to address the dearth of literature on bisexual, transgender, and LGBTQ+ people of color's experiences of being multiply marginalized and subject to within-group discrimination inside the LGBTQ+ community (Balsam et al., 2011; Biblars & Savci, 2010; Manning & Joyner, 2018).

LGBTQ+ DISCRIMINATION AND MINORITY STRESS

LGBTQ+ individuals are subject to discrimination, heterosexism, and homonegativity due to living in traditionally heteronormative societies (Ayhan et al., 2019; Center for the Study of Inequality at Cornell University, 2021). As a result, LGBTQ+ individuals experience oppression that is defined as "discrimination against and/or systematic denial of resources to members of groups who are identified as inferior or less deserving than others" (APA, 2018, p. 3). These oppressive experiences are associated with increased psychological vulnerability (i.e., higher risk of mental distress) and poorer mental health outcomes compared to those who identify as heterosexual and cisgender (DiPlacido & Fallahi, 2020). According to population-level data from those living the United States, LGBTQ+ individuals are nearly twice as likely to have a mental health disorder in their lifetime and are 2.5 times more likely to experience depression, anxiety, and substance misuse as compared with heterosexual individuals (American Psychiatric Association [APA], 2017).

Given these staggering statistics, it is common to question what accounts for such health disparities. Nearly 20 years ago, Meyer (2003) conceptualized LGBTQ+ individuals' psychological vulnerability in terms of *minority stress*. According to Meyer (2003), stigma, prejudice, and discrimination generate stressful social environments. Meyer's (2003) minority stress theory shows that the experience of *distal* stressors (e.g., prejudiced events such as discrimination and violence) leads to proximal stressors (e.g., expectations of rejection, concealment, internalized homophobia). Taken together, experiences of both distal and proximal minority stressors are associated with, or can lead to, negative mental health outcomes, such as emotion, social/interpersonal, and cognitive issues, conferring risk for psychopathology (Hatzenbuehler, 2009; King et al., 2008; Meyer, 2003).

Identity concealment is considered one source of minority stress (Haas & Stafford, 1998; Pachankis et al., 2020; Riggle et al., 2017; Rostosky & Riggle, 2017). While many definitions of identity concealment exist, it can be best understood as an umbrella term for behavioral and cognitive constructs related to the lack of disclosure/outness about one's identity (Pachankis et al., 2020). Depending on the situation, LGBTQ+ individuals may make the decision about whether to reveal or conceal their sexual orientation, gender identity, or relationship status to protect against discrimination (Haas & Stafford, 1998; Pachankis et al., 2020; Riggle et al., 2017; Rostosky & Riggle, 2017).

Cisgender and heterosexual people's attitudes toward LGBTQ+ people's identities and their relationship(s) may vary based on a range of demographic factors (e.g., age, gender, education, ethnicity, religiosity, political affiliation), which lend themselves to beliefs about whether sexual orientation is a choice (Costa et al., 2017; D'Amore et al., 2022). D'Amore et al. (2022) conducted a cross-national study, investigating attitudes toward same-sex marriage and lesbian and gay parenting in Belgium, France, Greece, Italy, Poland, Portugal, and Spain, The researchers found that sociopolitical context and legal status of LGBTQ+ relationships were associated with attitudes toward LGBTQ+ people. Furthermore, the study authors found that attitudinal variability exists between countries, despite many believing (or hoping) attitudes throughout Europe are changing. Attitudes toward LGBTQ+ issues were significantly more negative in Greece and Poland than of those living in other countries represented in the sample. Additional research is needed to understand the connections between sociopolitical context and people's attitudes toward LGBTQ+ relationships and families to assess LGBTQ+ stigmatization on an international scale.

COPING WITH LGBTQ+ DISCRIMINATION AND MINORITY STRESS: THE ROLE OF ONE'S ROMANTIC PARTNER

There has been considerable scholarly interest in exploring protective factors, including social support, given the negative association between LGBTQ+ discrimination and mental well-being (Hatzenbuehler, 2009; King et al., 2008; Meyer, 2003). More specifically, romantic relationship involvement has emerged in the literature as one social support factor that may protect psychological well-being (e.g., Haas, 2021; Haas & Lannutti, 2021). Being involved in a satisfying and healthy romantic relationship is considered a protective factor for mental health for all individuals (Loving & Slatcher, 2013), and some have argued being in a romantic relationship may have protective effects on the mental health of those who identify as LGBTQ+ (e.g., Whitton et al., 2021). Indeed, for those who identify as LGBTQ+, being in a committed romantic relationship is associated with lower depressive symptoms, anxiety symptoms, and substance use (Feinstein et al., 2016; Kornblith et al., 2016; Parsons et al., 2013; Whitton et al., 2021). Notably, LGBTQ+ people may experience same-gender or different-gender romantic relationships, and these relationships may or may not be legally recognized (i.e., marital or nonmarital).

PSYCHOSOCIAL IMPACTS OF LEGALLY RECOGNIZING LGBTQ+ RELATIONSHIPS

As of June 31, 2022, some countries have legalized same-sex marriage (Human Rights Campaign, 2022), and other countries (e.g., Czech Republic, Italy, and Taiwan) recognize same-sex relationships via legislation honoring civil unions (Council on Foreign Relations, 2021). Acknowledging the larger sociopolitical climate in which people live, it is important to consider the psychosocial impacts of governmental laws and policies that can impact LGBTQ+ individuals (e.g., equal marriage rights). Ogolsky and colleagues (2019) collected longitudinal data on the personal well-being of U.S. individuals in same-sex ($n = 279$) and different-sex ($n = 266$) relationships. Those in same-sex relationships experienced higher levels of stigma and psychological distress, prior to *Obergefell v. Hodges* (2015), the U.S. Supreme Court case decision that resulted in national same-sex marriage recognition. Following the ruling, over time, Ogolsky and colleagues (2019) found that levels of stigma decreased and life satisfaction increased. The study authors concluded that legal marriage recognition uniquely impacted discrimination and well-being for individuals in same-sex relationships.

In 2021, Drabble and colleagues conducted a scoping review of equal marriage rights' psychosocial impacts in medical, psychological, sociological, and other scholarly journals. The authors identified 59 empirical studies that were published from 2000 to 2019 and had explicitly focused on the psychosocial impacts of equal marriage rights and same-sex marriage on sexual minority adults. Across the articles included, positive psychosocial impacts of same-sex marriage were identified such as social acceptance and reduced stigma. Such impacts had been identified at individual, interpersonal (i.e., dyad, family), community, and societal levels. Some studies, however, found that sexual minority stigma persisted across all levels despite equal marriage rights (Drabble et al., 2021).

The expansion of LGBTQ+ rights has been globally unbalanced (Council on Foreign Relations, 2021), and discussions and debates over marriage equality are contextualized by the geopolitical landscape. Research to date has insufficiently examined diverse LGBTQ+ experiences across the globe, with limited attention to individuals outside the Global North. Future research is needed to identifying inequities that may exist based on sexual identity, gender identity, race, ethnicity, or other social, interactional factors (Drabble et al., 2021).

PURPOSE OF ENTRY

This entry reviews empirical literature that has been conducted with LGBTQ+ individuals in a romantic relationship, their experiences of stress, and associations with their relationship quality and functioning. Additionally, research is presented regarding LGBTQ+ relationship maintenance behaviors, namely dyadic coping, that may be beneficial in understanding ways LGBTQ+ couples can protect their relationship in times of duress. Lastly, a presentation of relationship education programs designed for queer relationships is provided.[3]

STRESS IN LGBTQ+ RELATIONSHIPS

Most research on LGBTQ+ stigma, prejudice, discrimination, and minority stress has examined the intersection of these experiences as they relate to individuals' health and well-being (e.g., Hatzenbuehler, 2009; King et al., 2008; Meyer, 2003). For example, research has shown that LGBT people are at higher risk of mental disorder, suicidal ideation, substance misuse, and deliberate self-harm (APA, 2017, 2021; King et al., 2008). However, it is important to consider that individuals exist in social systems and that one's experiences of stress may impact others around them, namely, one's romantic partner (for a discussion, see Randall & Bodenmann, 2017). Keeping this in mind allows researchers and the like to conceptualize stress as an interdependent and relational construct. Indeed, there is ample evidence to suggest LGBTQ+ individuals' experience of stress can negatively affect perceptions of romantic relationship well-being (e.g., Frost & LeBlanc, 2018; Frost et al., 2017; Mohr & Fassinger, 2006; Riggle et al., 2010; Rostosky et al., 2007).

Additionally, stigma aimed at LGBTQ+ parents can also affect their children's functioning. As an example, Bos and colleagues (2021) published a longitudinal study with 72 emerging adult children of lesbian parents. Results showed that 40.3% ($n = 29$) of study participants had experienced homophobic stigmatization that was indirectly associated with internalizing and externalizing problems during emerging adulthood. Being treated unfairly due to being raised by sexual minority parents was shown to have long-term effects. Bos and colleagues (2021) acknowledged the need for future research to address intervention strategies for school and community programs to prevent stigmatization. Acknowledging the interpersonal nature of stress in romantic relationships, models and theories that help to explain these associations are included in the relationship science literature.

MODELS THAT EXPLAIN STRESS IN LGBTQ+ RELATIONSHIPS

Karney and Bradbury's (1995) vulnerability–stress–adaptation model (VSA) provides a framework for understanding how individuals' enduring vulnerabilities, stressful life events, and adaptive processes are associated with relationship quality and stability. Enduring vulnerabilities are relatively stable traits that individuals bring with them into relationship (e.g., demographics, personality traits, attachment styles, and symptoms of psychopathology). The VSA proposes that individuals' enduring vulnerabilities predispose individuals to stress; ways of dealing with stress can impact their ways of handling conflict and disagreement within relationships, which can be either adaptive or maladaptive (Karney & Bradbury, 1995).

Applying the VSA model to empirical research with same-sex couples, Totenhagen et al. (2018) examined daily diaries from a community sample of 81 same-sex couples and found that individuals' reports of higher levels of enduring vulnerabilities (e.g., internalized homophobia, the internalization of negative societal beliefs about sexual identity by a sexual minority individual; Williamson, 2000) was associated with lower relationship quality and functioning. Results from Totenhagen et al. (2018) demonstrated that the VSA model (Karney & Bradbury, 1995) can be applied to understand LGBTQ+ couples' relational functioning in the context of minority stress. The VSA model helps explain the process by which minority stressors experienced at the individual level can lead to deleterious effects on relational wellbeing in LGBTQ+ couples.

STRESS AS AN INTERPERSONAL, DYAD-LEVEL CONSTRUCT

Akin to the VSA model in helping explain how experiences of stress can impact relationship functioning, Frost and colleagues (2017) acknowledge that sexual minority individuals entering in a same-sex relationship may become vulnerable to experiencing a new set of unique minority stressors. Such stressors include the family's devaluation of one's same-sex partnership (e.g., neglect to acknowledge or validate the relationship), or the stress of coming out as a couple and/or concealing one's same-sex relationship status.[4]

Acknowledging experiences of couple-level minority stressors, Frost and LeBlanc (2018) devised a couple-level minority stress framework to explain the ways in which minority stress experiences may influence same-gender relationships' quality and dissolution. This framework acknowledges how one partner's experience of stress can impact how they and their partner may cope with such experiences (LeBlanc et al., 2015), such as managing the visibility of their relationship (i.e., couple-level concealment), navigating lack of social support/acceptance, and facing legal barriers to adopting children (Frost & LeBlanc, 2018; Frost et al., 2017).

Experiencing and coping with minority stress can impact the emotional dynamics of LGBTQ+ individuals and their relationship. Romantic partners' experiences of stress are considered interwoven, given their shared interdependence (Kelley & Thibaut, 1978; Otis et al., 2006); as such, one partner's experience of stress can impact their partner's experience. Stress *spillover* and *crossover* are two processes by which an individual's stress levels can (negatively) impact their relationship couples (Randall & Bodenmann, 2017). *Stress spillover* occurs when one partner's stress influences their own perception of stress within their relationship (Buck & Neff, 2012). *Stress crossover* is a process by which stress becomes a dyadic phenomenon, wherein one's stress state impacts their behavior (e.g., less open, less communicative, more "on edge"), which in turn creates stress for the partner as well (Westman, 2001).

While stress spillover and crossover are characterized as universal relationship processes (i.e., applicable to all couples irrespective of identity status), early 21st-century research has highlighted how such processes may operate in the context of couples with varying sexual identities (LeBlanc et al., 2015; Meyer, 2003). For example, Feinstein et al. (2018) found that higher rates of minority stress were positively associated with negative relationship interactions in male couples (stress spillover). Additionally, using a sample of 81 same-sex couples, Cooper et al. (2019) found that individuals' perceived daily sexual minority stress was uniquely related to their partner's perception of relationship stress (stress crossover). Taken together, one partner's experience of stress can impact their partner's experience as well (e.g., Cao et al., 2017; Hatzenbuehler, 2009; Totenhagen et al., 2018).

Each partner in the dyad holds multiple statuses, and when one partner and/or both partners' gender/race/ethnicity/socioeconomic status/immigration status is marginalized, this can lead to unique forms of minority stress (Frost & LeBlanc, 2018). For example, Everett et al. (2019) found a difference in victimization, discrimination, and stigma consciousness rates between White sexual minority women and Black and Latina sexual minority women, depending on levels of masculinity and femininity. Black sexual minority women experience the "triple jeopardy" effect based on their intersecting marginalized identities (Calabrese et al., 2015). Because each person holds different intersecting identities, it is important that researchers, clinicians, and policymakers alike acknowledge the impact of intersecting identities on experiences of minority stress. By acknowledging each person's unique intersectionality, researchers and clinicians alike can begin to understand how an individual's identities may shape their experiences of stress, which can impact their partner's stress and their joint coping responses. There is a need for additional research that accounts for Black, Indigenous, and people of colors' sexual and gender minority individuals' mental health from a multidimensional minority stress perspective (for a discussion, see Abreu et al., 2022; Calabrese et al., 2015; Mosley et al., 2021).

LGBTQ+ PARTNERS COPING WITH STRESS

Just as partners' experiences of stress are interconnected, so are their coping responses (see Revenson et al., 2005). Therefore, partners' inability to cope with one another in the face of stress can lead to increased relationship conflict, intimacy problems, and disengagement from effective maintenance and ultimately relationship dissolution (Balsam et al., 2016; Doyle & Molix, 2015; Goldberg & Garcia, 2015; Goldberg et al., 2014; Mohr & Fassinger, 2006; Riggle et al., 2010; Rostosky et al., 2007). Relational maintenance behaviors, defined as processes in which romantic partners maintain their relationship (see Ogolsky & Monk, 2018), predict relational resilience and positive relational outcomes (e.g., commitment, satisfaction, control mutuality, and closeness) in queer romantic relationships (Haas & Lannutti, 2021). Relational resilience is the ability of the partners in a relationship to adapt positively to adversity. In a sample of 1,303 LGBTQ+ individuals, Haas and Lannutti (2021) found that people identifying as LGBTQ+ utilize a diverse range of positive relational maintenance behaviors to help promote relational resilience. For example, verbal and behavioral reaffirmations of commitment to the relationship (i.e., assurances of desire to be in the relationship) were found to be the primary predictor of relational resilience. Another impactful relational maintenance behavior is openness, that is, self-disclosing personal information about one's goals, needs, desires (Haas & Lannutti, 2021). Dyadic coping has also been defined as an important relationship maintenance behavior, which can help protect one's romantic relationship during times of duress in addition to increasing relationship longevity and satisfaction (Randall & Messerschmitt-Coen, 2019).

Dyadic coping is a process that conceptualizes how partners cope with stress in the context of their relationship (Bodenmann, 2005). Once a partner communicates their stress to their partner (stress communication), partners either respond positively or negatively. Research conducted with same-sex samples has found (positive) dyadic coping to be a protective factor in couples' experiences of sexual minority stress. For example, Randall et al. (2017b) found that the support of a romantic partner helped to buffer against individuals' negative minority stress experiences and anxiety symptoms. The researchers found that participants exhibited lower associations between workplace minority stress and anxiety when their partners reported higher levels of problem-focused and emotion-focused supportive dyadic coping. As noted by the study's authors, there remain scholarly gaps in understanding how social interactions with romantic partners are linked to mental health outcomes.

Apart from engaging in deliberate coping behaviors, LGBTQ+ individuals may benefit from making meaning from their minority stress experiences with their partner. Meaning making may involve reframing minority stress in a way that reaffirms commitment to their partner(s) (Frost 2011; Frost & LeBlanc, 2018; Rostosky & Riggle, 2017). As an example, a couple may discuss how their commitment to each other is further solidified by their ability to cope together with experiences of minority stress and in turn result in a stronger sense of commitment to the relationship. To understand more about how LGB individuals make meaning of and respond to minority stress in their everyday lives, Frost (2014) interviewed 99 individuals in same-sex relationships and conducted a narrative analysis. Frost (2014) found that sharing minority stress stories with one another allowed romantic partners to reflect on the importance of those events, to understand each other more deeply, and to reframe and reaffirm the notion that overcoming adversity leads greater strength (i.e., redemption stories). Frost (2014) found that when queer partners faced with minority stress participated together in "redemptive" meaning-making strategies, they experienced heightened closeness in their relationships (Frost, 2014). Lastly, LGBTQ+ individuals may also exercise "positive marginality" (i.e., reframing experiences of stigmatization as opportunities for activism and change), such as defining important relationship milestones for themselves rather than relying on heteronormative definitions of success in relationships (Frost, 2011; Frost & LeBlanc, 2018; Rostosky & Riggle, 2017).

As individuals in the LGBTQ+ community represent a diverse range of sexual and gender identities, roles, and expressions, it is important to consider the gendered context of couples coping with stress. For example, Meuwly et al. (2013) surveyed 82 Swiss women and compared relationship functioning among same-sex couples compared to heterosexual couples. Lesbian women in same-sex relationships reported receiving better support from, experiencing less conflict, and having better dyadic coping with their female partners. By comparing women's evaluations of female versus male partners, the authors provided some evidence that women may offer better relational support and thus be better equipped to reduce the possible spillovers effect from extradyadic stress (Meuwly et al., 2013).

Beyond the individual and dyadic level, community-level social support can be utilized as a coping factor for those in queer relationships. LeBlanc et al. (2015) found that community-level resilience factors, such as having a good support network of same-gender couples, could be helpful in buffering against the effects of couple-level minority stress. Additionally, available community resources that are LGBTQ+ focused or more generally focused may provide support (Eisenberg et al., 2017). These resources may be provided at the organizational level by LGBTQ+-serving organizations and sexual health service providers, and they may be community spaces where people gather informally to provide social support (e.g., coffee shops, bars). While there are many stories of churches and/or schools being unwelcoming (CITATIONS), these same spaces may also be helpful and positive, especially when LGBTQ+ community members are visibly represented, and affinity groups are embedded within (Eisenberg et al., 2017).

RELATIONSHIP EDUCATION PROGRAMS

Researchers and clinicians have begun to explore relationship education and clinical interventions that help LGBTQ+ couples navigate their relational experiences. As one example, the Affirming Couples Counseling to Engage Same-Sex partners (Pentel, 2021) program is geared toward same-sex female couples utilizing a cognitive behavioral therapy approach, which aims to treat relationship distress and increase couple coping. Another such program is the Strengthening Same-Sex Relationship (SSSR; Whitton et al., 2017) program that incorporates evidence-based relationship education curriculum into a culturally relevant framework geared specifically toward same-sex relationships. The SSSR program is the parent program to the SSSR-F and SSSR-M programs, designed for same-sex female and same-sex male relationships, respectively (Whitton et al., 2017). The aim of the programs is to teach the core tenets of relationship education programs (e.g., communication skills) while addressing potentially harmful programmatic effects such as unintentional increases in minority stress and heterosexist ideals (Whitton et al., 2017).

More recently, Arizona Board of Regents. (2021) have developed a relationship education program to teach sexual minority couples how to cope with stress in the context of their relationship. The Couples Coping Enhancement Training–Sexual Minority Stress (CCET-SMS) program is an adaptation of the original CCET program designed by Bodenmann and Shantinath (2004) based on stress and coping research and theory. The CCET-SMS program was developed to increase the cultural relevancy of the CCET by incorporating the minority stress model (Meyer, 2003). In doing so, CCET-SMS incorporates the unique experiences of sexual minority couples into the original CCET framework and is designed to help couples improve (minority) stress management; enhance their ability to cope as a couple; sensitize both partners to ideas of mutual fairness, equity, and respect; improve communication; and improve problem-solving skills. The CCET-SMS program's initial tests of efficacy, feasibility, and acceptability are ongoing and anticipated to be completed in 2022; pilot testing results are anticipated in early 2023. Beyond these prevention and intervention programs, additional research that can lend itself the development of such programming is needed especially for individuals and couples with diverse orientations and relationships (e.g., nonmonogamous relationships, polyamorous, etc.).

CONCLUSION

LGBTQ+ individuals face additional stressors above and beyond common stressors, which can impact their romantic relationship experience (see Cao et al., 2017; Meyer, 2003; Randall et al., 2017-a, 2017-b). Experiences of minority stressors associated with living in traditional, heteronormative societies (e.g., DiPlacido & Fallahi, 2020) have detrimental effects on both individual and relational well-being. Researchers have, however, identified key relationship maintenance behaviors that may help mitigate stress' deleterious effects, such as dyadic coping (e.g., Randall et al., 2017-a, 2017-b).

Beyond empirical research, there is an insurgence of relationship education programs designed to help LGBTQ+ couples identify and cope with experiences of minority stress (Pentel, 2021; Randall et al., 2022; Whitton et al., 2017). This insurgence is important, given the history of relationship education programs focusing primarily on heterosexual, cisgender relationships. Evaluating these and related clinical interventions with an eye toward addressing the growing needs of LGBTQ+ individuals and couples will continue to be important lines of research that will bridge empirical and clinical work for those working with these populations.

FURTHER READING

Brüderl, J., Drobnič, S., Hank, K., Neyer, F. J., Walper, S., Alt, P., Borschel, E., Bozoyan, C., Garrett, M., Geissler, S., Avilés, T. G., Gröpler, N., Hajek, K., Herzig, M., Huyer-May, B., Lenke, R., Lorenz, R., Lutz, K., Minkus, L.,...Wetzel, M. (2021). *The German Family Panel (pairfam)*. ZA5678 Data file Version 12.0.0. GESIS Data Archive. https://doi.org/10.4232/pairfam.5678.12.0.0

Harris, K. M., Halpern, C. T., Whitsel, E. A., Hussey, J. M., Killeya-Jones, L., Tabor, J., & Dean, S. C. (2019). Cohort profile: The National Longitudinal Study of Adolescent to Adult Health (Add Health). *International Journal of Epidemiology, 48*(5), 1415–1425. https://doi.org/10.1093/ije/dyz115

Kline, K., & Randall, A. K. (2021). The moderating effect of internalized transphobia on the association between gender congruence and sexual satisfaction for transgender men. *Journal of LGBT Issues in Counseling, 15*, 93–109. https://doi.org/10.1080/15538605.2021.1868378

Meyer, I. H. (2020). *Generations: A study of the life and health of LGB people in a changing society, United States, 2016–2019*. Inter-university Consortium for Political and Social Research [distributor]. https://doi.org/10.3886/ICPSR37166.v1

Meyer, I. H. (2021). *TransPop, United States, 2016–2018*. Inter-university Consortium for Political and Social Research [distributor]. https://doi.org/10.3886/ICPSR37938.v1

Randall, A. K., Tao, C., Totenhagen, C. J., Walsh, K. J., & Cooper, A. (2017). Associations between sexual orientation discrimination and depression among same-sex couples: Moderating effects of dyadic coping. *Journal of Couple and Relationship Therapy, 4*, 325–345. https://doi.org/10.1111/fare.12311

Rostosky, S. S. (2015). *Happy together: Thriving as a same-sex couple in your family, workplace, and community*. APA LifeTools.

Rostosky, S. S., & Riggle, E. D. (2017). Same-sex relationships and minority stress. *Current Opinion in Psychology, 13*, 29–38. https://doi.org/10.1016/j.copsyc.2016.04.011

Samrock, S., Kline, K., & Randall, A. K. (2021). Buffering against depression: Association between self-compassion, perceived family support, and age for transgender and non-binary individuals. *MDPI: International Journal of Environmental Research and Public Health, 18*, 7938. https://doi.org/10.3390/ijerph18157938

Statistics Canada. (2017, August). *Same-sex couples in Canada in 2016*.

Totenhagen, C. J., Randall, A. K., & Lloyd, K. (2018). Stress and relationship functioning in same-sex couples: The vulnerability of internalized homophobia. *Family Relations, 67*, 399–413. https://doi.org/10.1111/fare.12311

Umberson, D. (2022). *Health and Relationships Project, United States, 2014–2015*. Inter-university Consortium for Political and Social Research [distributor]. https://doi.org/10.3886/ICPSR37404.v2

U.S. Census Bureau. (2022, June 9). *Same-sex couples*. https://www.census.gov/topics/families/same-sex-couples.html

REFERENCES

Abreu, R. L., Townsend, D., Mitchell, Y., Ward, J., Audette, L., & Gonzalez, K. A. (2022). LGBTQ qualitative and mixed methods research in counseling psychology: A content analysis. *The Counseling Psychologist, 50*(5), 708–738. https://doi.org/10.1177/00110000221092481

American Psychiatric Association. (2017). *Mental health disparities: LGBTQ*. https://www.psychiatry.org/File%20Library/Psychiatrists/Cultural-Competency/Mental-Health-Disparities/Mental-Health-Facts-for-LGBTQ.pdf

American Psychological Association. (n.d.). *APA dictionary of psychology*. https://dictionary.apa.org/lgbtq

American Psychological Association, APA Task Force on Psychological Practice with Sexual Minority Persons. (2021). *Guidelines for psychological practice with sexual minority persons*. http://www.apa.org/about/policy/psychological-practice-sexual-minority-persons.pdf

American Psychological Association, Boys and Men Guidelines Group. (2018). *APA guidelines for psychological practice with boys and men*. http://www.apa.org/about/policy/psychological-practice-boys-men-guidelines.pdf

Arizona Board of Regents. (2021). *CCET-SMS Program Part 1: Towards the development of a couples coping program for same-gender couples*. Arizona State University. https://asu.pure.elsevier.com/en/projects/ccet-sms-program-part-1-towards-the-development-of-a-couples-copi

Atewologun, D. (2018). Intersectionality theory and practice. In *Oxford Research Encyclopedia of Business and Management*. https://doi.org/10.1093/acrefore/9780190224851.013.48

Ayhan, C. H. B., Bilgin, H., Uluman, O. T., Sukut, O., Yilmaz, S., & Buzlu, S. (2019). A systematic review of the discrimination against sexual and gender minority in health care settings. *International Journal of Health Services, 50*(1), 44–61. https://doi.org/10.1177/0020731419885093

Balsam, K. F., Molina, Y., Beadnell, B., Simoni, J., & Walters, K. (2011). Measuring multiple minority stress: The LGBT People of Color Microaggressions Scale. *Cultural Diversity & Ethnic Minority Psychology, 17*(2), 163–174. https://doi.org/10.1037/a0023244

Balsam, K. F., Rostosky, S. S., & Riggle, E. D. B. (2016). Breaking up is hard to do: Women's experience of dissolving their same-sex relationship. *Journal of Lesbian Studies, 21*, 30–46. https://doi.org/10.1080/10894160.2016.1165561

Bettergarcia, J., Matsuno, E., & Conover, K. J. (2021). Training mental health providers in queer-affirming care: A systematic review. *Psychology of Sexual Orientation and Gender Diversity, 8*(3), 365–377. https://doi.org/10.1037/sgd0000514

Biblarz, T. J., & Savci, E. (2010). Lesbian, gay, bisexual, and transgender families. *Journal of Marriage and Family, 72*(3), 480–497. https://doi.org/10.1111/j.1741-3737.2010.00714.x

Bodenmann, G., & Shantinath, S. D. (2004). The Couples Coping Enhancement Training (CCET): A new approach to prevention of marital distress based upon stress and coping. *Family Relations, 53*(5), 477–484. https://doi.org/10.1111/j.0197-6664.2004.00056.x

Bodenmann, G. (2005). Dyadic coping and its significance for marital functioning. In T. A. Revenson, K. Kayser, & G. Bodenmann (Eds.), *Couples coping with stress: Emerging perspectives on dyadic coping* (pp. 33–49). American Psychological Association. https://doi.org/10.1037/11031-002

Bos, H., Carone, N., Rothblum, E. D., Koh, A., & Gartrell, N. (2021). Long-term effects of homophobic stigmatization during adolescence on problem behavior in emerging adult offspring of lesbian parents. *Journal of Youth and Adolescence, 50,* 1114–1125. https://doi.org/10.1007/s10964-020-01364-1

Buck, A. A., & Neff, L. A. (2012). Stress spillover in early marriage: The role of self-regulatory depletion. *Journal of Family Psychology, 26*(5), 698. https://doi.org/10.1037/a0029260

Calabrese, S. K., Meyer, I. H., Overstreet, N. M., Haile, R., & Hansen, N. B. (2015). Exploring discrimination and mental health disparities faced by Black sexual minority women using a minority stress framework. *Psychology of Women Quarterly, 39*(3), 287–304. https://doi.org/10.1177/0361684314560730

Cao, H., Zhou, N., Fine, M., Liang, Y., Li, J., & Mills-Koonce, W. R. (2017). Sexual minority stress and same-sex relationship wellbeing: A meta-analysis of research prior to the U.S. nationwide legalization of same-sex marriage: stress and same-sex couple relationships. *Journal of Marriage and Family, 79,* 1258–1277. https://doi.org/10.1111/jomf.12415

Center for the Study of Inequality at Cornell University. (2021, August 3). *What does the scholarly research say about the effects of discrimination on the health of LGBT people? What We Know: The Public Policy Research Portal.* https://whatweknow.inequality.cornell.edu/topics/lgbt-equality/what-does-scholarly-research-say-about-the-effects-of-discrimination-on-the-health-of-lgbt-people/

Centers for Disease Control and Prevention (CDC). (n.d.-a). About LGBT health | lesbian, gay, bisexual, and transgender health. https://www.cdc.gov/lgbthealth/about.htm

Centers for Disease Control and Prevention (CDC). (n.d.-b). *Terminology | adolescent and school health.* https://www.cdc.gov/healthyyouth/terminology/sexual-and-gender-identity-terms.htm

Collins, P. H. (1990). *Black feminist thought: Knowledge, consciousness, and the politics of empowerment.* Routledge.

Cooper, A. N., Tao, C., Totenhagen, C. J., Randall, A. K., & Holley, S. R. (2019). Daily stress spillover and crossover: Moderating effects of difficulties in emotion regulation in same-sex couples. *Journal of Social and Personal Relationships, 37*(4), 1245–1267. https://doi.org/10.1177/0265407519891777

Costa, P. A., Carneiro, F., Esposito, F., D'Amore, S., & Green, R.-J. (2017). Sexual prejudice in Portugal: Results from the first wave European study on heterosexuals' attitudes toward gay and lesbian marriage and parenting. *Sexuality Research and Social Policy, 52,* 35–55. https://doi-org.ezproxy1.lib.asu.edu/10.1007/s13178-017-0292-y

Council on Foreign Relations. (2021, December). *Marriage equality: Global comparisons.* https://www.cfr.org/backgrounder/marriage-equality-global-comparisons

Crenshaw, K. (1989). *Demarginalizing the intersection of race and sex: A black feminist critique of antidiscrimination doctrine, feminist theory and antiracist politics* (Vol. 1989, Article 8). University of Chicago Legal Forum. https://chicagounbound.uchicago.edu/uclf/vol1989/iss1/8

D'Amore, S., Wollast, R., Green, R. J., Bouchat, P., Costa, P. A., Katuzny, K., Scali, T., Baiocco, R., Vecho, O., Mijas, M. E., Aparicio, M. E., Geroulanou, K., & Klein, O. (2022). Heterosexual university students' attitudes toward same-sex couples and parents across seven European countries. *Sexuality Research & Social Policy, 19,* 791–804. https://doi-org.ezproxy1.lib.asu.edu/10.1007/s13178-020-00511-4

DiPlacido, J., & Fallahi, C. R. (2020). Stigma and sexual and gender minority mental health. In Esther D. Rothblum (Ed.), *The Oxford handbook of sexual and gender minority mental health* (pp. 417–428). Oxford Academic. https://doi.org/10.1093/oxfordhb/9780190067991.013.37

Doyle, D. M., & Molix, L. (2015). Social stigma and sexual minorities' romantic relationship functioning. *Personality and Social Psychology Bulletin, 41*(10), 1363–1381. https://doi.org/10.1177/0146167215594592

Drabble, L. A., Wootton, A. R., Veldhuis, C. B., Riggle, E. D. B., Rostosky, S. S., Lannutti, P. J., Balsam, K. F., & Hughes, T. L. (2021). Perceived psychosocial impacts of legalized same-sex marriage: A scoping review of sexual minority adults' experiences. *PLOS ONE, 16*(5), e0249125. https://doi.org/10.1371/journal.pone.0249125

Eisenberg, M. E., Mehus, C. J., Saewyc, E. M., Corliss, H. L., Gower, A. L., Sullivan, R., & Porta, C. M. (2017). Helping young people stay afloat: A qualitative study of community resources and supports for LGBTQ adolescents in the United States and Canada. *Journal of Homosexuality, 65*(8), 969–989. https://doi.org/10.1080/00918369.2017.1364944

Everett, B. G., Steele, S. M., Matthews, A. K., & Hughes, T. L. (2019). Gender, race, and minority stress among sexual minority women: An intersectional approach. *Archives of Sexual Behavior, 48*(5), 1505–1517. https://doi.org/10.1007/s10508-019-1421-x

Feinstein, B., Latack, J., Bhatia, V., Davila, J., & Eaton, N. (2016). Romantic relationship involvement as a minority stress buffer in gay/lesbian versus bisexual individuals. *Journal of Gay and Lesbian Mental Health, 20*, 237–257. https://doi.org/10.1080/19359705.2016.1147401

Feinstein, B. A., McConnell, E., Dyar, C., Mustanski, B., & Newcomb, M. E. (2018). Minority stress and relationship functioning among young male same-sex couples: An examination of actor–partner interdependence models. *Journal of Consulting and Clinical Psychology, 86*, 416–426. https://doi.org/10.1037/ccp0000296

Frost, D. M. (2011). Social stigma and its consequences for the socially stigmatized. *Social and Personality Psychology Compass, 5*(11), 824–839. https://doi.org/10.1111/j.1751-9004.2011.00394.x

Frost, D. M. (2014). Redemptive framings of minority stress and their association with closeness in same-sex relationships. *Journal of Couple & Relationship Therapy, 13*(3), 219–239. https://doi.org/10.1080/15332691.2013.871616

Frost, D. M., & LeBlanc, A. J. (2018). Stress in the lives of same-sex couples: Implications for relationship dissolution and divorce. In Abbie E. Goldberg, & Adam P. Romero (Eds.), *LGBTQ divorce and relationship dissolution: Psychological and legal perspectives and implications for practice*. Oxford Academic.

Frost, D. M., LeBlanc, A. J., de Vries, B., Alston-Stepnitz, E., Stephenson, R., & Woodyatt, C. (2017). Couple-level minority stress: An examination of same-sex couples' unique experiences. *Journal of Health and Social Behavior, 58*(4), 455–472. https://doi.org/10.1177%2F0022146517736754

Goldberg, A. E., & Garcia, R. (2015). Predictors of relationship dissolution in lesbian, gay, and heterosexual adoptive parents. *Journal of Family Psychology, 29*(3), 394–404. https://doi.org/10.1037/fam0000095

Goldberg, A. E., Moyer, A. M., Black, K., & Henry, A. (2014). Lesbian and heterosexual adoptive mothers' experiences of relationship dissolution. *Sex Roles, 73*(3–4), 141–156. https://doi.org/10.1007/s11199-014-0432-2

Goldberg, A. E., & Romero, A. P. (2018). *LGBTQ divorce and relationship dissolution: Psychological and legal perspectives and implications for practice*. Oxford University Press.

Haas, S. M. (2021). Same-sex couple relationship maintenance. In *Oxford research encyclopedia of communication*. https://doi.org/10.1093/acrefore/9780190228613.013.1174

Haas, S. M., & Lannutti, P. J. (2022). Relationship maintenance behaviors, resilience, and relational quality in romantic relationships of LGBTQ+ people. *Couple and Family Psychology: Research and Practice, 11*(2), 117–131. https://doi.org/10.1037/cfp0000186

Haas, S. M., & Stafford, L. (1998). An initial examination of maintenance behaviors in gay and lesbian relationships. *Journal of Social and Personal Relationships, 15,* 846–855. https://doi.org/10.1177/0265407598156008

Hatzenbuehler, M. L. (2009). How does sexual minority stigma "get under the skin"? A psychological mediation framework. *Psychological Bulletin, 135,* 707–730. https://doi.org/10.1037/a0016441

Human Rights Campaign. (2022). *Marriage equality around the world.* https://www.hrc.org/resources/marriage-equality-around-the-world

Karney, B. R., & Bradbury, T. N. (1995). The longitudinal course of marital quality and stability: A review of theory, method, and research. *Psychological Bulletin, 118,* 3–34. https://doi.org/10.1037/0033-2909.118.1.3

Kelley, H. H., & Thibaut, J. W. (1978). *Interpersonal relations: A theory of interdependence.* Wiley.

King, M., Semlyen, J., Tai, S. S., Killaspy, H., Osborn, D., Popelyuk, D., & Nazareth, I. (2008). A systematic review of mental disorder, suicide, and deliberate self harm in lesbian, gay and bisexual people. *BMC Psychiatry, 8,* 1–17. https://doi.org/10.1186/1471-244x-8-70

Kornblith, E., Green, R.-J., Casey, S., & Tiet, Q. (2016). Marital status, social support, and depressive symptoms among lesbian and heterosexual women. *Journal of Lesbian Studies, 20,* 157–173. https://doi.org/10.1080/10894160.2015.1061882

Lazard, L., & McAvoy, J. (2020). Doing reflexivity in psychological research: What's the point? What's the practice? *Qualitative Research in Psychology, 17*(2), 159–177. https://doi.org/10.1080/14780887.2017.1400144

LeBlanc, A. J., Frost, D. M., & Wight, R. G. (2015). Minority stress and stress proliferation among same-sex and other marginalized couples. *Journal of Marriage and Family, 77,* 40–59. https://doi.org/10.1111/jomf.12160

Loving, T. J., & Slatcher, R. B. (2013). *Romantic relationships and health.* Oxford Handbooks Online. https://doi.org/10.1093/oxfordhb/9780195398694.013.0028

Manning, W. D., & Joyner, K. (2018). Demographic approaches to same-sex relationship dissolution and divorce: Research findings, data challenges, and implications for future research. In Abbie E. Goldberg & Adam P. Romero (Eds.), *LGBTQ divorce and relationship dissolution: Psychological and legal perspectives and implications for practice.* Oxford Academic.

Meuwly, N., Feinstein, B. A., Davila, J., Nuñez, D. G., & Bodenmann, G. (2013). Relationship quality among Swiss women in opposite-sex versus same-sex romantic relationships. *Swiss Journal of Psychology/Schweizerische Zeitschrift Fuer Psychologie, 72*(4), 229–233. https://doi.org/10.1024/1421-0185/a000115

Meyer, I. H. (2003). Prejudice, social stress, and mental health in lesbian, gay, and bisexual populations: Conceptual issues and research evidence. *Psychological Bulletin, 129*(5), 674–697. https://doi.org/10.1037/0033-2909.129.5.674

Mohr, J. J., & Fassinger, R. E. (2006). Sexual orientation identity and romantic relationship quality in same-sex couples. *Personality & Social Psychology Bulletin, 32*(8), 1085–1099. https://doi.org/10.1177/0146167206288281

Moradi, B., & Grzanka, P. R. (2017). Using intersectionality responsibly: Toward critical epistemology, structural analysis, and social justice activism. *Journal of Counseling Psychology, 64*(5), 500–513. https://doi.org/10.1037/cou0000203

Mosley, D. V., McNeil-Young, V., Bridges, B., Adam, S., Colson, A., Crowley, M., & Lee, L. (2021). Toward radical healing: A qualitative metasynthesis exploring oppression and liberation among Black queer people. *Psychology of Sexual Orientation and Gender Diversity, 8*(3), 292–313. https://doi.org/10.1037/sgd0000522

Obergefell v. Hodges, 576 U.S. ____ (2015). Supreme Court of the United States, https://www.supremecourt.gov/opinions/14pdf/14-556_3204.pdf

Ogolsky, B. G., & Monk, J. K. (2018). Maintaining relationships. In A. L. Vangelisti & D. Perlman (Eds.), *The Cambridge handbook of personal relationships* (pp. 523–537). Cambridge University Press. https://doi.org/10.1017/9781316417867.040

Ogolsky, B. G., Monk, J. K., Rice, T. M., & Oswald, R. F. (2019). Personal well-being across the transition to marriage equality: A longitudinal analysis. *Journal of Family Psychology, 33*(4), 422–432. https://doi.org/10.1037/fam0000504

Otis, M. D., Rostosky, S. S., Riggle, E. D. B., & Hamrin, R. (2006). Stress and relationship quality in same-sex couples. *Journal of Social and Personal Relationships, 23*(1), 81–99. https://doi.org/10.1177/0265407506060179

Pachankis, J. E., Mahon, C. P., Jackson, S. D., Fetzner, B. K., & Bränström, R. (2020). Sexual orientation concealment and mental health: A conceptual and meta-analytic review. *Psychological Bulletin, 146*(10), 831–871. https://doi.org/10.1037/bul0000271

Parsons, J. T., Starks, T. J., DuBois, S., Grov, C., & Golub, S. A. (2013). Alternatives to monogamy among gay male couples in a community survey: Implications for mental health and sexual risk. *Archives of Sexual Behavior, 42*(2), 303–312. https://doi.org/10.1007/s10508-011-9885-3

Pentel, K. Z. (2021). *Cognitive-behavioral couple therapy for same-sex female couples: A pilot study* [Unpublished doctoral dissertation]. University of North Carolina at Chapel Hill.

Randall, A. K., & Bodenmann, G. (2017). Stress and its associations with relationship satisfaction. *Current Opinion in Psychology, 13,* 96–106.

Randall, A. K., Donato, S., Neff, L. A., Totenhagen, C. J., Bodenmann, G., & Falconier, M. (2022). A scoping review on couples' stress and coping literature: Recognizing the need for inclusivity. *Journal of Social and Personal Relationships,* 026540752211019. https://doi.org/10.1177/02654075221101904

Randall, A. K., & Messerschmitt-Coen, S. (2019). Dyadic coping as relationship maintenance. In Brian G. Ogolsky & J. Kale Monk (Eds.), *Relationship maintenance: Theory, process, and context* (pp. 178–193). Cambridge University Press.

Randall, A. K., Tao, C., Totenhagen, C. J., Walsh, K. J., & Cooper, A. N. (2017a). Associations between sexual orientation discrimination and depression among same-sex couples: Moderating effects of dyadic coping. *Journal of Couple & Relationship Therapy, 16*(4), 325–345. https://doi.org/10.1080/15332691.2016.1253520

Randall, A. K., Totenhagen, C. J., Walsh, K. J., Adams, C., & Tao, C. (2017b). Coping with workplace minority stress: Associations between dyadic coping and anxiety among women in same-sex relationships. *Journal of Lesbian Studies, 21,* 70–87. https://doi.org/10.1080/10894160.2016.1142353

Régnier-Loilier, A. (2018). Are the generations and gender surveys well suited for studying same-sex couples? *European Journal of Population, 34*(4), 567–578. https://doi.org/10.1007/s10680-017-9440-6

Revenson, T. A., Kayser, K., & Bodenmann, G. (Eds.). (2005). *Couples coping with stress: Emerging perspectives on dyadic coping.* American Psychological Association. https://doi.org/10.1037/11031-000

Riggle, E. D., Rostosky, S. S., & Horne, S. G. (2010). Psychological distress, wellbeing, and legal recognition in same-sex couple relationships. *Journal of Family Psychology, 24,* 82–86. https://doi.org/10.1037/a0017942

Riggle, E. D. B., Rostosky, S. S., Black, W. W., & Rosenkrantz, D. E. (2017). Outness, concealment, and authenticity: Associations with LGB individuals' psychological distress and wellbeing. *Psychology of Sexual Orientation and Gender Diversity, 4,* 54–62. https://doi.org/10.1037/sgd0000202

Rosenfeld, M. J. (2014). Couple longevity in the era of same-sex marriage in the United States. *Journal of Marriage and Family, 76*(5), 905–918. https://doi.org/10.1111/jomf.12141

Rostosky, S. S., Riggle, E. D., Gray, B. E., & Hatton, R. L. (2007). Minority stress experiences in committed same-sex couple relationships. *Professional Psychology: Research and Practice, 38*(4), 392. https://doi.org/10.1037/0735-7028.38.4.392

Rostosky, S. S., & Riggle, E. D. B. (2017). Same-sex relationships and minority stress. *Current Opinion in Psychology, 13*, 29–38. https://doi.org/10.1016/j.copsyc.2016.04.011

Totenhagen, C. J., Randall, A. K., & Lloyd, K. (2018). Stress and relationship functioning in same-sex couples: The vulnerabilities of internalized homophobia and outness. *Family Relations, 67*(3), 399–413. https://doi.org/10.1111/fare.12311

Umberson, D., Thomeer, M. B., Kroeger, R. A., Lodge, A. C., & Xu, M. (2015). Challenges and opportunities for research on same-sex relationships. *Journal of Marriage and Family, 77*(1), 96–111. https://doi.org/10.1111/jomf.12155

Walker, L., & Taylor, D. (2021). *Same-sex couple households: 2019.* U.S. Census Bureau. https://www.census.gov/library/publications/2021/acs/acsbr-005.html

Westman, M. (2001). Stress and strain crossover. *Human Relations, 54*, 717–751. https://doi.org/10.1177/0018726701546002

Whitton, S. W., Dyar, C., Godfrey, L. M., & Newcomb, M. E. (2021). Within-person associations between romantic involvement and mental health among sexual and gender minorities assigned female-at-birth. *Journal of Family Psychology, 35*(5), 606–617. https://doi.org/10.1037/fam0000835

Whitton, S. W., Scott, S. B., Dyar, C., Weitbrecht, E. M., Hutsell, D. W., & Kuryluk, A. D. (2017). Piloting relationship education for female same-sex couples: Results of a small randomized waitlist-control trial. *Journal of Family Psychology, 31*(7), 878. https://doi.org/10.1037/fam0000337

Williamson, I. R. (2000). Internalized homophobia and health issues affecting lesbians and gay men. *Health Education Research, 15*, 97–107. https://doi.org/10.1093/her/15.1.97

NOTES

1. The authors acknowledge the terminology reflected in this entry likely does not reflect all possible identities within the LGBTQ+ community. For ease of interpretation, we have elected to refer to LGBTQ+ for individuals who do not identify as heterosexual and cisgender.
2. For notable examples of publicly disseminated data sets that researchers may use to count, characterize, or study the behaviors of LGBTQ+ couples, please see the Further Reading section.
3. Following Bettergarcia et al.'s (2021) recommendations, we use the term "queer" as an umbrella term to refer to people who identify as lesbian, gay, bisexual, pansexual, queer, or otherwise nonheterosexual. This includes transgender, cisgender, asexual, and allosexual people who also identify under the queer umbrella.
4. Throughout this text, "same sex" is used only when the cited research utilizes this language. Otherwise, "same gender" is used to reflect inclusivity and updated terminology; Frost et al. (2017) conducted research in Atlanta and San Francisco with 120 male and female same-sex couples whose relationships had endured from 6 months to over 7 years.

Steven Samrock, Kai Kline, and Ashley K. Randall

Queer Identities

ALTERNATIVES TO COMING-OUT DISCOURSES

INTRODUCTION

Coming-out discourse is an essential vehicle in Western LGBTQ movements in the past few decades (Boe, Maxey, & Bermudez, 2018; Gross, 1991; McLean, 2007; Rasmussen, 2004; Wei, 2006). As indicated in the phrase "come out of the closet," "coming out" and "closet" are twin tropes in contemporary queer discourse, narrating homosexuality as a tension between secrecy and disclosure, private and public (Martin, 2003; Ross, 2005; Sedgwick, 1990).

The gay liberation movement, for instance, was founded on the imperative of coming out (Gross, 1991; Ross, 2005). Coming out is repeatedly constructed as a milestone event in queer life, the failure of which is detrimental to one's sense of self (McLean, 2007; Mosher, 2001; Vargo, 1998). Every year, hundreds of U.S. schools and colleges join the National Coming Out Day program (Rasmussen, 2004) to reproduce a collective queerness that is narrated around the coming-out discourse. In everyday life, coming out of the closet is a central message in self-help guides (Osborn, 1996). It is constructed as a "salvational epistemologic certainty" (Sedgwick, 1990, p. 71), which produces a queer identity that is built on the disclosure imperative. Kenneth Plummer (1995), for example, summarizes the four processes of coming out: coming out to oneself, coming out privately, coming out publicly, and coming out politically which aims to catalyze social changes (pp. 57–58). In such a framework, coming out is narrated as liberatory, empowering (Rasmussen, 2004), and even heroic. Within this teleological discourse, coming out is considered as an indispensable element for "a consistent, integrated sense of a self" (Plummer, 1995, p. 86), which is the last stage that one needs to overcome in order to live a fully and happily queer life (Vargo, 1998, p. 45). Politically, coming out is narrated as "progress" (Ross, 2005), where levels of disclosure are seen as the measurement of commitment to queerness (Troiden, 1988, p. 55).

It is probably impossible to think about the discourse of coming out without addressing "the closet." The closet is imagined as the paradigmatic opposite of coming out. Fran Martin (2003) pointed out that the closet is "a spatial expression of, and a refuge for, the private inward depths of the monadic 'self' which is hidden and enclosed therein" (p. 198). Coming out of the closet is a rite of passage through which a queer subject becomes a "gay man" or a "lesbian." At a personal level, living in the closet is equated to a dishonest, unauthentic, and sexually repressed self (Boe et al., 2018; McLean, 2007; Rasmussen, 2004). Politically, not coming out is seen as a lack of commitment to the LGBTQ community (Rasmussen, 2004; Stewart, 1995). Mary Rasmussen (2004), for instance, observed that queer people who were not out were often silenced or shamed in the LGBTQ community. Contrary to the valorization of coming out, the closet is associated with "hiding" and "oppression" (Brown, 2000), "a place of denial and shameful secrecy" (Fisher, 2003, p. 179). The universalization of coming-out discourse positions coming out as mentally healthy, empowering, modern, and progressive and nondisclosure as repressed, premodern, and waiting to be liberated (McLean, 2007, p. 154).

HISTORICIZING COMING OUT

While coming out appears to be the code of conduct among queer people all over the world in the 21st century due to the transnational circulation of Euro-American LGBTQ discourse, the discourse of coming out has gained its dominance only in the past few decades. In fact, the term closet, which today is associated with hidden queer sexuality that is not "out," came to indicate "hidden, covert, or secret" sexuality only in the mid- to late 1960s (Barnhart, 1995; Chauncey, 1995).

As a key component in the gay and lesbian liberation movements in the United States (Bobker, 2015; Brown, 2000; D'Emilio, 1983), the ideological status of coming out is the result of a particular cultural and political context. It was, Michael Warner (1994) observed, "a political strategy without precedent or parallel" (p. xxv) that has rewritten the code of conduct among LGBTQ people in the United States (Gross, 1991, p. 377).

Larry Gross (1991) believed that the discourse of coming out in its current sense emerged in the 1950s and 1960s through the homophile movement in the United States (p. 356). By 1970, the slogan "Come out!" had served as a rallying cry in the gay liberation movement (Brown, 2000, p. 6). Coming out thus played a central role in building a then nascent gay liberation movement and creating a sense of community (Altman, 1993; D'Emilio, 1983; Murray, 1996). John D'Emilio (1983) noted: "Visible lesbians and gay men... served as magnets that draw others in. Furthermore, once out of the closet, they could not easily fade back in. Coming out provided gay liberation with an army of permanent enlistees" (pp. 235–236).

Moreover, the HIV-AIDS epidemic in the 1980s also produced a homosexuality that was visible to the public in order to participate in the public sphere (Snorton, 2014; Sullivan, 1996). By marking the gay body as an (over)sexed body, queer sexuality became licentious (Snorton, 2014, p. 11), where increased surveillance was made possible with such visibility.

Today, the discourse of coming out has become so prevalent in queer life in the United States that Warner (1994) argued that to some extent, a lesbian or gay identity is the product of the performative act of such discourse (p. xxv). The dominance of coming-out discourse results in a collective progress narrative—a unified "coming out story whereby isolated, alienated, closeted individuals are able to migrate to the largest urban centers in mass numbers... [to] form the new visible, militant gay, and to a lesser extent, lesbian ghettos awaiting them in the urban centers" (Ross, 2005, p. 143). In the mid-1990s, Glyn Davis and Gary Needham (2009) argued that the discourse of coming out assumed its current hegemonic status where the revelation of one's sexual identity became the only allowed narrative role for queer people.

COMPLICATING CLOSET OR COMING-OUT PROCESS

The Euro-American metaphor "closet" in the coming-out discourse suggests both clear spatial divisions and a spectacular but singular temporality. But queer spaces and timings are not so clean. Diana Fuss (1991), for instance, suggested that the boundary between "inside" and "outside" was porous, where "most of us are both inside and outside at the same time" (p. 5). Depending on one's location, many queer subjects constantly resituate themselves to be "out" to some people in some situations while staying closeted to others in other circumstances (Brown, 2000, p. 147).

Other queer scholars have complicated the process of coming out that privileges telling over feeling and voice over silence. Challenging the binary of "secrecy versus revelation" in the coming out narrative, Martin Manalansan (1995) argued that issues of sexuality can be communicated through feelings rather than verbalization of one's sexual identity: "Filipino gay men argue that identities are not just proclaimed verbally, but are 'felt' (*pakiramdaman*) or intuited as well" (p. 434). Such a nondeclaratory and nonconfrontational approach was affirmed by Liu Jen-peng and Ding Naifei's (2005) studies on the "reticent poetic" among Taiwanese queers and Wei Wei's (2006) studies of mainland Chinese gay men whose parents deployed the strategy of "acknowledging with silence." Here, the communication of sexuality has gone beyond explicit verbal messages. In such communication transactions, the process of interpretation depends on one's tacit knowledge and contextual sensibility. In other words, the register of "message" is not just verbal and symbolic language but also the context where communication happens. Verbal and nonverbal languages are not just informational registers that function on the cognitive level but also emotional registers that communicate through the feelings of people's bodies.

Marlon Ross (2005) also challenged the model of coming out by questioning its necessity. In a situation where one's queer sexuality is an open secret, Ross maintained, the performative act of disclosing one's queer desire by coming out will not be liberatory as prescribed in dominant closet and coming-out discourse (p. 145). In fact, there are debates over whether queer people should come out of the closet. Since the mid-1980s, Michael Brown (2000) observed, queer scholars like Gross (1993), Warner (1994), and McCarthy (1994) have questioned the equation between the closet and sexual oppression. Rather, the closet could serve as a place of safety where queer privacy is protected (Brown, 2000, p. 14) and a strategic resistance in a homophobic environment (p. 144). The closet, however temporary and compromised, functions as a tool that "destabilizes, subverts, and temporarily provides escape from the dominant ideology" (Fisher, 2003, p. 174). Cautious against the progress and liberation story in dominant coming-out discourse, Diana Fisher (2003) questioned the binary of closet versus coming out which valorizes disclosure and visibility in queer experience (p. 180). Questioning the presumption in coming-out discourse that the "outside" of the closet is less regulated, Riley Snorton (2014) argued that Black sexuality is figured within a "glass closet"—a space "marked by hypervisibility and confinement, spectacle, and speculation" (p. 4) and is thus subject to regulation and surveillance. The closet, Snorton (2014) concluded, could be protective to allow passing while facing the violence of racism and heteronormativity (p. 17). Therefore, closet space should be conceptualized as highly contextual, where cultural and material conditions determine the nature and value of the closet for queer subjects (Fisher, 2003, p. 180).

CRITIQUE OF COMING-OUT OR CLOSET PARADIGM

While the coming-out discourse has played an essential role in building and sustaining gay and lesbian movements in the United States, as discussed earlier in this article, many queer scholars are cautious of the assumptions in the coming-out discourse. Judith Butler (1993), for instance, asked: "Could it be that the subjection that subjectivates the gay and lesbian subject in some ways continues to oppress, or oppresses most insidiously, once 'outness' is claimed?" (p. 309). Warner (2002), however, challenged the paradigm of closet versus coming out by deconstructing the false dichotomy of the private and the public in the domain of sexuality. He also pointed out the individualistic framework in current coming-out discourse that emphasizes self-awareness and self-expression. Such a framework unwittingly positions queer people as being responsible for their invisibility while neglecting the cultural and institutional factors that condition the experience and expression of queer subjects.

Perhaps the most profound critique on the coming-out discourse is from queer of color critique and transnational queer theory that foreground race and geopolitics in queer studies. Ross (2005), for example, argued that Michel Foucault (1978) and Eve Sedgwick (1990)—two queer theorists who are often canonized in queer theory—were able to construct "a coherent epistemology of the closet as a ground for modern [sexual] identity" (p. 142) by bracketing race in their narratives. Queer of color critique and transnational queer theory argue that the prevalent discourse of coming out is built on a particular kind of queer experience and geography, which is usually from the standpoint of White, middle-class men of urban U.S. citizenship (e.g., Boe et al., 2018; Chávez, 2013; Huang & Brouwer, 2018a) and rarely consults the experience of queer people of color (Han, 2009; Rust, 2003) and non-Western queer subjects.

Against the backdrop of neoliberalism where queer issues are so often co-opted into nationalist and capitalist projects, queer of color critique and transnational queer theory further argue that coming-out discourse has increasingly become an assimilationist agent that erases differences (Bui, 2014; Manalansan, 1995; Ross, 2005). Utilized as a measurement of modern and progressive sexuality, the discourse of coming out has unwittingly privileged a queerness that is White, cosmopolitan, and U.S.-centric. Long Bui (2014), for instance, asserted that racial silences and violence are fueled by the discourse of coming out:

> The telos of gay coming out which begins with feelings of insecurity, trauma, and abjection to conclude with visibility and confidence offers an "emancipated" sexual world entailing the abandonment of the rigidity of Asian cultural parochialism for the "free" lifestyle of homo-cosmopolitanism. In this developmental paradigm, "race" and "sexuality" are set up as diametrically opposed with White gay modernity serving as the vehicle for liberation from the suffocating "closet" and closed-mindedness of Confucian patriarchal familism. (p. 136)

If the closet is seen as a cultural vehicle that conceals and makes queer people invisible and unintelligible (Brown, 2000, p. 141), the hypervisibility of the "out and proud" queers can ironically render other queer bodies—usually those who are more marginalized—being forced into the closet and thus staying unheard (Brown, 2000, p. 147). The dominance of the coming-out discourse thus becomes a regulatory force that pathologizes and erases different forms of queer relationalities.

ALTERNATIVES TO CLOSET OR COMING-OUT DISCOURSE

The Whiteness in dominant queer theory has obscured the ability to learn from the variations and discrepancies within and among diverse queer people (Liu, 2010; Ross, 2005; Snorton, 2014). The critical potential of queerness has been constrained by the narrow cultural context from which coming-out discourse is derived. Communication studies as well as queer theory must continue to interrogate the ideological construct of coming out in relation to different social locations such as race, gender, class, and nationality, and continue to investigate how alternatives to coming-out discourse can serve as useful queer tools to transform the landscapes of this field and society. The following text delineates some alternatives to the dominant discourse of coming out. The five alternatives presented demonstrate an intersectional and relational approach to understanding queerness, which recognizes differences that mark and position queer bodies in social hierarchies (LeMaster, 2017) and emphasizes interdependency and connectivity in queer worldmaking (Muñoz, 2009). They are not a comprehensive summary of alternative paradigms. Rather, they serve as epistemic tools that aim to revise the understanding of queer resistance and queer relationality and help people to go beyond the imagination of coming out as the only path for a livable queer future.

Down Low: Resistance to Sexual Surveillance and Regulation.

As mentioned in the previous section, coming-out discourse assumes that the outside of the closet is a more desirable space with less oppression and regulation. However, such an assumption overlooks the intersectionality of oppression. For queer subjects who face multiple marginalizations, not coming out of the closet could be a strategic resistance to the surveillance and regulation of queer subjects on the margin. In his study on the down low, Snorton (2014) interrogated the racialization of the closet and proposed a sexual politics of ignorance as opposed to the disclosure imperative in coming-out discourse. The down low, as defined by Snorton, refers to "black men who have sex with men and women and do not identify as gay, bisexual, or queer" (p. 6). The down low is usually used as a derogatory term in public discourse in the United States. Snorton observed that mainstream down low narratives are often constructed around safer sex in which Black queer sexuality is associated with the fear of sexual contagions (p. 8). Given that Black sexuality is always already marked by hypersexuality, Snorton pointed out that down low discourse is the effect of Black sexual hypervisibility that goes hand in hand with the racialized impulse to contain and regulate Black bodies. Mainstream down low discourse also reveals the cultural anxiety about "the possibility of refusing to comply with sexual identifications, of resisting being gay or even MSM" (p. 25). Within such discourse, Blackness is perceived as inherently homophobic; such perception distracts or even obscures the down low from the "truth" of Black sexuality, which is to identify as gay, bisexual, or queer. In the context of Black sexuality, according to Snorton, the down low could be read as a politics of ungovernability that resists forces of sexual categorization, which often entails surveillance and regulation. Therefore, in the context of Black sexuality, taking up the space of the closet no longer means concealment of one's queer desires. Rather, it is a refusal to comply with White sexual epistemology that positions Black bodies for observation and display. In this rendering, the ignorance of mainstream gay-bisexual-queer identification could be understood as a refusal to be governed and contained—"a performance and tactic that also taps into the affective and political possibilities for a body that is presumed to be known" (p. 154).

Fluid Closet: Moving Between the Center and Periphery. Centering the experience of Russian American immigrants who were queer identified, Fisher (2003) theorized an active closet among transnational queer subjects who saw the closet "as a fluid, dialogic and powerful tactical space" (p. 179). In Fisher's study, queer Russian immigrants often preferred an in-between position that was neither fully "out" nor totally "closeted." Resisting any fixed categorization, queer Russian immigrants used the closet as a site of contestation and negotiation, which allowed them to control the (re)presentations of their queer sexuality. Fisher believed the experience of queer Russian immigrants demonstrated a fluid and productive relationship between the closeted and the out sexuality. Focusing on the lives and experiences of transnational queer subjects, Fisher suggested a politics of discretion that emphasized contingency and ephemerality, affirming the possibility of queer agency that emerges from an unseen and transitory closet space deployed by some queer Russian immigrants.

As discussed earlier in this article, the dominant discourse of coming out valorizes the visibly out position as the designation that liberates queer subjects from repression and confinement. However, Fisher argued, the closet should not be "totalized or universally defined as a confined, powerless and isolated place" (p. 179). Rather, the experience of queer Russian immigrants suggests that the closet is a liminal space where needed invisibility is afforded through the negotiation between expectations and violations (p. 187). The tactical use of the closet allows queer subjects movements between the center and periphery to cope with heteronormative demands and cultural challenges particular to immigrant life. Rather than occupying a fixed sexual location, either as being closeted or out and visible, queer Russian immigrants gain agency through their perpetual motion that refuses to be fixed and contained. It is the constant movement in and out of the closet that allows queer immigrants to actively respond to heteronormativity and other cultural domination that comes with displacement. In a transnational context, the closet thus functions as a site of agency "where the power of movement challenges the power to fix" (p. 181). Refusing to settle in a marked sexual location, some queer Russian immigrants prefer the liminal space in and out of the closet—"an unseen and transitory space deployed as a tool to maneuver around stable designations and categorizations of sexual orientation" (p. 188).

Xianshen: Performing the Queer Face. With the transnational circulation of LGBTQ discourse, coming out in public has also become an important agenda in Taiwan. The issue of queer liberalism in Taiwan, Petrus Liu (2015) pointed out, is entwined with the geopolitics between Taiwan and mainland China, the economic and ideological fracturing created by the Cold War. Hijacked by "the US installment of a Cold War structure of feeling" (pp. 16–17), queer visibility is often attributed to liberal capitalism in Taiwan, in contrast to the "repressed queer subjects" in socialist China.

Focusing on the masking tactic deployed by local *tongzhi* activists, Martin (2003) theorized the model of *xianshen*, a local identity politics that questions the very conditions of visibility within authorized public space.[1] *Xianshen*, according to Martin, refers to an act of "showing" (*xian*) the body/self (*shen*) to the intended spectators, a social performance that emphasizes the situated enactment. Although *xianshen* seems to be similar to the politics of coming out at first glance, it functions very differently in Taiwanese society.

As a critical part of the Taiwanese activist effort to fight against homophobia that operates predominantly through shaming, public mask donning functions as a "collective coming out" to protest media voyeurism as well as a public display of *tongzhi* numbers in Taiwan (Martin, 2003, p. 191). Similar to the function that the closet serves in Anglo-American representations of gayness, the mask functions as a signifier of both the homophobic anxiety in Taiwan and "the corresponding desire [among *tongzhi*] to make it legible once and for all by removing the mask" (p. 191). Paradoxically, mask donning in public now becomes a sign of *tongzhi* identity in Taiwan, whereas revealing the face is regarded with suspicion by the *tongzhi* group. Here, the very marker of "authentic" *tongzhi* identity—the mask—is also a sign of its continuing concealment, rendering individual identity unreadable through concealment of the face (Martin, 2003, p. 195).

While the masking tactic appears to be similar to (and may be inspired by) the transnational discourse of the closet and coming out, the trope of mask draws on very different cultural knowledge in Taiwan. Emphasizing the socially performed character of queerness, Martin argued, the mask operates through the cultural citation of "face" (p. 196)—a central vehicle in Confucianism. In the discourse of coming out, queer subjectivity is articulated through the dichotomy of "true self versus false self," as well as the dyad of "private regime versus public regime." However, *xianshen* discourse in Taiwan operates through the affective construct of shame and social status (p. 198). Here, the mask in *xianshen* discourse is imagined as "a theatrical costume for the face, a disguise, [and] a false countenance" (p. 198). *Xianshen* discourse is organized through the performativity of the *tongzhi* mask rather than the ontology of queer identity. It is therefore less about a "true face" awaiting disclosure beneath the "false face." Rather, *xianshen* is about understanding and taking control of the social conditions that produce the "best/proper" face (p. 200), which implies a collective selfhood that is relational and interdependent. More than simply "resisting public voyeurism," the *tongzhi* masking tactic in *xianshen* discourse questions the very conditions of visibility in dominant coming-out discourse—"conditions which make it impossible for homosexuals to appear as complete or properly 'faced' social subjects" (p. 195).

Coming Home: A Decolonial Response to Coming Out.

Even among increasing forms of LGBTQ activism in China, contemporary Chinese queer subjects continue to negotiate between nonconflictual relations with their parents and efforts to create space for queer autonomy (Choi & Luo, 2016, p. 263). The dominant Euro-American discourse of coming out suggests that queer subjects should move away from the constraints of the "traditional" family and embrace their identities as LGBTQ in order to properly express their "free" modern sexuality (Blackwood, 2012). This approach in transnational LGBTQ movements was questioned in the press release for the 1998 Chinese *Tongzhi* Conference in Hong Kong: "Certain characteristics of confrontational politics, such as coming out and mass protests and parades, may not be the best way of achieving *tongzhi* liberation in family-centered, community-oriented Chinese societies which stress the importance of social harmony" (Chou, 2000, p. 278). The "best" way of achieving *tongzhi* liberation, Wah-shan Chou (2000) argued, is the "coming home" approach that emphasizes familial harmony and reticent practices to communicate queer sexuality.

Many Chinese queer subjects view coming home as both a historical practice and possibly the most common approach among Chinese queers. According to Chou (2000), Chinese queer subjects often "come out by bypassing the discussion of homosexuality" (p. 268):

> The usual practice is that a *tongzhi* maintains a loving relationship with the parents, then introduces his or her sexual partner into the family as a good friend...the *tongzhi* may then use quasi-kin categories such as half sister/brother to integrate the partner into the family. (p. 263)

This bypassing, Chou observes, is a culturally specific strategy to navigate between sexuality and kinship in family-centered, community-oriented Chinese society. The coming home approach emphasizes an expectation or obligation to remain close to the family and to maintain familial piety (especially to one's parents) and harmony by reining in and concealing queer desires. Foregrounding the relational existence of Chinese queers, Chou's coming home model suggests a selfhood that is defined by responsibilities and obligations, a queer subjectivity that is different from the independent and autonomous self implied in the dominant discourse of coming out.

Liu and Ding (2005) summarized the three characteristics of Chou's articulation of the coming home approach: "(1) non-conflictual harmonious relationships; (2) non-declarative practical everyday acts; [and] (3) a healthy personality that is not centered on sex(uality)" (p. 30). Different from the explicit, declarative style of communicating sexuality through coming out, in the coming home model, "reticence" (*hanxu*)—coding one's speech through indirect expression (Huang, 2011)—is the dominant aesthetic-ethical value that regulates the communication process of sexuality in a Chinese context (Chou, 2001; Kam, 2012; Liu & Ding, 2005; Wei, 2006).

Chou's articulation of coming home among Chinese queer subjects can be read as a decolonial response to the hegemony of Euro-American discourse of coming out. Chou (2000) observed that the main concern of Chinese parents is a Western identity label—lesbian or gay—that "privileges sexuality at the expense of his or her position in the family/kinship system, thus making the child a nonbeing in Chinese culture" (p. 96). This concern illustrates why the transnational discourses of identity-based homosexuality, especially the discourse of coming out, are perceived as threatening to parents and so difficult to navigate for queer subjects in Chinese societies. Emphasizing familial harmony and reticent practices of queer sexuality and de-emphasizing sexuality as a primary characteristic of individual identity (Huang & Brouwer, 2018a), the coming home approach promises to accommodate kinship and queer desires, which are so often antagonized in the dominant discourse of coming out.

Coming With: Disidentification With Coming Out. Several queer scholars (e.g., Engebretsen, 2009; Kam, 2012; Liu, 2010; Liu & Ding, 2005; Wei, 2006) have been skeptical of the innocent coming home approach that Chou proposed. In Chou's (2000, 2001) recuperation of coming home against the increasing imperative of coming out among Chinese queers, traditional Chinese culture is portrayed as showing tolerance and harmony toward same-sex desires. The underlying assumption of such an approach, Liu and Ding (2005) pointed out, is that homophobia is Western and therefore colonial (p. 31). The decolonial and nationalistic impulses in Chou's coming home model leaves both the family and national culture under-interrogated as sites of oppression (Huang, 2011; Kam, 2012; Liu & Ding, 2005). The "silent tolerance" in Chinese sexuality that Chou proposed is no more than a cultural myth: It is reticent homophobia complicit with heteronormativity through precisely the ordered conditions of silence (Huang, 2011, p. 10) that represses, disciplines, and keeps queer subjects in place (Liu & Ding, 2005).

Against either the confrontational, explicit, political visibility of coming-out discourse that privileges sexuality and the reticent, filial piety of the coming home approach that prioritizes family harmony, Huang and Brouwer (2018a) proposed an alternative "coming with" model to address the struggles of Chinese queers to disidentify with the family institution. The coming with approach shares the same commitment with coming home in harmonious familial relationships, especially with parents, seeing family as an indispensable network in queer lives. For Chinese queer subjects, Huang and Brouwer (2018a) argued, the most profound struggle is perhaps not in the public sociopolitical domain; instead, it is located in the private lives, in the precarious, lasting negotiations with their intimate families, especially with one's parents. The role of the family institution in queer life is amplified during China's recent postsocialist transition where the government withdraws from the welfare system and positions the family institution as the primary network for the care of the young and the aged (Huang & Brouwer, 2018b; Wong, 2007). For most Chinese queers, Huang and Brouwer (2018a) pointed out, the family is the space where negotiation and transformation happen. There is no "safe elsewhere" outside of the family space for such transformations to occur (Gopinath, 2005).

Unlike in the coming home strategy in Chou's definition, which implies bringing or even subsuming queer sexuality to the heteronormative home space, the coming with strategy attempts to engage the home space with queer desires, transforming the heteronormative family institution from within and redefining the meaning of queerness. Instead of coming out and turning away from their biogenetic family, as implied in the discourse of coming out, and instead of coming home and leaving the heteronormative family uncontested, as suggested in

Chou's version of coming home, some Chinese queer subjects deploy a coming with approach to integrate both familial belonging and sexual identification—a third path that is neither total rejection of nor total subsumption under the heteronormative family (Huang & Brouwer, 2018a). Embracing the politics of disidentification (Muñoz, 1999), coming with is a survival strategy that some Chinese queers deploy to rewrite different systems of belonging. For example, many Chinese queers today engage in a new form of marriage arrangement—queer *xinghun*, a marriage arrangement between a gay man and a lesbian woman that permits queer subjects to stay within the family kinship system (Huang & Brouwer, 2018b). While a *xinghun* marriage may seem like complete compliance to heteronormativity, it is also a way of preserving queer sexuality where the same-sex relationship is significantly sequestered away from surveillance by and interference from parents because of the public performance of "fake" heterosexuality through *xinghun* (Huang & Brouwer, 2018b). Through disidentification with the hegemonic forms of marriage, queer *xinghun* at once reinforces the roles of heterosexual marriage and family and contests the substance and effect of such heteronormative institutions.

CONCLUSION

The discourse of coming out has historically served as an effective vehicle to build and sustain LGBTQ movements, especially in the context of the United States. It has also been utilized as an empowering resource that enables queer people to establish a queer identity to fight against the violence of heteronormativity. That being said, the dominance of coming-out discourse today also serves as an assimilationist device that erases the underlying silences and violence through mandatory visibility and identification across race, ethnicity, and national borders (Bui, 2014). The alternative discourses to the model of coming out, which presents itself as predominantly White, cosmopolitan, and U.S.-centric, challenge the imagination of queer resistance and queer relationality. They also pose questions to the simple equation between "breaking silence" and empowerment (Rowe & Malhotra, 2013) in coming-out discourse. When emancipation is imagined as visibility and speaking up, silence and reticence appear as repression and failures of queer subjectivity (Huang & Brouwer, 2018a). However, "[t]here is not one but many silences, and they are an integral part of the strategies that underlie and permeate discourses" (Foucault, 1978, p. 27). The reductionist account in dominant coming-out discourse fails to capture the complexity of queer experiences and reflects the Euro-American bias in mainstream queer theory and politics.

FURTHER READING

Brown, M. (2000). *Closet space: Geographies of metaphor from the body to the globe.* Routledge.
Chou, W. (2000). *Tongzhi: Politics of same-sex eroticism in Chinese societies.* Haworth Press.
Eguchi, S., & Calafell, B. M. (Eds.). (2020). *Queer intercultural communication: The intersectional politics of belonging in and across differences.* Rowman & Littlefield.
Foucault, M. (1978). *The history of sexuality.* Penguin.
Gross, L. (1991). Contested closets: The ethics and politics of outing. *Critical Studies in Mass Communication, 8*, 352–388.

Huang, S., & Brouwer, D. (2018). Coming out, coming home, coming with: Models of queer sexuality in contemporary China. *Journal of International and Intercultural Communication, 11*(2), 97–116.

Martin, F. (2003). *Situating sexualities: Queer representation in Taiwanese fiction, film and public culture*. Hong Kong University Press.

McLean, K. (2007). Hiding in the closet? Bisexuals, coming out and the disclosure imperative. *Journal of Sociology, 43*(2), 151–166.

Ross, M. (2005). Beyond the closet as raceless paradigm. In E. Patrick Johnson & M. G. Henderson (Eds.), *Black queer studies: A critical anthology* (pp. 161–189). Duke University Press.

Sedgwick, E. K. (1990). *Epistemology of the closet*. University of California Press.

Snorton, C. R. (2014). *Nobody is supposed to know: Black sexuality on the down low*. University of Minnesota Press.

Yep, G. A., Lovaas, K. E., & Elia, J. P. (2003). *Queer theory and communication: From disciplining queers to queering the discipline*. Harrington Park Press.

REFERENCES

Altman, D. (1993). *Homosexual: Oppression and liberation*. New York University Press.

Barnhart, R. (1995). *Dictionary of etymology: The origins of American English words*. HarperCollins.

Blackwood, E. (2012). Queer Asian subjects: Transgressive sexualities and heteronormative meanings. *Asian Studies Review, 36*, 441–451.

Bobker, D. (2015). Coming out: Closet rhetoric and media publics. *History of the Present, 5*(1), 31–64.

Boe, J., Maxey, V. A., & Bermudez, J. M. (2018). Is the closet a closet? Decolonizing the coming out process with Latin@ adolescents and families. *Journal of Feminist Family Therapy, 30*(2), 90–108.

Brown, M. (2000). *Closet space: Geographies of metaphor from the body to the globe*. Routledge.

Bui, L. T. (2014). Breaking into the closet: Negotiating the queer boundaries of Asian American masculinity and domesticity. *Culture, Society and Masculinities, 6*(2), 129–149.

Butler, J. (1993). Imitation and gender insubordination. In H. Abelove, M. A. Barale, & D. M. Halperin (Eds.), *The lesbian and gay studies reader* (pp. 307–320). Routledge.

Chauncey, G. (1995). *Gay New York: Gender, urban culture, and the making of the gay male world 1890–1940*. Flamingo.

Chávez, K. R. (2013). *Queer migration politics: Activist rhetoric and coalitional possibilities*. University of Illinois Press.

Choi, S., & Luo, M. (2016). Performative family: Homosexuality, marriage, and intergenerational dynamics in China. *British Journal of Sociology, 67*(2), 260–280.

Chou, W. (2000). *Tongzhi: Politics of same-sex eroticism in Chinese societies*. Haworth Press.

Chou, W. (2001). Homosexuality and the cultural politics of *tongzhi* in Chinese societies. In G. Sullivan & P. A. Jackson (Eds.), *Gay and lesbian Asia: Culture, identity, community* (pp. 27–46). Haworth Press.

Davis, G., & Needham, G. (2009). Introduction: The pleasures of the tube. In G. Davis & G. Needham (Eds.), *Queer TV: Theories, histories, politics* (pp. 1–12). Routledge.

D'Emilio, J. (1983). Capitalism and gay identity. In A. B. Snitow, C. Stansell, & S. Thompson (Eds.), *Powers of desire: The politics of sexuality* (pp. 100–113). Monthly Review Press.

Engebretsen, E. (2009). Intimate practices, conjugal ideals: Affective ties and relationship strategies among *lala* (lesbian) women in contemporary Beijing. *Sexuality Research & Social Policy, 6*(3), 3–14.

Fisher, D. (2003). Immigrant closets: Tactical-micro-practices-in-the-hyphen. In G. A. Yep, K. E. Lovaas, & J. P. Elia (Eds.), *Queer theory and communication: From disciplining queers to queering the discipline* (pp. 171–192). Harrington Park Press.

Foucault, M. (1978). *The history of sexuality*. Penguin.

Fuss, D. (Ed.). (1991). *Inside/out: Lesbian theories, gay theories*. Routledge.

Gopinath, G. (2005). *Impossible desires: Queer desires and South Asian public cultures*. Duke University Press.
Gross, L. (1991). Contested closets: The ethics and politics of outing. *Critical Studies in Mass Communication, 8*, 352–388.
Gross, L. (1993). *Contested closets: The ethics and politics of outing*. University of Minnesota Press.
Han, C. (2009). Introduction to the special issue on GLBTQ of color. *Journal of Gay and Lesbian Social Services, 21*, 109–114.
Huang, H. T. (2011). *Queer politics and sexual modernity in Taiwan*. Hong Kong University Press.
Huang, S., & Brouwer, D. (2018a). Coming out, coming home, coming with: Models of queer sexuality in contemporary China. *Journal of International and Intercultural Communication, 11*(2), 97–116.
Huang, S., & Brouwer, D. (2018b). Negotiating performances of "real" marriage in Chinese queer *xinghun*. *Women's Studies in Communication, 41*(2), 140–158.
Kam, L. Y. L. (2012). *Shanghai lalas: Female tongzhi communities and politics in urban China*. Hong Kong University Press.
LeMaster, B. (2017). Notes on trans relationality. *QED: A Journal in GLBTQ Worldmaking, 4*(2), 84–92.
Liu, J., & Ding, N. (2005). Reticent poetics, queer politics. *Inter-Asia Cultural Studies, 6*(1), 30–55.
Liu, P. (2010). Why does queer theory need China? *Positions: East Asia Cultures Critique, 18*(2), 291–320.
Liu, P. (2015). *Queer Marxism in two Chinas*. Duke University Press.
Manalansan, M. (1995). In the shadows of Stonewall: Examining gay transnational politics and the diasporic dilemma. *GLQ: A Journal of Lesbian and Gay Studies, 2*(4), 425–438.
Martin, F. (2003). *Situating sexualities: Queer representation in Taiwanese fiction, film and public culture*. Hong Kong University Press.
McCarthy, J. (1994). The closet and the ethics of outing. *Journal of Homosexuality, 27*, 17–45.
McLean, K. (2007). Hiding in the closet? Bisexuals, coming out and the disclosure imperative. *Journal of Sociology, 43*(2), 151–166.
Mosher, C. (2001). The social implications of sexual identity formation and the coming-out process: A review of the theoretical and empirical literature. *The Family Journal, 9*(2), 164–173.
Muñoz, J. E. (1999). *Disidentifications: Queers of color and the performance of politics*. University of Minnesota Press.
Muñoz, J. E. (2009). *Cruising utopia: The then and there of queer futurity*. New York University Press.
Murray, S. O. (1996). *American gay*. University of Chicago Press.
Osborn, T. (1996). *Coming home: A roadmap to gay and lesbian empowerment*. St. Martin's Press.
Plummer, K. (1995). *Telling sexual stories: Power, change and social worlds*. Routledge.
Rasmussen, M. L. (2004). The problem of coming out. *Theory into Practice, 43*(2), 144–150.
Ross, M. (2005). Beyond the closet as raceless paradigm. In E. Patrick Johnson & M. G. Henderson (Eds.), *Black queer studies: A critical anthology* (pp. 161–189). Duke University Press.
Rowe, A. C., & Malhotra, S. (2013). Still the silence: Feminist reflections at the edges of sound. In S. Malhotra & A. C. Rowe (Eds.), *Silence, feminism, power: Reflections at the edges of sound* (pp. 1–22). Palgrave Macmillan.
Rust, P. C. (2003). Finding a sexual identity and community: Therapeutic implications and cultural assumptions in scientific models of coming out. In L. D. Garnets & D. C. Kimmel (Eds.), *Psychological perspectives on lesbian, gay, and bisexual experiences* (pp. 227–269). Columbia University Press.
Sedgwick, E. K. (1990). *Epistemology of the closet*. University of California Press.
Snorton, C. R. (2014). *Nobody is supposed to know: Black sexuality on the down low*. University of Minnesota Press.
Stewart, A. (1995). The early modern closet discovered. *Representations, 50*, 76–100.
Sullivan, A. (1996, November 10). When plagues end: Notes on the twilight of an epidemic. *New York Times Magazine* (pp. 55–62).

Troiden, R. (1988). *Gay and lesbian identity: A sociological analysis.* General Hall.
Vargo, M. (1998). *Acts of disclosure: The coming-out process of contemporary gay men.* Harrington Park Press.
Warner, M. (1994). Introduction. In M. Warner (Ed.), *Fear of a queer planet: Queer politics and social theory* (pp. vii–xxxi). University of Minnesota Press.
Warner, M. (2002). *Publics and counterpublics.* Zone Books.
Wei, W. (2006). *Going public: The production and transformation of queer spaces in postsocialist Chengdu, China* [Unpublished doctoral dissertation]. Retrieved from ProQuest Dissertations Publishing (UMI Number 3229807).
Wong, D. (2007). Rethinking the coming home alternative: Hybridization and coming out politics in Hong Kong's anti-homophobia parades. *Inter-Asia Cultural Studies, 8*(4), 600–616.

NOTE

1. *Tongzhi* literally means "common will." This is the Mandarin word for "comrade," which was famously used among the communists in mainland China. Now, in the 21st century, many gay, lesbian, and sometimes bisexual people in mainland China, Hong Kong, and Taiwan use *tongzhi* to refer to themselves.

Shuzhen Huang

COMING OUT IN INTERPERSONAL AND RELATIONAL PERSPECTIVES

INTRODUCTION

In a heteronormative society, coming out is a unique and critical experience for many sexual minority individuals. Based on a review of coming-out theoretical models and empirical studies related to sexual orientation disclosure, coming out through the lens of interpersonal and relational communication is discussed. The focuses are messages and message processes of coming out. Limitations of prior studies and suggestions for future research are also discussed.

TERMINOLOGY AND SCOPE

The acronym "LGBTQ+" has been commonly used to emphasize the diverse sexuality and gender identity of individuals, representing people who identify as lesbian, gay, bisexual, transgender, queer, and other sexual identities. However, transgender, or the "T," is an umbrella term for people whose gender identity or expression differs from cultural expectations based on their biological sex. Thus, transgender is not a form of sexual orientation. Transgender people may identify as heterosexual, gay, lesbian, or bisexual (American Psychological Association, 2008). Indeed, gender expression and sexual orientation disclosure are inherently different, and there are relatively limited studies on coming-out experiences of transgender individuals. Therefore, disclosing one's sexual orientation to others is the primary focus here. "LGBQ+" is utilized and considered interchangeable with "sexual minority."

THEORETICAL MODELS OF COMING OUT

While the metaphor "coming out (of the closet)" has been commonly used in people's daily conversations, there is no universal meaning of coming out among LGBQ+ individuals. In an interview study (Guittar, 2013), some participants considered "coming out" a personal journey of identity development, rather than revealing their sexual orientation to others. That is, "coming out is me accepting me—nobody else, just me" (p. 176). For other participants, coming out is sharing their identities with others, which means *either* the initial disclosure to family and close friends *or* the initial revelation and the everyday disclosure afterward (e.g., disclosing to a new colleague is also considered an instance of coming out to others). Thus, the two central meanings of coming out are coming out to oneself and coming out to others (Guittar, 2013). Indeed, prior theoretical work on coming out has also identified the two aspects of coming out; yet, the relationships between these two components differ across theoretical models.

The Homosexual Identity Model (HIM; Cass, 1979) has been the driving force for studies on coming out (Rust, 2003). Applied in a variety of disciplines, this model outlines six discrete stages utilized by LGBQ+ individuals who eventually achieve the goal of integrating the LGBQ+ identity into their overall self-concept, including identity confusion (i.e., individuals begin to wonder if same-sex attraction is personally relevant), identity comparison (i.e., people tentatively accept the possibility of being LGB), identity tolerance (i.e., individuals recognize that they are "not the only one" and search for peers in the LGBQ+ community to aid with isolation feelings), identity acceptance (i.e., individuals attach a positive connotation to their identity and become active in the LGBQ+ community), identity pride (i.e., people become immersed in LGBQ+ culture while minimizing contact with their heterosexual counterparts), and identity synthesis (i.e., people integrate their LGBQ+ identity with all other aspects of self).

The HIM is a helpful starting point to understand coming out, but the model has been criticized because of the assumption that people have to go through each of the six stages one by one (DeCecco & Shively, 2000; Rust, 2003). Indeed, individuals often experience elements of multiple stages simultaneously (Cass, 1990), and people go back and forth through various stages across their lifespan (Troiden, 1988, 1989). Thus, the HIM may not truly represent most LGBQ+ individuals' coming-out experiences. In addition, although the HIM suggests that coming out to others may occur at multiple stages, the terminate stage or ultimate goal is to come out to oneself. In other words, the HIM underestimates the role of coming out to others in people's everyday lives by viewing it just as one of many avenues that lead to coming out to oneself (Manning, 2015a; Rust, 2003).

Moving away from the stage approach, the Homosexual Lifespan Development Model (D'Augelli, 1994) highlights that LGBQ+ individuals need to come out repeatedly throughout their lives because of the evolving sociocultural contexts. Specifically, there are six developmental processes that occur multiple times or not at all as people develop, including exiting heterosexual identity (i.e., individuals realize the existence of alternative sexual orientation other than the "normal" heterosexuality), developing a personal LGBQ+ identity status (i.e., people come out to themselves and identify as LGBQ+), developing an LGBQ+ social identity (i.e., individuals come out to friends), becoming an LGBQ+ offspring (i.e., people come out to parents or guardians), developing a same-sex intimacy status (i.e., people develop intimate relationships with others of the same sex), and entering an LGBQ+ community (i.e., persons come out to multiple aspects of their social lives and become active within the LGBQ+ community).

This model highlights that coming out to oneself and coming out to others (e.g., parents, friends, romantic partners, and the public) are different aspects of an ongoing coming-out process. However, coming out to oneself and coming out to others are considered independent areas that do not influence one another (D'Augelli, 1994). In other words, the ongoing coming-out process is primarily driven by external cultural factors and has little to do with the internal aspects of the coming-out process. For instance, the model suggests that if people come out to their parents again, it is mainly because of cultural changes, rather than changes in how they view their sexual identities (i.e., coming out to oneself). Thus, while the model overcomes some issues of stages models, the interrelationships between coming out to oneself and coming out to others remain undefined.

Researchers have also pointed out that the aforementioned models often put a single person in the core of the analysis, overlooking the impact of interpersonal relationships on coming out (Diamond, 2003; Peplau & Garnets, 2000). In response to this criticism, the Constitutive Model of Coming Out (Manning, 2014, 2016) proposes that coming out occurs at three levels. At the cultural level, social norms and public discourses about sexual minority issues create frameworks for people to understand and communicate LGBQ+ identities. At the cognitive level, people realize, accept, and integrate their sexual orientation (i.e., coming out to oneself). The relational level connects the cognitive level with the cultural level, at which people share their sexual orientation with people in different relational contexts, such as family, friends, and at work (i.e., coming out to others). Thus, coming out to others is particularly important as it reflects both cultural and individual (i.e., coming out to oneself) understanding of sexuality.

Given the reciprocal relationships between perceptions and communication, between interpersonal relationships and communication, and between culture and communication (Gudykunst et al., 1988; Tracy, 2002), the process of coming out to others provides researchers with a valuable lens to understand the cognitive, relational, and cultural levels of coming out. However, existing theoretical work has often overlooked the roles of coming out to others, and even for Manning's theoretical model, the focal point is not sexual orientation disclosure per se. From a communication studies' perspective, LGBQ+ individuals' experiences of coming out to others is inherently communicative, and thereafter, coming out is discussed. Notably, while some LGBQ+ individuals use "coming out" to only refer to sexual orientation disclosure to parents and close friends, most people use the phrase more inclusively by involving all disclosure receivers (Adams, 2011; Guittar, 2013). Thus, coming out, or sexual orientation disclosure, includes LGBQ+ people revealing their sexual orientation to others in various relational contexts, such as family, friends, colleagues, and strangers.

EMPIRICAL STUDIES RELATED TO COMING OUT

Emerging research has focused on coming out in interpersonal and relational contexts. However, past studies rarely explore the communicative nature of sexual orientation disclosure. For instance, some studies investigated predictors and consequences of whether individuals reveal their sexual identities. Using population-based data, Pachankis et al. (2015) observed that closeted adult men were less likely to be depressed than their disclosed counterparts; in contrast, closeted adult women experience higher odds of depression than disclosed women. For sexual minority youths, levels of parental acceptance in childhood predict their decisions to come out to parents (D'Amico & Julien, 2012). In turn, disclosed youths reported lower levels of identity and psychological maladjustment and were less likely to engage in alcohol and drug consumption behaviors than undisclosed youths (D'Amico & Julien, 2012). In health care settings, sexual minority patients' age, education level, immigration status, medical history, and degree of internalized homophobia predicted whether they disclose to health care providers. One year later, disclosed patients reported better psychological well-being than those who did not disclose at baseline (Durso & Meyer, 2013). These three studies are representative of many that merely categorize individuals as "out" or not, oversimplifying coming out as a binary phenomenon.

Other studies have recognized that degrees of sexual orientation disclosure often vary among LGBQ+ individuals, but the communicative features of coming-out messages are still absent in the operationalization of coming out to others. For example, measuring the degrees of coming out to classmates as the number of years since youths first disclosed, researchers found that more disclosure was associated with increased verbal and physical victimization in high school, which predicted greater post-traumatic stress symptoms and suicidality (D'Augelli et al., 2002). While the results indicated that youths who have a longer disclosure history experience more negative consequences, little is known about how the adverse outcomes may vary as a function of different disclosure messages. For instance, posting a coming-out message online two years ago versus coming out by kissing a same-sex partner at school two years ago may yield different victimization and mental health consequences.

In the workplace, the perceived supportive environment and having a workplace nondiscrimination policy predicted greater degrees of coming out to colleagues (Ragins et al., 2007; Rostosky & Riggle, 2002), which were related to higher job satisfaction and lower job anxiety (Griffith & Hebl, 2002). The authors operationalized degrees of sexual orientation disclosure as the number of people who know the participants' sexual identities. Yet, one person may superficially disclose to everyone by displaying a rainbow flag on the desk, whereas another may talk to one or two colleagues in greater detail about their sexuality. Clearly, the two individuals' coming-out messages differ in disclosure breadth and depth, but those differences cannot be captured by how the aforementioned studies index coming out. Thus, although studies have documented that sexual orientation disclosure is a crucial experience for sexual minority individuals, much is to be known about the antecedents and outcomes of coming-out messages that differ in communicative features, such as breadth and depth.

Another body of research centering on disclosure receivers' reactions and the interpersonal contexts of sexual orientation disclosure found that only when LGB individuals disclosed in autonomy-supportive contexts was sexual orientation disclosure positively associated with people's psychological well-being (Legate et al., 2012, 2017). Similarly, receivers' negative reactions to people's initial sexual orientation disclosure were associated with LGB persons' current higher depression and lower self-esteem, suggesting that receivers' responses to the initial disclosure have long-lasting impacts on LGB people (Ryan et al., 2015). In line with the results, a population-based study also observed that parents' nonsupportive reactions to children's sexual orientation disclosure contributed to children's heightened odds of depressive symptoms and hazardous substance use (Rothman et al., 2012).

Thus, receivers' responses and the interpersonal context of the disclosure play a crucial role in people's disclosure experiences. However, prior studies have rarely measured sexual orientation disclosure, and even if they do, the majority employed the Outness Inventory (Mohr & Fassinger, 2000), which indeed indexes the consequences of coming out to others (i.e., how many people know a person's sexual orientation), rather than the disclosure per se (Meidlinger & Hope, 2014). Whether and how discloser–receiver relationships and coming-out messages influence one another is still unclear. Taken together, existing empirical studies on coming out often ignore and simplify the communicative features of sexual orientation disclosure as well as focus on variables related to but not the disclosure per se. The core of communication studies—messages and message processes—remain understudied. As an attempt to address the research gaps, communication scholars have started to focus on different types of coming-out conversations, contents, and strategies of coming out, and the motivations and antecedences to various degrees of coming out.

COMING OUT AS A COMMUNICATION BEHAVIOR

Coming out to others is inherently a communication behavior. LGBQ+ individuals create various coming-out messages across relational contexts. Existing research on coming-out conversations, contents, strategies, and goals is reviewed.

Coming-Out Conversations. A handful of studies explored different types of coming-out conversations and overall communication patterns of those interactions. Manning (2015a) examined coming-out narratives produced by LGB individuals and created a typology of coming-out conversations initiated in face-to-face settings. These categories include (1) *pre-planned* (i.e., a person decides they are going to come out to another in advance and prepares accordingly), (2) *emergent* (i.e., a person sees and takes an opportunity to introduce their sexual orientation into a conversation), (3) *coaxed* (i.e., a person is encouraged by others to share their sexual orientation), (4) *confrontational* (i.e., a person is demanded by others to come out), (5) *romantic/sexual* (i.e., a person comes out through romantic or sexual advances), and (6) *educational/activist* (i.e., a person comes out to a group of audience as a means of education or encouragement).

Another interview study of 130 LGB individuals identified several positive and negative communicative behaviors in coming-out conversations (Manning, 2015b). Specifically, positive behaviors for both disclosers and receivers included affirmations for love and relationships, open communication, laughter and joking, and nonverbal immediacy. Negative behaviors for sexual minority disclosers included indirectly approaching the topic, acting nervously, and lacking preparation. Negative behaviors for receivers encompassed engaging in religious talk, expressing refusal and denial, asking inappropriate questions and making improper comments, as well as verbally shaming and attacking the disclosers (Manning, 2015b).

In the health care context, Venetis et al. (2017) examined sexual minority patients' disclosure patterns of coming out to health care providers. The authors showed that sexual orientation disclosure often occurs around the initial contact with the provider or the practice.

Specifically, during customary greetings at the beginning of the visit, LGB patients often reveal their sexual orientation via introducing the present same-sex partner (e.g., a man said to his doctor, "this is my husband") or mentioning the absent partner (e.g., a woman told her provider, "My wife got a job at such and such"). The history-taking questionnaires and provider inquiries also provide LGB patients with opportunities to disclose their sexual orientation. In terms of disclosure styles, participants reported that their disclosures are basic in nature (i.e., revealing quickly and simply), casual (i.e., using a casual tone), and indirect (i.e., a woman using feminine pronouns to refer to her partner, rather than explicitly mentioning her sexual orientation). In short, coming out is not a "one-size-fits-all" experience. LGBQ+ individuals likely utilize different strategies and draft various messages to reveal their sexual orientation.

Coming-Out Strategies. Researchers have examined different types of disclosure strategies that individuals utilize to come out. Specifically, Afifi and Steuber (2009) outlined six communicative strategies for disclosing private information, including *preparation and rehearsal* (i.e., an individual prepares and practices revealing sensitive messages), *directness* (i.e., an individual discloses explicit information), *third-party disclosures* (i.e., the information owner shares the information with a third person so that they can inform the intended receiver of the information), *incremental disclosures* (i.e., an individual shares parts of the information in several disclosure episodes over time), *entrapment* (i.e., an individual feels compelled or forced to disclose), and *indirect mediums* (i.e., an individual discloses the information via a mediated channel such as text messages, emails, and social media). In the context of LGBQ+ children coming out to parents, Denes and Afifi (2014) found that children often employ multiple disclosure tactics, with the primary strategy being directness. They also tend to replicate their primary disclosure strategies when coming out the first and the second time.

Similarly, Li and Samp (2020) investigated coming-out strategies in mixed-orientation romantic relationships, in which one partner identifies as LGBQ+ and another partner is cisgender, heterosexual. Most LGBQ+ participants utilized preparation and rehearsal, and directness to reveal their sexual orientation to heterosexual partners. Yet, third-party disclosures were rarely employed (Li & Samp, 2020). Given the heteronormative ideology in society, the prominence of directness observed in prior studies is not surprising. Adams (2011) noted that sexual minority individuals, including those who are single, must confirm their sexual orientation via explicit disclosure, not to mention that if a person has been involved in a heterosexual relationship, that individual has to explicitly come out to confirm their sexual orientation with the heterosexual partner. The notion of self-confirming LGB identities also explains why few participants utilized third-party disclosures. In sum, while there are various disclosure strategies available, most sexual minority individuals tend to disclose explicit information when coming out to others.

Coming-Out Contents. In addition to how people say it (i.e., message strategies), what people say during coming-out conversations (i.e., message content) also received increasing attention from communication researchers. Specifically, Manning (2014) suggested that coming-out conversations, in general, tend to follow a particular script, which usually begins with an introduction, followed by the disclosure event, a reaction period, and a closing statement. In the context of initial coming out, Li and Samp (2020) identified eight common themes that occurred in coming-out conversations and further organized them into coming-out scripts for different coming-out interactions (see Figure 1).

In preplanned sexual orientation disclosure, sexual minority individuals usually initiate, prepare, reveal, elaborate, and conclude the interactions. *Initiating* refers to LGB individuals setting up a situation to start the sexual orientation disclosure (e.g., "I asked my mom if she wanted to grab some coffee at the Dunkin' Donuts up the street. So, we went and sat there"). *Preparing* represents people's efforts to prepare themselves and the receivers for the coming out, such as taking a deep breath, holding someone's hands, and saying, "I have something important to share with you." *Revealing* occurs when people disclose their sexual orientation verbally and nonverbally to others, including direct declaration (e.g., "I am lesbian/gay/bisexual"), indirect statement (e.g., "I like boys"), and softening statement (e.g., "I think/guess I am not straight."). *Elaborating* provides receivers with more details about what LGBQ+ individuals think and how they feel about their sexual orientation and the disclosure, as well as their future relationships with the receivers and relevant others. For instance, people may explain to their confidants that they are still the same person, and they can take care of themselves. Finally, *Concluding* is to end the sexual orientation disclosure.

In emergent coming out, where LGBQ+ people seize an opportunity to introduce their sexual orientation into a conversation, they usually start with conversing, followed by revealing, elaborating, and concluding. *Conversing* is when people start a daily conversation irrelevant to sexual orientation but as the interaction unfolds, topics related to sexuality emerge in the discussion. In confrontational coming out, when people are demanded by others to come out, the conversations usually begin with responding, followed by revealing, elaborating, and concluding. *Responding* occurs when sexual minority individuals answer receivers' questions and indirect hints of their sexual orientation. For instance, a mother asks her daughter if she finds other women attractive, and the daughter responds with a solid yes. Lastly, in romantic/sexual coming out, where people come out via romantic and sexual advances, the interactions usually start with *sexing*, in which disclosers and receivers engage in sexually intimate behaviors. Some people may discuss their sexual orientation with the confidants after sexing,

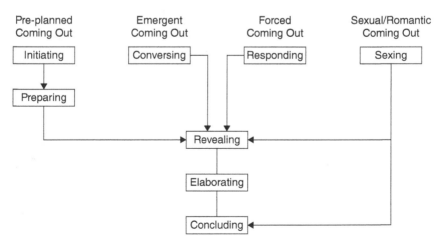

Figure 1. Theoretical scripts of different initial coming-out conversations
Source: Li & Samp, 2020.

following the sexing-revealing-elaborating-concluding pattern. Yet, many individuals may just end the interaction and believe that their sexual orientation is revealed via sexual activities.

Li and Samp's (2020) coming-out scripts provide a nuanced understanding of how different coming-out conversations unfold. The authors also found that the number of the elaborating theme identified in participants' responses was negatively correlated with self-reported depressive symptoms and psychological stress. That is, participants who talked about their thoughts and feelings about their sexual orientation, discussed future relationships with the receivers, and invited and answered receivers' questions tended to have better postdisclosure outcomes (Li & Samp, 2020). The results suggest that message content and features of coming out deserve scientific attention. In other words, how people say it and what they say during coming-out conversations matter.

Coming-Out Goals. Existing studies have demonstrated that coming-out messages often differ in aspects such as how private and intimate the information is (depth), how much information is shared (breadth), how much time is spent talking (duration), and how many emotions are expressed (emotional content) (Denes & Afifi, 2014; Li & Samp, 2020; Manning, 2015a). A related question is why people produce different coming-out messages across relational contexts and physical situations. Li and Samp (2020) developed a theory of coming-out message production (COMP) to explain how situational, personal, and relational factors may affect coming-out message production. Specifically, coming out is considered a goal-driven behavior in which people reveal their sexual orientation to achieve a range of specific objectives. COMP identifies five coming-out goals, namely self-oriented, disclosure target-oriented, nonromantic relational, romantic relational, and task goals (Li & Samp, 2020).

Self-oriented goals reflect the concerns about one's self-concept (i.e., how people define themselves) and self-image (i.e., how people want others to perceive them), as well as the desire to focus on one's own needs. For instance, people come out to be true about their identities (e.g., Boon & Miller, 1999; Cheah & Singaravelu, 2017) and to seek social support from others. *Disclosure target-oriented goals* indicate LGBQ+ individuals' efforts to satisfy disclosure receivers' interests and needs. For example, some college students come out to their roommates and friends (Evans & Broido, 1999) and some LGBQ+ youth reveal to their parents (Gattamorta & Quidley-Rodriguez, 2018) because the close others hint that they know the LGB persons' sexual orientation and want to receive confirmation from the disclosers. In these cases, people come out to meet the receivers' informational needs.

Nonromantic relational goals represent the desire to improve and maintain a nonromantic interpersonal bond between disclosers and receivers. Many LGBQ+ individuals come out to their families to improve family relationships (e.g., Boon & Miller, 1999; Scherrer, 2016). Some people also think that it is unfair to keep their friends ignorant and considered sexual orientation disclosure a touchstone of true friendships (Cheah & Singaravelu, 2017; Evans & Broido, 1999). Relatively, *romantic relational goals* reflect partnered LGBQ+ individuals' desire to improve and maintain their LGBQ+ romantic relationships. For instance, same-sex couples often come out to their family members and friends to show commitment to one another (LaSala, 2000; Rostosky et al., 2006). For many sexual minority individuals, coming out to others is a crucial way to validate and recognize their LGBQ+ romantic relationships.

Although receiving less attention, *task goals*, which refer to acquiring certain tangible resources or accomplishing specific objectives through communicative behaviors, also drive sexual orientation disclosure. For instance, college students sometimes come out to their roommates because they have LGBQ+ friends sleep over or because they want to host a pride event in the dormitory (Evans & Broido, 1999). In health care settings, sexual minority patients often revealed their sexual orientation to providers to receive relevant tests, medications, and services (Bjorkman & Malterud, 2007; Katz, 2011). These examples show that LGBQ+ individuals come out to accomplish practical or instrumental tasks.

Although discussed separately, the five types of coming-out goals are not mutually exclusive. Indeed, people frequently pursue multiple goals simultaneously (Caughlin, 2010). A sexual minority individual may come out to develop a closer relationship with their confidants (nonromantic relational goals) as well as to seek social support (self-oriented goals). COMP theorizes that when multiple coming-out goals become salient, people tend to disclose more, meaning that they reveal more topics, disclose more intimate information, talk longer, and express more emotions.

Notably, while salient disclosure goals often motivate coming out, other personal and relational factors may also affect people's coming-out messages. COMP proposes that when people have salient disclosure goals, those who experience lower levels of internalized homophobia and perceive more power over their disclosure receivers tend to disclose more (Li & Samp, 2020). In other words, disclosure goals, internalized homophobia, and relational power jointly affect people's coming-out message production. Research on initial coming out (Li & Samp, 2019) and sexual orientation disclosure to heterosexual partners (Li & Samp, 2021) support COMP's propositions.

Another noteworthy point is that people's coming-out message features seem to influence disclosure receivers' reactions to disclosure as well as the disclosers' personal and relational outcomes. For instance, Li and Samp (2019) found that higher degrees of initial sexual orientation disclosure are related to fewer postdisclosure depressive symptoms and higher self-esteem. In the context of coming out in mixed-orientation relationships, when LGBQ+ individuals engage in high levels of disclosure, their heterosexual partners react more positively, and the sexual minority people also report higher relationship satisfaction and lower depression (Li & Samp, 2021).

In short, coming out is purposeful and strategic. People disclose their sexual orientation to achieve various goals, either intentionally or unintentionally. The disclosure goals, coupled with personal factors such as internalized homophobia and relational factors like relational power, affect people's coming-out messages, which in turn predict disclosure receivers' reactions and disclosers' personal and relational outcomes.

SUGGESTIONS FOR FUTURE RESEARCH

Prior theoretical models of sexual identity development often view (initial) coming out a remarkable turning point of psychological development. Existing empirical studies usually focus on the processes and outcomes of people's disclosure decisions, overlooking the communicative features of coming out. What people say, how people say it, and why they say it remain largely understudied. Only until recently does emerging research shed light on messages and message processes of coming out. Yet, from communication studies' perspective, much is to be known. First, coming out is not a one-time event. People consistently need to disclose their sexual orientation in different relational and physical contexts. While studies have examined how personal, relational, and situational factors predict a particular coming-out scenario, future studies should explore how past coming-out experiences influence future disclosures. Researchers should also examine how people's disclosure goals change over different coming-out conversations, as well as how those changes affect coming-out messages and message outcomes.

Furthermore, many studies focus on lesbian, gay, and bisexual individuals' coming-out experiences, but less attention has been given to how transgender and gender nonbinary people express their gender identities and sexual orientation. The nuances of people's coming-out experiences have often been overlooked. In addition, much research focuses on White LGBTQ+ experiences. With few notable exceptions, such as Rosario et al. (2004) and Szymanski and Sung (2013), less is known about people of color's sexual identity development and coming-out experiences, especially from communication studies' perspective. Prior studies have also predominantly examined younger people's coming out. Less is known about how older adults manage their sexual and gender identities. Moreover, many studies either ignored or purposefully excluded participants residing outside of the United States, which limits the generalization of the results and leaves the role of culture in coming out underexplored. Therefore, future studies should include more diverse samples, focus more on marginalized members of the LGBTQ+ community, and explore how culture affects people's coming-out experiences.

In terms of research design, most studies of coming out are cross-sectional. More longitudinal studies are needed to understand the long-term impacts of coming out as well as how previous coming-out experiences affect future sexual orientation disclosure. Additionally, survey and interview studies have shown that coming-out message contents and features predict disclosure outcomes. Researchers should utilize experimental studies to further investigate how specific linguistic elements, message themes, and disclosure strategies may affect disclosure receivers' reactions and other message outcomes. Moreover, more individuals have utilized emerging social media and mediated channels to disclose their sexual orientation. Future studies should explore how media features and interpersonal factors affect people's coming-out messages and message processes.

FURTHER READING

Adams, T. E. (2011). *Narrating the closet: An autoethnography of same-sex attraction*. Left Coast Press.

Denes, A., & Afifi, T. D. (2014). Coming out again: Exploring GLBQ individuals' communication with their parents after the first coming out. *Journal of GLBT Family Studies, 10*(3), 298–325. https://doi.org/10.1080/1550428X.2013.838150

Li, Y., & Samp, J. A. (2019). Predictors and outcomes of initial coming out messages: Testing the theory of coming out message production. *Journal of Applied Communication Research, 47*(1), 69–89. https://doi.org/10.1080/00909882.2019.1566631

Li, Y., & Samp, J. A. (2020). *Navigating remarkable communication experiences of sexual minorities*. Lexington Books.

Li, Y., & Samp, J. A. (2021). Predictors and outcomes of LGB individuals' coming out to heterosexual romantic partners. *Journal of Applied Communication Research, 49*(1), 24–43. https://doi.org/10.1080/00909882.2020.1849769

Li, Y., & Samp, J. A. (2022). The impact of the COVID-19 pandemic on sexual orientation disclosure and post disclosure depression among US LGBQ individuals. *Journal of Applied Communication Research*. Advance online publication 50(5), 515–532. https://doi.org/10.1080/00909882.2022.2044503

Legate, N., Ryan, R. M., & Weinstein, N. (2012). Is coming out always a "good thing"? Exploring the relations of autonomy support, outness, and wellness for lesbian, gay, and bisexual individuals. *Social Psychological and Personality Science*, 3(2), 145–152. https://doi.org/10.1177/1948550611411929

Manning, J. (2014). Coming out conversations and gay/bisexual men's sexual health: A constitutive metamodel study. In V. L. Harvey & T. H. House (Eds.), *Health care disparities and the LGBT population* (pp. 27–54). Lexington Books.

Manning, J. (2015a). Communicating sexual identities: A typology of coming out. *Sexuality & Culture*, 19(1), 122–138. https://doi.org/10.1007/s12119-014-9251-4

Manning, J. (2015b). Positive and negative communicative behaviors in coming-out conversations. *Journal of Homosexuality*, 62(1), 67–97. https://doi.org/10.1080/00918369.2014.957127

Manning, J. (2016). Identity, relationships, and culture: A constitutive model of coming out. In J. Manning & C. Noland (Eds.), *Contemporary studies of sexuality & communication: Theoretical and applied perspectives* (pp. 93–108). Kendall Hunt Publishing.

Ryan, W. S., Legate, N., & Weinstein, N. (2015). Coming out as lesbian, gay, or bisexual: The lasting impact of initial disclosure experiences. *Self and Identity*, 14(5), 549–569. https://doi.org/10.1080/15298868.2015.1029516

Rosario, M., Schrimshaw, E. W., & Hunter, J. (2004). Ethnic/racial differences in the coming-out process of lesbian, gay, and bisexual youths: A comparison of sexual identity development over time. *Cultural Diversity and Ethnic Minority Psychology*, 10(3), 215–228. https://doi.org/10.1037/1099-9809.10.3.215

REFERENCES

Adams, T. E. (2011). *Narrating the closet: An autoethnography of same-sex attraction*. Left Coast Press.

Afifi, T. D., & Steuber, K. (2009). The revelation risk model (RRM): Factors that predict the revelation of secrets and the strategies used to reveal them. *Communication Monographs*, 76(2), 144–176. https://doi.org/10.1080/03637750902828412

American Psychological Association. (2008). *Answers to your questions: For a better understanding of sexual orientation and homosexuality*. https://www.apa.org/topics/lgbt/orientation.pdf

Bjorkman, M., & Malterud, K. (2007). Being lesbian—Does the doctor need to know? A qualitative study about the significance of disclosure in general practice. *Scandinavian Journal of Primary Health Care*, 25(1), 58–62. https://doi.org/10.1080/02813430601086178

Boon, S. D., & Miller, R. J. (1999). Exploring the links between interpersonal trust and the reasons underlying gay and bisexual males' disclosure of their sexual orientation to their mothers. *Journal of Homosexuality*, 37(3), 45–68. https://doi.org/10.1300/J082v37n03_04

Cass, V. C. (1979). Homosexuality identity formation: A theoretical model. *Journal of Homosexuality*, 4(3), 219–235. https://doi.org/10.1300/J082v04n03_01

Cass, V. C. (1990). The implications of homosexual identity formation for the Kinsey model and scale of sexual preference. In D. P. McWhirter, S. A. Sanders, & J. M. Reinisch (Eds.), *Homosexuality/heterosexuality: Concepts of sexual orientation* (pp. 239–266). Oxford University Press.

Caughlin, J. P. (2010). A multiple goals theory of personal relationships: Conceptual integration and program overview. *Journal of Social and Personal Relationships*, 27(6), 824–848. https://doi.org/10.1177/0265407510373262

Cheah, W. H., & Singaravelu, H. (2017). The coming-out process of gay and lesbian individuals from Islamic Malaysia: Communication strategies and motivations. *Journal of Intercultural Communication Research*, 46(5), 401–423. https://doi.org/10.1080/17475759.2017.1362460

D'Amico, E., & Julien, D. (2012). Disclosure of sexual orientation and gay, lesbian, and bisexual youths' adjustment: Associations with past and current parental acceptance and rejection. *Journal of GLBT Family Studies, 8*(3), 215–242.

D'Augelli, A. R. (1994). Identity development and sexual orientation: Toward a model of lesbian, gay, and bisexual development. In E. J. Trickett, R. J. Watts, & D. Birman (Eds.), *Human diversity: Perspectives on people in context* (pp. 312–333). Jossey-Bass.

D'Augelli, A. R., Pilkington, N. W., & Hershberger, S. L. (2002). Incidence and mental health impact of sexual orientation victimization of lesbian, gay, and bisexual youths in high school. *School Psychology Quarterly, 17*(2), 148–167. https://doi.org/10.1521/scpq.17.2.148.20854

DeCecco, J. P., & Shively, M. G. (2000). From sexual identity to sexual relationships: A contextual shift. In P. C. Rust (Ed.), *Bisexuality in the United States* (pp. 99–103). Columbia University Press.

Denes, A., & Afifi, T. D. (2014). Coming out again: Exploring GLBT individuals' communication with their parents after the first coming out. *Journal of GLBT Family Studies, 10*(3), 298–325. https://doi.org/10.1080/1550428X.2013.838150

Diamond, L. M. (2003). Was it a phase? Young women's relinquishment of lesbian/bisexual identities over a 5-year period. *Journal of Personality and Social Psychology, 84*(2), 352–364. https://doi.org/10.1037/0022-3514.84.2.352

Durso, L. E., & Meyer, I. H. (2013). Patterns and predictors of disclosure of sexual orientation to healthcare providers among lesbians, gay men, and bisexuals. *Sexuality Research and Social Policy, 10*(1), 35–42. https://doi.org/10.1007/s13178-012-0105-2

Evans, N. J., & Broido, E. M. (1999). Coming out in college residence halls: Negotiation, meaning making, challenges, supports. *Journal of College Student Development, 40*(6), 658–668.

Gattamorta, K., & Quidley-Rodriguez, N. (2018). Coming out experiences of Hispanic sexual minority young adults in South Florida. *Journal of Homosexuality, 65*(6), 741–765. https://doi.org/10.1080/00918369.2017.1364111

Griffith, K. H., & Hebl, M. R. (2002). The disclosure dilemma for gay men and lesbians: "Coming out" at work. *Journal of Applied Psychology, 87*(6), 1191–1199. https://doi.org/10.1037/0021-9010.87.6.1191

Gudykunst, W. B., Ting-Toomey, S., & Chua, E. (1988). *Culture and interpersonal communication.* SAGE.

Guittar, N. A. (2013). The meaning of coming out: From self-affirmation to full disclosure. *Qualitative Sociology Review, 9*(3), 168–187.

Katz, A. (2011). Gay and lesbian patients with cancer. In J. P. Mulhall, L. Incrocci, I. Goldstein, & R. Rosen (Eds.), *Cancer and sexual health* (pp. 397–403). Humana Press. https://doi.org/10.1007/978-1-60761-916-1_26

LaSala, M. C. (2000). Gay male couples: The importance of coming out and being out to parents. *Journal of Homosexuality, 39*(2), 47–71. https://doi.org/10.1300/J082v39n02_03

Legate, N., Ryan, R. M., & Rogge, R. D. (2017). Daily autonomy support and sexual identity disclosure predicts daily mental and physical health outcomes. *Personality and Social Psychology Bulletin, 43*(6), 860–873. https://doi.org/10.1177/0146167217700399

Legate, N., Ryan, R. M., & Weinstein, N. (2012). Is coming out always a "good thing"? Exploring the relations of autonomy support, outness, and wellness for lesbian, gay, and bisexual individuals. *Social Psychological and Personality Science, 3*(2), 145–152. https://doi.org/10.1177/1948550611411929

Li, Y., & Samp, J. A. (2019). Predictors and outcomes of initial coming out messages: Testing the theory of coming out message production. *Journal of Applied Communication Research, 47*(1), 69–89. https://doi.org/10.1080/00909882.2019.1566631

Li, Y., & Samp, J. A. (2020). *Navigating remarkable communication experiences of sexual minorities.* Lexington Books.

Li, Y., & Samp, J. A. (2021). Predictors and outcomes of LGB individuals' coming out to heterosexual romantic partners. *Journal of Applied Communication Research, 49*(1), 24–43. https://doi.org/10.1080/00909882.2020.1849769

Manning, J. (2014). Coming out conversations and gay/bisexual men's sexual health: A constitutive metamodel study. In V. L. Harvey & T. H. House (Eds.), *Health care disparities and the LGBT population* (pp. 27–54). Lexington Books.

Manning, J. (2015a). Communicating sexual identities: A typology of coming out. *Sexuality & Culture*, 19(1), 122–138. https://doi.org/10.1007/s12119-014-9251-4

Manning, J. (2015b). Positive and negative communicative behaviors in coming-out conversations. *Journal of Homosexuality*, 62(1), 67–97. https://doi.org/10.1080/00918369.2014.957127

Manning, J. (2016). Identity, relationships, and culture: A constitutive model of coming out. In J. Manning & C. Noland (Eds.), *Contemporary studies of sexuality & communication: Theoretical and applied perspectives* (pp. 93–108). Kendall Hunt Publishing.

Meidlinger, P. C., & Hope, D. A. (2014). Differentiating disclosure and concealment in measurement of outness for sexual minorities: The Nebraska Outness Scale. *Psychology of Sexual Orientation and Gender Diversity*, 1(4), 489–497. https://doi.org/10.1037/sgd0000080

Mohr, J. J., & Fassinger, R. (2000). Measuring dimensions of lesbian and gay male experience. *Measurement and Evaluation in Counseling and Development*, 33(2), 66–90. https://doi.org/10.1037/t07099-000

Pachankis, J. E., Cochran, S. D., & Mays, V. M. (2015). The mental health of sexual minority adults in and out of the closet: A population-based study. *Journal of Consulting and Clinical Psychology*, 83(5), 890–901. https://doi.org/10.1037/ccp0000047

Peplau, L. A., & Garnets, L. D. (2000). A new paradigm for understanding women's sexuality and sexual orientation. *Journal of Social Issues*, 56(2), 330–350. https://doi.org/10.1111/0022-4537.00169

Ragins, B. R., Singh, R., & Cornwell, J. M. (2007). Making the invisible visible: Fear and disclosure of sexual orientation at work. *Journal of Applied Psychology*, 92(4), 1103–1118. https://doi.org/10.1037/0021-9010.92.4.1103

Rosario, M., Schrimshaw, E. W., & Hunter, J. (2004). Ethnic/racial differences in the coming-out process of lesbian, gay, and bisexual youths: A comparison of sexual identity development over time. *Cultural Diversity and Ethnic Minority Psychology*, 10(3), 215–228. https://doi.org/10.1037/1099-9809.10.3.215

Rostosky, S. S., & Riggle, E. D. B. (2002). "Out" at work: The relation of actor and partner workplace policy and internalized homophobia to disclosure status. *Journal of Counseling Psychology*, 49(4), 411–419. https://doi.org/10.1037/0022-0167.49.4.411

Rostosky, S. S., Riggle, E. D. B., Dudley, M. G., & Wright, M. L. C. (2006). Commitment in same-sex relationships: A qualitative analysis of couples' conversations. *Journal of Homosexuality*, 51(3), 199–223. https://doi.org/10.1300/J082v51n03_10

Rothman, E. F., Sullivan, M., Keyes, S., & Boehmer, U. (2012). Parents' supportive reactions to sexual orientation disclosure associated with better health: Results from a population-based survey of LGB adults in Massachusetts. *Journal of Homosexuality*, 59(2), 186–200. https://doi.org/10.1080/00918369.2012.648878

Rust, P. C. (2003). Finding a sexual identity and community: Therapeutic implications and cultural assumptions in scientific models of coming out. In L. D. Garnets & D. C. Kimmel (Eds.), *Psychological perspectives on lesbian, gay and bisexual experiences* (2nd ed., pp. 227–269). Columbia University Press.

Ryan, W. S., Legate, N., & Weinstein, N. (2015). Coming out as lesbian, gay, or bisexual: The lasting impact of initial disclosure experiences. *Self and Identity*, 14(5), 549–569. https://doi.org/10.1080/15298868.2015.1029516

Scherrer, K. S. (2016). Gay, lesbian, bisexual, and queer grandchildren's disclosure process with grandparents. *Journal of Family Issues*, 37(6), 739–764. https://doi.org/10.1177/0192513X14526874

Szymanski, D. M., & Sung, M. R. (2013). Asian cultural values, internalized heterosexism, and sexual orientation disclosure among Asian American sexual minority persons. *Journal of LGBT Issues in Counseling*, 7(3), 257–273. https://doi.org/10.1080/15538605.2013.812930

Tracy, K. (2002). *Everyday talk: Building and reflecting identities*. Guilford Press.

Troiden, R. R. (1988). Homosexual identity development. *Journal of Adolescent Health Care, 9*(2), 105–113. https://doi.org/10.1016/0197-0070(88)90056-3

Troiden, R. R. (1989). The formation of homosexual identities. *Journal of Homosexuality, 17*(1–2), 43–74. https://doi.org/10.1300/J082v17n01_02

Venetis, M. K., Meyerson, B. E., Friley, L. B., Gillespie, A., Ohmit, A., & Shields, C. G. (2017). Characterizing sexual orientation disclosure to health care providers: Lesbian, gay, and bisexual perspectives. *Health Communication, 32*(5), 578–586. https://doi.org/10.1080/10410236.2016.1144147

Yachao Li

COMING OUT NARRATIVES IN AUDIOVISUAL CULTURE

INTRODUCTION: THE FAMILIAR SCRIPT

No matter how predictable, almost every narrative film has a script that structures and directs the action on screen. However, the genres that inform those scripts can become so reliant on the overly familiar that the two seem inseparable and other options appear to be excluded. *The Children's Hour* (Wyler, 1961) and *Advise and Consent* (Preminger, 1962) mark two of the starting points of the coming-out genre in classical Hollywood filmmaking. In that genre, where a LGBTQ+ sexual identity is acknowledged, the narrative is structured for an audience that seeks out a version of the well-worn drama with revelations that lead to explosive consequences. In these earlier films, a key element of the script is the death or suicide of the character who is marked as gay. Even though this script is familiar to contemporary audiences in the late 20th and 21st centuries, as well as in popular culture, it is now both ineffective and harmful. Its various iterations include such classic gay films as *The Boys in the Band* (Friedkin, 1970), *My Beautiful Laundrette* (Frears, 1985), and *Brokeback Mountain* (Lee, 2005). The genre that focuses on gay tragedy has given this narrative form a strong degree of predictability and foreclosed other queer options.[1] In those narratives, tragedy, death, or a simple lack of fulfillment in life because a protagonist identifies as gay structure the stories on screen. It is fruitful to explore alternatives without being trapped by the need to both identify another version of the coming-out narrative and then claim that once the newly identified model is incorporated, things will turn out alright in the end. It is necessary to propose a flexible and plural definition of coming out where reiteration, continual repetition, and open secrets structure the contours of the act.

The term *queer* is used here not as a substitute for the term LGBTQ+ but to embody acts of sexual, cultural, and political resistance by those who identify as LGBTQ+. Pioneering queer researcher Annamarie Jagose (1996) defined queer as "those gestures or analytical models which dramatize incoherencies in the allegedly stable relations between chromosomal sex, gender, and sexual desire" (p. 3). Jagose's definition emphasizes the ability of queer to illuminate and resist normative practices. The historical reality that structures coming out and its transformation into a normative practice is also at the heart of her analysis. She argued that from the 1970s onwards, there has been a strong liberationist focus within gay communities in Europe, North America, and Australia; in these communities coming out has been promoted as an act that can create social transformation and unambiguous identities, reduce individual shame, and pave the way for a recognition of legitimacy. She went on to point out that, beginning in the 1990s, queer researchers, as well as gays and lesbians themselves, began to "question and resist identity categories and their promise of unity and political effectiveness" (Jagose, 1996, p. 91). This transition documents one of the ways in which coming out has moved from being the metaphorical expression of queer liberation to the present moment where it has become a method for an enforcement of the normative, heteronormativity, and homonormativity.

Heteronormativity is defined by the ability to normalize the (re-)productive aspects of heterosexuality within the West. Queer studies specialists Lauren Berlant and Mark Warner (1998) defined heteronormativity as "the institutions, structures of understanding, and practical orientations that make heterosexuality seem not only coherent—that is, organized as a sexuality—but also privileged" (p. 548). They went on to define the privileged language that heteronormativity asserts in Western societies as the creation of a basic idiom, transmitted as a personal ideal, or even accomplishment. The combined concepts of naturalness and omnipresence that structure heteronormativity can also be extended to provide a definition for the related term, homonormativity. Queer political researcher Jasbir Puar (2007) pointed out that, in the era of late neoliberal capitalism, societal acceptance of the LGBTQ+ community in the West has become contingent on the "ever-narrowing parameters of white racial privilege, consumption capabilities, gender and kinship normativity, and bodily integrity" (p. xii). Puar (2007) clarified those parameters when she reminded her readers that those who are subject to hetero- and homonormativity are interwoven into "the bountiful market and the interstices of state benevolence" (p. xxvii). Acceptance of queer identities has become intimately tied with the requirement that those who identify as LGBTQ+ must conform to the structures and ideas of late capitalism.

The symbolic transformation from deviant to normative and from inside to outside are parts of the legacy that have shaped how the connection between coming out and the closet is perceived. In *Epistemology of the Closet*, Eve Kosofsky Sedgwick (1990) explained how the closet simultaneously both entraps and expels (p. 71). An essential step in the reevaluation of coming out and the closet is to see them as both unstable and multidirectional. Sedgwick's conceptual understanding about the intertwined nature of the closet and coming out reinforces the idea of their coexistence. She went on to discuss the fact that the closet and the exit from it "can bring about the revelation of a powerful unknowing *as* unknowing, not as a vacuum or as the blank it can pretend to be but as a weighty and occupied and consequential epistemological space" (Sedgwick, 1990, p. 77). Her comments communicate to the reader that exiting the closet can deliver the opposite of its presumed promises of clarity and identity.

The potential for the effects of the entanglements associated with coming out to be both dissident and subversive is examined by Judith Butler (1991) in "Imitation and Gender Insubordination," wherein she evaluated the connections between coming out, the closet, and opacity with a proposition:

> being "out" must produce the closet again and again in order to maintain itself as "out." In this sense, outness can only produce a new opacity; and the closet produces the promise of a disclosure that can, by definition, never come. (p. 16)

Her comments explore coming out and are an endorsement of it as a reiterative process. She did so when she argued that full disclosure can never happen; the act of revelation never reveals everything. She asked her readers to comfort themselves with the fact that whole truths are not always available. Sedgwick's idea that coming out is a kind of unknowing and Butler's notion of opacity suggest that coming out, being out, and the closet must be seen as reiterative, in that they are in a continual state of re-production and adaptation.

The scripting of coming out in audiovisual media as a reiterative act has become a complicated and, at times, impossible process. Richard Dyer (2003) illustrated how "it is much more difficult to show the process of CO [coming out]. It is only as one approaches dramatization that it becomes possible" (p. 236). He developed his point about the dramatic narrative potential of coming out with the assertion that "in the fiction films proper, CO is undoubtedly the narrative structure par excellence" (Dyer, 2003, p. 236). The allure of this dramatic narrative form has often created space only for that which could be considered canonical and the normative in coming-out narratives.

Coming out in contemporary film is often part of an attempt to achieve several objectives at the same time. This marks a change from conventional, mid-20th-century Hollywood films where an explosive revelation would lead to tragedy and the death of the gay character. In current audiovisual narratives, coming out serves as a depiction of LGBTQ+ identity, a political statement about the LGBTQ+ community, and as a visual narrative. Queer analyst Michael Bronski (2000) outlined how films such as *Beautiful Thing* (1996), *Edge of Seventeen* (1998), and *Head On* (1998), where coming out is a key narrative element, have failed to negotiate these challenges: "the coming out genre is symptomatic of a larger problem with films that are forced to carry the mantle of being 'overtly political' as well as being art" (p. 20). He went on to argue that these films present coming out as a "simple personal statement" (Bronski, 2000, p. 23). It is important to note that Bronski's assessment is focused on films produced in the late 1990s. Those films were part of the New Queer Cinema movement and focused on positive storylines where the protagonists eventually find love, belonging, and identity. This relentless quest to create a visible and positive difference from earlier Hollywood gay tragedies also motivates Bronski's analysis of the banal and positive representations of both coming out and LGBTQ+-identified characters in such films. He reminds his readers about what is missing in these films: "Coming out is essentially a complicated internal process, not a simple public act" (Bronski, 2000, p. 21). Through the simplification of complex personal narratives, the audiences of such films are forced onto a narrative track that leaves no room for the reiterative and adaptable elements within coming out. Beyond these narratives, where a singular and heroic statement often leads to a settled world, the genre often cuts off further analysis about the effects of the coming-out moment or whether it is, in fact, the end of the story. Bronski (2000) went on to propose that "coming out is nearly always the end point, never the beginning of the plot" (p. 23). Conventional coming-out films have relied so heavily on the restrictive nature of the genre's narrative structure, whether to set the stage for tragedy or a banal teenage love story, that the potential for alternative, or queered, realities of coming out are erased. Through a close study of four films, *Beautiful Thing* (Macdonald, 1996), *Summer Storm* (Kreuzpaintner, 2004), *Brotherhood* (Donato, 2009), and *North Sea Texas* (Defurne, 2011), alternative visions of coming out as an act and concept can be observed. These alternatives force the audience and popular culture's attention away from linear and normative forms of the act and toward an understanding of coming out as a reiterative moment that is continually present and endlessly adaptable.

These productions offer alternatives to normative coming-out scripts. Hettie Macdonald's *Beautiful Thing* weaves a coming-out narrative and a gay youth love story together. The visual narrative of this established film demonstrates the importance of the reiterative, adaptable, and unanticipated representation of the act in visual media. The characters Jamie and Ste come of age on a working-class public housing estate in London and each young man wrestles with issues of class, identity, and sexuality. Jamie's mother confronts her son about his identity and a dramatic, if unpredictable, moment of coming out follows. The established paradigm is subverted because the act is also presented as a reiterative moment. The acts of sexual self-identification in this film are the background to a sexual identity that is neither rejected nor heroically assumed.

In *Summer Storm*, coming out is intimately tied to ways in which secrets are revealed that everyone already knows. In this adolescent coming-out narrative, the principal protagonist is a Bavarian athlete who must balance his loyalties to his team, sport, and budding sexual desires. The character Tobi enacts coming-out moments that are structured around a secret that has been exposed. The continual acts of revelation are part of a process that is led both by himself and the other teenage athletes. This film illustrates that coming out and gay identification are not necessarily synonymous.

In *Brotherhood*, coming out is depicted by the ways in which identities are instantaneously accepted and rejected within a neo-Nazi subculture through a form of "un-coming out." In this narrative, a young, Danish neo-Nazi named Jimmy attempts to refuse both a minority sexual identity and a conventional coming-out moment. At the end, Jimmy is forced to publicly perform an un-coming out where he rapidly and violently alternates between refusals and acknowledgments of his sexual attraction to men. The end result is that all options lead to betrayal.

In *North Sea Texas*, the coming-out script is reimagined and reworked by two characters who decline any opportunity to clarify their identities. The plot is focused on the lives of two teenagers, Pim and Gino, who defy the scripts that could structure their identities and relationship. The ambivalence shown within the film's coming-out scenes steers the narrative away from the normative methods through which popular culture has come to view coming out. The film reorients the understanding of coming out toward an appreciation of the act as a time that is full of continual repetitions and variations.

Each production illustrates that coming out is continually repeated and endlessly adapted. To do so, all the narratives move away from normative coming-out stories where comedic, tragic, or even banal melodramatic moments accompany explosive revelations as well as the creation of stable and fixed identities. In these visual stories, acts of coming out occur incessantly and each new instance comes in the form of repetitions, adaptations, and evolutions from previous manifestations.

LOVE ON THE ESTATE: THE UNANTICIPATED COMING OUT IN *BEAUTIFUL THING*

The forms and reception of the coming-out narrative are the central themes in the gay youth love story that is depicted in *Beautiful Thing*. The film's visual narrative is focused on the adaptable and unanticipated representation of the act in practice. Both Jamie's coming-out moment with his mother and Sandra's response are emotionally poignant. However, their interaction redirects the storyline away from a banal moment of acceptance or rejection and toward a recognition of coming out as a continually rehearsed act that is never perfected.

The film, based on the stage play written by openly gay playwright Jonathan Harvey, presents a story of teenage love between two working-class boys on a council estate in London, England. Since its release, the film has become a research wellspring for contemporary queer film and narrative analysis. Israeli film researcher Gilad Padva (2004) summarized this narrative as the articulation of a "love story of two boys who live in a working-class neighborhood in East London: Jamie, a delicate boy who is bullied by his school-mates, and Ste, the football captain who is often beaten by his older brother, a drug dealer, and by his abusive father" (p. 358). Padva's brief summary elides the important role played by Jamie's mother, Sandra, who throughout the film remains concerned about her son. When she discovers that he has been taunted with homophobic abuse, she covertly trails after Jamie and Ste on their first visit to a gay bar. Back at home, she confronts Jamie and a dramatic, if unpredictable, moment of coming out ensues.

This narrative of youthful love, coming out, and acceptance is a story that does not end in shame, family breakup, or tragedy. It is described by Marxist queer analyst Bob Nowlan (2006) as a film that "explicitly takes the form of a 'fairy tale'" (p. 148). Despite the fairy tale nature of the love and teenage angst portrayed between Jamie and Ste, the narrative addresses a number of relevant sociological topics. Ste's father and brother are verbally and physically abusive. Eventually, Ste escapes to live with Jamie and his mother. Sandra is a single mother who struggles to establish security for herself and her family through her quest to become a pub manager. Race also plays a role in the narrative. Leah, the Afro-Caribbean straight teenage neighbor, regularly faces the brutal reality of racism. Her friendship with Jamie and Ste only confirms the minority status that each must confront. Harvey's adaptation of his stage work was attractive to Channel 4 Films as part of the company's mandate to "reflect public diversity" (Pullen, 2009, p. 175). In this film, diversity includes the challenging issues of class, race, sexual orientation, family dysfunction, and teenage life.

Scholarship about coming out often emphasizes how the act is structured by the linear and heroic narrative. Padva (2004) proposed that *Beautiful Thing* was part of a new wave of films focused on queer teenagers and demonstrated "the necessity to provide young queers with some form of representation of their life and possible life choice" (p. 357). This is a confirmation that from the mid-1990s onward, previous narrative patterns that always ended in gay tragedy were no longer acceptable to LGBTQ+ audiences. However, the move away from coming out and gay identity as a guarantee of a tragic ending has created a new dominant script about coming out, and one that Padva endorses. He interprets films, such as *Beautiful Thing*, where the coming-out narrative is a central theme, as an endorsement of the idea that "coming-out *is* difficult and painful but staying in the closet is much worse. Coming out is presented as the only way for a queer teenager to achieve his/her personal, social, cultural *and* sexual liberation" (Padva, 2004, p. 368). For Padva, coming out in film narrative has before and after moments and results in the adoption of a clearly defined gay identity where the queer teenager achieves personal and sexual liberation. His findings are based on his interpretation of how the protagonists adopt attitudes of "maturity, acceptance, pride, and happiness" (Padva, 2004, p. 369). These reflections on the narratives of films, including *Beautiful Thing*, construct coming out for the young male characters on screen, and the audience, as a necessary evil that is made unproblematic because it leads to an idealized form of liberation.

Nevertheless, he acknowledges that coming out in visual narratives can lead to the presentation of a narrow path that privileges a single discourse about gay youth and sexual identification. He does so when he posits that the "spectacular visualization of coming-out as the ideal solution for gay youth's agony is a naive illusion" (Padva, 2004, p. 369). Padva's comments reflect the reiterative nature of coming out and its presentation in visual narratives. On the one hand, the act is seen as a necessity, a liberation, and the conventional means to create both community and identity. On the other, coming out can never fully deliver its promises of liberation, identity, or an attachment to the LGBTQ+ community. Coming out remains adaptable, where the continual rehearsal of the act creates the possibility for a diversity of outcomes.

The narrative of *Beautiful Thing* has a strong homonormative element within the love storyline and the moments of coming out. The cinematography creates a story arc that can be seen as the establishment of a simplified and normative trajectory where the moment of coming out is constructed to be explosive, dramatic, and ultimately, successful. Each part of the story leads to what Nowlan (2006) described as the point where Jamie and Ste "develop the confidence to define themselves as gay and to commit themselves to each other" (p. 143). A series of successive elements gradually lead to the explosive moment of coming out. Leah repeatedly urges the boys to come out and threatens to expose them (00:50:39–00:52:19). Jamie's desire to explore his gay identity is made physically tangible when he steals a copy of the *Gay Times* from a local newsagent (00:44:20–00:44:50). The magazine becomes a talisman that symbolizes Jamie's, and later Ste's, first contact with the conventional LGBTQ+ community. Based on an advertisement therein, the two young lovers go out to their local gay pub, The Gloucester, to enjoy their first public evening out as a couple (01:02:40–01:04:59). From the moment they enter the pub, a dramatic coming out is preordained because Sandra has shadowed the two young men on their night out (01:02:35–01:02:40). Her confrontation with her son about the reality of his identity, something that she already knows, takes on an air of inevitability. Queer film researcher Fouz-Hernández (2008) argued that the film adopts "a more or less assimilationist approach whereby homosexuality would be accepted as a lifestyle and not just as a series of isolated acts" (p. 153). In a purely normative reading, the trajectory of the story that ends with the moment of explosive coming out can be observed as the completion of a simple, enclosed narrative. However, such a reading omits the reiterative and adaptable aspects of the coming out, which the audience confronts.

By looking closer at the moment when Jamie formally comes out to his mother, the reiterative nature of the act comes into focus. Jamie babbles while he explains his fears about being labeled as gay. He then describes himself in terms that are not merely about the present, but also a projection into an ominous future (01:07:25–01:10:30). As a result, the melodramatic declaration is neither a clear nor heroic statement where the young gay man proudly assumes the mantle of his sexual identity. At that moment, Sandra receives the already known news and does not reject her son when she states: "You think that you know all about me, don't you?" (01:09:46–01:09:50). Padva (2004) described how Sandra's actions within the storyline actualize the reiterative search for knowledge and understanding:

> This rhetorical question is an epistemological speech act because she refers to the interrelations of the known and the unknown, the explicit and the implicit, the recognized and the denied, the admitted and the repressed, the assumed and the guaranteed. (p. 360)

His comments confirm the observation that Sandra's preexisting knowledge and acceptance of her son is part of the visual representation of a reiterative coming out that weaves together both the known and unknown into a never finished search for knowledge and identity. Padva (2004) concluded that "Sandra was not angry at them because of their erotic identity but because they had lied to her and *pretended* to be straight" (p. 361). At that point in the film, coming out is both normative and subversive; and as a result, the depiction of coming out reveals how the act is always a reiterative rehearsal that is simultaneously both transparent and opaque. Jamie's declaration is neither heroic nor a disavowal based on a sense of self-hatred and shame. He releases his emotions and presumes that disaster lurks on the other side of the statement. However, the narrative is queered because the protagonist's expectations are defied. The act pivots on the fact that it is a disclosure of knowledge about which Sandra was already aware. Her acknowledgement and acceptance, of both her son and Ste's sexual identities and their shared love, are premised on the notion that honesty is the best policy. She leads the audience to prefer the adoption of a clear identity for the teenage boys.

The presentation of coming out in *Beautiful Thing* is part of established and conventional visual storytelling about the topic. In such depictions, the gay protagonist struggles with the explosive revelation of a secret that is disclosed in a dramatic moment of self-determination, affirmation, or even tragedy. Nevertheless, coming out in this film is also a queer act. The established paradigm is subverted because the audience is presented with a reiterative moment, where the adaptable nature of coming out is made visible through the revelation of a secret that everyone already knows. The film's coming-out storyline is the backdrop to a sexual identity that is neither rejected nor heroically assumed. The audience witnesses the articulation of coming out as the rehearsal of a search for identity and knowledge that is never-ending.

SUMMER STORM: SPORT, TEENAGERS, AND COMING OUT

In *Summersturm* (Marco Kreuzpaintner, 2004), coming out is presented as a time when secrets are revealed that everyone already knows and acknowledges. The film offers coming out as both a narrative and a script. That combination is made visible when the act creates a collective coming out where the teenage athletes demand that one of their own acknowledges a homosexual identity. Despite that peer pressure, Tobi chooses his own moment to rehearse and perform the secret in front of his friends and teammates. The film forces the audience to focus on the effects of the story: A coming out mediated as a secret that is both already known and forever being revealed.

The film was also released in English with the title *Summer Storm*; it is both a coming-out story and a coming-of-age story. It received a number of awards but was also criticized for its limitations.[2] The principal protagonist, Tobi, is a teenager from Bavaria who is slowly coming to terms with his homoerotic desires and the connection of those desires to a gay identity. In the first part of the film, Tobi makes gradual advances toward a full expression of his affection for his straight friend and fellow rower, Achim (00:05:50–00:07:49). The action accelerates once the scene shifts to a multiteam pre-competition rowing camp in the Bergisches region of northwestern Germany. There, the Bavarian rowers have their first encounter with a rowing team composed entirely of gay teenagers from Berlin. Team Queerstrokes is led by a toned, muscled, athletic, and emancipated character named Malte (00:22:29–00:24:49). Throughout the film, the fact that Malte does not recognize the existence of the closet is contrasted with Tobi's struggle about the secret of being gay. Tobi makes a final advance on Achim, only to be rejected (00:48:29–00:49:06). After that, he meets another member of Queerstrokes, Leo, and begins a sexual relationship with him (00:52:50–00:55:48). Leo is also out and his comfort with his sexual identity applies an additional layer of peer pressure on Tobi for intelligibility about the secret of his own sexuality. The existence of this pressure illustrates how the film makes coming out the only option for resolution, even though the narrative also shows how coming out is enacted without the adoption of a normative gay identity.

This film must be situated within the German context, where national and regional identities, along with the importance placed on physical and moral health, meet at the contested intersection of sport. German sport researcher Ilse Hartmann-Tews (2002) expanded on the links between sport and German culture by positing that "competition, performance and improvement are traditional values and orientations of the sports system in general and sports clubs in particular" (p. 160). In this film, the culture of German sports competition and personal improvement are central to the narrative and the coming-out story that is enacted.

In *Summer Storm*, the coming-out process is not binary, consisting of a before and after, but a flow of moments and actions. Theorist Ross Chambers (1981) argued that the biggest secret is that everyone knows both the existence of the secret and its contents. For Chambers, secrets are inherently open and public. He elaborated on this point when he wrote, "only the shared secret achieves full reality and performs the true function of secrecy, which is not private and personal, but public and social" (Chambers, 1981, p. 67). In the case of Tobi's secret, it is the various moments of revelation that matter. Just as importantly, the secret is already known in the public sphere before he denies the facts in the forest and when he later initiates his declaration of identity at breakfast. The film's narrative exposes a blurred border between being outed and coming out. With respect to being outed, the film portrays a group of teenagers who propel Tobi out of the closet with a relentless quest for intelligence about the secret of his homosexuality. The night before Tobi comes out to the whole group, the two teams search for a missing Bavarian team member in the forest (01:10:33–01:11:25). During the scene, Tobi is outed to both teams through moments of declaration and silence. However, the audience witnesses how he chooses moments in which to come out while declining others. Tobi demonstrates that gay identity and coming out coexist in an unstable relationship to one another. It is idealistic and naïve to assume that there are only ever singular and heroic moments of egress from a closet where an individually directed coming-out narrative exclusively structures the action.

In the narrative, the gay–straight alliance eventually gets the satisfaction of hearing Tobi come out. In one of the final scenes, the breakfast scene, Tobi formally comes out to his teammates and coach while in the presence of the Queerstrokes team. He does so when he says, "What's wrong? Can't I kiss girls anymore, just because I'm gay?" (01:23:11–01:23:16). The audience can easily view such a statement as a simple and singular revelation of his gay sexuality. If the audience only has a conventional understanding of coming out, this declaration serves as a simple moment of narrative closure. In fact, it is yet another of the multiple moments of coming out within the narrative. Although Tobi declares himself to be gay, he is seen to adopt a highly individualized gay identity that suits him. The audience bears witness to the fact that sexuality is not his priority. It also becomes clear that sports, his team, and the competition remain his overriding concerns. The storyline breaks with the possibility of a direct link between coming out and gay identity adoption. This particular moment can only lay claim to being the final point within the film where Tobi or members of both teams act on the already revealed secret. That being said, the revealed secret is central to Tobi's performance at the breakfast table.

The morning after the night in the forest, Tobi comes down to breakfast. Just before making his announcement, he sets up his own joke by kissing Anke on the cheek.

Anke serves as a foil throughout the storyline and Tobi pretends that he wants to be her boyfriend. Later, he tearfully confesses his gay identity during a secret lakeside assignation while the two are secluded in the reeds (00:56:30–00:59:26). Most importantly, Anke's silence serves to out Tobi during the confrontation between the teams in the forest (01:10:45–01:10:54). The kiss at breakfast is both platonic and an attempt to atone for his past behavior. However, Anke's facial reaction is one of discomfort and irritation (01:22:54). Tobi uses her presence and body to further his own ends. In this case, that objective is his moment of self-declaration. The narrative shows that affection can be expressed in a way that has nothing to do with sex or friendship. A gay man can always kiss a woman and a kiss does not always mean love or sex. In this case, he creates an uncomfortable moment that borders on harassment in order to set the stage for his planned performance.

Tobi's character adds another thread to the complicated fabric of coming-out moments. In the forest scene, his character rejected being labelled gay while not offering an alternative to his peer group or the audience. At breakfast, the film depicts him kissing a girl directly before making his declarative and personal coming-out statement. After the kiss, he comes out. However, it is done in such a way that the audience may not recognize it outside this particular context. Tobi performs a ritual statement that everyone will accept and understand, but which remains unique to the character and the circumstances. This moment of declaration is a performance. As an audience, it is assumed that both his speech act and the construction of an identity label mutually reinforce each other. In this case, the link is broken.

That broken link is made visible because Tobi almost immediately pivots back to the upcoming sports competition and urges the now reunited team to victory. Their reaction, or rather lack thereof, seems to confirm observations about the changing forms of homophobia in sports. British sports psychologist Brendan Gough (2007) pointed out, "Yet, when the athletes actually decide to tell their coming-out stories to their sports peers, they report few major problems" (p. 168). Furthermore, the narrative choice to have Tobi focus on the upcoming competition illustrates another trend that Gough (2007) has located in the coming-out stories of gay athletes, "Of those athletes who are out and accepted as gay, there seems to be a great effort to discount gay identities and a desire to be treated like (straight) peers" (pp. 168–169). Gough's comments are relevant because Tobi's character is shown to be keen to move away from a sexual focus just as he chooses to cast a spotlight on both his and the group's dedication to sport.

It would be equally valid to conclude that Tobi expresses a possible indifference to those around him or even about the secret itself, and it is useful to view Tobi as not exclusively oppressed by the secret. At breakfast, he is shown to embrace the open secret that he is gay. He has uttered words that matter, but the character has not changed within the narrative. At the very moment where his character performs a seemingly conventional act of coming out, the film privileges an effort by Tobi to refocus on the sports competition as a way to illustrate that the priorities of both the protagonist and the groups can shift to issues other than the coming-out drama and sexuality. In this coming-out narrative, there is no guarantee offered that the individual gay protagonist's sense of self would be altered. Tobi, as a character whose role is central to the film's storyline, does not change simply because he says that he is gay.

BROTHERHOOD AND COMING OUT

The coming-out story in film narratives must also be observed as a process of absence, refusal, and failure. Danish director Nicolo Donato's *Brotherhood* contains all these elements.[3] It is also a story of contested and tragic acknowledgement. A gay neo-Nazi is shown to engage in an "un-coming out," where homoerotic sexual desire is both violently refused and acknowledged.

On the surface, the film's narrative is a simple story of a secret love affair between two men, the principal protagonists, Jimmy and Lars. Lars is a former sergeant in the Danish Army who is invited to join his local branch of the neo-Nazi party. Jimmy is instructed by party leader Michael to indoctrinate Lars. Shortly after they start living together, Jimmy and his protégé begin an intense sexual relationship. Jimmy avoids any open acknowledgement of his relationship to Lars and his own sexual identity until the very end of the film. Jimmy's resistant script not only involves his homoerotic desires and his affiliation to the neo-Nazi movement, but also his relationship to his brother, Patrick. Patrick is depicted as a drug addict and someone whom Jimmy must frequently rescue. When Patrick secretly observes his brother and Lars cuddling on a bed, Patrick goes into a rage that leads him to reveal to the party elders that his brother and Lars are homosexuals.

The film's storyline forces the audience to reflect on the collision of the homosocial and the homoerotic in a fictionalized neo-Nazi gang. As Sedgwick (2015) argued, the social bonds between men that define the homosocial are a "neologism, obviously formed by analogy with 'homosexual,' and just as obviously meant to be distinguished from 'homosexual'" (p. 1). The homosocial world is both connected to and radically distinct from the realities of homosexuality and homoeroticism. Sedgwick went on to offer an example of the homosocial and one that is relevant to this article on coming out within in a fictionalized hyper-masculine neo-Nazi group as it is portrayed on screen. She pointed out that the desire among men for each other, and for the activities they engage in together, cannot be compartmentalized. To do so, she put forward the hypothesis that there exists "the potential unbrokenness of a continuum between homosocial and homosexual—a continuum whose visibility, for men, in our society, is radically disrupted" (Sedgwick, 2015, pp. 1–2). In *Brotherhood*, that continuum is presented in the form of a violent and hyper-masculine neo-Nazi gang that chooses to bond over their camaraderie, shared ideology, and homophobia.

Homosociality and homosexuality are on the menu in a scene from the film where the gang members partake of an informal dinner (01:04:31–01:05:25). In a classroom-like setting, the men crowd around a table and the militaristic Kenneth is berated as a faggot for examining himself in a nearby mirror (01:04:32). He then nearly instigates a brawl to counteract the threat to his masculinity. In answer to the conflict involving Kenneth, Lars mentions Ernst Röhm, the leader of the Sturmabteilung (SA) who was both a Nazi and a homosexual. Lars says, "He was queer. He was. That's why Hitler had him executed" (01:05:14–01:05:16). At that moment, Lars risks outing himself, Jimmy, and indirectly, the whole movement as a dedicated club of violent hyper-masculine, fascist homosexuals. Michael takes the role of a knowledgeable teacher, in an attempt to set the record straight: "He wasn't necessarily a faggot, but he got too powerful, so they shot him" (01:05:14–01:05:16). The response from the other men, while they devour their food, comes in the form of a statement that one of them yells out: "Who cares why? The main thing is they wasted him." The comment offers a display of violence and bravado at the expense of understanding the movement's own history. As European political scientist Anna Krasteva (2016) argued about the young men involved in far-right movements, "violence is so important that it is shown off like a badge of honour, a supreme distinction" (p. 159). The gang members luxuriate in all forms of violence, even violence directed against one of the pillars of German National Socialism. At the end of this moment in the visual narrative, it becomes clear to the audience—by all their facial expressions—that the gang now harbor suspicions about Lars' sexuality and his ability to be a loyal team member.

Gay neo-Nazis are an issue that has, for some time, fascinated sociologists and theorists alike. However, it is important to draw some distinctions. Not all skinheads are neo-Nazis and a constellation of skinheads, neo-Nazi skinheads, gay skinheads, and gay neo-Nazis exist. Criminal justice researcher Kevin Borgeson and hate-crimes researcher Robin Valeri (2005) analyzed the connections between skinhead culture and gay men. They pointed out that, "for gay men who were dissatisfied with the then current image of homosexual men as effeminate or 'queens,' the strong masculinity asserted by skinheads was appealing" (Borgeson & Valeri, 2005, p. 45). In their findings, the researchers point to the fact that some gay men crave defined forms of traditional masculinity. To achieve that masculine status, these gay men observed, adapted, and adopted the ways that straight men used the skinhead movement to define themselves. Nevertheless, the forms of traditional masculinity adopted by both gay and straight skinheads are intimately tied to acts of violence. Journalist Michael Kimmel (2018) argued that, for neo-Nazi skinheads, "the group's dynamics—the intense bonding, the camaraderie, the parties, the fights—forms much of the glue that keeps the groups together. Ideology comes later, if at all" (p. 23). These comments are particularly relevant to any assessment of neo-Nazi skinheads, where the combination of homosocial camaraderie and violence are often more important than a sense of racial superiority. The targets of their violence are men who are deemed less masculine than themselves. Jimmy's behavior in the film represents a conformation of the analysis from these researchers. The defensive position of the skinheads—whether gay or straight—frequently rests on the choice to prove masculinity through violence.

In the film, the struggle to reconcile his alliances and desires ends in violent failure for Jimmy. After a confrontation with his brother, Patrick goes to party leader Michael's home in order to reveal what he knows about his brother's sexual conduct (01:17:55–01:18:12). Patrick's actions set the stage for the punishment that follows. Once he learns about the conduct of Jimmy and Lars, Michael summons the members to a meeting at which he delivers a coded speech and then announces that he has a surprise for Jimmy and Lars. Unbeknownst to the two lovers, they are driven to a water tower on the town's outskirts where Lars is to be bashed (01:22:40–01:23:43).

The results of Patrick's confessional act are moments of ultimatum, gay-bashing, and an uncoming out where identity is instantaneously refused, rejected, and accepted through acts of violence. Jimmy is forced—through the violence of Michael's ultimatum—to make an impossible choice. He is told to either renounce being gay or neo-Nazism. Jimmy is seen to undo his avoidance of his own coming-out story when he is instructed to physically attack his lover in a ritual that Michael carefully orchestrates. Within this scene, Jimmy's relationships and alliances to Michael, his fellow neo-Nazis, and his lover are governed by shame and betrayal. Sedgwick (2003) highlighted the destructive role that shame and anger can play when she underscores "the double movement shame makes: toward painful individuation, toward uncontrollable relationality" (p. 37). Michael's ritual forces Jimmy into an unwanted spotlight. Jimmy's painful individuation as the "outed" homosexual within the gang is accompanied by the total destruction of his relationships with all those present in the scene. At this point in the film, the audience is forced to watch the ways in which a ritual, an ultimatum, and an un-coming out are enacted.

During the bashing scene, in his capacity as the high priest of this ritualistic sacrifice, Michael gives Jimmy a final choice which turns out to be no choice at all. He reveals that he knows everything when he says to Jimmy, "You can't have it all, so you have to choose. It either ends here for the both of you or else you show Lars what we do with fucking faggots like him" (01:24:42–01:24:59). Michael's sense of betrayal at the sexual behavior of the lovers results in a statement that must be read as an implied death threat. Even if Jimmy accepted Michael's offer and were to kill Lars, Jimmy's homosexual desires would still be present. The audience can speculate that if Jimmy chose to engage in such deadly violence, the act would not achieve the desired result. The other members of the gang recognize Jimmy's actions as part of an un-coming out and a poisonous suspicion of their comrade remains intact. Jimmy chooses to attack his lover (01:25:15). However, he proves unable to complete the task and sinks to the ground in order to comfort the wounded Lars (01:28:18–01:28:21). His actions represent another part of how the un-coming out drama is made visible. In effect, Jimmy goes on to adopt the very homosexual identity that he initially rejected. The other gang members, including Patrick, exit the scene having been able to "out," categorize, discipline, and expel both Jimmy and Lars.

Jimmy's struggles to choose, or privilege, being a neo-Nazi over his sexual relationship with another man and the effort to guard that secret end in violent failure. At the end, as Jimmy and Lars try to escape into the night, the gay man whom Jimmy beat up in the opening scene emerges from the darkness to stab Jimmy in the stomach (01:29:22–01:29:44). Within the storyline, Jimmy has neither directly comes out nor has he asserted a homosexual identity. However, the audience observes that he now classifies himself, just as the neo-Nazis classify him, as a homosexual. By the same token, he can no longer remain a neo-Nazi. He betrays his love and his political cause. One of the most generous interpretations of the film is that it shows the audience that all positions are untenable because Jimmy loses everything, and is gravely wounded, even when he is forced to make a choice.

UIT: QUEER REALITIES IN *NORTH SEA TEXAS*

The LGBTQ+ characters in Flemish audiovisual culture embody many aspects of the normative. These characters have been a presence in Flemish television and film since the 1990s, but are often presented exclusively within banal contexts where storylines privilege those who are almost indiscernible from their straight counterparts (Vanlee, 2019). Flemish filmmaker Bavo Defurne pushes back against that static reality in *North Sea Texas*.[4] In the film's final scene, a moment of coming out that both takes place and does not happen is made visible to the audience. The film broadens the presentation of queer realities to include an unconventional approach to coming out, LGBTQ+ identity, as well as Flemish cultural and linguistic identity.

The conflicts surrounding both queer identity and coming out are demonstrably visible within Belgian film and television production. The visibility of LGBTQ+ characters, storylines, and themes is directly influenced by the social and culture context of LGBTQ+ life in the Flemish region of Belgium. Belgium is perceived globally as a leader in equality rights and recognition for those who identify as LGBTQ+. The country adopted same-sex marriage in 2003 and, since 2007, Belgians may legally change their gender. As Flemish sociologists Saskia Aerts et al. (2012) noted, "research also shows quite positive attitudes among the Flemish population toward LGBs and LGB rights, especially compared with the attitudes in most other European countries (p. 91). Nevertheless, the acceptance of LGBTQ+ communities into the mainstream of Belgian life does not necessarily mean complete societal tolerance. Flemish psychology researchers Alexis DeWaele et al. (2014) described a societal climate in Flanders that is premised on: "attitudes that can be characterized as superficially tolerant; that is, attitudes are positive as long as homosexuality or bisexuality does not become too visible" (p. 312). Despite legal progress for rights and legal recognition, acceptance for the LGBTQ+ community in Flanders is structured by the pressure on the various elements of the community to conform to normative values.

The mixture of homonormative acceptance and normative values are represented by many of the LGBTQ+ characters who appear on Flemish television and their storylines. Vanlee (2019) posit that Flemish television production privileges "gay and lesbian characters conforming to traditional gender scripts or heterosexual cultural institutions like marriage or procreation" (p. 521). In this way, the queer characters take on the mantle of the homonormative, in that they rarely deviate from what Jasbir Puar (2007) called the "disciplinary queer (liberal, homonormative, diasporic) subject" (p. xxvii). The omnipresent obedience to a neoliberal and homonormative approach to queer realities is at the heart of Vanlee's contention that the "presence of LGBT+ characters in Flemish fiction series borders on banal. But, banality in this context appears synonymous to homogeneity" (p. 522). In Flemish television, LGBTQ+ characters appear on screen, so long as they embrace the norms of gender, race, and sexuality itself. The combination of acceptance, visibility, and the pressure for an adherence to normative values is visible in the television series, *Thuis*, where a queer character is part of the ongoing narrative and that character abides by conventional normative expectations about Trans* identity. Vanlee et al. (2020) made it clear that the presence of the trans character Kat is conditional on their compliance with broader Flemish expectations that trans people will, "complete physical and performative transition from one binary constructed gender to its counterpart" (p. 109). The juxtaposition of realities in Flemish television narratives is made clear by this example. The diversity of the LGBTQ+ community can be represented in audiovisual storylines, only so long as normative expectations are reinforced. Vanlee et al. (2020) concluded that "rather, non-heterosexual and—more recently—non-cisgender characters are inconspicuously introduced in stories that revolve around less overtly identitarian arcs" (p. 112). Flemish audiovisual culture has incorporated queer realities and has been doing so for nearly a generation. However, the boundaries of inclusivity have not been expanded and Flemish audiences are presented with static and normative LGBTQ+ characters.

The film's protagonists openly adapt gender roles and binary notions of sexuality. For instance, Pim, one of the youthful protagonists, is portrayed as a queer figure in the film's first scenes. During a childhood flashback, the audience witnesses the pre-adolescent Pim as he sneaks into his mother's room to adorn himself with a tiara and other trappings from her period as a beauty pageant contestant (00:03:04–00:06:05). Eventually, Pim is interrupted by his mother, Yvette, and she expresses little reaction to her son's behavior.

As Pim grows up, he lives in a world built around a longing for his neighbor, a swarthy young man in his late teens named Gino. The film focuses on Pim's story during his mid-teenage years in a suburban town along the West Flemish coast. In the first part of the narrative, the audience watches as Pim's friendship with Gino deepens into a sexual relationship; neither character expresses any sense of self-hatred or internalized homophobia. The audience witnesses two characters who exhibit affection for each other, engage in sexual relations, but who never show any desire to perform a conventional coming-out act or adopt gay identities. After an extensive period where Pim and Gino hang out together and regularly have sex, Gino breaks off their relationship in order to begin anew with a teenage French girl who never appears on screen. At the end of the film, Pim and Gino rekindle their sexual and romantic relationship.

What makes Defurne's film queer is that it creates a new space for otherness that is situated between the extremes of banality and the celebration of marginality. The director resisted efforts to cast the film as exclusively Flemish through his choice to use Algemeen Nederlands (standard Dutch) for the dialogue. His choice was a deliberate effort to both broaden the film's appeal and to avoid the creation of a distraction with local Flemish dialects. Nevertheless, the use of standard Dutch aided in the film's nostalgic tone (Hartford, 2017, p. 240). The language choice further queered the film because it helped to universalize a narrative based in Flanders that could not be overtaken by the charged political, cultural, and linguistic realities of the region. To address that choice, researcher Jason Hartford (2017) illustrated how "the film resists identity categorization, with explicit identity markers missing or suppressed even as the setting and topics are clearly identifiable. In short, it queers Belgianness" (p. 241). In the film, Flemish and gay identities are both invisible and omnipresent as the narrative resists easy modes of classification.

The film addresses the reality of coming out in much the same way that it manages the linguistic and cultural realities of Flanders: It charts a new course. There is no clear-cut moment of coming out or gay identity adoption because Pim and Gino do not hide in plain sight, their stories are not banal, and there is no reversion to normative discourses about gay identity adoption. Neither Pim nor Gino ever enact a conventional coming-out moment within the film's narrative. That absence enables the audience to witness how the act can lose its privileged status as the essential, singular, and heroic undertaking that is necessary to become gay.

During the film's final moments, Pim and Gino acknowledge their shared sexual experiences and continuing desires. However, the acknowledgment and mutual recognition does not metamorphose into a time for normative and declarative statements about sexual identity. At the film's end, Pim is shown to be living entirely at Gino's family home. Pim's choice of where to live is influenced by several factors. By the end of the narrative, his mother has fled for a romantic life on the road with a Roma carny (01:12:46). After Yvette's departure, Gino's mother Marcella insists that Pim move in with her family (01:13:20–01:14:51). Marcella's support also includes a final act of acknowledgement—just before she dies—of the love and affection she believes that Pim and Gino share (01:21:28). The two young men decline the offer of recognition and postpone any definitive narrative action (01:21:32–01:21:36).

The two young men demonstrate for the audience that different forms of performative actions can take place on screen about sexuality and identity adoption. Periperformative actions and statements evade the moment of normative consensus. In the storyline, the care, longing, and affection that Pim offers to Gino creates multiple opportunities for acts of interpretation by the audience. This final scene offers moments of variation that do not rely on an "assumption of consensus" (Poletti, 2016, p. 362) from the audience. The audience's expectations of a normative romantic conclusion that would result in either Pim or Gino saying that they are gay or adopting a gay identity are pushed aside. As a result, the audience's struggle to interpret and understand what is taking place also ensures that these moments in the storyline are invested with periperformative aspects that help illustrate how change, control, and adaptation can function. Sedgwick (1994) defined the power of periperformative statements when she highlighted how "they dramatize... the pathos of uncertain agency, rather than occluding it as the explicit performative almost must" (p. 76). The power of the periperformative thus lies in the fact that it creates options where various discourse acts remain in tension because no options are precluded, either for the characters or the audience. The periperformative helps to illuminate this film's final scene because the audience serves as a witness to actions on screen that do not showcase direct declarations of love, or identity adoption, or even coming out, but a bundle of actions and statements that surround such concepts without any options having been excluded.

The final scene begins with Gino's arrival during a heavy rainstorm. The two young men renew their sexual relationship through the creation of a new ritual: The exchange of a semen-soaked handkerchief. As the scene opens, Pim offers a generic act of hospitality to Gino that serves as a prelude to an intimate demonstration of his continuing attachment. In this scene, the actions and sparse conversation that take place are always an allusion to what is not directly said or declared. As such, this scene demonstrates the ways in which the two protagonists rekindle their friendship and sexual relationship through a series of periperformative moments that require close reading and analysis.

During the first part of this scene, Pim plays the role of a homemaker and caregiver. When Pim hands his lover a towel and a beer, he is not merely engaged in a banal act of assistance; his actions represent his own way of expressing his continuing love for Gino. What both Pim and Gino say to each other always indirectly alludes to what the audience perceives to be their feelings for one another. Despite the clarity of the actions on screen, there are no clear or normative clues about the meaning of what has just been depicted.

In the second part of the scene, Gino responds to Pim through the creation of a new ritual. He does so when he tucks the soiled handkerchief that Pim preserved as a memento of the first time that he and Gino engaged in mutual masturbation (00:13:30–00:14:56) back into Pim's hands (01:29:16–01:29:22). In a moment that can be read as an implied acknowledgement of both his own homosexual desires, and those of Pim, Gino says, "Tie a knot in it, so you won't forget me." This child-like ritual can also be understood as a way in which the two "tie the knot" and get married. The audience witnesses how the handkerchief is transformed into a keepsake connoting the desire that the two young men share. In response to Gino's comment, the audience sees the two young men begin intense kissing and foreplay. Through his words, Gino has offered Pim a form of periperformative acknowledgement that elides a simple validation and recognition of their shared sexual experiences.

The dry, sperm-laden handkerchief that passes from hand to hand is not only the physical manifestation of a memory but also a piece of evidence of their shared desire. The cloth, and the actions performed with it, represents something that is not easily acknowledged. As cultural analyst Murat Aydemir (2007) pointed out, "ejaculation forges narrative" (p. xix). Aydemir (2007) went on to argue that ejaculation must be seen "as an irreducible happening, bringing about change and consequence, it forces narrators, focalizers, and characters to come up with accounts of what is about to happen, what is happening, and what has happened" (p. xix). The handkerchief is evidence of a narrative and a relationship that combines elements of rehearsal and adaptation. The audience may cast a judgment that the object is obscene and should be hidden. What is received is an "in your face," and almost pornographic, admission of an "irreducible happening," the first time the boys ejaculated together. Their rekindled relationship demonstrates how the effects of that first event require an ongoing accounting of the past, present, and future. The passing of the handkerchief from hand to hand also reveals a moment of "change and consequence" about how desire can be expressed as a souvenir of futures to come.

However, Pim problematizes the moment of passion. In the final seconds of the film, while the two lovers are engaged in oral foreplay, Pim says, "Stay" (01:29:47). The statement has multiple interpretations. It is both a question and a demand. The fluctuating nature of the relationship between Pim and Gino is never resolved for the audience. The moment of periperformative acknowledgement is structured around the ways in which the lovers seek and receive recognition from each other. In the film's final scene, Gino acknowledges their shared carnal desire without a coming-out moment or the adoption of a gay identity. The words they share before they engage in sexual relations constitute an ambiguous act of recognition that both validates the homosexual desires of each young man and omits any possible normative conclusion.

CONCLUSION

The relaxed logic and apparent stability of the words "coming out" become unstable through points of contrast, such as the ideas of presence and loss; knowing and not knowing; and even desire and its absence. These contrasts form the background of the ways in which coming out is scripted in audiovisual media. Coming-out scripts can revolve around the revelation of a deeply held secret and the ongoing rehearsal of information that is always, already known. Coming out also straddles moments of revelation and the never-ending repetition of memories and facts. Most importantly, the act of coming out is forever engaged in a struggle regarding questions of political ambivalence, visibility, and identity.

The films that have been analyzed in this article offer alternatives to a normative coming-out script. *Beautiful Thing* weaves together the coming-out narrative and a gay youth love story. The acceptance that Sandra offers to Jamie and Ste authors a coming-out storyline that is the background to a sexual identity that is neither rejected nor heroically assumed. In *Summer Storm*, coming out comprises a script where secrets are revealed that everyone already knows. When Tobi enacts his own coming-out moments, they are structured around the fact that the secret is already out. The continual acts of revelation are part of a process that is propelled both by himself and the other teenage athletes. In *Brotherhood*, coming out is depicted by the ways in which identities are instantaneously accepted and rejected within a neo-Nazi subculture. Jimmy's un-coming out illustrates how he rapidly and violently vacillates between a refusal and acknowledgement of his sexual attraction to men. The end result is that all options lead to betrayal and failure. In *North Sea Texas*, the script of coming out is reimagined and reworked by two characters, Pim and Gino, who decline any opportunity to clarify their identities. The film contains a narrative where the principal protagonists present an ambivalence about coming out that is exhibited by the ways in which their actions allude to, but never fully address, their shared love and sexual identity. The presence of these characteristics within each narrative emphasizes the reiterative nature of the act and enables the audience to witness how coming out is both indispensable and how the act is forever opaque.

The desire for queer audiences to find visual narratives about coming out that reflect and resonate with their lives is one of the reasons that this particular genre remains adaptable. Film theorist Janet Harbord (2002) discussed the importance of the background that individuals bring to the films they view when she wrote: "We bring to film, and what brings us to film, is our own individual histories... our broader positioning of dispositions more generally, lead us to the social comfort and ease of certain texts and locations and the rejection of others" (p. 2).

The stories of coming out in audiovisual media present both a comfort and challenge to the audience. Harbord (2002) went on to note that the interplay of representation and language in film is a flexible field of discourse. To that end, she highlights how "filmic representation is precisely re-presentation, a fabrication, a replaying of stories, images and conventions; it is the replay of a language rather than a replay of the 'real'" (Harbord, 2002, p. 128). Her faith in the power of engagement with filmic language and narrative is also a belief that these devices create spaces for ruptures and new performances. These flexible ways, in which to enact identification, are central to reiterative coming-out narratives in film. The normative representation of coming out, such as that which is presented in Lee's *Brokeback Mountain*, have attempted to reinforce a "replay of the real" based on a set of normative conventions and expectations about how coming out is supposed to look and operate. *Beautiful Thing*, *Summer Storm*, *Brotherhood*, and *North Sea Texas* offer their audiences narratives that deviate from the normative and where stories of gay identity are rehearsed, replayed, and then reconstructed.

It would be absurd to claim that the films discussed in this analysis represent an exclusive and encyclopaedic list that contains the perfected models of the coming-out script in audiovisual media. The point of this research is not to try and fine-tune the genre, but to illustrate how a diverse agglomeration of stories, storytelling, moments of revelation, and instances when nothing is revealed work both with and against each other. The narratives discussed are not representative of a singular or unified genre, but instead form a symptomatic collection of coming-out scripts. Therefore, each makes the creation of a broader model impossible. Because of that impossibility, these narratives are available to help develop a more plural understanding of coming out as an act that is endlessly repeated but is adapted and changed each time it occurs or does not. The analysis of these narratives offers new interpretive strategies about coming out. As objects, they represent a way forward and offer plural definitions of coming out where that which does not fit can be given a place, and to illustrate how adaptation is made a central theme.

REFERENCES

Aerts, S., Van Houtte, M., Dewaele, A., Cox, N., & Vincke, J. (2012). Sense of belonging in secondary schools: A survey of LGB and heterosexual students in Flanders. *Journal of Homosexuality, 59*(1), 90–113. https://doi.org/10.1080/00918369.2012.638548

Arellano, L. (2007). The "gay film" that wasn't: The heterosexual supplement in *Brokeback Mountain*. In J. Stacy (Ed.), *Reading Brokeback Mountain: Essays on the story and the film* (pp. 59–70). McFarland.

Aydemir, M. (2007). *Images of bliss: Ejaculation, masculinity, meaning*. University of Minnesota Press.

Berlant, L., & Warner, M. (1998). Sex in public. *Critical Inquiry, 2*(24), 547–566.

Borgeson, K., & Valeri, R. (2005). Examining differences in skinhead ideology and culture through an analysis of skinhead websites. *Michigan Sociological Review, 19*, 45–62.

Bronski, M. (2000). Positive images & the coming out film: The art and politics of gay and lesbian cinema. *Cineaste, 26*(1), 20–26.

Bui, L. T. (2007). Whiteness of a different kind of love: Letting race and sexuality talk. In J. Stacy (Ed.), *Reading Brokeback Mountain: Essays on the story and the film* (pp. 152–162). McFarland.

Butler, J. (1991). Imitation and gender insubordination. In D. Fuss (Ed.), *Inside/Out: Lesbian theories, gay theories* (pp. 13–31). Routledge.

Chambers, R. (1981). Histoire d'oeuf: Secrets and secrecy in a La Fontaine fable. *SubStance, 10*(3), 65–74.

Defurne, B. (Director). (2011). *Noordzee, Texas* [*North Sea Texas*] [Film]. Indeed Films; Mollywood; Eén; Vlaams Audiovisueel Fonds.

Dewaele, A., Caen, M., & Buysse, A. (2014). Comparing survey and sampling methods for reaching sexual minority individuals in Flanders. *Versita: Journal of Official Statistics, 30*(2), 251–275. https://doi.org/10.2478/jos-2014-0016

Donato, N. (2009). *Brøderskab* [*Brotherhood*] [Film]. Asta Film; Film i Väst; Det Danske Filminstitut; Dansk Råfilm; FilmFyn; Danmarks Radio (DR).

Dyer, R. (2003). *Now you see it: Studies in lesbian and gay film* (2nd ed.) Routledge.

Enghien, W., Baert, K., Baras, M., Roggen, L., Kleynen, E., Schellekens, P., Mouton, A., Haegemans, D., Janssen, W., & Roggen, H. (Producers). (1995–present). *Thuis* [Television series]. Vlaamse Radio- en Televisieomroeporganisatie (VRT).

Fouz-Hernández, S. (2008). School is out: British "coming out" films in the 1990s. In R. Griffiths (Ed.), *Queer cinema in Europe* (pp. 145–164). Intellect Books.

Frears, S. (Director). (1985). *My beautiful laundrette* [Film]. Channel 4 Films; Working Title Films; SAF Productions.

Friedkin, W. (Director). (1970). *The boys in the band* [Film]. National General Pictures; Cinema Center Films; Leo Films.

Gough, B. (2007). Coming out in a heterosexist world of sport: Qualitative of web posting by gay athletes. *Journal of Gay and Lesbian Psychotherapy, 30*(2), 135–151. https://doi.org/10.1300/J236v11n01_11

Harbord, J. (2002). *Film cultures*. SAGE.

Hartford, J. (2017). Implicitly Queer Belgian cinema: *Noordzee, Texas* (Bavo Defurne, 2011). *Studies in European Cinema, 14*(3), 231–248.

Hartmann-Tews, I. (2002). Sport for all: System and policy. In K. Hardman & R. Naul (Eds.), *Sport and physical education in Germany* (pp. 153–164). Routledge.

Harvey, D. (2004, September 29). Review: Summer storm. *Variety*. https://variety.com/2004/film/reviews/summer-storm-2-1200530609/

Jagose, A. (1996). *Queer theory: An introduction*. Melbourne University Press.

Kimmel, M. (2018). *Healing from hate: How young men get into and out of violent extremism*. University of California Press.

Kokkinos, A. (1998). *Head on*. [Film]. Australian Film Finance Corporation (AFFC); Great Scott Productions Pty; Film Victoria; Head on Productions; Palace Films; Strand Releasing.

Krasteva, A. (2016). Re/de/constructing far-right youth: Between the lost generation and contestatory citizenship. In G. Lazaridis & G. Campani (Eds.), *Understanding the populist shift: Othering in a Europe in crisis* (pp. 150–178). Routledge. https://doi.org/10.4324/9781315656779

Kreuzpaintner, M. (Director). (2004). *Sommersturm* [Summer storm] [Film]. X Verleih AG; Claussen & Wöbke Filmproduktion; ProSieben Entertainment; SevenPictures Film.

Lee, A. (Director). (2005). *Brokeback Mountain* [Film]. Focus Features; River Road Entertainment; Alberta Film Entertainment; Good Machine.

Macdonald, H. (Director). (1996). *Beautiful thing* [Film]. Channel 4 Films; World Productions.

Moreton, D. (1998). *Edge of seventeen*. [Film]. Blue Streak Films; Luna Pictures; Strand Releasing.

Mosse, G. (1997). *Nationalism and sexuality: Respectability and abnormal sexuality in modern Europe*. Howard Fertig.

Nowlan, B. (2006). The politics of love in three recent U.S. and U.K. films of young gay romance: A symptomatic reading of *Beautiful Thing, Get Real*, and *Edge of Seventeen. Journal of Homosexuality, 50*(4), 141–182. https://doi.org/10.1300/J082v50n04_07

Padva, G. (2004). Edge of seventeen: Melodramatic coming-out in new Queer adolescence films. *Communication and Critical/Cultural Studies, 4*(1), 355–372. https://doi.org/10.1080/1479142042000244961

Poletti, A. (2016). Periperformative life narrative: Queer collages. *GLQ: A Journal of Lesbian and Gay Studies, 22*(3), 359–379.

Preminger, O. (Director). (1962). *Advise and consent* [Film]. Columbia Pictures Corporation; Sigma Productions; Alpha Alpina.

Puar, J. (2007). *Terrorist assemblages: Homonationalism in queer times*. Duke University Press.

Pullen, C. (2009). *Gay identity, new storytelling and the media*. Palgrave Macmillan.

Sedgwick, E. K. (1994). *Tendencies*. Routledge.

Sedgwick, E. K. (2003). *Touching, feeling: Affect, pedagogy, performance*. Duke University Press.

Sedgwick, E. K. (1990). *Epistemology of the closet* (2nd ed.). University of California Press.

Sedgwick, E. K. (2015). *Between men: English literature and male homosocial desire* (3rd. ed.). Columbia University Press.

Simon, A. (2011, August 29). Review: North Sea Texas. *Variety*. https://variety.com/2011/film/reviews/north-sea-texas-111794589

Theweleit, K. (1989). *Male fantasies: Volume 2 male bodies–Psychoanalyzing the white terror* (E. Carter, C. Turner, & S. Conway, Trans.). University of Minnesota Press.

Vanlee, F. (2019). Acknowledging/denying LBGT+ difference: Understanding homonormativity and LGBT+ homogeneity in Flemish TV fiction through production research. *European Journal of Communication, 34*(5), 520–534. https://doi.org/10.1177/0267323119874250

Vanlee, F., Dhaenens, F., & Van Bauwel, S. (2018). Understanding queer normality: LGBT+ representations on millennial Flemish television fiction. *Television & New Media, 19*(7), 610–625. https://doi.org/10.1177/1527476417748431

Vanlee, F., Dhaenens, F., & Van Bauwel, S. (2020). Indifference and queer television studies: Distinguishing norms of existence and coexistence. *Critical Studies in Media Communication, 37*(2), 105–119. https://doi.org/10.1080/15295036.2020.1714070

Vivarelli, N. (2009, October 23). Rome fest embraces "Brotherhood". *Variety*. https://variety.com/2009/biz/markets-festivals/rome-fest-embraces-brotherhood-1118010342/

Weissberg, J. (2009, October 26). Review: Brotherhood. *Variety*. https://variety.com/2009/film/markets-festivals/brotherhood-3-1200476663/

Wyler, W. (Director). (1961). *The Children's Hour* [Film]. The Mirisch Company; United Artists.

NOTES

1. For a critical response to Lee's *Brokeback Mountain,* see Arellano (2007) and Bui (2007).
2. The film was released in 2004 and went on to win the 2004 Audience Award at the 2004 Munich Film Festival and Best Director award at the 2005 New Faces Awards in Germany. However, praise was limited for the film. *Variety* critic Dennis Harvey (2004) noted in his review that "the pic is visually undistinguished for the most part, with a TV-movie feel overall and lame use of freeze frames at fadeout. But the banality it skirts in general outline and presentation are compensated for by incisive scene-by-scene writing, perfs and direction" (n.p.).
3. For additional analyses about the commercial and cultural reception of *Brotherhood,* see Vivarelli (2009) and Weissberg (2009).
4. The film won the 2011 FIPRESCI Award for a first film and the Silver Zenith at the 2011 Montreal World Film Festival. In 2011, it would also go on to win the Alice in the City Prize at the Rome Film Festival. *Variety* film critic Alissa Simon noted in her review that the film's cast of relative newcomers provide the audience with: "emotionally truthful performances" (Simon, 2011).

Paris S. Cameron-Gardos

GAY AGING AND DISCOURSES OF FUTURE

CONSTRUCTING THE FUTURE

The future is not known to anyone. Humans, through our use of symbols and communication, can contemplate future outcomes and possibilities, yet this work is achieved solely through a mapping of past and present understandings (however limited they may be) onto the yet-to-occur. There is no guarantee that one's sexual desires, partners, or preferences will or will not determine their capacity for health, happiness, joy, relational bonds, or satisfaction. Thus, the future is a discursive construct, produced within systems of power, to naturalize and normalize certain identities and relational formations. Heteronormativity defines the hegemonic ideal from which narratives of proper aging, success, and future happiness are often scripted. "Acting one's age" and "preparing for the future" conjure certain adherences to norms of maturation and a series of idealized images of what one's family, life, and behavior ought to aspire.

Contingent to the story of heteronormative correctness are cautionary tales of the aging queer—a figure that has been constructed in mainstream discourse to discipline and vilify gay aging and the possibility of queer future. The most demonizing representations and cultural scripts move beyond queers being merely without future (Muñoz, 2006), wherein queers are constructed as anti-future, an actual antagonistic threat to "our" collective future, who are actively fighting against the future (Edelman, 2004). Herein mythologies of queer recruitment, predation, and discourses of sin weave together stories of LGBT persons being a threat to "our" children. Metaphors of illness and infection have been used to demonize the "dangerous" effect that queerness has on the lives of the good and righteous (code for heterosexual). It is a story that has been retold for decades, fueling Anita Bryant's "Save the Children" campaign and long-justifying political oppositions to gay marriage, gay adoption, and the "threat" of "exposing" kids to anything queer (it will confuse them!). Mythologies of pedophilia and hypersexualization fuel these cautionary tales, where homosexuals are "modern vampires who must create new victims in order to survive" (Russo, 1987, p. 236).

This article begins by tracing the construction of the tragic and futureless queer through media representation and cultural discourse. Next, it traces the impact of HIV/AIDS on the discourses of gay aging and future and also the emergence of queer media criticism in communication studies. The cultural script of the "harder path" is then examined through interdisciplinary research on gay and lesbian aging populations, exploring how the meanings, values, and scripts of gay aging, intergenerational relations, and queer future are being interrogated and reimagined in the field of communication.

THE DISCURSIVE CONSTRUCTION OF QUEER DOOM

By definition, queerness marks that which is at odds or in tension with the normative, and cultural narratives of aging and future have long been in tension with queer lives, queer bodies, and queer relations. There is a long history of stories of queers being punished, sad, and doomed (Fejes & Petrich, 1993; Goltz, 2010; Gross, 1994; Russo, 1987; Seidman, 2002; Walters, 2001)—cautionary tales of failed maturation that operate to reify the correctness of heterosexuality, the correctness of White–masculine–ableist modes of time, and the dangers of its departures. Master narratives of the futureless queer and the "inevitability" of queer misery can be traced across our culture and history, from religious discourses, the arts, theater, politics, and popular culture (Corey, 1998).

Contemporary research on queer representation in media and popular culture can be traced back to the foundational work of Vito Russo. Although not explicitly framed as "queer media criticism" (Erni, 1998) until the late 1990s, this critical project sought to understand the complex ways that LGBT persons were being represented in mainstream media. Russo, followed by a new generation of LGBT scholars, traced how LGBT stories and characters were narrated within scripts of survival, punishment, happiness, success, and future—setting the theoretical foundation for examining the relationship between queerness, representation, and age.

In the early 1980s, Russo's work focused primarily on the historical depiction of gay and lesbian characters in Hollywood. Since the early days of film, queers were commonly painted as outliers and deviants to the conventions of the heteronormative narrative. Queerness was a problem to be addressed, corrected, or eliminated. A key finding across representation from the 1930s forward was the recurrent positioning of queer characters within narratives of punishment. Russo (1987) states, "The essence of homosexuality as predatory weakness permeated the depiction of gay characters in horror films" (p. 49). Homosexuals were cast as monstrous "twilight creatures," often framed as mentally ill, morally depraved, and a threat to the natural order. In these stories, time, age, and future worked together as systems to punish queer bodies, mark them as socially deviant, and position them within cautionary tales that reify heteronormative correctness—the good life, the happy family, and the righteous mainstream. Strict enforcement of the Hays Code began around 1934, and up to the late 1950s and early 1960s, careful monitoring of these censoring standards of "don'ts" and "be carefuls" worked to contain and limit explicit representation of homosexuality in Hollywood to ambiguous gestures, filmic whisper, and subtext for the audience to read, trace, and piece together. In what Russo calls "the invisible years," the Hays Code marked a period in which queerness was surely present in film but could not be named explicitly.

As enforcement of the Hays Code softened, and gay and lesbian content became more open and visible in the late 1950s and 1960s, narratives of queer developmental failure and punishment proliferated. With greater visibility, the queer became a common scapegoat and villain for mainstream audience consumption. Russo's research on the 32 films with major homosexual representations from 1961 to 1976 identified the depiction of 13 suicides, 18 murders, and 1 castration (cited in Fejes & Petrich, 1993, p. 413). For the representation of queerness, "violence comes with the territory" (Russo, 1987, p. 91) because the "homosexual subculture equals violence" (p. 91). In his analysis of 1967's *Reflections in a Golden Eye* and 1968's *The Sergeant*, Russo argues the gay characters are reduced to spiteful manipulations and self-loathing, where "both films insist that there is no option, no way out for these doomed people" (p. 167). Homosexuality in films "was clearly only for villains" (p. 135) and was "treated like a dread disease" (p. 116). Championing heterosexuality as the noble, the preferred, and the correct way of living, "the intrinsically pathological and destructive nature of homosexuality" (Porfido, 2007, p. 60) became the premise for the new Hollywood monster of the 1960s (see also Baker, 2012; Benshoff, 1997, 2005). "Homosexuality was portrayed at best as unhappiness, sickness, and marginality, and at worst perversion and an evil to be destroyed" (Fejes & Petrich, 1993, p. 398). Films such as *Freebie and the Bean* and *Midnight Cowboy* exemplify this form of cinematic punishment, where audiences are witness to, and positioned as supportive of, violence enacted upon queer bodies. Narratively, queerness was communicated as a threat, a threat to be defeated, or an illness in need of eradication. Russo quotes screenwriter Abby Mann in 1967, who breaks down the cultural vice grip of writing gay characters for film, stating, "it's easier to be accepted in our society as a murderer, than a homosexual" (p. 169). Even when sympathetic (i.e., Montgomery in Alan Parker's musical smash *Fame*), the queer figure is isolated and broken, the "sad frustrated lone gay student" (p. 88).

George Gerbner and Larry Gross (1976) famously argued, "Representation in the fictional world signifies social existence; absence means symbolic annihilation" (p. 182). Fejes and Petrich (1993) elaborate on the unique importance of LGBT representation as most LGBT youth (particularly before the 1990s) will be raised in a culture that provides "little or no help in understanding or defining themselves as gay or lesbian" (p. 396). LGBT kids rarely are raised in LGBT families, lacking immediate role models and scripts to understand what it is (and what it might be) to grow up as an LGBT person. Mediated images, in this void, take on a significant role (Gross, 2001). The communicative power of these images, and the stories they reinscribe, comes to dominate understandings of who queer people were—both for mainstream audiences and for queer folk. For example, films with major releases such as *The Boys in the Band* were so important because audiences took them as "definitive portraits of gay life" (Russo, 1987, p. 170). Lacking visible role models, the very understanding or imagination of what one's future can or might look like, as an LGBTQ person, presents unique obstacles and absences. Models are limited, and so where and when stories and images are available for LGBT persons to glimpse into what their life could be, they take on greater significance. They work to make sense of the unknown. Gloomy and depressed images framing gay aging serve as "a social control function" (Berger, 1982, p. 15) to mark queerness as something to be avoided.

AIDS AND QUEER ACTIVISM IN DISCOURSES OF FUTURE

The initial outbreak of the AIDS pandemic in the 1980s and early 1990s was highly influential, if not directly tied, to contemporary understandings of gay aging and discourses of future. Although queers, historically, have regularly experienced a form of alienation from discourses of future, the 1980s and the outbreak of the AIDS pandemic marked a significant moment of temporal interruption and vilification. Young gay men were dying, and narratives around gay life span, aging, and future were radically impacted. What it meant to age, to live, and to mature as a gay male came undone in the face of the plague. As gayness and AIDS were sutured together in discourse and in the minds of the broader culture, the very understanding of being a gay man was linked to the virus, abbreviated life span, and the recurrent images of death and dying. This "epidemic of signification" (Treichler, 2004, p. 109) worked to construct the "'gay' nature of AIDS" in research, testing, and larger discourse (p. 111). Thus, AIDS has a "dual life as both a material and linguistic entity" (p. 131), attaching itself to previous systems of meanings already in the culture that worked to organize social constructions of goodness, sin, othering, innocence, victims, and a complex network of meanings Treichler maps in relations to the word "AIDS."

"Living with AIDS was tantamount to 'being-not-one of time... no longer part of a coherent and continuous time' but in limbo where a generation of young men waited to die before-one's-time" (Duttman, 1996, as cited in Dunn, 2015, p. 134). For the men of that generation who did survive, there was a complicated negotiation and question of "Why me?" For the next generation, those who grew up only understanding gayness in relation to AIDS and images of death, a logic of "not if, but when" haunted. This "cultural logic of inevitability" (Román, 1997, p. 164) was tied to a shifting in one's orientation toward life, understanding of aging, and future, ranging in responses from "trauma and guilt, others forgetting or preventing, and still others in defiance of the demands placed on them by both time and the disease" (Dunn, 2015, p. 134). Regardless of one's HIV status, HIV/AIDS greatly informed what it meant to be queer into the 1990s. "All the ways HIV-negatives are represented in public culture are extremely depressing, and consequently, offer little incentive to imagine a life worth living" (Román, 1997, p. 166). Thus, alongside what can be described as survivor guilt is also a dooming perpetuated narrative that is constructed around queer experience, tied with illness, doom, misery, and sadness. For example, in *Banning Queer Blood*, Bennett (2015) demonstrates how images and narratives of gay men as menacing and contagious, counter to the narrative of proper and healthy civic life, were—and continue to be—perpetuated by government agencies.

In the mid-1980s to the early 1990s, gay representation was continually tied to HIV/AIDS, and narratives of death and dying were rescripted through the HIV/AIDS stories. Although gay men were still dying in large numbers on the cultural screen, these images were more sympathetic and less vilifying. From more independent classics such as *Tongues Untied*, *Buddies*, or *Parting Glances* to larger Hollywood productions such as *Philadelphia* and *Longtime Companion*, the representation of gay men at this time was linked to visuals of hospitals, emaciation, and death. Gay aging was no longer just scripted as a life defined by misery but also conjured immediate discursive linkages of inevitability to HIV and AIDS (i.e., not *if* positive, but when).

In response to sensationalist, homophobic, and inaccurate media coverage, GLAAD (Gay and Lesbian Alliance Against Defamation) was formed in 1985—of which Vito Russo was a founding member. In response to the despicable government silence and bureaucracy, as thousands of Americans were sick and dying, activist organizations, most notably ACT-UP (AIDS Coalition to Unleash Power), took to the streets and direct action to protest and change governmental policies. In addition, in response to mounting homophobic violence and discrimination, and a refusal to be silenced or apologetic, the direct actions of Queer Nation—an anti-assimilationist decentralized collection of protest activities—gave voice to a mounting anger and anti-normative sentiment in LGBT communities. Concurrently, in the academy, the emergence of a diverse body of critical ideas under the umbrella of "queer theory" began to take shape. Reappropriating the term "queer" from a tool of degradation to one of self-proclaimed difference—a loud and proud defector from the bounds of normativity—queer theory emerged as a critical project to interrogate and destabilize the categories of gender and sexual identity and expose the violent limitation and foreclosures of heteronormativity. As the assumed centeredness and correctness of heteronormative institutions came under scrutiny, queer theorists further examined the perpetuation, historical production, and limitations of the cornerstones of compulsive heteronormativity—sex and gender binaries, gender roles, fixed sexual identity, systems of marriage, monogamy, and procreation. In this interrogation of heteronormativity, the foundational work of queer media criticism, and specifically its examinations of age and future in communication, began to take shape.

THE 1990S, QUEER MEDIA CRITICISM, AND A MORE "POSITIVE" FUTURE

Within communication studies, under the name of "queer media criticism," mainstream representation of lesbian and gay characters in the 1990s has generated a large body of research, mapping the strategies and approaches to how queer lives were being mainstreamed into the culture. In a shift from the totalizing doom and misery that defined early queer representation, the 1990s marked a period of significant increase in representation and assimilation of (primarily cis, White, middle-class, able-bodied) gay and lesbian characters into the dominant cultural story. The queer analysis of television shows such as *Ellen* (Dow, 2001) and *Will & Grace* (Battles & Hilton-Morrow, 2002; Shugart, 2003) and films such as *Philadelphia* (Brookey, 1996) and *To Wong Foo Thanks for Everything! Julie Newmar* (Brookey & Westerfelhaus, 2001) mapped a recurrent pattern of normative impulses and systems being reified within the project of "positive" gay representation. Regarding aging and future, these storylines worked to rhetorically bridge gay and lesbian characters with mainstream audience sensibilities of proper maturation and normative familial commitments. In a recurrent trope of "the normal gay," these newly acceptable and consumable gay and lesbian characters provided what Fejes and Petrich (1993) describe as "a heterosexual view of homosexuality" (p. 401). Here, gay and lesbian characters appeared in primarily straight contexts, with straight families and friends, living (and/or aspiring for) essentially straight lives (and straight-looking futures). Exemplars of this period range from *Ellen* to *Melrose Place* and *Dawson's Creek*, in which gay and lesbian characters desperately wanted "to just be normal," insisted gayness is not a big part of who they are, and were primarily represented outside of (and often with expressed disinterest in) queer spaces. Wherein, historically queer characters were written out of the future, this new trend in mainstreamed gay and lesbian characters offered up "the good gay" (Seidman, 2002). Outside of their singular normative deviation (their sexual identity), these representations were remarkably (if not excessively) normative in every manner, exemplifying Duggan's (2002) conceptualization of privatized and neoliberal homonormativity. In order to make it on Must See TV, most traces of their queerness would have to be filed down or fully evacuated. These characters stood before the mainstream audiences and pledged allegiance to the tenants of straight time (Halberstam, 2005)—declaring unwavering commitment to systems of marriage, love of children, and their refusal to identify with anything too queer, too political, too sexual, or too out of the norm.

By the 1990s, many would believe the cautionary narrative of the futureless and doomed queer was now a historical footnote in the dark corners of Hollywood history—washed away in this wave of "positive" representation. Although repackaged for contemporary audiences, many of the tragic narratives continued to replay within mainstream film and television well into the new millennium. In analyzing more than 100 films and 25 television series released between 2000 and 2007, Goltz (2010) studied how the experience of aging and future was narrated in relationship to gay male characters. Although more sympathetic in their construction, many of the punishing scripts present in Russo's earlier work continued to circulate. "The heteronormative tragedy" of contemporary representation repeats scripts of queer brutality and punishment, "reaffirming the misery attached to heteronormative deviance—and constituting life, progress, health, and future within the path of heterosexuality" (p. 56). From films such as *Brokeback Mountain* and *The Mexican* to television series such as *Queer as Folk* or *The Sopranos*, queer characters (especially older characters) routinely faced doomed futures and violent ends (pp. 49–56).

Coupled with the perpetual storying of external violence (i.e., hate crimes and queer attacks) was a recurrent degradation of gay aging and a gay devaluation of future (Goltz, 2010). There once was a time when queer teens in media were nearly absent (Fejes & Petrich, 1993; Gross, 2007), but in more recent representations, queers in their teens, 20s, and early 30s were the predominant images being depicted. Alongside this broad range of intersecting normative identifications being depicted (sex, race, gender, class, apolitical, and able-bodied), youth appeared as a recurrent strategy to make gay and lesbian representations more acceptable and less scary. The threat of queerness, as seen in mainstream representation, is coded with age (Goltz, 2010). Berger (1982) coined the term "youthism" to mark the extreme degree that youth and beauty were overly linked to value within gay male culture. Wherein the aging gay male is often devalued, if not degraded, in the youthist economy of many gay cultural spaces, youthfulness has been overcelebrated as a powerful commodity. Gay cultural youthism works in opposition to the threat of queerness, where younger gays and lesbians are seen as more innocent, less threatening, and, perhaps, redeemable to the logics of heteronormativity. This concept is exemplified in several mediated texts representing gay male culture (i.e., *Broken Hearts Club* and *Dante's Cove*) in which the story is framed around and driven by the arrival and experiences of the younger (and so, attractive and desirable) "golden boy" (Goltz, 2010). Cast as the object of desire and jealousy, he is constructed as sexualized, idealized "newbie," and his beauty is translated into power in that space and in relationship with the older gay men. For the constructed audience, they are routinely called to identify with the younger character and see the story, queer culture, and the unfolding narrative through their eyes and perspective. These youth-centered mainstreaming strategies of gay and lesbian youth were also being deployed beyond film and television. In their analysis of the coverage of the brutal murder of Matthew Shepard and the public outcry that followed, Ott and Aoki (2002) argue how Shepard's identity as both a younger and White gay man was used to frame him for audiences as innocent and unthreatening.

In queer representation in the 2000s, while repeating some familiar tropes of developmentally stagnant, predatory, sad, miserable, and alone (Corey, 1998; Gross, 2001), older gay representation was infrequent. Because younger characters were more commonly represented in this time, the discursive production of meanings around queer age and future were primarily crafted through the younger, centralized characters—how they talked about aging and future. An ideological analysis of *Instinct Magazine*, a glossy gay magazine geared toward gay youth in the early 2000s, examined the construction of meanings around "young" and "old" and "future" over seven years of publication (Goltz, 2007). The magazine constructed a voice of a hypermasculine queerness that called its critics "sad losers"; reaffirmed youthist narratives of power; and distanced itself from anxieties around aging and future through sarcasm, ironic dismissals, and a "live for today" focus (Goltz, 2007). Although narratives of the older gay male posing a sexual threat were present, if it was the younger hypermasculine queer asserting and controlling their sexualization—the claiming of youth power through "sexualizing daddy"—then it could be "hot." But if it was not initiated by the youth, and the older man was sexual on his own terms, it was deemed creepy and predatory.

This dread of future and devaluation/disinterest in aging is also linked to another recurrent and tragic plotline in queer cultural narratives. Summarized succinctly in the title *I Thought People Like That Killed Themselves* (Rofes, 1983), there remains a troubling linkage and causation drawn in discourse between homosexuality, fear of aging, and self-destructive behavior. For example, in *Queer as Folk*, Brian Kinney's "Death Day Party," for his 30th birthday, was celebrated with a gravestone cake, marking his entrance into "The Dead Faggot's Society." His dreaded birthday concludes with an auto-asphyxiation/suicidal ideation episode with a new silk scarf he bought himself for his birthday. Herein, the recurrent themes of youthism, fear of aging, queer doom, and the normalization of suicide all interanimate in a singular text. Describing what Rofes refers to as the "dual myth of homosexual suicide" (p. 3), the myth argues both that LGBT persons commit suicide at accelerated rates and that one's queerness is "itself the source of self-destructiveness" (p. 3). Blackman (2011) refers to this as the "paradox of queerness," in which discourses of queer health and happiness are co-promoted among stories of queer depression, substance abuse, and illness. Russo (1987) noted that in 1960s Hollywood, once visible, gays "dropped like flies, usually by their own hand" (p. 52). The trope of the suicidal queer has become so normalized and routinized in mainstream representation that audiences only need the smallest gesture or camera shot to connect suicidal ideation and motive with queer characters. In film and television, when queer coded characters stare sadly into a mirror, gaze out over passing traffic or an overpass, or look out at the ocean, audiences have been trained to "shorthand" queer pain and sadness with suicidal storylines. This narrative shorthand of "sensible suicides" (Goltz, 2013, 2015) reproduces a dangerous and destructive story that queer suicide is logical, expected, and even anticipated. Rather than questioning why a queer character might take their own life, in these tacit narrative assumptions, queerness *is* the implicit "why" or justification—fusing one's sexuality with suicidal tendencies. The image of queer characters taking their own life is so entrenched in popular culture that it has become overly typical, a cliché, and a comedic punchline. This can be seen in a broad range of comedic texts, such as *South Park* or *Drawn Together*, in which the absence of queer future and the inevitability of queer suicide fuel the humor of a joke, banking on this shared audience expectation (Goltz, 2010, p. 52). Herein marks an ongoing tension between creating awareness of the crisis of LGBTQ suicide and the normalization of LGBTQ suicide in the media. This extends to a broader tension between the LGBTQ narratives represented in the media and the reported, felt, and lived experiences of LGBTQ persons.

THE HARDER PATH? RESEARCH ON LGBTQ AGING

Although social science research on aging gay and lesbian populations details a range of distinct challenges, the perpetuated narrative of the sad, miserable, lonely queer has been continually challenged in research. The relationship between queers and time, with respect to age, does pose many questions, as the study of gay and lesbian aging marks unchartered territory for many researchers (de Vries & Blando, 2004, p. 21). Prior to 1990, handbooks and standardized textbooks on age and aging "made no mention of homosexuality, and studies of sexuality routinely lacked a focus on people 60 years or more" (Barker, 2004, p. 30; see also Cruikshank, 1990, p. 77). Since then, although there is an increasing breadth of study, the majority of the research on queer aging has still specifically examined the aging processes of gay male and lesbian female communities. Many LGBT elders were raised in a society in which homosexuality was "classified as mentally ill, and they were thereby stigmatized and assigned to a low status" (Grossman et al., 2001). There are stressors that aging gay populations face, such as the stress of living in the minority, systemic issues, lack of legal protections (job, custody, and home), and daily stressors of harassment threat and always being on watch (p. 36). Aging lesbian populations face what has been called a triple invisibility (Barker, 2004, p. 3) because they are older, female, and lesbian. Weinstock's (2004) research on aging lesbians calls into question the function of the phrase "friends as family" and challenges dominant assumptions about what is the correct or "proper" place of one's partner, friend, children, and family of origin, as well as the "proper" structure and function of particular relationships. However, the aging process and the valuation of youth operate differently in gay and lesbian communities, as "lesbians are said to not glorify either their early adult years or the corporeal ideals commonly ascribed for females" (Barker, 2004, p. 48). With these very real struggles and stressors, research continually suggests older gay and lesbian populations do okay, wherein social support and positive self-image are shown to be significant in mitigating the diverse effects of homophobia, heteronormativity, and aging (p. 36).

Although the research on gay and lesbian populations is still fairly new, research on trans aging is currently lacking. Yet, when considering the added impact of cisgenderism, there are distinct obstacles facing the trans* community with regard to aging and future. Donovan (2000) reflects on the distinct aging obstacles they have witnessed, such as material constraints, financial constraints, and substance abuse. Yet, they also underscore that "coping with the medical establishment has been a living hell" (p. 20), marking the struggle of navigating the threats of health care workers as well as the access and availability of care. In addition, dominant discourse frames the achievement of maturation, growth, and development within rigid binary frames of gender. These developmental scripts normalize linear narratives of transition from one gender to another, in a unidirectional sequence of progressive events that operate to preserve discrete gender binary formations. In turn, these straight narratives work to erase or invalidate "non-linear narratives that more accurately account for felt gender, felt maturation, and felt experience" (King, 2022). In a scholar roundtable about transgender media representation, Whitestone (Billard et al., 2020) discusses her research with aging trans populations, noting "the disturbing practice of detransitioning trans people after their deaths—that is, of erasing their transgender identity and presenting them in the gender they were assigned at birth" (p. 4497). She laments how after facing decades of demeaning trans images perpetuated across the culture in mass media, even "a coffin is not a safe space," marking the future as a space of struggle over maintaining one's identity (p. 4497).

Whether queer violence is enacted from others or toward oneself, queers have been cast out of the possibility of future by the confines of what is deemed (or constructed) as imaginable—although most of the research on this has been primarily focused on gay male communities. Threads of this internalized set of scripts in which gay men understand themselves as "old" at younger ages or what has been theorized in gerontology (and also challenged) as the "accelerated aging hypothesis" are also demonstrated (Barker, 2004; Bennett & Thompson, 1991; Brown et al., 2001; Hostetler, 2004). Examination of these meanings may also be traced across a range of qualitative, poetic, narrative, and autoethnographic queer work (Adams, 2021; Fox, 2007; Goltz, 2009, 2015, 2021; Hajek, 2015, 2018; Oswald, 2019). In an autoethnographic essay, Adams (2021) reflects on the memory of an ex-partner and friend, Brett, who, upon meeting him at age 26 years, routinely declared "I'll be dead by 30." Tragically, this was the case, as he died 6 months before his 30th birthday. Elaborating on his understanding of youthism and the threat of gay aging, Adams recalls his words: "Gays are vicious and live for youth. After 30 you won't be wanted or attractive." Corey and Nakayama (2012) succinctly mark the exhaustive repetition and constitution of these damning stories, eye-rolling at "the nonnewness of queerness with a future under scrutiny" (p. 18). There are certain "logics" that are routinely communicated in the culture, which work to discursively sever queerness from the concept of future. Historically, queerness has been discursively produced as a warning, as "A Harder Life" and "The Harder Path," and is narrated as an inevitable place of struggle and hardship. The linkage between struggle, pain, failure, and queerness is so normalized within cultural discourse that the reproduction of the "harder life" narrative is commonly regurgitated as if it were inevitable truth, even with the best of intentions. Statements such as "It's not the life I wanted for you" or "I don't want you to be lonely" mark common cultural scripts from parents and loved ones, often well-meaning and sincere, yet unquestioning in their linkage between queerness and struggle. Examining the creative strategies to positively negotiate their identities in the face of negative meanings, Hajek's (2016) study on resolving identity conflict identified three creative social strategies enlisted by gay men at midlife: shifting the power center from external worth to internal, resolving one's identity conflict, and transcending the negative identity of gay aging by embracing age and the role of elder. In a creative focus group project (Goltz, 2009), queer participants reflected and interrogated their lived understandings of queer age, aging, and future through performance, writing, and discussion. Although negative myths assigned to queer aging and the expectation of "the harder road" were noted across the entire group, regardless of gender, the myth tended to be more prominent in the gay men's discussion of aging, reflecting a greater struggle to think of aging in positive terms and a more bitter and sarcastic approach to their future. As a creative intervention, seeking out more positive and liberatory ways to think about future beyond negative queer mythologies or heteronormative life scripts, the focus group project set forth a series of alternative meanings for what "successful" aging and meaning could be, including being a queer role model, queer community engagement, "the erotic" as meaning, meaning through work in social justice, and the rejection of coupling through the "I complete me" script. Work in queer scripts of future calls for a reimagining of systems of generativity (Hostetler, 2009), beyond the heteronormative scripts of aging and future that work to narrate meaning in very limited (and exclusionary) ways. Although generativity has traditionally been confined in its understanding to childbearing and raising, Hostetler works to explore additional ways queer populations can contribute and "pay it forward" as a means of framing meaning and value—opening a space of a more queered generativity (Goltz, 2015). Herein, creative interventions, performance works, and creative methodologies open a space for thinking about queer future in more inclusive (Sandberg & Marshall, 2017) and creative projects (Farrier, 2015).

INTERGENERATIONAL COMMUNICATION

One of the most significant ways to challenge aging myths is through intergenerational connections, sharing, and the presence of queer role models. Many of the demonizing scripts actively work to impede queer intergenerational connections and relationships, perpetuating myths that challenge the possibility for older and younger members of the queer community to forge bonds, share experiences, and co-create more positive understandings of queer living and queer future. These cross-generational relationships become vitally important for challenging and disrupting the lingering negative assumptions about queer aging and the social scripts that insist the queer future is equated to punishment. Yet in the media, intergenerational gay and lesbian relationships are often framed around these lingering mythologies of abuse. In his analysis of the film *Gods and Monsters*, Yoakam (2001) notes,

> When one sees an intergenerational male relationship it can stir up a powerful mixture of homophobia and ageism in a culture that assumes heterosexuality as the norm and regards intergenerational sexual relationships, be they homosexual or heterosexual, as inappropriate and exploitative. (p. 66)

In these depictions, "The elder is believed to be love starved and eager to recapture lost youth" (p. 66). This theme of using aging queer bodies and queer spaces to signify threat, sadness, or desperation is a common trope used in dramatic films (e.g., *L.I.E.* and *Mysterious Skin*) or comedies (e.g., *Boat Trip* and *Nine Dead Gay Guys*). This trope of queer bars signaling both narratively and developmentally that "you're in the wrong place" is played for both threat and humor, marking queer bodies as both dangerous and ridiculous. For example, in a recurrent site gag in the 1980s comedy franchise *Police Academy*, characters would accidentally stumble into The Blue Oyster Bar, a gay bar in which men wore leather and uniform fetish outfits. The tune "El Bimbo" by Jean-Marc Dompierre would play as the door opened, and whoever was the unsuspecting visitor was forced to slow dance with the patrons in a recurring site gag.

In communication, a number of qualitative studies have specifically examined cross-generational experiences yet have focused primarily on the gay male community (Fox, 2007; Goltz, 2014; Hajek, 2014, 2018; Hajek & Gilles, 2002). Hajek and Gilles examined the recurrent degradation of older gay men by younger gay men through the lens of social identity theory and the black sheep effect, wherein older gay members are seen to "negatively contribute to social identity, or detract from the group's sense of positive distinctiveness, [and] are purged in the interest of protecting the group's positive identity" (p. 706). They argue this is tied to the notions of the appearance-conscious cultural ideal of gayness as attractive and young and that older gays represent "bad gays" who deviate from and challenge this norm. They also argue how "younger gays may fear the proximity of aging to such an extent that they discriminate against older gay men in order to distance themselves from the aging process" (p. 707). This fear is fueled by lingering stereotypes, the invisibility of older gay men in (youthist) gay cultural spaces, and the perception of older gays as being alienated and at odds with temporal norms of future and success. Fox's (2007) qualitative study of The Primetimers, a social organization for older gay men, further examined how language operates to reflect attitudes and understanding of their identities and their relationship to younger gay men. For example, the use of age-specific metaphors by the older gay men, such as "chicken" and "troll," operates to perpetuate rifts in intergenerational community, reifying stereotypes of youth consumption and older gay male sexual predation (p. 55). Hajek (2014) also found aging metaphors to be important ways of negotiating age and negotiating in-group and out-group management. In an interview study of 40 gay men aged 40–53 years, Hajek examined how language and communicative behaviors of early midlife gay men reflected their experiences with age, identity, and relationships with younger gay men. Although many men expressed pressures and desires to act and appear younger, and looked fondly upon their younger selves, midlife offered a creative opportunity for rethinking one's self and one's community beyond the confines of normative aging or the trappings of youth-centrism.

Hajek's (2014) work has continued to examine gay male identity management at midlife, specifically examining linguistic labels, peer communication, and intergenerational communication within gay culture. Using identity process theory, Hajek (2018) focuses on positive perceptions of gay men at midlife by examining generational communicational differences. His interview analysis brought forward three themes of generational communication differences, including older participants' fluency in communicative finesse and the history and practice of face-to-face communication—something less common in the age of increasing mediated communication.

Gross (2007) asked what the new cohorts will be like in a world so fundamentally different with the internet, representation, coming out earlier, and more social support. Queer communities have shifted greatly in recent years, during which the internet has taken on a far greater role of mentorship and queer cultural connection and introduction (Harper et al., 2009). These shifts challenge and change how intergenerational interaction functions in queer communities, in which older members of the community were once central to introducing and enculturating younger queers into the subculture. Through a series of intergenerational workshops, Goltz (2015) worked with gay male participants to creatively reflect on, write about, and discuss their experiences of gay aging and shifting intergenerational dynamics in gay culture. Using prompts such as "What does it mean to age successfully?" and "What are the best and worst parts of being older?," invited creative writing and the crafting of participant personal narratives and poems. The recurrent theme of youth = power and the "dirty old man" stereotypes commonly once again appeared. However, the project reflected a shift across the different age groups about the meanings and understandings they had about queer identity and community (see also Westrate & McLean, 2010). In their stories and narratives, the older participants narrated gay culture in spatial terms, such as a bar one found or a location to be sought out—a refuge removed from the straight world (like the mystical land of Oz). Younger queers, however, did not have to "find" queerness and did not think of it so much as a location because it was more pervasive and ever present in media and online. Rather than coming out into a space, to find oneself, they discussed having to come out in relation to a broad set of meanings already in the discourse, needing to negotiate themselves.

THE QUEER FUTURE

The shifting of meanings between age cohorts, understandings of sexual identity (and its fictions), and a range of movements within queer communities and research will continue to change how people think about and research LGBTQ aging and future. Although LGBTQ aging is a rapidly expanding field in gerontology (Fabbre et al., 2019), there remains a large amount of work to be examined through a communication framework. A broad range of practitioners in queer performance research continue to provide a laboratory to examine how the queer body is audienced, how queer narratives are mapped upon bodies, and how bodies negotiate these meanings. While working from a long-sedimented series of damning scripts, more recent research has worked to directly disrupt and reimagine the ways "older," "Youth," and "aging" are constructed and performed in cultural discourse. Ramirez-Valles (2016), in his collection of narratives of "gayby boomers," argues his interviewees' experiences "are not confined to illness, disease, or stigmatization" (p. 19). Ramierez-Valles' text works alongside several other projects during the past two decades that work to bridge a dialogue with communication, queer theory and gerontology, and challenge ongoing research on LGBTQ aging to engage in more intersectional engagement with race, class, and gender. In recent years, queer media research has come to reflect a diversification of mainstream stories around LGBTQ aging that offer more celebratory images of LGBTQ aging with texts such as *Tales of the City, Carol, It's a Sin, Looking, The Beginners, Pose,* and *Transparent*. The media landscape is shifting as rapidly as understandings and meanings around sexuality and sexual identity. What does it mean to age, in the face of these shifts? What can it mean to age more queerly? These ongoing questions work to bridge this body of research on gay aging and future with the projects of queer worldmaking and research in queer temporalities.

FURTHER READING

Baker, D. (2012). Seduced and abandoned: Lesbian vampires on screen 1968–74. *Continuum, 26*(4), 553–563.

Benshoff, H. M. (1997). *Monsters in the closet: Homosexuality and the horror film.* Manchester University Press.

Bersani, L. (2010). *Is the rectum a grave? And other essays.* University of Chicago Press.

Billard, T. J., Abbott, T. B., Haimson, O. L., Whipple, K. N., Whitestone, S. B., & Zhang, E. (2020). Rethinking (and retheorizing) transgender media representation: A roundtable discussion. *International Journal of Communication, 14*, 4494–4507.

Brown, A., Conrad, R., Gresham, R., Kenney, J., Stabnicki, T., & Walton, D. (2011). *Our legacies: Writings from Chicago's older gay men*. iUniverse.

Cruikshank, M. (1990). Lavender and gray: A brief survey of lesbian and gay aging studies. In J. A. Lee (Ed.), *Gay midlife and maturity* (pp. 77–88). Haworth Press.

Hajek, C. (2015). Gay men in early midlife: Intergenerational accommodation for approval, reclaimed status, and distinctiveness. *Language & Communication, 41*, 46–56.

Hajek, C. (2018). Distinguished... or dissonant: Gay male midlife identity as emergent in intergenerational communication with younger gay men. *Journal of Social and Personal Relationships, 35*(3), 329–347. https://doi.org/10.1177/0265407516689309

Herdt, G., & de Vries, B. (2004). *Gay and lesbian aging*. Springer.

Gabbay, S. G., & Wahler, J. W. (2002). Lesbian aging: Review of a growing literature. *Journal of Gay and Lesbian Social Sciences, 14*(3), 1–21.

Goltz, D. B. (2012). Blasphemies on forever: Remembering queer futures. *Liminalities, 8*(2). http://liminalities.net/8-2/blasphemies.pdf

Goltz, D. B. (2015). Overcoming the villainous monster: The beginnings of heroic gay male aging. In N. Jones & B. Batchelor (Eds.), *Aging heroes: Growing old in popular culture* (pp. 77–87). Rowman & Littlefield.

Goltz, D. B. (2020). Fred Astaire's dancing lessons. *Liminalities, 16*(3). http://liminalities.net/16-3/fredastaire.html

Goltz, D. B. (2021). Framing our story: Youthist and queer temporalities in Lopez's *The Inheritance*. *QED, 8*(1), 1–24.

Hess, L. (2017). My whole life I've been dressing up like a man: Negotiations of queer aging and queer temporality in the TV series *Transparent*. *European Journal of American Studies, 11*(3), 1–19.

Kimmel, D. C., & Sang, B. E. (1995). Lesbians and gay men in midlife. In A. R. D'Augelli & C. J. Patterson (Eds.), *Lesbian, gay, and bisexual identities over the lifespan: Psychological perspectives* (pp. 190–214). Oxford University Press.

Kooden, H. (1997). Successful aging in the middle-aged gay man: A contribution to developmental theory. *Journal of Gay and Lesbian Social Services, 6*, 21–43.

Russo, V. (1987). *The celluloid closet: Homosexuality in the movies* (Rev. ed.). Harper & Row.

REFERENCES

Adams, T. E. (2021). On (not) living past 30. In E. Rodríguez-Dorans & J. Holmes (Eds.), *The everyday lives of gay men: Autoethnographies of the ordinary*. Routledge.

Barker, J. (2004). Lesbian aging: An agenda for social research. In G. Herdt and B. de Vries (Eds.), *Gay and lesbian aging: Research and future directions* (pp. 29–72). Springer Publishing.

Battles, K., & Hilton-Morrow, W. (2002). Gay characters in conventional spaces: *Will & Grace* and the conventional comedy genre. *Critical Studies in Media Communication, 19*(1), 87–105.

Bennett, J. A. (2015). *Banning queer blood: Rhetorics of citizenship, contagion, and resistance*. University of Alabama Press.

Bennett, K. C., & Thompson, N. L. (1991). Accelerated aging and male homosexuality: Australian evidence in a continuing debate. In J. A. Lee (Ed.), *Gay midlife and maturity* (pp. 65–76). Hayworth.

Benshoff, G. (2005). *Queer images: A history of gay and lesbian film in America*. Rowan & Littlefield.

Berger, R. M. (1982). *Gay and gray: The older homosexual man*. University of Illinois Press.

Blackman, L. (2011). Affect, performance, and queer subjectivities. *Cultural Studies, 25*(2), 183–199.
Brookey, R. A. (1996). A community like *Philadelphia*. *Western Journal of Communication, 60*(1), 40–56.
Brookey, R. A., & Westerfelhaus, R. (2001). Pistols and petticoats, piety and purity: *To Wong Foo* the queering of the American monomyth, and the marginalizing discourse of deification. *Critical Studies in Media Communication, 18*(2), 141–156.
Brown, L. B., Alley, G. R., Sarosy, S., Quarto, G., & Cook, T. (2001). Gay men: Aging well! In D. C. Kimmel & D. L. Martin (Eds.), *Midlife and aging in gay America* (pp. 41–54). Harrington Park Press.
Corey, F. C. (1998). The personal: Against the master narrative. In S. J. Dailey (Ed.), *The future of performance studies: Visions and revisions* (pp. 249–253). National Communication Association.
Corey, F., & Nakayama, T. (2012). deathTEXT. *Western Journal of Communication, 76*(1), 17–23.
De Vries, B., & Blando, J. A. (2004). The study of gay and lesbian aging: Lessons for social gerontology. In G. Herdt & B. de Vries (Eds.), *Gay and lesbian aging* (pp. 3–28). Springer.
Donovan, T. (2000). Being transgender and older: A first person account. In D. C. Kimmel & D. L. Martin (Eds.), *Midlife and aging in gay America* (pp. 19–22). Harrington Park Press.
Dow, B. J. (2001). *Ellen*, television, and the politics of gay and lesbian visibility. *Critical Studies in Media Communication, 18*(2), 123–140.
Duggan, L. (2002). The new homonormativity: The sexual politics of neoliberalism. In R. Castronovo & D. D. Nelson (Eds.), *Materializing democracy: Towards a revitalized cultural politics* (pp. 175–194). Duke University Press.
Dunn, T. R. (2015). (Queer) family time: *Brothers & Sisters* and managing temporal anxieties. *Western Journal of Communication, 79*(2), 133–150.
Duttmann, A. G. (1996). *At odds with AIDS: Thinking and talking about a virus*. Stanford University Press.
Edelman, L. (2004). *No future: Queer theory and the death drive*. Duke University Press.
Erni, J. N. (1998). Queer figurations in the media: Critical reflections on the Michael Jackson sex scandal. *Critical Studies in Media Communication, 15*(2), 158–180.
Fabbre, V. D., Jen, S., & Fredriksen-Goldsen, K. (2019). The state of theory in LGBTQ aging: Implications for gerontological scholarship. *Research on Aging, 41*(5), 495–518.
Farrier, S. (2015). Playing with time: Gay intergenerational performance work and the productive possibilities of queer temporalities. *Journal of Homosexuality, 62*(10), 1398–1418.
Fejes, F., & Petrich, K. (1993). Invisibility, homophobia, and heterosexism: Lesbians, gays and the media. *Critical Studies in Media Communication, 10*(4), 395–422.
Fox, R. C. (2007). Gay grows up: An interpretive study on aging metaphors and queer identity. *Journal of Homosexuality, 52*(3–4), 33–61.
Gerbner, G., & Gross, L. (1976). Living with television: The violence profile. *Journal of Communication, 26*(2), 173–199.
Goltz, D. B. (2007). Laughing at absence: *Instinct* magazine and the hyper-masculine gay future? *Western Journal of Communication, 71*(2), 93–113.
Goltz, D. B. (2009). Investigating queer future meanings: Destructive perceptions of "the harder path." *Qualitative Inquiry, 15*(3), 561–586.
Goltz, D. B. (2010). *Queer temporalities in gay male representation: Tragedy, normativity, and futurity*. Routledge.
Goltz, D. B. (2013). "Sensible" suicides, brutal selfishness, and John Hughes's queer bonds. *Cultural Studies ↔ Critical Methodologies, 13*(2), 99–109.
Goltz, D. B. (2014). We're not in Oz anymore: Shifting generational perspectives and tensions of gay community, identity, and future. *Journal of Homosexuality, 61*(11), 1503–1528.
Goltz, D. B. (2015). "On ~~my~~ our way": Gay suicidal logics and queer survival on *Glee*. In B. C. Johnson & D. Faill (Eds.), *Glee's new directions for social change* (pp. 173–84). Sense.

Goltz, D. B. (2021). Framing our story: Youthist and queer temporalities in Lopez's *The Inheritance*. *QED*, *8*(1), 1–24.
Gross, L. (1994). What is wrong with this picture? Lesbian women and gay men on television. In J. Ringer (Ed.), *Queer words, queer images: Communication and the construction of homosexuality* (pp. 143–158). New York University Press.
Gross, L. (2001). *Up from invisibility*. Columbia University Press.
Gross, L. (2007). Gideon who will be 25 in the year 2012: Growing up gay today. *International Journal of Communication*, *1*, 121–138.
Grossman, A. H., D'Augelli, A. R., & O'Connell, T. S. (2001). Being lesbian, gay, bisexual, and 60 or older in North America. In D. C. Kimmel & D. L. Martin (Eds.), *Midlife and aging in gay America* (pp. 23–40). Harrington Park Press.
Hajek, C. (2014). Gay men at midlife: A grounded theory of social identity management through linguistic labeling and intra- and intergenerational talk. *Journal of Language and Social Psychology*, *33*, 606–631.
Hajek, C. (2015). Gay men in early midlife: Intergenerational accommodation for approval, reclaimed status, and distinctiveness. *Language & Communication*, *41*, 46–56.
Hajek, C. (2016). Social and psychological creativity in gay male midlife identity management. *British Journal of Social Psychology*, *55*, 227–243.
Hajek, C. (2018). The role of generational communication differences in the development of a positive gay midlife identity. *Communication Quarterly*, *66*(4), 345–362.
Hajek, C., & Giles, H. (2002). The old man out: An intergroup analysis of intergenerational communication among gay men. *Journal of Communication*, *52*(4), 698–714.
Halberstam, J. (2005). *In a queer time & place: Transgender bodies, subcultural lives*. New York University Press.
Harper, G. W., Bruce, D., Serrano, P., & Jamil, O. B. (2009). The role of the internet in the sexual identity development of gay and bisexual male adolescents. In P. M. Hammack & B. J. Cohler (Eds.), *The story of sexual identity: Narrative perspectives on the gay and lesbian life course* (pp. 297–326). Oxford University Press.
Hostetler, A. J. (2004). Old, gay, and alone? The ecology of well-being among middle-aged and older single gay men. In G. Herdt & B. de Vries (Eds.), *Gay and lesbian aging: Research and future directions* (pp. 143–176). Springer.
Hostetler, A. J. (2009). Generativity and time in gay men's life stories. In P. M. Hammack & B. J. Cohler (Eds.), *The story of sexual identity: Narrative perspectives on the gay and lesbian life course* (pp. 397–424). Oxford University Press.
King, J. (2022). *Inclusive screenwriting for film and television*. Routledge.
Muñoz, J. E. (2006). Stages: Punks, queers, and the utopian performance. In D. S. Madison & J. Hamera (Eds.), *The SAGE handbook of performance studies* (pp. 9–20). SAGE.
Oswald, A. G. (2019). A poetic gaze into gay aging. *The Qualitative Report*, *24*(7), 1610–1617.
Ott, B. L., & Aoki, E. (2002). The politics of negotiating public tragedy: The media framing of the Matthew Shepard murder. *Rhetoric and Public Affairs*, *5*(3), 483–505.
Porfido, G. (2007). *Queer as Folk* and the spectacularization of gay identity. In T. Peele (Ed.), *Queer popular culture: Literature, media, film, and television* (pp. 57–70). Palgrave Macmillan.
Ramirez-Valles, J. (2016). *Queer aging: The gayby boomers and the new frontier for gerontology*. Oxford University Press.
Rofes, E. E. (1983). *I thought people like that killed themselves: Lesbians, gay men, and suicide*. Grey Fox Press.
Román, D. (1997). Negative identifications: HIV-negative gay men in representation and performance. In M. Duberman (Ed.), *Queer representations: Reading lives, reading cultures* (pp. 162–176). New York University Press.

Russo, V. (1987). *The celluloid closet: Homosexuality in the movies* (Rev. ed.). Harper & Row.
Sandberg, L. J., & Marshall, B. L. (2017). Queering aging futures. *Societies, 7*(3), 21. https://www.mdpi.com/2075-4698/7/3/21/htm
Seidman, S. (2002). *Beyond the closet: The transformation of gay and lesbian life*. Routledge.
Shugart, H. A. (2003). Reinventing privilege: The new (gay) man in contemporary popular media. *Critical Studies in Media Communication, 20*(1), 67–91.
Treichler, P. (2004). AIDS, homophobia, and biomedical discourse: An epidemic of signification. In D. Carlin (Ed.), *Queer cultures* (pp. 101–37). Pearson.
Walters, S. D. (2001). *All the rage: The story of gay visibility in America*. University of Chicago Press.
Weinstock, J. S. (2004). Lesbian friendships at and beyond midlife: Patterns and possibilities for the 21st century. In G. Herdt & B. de Vries (Eds.), *Gay and lesbian aging* (pp. 177–210). Springer.
Westrate, N. M., & Mclean, K. C. (2010). The rise and fall of gay: A cultural-historical approach to gay identity development. *Memory, 18*, 225–240.
Yoakam, J. R. (2001). Gods or monsters: A critique of representations in film and literature of relationships between older gay men and younger men. In D. C. Kimmel & D. L. Martin Eds.), *Midlife and aging in gay America* (pp. 65–80). Harrington Park Press.

Dustin Goltz

JOTERÍA STUDIES AND/IN COMMUNICATION

DEFINITIONS OF JOTERÍA

The term *Jotería* has a unique etymology and many variations, including its root words, *Joto* or *Jota*. *Joto* and *Jota* were originally pejorative terms that loosely translate to "faggot" or "sissy" and are used by Spanish-speaking Latina/o/x, Chicana/o/x, and mestiza/o/x communities against gay and queer people. The original connotations were negative as they implied perversion, immorality, and degeneracy that were scripted onto Jota/o/x bodies. Although the birth of the terminology is not fully certain, scholars argue that the term *joto* "derives... from Jota (Cell Block J) of the Lecumberri federal penitentiary—in existence from 1900 to 1976—in Mexico City, where prison authorities kept effeminate men isolated from the rest of the prison population starting in the early part of the twentieth century" (Alvarez & Estrada, 2019, p. 863). Three predominant definitions of Jotería show its productive function and make it a very complex and phenomenal term. This section will explain the three distinct definitions, which suggest that there is an interplay between singular and general group processes in the study of Jotería.

One definition of Jotería is that of an umbrella noun for singular people who self-identify as Jotas, Jotos, or Jotxs. As mentioned previously, the terms arose first as derogatory terms, but some Latina/o/x, Chicana/o/x, and mestiza/o/x persons reappropriate the terms positively. More than reappropriation, Bañales (2014) views the reclamation of the terms as a "resignification" (p. 156), which takes the originally negative sign and turns it into a signifier for collective empowerment and transformative movement. Jota/o/x identities are not static because they include variant genders and sexualities, including trans and gender-nonconforming identities, and every person uniquely performs their sex and gender differently. Also, scholars note that jota/o/x identities are not reducible to gender and sexuality because the terms also denote an intersection with Latina/o/x, Chicana/o/x, and mestiza/o/x ethnic and racialized identities (Hames-García, 2014). Importantly, Alvarez and Estrada (2019) explain that the use of the terminology is still largely contested among scholars and activists, and although queers and trans persons may identify as Latina/o/x, Chicana/o/x, and mestiza/o/x, they may not self-identify or accept the Jota/o/x terms.

Jotería can also be defined as an adjective used to describe behaviors, performances, or aesthetics by Jota/o/xs. In other words, another way to understand Jotería is not as a noun but as a complex adjective that refers to the trends and performances exhibited in the group. Jotería descriptors are found in the everyday, or mundane, actions, rituals, and behaviors—performances—of people who self-identify as Jota/o/xs or others in the Jotería community and in different contexts, ranging from dance clubs, homes, educational settings, and other public or private domains. It is no surprise, then, that Jotería Studies scholars study poetry, art, music, dancing, queer spaces, photography, fashion, writing, history, mannerisms, and other behaviors that are found in or organically nascent to Jota/o/xs. In describing the adjective functions of the term, scholars have viewed Jotería, for instance, as a blend between modern, postmodern, ethnic and/or nationalistic, mariposa (butterfly), rasquache, and other aesthetics or sensibilities (Calvo-Quirós, 2014; Pérez, 2014b). A more thorough description of Jotería aesthetics is provided in the section on methodologies.

The last definition of Jotería is that of an abstract noun referencing a subculture or community. As Hames-García (2014) explains, Jotería is "a group of people of Chicana/o or Mexicana/o descent whose lives include dissident practices of gender and sexuality. While some authors draw close comparisons with terms like *lesbian*, *gay*, *bisexual*, *trans**, and *queer*, others suggest that historical, geographic, and cultural contexts make jotería not equivalent to any of these North American terms" (p. 139). As a subculture, Jotería identities are inherently intersectional because their Latina/o/x, Chicana/o/x, and mestiza/o/x backgrounds intersect with their genders, sexualities, religions, classes, citizenship, migration, abilities, indigeneity, and other layers of identity that influence identity formation and survival. The subculture, as Pérez (2014a), suggests, "can be considered a critical site of inquiry that centers on noncisheteronormative gender and sexuality as related to mestiza/o subjectivities" (p. 143). Alvarez and Estrada (2019) indicate that the subculture is part of a decolonial project because it challenges normative conceptions of identity and gender traditionally found in Western society and "jotería identity and consciousness [tenets]... include radical queer love, commitment to multidimensional social justice, and rejection of racism and colonization" (p. 864). To view Jotería as a subculture means that we can understand it as a collective and a combination of resistant, particularized, or micro processes, and broader, collective, or macro processes, of becoming and transformation.

A BRIEF HISTORICAL ACCOUNT OF JOTERÍA STUDIES

When did Jotería studies begin? Hames-García (2014) describes that "jotería studies is not something new. It feels old, continuous with years of organizing, reading, writing, and activism" (p. 137). As the definitions suggest, Jotería studies attempt to avoid generalization or essentialism and embrace continual shifts, transformations, and indeterminacy of Jotería identities. Perhaps this indeterminacy is also the case because Jotería have existed for hundreds of years, whether in the public eye or in their homes, and they have not always fit neatly in socially constructed identity categories. The terminology itself may seem anachronistic given that Latina/o/x, Chicana/o/x, and mestiza/o/x noncisheteronormative and gender-nonconforming persons predate formal study. The formal study of Jotería is relatively modern, although its roots extend back to the rise of other important ethnic and gender studies. This section provides a brief historical account of formal Jotería studies. One important goal of this section is to show how Jotería worked alongside women of color feminist groups to create their own liberation, spaces, and homes when they felt excluded and silenced by mainstream civil rights groups. In addition, this section also spotlights the formal creation of the Association for Jotería Arts, Activism, and Scholarship (AJAAS); important work presented in a 2014 *Aztlán* issue; and other foundational works in the subdiscipline.

In the 1960s and 1970s, important revolutionary groups emerged alongside each other. The civil rights, feminist, environmental, antiwar, and more particularized indigenous rights, Chicano rights, and farmworkers rights movements altogether exposed inequalities and oppressive conditions in the United States and internationally. However, individuals soon realized that the internal structures and interpersonal dimensions of many of these revolutionary groups, including the civil rights movement and the Chicano rights movement, perpetuated heteronormative and patriarchal structures and behaviors. Other movements, such as the mainstream feminist and LGBTQ+ movements, perpetuated white supremacy and coloniality that silenced women of color, including lesbians, queer, and trans persons. Hence, activists like Audre Lorde, Angela Davis, Gloria Anzaldúa, Cherríe Moraga, Dolores Huerta, and others created groups and spaces that focused on women of color and indigenous issues, struggles, rights, and activism. From this energy also emerged the recognition of Jota/o/xs by authors like Anzaldúa (1987), who once proclaimed, "People, listen to what your *jotería* is saying" (p. 85) in her acclaimed *Borderlands: La Frontera*. Researchers point to this time in history as the nascent point for formal Jotería studies (Alvarez & Estrada, 2019; Pérez, 2014a). Inspired by the aforementioned feminists of color, Jotería studies focused on the lived experiences of noncisheteronormative and gender-nonconforming people who were marginalized by mainstream movements (Revilla, 2014). In all, new Black and Brown women groups recognized the factionalism of earlier movements and, consequently, fought for new spaces to celebrate multiplicitous and intersectional identities, including trans, gender-nonconforming, and other fluid identities.

Any historical account or genealogy of Jotería studies, which includes the extensive study of Latina/o/x, Chicana/o/x, mestiza/o/x, and indigenous noncisheteronormative and gender-nonconforming identities in many fields and in fictional and nonfictional works, risks incompletion or omission of important voices. In fact, a summary of all Jotería studies authors would be impossible for an essay like this. As Hames-García (2014) describes, Jotería studies technically include all writings by and from Latina/o/x, Chicana/o/x, and mestiza/o/x LGBTQ+ members, even when they do not self-identify as Jota/o/xs, because their writings add to the understandings of the ever-changing and complex identities of the subculture. Important works include but are not limited to *This Bridge Called My Back: Radical Writings by Women of Color* (Anzaldúa & Moraga, 1983); *Borderlands/La Frontera* (Anzaldúa, 1987); *The Last Generation: Prose and Poetry* (Moraga, 1993); *Disidentifications: Queers of Color and the*

Performance of Politics (Muñoz, 1999); *The Decolonial Imaginary: Writing Chicanas Into History* (Pérez, 1999); *Virgins, Guerrillas, and Locas: Gay Latino Men Write About Love* (Cortez, 1999); *Gay Latino Studies: A Critical Reader* (Hames-García & Martínez, 2011); and others. *This Bridge Called My Back: Radical Writings by Women of Color* (Anzaldúa & Moraga, 1983) is a foundational anthology of essays and poetry by women of color feminists that criticized the oppressive conditions at home, academia, and other contexts and openly discussed different matters, including sexuality. One goal of the writers was to create transformative coalitions and change within and outside women of color spaces. Many decades later, in *Gay Latino Studies: A Critical Reader*, the editors, Hames-García and Martínez (2011), compiled a collection of essays by and/or for the understanding of complex gay Latino males, or Jotos. Although the editors noted the potentially dangerous masculinist or meninist consequences of curating such an unprecedented collection, the scholars argued that it was timely to archive essays by Jotos that were largely absent in academia or obfuscated by white queer theory. Hames-García and Martínez (2011) also had the goal of showing the ongoing debates about the negotiation, formation, and emergence of gay and Joto Latinidad. *This Bridge* and *Gay Latino Studies* show divergent foci, despite similar goals.

Additional writings are foundational in Jotería studies. In 2014, *Aztlán: A Journal of Chicano Studies* published a collection of essays entirely focused on the emergence, contributions, and future possibilities of Jotería studies, including a focus on different types of Jota/o/xs, not just Latino gay men. These works theorized on the ongoing definitions and often contradictory, antagonistic, or oppositional nature(s) of Jotería identities. The special issue was perhaps the first time a journal centered its attention on the history and possibilities of the subdiscipline. The works of other scholars are also important. For example, Horacio N. Roque Ramírez (2002, 2013) utilized oral history to describe the painful and traumatic aspects of the methodology, the author's migration from El Salvador to the United States, and struggles navigating the San Francisco queer scene and the AIDS pandemic. The works of David Román (1998, 2005) revealed the power of Latina/o/x queer performances to shape culture; provide opportunities to memorialize the dead, particularly during and after the AIDS crisis; and challenge dominant imaginaries of immigration and citizenship. As Pérez (2014a) suggests, Jotería studies is a "generative space" because there is room to develop new areas of critical inquiry, including "consciousness, mariposa theory, xueer theory, the undocuqueer movement, putería studies, and more" (p. 145). The aforementioned works are often cited and referenced in Jotería Studies.

The Need to Document and Fight Oppression. A long history of persecution informs and encourages Jotería studies; in fact, one reason Jotería Studies emerged was to archive the unique oppressions they face. Gloria Anzaldúa's (1987) work here is critical. In *Borderlands/La Frontera* she discussed the ways white colonizers inhabited the land along the United States-Mexico border forcefully and how religion and dogmatic morality became a root for violence against diverse queers and lesbians in different borderlands, or physical and/or liminal spaces where such violence happens. This violence is also what caused her psychic pain and transitory states of fragmentation or dislocation. When she suggested that people listen to the Jotería, this call to action was a demand to pay dual attention to their pain and survival and healing mechanisms. In "The Coloniality of Gender," Maria Lugones (2016) provided a history of the rise of white, Eurocentric, compulsory heterosexuality against colonized peoples since the times of colonization of the Americas. Lugones's essay was important because it provided useful historical analysis for Jotería scholars to trace how the modern/colonial gender systems still operate to oppress women of color and indigenous noncisheteronormative and gender-nonconforming people. In addition, scholars have turned to specific historical incidents, such as the punishments and burnings of indigenous persons under Inca and Aztec laws (Greenberg, 1988); the arrests of The Famous 41, men who held a dance party that included crossdressing in Mexico City in 1901 (Irwin, 2003); the involvement of Jotería in the Stonewall riots who fought against police brutality; and other events as historically significant (Pérez, 2014a). These works and events provide mappings and understandings to the particularized and systematic violence against Jota/o/xs due to their nonconformance to the modern/colonial gender systems and rules, laws, and expectations. The study of ongoing violence motivates one telos: the urgent need to resist past, present, and future violence that is syphoned against this particular subculture and its members.

The Need for Safe Space(s). The rise of formal Jotería studies coincides with the autonomization of the field from dominant academic organizations and the formation of new and urgent safe space(s). In 2007, the Joto Caucus of the National Association for Chicana and Chicano Studies (NACCS) envisioned a conference to be held separately to focus entirely on Jotería Studies alongside the Lesbian, BiMujeres, and Trans Caucus (Alvarez & Estrada, 2019). According to Revilla (2014), "While NACCS had officially incorporated feminist and queer themes into its agenda, there was still a desire for a space that was wholly committed to these topics and struggles, in and outside of academia" (p. 254). The very first independent conference by and for Jotería, spearheaded by former NACCS members, was named "Towards a Queer Homeland: Bridging Communities and Resisting Hate" and happened at the University of Nevada, Las Vegas in late 2007. This initial conference became a motivational pivot point to hold annual conferences thereafter. Furthermore, in 2011, former members of the NACCS, including the Joto Caucus, and other organizations, such as the Young Queers United for Empowerment, established the AJAAS. The AJAAS became a space that disrupted the largely cisheteronormative environment of the NACCS. Under a new organizational name, the first AJAAS conference was held in late 2012 and was titled "We Speak for Ourselves: Decolonizing Nuestr@s Conciencias, Cuerpos, La Tierra y el Alma." The AJAAS became a space for Jotería to "work together on much larger projects: scholarship, mentorship, healing, activism, artistry, professional development, and more" (Pérez, 2014a, p. 151). Part of the original AJAAS mission statement read, "For AJAAS, 'Jotería' represents a decolonizing Latina/o-Chicana/o feminist, queer consciousness and praxis. By way of community-building and knowledge sharing, we facilitate a generative and communal space to map and shape our stories toward a Jotería homeland" (Revilla, 2014, p. 253). Today, the AJAAS continues to hold conferences and involves many self-proclaimed Jotería studies scholars, activists, and artists. Jotería studies scholars and activists often form part of conferences and organizations, including the NACCS, the Modern Language Association, Latin American Studies Association, and, most recently, the National Communication Association (NCA).

The Need for Praxis and Transformation. Jotería studies, including the work that occurs with and through the AJAAS, is committed to praxis and activism beyond academia; this approach is descriptive of a need for broader sociopolitical transformation. For example, in recent decades, migrant Jota/o/x and queer students have led the Undocuqueer movement across the United States and internationally; their aim is to spotlight the lived experiences and continued marginalization of undocumented *and* Jota/o/x students while also fighting for legislative, educational, and sociopolitical changes. The Undocuqueer movement works alongside other movements, including the Dreamers, to create coalitions around immigrant rights; to participate in protests and marches, especially against anti-immigration and racist policies; and to build networks with other movements to increase consciousness in local and international communities. Additionally, the activism of Bamby Salcedo, the founder of the TransLatin@ Coalition, and Jennicet Gutiérrez, a founder of La Familia: Trans Queer Liberation Movement, often inform the works and ideals of Jotería studies because they are examples of the need to fight for trans rights and inclusion in Jotería and other spaces. Salcedo and Gutierrez's work is vital and urgent given that, as Galarte (2014) illustrated, one ongoing struggle has been the inclusion of and attention given to transgender members in white, Chicano, and mainstream queer spaces. Moreover, the poetry and prose of Maya Chinchilla and Yosimar Reyes, as well as the art of Julio Salgado, frequently focus on the joys, struggles, and experiences of Jota/o/xs. Via artistic methodologies, they present their works in intimate and public places to reach audiences beyond academia. These activists participate in workshops, community efforts, and events beyond the yearly AJAAS academic conference. Moreover, Guillermo Gomez Peña and La Pocha Nostra, Vaginal Davis, and Carmelita Tropicana are activist performance artists that utilize drag, props, poetry, and their bodies in clubs and on the streets to shock audiences into positive transformational change and increase consciousness about violence against Latina/o/x and queer communities. Although the list of Jota/o/x activists, poets, and artists is endless, they commonly reveal the entrenched nature of Jotería studies in transformative change and community building. A key takeaway in Jotería studies is that the line between scholarship and activism is not clear-cut—it is blurred. Although work happens inside the academy, it also occurs on the streets, but sometimes the same agents do both. Practice meets theory and vice versa. And both theory and community activism are made accessible for all Jotería and allies to form emancipatory collective consciousness.

JOTERÍA STUDIES' ENTRY INTO AND INFLUENCE ON COMMUNICATION

It is hard to say when Jotería studies entered the field of Communication because, like Hames-García (2014) argued, there have been tangential and complementary analyses of Latina/o/x, Chicana/o/x, and mestiza/o/x queer, noncisheteronormative, and/or gender-nonconforming identities in many fields, including Communication, for many years. Undeniably, however, there are research trends in Communication that either motivated the emergence of Jotería studies or intentionally adopted the subdiscipline in the field.

Several early trends in Communication planted important seeds for Jotería studies in the field. In the 1990s and 2000s, scholars, such as Bernadette Calafell, Fernando P. Delgado,

Sarah Amira De La Garza, Lisa A. Flores, and Michelle A. Holling, and books, such as *Shifting Borders: Rhetoric, Immigration, and California's Proposition 187* (Ono & Sloop, 2002), *Latina/o Communication Studies Today* (Valdivia, 2008), and *Latina/o Discourse in Vernacular Spaces: Somos de una Voz?* (Holling & Calafell, 2011), investigated Latina/o/x and Chicana/o/x identities in relation to the following nonexhaustive concepts: assimilation, coalition building, colonization, citizenship, cultural belonging or preservation, gender, immigration, nationalism, performance, racialization processes, sex and sexuality, and other topics. Some scholars focused entirely on personal reflections and self-transformation. For example, Erik Aoki (2017) utilized autoethnography and personal narrative to discuss the liminal nature of gay male identity and the struggles of losing or searching for one's ethnic identity. Other works provided historical and structural analyses pertinent to the complex intersections between Latina/o/x and gender identities. For example, in Flores's (1996, 2000) early work, she introduced a Chicana feminist epistemological framework to dually criticize Chicano movements and academia as exclusionary and sexist. In *Queer Migration Politics: Activist Rhetoric and Coalitional Possibilities*, Chávez (2013b) offered a historical analysis of laws that targeted and marginalized queers/migrants. Chávez also criticized modern LGBTQ+ movements that seek inclusion into statist frameworks, such as the fight for same-sex marriage, and any coalitions that are grounded in normative understandings of gender, law, or politics that are utopian without having grounding in "the dirt and concrete where people live, work, and play" (p. 7). Aimee Carrillo Rowe (2008) combined personal reflection and macro-historical analyses to discuss the complexities of living as a queer Chicana raised in a middle-class family and confronting whiteness, hybridity, power, dislocation, a lack of belonging, and settler colonial identity. Carrillo Rowe (2008) also criticized mainstream feminist movements that reinforce white supremacy and settler colonial logics in academia and society.

Communication scholars have provided even more specific investigations of Latina/o/x queer identities and their experiences in or relationships to many areas and contexts. Such areas or contexts include academia and education (Aoki, 2003; Calafell & Moreman, 2009; Moreman, 2019c), aesthetics (Muñoz, 2009; Rivera-Servera, 2012), Blacktino identity (Johnson & Rivera-Servera, 2016), Chicana feminisms (Calafell, 2007; Carrillo Rowe, 2008), coalitions and alliances (Chávez, 2013b; Carrillo Rowe, 2008), disability (Moreman, 2019a; Moreman & Briones, 2018), family (Calafell, 2007; Martinez, 2003), futurity (Moreman, 2019b, 2020; Muñoz, 2009), home/homeland (Calafell, 2007; Carrillo Rowe, 2008), indigeneity and settler colonialism (Chávez, 2013a), liminality (Aoki, 2017; Carrillo Rowe, 2017), mestiza/o/x and/or hybrid identity (Calafell, 2007; Carrillo Rowe, 2017; Moreman, 2009a), migration (Chávez, 2013b; Moreman & Non Grata, 2011), performance and performativity (Calafell, 2007; Moreman & McIntosh, 2010; Muñoz, 1999, 2009; Pérez & Goltz, 2010; Rivera-Servera, 2012), space and spatiality (e.g., clubs, bars, etc.; Rivera Servera, 2012), and many others. Much of this work has emerged alongside the works of critical/cultural intercultural scholars and other Communication scholars of color, such as Bryant Keith Alexander, Myron Beasley, Joshua Chambers-Letson, E. Patrick Johnson, Jeffrey Q. McCune, Thomas Nakayama, and Wenshu Lee. In recent years, the publication of *Latina/o/x Communication Studies: Theories, Methods, and Practice* (Hernández et al., 2019) and *This Bridge We Call Communication: Anzaldúan Approaches to Theory, Method, and Praxis* (Hernández & Gutierrez-Perez, 2019) placed an updated spotlight on the complexity and dynamics of Latina/o/x identities. Although many of the aforementioned scholars may not have mentioned Jotería directly, it is their works that inform and motivate future Jotería scholars in and beyond the field.

Several Communication scholars have intentionally theorized on Jotería identities. The works of Moreman (2009b), Andrade (2019, 2020), Gutierrez-Perez (2015, 2016, 2021), and collaborative works (Andrade & Gutierrez-Perez, 2017) directly named and focused on Jotería. A closer look at Shane T. Moreman's scholarship is appropriate given that the author first introduced the concepts of "joto" and "jotería" in the field (Moreman, 2009b). In "Rethinking Conquergood: Toward an Unstated Cultural Politics," Moreman (2009b) offered a constructive criticism, or reimagination, of Dwight Conquergood's theorizations on performance, as well as queer theory in general, to open space for his "joto" identity. Moreman (2009b) used the term *joto* to show how such an intersectional identity, "Latino + gay + male" (p. 5), challenges dominant discourses surrounding Latino masculinity and citizenship and to illustrate that Communication understudied the precise identity formation of Latino gay males prior to Moreman's essay. In the same essay, Moreman (2009b) proclaimed, "To embrace such an identity [of joto] is to claim the inhospitableness of (white) (straight) queer space" (p. 12). Although Moreman (2009b) centered his analysis of joto on his experiences as a Latino male, in "Brown Scriptings and Rescriptings: A Critical Performance Ethnography of Latina Drag Queens," Moreman and McIntosh (2010) explained that "jotita" was an appropriate reference to lesbian or gay women. Andrade (2019, 2020) looked at the intersection between Jota/o/x identities and undocumented status by illustrating the ways that Jota/o/x migrants seek life-affirming coping mechanisms, as well as embody resistant protest tactics that deterritorialize statist norms or exclusionary limits in spaces, such as museums, clubs, and other spaces. Moreover, in *Jotería Communication Studies: Narrating Theories of Resistance*, Gutierrez-Perez (2021) provided glimpses into his experiences as a queer Chicanx academic and family member and utilized poetry, prose, and academic language to do so. Gutierrez-Perez also looked at the performances, narratives, and *consejos* (advice) of Jota/o/xs in the Southwest United States and their embodied experiences in the borderlands to show how their narratives enable decolonial acts on a daily basis. These authors blend many research methodologies and frameworks from the fields of Communication and Jotería studies, including, but not limited to, critical (auto)ethnography, oral history, rhetorical criticism, performance, poetry, and archival analyses.

Why is the Communication approach to Jotería important or unique? First and foremost, scholars have documented a history of racism and struggles to create spaces uniquely devoted to people of color, such as the Latina/o Communication Studies Division and La Raza Caucus, in the NCA (González et al., 2014). In 1977, members of the NCA formed the Caucus on Lesbian, Gay, Bisexual, Transgender, and Queer Concerns. In 1997, members also formed the Gay, Lesbian, Bisexual, Transgender, and Queer Communication Studies Division for scholars to share their research and projects at the yearly NCA conference. The emergence of the Caucus and Division were important to officially recognize the divergent, diverse, and intricate scholarship from and about GLBTQ members (Yep et al., 2003). Despite the emergence of these formal groups, Yep et al. (2003) published a volume, in which they explained, "much of the scholarly work on sexuality, either consciously or unconsciously, participates in, contributes to, and affirms the normalization of hegemonic heterosexuality as invisible, natural, given, and taken for granted" (p. 2). In that same volume, Jacqueline M. Martinez (2003) offered a semiotic phenomenology of her lived experiences and likened the ways she was culturally pressured to be white and heterosexual at home in the same way that queer theory and other contemporary scholarship overlooked the fleshed, lived experiences of Chicanas and lesbians of color. Years after that volume, West (2018) noted the erasure of queer theory/studies within mainstream GLBTQ studies; Chávez (2013a) found that no journals in communication studies ever published any volumes centered on "lesbian, trans, or queer of color themes" (p. 83); and Gutierrez-Perez and Andrade (2020) revealed that scant research exists that intentionally uses the verbiage of or advances Jotería studies in communication, particularly within intercultural communication. The aforementioned history suggests that the entry of Jotería studies in communication is important to resist obfuscation and erasure within current formal academic spaces and scholarship.

Moreover, although many scholars outside of the field of Communication have paid attention to performance and communication of Jotería (Alvarez, 2014; Pérez, 2014a), the aim of Communication scholars is that of expanding the scope, focus, and deeper analysis of language, discourse, words, rhetorical devices, and semiotics in Jotería identity, community, and becoming (Andrade, 2019, 2020; Gutierrez-Perez, 2015, 2016, 2021; Moreman, 2009a). The works of Jotería Communication scholars show that modern/colonial systems oppress in similar and different violent ways, especially in the white supremacist colonial environments that Anzaldúa (1987) identifies and the compulsory heteronormativity that Lugones (2016) describes. Therefore, Jotería Communication scholars also have precise goals to expose modern/colonial gendered systems and assumptions in the history of the field, the micro- and macro-aggressions that occur against noncisheteronormative and/or gender-nonconforming persons, and mechanisms for survival, including the vernacular discourses of Jotería persons. Despite the uniqueness of Jotería Communication and the emergent space to share scholarship, it is incredibly important to invoke Hames-García's (2014) warning not to equivocate Jotería experiences or scholarship. The goal is not to homogenize Jotería but to celebrate the unique, different, and creative communicative approaches to the subgroup and subdiscipline.

JOTERÍA STUDIES METHODOLOGIES

This section explains three popular Jotería studies methodologies, including those used by scholars in Communication. The three methodologies are personal stories/autohistorias/testimonios, theories in the flesh, and Jotería aesthetics. Although these methodologies strongly resemble methods from other ethnic and gender studies disciplines, the section describes how the methodologies uniquely enhance our understanding of the complex and often antagonistic Jotería identities.

The Personal: Stories, Autohistorias, Testimonios.
One outstanding characteristic of Jotería studies methodologies is the use of personal stories and similar other frames, which are grounded in an underlying belief that "the personal is political." This belief emerges from feminist philosophies of the 1960s and 1970s. As Hames-García (2014) explains, "personal experiences—of serving their brothers at home, of experiencing violence at the hands of men, of desiring other women, of being cast out by their own people—were political subjects

worthy of theorization. These experiences could be the starting point for theory, and their own personal responses to them were, in fact, *theory*" (p. 135). In reflecting on the history of the AJAAS, Revilla (2014) notes that the story of the organization, similar to the scholarship by and about Jotería, "is mainly undocumented and lives in the oral testimonies of our ancestors, elders, and *comunidad*, and among activists, artists, and poets" (p. 253) and, hence, telling stories, autohistorias, testimonios, and similar methodologies is vital for their survival.

By using personal experience and stories, or what Anzaldúa (2002) refers to as *autohistoria* and what Pérez (2014a) refers to as *joteríastoria*, and testimonios, Jota/o/xs shed light on the complexities of their intersectional identities and illustrate experiences living in modern/colonial gender systems. In reflecting on the reasons why personal experience and storytelling is urgent and essential, Anzaldúa (2015) explains,

> In formulating new ways of knowing, new objects of knowledge, new perspectives, and new orderings of experiences, I grapple, half-unconsciously, with a new methodology—one that I hope does not reinforce prevailing modes.... I cannot use the old critical language to describe, address, or contain the new subjectivities.... I scrutinize my wounds, touch the scars, map the nature of my conflicts, croon to las muses (the muses) that I coax to inspire me, crawl into the shapes the shadow takes, and try to speak with them. (p. 4)

This quotation also captures Jotería scholars' aims to include an interplay of experiences linked to bodily movement, visceral reactions, poetry, spirituality, and new onto-epistemological ways of reading, writing, and expressing the world. In addition, scholars realize that identity is fragmented or in hybridization processes. Such is the case for most people of color and colonized subjects that are wounded and harmed by oppressive institutions and forces, but the goal is to heal and foment community transformation (Anzaldúa, 1987).

Other broader goals include reshifting paradigms to create new understandings of culture that white supremacist and Eurocentric methodologies have ignored or made unintelligible. For example, the method of *autohistoria*, coined by Gloria Anzaldúa, is about understanding the self by piecing memories, psychic thoughts, and history together as a mechanism for empowerment. In Communication, Gutierrez Perez (2016) has used autohistoria methodology to describe the specificity of the Jota/o/x lived experience in what the author describes as *Jotería-historia* that spotlights violence against and resistance tactics of Jota/o/xs. Another specific example of a methodology that is grounded in personal experience is that of *testimonios* (testimony). Many scholars, including Communication researchers, have pointed to a long history of and importance of testimonios. The methodology arose during the Chicana/o rights movements of the 1960s and 1970s (Delgado Bernal et al., 2012) because activists sought to provide standpoints and perspectives of oppression that the government and society had previously silenced. Researchers have applied testimonios to understand concepts, such as femicide (Holling, 2014) and the struggles of indigenous peoples (Delgado, 1999), and to uncover racial injustice and violence. In the context of Jotería, testimonios are a mechanism by which members of the community tell and share counterhegemonic stories and provide new decolonial understandings (Gutierrez-Perez, 2016).

In groundbreaking works, like *This Bridge Called My Back*, *Borderlands/La Frontera*, and other early essays, there are trends that emerge, whether by coincidence or because of collaborative academic influence, including that of decoloniality and intersectionality. Decoloniality is the active attempt and combination of methodological approaches to interrogate or dismantle settler colonial logic and processes, as well as attendant matrices of power, including racism, anti-Blackness, classism, and gendered structures. Intersectionality is a concept developed by Kimberlé Crenshaw (1989) that refers to the idea that individual identities are composed of different layers that intersect and often magnify oppressive circumstances, such as the case of Black women, who often face discrimination because of their Black *and* woman identities. Concurrently, these trends resemble the visions and tenets of *womanism*, the term that is derived from Alice Walker's (1981) reference to "womanist" in her early writings (p. 100), and third world feminism, which focused on experiences of Black and indigenous women, their needs, and struggles in the United States and abroad (Mohanty, 2003). Tijerina-Revilla (2009) explains another organic feminism that emerged since the early 1990s, muxerista consciousness, which placed the experiences of "Raza Womyn," Chicanas/Latinas, and "nongender conforming, transgender, Queer-gendered, and/or males" (p. 49) at the forefront of academic and activist discussions to disrupt the sexism and heteronormativity of earlier movements. It is the philosophical tenets of the aforementioned traditions—love, healing, and transformation—that encourage researchers to rely on voice, vernacular discourse, social location, and discussion of bodily, visceral experiences as the starting point of theory.

Theories in the Flesh. Another example of a recurrent Jotería studies methodology is that of theories in the flesh (Anzaldúa & Moraga, 1983). Many scholars in different disciplines, including Communication scholars, like Calafell (2007, 2019) and Gutierrez-Perez (2016), use "theories in the flesh" as a methodology to theorize Latina/o/x identity, hybridity, fragmentation, coalition building, trans politics, and other important concepts that are interrelated with Jotería studies (Hurtado, 2003). Jotería studies scholars use this methodology because of an understanding that new knowledge happens from and through the body and its interconnectedness with the spirit, surroundings/environment, affect, and others. The body stores experience that scholars unpack, albeit the difficult processes of confronting (un)conscious trauma and memories as they do so. As Anzaldúa and Moraga (1983) describe it, "A theory in the flesh means one where the physical realities of our lives—our skin color, the land and concrete we grew up on, our sexual longings—all fuse to create a politic born out of necessity. Here we attempt to bridge the contradictions of our experience.... We do this bridging by naming our selves and by telling our stories in our own words" (p. 23). In describing the importance of "theory in the flesh," Calafell (2019) adds, "Queer women of color have drawn upon experience as a way to reclaim the abjection of the raced and queer body in traditional social scientific and postpositivist methods and knowledge production. This work embraces the so-called excess of the body as radical sites of potential for knowledge creation and theorizing. It also disrupts discourses privileging so-called rationality against the emotional body" (p. 31). For Jotería studies, in particular, theory in the flesh is useful because, as Gutierrez-Perez (2016) describes it, many Jota/o/xs experience physical, mental, and emotional violence, and they carry such trauma on their bodies that is important to investigate, reflect on, and archive. As an example, Moreman and Non Grata (2011) described the ways that academic spaces are often violent against undocumented students, but it is through theory in the flesh that the authors illustrated the power of mentorship relationships to resist ideologies that seek to remove undocumented and Latina/o/x bodies from academic and sociopolitical spaces. Utilizing theory in the flesh allowed Non Grata to discuss her lived experiences as a person in constant transit, moving through borders, and surviving academia. In all, theories in the flesh emanate from bodies, and these deserve important attention to understand the condition of living in the world as Jota/o/xs.

Jotería Aesthetics. Another methodology that is frequently used in Jotería studies is that of Jotería aesthetics. The study of aesthetics is centuries long, and different fields of study, ranging from philosophy, sociology, the arts, and others, have dedicated extensive time and writings to the evolution, complexities, and different meanings of the concept. Unlike their predecessors and contemporary aesthetics scholars, Jotería scholars criticize Western aesthetics and focus on the particularities of art and performances that uniquely describe or are part of the subculture. Jotería scholars, including several in Communication, explore and illustrate variations of what Calvo-Quirós (2014) refers to as a "jotería aesthetic" (p. 182). What is a "jotería aesthetic"? The answer is complex. In fact, Calvo-Quirós argues that to provide static definitions of aesthetics risks *"oppressive epistemologies of taste,"* especially litmus tests that have been handed down by modern/colonial systems and used to center cisheteronormative values (p. 182). Therefore, to describe a Jotería aesthetic necessitates ongoing critical reflexivity and a commitment to decolonial imaginaries and thought (Pérez, 1999). With reflexive and decolonial frames in mind, Jotería studies scholars depict shifting, hybrid, colorful, and culturally relevant performative aesthetics in poetry, art, music, dancing, drag, queer spaces, photography, fashion, writing, history, mannerisms, artifacts, and other contexts. And Jotería aesthetics are influenced by Latina/o/x and Chicana/o/x culture, indigeneity, citizenship, class, sexuality, and other variant cultural elements. Studying different contexts, scholars point to the ways different mediums help transgress, subvert, or expose white supremacist, racist, cisheteronormative, patriarchal, ableist, and other oppressive tastes, values, attitudes, and structures. Jotería studies also repeatedly describe Jotería aesthetics as founded on love, community, interconnectedness with nature and others, and activism for change.

Jotería and Communication scholars advance important theorizations on Jotería aesthetics that are noteworthy. For example, Calvo-Quirós (2014) and Pérez (2014b) both provide an example of a Jotería aesthetic found in mariposa aesthetics/consciousness. Similar to the terminology/etymology of Jotería that emerged with negative connotations, the term *mariposa* is often negatively used by Latina/o/x communities to negatively chastise queer, noncisheteronormative, and/or gender-nonconforming persons as feminine. However, Calvo-Quirós (2014) and Pérez (2014b) describe Jotería's reappropriation of the symbol of the butterfly as a positively transformative one—an empowerment mind-set. The mariposa represents free, colorful winged creatures, worshipped by ancestors as representatives of divine figures, such as Xochipilli, that are/were important for the continuation of natural environments. Pérez (2014b) explains, "The ancient mariposa warriors can be considered an integral part of a lengthy history of fierce mariposa warriors struggling to build a Mariposa Nation" (p. 116). Other scholars positively reappropriate what Western aesthetics deprecate. Such is the case with Calafell's (2015) conceptual framework of monstrosity, a "theory in the flesh," which begins with an understanding that Western media and oppressive institutions, including academia, have historically depicted people of color, especially queer women, as monsters, but Calafell reappropriates such monstrosity as a mechanism for self-empowerment. As the author explains, "My monstrosity has become a space of activity and possibility" (p. 3). Power lies in affirming the grotesque and the monstrous because, as queers of color, monsters begin to create affective, productive relationships with self and others that are reviled, similarly. Lastly, some authors point to symbols and artifacts as sites of aesthetic revolution. For instance, Gutierrez-Perez and Andrade (2020) analyze *Jotería*, a game created by Antonio Castellanos that reimagines the original Lotería game, a table card game traditionally played in Latina/o/x communities/households, by changing the originally cisheteronormative and racist symbols on the cards to reflect Latina/o/x noncisheteronormative and/or gender-nonconforming persons in a positively creative way. The authors view the *Jotería* game as an example of Jotería aesthetics that rupture traditional heteronormative and modern/colonial gendered systems' cultural aesthetics while also creating a new praxis to bring awareness about the realities of Jota/o/xs in a game. The mariposa, monstrosity, and game of *Jotería* reveal that, just like identities shift and change, Jotería aesthetics merge postmodern, decolonial, deconstructive, and resistant attitudes, values, actions, performances, and expressions that resist Western aesthetics. In sum, Jotería scholars reappropriate what it means to study aesthetics to decolonize the historically predominantly Western and Eurocentric frameworks.

CONCLUSION

Jotería studies emerged as a subdiscipline during tumultuous sociopolitical shifts in the United States to spotlight the plight of Jotería and to create transformational change. However, due to the proliferation of writing, activism, and work by Jotería, it resists being a *sub*discipline, especially because of the creation of the independent AJAAS as well as the direct influence of scholars/activists on their communities and academia that make it a discipline worthy of attention and respect. To this end, Communication scholars, faculty, and students would benefit greatly by introducing and using Jotería studies works into and in all subdisciplines of the field, including intercultural, interpersonal, organizational, and protest/agitational Communication courses. Jotería studies are a bridge and a pedagogical tool for those committed to social and racial justice and to reach those who can see themselves in the lived experiences and methodologies of the discipline (Alvarez, 2014).

Undeniably, Jotería studies have grown enough to influence many fields, including Communication. Hence, Communication scholars continue to enhance the theories and methodologies because, from a Communication angle, expanding the scope and application of Jotería studies methods to different segments of the Jotería subculture is a fruitful endeavor for the field and our communities writ large. Nonetheless, important future work is needed at the intersection of Jotería and communication studies, including a response to and potential urgency to discuss current world happenings. For example, Jotería scholars and activists are poised to address the ongoing violence and detentions by immigration and customs enforcement, the disproportionate impact of COVID-19, and increasing xenophobia and racism within the Latinx and other communities before and after Donald J. Trump's presidency.

Moreover, recent Black Lives Matter, indigenous, and racial violence protests require that all strata of society and academia continuously confront anti-Blackness, anti-indigeneity, and the resurgence of white supremacist, active groups. The question is, how can Jotería studies take on these calls? The goal of Jotería studies has always been to understand the micro, particular processes of and the macro, universal forces and contexts that shape Jotería and identity formation; hence, the goal remains to adapt and resist the perpetual intensification of modern/colonial systems' violence against Jotería communities. Pushing epistemological boundaries is important for the discipline, and consequently, the rise of new technologies, media, and sociopolitical realities, including neoconservative sources of violence, will require Jotería studies to keep up with the times and further join academic and activist forces to address trauma, physical violence, and oppression in the current moment and the future.

Moreover, Jotería studies must expand their analysis of specific Jotería, such as those from many understudied Latin American countries and geographies, mixed identities (e.g., Afro-Latina/o/x Jotería), indigenous global and local communities, and trans communities. If critical reflexivity is an essential aspect of Jotería studies, then this must persist to avoid amalgamation, essentialism, or conflation of ever-changing Jotería identities in the present and future. As shown in critical/cultural research studies, identities are in constant flux, and this includes their nuanced performances, lifestyles, and expressions. Lastly, Jotería studies have a responsibility to craft scholarship and activism that does not forget a spirit of revolutionary praxis. As Hurtado (2003) warns, "The cycle of deconstruction as a means to make a splash many times circumvents issues of advocacy, influencing policy, or providing direction for practitioners and activists" (p. 222). As such, Jotería and/in communication studies should continue to promote community, policy, and self-collective change to continuously advance the needs and survival of all Jotería.

FURTHER READING

Alexander, B. K. (2006). *Performing Black masculinity: Race, culture, and queer identity*. AltaMira Press.

Chambers-Letson, J. (2018). *After the party: A manifesto for queer of color life*. New York University Press.

Galarte, F. J. (2021). *Brown trans figurations: Rethinking race, gender, and sexuality in Chicanx/Latinx Studies*. University of Texas Press.

Johnson, E. P. (2001). "Quare" studies, or (almost) everything I know about queer studies I learned from my grandmother. *Text and Performance Quarterly, 21*(1), 1–25.

McCune, J. Q., Jr. (2015). The queerness of Blackness. *QED: A Journal in GLBTQ Worldmaking, 2*(2), 173–176.

Moreman, S. T., & Calafell, B. M. (2008). Buscando para nuestros hijos: Utilizing la llorona for cultural critique. *Journal of International and Intercultural Communication, 1*(4), 309–326.

Nakayama, T. K. (1994). Show/down time: "Race," gender, sexuality, and popular culture. *Critical Studies in Media Communication, 11*(2), 162–179.

Pérez, K. (2012). Blasphemies and queer potentiality: Performance and/as relation. *Liminalities: A Journal of Performance Studies, 8*(2), 1–10.

Valdivia, A. N. (2020). *The gender of Latinidad: Uses and abuses of hybridity*. John Wiley.

Yep, G. A. (2003). The violence of heteronormativity in communication studies: Notes on injury, healing, and queer world-making. *Journal of Homosexuality, 45*(2–4), 11–59.

REFERENCES

Alvarez, E. F., Jr. (2014). Jotería pedagogy, SWAPA, and Sandovalian approaches to liberation. *Aztlán: A Journal of Chicano Studies, 39*(1), 215–228.

Alvarez, E. F., Jr., & Estrada, J. (2019). Jotería Studies. In H. Chiang, A. Arondekar, M. Epprecht, J. Evans, R. G. Forman, H. Al-Samman, E. Skidmore, & Z. Tortorici (Eds.), *Global encyclopedia of lesbian, gay, bisexual, transgender, and queer (LGBTQ) history* (pp. 863–867). Charles Scribner's Sons.

Andrade, L. M. (2019). CAUTION: On the many, unpredictable iterations of a yellow border sign ideograph and migrant/queer world-making. *Text and Performance Quarterly, 39*(3), 203–228.

Andrade, L. M. (2020). "Vale Verga" ("it's worth a cock (nothing)"): The queer of color world-making consejos of Fernanda, an aging undocumented muxer/jota *Text and Performance Quarterly, 40*(3), 1–19.

Andrade, L. M., & Gutierrez-Perez, R. (2017). Bailando con las sombras: Spiritual activism and soul healing in the war years. *Qualitative Inquiry, 23*(7), 502–504.

Anzaldúa, G. (1987). *Borderlands/La Frontera: The new mestiza*. Aunt Lute.

Anzaldúa, G. E. (2002). Now let us shift…the path of conocimiento…inner work, public acts. In G. E. Anzaldúa & A. Keating (Eds.), *This bridge we call home: Radical visions for transformation* (pp. 540–578). Routledge.

Anzaldúa, G. (2015). *Light in the dark/Luz en lo oscuro: Rewriting identity, spirituality, reality*. Duke University Press.

Anzaldúa, G., & Moraga, C. (Eds.). (1983). *This bridge called my back: Radical writings by women of color*. Kitchen Table Press.

Aoki, E. (2003). "Making space in the classroom for my gay identity: A letter I've been wanting to write." In B. Timpson, S. Canetto, E. Borrayo, & R. Yang (Eds.), *Teaching diversity: Challenges and complexities, identities and integrity* (pp. 91–102). Atwood.

Aoki, E. (2017). Strategic liminality and trans-regional mobility: Engaging diverse city spaces to constitute and negotiate intersectional identities of newfound class privilege, repressed ethnic anger, and the (in)visibility of gay (male) life. In A. Atay & J. Brower (Eds.), *Communication, culture, and making meaning in the city: Ethnographic engagements in urban environments* (pp. 197–216). Lexington Books.

Bañales, X. (2014). Jotería: A decolonizing political project. *Aztlán: A Journal of Chicano Studies, 39*(1), 155–166.

Calafell, B. M. (2007). *Latina/o communication studies: Theorizing performance*. Peter Lang.

Calafell, B. M. (2015). *Monstrosity, race, and performance in contemporary culture*. Peter Lang.

Calafell, B. M. (2019). Narrative authority, theory in the flesh, and the fight over the death and life of Marsha P. Johnson. *QED: A Journal in GLBTQ Worldmaking, 6*(2), 26–39.

Calafell, B. M., & Moreman, S. T. (2009). Envisioning an academic readership: Latina/o performativities per the form of publication. *Text and Performance Quarterly, 29*(2), 123–130.

Calvo-Quirós, W. A. (2014). The aesthetics of healing and love: An epistemic genealogy of Jota/o aesthetic traditions. *Aztlán: A Journal of Chicano Studies, 39*(1), 181–195.

Carrillo Rowe, A. (2008). *Power lines: On the subject of feminist alliances*. Duke University Press.

Carrillo Rowe, A. (2017). Settler Xicana: Postcolonial and decolonial reflections on incommensurability. *Feminist Studies, 43*(3), 525–536.

Chávez, K. R. (2013a). Pushing boundaries: Queer intercultural communication. *Journal of International and Intercultural Communication, 6*(2), 83–95.

Chávez, K. R. (2013b). *Queer migration politics: Activist rhetoric and coalitional possibilities*. University of Illinois Press.

Cortez, J. (Ed.). (1999). *Virgins, guerrillas & locas: Gay Latinos writing on love*. Cleis Press.

Crenshaw, K. (1989). Demarginalizing the intersection of race and sex: A Black feminist critique of antidiscrimination doctrine, feminist theory and antiracist politics. *University of Chicago Legal Forum, 1989*, 139–167.

Delgado, F. (1999). Rigoberta Menchú and testimonial discourse: Collectivist rhetoric and rhetorical criticism. *World Communication, 28*(1), 17–29.

Delgado Bernal, D., Burciaga, R., & Flores Carmona, J. (2012). Chicana/Latina testimonios: Mapping the methodological, pedagogical, and political. *Equity & Excellence in Education, 45*(3), 363–372.

Flores, L. A. (1996). Creating discursive space through a rhetoric of difference: Chicana feminists craft a homeland. *Quarterly Journal of Speech, 82*(2), 142–156.

Flores, L. A. (2000). Reclaiming the "other": Toward a Chicana feminist critical perspective. *International Journal of Intercultural Relations, 24*(5), 687–705.

Galarte, F. (2014). On trans* chican@ s: Amor, justicia, y dignidad. *Aztlán: A Journal of Chicano Studies, 39*(1), 229–236.

González, A., Calafell, B. M., & Avant-Mier, R. (2014). An LCSD & La Raza microhistory: The Latina/o Communication Studies Division & La Raza Caucus of the National Communication Association. *Review of Communication, 14*(2), 125–137.

Greenberg, D. F. (1988). *The construction of homosexuality*. University of Chicago Press.

Gutierrez-Perez, R. M. (2015). Disruptive ambiguities: The potentiality of jotería critique in communication studies. *Kaleidoscope: A Graduate Journal of Qualitative Communication Research, 14*(1), 10.

Gutierrez-Perez, R. (2016). *Jotería-Historias: Theories from the fringes*. University of Denver.

Gutierrez-Perez, R. (2021). *Jotería communication studies: Narrating theories of resistance*. Peter Lang.

Gutierrez-Perez, R. M., & Andrade, L. M. (2020). How queer (of color) is intercultural communication? Then and there, Jotería the game as a praxis of queerness, advocacy, and utopian aesthetics. In S. Eguchi & B. M. Calafell (Eds.), *Queer intercultural communication: The intersectional politics of belonging in and across differences* (pp. 179–194). Rowman & Littlefield.

Hernández, L. H., Bowen, D. I., Upton, S. D., & Martinez, A. R. (Eds.). (2019). *Latina/o/x communication studies: Theories, methods, and practice*. Lexington Books.

Hernández, L. H., & Gutierrez-Perez, R. (Eds.). (2019). *This bridge we call communication: Anzaldúan approaches to theory, method, and praxis*. Lexington Books.

Hames-García, M. (2014). Jotería studies, or the political is personal. *Aztlán: A Journal of Chicano Studies, 39*(1), 135–142.

Hames-García, M., & Martínez, E. J. (Eds.). (2011). *Gay Latino studies: A critical reader*. Duke University Press.

Holling, M. A. (2014). "So my name is Alma, and I am the sister of…": A feminicidio testimonio of violence and violent identifications. *Women's Studies in Communication, 37*(3), 313–338.

Holling, M. A., & Calafell, B. M. (2011). *Latina/o discourse in vernacular spaces: Somos de una voz?* Lexington Books.

Hurtado, A. (2003). Theory in the flesh: Toward an endarkened epistemology. *International Journal of Qualitative Studies in Education, 16*(2), 215–225.

Irwin, R. M. (2003). *Mexican masculinities*. University of Minnesota Press.

Johnson, E. P., & Rivera-Servera, R. (2016). *Blacktino queer performance*. Duke University Press.

Lugones, M. (2016). The coloniality of gender. In W. Harcourt (Ed.), *The Palgrave handbook of gender and development* (pp. 13–33). Springer.

Martinez, J. M. (2003). Racisms, heterosexisms, and identities: A semiotic phenomenology of self-understanding. *Journal of Homosexuality, 45*(2–4), 109–127.

Mohanty, C. T. (2003). *Feminism without borders: Decolonizing theory, practicing solidarity*. Duke University Press.

Moraga, C. (1993). *The last generation: Prose and poetry*. University of California Press.

Moreman, S. T. (2009a). Memoir as performance: Strategies of hybrid ethnic identity. *Text and Performance Quarterly, 29*(4), 346–366.

Moreman, S. T. (2009b). Rethinking Conquergood: Toward an unstated cultural politics. *Liminalities: A Journal of Performance Studies, 5*(5), 0–12.

Moreman, S. T. (2019a). Accommodating desires of disability: A multi-modal methodological approach to Terry Galloway and the Mickee Faust Club. *QED: A Journal in GLBTQ Worldmaking, 6*(3), 149–162.

Moreman, S. T. (2019b). A queer futurity autofantasía: Contouring discourses of Latinx through memory and queer youth literature. *Text and Performance Quarterly, 39*(3), 185–202.

Moreman, S. T. (2019c). The Hispanic-serving institution: Communicating a future with or without a past. *Communication Education, 68*(4), 509–516.

Moreman, S. T. (2020). Narrative embodiment of Latinx queer futurity: Pause for dramatic affect. In A. L. Johnson, & B. LeMaster (Eds.), *Gender futurity, intersectional autoethnography* (pp. 223–236). Routledge.

Moreman, S. T., & McIntosh, D. M. (2010). Brown scriptings and rescriptings: A critical performance ethnography of Latina drag queens. *Communication and Critical/Cultural Studies, 7*(2), 115–135.

Moreman, S. T., & Non Grata, P. (2011). Learning from and mentoring the undocumented AB540 student: Hearing an unheard voice. *Text and Performance Quarterly, 31*(3), 303–320.

Moreman, S. T., & Briones, S. R. (2018). Deaf Queer world-making: A thick intersectional analysis of the mediated cultural body. *Journal of International and Intercultural Communication, 11*(3), 216–232.

Muñoz, J. E. (1999). *Disidentifications: Queers of color and the performance of politics* (Vol. 2). University of Minnesota Press.

Muñoz, J. E. (2009). *Cruising utopia: The then and there of queer futurity*. New York University Press.

Ono, K. A., & Sloop, J. M. (2002). *Shifting borders: Rhetoric, immigration, and California's Proposition 187* (Vol. 15). Temple University Press.

Pérez, D. E. (2014a). Jotería epistemologies: Mapping a research agenda, unearthing a lost heritage, and building. *Aztlán: A Journal of Chicano Studies, 39*(1), 143–154.

Pérez, D. E. (2014b). Toward a mariposa consciousness: Reimagining queer Chicano and Latino identities. *Aztlán: A Journal of Chicano Studies, 39*(2), 95–127.

Pérez, E. (1999). *The decolonial imaginary: Writing Chicanas into history*. Indiana University Press.

Pérez, K., & Goltz, D. B. (2010). Treading across lines in the sand: Performing bodies in coalitional subjectivity. *Text and Performance Quarterly, 30*(3), 247–268.

Revilla, A. (2014). The association for Jotería arts, activism, and scholarship: A movimiento for queer Chicana/os and Latina/os. *Aztlán: A Journal of Chicano Studies, 39*(1), 253–260.

Rivera-Servera, R. (2012). *Performing queer latinidad: Dance, sexuality, politics*. University of Michigan Press.

Román, D. (1998). *Acts of intervention: Performance, gay culture, and AIDS*. Indiana University Press.

Román, D. (2005). *Performance in America: Contemporary U.S. culture and the performing arts*. Duke University Press.

Roque Ramírez, H. N. (2002). My community, my history, my practice. *The Oral History Review, 29*(2), 87–91.

Roque-Ramirez, H. N. (2013). *Queer Latino San Francisco: An oral history, 1960s–1990s*. Palgrave Macmillan.

Tijerina-Revilla, A. (2009). Are all Raza womyn queer? An exploration of sexual identity in a Chicana/Latina student organization. *NWSA Journal, 21*(3), 46–62.

Valdivia, A. N. (2008). *Latina/o communication studies today*. Peter Lang.

Walker, A. (1981). *You can't keep a good woman down*. Harcourt Brace Jovanovich.

West, I. (2018). Queer studies in critical and cultural communication. In D. L. Cloud (Ed.), *Oxford research encyclopedia of communication* (pp. 1–29). Oxford University Press. https://doi.org/10.1093/acrefore/9780190228613.013.625

Yep, G. A., Lovaas, K. E., & Elia, J. P. (2003). Introduction: Queering communication: Starting the conversation. *Journal of Homosexuality, 45*(2–4), 1–10.

Luis M. Andrade

KUAER THEORY

FIRST-GENERATION QUEER THEORY AND ITS CONSPICUOUS OMISSIONS

In addition to being influenced by the writing and theorizing of James Baldwin, poststructuralism, and existential philosophy, queer theory was very profoundly influenced by Black and womanist feminists such as Alice Walker, Audre Lorde, bell hooks, Cherríe Moraga, and Gloria Anzaldúa (Barker & Scheele, 2016). Anzaldúa, for example, theorized *mestiza queer* in the 1980s prior to what is perceived as the "official" origin of queer theory, which is something that tends to be omitted when histories of queer theory are presented (Amin, 2016). Indeed, queer theory has multiple influences and origin points, but the massive contributions of Black feminists and feminists of color are often left out of its "official" origin story, which typically cites Teresa de Lauretis's (1991) conceptualization of queer theory as *the* foundational moment in the development of queer theory as it is currently known (Barker & Scheele, 2016; West, 2018; Yep et al., 2003). In her introduction to the 1991 queer theory special issue of the scholarly journal *differences*, de Lauretis directly calls for queer theorists to address the ways in which sexuality intersects with other identity categories such as gender and race (Barker & Scheele, 2016). The politics of de Lauretis's call is aligned with the intersectional politics of the Black feminist and womanist theorizing that influenced the development of queer theory more generally. Unfortunately, this call and its politics went largely unheeded as "first generation" (Yep et al., 2012, p. 125) queer theory become more popular and established in academic contexts throughout the 1990s (Johnson, 2001; Yep et al., 2003). Because first-generation queer theorists tended to theorize about sexuality without thoroughly describing its relationships with other identity categories and because many of the prominent queer theorists who were producing scholarship at the time were very privileged in an intersectional sense, popular first-generation queer theory tended to construct a problematically universalized understanding of a "default queer subject." Even though queer theory emerged from fields that prioritize radical social change and emphasize intersectionality such as Black feminism, womanism, gay and lesbian studies, and women and gender studies, this default queer subject of popular 1990s scholarship ultimately tended to become a White, affluent, able-bodied, United States–based cisgender man. Queer individuals who did not fit into this very narrow and privileged mold were largely absent from popular queer scholarship at the time. This omission is obviously problematic, but it is especially notable for happening in relation to queer theory, which aims to be a theoretical tradition that is centered around anti-normativity, troubling the status quo, and dismantling hierarchies of power.

First-generation queer theory's normative dynamics and its general lack of attention to intersectionality was profoundly challenged by E. Patrick Johnson in a 2001 scholarly journal article published in *Text and Performance Quarterly*. In this article, Johnson challenged queer theorists to center the interconnectedness of sexuality, race, socioeconomic class, and gender when producing queer scholarship. Johnson advances the theory of quare studies as a challenge to the overwhelming, yet underacknowledged whiteness of first-generation queer theory. Quare studies challenges queer theory to be richly intersectional and to avoid and contest attempts to construct universal queer subject positions that erase the experiences and subjectivities of queer people who do not fit a very privileged mold in an intersectional sense (Yep et al., 2003). Quare studies specifically encourages centering the experiences of Black queer people, low-income queer people, and queer people of color. Additionally, Johnson argues that queer theorizing must avoid assuming that people will automatically have stereotypical subjectivities or experiences simply because they identify with a certain set of identity categories. Instead, Johnson's quare studies pushes queer theory to center and celebrate the diversity of queer subjectivities, lived experiences, and material circumstances while simultaneously contextualizing how all of this relates to power at multiple levels in specific cultural and historical contexts.

While quare studies, Black feminism, and Alice Walker's (1983) womanism are the most direct and significant influences on Wenshu Lee's (2003) kuaer theory, kuaer theory is also substantially informed by scholarship and activism in the fields of postcolonialism and critical intercultural communication. Like quare studies, kuaer theory contends that it is crucial for queer theorists to take an intersectional approach to analyzing sexuality by emphasizing its interrelatedness to other identity categories such as race, gender, and class. However, kuaer theory adds another dimension, ultimately arguing that it is also necessary for queer theorists to contextually consider sexuality in relation to national identity, colonialism, imperialism, language, and local and global hierarchies of power (Yep, 2013). In other words, as Lee puts it, kuaer theory can be understood as "transnational womanist quare studies" (Lee, 2003, p. 161).

While advancing kuaer theory, Lee heeds Johnson's call to centralize queer subjectivities and experiences that had often been absent from popular first-generation queer scholarship. In the 2003 article where she initially advanced kuaer theory, Lee refers to her writing as a "bilingual and multi-styled journal" (p. 148) that contains a combination of italicized personal reflections and ruminations along with a more traditional nonitalicized historical and rhetorical analysis. As a result of this combination, Lee's article breathes life into theory in the spirit of theorists such as E. Patrick Johnson, Gloria Anzaldúa, and Gayatri Chakravorty Spivak, ultimately challenging the normative conventions of scholarship. Lee's article seems to be a precursor to contemporary queer autoethnographic scholarship in that Lee offers the reader a striking amount of insight into her thoughts, her experiences, and how her scholarship connects with her identity. This is largely accomplished through Lee's employment of Michael Awkward's concept of *autocritography*, which Awkward defines as "an account of individual, social, and institutional conditions that help to produce a scholar and, hence, his or her professional concerns" (Awkward, 1999, p. 7).

Lee's autocritography opens with a rich and reflexive exploration of her internalization of various hegemonic racial, gendered, and sexual ideologies as well as her ongoing process of critically examining and ultimately transforming these internalizations. She describes her multicultural and multilingual identity and how she perceives and navigates her identity fluidly while moving between cultural contexts in Taipei, Taiwan and San Jose, California. Lee shares three moments that have led her to profoundly expand her engagement with sexuality beyond a hegemonic Eurocentric, Anglocentric, and generally heteropatriarchal understanding. Lee notes that these three moments have "awakened her consciousness" (p. 151) and, as such, refers to them as *awakenings*.

LEE'S THREE AWAKENINGS

The three awakenings that Lee describes in her 2003 article involve wordplay in the Mandarin language as well as various historical feminist queer practices within Taiwan and China. In her first awakening, Lee explores various historical Chinese queer feminisms, namely *jin lan hui* (golden orchid association), which Lee describes a sisterhood of marriage resisters in 19th-century Canton. In her second awakening, Lee conducts a rhetorical analysis of the title of Taiwan's first officially registered lesbian publication, which is called *Ai Fu Hao Zi Zai Bao* (love, luck, good, self-at-ease newspaper) and argues that this title rhetorically constitutes a subtle but subversive challenge to heteropatriarchy in Taiwanese culture. In her third awakening, Lee synthesizes multiple theoretical traditions, specifically quare studies, womanism, and postcolonialism, to ultimately advance kuaer theory and its core principles.

In her first awakening, Lee focuses on historical Chinese feminist queer practices that tend not to be focused on in Western queer scholarship. Lee describes coming across the term *jin lan hui* (golden orchid association) when researching Chinese feminisms and having this experience break "the massive silence on Chinese lesbianism" (p. 151) for her. Lee engages in a dialectical analysis of Chen Dongyuan's (1928/1994) writing about Chinese women's history, arguing that Chen stigmatizes feminine queerness even as he is critical of patriarchy in China. Lee specifically notes that Chen endorses historical Chinese performances of feminine queerness that incorporate elements of Western relationship structures such as free love and monogamy while he stigmatizes feminine queer practices, such as *jin lan hui*, that involve marriage resistance and tend to be anti-heteropatriarchal.

Citing Topley (1975), Lee also describes two more terms that relate to marriage resistance: *zi shu nu* and *buo luo jia*. Lee notes that "there was a hairdressing ritual for a bride before marriage" (p. 152) and that *zi shu nu* refers to "self-brushing [the hair] women" (p. 152) who would choose not to marry and would engage in this hairdressing ritual alone to signify "entering a new stage of life along, henceforth the term *zi* (self) *shu* (brushing) *nu* (female)" (p. 152). *Buo luo jia* refers to women who married their husbands but ultimately did not consummate their relationship. Lee explains *buo luo jia* more fully:

> Three days after the wedding, the bride would be accompanied by the groom to pay a ritual visit to her natal family, called *gui ning*. *Gui* means returning and *ning* means safe/peaceful. Together, it means the bride returns home to wish her parents a safe and healthy life. The unwilling bride during the resistance era would take advantage of this ritual, refusing to return to the husband's family. (pp. 152–153)

Lee describes *zi shu nu* and *buo luo jia* as being specific forms of *jin lan hui*, which she summarizes as "a 19th century Chinese vocabulary for *nu nu* connections in Canton" (p. 153). Lee notes that marriage resistance declined in the 1930s and became a relatively unknown hidden history shortly thereafter. At the end of her description of her first awakening, Lee reflects on the personal dimensions of her research and her feelings of connectedness to the lives and subjectivities of the women that she grew to know through researching *jin lan hui*.

In her second awakening, Lee analyzes the title of Taiwan's first officially registered lesbian publication, *Ai Fu Hao Zi Zai Bao*, and explores how it engages in rhetorical invention through its use of playful and subversive wordplay. Lee describes being in Taiwan in the early 1990s and witnessing the spirited theoretical debate between Taiwanese lesbian feminists who advocated for an intersectional approach to analyzing sexuality and "heterosexually unconscious" (p. 154) Taiwanese feminists who neither paid very much attention to the relationships between gender and sexuality nor how heteronormativity and heterosexual privilege framed their feminist politics. Lee notes that her professor friends in Taiwan considered the publication of *Ai Fu Hao Zi Zai Bao*, or as it is commonly abbreviated, *Ai Bao* (the love magazine/love paper), to be a breakthrough for lesbian activism and theorizing in Taiwan.

Lee explains that wordplay is often used to advance multiple meanings in Mandarin in a way that is different from English and that *Ai Bao*'s title exemplifies this. To demonstrate this, Lee utilizes the style of postmodern cultural studies theorists such as Stuart Hall (1980) and offers multiple interpretations, or "takes," of the meaning of *Ai Bao*'s full name. Lee argues that *Ai Bao*'s full title can be interpreted in multiple ways, some of which are likely to be perceived as relatively "traditional" and aligned with normative cultural values and some of which are likely to be perceived as "radical" for their challenge to the status quo. In other words, Lee notes that the abbreviated name, *Ai Bao*, "is a non-threatening title for those who endorse heteropatriarchy" (p. 157), while the radical ways in which the full title can be interpreted have the effect of rejecting the male gaze and endorsing love and sexuality between women. Through wordplay, Lee notes that the full title of *Ai Bao* is likely going to be interpreted very differently by audiences because of their standpoint. This is a clever, subversive, and undeniably queer rhetorical move that exemplifies de Certeau's (1980/2011) notion of tactics and evokes the covert semiotics that have traditionally been employed by queer communities as noted by Muñoz (1996) as well as by members of subcultural groups more generally as noted by Hebdige (1979).

Lee offers several possible takes for interpreting *Ai Bao*'s full title. The first take is a literal one that means "love, luck, good, self at ease newspaper/magazine" (p. 155). Lee notes that, when placed together, *Zi Zai* and *Ai Fu Hao* "create a perfectly traditional, innocent and positive title for the new magazine; that is, the title is not only familiar, but also good" (p. 156). She notes that this meaning is a very persuasive one that is likely to be discursively deemed nonthreatening to power structures, which ultimately creates space for the more subversive meanings to circulate within. The second take of *Ai Bao*'s full title is, according to Lee, more "risqué" and overtly queer than the first and can be understood as meaning "caress/foreplay is so very great/free" (p. 156). The third take can be understood as blending the name of a commercial herbal drink that is marketed as facilitating masculine heterosexual virility with a brand of imported sanitary napkins. Lee notes that this take can be understood as meaning "Chinese traditional potency drinks for men and female sanitary napkins from the U.S." (p. 156). The fourth and fifth takes emerge somewhat from the third take and can respectively be understood as "'caress/foreplay and United Statesian sanitary napkins/feel great/make people self-at-ease' and 'traditional Chinese potency drinks for men feel great/make people self-at-ease'" (p. 157).

In her third and final awakening, Lee critiques the intersectional omissions of queer theory before ultimately describing and advancing kuaer theory. Lee cites Barbara Smith, Vera Miao, and E. Patrick Johnson to illustrate the ways in which queer theory often reproduces hierarchies of power in relation to race, gender, and socioeconomic class while attempting to dismantle hierarchies of sexuality. Like the scholars she cites, Lee notes that these hierarchies are inseparable. Lee explains what she means by describing kuaer theory as "transnational womanist quare studies" (p. 161). She states:

> My rearticulation is "womanist" because I insist on noting gendered and racialized women of color who have taught me many important lessons. My rearticulation is

"quare" because, like Johnson, I can no longer stomach the naturalized presence of homophobia in heteronormative communities or whiteness in queer communities. Finally, my rearticulation is also "transnational" because I live in an increasingly globalized world that is desperately in need of critical praxis. (p. 161)

Like *Ai Fu Hao Zi Zai Bao*, the term *kuaer* itself is an example of wordplay. Lee explains that kuaer is a combination of *kua*, which means crossing, praised, and proud or boastful, and *er*, which means child or children and is a diminutive that has a similar effect as adding a *y* to the end of a person's name in English. Therefore, kuaer refers to children who cross horizons, children who are praised, children who are proud or boastful, or children who cross worlds and embody womanist and quare politics. Kuaer theory responds to E. Patrick Johnson's quare studies and applies quare ideas to transnational contexts, exploring the specific ways in which the lived experiences of individuals relate to and are shaped by power at the global level. Kuaer theory also specifically calls for analyzing sexualities and queerness outside of the United States while also avoiding doing so through Eurocentric and Anglocentric lenses. Furthermore, kuaer theory criticizes popular queer theory for advancing imperialism through theory, arguing that queer theorists must be more attentive to the ways in which their theorizing reflects and reproduces cultural hierarchies at the global level. As Lee puts it, "I resist the technologies of global domination on the Third World, wittingly or unwittingly exercised by First World *identity academicians*" (p. 161). Finally, kuaer theory highlights the individuals and subjectivities that are often absent from queer scholarship and communication research more generally, interrogating the ways in which this absence relates to power at global and local levels, socioeconomic class, and education.

THE ENDURING INFLUENCE OF KUAER THEORY

In the time since Lee first advanced kuaer theory in 2003, it has continued to be an influential concept in several disciplines and different strands of queer scholarship. It is an important development in womanist theorizing and was reprinted in *The Womanist Reader* in 2006. Lee's use of autocritography in her discussion of kuaer theory has inspired queer scholarship that uses similar autoethnographic methods (e.g., Asante, 2015; Holman Jones & Adams, 2010; Johnson, 2014). Additionally, kuaer theory significantly informs contemporary queer of color critique and similar fields of queer scholarship that continue to push queer theory to be more intersectional, diverse, inclusive, equitable, and anti-normative. In an article advocating for greater intersectional inclusivity in queer theoretical spaces as well as calling more generally for expanding what is understood to "count" as queer in the first place, Amber Johnson (2018) finds clear influence in the inclusivity that kuaer theory advocates for. Similarly, LeMaster (2014) references kuaer theory when calling for queer theory to be more attentive to race and the diversity of queer embodiment. In an article calling for further attention to be paid to queer diasporas, Parker (2011) cites kuaer theory in relation to her exploration of the subjectivities of diasporic queer Jewish women. Additionally, Panfil (2020) cites kuaer theory in an article involving interviews with young LGBTQ people of color about their engagement with the term *queer*. Here, Panfil notes that both quare studies and kuaer theory "seek not just to address omissions in queer theory, but also to draw out specific examples of queer (or quare or kuaer) ways of knowing that exist within communities of color" (p. 1717).

Because of kuaer theory's transnational focus (Coffey, 2014), its emphasis on non-Western queer ontologies and epistemologies, and its emphasis on critiquing Eurocentrism, Anglocentrism, and imperialism, it has also been influential in the fields of critical intercultural communication and the emerging field of queer intercultural communication (e.g., Eguchi & Calafell, 2020; Huang, 2023). In her introduction to the 2014 transnational feminism special issue of the scholarly journal *Wagadu*, Kathryn Coffey cites kuaer theory along with quare studies as being rare examples of inclusive queer theorizing that "speak to the critiques of queer theory being by and about a homogenous population" (p. 3). Similarly, Eguchi (2015) cites Lee's (2003) article when critiquing the hegemony of affluent white gay normativity at the global level and its imperialistic influence on localized queer epistemologies and ontologies. Yep and Lescure (2014) employ kuaer theory as a theoretical framework for their critique of the global hegemony of the western closet metaphor and their exploration of the representation of racialized and gendered queer sexualities in Taiwan and U.S. cultural contexts in Ang Lee's film *The Wedding Banquet*. Finally, in their chapter offering guidance for queer intercultural communication scholars to engage with while conducting research, Yep et al. (2020) find substantial influence in kuaer theory's emphasis on centering local examples of queerness in the context of transnational power dynamics while also critiquing and destabilizing the hegemony of Eurocentric and Anglocentric frameworks for interpreting sexualities.

FURTHER READING

Johnson, E. P. (2001). "Quare" studies, or (almost) everything I know about queer studies I learned from my grandmother. *Text and Performance Quarterly, 21*(1), 1–25. https://doi.org/10.1080/10462930128119

LeMaster, B. (2014). Telling multiracial tales: An autoethnography of coming out home. *Qualitative Inquiry, 20*(1), 51–60. https://doi.org/10.1177/1077800413508532

Lorde, A. (1983). There is no hierarchy of oppressions. *Interracial Books for Children Bulletin: Homophobia and Education, 14*(3/4), 9.

Yep, G. A. (2013). Queering/quaring/kauering/crippin'/transing "other bodies" in intercultural communication. *Journal of International and Intercultural Communication, 6*(2), 118–126. https://doi.org/10.1080/17513057.2013.777087

Yep, G. A., & Lescure, R. (2014). Kuaering "home" in Ang Lee's *The Wedding Banquet*. In E. Patton & M. Choi (Eds.), *Home sweat home: Perspectives on housework and modern relationships* (pp. 167–182). Rowman & Littlefield.

REFERENCES

Amin, K. (2016). Haunted by the 1990s: Queer theory's affective histories. *WSQ: Women's Studies Quarterly, 43*(3/4), 173–189.

Asante, G. A. (2015). (De)stabilizing the normative: Using critical autoethnography as intersectional praxis to (re)conceptualize identity performances of Black queer immigrants. *Kaleidoscope: A Graduate Journal of Qualitative Communication Research, 14*, 83–88.

Awkward, M. (1999). *Scenes of instruction: A memoir*. Duke University Press.

Barker, M., & Scheele, J. (2016). *Queer: A graphic history*. Icon Books.

Chen, D. Y. (1994). *Zhongguo funu shenghuo shi* [A history of the lives of Chinese women]. Chinese Commercial Press. (Original work published 1928)

Coffey, K. (2014). Queering borders: Transnational feminist perspective on global heterosexism. *Wagadu: A Journal of Transnational Women's and Gender Studies, 12*, 1–14.

de Certeau, M. (2011). *The practice of everyday life* (3rd ed., S. Rendell, Trans.). University of California Press. (Original work published 1980).

de Lauretis, T. (1991). Queer theory: Lesbian and gay sexualities, an introduction. *differences, 3*(2), iii–xviii.

Eguchi, S. (2015). Queer intercultural relationality: An autoethnography of Asian-Black (dis)connections in white gay America. *Journal of International and Intercultural Communication, 8*(1), 27–43. https://doi.org/10.1080/17513057.2015.991077

Eguchi, S., & Calafell, B. M. (2020). Introduction: Reorienting queer intercultural communication. In S. Eguchi & B. M. Calafell (Eds.), *Queer intercultural communication: The intersectional politics of belonging in and across differences* (pp. 1–18). Rowman & Littlefield.

Hall, S. (1980). Encoding/decoding. In S. Hall, D. Hobson, A. Love, & P. Willis (Eds.), *Culture, media, language* (pp. 128–138). Hutchinson.

Hebdige, D. (1979). *Subculture: The meaning of style*. Routledge.

Holman Jones, S., & Adams, T. E. (2010). Autoethnography and queer theory: Making possibilities. In N. K. Denzin & M. D. Giardina (Eds.), *Qualitative inquiry and human rights* (pp. 136–157). Routledge. https://doi.org/10.4324/9781315421575

Huang, S. (2023). Reclaiming family, reimagining queer relationality. *Journal of Homosexuality, 70*(1), 17–34. https://doi.org/10.1080/00918369.2022.2106466

Johnson, A. (2014). Confessions of a video vixen: My autocritography of sexuality, desire, and memory. *Text and Performance Quarterly, 34*(2), 182–200. https://doi.org/10.1080/10462937.2013.879991

Johnson, A. (2018). Quare/kuaer/queer/(e)ntersectionality. *CrossCurrents, 68*(4), 500–541. https://doi.org/10.1111/cros.12338

Johnson, E. P. (2001). "Quare" studies, or (almost) everything I know about queer studies I learned from my grandmother. *Text and Performance Quarterly, 21*(1), 1–25. https://doi.org/10.1080/10462930128119

Lee, W. (2003). Kuaering queer theory: My autocritography and a race-conscious, womanist, transnational turn. *Journal of Homosexuality, 45*(2–4), 147–170. https://doi.org/10.1300/J082v45n02_07

LeMaster, B. (2014). Telling multiracial tales: An autoethnography of coming out home. *Qualitative Inquiry, 20*(1), 51–60. https://doi.org/10.1177/1077800413508532

Muñoz, J. E. (1996). Ephemera as evidence: Introductory notes to queer acts. *Women & Performance: A Journal of Feminist Theory, 8*(2), 5–16.

Panfil, V. R. (2020). "Nobody don't really know what that mean": Understandings of "queer" among urban LGBTQ young people of color. *Journal of Homosexuality, 67*(12), 1713–1735. https://doi.org/10.1080/00918369.2019.1613855

Parker, R. (2011). Introduction: Queer, there, and everywhere. *Textual Practice, 25*(4), 639–647. https://doi.org/10.1080/0950236X.2011.586773

Philips, L. (Ed.). (2006). *The womanist reader: The first quarter century of womanist thought*. Routledge. https://doi.org/10.4324/9780203943670

Topley, M. (1975). Marriage resistance in rural Kwangtung. In M. Wolf & R. Witke (Eds.), *Women in Chinese society* (pp. 111–142). Stanford University Press.

Walker, A. (1983). *In search of our mothers' gardens: Womanist prose*. Harcourt Brace Jovanovich.

West, I. (2018, February 26). Queer perspectives in communication studies. *Oxford Research Encyclopedia of Communication*. https://doi.org/10.1093/acrefore/9780190228613.013.81

Yep, G. A. (2013). Queering/quaring/kauering/crippin'/transing "other bodies" in intercultural communication. *Journal of International and Intercultural Communication, 6*(2), 118–126. https://doi.org/10.1080/17513057.2013.777087

Yep, G. A., Alaoui, F. Z. C., & Lescure, R. M. (2020). Relationalities in/through difference: Explorations in queer intercultural communication. In S. Eguchi & B. M. Calafell (Eds.), *Queer intercultural communication: The intersectional politics of belonging in and across differences* (pp. 19–46). Rowman & Littlefield.

Yep, G. A., & Lescure, R. (2014). Kuaering "home" in Ang Lee's *The Wedding Banquet*. In E. Patton & M. Choi (Eds.), *Home sweat home: Perspectives on housework and modern relationships* (pp. 167–182). Rowman & Littlefield.

Yep, G. A., Lovaas, K. E., & Elia, J. P. (2003). Introduction: Queering communication: Starting the conversation. In G. A. Yep, K. E. Lovaas, & J. P. Elia (Eds.), *Queer theory and communication: From disciplining queers to queering the discipline(s)* (pp. 1–60). Harrington Park Press. https://doi.org/10.4324/9781315864075

Yep, G. A., Olzman, M., & Conkle, A. (2012). Seven stories from the "It Gets Better" Project: Progress narratives, politics of affect, and the question of queer world-making. In R. A. Lind (Ed.), *Produsing theory in a digital world: The intersection of audiences and production in contemporary theory* (3rd ed., pp. 120–141). Peter Lang. https://doi.org/10.3726/b13192

Ryan M. Lescure

LGBTQ+ WORKERS

INTRODUCTION

Communication studies and affiliated disciplines investigate the lived experiences of LGBTQ+ workers.[1] As Compton (2016) has theorized, "Managing sexual identities is inherently a communicative process" (p. 416), and this article connects extensive research on communicating sexuality, gender identity, and intersectionality at work. It reviews how communication at and about work impacts identification, socialization, relationships, work-life, organizing, and health for LGBTQ+ workers. Organizations are structured on discrimination and normativity often invisible to cisgender and/or heterosexual people. This article surfaces, critiques, and resists heteronormativity, transphobia, and cissexism in organizations and their intersections with racism, ableism, colonialism, and capitalism.

McKenna-Buchanan and Baker (2016) defined heteronormativity at work as "organizations' structures and processes [that] uphold heterosexuality as the norm, the presumed sexual orientation of their workers" (p. 309). Heteronormativity impacts organizational communication, culture, and structure. Workers who attempt to surface heteronormativity may be met with silence and dismissal, especially if coworkers and supervisors' own communication is called into question. Calafell (2017) explained such silencing within academia as follows: "My critique of heteronormativity causes discomfort. Perhaps it hits too close to home? I sit in the silence as we move on quickly to the next agenda item" (p. 6). Heteronormativity is rendered invisible to those not experiencing its material impacts. It is "engrained" with an "overwhelming presence [that] is frequently interpreted as absence" (Fox, 2013, p. 59).

We use LeMaster's (2017) definition of cissexism as "the systemic privileging of cisgender and cissexual— nontrans—bodies, identities, and subjectivities" (p. 129). Cissexism also structures transphobia, where violence is enacted on trans and nonbinary people. While some organizational members are learning to challenge heteronormativity, transphobia "can still be a matter of practice" (McKenna-Buchanan & Baker, 2016, p. 315). The violence of the gender binary is perpetuated in organizations that institutionalize cissexism. For example, organizations enforce "the male/female binary includ[ing] gendered restrooms, he/she pronoun usage on forms and paperwork, and the usage of legal name on office documentation such as e-mail addresses and nametags" (Resnick & Galupo, 2019, p. 1383).

Cissexism and heteronormativity coalesce together. Because of these inseparable entanglements, scholars employ the term cisheteronormativity to communicate their interconnections (see LeMaster, 2017), how they are shaped by difference (i.e., race, class, size), and the potential of the "processual unlearning of cisheteronormativity across time and space in our relational context" (LeMaster et al., 2019, p. 2).

This article investigates the structures and cultures of cisheteronormativity at work, its constraints, and resistance to its violence. It examines LGBTQ+ workers' organizational communication and experiences by reviewing five central areas of literature: (1) workplace discrimination, (2) disclosure at work, (3) navigating interpersonal relationships at work, (4) inclusive and exclusive policies, and (5) intersectional work experiences and organizing. It ends with envisioning futures for queer, trans, and intersex workers and recommends future communication studies scholarship.

WORKPLACE DISCRIMINATION

In the United States, "[w]orkplace discrimination against lesbian, gay, bisexual, and trans (LGBT) employees is commonplace" (Resnick & Galupo, 2019, p. 1380). Communication studies and related fields examine discrimination that LGBTQ+ workers face in their organizational communication. In a review of the literature, four themes emerged: (1) microaggressions, (2) worker protection laws, (3) material consequences, and (4) actions for change.

Microaggressions. There is robust interdisciplinary inquiry into microaggressions, largely in psychology and education, which predominantly focuses on racial microaggressions. Yep and Lescure (2019) reviewed microaggression research historically and in communication studies, and they proposed intersectional microaggression analyses. Interdisciplinary scholarship further examines microaggressions that LGBTQ+ people encounter at work (Galupo & Resnick, 2016; McKenna-Buchanan & Baker, 2016; Resnik & Galupo, 2019).

Galupo and Resnick (2016) theorized three forms of LGBTQ+ workplace microaggressions, including "microassaults, microinsults, and microinvalidations" (p. 272) following Sue et al.'s (2007) classification of microaggressions. Galupo and Resnick situated microassaults as "most closely aligned with 'traditional' forms of heterosexism. Referring to a colleague as a 'fag,' 'dyke,' or 'tranny' are examples of microassaults" (p. 272). Microinsults would be "communications that convey rudeness or insensitivity and demean a person's identity" (p. 272), like a supervisor continuing to dismiss their queer employees' ideas. Microinvalidations "negate or nullify the psychological thoughts, feelings, or experiential reality of the marginalized group" (p. 272), such as saying "You don't sound gay" to a coworker.

Galupo and Resnick (2016) identified these three forms of microaggressions with 100 LGBTQ+ participants through open-ended questionnaires. Their participants revealed three common organizational challenges: workplace climate, organizational structure, and workplace policy (Galupo & Resnick, 2016, p. 277). For workplace climate, participants reported communication such as purposeful misgendering, exclusion, and feeling unsafe to be out at work. Workers that were out also faced microaggressions directed at them specifically, such as one social service worker with almost an entirely queer staff serving LGBTQ+ people where others called them "the fag group" (p. 279). Similarly, employees experienced isolation and being called "gross" when coworkers found out about their queer relationships (p. 279). Here, microaggressions shaped organizational culture and communication whether or not workers shared their LGBTQ+ identities at work.

Second, Galupo and Resnick's (2016) participants focused on organizational structure that "reflected the power dynamic inherent to the employees' position... [and was] often experienced within an employee-supervisor or employee-client relationship" (pp. 279–280). For example, when an educator served on an LGBT commission for their university, their chancellor would say "you people" when describing queer and trans employees. When the employee complained to their diversity vice-chancellor, they suggested "we just be more understanding of the chancellor's age and background as a wealthy white heterosexual male" (Galupo & Resnick, 2016, p. 280). This example illustrated how LGBTQ+ workers are expected to cater and submit to those emboldened by white, upper-class heteronormativity, especially in queer, trans, and intersex service roles that can be tokenizing.

Third, Galupo and Resnick (2016) identified workplace policies as a central space where microaggressions are communicated. Importantly policy absence also enabled LGBTQ+ microaggressions (Galupo & Resnick, 2016, p. 281). Stories from these participants included binary-gendered dress codes, disclosing trans surgery history in violation of HIPAA in front of coworkers, and domestic partnerships from another state not being recognized by their employer. One participant critiqued the structural barriers of name changes; when they took their required documentation to IT to change their email, the cisgender IT worker "told me that he wouldn't be allowed to change his name to Batman (a fictional cartoon character), so I shouldn't expect him to change my legal name to my real name" (p. 282). Here, even when policies were in place, other employees communicated microaggressions and violated inclusive policies (see also Patterson and Hsu's [2020] discussion of digital personhood). Even with so-called inclusive policies, LGBTQ+ people risk workplace discrimination, especially when microaggressions "may not be covered under conventional non-discrimination policies" (Galupo & Resnick, 2016, p. 273). Policies will be examined in more depth below in the section "Inclusive and Exclusive Policies."

In communication studies, McKenna-Buchanan and Baker (2016) theorized "how four LGB/TQ-based microaggressions (endorsement, heterosexism, exoticization, and denial) are communicated in the workplace" (p. 307) using vignettes. First, they identified endorsement when employees conformed to cisgender normativity for their own safety (p. 308). Because of past cissexist violence, trans and nonbinary people may use endorsement to try to stay safer at work. Second, heterosexism occurred when people use language that demeans LGBTQ+ workers' experiences. In this vignette, co-workers discussed the use of homophobic language on their softball team including "sissy," "that's so gay," and "no homo" (p. 310). McKenna-Buchanan and Baker addressed how such language was dismissed as "unintentional." Yet:

> Even if it is not intended, heterosexist language still communicates the message that "heterosexuality is normal" and that it is okay to talk negatively about LGB/TQ

sexualities. Heterosexist language is a difficult microaggression to combat because sexual orientation/identity is not always readily apparent, it is (in)visible. (p. 311)

The third microaggression was exoticization, and the vignette introduced a supervisor dismissing an employee's bisexuality, sexualizing her by taking her to a strip club, and calling bisexuality "a phase." Fourth, McKenna-Buchanan and Baker presented denial where employees' identities were silenced or ignored in practices and policies. The vignette focused on a narrative of a trans man who was pregnant and how the company had "inclusive" policies about sexuality but nothing about gender identity to support the man's experiences. Because of this, he experienced "a *denial* of both societal and individual transphobia…gender identity is absent from the conversation. This denial communicates transphobia through the absence of recognition" (McKenna-Buchanan & Baker, 2016, p. 315).

While the literature labels such communication as microaggressions, Calafell argued that queer people of color face them as, "Micro attacks. Macro assaults" (2017, p. 6). Similarly, Yep and Lescure's (2019) thick intersectional (TI) microaggression communication theory connects the micro and macro. They explained the importance of TI to "confront relations of power in a culture. Microaggressions not only create and maintain social inequalities but such inequalities continue to fuel microaggressions in a seemingly endless feedback loop" (p. 122). As researchers study microaggressions, they should address how communication framed as "micro" has continuous, systemic violent impacts on queer, trans, and intersex workers, especially workers experiencing attacks from intersections of race, ethnicity, disability, class, and more. Treating any microaggressions as only focused on one category of identity misses overlapping discrimination (Yep & Lescure, 2019). Yep and Lescure (2019) also cautioned researchers from creating a new violence of the "homogenization of identities and symbolic erasure of individual experiences—while attempting to understand and mitigate their effects" (pp. 115–116). In other words, essentializing and grouping shared identity experiences can create new violence. Like everyday microaggressions, workplace discrimination is also structured through worker protection laws and their inconsistent enactment.

Worker Protection Laws. Complicated state and federal worker protection laws continue to permit discrimination and violence against LGBTQ+ workers. While some states offer protections around sexual orientation and/or gender identity, many allow for the firing of and discrimination against queer, trans, and intersex workers. When no policy exists at state or organizational levels, "the choice to report discrimination to a supervisor or to Human Resources becomes a difficult and uncertain one. The organization could dismiss the claims entirely or they could choose to fire the employee because of the conflict the employee's claims articulated, both of which would be legal" (Resnick & Galupo, 2019, p. 1382).

The role of federal protections continues to be precarious and at the whim of politics and new rulings, elections, and administrators. Resnick and Galupo (2019) reviewed the U.S. Equal Employment Opportunity Commission (EEOC) ruling during Obama's administration for the illegality of sexual orientation discrimination. Then, Trump reversed this ruling where:

In addition to placing LGBT employees in a vulnerable position within the workplace, the message from the [Trump] administration is one that implies that LGBT people do not deserve the same protections as other Americans and are valued less than heterosexual and cisgender employees. (p. 1382)

Since the publication of Resnick and Galupo's (2019) essay, two primary national impacts on employee protections were *reversed again* with a Supreme Court ruling and President Biden's executive order. On June 15, 2020, the Supreme Court announced their ruling on *R.G. & G.R. Harris Funeral Homes Inc. v. Equal Employment Opportunity Commission* to protect transgender and queer employees from discriminatory firing. The plaintiff, Aimee Stephens, was fired from R.G. & G.R. Harris Funeral Homes after disclosing she was a transgender woman (ACLU, 2020). "In March of 2018, the Sixth Circuit Court of Appeals ruled that Aimee was unlawfully fired and that federal sex discrimination laws protect transgender people" (ACLU, 2020). Tragically, Aimee died before her case was won from kidney failure after losing her health insurance. Firing workers for their LGBTQ+ identities was deemed unlawful with the Supreme Court ruling.

Additionally, in an executive order signed the first day of his presidency, Biden reversed Trump's reversal of the EEOC ruling under Obama's inclusion of sexuality and gender identity in workplace protections. Biden's order (Exec. Order No. 13988, 2021) stated, "Adults should be able to earn a living and pursue a vocation knowing that they will not be fired, demoted, or mistreated because of whom they go home to or because how they dress does not conform to sex-based stereotypes." His executive order also addressed intersections of discrimination that LGBTQ+ people face, including a specific section on violence against Black transgender people. The order pledged:

> It is the policy of my Administration to prevent and combat discrimination on the basis of gender identity or sexual orientation, and to fully enforce Title VII and other laws that prohibit discrimination on the basis of gender identity or sexual orientation. It is also the policy of my Administration to address overlapping forms of discrimination.

How the Supreme Court ruling and the Biden executive order will be enforced in practice—especially in states, regions, and organizations that are writing bills to attack queer, trans, and intersex people—remains to be seen and is an important need area for scholarship and activism. Protections for LGBTQ+ workers remain precarious and at the whim of politicians' decision-making, organizational practices, and societal injustice. Reports such as the Movement Advancement Project and peer organizations' *A Broken Bargain for LGBT Workers of Color* (2013) (hereafter *A Broken Bargain*) presented recommendations for federal and state policy, especially for LGBTQ+ workers of color and immigrant workers (A further discussion is provided in section "Material Consequences").

Additionally, utilizing workplace discrimination laws creates enormous burdens on LGBTQ+ people to prove discrimination for organizations and courts alike, which is costly and assumes educational, class, and citizenship privilege to navigate legal proceedings. This is complicated by unequal understandings of workplace discrimination when it is enacted in organizations, creating departing narratives of "what happened." For example, new research from the Williams Institute illustrates how cisgender and heterosexual employees perceive LGBTQ+ discrimination differently than LGBTQ+ employees across public and private sectors (Sears et al., 2021). Sears et al. (2021) surveyed over 2200 people across states and sectors in 2019 and found that "LGBT employees (53%) are twice as likely to feel that LGBTQ people are treated worse across the nation than non-LGBT employees (23%)" (p. 2). This is despite the fact that more than "45% of all employees (both LGBT and non-LGBT) report hearing anti-LGBT remarks in the workplace across employer types" (p. 2). Religious institutions can also buttress dangerous rhetoric, as "27.3% of Americans believe that employers should have the right to fire an LGBTQ employee based on a religious objection" (Sears et al., 2021, p. 8). Such laws, difficulties tracking and proving injustice, and uncertain legal futures are just one piece of the material impacts LGBTQ+ workers face.

Material Consequences. LGBTQ+ workers face employment discrimination and violence from job searching to hiring to promotion to exit. This results in material consequences impacting people's lives including unemployment, underemployment, discrimination, firing, violence, housing, and healthcare. Trans and nonbinary workers face disparate material consequences of discrimination (Eger, 2018; James et al., 2016; LeMaster, 2015).

McFadden and Crowley-Henry (2016) reviewed 30 articles on literature about trans people's organizational experiences in Western countries (25 in the United States) across the work timeline. They identified challenges of job searching for transgender workers to "fully show their experience and skills built up during their career, a person may have to disclose their trans* status to the potential employer, running the risk of discrimination and stigma, and ruling out the possibility of a completely fresh start in their new gender expression" (McFadden & Crowley-Henry, 2016, pp. 14–15). Eger (2018) examined job-seeking communication of trans and nonbinary workers in the southwestern United States. Participant "Brooks (a White transman in his 40s) explained, 'We see people look for jobs for 3–4 years, and they tell us that they've seen people throw out their application when they leave because they are trans people of color'" (p. 278). Similarly, LeMaster wrote about their partner (a transgender woman's) job application process with zero interview call backs:

(1) Approach the counter
(2) Ask for a manager
(3) Submit job application to the manager
(4) Exude confidence as the manager and employees giggle and point
(5) Perform poise as the manager:
   a) Throws the application, and your labor, away
   b) Tears the job application up, and/or
   c) Claims to file the application in a filing cabinet (that doesn't exist)
   d) Repeat. (2015, p. 85)

Unemployment and underemployment becomes normative for many trans and nonbinary workers facing immediate transphobia and violent erasure in hiring.

The most comprehensive research on trans, Two-Spirit, nonbinary, and gender nonconforming workers comes from the National Center for Transgender Equity's U.S. Transgender Survey (USTS), a nationally representative survey of over 27,000 respondents (James et al., 2016). The USTS documents immense intersectional injustice against trans and nonbinary workers, especially workers of color, workers with disabilities, and immigrant workers. The unemployment rate for USTS respondents was:

15%, three times the U.S. unemployment rate at the time of the survey (5%). Nearly one-half (49%) of undocumented residents were unemployed. The unemployment rate was also higher among people with disabilities (24%) and people of color, with Middle Eastern (35%), American Indian (23%), multiracial (22%), Latino/a (21%), and Black (20%) respondents being more likely to be unemployed. (James et al., 2016, p. 147)

In addition to disproportionately high unemployment, trans and nonbinary (sometimes referred to as enby) workers experienced firing, discrimination, and violence when employed. "One in six (16%) respondents who have been employed reported that they had lost a job because of their gender identity or expression" (James et al., 2016, p. 149). This was complicated by race and other intersections, as "American Indian (21%), multiracial (18%), and Black (17%) respondents were more likely than the overall sample to have lost a job because of their gender identity or expression" (p. 150).

Additionally, 30% of participants reported mistreatment, discrimination, and violence at work in the last year (p. 148), including 15% experiencing verbal, physical, or sexual assault at work due to "gender identity or expression" (p. 148). Because of this incredible violence, "more than three-quarters (77%) of respondents who had a job in the past year took steps to avoid mistreatment in the workplace, such as hiding or delaying their gender transition or quitting their job" (James et al., 2016, p. 148). Systemic unemployment, underemployment, and discrimination compounds for trans and nonbinary people impacting their access to safe housing, healthcare, and other social services tied to employment.

Relatedly, *A Broken Bargain* (Movement Advancement Project et al., 2013) presented the overlapping systemic barriers that United States LGBTQ+ workers of color face. The report identified core problems of: (1) educational barriers, (2) hiring bias and on-the-job discrimination, and (3) unequal pay, benefits, and taxation (p. 7). They reviewed extensive literature and public reports across national studies and surveys. They combined multiple studies that showed "between 75–82% of API LGBT people said they had been discriminated against at work because of their sexual orientation. Surveys of Black LGBT people put rates of employment discrimination closer to 50%" (p. 29; see *A Broken Bargain* references for more statistics). Such discrimination heightened poverty, especially as people of color in same-sex relationships experienced disproportionate poverty. For example, "Black men in same-sex couples are more than six times more likely to be poor than white men in same-sex couples (19% vs. 3%); and black women in same-sex couples are more than three times more likely to be poor than white women in same-sex couples (18% vs. 6%)" (p. 5).

A Broken Bargain also presented the experiences of undocumented LGBTQ+ people, many of whom are people of color. They explained:

Many undocumented workers have few options aside from minimum-wage jobs and jobs that do not provide any benefits. They may be afraid to speak up when they see or experience legal violations, such as unsafe working conditions or unfair wages, out of fear of being deported. (p. 37)

In summary, workers living at the intersections of undocumented, immigrant, queer, and trans identities encounter immense, material systemic violence.

Actions for Change. Because of the violence of microaggressions, legal complexities, and material consequences, scholars have recommended some actions for change to combat workplace discrimination. After examining LGBTQ+ microaggressions, McKenna-Buchanan and Baker (2016) offered four practices to enact immediate change, which can be linked to other researchers' practical recommendations. First, because of cisheteronormativity and cissexism at work, organizations need to rethink the roles and purposes of dress codes. As Resnick and Galupo (2019) explained, "adhering to a formal or informal dress code according to assigned sex is an example of behavior that is supported by the dominant group and endorses cisnormative behavior" (p. 1382). McKenna-Buchanan and Baker suggest that both leaders and human resource (HR) professionals should open dress codes to "give employees space to dress in the ways that are most comfortable to them" (2016, p. 316). The openness of dress codes should be written in policy, enacted in practice, and supported in casual conversations from supervisors and mentors. They recommended that employees "look at the current dress code and create recommendations for how it can be amended to create a more affirming and comfortable workplace. Gather the support of your peers (e.g., petition, survey, etc.) and present your recommendations to the leadership" (McKenna-Buchanan & Baker, 2016, p. 316).

In addition to occupations with specific dress codes, many occupations use binary norms of "professionalism" and "professional dress" to limit queer, trans, and nonbinary workers' dress and embodiment. This shows up in "dress for success" discourses where Leslie (2020) argued, "the weight of it falls most heavily on bodies deemed by race, size, gender, and gender expression to be Other" (2020, p. 133). Similarly, Patterson and Hsu's (2020) exemplars visualized how nonbinary workers are disciplined through professionalism in job-seeking and at work. They suggested using "undressing" as heuristic to strip "away the language of decorum and respectability in which discriminatory patterns are often enshrouded" (Patterson & Hsu, 2020, pp. 108–109). Thus, in addition to specific dress code changes, disrupting professionalism communication and professional dress norms is integral for LGBTQ+ people to experience comfort in their bodies at work.

Returning to McKenna-Buchanan and Baker (2016), their second recommendation is to create awareness and corrections for "heterosexist and transphobic terminology" in microaggressions, which included avoiding derogatory language like "that's so gay" and also using inclusive language like "partner" when referring to all romantic relationships or using "they" pronouns. Implementing language changes and training on inclusive communication can therefore disrupt cisheteronormative microaggressions. Their third recommendation is to avoid asking "prying questions" of LGBTQ+ workers (p. 316) and avoiding assuming someone's sexuality. As an example, bisexual, pansexual, aromantic, asexual, or queer employees may be presumed heterosexual because of their current romantic or sexual relationship(s) and/or not being in relationship(s). Thus, avoiding assumptions and invasive questioning are integral communication practices for preventing workplace discrimination. Fourth, McKenna-Buchanan and Baker remind us we cannot deny structures of exclusion, as:

> We live in a society that privileges heterosexuality and cisgender identities. It is up to us to be aware of these structures and, through our communicative actions, seek to tear down these divisions and create the policies and practices that provide space for diverse sexualities and genders in the workplace and in society. (2016, p. 317)

Therefore, even in organizations that attempt to avoid LGBTQ+ discrimination in their structures and cultures, there is always work to do to sustain inclusion.

Other research identified further best practices of honoring personal pasts and privacy (McFadden & Crowley-Henry, 2016) and gathering data for change (Resnick & Galupo, 2019). For trans and nonbinary workers, HR professionals play an important role in recognizing workers' personal pasts and protecting them from disclosure if they do not choose to communicate about their gender identity at work. McFadden and Crowley-Henry (2016) called for HR professionals to understand how trans workers' resumes and references may use former names, and for them to use gender affirming dialogue with trans workers. For example, in checking references, HR professionals should ask "the candidate if their referees know them by a different name, in case they inadvertently 'out' them, harming interpersonal relations and the candidate's career capital" (p. 20).

Moreover, to combat workplace discrimination, organizations should gather data to understand LGBTQ+ workers' experiences. While organizations may claim to be inclusive, workers' *actual* experiences must be collected and understood. Resnick and Galupo (2019) created scales to measure three common microaggressions against LGBTQ+ workers: (1) workplace values (or how the culture impacted their experiences), (2) heteronormative assumptions (such as asking workers to speak on behalf of all queer or trans people), and (3) cisnormative culture (Resnick & Galupo, 2019, pp. 1394–1395). They argue that "assessing microaggressions will allow employers to develop targeted trainings and interventions to increase productivity and job satisfaction in relation to workplace values, heteronormative assumptions, and cisnormative culture" (p. 1397). Taking time to gather employees' experiences, is only a first step toward increasing inclusion. Organizations should then implement regular microaggressions trainings, like sexual harassment trainings. They also encourage missions, values, and visions that include "pluralistic, trans, and genderfluid identities" (p. 1397) and everyone using pronouns in emails and on nametags (p. 1398). Given the extensive experiences of workplace discrimination, this creates communication challenges for workers considering disclosing sexuality and/or gender identities at work.

DISCLOSURE AT WORK

Communication studies researchers address the complexities of workplace disclosure of LGBTQ+ identities, including through closeting, passing, and outing communication. Workplace identity disclosures are challenging and uncertain to navigate. Compton and Dougherty (2017) showcased how sexuality norms and normativity impact being silenced or silencing oneself as organizational communication processes (p. 890). As scholars theorize communication disclosure at work, they must be careful to avoid blaming individuals for how or if they communicate their identities but instead critique "systems and institutions that performatively discipline all bodies, identities, and subjectivities to acquiesce to normative formations" (LeMaster, 2017, p. 129). Thus, LGBTQ+ workers engage in potential disclosure(s) that inform others of their sexuality and gender identities via communication through: (1) closeting, (2) passing, (3) outing, and (4) navigating disclosure complexities at work.

Closeting. Queer and trans research uses the closet metaphor to communicate about concealing LGBTQ+ identities, thus avoiding identity disclosure. This metaphor visualizes the process of workers navigating safety from potential physical violence, discrimination, and/or stigma associated with communicating their queer, trans, and intersex identities, experiences, and politics. Closeting is sometimes seen by organizational members as intentionally deceptive and negative, potentially originating from the Western phrase of shameful or embarrassing "skeletons in the closet" and connecting back to historical events of gay rights organizing using such phrases (Cox, 2019). The closet has been expanded as a metaphor to examine other intersections of difference and disclosure in organizational communication (Dixon, 2018; Eger, 2018; Ferguson, 2018; Harris & McDonald, 2018; McDonald et al., 2020).

Cox theorizes a "working closet" to understand LGBTQ+ workers' closeting communication. Working closets function when workers "either by choice or by situational exigency, conceal or volunteer (even partially) their sexual orientation, thereby remaining disjointed and fractured in their identities... [W]orking closets enable LGBT professionals to negotiate, challenge, and disrupt dominant discourses" (Cox, 2019, p. 4). Their fragmentation ties to working closets as articulations because "closets might be needed one moment and not be needed (in nearly identical situations) later" (Cox, 2019, p. 5). The closet at work is therefore theorized as complex and ongoing identity management rather than a one-time occurrence (see Dixon, 2013; Eger, 2018). Eger frames closeting communication at work as "an ongoing communication process where individuals continuously navigate potential disclosures of their identities" (2018, p. 276). Closeting for LGBTQ+ workers, then, is always ongoing and navigated differently in new relationships, organizations, and conversations.

Closeting communication may also involve concealing information about personal and family relationships at work. In past organizational communication research, Hoffman and Cowan (2008) examined how work–life balance operates within corporate settings to privilege nuclear families. The authors concluded that a core theme heavily emphasized "life means family," and "work is the most important element of life" (Hoffman & Cowan, 2008, p. 233). The symbolic representation of a nuclear family at work is a key component for workers to connect and identify with others and work itself. Additionally, Dixon (2018) explained that employees navigate the recognizability of their family in their organizational cultures unfamiliar with families beyond "straight couple with children;" here closeting may be preferred to the processes where "one is not simply attempting to communicate family into being, but arguing that said family is just as worthy of regard as any more widely recognizable family structure" (p. 273). The lack of a visible family can exclude all single and nonnormative family dynamics, especially for those LGBTQ+ individuals that are not comprised of two heterosexual partners. Therefore, the closet is both a space and process for LGBTQ+ workers navigating their disclosure(s) and protecting themselves, which can require hyper-awareness and hyper-vigilance. Other workers may also pass as cisgender and/or heterosexual at work.

Passing. Passing is one of the earliest LGBTQ+ organizational communication practices researched in communication studies. Passing is best understood as "how one conceals *normal* information about oneself to preserve, sustain, and encourage others' predisposed assumptions about one's identity... [with] emphasis... [on] the word *normal*" (Spradlin, 1998, p. 598).

Spradlin's (1998) essay was also one of the first to examine lesbian workers' organizational communication. She emphasized how the labor of passing forces "suppression of normal exchanges of information … [and] is an oppressive task that requires constant and careful attention by self-monitoring conversations and behaviors" (pp. 598–599). Her analysis linked passing to United States institutional reinforcement of "don't ask, don't tell policies in civilian work environments" (Spradlin, 1998, p. 598). Spradlin presented six passing strategies: distancing (avoiding personal information routinely during informal everyday conversations), dodging (shifting and avoiding topics to prevent identity disclosure), dissociating (rejecting queer associations and attempting to present as heterosexual), distracting (using ambiguous messages that confuse the determination of sexual identity), denial (utilizing ambiguous lack of confirmation), and deceiving (intentionally presenting as heteronormative). Similar to closeting, passing can also be perceived as a deceptive tactic by others at work.

Internationally, Mitra and Doctor (2016) more recently examined passing in corporations through experiences of 14 gay men in India. They utilized a constant comparative approach that found distanciation (distancing oneself from work culture and socialization), concealment (performing within heteronormative expectations), reframing (emphasizing their other attributes that cannot be stigmatized to quiet questions about their queer sexuality), appropriating lesser stigmas (using other aspects of life to remove or minimize discussions of queerness and explain behavior), and partitioning (strategically communicating queer identity to certain groups) as passing strategies used by gay men in India.

Additionally, closeting and passing complicate the politics of visibility, questions who gets to be (or *wants* to be) visible at work, and the safety of that visibility. The ideas of closeting and passing are framed in whiteness and can erase experiences of some queer and trans people of color (QTPOC), such as Black men who have sex with men on the DL, or "down-low," who sustain public heterosexual relationships (McCune, 2014). While LGBTQ+ workers navigate closeting and passing, some choose to disclose their LGBTQ+ identities by "coming out" at work. Others face forced disclosure when another organizational member "outs" them.

Outing. Outing traditionally refers to the consensual or nonconsensual identity disclosure from oneself or others. Outing makes LGBTQ+ identities readily visible when workers are "out of the closet" when considering the working closet metaphor. Like closeting and passing, outing is navigated across organizational contexts, times, and relationships. Outing is never finished as a process for LGBTQ+ employees.

Coming out at work involves strategic organizational communication. McKenna-Buchanan et al. (2015) investigated how lesbian, gay, and queer teachers strategically navigated complex interworking between "cultural, gender, contextual, risk-benefit, and motivational criteria to decide whether to reveal or conceal their sexual orientation" (p. 294). Their research theorized coming out via communication privacy management theory. Furthermore, faculty may make decisions about being out in the classroom in relationship to students' perceptions. Boren and McPherson (2018) replicated a previous 2002 study where students perceived lower credibility and reported learning less from gay teachers. In contrast, Boren and McPherson's (2018) research conducted at a new location 15 years later no longer matched these original findings. Instead "students rated the gay instructor as higher in the credibility dimension of goodwill/caring than the straight instructor" (p. 247), and there were no cognitive or affective learning differences. The authors suggest these changes as likely connected to activism and legal protective rights for queer people within the United States, such as legalized gay marriage, especially as their study was based in a more progressive region. Thus, understanding the politics of being out in the classroom and LGBTQ+ teachers' strategic communication with students should be researched in the future across regions and institutional types and include other intersecting identities.

Furthermore, queer workers use delicate maneuvering when outing themselves (or not) with other organizational members. Cox (2019) presented code-switching as a tactic for managing how "the working closet exists in myriad moments, places, and situations" (p. 6). Through code-switching, LGBTQ+ workers can intentionally disclose or hide their identities with others. Additionally, Greene's (2009) disclosure-decision-making model theorized the intersection of disclosure and nondisclosure specifically regarding medical diagnoses typically associated with stigma. Greene's research points to how queer, trans, and intersex workers may contemplate disclosure or nondisclosure and the effects on personal relationships.

Finally, people may be out in some contexts but not others in their lives and work. For example, Capous-Desyllas and Loy's (2020) trans sex worker participants navigated if they were out about their trans identities in their sex work and also if they were out about their sex work in their personal lives. Outing can also include intentional disclosure from others about queer, trans, or intersex workers' identities without their consent. Such nonconsensual outing forcibly removes working closet protections. Thus, as Eger (2018) argued, "we need additional inquiry into closeting communication, consent, and outing" (p. 280). Consent is just one example of navigating disclosure complexities.

Navigating Disclosure Complexities. Overall, LGBTQ+ individuals experience diverse challenges with identity navigation at work amidst cisheteronormative organizational expectations. Researchers suggest that the strategies that workers utilize will alter depending on context and identity perceptions. For example, lesbians navigated their identities differently through passing strategies that typically led to negative organizational and individual impacts by their rejecting heteronormativity and suffering from patriarchal expectations (Spradlin, 1998). Horan and Chory (2013) showed that gay men involved in work relationships are seen as more competent and caring compared to their female counterparts. Despite this, gay men still must engage in identity management. By rejecting hegemonic masculinity by not dating women, gay men may be constructed by others at work to be effeminate, including by other gay men. Eguchi (2009) referred to this as sissyphobia, where gay men find "nonmasculine" men unattractive, in response to aiming to achieve ideal hegemonic masculinity and to shield their queer identities. Specifically, gay men were sometimes "not considered masculine enough because they break the boundary of heteronormativity-heterosexuality as normal. Thus, society pressures gay men to negotiate who they are according to hegemonic masculinity to compensate for their same-sex preference" (Eguchi, 2009, p. 194). Because of the ways hegemonic masculinity is rewarded in all institutions, gay, queer, bisexual, and trans men may face exclusion as they consider disclosing identities and for how they perform masculinity at work.

Bisexual individuals navigate their sexuality differently compared to lesbian and gay workers, despite sharing experiences of workplace discrimination. Some research showed lower rates of tolerance and stability perceived for bisexual workers compared to gay or lesbian workers (Arena & Jones, 2017). Arena and Jones (2017) identified bisexual identity disclosure as a unique process because "bisexual employees are less open about their sexual orientation at work and are less likely to disclose their sexual orientation at work as compared to gay or lesbian employees" (p. 94). They theorized that this difference occurred in response to potential bisexual stigma and/or discrimination. Additionally, job applicants who disclosed their bisexual identity were given lower entry salary rates compared to gay applicants (Arena & Jones, 2017). Bisexual women also faced unique challenges as they communicated nuanced and indirect identity disclosures (Helens-Hart, 2017).

Transgender and nonbinary workers encountered compounding oppressions with disclosure at work, especially trans and nonbinary people of color, trans sex workers, and those who were outed by others (Eger, 2018). As theorized with workplace discrimination above, many trans and nonbinary people choose to closet their trans identities at work for their safety (James et al., 2016). Stealth is a unique "transgender vernacular term sometimes used to signify not disclosing transition" (Eger, 2018, p. 277) that allows transgender workers to navigate the potential policies, practices, and communication that can target them. Like closeting, living stealth can include the possibility of nonconsensual outings by managers or coworkers. Eger's ethnographic research revealed how trans and nonbinary people:

> frequently processed job-seeking ambiguity and retrospectively questioned their closeting communication challenges, especially through possible "outing" of their identities without their consent, including potential employers reading their bodies and/or speech in interviews, background checks revealing former names, and having inconsistent gender markers on identification documents. (2018, p. 278)

Participants in Eger's research surfaced issues of consent when it came to closeting, passing, and outing, and how texts, work histories, and others outed jobseekers' gender identity without their knowledge or permission. Additionally, the USTS surveyed trans and nonbinary workers who concealed their genders to protect themselves from discrimination, especially across intersectional identities for respondents "who were living in poverty (82%), non-binary respondents (81%), and people with disabilities (81%) were more likely to take...steps to avoid discrimination" (James et al., 2016, p. 154), such as delaying gender transition and avoiding asking for their pronouns to be used.

Communication studies scholarship has rarely, and in some cases never, specifically researched queer, questioning, intersex, asexual, aromantic, demisexual, polyamorous, pansexual, Two-Spirit, and other identity disclosures at work. Further research is needed to examine both the breadth and depth of LGBTQ+ work disclosures. All LGBTQ+ workers have unique experiences not only within but also across their identities. Intersectionality impacts disclosure complexities, and one worker's disclosure communication is not a blanket experience for all queer, trans, or intersex workers.

Disclosure and privacy are complicated by how identities and experiences are compounding and inseparable for workers. For example, "transgender jobseekers' closeting communication involves multiple identities interacting" (Eger, 2018, p. 279), such as people sharing their trans identities at work but closeting their incarceration histories or homelessness. Closeting communication as theorized by Eger is transformed from a "container for simply concealing gender identity into an *intersectional* process where individuals navigate communication of their diverse, overlapping identities" (p. 280). Also, queer women may avoid coming out because of their "minority sexual identities" as both women and queer (Helens-Hart, 2017); thus, queer women utilized indirect messages and strategic ambiguity because of the intersections of their gender and sexuality. Research illustrates that workers with compounding experiences of marginalization face more risks with their identity (non)disclosure(s). Because closeting and disclosure are intersectional processes, workers' unique, overlapping experiences of privilege and oppression may shape their willingness to share themselves at work, including in workplace relationships.

NAVIGATING INTERPERSONAL RELATIONSHIPS AT WORK

Scholars examine how LGBTQ+ people negotiate workplace relationships, in particular with heterosexual and/or cisgender coworkers and managers and in organizations that assume cisheteronormativity. Looking at micro discourses and relationships among coworkers, supervisors, and workplace romantic relationships between employees is important because microaggressions are co-created through discourses that highlight homophobia and anti-queer ideologies (Chevrette & Eguchi, 2020, p. 56). Dixon (2013) theorized the challenges and uncertainty LGBTQ+ workers face where "determining relationships can be a daunting task" (p. 69). This section illustrates how (1) cisheteronormativity structures work relationships and (2) how workers communicate their LGBTQ+ identities in interpersonal work relationships.

Cisheteronormativity Structures Work Relationships.
Chevrette and Eguchi (2020) outlined how heteronormativity functions as a "structural force" that "continues to organize the ideological, institutional and everyday interaction and relational contexts in which LGBTQ people are positioned" (p. 55). They described the insidious nature of heteronormativity through a logic of colorblindness that allows individuals to "not see LGBTQ differences," which inherently reproduces cisheteronormativity in relationships (Chevrette & Eguchi, 2020, p. 55). Furthermore, McKenna-Buchanan (2017) theorized organizations as visible sites saturated with gendered and sexualized scripts, such as expecting cisgender, heterosexual, and monogamous partnerships.

Communicating about family and romantic relationships can both build workplace relationships and reinscribe cisheteronormativity. Dixon's (2013, 2015, 2018) extensive research illustrates how communication about work-life and family is a primary organizational socialization experience shaped by sexuality, gender identity, and heteronormativity. This included communicating diverse family structures (Dixon, 2018) and how work-family policy is organized "around the compulsory traditional family" (Dixon & Dougherty, 2014, p. 11). Dixon and Dougherty (2014) interviewed 60 participants to understand how family policies are communicated and implemented in organizations to reinforce heteronormative familial structures and make queer workers invisible. This mirrors Hoffman and Cowan's (2008) earlier research that found strong correlations between the concept of life and family. When work and family are seen as one, the lack of the latter—a traditional heterosexual family—can lead to the closeting techniques (discussed in the "Closeting" section) that protect LGBTQ+ individuals from negative perceptions and discrimination by their coworkers, superiors, and organizations. Organizational cisheteronormativity, then, is structured into policies and practices that in turn shape workplace interpersonal relationships.

Communicating LGBTQ+ Identities in Interpersonal Work Relationships. Although LGBTQ+ workers navigate disclosure frequently during working hours (as reviewed in the "Closeting" section), managing disclosure often occurs in other spaces, such as mandatory work events and socializing outside of work (Dixon, 2013). Communication can comprise partner identification, relationship status, and normative conceptions of what to communicate in social functions with colleagues (Dixon, 2013). For example, coworkers commonly communicate about marriage at work. Although legally LGBTQ+ people can marry in the United States since 2015, "this does not undo the cissexist and heterosexist values the institution upholds" (Chevrette & Eguchi, 2020, p. 56). Communicating informally to build personal relationships at work, then, may require navigating not only decision-making about disclosure but also coworkers' or supervisors' judgments.

If coworkers and superiors disclose queer or trans identities, other LGBTQ+ workers may feel more inclined to be out as well (Dixon & Dougherty, 2014). Additionally, coworker conversations impact experiences of LGBTQ+ inclusion and exclusion (Compton, 2016) and interpersonal relational risk upon disclosing sexuality and gender identity (Helens-Hart, 2017). Compton (2016) utilized the communication theory of identity (CTI) to analyze how micro discourses, such as communication with coworkers and supervisors, impacted the construction of sexuality in organizations. In 20 interviews with gay or lesbian people, Compton's (2016) participants framed coworker conversations as spaces where workers could feel comfortable with their sexuality at work. Dixon (2013) found that while all LGBTQ+ workers with same-sex partners experienced anxiety, there were also participants who brought their partners to social events after "seeing one or more coworkers or boss communicate sexual orientation without (negative) consequence" (p. 67).

Just as coworkers can build inclusive workplaces, they can create exclusionary cultures. Galupo and Resnick's (2016) participants:

> described their coworkers and supervisors misgendering them, tokenizing/exoticizing their identities, using derogatory language when referring to members of LGBT communities in general, not acknowledging the relationships and families of LGBT employees, and excluding LGBT employees from the social environment within the workplace. (pp. 277–278)

Similarly, a USTS trans respondent shared the devastating impact of coworker communication where "coworkers felt they had the right to disrespect me because the owners set the tone. I became a spectacle in my own workplace" (James et al., 2016, p. 151). Because of discrimination and violence in organizational communication, 42% of trans and nonbinary respondents did not tell their coworkers about their gender identity, and 49% did not tell their supervisors (p. 51).

Likewise, Jones (2020) discussed how trans workers often face hostile communication from coworkers and supervisors after disclosing their gender identity. Trans participants also noted that if they more frequently interacted with coworkers or customers due to their occupation, their "risk of being misgendered or otherwise discriminated against are exponential and the consequences are infinite" (Jones, 2020, p. 267). Colleagues' unwillingness to respect them impacted not only possible personal relationships but also professional interactions. For example, participant Lana shared that "when two co-workers refused to call her by her name, she was quick to act: 'I told you my name has changed... If you don't have the common decency to respect that, then don't talk to me.' After that, she said, 'they didn't mess with me anymore'" (Jones, 2020, p. 262). Coworkers and supervisors can thus influence whether queer and trans workers build or avoid personal workplace relationships.

Through organizational communication, workers also build relationships as colleagues, friends, and romantic partners. Rumens's (2008) qualitative analysis on gay men's workplace friendships highlighted the importance of intimacy and friendship as emotional support in the workplace. Heteronormative workplaces functioned as a site of anxiety for gay men's friendships, especially with straight men; thus, participants in Rumens's (2008) study revealed creative ways gay men sustain work friendships.

While work friends may discuss sex or sexuality with their colleagues, when dating or sexuality is discussed in organizations, there is an underlying assumption that employees are in (or should be in) heterosexual and monogamous relationships (Compton, 2016). Rothblum et al. (2019) interviewed 27 asexual individuals, three who identified as nonbinary, about their organizational experiences. The majority of the asexual participants said that sex and sexuality were not a common talking point at work. However, those who experienced discussions of relationships and sex in their organization felt left out, anxious, or different (Rothblum et al., 2019, p. 92), as they are often "judged by their own sexual attractiveness, and asked about their romantic interests" (p. 92). The authors highlight how heteronormativity also functions to silence or render those who are asexual as different by not being able to contribute to conversations regarding dating and relationships.

Moreover, Horan and Chory (2013) examined how employees in same sex work relationships were deemed as less competent to coworkers than those in opposite sex relationships. They analyzed perceptions of same sex work relationships through five variables: trust, deception, competence, caring, and character. They surveyed 147 participants on their perceptions of same sex office relationships versus opposite sex relationships, and their findings indicated that those who are in same sex relationships were perceived as less trustworthy. The lack of trust and perception of deception came from an assumption that same sex partnerships between superiors and employees were derived less from mutual liking and more so to maintain an organizational position. However, Horan and Chory (2013) also found that coworkers are more likely to view gay and lesbian peers as more caring and of higher character than those in workplace heterosexual relationships (p. 180). More recently, Horan et al. (2021) noted further complexities of communicating personal workplace relationships, including same sex coworker relationships being read as platonic that may be romantic and/or sexual because a coworker's bisexuality is not known. Horan et al. (2021) also suggested that coworkers may perceive workplace romances as infidelity because they are unaware of their coworkers' polyamorous and non-monogamous relationships. Thus, some LGBTQ+ personal workplace relationships remain understudied, such as polyamorous, bisexual, and pansexual workers' experiences.

Communication about sexuality at work in interpersonal relationships may also be viewed as unprofessional, thus influencing queer workers to silence themselves and creating an overarching assumption of heteronormativity. Compton's (2020) Midwest study found that participants often point to religion in performing heterosexuality at work, which she argued can be expanded to other U.S. states and regions. Discussing any queer sexuality display was considered against the moral code set, with workers fearing potentially being fired if they communicated their LGBTQ+ identities (Compton, 2020). Similarly, Fox (2013) detailed his experience as an assistant professor preparing to go up for tenure when a colleague asked him to take down where he referred to himself as a bottom on social media so no "students will be exposed to it" (p. 67). He argued:

> Implicit in my well-intended colleague's request is the notion that my sexual and social identity might expose students in our department to contaminative sexual knowledge... [and] is a disciplinary exercise in gay containment and erasure. Heterosexual sex is not subject to the same scope of corrective measures. (p. 68)

Dixon (2013) similarly surfaced heterosexist expectations of bringing only opposite sex partners to work events (See also Helens-Hart, 2017 on professionalism).

Overall, LGBTQ+ workers often are pressured to conform to cisheteronormativity to fit in and be accepted by coworkers and supervisors, or they risk stigma or exclusion for challenging normativities. Thus, LGBTQ+ individuals are forced to choose between themselves and their relationships versus the collective organizational culture (Dixon, 2013). In contrast, Ragins et al. (2007) evidenced that organizations with gay-friendly workplace cultures are more successful at reducing perceived workplace discrimination than state-level legislation barring discrimination against LGB employees. In other words, cultures that center LGBTQ+ people as a part of the organization and invite them to have authentic relationships may make a difference in not only interpersonal communication but also disrupting discrimination and violence. McKenna-Buchanan (2017) furthered this notion by recognizing that sharing stories about cisheteronormativity allows coworkers and supervisors to "learn from the discursive struggle embedded within these narratives and others" (p. 25) in a transformative manner. Otherwise, cisheteronormativity will be (re)produced and (co)constructed differently in explicit and/or nuanced practices (McKenna-Buchanan, 2017) that influence LGBTQ+ workers and their professional and professional workplace relationships. Another space for dismantling such structures occurs via policies.

INCLUSIVE AND EXCLUSIVE POLICIES

Policies within organizations, institutions, and online spaces impact LGBTQ+ workers both positively and negatively, sometimes simultaneously. Creating inclusive policies can have lasting influences such as low turnover rates and employee comfortability with disclosing their sexuality and/or gender identity. Furthermore, much like specific policies impacting LGBTQ+ individuals, work-life policies overall can limit employees' discretion for how they define both "life" and "family" (Hoffman & Cowan, 2008). Organizational work-life policies further hinder LGBTQ+ workers because of the heteronormative definitions that constitute family within these policies (Compton, 2016).

Organizations can counteract workplace discrimination, turbulent laws, and microaggression communication with their own policies. Resnick and Galupo (2019) explained:

> Even if an organization is located within a state without workplace protections for LGBT people, the organization can be autonomous and push back against the broader norms in the state by enforcing policies that protect LGBT employees. While policies may not cover all workplace microaggressions, the inclusion of a policy and a verbalized message of inclusivity as an espoused value signifies to employees the type of behavior that is expected in the organization—that is, the cultural norms are established. (p. 1397)

Thus, organizational policies and practices have incredible impacts for inclusion when embraced. However, the literature reflects that institutional, organizational, and media policies often violently reinforce cisheteronormativity, thereby excluding and harming LGBTQ+ workers. This reveals tensions between (1) inclusive policies and positive impacts and (2) exclusive policies and negative impacts.

Inclusive Policies and Positive Impacts. Implementing inclusive policies creates organizational benefits for both LGBTQ+ individuals and organizations. Scholarship primarily focuses on LGB-inclusive policies, showcasing a need for other queer, trans, and intersex identities and affirming policies to be researched. Huffman et al. (2008) defined LGB-supportive organizations as rejecting heterosexist policies and instituting gay-supportive policies that welcome sexual orientation diversity. Gay-supportive policies may include same-sex partner benefits, nondiscrimination policies, and zero tolerance for heterosexist acts (Huffman et al., 2008, p. 247). Queer-friendly policies can positively impact not only work but also health, as studies show that LGB employees who fear workplace discrimination report adverse health outcomes (Ragins et al., 2007), and policies are one pragmatic way organizations can become more inclusive (Badgett et al., 2013), thereby reducing discrimination and impacting the health of LGBTQ+ workers as whole people.

Research investigates how supportive and inclusive policies relate to LGB employees' job satisfaction and result in fewer discrimination reports (Button, 2001; Ragins & Cornwell, 2001). Badgett et al.'s (2013) literature synthesis of 36 studies of LGBT-supportive policies analyzed how policies and workplace climates impact business outcomes. They showcased positive links between LBGT supportive work policies and climates that benefit employers. Badgett et al.'s (2013) most significant finding was that LGBT-supportive policies and organizational climates were most strongly linked to openness to being LGBT. Inclusive policies thus created feelings of safety for LGBTQ+ workers to be out. Furthermore, numerous studies illustrated that LGB people are more likely to disclose their sexual orientation when their employer has an LGBT-inclusive nondiscrimination policy and/or a domestic partner benefits policy (Button, 2001; Ragins & Cornwell, 2001; Rostosky & Riggle, 2002; Tejada, 2006). In contrast, employees who have to hide their sexuality within their workplace are more likely to feel uncomfortable or exit the organization (Badgett et al., 2013).

Therefore, gay-friendly policies directly impact turnover within organizations, indicating that such policies not only include LGBTQ+ employees but also help organizations retain them. Using a national survey of 534 gay and lesbian employees, Ragins and Cornwell (2001) discussed how supportive workplace policies directly affected their turnover intentions and cultivated workers' substantially higher commitment to their employers and careers. These employees were also less likely to report that they planned to leave their jobs than those not covered by an LGBT-supportive policy (Ragins & Cornwell, 2001). Sabharwal et al.'s more recent review (2019) echoes Ragins and Cornwell's (2001) findings by looking at how policies impact federal agency practices. Sabharwal et al. (2019) surveyed over 400,000 employees from 82 federal agencies; while only 3% of this population identified as LGBT, this study reflects how policies impact LGBT workers within federal organizations. When federal agencies have LGBT inclusive policies and practices, LGBT employees were significantly more likely to stay. However, regardless of whether policies were implemented, LGBT employees were likely to experience higher turnover than non-LGBT employees, indicating that policies are just one step in the process of creating inclusive workplaces (Sabhwaral et al., 2019).

Scholars also emphasize how incorporating training and inclusive language with implementation of LGBTQ+ policies can foster positive change. Dixon and Dougherty (2014) recommended that organizations should consider changing their trainings to provide a better link between policy and member discourse about that policy. As theorized previously, the word "family" can function as a means to discipline those who do not have normative families or who are single workers. Using "family" in policies can privilege those with children over other nonnormative definitions of family (Hoffman & Cowan, 2008; Kirby et al., 2003). Therefore, organizations should create inclusive meanings to account for all notions of family and ensure all employees are included in work-life discourses.

For gender identity, Elias et al.'s (2018) findings demonstrated that every agency should create and implement a transgender policy to support trans employees. Their study suggested that an inclusive transgender policy should include the following: a detailed transition process, inclusive language throughout the policy that prohibits harassment and discrimination, and explicit restroom and locker room use guidance (p. 72). Galupo and Resnick (2016) also recommended frequent language evaluations in policies and practices. They wrote, "For instance, sex assigned at birth, gender identity, and gender expression have different implications for individuals and thus, each should be addressed in written policy and practice" (p. 284). Then, updating language frequently in consultation with LGBTQ+ experts will help organizations progress as sexuality and gender identity communication evolves.

Exclusive Policies and Negative Impacts. Despite the potential for inclusion, queer and trans friendly policies may also simultaneously reproduce cisheteronormativity, constitute what we understand as family and relationships, and impact the material experiences of LGBTQ+ workers. Policies can create and sustain insidious impacts in federal institutions, organizations, and media.

Just because an organization has a policy does not mean that workers feel protected and supported. Organizations must move beyond policy creation to disseminating policies and ensuring their enactment and enforcement (Galupo & Resnick, 2016). Lloren and Parini (2017) surveyed 1065 Swiss participants to analyze inclusive policies impacting LGB workers. Results indicated that even though 65% of companies enacted LGB-supportive policies, only 5% of participants believed these policies were internally communicated. Participants viewed policies as rhetorical and as a means of public relations. Performative LGBTQ+ policies highlight Tejeda's (2006) findings wherein workers covered by an LGBT-inclusive nondiscrimination policy still rated their employers as significantly more hostile than workers not covered by a policy. Thus, further scholarship on performative policies is needed.

Past communication research also reveals how "gay-friendly" workplace policies often use mixed messages (Compton, 2016) and how written policies are not implemented in practice (Kirby & Krone, 2002). Compton (2016) interviewed gay and lesbian employees in organizations to analyze how gay-friendly workplace policies influenced employees' work disclosures of sexual identity. Compton (2016) built upon Gusmano's (2008) and Kirby and Krone's (2002) theorizations of how the existence of policies does not mean that workers can actually use or feel protected by these policies. Compton (2016) discussed the need for coworkers, and especially supervisors, to support these policies. Furthermore, Boren and Johnson (2013) examined how interpersonal relationships and tensions impact work-life policy use in organizations. Their findings indicated that peer resentment messages, guilt, and job burnout were associated with whether or not workers perceived that they could use work-life policies. In other words, the organizational communication practices matter as much as "inclusive" policies so that policies are actually enacted, supported, and affirmed.

Relatedly, Elias et al. (2018) studied how agencies that did include policies discussing repercussions of harassment and discipline of LGBT workers often lack clear and inclusive language. Lack of examples of harassment and discipline led to uncertainty for behaviors; thus, failing to identify harassment can create manipulations and misinterpretations. Galupo and Resnick (2016) also argued that broad definitions, inconsistencies, grey areas, and disconnects "leave discrimination up for interpretation depending on the reader" (p. 283), making clear, inclusive, and actionable language in policies to be of the utmost importance.

Policies can also alienate queer, trans, and intersex employees through the reinforcement of cisheteronormativity. Policies that benefit families and try to exhibit a healthier work-life negotiation for employees may alienate LGBTQ+ employees (Dixon & Dougherty, 2014). Elias et al.'s (2018) qualitative content analysis on nine transgender policies from federal agencies focused on the potential material consequences for trans employees. Despite trans-friendly policies being implemented in federal agencies, many of these policies harmed transgender employees. They showcased how so-called "trans-inclusive" policies actually can reinforce a gender binary without including individuals who may be nonbinary, gender-neutral, agender, genderqueer, or other gender nonconforming people (p. 73).

Policies also have the power to reinforce and enact normativity that can have violent consequences for workers whose sexuality and gender identities are deemed nonnormative. Through policy institutionalization, queer, trans, and intersex bodies are rendered as suspect and predatory. Examples include the U.S. military's "Don't Ask, Don't Tell" (DADT) (Rich et al., 2012), and social media and organizational policies that surveil and dismiss the "realness" of queer and trans identities (MacAulay & Moldes, 2016). MacAulay and Moldes (2016) frame Facebook's real names policy as a queer and trans issue, as users marked as not providing a "real" name—that is within the confines of a normative cisgender name—to Facebook were locked out of their accounts. Drag queens and other gender nonconforming names were deemed inauthentic or "illegal" names and accounts. MacAulay and Moldes (2016) argued that restricting names to individuals' legal IDs or being "authentic" reinforced how state and market actors use technology and policy to uphold normativity. Similarly, Beauchamp (2009) investigated how problematic national and state policies like U.S. Department of Homeland

Security Advisory letters, the Real ID Act, and the Social Security Administration (SSA) no-match letters frame the biomedically-managed trans citizen as safe while positioning other nonnormative identities as suspicious, risky, and threatening (p. 360). These kinds of policies have the power to require employees to submit gender classification to the SSA to verify employment (Beauchamp, 2009, p. 632), which invades the privacy of trans, queer, and intersex people.

Lack of policies also have the power to enforce normativity. Rich et al. (2012) looked at the U.S. military's "Don't Ask Don't Tell" (DADT) and the Department of Defense's recommending this policy's repeal. Their argument centered on the rhetoric used for support of a DADT repeal and how the policy framed gay soldiers as predatory in the hypermasculine military culture. The policy repeal suggested that queer folks should and will continue to refrain from disclosure because of fear of negative repercussions from hegemonic and toxic masculine military cultures (Rich et al., 2012). Numerous anti-LGBTQ+ military policies, including the DADT policy, were reinstated by Trump; however, Biden rolled back these discriminatory military policies including for trans and nonbinary people (National Center of Transgender Equality, 2021). In closing, then, policies can impact workers across their organizations and interactions with broader institutions, which are exacerbated by overlapping experiences of oppression.

INTERSECTIONAL WORK EXPERIENCES AND ORGANIZING

Although the previous sections have included intersectional experiences that LGBTQ+ workers face, this section specifically reviews literature addressing how gender identity and sexuality are interwoven with race, class, disability, nation, age, and more, and how such intersections shape the lived experiences of oppression, violence, and/or privilege for LGBTQ+ workers and organizations. Intersectionality shapes work experiences including: the complexities of nation and citizenship (Chávez, 2010, 2017), queer brown bodies in the academy (Calafell, 2017), familial histories of working class and immigrant labor impacting queer and trans people (LeMaster, 2017), and closeting intersectional identities (Eger, 2018).

Importantly, research also examines how LGBTQ+ intersectional organizing responds to work and organizational tensions, including immigrant and LGBTQ+ belonging (Chávez, 2010), outreach organizing in conservative rural/urban areas (e.g., urban areas with larger surrounding rural communities) (Drumheller & McQuay, 2010), and nonprofits advancing "chosen family" identities (Eger, 2021). Theorizing queer and trans justice in organizing and work requires critiques of not only cisheteronormativity but also classism, racism, ableism, xenophobia, capitalism, colonization, sexism, and other structures of injustice (see LeMaster et al., 2019; Patterson & Hsu, 2020; Yep & Lescure, 2019). The following subsections examine: (1) LGBTQ+ workers and intersectionality; and (2) intersectional LGBTQ+ organizing.

LGBTQ+ Workers and Intersectionality. Scholars theorizing intersectionality may examine how identities coalesce and inform one other and/or how intersections are experienced beyond identity categories. Importantly, theorizing intersectionality should not falsely group shared experiences as universal or use additive approaches. This is why some queer studies scholarship utilizes an anticategorical intersectional approach (McDonald, 2015). Yep and

Lescure (2019) argued that researchers cannot look at microaggressions as additive and should avoid the tendency to "homogenize individuals inhabiting similar intersections" as this erases "their unique subjectivities and experiences" (p. 115). Using Yep's thick intersectionalities, they push for scholarship that "works against simply listing identity categories—the roster-like approach to intersectionality…Instead, it attends to the messiness, multidimensionality, and voluptuousness of identities as they are lived, expressed, and embodied" (p. 116). This section focuses on research about the multidimensionality across LGBTQ+ workers' lives including experiences of racism, transphobia, undocumented work, sex work, age, immigration, homelessness, and more.

Theorizing LGBTQ+ workers must include not only white-collar or blue-collar organizations with formal policies but also undocumented work, street survival work, and sex work. Capous-Desyllas and Loy (2020) used an interview timeline approach to understand the complexities of sex work for trans and nonbinary sex workers. Their participants pushed against narratives of sex work as only forced or for survival, and they addressed interlacing experiences of empowerment, violence, toxic masculinity, fetishizing, bodily control, agency, and affirmation. They argued:

> For many trans and gender-fluid people, the sex trade can offer greater autonomy, control, agency, a sense of empowerment, and financial stability, in comparison with other forms of employment, as well as fewer barriers to entry and engagement. However, one's intersecting identities can play a role in their experiences in the sex trade, especially for poor trans women of color. (p. 365)

Communication studies scholarship should further contribute to understanding sex work as work, organizational communication and sex work, and how LGBTQ+ people may find both violence and empowerment in sex work. For example, Capous-Desyllas and Loy (2020) wrote that "the importance of having control over one's own body, especially within a culture that polices trans bodies, was commonly expressed among the participants" from their study of trans and nonbinary people who have engaged or are engaging in sex work (p. 357). Participants also shared differing experiences of safety and fear as shaped by their other intersectional identities like being undocumented, people of color, or women. Eger's research (2018) worked with trans people who experienced unemployment and reported turning to sex work for income when they faced occupational segregation, such as one participant, Aron, who was turned away by employers as an indigenous trans woman. Other participants discussed engaging in sex work only for survival and the loneliness of what participant Alyce (who was also an indigenous trans woman) called "making money for a living" (Eger, 2021, p. 265).

LeMaster (2015) addressed how those who do not consider sex and underground economy work as labor do so from locations of cisgender, class, racial, and other privilege. She wrote:

> I am not privileged enough to think labor does not matter or that labor fixes everything. The material reality is also this: we, like so many others, are coerced into taking the work that we can find: Legitimate work. Questionable work. Il/legal work. Union work. Scab work. (p. 86)

LeMaster's poetic autoethnography traced the intersectional violence and possibilities of labor, including complexities of union strikes with poverty, job seeking experiences of her trans partner, and immigrant and family work and health needs.

In theorizing migration for queer and trans workers, Karma Chávez's research is instrumental for understanding workers' intersectional experiences in society, organizations, rhetoric, and relationships. Chávez (2010) carefully traced how LGBT organizations utilized immigrant queers only to embolden homonationalism narratives and then quickly forgot and erased their needs. She argued that "large, national and mainstream LGBT, immigrant and human rights organizations enact a particular kind of cultural citizenship that attempts to ameliorate the threat LGBT people and their immigrant partners pose by utilizing normalizing discourses of belonging to frame the issues—a strategic move with potentially significant consequences" (Chávez, 2010, p. 137). Chávez's review of organizational texts positions work as an "acceptable" pathway of citizenship for undocuqueers. She explicated:

> Characteristics such as personal responsibility and financial stability/ability as well as a desire to exist within the mainstream are all hallmarks of good citizenship. A number of the narratives express upholding these values at the same time that they reject undesirable qualities that would disqualify them from belonging as good citizens. These narratives are both racializing and class-based. (p. 143)

Chávez also reviewed organizing documents from Queers for Economic Justice (QEJ) that instead used solidarity with U.S. citizen and immigrant laborers impacted by low wages and centered relationality (p. 149). She established the need for intersectional and coalitional organizations supporting queer migrants.

In 2017, Chávez continued to call for new queer worldmaking for immigrant justice. She credited "undocuqueer" leaders for "illuminating the fact that immigration is a queer issue" (p. 132). She noted how mainstream queer organizations continuously ignore intersections that immigrants face around nation, poverty, racism, and more. Chávez cautioned against LGBTQ+ organizing that does not center immigrant intersections, such as tracing the violence enacted by the 2016 Creating Change Conference hosted by the National LGBTQ Task Force who invited U.S. Immigration and Customs Enforcement (ICE) as a panelist. She explained why their apologies and removal of ICE from the conference were not enough because of their participation in "other kinds of violence named in the refusal-deportations, financial insecurity, and invisibility of LGBTQ immigrants" (2017, p. 134). Thus, future scholarship must examine undocuqueer workers, support immigrant queer and trans people, and theorize how organizing and rhetoric can be instrumental in queer and trans worldmaking.

Another important intersection for LGBTQ+ workers is age (Croghan et al., 2015; Drumheller & McQuay, 2010; Meyer, 2009). Meyer (2009) revealed the organizational communication tensions faced by LGBT college students as younger adults, including three themes of unity/difference, commitment/apathy, and empowerment/disempowerment from ethnographic research on one university with three LGBT organizations. For example, "participants noted that they could finally 'be themselves' once they affiliated with one or several of the three organizations, and frequently indicated that they 'felt good' about their contributions to the LGBT community" (Meyer, 2009, p. 508). In contrast, students experienced disempowerment bound in heteronormativity. One participant attributed being out in the student LGBT organizations as making "her subject to talk and rumors that she would not have dealt with prior to affiliating with the organization" (p. 509). They called for further research on organizations as communities.

Croghan et al. (2015) advanced an understudied area of age, sexuality, and gender identity intersections by looking at LGBTQ+ elders. They questioned, "How best do health and human services providers communicate readiness to work with a community that has a history of significant discrimination?" (p. 648). Their survey of 327 LGBT baby boomers and older adults focused on what organizations (particularly social service organizations and service workers) could do to communicate inclusion to older adults. Importantly, older adults responded to organizations who actually employed LGBT service workers, explaining "it is difficult to convey a welcoming environment to the public if an organization's staff does not feel welcome and safe enough to be out on the job" (Croghan et al., 2015, p. 647). They also valued physical artifacts being displayed like "general signage and the rainbow flag, and using inclusive language on forms" (p. 647). Beyond artifacts, LGBT older adults reported that employees' inclusive language use communicated welcoming environments. Organizations should not only utilize artifacts of acceptance on display but also employ queer, trans, and intersex people and train all for inclusive communication to support older adults. Like with LGBTQ+ elders' communication needs, LGBTQ+ organizations and organizing must respond to complex needs across workers' intersectional experiences.

Intersectional LGBTQ+ Organizing. Research examining intersectionality also focused on the benefits and challenges of LGBTQ+ organizing and organizations. From tensions in student organizing (Meyer, 2009) to queer immigrant organizing (Chávez, 2010, 2017) to intersectional grassroots organizing (Eger, 2021) to regional complexities (Drumheller & McQuay, 2010) to intersectional media organizing (Costanza-Chock et al., 2017), theorizing LGBTQ+ organizing is an area of vibrant inquiry in communication studies that impacts workers and those served by intersectional outreach.

Drumheller and McQuay (2010) focused on LGBT organizing in conservative areas in the United States by specifically focusing on a rural/urban outreach center in the Bible Belt. Their project demonstrated how regional identity and religion impacts work and organizing experiences. They explained that "in an area where religious dogma supersedes social justice, it might be difficult for community members to even admit they are LGBT much less seek out needed services such as counseling, networking, social events, or anything else that heterosexuals likely take for granted" (Drumheller & McQuay, 2010, p. 71). Their focus organization, LGBT Outreach Center (LOC), faced challenges of organizational commitments (similar to those faced in Meyer, 2009), marketing and fundraising tensions, and membership. Drumheller and McQuay's (2010) focus groups revealed three themes of life as: struggle, apathy, and compartmentalization. For life as struggle, they traced how in moving "into this community, gay males and lesbians are quick to find what one participant referred to as 'heterophobia,' making them fearful of the response of conservative heterosexuals. Further, participants felt that most were fearful of their families more than anyone else" (p. 76). Because of the fear of coworkers, community members, and even family members, identifying with the organization and receiving outreach became a barrier. This also led to the second theme of life as apathy when it became difficult to unify around a common LGBT cause.

Third, members faced compartmentalizing in two important ways: (1) LGBT people were forced to compartmentalize their sexuality and gender identities, and (2) heterosexual and cisgender people used compartmentalization to cause violence. LGBT people in the urban/rural region were forced to often comply with "Don't Ask, Don't Tell" community and organizational policies and norms. This created contradictions where "LGBT participants of the focus groups would talk about how safe they felt in the city, on the one hand, and then tell tales of those fearful of losing their jobs if they came out" (p. 79). Similarly, heterosexual friends or coworkers said, "Community members engage in compartmentalization as they place the gay individuals they know into a separate category from the LGBT community as a whole, thus accepting the individual but denying the larger group" (p. 80). Drumheller and McQuay (2010) thus surfaced important challenges LGBTQ+ organizing must address for creating inclusion across U.S. regions and organizations.

While many LGBTQ+ people struggle to find belonging at work and in community organizations (even in queer, trans, and intersex ones), other organizations driven by grassroots and intersectional organizing present welcoming alternatives. Costanza-Chock et al. (2017) surveyed 231 LGBTQ and Two-Spirit organizations to explore their media and communication challenges and strengths. Their article tracked powerful exemplars of "transformative" media as intersectional by LGBTQ and Two-Spirit organizations. However, their analysis revealed that organizations using intersectional, multi-issue approaches were largely excluded in "mainstream media coverage," which instead "are often narrowly focused on single issues" (p. 167). This lack of mainstream coverage impacted intersectional LGBTQ and Two-Spirit organizers' access to funding, visibility, and resources.

Eger (2021)'s three-year ethnography and volunteering with the Transgender Resource Center of New Mexico (TGRC) centered grassroots, intersectional transgender organizing to combat:

> systemic discrimination transgender people face not only for their gender identities but also other identities including race, age, disability, citizenship, sexuality, and more. TGRC specifically serves large populations of transgender women of color (particularly indigenous trans women) as well as transgender people experiencing addiction, engaging in survival sex work, and experiencing chronic homelessness. (p. 260)

Eger revealed how using "chosen family" communication as an organizational identity shaped how participants understood their inclusion and TGRC's communication of radical acceptance. For example, Theresa a "Black, trans woman in her early 40s who identified as homeless, worked in sex work, and experienced addiction" (p. 267) explained how TGRC's intersectional organizing was unique and affirmed her as a whole person. She said that TGRC:

> stands out because they really show you that they care. I mean, a lot of organizations will say this or say that but the Transgender Resource, it stands out because they show it. They just don't talk about it. They really *be* about it, and they do care. (p. 268)

One of the directors of TGRC, Henry (a white, housed trans man in his 40s), focused on the importance of intersectional trans organizations using love and family throughout their organizing. Even without sustained funding for TGRC in their early years, Henry "described the incredible life-saving importance of love to create a chosen family" (Eger, 2021, p. 268). The family organizational identity was not without challenges, however, with volunteer staff turnover, spatial and rule tensions, and tensions when a community member experiencing addiction who used violence against staff created turbulent navigation for keeping them in the family. Yet, despite the inclusion of the family and the immense impacts of TGRC's organizing, trans and nonbinary people still faced systemic barriers in seeking employment, social services, and housing because of intersectional violence (see Eger, 2018, 2021). Combatting daily embodied violence made the importance of family-based organizing like TGRC all the more important for trans survival (Eger, 2021). Organizing for justice for LGBTQ+ workers, then, must include action across intersectional experiences.

FUTURE RESEARCH

While there is growing research on LGBTQ+ workers in communication studies, our discipline requires sustained scholarship and new foci for the future. First, future research should center LGBTQ+ workers' voices and their intersectional organizational experiences, such as age, citizenship, race, region, disability, education level, social class, and more. One needed area is on the experiences of Queer and Trans People of Color (QTPOC) at work, especially researched by QTPOC scholars. Theorizing intersections of racism and cisheteronormativity in organizational communication, cultures, and structures that impact QTPOC workers' livelihoods is vital to not continue to reinscribe whiteness. This follows ongoing calls to disrupt the whitening of queer and intersectionality theorizing in communication studies (see Eguchi et al., 2020). Applied communication policies and practices research is also needed to support not just LGBTQ+ workers' sexuality or gender identities but them as whole people with complex, interconnected lives. One place communication studies can contribute is in more development on language, rhetoric, and policies. For example, organizations may share policies and practices against homophobia or transphobia, but simultaneously lack policies addressing LGBTQ+ workers' experiences of racism, ableism, or languages spoken. Researchers should explore what decolonial, queer, trans, and crip futures can be imagined, created, and enacted for LGBTQ+ workers and organizations. Theorizing leadership and diversity management of intersectional identities of LGBTQ+ workers could also enrich future scholarship and praxis.

Second, LGBTQ+ people are not monoliths; thus, we need to understand the complexities of sexuality, gender expression, sexual identities, and gender identities across queer, trans, and intersex workers. This calls for research to have more inclusion of trans, nonbinary, Two-Spirit, and other gender nonconforming workers' experiences and avoid leaving the "T" out of research. Throughout the literature reviewed previously, certain workers are included more than others, so researchers should specifically investigate how pansexual, bisexual, queer, asexual, aromantic, intersex, Two-Spirit, demisexual, polyamorous, questioning, and more workers face unique barriers and joys at work as they transverse cisheteronormativity at work.

Third, past research surfaces queer and trans workers critiques of their own and others' experiences in academia, which is important to mark and dismantle violence in our own institutions. To build upon this scholarship, we need further inquiry into all forms of work beyond academic and white-collar labor to including blue-collar work, manual labor, undocumented work, sex work, underground work, and more. Because the field often privileges white-collar work overall, the experiences of other workers are marginalized and are needed for justice in our organizational communication praxis.

Fourth, to better conceptualize workplace disclosure complexities, we need further research on closeting communication across sexualities, gender identities, and intersections. For example, how one discloses their sexuality and/or gender identity can play an important role regarding communication and relationships with coworkers. Disclosure communication can function to completely alter the communicative situation as a whole. This has been shown in past research on cancer disclosure at work to peers (Wittenberg-Lyles & Villagran, 2006) and personal health information to supervisors (Westerman et al., 2017). Thus, deeper understanding of the different ways to disclose (or not disclose) sexuality and gender identity could offer insight into strategies workers attempt in these interactions and how their communication shapes these very relationships and organizations. Communication studies could provide an opportunity to understand workers' affirming experiences of disclosure while also reducing adverse reactions and outcomes for LGBTQ+ workers when facing cisheteronormativity and violence at work.

While some closeting communication research examines gender identity, further theorizing of the continuous processes of coming out as trans, nonbinary, Two-Spirit, or gender nonconforming at work is needed. As trans and nonbinary workers face systemic discrimination, especially trans and enby women, immigrants, people of color, and people with disabilities, theorizing how they navigate disclosure and creating better best practices for hiring, promoting, and retaining them is essential. Researchers might examine: How do coming out experiences for gender identity connect to or differ from sexuality? How is closeting communication complicated by intersectional identities (see Eger, 2018)? When is closeting or passing inadequate as a frame (see McCune, 2014)? Additionally, how does already being established within an organization impact the experience and communication of coming out as trans or nonbinary (see Schilt, 2011)? How can we better theorize consent and closeting communication (Eger, 2018)? How can we understand closeting communication through an anticategorical, intersectional approach?

Fifth, we must not only contend with whiteness in organizational communication scholarship but also the U.S. dominance in the literature. This article focused predominantly on U.S. LGBTQ+ workers based on what current literature is available to read in the discipline. There is an urgent need for more international foci on LGBTQ+ workers' communication from more countries and their experiences (see exceptions from Mitra & Doctor, 2016; Lloren & Parini, 2017; and see further readings from sister disciplines). Organizational cultures impact policies and interpersonal interactions for international coworkers and supervisors. Researchers may question how companies with varying workplace cultures, located internationally, with different societal expectations and norms, impact the work-life experience of LGBTQ+ workers. Additionally, how do LGBTQ+ workers face inclusion and/or exclusion in different countries and regions? How do language, laws, rhetoric, borders, and structures shape LGBTQ+ workers' experiences across the globe? How can decolonial theorizing connect to queer, trans, and intersex theorizing across locations and spaces? What decolonial LGBTQ+ working futures can we imagine and build?

Sixth, while some research examines workplace relationships with supervisors and coworkers, further inquiry connecting interpersonal and organizational communication for LGBTQ+

workers is needed on workplace relationships and romances for queer, trans, and intersex workers. This may include areas such as: romances where one partner is trans or nonbinary and how that impacts their personal relationships at work; relationships where two or more LGBTQ+ partners are polyamorous and how this frames their disclosure, friendships, and relationships at work; or LGBTQ+ coworkers' romantic relationships and hook-ups. Additionally, interpersonal relationships with supportive supervisors are needed to theorize best practices for inclusion. Research could also investigate cisgender or heterosexual workers who identify as "allies," and pair interviews or surveys with their LGBTQ+ coworkers to distinguish between claiming ally identity and actually enacting allyship.

Seventh and finally, there is a plethora of research on discrimination and resiliency strategies for LGBTQ+ workers attempting to assuage the effects of harmful and violent organizational communication. There is not enough research on the ways in which supervisors, employees, and coworkers can help to remove or alleviate such violence for LGBTQ+ workers. Research should focus on ways to increase retention and structural inclusion and put the onus on cisgender and heterosexual people to do *the work* for change, rather than LGBTQ+ workers always laboring for and championing their own organizational survival. Such research should not only be critiques using queer and trans theory but also practical, applied guidance for practitioners who can utilize new communication lenses to create justice at work. Further inquiry into LGBTQ+ organizing for justice is needed to realize how queer, trans, and intersex collectives can best serve their communities. More scholarship on joy, queer and trans worldmaking, and justice at work is also necessary. May the communication studies discipline become a catalyst for radical changes that increase not only the survival of LGBTQ+ workers in their organizations but also support them to thrive at work.

FURTHER READINGS

Asante, G. A. (2020). Anti-LGBT violence and the ambivalent (colonial) discourses of Ghanaian Pentecostalist-Charismatic church leaders. *Howard Journal of Communications, 31*(1), 20–34. https://doi.org/10.1080/10646175.2019.1590255

Bruni, A. (2006). "Have you got a boyfriend or are you single?" On the importance of being "straight" in organizational research. *Gender, Work and Organization, 13*(3), 299–316. https://doi.org/10.1111/j.1468-0432.2006.00309.x

Chin, M. (2018). Making queer and trans of color counterpublics: Disability, accessibility, and the politics of inclusion. *Affilia, 33*(1), 8–23. https://journals.sagepub.com/doi/10.1177/0886109917729666

Cook, A., & Glass, C. (2016). Do women advance equity? The effect of gender leadership composition on LGBT-friendly policies in American firms. *Human Relations, 69*(7), 1431–1456. https://doi.org/10.1177/0018726715611734

Cornejo Salinas, G., Martínez, J., & Vidal-Ortiz, S. (2020). LGBT studies without LGBT studies: Mapping alternative pathways in Perú and Colombia. *Journal of Homosexuality, 67*(3), 417–434. https://www.tandfonline.com/doi/full/10.1080/00918369.2018.1534411

DeSouza, E. R., Wesselmann, E. D., & Ispas, D. (2017). Workplace discrimination against sexual minorities: Subtle and not-so-subtle. *Canadian Journal of Administrative Sciences/Revue Canadienne Des Sciences de l'Administration, 34*(2), 121–132. https://doi.org/10.1002/cjas.1438

Goldberg, A. E., Beemyn, G., & Smith, J. Z. (2018). What is needed, what is valued: Trans students' perspectives on trans-inclusive policies and practices in higher education. *Journal of Educational and Psychological Consultation, 29*(1), 27–67. https://doi.org/10.1080/10474412.2018.1480376

Hollis, L. P., & McCalla, S. A. (2013). Bullied back in the closet: Disengagement of LGBT employees facing workplace bullying. *Journal of Psychological Issues in Organizational Culture, 4*(2), 6–16. https://doi.org/10.1002/jpoc.21109

Kelly, M., Carathers, J., & Kade, T. (2020). Beyond tolerance: Policies, practices, and ideologies of queer-friendly workplaces. *Sexuality Research and Social Policy, 18*, 1078–1093. https://doi.org/10.1007/s13178-020-00512-3

Köllen, T. (2013). Bisexuality and diversity management: Addressing the B in LGBT as a relevant "sexual orientation" in the workplace. *Journal of Bisexuality, 13*(1), 122–137. https://www.tandfonline.com/doi/abs/10.1080/15299716.2013.755728

Nadal, K. L., Issa, M. A., Leon, J., Meterko, V., Wideman, M., & Wong, Y. (2011). Sexual orientation microaggression: "Death by a thousand cuts" for lesbian, gay, and bisexual youth. *Journal of LGBT Youth, 8*(3), 234–259. https://www.tandfonline.com/doi/abs/10.1080/19361653.2011.584204

Nadal, K. L., Rivera, D. P., & Corpus, M. J. H. (2010). Sexual orientation and transgender microaggressions in everyday life: Experiences of lesbians, gays, bisexuals, and transgender individuals. In D. W. Sue (Ed.), *Microaggressions and marginality: Manifestation, dynamics, and impact* (pp. 217–240). Wiley.

O'Brien, A., & Kerrigan, P. (2020). Gay the right way? Roles and routines of Irish media production among gay and lesbian workers. *European Journal of Communication, 35*(4), 355–369. https://doi.org/10.1177/0267323120903684

Pomeranz, J. L. (2018). Challenging and preventing policies that prohibit local civil rights protections for lesbian, gay, bisexual, transgender and queer people. *American Journal of Public Health, 108*(1), 67–72. https://doi.org/10.2105/AJPH.2017.304116

Popova, M. (2018). Inactionable/unspeakable: Bisexuality in the workplace. *Journal of Bisexuality, 18*(1), 54–66. https://doi.org/10.1080/15299716.2017.1383334

Robinson, C. S. (2018). Hiding in plain sight: Early career experiences of a non-binary, queer faculty member. *Women & Language, 41*(1), 110–127.

Spade, D. (2015). *Normal life: Administrative violence, critical trans politics, and the limits of law* (Rev. and expanded ed.). Duke University Press.

REFERENCES

ACLU. (2020). *R.G. & G.R. Harris Funeral Homes V EEOC & Aimee Stephens.* https://www.aclu.org/cases/rg-gr-harris-funeral-homes-v-eeoc-aimee-stephens

Arena, D. F., & Jones, K. P. (2017). To "B" or not to "B": Assessing the disclosure dilemma of bisexual individuals at work. *Journal of Vocational Behavior, 103*, 86–98. https://doi.org/10.1016/j.jvb.2017.08.009

Badgett, M. V. L., Duso, L. E., Mallory, C., & Kastanis, A. (2013). *The business impact of LGBT-supportive policies.* Williams Institute. https://williamsinstitute.law.ucla.edu/publications/impact-lgbt-supportive-workplaces/

Beauchamp, T. (2009). Artful concealment and strategic visibility: Transgender bodies and U.S. state surveillance after 9/11. *Surveillance and Society, 6*(4), 356–366. https://doi.org/10.24908/ss.v6i4.3267

Boren, J. P., & Johnson, S. L. (2013). Examining the relationships among peer resentment messages overheard, state guilt, and employees' perceived ability to use work/family policies. *Southern Communication Journal, 78*(2), 128–145. https://doi.org/10.1080/1041794X.2012.736008

Boren, J. P., & McPherson, M. B. (2018). Is coming out in the classroom still an occupational hazard? A replication of Russ, Simonds, and Hunt (2002). *Communication Studies, 69*(3), 242–250. https://www.tandfonline.com/doi/full/10.1080/10510974.2018.1466719

Button, S. B. (2001). Organizational efforts to affirm sexual diversity: A cross-level examination. *Journal of Applied Psychology, 86*(1), 17–28. https://doi.org/10.1037/0021-9010.86.1.17

Calafell, B. M. (2017). When depression is in the job description #realacademicbios. *Departures in Critical Qualitative Research*, 6(1), 5–10. https://doi.org/10.1525/dcqr.2017.6.1.5

Capous-Desyllas, M., & Loy, V. (2020). Navigating intersecting identities, self-representation, and relationships: A qualitative study with trans sex workers living and working in Los Angeles, CA. *Sociological Inquiry*, 90(2), 339–370. https://doi.org/10.1111/soin.12350

Chávez, K. R. (2010). Border (in)securities: Normative and differential belonging in LGBTQ and immigrant rights discourse. *Communication and Critical/Cultural Studies*, 7(2), 136–155. https://doi.org/10.1080/14791421003763291

Chávez, K. R. (2017). Homonormativity and violence against immigrants. *QED: A Journal in GLBTQ Worldmaking*, 4(2), 131–136. https://doi.org/10.14321/qed.4.2.0131

Chevrette, R., & Eguchi, S. (2020). "We don't see LGBTQ differences": Cisheteronormativity and concealing phobias and irrational fears behind rhetorics of acceptance. *QED: A Journal in GLBTQ Worldmaking*, 7(1), 55–59.

Compton, C. A. (2016). Managing mixed messages: Sexual identity management in a changing U.S. workplace. *Management Communication Quarterly*, 30(4), 415–440. https://www.doi.org/10.1177/0893318916641215

Compton, C. A. (2020). Co-sexuality and organizing: The master narrative of "normal" sexuality in the midwestern workplace. *Journal of Homosexuality*, 67(7), 1013–1039. https://doi.org/10.1080/00918369.2019.1582220

Compton, C. A., & Dougherty, D. S. (2017). Organizing sexuality: Silencing and the push-pull process of co-sexuality in the workplace: Co-sexuality and silence. *Journal of Communication*, 67(6), 874–896. https://doi.org/10.1111/jcom.12336

Costanza-Chock, S., Schweidler, C., & Toward Transformative Media Organizing Project. (2017). Toward transformative media organizing: LGBTQ and Two-Spirit media work in the United States. *Media, Culture & Society*, 39(2), 159–184. https://journals.sagepub.com/doi/10.1177/0163443716674360

Cox, M. B. (2019). Working closets: Mapping queer professional discourses and why professional communication studies need queer rhetorics. *Journal of Business and Technical Communication*, 33(1), 1–25. https://doi.org/10.1177/1050651918798691

Croghan, C. F., Moone, R. P., & Olson, A. M. (2015). Working with LGBT baby boomers and older adults: Factors that signal a welcoming service environment. *Journal of Gerontological Social Work*, 58(6), 637–651. https://doi.org/10.1080/01634372.2015.1072759

Dixon, J. (2013). Uneasy recreation: Workplace social events as problematic sites for communicating sexual orientation. *Florida Communication Journal*, 41(1), 63–71.

Dixon, J. (2015). Organizational communication: The workplace socialization of gender identity: A phenomenological exploration of being transgender at work. In L. G. Spencer IV & J. C. Capuzza (Eds.), *Transgender communication studies: Histories, trends, and trajectories* (pp. 19–31). Lexington Books.

Dixon, J. (2018). Looking out from the family closet: Discourse dependence and queer family identity in workplace conversation. *Management Communication Quarterly*, 32(2), 271–275. https://doi.org/10.1177/0893318917744067

Dixon, J., & Dougherty, D. S. (2014). A language convergence/meaning divergence analysis exploring how LGBTQ and single employees manage traditional family expectations in the workplace. *Journal of Applied Communication Research*, 42(1), 1–19. https://www.tandfonline.com/doi/abs/10.1080/00909882.2013.847275

Drumheller, K., & McQuay, B. (2010). Living in the buckle: Promoting LGBT outreach services in conservative urban/rural centers. *Communication Studies*, 61(1), 70–86. https://doi.org/10.1080/10510970903398010

Eger, E. K. (2018). Transgender jobseekers navigating closeting communication. *Management Communication Quarterly*, 32(2), 276–281. https://doi.org/10.1177/0893318917740226

Eger, E. K. (2021). Co-constructing organizational identity and culture with those we serve: An ethnography of a transgender nonprofit organization communicating family identity and identification. *International Journal of Business Communication, 58*(2), 254–281. https://journals.sagepub.com/doi/abs/10.1177/2329488419893738

Eguchi, S. (2009). Negotiating hegemonic masculinity: The rhetorical strategy of "straight-acting" among gay men. *Journal of Intercultural Communication Research, 38*(3), 193–209. https://doi.org/10.1080/17475759.2009.508892

Eguchi, S., Calafell, B. M., & Abdi, S. (Eds.). (2020). *De-whitening intersectionality: Race, intercultural communication, and politics.* Lexington Books.

Elias, N. M., Johnson, R., Ovando, D., & Ramirez, J. (2018). Improving transgender policy for a more equitable workplace. *Journal of Public Management & Social Policy, 24*(2), 53–81. https://digitalscholarship.tsu.edu/jpmsp/vol24/iss2/7

Exec. Order No. 13988, 3 C.F.R. page (2021), https://www.whitehouse.gov/briefing-room/presidential-actions/2021/01/20/executive-order-preventing-and-combating-discrimination-on-basis-of-gender-identity-or-sexual-orientation/

Ferguson, M. W. (2018). (Re)negotiating organizational socialization: Black male scholarship and the closet. *Management Communication Quarterly, 32*(2), 282–286. https://doi.org/10.1177/0893318917741990

Fox, R. (2013). "Homo"-work: Queering academic communication and communicating queer in academia. *Text and Performance Quarterly, 33*(1), 58–76. https://doi.org/10.1080/10462937.2012.744462

Galupo, M. P., & Resnick, C. A. (2016). Experiences of LGBT microaggressions in the workplace: Implications for policy. In T. Köllen (Ed.), *Sexual orientation and transgender issues in organizations* (pp. 271–287). Springer International Publishing.

Greene, K. (2009). An integrated model of health disclosure decision-making. In T. D. Afifi & W. A. Afifi (Eds.), *Uncertainty, information management, and disclosure decisions: Theories and applications* (pp. 226–253). Routledge/Taylor & Francis Group.

Gusmano, B. (2008). Coming out or not? How nonheterosexual people manage their sexual identity at work. *Journal of Workplace Rights, 13,* 473–496. http://mr.crossref.org/iPage?doi=10.2190%2FWR.13.4.g

Harris, K. L., & McDonald, J. (2018). Forum introduction: Queering the "closet" at work. *Management Communication Quarterly, 32*(2), 265–270. https://journals.sagepub.com/doi/10.1177/0893318917742517

Helens-Hart, R. (2017). Females' (non)disclosure of minority sexual identities in the workplace from a communication privacy management perspective. *Communication Studies, 68*(5), 607–623. https://doi.org/10.1080/10510974.2017.1388827

Hoffman, M. F., & Cowan, R. L. (2008). The meaning of work/life: A corporate ideology of work/life balance. *Communication Quarterly, 56*(3), 227–246. https://www.doi.org/10.1080/01463370802251053

Horan, S. M., & Chory, R. M. (2013). Relational implications of gay and lesbian workplace romances: Understanding trust, deception, and credibility. *Journal of Business Communication, 50*(2), 170–189. https://journals.sagepub.com/doi/abs/10.1177/0021943612474993

Horan, S. M., Chory, R. M., Craw, E. S., & Jones, H. E. (2021). Blended work/life relationships: Organizational communication involving workplace peers, friends, and lovers. *Communication Research Trends, 40*(2), 3–47.

Huffman, A. H., Watrous-Rodriguez, K. M., & King, E. B. (2008). Supporting a diverse workforce: What type of support is most meaningful for lesbian and gay employees? *Human Resource Management, 47*(2), 237–253. https://www.doi.org/10.1002/hrm.20210

James, S. E., Herman, J. L., Rankin, S., Keisling, M., Mottet, L., & Anafi, M. (2016). *The Report of the 2015 U.S. Transgender Survey.* National Center for Transgender Equality. https://transequality.org/sites/default/files/docs/usts/USTS-Full-Report-Dec17.pdf

Jones, S. E. (2020). Negotiating transgender identity at work: A movement to theorize a transgender standpoint epistemology. *Management Communication Quarterly, 34*(2), 251–278. https://doi.org/10.1177/0893318919898170

Kirby, E. L., & Krone, K. J. (2002). "The policy exists but you can't really use it": Communication and the structuration of work-family policies. *Journal of Applied Communication Research, 30*(1), 50–77. https://www.doi.org/10.1080/00909880216577

Kirby, E. L., Golden, A. G., Medved, C. E., Jorgenson, J., & Buzzanell, P. M. (2003). An organizational communication challenge to the discourse of work and family research: From problematics to empowerment. In P. J. Kalbfleishch (Ed.), *Communication yearbook 27* (pp. 1–43). Lawrence Erlbaum Associates. https://www.doi.org/10.1016/j.jvb.2011.03.018

LeMaster, B. (2015). On strike! A poetic autoethnography of labor. *Departures in Critical Qualitative Research, 4*(2), 83–95. https://doi.org/10.1525/dcqr.2015.4.2.83

LeMaster, B. (2017). Unlearning the violence of the normative. *QED: A Journal in GLBTQ Worldmaking, 4*(2), 123–130. https://doi.org/10.14321/qed.4.2.0123

LeMaster, B., Shultz, D., McNeill, J., Bowers, G., & Rust, R. (2019). Unlearning cisheteronormativity at the intersections of difference: Performing queer worldmaking through collaged relational autoethnography. *Text and Performance Quarterly, 39*(4), 341–370. https://www.tandfonline.com/doi/full/10.1080/10462937.2019.1672885

Leslie, K. J. (2020). Scenes from the margins. *Departures in Critical Qualitative Research, 9*(2), 133–136. https://doi.org/10.1525/dcqr.2020.9.2.133

Lloren, A., & Parini, L. (2017). How LGBT-supportive workplace policies shape the experience of lesbian, gay men, and bisexual employees. *Sexuality Research and Social Policy, 14*(3), 289–299. https://doi.org/10.1007/s13178-016-0253-x

MacAulay, M., & Moldes, M. D. (2016). Queen don't compute: Reading and casting shade on Facebook's real names policy. *Critical Studies in Media Communication, 33*(1), 6–22. https://doi.org/10.1080/15295036.2015.1129430

McCune, J. Q. (2014). *Sexual discretion: Black masculinity and the politics of passing*. The University of Chicago Press.

McDonald, J. (2015). Organizational communication meets queer theory: Theorizing relations of "difference" differently. *Communication Theory, 25*(3), 310–329. https://doi.org/10.1111/comt.12060

McDonald, J., Harris, K. L., & Ramirez, J. (2020). Revealing and concealing difference: A critical approach to disclosure and an intersectional theory of "closeting." *Communication Theory, 30*(1), 84–104. https://doi.org/10.1093/ct/qtz017

McFadden, C., & Crowley-Henry, M. (2016). A systematic literature review of trans* careers and workplace experiences. In T. Köllen (Ed.), *Sexual orientation and transgender issues in organizations* (pp. 63–82). Springer International Publishing.

McKenna-Buchanan, T. (2017). It's not all "one" story: A narrative exploration of heteronormativity at work. *Departures in Critical Qualitative Research, 6*(1), 11–29. https://doi.org/10.1525/dcqr.2017.6.1.11

McKenna-Buchanan, T., & Baker, S. (2016). "You are on your own": Magnifying co-cultural LGB/TQ microaggressions in the workplace. In J. Manning & C. M. Noland (Eds.), *Contemporary studies of sexuality & communication: Theoretical and applied perspectives* (pp. 305–320). Kendall Hunt Publishing.

McKenna-Buchanan, T., Munz, S., & Rudnick, J. (2015). To be or not to be out in the classroom: Exploring communication privacy management strategies of lesbian, gay, and queer college teachers. *Communication Education, 64*(3), 280–300. https://www.tandfonline.com/doi/full/10.1080/03634523.2015.1014385

Meyer, M. D. E. (2009). "We're too afraid of these imaginary tensions": Student organizing in lesbian, gay, bisexual and transgender campus communities. *Communication Studies, 55*(4), 499–514. https://www.tandfonline.com/doi/abs/10.1080/10510970409388635

Mitra, R., & Doctor, V. (2016). Passing in corporate India: Problematizing disclosure of homosexuality at the workplace. In T. Köllen (Ed.), *Sexual orientation and transgender issues in organizations* (pp. 307–320). Springer International Publishing.

Movement Advancement Project, Center for American Progress, Human Rights Campaign, Freedom to Work, and National Black Justice Coalition. (2013, November). *A broken bargain for LGBT workers of color*. https://www.lgbtmap.org/workers-of-color

National Center for Transgender Equality. (2021). The discrimination administration: Trump's anti-LGBT record. https://transequality.org/the-discrimination-administration

Patterson, G., & Hsu, V. J. (2020). Exposing the seams: Professional dress & the disciplining of nonbinary trans bodies. *The Journal of Multimodal Rhetorics, 3*(2), 90–111. http://journalofmultimodalrhetorics.com/3-2-issue-patterson-and-hsu

Ragins, B. R., & Cornwell, J. M. (2001). Pink triangles: Antecedents and consequences of perceived workplace discrimination against gay and lesbian employees. *Journal of Applied Psychology, 86*, 1244–1261. https://www.doi.org/10.1037/0021-9010.86.6.1244

Ragins, B. R., Singh, R., & Cornwell, J. M. (2007). Making the invisible visible: Fear and disclosure of sexual orientation at work. *Journal of Applied Psychology 92*(4), 1103–1118. https://doi.apa.org/doiLanding?doi=10.1037%2F0021-9010.92.4.1103

Rich, C., Schutten, J. K., & Rogers, R. A. (2012). "Don't drop the soap": Organizing sexualities in the repeal of the US military's "Don't Ask, Don't Tell" policy. *Communication Monographs, 79*(3), 269–291. https://doi.org/10.1080/03637751.2012.697633

Resnick, C. A., & Galupo, M. P. (2019). Assessing experiences with LGBT microaggressions in the workplace: Development and validation of the microaggression experiences at work scale. *Journal of Homosexuality, 66*(10), 1380–1403. https://doi.org/10.1080/00918369.2018.1542207

Rostosky, S. S., & Riggle, E. D. B. (2002). "Out" at work: The relation of actor and partner workplace policy and internalized homophobia to disclosure status. *Journal of Counseling Psychology, 49*, 411–419. https://doi.apa.org/doiLanding?doi=10.1037%2F0022-0167.49.4.411

Rothblum, E. D., Heimann, K., & Carpenter, K. (2019). The lives of asexual individuals outside of sexual and romantic relationships: Education, occupation, religion and community. *Psychology & Sexuality, 10*(1), 83–93. https://doi.org/10.1080/19419899.2018.1552186

Rumens, N. (2008). Working at intimacy: Gay men's workplace friendships. *Gender, Work and Organization, 15*(1), 9–30. https://www.doi.org/10.1111/j.1468-0432.2007.00364.x

Sabharwal, M., Levine, H., D'Agostino, M., & Nguyen, T. (2019). Inclusive work practices: Turnover intentions among LGBT employees of the U.S. federal government. *The American Review of Public Administration, 49*(4), 482–494. https://doi.org/10.1177/0275074018817376

Schilt, K. (2011). *Just one of the guys? Transgender men and the persistence of gender inequality*. University of Chicago Press.

Sears, B., Mallory, C., & Luhur, W. (2021, April). *Public and private sector employees' perceptions of discrimination against LGBTQ people*. The Williams Institute. https://williamsinstitute.law.ucla.edu/publications/employee-perception-discrim/

Spradlin, A. L. (1998). The price of "passing": A lesbian perspective on authenticity in organizations. *Management Communication Quarterly, 11*(4), 598–605. https://doi.org/10.1177/0893318998114006

Sue, D. W., Capodilupo, C. M., Torino, G. C., Bucceri, J. M., Holder, A. M. B., Nadal, K. L., & Esquilin, M. (2007). Racial microaggressions in everyday life: Implications for clinical practice. *American Psychologist, 62*(4), 271–286. http://doi.org/10.1037/0003-066X.62.4.271

Tejeda, M. J. (2006). Nondiscrimination policies and sexual identity disclosure: Do they make a difference in employee outcomes? *Employee Responsibilities and Rights Journal, 18*(1), 45–59. https://www.doi.org/10.1007/s10672-005-9004-5

Westerman, C. Y. K., Currie-Mueller, J. L., Motto, J. S., & Curti, L. C. (2017). How supervisor relationships and protection rules affect employees' attempts to manage health information at work. *Health Communication, 32*(12), 1520–1528. https://doi.org/10.1080/10410236.2016.1234538

Wittenberg-Lyles, E. M., & Villagran, M. M. (2006). Disclosure of a cancer diagnosis in organizational peer relationships. *Communication Research Reports, 23*(4), 251–257. https://doi.org/10.1080/08824090600962383

Yep, G. A., & Lescure, R. (2019). A thick intersectional approach to microaggressions. *Southern Communication Journal, 84*(2), 113–126. https://doi.org/10.1080/1041794X.2018.1511749

NOTE

1. We use the acronym LGBTQ+ to include workers' queer, trans, and intersex identities and namings. This acronym stands for: Lesbian, Gay, Bisexual, Trans, Queer, and Questioning. The + symbolizes that naming is a complex practice, and not all community or individual namings are listed by letter in this acronym. This is not to erase those identities or experiences but instead point to how current communication studies research has predominantly examined LG workers (and sometimes BTQ+ workers). Throughout this article, we use language from researchers and their participants, and we call for more inclusive and extensive research on underrepresented workers including nonbinary, QTPOC, Two-Spirit, pansexual, intersex, asexual, aromantic, demisexual, polyamorous, and more LGBTQ+ intersectional experiences.

Elizabeth K. Eger, Morgan L. Litrenta, Sierra R. Kane, and Lace D. Senegal

PERFORMANCE OF BROWN SEXUALITIES

INTRODUCTION

Understanding the "performance of Brown sexualities" requires individually understanding three main words—"performance," "Brown," and "sexualities." All three words are instable English-language referents that combine across one another to potentially evoke the wonder of scholarly curiosity or even to potentially provoke the taboo of explicit fantasy. In Derridean différance fashion (Derrida, 1982), all three words consort with the adjoining terms to help define them; also, all three words dissociate with the other terms for their own refinement. Even a slight altering of the reference of one term can radically shift the interpretation of the full phrase. The three words influence one another's connotations, offer a confluence of larger denotative meanings, and provide an effluence toward yet-to-be created interpretations. Perhaps, of the three words, "Brown" is the least often academically defined term, while "performance" and "sexualities" have both inspired tomes. To help explain Brown, José Esteban Muñoz avoided ancestral genetics and embraced the experience of heritage. Muñoz (2020) provided an expansive and inclusive affective definition of Brown that also moves away from visuality and toward an embodiment of social forces: "uneven distribution of resources; systematic race-, nation-, and language-based bias; unjust and phobic immigration policies; and a general tendency to be scapegoated during a nation-state's moments of economic or cultural instability" (p. 101). Of note, he also avoided tracing the term through non-English languages like Spanish, French, and native languages like Nahuatl or Quechua but instead focused on an Anglo-phonic articulation of the concept. As such, for this article, a Muñozian approach to

Brown (with all its limitations) will anchor the interfluence of "performance of Brown sexualities." In relation to Brown, performance and sexualities will be determined with the overall goal of understanding the theoretical and material possibilities of the performance of Brown sexualities.

A historiography of the performance of Brown sexualities is challenging because of the digressive contexts in which it derived. For example, the communication discipline has both a long history (e.g., Aristotle) and a short one (e.g., division from English literature departments)—and either history can be a contested one. Similarly, performance studies, as located within the communication discipline, can also have a contested history. Then, when seeking to locate scholars of color within either or both histories, the archival records certainly become, if not more contested, then definitely more obscured. A history of the scholarship of performance studies by Brown scholars that has a sexuality focus has sometimes been indirectly chronicled in academic literature reviews like Latina/o communication studies (González et al., 2014), rhetoric (Holling, 2008), Chicana feminism (Holling, 2020), and critical/cultural studies (Mejia, 2020). Without a doubt, directly locating the scholarship of Brown performance studies with a focus on sexuality is necessary for the citational, factual documentation such a history provides. With more of the history told, we better know what this scholarship has offered in the past and what we should or could be building toward for the future. Importantly, we can reject the political alienation that comes with being considered academically novel or only recently discovered (Ahmed, 2017; Calafell & Moreman, 2009; Gómez-Peña, 1996; Moreman & Xiong, 2022; Valdivia, 2013). Perhaps most relevant to scholars of performance of Brown sexualities studies, documenting our work offers appreciation for the influential ways we have complexified and continue to complexify the ontological, epistemological, and heuristic offerings of performance studies in communication.

To give form to the abstract and ephemeral meanings of Brown, Latino/a/x scholarship that engages with sexual expression as constituted through the practice and the theory of performance studies in communication is joined together here. For this article, Brown is a subject, not just an object and definitely more than the abject. Brown is agentic, and Brown draws its agency from its *mestizaje* subjectivity—a subject positionality that both rejects and acknowledges Brown's relationship to settler colonialism. For many essays of this type, scholars use the map as a metaphor to reveal historical intellectual lineage or conceptual theoretical categorizations. For example, in her essential-reading book on performance studies, Jackson (2004) reconsidered previous mappings of the academic area and sojourned into the castle-like dwellings (i.e., schools and departments) within these charted territories. Similarly, in their future-oriented archival essay, Simmons and Brisini (2020) metaphorically navigated the archipelagos of performance studies in communication and then playfully collapsed the map and the land to better equate the theoretical trajectories with the scholars-in-action. Brown communities are *mestiza* communities, and the synthesizing between the map and the people, the map and the land, and the people and the land have always been recognized. As border people, Brown persons are consistently in interpretive flux: "a constant changing of forms, *renacimientos de la tierra madre*" (Anzaldúa, 2012a, p. 313). Brown has a problematic relationship to cartographical metaphors. Indeed, maps have been drawn to justify how to create, to alienate, and to expatriate Brown people. As such, Anzaldúa (2012a) offered forth the border as a metaphor that subverts the cultural norms that dominate Brown lives. Quite ingeniously, the border metaphor becomes an inspiring symbol that delineates dominant cultural discourses and in turn suggests ways to affect social change. "For the mestiza our strength lies in our ability to negotiate borders, to mediate, to move between identities and positions. Mestizas function disruptively, making definitions of otherness hard to sustain" (Anzaldúa, 2012b, p. 50). Brown performance of sexualities is one such key example of our disruptive ability at negotiation, mediation, and movement among our dynamic otherness. This article further expounds upon the capacious qualities of Brown and more fully links Brown to communication studies. To consider the range of ways we perform Brown sexualities, two broad types of performance, stage and everyday, will be focused on. A projection about the futurity of the performance of Brown sexualities will be presented.

EL MAPA IS NOT THE TERRITORY

The performance of Brown sexualities can be best understood as ritualized relations of kinship. This understanding does not invoke the concept of inheritance rights tied to patriarchal lineage nor promote the advantages of societal prestige tied to familial legitimacy. Indeed, the scholars of the performance of Brown sexualities are more like illegitimate children who are born into a legacy of innovation without the stability of birthright entitlements. R. R. Flores (1997) explained how Latinx communities perform public rituals that maintain our cultural legacy while also welcoming participants into a community. Through these ceremonies we gather one another to produce associations that are very often built upon genealogical links. However, these same ceremonies then create kindred with one another who may or may not be blood-related. Connective affects become vernacularized through terms like *la familia, la raza*, and *mi gente* that accept one another into a family body politic. By shifting inclusion away from patrilineal, heterosexual reproduction and more toward ritualized relations, generational production becomes a queer iterative practice toward creating Latinidad. This Latinidad gathers outsider members (e.g., Muslim, trans-identified, Crip, undocumented) for the creation of an inclusive collective of politically minded survivors. Performing Brownness with one another, we transform one another into family as we renew how cultural endurance can improve current and future societies. One way Brownness is performed is through the process and the product of writing and reading (Moreman, 2009a). The process and the product of this article, then, is a performance of Brown sexualities that is realized through the performance ritual of writing and reading that maintains kinship into *la familia* of the performance of Brown sexualities while also inviting others into this kindred circle.

In order to explain the performance of Brown sexualities, Brown is offered as a concept expressed through performance that intentionally intersects with gender and sexual expression. "Identity is indeed a problematic term when applied to Latinas/os—groups who do not cohere along the lines of race, nation, language, or any other conventional demarcation of difference" (Muñoz, 2020, p. 38). Brown, as an identity grouping that names Latinxs, is first understood by its lack of easy correlation to normativity and the terms for these normativities. The synonyms with Brown carry their own connotative misjoinders that further challenge normative cultural identifiers and therefore normative discursive practices, for example, Hispanic, Latina, Latino, Latinx, Latine, Latinidad, Chicana, Chicano, Chicanx, Chicane, and chicanidad. Further, Brown signifies beyond Latin American and *mestizx* ancestry and spans to include people and cultures from South Asia, the Middle East, North Africa, the Pacific Islands, and more. "Brownness is coexistent, affiliates, and intermeshes with blackness, Asianness, indigenousness, and other terms that manifest descriptive force to render the particularities of various modes of striving in the world" (Muñoz, 2020, p. 138). Brown is a term that accepts and includes difference that comes from being marginalized from more dominant constructs of culture. Through a performance of Brown, we defer to continually negotiating our cultural complexities within public and private performance sites that express our presence and our belonging. The performance of Brown sexualities becomes a type of performance that validates how we collectively constitute ourselves across nonnormative embodied experiences to generate cultural knowledge. In performances, whether they be on the stage, within the everyday, or even as writing and reading, we make sense of our worlds by self-valuing our physical and emotional presence. Expressions are shared with each other for the co-creation of community that honors alliances with each other's difference as a strategy to improve uncontrollable but commutable cultures. Brown will continue to be defined here from a Muñozian perspective and then that perspective will be extended into a performance studies in communication perspective.

BROWN IN PERFORMANCE STUDIES IN COMMUNICATION

José Esteban Muñoz profoundly impacted the performance of Brown sexualities within the communication discipline. After Muñoz's passing, *QED* published a spotlight on the effect of Muñoz upon scholars mostly within communication but also from sister disciplines (Calafell, 2014; Chávez, 2014; Corey, 2014; McIntosh, 2014; Rivera-Servera, 2014; Tropicana, 2014). In a simple statement, Calafell captured the importance of Muñoz's scholarship: "It has created a lifeline for many of us in the academy" (p. 135). Muñoz had multiple journal articles and book chapters, and two edited books, but it is his three solo authored books that have had and will continue to provide a lifeline across all academic disciplines interested in how culture is aesthetically embodied and transformed. Those three books are *Disidentifications: Queers of Color and the Performance of Politics* (Muñoz, 1999), *Cruising Utopia: The Then and Now of Queer Futurity* (Muñoz, 2009), and *The Sense of Brown* (Muñoz, 2020). His first book, *Disidentifications*, honored queer of color aesthetic performances as strategies to change society. *Cruising Utopia* further examined how queer is a creative endeavor that is future focused in its aspirations for a more hopeful political hereafter. *The Sense of Brown*, posthumously published, is an aggregated musing upon Brown embodiment that postulated how alienation catalyzes survival. Across all of his works, Muñoz dignified Brown agency while rejecting an "according to" determination and embracing an "in accord with" process. He never denied the violence and harms of dominant discourses on Brown cultures and peoples. However, he modeled how to cultivate endurance through appreciating societal aesthetics and attending to corporeal senses so as to progress within the logics of dominant ideologies. Rather than existing according to the world, Brown exists in accord with the world so as to thrive in a future-forward survivalist shaping of the world.

Within the larger communication discipline, performance studies is a specialized area of study and practice. Offering a name for the scholarly community and works at the fusion of the two areas, Bell (2008) used the term "Performance Studies in Communication (PSC)."

To help specify the scholars and scholarship of PSC, Bell overlapped the axiological affinities of communication and performance studies; that is, both conspicuously value inquiry and meaning as being constitutive, epistemic, and critical. Within the larger communication discipline, communication scholars study how humans use symbols to transmit information, represent reality, and transform meaning. PSC scholars carry those same general goals but frame symbol usage through embodied, presentational offerings. Both Brown and sexualities come to PSC as epistemic concepts that offer language for critiques of the ways we all live while also proposing better ways of living. Dynamic and situated, Brown and sexualities productively respond to the limits of normativity through their intersectional demands on meaning. Sexuality recognizes discursive constructs of desire within the matrix of sexes and genders. Brown recognizes the discursive constructs of agency within the matrix of culture, race, and ethnicity. Indeed, intersectionality effectively offers forth the oscillating power relations Brown and sexualities endure within normative discourses (Calafell, 2010; Crenshaw, 1989, 1991; Moreno Tabarez, 2012; Yep, 2010, 2016). However, PSC best provides the theories, methods, and practices for thinking through the complicated abstract and material realities of the lived experience of the performance of Brown sexualities. Brown is socially manifested through visual and affective recognition and rejection. Both staged performances and the performance of everyday life are rendered and revised along a spectrum of acceptance and rejection. Whether Brown performances are on the stage or in everyday lives, we negotiate and then modify performances along a spectrum of belonging. Brown sexualities on the stage are considered, with an emphasis on how communication scholars have framed these performances.

TEATRO PERFORMANCE OF BROWN SEXUALITIES

To broaden the stage of the performance of Brown sexualities in communication, the stage of theater and dance is included. Both of these staged performances are marked by their intentional practice of providing a narrative for a live audience. Beyond the communication discipline, scholars offer multiple examples of analyses of theatrically staged performances of Brown sexualities (Román, 2005; Santana, 2018; Taylor, 2014, 2020). Within the communication discipline, there are fewer instances of formal analyses. For example, both Moreman (2019b) and Rodríguez-Dorans (2020) provided considerations that include Latinx stages, Latinx actors, and Latinx references; however, neither analysis centered Brown as the driving concept. Similarly, Calafell and Moreman (2010) focused upon an El Teatro Campesino production, but it is one part of a larger analytical arc. In a more extensive staged theater analysis, Spangler (2013) submitted his adaptation of *Tortilla Curtain* from Boyle's novel (1995) of the same name. While five scholars reflected upon the staging of his play, only B. Chávez (2013) directly brought sexuality to fore. She analyzed the ways the play intentionally exacerbates a tension between the disruption of a White, heterosexual, upper-middle class, straight family-oriented neighborhood and the presence of an undocumented, heterosexual Brown couple and their newborn. She reconfigures the play's tragic denouement by reading it through a performance of Brown queer lens: "Here, futurity begins in darkness, in the belly of the serpent, where only slivers of light can be found. It is in this space that a new present can be crafted—one we *desperately* need" (p. 189). B. Chávez's belly invocation becomes metaphorical for

Brown queer *arrasandos* that provide the possibility of new futures. Documenting a Chicana/o presence in theater, Holling and Calafell (2007) assembled a focused overview that spans from *carpa* to El Teatro Campesino to a consideration of Guillermo Gómez Peña and *Culture Clash*'s Richard Montoya. Rightfully so, Holling and Calafell critiqued the erasure of women in Chicanx history and, more recently, scholars like Sowards (2019) have rewritten women into that history. There has also been a concern for the erasure of nonnormative sexualities, as well. Holling and Calafell insightfully detailed how Brown performance provides opportunities for future subjectivities to be expressed and accepted. Richard Montoya and *Culture Clash* provided comic satire and visibility for Latinx culture within a post–civil rights 1980s and they certainly deserve canonical embrace. Not more important but differently important, Guillermo Gómez Peña (1986, 1993, 1996, 2000, 2021) is a Mexican-born and U.S.–based performance artist with a 40-plus-year career who continues performing to this day. He summarizes the core of his performance artist reputation: "I developed a reputation as an iconoclast by engaging in symbolic acts of transgression that explored and exposed sources of racism and nationalism" (Gómez-Peña, 2006, p. 150). While his transgressive acts have never fixated on sexualities, they always included sexualities as part of his artistic transgressive practices.

While not consistently staged, dance is an important formalized cultural practice for the performance of Brown sexualities. Dance spans from strict choreography to mediated artifact and is resistant to being limited to a theatrical dais. "Dance choreography is a good example of performance that can be based on pre-text (dance notions written down and used to guide performance), improvisation (dance is created in the moment in and through bodies), or post-text (the performance is coded and recorded after the performance)" (Bell, 2008, p. 73). Certainly explored outside the communication discipline (McMains, 2001; Power-Sotomayor, 2020; Román, 2003), the link between dance and Brown sexualities has been explored within the discipline as well. For Rivera-Servera (2012), dance of queer Latinxs is both "a social situation always already embedded in the political and a technology for achieving political interventions" (p. 32). Sometimes those political interventions are not found within the art form but within the community that is brought together to honor the art form. For example, through heterosexual overtones, Willis (1997) ethnographically explained "Latino night" as a constructed cultural space in the U.S. Midwest. Then, highlighting the Brown queer body in a queer bar and more specifically in a Brown queer bar, Calafell (2009, 2017a) and Moreman (2008, 2009b, 2020) demonstrated how these spaces offer important resources for understanding the interstices of minoritarian belongings. Moreman and McIntosh (2010) emphasized how, on "Latin drag night," Brown agentic subjects create a Brown hybrid context where a range of identificatory, intersectional possibilities become realized. Fraser Delgado and Muñoz (1997) directly linked Latinidad to dance and how both liberate one another. "Latin/o bodies serve as the site of a long history of racial, cultural, and economic conflict. Dance promises the potential reinscription of those bodies with alternate interpretations of that history. Magnificent against the monotonous repetition of everyday oppressions, dance incites rebellions of everynight life" (p. 10). To proactively reframe the Orlando Pulse tragedy, two separate journal forums reclaimed the physical joys and conceptual bounties of the Brown queer dance club. Sloop and Morris (2017) organized a forum in *Communication and Critical/Cultural Studies* that included scholars like Calafell (2017b), Ganesh (2017), and Gutierrez-Perez (2017). Alexander and Weems (2017) organized a four-part forum in *Qualitative Inquiry* that included scholars like Andrade and Gutierrez-Perez (2017), Johnson (2017), and Masango Chéry (2017). Ways that the performance of Brown sexualities is embodied in the mundane of our everyday lives are examined.

BROWN IN EVERYDAY LIFE, ¡Y OJO!

The performance of Brown sexualities provides examples of a type of self-performance in which the scripts of society's normative discourses are enacted and resisted. Performing the self is, in most ways, a quotidian awareness among most everyone. Calafell's self-awareness could easily be an example of a common sense that most people have about their own everyday performances: "I have been thinking about Latina/o performance for quite some time, even before I knew that that object of my affection was performance" (2007, p. 1). Academics stylize the techniques and language for understanding self-performance, similarly to how artists stylize the techniques and language of the performing arts. Whether it is performance mode, sexuality desires, or Brown recognitions, we adapt to our changing needs for survivalist reasons. De la Garza (2004, 2007, 2014a, 2014b, 2018) elucidated and explained how Latinidad is more than just survival, it is a source for thriving that allows us to locate and attract communal acceptance. The everyday performance of Brown sexualities, while capacious in meaning and form, follows a common theme of respected belonging. For many scholars, the educational space is a key context for the consideration for the regulation of the performance of Brown sexualities (De La Garza & Spieldenner, 2020; Juárez, 2019, 2020; Moreman & Non Grata, 2011). For example, Chawla (2011) and Cruz (2010, 2018) explained how their Brownness intersects with their other positionalities (e.g., citizenship, sexuality, gender) and how these intersections are complicated and often academically dismissed due to their Brownness. "As a woman from the global south and faculty of color in a Midwest college town, walking around in Brown skin can be/is uncomfortable" (Chawla, 2011, p. 53). "But, but [pause] my C.V. reads French and Ivorian / Not American / I did not pretend to be non-alien" (Cruz, 2018, pp. 363–364). In seeking alliances with Whiteness, Carrillo Rowe (2008) and Pérez and Goltz (2010) have theorized and analyzed the ways that Brown queer women have been both separated from and sometimes sought connection to Whiteness. Other scholars have turned away from partnering with Whiteness in their considerations for more liberatory spaces. For example, Chakravartty et al. (2018) denounced the unacknowledged White-centeredness of universities as racism. "This historical grounding of modern European racism allows for more analytic clarity on how race is normalized and institutionally rearticulated in the present, whether through the split between West/non-West, White, Black, and Brown, or citizen/foreigner" (p. 255). Brown performative alliances among each other allow for intellectual melding that results in coalitional knowledge creation. An early result of Brown alliances is the recognition of and support for intellectual courageousness that rejects frameworks that depict Brown work as being too castigating or overly trivial. For example, Calafell and Gutierrez-Perez (2018), Calvante et al. (2020), Ghabra and Calafell (2018), and Gutierrez-Perez and Andrade (2018) allowed their vulnerable queer Brown lived histories to be presented as possibilities for ways to redefine academic and non-academic Brown relationships and therefore redefine knowledge creation.

The performance of Brown sexualities, as an everyday practice, helps create a space for those seeking to better understand the complexities of belonging. Within the 21st century, "Latinx" has emerged as a term of inclusivity for Brown gender and sexual flexibility that affirms multiplicities of ethnic intersectionality but also offers affinity with wider social justice movements. As Latinx spans gender and sexuality, it also spans the affinitive possibilities of race and ethnicity (Dame-Griff, 2022; de Onís, 2017; Moreman, 2019a). "Latinx refers foremost to an ethnic identity that is often associated with a [B]rown racial identity, but it can also refer to a white or black racial identity, as well as an indigenous identity (not to mention how multiraciality complicates this simple schema)" (Soto Vega & Chávez, 2018, p. 320). Early on in PSC, Conquergood (1992, 1994a, 1994b, 1997, 2002) explored cultural performance, specifically Latinxs who sought community inclusion and fought social persecution. More recently, Brown has again become an important identity marker for those seeking to name and critique how nation-states police citizenship. Silva (2016) and Mudambi (2015) illustrated how racial profiling unites Brown ethnic groups across one another in a way that gives them belonging with one another, even if that belonging is a commonality of oppression. K. R. Chávez (2009a, 2009b, 2010a, 2010b) interceded between the capaciousness of nonnormative sexualities and Brown to consider queer migrations. She understood the variabilities of the performance of Brown sexualities as an opportunity for coalition (K. R. Chávez, 2013). However, she was cautious to not overly celebrate coalition as a finalized solution. Also, she warned against too quickly aligning coalition goals toward nationalist aspirations. She emphasized that local communities should always be the source for imagining liberatory possibility and emancipatory goals. Through the performance of Brown sexualities as located within family, Andrade (2018, 2020) and Moreman (2020) performed liberatory possibility and presented emancipatory goals. Andrade (2020), in particular, wrote about himself and his family in ways that point to the toll of seeking belonging within violent discourses of nationality, ethnicity, gender, and sexuality. In reference to Fernanda, his muxer, jota/o/x family member, he stated: "Seeking queer of color consejos that will equip us with ways to pessimistically affirm life, indigenous people, and assaults on jota/o/xs and queers also makes me realize that we need to find tactical consejos that will equip us with ways to pessimistically affirm life, community, and others from our queer migrants and others that survive our current dystopias in the shadows" (p. 246). For Andrade, Fernanda's contradictions are manifested from the performance of Brown sexuality and, rather than being problems of confusion, they are lessons for the creative survival.

CONCLUSION

The performance of Brown sexualities is vibrant within performance studies in communication. Over a decade ago, Calafell and Moreman (2009) introduced the benefits of Latinx alliance work with a special issue of *Text and Performance Quarterly* on Latina/o performativities (Chávez, 2009c; Delgado, 2009; Pineda, 2009; Rivera-Servera, 2009). The introductory essay was intentional in its stated intervention to offer a Latinx perspective to performance studies in communication and to academic publishing, but additionally the introductory essay was intentional in its acknowledgement and confirmation of a Latinx academic audience. "Per the form of publication in this special issue on Latina/o performativities, they offer us the possibility to conceptually imagine what materially might be and what physically could be. And they do this all the while envisioning their audience—you" (Calafell & Moreman, 2009, p. 130). Since that special issue, the scholarship of the performance of Brown sexualities has been robust and meaningful, but that does not mean that it has always been supported or endorsed. Universities, even culturally identified universities like Hispanic-serving institutions, still struggle to understand how to serve non-White students and their faculty (Moreman, 2019c). Scholars of color still struggle against unwelcoming educational spaces, and the need for solidarity has never been greater: "I performatively and vulnerably ask readers to be implicated or intercede in hostile academic spaces that continue to Other women of color" (Calafell, 2015, p. 30). The work of the performance of Brown sexualities effectively destabilizes normative discourses while simultaneously provoking and inviting new individual and community subjectivities. However, the work of the performance of Brown sexualities is never beyond contexts of co-performance with oppressive subjectivities and always potentially implicated in oppressing emerging subjectivities. Indeed, anti-Black and anti-Indigenous racism is always a potentiality within the performance of Brown sexualities. For example, Valdivia (2020) warned against light-skin Latina representation being utilized as the diversity element within all White media contexts. Also, Chávez (2021) rebuked casual usage of "person of color" to deeply consider whether our situated positions really work in communities toward Black and Indigenous social justice issues. Johnson and Rivera-Servera (2016) showcased the conceptual and practical value of beginning with and developing method from the experiences of Blatino queer performance studies scholars and critics. And, arguably, all of these aforementioned progressive efforts are borne from valuing the complex and sophisticated every day, non-academic experiences of the performance of Brown sexualities. José Esteban Muñoz established how to use the performance of Brown sexualities to dismantle normative discourses and then how to use the performance of Brown sexualities to offer forth nonnormative inclusivity. This type of work requires the unguaranteed risk of vulnerability matched with the non-shaming acceptance of pleasure. Most important, this type of work requires the intentionality of coalitional work toward social justice. However, those who embrace the work of the performance of Brown sexualities, join a dynamic and inchoate *familia* of practitioners who—though often left out of official normative historical and regulative canonical lists (even sometimes by one another)—continue to transgress and transcend. With our Jotería, somxs pocxs, pero locxs.

FURTHER READING

Chávez, K. R. (2021). *The borders of AIDS: Race, quarantine, and resistance*. University of Washington Press.
Galarte, F. J. (2021). *Brown trans figurations: Rethinking race, gender, and sexuality in Chicanx/Latinx studies*. University of Texas Press.
Gutierrez-Perez, R. (2021). *Jotería communication studies: Narrating theories of resistance*. Peter Lang.
La Fountain-Stokes, L. (2021). *Translocas: The politics of Puerto Rican drag and trans performance*. The University of Michigan Press.
Moreira, R. (2021). *Bitches unleashed: Performance and embodied politics in favela funk*. Peter Lang.
Muñoz, J. E. (2020). *The sense of Brown* (J. Chambers-Letson & T. Nyong'o, Eds.). Duke University Press.

REFERENCES

Ahmed, S. (2017). *Living a feminist life*. Duke University Press.
Alexander, B. K., & Weems, M. E. (2017). June 12, 2016: Terrorism and hate in Orlando, America—Poetic and performative responses. *Qualitative Inquiry*, 23(7), 483–487. https://doi.org/10.1177/1077800417718282

Andrade, L. M. (2018). On the death of *mi madre*, hauntings, and ethnic mourning. *Text and Performance Quarterly, 38*(3), 136–152. https://doi.org/10.1080/10462937.2018.1468572

Andrade, L. M. (2020). "*Vale verga*" ("It's worth a cock (Nothing)"): The queer of color world-making *consejos* of Fernanda, an again undocumented *muxer/jota*. *Text and Performance Quarterly, 40*(3), 231–249. https://doi.org/10.1080/10462937.2020.1788134

Andrade, L. M., & Gutierrez-Perez, R. (2017). *Bailando con las sombras*: Spiritual activism and soul healing in the war years. *Qualitative Inquiry, 23*(7), 502–504. https://doi.org/10.1177/1077800417718287

Anzaldúa, G. (2012a). *Borderlands/La frontera: The new* mestiza (4th ed.). Aunt Lute Books.

Anzaldúa, G. (2012b). Geographies of self—Re-imagining identity: *Nos/otras* (us/other) and the new tribalism. In A. N. Valdivia & M. García (Eds.), In *Mapping Latina/o studies: An interdisciplinary reader* (pp. 39–61). Peter Lang.

Bell, E. (2008). *Theories of performance*. SAGE.

Boyle, T. C. (1995). *The tortilla curtain*. Viking.

Calafell, B. M. (2007). *Latina/o communication studies: Theorizing performance*. Peter Lang.

Calafell, B. M. (2009). She ain't no diva!: Reflections on in/hospitable guests/hosts, reciprocity, and desire. *Liminalities: A Journal of Performance Studies, 5*(5), 1–18.

Calafell, B. M. (2010). When will we all matter?: Exploring race, pedagogy, and sustained hope for the academy. In D. L. Fassett & J. T. Warren (Eds.), *The SAGE handbook of communication and instruction* (pp. 343–359). SAGE.

Calafell, B. M. (2014). "Feeling brown, feeling down": Honoring the life and legacy of José Esteban Muñoz. *QED: A Journal of GLBTQ Worldmaking, 1*(3), 133–137.

Calafell, B. M. (2015). *Monstrosity, performance, and race in contemporary culture*. Peter Lang.

Calafell, B. M. (2017a). Brown queer bodies. *Qualitative Inquiry, 23*(7), 511–512. https://doi.org/10.1177/1077800417718290

Calafell, B. M. (2017b). Brownness, kissing, and US imperialism: Contextualizing the Orlando Massacre. *Communication and Critical/Cultural Studies, 14*(2), 198–202. https://doi.org/10.1080/14791420.2017.1293957

Calafell, B. M., & Gutierrez-Perez, R. (2018). (Critical) love is a battlefield: Implications for a critical intercultural pedagogical approach. In A. Atay & S. Toyosaki (Eds.), *Critical intercultural communication pedagogy* (pp. 49–63). Lexington Books.

Calafell, B. M., & Moreman, S. T. (2009). Envisioning an academic readership: Latina/o performativities per the form of publication. *Text and Performance Quarterly, 29*(2), 123–130. https://doi.org/10.1080/10462930902774833

Calafell, B. M., & Moreman, S. T. (2010). Iterative hesitancies and Latinidad: The reverberances of raciality. In T. K. Nakayama & R. T. Halualani (Eds.), *The handbook of critical intercultural communication* (pp. 400–416). Blackwell.

Calvante, L. B. Y., Calafell, B. M., & Chávez, K. R. (2020). Here is something you can't understand: The suffocating Whiteness of communication studies. *Communication and Critical/Cultural Studies, 17*(2), 202–209. https://doi.org/10.1080/14791420.2020.1770823

Carrillo Rowe, A. (2008). *Power lines: On the subject of feminist alliances*. Duke University Press.

Chakravartty, P., Kuo, R., Grubbs, V., & McIlwain, C. (2018). #CommunicationSoWhite. *Journal of Communication, 68*(2), 254–266. https://doi.org/10.1093/joc/jqy003

Chávez, B. (2013). Performing the border: A queer of color artist-scholar and ally response to *Tortilla Curtain*. *Text and Performance Quarterly, 33*(2), 184–190. https://doi.org/10.1080/10462937.2013.770911

Chávez, B. (2014). A living legacy: What disidentification will continue to mean for queer performance artists of color. *QED: A Journal in GLBTQ Worldmaking, 1*(3), 150. https://doi.org/10.14321/qed.1.3.0150

Chávez, K. R. (2009a). Exploring the defeat of Arizona's marriage amendment and the specter of the immigrant as queer. *Southern Communication Journal, 74*(3), 314–324. https://doi.org/10.1080/10417940903060930

Chávez, K. R. (2009b). Embodied translation: Dominant discourse and communication with migrant bodies-as-text. *The Howard Journal of Communications, 20*(1), 18–36. https://doi.org/10.1080/10646170802664912

Chávez, K. R. (2009c). Remapping Latinidad: A performance cartography of Latina/o identity. *Text and Performance Quarterly, 29*(2), 165–182. https://doi.org/10.1080/10462930902774866

Chávez, K. R. (2010a). Border (in)securities: Normative and differential belonging in LGBTQ and immigrant rights discourse. *Communication and Critical/Cultural Studies, 7*(2), 136–155. https://doi.org/10.1080/14791421003763291

Chávez, K. R. (2010b). Spatializing gender performativity: Ecstasy and possibilities for livable life in the tragic case of Victoria Arellano. *Women's Studies in Communication, 33*(1), 1–15. https://doi.org/10.1080/07491401003669729

Chávez, K. R. (2013). *Queer migration politics: Activist rhetoric and coalitional possibilities*. University of Illinois Press.

Chávez, K. R. (2021). Bridge work: A radical subject in the community and new ways of knowing. *Journal of Autoethnography, 2*(1), 119–122. https://doi.org/10.1525/joae.2021.2.1.119

Chawla, D. (2011). Between solids/monologues in Brown: A mystory performance. *Critical Studies/Critical Methodologies, 11*(1), 47–58. https://doi.org/10.1177/1532708610386921

Conquergood, D. (1992). Life in Big Red: Struggle and accommodations in a Chicago polyethnic tenement. In L. Lamphere (Ed.), *Structuring diversity: Ethnographic perspectives on the new immigration* (pp. 95–144). The University of Chicago Press.

Conquergood, D. (1994a). For the nation!: How street gangs problematize patriotism. In H. W. Simons & M. Billig (Eds.), *After postmodernism: Reconstructing ideology critique* (pp. 200–221). SAGE.

Conquergood, D. (1994b). Homeboys and hoods: Gang communication and cultural space. In L. R. Frey (Ed.), *Group communication in context: Studies in natural context* (pp. 23–55). Erlbaum.

Conquergood, D. (1997). Street literacy. In J. Flood, S. Brice Heath, & D. Lapp (Eds.), *Handbook of research on teaching literacy through communicative and visual arts* (pp. 354–375). Macmillan.

Conquergood, D. (2002). Lethal theatre: Performance, punishment, and the death penalty. *Theatre Journal, 54*(3), 339–367. https://doi.org/10.1353/tj.2002.0077

Corey, F. (2014). A queer divine dissatisfaction. *QED: A Journal in GLBTQ Worldmaking, 1*(3), 142. https://doi.org/10.14321/qed.1.3.0142

Crenshaw, K. (1989). Demarginalizing the intersection of race and sex: A black feminist critique of antidiscrimination doctrine, feminist theory and antiracist politics. *The University of Chicago Legal Forum, 1989*(1), 130–167.

Crenshaw, K. (1991). Mapping the margins: Intersectionality, identity politics, and violence against women of color. *Stanford Law Review, 43*(6), 1241–1299. https://doi.org/10.2307/1229039

Cruz, J. (2010). This ain't Paris sweetie: Exploring West African and French identity in the southern United States. *Qualitative Inquiry, 16*(10), 792–800. https://doi.org/10.1177/1077800410383125

Cruz, J. M. (2018). Brown body of knowledge: A tale of erasure. *Critical Studies/Critical Methodologies, 18*(5), 363–365. https://doi.org/10.1177/1532708617735131

Dame-Griff, E. C. (2022). What *do* we mean when we say "Latinx?": Definitional power, the limits of inclusivity, and the (un/re)constitution of an identity category. *Journal of International and Intercultural Communication, 15*(2), 119–131. https://doi.org/10.1080/17513057.2021.1901957

De La Garza, A. T., & Spieldenner, A. R. (2020). "Bad hombre" in the classroom: Pedagogical politics in performing "brown man" in a conservative time. In D. S. Strasser (Ed.), *Communication and identity in the classroom: Intersectional perspectives of critical pedagogy* (pp. 59–70). Lexington Books.

de la Garza, S. A. (2004). *Maria speaks: Journeys into the mysteries of the mother in my life as a Chicana*. Peter Lang.

de la Garza, S. A. (2007). The integrated self crosses borders daily: Inviting the mystical realism of the integrated scholar. *Issues in Integrative Studies, 25*, 156–168.

de la Garza, S. A. (2014a). Mindful heresy, *holo-expression*, and poiesis: An autoethnographic response to the orthodoxies of interpersonal & cultural life. In R. M. Boylorn & M. P. Orbe (Eds.), *Critical autoethnography: Intersecting cultural identities in everyday life* (pp. 209–221). Routledge.

de la Garza, S. A. (2014b). The four seasons of ethnography: A creation-centered ontology of ethnography. In M. K. Asante, Y. Miike, & J. Yin (Eds.), *The global intercultural communication reader* (2nd ed., pp. 151–173). Routledge.

de la Garza, S. A. (2018). Challenges of de-/pre-colonial ontologies. *Journal of Multicultural Discourses, 13*(3), 226–231. https://doi.org/10.1080/17447143.2018.1519886

de Onís, C. (2017). What's in an "x"?: An exchange about the politics of "Latinx". *Chiricú Journal: Latina/o Literatures, Arts, and Cultures, 1*(2), 78–91. https://doi.org/10.2979/chiricu.1.2.07

Delgado, F. P. (2009). Reflections on being/performing Latino in the academy. *Text and Performance Quarterly, 29*(2), 149–164. https://doi.org/10.1080/10462930902774858

Derrida, J. (1982). *Margins of philosophy* (A. Bass, Trans.). The University of Chicago Press.

Flores, R. R. (1997). Aesthetic process and cultural citizenship: The membering of a social body in San Antonio. In W. V. Flores & R. Benyamor (Eds.), *Latino cultural citizenship: Claiming identity, space, and rights* (pp. 124–151). Beacon Press.

Fraser Delgado, C., & Muñoz, J. E. (1997). Rebellions of everynight life. In C. Fraser Delgado & J. E. Muñoz (Eds.), In *Everynight life: Culture and dance in Latin/o America* (pp. 9–32). Duke University Press.

Ganesh, S. (2017). The Orlando shootings as a mobilizing event: Against reductionism in social movement studies. *Communication and Critical/Cultural Studies, 14*(2), 193–197. https://doi.org/10.1080/14791420.2017.1293956

Ghabra, H., & Calafell, B. M. (2018). From failure and allyship to feminist solidarities: Negotiating our privileges and oppressions across borders. *Text and Performance Quarterly, 38*(1–2), 38–54. https://doi.org/10.1080/10462937.2018.1457173

Gómez-Peña, G. (1986). *Border culture: A process of negotiation toward utopia*, La linea quebrada = *The broken line*. Centro Cultural de La Raza.

Gómez-Peña, G. (1993). *Warrior for gringostroika: Essays, performance texts, and poetry*. Graywolf Press.

Gómez-Peña, G. (1996). *The new world border: Prophecies, poems, & loqueras for the end of the century*. City Lights.

Gómez-Peña, G. (2000). *Dangerous border crossers: The artist talks back*. Routledge.

Gómez-Peña, G. (2006). Disclaimer. *TDR: The Drama Review, 50*(1), 149–158.

Gómez-Peña, G. (2021). *Gómez-Peña unplugged: Texts on live art, social practice and imaginary activism (2008-2019)*. In B. Gómez, E. Tramposch, W. Stark, & E. A. Peña, (Eds.). Routledge.

González, A., Calafell, B. M., & Avant-Mier, R. (2014). An LCSD & La Raza microhistory: The Latina/o communication studies division & La Raza caucus of the National Communication Association. *Review of Communication, 14*(2), 125–137. https://doi.org/10.1080/15358593.2014.939706

Gutierrez-Perez, R. (2017). A journey to El Mundo Zurdo: Queer temporality, queer of color cultural heritages. *Communication and Critical/Cultural Studies, 14*(2), 177–181. https://doi.org/10.1080/14791420.2017.1293947

Gutierrez-Perez, R., & Andrade, L. M. (2018). Queer of color worldmaking: In the rhetorical archive and the embodied repertoire. *Text and Performance Quarterly, 38*(1–2), 1–18. https://doi.org/10.1080/10462937.2018.1435130

Holling, M. A. (2008). Retrospective on Latin@ rhetorical performance scholarship: From "Chicano communication" to "Latina/o communication?" *The Communication Review, 11*(4), 293–322. https://doi.org/10.1080/10714420802511218

Holling, M. A. (2020). Intersectionalities in the fields of Chicana feminism: Pursuing decolonization through Xicanisma's "Resurrection of the Dreamers." In B. M. Calafell, S. Eguchi, & S. Abdi (Eds.), *Dewhitening intersectionality: Race, intercultural communication, and politics* (pp. 3–24). Lexington Books.

Holling, M. A., & Calafell, B. M. (2007). Identities on stage and staging identities: ChicanoBrujo performances as emancipatory practices. *Text and Performance Quarterly, 27*(1), 58–83. https://doi.org/10.1080/10462930601046053

Jackson, S. (2004). *Professing performance: Theatre in the academy from philogoy to performativity*. Cambridge University Press.

Johnson, A. (2017). Pulse: From death to resurrection and back again. *Qualitative Inquiry, 23*(7), 515–518. https://doi.org/10.1177/1077800417718292

Johnson, E. P., & Rivera-Servera, R. H. (2016). *Blatino queer performance*. Duke University Press.

Juárez, S. F. (2019). Chicana feminist ontologies and the social process of constructing knowledge. *Review of Communication, 19*(4), 291–308. https://doi.org/10.1080/15358593.2019.1667520

Juárez, S. F. (2020). Family stories, pedagogy, inclusive practices, and autohistoria. In D. S. Strasser (Ed.), *Communication and identity in the classroom: Intersectional perspectives of critical pedagogy* (pp. 141–154). Lexington Books.

Masango Chéry, T. (2017). "No one shakes me:" Rejected queer identities and the creation of sacred Ugandan spaces in honor of the Orlando massacre. *Qualitative Inquiry, 23*(7), 550–556. https://doi.org/10.1177/1077800417718302

McIntosh, D. M. D. (2014). White feelings, feeling straight: Cultivating affective attentiveness for queer futurities. *QED: A Journal in GLBTQ Worldmaking, 1*(3), 154. https://doi.org/10.14321/qed.1.3.0154

McMains, J. (2001). Brownface: Representations of Latin-ness in dancesport. *Dance Research Journal, 33*(2), 54–71. https://doi.org/10.2307/1477804

Mejia, R. (2020). Forum introduction: Communication and the politics of survival. *Communication and Critical/Cultural Studies, 17*(4), 360–368. https://doi.org/10.1080/14791420.2020.1829657

Moreman, S. T. (2008). Hybrid performativity, South and North of the border: *Entre la teoría y la materialidad de hibridación*. In A. N. Valdivia (Ed.), *Latina/o communication studies today* (pp. 91–111). Peter Lang.

Moreman, S. T. (2009a). Memoir as performance: Strategies of hybrid ethnic identity. *Text and Performance Quarterly, 29*(4), 350–370. https://doi.org/10.1080/10462930903242855

Moreman, S. T. (2009b). Rethinking Dwight Conquergood: Toward an unstated cultural politics. *Liminalities: A Journal of Performance Studies, 5*(5), 1–13.

Moreman, S. T. (2019a). A queer futurity autofantasía: Contouring discourses of Latinx through memory and queer youth literature. *Text and Performance Quarterly, 39*(3), 185–202. https://doi.org/10.1080/10462937.2019.1620959

Moreman, S. T. (2019b). Accommodating desires of disability: A multi-modal approach to Terry Galloway and the Mickee Faust Club. *QED: A Journal of GLBTQ Worldmaking, 6*(3), 149–162. https://doi.org/10.14321/qed.6.3.0149

Moreman, S. T. (2019c). The Hispanic-serving institution: Communicating a future with or without a past. *Communication Education, 68*(4), 509–516. https://doi.org/10.1080/03634523.2019.1646429

Moreman, S. T. (2020). Narrative embodiment of Latinx queer futurity: Pause for dramatic affect. In A. L. Johnson & B. LeMaster (Eds.), *Gender futurity, intersectional autoethnography: Embodied theorizing from the margins* (pp. 223–236). Routledge.

Moreman, S. T., & McIntosh, D. M. (2010). Brown scriptings and rescriptings: A critical performance ethnography of Latina drag queens. *Communication and Critical/Cultural Studies, 7*(2), 115–135. https://doi.org/10.1080/14791421003767912

Moreman, S. T., & Non Grata, P. (2011). Learning from and mentoring the undocumented AB540 student: Hearing an unheard voice. *Text and Performance Quarterly, 31*(3), 303–320. https://doi.org/10.1080/10462937.2011.573949

Moreman, S. T., & Xiong, C. N. (2022). Conquergood's other: Materializing the cultural text of Hmong and Latinx. *Text and Performance Quarterly, 41*(3–4), 187–203. https://doi.org/10.1080/10462937.2021.2024245

Moreno Tabarez, U. (2012). Trafficking across dangerous borders (shores): An open letter to a brother. *Text and Performance Quarterly, 32*(3), 227–243. https://doi.org/10.1080/10462937.2012.691331

Mudambi, A. (2015). The construction of brownness: Latino/a and South Asian bloggers' responses to SB 1070. *Journal of International and Intercultural Communication, 8*(1), 44–62. https://doi.org/10.1080/17513057.2015.991079

Muñoz, J. E. (1999). *Disidentifications: Queers of color and the performance of politics*. University of Minnesota Press.

Muñoz, J. E. (2009). *Cruising utopia: The then and there of queer futurity*. New York University Press.

Muñoz, J. E. (2020). *The sense of Brown*. In J. Chambers-Letson & T. Nyong'o (Eds.), Perverse modernities: A series. Duke University Press.

Pérez, K., & Goltz, D. B. (2010). Treading across lines in the sand: Performing bodies in coalitional subjectivity. *Text and Performance Quarterly, 30*(3), 247–268. https://doi.org/10.1080/10462937.2010.481797

Pineda, R. D. (2009). Will they see me coming? Do they know I'm running? Los Lobos and the performance of *mestizaje* identity through journey. *Text and Performance Quarterly, 29*(2), 183–200. https://doi.org/10.1080/10462930902774874

Power-Sotomayor, J. (2020). Moving borders and dancing in place: Son Jarocho's speaking bodies at the Fandango Fronterizo. *TDR: The Drama Review, 64*(4), 84–107.

Rivera-Servera, R. H. (2009). Exhibiting voice/narrating migration: Performance-based curatorial practice in ¡Azúcar! The life and music of Celia Cruz. *Text and Performance Quarterly, 29*(2), 131–148. https://doi.org/10.1080/10462930902774841

Rivera-Servera, R. H. (2012). *Performing queer Latinidad: Dance, sexuality, politics*. The University of Michigan Press.

Rivera-Servera, R. H. (2014). José E. Muñoz's queer gestures. *QED: A Journal in GLBTQ Worldmaking, 1*(3), 146. https://doi.org/10.14321/qed.1.3.0146

Rodríguez-Dorans, E. (2020). With our clipped wings: A research-based performance on gay men's identities devised through narrative portraiture. *Text and Performance Quarterly, 40*(2), 190–209. https://doi.org/10.1080/10462937.2020.1752931

Román, D. (2003). Theatre Journals: Dance liberation. *Theatre Journal, 55*(3), 377–394.

Román, D. (2005). *Performance in America: Contemporary U.S. culture and the performing arts*. Duke University Press.

Santana, A. (2018). *Freak performances: Dissidence in Latin American theater*. The University of Michigan Press.

Silva, K. (2016). *Brown threat: Identification in the security state*. University of Minnesota Press.

Simmons, J., & Brisini, T. (2020). Performance studies in communication. *Text and Performance Quarterly, 40*(1), 1–48. https://doi.org/10.1080/10462937.2020.1725726

Sloop, J. M., & Morris, C. E. (2017). Feeling for the pulse after Orlando. *Communication and Critical/Cultural Studies, 14*(2), 176. https://doi.org/10.1080/14791420.2017.1293944

Soto Vega, K., & Chávez, K. R. (2018). Latinx rhetoric and intersectionality in racial rhetorical criticism. *Communication and Critical/Cultural Studies, 15*(4), 319–325. https://doi.org/10.1080/14791420.2018.1533642

Sowards, S. K. (2019). ¡Sí, ella puede!: The rhetorical legacy of Dolores Huerta and the United Farm Workers. University of Texas Press.
Spangler, M. (2013). Artist's statement: Adapting T. C. Boyle's novel *The Tortilla Curtain* and subsequent production by the San Diego Repertory Theatre. *Text and Performance Quarterly*, 33(2), 151–167. https://doi.org/10.1080/10462937.2013.769061
Taylor, D. (2014). *Theatre of crisis: Drama and politics in Latin America*. The University Press of Kentucky.
Taylor, D. (2020). *¡Presente!: The politics of presence*. Duke University Press.
Tropicana, C. (2014). A queer friendship. *QED: A Journal in GLBTQ Worldmaking*, 1(3), 138–141. https://doi.org/10.14321/qed.1.3.0138
Valdivia, A. N. (2013). Amnesia and the myth of discovery: Lessons from transnational and women of color communication scholars. *Communication and Critical/Cultural Studies*, 10(2–3), 329–332. https://doi.org/10.1080/14791420.2013.812599
Valdivia, A. N. (2020). *The gender of Latinidad: Uses and abuses of hybridity*. Wiley-Blackwell.
Willis, J. L. (1997). "Latino night:" Performances of Latino/a culture in northwest Ohio. *Communication Quarterly*, 45(4), 335–354. https://doi.org/10.1080/01463379709370070
Yep, G. A. (2010). Toward the de-subjugation of racially marked knowledges in communication. *Southern Communication Journal*, 75(2), 171–175. https://doi.org/10.1080/10417941003613263
Yep, G. A. (2016). Toward thick(er) intersectionalities: Theorizing, researching, and activating the complexities of communication and identities. In K. Sorrells & S. Sekimoto (Eds.), *Globalizing intercultural communication: A reader* (pp. 85–93). SAGE.

Shane Moreman

QUEER INTERCULTURAL COMMUNICATION: SEXUALITY AND INTERCULTURAL COMMUNICATION

INTRODUCTION

Queer intercultural communication as a subfield of communication is a relatively new area of study (Chávez, 2013), although the study of sexuality within intercultural communication has existed at various intersections for some time in the work of scholars such as Bernadette M. Calafell (2007), Shane T. Moreman and Bernadette Marie Calafell (2008), Shane T. Moreman and Dawn M. McIntosh (2010), Shinsuke Eguchi and Godfried Asante (2016), and Thomas K. Nakayama (1994). Calafell (2020) has argued that, in the move from postpositivism, to interpretativism, to critical rhetoric, and finally to performance, critical intercultural communication has found a home in the latter two, which include queer intercultural communication because of its focus on the body or embodiment. Certainly, queer intercultural communication would not have existed without the shift to critical intercultural communication in the 1990s.

The groundbreaking special issue of the *Journal of International and Intercultural Communication* on queer intercultural communication called "to the forefront counternormative productions of sexual and gender knowledge(s) associated with being *queer* to interrogate the intersections of between/among culture, identity and power" (Eguchi & Calafell, 2020, p. 3). Karma R. Chávez (2013) provocatively asked, "What would a queer or trans critique of intercultural communication scholarship entail and reveal?" (p. 84). Building on Chávez (2013), who identified the need for the area of study of queer intercultural communication, Eguchi (2016) noted that research on sexuality and communication bypassed the impact of culture on sexuality, as intercultural communication scholarship left the critical roles of sexuality and sex/gender in praxis of cultural identity unattended. Likewise, Eguchi and Asante (2016) argued for the necessity of queer intercultural communication in order to critique the Westernization of the experiences of queer people of color both locally and transnationally. In doing so, they decentered "white/Western capitalistic hetero-homonormative distribution of power" (Eguchi & Asante, 2016, p. 175), revealing the complexity of sex, gender, and sexuality. Eguchi and Calafell (2020) understood that centering queerness disrupts normative knowledge production in the field of intercultural communication. Hence, queer intercultural communication aims for new ways of knowing, being, and performing in resistance to mainstream belongings throughout local, national, and global contexts.

In their article "Queer Intercultural Communication," Gust Yep et al. suggested:

> Indeed, queer intercultural communication offers the great promise to advance communication—academically, culturally, and politically—not only for sexual and gender minority communities across the globe but for all communities as they grapple with questions of identity and difference in an increasingly neoliberal and global social world. (p. 2)

Yep et al. further argued that queer intercultural communication "offers ways to produce deeper and more nuanced understanding of communication within and between the intersections of culture and sexuality" (p. 3) while potentially guarding against Western imperialism. They offered four themes underlying queer intercultural communication: culture, history, geography, and power. The article "Queer Intercultural Communication (https://doi.org/10.1093/acrefore/9780190228613.013.170)" also provided a mapping or model of queer intercultural communication that allows scholars to examine how research breaks down sexual systems into various cultural contexts to handle the symbolic, material, and theoretical conclusions of queer intercultural communication scholarship. This model considers microscopic, mesoscopic, and macroscopic lenses or approaches to queer intercultural communication.

Eguchi and Calafell (2020) identified themes of intersectionality, belonging, and difference as being key to queer intercultural communication. Additionally, Andrew Spieldenner and Deion Hawkins (2020) recognized critical awareness, praxis, and history as significant to queer intercultural communication. They upheld the connection between queer of color critique and queer intercultural communication through naming, expanded knowledge production, and community identification. These scholars use queer intercultural communication to unpack how Black and brown queer men are represented and disciplined in the HIV prevention social marketing of pre-exposure prophylaxis (PrEP) in the U.S. healthcare system. Spieldenner and Hawkins (2020) claimed that queer intercultural communication reveals community discourse, meaning making, and norms. Criticality is central to such revelations and to queer intercultural communication praxis (Calafell, 2020). Calafell (2020) noted that criticality is important to intersectional approaches seeking distance from nationalist, traditional intercultural scholarship that lacks the feminist, queer, and performative lens. Specifically, she insisted that critical intercultural communication should be more praxis oriented, which leaves room for inclusive methodologies, essentially queering the field. Her suggestions are predicated on centering intersectionality within critical intercultural communication.

This article shares a brief history of the ways intercultural communication or the study of sexuality in intercultural communication has been queered. Following this history, the article breaks down queer intercultural communication into three areas: intersectionality, embodiment, and power. These three themes represent the past, present, and necessary future of queer intercultural communication.

INTERSECTIONALITY

Intersectionality is a relevant theme for queer intercultural communication because it has the potential to destabilize static notions of sex, gender, and sexuality across sociopolitical and postcolonial contexts (Asante, 2020). Amber Johnson (2019) wrote that queer intersectionality avoids creating identity hierarchies or relying on silencing binaries. Queer intersectionality imagines new discourse and understandings outside oppressive rigidity in its engagement with multifaceted identities. It "invites multiple stories of sexuality and gender that don't fit neatly into categories like lesbian, gay, bisexual, transgender, cisgender, queer, heterosexual, asexual, or intersexed" (Johnson, 2019, p. 503). Kimberlé Crenshaw (1989, 1991) proposed intersectionality as a tool for understanding how race, gender, and class co-produce lived experiences for women of color. Moving away from identity theorizing that focused on one identity vector, Crenshaw (1989, 1991) offered intersectionality, which instead sought to explore race along with other identities that simultaneously shape people's experiences. Asante (2020) stated that intersectionality "provides counternarratives of resistance and critique of the singularity of experience" (p. 163). In line with Crenshaw, he argued that intersectionality scholars investigate interlocking systems of power to understand social phenomena and social inequities.

Asante (2020) applied a transnational lens to the intersectional theorizing of people on the margins, outside the Western gaze. Asante (2020) claimed that intersectionality is used "to disentangle the complex layers of identity, categories, and experiences that form the everyday life of Sasso in Ghana" (p. 173). His work examined African articulations of decolonial queer theory as resistance to categorization and universalism. Asante (2020) insisted that exploring others' perspectives creates new ways to articulate and imagine intercultural communication. In writing about queerness and intercultural communication, Calafell (2020) implored scholars to think and theorize from an *Other* perspective, which is an avenue for decolonizing restrictive categorization and shifting the intercultural imagination.

Similarly, Nicole Files-Thompson and Melina McConatha (2020) used intersectionality to confront normative gender constructs outside "patriarchal hegemony of femininity to deconstruct power hierarchies" (p. 240). In their analysis of the #sayhername online campaign, they investigated how performing intersectional allyship with trans Black women impacted by violence in digital storytelling influenced the mobilization of intercultural communities. They wrote, "Intersectionality serves as a foundational framework in the development of more nuanced theoretical interrogations across intersectional oppressions" (Files-Thompson &

McConatha, 2020, p. 241). Like Johnson (2013), they argued for the importance of centering the experiences of trans folks in intercultural communication. Specifically, Johnson (2013) contended that intercultural communication needs trans studies in order to fully understand issues of power and intersectionality when it comes to queerness.

Sheena Howard (2020) interrogated the film *Pariah* (Universal Pictures [Firm], 2012), arguing that the queer film resists normative representations and exclusionary politics of the gay rights movement while pushing back against boundaries of belonging to reject LGBTQ normativity. #sayhername and *Pariah* are concerned with demonstrating how the nature of interlocking oppressions necessitates an intersectional lens for theorizing and methodological analyses of queer and women of color, specifically, and all bodies on the margins, broadly. The works discussed thus far are attentive to the compounded experiences by those on the margins and seeks to decolonize, disrupt, and queer the boundaries of intercultural communication.

Extending intersectionality beyond theory, Eguchi and Calafell (2020) wrote that "intersectionality is a methodology identifying with and critiquing the complex particularities of tensions between macro structural and systemic forces and micro acts and processes of identity and performance" (p. 9). Thus, queer intercultural communication is concerned with how multiple streams of power create continuous intersectional tensions between privilege and oppression (Eguchi & Calafell, 2020, p. 8). Benny LeMaster and Meggie Mapes (2020) understood intersectionality to be a focal point of queer intercultural communication because it "reveals the performative and material constitution of cultural power at the intersections of difference" (p. 67). Further, they proposed that intersectionality "disrupts normativity by affirming the concurrent embodiment and navigation of privilege and disadvantage while refusing to acquiesce to reductive articulations of identity and embodiment" (LeMaster & Mapes, 2020, p. 67). Chávez (2013) recalled Sirma Bilge's push for queer theorists to combat this reductive "'whitening of intersectionality' that pilfers ideas from intersectional thinking while marginalizing queer and women of color scholarship" (p. 90). Asante (2020, p. 159) upheld this push, calling on queer intercultural academics to demonstrate how non-Western racialized, gendered, and sexual identities contest and perform identities across their national boundaries. Taken together, this performative shift centering embodiment becomes the outline for intersectionality as praxis. Clearly, queer sexual bodies rupture binaristic normative White, Western imperialist frames. Eguchi and Long (2019) explained that, as "we write the personal, we need to step out of our comfort zones to interrogate complex and contradictory experiences of becoming and being femmes created by intersectionality—a simultaneous function of race, ethnicity, gender, sexuality, class, empire, and the body in and across historical and ideological contexts" (p. 1593). However, flattening intersectional approaches to speaking with these bodies remains an issue for intercultural communication and queer studies with few exceptions.

To avoid flattening the potential of intersectionality, Yep (2013) deployed thick intersectionalities as a thorough, embodied exploration of the racial, sexual, gender, and class multiplicity of people's lives and identities in time and space. He petitioned scholars to maintain the integrity of intersectional experiences "and biographies of the persons inhabiting a particular intersection" (Yep, 2013, p. 123). In accordance, Asante (2020) stated, "writing about queerness from the margins and especially from a postcolonial space is essential to furthering the critical impulse of queer intercultural communication" (p. 159). Shadee Abdi and Bobbi Van

Gilder (2016) heeded this call in their work examining queer Iranian women's identity narratives. They looked at how the women manage stigma around their sexual identities in their ethnic communities (p. 83), giving them space to share and center their stories (see also Abdi & Van Gilder, 2016). Writing from the margins in this way opens possibilities for decentering homonormative queerness (Asante, 2020). This decentering is significant because "homonormativity is always driven by ideologies of whiteness" (McIntosh, 2020, p. 119) and has a kinship with heteronormative, White, U.S. nationalism, according to Calafell and Nakayama (2020). For McIntosh (2020), the critique of homonormativity demonstrates the importance of using intersectionality for queer intercultural communication scholars when analyzing sexuality.

EMBODIMENT

> As a complex sociocultural construction, the body is a powerful set of signifiers in social relations. (Yep, 2013, p. 118)

Calafell (2020) noted that queerness involves the body, embodiment, and possibilities. This is significant as mainstream queer theory has often ignored embodiment through theories focused on abstraction. However, scholars such as José Esteban Muñoz (1999) have demonstrated the importance of centering the body in queer theory through examinations of the lived experiences and performances of queer people of color. Moraga and Anzaldúa (2015) argued for a theory in flesh, which they defined in the following way:

> A theory in flesh means one where the physical realities of our lives—our skin color, the land or concrete we grew up on, our sexual longings—all fuse to create a politic born out of necessity. Here, we attempt to bridge the contradictions in our experience. (p. 19)

This theory in the flesh is central to the concept of embodiment. Embodiment is the second aspect of queer intercultural communication. Ghabra and Calafell (2018) stated that "it is vital to situate our intersections cross-culturally and transnationally" (p. 41) when writing about embodiment and allyship. This application of embodiment and intersections cross-culturally and transnationally are demonstrating a deeper understanding of embodiment through intersectional identities. McIntosh (2020) stated that it is through the material realities of the body one come to know their identities. Accordingly, "performance makes the body present, and the racialized body holds queerness accountable to issues of power" (Calafell, 2020, p. 259). Giorgia Aiello et al. (2013) asserted, "Bodies are always inseparable from race and ethnicity" (p. 107). Therefore, McIntosh (2020) believed that, across social-isms, "Queer intercultural communication scholarship is ethically responsible for understanding embodied politics" (p. 120). She argued that the criticality needed to handle interlocking oppression must center the body. The body is a "visual register, affective producer, and site of relation, difference, and complex belonging" (Aiello et al., 2013, p. 115).

It is in day-to-day moments that one can hone in on the importance of embodiment for queer intercultural communication. Like Moraga and Anzaldúa (2015), Calafell (2020) understood the importance of the body, describing queerness as "everyday lived experiences and actions that allow us to thrive, survive, and resist" (p. 260). In agreement, Aiello et al. (2013) took issue with queer theorists who erase class, race, and gender as they assumed queer bodies to be "white and marked by class privilege, but also 'unmarked' by language and flesh alike" (p. 114). This unmarkedness is counterintuitive to queerness and the process of queering. Nikki Lane (2016) aimed to intervene in queer theorizing of sexuality. In discussing bodies, she said, "flesh refers simultaneously to issues of embodiment and the way bodies are engaged in theory and practice" (Lane, 2016, p. 648). Lane (2016) noted that to study flesh you must involve the people who are living through the experiences and allow them to guide the research. Moreover, researchers simultaneously talk about themselves and how their bodies shape what they know and how they experience the world (Lane, 2016). Embodiment is also central to Eguchi (2020), whose work explores Asian men loving Asian men, or what is termed *sticky rice*. Queer kinship and relationality are at the heart of embodiment in Eguchi (2020). This reflexivity about the body, and thus embodiment, is central to queer intercultural communication and to queering scholarship.

Yep (2013) defined queering as "an active process of making an unquestioned and taken-for-granted idea or social relation. It offers possibilities of resistance and other ways of thinking, doing, living, and loving" (p. 119). Queering is thus important for rendering bodies visible, which is a key component of embodiment. Gutierrez-Perez and Andrade (2020) viewed queering as a mode of educating and structuring desire that shifts visions and emotions outside the status quo. For Aiello et al. (2013), queering satisfies its goals through "embodied social articulations of difference" (p. 115) that are often pushed to the margins. Queering continues to be a powerful tool for understanding how identities and social institutions are constituted (Yep et al., 2019).

In his discussion of African cultural citizenship, Asante (2020) reminded queer intercultural communication scholars that the material realities of other bodies are imbued with the theorizing power to resist heteropatriarchal coloniality. He invited these scholars to focus on the everyday as a postcolonial space for queerness to reshape political and relational practices of resistance. Robert Gutierrez-Perez and Luis Andrade (2020) focused on the body to resist dominant logics of knowledge production and queerness rooted in coloniality, racism, cisheteronormativity, and sexism in their queer of color intercultural *Jotería* project, which centers on the experiences of queer Latinx folks. They argued that the potential of resistance for queer intercultural communication lies in queer of color aesthetics through performative scholarship, personal narratives, and image-making. Gutierrez-Perez and Andrade (2020) emphasized that resistive potentiality imagines radical, decolonial praxis that increases embodied knowledge. Asante (2020) explained that the focus on how the body resists normativities within queer intercultural communication helps postcolonial sexual subjects push back against geopolitical erasures.

Sara Ahmed (2014) posited that sexuality positions the body toward and away from others, impacting movement throughout social spaces. Abdi (2020) understood this as a liminal space of possibilities where unheard stories are told. She shared her personal experiences of negotiating her identity as an Iranian lesbian with family members (Abdi, 2014). Specifically, her scholarship calls for "awareness of the complexities of being (in)visibly queer within both the Iranian/Iranian American communities as well as within a majority of queer/queer of color contexts" (Abdi, 2020, p. 48). She provoked her reader to move beyond hetero/homonormativity to make room for embodied conversations in queer intercultural communication. She wrote that queerness is "undefined, unrefined, and unpredictable" (Abdi, 2020, p. 48). Abdi (2020) used personal stories as a method of bridging the political with the personal. This creates space for marginalized bodies to disrupt dominance. In conjunction with Gutierrez-Perez and Andrade (2020) and Asante (2020), Abdi offers ways that queer intercultural scholars can trouble normative identity categorizations and shift toward new cultural dimensions of embodiment.

Embodied Translation. Yep (2013) insisted on using embodied translation in approaches to speaking with bodies on the margins. For Yep (2013), such translation holds constant the contexts in which subjects exist. Chávez (2009) defined embodied translation as the decoding and encoding process of rendering "other bodies" legible through examining the cultural scapes or contexts in which those bodies exist. Further, "embodied translation provides a way to view which scapes people (c)overtly rely upon" (Chávez, 2009, p. 25). Yep (2013) added that embodied translation reads "cultural systems of body normativity in their respective cultural and geopolitical contexts" (p. 120). The translation process encompasses "verbal, nonverbal, and metaphysical communication, primary and historical contexts, and textual signifiers of the body" (Yep, 2013, pp. 120–121). For Yep (2013), embodied translation, engaged with the tools queering/quaring/kauering/crippin'/transing, contributes to intercultural communication research by unpacking cultural normativity constructs. Yep (2013) drew on the work of Johnson (2001), Lee (2003), and McRuer (2006). Each tool explicates dominant, harmful constructs of the body to reread social systems related to race, gender, class, ability, and sexuality (Yep, 2013). This embodied approach holds space for the translation of perspectives outside restrictive normativity. Yep (2013) aimed to read transgender, queer, and intercultural communication together, highlighting the body as central to knowledge production and privileging the vernacular or local cultural understandings of sexualities. Moreman and Stephanie Briones (2018) similarly drew on crip theory in their reading of Nyle Dimarco, a sexually fluid deaf public figure, to examine how he resisted the homonormative and offered what they termed *deaf queer world-making*.

Atay (2020) drew on his queer, Turkish Cypriot subjectivity to demonstrate how intercultural research fails to account for the experiences of transnational queers. He recognized the scholarship's limitation on international, immigrant, and diasporic identities as a queer intercultural slippage. Slippage is an experience, a meaning, and a cultural–linguistic in-betweenness (Atay, 2020, p. 141). This critical autoethnography analyzed international queer slippages and translations in intercultural communication. Atay (2020) sought to decolonize and queer intercultural scholarship by decentering dominant U.S. normativities that limit transnational queer sexualities. Using four vignettes about finding a queer home, he challenged traditional intercultural communication to be intersectional and queer its methodologies, theories, discourse, and texts. The space from which he wrote is indicative of queer embodied translation whereby a transnational perspective outside the confines of White, Western academic normativity was provided. He wrote, "I live between nations and continents. I write about peripheries, queer intercultural experiences and lives, and non-normative and 'othered' queers.... I theorize from the academic sidelines" (Atay, 2020, pp. 144–145). Decolonizing and queering intercultural communication creates space for the theories and stories that Atay (2020) believed will shift the field in ways that "allow marginalized voices to be empowered within the IC [intercultural communication] discourse" (p. 151).

Files-Thompson and McConatha (2020) said that queering/quaring/transing uses intersectionality to trouble and expand analysis of "other bodies" in the interconnected, conflation of gender and sexuality. For instance, transing challenges simplistic understandings that limit gender to a spectrum confining masculine–feminine to a binary (Eguchi et al., 2020). Yep (2013) said that transing involves "examining gender embodiment in relation to other modes of difference through new forms of biomedical and communication technologies that circulate in the global world" (p. 120). Spieldenner and Hawkins (2020) noted that queer intercultural scholars must account for embodied knowledge to arise through experiences with colonialism, racism, and other -isms to highlight the social values of communities and people. Each example aims to illustrate how bodies are translated and issues surrounding translation. Chávez (2009) stated that the embodied translation framework can analyze power dynamics during interactions between those with perceived differences. It helps people push back against dominant, oppressive discourse and understand how communication scapes apply meaning to bodies (Chávez, 2009). The framework is valuable for queer interculturalists as it addresses the complex nature of theorizing and using methods equipped for centering people in the margins.

POWER

Decoloniality is an important requirement of queer intercultural communication, both conceptually and methodologically (Eguchi et al., 2020). It offers a way to address social oppression (Spieldenner & Hawkins, 2020). Addressing social oppression and power is the third aspect of queer intercultural communication. As a social construct, sexuality is produced and constituted by power and knowledge (Yep et al., 2020). With this, identity categories become positioned higher or lower along an axis of power (Howard, 2020, p. 231). Eguchi and Calafell (2020) believed that socially constructed differences are significant to material realities because relationships between power and identity map intersectional differences onto the body. They understood how meanings and power intersect on bodies and mark them as Other.

Because concepts of sexuality and difference are unequally distributed in and across cultures, Yep et al. (2020) turned their attention to hegemonic power. They viewed hegemonic power as "the social, cultural, political, structural, and institutional resources and dominance of one identity, practice, or conceptualization over others" (Yep et al., 2020, p. 31). Their work on relationalities in and through difference unpacks the significance of power in creating a hierarchy of dominance of ideas. The scholars maintain that hegemonic power conceals sexuality in a heterosexual–homosexual binary where the latter is most often forced into a nonnormative positionality. White and Western cisheteronormative notions of sexuality steeped in colonialism and imperialism permeate and erase other cultural, sexual knowledges (Yep et al., 2020). For instance, Yep et al. (2020) examined changes in Indigenous sexualities after exposure to Western hegemony, finding that, prior to Western imposition, diversity of sexualities was a normalized part of Indigenous community and culture. This erasure and discussion of power is an important reminder for queer intercultural communication scholars to center the voices of those under study and interrogate on-the-ground, everyday experiences in analyses of sexuality and normativity (Yep et al., 2020).

Calafell and Nakayama (2020) wanted queer intercultural scholars to understand institutional powers working to oppress LGBTQ people globally as this area of scholarship is still lacking, despite the work of scholars like Eguchi (2020) and Atay (2020). Currently, sexually dissident and gender non-conforming subjects experience pressure to follow the standard, Western queer sex and gender identity norms, performances, and politics (Eguchi et al., 2020). In their work on queer intercultural relationality, Eguchi et al. (2020) interrogated White, gay homonormativity in various queer identities and terrains using an autoethnographic retelling of personal relationships and experiences in the queer scene. They critiqued U.S. assumptions of Asian gay men as "bottoms," perpetual foreigners, or submissive femmes as these evidence White Western imperialism. By recalling conversations with friends about dating and race, Eguchi et al. (2020) interrogated their own views of attractions and desire, noting how they disidentified from Asian–White colonial encounters through enacting a different gay cultural performance.

Spieldenner and Hawkins (2020) looked at the power of naming and being able to name oneself. They believed that queer people of color are not afforded agency to name themselves through community media narratives. Connectedly, the White, dominant LGBTQ community's gaze on people of color is monolithic. People of color are either fetishized or stereotyped through this gaze (Spieldenner & Hawkins, 2020). Ultimately, naming is connected to power relations because it proposes questions about recognizing whose notion of truth is centered, how people understand the world around them, and what matters in evidencing truth (Spieldenner & Hawkins, 2020).

CONCLUSION

Queer intercultural communication, or the study of sexuality in intercultural communication, is a critical, interdisciplinary field of study that explores identity (i.e., race, gender, sexuality, nationality, and class) across political, historical, transnational, and social spheres. This article locates intersectionality, embodiment, and power as prominent themes guiding queer interculturalist analyses. As a newer field connecting intercultural communication with queer studies, it is concerned with empowering voices and stories of those in the margins by challenging cisgender, White U.S. heteronormative knowledge production.

"Queer theory has been limiting in terms of race, class, and gender futurity, repositioning queer as another normative theoretical frame that restricts identity" (Johnson, 2019, p. 510). Intercultural communication has struggled to include intersectional works that center queer and transgender voices, methodologies, and theories. In response to these gaps in scholarship around sexuality, Johnson (2019) felt that people have a duty to push for a quare/kuaer/queer rhetoric that is welcoming of embodiment, personal narratives, and intersectional self-reflexivity. They believed this rhetoric must celebrate difference while it makes room for the development of a new self, community, and social relations. Similarly, Muñoz (2009) reminded his reader to think of queerness as the reason one wishes for something else—something beyond current normativities—to insist on the potentiality for a different world. Embodiment and intersectionality provide people with new ways to think about complex identities and issues such as globalization, queer and transgender identity, homonormativity, and diaspora (Calafell, 2020). Queer intercultural communication therefore moves people toward theoretical approaches that encompass the worldmaking that Johnson (2019), Muñoz (2009), and Calafell (2020) suggested to account for multifaceted positionalities. As this work continues, scholarship on sexualities must remain open to broadening discourse, theory, and methodologies that are inclusive of multiple stories that evoke queer possibilities.

FURTHER READING

Abdi, S. (2014). Staying I(ra)n: Narrating queer identity from within the Persian closet. *Liminalities: A Journal of Performance Studies, 10*(2), 1–19. https://www.proquest.com/openview/75bc257e21c33eca9fd030ed0c04cb15/1

Ahmet, A. (2021). Charting the future of queer studies in communication and critical/cultural studies: New directions and pathways. *Communication and Critical/Cultural Studies.* https://doi.org/10.1080/14791420.2021.1907847

Asante, G., & Handchey, J. N. (2021). Decolonizing queer modernities: The case for queer (post)colonial studies in critical/cultural communication. *Communication and Critical/Cultural Studies, 18*(2), 212–220. https://doi.org/10.1080/14791420.2021.1907849

Atay, A., & Pensoneau-Conway, S. L. (2019). *Queer communication pedagogy.* Routledge.

Calafell, B., & Eguchi, S. (2020). *Queer intercultural communication: The intersectional politics of belonging in and across differences.* Rowman & Littlefield.

Eguchi, S., & Long, H. R. (2019). Queer relationality as family: Yas fats! Yas femmes! Yas Asians! *Journal of Homosexuality, 66*(11), 1589–1608. https://doi.org/10.1080/00918369.2018.1505756

Gutierrez-Perez, R. M. (2020). A return to El Mundo Zurdo: Anzaldúan approaches to queer of color worldmaking and the violence of intersectional heteronormativity. *Women's Studies in Communication, 43*(4), 384–399.

Johnson, A., & LeMaster, B. (2020). *Gender futurity, intersectional autoethnography: Embodied theorizing from the margins.* Routledge.

Johnson, E. P. (2016). *No tea, no shade: New writings in Black queer studies.* Duke University Press.

LeMaster, B. (2018). Pedagogies of failure. In A. Atay & S. Toyosaki (Eds.), *Critical intercultural communication pedagogy* (pp. 81–96). Lexington.

REFERENCES

Abdi, S. (2014). Staying I(ra)n: Narrating queer identity from within the Persian closet. *Liminalities: A Journal of Performance Studies, 10*(2), 1–19. https://www.proquest.com/openview/75bc257e21c33eca9fd030ed0c04cb15/1

Abdi, S. (2020). Revisiting a letter for someday: Writing toward a queer Iranian diasporic potentiality. In S. Eguchi & B. M. Calafell (Eds.), *Queer intercultural communication: The intersectional politics of belonging in and across difference* (pp. 47–61). Rowman & Littlefield.

Abdi, S., & Van Gilder, B. (2016). Cultural (in)visibility and identity dissonance: Queer Iranian-American women and their negotiation of existence. *Journal of International and Intercultural Communication, 9*(1), 69–86. https://doi.org/10.1080/17513057.2016.1120850

Ahmed, S. (2014). *The cultural politics of emotion.* Edinburgh University Press.

Aiello, G., Bakshi, S., Bilge, S., Hall, S. K., Johnston, L., Perez, K., & Chávez, K. (2013). Here, and not yet here: A dialogue at the intersection of queer, trans, and culture. *Journal of International and Intercultural Communication, 6*(2), 96–117. https://doi.org/10.1080/17513057.2013.778155

Asante, G. A. (2020). "Queerly ambivalent": Navigating global and local normativities in postcolonial Ghana. In S. Eguchi & B. M. Calafell (Eds.), *Queer intercultural communication: The intersectional politics of belonging in and across difference* (pp. 157–176). Rowman & Littlefield.

Atay, A. (2020). Intercultural queer slippages and translations. In S. Eguchi & B. M. Calafell (Eds.), *Queer intercultural communication: The intersectional politics of belonging in and across difference* (pp. 141–156). Rowman & Littlefield.

Calafell, B. M. (2007). *Latina/o communication studies: Theorizing performance*. Peter Lang.

Calafell, B. M. (2020). The critical performative turn in intercultural communication. *Journal of International and Intercultural Research, 49*(5), 410–415. https://doi.org/10.1080/17475759.2020.1740292

Calafell, B. M., & Nakayama, T. K. (2020). Dialoguing about the nexus of queer studies and intercultural communication. In S. Eguchi & B. M. Calafell (Eds.), *Queer intercultural communication: The intersectional politics of belonging in and across difference* (pp. 259–266). Rowman & Littlefield.

Chávez, K. R. (2009). Embodied translation: Dominant discourse and communication with migrant bodies-as-text. *Howard Journal of Communication, 20*(1), 18–36. https://doi.org/10.1080/10646170802664912

Chávez, K. R. (2013). Pushing boundaries: Queer intercultural communication. *Journal of International and Intercultural Communication, 6*(2), 83–95. https://doi.org/10.1080/17513057.2013.777506

Crenshaw, K. (1989). Demarginalizing the intersection of race and sex: A Black feminist critique of antidiscrimination doctrine, feminist theory and antiracist politics. *University of Chicago Legal Forum, 1*, 139–167. https://chicagounbound.uchicago.edu/uclf/vol1989/iss1/8

Crenshaw, K. (1991). Mapping the margins: Intersectionality, identity politics, and violence against women of color. *Stanford Law Review, 43*(26), 1241–1299. https://doi.org/10.2307/1229039

Eguchi, S. (2016). Queer foreignness and intersectionality: A case for "doing" sexual and cultural mixing and mingling across borders. In J. Manning & C. Noland (Eds.), *Contemporary studies of sexuality & communication: Theory and practice* (pp. 291–304). Kendall Hunt.

Eguchi, S. (2020). Sticky rice politics: Impossible possibilities of queerness in and across yellow fever and front cover. *Women's Studies in Communication, 23*(1), 67–84. https://doi.org/10.1080/07491409.2019.1696435

Eguchi, S., & Asante, G. (2016). Disidentifications revisited: Queer(y)ing intercultural communication theory. *Communication Theory, 26*(2), 171–189. https://doi.org/10.1111/comt.12086

Eguchi, S., & Calafell, B. M. (2020). Introduction: Reorienting queer intercultural communication. In S. Eguchi & B. M. Calafell (Eds.), *Queer intercultural communication: The intersectional politics of belonging in and across difference* (pp. 1–16). Rowman & Littlefield.

Eguchi, S., Jones, S., Long, H., & Zarinana, A. (2020). Closing thoughts: The future of queer intercultural communication. In S. Eguchi & B. M. Calafell (Eds.), *Queer intercultural communication: The intersectional politics of belonging in and across difference* (pp. 267–279). Rowman & Littlefield.

Eguchi, S., & Long, H. R. (2019). Queer relationality as family: Yas fats! Yas femmes! Yas Asians! *Journal of Homosexuality, 66*(11), 1589–1608. https://doi.org/10.1080/00918369.2018.1505756

Files-Thompson, N., & McConatha, M. (2020). Mobilizing allies for Black transgender women: Digital stories, intersectionality, and #sayhername. In S. Eguchi & B. M. Calafell (Eds.), *Queer intercultural communication: The intersectional politics of belonging in and across difference* (pp. 239–257). Rowman & Littlefield.

Ghabra, H., & Calafell, B. M. (2018). From failure and allyship to feminist solidarities: Negotiating our privileges and oppressions across borders. *Text and Performance Quarterly, 38*(1–2), 38–54. https://doi.org/10.1080/10462937.2018.1457173

Gutierrez-Perez, R., & Andrade, L. (2020). How queer (of color) is intercultural communication? Then and there, Joteria, the game as a praxis of queerness, advocacy, and utopian aesthetics. In S. Eguchi & B. M. Calafell (Eds.), *Queer intercultural communication: The intersectional politics of belonging in and across difference* (pp. 179–193). Rowman & Littlefield.

Howard, S. (2020). (Re)defining boundaries and the politics of belonging in the film *Pariah*. In S. Eguchi & B. M. Calafell (Eds.), *Queer intercultural communication: The intersectional politics of belonging in and across difference* (pp. 217–237). Rowman & Littlefield.

Johnson, A. (2019). Quare/Kuaer/Queer/(E)ntersectionality: An invitational rhetoric of possibility. *CrossCurrents, 68*(4), 500–514. https://www.jstor.org/stable/26756881

Johnson, E. P. (2001). "Quare" studies or (almost) everything I know about queer studies I learned from my grandmother. *Text and Performance Quarterly, 21*(1), 1–25. https://doi.org/10.1080/10462930128119

Johnson, J. R. (2013). Cisgender privilege, intersectionality, and the criminalization of CeCe McDonald: Why intercultural communication needs transgender studies. *Journal of International and Intercultural Communication, 6*(2), 135–144. https://doi.org/10.1080/17513057.2013.776094

Lane, N. (2016). Bringing flesh to theory: Ethnography, Black queer theory, and studying Black sexualities. *Feminist Studies, 42*(3), 632–648. https://doi.org/10.15767/feministstudies.42.3.0632

Lee, W. (2003). Kauering queer theory: My autocritography and a race-conscious womanist, transnational turn. In G. A. Yep, K. E. Lovaas, & J. P. Elia (Eds.), *Queer theory and communication: From disciplining queers to queering the discipline(s)* (pp. 147–170). Harrington Park Press.

LeMaster, B., & Mapes, M. (2020). Embracing the criminal: Queer and trans relational liberatory pedagogies. In S. Eguchi & B. M. Calafell (Eds.), *Queer intercultural communication: The intersectional politics of belonging in and across difference* (pp. 63–77). Rowman & Littlefield.

McIntosh, D. M. (2020). Ain't my first rodeo in homonormative whiteness: Queer intercultural lessons from the international gay rodeo community. In S. Eguchi & B. M. Calafell (Eds.), *Queer intercultural communication: The intersectional politics of belonging in and across difference* (pp. 117–140). Rowman & Littlefield.

McRuer, R. (2006). *Crip theory: Cultural signs of queerness and disability*. New York University Press.

Moraga, C., & Anzaldúa, G. (2015). Theory in the flesh. In C. Moraga & G. Anzaldúa (Eds.), *This bridge called my back: Writings by radical women of color* (4th ed., p. 19). SUNY Press.

Moreman, S. T., & Briones, S. R. (2018). Deaf queer world-making: A thick intersectional analysis of the mediated cultural body. *Journal of International and Intercultural Communication, 11*(3), 216–232. https://doi.org/10.1080/17513057.2018.1456557

Moreman, S. T., & Calafell, B. M. (2008). *Buscando para nuestros hijos*: Utilizing *La Llorona* for cultural critique. *Journal of International and Intercultural Communication, 1*(4), 309–326. https://doi.org/10.1080/17513050802344647

Moreman, S. T., & McIntosh, D. M. (2010). Brown scriptings and rescriptings: A critical performance ethnography of Latina drag queens. *Communication and Critical Cultural Studies, 7*(2), 115–135. https://doi.org/10.1080/14791421003767912

Muñoz, J. E. (1999). *Disidentifications: Queers of color and the performance of politics*. University of Minnesota Press.

Muñoz, J. E. (2009). *Cruising utopia: The then and there of queer futurity*. Duke University Press.

Nakayama, T. K. (1994). Show/down time: "Race,"; gender, sexuality, and popular culture. *Critical Studies in Media Communication, 11*(2), 162–179. https://doi.org/10.1080/15295039409366893

Spieldenner, A., & Hawkins, D. (2020). Queerying race, culture, and sex: Examining HIV pre-exposure prophylaxis (PrEP) social marketing for African American and Latinx gay and bisexual men. In S. Eguchi & B. M. Calafell (Eds.), *Queer intercultural communication: The intersectional politics of belonging in and across difference* (pp. 195–215). Rowman & Littlefield.

Universal Pictures (Firm). (2012). *Pariah*. Alliance (UHV) Alliance / Universal.

Van Gilder, B., & Abdi, S. (2014). Identity management and the fostering of network ignorance: Accounts of queer Iranian women in the United States. *Journal of Intercultural Communication Research*, 43(2), 151–170. https://doi.org/10.1080/17475759.2014.892895

Yep, G. A. (2013). Queering/quaring/kauering/crippin'/transing "Other Bodies" in intercultural communication. *Journal of International and Intercultural Communication*, 6(2), 118–126. https://doi.org/10.1080/17513057.2013.777087

Yep, G. A., Alaoui, F. Z. C., & Lescure, R. (2020). Relationalities in/through difference: Explorations in queer intercultural communication. In S. Eguchi & B. M. Calafell (Eds.), *Queer intercultural communication: The intersectional politics of belonging in and across difference* (pp. 19–45). Rowman & Littlefield.

Yep, G. A. Lescure, R. & Russo, S. (2019). Queer intercultural communication. In J. Nussbaum (Ed.), *Oxford Research Encyclopedia of Communication*. https://doi.org/10.1093/acrefore/9780190228613.013.170

Taisha McMickens, Miranda Dottie Olzman, and Bernadette Marie Calafell

QUEER MEN'S BODIES AND DIGITAL MEDIA

INTRODUCTION

The politics of queer men's bodies had been a site of contestation long before the internet started to be taken up in everyday life. Yet the advent of the more widespread use of networked media has reconfigured these politics and their possibilities in significant ways. Before discussing these, it is necessary to clarify this article's key terms.

Historically, scholarship on "queer men" has centered cisgender, gay men, and although this article inevitably includes this literature, it discusses research on trans men too. The term "bodies" is similarly broad, potentially including questions relating to medicine and health. This article, however, focuses on what psychologists refer to as "body image" and media, cultural, and communications studies often think of as "beauty politics"—that is, how media help establish the parameters for what bodies come to be understood as beautiful and/or desirable in contemporary culture. When referring to "digital media," this article refers mostly to the "digital intimate publics"(Carah et al., 2018) afforded by networked media such as Internet Relay Chats (IRCs), websites, social media platforms, and smartphones and their applications, all of which publicly mediate domains of human experience historically understood to be intimate and private. This article does not refer to psychology literature, which often finds a negative correlation between digital media and queer men's body image (e.g., Acic et al., 2021), but instead engages with the media, cultural, and communication studies literature, which, as a field, presumes a more complex, ambivalent, and shifting relationship between digital media, queer men, and their bodies.

Indeed, ambivalence is arguably what defines the politics of queer men's bodies and their relationship to digital media. Although these politics continue to be hegemonized by a very narrowly defined "gay beauty ideal" (see the section on "'Gay Beauty Ideal' in Predigital Media Cultures"), the function of this ideal—its meanings, ethics, and politics—shifts across the various contexts in which it operates. In some spaces, this ideal renders entire social groups as somehow less than human. In others, *desire for* this ideal can create subcultural networks of safety, belonging, and pleasure in otherwise homophobic and transphobic cultures. The development of the internet during the past 30 years also changes the uses to which this ideal is put, while proliferating the amount of mediated spaces where new ideals, with their own ambivalences, flourish. Before unpacking these ambivalences, the article discusses how this ideal was formed in predigital media cultures.

THE "GAY BEAUTY IDEAL" IN PREDIGITAL MEDIA CULTURES

Since the advent of mass media in the Global North, the body type considered most desirable in queer men's cultures has been of a highly specific type: white, cisgender, able-bodied, and masculine. To be more specific still, this type is often lean and/or muscular, youthful, and, especially in the Anglo-American and Northern European contexts, hairless. This ideal draws on archetypes prevalent in the history of Western art whereby this body type is made to signify spiritual, political, or national purity (Barcan, 2004). This type can be seen across the media that queer men have consumed, whether they were constructed with queer men's consumption in mind (e.g., pornography, the promotional materials used by gay businesses, and gay cinema) or they are mainstream texts that have been appropriated by queer men for their visual pleasure (J. Mercer, 2017; Waugh, 1996). For brevity, this ideal body type is called the "gay beauty ideal."

It is also important to note, however, that there has been and continues to be space within queer men's cultures for body types that deviate from the gay beauty ideal but are still considered beautiful and/or desirable. For example, the term "bear" evokes male bodies that are "stocky and hirsute" (J. Mercer, 2017, p. 128). The term "daddy" "simultaneously refers to a broad generational category (men over 30), to a physicality (frequently mesomorphic and sometimes herculean in stature)" (J. Mercer, 2017, p. 100). In gay male subcultures, there are also racist categorizations of desire for racialized groups such as, in the United Kingdom, "curry queen"—a gay man who claims a sexual preference for South Asian men—and "rice queen"—a gay man who claims sexual preference for Southeast Asian men.

The politics of the gay beauty ideal and its subsidiary categories are contested in the academic literature. Broadly, the most common critique is that the overrepresentation of the gay beauty ideal in queer men's media cultures produces exclusions along lines of race, gender, and able-bodiedness. It renders anybody who deviates from this ideal invisible in these media cultures, of diminished value in economies of sex and intimacy, anxiety-ridden, symbolically less-than-human, or all of these. There are, however, other scholars who, while not negating these critiques, do point to the audience subcultures that can emerge in relation to mediations of the gay beauty ideal. For instance, Thomas Waugh (1996) has argued that networks of communication and belonging existed in relation to the circulation of gay erotica (where the gay beauty ideal was lionized) in profoundly homophobic early-20th-century America. Similarly, in reference to a slightly later historical period, Samuel Delany (1999) has written about the cross-class, "interracial" modes of sexual and nonsexual collectivity that were produced in the porn cinemas of New York City's Time Square area—again, where images of the gay beauty ideal dominated.

These are the parameters that define the debates on the body politics of queer men's media cultures, digital or otherwise. On the one hand, they are understood to reinforce a series of exclusions that render some social groups less than human. On the other hand, these cultures have also been understood to legitimate queer desire, as well as create a more general sense of belonging in cultures marked by profound transphobia and homophobia.

THE INTERNET

These politics do not fundamentally alter amid the historical changes that have occurred with the popularization of the internet. They do, however, take on different emphases and inflections. When internet studies was a nascent field in the 1990s and 2000s, there was a strong "cyber-utopian" tendency that imagined that the wider adoption of this form of networked communication could bypass the hierarchies of body politics entirely (Bruckman, 1996; Rheingold, 2000; Turkle, 1995). This argument was based on an internet that (1) provided mediated spaces for globally dispersed minorities who were considered too niche to profitably cater for in a pre-internet mediascape; and (2) was primarily text based because dial-up connections made downloading images highly cumbersome. These scholars argued that the body-based differences that sort social groups into exclusionary hierarchies were rendered all but meaningless in these text-based networked spaces (primarily Multiple-User Dimensions and Internet Relay Chats [IRCs]) and in fact could lead to radical forms of identity experimentation—for example, men participating in these spaces "as women."

This argument was called the "online disembodiment thesis" in the first book-length study to examine gay men's body politics and the internet—*Getting It on Online: Cyberspace, Gay Male Sexuality, and Embodied Identity* by John Edward Campbell (2004). The book, a rebuttal of the online disembodiment thesis, is based on a virtual ethnography of three IRC communities:

> #gaymuscle, a community formulated around images of the muscular male body; #gaychub, a community celebrating male obesity, where—in diametric opposition to #gaymuscle—fatness holds considerable value; and finally, #gaymusclebears, a space representing the erotic convergence of the obese and muscular male body emerging out of the gay male "bear" subculture. (p. 6)

As primarily text-based chat rooms where images of bodies were difficult to share, one might presume that the exclusionary politics of the gay beauty ideal would evaporate. Campbell (2004) shows that this is demonstrably not the case, arguing that "bodies remain very much a part of the experience of the virtual" (p. 4). He uses a post-structuralist understanding of the body to make this argument, one that understands "the body" to be as much a discursive as a material phenomenon. For Campbell, the body comes to matter in these digital spaces through the language used to organize them—that is, the names of the IRCs, the handles adopted by their users, and the nature of the chat in which they engage.

Regarding the politics of these spaces, Campbell (2004) is attentive to their contradictions. Aside from perhaps #gaymuscle, the users of the IRCs come to them "to find or construct representations of the attractive and desirable male body that do not conform to (or reject outright) those images presented in the mainstream media" (p. 163). It therefore becomes "possible to view these particular channels as resistive efforts to broaden cultural understandings of what constitutes the attractive, the healthy, and the erotic male body" (p. 164). However, Campbell also notes that in creating virtual spaces around highly specific body types, the concept of a beauty ideal and the problems that inhere within it are not transcended entirely. Instead, "what is in fact taking place is a proliferation of competing beauty myths" (p. 157) in which "individuals construct new models of the desirable body that are often just as constraining" (p. 190). In his groundbreaking book, Campbell is keenly aware of the ambivalences of this form of digital media's impact on gay beauty politics. Although the internet has enabled an escape from the hegemonic beauty ideal long prevalent in gay culture, it has also helped facilitate the more sustained exploration of other beauty ideals. These beauty ideals have their own problems but can also form the basis of digitally mediated spaces that provide senses of safety, belonging, pleasure, and self-experimentation.

Equally as significant is Sharif Mowlabocus's (2010) *Gaydar Culture: Gay Men, Technology and Embodiment in the Digital Age*, which is the first book-length study of the next phase of the internet's development—the commercial website—and its impact on gay men's body politics. More widely used than IRCs, commercial websites also have far greater capacity to include visual imagery, whether commissioned by the website or uploaded by its users. Gaydar was the most popular "gay dating" website in the 2000s. It allowed users to create profiles where they could upload images (often sexually explicit), send each other private messages, and enter chat rooms, mostly with the intention of organizing dates, casual sex, or "cyber" sex encounters, although the website was used for other purposes too.

Mowlabocus (2010) undertakes a discourse analysis of Gaydar, paying particular attention to its visual culture. He names the discourse underpinning the website "cybercarnality," which he argues is defined by two tropes: "a) the pornographic remediation of the gay male body and b) technologies of self-surveillance and corporeal regulation" (p. 58). What this means is that when the website's users produced images of themselves to upload onto their profiles, more often than not they drew on the hegemonic codes of gay pornography (and hence the gay beauty ideal) to represent their bodies. One way he evidences this is by analyzing the images submitted to the website's Sex Factor competition where users could vote on which Gaydar profile they thought was the most desirable. He shows that despite the various gay subcultural categories in which users can compete, the majority of the Sex Factor's top-ranked images all adhere to

> a particular aesthetic—a particular masculinity—that continues to be cultivated within metropolitan gay culture and which permeates Gaydar and similar dating/sex websites. For example, many of the top profiles feature men with remarkably similar bodies: toned, developed muscles, evenly tanned and (save for the bears and cubs) hairless. (p. 112)

Moreover, because the website facilitates the possibility of all its users uploading images, a form of "corporeal regulation" is also at play whereby users feel compelled to regulate their self-representation in line with these codes. This is the nub of *cyber*carnality: the digital's facilitation of self-representation in newly public domains, and the regulatory effects this has in the realm of beauty politics. According to Mowlabocus, the increased capacity for uploading and storing images at this point in the internet's history helped reinforce the most exclusionary tendencies of gay men's beauty politics.

HOOKUP APPS AND THE GAY BEAUTY IDEAL

The next development in dating technologies did little to challenge the hegemony of the gay beauty ideal. The early part of the new millennium was dominated by websites such as Gaydar, but by the 2010s smartphone "hookup" applications (apps) became the most common technology used by gay men for the purposes of dating and casual sex. Grindr remains the market leader, but there are a wide range of apps in use, each with different unique selling points, some which focus on body types. For example, Scruff has been designed and marketed with "bears" in mind. Although these hookup apps have a range of affordances that distinguish them from each other, most of them share two distinctive features which mark them out from their predecessors. The first is that they exist on *mobile* phones and therefore can be accessed all the time, providing what Lisa Reichelt (2007) termed "ambient intimacy"—constant access to potential and existing intimate partners. The second is that they are geolocational, and therefore able to organize users on their interfaces through proximity to each other more efficiently than websites—increasing the possibilities for users to meet offline. Arguably, images play an even more important role on hookup app profiles because they take up a greater proportion of the space in comparison to dating website profiles.

One of the major principles of "hookup app studies" (a significant subfield of internet studies) is that hookup apps are frequently used for more than hooking up—for example, for friendship (Byron & Møller, 2021) and for migrants to establish themselves in the locales to which they have migrated (Shield, 2019). Despite the unexpected uses of these technologies, their body politics have a tendency to be hegemonized by the gay beauty ideal. In a study of Grindr use in Newcastle, UK, Carl Bonner-Thompson (2017) argues that "hyper-masculinity" is a dominant tendency present in the Grindr profiles visible in the UK city: "Hypersexualised masculinities are produced through photos that focus on bodies and exposed flesh and skin. In these pictures the context of the image is blurred or the body takes up all space obscuring the background" (p. 1613). These bodies are mostly those which are "lean and muscular and have little or no chest hair [the types that] dominate media and advertising culture" (p. 1618). They are also predominantly White, the significance of which will be reflected on in the section on "Race, Racism, Dating Websites, and Hookup Apps." Evangelos Tziallas (2015) discerns similar patterns of mediation in an earlier article compounding Mowlabocus's cybercanality thesis, arguing that these applications are part of the continual "pornification of gay male culture" (p. 772). Begonya Enguix and Erick Gomez-Narvaez (2018) similarly notice an overrepresentation of muscular bodies among Grindr users in Spain.

RACE, RACISM, DATING WEBSITES, AND HOOKUP APPS

The ethical problems of how dating websites and hookup apps intersect with queer men's body politics only intensify when their racial dynamics are considered. Again, the issues raised by the presence of bodies of color in White majority Global North gay cultures had been interrogated in media, communication, and cultural studies long before the internet penetrated everyday life. The broad parameters of this scholarship are that when these bodies achieved visibility in these cultures, they were either represented as sexually abject or, conversely, fetishized as excessively sexual—both tactics of dehumanization (e.g., Fung, 2007;

K. Mercer, 1994). With regard to websites and hookup apps, these predigital racial dynamics persist but become rearticulated in different ways in these new technological contexts.

This is neatly evidenced through an experiment carried out by legal scholar Russell Robinson (2008) on gay dating website Adam4Adam. This experiment involved opening a series of dating profiles that each used the same image of a topless Latino fitness trainer and included all the same information in the profile bios except in the "race" and "sexual position" categories. All of the profiles were located in the same White majority neighborhood in the United States. The objective of the experiment was to determine how the attractiveness of someone who is "racially ambiguous" increases or diminishes when they are attributed different ethnic identities and sexual positions on the same dating website. This was achieved by counting the messages each of the profiles received over a specific period of time. It was found that the White and Latino profiles received the most emails and the Black and Asian profiles received the least—gesturing toward the racialized beauty hierarchies of American gay culture at play on these platforms more generally.

Shaka McGlotten's (2014) *Virtual Intimacies: Media, Affect and Queer Sociality* was the first book-length study that brought queer of color critique, as well as affect theory, to bear on different digital media spaces. The chapter on Grindr beautifully explicates the ambivalences that queer men of color experience pursuing sex and intimacy on the app. Drawing on both autoethnography of their own Grindr use and interviews they carried out during fieldwork in Austin, Texas, in the 2000s, McGlotten argues that queer men of color's Grindr use is primarily defined by three affects: anxiety, paranoia, and optimism. Anxiety emerges in anticipation of what queer men of color may encounter when they enter such a highly racialized sexual marketplace, "in which whiteness enjoys dominance, blackness generally possesses less value...while at other times it achieves worth through fetishization" (p. 68). This anxiety can turn into paranoia when it becomes impossible to know if an encounter, or indeed an encounter that fails to materialize, is *not* tainted by the specter of racism. Optimism arises when queer men of color can imagine, perhaps not a way out, but at least a way through this sexual marketplace that does not consume them with either anxiety or paranoia. As an example of this, McGlotten uses one of their interviewee's anecdotes in which the interviewee confounded his partner's racialized sexual expectations, with both enjoying the encounter in the process.

One of the features of Grindr that produced anxiety in McGlotten and the interviewees is the "race" category in the drop-down menu that Grindr provides for its users to construct their bios. The other feature of hookup apps that is most commonly discussed in the academic literature is the ethnicity filter, which enables users to find or block other users identifying on the app using a particular racial or ethnic category. Mowlabocus (2021) interrogates the politics of Grindr's ethnicity filters as part of a larger critique he makes of the app's Kindr initiative, which introduced a series of measures to counter various types of discrimination on the app. These measures included updating the brand's image, changing the community guidelines, and exhorting users to report discriminatory behavior. What Grindr failed to do was remove its ethnicity filters. Mowlabocus argues that this is a major failing of the Kindr campaign because these ethnicity filters are used to exclude ethnic groups from users' Grindr cascades and therefore create "networks of exclusion" (p. 123). He writes,

It is not just the white supremacists, the misogynists and the body fascists who seek to marginalise, silence and exclude particular identities and communities on Grindr; the very infrastructure of the platform affords the ring-fencing, screening out and segregation of those it claimed to be advocating on behalf of in the Kindr campaign. In identifying race, but also weight, age, body type and height, as potential filters that can be imposed on the database, Grindr validates and reproduces the very inequalities it allegedly seeks to combat. (pp. 124–125)

Although Mowlabocus makes a persuasive argument for the racist uses to which the ethnicity filters can be put, other uses were publicly discussed after Grindr eventually did remove them in response to the explosion of #blacklivesmatter in 2020. Many activists and users of color took to social media to express their disappointment at the removal of the ethnicity filters because they had been using these filters to find other men of color in an attempt to avoid racism on the app. Again, this demonstrates a feature of queer men's mediated cultures being used to exacerbate body-based exclusions while simultaneously creating spaces of safety, belonging, and the legitimation of otherwise marginalized forms of desire.

INSTAGRAM AND #INSTAGAYS

As the most popular image-based social media platform, Instagram has reshaped the particular ambivalences discussed in the section on "Race, Racism, Dating Websites, and Hookup Apps" in both predictable and unexpected ways. Much that has been written on Instagram shows how the platform's queer male visual culture is informed by similar tendencies to those that Mowlabocus (2010) identified on Gaydar. This is not only because of the platform's emphasis on photography but also because Instagram achieved its popularity during a period when social media more generally had evolved from being dominated by amateurish user-generated content to becoming the cutting edge of global capitalism (Little & Winch, 2021; Srnicek, 2017). Some of the most famous people in the world have achieved their celebrity through the architecture of this form of social media (Abidin, 2018). The profitability of these platforms, and the success of these influencers, has in part been achieved through the use of algorithms that prioritize the most liked, shared, and commented on, and therefore most normative, content into users' feeds. In terms of the politics of beauty, this means that the most successful influencers are the most conventionally beautiful. Moreover, they frequently use the glossy photographic styles historically found in high-end magazines and advertising campaigns. According to the research on queer men's Instagram cultures, these styles are apparent in many of the images that aggregate around the most widely used gay hashtags. This has a predictable effect on gay men's body politics, intensifying the hegemony of the gay beauty ideal.

Tyler Quick (2021) explores this in an article that unpacks the "representational anxieties" (p. 4938) of the "Instagay" phenomenon on Instagram. Beginning life as a hashtag, the term Instagay has now entered gay vernacular to mean "gay influencers who specialize in homoerotic self-representation and are among the most followed LGBTQ people on Instagram" (p. 4935). As influencers, these Instagays very often post paid-for content promoting products targeting gay men (e.g., grooming products and sex toys) in aspirational settings commonly found in gay men's lifestyles magazines (e.g., beaches and gay bars). Quick spent a month observing different media content relating to the hashtag #Instagay. He notes that two-thirds of the images posted using the hashtag were "thirst traps"—"a term describing erotic self-portraiture whose aim is to solicit attention in the form of quantifiable metrics from their followers" (p. 4941). Regarding the body types represented in this thirst trap content, "audiences and algorithms alike seem to privilege physicality, especially that which conforms to the Eurocentric, muscle-obsessed, hegemonic gay beauty standard" (p. 4940).

Quick's (2021) findings are confirmed by Adrián Gras-Velázquez and Antoni Maestre-Brotons's (2021) analysis of the Instagram hashtag "#gayspain," through which very similar visual content to #Instagay is aggregated. According to the authors, users who post content under #gayspain perpetuate "an online self-narrative of success and communicate a particular type of 'impression' to their followers that entails sculpting their bodies at the gym, eating healthy food, traveling to gay holiday destinations, wearing fashionable clothes, and attending trendy venues" (p. 7). And perhaps unsurprisingly, the body type that ends up being "used to communicate this impression is the one who shapes and displays a fit masculine body and performance—while excluding others with a feminine, queer, or unfit look" (p. 10), producing the exclusions associated with the gay beauty ideal. Gras-Velasquez and Maestre-Brotons's interpretation of these representational tropes is explicitly political—situating them within the neoliberal, homonormative tendencies that have grown stronger in culture more generally and have begun to shape so much cultural production since Instagram became one of the most popular social media platforms in the world (Hakim, 2020). Gras-Velasquez and Maestre-Brotons are firm in their argument against the possibility that the #gayspain content might resist these hegemonic tendencies and their representation through the fit, muscular, White body. They write, "We have not found any counter-discourse in the posts under the hashtag #gayspain that fight against self-branding and self-promotion in accordance with a neoliberal understanding of subjectivity and the body" (p. 7). This claim contradicts the argument made by Enguix and Gomez-Narvaez (2018). Although not focusing on this hashtag specifically, they found the gay beauty ideal more prevalent among Spanish Grindr users than among Spanish users on Instagram, where different body types were visible in the gay content posted. They pay particular attention to the images posted by trans men on Instagram, who represent their bodies in order to visually evidence different aspects of their transition processes. The social media use of trans men is different enough from that of cis-gay men to warrant a separate discussion.

TRANS MEN AND SOCIAL MEDIA

A significant growth area in queer digital media studies concerns trans use of digital media. It is difficult to overstate the effect of the internet on trans visibility, culture, and politics (Haimson et al., 2021; Horak, 2014; Jenzen, 2017). As Andre Cavalcante's (2016) trans participant states in an article on the effects of the internet on trans everyday life, "I did it all online" (p. 191). Whereas gay men and lesbians were comparatively well served by the post-gay rights, pre-internet mediascape, trans folk were considered too niche an audience to profitably cater for. The internet therefore provided an infrastructure to network this otherwise geographically dispersed group of people and enabled them to communicate, share information, and create culture in ways that were not possible to anywhere near the same extent before. There are now online forums for different trans and gender nonconforming users, particular genres of trans social media content, and increasingly trans influencers who have visibility to even non-trans audiences. Given the critical place of the body and embodiment to trans culture and identity, there is a growing academic literature on trans male online body politics.

The gay beauty ideal is an important presence within these online cultures, but it is articulated in subtly different ways. In the research carried out on online trans male bodies, most of the literature has had to engage with visual and textual representations of the fit, White, muscular body. Each of the scholars attributes a similar meaning to these representations: It becomes the ideal for many trans men because it is the body type that is most immediately recognizable as masculine in contemporary culture, which many trans men are anxious to achieve. This involves different processes of embodiment to cisgender gay men as well as different sorts of mediation.

In *Out Online: Trans Self-Representation and Community Building on YouTube*, Tobias Raun (2016) argues that the internet has been critical for creating and affirming contemporary trans cultures. Raun analyzes the content of four transmasculine YouTube vloggers, paying particular attention to how transmasculinity is represented and embodied. He finds that each of the vloggers is invested to a greater or lesser extent in this hegemonic mode of masculine embodiment. For people assigned female at birth, this is achieved differently to those assigned male, and these differences are key features of the vlogs. For instance, discussions of top surgery, taking testosterone, and standing-to-pee devices are distinctive to this genre of YouTube vlog. Similarly, the gym workouts are given different meanings to similar online content posted by their cisgender counterparts. Although both want to achieve "a lean and muscular male body" (p. 48), the trans masc vloggers narrate the processes they use to achieve this body in terms of transitioning. This includes weight training at gyms to, for instance, build muscular shoulders and chests to make "feminine" hips look narrower.

For Raun (2016), the representation of the bare chest is the privileged site of masculinity in this genre of social media content:

Working out and sculpting the torso are some of the most frequently discussed topics in the vlogs. Generally, the upper body is a prime point of focus and labor, often overtly worked on through weight-lifting, or at least talked about as the important site of workout. Working out after surgery seems to be a way to (re)claim and (re)connect with one's (upper) body after years of dissatisfaction with that same body and after medical intervention. It seems part of an empowering process of (re)claiming and self-creation. (pp. 67–68)

In this context, representing lean muscular torsos on the internet is not simply a case of reinforcing the exclusions of the gay beauty ideal. It becomes a critical component of the project of trans visibility:

> Muscles are one of a number of ways to produce masculinity—a way to produce male "realness" through the bodily feeling and/or visual appearance of strength. They become a way of controlling representation and visibility, making bodies intelligible as male bodies. (p. 69)

In an article co-authored with Cael M. Keegan, Raun further extends this argument through analyzing a composite of two nude images—one of cisgender, white, muscular pop star Adam Levine and the other of trans masc bodybuilder Aydian Dowling mirroring Levine's pose. Raun and Keegan argue that comparing cis and trans muscularity in this way works to deconstruct hegemonic masculine body ideals altogether, exposing both as processes of gender construction.

Despite the strong argument that Raun (2016) makes for the role that representations of the lean/muscular male body play in the project of trans male visibility, he also writes about its ambivalences. The YouTube vloggers whose vlogs he analyzed frequently talked about the anxiety they experienced in relation to not being able to achieve masculinity "proper" through these processes, something that was still defined in a cis-normative culture by being medically recognized as male at birth.

GAY MALE BEAUTY INFLUENCERS

The final type of online content where body politics is invoked in relation to queer masculinity is in the increasingly famous figure of the "beauty influencer"—influencers who promote beauty brands and post makeup routines on social media platforms. Although mostly dominated by cisgender females, there are certain gay men who are highly prominent in the field—for example, Jeffree Star, James Charles, Bretman Rock, and Patrick Starrr. These four, in particular, are the focus of an article titled "Authenticity, Uniqueness and Talent: Gay Male Beauty Influencers in Post-Queer, Postfeminist Instagram Beauty Culture" by Shirley Xue Chen and Akane Kanai (2022). In terms of the beauty politics under discussion, these influencers offer the most significant departure from the hegemonic framing of the gay beauty ideal. Wearing women's makeup and very often feminine clothes in the content they post, Chen and Kanai are interested in the *femininities* being constructed by these gay male influencers. Although gay men constructing femininity in this way could arguably be seen as queering the gendered body norms that gay men have long been expected to adhere to, the type of femininity these influencers construct draws heavily on the postfeminist beauty ideals that have been a mainstay of corporate content since at least the 1990s and that the capitalist beauty–industrial complex has long used to extract value from feminine bodies. The adoption of these aesthetics by gay male beauty influencers partially explains their significant success in this context. But it also raises political conundrums that confound a straightforward interpretation of these aesthetics as radical or queer. Gender binaries are clearly disrupted when self-identified men use such highly feminine aesthetics in their gender presentation, but they are also strengthened when they feed into circuits of power that many feminists argue have long worked to constrain the possibilities of cisgender female embodiment.

CONCLUSION

The politics of queer men's bodies as they relate to digital media are fraught with ambivalence. Although hegemonized by a very narrowly defined gay beauty ideal—White, masculine, able-bodied, lean/muscular, youthful, and hairless—the resonances of this ideal shift as it moves across different contexts. The continued mediation of this ideal across a variety of digital platforms has had the effect of intensifying the body-based exclusions that have defined queer men's cultures long before the popularization of the internet, reproducing age-old racist, sexist, ageist, and ableist structures that discursively render entire social groups less-than-human (e.g., Mowlabocus, 2010; Quick, 2021). Research shows, however, that this same ideal has also had the effect of producing networks of belonging, safety, pleasure, and experimentation for groups of people for whom their desire for this ideal, in other bodies or in their own, has itself been the basis on which they can be violently excluded from the prevailing symbolic order. This can be seen in the porn cinemas of New York's Time Square in the 20th century, in the Internet Relay Chats of the early internet, and in trans men's use of more recent social media platforms. Whether these networks can *only* be produced in relation to this highly specific ideal is another question, but so too is the question of whether the existence of new ideals creates more egalitarian networks or just further exclusions (Campbell, 2004; Chen & Kanai, 2022; J. Mercer, 2017) The problem is that ideals, types, categories, and taxonomies are by their very nature exclusionary, and yet culture and people's ability to make sense of it cannot operate without them. Furthermore, the immensely complex architecture of the internet has exponentially proliferated the possibility of categories *as such* through the multiplicity of interconnected spaces it has created and the cultures they produce. The creative, unpredictable, and even radical uses to which these spaces can be put should provide cause for, in McGlotten's (2014) terms, optimism.

What is the future of research on the politics of queer men's bodies and digital media? This article has focused on the Global North, often the Anglo-American context, because with regard to the Anglophone internet, these are the cultures that dominate. This hegemony is no longer guaranteed (if it ever was) and is being challenged by other geopolitical blocs. What this means in terms of popular culture is that Anglophone audiences are being exposed to a greater number of cultural forms from different areas of the world. For instance, Korean K-Pop band BTS (with its distinctive brand of male embodiment) spent 10 weeks in the number 1 position on the U.S. Billboard Hot 100 singles chart. The globalization of culture is not new, but aspects of it are being intensified by the fact that the networking capabilities of internet technologies can bypass the gatekept, nation-focused, nature of the mass media era. More English language research into this area is necessary, be it original or in translation. Some of this work already exists. For instance, Lik Sam Chan's (2021) *The Politics of Dating Apps: Gender, Sexuality, and Emergent Publics in Urban China* outlines dating app use in China, with sections on masculine body ideals that clearly depart from those under discussion here. Similarly, *Queer Sites in Global Contexts Technologies, Spaces, and Otherness*, edited by Regner Ramos and Sharif Mowlabocus (2021), includes research on race and gay digital media use in China too.

Finally, the hegemony of neoliberalism also appears to be waning in the Global North and with it, its culture of entrepreneurialism, self-branding, and beautifying the body as a form of optimizing human capital (Gras-Velázquez & Maestre-Brotons, 2021; Hakim, 2020). Different body projects are emerging across digital platforms in response, and these require scholarly analysis. For instance, there are a new generation of QTIPOC (queer, trans. and intersex people of color) "activist/influencers" with a large amount of public recognition who are using social media platforms to challenge Eurocentric, hetero- and cis-normative beauty ideals. For example, Alok V. Menon frequently uses images of their own body captioned by queer and queer of color critique. This is just one example. The internet is teeming with similar projects, across the political spectrum, some more organized than others. The hegemonic struggle in the domain of body politics continues, and the digital is now where much of this struggle is taking place.

FURTHER READING

Bonner-Thompson, C. (2017). "The meat market": Production and regulation of masculinities on the Grindr grid in Newcastle-upon-Tyne, UK. *Gender, Place & Culture, 24*(11), 1611–1625. https://doi.org/10.1080/0966369X.2017.1356270

Campbell, J. E. (2004). *Getting it on online: Cyberspace, gay male sexuality, and embodied identity*. Harrington Park Press.

Chan, L. S. (2021). *The politics of dating apps: Gender, sexuality, and emergent publics in urban China*. MIT Press.

Chen, S. X., & Kanai, A. (2022). Authenticity, uniqueness and talent: Gay male beauty influencers in post-queer, postfeminist Instagram beauty culture. *European Journal of Cultural Studies, 25*(1), 97–116. https://doi.org/10.1177/1367549421988966

Enguix, B., & Gómez-Narváez, E. (2018). Masculine bodies, selfies, and the (re)configurations of intimacy. *Men and Masculinities, 21*(1), 112–130. https://doi.org/10.1177/1097184X17696168

Gras-Velázquez, A., & Maestre-Brotons, A. (2021). Spanish gay male subjectivity, body, intimacy, and affect on Instagram. *Sexualities*. https://doi.org/10.1177/13634607211031418

Hakim, J. (2020). *Work that body: Male bodies in digital culture*. Rowman & Littlefield.

McGlotten, S. (2014). *Virtual intimacies: Media, affect, and queer sociality*. State University of New York Press.

Mercer, J. (2017). *Gay pornography: Representations of sexuality and masculinity*. Tauris.

Mowlabocus, S. (2010). *Gaydar culture: Gay men, technology and embodiment in the digital age*. Ashgate.

Mowlabocus, S. (2021). *Interrogating homonormativity: Gay men, identity and everyday life*. Springer.

Quick, T. (2021). #GaysOverCOVID: The social drama of LGBTQ representation on Instagram. *International Journal of Communication, 15*, 4934–4955.

Raun, T. (2016). *Out online: Trans self-representation and community building on YouTube*. Routledge.

Tziallas, E. (2015). Gamified eroticism: Gay male "social networking" applications and self-pornography. *Sexuality & Culture, 19*(4), 759–775. https://doi.org/10.1007/s12119-015-9288-z

REFERENCES

Abidin, C. (2018). *Internet celebrity: Understanding fame online*. Emerald.

Acic, I., Stevens, H., Yu, X., & Taylor, L. D. (2021). How gay men discuss their bodies online. *Communication Research Reports, 38*(5), 325–335.

Barcan, R. (2004). *Nudity: A cultural anatomy*. Berg.

Bonner-Thompson, C. (2017). "The meat market": Production and regulation of masculinities on the Grindr grid in Newcastle-upon-Tyne, UK. *Gender, Place & Culture, 24*(11), 1611–1625. https://doi.org/10.1080/0966369X.2017.1356270

Bruckman, A. (1996). Gender swapping on the Internet. In *High noon on the electronic frontier: Conceptual issues in cyberspace* (pp. 317–326). MIT Press.

Byron, P., & Møller, K. (2021). Flirting and friendship at the periphery of hook-up app research. *Lambda Nordica*, 26(1), 23–52. https://doi.org/10.34041/ln.v26.720

Campbell, J. E. (2004). *Getting it on online: Cyberspace, gay male sexuality, and embodied identity*. Harrington Park Press.

Carah, N., Dobson, A. S., & Robards, B. (Eds.). (2018). *Digital intimate publics and social media*. Springer. https://doi.org/10.1007/978-3-319-97607-5

Cavalcante, A. (2016). "I did it all online": Transgender identity and the management of everyday life. *Critical Studies in Media Communication*, 33(1), 109–122. https://doi.org/10.1080/15295036.2015.1129065

Chan, L. S. (2021). *The politics of dating apps: Gender, sexuality, and emergent publics in urban China*. MIT Press.

Chen, S. X., & Kanai, A. (2022). Authenticity, uniqueness and talent: Gay male beauty influencers in post-queer, postfeminist Instagram beauty culture. *European Journal of Cultural Studies*, 25(1), 97–116. https://doi.org/10.1177/1367549421988966

Delany, S. R. (1999). *Times Square red, Times Square blue*. New York University Press.

Enguix, B., & Gómez-Narváez, E. (2018). Masculine bodies, selfies, and the (re)configurations of intimacy. *Men and Masculinities*, 21(1), 112–130. https://doi.org/10.1177/1097184X17696168

Fung, R. (2007). Looking for my penis: The eroticized Asian in gay video porn. In K. A. Ono (Ed.), *A companion to Asian American studies* (pp. 235–253). Blackwell. https://doi.org/10.1002/9780470996928.ch15

Gras-Velázquez, A., & Maestre-Brotons, A. (2021). Spanish gay male subjectivity, body, intimacy, and affect on Instagram. *Sexualities*. https://doi.org/10.1177/13634607211031418

Haimson, O. L., Dame-Griff, A., Capello, E., & Richter, Z. (2021). Tumblr was a trans technology: The meaning, importance, history, and future of trans technologies. *Feminist Media Studies*, 21(3), 345–361. https://doi.org/10.1080/14680777.2019.1678505

Hakim, J. (2020). *Work that body: Male bodies in digital culture*. Rowman & Littlefield.

Horak, L. (2014). Trans on YouTube: Intimacy, visibility, temporality. *Transgender Studies Quarterly*, 1(4), 572–585. https://doi.org/10.1215/23289252-2815255

Jenzen, O. (2017). Trans youth and social media: Moving between counterpublics and the wider web. *Gender, Place & Culture*, 24(11), 1626–1641. https://doi.org/10.1080/0966369X.2017.1396204

Little, B., & Winch, A. (2021). *The new patriarchs of digital capitalism: Celebrity tech founders and networks of power*. Routledge.

McGlotten, S. (2014). *Virtual intimacies: Media, affect, and queer sociality*. State University of New York Press.

Mercer, J. (2017). *Gay pornography: Representations of sexuality and masculinity*. Tauris.

Mercer, K. (1994). *Welcome to the jungle: New positions in Black cultural studies*. Routledge.

Mowlabocus, S. (2010). *Gaydar culture: Gay men, technology and embodiment in the digital age*. Ashgate.

Mowlabocus, S. (2021). *Interrogating homonormativity: Gay men, identity and everyday life*. Springer.

Quick, T. (2021). #GaysOverCOVID: The social drama of LGBTQ representation on Instagram. *International Journal of Communication*, 15, 4934–4955.

Ramos, R., & Mowlabocus, S. (Eds.). (2021). *Queer sites in global contexts: Technologies, spaces, and otherness*. Routledge.

Raun, T. (2016). *Out online: Trans self-representation and community building on YouTube*. Routledge.

Reichelt, L. (2007, March 1). Ambient intimacy. *Disambiguity*. http://www.disambiguity.com/ambient-intimacy/

Rheingold, H. (2000). *The virtual community: Homesteading on the electronic frontier* (Rev. ed.). MIT Press.

Robinson, R. K. (2008). Structural dimensions of romantic preferences. *Fordham Law Review*, 76(6), 2787–2819.
Shield, A. D. (2019). *Immigrants on Grindr: Race, sexuality and belonging online*. Palgrave Macmillan.
Srnicek, N. (2017). *Platform capitalism*. Polity.
Turkle, S. (1995). *Life on the screen: Identity in the age of the Internet*. Simon & Schuster.
Tziallas, E. (2015). Gamified eroticism: Gay male "social networking" applications and self-pornography. *Sexuality & Culture*, 19(4), 759–775. https://doi.org/10.1007/s12119-015-9288-z
Waugh, T. (1996). *Hard to imagine: Gay male eroticism in photography and film from their beginnings to Stonewall*. Columbia University Press.

Jamie Hakim

TRANSFEMINISMS

WHERE CAN WE BEGIN? BY WAY OF INTRODUCTION

To understand the vicissitudes of transfeminism(s) is to listen to a polyvocal palimpsest of voices from varying geopolitical locations with prerogatives emerging from local and global struggles. Geopolitically, the cultural and intellectual production that can be called transfeminism and that calls itself transfeminism cannot be flattened to dismiss the work coming out of the United States or Spain, for instance, because the transfeminist work we will concern ourselves with here begins at the margins and the periphery of hegemonic subject (and at time subjectless) positions. (More on the latter shortly). In this way, even transfeminism that does not reckon fully with its whiteness understands how the production of a supposed "third world" in these "First Worlds" generated internationally significant bodies of literature from "women of color," "third world women of color," and "women of color" feminisms that they benefit from. Simultaneously, we must acknowledge how the global network of neoliberal power regimes makes certain work circulate more than other works and prioritizes certain people as more important interlocutors because of their geopolitical locations. Other times it is a crisis of translation where work is directed to monolingual Anglophone audiences making it easier for such populations to not engage in the work of learning languages outside of English for the purposes of dialoguing with communities and scholarship outside of known canons and taking their contributions just as seriously. In part because of hegemony's hold on the global circulation of knowledges, transfeminism has traveled far and wide, but not uncritically. It has been reappropriated and used in contextual ways that aim to create spaces and improve the conditions of people whose realities are made precarious by the state and its social mechanisms for reinforcing power. It has also been named as an activist strategy and practice of analysis in spaces that previously may not have had the language of transfeminism to name their interventions.

An all-encompassing purview of transfeminisms is outside the scope of this article. What the author of this article aims to do—situated from a Black transfeminist artist-activist scholar positionality—is to provide articulations of some of the nuances of the crucial activist–intellectual–artistic work of transfeminists and transfeminism and the work that informs it. The aim is for the article to be intellectually useful and to provide multiple apertures through which much lengthier investigations can arise. True to the reticular nature and plurality of transfeminisms, this article will account for some of the geopolitically specific queries, some of which are informed by questions of genealogy. However, this article has been organized more in a teleological fashion rather than a temporally linear narration. This teleology is one that spans five decades of work, whose temporal unboundedness is directed by the ever-changing conditions under late neoliberal colonial racial capitalism. To place a claim on who began the discourse of transfeminism and where is to have misunderstood the cartography of transfeminisms and the ongoing networks of its sustenance.[1] With this, it is also the author's hope that some of the work in this article might encourage a critical transfeminisms international archive. In working this way, we honor the trans analytic by leaning into its ongoing openings where no notion of a totality can conceal its borders.

If we are to situate some of the best that transfeminism has to offer (though this article will not shy away from the critiques), it is suggested that we center transfeminism that does not result from nor get its fire from injury, as in weaponizing abjection, individualizing stories-as-gratuitous-oppression Olympics, and spectacularizing death as the tool through which to garner particular types of support and sympathy.[2] Turning away from injury as the emergence of trans subjectivity also moves us away from overemphasis on the spectacularity of trans brutality, particularly by those who do not experience it (more on this shortly). Secondarily, moving with the best of transfeminisms also means attending to the openness of their trans* horizons and not limiting them to an additive genealogy of inserting transness and trans people (usually referring to transwomen) into feminisms.[3] Refusing an additive logic also uncouples trans becomings from transnormativity because it leaves room to interrogate "biomedical, neoliberal, racist, and imperialist projects" that are the investments of the state (Varun Chaudhry, 2020, p. 67). Expounding upon the limitations of the additive logic, Kai M. Green in conversation with Marquis Bey (2017) explains:

> As our grammars shift and change to be more inclusive, particularly when it comes to a Black queer feminist politic that consciously names "cis and trans" as a modifier of "woman," we must be careful about what the *and* then dislodges. It is not productive to simply add transgender women to the category of woman without thinking through the ways that transgender women force us to consider again how "woman" as a category is a failure. (p. 441)

This latter point is where this article will begin the larger conversation.

In what follows, this article breaks (what the author hopes will be) a capacious definitional space of transfeminisms into five main sections in addition to this introduction. "Transgender Studies' Need to Reckon Fully with Black Feminisms" addresses the Black feminist history of transfeminisms and why their imbrication and relationality is historically and theoretically deciding. It also addresses how intersectionality has become a type of trope and dehistoricized from its Black feminist foundations. "Shared Corporeal Quandaries of Blackness and Transness" expands upon this by situating the relation between blackness and transness, especially as they traffic in questions of ontology and necropolitics. The uptake of necropolitics in different geo-locals instantiates Black theorizing foundations of transfeminisms. "Trans* Movements, Decolonial Feminisms, Indigenous Feminisms" addresses how transness has an anoriginal ontology that troubles genesis and biologist notions of gender stasis. This section addresses decolonial feminist and Indigenous feminist projects as rejoinders to the idea of being transgender as a mutation from what is "normal." "Refusing Neoliberal Capitalist Logics of Nation-Statehood" speaks to transfeminism as a mobilization of dissident bodies beyond state inclusionary logics while also acknowledging how some transfeminist issues have utilized the state strategically. Within this, it also addresses how certain transfeminist corporal practices are part of an antistate network of living. In "Subversive Grammars of Transness," the article finalizes this trajectory by addressing inventive grammars of transwomen, travestis, and travas in the "Global South" whose transfeminist practices continue to destabilize feminine categorizations.

TRANSGENDER STUDIES' NEED TO RECKON FULLY WITH BLACK FEMINISMS

In a conversation with Kai M. Green, Marquis Bey (2017) writes:

> To speak of Black feminism and trans feminism is to submerge oneself in a kind of study of life's interstices. They both name, in different ways and by different inflections, the refusal of racialized sexism, transantagonism, anti-Blackness, the gender binary, and a range of other identificatory and sociohistorical vectors tied to hierarchical and hegemonic regimes. (p. 439)

In this conversation, what Bey makes clear is that there is a way to read Black feminism and trans feminisms as not "mutually exclusive" but rather, constitutive of one another (pp. 438–439). Not only does this engage their "referential overlap" but this puts a pin in their coconstitutive histories, theorizations, and genealogies. What we must hold in tension here is how some Black feminisms struggle with trans, nonbinary, and other gender nonconforming identities, while some transfeminisms make only performative gestures to Black feminisms (often collapsed into women of color feminisms) without engaging in the substantive critiques of the gender binary that were not invented by trans studies but rather by Black feminist thought. In this instance, how "woman" was not an available category to Black women because of the property status instilled through the plantation economy in the United States. These critiques have been some of the underlying basis of the critique of liberal humanism as well.

As many have pointed out, a foundational text to transfeminist thought at its intersection with Black feminisms is Hortense Spillers's (1987) "Mama's baby, Papa's maybe: An American grammar book" (Bey, 2017; Coleman, 2020; Day, 2021; Snorton, 2017). In this field-defining article, Spillers explicates how the law of *partus sequitur ventrem* meant that all people born to enslaved women inherited the legal status of their mothers—or the status of nonperson (Spillers, 1987). Enslaved women, particularly in the American South, were used as reproductive agents once the United States banned further importation of enslaved people from the African continent. In this process, the birth of American gynecology was born of white Southern doctors in order to repair fistulas and other health issues that arose during pregnancy or childbirth so that these women could continue to reproduce for the state.[4] Given this reality, Spillers's attention was drawn to the role of the mother and the Black woman in this scenario and its ongoing consequences in slavery's afterlives. If the Black woman is the place through whom all others earned their status, it is to this history of the Black woman that we must return.

As Iyko Day (2021) so trenchantly observes, in Spillers's work, the Black woman's reproductive labor was continual whereas her physical labor was about temporary surplus value (p. 74). We can read enslaved women's reproduction, then, as "the technology that could generate relative surplus value and decrease the value of commodities and the labor expressed in it" by virtue of producing more for less (Day, 2021, p. 75). Agreeing with Day's (2021) logic, the enslaved Black woman passed on two things to her progenitors: devaluation and disinheritance (p. 75). Given this, the stakes of disavowing or bypassing the Black woman as marked by the laws of enslavement and all of their modern-day afterlives and echoes is to negate what has structured forms of Black gender in this country, troubling any notion of the "all" of gender. Enslaved women, for Spillers (1987), became "ungendered flesh" in their role as those who would reproduce those to produce surplus labor (p. 77). Being Black and having a Black mother *means something* in the United States because of this history.

What serves as the linchpin of Spillers's (1987) argument and its uptake in trans studies is Spillers's (1987) articulation of the dispossession from the self-as-mother (and therefore woman wherein woman in the Western cosmology meant the capacity to be a mother) experienced by the enslaved Black woman such that dispossession meant a "loss of gender" since women's reproductive capacity for their master was their only value, akin to the life of animals (p. 77). For Spillers (1987), gendering and ungendering are intimately linked to the disavowal of motherhood that, to the present day, troubles facile or essentialist feminist assumptions about gendered beings (p. 78). Since "[femininity] loses its sacredness in slavery," to name the gender of Black women is to name a gender that never existed for Black women in the way that it did for white women (p. 156).[5] The Black woman's gender was already queered, odd, slippery, and not capturable by the grammars of the colonial world. The Black enslaved woman's gender/ungendering as fungible flesh that exists in two modes of production troubles any way of thinking about transness that assumes abstract universals for normative gender identity because these, by default, assume white Western gender constructs as abstract universals.[6] Therefore, transfeminisms and trans studies cannot simply instrumentalize the contributions of Black feminism but actually have to be in full dialogue with them.

Intersectionality and Beyond. The concept of intersectionality, though explicated and utilized before the 1989 work of Kimberlé Crenshaw, was one theoretical intervention meant to name the social ills caused by the impossibility of the intersection of Black and woman, stemming from this foundational history of dispossession.[7] The popularly recognized coining of the term by Kimberlé Crenshaw comes from legal scholarship and what became known as "critical race theory" through looking at discrimination court cases where Black women were the plaintiffs. Crenshaw (1989) recognized how Black women were being excluded from both feminist theory and antiracist policy because feminist theory was driven by an ostensible universal experience of the gender "woman" (read: white) and antiracist theory was driven by an ostensible universal experience of the race "Black" (read: male; p. 140). Intersectionality became the language through which to articulate the overlapping and compounding axes of discrimination faced by Black women when confronting hegemonic power.[8]

Scholars like Jennifer C. Nash (2019) have more recently taken up and troubled the cache that intersectionality holds at universities and in mainstream spaces, particularly how the Black woman's body oftentimes "haunts the analytic" even if its history makes this analytic central to naming Black women's lives (p. 2). Nash is concerned with the institutional life of intersectionality and how it has helped to build women's studies programs across the United States. She asks crucial questions about how Black women have handled intersectionality's popularization and the evacuation of Black women's stories from its theorizations. In this way, Nash's project is invested in the affect of Black women and, in particular, their defensiveness around the proprietary issues tracked by the widespread uptake of intersectionality. What is so interesting about this work is that it at once troubles the delinking of intersectionality from Black feminism and Black gender(s) and it also remains critical about proprietary conservativeness in that it might hinder the Black feminist project's full influence over a vast array of disciplinary analytics. What is particularly problematic is how Black feminist theories like intersectionality get mobilized by institutions as "novel" concepts meant to remedy canons and White feminism (Nash, 2019). What this does not remedy is the erasure of Black women's embodied lives and their intellectual contributions as foundational rather than, again, as additive.

To take Black feminism as one of the foundations of transfeminism, then, is to read the capaciousness of Black gendering/ungendering in the context of the African American experience and the transatlantic slave trade and to also ask wider questions about Black gender in the diaspora, acknowledging the endless multiplicity of blackness, not only predicated on its relationship to Western modernity and hegemonic hemispheres. Oyèrónkẹ́ Oyěwùmí's (1997) work discusses how Yoruba common sense about gender reveals Western assumptions about gender logics. Oyěwùmí's (1997) work provides an epistemological lens through which to shift our ideas about where knowledge produced about gender comes from rather than assume stable givens that can only be true for certain white Western subjects. Oyèrónkẹ́ Oyěwùmí (1997) began this investigation noting how the Western concept of "woman" did not exist in Yorubaland prior to the encounter with the West (p. ix). Oyěwùmí (1997) takes issue with the givenness of what has come to be called "sex" and its conflation with gender.

Oyěwùmí's (1997) major contribution to theorizing gender otherwise comes in her analysis of the Western gender system as a form of biological determinism or "the concept that biology provides the rationale for the organization of the social world" (p. ix).[9] She calls this form of biological determinism a "bio-logic" where the gender "woman" must exist in opposition to her supposed biological antithesis "man" (pp. ix–x). Oyěwùmí (1997) explains that in order to apply this bio-logic to Yorubaland, the category of "woman" would first have to be invented (p. x). What is crucial to this bio-logic that determines the social order in the Western world is its basis on bodily organs (p. x). However, the body in Yorubaland is not what determined gender, social roles, or society structure. Oyěwùmí's (1997) work in Yorubaland contests all notions of a stable gender as determined by the West and that gender legislated in such way is "fundamental organizing principle" of all studies, derailing some of the founding assumptions of Western feminisms.

Transfeminisms, then, step into this legacy of Black feminisms troubling Western relationships to gender through dispossession and through cultural notions of gender that had entirely different lives prior to colonial encounters with the West. What transfeminisms can do is to reignite these spaces of excess, refusing an abstract universal bio-logic through which to come to know gender of all kinds. Transfeminisms can account for these subjugated ungenderings that unsettle universal gender theories. Transfeminisms are also interested in the subjectivities that are critical of all of these historicities and who position themselves in relation to them.

SHARED CORPOREAL QUANDARIES OF BLACKNESS AND TRANSNESS

To build upon what we have just looked at, blackness, as a concept, adds another layer to the trans question of transfeminism and that which becomes ungendered or that which cannot be named through Western bio-logics. The "problem of blackness" and the "problem of transness" lie in their inherent instabilities in the Western colonial world system. That is to say, some theorists argue that for humans who cannot have full subjectivity under Western modernity, blackness is not a choice but a projection onto the Black person that marks them as other so that whiteness might be human. And, following the previously mentioned Black feminist work, how can one "be" trans if historical access to gendered subjectivity is not available or if gendered categories used by the West do not apply to certain cultural logics? Transfeminisms need attend to the logics of the human and the logics of race in order to understand what openings become available.

A Brief Word on Ontology.   Ontology, or that sticky Western metaphysical science that asks questions about "being," has become a dividing force along disciplinary lines in Black thought.[10] Afro-pessimists, or Black theorists who understand the world would have to end for Black people to ever experience ontology, are the ground zero for the limitations of ontology conceived from a Western metaphysical standpoint. Iyko Day (2021) also exposes Afro-pessimism's heterosexist masculinist problem by refusing to begin its theorization from its "critical inheritance" of "Afro-feminism" (p. 62).[11] Afro-pessimism has benefited from Black feminist theorizing yet uses it "to write through" while continuing to negate "the mother" (Day, 2021, p. 62). In Afro-pessimism's totalizing argument that positions "Blackness outside of humanist material relations and as a condition of ontological death" there is no room from which to think Black woman's material lives, for material life is foreclosed upon as an impossibility to think from. Black women get erased within the "rigid Afropessimist frame, in which the history and politics are collapsed into a metaphysical plea for the end of the world" (p. 80).

The limitations here become obvious in the totalizing arguments that hold Afro-pessimism together. The author sees this perhaps most poignantly in Calvin Warren's takedown of Kai M. Green and Treva Ellison's concept of "tranifestation." Tranifestation is, arguably, a Black transfeminist epistemological intervention that means to transformatively manifest. Tranifesting, in the words of the authors,

> is meant to call attention to the ways in which black feminism and transgender studies are similarly yet differentially capable of mediating particular individual experiences and operationalizing identity–not as ends in themselves but as places from which to generate transformative politics. (Green & Ellison, 2014, p. 223)

They acknowledge how both Black feminism and transgender studies challenge the ontological givenness of the subjects of "woman" and "man" and therefore have the potential to call in collective forms of gender self-determination (pp. 223–224).

Warren (2017), though intellectually generous in his critique, runs the risk of obliterating transness through his totalizing entrenchment in his Afro-pessimist paradigm. At the same time, the limitations of tranifesting, for Warren, are also what make it such a crucial intervention and what Black trans studies does to destabilize the category of the human.[12] He argues that "we can reconceptualize black trans not as an ontological formation (i.e., nonnormative human subjects) but as a speculative or philosophical enterprise—one designed to devastate ontological humanism" (Warren, 2017, p. 267). The two arguments that leave us with no conclusions but Warren's are that "the black never manifests in an antiblack world since blackness lacks being" and "Blacks can experience trans violence, but this experience does not translate into being trans" (p. 267). Where Warren (2017) gets trapped and where the limits of ontology show up is that if neither blackness nor transness can exist ontologically, no amount of theorizing, manifesting, or political calling-into-being will give them being.

Ontology, then, and the Afro-pessimist critique of Black transfeminism falls flat when we consider possible original elements of blackness and transness that do not begin with the transatlantic slave trade and that do not belong to a singular cosmology through which to name the world. The author would argue that this entrapment in Western metaphysical definitions of ontology surrenders itself to the concept of a singular and totalizing cosmology through which people live and name their lives, forgetting that power does not and cannot erase cosmology and the existence of many worlds in this one. It is the work of Black transfeminism to keep tranifesting so that the trappings of Western metaphysics and its limited concepts of ontology do not hold us in place as nonagents of an inevitable nonpresent and nonfuture.

Necropolitics and Trans Activism. This brings us to the activism and cultural work that we can name as transfeminist and that names itself as such. Moving away from philosophical or academic trappings is to acknowledge the role that activism has in producing material culture and in moving lives. It is to have endless places from which to start. It is also to name possible counter-archives that might get overlooked as transfeminist foundations and to not rely solely on academic trajectories. As Elías Cosenza Krell (2017) mentions, this might include the work of transcestors like Marsha P. Johnson and Sylvia Rivera and their Street Transvestite Action Revolutionaries, Angelica Ross's TransTech, Ignacio Rivera's HEAL Project, or Suzy Shock's performances (p. 237). What arises when we begin to name these alternative archives of transfeminist labor is that we must traffic with death and the role the state has in living and dying. This "necropolitical" truth means that activism also exists in a complex set of relations that is not inherently more anti-institutional than university spaces.

C. Riley Snorton and Jin Haritaworn (2013) explain that "trans deaths—and most frequently the deaths of trans women and trans-feminine people of color—act as a resource for the development and dissemination of many different agendas" (p. 66). They question the idea of "transgender as first and foremost victimized" and how this actually supports the "value extracted from trans of color death" (p. 67). Brilliantly, they articulate that [for more precarious trans people] "while those multiple vulnerabilities lend the moral panic its spectacularly violated bodies are continually reinscribed as degenerate and killable, the same processes secures a newly professionalizing class of experts in the realm of life" (p. 67). They are challenging the hyper-emphasis on trans women of color's death and dying as what mobilizes a lot of funding for LGBTQ organizations and also what structures a lot of academic writing about trans studies. What can appear as a loving gesture of remembering the dead actually becomes a performative strategy for demonstrating trans "wokeness." Snorton and Haritaworn (2013) are concerned with how the global rise in trans politics has also been about these "technologies of value extraction" mediated by necropolitics (p. 68). This behavior becomes a type of "murderous inclusion" (p. 74). This is particularly common in overly-White spaces around the world where a "parasitic" relationship to the death of trans people of color is developed (pp. 67, 74).[13]

Snorton and Haritaworn (2013) define necropolitics according to scholar Achille Mbembe's (2003) conception of necropolitics (mobilized in the context of neoliberal accumulation). Necropolitics is essential to Snorton and Haritaworn's engagement with transnational trans/feminisms. Necropolitics "describes a form of power that marks some fraction of a population for death even while it deems other fractions suitable for life enhancing investment" (p. 66). It is used to understand "the centrality of death in social life" (p. 66). What necropolitics also offers them is a vision of "how biopower—the carving out of subjects and populations (Foucault 1978)—can profess itself at the service of life and yet generate death, in both quotidian and spectacular forms" (p. 66). Necropolitics is not only crucial to the circulation of trans death but also to question what requires death for its flourishing in contemporary neoliberal life.

Mexican transfeminist scholar Sayak Valencia (2018) also takes up Mbembe's (2003) necropolitics in her transfeminist theorizations from México coming out of performance work, organizing communities, and intellectual lives in México and Spain. She says, "I say the word death and then the word feminisms appears…" (p. 30). Valencia theorizes necropolitics in two primary ways: (1) How cis-normative White feminisms actually cosign on necropolitical regimes and realities by engaging in the modern colonial gender systems bio-logic, also hurting themselves, and (2) How the neoliberal capitalist machine actually requires and directs precarious and marginalized bodies toward death—literal blood is its sustenance (see Valencia, 2018, 2019). These two goals of her work (one more specifically about trans people and gender in society and the other invested in an articulation of how systems of oppression can be read through transfeminism) exemplify the tracks of transfeminist thought.

Operating in these ways, Valencia gives us a transnational definition for transfeminisms as an "epistemological tool." She explains:

> [transfeminism] cannot be reduced to trans incorporation into feminist discourse. Instead, it is about a web that considers the state of gender transition, of migration, of mixed-raceness (via mestizaje), of vulnerability, of race and of class, to articulate ourselves from the heirs of historical memory of social movements of insurrection. (p. 31)

Valencia (2018) then provides examples of what local transfeminist work can include: "destigmatization of sex work, depathologization of trans bodies, expanding the political subject of feminisms, intersectionality, coloniality, systemic violence, extractivism, buen vivir (good living)" are all examples of what local contemporary realities need from transfeminist work (p. 33).

Valencia addresses the problematics of trans-exclusionary radical feminist (TERF) arguments coming out of a critique that transfeminism is "genderism" where the fear is the erasure of the category of "woman" with real social consequences in the world (Valencia, 2018a). Nevertheless, Valencia (2018) poignantly argues, "to think of oneself as a feminist and to profess a trans-exclusionary positionality is to make pacts with the necro-patriarchal State, pimp and feminicidal that reappropriates our struggles through separatism and the destruction of the common good" (p. 36). Valencia notes that this kind of feminism attempts to "institutionalize the language of protest." In contradistinction, transfeminisms, in their "contradictory multitudes... have in common to not subscribing to, not embodying, and not reproducing the promises of the modern Nation State; that is to say, to make our leave of absence a political practice of dissidences" (p. 39).[14]

Transfeminisms, in their transnational theorization emerging from collectives and thinkers of the "Global South," promote and analyze queer/cuir and dissident ways of loving, living, forming kinship, practicing art and activism, having sex, making a living, etc. that do not seek valorization from the Nation State in order to legitimize their existence.[15] This means that transfeminisms are the production of, archiving of, and storying of queer/dissident cultures where people outside of the normative constraints of the hegemon make their lives. Concomitantly, it is the analysis of the systems that created the hegemon and its exclusions in the first place.

TRANS* MOVEMENTS, DECOLONIAL FEMINISMS, INDIGENOUS FEMINISMS

Transfeminisms have, as a tall order, to act and theorize from and through the possibility trans* enables, while simultaneously holding that the very need for the existence of transgender as a category is thanks to the coloniality of gender in the present modern colonial world system. To hold both simultaneously requires an understanding of the mutability of sex and gender, from *genesis*, that trans* enables.

Claire Colebrook cited as part of the prologue of Marquis Bey's article (2017) explains:

> I want to argue that "in the beginning is 'trans'": that what is original or primary is a not-yet-differentiated singularity from which distinct genders, race, species, sexes and sexualities are generated in a form of relative stability... Freed kinds such as the transgendered, trans-sexual, or trans-animal body are expressions of a more profound transitivity that is the condition for what becomes known as the human. (p. 276)

Colebrook's work, as explicated by Bey, seems to follow after Julian Gill-Peterson's (2014) work that doesn't want to "restrict trans agency to psychic identity" because this leaves far too much room for transphobic logics of biological essentialisms to take root (pp. 405–406). Gill-Peterson (2014) instead follows the work of Nikki Sullivan and Susan Stryker (2009) "in proposing trans as an expression of the originary technicity of the body" (p. 406). She elaborates, "If forms of trans embodiment are expressions of the originary technicity of the body, then body modification cannot be transphobically exceptionalized as a betrayal of the human's integrity" (p. 407). This means that elective, "medically necessary," or otherwise categorized surgeries and interventions to the trans body "are a participation in the body's open-ended technical capacities, the ways in which its physical matter, biological systems, and affective components exceed conscious will through receptiveness to change as difference, as nonidentity" (p. 407). This means we might transsexualize the category of human so as to rupture the modern colonial gender categories that cannot actually hold it.

Gill-Peterson (2014) builds on the early work of endocrinologists who discovered in the early 20th century that hormones had a certain plasticity separate from the function of the gametes which meant that "sex" could be modified by "removing or transplanting gonads" as the "medical intervention to the body's technicity" (p. 407). Similarly, in her transfeminist analysis and following of the hormone testosterone, she also observes how race has also become a technique through which the Western people called "humans" could cohere. In a social constructivist vein, we can understand that "Race has not always existed; it is not required for human life. Indeed, race is literally no-thing" (p. 411). Since race and puberty have always experienced entanglement because of the technical capacities of the body, the body then holds the potential to undo/unlearn in spaces of antiracist gender autonomy (p. 411).

To perceive the body's technicity as its original inheritance is to bring intersex questions and transgender questions into conversation. In a crucial intervention by an intersex thinker, "The missing vagina monologue... and beyond," Esther Morris Leidolf (2006) troubles some of the gender and genital-essentialist as well as White feminist foundations of the original *Vagina Monologues* (Eve Ensler, 1998). Leidolf is an intersex woman who was diagnosed with the condition MRKH or Mayer–Rokitansky–Küster–Hauser syndrome. At 13, after a bout of severe abdominal cramps, the doctors discovered that she had a vaginal dimple rather than a vagina and no uterus (Leidolf, 2006, p. 78). Since Leidolf had secondary sex characteristics, doctors assumed she also had ovaries (p. 78). However, MRKH syndrome meant that it took many specialists to physically identify the location of her ovaries given the absence of a uterus (p. 78). Though Leidolf (2006) quickly realized that the absence of a vagina did not faze her, doctors and other medical professionals continued to probe her and made decisions about her body and her future (p. 80). This included vaginal dilation with the intention of a penis fitting into her vaginal dimple so that she "could have sex with her husband"—assuming heterosexuality and prescriptions about how sex is practiced (pp. 80–87). Denying the intersex body its agency (in the 33 possible variations) is to negate the original technicity of our bodies to begin with. To paraphrase Leidolf (2006), the problem was not that she did not have a vagina but that she needed to have one (p. 86). For biologically essentialist Western colonial feminisms, intersex people are simply aberrations for "normal biology." Here is where transfeminist technicity intervenes.[16]

María Lugones's (2010) work furthers this idea of what preceded the colonial encounter, offering us feminist definitions for the coloniality of gender and for decolonial feminism; both are part of transfeminism's work.[17] Lugones proposes that the "modern colonial gender system" is "a lens through which to theorize further the oppressive logic of colonial modernity, its use of hierarchical dichotomies and categorical logic" (p. 743). By working through this lens, she also argues that women of color and third world women's feminisms understand how particular intersections of categories like race, class, sexuality, and gender "exceed the categories of modernity" (p. 743). The various intersections that compound to produce multiple marginalizations are not legible under the modern colonial gender system. That is to say that in the modern colonial gender system, "the colonial answer to Sojourner Truth is clearly, 'no'" (p. 745).[18]

Lugones lays out for us, following the work of scholars like Sylvia Wynter, how the binary hierarchies set up in colonial modernity to distinguish the human from the nonhuman was an imposition "in the service of Western man" (p. 743). In this hierarchical structure that organized social life, "Indigenous peoples of the Americas and enslaved Africans were classified as non-human in species—as animals, uncontrollably sexual and wild" (p. 743). Within this modern world order, the European Christian bourgeois colonial and modern heterosexual man became the pinnacle of civilization fit to rule over others and act as a public agent. The European woman was "not seen as his complement" but rather, "as someone who reproduced race and capital through her sexual purity, passivity, and being home-bound in the service of the white European bourgeois man" (p. 743). Within this gendered framework, only the European bourgeois could be fully human. In this order, intersex people, gay people (deemed sodomites), "viragos," and others were seen as "aberrations of male perfection" (p. 743).

What Lugones calls the colonial "civilizing mission" was full of "brutal access to people's bodies" where rape and other forms of violation and torture, the biopolitical control of reproduction, and other forms of terror were utilized to subjugate all others into this gendered system. Within this system "turning the colonized into human beings is not a colonial goal" (p. 744). Along with the development of anthropological sciences of colonial observation, this binary gender system was read onto Indigenous societies who were gendered according to what roles Western Europeans saw them performing in their cultures. Here, the bio-logic of Western gender essentialism was extrapolated and projected onto the cultures they encountered; the colonized were then forced to assimilate to this colonial gendered projection. Of the consequences of the civilizing mission include a total transformation in the nature of life itself and in identity (p. 745). This means that various aspects of life were colonized: memory as well as "people's senses of self, of intersubjective relation, of their relation to the spirit world, to land, to the very fabric of their conception of reality, identity, and social, ecological, and cosmological organization" (p. 745). The civilizing mission was a dehumanizing process that also had a "semantic consequence." Said differently, "no women are colonized; no colonized females are women" (p. 745).

What is perhaps most important in the contribution of María Lugones to decolonial feminist thinking and the coloniality of gender is to understand the following: "The suggestion is not to search for a non-colonized construction of gender in indigenous organizations of the social. There is no such thing; 'gender' does not travel away from colonial modernity" (p. 746). If we follow Lugones's argument to its logical ends, we understand that her project and others of the decolonial vein (including the Black feminist understanding of ungendering) are not recuperative projects harkening back to idealized Indigenous notions of a genderless utopia. Instead, we must understand that prior to the colonial encounter, many Indigenous communities around the world did not have the Western colonial gender system that dichotomizes "men" and "women" and conflates "sex" and "gender" that we have today. This is not to say that these societies did not have gender but the current system we are entrenched in was not what they had nor what it was called. It also did not organize society as it does today because many societies conceived of concepts akin to ideas of "gender" as part of an entire cosmological system and integral to life in alignment with all of life. Also important here, that Lugones (2010) notes in an endnote, is that she agrees with Oyěwùmí (1997) that gender is a colonial imposition but argues that so is "sex" since the conflation of gender and sex as determined by genitalia, then predetermining social roles and function in Western modernity, is yet another colonial imposition (p. 758). The imposition of a dichotomous gender system of "men" and "women" as it confronts other systems usually deemed "nonmodern" is what Lugones calls a "colonial difference" (p. 749).

What is also important for transfeminism(s) about Lugones's work is how the imposed sex–gender binary system and the various consequences of the worldview of the "civilizing mission" created fractured selves in colonized people where people were (and continue to be) forced to name themselves in the terms of the colonizer in order to be afforded recognition in the modern world, even if this does not afford them/us access to full humanity. The colonial difference requires it of them. Lugones (2010) is interested in how this makes subjugated people turn to resistance work and what she terms the "infra-politics"—the inward turn as an integral part of the work toward liberation (p. 746). Lugones (2010) explains of infra-politics: "It shows the power of communities of oppressed in constituting resistant meaning and social organization by power. In our colonized, racially gendered, oppressed existences we are other than what the hegemon makes us to be" (p. 746). Lugones's work here is not only an indispensable aperture for transfeminist theorizing, it is also a way out of some of the Western metaphysical trappings of lines of thought like Afro-pessimism. What she is saying here is that form of intra-political resistance that oppressed people enact, including naming their own genders or returning to community names for genders and sexualities, means that they are not only how they are perceived by the hegemonic modern colonial gender system.

One can see Lugones's argument here to work in alignment with the game-changing epistemic work of Arturo Escobar (2020), Marisol de la Cadena and Mario Blaser (2018) who offer the decolonizing of all forms of universal thought that stems from a Western cosmology that understands that there is one world (what they call, after John Law, the "OWW" or One World World). Instead, pluriversality, inspired by Zapatista thought like "un mundo donde quepan muchos mundos" or "a world in which many worlds fit," is the foundation of the intra-political work where one knows that they are not defined merely by the hegemon. Pluriversality is the vision through which we can see the limitations of Western metaphysics in that they refuse to apprehend multiple realities, multiple worlds, and various cosmologies as coeval. Transfeminism (again, in its best form) is seeking pluriversality. Expanding and confounding normative notions of gender is only one aspect of this pluriversality. Transfeminist resistance is appropriating namings like "transgender" because they are what is available in the modern colonial gender system, while living in community as a Two-Spirit teacher-healer following the cosmology of your people.

REFUSING NEOLIBERAL CAPITALIST LOGICS OF NATION-STATEHOOD

In the political sphere of nation-states, Agathangelou et al. (2008) turn to readings of empire and imperial projects that kill "those at the margins of liberal and neoliberal sovereignty" that "continues to be glamorized and fetishized in the name of 'democracy'" (p. 120). In these societies, those "most killable" are "seduced" into performing murder (p. 120). The fact that marginalized LGBTQ people are executing murder, to Agathangelou et al. (2008), means that homonormative politics that are state-sanctioned and afforded privacy actually participated in the further marginalization of queer people, particularly queer people of color who do not have access to or have no desire to assimilate to neoliberal self-possessed personhood (pp. 121–122). The "homonormative" turn of neoliberal gayness in the three decades prior to 2008 was met with a three-hundred-fold increase in incarcerated Black, brown, and other people of color (p. 122). This relationship is not incidental but rather constitutive. Normative "gayness" that can be subsumed into cisheterosexist colonial white supremacist culture makes that mainstream culture feel better about its norms because even those on the margins come to replicate it. In such circumstances, Black, brown, and queer people of color, poor people, disabled people and others become an increasing nuisance to the state as unassimilable and disruptive outsiders.

Transfeminist scholarship by the likes of Morgan Bassichis and Dean Spade (2014) understands that homonormative (and by extension transnormative) LGBTQ politics are inherently anti-Black given that antiblackness is the foundation upon which the formation of the U.S. nation state occurred. These mainstream politics fall into this trap by being satisfied with the access they have to the priorities of the nation-state and all that this affords them with little regard to what has buttressed and continue to fill the coffers of this access. For example, to uplift the sexual trauma of cisgender gay homosexual men over that of the perpetual rape of the Black woman through the system of chattel slavery and its multiple afterlives is to steep gay politics in anti-Black analytics. Bassichis and Spade (2014) argue that white gay and lesbian people who liken their struggles to "African American Civil Rights," conceiving of civil rights as a done deal, cannot comprehend the afterlives of enslavement (2013). White gay and lesbian people seeking to "achieve" the same "rights" that Black people have supposedly now been afforded do not understand the colonial condition that people other than them find themselves in (pp. 200–201).[19]

International Dissidence and Corporeal Refusals. Transfeminist analyses and practices that challenge mainstream trans and other forms of queer incorporation into state politics have meant the birth of a multitude of radical queer and trans, DIY, and underground activisms, practices, and convivialities around the world, while hacking the systems in place to gain access to basic needs. In the subaltern communities of Spain, particularly in Barcelona and Madrid, transfeminist activism has meant a radical shift in the cultures around the pathologizing of trans identities and embodiments; a massive postpornography scene; a community of radical intellectuals working both within and outside of the universities; coalitions between migrant and refugee communities and the trans and queer community around forms of state repression; transnational mobilizations between Spain and countries in Latin America to change the gender requirements for Latin American trans migrants; an interrogation of the many racisms of Western feminisms; transnational and American hemispheric conversations across third world women of color feminisms, Black feminisms from the Global Norths and Souths; reformations in disability activism as it intersects trans politics; and radical relationships to queer, trans, Black, brown, fat, disabled, nonbinary, and gender nonconforming bodies (see Egaña & Solá, 2016; Garaizabal, 2013; Post-Op, 2013; Rojas & Aguirre, 2013; Sentamans, 2013; Trujillo, 2020).

What the work in Madrid and Barcelona has drawn particular transnational attention to is postporn as a global practice of dissident bodies stepping into the fullness of their sexual lives and pleasure. Postporn practices are not limited to Spain nor were they invented by Spain. The collective Post-Op has defined and delimited some of the characteristics of postporn in the following way:

> Postporn is of the monsters. Postporn is by the empowered monsters that show their sexuality without modesty or taboos, that show their battle scars, that show what high thinking society has asked them to hide. It shows bodies that break with the binary sex–gender system, with the categories of sexual orientation, of corporeal normality and able-bodiedness... and it is not only looking for sexual arousal, but it is also looking for this arousal to also be produced from humor, irony, and critical discourse. (Post-Op, 2013, p. 198)

Postporn, in the case of Spain, has been interested in what transfeminist sexual liberation practices might bring to the disability movement when advocating for those with "cognitive and functional diversity" to be full agents of their sexual lives and pleasure. Working through the commonality between trans people's embodiments and people with disabilities as having deviant sexualities, whose sexualities are seen as for someone else's pleasure rather than deserving of their own, this unfamiliar coalition has led to much important work for the local communities and for transnational sexual assistance and sex work.[20]

Transfeminist postporn includes seeing trans, gender-variant Black, brown, and other global majority bodies; disabled; fat; hairy; and nonnormative people engaged in sex acts, BDSM, role-play, performative and performance scenes, kink, and other forms of sexual and physical expression through their/our eyes and with one another. In the United States, feminist postporn sites like CrashPad have served what others call "dissident" communities. CrashPad is filmed by and for the community and aims to produce ethical porn from a literal feminist lens. Porn practices out of the postporn scene in the United States have included the production of documentaries like "Trans Entities: The Nasty Love of Papí and Wil" where feminist postporn lovers Papí Coxx and Wil Thrustwell take us through their Black trans/masculine-of-center and fluid love, relationships, polyamory, and kinky sex. At the time of its creation, the postporn scene in the United States was unaccustomed to seeing trans-identified non-op Black queer people on screen in this way. In the final scene, as a lot of transfeminist postporn likes to display, Papí and Wil engage in a long and emotionally charged role-play that culminates in a tender scene of aftercare.[21]

In Ecuador, the transfeminist postporn film "Obito travesti" by Eunuka Posporno shows two gender nonconforming people in a loving and felt bondage scene/exchange set to spoken text that challenges the regimens that delimit proper sexual practice and by which bodies. The performance for video understands itself as utilizing ritualized sexual actions to atone for gender mandates and the violence inflicted on those who disobey them. Postporn in this form crosses the realms of performance and sexual play, usually set for a live audience. Here, bodies that are not normally centered are the loci from which this political work is done. The artists of Eunuka Posporno explain that their work comes "from fury" and that they are "naming the violences, fears, and guilts that are inflicted on them daily by the patriarchal order." Finally, that they "seek vengeance from the mandates of domestication" (Eunuka Posporno, 2020). Transfeminism performed through postporn dissidence rewrites the position of sexual agency for transgender and gender nonconforming people.

Alongside these dissident practices, it is important to also name transfeminist practices of radical tenderness-as-dissidence and not only practices that more normatively hold the category of "radical." Radical tenderness is a term that was coined by Lia La Novia Sirena or Lía Garcia in 2009. She embodies radical tenderness in her performance-pedagogy. Lia García is a transfeminist transwoman performance artist from México City. She does not call her performance work "performances," but rather "affective encounters" because her work is pedagogically invested in the affective exchange between herself and her audience members. Her performance work moves with tropes of femininity like the bride, the *quinceañera*, and the mermaid in ways that intend to serve a "counterintuitive function" in that they destabilize normative ideas around gender and sexuality, also revealing our "complicity around these fantasies" (Delgado Huitrón, 2019, p. 166). García has long used her process of social transition as a trans woman to parallel a transition that she makes with society. For this reason, a lot of her performances occur in places like the busy public metro, famous and infamous streets and plazas found in México City and in other parts of the world, and public institutions. Her performances (and pedagogical workshops-as-performances) invite the participants into transitioning with her in their thoughts and perhaps long-held beliefs about trans women and other trans people, gender roles, attraction/repulsion, sexuality and desire, and rigid ideas about gender, to name just part of what her work destabilizes for others.

Cynthia Citlallin Delgado Huitrón (2019) recounts Lia's pedagogical work in a men's prison in México City, "Reclusorio Norte." In 2016, García was working with a group of men in the queer wing of the prison, in the dorm 10Bis. She called the project "Proyecto 10Bis." Huitrón offers a transfeminist analysis of Lia's transfeminist pedagogical and political performance project through first reading an image of García with one of the incarcerated men and then describing the work of the performance/pedagogy itself over the life of the project. It is essential to highlight this work also because it shows the scholarship possible through the collaboration of transfeminist scholars and the artists that they represent.

In the performance/pedagogy workshop, Proyecto 10Bis was a long-term intervention where Lia worked weekly with the group of eight cis-men who belonged to this dormitory (Delgado Huitrón, 2019, p. 170). García used a variety of strategies including conversation circles, workshops, and performance actions where, thinking of her own body as an archive, Lia used personal images, objects, and stories to share with those on the inside about what transition has been like for her on the outside (p. 170). During the work, García is careful to give her undivided attention to these men, using prolonged eye contact, handholding, hugging, whispers, soft caresses, and her form of "seduction" to get people to think about trans womanhood in new ways and in turn, to question their assumptions about gender and sexuality (p. 170). This work is particularly salient in a men's prison, where, as Delgado Huitrón (2019) rightly dictates, they are Valencia's version of "endriago subjects." Huitrón argues that Lia's work uses these forms of touch and other sensory encounters (or "haptic" encounters) to counter the violence of the state that is then embodied in these prisoners. Delgado Huitrón (2019) identifies the various types of physical touch and bodily intimacy as belonging to the "haptic" where the object of concern—the Mexican state—and its deeply interwoven narco reality are subverted by Lia's work with these men. Delgado Huitrón (2019) asks, "In a world reigned by a touch that strikes, what may be engendered by a touch that strokes? Through this caress the law itself is reordered" (p. 175).[22]

SUBVERSIVE GRAMMARS OF TRANSNESS

Confronting the normalization of the state apparatus and the whiteness of transmisogyny—see Cosenza Krell's (2017) critique of Julia Serano (2007)—women and gender nonconforming people of trans experience, particularly Black, Latin/x American, and Native/Indigenous women in the Americas (and elsewhere) have taken to revitalizing, inventing, and reinventing transfeminist and culturally specific and appropriate ways of naming their transfeminine genders against normalizing necropolitical and neoliberal forces.[23] The article ends with this because the problem that transfeminism must constantly confront is the limited discursive enclosures through which so many are trying to feel legitimized as gendered subjects. The article would like to signal just a few of the grammars that women of trans experience have used/are using to move beyond how hegemony would name them.

P. J. DiPietro (2016) "enacts transing methodologies" by determining how linguistic practices that are culturally particular to the Andes allow us to see the decolonizing work of travesti naming their embodiments and social ontological positions—how they use transing methodology (p. 66). DiPietro (2016) notes how famous Argentinian travesti Lohana Berkins claimed travesti embodiments not as replicas of femininity nor a marking of the flesh through particular surgical modifications, but rather, "intersubjective" interdiction into transnormative corporeal project that she instead refers to as "así" or "like that" (p. 69). Berkins would signal aspects of feminine embodiment that resonated for her, saying "así" or "like that" as in "I'm a bit like this and a bit like that." In this way, Berkins's transing methodology utilizes culturally derived language to name another way of contemplating travesti embodiment practice for Andean subjects.

Silva and Ornat (2016) explain how in Brazil, "travesti" has pushed up against the Anglophone cannon of trans studies and has done important decolonizing work (p. 221). Some travesties distance themselves from transsexual women saying that the difference is their relationship to genitalia. In this case, travesties may care less about gender affirming surgeries because their racial and class status tend to disallow such interventions (p. 223). Others disagree with such demarcations—it tends to vary person to person. What is crucial in the case of Brazil is how travesti is contextually located. They explain, "Brazilian travesties are historically and politically situated individuals who construct their subjectivities by assigning meanings to themselves and others" (p. 224).

Muxe Mexican performance artist Lukas Avendaño from Oaxaca pushes the boundaries and borders around Muxe identity in the Isthmus of Tehuantepec through their performance work. Avendaño is a Native/Indigenous dmab (designated male at birth) Zapotec muxe person. Avendaño uses large-scale performance work to define "muxeidad" as queer-po (a play-on-words of the Spanish word for body "cuerpo"). Avendaño (2019) has felt the need to respond to "muxeidad on the Isthmus of Tehuantepec" because of its role as "a distinctive cultural gesture from the age-old zaa culture (Zapotec/binni zaa/zaa)." Avendaño (2019) reflects on how muxes, historically revered in the Isthmus, become "homosexuals and fags" when not physically there. Muxeidad is an experience of revered gender transgression, at once, and an erasure of sexuality, on the other side. Instead of locating muxeidad strictly within gender and/or sexuality, Avendaño instead imagines muxeidad as a "total social fact" (Avendaño, 2019).

By way of a final example of the infinite, Afro-Brazilian transwoman scholar Santana (2019) puts forward the Brazilian Portuguese phrase "mais viva" or "being-alive-savvy" as a term to name a counter-erotics of Black trans womanhood to counter the overemphasis on necropolitics and death (p. 215). "Mais viva" becomes an antidote to what Santana fears that "trans women, especially black trans women, are discussed only as corpse" (p. 215). "Mais viva" calls upon "an Afro-diasporic rhythm and imaginary" that celebrates the micropolitical moments of joy, support, and community that Black trans women and travestis also experience.

CONCLUSION AND PEDAGOGICAL IMPERATIVES

The aim of this article was to trace *an* ecology of transfeminisms as a plural and transnational web of practices, epistemologies, activisms, and forms of theoretical analysis. While certainly not comprehensive nor able to account for a perfectly decentered North American academy, the teleology traced here attended to the complexities of the geopolitical webs through which this transfeminism is wound. By moving from the perspective of teleology, the article walked through transfeminism's foundation in Black feminisms and how Black feminisms essentially brought trans studies forth. It then addressed the issue with intersectionality as it has been institutionally mobilized. The article then expounded upon the theorists thinking through the blackness of transness and the transness of blackness. Within this query, the limitations and implications of ontology were cited, finishing with the necropolitics that transfeminist trans activism attends to. Then, the article opened up some theorists' arguments about transness as a possible anoriginal to the Western gender system. Following this, it explicated the contribution of decolonial feminists like María Lugones to gender undecidability through colonization and its ongoing afterlives of coloniality. In the last two sections, the article explained how transfeminisms have made way for various forms of dissident practices and how they have also led to new grammars for naming gendered lives that are geopolitically emergent.

For the student of transfeminisms and transfeminist analysis, it is important to understand that their genealogy is reticular in form and should not be nailed down based on geopolitical location given the epistemological flows of the work. Transfeminism does not belong to bifurcated spaces of either the academy or activism or performance, but rather endlessly crosses any divides that might continue to separate these deeply entrenched spaces. Transfeminism's capaciousness remains its analytical weapon and gift.

FURTHER READING

Ahmed, S. (2017). An affinity of hammers. In R. Gosset, E. R. Stanley, & J. Burton (Eds.), *Trap door: Trans cultural production and the politics of visibility* (pp. 221–234). MIT Press.

Bey, M. (2017). The trans*-ness of blackness and the blackness of trans*-ness. *Transgender Studies Quarterly*, 4(2), 275–295.

Bey, M. (2022). *Black trans feminism*. Duke University Press.

Bey, M., & Green, K. (2017). Where Black feminist thought and trans* feminism meet: A conversation. *Souls: A Critical Journal of Black Politics, Culture, and Society*, 19(4), 438–454.

Coleman, D. (2019). Cuerpos y existencias cotidianas trans* como ruptura, abertura, e invitación [Bodies and quotidian trans existences and rupture, opening and invitation]. In X. Leyva Solano & R. Icaza (Eds.), *En tiempos de muerte: Cuerpos, rebeldías, existencias* [*In times of death: Bodies, rebellions, and existences*] (pp. 221–238). CLACSO.

Garriga-López, C. S. (2016). Transfeminist crossroads: Reimagining the Ecuadorian state. *Transgender Studies Quarterly*, 3(1–2), 104–119.

Garriga-López, C. S. (2019). Transfeminism. *Global Encyclopedia of Lesbian, Gay, Bisexual, Transgender and Queer History*, 3(P–Z), 1619–1623.

Keegan, C. M. (2016). On being the object of compromise. *Transgender Studies Quarterly*, 3(1–2), 150–157.

Lugones, M. (2010). Toward a decolonial feminism. *Hypatia*, 25(4), 742–759.

Morgensen, S. L. (2016). Conditions of critique: Responding to indigenous resurgence within gender studies. *Transgender Studies Quarterly*, 3(1–2), 192–201.

Serano, J. (2007). *Whipping girl: A transsexual woman on sexism and the scapegoating of femininity*. Seal Press.

Silva, J. M., & Ornat, M. J. (2016). Transfeminism and decolonial thought: The contribution of Brazilian travestis. *Transgender Studies Quarterly*, 3(1–2), 220–227.

Spillers, H. (1987). Mama's baby, Papa's maybe: An American grammar book. *Diacritics*, 17(2), 64–81.

Stryker, S., & Bettcher, T. M. (2016). Introduction: Trans/feminisms. *Transgender Studies Quarterly*, 3(1–2), 5–14.

Valencia, S. (2018a). Interferencias transfeministas y pospornográficas a *la colonialidad del ver* [Transfeminist interferences in the coloniality of sight]. *E-misférica*, 11(1).

Valencia, S. (2018b). *Gore capitalism* (J. Pluecker, Trans.). Semiotext(e).

Valencia, S. (2019). Necropolitics, postmortem/transmortem politics, and transfeminisms in the sexual economies of death. *Transgender Studies Quarterly*, 6(2), 180–193. (O. Arnaiz Zhuravleva, Trans.)

Williams, C. (2016). Radical inclusion: Recounting the trans inclusive history of radical feminism. *Transgender Studies Quarterly*, 3(1–2), 254–258.

REFERENCES

Ahmed, S. (2017). An affinity of hammers. In R. Gosset, E. R. Stanley, & J. Burton (Eds.), *Trap door: Trans cultural production and the politics of visibility* (pp. 221–234). MIT Press.

Aizura, A. Z., Cotten, T., Balzer, C., Ochoa, M., & Vidal-Ortiz, S. (2014). Introduction to decolonizing the transgender imaginary. *Transgender Studies Quarterly*, 1(3), 308–319.

Agathangelou, A., Bassichis, D., & Spira, T.L, (2008). Intimate Investments: Homonormativity, Global Lockdown, and the Seductions of Empire. *Radical History Review 100*, 120–145.

Ausserer, C. (2016, May). *Mauro Cabral: "We need an intersex version of the principles."* The Green Political Foundation.

Avendaño, L. (2019, May). *Queer: No. Queer-po muxe: Yes* (R. Myers, Trans.). Goethe Institut. https://www.goethe.de/ins/us/en/kul/wir/swl/qpe/21586998.html

Bassichis, M., & Spade, D. (2014). Queer politics and anti-blackness. In J. Haritaworn, A. Kuntsman, & S. Posocco (Eds.), *Queer necropolitics* (pp. 191–210). Routledge.

Bey, M. (2017). The trans*-ness of blackness and the blackness of trans*-ness. *Transgender Studies Quarterly*, 4(2), 275–295.

Bey, M., & Green, K. (2017). Where Black feminist thought and trans* feminism meet: A conversation. *Souls: A Critical Journal of Black Politics, Culture, and Society*, 19(4), 438–454.

Cabral, M. (2015, October). *The marks on our bodies*. Intersex Human Rights Australia.

Coleman, D. B. (2020). If rigor is our dream: Theorizing Black transmasculine futures through ancestral erotics. In L. Lemaster & C. A. Johnson (Eds.), *Gender futurity, intersectional autoethnography: Embodied theorizing from the margins* (pp. 151–164). Routledge.

Combahee River Collective. (1983). The Combahee River Collective statement. In B. Smith (Ed.), *Home girls: A Black feminist anthology* (pp. 264–274). Rutgers University Press.

Cooper Owens, D. (2017). *Medical bondage: Race, gender, and the origins of American gynecology*. University of Georgia Press.

Cosenza Krell, E. (2017). Is transmisogyny killing trans women of color? Black trans feminisms and the exigencies of white femininity. *Transgender Studies Quarterly*, 4(2), 226–242.

Crenshaw, K. (1989). Demarginalizing the intersection of race and sex: A Black feminist critique of antidiscrimination doctrine, feminist theory, and antiracist politics. *University of Chicago Legal Forum*, 1(8), 139–167.

Day, I. (2021). Afro-feminism before Afropessimism: Meditations on gender and ontology. In M.-K. Jung & J. M. C. Vargas (Eds.), *Antiblackness* (pp. 60–81). Duke University Press.

De la Cadena, M., & Blaser, M. (2018). Introduction, pluriverse: Proposals for a world of many worlds. In M. De la Cadena & M. Blaser (Eds.), *A world of many worlds* (pp. 1–22). Duke University Press.

Delgado Huitrón, C. C. (2019). Haptic tactic: Hypertenderness for the [Mexican] state and the performances of Lia García. *Transgender Studies Quarterly*, 6(2), 164–179.

DiPietro, P. J. (2016). Of Huachería, Así, and M'E Mati: Decolonizing transing methodologies. *Transgender Studies Quarterly*, 3(1–2), 65–73.

Egaña, L., & Solá, M. (2016). Hacking the body: A transfeminist war machine. *Transgender Studies Quarterly*, 3(1–2), 74–80.

Ensler, E. (1998). *The Vagina Monologues*. Villard Books.

Escobar, A. (2020). *Pluriversal politics: The real and the possible*. Duke University Press.

Eunuca Posporno. (2020, November 2). Obito Travesti—Un video performance de Eunuka Posporno. *Hysteria Revista*, 33. https://hysteria.mx/obito-travesti-un-videoperformance-de-eunuka-posporno/

Foucault, M. (1978). *The History of Sexuality: An Introduction*. R. Hurley (Trans.). Vintage Books

Garaizabal, C. (2013). Feminismos, sexualidades, trabajo sexual [Feminisms, sexualities, sex work]. In M. Solá & E. Urko (Eds.), *Transfeminismos: Epistemes, fricciones y flujos* [*Transfeminisms: Epistemies, frictions, and flows*] (pp. 59–72). Txalaparta.

Garriga-López, C. S. (2016). Transfeminist crossroads: Reimagining the Ecuadorian state. *Transgender Studies Quarterly*, 3(1–2), 104–119.

Garriga-López, C. S. (2019). Transfeminism. *Global Encyclopedia of Lesbian, Gay, Bisexual, Transgender and Queer History*, 3(P–Z), 1619–1623.

Gill-Peterson, J. (2014). The technical capacities of the body: Assembling race, technology, and transgender. *Transgender Studies Quarterly*, 1(3), 402–418.

Green, K. M. (2015). The essential I/eye in we: A Black transfeminist approach to ethnographic film. *Black Camera*, 6(2), 187–200.

Green, K. M., & Ellison, T. (2014). Tranifest. *Transgender Studies Quarterly*, 1(1–2), 222–225.

Hartman, S. (1997). *Scenes of subjection: Terror, slavery, and self-making in nineteenth-century America*. Oxford University Press.

Leidolf, E. M. (2006). The missing vagina monologue…and beyond. *Journal of Gay and Lesbian Psychotherapy*, 10(2), 77–92.

LeMaster, L. (2017). Unlearning the violence of the normative. *QED: A Journal in GLBTQ Worldmaking*, 4(2), 123–130.

Lugones, M. (2008). The coloniality of gender. In W. Mignolo & A. Escobar (Eds.), *Worlds and knowledges otherwise* (pp. 1–17). Springer.

Lugones, M. (2010). Toward a decolonial feminism. *Hypatia*, 25(4), 742–759.

Mbembe, A. (2003). Necropolitics. *Public Culture* 15(1), 11–40.

Nash, J. C. (2019). *Black feminism reimagined: After intersectionality*. Duke University Press.

Oyěwùmí, O. (1997). *The invention of women: Making an African sense of Western gender discourses*. University of Minnesota Press.

Pearce, R., Erikainen, S., & Vincent, B. (2020). TERF wars: An introduction. *The Sociological Review Monographs*, 68(4), 677–698.

Post-Op. (2013). De placeres y monstruos: Interrogantes en torno al posporno [Of pleasures and monsters: Questions about post porn]. In M. Solá & E. Urko (Eds.), *Transfeminismos: Epistemes, fricciones y flujos* [*Transfeminisms: Epistemies, frictions, and flows*] (pp. 193–210). Txalaparta.

Rojas, L., & Aguirre, A. (2013). *Políticas trans-feministas y trans-fronterizas desde las diásporas trans migrantes* [Trans-feminist and trans-border politics from trans migrant diasporas]. In M. Solá & E. Urko (Eds.), *Transfeminismos: Epistemes, fricciones y flujos* [*Transfeminisms: Epistemies, frictions, and flows*] (pp. 127–140). Txalaparta.

Santana, D. S. (2019). Mais viva! Reassembling transness, blackness, and feminism. *Transgender Studies Quarterly, 6*(2), 210–222.

Sentamans, T. (2013). Redes transfeministas y nuevas políticas de representación sexual (II). In M. Solá & E. Urko (Eds.), *Transfeminismos: Epistemes, fricciones y flujos* [*Transfeminisms: Epistemies, frictions, and flows*] (pp. 177–192). Txalaparta.

Serano, J. (2007). *Whipping girl: A transsexual woman on sexism and the scapegoating of femininity*. Seal Press.

Silva, J. M., & Ornat, M. J. (2016). Transfeminism and decolonial thought: The contribution of Brazilian travestis. *Transgender Studies Quarterly, 3*(1–2), 220–227.

Snorton, C. R. (2017). *Black on both sides: A racial history of trans identity*. University of Minnesota Press.

Snorton, C. R., & Haritaworn, J. (2013). Trans necropolitics: A transnational reflection on violence, death, and the trans of color afterlife. In S. Stryker & A. Z. Aizura (Eds.), *The transgender studies reader 2* (pp. 6676). Routledge.

Spillers, H. (1987). Mama's baby, Papa's maybe: An American grammar book. *Diacritics, 17*(2), 64–81.

Stanley, E. (2011). Near life, queer death: Overkill and ontological capture. *Social Text, 29*(2), 1–19.

Stryker, S. and Sullivan, N. (2009). King's member, queen's body: Transsexual surgery, self-demand amputation, and the somatechnics of sovereign power. In N. Sullivan & S. Murray (Eds.), *Somatechnics: Queering theh Technologisation of Bodies* (pp. 49–64). Ashgate.

Trujillo, R. V. (2020, November 20). Cuir: Pistas para la construcción de una historia transfeminista en América Latina [Cuir: Steps toward the construction of a transfeminist history in Latin America]. *Hysteria Revista, 33*. https://hysteria.mx/cuir-pistas-para-la-construccion-de-una-historia-transfeminista-en-america-latina/

Valencia, S. (2018). El feminismo no es un generismo [Feminism is not genderism]. *Pléyade Revista de Humanidades y Ciencias Sociales* [Pléyade Journal of Humanities and Social Sciences], 22(July–December), 22–43.

Valencia, S. (2019). Necropolitics, postmortem/transmortem politics, and transfeminisms in the sexual economies of death. *Transgender Studies Quarterly, 6*(2), 180–193.

Varun Chaudhry, V. (2020). On trans dissemblance: Or, why trans studies needs Black feminism. *Signs: Journal of Women and Culture in Society, 45*(3), 529–535.

Warren, C. (2017). Calling into being: Tranifestation, Black trans, and the problem of ontology. *Transgender Studies Quarterly, 4*(2), 266–274.

NOTES

1. Here, the article does not wish to undermine the work of scholars like Claudia Sofía Garriga-López (2019) in her short encyclopedia entry on transfeminisms. In fact, it has been included here because it is an incredibly helpful gloss of some of the primary prerogatives of transfeminisms. Where the article parts ways with it is the claim that transfeminisms originated in Spain since we cannot create geopolitical-temporal proof of this and because transfeminist practices have been occurring since long before they were read through transfeminism. The article also wants to resist any academic impulses that try to canonize social movements and phenomena, similar to what the "feminist waves" do.
2. In its critique of mobilizing injury as the source of work, the article does not mean that attending to injury is not feminist work nor is it always problematic in the ways it is naming here. To see an example of powerful use of injury, it recommends visiting the work of Lore LeMaster (2017) where she discusses

the consciousness-raising group of trans and other gender nonconforming students that she held at the university she was teaching, at the time. Utilizing Gust Yep's notion of injury, LeMaster discusses the important work of relationship that the disclosure of injury did for the group.

3. A note on symbols: The author prefers the use of trans* as an asterisked prefix as utilized by Marshall (Kai M.) Green (2017) in his conversation with Marquis Bey, who says trans* is "a disruptive orientation… [that is not] specific to transgender bodies, it is rather a method of mode of engaging time, history, people, things, places with an openness and acceptance of the excesses that are constantly being created and accounted for" (p. 448) That is to say, this work is always about the impossibilities of apprehending wholeness that concretized markers foreclose upon and about our necessity of utilizing these markers in order to strive for more livable existence—it is the author's understanding that this is some of the best of what transfeminisms offer.
4. For an excellent and full accounting of this history, the author recommends Deirdre Cooper Owen's (2017) book *Medical Bondage: Race, Gender, and the Origins of American Gynecology*.
5. C. Riley Snorton's (2017) paradigm-shifting work in *Black on Both Sides: A Racial History of Trans Identity* also takes an incredibly in-depth look at the historical realities of enslaved women and their doctors that have created these analyses.
6. Numerous Black scholars have used the notion of "fungibility" to explain the interchangeability of Black flesh when utilized for commodity production. Black nonsubjects were interminably fungible given their productive status under the plantation design and their use value in surplus production (see Hartman, 1997; Snorton, 2017; Spillers, 1987).
7. The Combahee River Collective Statement (1983) was one of the earlier iterations of intersectional analysis that did not call itself that and yet defined itself in what we would now call intersectional terms.
8. For more on the court cases that Crenshaw (1989) intersectionally analyzed, the author recommends the full article.
9. Since this work, we have come to trouble the concept of biology in gender studies as something that relates to "natural" as opposed to something that is simply "living."
10. Ontological questions are most often cited as arising from the work of Martin Heidegger. For the pedagogical purposes of this article, the author has pulled what is important to know about ontology rather than go into Heidegger's oeuvre, particularly because one of its limitations, even in Black thought, is the worldview that it relies upon.
11. Day (2021) notes that she uses "Afro-feminism" as a "neologism or catachresis" to expose how Black feminism has shifted with the introduction of Afro-pessimism (p. 62).
12. Perhaps some of the most important work on destabilizing the Western modern construction of "the human" and "humanity" exists in Sylvia Wynter's opus.
13. Stanley's (2011) work on overkill and ontological capture might signal why trafficking with necropolitics in this way is just a reinforcement of death rather than a celebration of trans life. "Overkill" is the term he uses to describe the extreme violence that ends many Black trans women's lives—a violence that exceeds death (p. 9).
14. A comprehensive overview of TERF ideology is outside the scope of this article. However, for a fairly robust account of this ideology in the United States, see Pearce et al. (2020).
15. The article uses queer/cuir here because in Abya Yala/Latin America, there has been a real resentment about how white queer thinking in the United States circulated throughout Latin America in ways that were colonialist and imperialist as well as white supremacist and U.S. exceptionalist. Cuir has been a critical reappropriation about dissident gender and sexual practices emerging from and situated in Latin America.
16. The work of Mauro Cabral (2015) in Argentina, a foremost intersex and transmasculine activist and thinker, is an excellent example of the overlaps between intersex and trans identities. Cabral often laments that the too-flattened and bio-logic understandings of gender and sex are too limited to understand how intersex people can be trans and how trans people can be intersex.

17. Lugones (2010) says, "I call the analysis of racialized capitalist, gender oppression 'the coloniality of gender.' I call the possibility of overcoming the coloniality of gender 'decolonial feminism'" (p. 747).
18. Here, Lugones is referring to the famous speech "Ain't I a Woman? (https://thehermitage.com/wp-content/uploads/2016/02/Sojourner-Truth_Aint-I-a-Woman_1851.pdf)" delivered by Sojourner Truth at the Ohio Women's Rights Convention, May 1851.
19. Claudia Sofía Garriga-López's (2016) work in Ecuador is a great example of how transfeminists strategically utilized state politics to secure their gender on their ID in order to access some of the basic human services that require having an ID like housing, education, and jobs.
20. The documentary "Yes, We Fuck!" serves as a transfeminist, sex positive, and disability-centered film that chronicles the lives of various people with cognitive and physical disabilities. Spain has also led the way in refusing the word "discapacidad" in Spanish for all of its derogatory connotations and instead has moved to "cognitive and functional diversity" to take seriously the full lives, desires, genders, and sexualities of disabled people. What is so revolutionary about this documentary is that it highlights the coalitions that are possible with transfeminism where the experience of being othered as trans and gender nonconforming people invites folks to engage with disabled people in intentional ways. A number of trans, queer, and other gender diverse transfeminists have engaged in types of sex work and sexual assistance for people with a variety of disabilities. This is a prominent feature of the documentary and has sparked a plethora of conversations about the lines between sexual assistance and sex work. The transfeminist community in Spain has made it a prerogative of theirs to be on the frontlines of activism for disabled people to be treated as whole human beings, including with access to the full range of their pleasure possibilities as an essential site of activism.
21. By "scene," the author refers to the planned beginning, middle, and end of a bondage and discipline, dominance and submission, and/or sadism and masochism play between consenting people. A "scene" does not need to include BDSM at all but might instead include things like age play, humiliation, or other forms of sexual and corporal pleasures that have historically been deemed to be "deviant" practices. When genders, sexualities, and races that have already been deemed "deviant" reclaim the space of these practices, there is important decolonizing work that is done here.
22. To read Lia in her own words about her work, see "Diarios de una novia en acción: Más allá del beso se dislocan los sentidos" [Diaries of a bride in action: Beyond the kiss senses are dislocated] (https://hysteria.mx/diarios-de-una-novia-en-accion-mas-alla-del-beso-dislocar-lo-sentidos/).
23. Cosenza Krell (2017) notes that the way Serano (2007) deals with and defines transmisogyny as a particular form of sexism unique to trans women has no racial analysis whatsoever, assuming the white subject as the abstract universal of trans womanhood. In this way, white exceptionalism and trans womanism become dangerous bedfellows when white transwomen are assumed to experience more abjection than cisgender women of color always (pp. 232–235).

Daniel Coleman

Queer Intimacies

LGBTQ+ MARRIAGE: RELATIONAL COMMUNICATION PERSPECTIVES

INTRODUCTION

This article discusses research on the effects of legally recognized marriage on experiences of and communication within relational lives of LGBTQ+ people. Limitations of the current research and suggestions for future research are also discussed.

Terminology and Scope. This article uses the acronym LGBTQ+ as a shorter version of LGBTQQIPAA, which is used to represent people who identify as lesbian, gay, bisexual, transgender, queer, questioning, intersex, pansexual, asexual, and ally. The article uses LGBTQ+ marriage to indicate legally recognized marriage between two members of the LGBTQ+ community and to distinguish these relationships from legally recognized marriage between two people who are generally assumed to be a heterosexual cisgender man and a heterosexual cisgender woman. Most of the research on LGBTQ+ marriage uses the term "same-sex marriage" to refer to these relationships and in doing so either assumes or assesses that the partners are both cisgender. Thus, the article indicates when a study had significant participation from transgender or gender nonbinary participants. Additionally, because the vast majority of research on LGBTQ+ marriage focuses on the marriage of a couple rather than a polyamorous family, this article does so as well. It is also important to note that members of the LGBTQ+ community engaged in various ways of marking and communicating their commitment before legal marriage was available, such as commitment ceremonies (see Stiers, 1999), and many continue to do so. However, the scope of this article is limited to legally recognized LGBTQ+ marriage. Further, because relational termination and divorce are covered elsewhere in this encyclopedia, this article does not review research on these topics.

Brief Background of LGBTQ+ Marriage. Historically, the availability of LGBTQ+ marriage has differed between countries and regions within countries. Regions of the world that tend to be conservative, such as Islamic theocracies and parts of Asia and Africa, have not recognized LGBTQ+ marriage and often have laws against LGBTQ+ relationships. Although there have been some earlier examples of legal recognition for LGBTQ+ relationships, in the late 20th century, countries in northern Europe (e.g., Denmark, Sweden, Norway), and other regions (e.g., Israel), made legal status available for LGBTQ+ partnerships. During the first two decades of the 21st century, more countries in more regions legally recognized LGBTQ+ partnerships, including countries in Africa, Oceania, South America, and North America.

Although changes to expand recognition for LGBTQ+ relationships were taking place, there were also moves to prevent, limit, and abolish LGBTQ+ marriage in many regions and countries. In some cases, a region or country would have attempts to expand and attempts to prevent, limit, or abolish LGBTQ+ marriage occurring simultaneously. For example, in the United States in 2014, LGBTQ+ marriage was available in a number of states and jurisdictions such that 70% of the U.S. population lived in a place where LGBTQ+ marriage existed. Much of the remaining 30% of the U.S. population lived in an area that had banned or restricted LGBTQ+ marriage. Two cases before the Supreme Court of the United States (SCOTUS) were significant for LGBTQ+ marriage. In 2013, SCOTUS ruled in *United States v. Windsor* and struck down the law barring federal recognition of LGBTQ+ marriage. In 2015, SCOTUS ruled in *Obergefell v. Hodges* and struck down all state LGBTQ+ marriage bans making LGBTQ+ marriage legal in all 50 states and the District of Columbia. Yet, since the 2015 SCOTUS ruling, there have been attempts to limit and/or overturn legal recognition of SSM at the federal and various state levels.

Given the shifting legal and cultural landscape of LGBTQ+ marriage in a variety of locations, LGBTQ+ marriage should be understood as a sociopolitical context that influences relationships and communication of LGBTQ+ people and their social networks rather than just as a means to formally institutionalize a relationship (Lannutti, 2014a). In this article, we review the relevant literature on LGBTQ+ marriage as it relates to the relationships and communication of LGBTQ+ individuals. We also offer a critique of the existing literature and suggestions for future research.

LGBTQ+ MARRIAGE AND LGBTQ+ INDIVIDUALS

Research has shown that the availability of legally recognized LGBTQ+ marriage has influenced the communication and relational experiences of LGBTQ+ individuals. Specifically, LGBTQ+ marriage has been shown to have psychological impacts on LGBTQ+ individuals and effects on LGBTQ+ individual's perceptions of their identity and how it relates to LGBTQ+ communities.

Psychological Impacts of LGBTQ+ Marriage on LGBTQ+ Individuals. The overall trend among studies that examine the effect of LGBTQ+ marriage is that the availability of LGBTQ+ marriage has a positive impact on LGBTQ+ people. In a study conducted soon after Massachusetts became the first U.S. state to recognize LGBTQ+ marriage, Lannutti (2005) found that LGBTQ+ people felt a sense of social acceptance and validation as a result of legal marriage. Other studies have also shown an increased sense of social acceptance and social inclusion for LGBTQ+ people as a result of LGBTQ+ marriage availability (Badgett, 2011; Lannutti, 2011a; Metheny & Stephenson, 2019; Riggle et al., 2017). Riggle et al. (2017) demonstrated a communicative outcome of LGBTQ+ people's increased sense of social acceptance as a result of LGBTQ+ marriage being available. Their study was conducted when some U.S. states had legally recognized LGBTQ+ marriage and other states did not. In states where legal LGBTQ+ marriage was available, LGBTQ+ people reported significantly less concealment of their LGBTQ+ identity, less vigilance behaviors, and less isolation than did those in states where LGBTQ+ marriage was not available. Greater amounts of LGBTQ+ identity disclosure in areas where LGBTQ+ marriage is available than where it is not were also found in a study by Charlton et al. (2016). Ogolsky et al. (2019) also found that LGBTQ+ people who lived in areas where LGBTQ+ marriage is available experienced lower stress and stigma and higher life satisfaction than those who did not live in such an area.

The majority of studies of LGBTQ+ marriage have included samples whose majority is White. One exception is a study conducted by Lee (2018) who found that Black lesbian, gay, and bisexual (LGB) participants may perceive LGBTQ+ marriage as an important tool to gain social acceptance because being married has a high social status within Black communities. However, the increased sense of social inclusion associated with LGBTQ+ marriage may differ depending on the intersection of individuals' identities. Badgett (2011) found that White LGBTQ+ people reported greater social inclusion than did BIPOC LGBTQ+ people as a result of marriage equality. Conversely, other studies have suggested that BIPOC LGBTQ+ people report higher degrees of positive outcomes of marriage equality, including lower stigma consciousness and increased social inclusion, than do White LGBTQ+ people (Everett et al., 2016; Metheny & Stephenson, 2019). Thus, the intersectionality of sexual, gender, racial, and ethnic identities should be considered when assessing the positivity of the impact of LGBTQ+ marriage on LGBTQ+ individuals.

Although there is an overall trend that LGBTQ+ marriage availability has a positive impact on LGBTQ+ individuals in the research literature, it is also important to recognize that negative impacts on LGBTQ+ people as a result of legal marriage have been found. The road to legal marriage has not been smooth, straightforward, or linear in many locations. The debates over marriage legalization and legal efforts to ban, retract, or limit LGBTQ+ marriage have been shown to negatively affect LGBTQ+ individuals. For example, in 2006 a backlash against expanding marriage equality in the United States culminated in many locations in the United States passing or attempting to pass legislation limiting or banning LGBTQ+ marriage. Riggle et al. (2009) found that LGBTQ+ people in areas where anti-LGBTQ+ legislation was being considered experienced increases in negative messages about themselves and their relationships and experienced increases in negative psychological effects such as stress. Similarly, Maisel and Fingerhut (2011) found that LGBTQ+ people living in California when anti-LGBTQ+ marriage legislation was being considered reported increases in negative emotions and negative effects on their social relationships. Further, Ecker et al. (2019) found that LGBTQ+ Australians experienced harm as a result of national debates over LGBTQ+ marriage.

Focusing on communication more specifically, Lannutti (2011b) examined interactions that LGBTQ+ people living where anti-LGBTQ+ marriage legislation was being considered had with extended social network members (defined as acquaintances, neighbors, coworkers who are not close friends or family). Lannutti (2011b) found that LGBTQ+ people reported disconfirming interactions with those who supported anti-LGBTQ+ marriage legislation, but that LGBTQ+ people also experienced support and solidarity in interactions with those who supported LGBTQ+ marriage. The idea that anti-LGBTQ+ marriage legislation could have both negative effects on LGBTQ+ people but also some areas of positive consequence on them, their relationships, and their interactions through expressions of support and feelings of empowerment is echoed in findings of Maisel and Fingerhut (2011). Interestingly, this mix of increases in negative outcomes such as increased minority stress and increased feelings of social isolation and positive outcomes such as increases in feelings of empowerment and resiliency experienced by LGBTQ+ people when anti-LGBTQ+ marriage legislation was being considered were also found to be experienced by LGBTQ+ people after the 2016 election of Donald Trump as U.S. president (Brown & Keller, 2018; Gonzalez et al., 2018; Riggle et al., 2018). This may be because the Trump/Pence administration was understood to be a threat to LGBTQ+ rights, including LGBTQ+ marriage. In fact, Lannutti (2018b) found that some LGBTQ+ couples were partially motivated to marry after the 2106 U.S. presidential election because of fear that marriage equality may be eliminated in the United States. Yet, even the LGBTQ+ couples, in the study by Lannutti (2018b), that were partially motivated to marry because of concerns brought upon by the election of Trump/Pence also reported feelings of hope and empowerment associated with getting married.

LGBTQ+ Marriage and Identity. We have discussed negative and positive impacts of LGBTQ+ marriage availability for LGBTQ+ individuals, but the research literature also indicates a sense of ambivalence for some LGBTQ+ people toward LGBTQ+ marriage. This sense of ambivalence is often rooted in LGBTQ+ people's perceptions of the intersectionality of their sexual and gender identity with other aspects of their identity, and their perceptions of the LGBTQ+ community as they experience it. Even with legal LGBTQ+ marriage available, LGBTQ+ individuals continue to experience stigma and discrimination interpersonally and institutionally that has not been alleviated by marriage equality (Reynolds & Robinson, 2019). Ambivalence toward LGBTQ+ marriage, in part because it does not erase the stigma and discrimination faced by LGBTQ+ people, may be stronger for LGBTQ+ people who also experience discrimination based on their racial and ethnic identities. For example, in a study of Black LGBT participant's perceptions of LGBTQ+ marriage, McGuffey (2018) found that although many participants expressed support of LGBTQ+ marriage as a civil right, they also were concerned that the focus on gaining marriage equality deprioritized focusing on racism, economic injustice, and transgender inclusion for the LGBTQ+ community. Further, Drabble et al.

(2020) found that among their sample of sexual minority women and gender diverse individuals, gender nonbinary people in particular expressed concerns about a focus on marriage diverting attention from other important issues of safety and rights for LGBTQ+ people. Some LGBTQ+ people have even reported concerns about increased stigma and discrimination as a result of LGBTQ+ marriage itself. In a study with a sample of older LGBTQ+ individuals (Lannutti, 2011a), participants expressed concerns that getting married makes a person's LGBTQ+ identity public which may make that person a target for harassment, discrimination, or physical harm.

LGBTQ+ people's understanding and experience of their own sexual and/or gender identity are often tied to their perceptions of LGBTQ+ communities. LGBTQ+ marriage has been shown to have an impact here as well. Multiple studies have reported that LGBTQ+ participants express concerns about LGBTQ+ marriage because marriage has been a heteronormative institution that has historically been a source of oppression for women and because marriage may be seen as a means of assimilation of LGBTQ+ people to heterosexist norms (Drabble et al., 2020; Hull, 2019; Lannutti, 2014a; Philpot et al., 2016). These concerns about the heteronormative and assimilationist aspects of marriage are linked to concerns that LGBTQ+ marriage will make LGBTQ+ communities less vibrant, less unique, more divided, and weaker (Hull, 2019; Lannutti, 2005). Conversely, some LGBTQ+ people believe LGBTQ+ marriage makes LGBTQ+ communities stronger and more resilient, in part because gaining marriage equality shows the political power of the LGBTQ+ community (Drabble et al., 2020; Lannutti, 2005, 2011a).

Concerns about inclusiveness of various sexual and gender identities as well as racial and ethnic identities within LGBTQ+ communities are common. Some research has reflected these concerns. Lannutti (2007a) examined the relationships and communication about marriage for lesbian-bisexual cisgender female-female couples and found that these couples had positive experiences of increased support and validation as well as negative experiences including challenges to the bisexual partners' identity as a result of marrying a woman. Still, in the data provided by Lannutti (2007a), many of the lesbian-bisexual couple participants described feeling a greater sense of connection to the LGBTQ+ community as a result of LGBTQ+ marriage. The study is relatively rare in its focus on bisexual people and LGBTQ+ marriage. Similarly, the experiences of transgender and gender nonbinary people in relation to LGBTQ+ marriage is also understudied. Further, research focusing on the experiences of BIPOC LGBTQ+ people related to marriage are also scant. Studies by Lee (2018) and McGuffey (2018) suggest that Black LGBTQ+ people may experience marriage in distinct ways linked to the intersection of their sexual and gender identities and racial identities, but more research in this area is needed. Overall, there is a need for more research on LGBTQ+ marriage that fully considers the positionality of various sexual and gender identities and the intersection of LGBTQ+ identity with racial and ethnic identities.

LGBTQ+ MARRIAGE AND RELATIONSHIPS

Research has also investigated the effects of LGBTQ+ marriage on the romantic relationships of LGTBQ+ people. Again, the majority of studies in this area has focused on relationships between two people rather than polyamorous relationships. Studies have investigated the effects of LGBTQ+ marriage on relationship-related perceptions as well as experiences within relationships.

LGBTQ+ Marriage and Relationship-Related Perceptions. LGBTQ+ marriage has been shown to have an effect on the relationship-related perceptions of LGBTQ+ people, even those who are not currently involved in a relationship. Depending on age and location, a LGBTQ+ person may have grown into adulthood, come to terms with their sexual and gender identity, and formed romantic relationships when LGBTQ+ marriage was available or when it was not. Thus, many LGBTQ+ adults may have formed their understanding of relationship expectancies, relationship milestones and turning points, and ways of communicating relational commitment internally and externally without the option of marriage, and they may have had to reconsider these ways of relational understanding and communication when marriage became available (Lannutti, 2014a). This shift in relational perceptions and communication has been demonstrated to affect attitudes about partner desirability and relationship goals. For example, some LGBTQ+ people described a change in the attributes they desire in a partner as a result of the possibility of legal marriage such that they sought partners who would make "marriage material" (Lannutti, 2007b). Further, many participants in the study by Lannutti (2007b) reported a reevaluation of their relational goals and expressed a new, and surprising, desire to ritualize their commitment by marrying a partner in the future when they had previously not had a desire to engage in other commitment-signaling rituals such as commitment ceremonies. In a study of Canadian same-sex couples, MacIntosh et al. (2010) also found that marriage availability affected relational goals in that couples reported a greater desire to have children together as a result of LGBTQ+ marriage. Haas and Whitton (2015) point out that LGBTQ+ marriage may be considered an important option for committed LGBTQ+ couples, but that living together is still considered to be a significant way of symbolizing relational commitment among same-sex couples.

LGBTQ+ Marriage and Experiences Within Relationships. In addition to marriage-related perceptions, research has examined couples' experiences and communication surrounding LGBTQ+ marriage. First, there has been significant research examining LGBTQ+ couples' decision processes regarding whether to get married or not. Second, studies have examined the impact of getting married on the LGBTQ+ couple's romantic relationship.

Deciding to Marry or Not. As with all couples, the decision to marry or not is often a complex one for LGBTQ+ couples. Because the option to legally marry is relatively new for LGBTQ+ couples in most regions, some couples will have formed and developed their relationship with the possibility of legal marriage having always been available to them while others may have formed, developed, and possibly taken steps to symbolically and legally commit to their relationship without legal marriage having been an option. These two types of LGBTQ+ couples may share some similar considerations when deciding to marry or not such as their love for one another, their desire to build a family together, legal protections for their relationship, and financial considerations. However, LGBTQ+ couples who have been enacting their committed relationships before legal marriage was available to them may have some considerations that differ from those couples who always had the option marry during the lifespan of their relationship, including whether marriage would be redundant with legal measures they may have already taken to protect their relationship and symbolic steps they took to express their commitment to each other and others. With the possibly differing experiences of these two types of LGBTQ+ couples in mind, we review the major factors that have been identified in studies of LGBTQ+ couples' deliberations about getting married.

Although there are certainly unique factors that any LGBTQ+ couple may consider when deliberating about marriage, the research literature has identified some common reasons that LGBTQ+ couples have decided to marry. Civil equality reasons to marry include the ability to gain legal protections for LGBTQ+ couples and their family, insurance benefits, shared property benefits, ability to make proxy medical decisions, tax benefits, and similar benefits as a result of marrying. In a study of married and engaged LGBTQ+ couples in Massachusetts, Lannutti (2008) found that these types of civil benefits were the most common reasons couples gave for getting married. Similarly, 91% of LGBTQ+ participants in a study by Haas and Whitton (2015) identified civil equality as a reason marriage was important for LGBTQ+ people. Relatedly, when LGBTQ+ marriage was available in some U.S. states but not in others, LGBTQ+ couples commonly described the limited scope of the civil equality protections of marriage as a concern that made them cautious about marrying or to postpone marrying (Haas & Whitton, 2015; Lannutti, 2008).

Another common reason to marry for LGBTQ+ couples relates to parenting. LGBTQ+ families are often formed through adoption, surrogacy, sperm donations, and other nontraditional methods. Being married is perceived to make building families for LGBTQ+ people easier and protecting those families once formed more secure (Lannutti, 2008). LGBTQ+ people also perceive social benefits for parents as a result of being married because marriage makes LGBTQ+ parents more visible and more accepted by society (Badgett, 2009; Lannutti, 2014a). Further, having married parents is believed by LGBTQ+ people to benefit their children because their family will be more easily defined, accepted, and supported by peers and society in general (Badgett, 2009; Lannutti, 2014a; Ramos et al., 2009).

Political reasons are also common factors in LGBTQ+ people's deliberations about marriage. For many LGBTQ+ people, gaining marriage equality is seen as an important part of the overall political and social movement in favor of LGBTQ+ civil rights and they wish to marry to be a part of this movement (Haas & Whitton, 2015; Lannutti, 2011a, 2014a). This desire to marry, in part, as a political act may be especially salient for LGBTQ+ couples in regions where legislation to ban or limit LGBTQ+ marriage is being considered (Lannutti, 2011a) or when political outcomes are perceived as threatening to LGBTQ+ marriage (Lannutti, 2018b). Conversely, LGBTQ+ people have cited their own political disagreements with what they perceive to be too large a focus on marriage equality in the LGBTQ+ civil rights movement to the detriment of focusing on other important aspects of LGBTQ+ discrimination as a reason not to marry (Lannutti, 2018a). Further, LGBTQ+ people have described political objections to marriage as heteronormative and misogynist as reasons not to marry (Drabble et al., 2020; Lannutti, 2008, 2018a).

LGBTQ+ couples have also described social factors as part of their marriage deliberations. These social factors relate to perceptions of and meaning assigned to LGBTQ+ relationships within social networks and society in general. One social benefit of LGBTQ+ marriage discussed by LGBTQ+ couples is that marriage helps define them as a committed couple to people they know and society in general (Lannutti, 2008). Baxter et al. (2009) and Galvin (2006) point out that nontraditional families are often not recognized as families and therefore must use discursive strategies to communicate their family identity to themselves and others. Legal marriage may alleviate some of LGBTQ+ couples' need to explain, legitimize, and defend their family identity (Lannutti, 2014b). Couples deliberating LGBTQ+ marriage have also indicated that getting married is a means to greater acceptance of their LGBTQ+ identities and relationship from their families, friends, and other social network members (Lannutti, 2007a, 2008). Relatedly, opposition to their marriage from social network members, especially family members, has been cited by LGBTQ+ couples as an obstacle to getting married (Lannutti, 2008, 2013). Some LGBTQ+ couples considering marriage expressed hurt and surprise because family members who expressed acceptance and support for their relationships were sometimes opposed to the couple's getting married, often because it created a privacy management dilemma for family members now forced to share information about having an LGBTQ+ child or sibling in ways they had previously avoided (Lannutti, 2013).

LGBTQ+ couples considering marriage also describe interpersonal factors that are part of their decision making. Feelings of love for each other have frequently been cited as reasons that LGBTQ+ couples decide to marry (Haas & Whitton, 2015; Lannutti, 2008). Interestingly, in a study that asked married and engaged LGBTQ+ people about their reasons for marrying, 15% of participants mentioned feelings for their partner as a factor when in the same study, 57% of participants mentioned civil equality reasons for marrying (Lannutti, 2008). The relatively low frequency of mentions of interpersonal feelings in comparison to civil equality factors is likely less indicative of a lack of love among these couples and more indicative of the strong link between legal marriage and civil protections and rights for LGBTQ+ people. Some LGBTQ+ people have also indicated that they chose to marry for religious reasons (Haas & Whitton, 2015; Lannutti, 2008), to fulfill desires for romantic aspects of weddings and marriage (Haas & Whitton, 2015; Lannutti, 2007b), and to move their relationship to a new level of commitment (Haas & Whitton, 2015).

Studies have also investigated the experiences of LGBTQ+ couples who have decided not to marry. Lannutti (2014a) examined the marriage deliberations of LGBTQ+ couples who identified themselves as "committed, unmarried" couples. Committed, unmarried couples in the study by Lannutti (2014a) fell in two categories: those who had decided to never marry and those who had decided not to marry but might reconsider in the future. Six reasons not to marry were described by both types of couples: disapproval from their families, concerns about negative effects of LGBTQ+ marriage on LGBTQ+ culture, concerns about having to be more "out" than they wanted if they got married, negative financial outcomes as a result of marrying, feeling marriage was not needed to strengthen their commitment to each other, and concerns about the limitations of and future of LGBTQ+ marriage. Lannutti (2018a) again examined the experiences of committed, unmarried LGBTQ+ couples and found that these couples felt that they were perceived as less committed to their relationship by family and friends and received less support for their relationship from family and friends because they were not married. Committed, unmarried LGBTQ+ couples described engaging in a variety of discursive strategies to explain, legitimize, and defend their relationship as committed yet unmarried and to avoid having to discuss their committed but unmarried status (Lannutti, 2018a). For example, committed unmarried LGBTQ+ couples would use avoidance strategies by not correcting people who assumed they were married and legitimizing strategies by pointing out that they engaged in commitment practices like shared home ownership even though they were not married. Unmarried, committed LGBTQ+ couples described the ironic nature of legal marriage for them: They found themselves feeling less supported and having to justify their relationship more than they would otherwise because a legal option to support and validate LGBTQ+ relationships existed but they opted not to use it (Lannutti, 2018a).

Impact of Getting Married on LGBTQ+ Couple Relationships. Married LGBTQ+ couples have described several ways in which getting married has impacted their relationship with one another. Married LGBTQ+ couples have reported that their relationship felt more legitimate, protected, serious, and solid as a result of getting married (Badgett, 2009; Haas & Whitton, 2015; Richman, 2013). Further, LGBTQ+ couples report that their relationship is more recognized, supported, and accepted by others in their families and communities as a result of getting married (Haas & Whitton, 2015; Lannutti, 2014a; Ramos et al., 2009; Rostosky et al., 2016). Ramos et al. (2009) found that married LGBTQ+ couples were more "out" as a result of getting married. Increased feelings of relational commitment, relational satisfaction, partner support, and intimacy have also been associated with getting married for LGBTQ+ couples (Badgett, 2009; Lannutti, 2014a; Ramos et al., 2009; Riggle et al., 2017). Further, married LGBTQ+ people report that because of getting married, they have gained health insurance benefits and worry less about legal and financial issues (Lannutti, 2011a; Ramos et al., 2009). Older LGBTQ+ people described the importance of having more control over health and end-of-life decisions for their partners as a result of getting married (Haas & Whitton, 2015; Lannutti, 2011a). Further, older LGBTQ+ people feel that being married will lead to more support for a widow when a partner dies (Lannutti, 2011a). Thus, the research literature suggests that the impact of getting married on LGBTQ+ couples is positive overall.

LGBTQ+ Marriage and Relationships With Friends and Families. In addition to investigating the ways that LGBTQ+ marriage influences couples, research has examined the impact of LGBTQ+ marriage on the friendships and family relationships of LGBTQ+ people. Overall, friends have been found to be supportive of LGBTQ+ people's marriages, often more supportive than family members (Lannutti, 2008). In some cases, support from friends for LGBTQ+ people has been described as weakening after LGBTQ+ marriage became available (Ogolsky et al., 2019). Committed, unmarried LGBTQ+ couples report less support for their relationship from friends because they are not married (Lannutti, 2018a), and lesbian-bisexual couples have reported challenges from lesbian friends directed to the legitimacy of the bisexual partner's identity as a result of deciding to marry (Lannutti, 2007a). Several studies have extended the definition of friendships to include extended social network members such as acquaintances, coworkers, neighbors, and the like. In a study in the Netherlands, Badgett (2011) found that LGBTQ+ people's sense of increase social inclusion associated with LGBTQ+ marriage increased at the extended social network level. Wootton et al. (2019) found that LGBTQ+ experienced neutral, positive, and negative interactions with extended social network members as a result of LGBTQ+ marriage availability. For example, LGBTQ+

people reported positive conversations with coworkers and being more "out" at work after LGBTQ+ marriage became available nationally in the United States (Wootton et al., 2019).

Although friends have been shown to have been mostly supportive of LGBTQ+ people's marriages, the research on family-of-origin relationships and LGBTQ+ marriage is more mixed. Whereas many LGBTQ+ people report support for LGBTQ+ marriage from family members, the same studies often show that other LGBTQ+ people experience lack of support for their marriage from family members (Clark et al., 2015; Lannutti, 2008, 2013). LGBTQ+ couples who experience support from their families for their marriages report greater overall well-being and a stronger sense of overall social acceptance than those that do not experience family support (Badgett, 2011; Kennedy et al., 2018). Research has shown that participating in LGBTQ+ marriages allows family members to demonstrate support and solidarity for the LGBTQ+ couple (Lannutti, 2014). Studies have shown that some family members are supportive of the LGBTQ+ couple but not their marriage per se (Lannutti, 2013; Ocobock, 2013). Lannutti (2013) found that an LGBTQ couple's decision to marry led some families to experience privacy management turbulence about the couples' sexual and gender identities as well as private information about the couple. In some cases, getting married led family members to try to limit the amount of people who knew about the marriage while other family members took the couples' decision to marry as permission to ask for and share private information about the couple (Lannutti, 2013).

LGBTQ+ marriage has an impact on the families that LGBTQ+ people build as well. LGBTQ+ people often consider parenting and family-building desires in their marriage deliberations and are attracted to marriage because it provides protections for existing families and eases the path to build families. Lesbian couples are more likely than gay male couples to have children (Kimport, 2013; Rothblum et al., 2008; Solomon et al., 2004). In the United States, lesbian couples are also more likely to marry than are gay male couples. Kimport (2013) argues that the U.S. "gender gap" between lesbian couples and gay male couples in getting married is actually a "parenthood gap" in that lesbian couples seek marriage to help build and protect the families they build together. However, in many European countries gay male couples are more likely to formalize their relationships through marriage and civil unions than are lesbian couples which the argument by Kimport (2013) does not account for (Bernstein et al., 2016). Wall (2011) points out that lesbian couples see value in marriage when family building because it may help eliminate the need for nonbiological mother adoptions. In a cross-national analysis, Bernstein et al. (2016) found mixed results for the ability of LGBTQ+ marriage to make legal aspects of family building for LGBTQ+ couples easier. Chauveron et al. (2017) found the same mixed results across various U.S. states. Despite mixed results regarding the legal implications for LGBTQ+ marriage and family building, the symbolic power of marriage for communicating family identity within the family and to those outside the family is perceived as strong by many LGBTQ+ people (Lannutti, 2014b).

CRITIQUE AND FUTURE DIRECTIONS

Research has shed important light on LGBTQ+ marriage and its impact on LGBTQ+ individuals and their relationships. However, it is largely White LGBTQ+ experiences that are represented. With the notable exceptions of McGuffey (2018) and Lee (2018), whose research focuses on Black LGBTQ+ individuals, most of the research uses samples that are majority White. Further research that focuses on BIPOC LGBTQ+ individuals and communities is needed to understand these unique experiences. Furthermore, transgender and gender nonbinary people are either ignored or purposefully excluded from the vast majority of this literature. Even the term "same-sex marriage," which is prominently used in the literature, excludes and erases transgender and gender nonbinary individuals. As Greenberg (2000, 2012) explains, marriage rights for transgender and gender nonbinary individuals may not have followed the same path as for cisgender people wishing to marry a cisgender same-sex partner. Thus, the experiences of transgender and gender nonbinary individuals with legal marriage should be specifically investigated in future research. Although they have received more attention from LGBTQ+ marriage researchers than transgender and gender nonbinary individuals (see Galupo, 2008), bisexual people are another population that has been mostly overlooked in the research. Overall, the research focuses on the White, cisgender, gay- or lesbian-identified members of the LGBTQ+ community, excluding the most marginalized members. More diverse samples that include BIPOC, bisexual, transgender, and gender nonbinary participants are needed in addition to research studies that focus specifically on these marginalized populations. Polyamorous individuals and families are also excluded from the LGBTQ+ marriage literature. Monogamy is the dominant couple and family structure that is studied, despite the existence of LGBTQ+ polyamorous relationships and families. Research should specifically look at the impacts of LGBTQ+ marriage for individuals who do not practice monogamy.

In terms of research design, most studies of LGBTQ+ marriage are cross-sectional. More longitudinal studies are needed to understand both the long-term impact of LGBTQ+ marriage on individuals and their relationships and how the effects of LGBTQ+ marriage influence relational communication through the lifespan of relationships. As many locations transitioned to recognizing LGBTQ+ marriage throughout the first two decades of the 21st century, the research on LGBTQ+ marriage also mostly focused on the effects of this transition on LGBTQ+ people and their relationships. Future directions in LGBTQ+ marriage research should focus on understanding more about the functioning and communication within LGBTQ+ marriages by conducting studies with samples composed of LGBTQ+ married people as well as better incorporating married LGBTQ+ people into all studies of relational communication in marriages and families.

FURTHER READING

Badgett, M. V. L. (2009). *When gay people get married: What happens when societies legalize same-sex marriage*. New York University Press.

Lannutti, P. J. (2014). *Experiencing same-sex marriage: Individuals, couples, and social networks*. Peter Lang.

Lannutti, P. J., & Galupo, M. P. (Eds.). (2019). *The 2016 U. S. Presidential election and the LGBTQ community*. Routledge.

Richman, K. D. (2013). *License to wed: What legal marriage means to same-sex couples*. New York University Press.

REFERENCES

Badgett, M. V. L. (2009). *When gay people get married: What happens when societies legalize same-sex marriage*. New York University Press.

Badgett, M. V. L. (2011). Social inclusion and the value of marriage equality in Massachusetts and the Netherlands. *Journal of Social Issues, 67*(2), 316–334. https://doi.org/10.1111/j.1540-4560.2011.01700.x

Baxter, L. A., Henauw, C., Huisman, D., Livesay, C. B., Norwood, K., Su, H., Wolf, B., & Young, B. (2009). Lay conceptions of "family": A replication and extension. *Journal of Family Communication, 9,* 179–189.

Bernstein, M., Naples, N. A., & Harvey, B. (2016). The meaning of marriage to same-sex families: Formal partnership, parenthood, gender, and the welfare state in international perspective. *Social Politics: International Studies in Gender, State & Society, 23*(1), 3–39. https://doi.org/10.1093/sp/jxv002

Brown, C., & Keller, C. J. (2018). The 2016 Presidential election outcome: Fears, tension, and resiliency of GLBTQ communities. *Journal of GLBT Family Studies, 14*(1–2), 101–129.

Charlton, B. M., Corliss, H. L., Spiegelman, D., Williams, K., & Austin, S. B. (2016). Changes in reported sexual orientation following US states recognition of same-sex couples. *American Journal of Public Health, 106*(12), 2202–2204. https://doi.org/10.2105/AJPH.2016.303449

Chauveron, L. M., Alvarez, A., & van Eeden-Moorefield, B. (2017). The co-evolution of marriage and parental rights of gays and lesbians. *Journal of GLBT Family Studies, 13*(2), 114–136. https://doi.org/10.1080/1550428X.2016.1187105

Clark, J. B., Riggle, E. D. B., Rostosky, S. S., Rothblum, E. D., & Balsam, K. F. (2015). Windsor and Perry: Reactions of siblings in same-sex and heterosexual couples. *Journal of Homosexuality, 62*(8), 993–1008. https://doi.org/10.1080/00918369.2015.1039360

Drabble, L. A., Wooton, A. R., Veldhuis, C. B., Perry, E., Riggle, E. D. B., Trocki, K. E., & Hughes, T. L. (2020). It's complicated: The impact of marriage legalization among sexual minority women and gender diverse individuals in the United States. *Psychology of Sexual Orientation and Gender Diversity.* https://doi.org/10.1037/sgd0000375

Ecker, S., Rostosky, S. S., Riggle, E. D. B., Riley, E. A., & Byrnes, J. M. (2019). The Australian marriage equality debate: A qualitative analysis of the self-reported lived experience of lesbian, gay, bisexual, transgender, intersex, and queer (LGBTIQ) people. *International Perspectives in Psychology: Research, Practice, Consultation, 8*(4), 212–226. https://doi.org/10.1037/ipp0000116

Everett, B. G., Hatzenbuehler, M. L., & Hughes, T. L. (2016). The impact of civil union legislation on minority stress, depression, and hazardous drinking in a diverse sample of sexual-minority women: A quasi-natural experiment. *Social Science & Medicine, 169,* 180–190. https://doi.org/10.1016/j.socscimed.2016.09.036

Galupo, M. P. (Ed.). (2008). *Bisexuality and same-sex marriage.* Routledge.

Galvin, K. M. (2006). Diversity's impact on defining the family: Discourse-dependence and identity. In L. H. Turner & R. West (Eds.), *The family communication sourcebook* (pp. 3–20). SAGE.

Gonzalez, K. A., Pulice-Farrow, L., & Galupo, M. P. (2018). "My aunt unfriended me:" Narratives of GLBTQ family relationships post 2016 Presidential election. *Journal of GLBT Family Studies, 14*(1–2), 61–84.

Greenberg, J. A. (2000). When is a man a man, and when is a woman a woman? *Florida Law Review, 52,* 745–768.

Greenberg, J. A. (2012). *Intersexuality and the law.* New York University Press.

Haas, S. M., & Whitton, S. W. (2015). The significance of living together and importance of marriage in same-sex couples. *Journal of Homosexuality, 62*(9), 1241–1263. https://doi.org/10.1080/00918369.2015.1037137

Hull, K. E. (2019). Same-sex marriage: Principle versus practice. *International Journal of Law, Policy & the Family, 33*(1), 51–74. https://doi.org/10.1093/lawfam/eby018

Kennedy, H. R., Dalla, R., & Dreesman, S. (2018). "We are two of the lucky ones": Experiences with marriage and wellbeing for same-sex couples. *Journal of Homosexuality, 65*(9), 1207–1231. https://doi.org/10.1080/00918369.2017.1407612

Kimport, K. (2013). Marrying for the kids: Gender, sexual identity, and family in same-sex marriage. *Advances in Gender Research, 17,* 67–88.

Lannutti, P. J. (2005). For better or worse: Exploring the meanings of same-sex marriage within the lesbian, gay, bisexual and transgendered community. *Journal of Social and Personal Relationships, 22*(1), 5–18. https://doi.org/10.1177/0265407505049319

Lannutti, P. J. (2007a). "This is not a lesbian wedding": Examining same-sex marriage and bisexual-lesbian couples. *Journal of Bisexuality, 7*(3–4), 237–260. https://doi.org/10.1080/15299710802171316

Lannutti, P. J. (2007b). The influence of same-sex marriage on the understanding of same-sex relationships. *Journal of Homosexuality, 53*, 135–151. https://doi.org/10.1300/J082v53n03_08

Lannutti, P. J. (2008). Attractions and obstacles while considering legally recognized same-sex marriage. *Journal of GLBT Family Studies, 4*(2), 245–264. https://doi.org/10.1080/15504280802096914

Lannutti, P. J. (2011a). Security, recognition, and misgivings: Exploring older same-sex couples' experiences of legally recognized same-sex marriage. *Journal of Social and Personal Relationships, 28*(1), 64–82. https://doi.org/10.1177/0265407510386136

Lannutti, P. J. (2011b). Examining communication about marriage amendments: Same-sex couples and their extended social networks. *Journal of Social Issues, 67*(2), 264–281. https://doi.org/10.1111/j.1540-4560.2011.01697.x

Lannutti, P. J. (2013). Same-sex marriage and privacy management: Examining couples' communication with family members. *Journal of Family Communication, 13*(1), 60–75. https://doi.org/10.1080/15267431.2012.742088

Lannutti, P. J. (2014a). *Experiencing same-sex marriage: Individuals, couples, and social networks*. Peter Lang.

Lannutti, P. J. (2014b). Families centered upon a same-sex relationship: Identity construction and maintenance in the context created by legally recognized same-sex marriage. In L. A. Baxter (Ed.), *Remaking "family" communicatively* (pp. 51–68). Peter Lang.

Lannutti, P. J. (2018a). Committed, unmarried same-sex couples and their social networks in the United States: Relationships and discursive strategies. *Journal of Homosexuality, 65*(9), 1232–1248. https://doi.org/10.1080/00918369.2017.1411690

Lannutti, P. J. (2018b). GLBTQ people who decided to marry after the 2016 U.S. election: Reasons for and meanings of marriage. *Journal of GLBT Family Studies, 14*(1–2), 85–100. https://doi.org/10.1080/1550428X.2017.1420846

Lee, J. (2018). Black LGB identities and perceptions of same-sex marriage. *Journal of Homosexuality, 65*(14), 2005–2027. https://doi.org/10.1080/00918369.2017.1423214

MacIntosh, H., Reissing, E. D., & Andruff, H. (2010). Same-sex marriage in Canada: The impact of legal marriage on the first cohort of gay and lesbian Canadians to wed. *Canadian Journal of Human Sexuality, 19*(3), 79–90.

Maisel, N. C., & Fingerhut, A. W. (2011). California's ban on same-sex marriage: The campaign and its effects on gay, lesbian, and bisexual individuals. *Journal of Social Issues, 67*, 242–263.

McGuffey, C. S. (2018). Intersectionality, cognition, disclosure and Black LGBT views on civil rights and marriage equality: Is gay the new Black? *Du Bois Review: Social Science Research on Race, 15*(2), 441–465. https://doi.org/10.1017/S1742058X18000218

Metheny, N., & Stephenson, R. (2019). Political environment and perceptions of social inclusion after nationwide marriage equality among partnered men who have sex with men in the USA. *Sexuality Research & Social Policy: Journal of NSRC, 16*(4), 521–528. https://doi.org/10.1007/s13178-018-0357-6

Ocobock, A. (2013). The power and limits of marriage: Married gay men's family relationships. *Journal of Marriage and Family, 75*(1), 191–205. http://www.jstor.org/stable/23440769

Ogolsky, B. G., Monk, J. K., Rice, T. M., & Oswald, R. F. (2019). Personal well-being across the transition to marriage equality: A longitudinal analysis. *Journal of Family Psychology, 33*(4), 422–432. https://doi.org/10.1037/fam0000504

Philpot, S. P., Ellard, J., Duncan, D., Dowsett, G. W., Bavinton, B. R., Down, I., Keen, P., Hammoud, M. A., & Prestage, G. (2016). Gay and bisexual men's interest in marriage: An Australian perspective. *Culture, Health & Sexuality, 18*(12), 1347–1362. https://doi.org/10.1080/13691058.2016.1184314

Ramos, C., Goldberg, N. G., & Badgett, M. V. L. (2009). *The effects of marriage equality in Massachusetts: A survey of the experiences and impact of marriage on same-sex couples.* The Williams Institute, UCLA.

Reynolds, R., & Robinson, S. (2019). Marriage as a marker of secular inclusion? Oral history and lesbian and gay narratives on marriage in contemporary Australia. *Journal of Religious History, 43*(2), 269–284. https://doi.org/10.1111/1467-9809.12591

Richman, K. D. (2013). *License to wed: What legal marriage means to same-sex couples.* New York University Press.

Riggle, E. D. B., Rostosky, S. S., Drabble, L., Veldhuis, C. B., & Hughes, T. L. (2018). Sexual minority women's and gender-diverse individuals' hope and empowerment responses to the 2016 Presidential election. *Journal of GLBT Family Studies, 14*(1–2), 152–174.

Riggle, E. D. B., Rostosky, S. S., & Horne, S. G. (2009). Marriage amendments and lesbian, gay, and bisexual individuals in the 2006 election. *Sexuality Research & Social Policy, 6,* 80–89. https://doi.org/10.1525/srsp.2009.6.1.80

Riggle, E. D. B., Wickham, R. E., Rostosky, S. S., Rothblum, E. D., & Balsam, K. F. (2017). Impact of civil marriage recognition for long-term same-sex couples. *Sexuality Research & Social Policy: A Journal of the NSRC, 14*(2), 223–232.

Rostosky, S. S., Riggle, E. D. B., Rothblum, E. D., & Balsam, K. F. (2016). Same-sex couples' decisions and experiences of marriage in the context of minority stress: Interviews from a population-based longitudinal study. *Journal of Homosexuality, 63*(8), 1019–1040. https://doi.org/10.1080/00918369.2016.1191232

Rothblum, E. D., Balsam, K. F., & Solomon, S. F. (2008). Comparison of same-sex couples who were married in Massachusetts, had domestic partnerships in California, or had civil unions in Vermont. *Journal of Family Issues, 29*(1), 48–78.

Solomon, S. E., Rothblum, E. D., & Balsam, K. F. (2004). Pioneers in partnership: Lesbian and gay couples in civil unions compared with those not in civil unions and married heterosexual siblings. *Journal of Family Psychology, 18*(2), 275–86.

Stiers, G. (1999). *From this day forward: Commitment, marriage, and family in lesbian and gay relationships.* St. Martin's Press.

Wall, M. (2011). Hearing the voices of lesbian women having children. *Journal of GLBT Family Studies, 7*(1–2), 93–108.

Wootton, A. R., Drabble, L. A., Riggle, E. D. B., Veldhuis, C. B., Bitcon, C., Trocki, K. F., & Hughes, T. L. (2019). Impacts of marriage legalization on the experiences of sexual minority women in work and community contexts. *Journal of GLBT Family Studies, 15*(3), 211–234. https://doi.org/10.1080/1550428X.2018.1474829

Pamela J. Lannutti and Hilary Wermers

MOLECULAR IMAGES, LEAKY MASCULINITIES: PAIN, PHOTOGRAPHY, AND QUEER DESIRE

INTRODUCTION

The process of normalization (assignment, reassignment) that could be accomplished only by discursive or photographic representation in the past is now inscribed within the very structure of the living being by surgical, endocrinological, and even genetic techniques. (Preciado, 2013, p. 112)

In this passage, Paul B. Preciado describes a change of register that not only allowed the relationship between materiality (sex) and culture (gender), much discussed in gender and queer studies, to be revived, but also raises the question of the meaning of photographic representation.[1] While photography has played a decisive role in the production of the sexual subject and its visual truth since its invention in the 19th century, according to Preciado it seems to have shrunk in its importance for determining gender. Instead, it is molecules, genes, and hormones that produce gender (Preciado, 2013, p. 111).

> Although the visual criteria for sex assignment may not seem to have changed very much since the end of the nineteenth century, the current technical possibilities of body modification are introducing substantial differences in the process of the assignment and production of femininity and masculinity. (Preciado, 2013, p. 112)

Contrary to the assumption of (image-)discursive construction, which has long been common in gender and queer studies, it is the technical possibilities of, for example, hormone intake that generates sexual subjects. Preciado gained the insight that substances such as hormones are the productive force of gender in a self-experiment of guided hormone ingestion, whose effects on gender(-perception) he described in *Testo Junkie* in 2013. The realization of the productive force is all the more remarkable as it goes back to a genealogical paradox that directs the focus to a historically neglected epoch of gender and queer studies: The first time, in 1955, that gender was mentioned in the sense of a category based on the constructedness of gender was when intersexual babies were administered hormones to normalize them (Preciado, 2013, p. 99). Gender was conceived as a biotechnological artifact at the moment when attempts were made to bridge the gap between biological and cultural gender, and the body became a biopolitical gender regime (Preciado, 2013, p. 100). Gender can be understood as changeable and unstable and dependent upon various hormone levels, and hormones were used in the sign of normative gender conceptions. In the 1950s, hormones were nowhere near ready to be hacked by testosterone users like Preciado to resist the normative demands on gender. Thus photography in 1955—as we will see—plays a decisive role. Although at the moment of visualizing gender it always means regulating it, gender hacking goes hand in hand with the molecularization of photography, which is illustrated in this article by the molecules of "dirt."

Albrecht Becker's photography can be used as an example to show how photography interacts with the pharmacopornographic turn in the 1950s, and to what extent moments of queer hacking can be discerned. His photography is an example of queer media use at a time that was very much characterized by homonormative aesthetics due to homophobic resentment. Becker's photography therefore anticipates his time in terms of counterhegemonic queer articulations of gender, sexuality, and the body.

The molecularization of photography in Becker began at the same time as the pharmacopornographization of society; it allows for moments of queer critique through media usage at a time when neither queer theory nor practices of hormonal gender hacking could be spoken of. Through this use of photography, it is argued that what Preciado conceptualizes as *biodrag* in the sense of queer critique was already articulated in the 1950s. Critique in the sense of "queer" here means using the imitation game of substances affirmatively to point out that gender is also a somatic fiction—that is, an idea generated with the help of molecules (Preciado, 2013, p. 191). Molecules in this function of drag are already embraced in Becker's photography to question normative settings of *white*[2] bourgeois homosexual masculinity.[3] In this context of molecularization, Becker's photography is conceived as *minor photography* based on Gilles Deleuze and Felíx Guattari's concept of *minor literature* (Deleuze & Guattari, 2012). This means to discuss the queer-political dimension of vernacular media practices, since the concept of *minor literature* has been developed in the realm of the politics of private and everyday contexts. *Minor* hints to the political potential of hidden places and practices, which because of their marginality have an even greater impact on the transformation of society's norms.

The section "Albrecht Becker: A Short Photographic Biography" discusses Albrecht Becker's photographic work, and the mutually informing strands of argumentation of molecularization and vernacularization. In particular, Albrecht Becker's stagings in worker drag will be the focus of the analysis, with a special emphasis on the twofold meaning of "dirt." Dirt in Becker's photography is not only significant in terms of its cultural semantics, but dirt as a material signifier also points to gender as a somatic fiction, and even reworks heteronormative devaluations of homosexuals as the "dirt of society" in such a way that a different relationship between queer sexuality and dirt becomes conceivable: A relationship of desire and connection.

ALBRECHT BECKER: A SHORT PHOTOGRAPHIC BIOGRAPHY

Albrecht Becker was born in a small German town in 1906. He initially trained as a tailor in Quedlinburg, but was imprisoned under National Socialism in accordance with paragraph 175 of the Criminal Code for the German Reich.[4] After his release, he was employed in the Federal Republic as a stage designer for film, and then later for television. He photographed himself throughout his life—up to the ripe old age of 90—which was marked by persecution, stigmatization, and discrimination due to his homosexuality, and what later came to be known as BDSM passion. His photographs, which he handed over to the archive of the Gay Museum in Berlin in the 1990s (at the age of 80), could certainly be read as testimonies of introjected social hatred or of working through the trauma of his imprisonment during National Socialism.[5] The photographs depict many things, including pain, insignia of becoming a man (such as steely glances), rational central perspectives, or the enlargement—potentiation—of his genitals caused by modifications such as paraffin injections. These body-modifying interventions, which inform the use of media as well as the material alterations of the image, nevertheless enable an alternative reading of Becker's photographs. In dealing with his visualizations, Köppert (2021) explores the significance of the opulent visual production of pain for the history of homosexuality in the 20th century, on the one hand, and the theoretical question of the queer politics of negative feelings or affects, on the other (Köppert, 2021). This article narrows the question somewhat further and refers, in particular, to the use of molecules, like kerosene and tar, and especially particles like dust and dirt, for the modification of body and image.

Becker's approximately 100,000 self-portraits (of an estimated 300,000–500,000 photographs of Becker in total, Regener, 2016, p. 43) were taken throughout the entire 20th century and, due to their large number alone, give an impression of the importance that photographic pain production must have had for Becker. But the visual and sensual aesthetics of pain in his photographs also stand out from the history of private photography. In this respect, they represent an extraordinary and, as far as I know, not really representative fund for his time.

Already during his imprisonment under the Nazi regime and the highly stressful psycho-emotional situation of being stationed on the Eastern Front during World War II, his imagery counters the canon. After his release, a radical change in Becker's aesthetic expression can be reconstructed.[6] His closed body surfaces increasingly break up, and dirt and ink replace the oil that had gloriously accentuated his body during the Weimar period. During his imprisonment, Becker begins to paint, puncture, and stab his body using the cultural technique of tattooing. While stationed at the Eastern Front, he drew a curtain in front of his bed in the bunker to tattoo himself secretly with self-made utensils (Sternweiler, 1993, p. 53). After 1945, Becker's photographic practice was restricted to these painful self-experiments that began during National Socialism. From that point on, the emphasis of his aesthetic practice is less on accentuating his body or his skin, which constitutes the wholeness of the body-ego.[7] Instead, the tattoos stand for a visio-material, repetitive, and experimental practice of a pain that decomposes the body surface. These experiments anticipate new grids of the intelligibility of gay sexuality, which can be understood as a form of queer desire expanded to include pain as well as media and cultural techniques of pain production. In the 1980s, this became recognized as a practice of BDSM in gay contexts. From these grids arises the question of new and queer embodiments of gay masculinity in the otherwise rather homonormative epoch of the 1950s (Duggan, 2002). Homosexual masculinity, which began to become increasingly masculinized in the 1950s, was decomposed—as Becker's photographs make clear—through fragmentation associated with pain practices. Becker's photographs from 1945 are depictions of the direct effects of pain—caused by piercings, genital weightings, and body-modifying interventions—that constitute masculinity as porous, as leaky.[8] In the midst of the pathologizing and marginalizing discourse of the postwar period, Becker develops a visual expression of pain which is neither psychologizing in the sense of a self-victimization, nor self-referential in the sense of an individualistic isolation and desolidarized claim of pain. Thus, instead of staging individualized victimhood to the discriminating or derealizing medical and legal discourses, pain in his photography and through its media usage functions as a mode of queer critique.[9]

MOLECULARIZATION: DRAGZ-IMAGES

Dirt is one of the molecules Becker not only uses for a certain depiction of him in worker drag, but as the material force to decompose homonormative masculinity—as a queer form of *biodrag* so to speak. Mary Douglas's and Judith Butler's concepts of dirt help to reconceptualize dirt in terms of *biodrag* with regard to Becker's photography.

The majority of his self-portraits from 1945 are taken from the central perspective, and Becker is mostly seen from the front in a partial or half-body shot.[10] His pictures are littered with insignia and agents that, in many cases, undermine the goal of portrait photography, which is to help to gain power and status or to establish self-reference (Tagg, 1993, p. 37).

In one image Becker's face is deformed by nose braces; needles massacre his sex; in another image, paint, ink, and soot make his skin appear dirty, washed out, and fragile (see Figure 1).

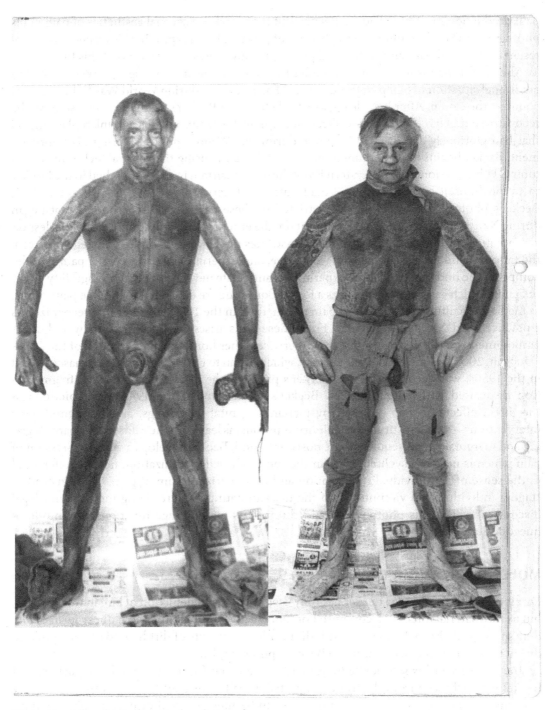

Figure 1. Albrecht Becker: Becker dirty, n.d.
Source: AB_Selbst_Ordner_Original_1960–1970 (Folder_B_1938_1944_1970 (1970)).

Fluff, scratches, and stains as well as gradients, blurring, and smears indicate that the photographer worked with little sterility and little accuracy when photographing, developing, and peeling. Holes, cuts, ink, and pencil applications or cracks in the photo paper surfaces suggest that the images were either further processed or poorly stored (see Figure 2).

In short: Immaculate idealized masculinity is defiled, becomes brittle and leaky in the process of photographic representation. Homosexual masculinity—which until 1969, the year of breaking free, emancipation, and political reinvention, sought primarily to adapt itself to the bourgeois middle class in order not to attract attention—is being challenged in Becker's private photography. The molecularization of the body is directly transferred to the ways in which photography is used in its production, as well as in its further processing in the form of montages, photo folders, or scrapbooks. This is to be made clear in an exemplary way by Becker's staging of himself as a dirty worker. Dirt is the productive force of queer masculinity.

A further image shows Becker standing in front of a white wall in a workman's uniform, casting a shadow that stands in stark contrast to the wall; he is turned sideways and looking into the camera (see Figure 3).

His face, his upper body, and his penis—sticking out of his fly—are smeared and sooty. The dirt on Becker's body makes his tattoos almost unrecognizable. The chains attached to the sides of his trousers suggest that the uniform is that of a chimney sweep. In the picture, Becker's pert look and his seemingly pert facial expression, which seems to be perky due to the advanced

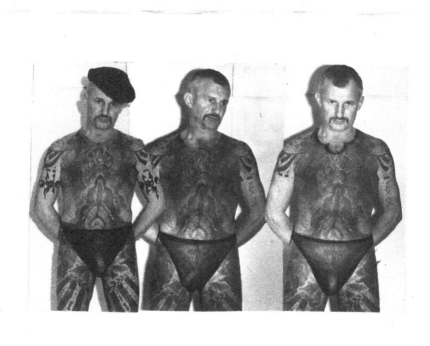

Figure 2. Albrecht Becker: Cuts, montages, paintings, 1961.
Source: AB_Selbst_Tatoo_Alben_Original_1960–1970 (Folder with Phallus (oJ)).

Figure 3. Albrecht Becker: The big pisser is only pretending, n.d. Subtitled "He pretends to be very common."
Source: AB_Selbst_Ordner_Original_1960–1970 (Folder_B_1938_1944_1970 (oJ)).

lower lip, correspond with the photo's caption: "[H]e pretends to be very common." Through gaze, facial expression, and the description "pretends," Becker propagates the assumption that he can be regarded as part of the common, which has become as self-evident as common sense. With the technique of imitation, Becker pretends to belong to an ideology and political order that claims to be self-evident. The process of imitation reveals that which "goes without saying" (Barthes, 2003, p. 7); it is a process of constructing "common sense."

Becker's estate contains numerous images of imitation. These suggest an "epistemology of the wardrobe" (Halberstam, 1998, p. 99), an epistemology of drag, as it can be thematized in terms of the question of performative masquerade in Becker's depictions. However, in many of Becker's photographs, a function of drag is articulated, which, together with the dirt as a material particle, in the context of photographic practices, represents an early version of the queer strategy of *biodrag* after Preciado. Therefore, I do not speak of drag images, but of "dragz-images," since its pronunciation with the "z" sounds like the German word for dirt (*Drecksbilder*).

Following Mary Douglas's study "Purity and Endangerment," which is central to the scientific debate, dirt can be understood as a historically and socially produced scheme that itself refers to an order, a system (Douglas, 1985, p. 52). In addition, dirt is a culturally effective means of deconstruction and deregulation, as Judith Butler expresses it (Butler, 1993, pp. 193–194). Once again, briefly referring to Figure 3: Becker's claim to be common is then countered not only by the word "pretends," but by the dirt in the image. The second line of the caption, "The big pisser," also reads as a caricature of the desire to be common in the sense of bourgeois norms. The dirt, excrement, urine, and filth become visual metaphors of the threat to the bourgeois good life, which has been normalized as common sense, as Lauren Berlant formulates it in reference to Barthes.[11] As a background, it should be mentioned that the removal of filth was one of the defining narratives of the reconstitution of a postwar West-German "white vest." In the context of the effort to achieve a "clean youth leadership," against the background of the misguidance by National Socialism, for example, the censorship of so-called pulp fiction and trashy literature, which were allegedly harmful to young people, was at the center of public discourse.[12] Added to this were narratives that linked the body of nations, which was to be restored in the postwar period, to concepts of purity and Whiteness. In so far as the symbolic threatening gesture of filth was of high relevance, especially in the postwar period, I am interested in the deconstructive potential of cultural filth from a queer perspective. As such, I understand dirt—as Butler does—as a demarcation of the body, as a culturally constructed coherence. Dirt, according to Butler, is in this respect itself a cultural form of designation and relational practice. As a cultural means, dirt is interchangeable with other metaphors of contamination and "disorder" (Butler, 1993, pp. 190–208). In this context, Butler examines the examples of parody, travesty, and drag as "disorder" (Butler, 1993, p. 196). Against this background, "drag" and "dirt" can be regarded as synonyms. Butler thus contradicts the assumption that dirt is a "pre-discursive...multiplicity of physical forces that break through the surface of the body and disturb the regulatory procedures of cultural coherence" (Butler, 1993, p. 193).[13]

But dirt is also drag in the sense of its material effectiveness. We are dealing with dirt not only on a symbolic level, but as an actual material technique of contamination—in so far as the body and photography as a material carrier become dirty. Therefore, it has to be asked, whether dirt operates here exclusively as a semantic designation structure, as Butler discusses it. Although such a structure is connected with physical and spatial practices (Butler, 1997), it cannot be a purely physical and material structure of meaning production. In other words, according to Butler, dirt does not have the potential to produce meaning as materiality or to transform boundaries of meaning. With regard to Becker's photography, however, it is this potential of the discursive and yet nondiscursive effectiveness of dirt that creates a situation of drag, of irregularity and hybridization. Connected with this is the assessment that Becker affirms dirt in the photographic process as something that produces effects as a material particle, as a physical trace or actual discoloration, and as a "creative material" that produces unforeseen reactions (Zimmermann, 2003). With his photographic dragz-images, Becker senses from the place of the private sphere a world that lies in the uncertain, away from the self-evident, the standardized, the commonsense.

In other images, Becker poses with a slider cap, rolled up sleeves, and a dirty face, this time as a worker in a private studio that he has created (see Figures 4 and 5, especially the image on the lower right).[14] With the scene-like staging of a photo studio, Becker refers to the artificiality of the shooting situation.

Despite the sometimes very elaborate disguise as a masculine worker, Becker stages himself neither as a social documentary photographer nor as a socially committed amateur worker

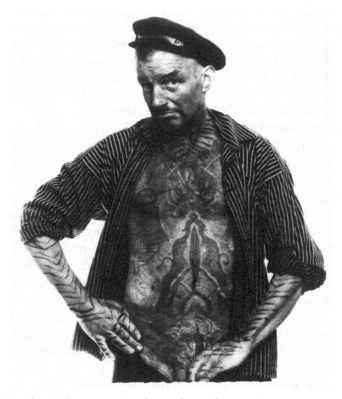

Figure 4. Albrecht Becker: When posing as the worker, n.d.
Source: AB_Fotos_Selbst_Tatoo_1960–1966 (Folder_AB_Self_Tattooed_1960–66 (1962)).

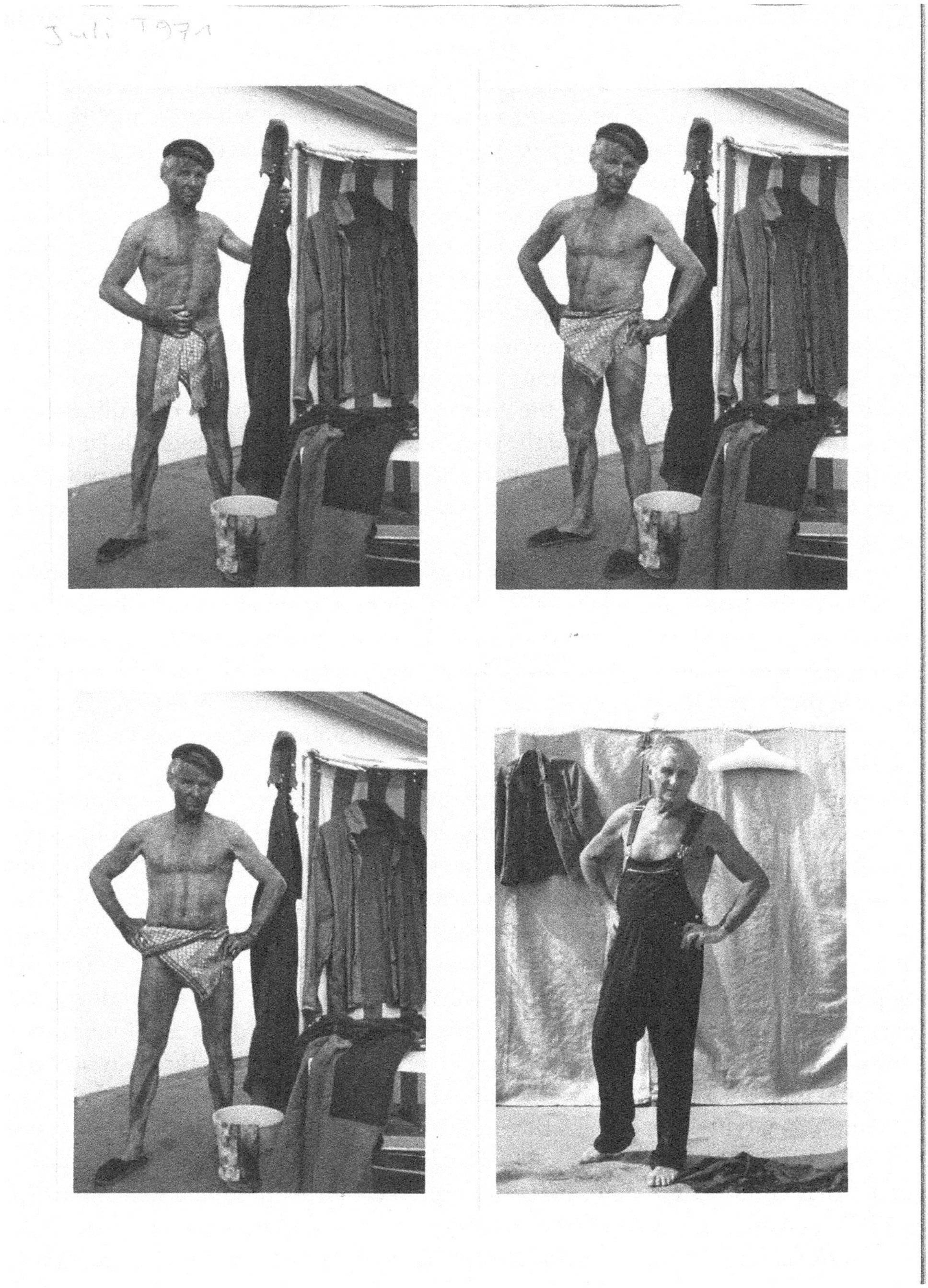

Figure 5. Albrecht Becker: Workers' backdrops, 1971.
Source: AB_Selbst_Ordner_Original_1960–1970 (Folder_W_1970–71 (July_1971)).

photographer. Rather, his staffage of the worker contradict the claim to pursue sociopolitical enlightenment from the place of the public sphere. Instead, Becker uses techniques of drag and imitation to reveal that the aforementioned genres of photography are a form of minework, a form of "extraction" of images of social disadvantage or self-referential reassurance, rather than the mere disclosure of supposedly natural content. Becker's photography does not follow the desire to realize political programs. It does not want to bring out the dirt of society in order to typologize, regulate, or mobilize it in a party-political way. This by no means implies that his photography is apolitical. Nevertheless, it must be distinguished from the purpose-bound, emotionalizing, and self-referential politics of the public spectacle of social documentation and workers' photography. This difference also has to do with the fact that the starting point of his photography is simultaneously the redefinition of its function of depicting workers. For Becker, photographing himself as a worker is an occasion to get dirty in a private setting, to humiliate himself through the contamination, to dissolve at the culturally drawn and "pure" boundaries of the body and the self. In and on Becker's photographs, it soothes or, as Christian Enzensberger (1980, p. 17) writes, slips, gnashes, and splashes. Streaky traces of paint (see Figure 1), oily tar (see Figure 3), or bodies and body shells, which have been licked by dirt, can be seen and felt (see Figure 6).

Becker's images, following Enzensberger, mark the border to the great landscape of the moist and oily (Enzensberger, 1980, p. 17). With their profane function of being able to make himself and the picture dirty, images are small and minor. Small because they do not serve the large landscape of dirt—that is, the cultural, social, and political-public meanings of dirt—but also because they stand for the vernacular way of dealing with dirt. Following Deleuze and Guattari (2012, p. 24), I therefore regard them as a minor attempt at the great landscape of dirt (Enzensberger, 1980, p. 17).

In this sense, photography becomes a dirty medium for Becker. Dirt and photography interact with each other; even more, dirt is as much an inherent part of photography as photography is an inherent part of dirt. Every particle of dirt can only be experienced through photography, and photography only experienced as dirt or the process of contaminating the world, body, everyday life. The dirt, which until now has served as a cultural taboo and as a deregulation of a society in which the structural lines are clearly defined (Douglas, 1985, p. 149), to catalog people, to produce empathy, and to construct the project of a "social documentary." Photography, as part of the humanitarian policy of prevention and the abolition of poverty, takes on a different dimension here. Dirt should be dirty, should sully the body and the self-image, should molecularize the body. Dirt should affect more than it represents.

In its unpredictability, dirt attacks the body, makes skin porous, and turns into an open wound. Dirt particles become part of the body, so that dirt in its cultural meanings is travested—that is, distorted, deformed, and changed by this modified and molecularized body. Dirt is then no longer pejorative or, as the example of working-class photography makes clear, heroically connoted, but in its travesty forms the potential to recognize the humiliation and also the physical pain associated with dirt as an ability to understand oneself on the threshold and to see oneself as a relational being. Thus, if the reason for photography is no longer to constitute itself as a molar entity—that is, as a self-contained functional unit—but to become dirty in order to become small, liminal, and relational, the function and politics of photography also change. Becker's everyday photography does not pretend to depict the

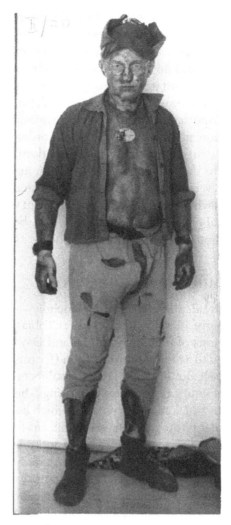

Figure 6. Albrecht Becker: Trouser fly, 1970.
Source: AB_Fotos_Folder_Original_Tätoo_Collected Tattoo (Folder_MAS (oJ)).

reality of the worker. In the form of the artistic stage in the middle of the everyday life of Becker's house, it consciously creates a distance to the topos of politically ambitious amateur or social photography. In this context, dirt is not a political declamatory statement about the well-being or non-well-being of the worker. Dirt is rather the materialistic side of drag (Rebentisch, 2013)—that is, the side of the photographic worker's experiments that is effective on the level of physical affection.

This analysis of drag images is in contrast to fetishist representations of *white* workers.[15] It understands Becker's dragz-images as examples of becoming small, of becoming "minor" in the sense Deleuze and Guattari use the term. This reading should motivate us to perceive the minorizing potential of dirt in Becker's photographs. Becoming minor favors a minorization of *white* homonormative masculinity. Deleuze and Guattari emphasized that this is not about becoming a minority in the sense of a fixed and thus objectifiable state of aggregation (Deleuze & Guattari, 1992, pp. 341–342). Instead, it is a matter of becoming liminal and thresholded. The concept of the minority should not negate the comprehensible and necessary efforts of those who struggle for recognition and status as marginalized. Following on from Deleuze and Guattari, becoming a minority can be understood as a project for society as a whole, regardless of one's own position.[16] It is important to keep becoming a minority as a horizon of thought in the struggle for self-justification and recognition. Thus, in order not to become a function of hegemonic structures in the struggle for recognition (Braidotti, 2003, p. 50), there must be the prospect of retreating into the "narrow space" in becoming a subject, in which politics becomes molecular, that is, very "small," but very urgent and thus effective (Deleuze & Guattari, 2012, p. 129). This is what Deleuze and Guattari meant when they wrote about minor literature and this has parallels in photography, as will be further illustrated in the "Vernacularization: Minor Photography" section.

VERNACULARIZATION: MINOR PHOTOGRAPHY

Through Becker's photography, depictions of gay melancholy—which in the postwar period, for example, in works by George Platt Lynes or Herbert Tobias, echo motifs in the pictorial and art-photographic depictions of pain by Fred Holland Day from the late 19th and early 20th centuries—are subjected to a radical reformulation (Crimp, 2002, p. 152). Pain is visualized less in the canonized spectrum of the longing for subjection connoted with desire, but rather through an aesthetic of injury as a practice of relating. The relevance of photography as a relational medium must thus be taken into account—which leads directly to the question as to why the focus on vernacular photography is so significant for the reconceptualization of queer critique: queer critique is linked to private space and minor media practices, through which relations to an alternative public sphere are established.

Since the end of the 19th century in homosocial and homosexual iconography, pain, ritualized due to repeated discrimination, found its way into visual culture also for the symbolic purpose of sacrifice and the promise of salvation detached from the secular body. Pictorialists, such as Fred Holland Day, Adolphe de Meyer, and Thomas Eakins, recreated the painful Passion of Christ in order to, in a theoretically highly conservative manner, grant photography and the amateurs working with it recognition as art and artists (Stiegler, 2011, p. 49). This was accompanied by a reference to the homosexual self that could fit into the ideal of Western subjectivity. At the same time—denying the use of photographic means—reference was made to an Impressionist visual language that was supposed to make it possible to sublimate the motif of suffering. The social hatred of homosexuality was transformed into a form of self-affirmation of pain in order to be able to transcend itself. George Platt Lynes and Tobias Herbert included the motif of martyrdom in their visual language and mixed it with the neoclassical or morbid expression of gothic. In doing so, they moved to two ends of the same ideal. While one used stylistic devices, such as clear lines and contrasting surfaces, to abstract the image of the subject for his visualization of transcending pain, the other let pain settle in the midst of the ruined romanticism of the postwar period. Herbert Tobias and George Platt Lynes can be described as two aesthetic positions that were exemplary in the immediate postwar period. Both developed an euphemized image of injured masculinity. This calls up the image program of the Man of Sorrows in Christian art history par excellence: Jesus Christ.[17] To imitate the Passion of Christ meant to give meaning to the pain in this postwar period of privation, to which the images of ruin and neglect—in Tobias's images—bear witness. The earthly and physical, including homosexual desire, was to be overcome in favor of attaining sublimity. This iconography, transcending the sexually desiring body, played a considerable role in determining the political program of the homophile movement, which was adapted to bourgeois values.[18] As a result, their press either did not contain any images of naked masculinity at all, or only those characterized by art-historical intelligibility, including images of Jesus Christ, St. Sebastian, or antique athletes. The iconographic tradition of Christian symbolism did not pass Becker by either, but is very distorted in his images. There can be no question that Becker has quoted the aesthetic program of these photographic positions in the 1950s and 1960s with blatant breaks. Until the late 1990s, Becker rather designed a visual program that does not romanticize pain for the purpose of transcendence, but rather trivializes pain. To this end, he uses not only dirt particles, tarry molecules, and secretions of the intimate sphere of the body and sexuality, such as sperm, but also those from everyday culture, such as needles, scissors, and pens. Pain is thus articulated less as a grand gesture, as a wound, but as a minor form of the everyday, the vernacular.[19]

The term "vernacular" here refers to "vernacular culture," which describes cultural artifacts of everyday production and the use of photographs and pop-cultural images, such as family snapshots, photo albums, scrapbooks, collectibles, souvenirs, and postcard images (McCarroll Cutshaw & Barrett, 2008, p. 8). This description implies that these are not only artifacts, but also media practices of snapping and sloppy developing, snipping and cutting, arranging and assembling, scraping. In the context of these media practices, the interest is focused on the production, use, and reception of visual products in everyday and private life. Consequently, the concept of vernacular culture has become especially significant in the context of visual culture studies. Cultural studies, after Richard Hoggart and Stuart Hall (2000), which had a decisive influence on the studies of visual culture, have since the 1960s contributed to an expansion of the concept of culture, previously limited to "high culture," to include aspects of everyday, mass, and subculture (Schade & Wenk, 2011, p. 57).[20] The aim is not to draw a line between everyday and amateur photography, on the one hand, and art photography, on the other. Rather, the aim is to draw attention to the private, intimate, and everyday in creative and artistic expression—that is, to a dimension that is of interest within the history of art. This focus results in a reformulation of the private as art. Becker's photography can thus be placed in a series of artistic works of the queer subculture, which did not become public until the late 1980s (other examples include works by Mark Morrisroe, Jürgen Baldiga, Ron Athey, and Bob Flanagan). Becker was a role model for many of these artists, but not because his art had already become public before or was aimed at the public. The artistic significance of Becker's photographs ties in with the private. Becker's series of images of pain allow us to view the private as artistic and the artistic as private. The question of how political the private is also plays a decisive role.

Becker photographed himself in private since moving to Hamburg in 1949; first in a small apartment that he rented alone, later in the house he built himself, which he lived in with his long-time partner, Herbert Kirchhoff. By using the secret and heterotopic places of this house, such as the cellar or the attic, as stages for his productions, he emphasized the private as a political place.[21] The fact that Becker accepted and shaped the private as a potential for artistic expression and micropolitical alliances is also confirmed by the fact that he made no great effort to publish his photographs. Only in the 1990s did he hand them over to the archive of the Gay Museum in Berlin (Sternweiler, 1993, p. 96).

In an analogous way to Deleuze and Guattari's characterization of *minor literature* (Deleuze & Guattari, 2012), Becker's pictures can be characterized as *minor photographs*, and the private nature of his photography marks not only a political but also a collective place. In reference to Franz Kafka, Deleuze and Guattari spoke of minor literature and pointed to the political potential of the place they considered to be a "dead end."[22] In Kafka's case, the impasse is the simultaneity of two impossibilities: the inconceivability of anything to prevent him from writing, and the impossibility of being an author at all due to the rampant anti-Semitism as a German Jew in Prague.[23] Translated to Becker's positioning, this would mean: the simultaneity of the impossibility of being able to do without photography, and the inconceivability of becoming publicly perceivable with his photographs as a homosexual man in a heteronormative visual culture. The deterritorialized visual language of homosexual BDSM masculinity in the territoriality of the heterosexual dominant culture of the postwar period only offered itself to Becker for small uses in the confined space of private seclusion (Deleuze & Guattari, 2012, p. 25). This narrow space, however, has the effect that every individual affair is linked to politics, and becomes all the more necessary and indispensable the more a completely different history other than the individual history takes place in it (Deleuze & Guattari, 2012, p. 25). The late capitalist, heteronormative, family-centered history of the Federal Republic of Germany (of the 1950s), which occurs in the individual affairs of Becker's sexuality and his body, takes on an existential and thus politically more urgent meaning in the narrow space of his photographic expression than in the wide space of the public sphere, in which everything is somehow and momentarily connected.[24]

The finding that everything is politically more urgent in the confined space does not yet say anything about what form of the political we are dealing with or what politics is indispensably articulated in Becker's photographic space. Deleuze and Guattari point out that in minor literatures, due to the lack of great talents, the conditions for individual statements are missing. Therefore, it is precisely here that something collective, something that undermines the narrative of great "masters," can be articulated (Deleuze & Guattari, 2012, p. 25). Following this thesis, I understand Becker's photography as a subversive collective, as a moment of queer politics. A queer moment begins where the system of a society focused on individual subjects and subjective rights reaches its limits (Hark, 2017, p. 27), where the individualization that took hold under capitalism no longer falls on fertile ground. Becker's minor photographs, which were not suitable for his invention as a "master" at the time, form the queer moment of a sociality based on a subjectivity permeated by the Other. Pain plays a decisive role in the interaction with the molecularization and vernacularization of photography. It is thus no longer merely an expression of oppression, but an agent of a speculative future of liberation.

FURTHER READING

Köppert, K. (2021). *Queer pain: Schmerz als Solidarisierung, Fotografie als Affizierung: Zu den Fotografien von Albrecht Becker aus den 1920er bis 1990er Jahren*. Neofelis Verlag.

Köppert, K. (2017). The Tableau Vivant as a plateau of pain and queer temporality in photography as cinema. In B. Paul, J. Hoenes, A. I. Beyer, N. Frankenberg, & R. Onat (Eds.), *Perverse assemblages: Queering heteronormativity inter/medially* (pp. 93–105). Revolver Verlag.
Lorenz, R. (2009). *Aufwändige durchquerungen: Subjektivität als sexuelle Arbeit*. Transcript.
Musser, A. (2014). *Sensational flesh: Race, power and masochism*. New York University Press.
Ngai, S. (2005). *Ugly feelings*. Harvard University Press.

REFERENCES

Anzieu, D. (1996). *Das Haut-Ich*. Suhrkamp.
Barthes, R. (2003). *Mythen des Alltags*. Suhrkamp.
Berlant, L. (2016). The commons: Infrastructures for troubling times. *Society and Space, 34*(3), 393–419.
Braidotti, R. (2003). Becoming woman, or sexual difference revisited. *Theory, Culture & Society, 20*(3), 43–64.
Brown, W. (1995). Rights and identity in late modernity: Revisiting the "Jewish Question." In A. Sarat & T. Kearns (Eds.), *Identities, politics, and rights* (pp. 85–130). Michigan University Press.
Butler, J. (1993). *Das Unbehagen der Geschlechter*. Suhrkamp.
Butler, J. (1997). *Körper von Gewicht: Die diskursiven Grenzen des Geschlechts*. Suhrkamp.
Butler, J. (2005). *Gefährdetes Leben: Politische essays*. Suhrkamp.
Butler, J. (2010). *Raster des Krieges: Warum wir nicht jedes Leben beklagen*. Campus.
Connell, R. W. (2006). *Der gemachte Mann: Konstruktion und Krise von Männlichkeiten*. VS Verlag.
Crimp, D. (2002). The boys in my bedroom. In D. Crimp (Ed.), *Melancholia and moralism: Essays on AIDS and queer politics* (pp. 151–163). MIT Press.
Deleuze, G., & Guattari, F. (1975). *Kafka: Pour une littérature mineure*. Minuit.
Deleuze, G., & Guattari, F. (1986). *Kafka: Toward a minor literature*. Minnesota University Press.
Deleuze, G., & Guattari, F. (1992). *Tausend plateaus: Kapitalismus und schizophrenie*. Merve.
Deleuze, G., & Guattari, F. (2012). *Kafka: Für eine kleine Literatur*. Suhrkamp.
Deutsches Institut für Medizinische Dokumentation und Information. (2016).
Douglas, M. (1985). *Reinheit und Gefährdung: Eine Studie zu Vorstellungen von Verunreinigung und Tabu*. Dietrich Reimer Verlag.
Duggan, L. (2002). The new homonormativity: The sexual politics of neoliberalism. In D. D. Nelson & R. Castronovo (Eds.), *Materializing democracy: Toward a revitalized cultural politics* (pp. 175–194). Duke University Press.
Eggers, M. M., Kilomba, G., Piesche, P., & Arndt, S. (Eds.). (2005). *Mythen, Masken und Subjekte. Kritische Weißseinsforschung in Deutschland*. Unrast Verlag.
Elkins, J. (2003). *Visual studies: A sceptical introduction*. Routledge.
Enzensberger, C. (1980). *Größerer Versuch über den Schmutz*. Ullstein.
Finger, J. D. (2015). *Homophobie und Strafrecht: Eine strafrechtliche Untersuchung homophober Äußerungen und Äußerungen in Bezug auf Homosexualität*. Berliner Wissenschafts-Verlag.
Foucault, M. (1978). Nietzsche, die Genealogie, die Historie. In M. Foucault (Ed.), *Von der Subversion des Wissens* (pp. 83–109). Ullstein.
Foucault, M. (1992). *Andere Räume*. Reclam.
Halberstam, J. (1998). *Female masculinity*. Duke University Press.
Hall, S. (2000). *Ausgewählte Schriften 3: Cultural studies—Ein politisches Theorieprojekt*. Argument Verlag.
Hark, S. (2017). *Koalitionen des Überlebens: Queere Bündnispolitiken im 21; Jahrhundert*. Wallstein Verlag.
Herzog, D. (2005). *Die Politisierung der Lust: Sexualität in der deutschen Geschichte des zwanzigsten Jahrhunderts*. Siedler Verlag.

Köppert, K. (2021). *Queer pain: Schmerz als Solidarisierung, Fotografie als Affizierung: Zu den Fotografien von Albrecht Becker aus den 1920er bis 1990er Jahren*. Neofelis Verlag.

Langham, J. (2015). *Under the shadow of paragraph 175: Part 1: Albrecht Becker*. USC Shoah Foundation. https://sfi.usc.edu/blog/jeffrey-langham/under-shadow-paragraph-175-part-1-albrecht-becker

McCarroll Cutshaw, S., & Barrett, R. (2008). *In the vernacular: Photography of the everyday*. Boston University Art Gallery.

Preciado, P. B. (2013). *Testo junkie: Sex, drugs, and biopolitics in the pharmacopornographic era*. Feminist Press.

Rebentisch, J. (2013). Über eine materialistische Seite von Camp: Naturgeschichte bei Jack Smith. *ZfM Zeitschrift für Medienwissenschaft, 5*(8), 165–178.

Regener, S. (2016). Fotoarchiv der emotionen: Fotografien von homosexuellen Männern und ihre Archivierung. In S. Regener, W. Ernst, K. Ebeling, & K. Hasenpflug (Eds.), *Atelier der Erinnerung—Aspekte des Archivarischen als Ausgangspunkt künstlerischer Fotografie* (pp. 37–47). Wüstenrot Verlag.

Schade, S., & Wenk, S. (2011). *Studien zur visuellen Kultur: Einführung in ein transdisziplinäres Forschungsfeld*. Transcript.

Schulz, C. (1994). *Paragraph 175. (abgewickelt): Homosexualität und Strafrecht im Nachkriegsdeutschland: Rechtsprechung, juristische Diskussionen und Reformen seit 1945*. Männerschwarm Verlag.

Schuster, P.-K. (2007). Der Künstler als Christus: Zur Wiederherstellung der Gottebenbildlichkeit aus dem Geist der Passion. In E. Blume, A. Hürlimann, T. Schnalke, & D. Tyradellis (Eds.), *Schmerz: Kunst + Wissenschaft* (pp. 127–135). DuMont.

Shildrick, M. (2009). Prosthetic performativity: Deleuzian connections and queer corporealities. In C. Nigianni & M. Storr (Eds.), *Deleuze and queer theory* (pp. 115–133). Edinburgh University Press.

Sternweiler, A. (1993). *Fotos sind mein Leben: Albrecht Becker*. Rosa Winkel.

Stiegler, B. (2011). Orthofotografie: Kleine fotografische Fehlerkunde. *Fotogeschichte, 31*(122), 41–50.

Tagg, J. (1993). *The burden of representation: Essays on photographies and histories*. Minnesota University Press.

Theweleit, K. (2005). *Männerphantasien*. Piper.

Wolfert, R. (2014). Zwischen den Stühlen—die deutsche Homophilenbewegung der 1950er Jahre. In Bundesstiftung Magnus Hirschfeld (Ed.), *Forschung im Queerformat: Aktuelle Beiträge der LSBTI*-, Queer- und Geschlechterforschung* (pp. 87–104). Transcript.

Zimmermann, A. (2003). Von Produktion und Produktivität: Blut und Sperma als Kreativstoffe in der Kunst um 1960. In R. Fayet (Ed.), *Verlangen nach Reinheit oder Lust auf Schmutz? Gestaltungskonzepte zwischen rein und unrein* (pp. 97–114). Passagen Verlag.

NOTES

1. This contribution is a translated excerpt from my monograph (Köppert, 2021).
2. Following Eggers et al. (2005), I capitalize Black in order to emphasize the resistance of Black subjects against the de-subjectifying constructions. In contrast, I write *white* in italics, which is meant to mark the constructional nature of the category.
3. According to Connell (2006), homosexual masculinity should not be understood here as the opposite of hegemonic masculinity *per se*. According to this definition, homosexual masculinity would be a deviation from hegemonic masculinity, which separates it from hegemonic masculinity for its own reassurance. However, as studies on homonormativity have shown (Duggan, 2002), specific manifestations of homosexual masculinity can also bring about a balance between a cultural ideal (e.g., virility) and institutional power (e.g., political power). For this reason and the fact that homosexuality is often used as a fixing identification marker in the description of self and others, I use the terminology of homosexual masculinity only to suggest that Becker practiced male-male sex. Beyond that, however, I argue that he differs from

the homosexual-masculinity model in his gender- and body-related practices. The homosexual-masculinity model thus provides the contrast for the discussion of queer gender and sexuality modes.
4. Albrecht Becker was arrested in early 1935 for offences against §175 of the Criminal Code for the German Reich (RStGB); he was interrogated and sentenced to three years in prison. Even in his old age, Becker reflected that he would have died in a concentration camp if he had challenged the sentence like his acquaintances (Langham, 2015). The §175 Strafgesetzbuch made sexual acts between persons of male sex punishable. The paragraph was incorporated into the RStGB in 1871, and was tightened in 1935, during the National Socialist era. In the Federal Republic of Germany, it was retained in this tightened version until 1969. The paragraph was only deleted in 1994 without any replacement. In 2017, the Bundestag then passed the bill to repeal all sentences passed on the basis of §175 StGB (Finger, 2015; Schulz, 1994).
5. After the Gay Museum in Berlin expressed an interest, Becker handed over the majority of his private photographs to its archive in 1993. Since no official contract for the transfer was concluded, it is no longer possible to trace the public to which Becker wanted to make his materials available, at what time (during his lifetime or posthumously), and under what conditions.
6. This can be reconstructed on the basis of the numerous interviews that were created for the exhibition on Albrecht Becker's life's work, in the Gay Museum, Berlin, in 1993 (Sternweiler, 1993).
7. Didier Anzieu describes a development in the 20th century according to which, contrary to the modern understanding of a self that resides inside the body, the limitation of the body—i.e., the skin—becomes decisive for the constitution of the ego (Anzieu, 1996). Klaus Theweleit discusses the outer body armor as the stabilizing function of the psychological instance of the ego (Theweleit, 2005).
8. These interventions must be viewed against the background of §175, in the version tightened by the Nazis, and incorporated into the Criminal Code of the Federal Republic (StGB), where it remained in force until 1969. The paragraph was only deleted in 1994, without replacement. It should also be noted that at this time (and right up until 1992), homosexuality was pathologized according to the International Classification of Diseases (ICD) of the World Health Organization. Given that Becker's photographs since 1945 are depictions of the direct effects of pain—caused by piercings, genital weights, body-modifying interventions, and much more—the effectiveness of the discourse of identifying self-harming actions with masochism must also be taken into account. As of 2021, the ICD still has an entry on masochism as a disturbance of sexual preference. According to ICD-10 F65.5 of the WHO (from 2016), masochism is still considered a disorder. In contrast, since 1994, the *Diagnostic and Statistical Manual of Mental Disorders* (DSM IV), of the American Psychiatric Association, no longer considers the preference for masochistic practices a disorder in the narrower sense (Deutsches Institut für Medizinische Dokumentation und Information, 2016).
9. Derealization means that specific lives cannot be perceived as destroyed, because they are not perceived as alive—i.e., not real. This selective violence that affects only specific lives is the result of cultural formations (Butler, 2005, 2010).
10. It is known that Becker continued to take photographs with a Leica after World War II. Since he used a tripod camera with a time-mechanical shutter release to create his self-portraits, it is likely that he photographed himself with the 1950 model IIIf.
11. To go back to Barthes again here may be revealing: Capitalism is not easily recognizable as a political system. As an economic system, however, capitalism is not a taboo: there is an impudent commitment to the good life under capitalism (Barthes, 2003, p. 124; Berlant, 2016).
12. The attack of pornography on the minds of the youth was stopped with the Law on the Dissemination of Publications Harmful to Young Persons (Gesetz über die Verbreitung jugendgefährdender Schriften in 1953 (Herzog, 2005, p. 141).
13. Here Butler takes a critical look at Foucault, who actually assumed that dirt is prediscursive (Foucault, 1978, pp. 91–93).

14. The design of the private space as a studio becomes particularly clear on the background screen, which is typical for studio photography. In the early days of studio photography, canvases were hung in the background to give the impression that the person was either in the middle of a private, middle-class setting or in nature. Becker takes up the disturbance of this illusion, which often resulted from a faulty transition to the ground or from waves in the canvas, to the extent that he often inserts his canvases incorrectly into the picture.
15. By speaking of *white* workers, I want to contradict the practice of ignoring Whiteness as a structuring category in the general discussion about workers, working class, and class struggle. I emphasize Whiteness as a category, not because I believe that there are no Black workers, but to emphasize that the discourses I discuss around the aspect of class are here those that revolve around *white* workers.
16. As Margit Shildrick put it: "[N]otions of becoming-woman, becoming-animal or becoming-minoritarian are not simply conceptually unattached to the groupings named and open to all, but refer to processes that operate only through the assemblages temporarily brought about by radically disparate machinic connections" (Shildrick, 2009, p. 129).
17. Albrecht Dürer's drawings, which show Jesus Christ as the Man of Sorrows with a whip and scourge rod, among other things, are an art-historically important marker of alignment with Christ as the result of a creative effort to become the image of God (Schuster, 2007).
18. In West-Germany—as in many other European countries and the United States—so-called homophile groups began to establish themselves after 1945. The central concern of these organizations was the fight against legal and social discrimination. This struggle was not only highly masculinized, but also characterized by a high degree of adaptation to the prevailing conditions (Wolfert, 2014, pp. 87–88).
19. Wendy Brown criticizes the overvaluation of the wound to the extent that it is fetishized as proof of identity (Brown, 1995).
20. Hoggart founded the Birmingham Center for Contemporary Cultural Studies in 1964. James Elkins points out that cultural studies was a prerequisite for the emergence of visual culture studies from about 1990 (Elkins, 2003, pp. 4–6).
21. Foucault understands heterotopic places as spaces that represent actually realized utopias—i.e., counterplacements to places valid within culture (Foucault, 1992, p. 39).
22. The term is *"littérature mineure"* in the original French and has been translated into English as "minor literature." The translator of the German version therefore notes that minor literature can also be translated as "kleine Literatur" (Deleuze & Guattari, 1975, 1986, 2012).
23. Deleuze and Guattari explain this by saying that Kafka, as a German-writing Jew in Prague, could not be part of either the Czech nationality or the German minority, since Jews were excluded from the latter (Deleuze & Guattari, 2012, p. 24).
24. Deleuze and Guattari claim that the current convergence of individual and social affairs, unlike in the "wide space" of great literature, means the decision of life and death in the "narrow space" of minor literature. (Deleuze & Guattari, 2012, p. 25).

Katrin Köppert

RELATIONAL COMMUNICATION AND CONSENSUAL NON-MONOGAMY

CONSENSUALLY NON-MONOGAMOUS RELATIONSHIPS

Increased attention from the entertainment and news media (Moors et al., 2015) and the social sciences, including the development of the Consensual Non-Monogamy Attitude Scale

(Cohen & Wilson, 2017) and Willingness to Engage in Consensual Non-Monogamy Scale (Sizemore & Olmstead, 2017), have highlighted the existence of consensually non-monogamous relationships, people, and their relevance and connection to communication. Consensual non-monogamy (CNM) includes a range of relational dynamics that allow, to some degree, for the romantic or sexual inclusion of extradyadic relationships. Many people practice some form of CNM at some point in time (Moors et al., 2015), with some estimates suggesting that approximately one in five people is involved in CNM at some point in their life (Haupert et al., 2017). In general, the proportion of the population that practices CNM remains consistent across education level, income, age, religion, political affiliation, region, and race, with some variation by gender and sexual orientation (Haupert et al., 2017). This article begins by explaining the different types of CNM and defining the academic and community terminology relevant to CNM. It then examines the interdisciplinary research literature about CNM and relational communication, highlighting common findings and conclusions.

CONSENSUAL NON-MONOGAMY: TERMS AND DEFINITIONS

The differences between types of consensually non-monogamous (CNM) relationships are nuanced but important in their distinctions within sexual boundaries, relationship agreements, and communication. The differing structures help navigate the unique changes and challenges that occur within each type of CNM relationship. The following sections highlight what current research has indicated about the similarities and differences between three broadly defined CNM relationships—swinging, open, and polyamorous. This section describes intersections between CNM relationships and the LGBTQ community and the bondage, domination, and sadomasochist (BDSM) community.

Swinging Relationships. *Swinging relationships* are defined as established romantic dyads where members engage in sexual activity outside of the dyadic relationship for generally recreational purposes (Kimberly & Hans, 2017; Vaillancourt & Few-Demo, 2014). Sexual encounters that contribute to a swinging relationship commonly occur at the same time, with the couple engaging in sexual activity with either a single other person or another couple (Vaillancourt & Few-Demo, 2014). In addition, for couples who wish to engage in CNM sexual encounters, they may locate their external partners in either swinger-specific clubs (Bentzen & Træen, 2014) or by hiring sex workers (Kimberly & Hans, 2017). Although swinging relationships may comprise various combinations, their defining feature is external sexual activity for recreation or exploration and minimal emotional connection with anyone outside of the established dyadic relationship.

Swingers, as opposed to other CNM relationships, define their relationship through sexual engagements with others rather than the emotional ties they have with other relational partners. These behaviors, documented both in lived experiences from swingers and in scholarly research, may be considered a "lifestyle" rather than an identity (Bentzen & Træen, 2014), with the idea that the dyadic couple can cease the swinging, an activity rather than core identity, at any point with the ramifications affecting only the dyad and not anyone external to them. Although there are some parallels between swinging and some polyamorous relationships, where certain partners may view their behavior as a lifestyle, the activity rather than identity mentality may be more notably present within the swinger culture (Bentzen & Træen, 2014).

Considering the scholarly research on CNM relationships over the years, swinging relationships have received the most attention. Because, by definition, swinging relationships require an established dyad, married or unmarried committed couples are typically researched (Jenks, 1998). Research targeting swinging couples predominantly focuses on heterosexual couples' swinging behaviors. Topics that specifically focus on the experiences of swinging relationships include privacy management about swinging with outsiders (Kimberly & Hans, 2017; Vaillancourt & Few-Demo, 2014), fulfillment of sexual fantasies (Bentzen & Træen, 2014; Kimberly & Hans, 2017), and rules or boundaries to protect the dyadic relationship (Harviainen & Frank, 2018; Kimberly & Hans, 2017). Research methods within swinging literature tend to lean toward qualitative methods such as in-depth interviews (Bentzen & Træen, 2014; Kimberly & Hans, 2017) and case studies (Vaillancourt & Few-Demo, 2014), with some studies using quantitative measurements (Kimberly, 2019).

Open Relationships. Swinging and open relationships share a few similarities in terms of their relationship dynamics. Like swinging, people in open relationships engage in extradyadic sexual activity for recreational purposes (Adam, 2006). The unique distinction for open relationships is that the sexual activity within open relationships typically occurs outside of the presence of one member of the dyad and within the separate, independent relationship of the other. Thus, open relationships are loosely defined as a dyadic relationship with the option for extradyadic partners for recreational sexual activity (Grunt-Mejer & Campbell, 2016). The primary distinction between swinging and open relationships is that with individuals who consider themselves to have an open relationship, sexual activity does not occur in the presence of the other partner. Thus, while swinging may be thought of as a couple activity, open relationships may be considered a relational type. Within open relationships, extradyadic relations are independent of each member of the couple, thus not a couple activity, but the pursuance of those relations is characteristic of the dyadic relationship. Further, for open relationships, extradyadic partners might be considered "friends-with-benefits" (Ritchie & Barker, 2006). Both swinging and open relationships share the commonality of emotional fidelity within the dyadic relationship, whereas polyamorous relationships allow for multiple simultaneous romantic relationships (Klesse, 2006). Aside from the shared emphasis on emotional fidelity with a primary partner, there is a significant definitional overlap between swinging and open relationships. However, both are closely connected to the absence of the allowance of external emotional connections, unlike the polyamorous CNM relationship type, which allows such connections to occur.

Research on open relationships often focuses on gay men's relationships (Adam, 2006; Coelho, 2011; Hosking, 2014). Topics that specifically focus on the experiences of open relationships include more complex situations regarding jealousy (Hosking, 2014), specific rules for sexual engagement with regard to external partners (Coelho, 2011), and exploring what monogamy means within gay male relationships (Adam, 2006). Research methods within the open relationship literature range from quantitative survey data (Hosking, 2014) to qualitative interview data (Adam, 2006; Coelho, 2011). Only a few research studies have focused specifically on open relationships, perhaps due to another type of CNM relationship gaining attention and popularity: polyamory.

Polyamory. Along the CNM spectrum, an undercurrent of degrees of acceptable emotional attachment to extradyadic partners may be considered a definitional sticking point. Swinging and open relationships purposefully define their extradyadic sexual encounters as "just sex," purely sexual activity for the purpose recreation or sexual fulfillment, and do not allow for the possibility of forming emotional connection or attachment to people outside of the romantic dyad. Polyamorous relationships are different in that, unless otherwise specified, there is an allowance for multiple emotional connections. There are many nuances and dynamics within polyamorous relationships, but the overarching commonality surrounding these relationships is the ability to form multiple emotional connections. Thus, *polyamory* is defined as a type of CNM relationship that allows for the possibility or exploration of multiple, simultaneous romantic or sexual relationships with an emphasis on openness and honesty for those involved (Dixon, 2016; Haritaworn et al., 2006; Klesse, 2006).

Although the definition of polyamory may be simplified to mean allowance for multiple romantic relationships, the concept of polyamory extends beyond the sexual behaviors permitted within these relationships. The additional entities of emotional connection and love separate polyamory from other CNM relationships (Klesse, 2006). Polyamory is conceptualized as multiple romantic relationships and everything it entails, whereas swinging and open relationships focus primarily on extradyadic sexual activity. Therefore, love is centralized in polyamory, whereas sex is centralized in swinging and open relationships (Klesse, 2006).

The difficulty in defining polyamory, however, lies in the ways in which it is practiced. The scripts for swinging and open relationships are born out of a monogamous script of a dyadic relationship with the practice of sexual activity outside of a relationship being the defining feature of what separates these relationships from traditional monogamous relationships. Within polyamorous relationships, the option for "swinging" or "open" types of relationships (often referred to as polyfidelitious relationships where there are sexual restrictions placed upon the members within the relationship; West, 1996) can occur; and yet, individuals who practice those relational dynamics may still identify as polyamorous. Defining polyamory is then extended beyond the sexual behaviors within relationships and into the concepts of love, emotion, and relationships, but not everyone who practices polyamory may identify with that conceptualization (West, 1996). Further, a number of relational dynamics may compose polyamorous relationships. For instance, polyfidelitious relationships mirror swinging and open relationships in many ways (West, 1996), generally focusing on a dyadic relationship with extradyadic sexual activity. Other hierarchical dynamics may include a primary dyadic relationship, with secondary and sometimes tertiary relationships (Barker & Langridge, 2010). Alternatively, others may completely reject hierarchical relational structure that inhibits the freedom to form authentic connection with other people, considering it a byproduct, often harmfully so, of monogamous scripts (Barker & Langridge, 2010). Further still, dynamics such as "V"s, in which one person may have two otherwise equal relationships, triads, in which three people may be in an otherwise emotionally or sexually fidelitous dynamic, or more elaborate "polycules," consisting of more extensive networks of romantic or sexual relationships, may be considered polyamorous (Barker & Langridge, 2010; Klesse, 2006; Rubinsky, 2018b). The differences between these relational makeups are substantial, but all may fall under the umbrella of polyamory.

Due to this more nuanced definition of polyamory to go beyond sexual behaviors within relationships, polyamory has been theorized within research to be an orientation (Klesse, 2014) or a community with its own constructed terminology (Ritchie & Barker, 2006). By contrast, swinging and open relationships still follow the normative rules set forth by monogamous culture (specifically, the focus on a central dyad), whereas polyamory as a concept typically rejects the notion of a singular central dyad and instead opts for multiple dyads with differing levels of involvement or connection.

Another defining characteristic of polyamory is the emphasis on "openness" and "honesty." Nearly any research study or popular press material about polyamory will highlight the phrase "open and honest" when describing polyamory (Rubinsky, 2018b; Wosick-Correa, 2010, among others). Communicating needs, boundaries, and negotiating an agreement for the determined relational structure are characteristics of polyamory.

Interest in polyamorous relationships among researchers, entertainment media, and the popular press (Moors, 2017) has increased. Considering the complexity of polyamory, concepts such as identity (Barker, 2005; Robinson, 2013), sexual orientation (Klesse, 2014), and language construction (Ritchie & Barker, 2006) have been the focus of scholarly attention. Scholars have also gained interest in viewing and deconstructing polyamory under critical lenses such as intersectionality (Haritaworn et al., 2006) and feminism (Aguilar, 2013), as well as challenging the polyamory self-help literature with regard to perpetuating certain oppressions (Haritaworn, et al., 2006). Additionally, there have been increased calls for the recognition of polyamory's legitimacy within mental health professions (Graham, 2014; Jordan et al., 2017; Williams & Prior, 2015). In the communication discipline, polyamory has received some attention, specifically focusing on communication surrounding jealousy (Rubinsky, 2018a, 2019c), disclosure of polyamorous identity (Rubinsky, 2018b), and intercultural communication in polyamorous communities (Table et al., 2017). Research methods regarding polyamory have ranged from qualitative ethnographies (Aguilar, 2013) and interviews (Barker, 2005; Robinson, 2013) to quantitative surveys (Balzarini et al., 2017; Manley et al., 2015).

Overall, within CNM scholarly literature, researchers tend to focus on a specific CNM relationship (swinging, open, or polyamorous) or compare CNM to monogamous relationships, rather than comparing the different types of CNM (Barker & Langdridge, 2010), with a few notable exceptions (e.g., Matsick et al., 2014). Comparative CNM research generally focuses on either demographic information (Jenks, 2014; Levine et al., 2018) or meta-analyses (Rubel & Bogaert, 2015).

CNM and LGBTQ Communities. Although they can be independent of other relational practices and sexual identities, CNM relationships share a few parallels with the LGBTQ community. An intersection between CNM and the LGBTQ community is the distinction between a "lifestyle," an identity, and an orientation. Parallel to early research on nonheterosexual sexualities, research into CNM relationships explores whether the various types are better understood as a lifestyle, activity, or as an identity. While individuals in swinging culture tend to view their behaviors as a lifestyle (Kimberly & Hans, 2017; Vaillancourt & Few-Demo, 2014), the polyamorous community, more often, tends to view their relational practices as an identity (Barker, 2005). Some swinging couples indicate that there is an ability to stop swinging and "take a vacation" if it ends up taking over their lives (Vaillancourt & Few-Demo, 2014), whereas some polyamorous individuals indicate that they cannot stop being polyamorous because it is a part of who they are (Barker, 2005). Connecting further with the LGBTQ community is the argument of polyamory as a sexual orientation (see Klesse, 2014). However, Klesse (2016) cautioned against polyamorous advocates who try to position polyamory as a sexual orientation similar to other LGBQ identities, noting that such a model may reduce the transformative potential for polyamorous intimacy and limit the reach of any potential legislation that may legalize marital opportunities for multiple partner dynamics. Thus, although outside the scope of this entry, where or if polyamory fits under a queer umbrella or acronym may be debated both within and outside of CNM communities.

Other research has explored overlaps between bisexual and polyamorous communities. Robinson (2013) argued that polyamory may be considered a strategy of sexual expression rather than a stable orientation, which may enable bisexual women to manage their bisexual visibility. Research on queer polyfamilies notes the overlap on managing both heteronormative and mononormative cultural constructions of family (Pain, 2019). Other work has explored the intersections of polyamory and bisexuality (Gusmano, 2018) and comparisons between disclosing an LGBQ identity with disclosing a polyamorous identity (Rubinsky, 2018b). Despite stereotypes of CNM as a "gay male thing" among sexual minority men and women, there are no real differences in attitudes and interest in CNM (Moors et al., 2014).

CNM and BDSM. In addition to the LGBTQ communities, the BDSM culture and CNM relationships share a connection in that it is not uncommon that individuals engage in both communities simultaneously (Klesse, 2006). Those who are in CNM relationships, specifically polyamorous relationships, have been shown to also engage or at least demonstrate knowledge of the BDSM culture (Pitagora, 2016). Little research has explored this intersection in depth, but many studies have included both polyamorous and kinky or BDSM practicing persons in their samples (Kattari, 2015; Rubinsky, 2019a; Sheff & Hammers, 2011, among others).

COMMUNICATION AND RELATIONAL MAINTENANCE

While only a handful of scholarly studies come explicitly from the field of communication studies or utilize communication theory in exploring CNM relational practices, the term communication and a variety of communication constructs can be found in nearly all research and writing about CNM people, communities, and relationships. When it comes to relationships, much of this research focuses on the relational maintenance practices that take place across multiple relationships and interpersonal communication skills emphasized in these communities. This section explores the interdisciplinary literature on relational maintenance and interpersonal skills in CNM relational communication, and specifically the research concerning jealousy communication and CNM relationships.

Interpersonal Skills in CNM Communities. Despite popular perceptions of consensual non-monogamy as relationally irresponsible, scholarly, applied, and popular work on

CNM relationship communication consistently finds a communal emphasis on interpersonal skill-building and responsible relationship communication practices. Conley and Moors (2014) argued that adopting the communication practices encouraged by the polyamorous community specifically may be beneficial to monogamous couples as well, highlighting the emphasis on interpersonal skills encouraged by the polyamorous community.

Specifically, Conley and Moors (2014) noted five general principles derived from previous research (Barker, 2005, 2013; Hardy & Easton, 2017, among others) about polyamorous relationships that may be psychologically helpful relational practices across a variety of monogamous and non-monogamous relational dynamics:

1. Individuals should not expect one person to be able to meet all of their needs.
2. One should not assume they will consistently be completely and solely sexually attracted to a single partner throughout the entire course of a relationship.
3. Engaging in multiple loving relationships (sexual and non-sexual) with other people is healthy and beneficial to both the individual and the relationship.
4. Communicating and openness with all partners is a key to having an ethical and successful relationship.
5. Individuals should both learn how to talk effectively about the relationship itself and schedule time to talk about the relationship(s) (Conley & Moors, 2014).

Of these items, 4 and 5 are explicitly geared toward communication practices embedded in the polyamorous community, including notions of openness, a relational maintenance behavior pivotal to relational success, and explicitly engaging in a taboo relational topic—the status of the relationship itself—with regularity.

Identity gaps, from the Communication Theory of Identity, are affective, cognitive, or behavioral discrepancies among or between layers of the self (i.e., personal, relational, enacted, or communal; see Jung & Hecht, 2004). Generally, identity gaps have a negative relationship with outcomes like relational satisfaction and resilience, but for individuals in polyamorous relationships the enactment of these prosocial maintenance behaviors tends to weaken that relationship (Rubinsky, 2019b). Rubinsky (2019b) investigated the moderating role of relational maintenance behaviors on the effect of identity gaps on relational satisfaction and resilience and found the presence of multiple prosocial or positive maintenance behaviors in polyamorous relationships. This included expanded access and involvement in social networks, advice, positivity, openness, and shared tasks, all of which weaken the negative effect of personal-relational identity gaps on resilience (Rubinsky, 2019b).

In addition to the interpersonal skills necessary for relational maintenance, work from outside the field of communication studies has investigated needs-communication and boundary setting as common practices in the polyamorous community. In a large-scale study of intimate relationships, Wosick-Correa (2010) introduced the notion of *agentic fidelity* to describe a form of commitment outside traditional notions of sexual fidelity that emphasizes ideas of choice and the ability to express boundaries and needs to one's partner(s). That is, agentic fidelity might describe a type of fidelity to the relational communication process, or loyalty to the process of establishing rules, agreements, and boundaries between one's self and one's partners (Wosick-Correa, 2010). Thus, boundary setting and the process of negotiating agreements between relational partners requires explicit interpersonal communication about the status of the relationship, as well as a high degree of openness. In sum, research on CNM communities and relational communication highlights the role of interpersonal skills and explicit emphasis on relational maintenance behaviors like openness.

"Don't You Get Jealous?" CNM and Jealousy Communication.

Much of the research on polyamory and communication both from within and outside the field of communication studies concerns conceptualization, communication, and relational maintenance around issues of jealousy. A well-documented response from friends, family, and society at large to an individual's disclosure of a polyamorous identity involves questions about relational jealousy (Deri, 2015; Mint, 2010; Rubinsky, 2018a). First, we will discuss how jealousy is conceptualized in CNM communities in light of compersion.

Conceptualizing Jealousy and Compersion. By most scholarly and popular accounts, jealousy is understood through a monogamous model that assumes the perception of a third party as a threat to perceptions of exclusivity in a romantic relationship (Deri, 2015; Easton et al., 1997; Mint, 2010; Rubinsky, 2018a; Wolfe, 2003). However, Ritchie and Barker (2006) found that polyamorous, bisexual individuals noted that the term "jealousy" seemed inadequate for how they understood and experienced this sensation. Polyamorous individuals still experience jealousy (Mint, 2010), but likely not as a result of the presence of a third party (Rubinsky, 2019a). In a qualitative study of 423 open-ended responses, Rubinsky (2018a) found that polyamorous individuals understood jealousy as an umbrella term for insecurity, possessiveness, or certain needs not being met within a particular relationship. Criticism of perceptions of monogamous persons as tolerating possessiveness as an acceptable relational behavior permeate CNM conceptualizations of jealousy. Specifically, participants in that study conceptualized monogamous understandings of jealousy as rooted in the idea that people are possessions, a problematic notion they believed was grounded in personal insecurity, and one that should be rejected. In addition, CNM participants noted that often jealousy was simply the feeling of not having a particular need met. For example, one might call the sensation of feeling like they are not receiving enough time or attention "jealousy" (Rubinsky, 2018a).

An important emotional response that may occur in polyamorous relationships either counter to feelings of jealousy or simultaneously with feelings of jealousy is *compersion*. The polyamorous community describes compersion as a positive emotional response elicited by a partner's happiness with another partner (Wolfe, 2003). The extent to which polyamorous individuals may experience the negative emotions associated with jealousy, such as anxiety, may be moderated by feelings of compersion and involvement in the polyamorous community (Duma, 2009; Wolfe, 2003). Mogilski et al. (2019) explored differences in mate-guarding behaviors as a response to jealousy in monogamous compared to CNM relationships, and suggested that CNM individuals may experience relational benefits from extradyadic interactions. Feelings of compersion in that sense may positively impact the initial relationship as well as extend positive feelings to other relational encounters. Exact conceptualizations of compersion and its relationship to jealousy are still being debated, but empirical work seems to suggest that compersion is overall a beneficial sensation. For example, sexual or relational encounters outside of a primary relationship may satisfy a person's desire for sexual novelty or increase the couple's social network, thereby benefiting both members of the pair (Mogilski et al., 2019).

Communicating Jealousy. Importantly, much of the research on polyamory and jealousy emphasizes the communicative nature of both polyamorous relationships and responses to jealousy. That is, individuals in polyamorous relationships seem both likely to discuss jealousy with their partner(s) and to have some tools from their community to help them engage these discussions in ways that are productive.

Polyamorous individuals sometimes discuss jealousy by explicitly seeking validation, affirmation, or acknowledgment. Rubinsky (2018a) found that polyamorous individuals described talking to their partner about jealousy not necessarily in an effort to change any behavior, especially toward third parties, but rather to seek validation that they and their relationship remain important to the person. In addition, polyamorous individuals describe discussing jealousy with their partner(s) in the context of negotiated agreements to add or remove an additional partner. In a study of swinging couples in southern England, de Visser and McDonald (2010) found that jealousy management involved discussion and negotiation, the development of a shared couple identity, and explicitly developing and communicating shared rules and boundaries. For swinging couples in the United Kingdom, feelings of jealousy may occur, but individuals in those relationships may not attempt to eliminate them entirely, preferring instead to manage them and encourage satisfying communication interactions (de Visser & McDonald, 2010). Scoats and Anderson (2019) investigated jealousy in mixed-sex threesomes and found that open communication was a method by which couples attempted to mitigate the negative effects of feelings of exclusion and jealousy. In addition, those from the study who were in a committed relationship identified the importance of establishing rules and reassuring their partner of the specialness of their primary relationship (Scoats & Anderson, 2019). Thus, qualitative research describes, in multiple CNM dynamics, the presence of conversations that explicitly acknowledge the occurrence of jealousy and relational communication that highlights the individual's needs and wants, rather than trying to alter their partner's behavior toward the third party.

Rubinsky (2019c) examined how identity gaps may explain some of the variation in relational or communication satisfaction attributed to jealousy for polyamorous individuals. In regression models, identity gaps and jealousy work together to predict changes in communication and relational satisfaction for individuals in polyamorous relationships (Rubinsky, 2019c). Thus, while it seems likely that productive conversations about jealousy may take place among CNM relationships, those conversations may also be highly connected to identity work. As with jealousy, compersion and how to have conversations about it are a part of polyamorous communal discourse, and people who identify as a part of that community may feel that these conversations not only impact their relationships but also reflect their participation in these social networks and communal identities (Rubinsky, 2019c).

COMMUNICATION, IDENTITY, AND POLYAMORY

All forms of CNM involve explicit communication by definition: achieving a state of the nonmonogamy being consensual involves communicating this. Polyamory specifically is often described as a communicated identity (Klesse, 2006; Ritchie & Barker, 2006; Table et al., 2017). As such, theories and research specific to the intersection of communication and identity have been usefully applied to polyamorous communication and relationships. In addition, identity theories may prove a useful direction for future research about communication and consensual non-monogamy. In previous research, the Communication Theory of Identity and Identity Management Theory have been applied to CNM and polyamorous research. The utility of these theories has helped advance understanding about the intercultural and intergroup nature of communication between monogamous and non-monogamous peoples and has furthered our understanding of the dynamics of CNM relationships. This section explores two particular studies that centered questions about communication and identity in research about CNM relationships.

Although less work has examined the intersections of nonpolyamorous forms of CNM and identity with communication, several studies have addressed the uniquely communicative nature of polyamory as an identity. Polyamorous relationships are considered sites of intercultural and intergroup communication (Table et al., 2017), in that "polyamorous culture shares not only a common language to describe their relationships but also an understanding of how relationships should work. When interacting with individuals who are monogamous about relationship-related topics, intercultural communication across these social groups occurs" (Table et al., 2017, p. 278). Polyamory may be thought of as a co-culture, or a cultural group outside of the dominant culture of monogamy (Orbe, 1998; Table et al., 2017). As a cultural group, polyamorous people manage a stigmatized identity (Anderson, 2010; Table et al., 2017). Although perhaps more accepted than other forms of CNM, like swinging (Matsick et al., 2014), polyamory is still viewed as a deviation from the norm, and people who are polyamorous report experiences with job loss and rejection from families, among other concerns (Rubinsky, 2018b; Sheff, 2005). At minimum, polyamorous identities counter normative understandings of what it means to be in a relationship, and those in polyamorous relationships engage in discursive work to legitimize their relationships to external parties (Dixon, 2016; Rubinsky, 2018b; Sheff, 2013).

In an interview study employing Identity Management Theory, Table et al. (2017) explored the interpersonal communication, identity management practices, and intercultural negotiations for polyamorous individuals situated within an otherwise mononormative and heteronormative culture in which their relational culture is often neglected. Polyamorous participants in this study all identified experiences with monogamous people reacting to their identity disclosure with stereotypical information that was often offensive (Table et al., 2017). Stereotypes of polyamorous individuals that they encountered as a response to their identity disclosures included polyamorous people as sexually deviant, selfish, less commitment-oriented, or unsustainable (Table et al., 2017). In addition, polyamorous individuals identified self-censoring in professional settings and evaluating the degree of risk and stigma associated with a disclosure as factors that filter selective self-disclosure decisions (Table et al., 2017). Responses to polyamorous disclosures that involve stereotyping or even intense curiosity can be face-threatening (Table et al., 2017). These challenges may emerge in a number of communication settings, including the workplace, friendships, romantic relationships, and the family.

Research on polyamorous family dynamics often explores identity and cultural communication needs as central concerns for those families. For instance, parents who are polyamorous identify disclosing their identity to their children, structural issues such as employment, and their relationships with extended family and friendship networks as salient concerns (Pallotta-Chiarolli et al., 2013). In another study that included both open-ended survey data and interviews with polyamorous people, reports of selective identity disclosure again suggested that polyamorous individuals are well aware of the consequences of their sometimes stigmatized identity, and the risks that disclosing that identity could involve, even in the family (Rubinsky, 2018b). Framed through Communication Privacy Management Theory (Petronio, 2002), the coming out literature, and research on discourse-dependent families (Galvin, 2006), Rubinsky (2018b) investigated the communication processes central to privacy negotiation for polyamorous individuals managing disclosure decisions and boundary negotiation across multiple generations of families including their siblings or peers, their own children, and their parents. Polyamorous people, especially those who also shared LGBTQ identities, sometimes compared the process of disclosing polyamorous identity to coming out as an LGBTQ identity (Rubinsky, 2018b).

Although understudied, insights into family communication in polyamorous and other CNM family dynamics may be insightful, as popular press and social psychology research suggest that polyamorous relationships promote healthy relationship practices and may even curb abuse (Klesse, 2006; Ritchie & Barker, 2006; Sheff, 2013). How these efforts may be accomplished by families whose members' identities must be "discovered, disclosed, and often defended" can offer insights for family and relational communication across the board (Rubinsky, 2018b, p. 22).

Findings from the family disclosure study included a typology of polyamorous disclosure within the family that ranged from not at all disclosed, minimally disclosed, selectively disclosed, mostly disclosed, to completely open with family (Rubinsky, 2018b). Importantly, findings also revealed that in determining rules for boundary management around their polyamorous identity disclosures, polyamorous individuals examined cultural norms and compatibilities between their polyamorous communities and their family of origin communities. Specifically, privacy rule decisions for those who can co-own information about their polyamory was often motivated by the degree of discrepancy between their polyamorous culture, often perceived as liberal, educated, and areligious, and their family-of-origin culture, which varied in their political orientation, religious orientation, and education. The most incompatible cultures occurred in families that participants described as highly conservative and Catholic. Polyamorous participants attributed the degree to which their cultures were in tension to their disclosure choices, often indicating that they were more selective or minimal in their disclosure when they believed their family culture was incompatible with their polyamorous culture. Similarly, participants whose families were perceived as more liberal and more accepting were more willing to disclose their identity mostly or fully. Specifically, participants often pointed to how a family treated members of the lesbian, gay, bisexual, transgender, and queer (LGBTQ) community or reacted to other family members coming out with an LGBTQ identity as an indicator of how they may react to polyamorous disclosures. Similar to Table et al. (2017), Rubinsky (2018b) concluded that polyamorous people largely consider their identity to be stigmatized, and, while the degree to which they consider their identity as private varied, even those who were very publicly polyamorous (e.g., activists and community organizers) generally understood the risk and stigma involved in revealing their identity to others (Rubinsky, 2018b) and assumed that how someone responded to other marginalized sexual and gender identities, like LGBTQ identities, might predict their reaction to a polyamorous disclosure.

Findings from research that explores the intersections of identity, communication, and CNM, focused mostly on polyamory specifically, generally suggest that managing a stigmatized identity that necessitates disclosure can result in cultural and personal dilemmas for those involved. Polyamorous people selectively disclose their identity and relationships based on a number of cultural cues that suggest how accepting the receiver might be, as well as the potential consequences of a negative reaction.

AREAS FOR FUTURE RESEARCH

Despite advances in research at the intersection of relational communication and CNM, overall the work that has been done is exploratory. CNM communities are highly underrepresented in the interpersonal communication literature, which tends to assume monogamy as a characteristic of romantic relationships. Thus, relational communication research attending to practices in CNM communities is warranted, and there is much work to be done.

Broadly speaking, many relational communication constructs would warrant exploration within CNM communities. While some recent work has explored the conceptualization and communication of jealousy in polyamorous communities, this work is exploratory in nature and requires further research. Future research may investigate questions such as how communal identity discourses interact with interpersonal relational communication about jealousy in CNM communities. In addition, the question remains of how the experiences and communication of compersion and jealousy coexist or contradict one another, and with what consequences, for individuals in CNM relationships. Communication research is well positioned to explore these and other questions. Further, the intersections of LGBTQ identities, polyamory, and jealousy communication are underexplored, with sexual identity usually only mentioned as a demographic detail in those studies. Future research might be well suited to explore these intersections in greater depth.

Despite reference to relational maintenance strategies across CNM relationships, only one study explicitly explored the presence and impact of relational maintenance strategies in CNM communities, focusing explicitly on polyamorous relationships (Rubinsky, 2019b). Future communication research may be well suited to explore what varied relational maintenance strategies look like in polyamorous communities. Although initial investigations suggest that polyamorous relationships are relatively independent of one another (Mitchell et al., 2014), more work investigating how communication in one relationship affects another might also be worthwhile.

Only a small body of literature has looked at sexual communication in CNM communities (see Dixon, 2016), and polyamorous folks are generally combined with other sexual minority groups (e.g., Kattari, 2015; Rubinsky, 2019a). Sexual communication is an important facet of relational communication. CNM communities may benefit from increased attention to issues like boundary negotiation and relational openness (Wosick-Korea, 2010), but little work has explicitly explored how CNM relationships discuss issues relating to sexual activity or sexual health. This is a meaningful area for future research. In addition, although swinging relationships have received attention from researchers studying CNM dynamics, they predominantly focus on heterosexual couples. Further research may benefit from exploring the intersections of swinging and LGBTQ communities.

In addition, reflecting a limitation of CNM research in many pockets of the community, such as polyamorous communities, much of the scholarship on CNM relational communication focuses on extremely White samples. Exploring how similar or dissimilar practices emerge and to what end in CNM communities of color warrants focused attention (see Sheff & Hammers, 2011, for a more thorough discussion of Whiteness and increasing representation in samples targeting polyamorists and people who practice BDSM).

CONCLUSION

Relationship communication research surrounding CNM communities is limited, and the studies that exist have focused primarily on only one form of CNM: polyamory. This research is generally limited by sample and methodology. From the work that has been done, it can be surmised that CNM relationships emphasize communication about needs and boundaries, compersion and jealousy management, and increased social networks. Despite the positivity that might characterize the communication within CNM relationships, communication about CNM relationships, particularly to monogamous peoples, remains highly stigmatized and often results in emotional and material consequences.

FURTHER READING

Barker, M. (2005). On tops, bottoms and ethical sluts: The place of BDSM and polyamory in lesbian and gay psychology. *Lesbian and Gay Psychology Review*, 6(2), 124–129. http://oro.open.ac.uk/17267/2/5470e82f.pdf

Easton, D. (2010). Making friends with jealousy. In M. Barker & D. Langdridge (Eds.), *Understanding non-monogamies* (pp. 207–211). Routledge.

Sheff, E. (2013). *The polyamorists next door: Inside multiple-partner relationships and families*. Rowman & Littlefield.

Sheff, E., & Hammers, C. (2011). The privilege of perversities: Race, class, and education among polyamorists and kinksters. *Psychology and Sexuality*, 3, 198–223. http://doi.org/10.1080/19419899.2010.537674

REFERENCES

Adam, B. D. (2006). Relationship innovation in male couples. *Sexualities*, 9(1), 5–26. http://doi.org/10.1177/1363460706060685

Aguilar, J. (2013). Situational sexual behaviors: The ideological work of moving toward polyamory in communal living groups. *Journal of Contemporary Ethnography*, 42(1), 104–129. http://doi.org/10.1177/0891241612464886

Anderson, E. (2010). "At least with cheating there is an attempt at monogamy": Cheating and monogamism among undergraduate heterosexual men. *Journal of Social and Personal Relationships*, 27, 851–872. http://doi.org/10.1177/0265407510373908

Balzarini, R. N., Campbell, L., Kohut, T., Holmes, B. M., Lehmiller, J. J., Harman, J. J., & Atkins, N. (2017). Perceptions of primary and secondary relationships in polyamory. *PLOS One*, 12(5), e0177841. https://doi.org/10.1371/journal.pone.0177841

Barker, M. (2005). This is my partner, and this is my partner's partner: Constructing a polyamorous identity in a monogamous world. *Journal of Constructivist Psychology, 18*, 75–88. http://doi.org/10.1080/10720530590523107

Barker, M. (2013). *Rewriting the rules: An integrative guide to love, sex and relationships*. Routledge.

Barker, M., & Langdridge, D. (2010). Whatever happened to non-monogamies? Critical reflections on recent research and theory. *Sexualities, 13*(6), 748–772. http://doi.org/10.1177/1363460710384645

Bentzen, A., & Træen, B. (2014). Swinging in Norway in the context of sexual health. *Sexuality and Culture, 18*, 132–148. http://doi.org/10.1007/s12119-013-9181-6

Coelho, T. (2011). Hearts, groins and the intricacies of gay male open relationships: Sexual desire and liberation revisited. *Sexualities, 14*(6), 653–668. http://doi.org/10.1177/1363460711422306

Cohen, M. T., & Wilson, K. (2017). Development of the consensual non-monogamy attitude scale (CNAS). *Sexuality and Culture, 21*(1), 1–14. http://doi.org/10.1007/s12119-016-9395-5

Conley, T. D., & Moors, A. C. (2014). More oxygen please! How polyamorous relationship strategies might oxygenate marriage. *Psychological Inquiry, 25*, 56–63. http://doi.org/10.1080/1047840X.2014.876908

Deri, J. (2015). *Love's refraction: Jealousy and compersion in queer women's polyamorous relationships*. University of Toronto Press.

de Visser, R., & McDonald, D. (2010). Swings and roundabouts: Management of jealousy in heterosexual "swinging" couples. *British Journal of Social Psychology, 46*(2), 459–476. http://doi.org/10.1348/014466606X143153

Dixon, J. (2016). Polyamory, sex, and the communication of commitment. In J. Manning & C. Noland (Eds.), *Contemporary studies of sexuality and communication: Theoretical and applied perspectives* (pp. 143–154). Kendall Hunt.

Duma, U. (2009). *Jealousy and compersion in close relationships: Coping styles by relationship types*. GRIN Verlag.

Easton, D., Liszt, C. A., Dodson, B., Nearing, R., Magazine, L. M., Anapol, D., & Stan Dale, D. H. S. (1997). *The ethical slut: A practical guide to polyamory, open relationships and other adventures*. Greenery Press.

Galvin, K. M. (2006). Diversity's impact on defining the family. In L. Turner & R. West (Eds.), *The family communication sourcebook* (pp. 3–19). SAGE.

Graham, N. (2014). Polyamory: A call for increased mental health professional awareness. *Archives of Sexual Behavior, 43*, 1031–1034. http://doi.org/10.1007/s10508-014-0321-3

Grunt-Mejer, K., & Campbell, C. (2016). Around consensual nonmonogamies: Assessing attitudes toward nonexclusive relationships. *Journal of Sex Research, 53*(1), 45–53. https://doi.org/10.1080/00224499.2015.1010193

Gusmano, B. (2018). Coming out through an intersectional perspective: Narratives of bisexuality and polyamory in Italy. *Journal of Bisexuality, 18*(1), 15–34. http://doi.org/10.1080/15299716.2017.1416510

Hardy, J. W., & Easton, D. (2017). *The ethical slut: A practical guide to polyamory, open relationships, and other freedoms in sex and love*. Ten Speed Press.

Haritaworn, J., Lin, C., & Klesse, C. (2006). Poly/logue: A critical introduction to polyamory. *Sexualities, 9*(5), 515–529. http://doi.org/10.1177/1363460706069963

Harviainen, J. T., & Frank, K. (2018). Group sex as play: Rules and transgression in shared non-monogamy. *Games and Culture, 13*(3), 220–239. http://doi.org/10.1177/1555412016659835

Haupert, M. L., Gesselman, A. N., Moors, A. C., Fisher, H. E., & Garcia, J. R. (2017). Prevalence of experiences with consensual nonmonogamous relationships: Findings from two national samples of single Americans. *Journal of Sex and Marital Therapy, 43*(5), 424–440. http://doi.org/10.1080/0092623X.2016.1178675

Hosking, W. (2014). Australian gay men's satisfaction with sexual agreements: The roles of relationship quality, jealousy, and monogamy attitudes. *Archives of Sexual Behavior, 43*, 823–832. http://doi.org/10.1007/s10508-013-0197-7

Jenks, R. J. (1998). Swinging: A review of the literature. *Archives of Sexual Behavior, 27*(5), 507–521. http://doi.org/10.1023/A:1018708730945

Jenks, R. J. (2014). An online survey comparing swingers and polyamorists. *Electronic Journal of Human Sexuality, 17*. http://www.ejhs.org/volume17/swing.html

Jordan, L. S., Grogan, C., Muruthi, B., & Bermúdez, J. M. (2017). Polyamory: Experiences of power from without, from within, and in between. *Journal of Couple and Relationship Therapy, 16*(1), 1–19. http://doi.org/10.1080/15332691.2016.1141135

Jung, E., & Hecht, M. L. (2004). Elaborating the communication theory of identity: Identity gaps and communication outcomes. *Communication Quarterly, 52*, 265–283. http://doi.org/10.1080/01463370409370197

Kattari, S. K. (2015). "Getting it": Identity and sexual communication for sexual and gender minorities with physical disabilities. *Sexuality and Culture, 19*(4), 882–899. http://doi.org/10.1007/s12119-015-9298-x

Kimberly, C. (2019). A measurement to assess transition, maintenance and satisfaction in the swinging lifestyle. *Journal of Family Therapy, 41*, 559–581. http://doi.org/10.1111/1467-6427.12239

Kimberly, C., & Hans, J. D. (2017). From fantasy to reality: A grounded theory of experiences in the swinging lifestyle. *Archives of Sexual Behavior, 46*, 789–799. http://doi.org/10.1007/s10508-015-0621-2

Klesse, C. (2006). Polyamory and its "others": Contesting the terms of non-monogamy. *Sexualities, 9*(5), 565–583. http://doi.org/10.1177/1363460706069986

Klesse, C. (2014). Polyamory: Intimate practice, identity or sexual orientation? *Sexualities, 17*(1/2), 81–99. http://doi.org/10.1177/1363460713511096

Klesse, C. (2016). Marriage, law and polyamory: Rebutting mononormativity with sexual orientation discourse?. *Oñati Socio-Legal Series, 6*(6). https://papers.ssrn.com/sol3/papers.cfm?abstract_id=2891035

Levine, E. C., Herbenick, D., Martinez, O., Fu, T. C., & Dodge, B. (2018). Open relationships, nonconsensual nonmonogamy, and monogamy among U.S. adults: Findings from the 2012 national survey of sexual health and behavior. *Archives of Sexual Behavior, 47*, 1439–1450. http://doi.org/10.1007/s10508-018-1178-7

Manley, M. H., Diamond, L. M., & van Anders, S. M. (2015). Polyamory, monoamory, and sexual fluidity: A longitudinal study of identity and sexual trajectories. *Psychology of Sexual Orientation and Gender Diversity, 2*(2), 168–180. http://doi.org/10.1037/sgd0000098

Matsick, J. L., Conley, T. D., Ziegler, A., Moors, A. C., & Rubin, J. D. (2014). Love and sex: Polyamorous relationships are perceived more favourably than swinging and open relationships. *Psychology and Sexuality, 5*(4), 339–348. http://doi.org/10.1080/19419899.2013.832934

Mint, P. (2010). The power mechanisms of jealousy. In M. Barker & D. Langdridge (Eds.), *Understanding non-monogamies* (pp. 201–206). Routledge.

Mitchell, M. E., Bartholomew, K., & Cobb, R. J. (2014). Need fulfillment in polyamorous relationships. *Journal of Sex Research, 51*(3), 329–339. http://doi.org/10.1080/00224499.2012.742998

Mogilski, J. K., Reeve, S. D., Nicolas, S. C., Donaldson, S. H., Mitchell, V. E., & Welling, L. L. (2019). Jealousy, consent, and compersion within monogamous and consensually non-monogamous romantic relationships. *Archives of Sexual Behavior, 48*(6), 1811–1828. http://doi.org/10.1007/s10508-018-1286-4

Moors, A. C. (2017). Has the American public's interest in information related to relationships beyond "the couple" increased over time? *Journal of Sex Research, 54*(6), 677–684. http://doi.org/10.1080/00224499.2016.1178208

Moors, A. C., Conley, T. D., Edelstein, R. S., & Chopik, W. J. (2015). Attached to monogamy? Avoidance predicts willingness to engage (but not actual engagement) in consensual non-monogamy. *Journal of Social and Personal Relationships, 32*(2), 222–240. http://doi.org/10.1177/0265407514529065

Moors, A. C., Rubin, J. D., Matsick, J. L., Ziegler, A., & Conley, T. D. (2014). It's not just a gay male thing: Sexual minority women and men are equally attracted to consensual non-monogamy. *Journal für Psychologie, 22*(1), 38–51. https://digitalcommons.chapman.edu/psychology_articles/132/

Orbe, M. P. (1998). From the standpoint(s) of traditionally muted groups: Explicating a co-cultural communication theoretical model. *Communication Theory, 8*(1), 1–26. https://doi.org/10.1111/j.1468-2885.1998.tb00209.x

Pain, E. (2019). Queer polyfamily performativity: Family practices and adaptive strategies among LGBTQ+ polyamorists. *Journal of GLBT Family Studies, 16*(3), 277–292. http://doi.org/10.1080/1550428X.2019.1596858

Pallotta-Chiarolli, M., Haydon, P., & Hunter, A. (2013). "These are our children": Polyamorous parenting. In A. E. Goldberg & K. R. Allen (Eds.), *LGBT-parent families* (pp. 117–131). Springer.

Petronio, S. (2002). *Boundaries of privacy: Dialectics of disclosure*. State University of New York Press.

Pitagora, D. (2016). The kink-poly confluence: Relationship intersectionality in marginalized communities. *Sexual and Relationship Therapy, 31*(3), 391–405. http://doi.org/10.1080/14681994.2016.1156081

Ritchie, A., & Barker, M. (2006). "There aren't words for what we do or how we feel so we have to make them up": Constructing polyamorous languages in a culture of compulsory monogamy. *Sexualities, 9*(5), 584–601. http://doi.org/10.1177/1363460706069987

Robinson, M. (2013). Polyamory and monogamy as strategic identities. *Journal of Bisexuality, 13*, 21–38. http://doi.org/10.1080/15299716.2013.755731

Rubel, A. N., & Bogaert, A. F. (2015). Consensual nonmonogamy: Psychological well-being and relationship quality correlates. *Journal of Sex Research, 52*(9), 961–982. http://doi.org/10.1080/00224499.2014.942722

Rubinsky, V. (2018a). Bringing up the green-eyed monster: Conceptualizing and communicating jealousy with a partner who has other partners. *Qualitative Report, 23*, 1441–1455. https://nsuworks.nova.edu/tqr/vol23/iss6/11/

Rubinsky, V. (2018b). Revealing or concealing polyamory in the family: Cultural rules for communicating polyamory to family members. *Women and Language, 41*, 16–38.

Rubinsky, V. (2019a). *Extending sex as an intergroup arena: Testing the mediating role and management of identity gaps in sexual communication on relational, sexual, and health outcomes in "non-normative" relationships* (Doctoral dissertation, Ohio University).

Rubinsky, V. (2019b). Extending the theory of resilience and relational load into polyamorous relationships. *Interpersona, 13*, 144–170. http://doi.org/10.5964/ijpr.v13i2.364

Rubinsky, V. (2019c). Identity gaps and jealousy as predictors of satisfaction in polyamorous relationships. *Southern Communication Journal, 84*, 17–29. http://doi.org/10.1080/1041794X.2018.1531916

Scoats, R., & Anderson, E. (2019). "My partner was just all over her": Jealousy, communication and rules in mixed-sex threesomes. *Culture, Health and Sexuality, 21*(2), 134–146. http://doi.org/10.1080/13691058.2018.1453088

Sheff, E. (2005). Polyamorous women, sexual subjectivity, and power. *Journal of Contemporary Ethnography, 34*, 251–283. http://doi.org/10.1037/e512142015-905

Sheff, E. (2013). *The polyamorists next door: Inside multiple-partner relationships and families*. Rowman & Littlefield.

Sheff, E., & Hammers, C. (2011). The privilege of perversities: Race, class, and education among polyamorists and kinksters. *Psychology and Sexuality, 3*, 198–223. http://doi.org/10.1080/19419899.2010.537674

Sizemore, K. M., & Olmstead, S. B. (2017). Testing the validity and factor structure of the willingness to engage in consensual non-monogamy scale among college men and women. *Sexuality Research and Social Policy, 14*, 182–191. http://doi.org/10.1007/s13178-016-0263-8

Table, B., Sandoval, J. A., & Weger, H. (2017). Transitions in polyamorous identity and intercultural communication: An application of identity management theory. *Journal of Bisexuality, 17*(3), 277–299. http://doi.org/10.1080/15299716.2017.1350897

Vaillancourt, K. T., & Few-Demo, A. L. (2014). Relational dynamics of swinging relationships: An exploratory study. *Family Journal, 22*(3), 311–320. http://doi.org/10.1177/1066480714529742

West, C. (1996). *Lesbian polyfidelity*. Booklegger Publishing.
Williams, D. J., & Prior, E. E. (2015). Contemporary polyamory: A call for awareness and sensitivity in social work. *Social Work, 60*(3), 268–270. http://doi.org/10.1093/sw/swv012
Wolfe, L. (2003). *Jealousy and transformation in polyamorous relationships* (Unpublished manuscript). Institute for Advanced Study of Human Sexuality, San Francisco, CA.
Wosick-Correa, K. (2010). Agreements, rules and agentic fidelity in polyamorous relationships. *Psychology and Sexuality, 1*, 44–61. http://doi.org/10.1080/19419891003634471

Valerie Rubinsky and Lucy C. Niess

SEX WORK, QUEER ECONOMIC JUSTICE, AND COMMUNICATIVE ETHICS

SEX WORK IN COMMUNICATION STUDIES

The year 2020 was a transformative year for the digital sex industry. Amid a pandemic, disruptions to the global supply chain, devastating climate disasters, a tanking economy, and surges of political violence, 136 million people still visited PornHub on a daily basis (PornHub, 2020). In fact, when the initial waves of coronavirus shutdowns hit early in the year, regions that implemented stay-at-home orders witnessed a massive spike in consumption through the site (PornHub, 2020). Meanwhile, this very same cocktail of conditions led to massive unemployment for workers in several sectors. In early April, the adult media platform OnlyFans saw a 75% increase in new content creators looking to generate income (Lòpez, 2020). In addition to industry newcomers, sex workers who typically relied on face-to-face interactions such as in strip clubs, red light districts, or escort services were forced to reevaluate; for many, moving online was the safest choice. While digital pornography, webcam modeling, and other online adult entertainment practices have existed for decades, the exceptional conditions of the pandemic revealed how crucial the sex industry is for creating and sustaining forms of human connection, especially when conventional means of connection become unavailable.

Even with this mainstreaming of digital sex work, communicating about sex work can be fraught with controversy. Debates about the ethical and ideological implications of sex work are long-standing and difficult to resolve given the diversity of practices that might be called sex work. For the purposes of this article, the term "sex work" is meant in its broadest sense to mean any form of exchange in which money, gifts, or resources are traded for a sexual or erotic experience. Sex work thus encompasses activities that are legal and illegal, consensual and nonconsensual, mutually beneficial and exploitative (Weitzer, 2012, p. 3). Similarly, the term "sex worker" is meant to implicate anyone who participates in the industry as a provider, including performers, models, producers, staff, and third parties who facilitate these exchanges. The ambiguity of sex work and sex worker has some tactical communicative advantage in that the terms can unite different parts of the industry under a shared identity and constitute a community to which individuals can turn for help and resources. Learning how to communicate about sex work is a vital part of making the industry safer for everyone involved. As discourse about sex work continues to proliferate, communication studies scholars can help bridge gaps of understanding by critically examining the language that shapes their perceptions.

One communication strategy that can reduce the stigma about sex work is to consider it from the perspective of economic justice. Economic justice is a perspective that acknowledges and responds to the exploitation intrinsic to present systems by exploring the means of resistance. In the long term, those committed to economic justice envision forms of distribution and exchange that ensure everyone's needs are met without privileging profit over people. In the short term, economic justice aims to provide mutual aid and other forms of immediate relief to individuals and communities in need of material support. Economic justice can take on many forms and often requires multiple tactics and avenues of change. Rather than communicating about economic justice monolithically, it is helpful to make meaning of it in specific contexts, as it might pertain to particular industries, populations, and commodities.

In a contemporary context, the concept of queer economic justice emerged in response to the marginalization of class struggle in the mainstream LGBT movement. From 2002 to 2014, an activist organization in New York City, "Queers for Economic Justice," worked to address issues such as poverty, addiction, and homelessness in the queer and trans communities—but, of course, a lack of financial support seriously hindered these efforts, and the organization eventually closed (Lefkowitz, 2017). Therefore, in addition to practicing economic justice to make sure that queer people are fed, housed, and provided opportunity in the short term, the attendant long-term project must involve a critique of the economic rationalities of success. Without an intersectional, queer-of-color critique of what counts as economic justice, the multidimensionality of queerness becomes flattened into an umbrella LGBT identity (Ferguson, 2019). Nothing could be more fatal to the principle of queer economic justice than its assimilation into current structures of wealth and white supremacy at the expense of the working class and communities of color. Queer economic justice is a decidedly intersectional endeavor.

The discussion of sex work in the communication studies discipline is not new; however, much of the emphasis of this discussion has focused on nonconsensual forms of sex work such as sex trafficking and commercial exploitation (Anderson, 2013; Hill, 2019; Palczewski, 1995). Examining the communicative dimensions of sex trafficking as a phenomenon equips scholars to better understand how dominant frames can efface or enable the experiences of victims and survivors and how the framings of that violence impact the culture more broadly. Although scholars may focus on one aspect of the sex industry or another, a complete understanding of the field requires acknowledgment that there is a broad range of possible experiences with consent in the industry. There is a gulf of difference between consensual sex work and commodified sexual violence, and yet both are components of the same global sex industry and share some of the same issues in terms of how they are legislated and policed, which creates problems for both consenting sex workers and victims of trafficking. Conversations about sex work must be nuanced by this distinction, which requires an eye toward the ethical dimensions of a given context and situation. Thus, ethics are often a central component to research on sex work.

There are innumerable perspectives on what kinds of sexual acts, desires, and relations are ethical; rather than sort through these ethics one by one, a broader perspective may consider the process by which ethics are created, maintained, and shifted. Historically, LGBT and other sexual minorities have experienced marginalization on the basis of a normalizing ethic, which uses monogamous cisheteronormativity and the sexual practices implicit in such an arrangement as an ideal against which all others are stigmatized. The taboo against discussing sexuality bolsters these homogenizing norms, encouraging a divide between private and public life.

As an alternative to a normalizing ethic, a communicative ethic "shifts moral judgements about the character of sexual desires and acts to the qualities of the social exchange and communication encounter, such as mutual consent, responsibility, respect, and reciprocity" (Yep, 2003, p. 47). Focusing on the contexts that frame the sexual exchange rather than exclusively on the nature of the sexual exchange helps articulate broader social forces that set up the field of possibilities for consent. A communicative ethic is not an absence of ethical discernment nor is it blanket relativism—on the contrary, it requires an appreciation of the multidimensionality of gendered and sexual relations, an attunement to the needs and desires of all, and a keen eye toward the ways in which prevailing systems of oppression inflect intimate interactions. From such a perspective, there is nothing inherently wrong with monetary sexual exchange between consenting adults, and there can be no justification for slavery, violence, or coercion.

Although some forms of consensual sex work have become more widespread and normalized, there are still considerable social and legal barriers for sex workers around the world seeking to secure their rights and safety. Laws that govern sex work vary from nation to nation and from municipality to municipality. Ranging from criminalization to legalization, systems that regulate the sex industry intervene in the market and determine the ways in which capital can or cannot flow legally. An illegal sex trade may coexist with legal sex work if the legal models are insufficient to fulfill market needs or if they overly complicate processes like business licensing. Due to the harmful ways in which the criminalization of sex work compounds existing social inequities along lines of race, class, and gender, imagining alternative communicative frameworks beyond carceral punishment is a way to address interlocking structures of oppression that threaten sex workers' lives and livelihoods.

As a primer to the critical study of sex work, this article first offers a historiography of the academic debates on sex work and pornography in feminist academic discourse during the "sex wars" of the 1970s and 1980s. Updating the terms of this debate to conditions of the present and future, three interconnected topics are further detailed over the course of this article: the labor framing of sex work, sex work under the conditions of neoliberalism, and alternatives to the criminalization of sex work,. Altogether, this summary of conceptual conversations aims to inspire new questions and novel forms of communicating about sex work and economic justice that reject prevailing frameworks in order to bring forth a world that is more hospitable to queer bodies and practices.

HISTORIOGRAPHY: THE SEX WARS

Although public discourse about the ethics of sex work might be traced in a number of ways, general perspectives on the issue in academia are still informed by feminist debates on sexuality during the Women's Liberation Movement. After the sexual revolution, when the birth control pill became widely available and heterosexual norms were being openly called into question, feminist theorists sought to better understand the ways in which sex was articulated with broader gender relations. When it came to sex work in particular, theorists were polarized on whether sex work was inherently a form of patriarchal domination that should be prohibited or a nonnormative means of income that should be destigmatized. This fissure in opinion came to be known colloquially as the sex wars.

Pornography was a major area of contestation that structured these debates and remains a major focus of scholarship on sex work. Over the course of the 20th century, the growth of media technologies made pornography increasingly accessible in a variety of formats such as magazines, movies, posters, and eventually digital content. In addition to format, the style and content of pornography changed as the viewership moved from topless centerfolds to full-length films, with a proliferation of materials catering to specific kinks and niche audiences. As the pornography industry expanded, feminist critics voiced their critiques and concerns regarding the impact of pornography on gender relations and sexuality. Although a number of perspectives on pornography and feminism existed then and persist today, this historiography provides a brief overview of some of the major voices in the sex wars in order to primarily illustrate the contrast among stances.

During the late 1970s and 1980s, antipornography activism became more pronounced within the Women's Liberation Movement. In 1976, the release of Michael Finlay's grindhouse film *Snuff*, which was marketed as depicting the actual murder and dismemberment of a pregnant woman, prompted movie theater protests in Los Angeles. Activist Marcia Womongold worked to organize a coalition called Women Against Violence Against Women (WAVAW), which successfully campaigned to end circulation of the film in theaters in southern California. WAVAW's strategy was not to advocate for censorship of pornography outright but to take objection to particularly sexist and violent imagery wherever it appeared in media, pressuring corporations to act responsibly in discerning the images they reproduced and distributed (Comella, 2015, pp. 445–446).

Meanwhile, another California-based group, Women Against Violence in Pornography and Media (WAVMP), took a more radical stance that condemned pornography as a precursor of rape and focused on protesting in overtly sexualized urban spaces in the San Francisco area, such as the Mitchell Brothers Theater, which offered live sex shows, as well as massage parlors and pornography shops (Comella, 2015, p. 447). Concurrently with the release of *Snuff*, a group of antipornography feminists known as Women Against Pornography (WAP) formed in New York City. WAP would go on to use materials and strategies from both California organizations to push for similar goals (Comella, 2015, p. 450). Although WAVAW, WAVMP, and WAP cautioned that pornography could be linked to violence, WAVAW's focus was on the violence of content, not sexual obscenity; by comparison, WAP and WAVMP opposed forms of sexual expression that included consensual practice. This ideological split between activists who saw all pornography as intrinsically problematic and those who only took issue with particularly violent forms was a distinctive characteristic of this period of antipornography feminism.

Criticism of antipornography rhetoric echoed from queer and kink communities who took issue with these organizations' aims to sanitize the city streets of overtly erotic spaces and censor consensual forms of expression, taking away the little visibility that sexual minorities had recently gained. One particularly audible voice of opposition came from Samois, a San Francisco-based organization devoted to supporting lesbian sadomasochism. Samois posited that the principles of feminism and sadomasochism could be in consistency as long as those practices were safe, consensual, and mutually fulfilling (Rubin, 2003, p. 4). Rather than framing their politics and critique of antipornography activism in feminist terms, Samois "was instead groping toward a proto-queer politics that contained a broader and more inclusive sense of sexual oppression based on specifically sexual inequalities" (Rubin, 2003, p. 4). By staking a claim not only with "women" as broadly constructed but also on an axis of sexual oppression—which affects more than only women—Samois publicly represented a sex-positive or pro-sex position that opened feminism up to the issues and interests of the kink, queer, and sex worker communities.

If these 20th-century debates around pornography, sadomasochism, and other forms of nonnormative sex have been remembered as a "war," then the April 1982 conference at Barnard College in New York City, entitled "Towards a Politics of Sexuality," was perhaps the most decisive battle among these major players (Stein & Press, 1985, p. 205). During the planning stages, conference organizers sought to center more sex-positive voices rather than give antipornography feminism an additional platform, which led a certain "Coalition of Women for a Feminist Sexuality and Against Sadomasochism" to picket outside of the conference, passing out leaflets that objected to their exclusion from conference planning and that condemned sadomasochism as irredeemably patriarchal (Wilson, 1983, p. 37). Indeed, the conference was intended to exclude these perspectives not merely by oversight, but because organizers wanted to "challenge the conservative feminist sexual discourse that held sway in the women's movement" (Comella, 2015, p. 452). Given how intelligibly antipornography feminism already fit within the puritanical traditions of sexual discourse in the United States, excluding antipornography feminists in favor of a more sex-positive platform was extremely bold, especially for the time.

Of the many papers presented at the conference, one of the best remembered was entitled "Thinking Sex: Notes for a Radical Theory of the Politics of Sexuality," by Gayle Rubin (Rubin, 1984). Combining historical and contemporary examples of the hierarchal disciplining of sexual deviance, the article detailed how "sex is a vector of oppression" (Rubin, 1984, p. 2). The author listed and detailed five ideological formations that structured discourse at the expense of sexual minorities: "sex negativity, the fallacy of the misplaced scale, the hierarchal valuation of sex acts, the domino theory of sexual peril, and the lack of a concept of benign sexual variation" (Rubin, 1984, p. 11). The first two of these formations essentially conveyed that the puritanical sexual culture that emerged from Christian traditions viewed sex as inherently sinful and put a great deal of misplaced significance on sexuality. The article expressed the hierarchal valuation of sex acts by contrasting a "charmed circle" of sanctified acts (e.g., married, monogamous, vanilla, heterosexual) with "the outer limits" of sinful sexuality (e.g., nonmarried, polyamorous, sadomasochistic, homosexual), and connected this valuation with the privileges that came to those who remained within the charmed circle (Rubin, 1984, p. 13). The final two of these formations suggested that once a person crossed a line from sanctioned to nonnormative sexual acts, their deviance was bound to slip out of their control, and any variation from the sanctioned acts signaled danger. The essay moved from theoretical discussions about sexual oppression to contemporary applications that signaled how antipornography and antiprostitution legislation—what the author referred to as "sex law"—actually harmed communities by enabling criminalization, social stratification, and innumerable forms of marginalization of sexual minorities. In the concluding pages, Rubin referenced "the current right-wing sexual counter-offensive" as a reaction to the sexual revolution of the 1960s and hopefully remarked that the discourse that were emerging from "the sex wars out on the streets" were "provoking a new intellectual focus on sexuality" (Rubin, 1984, p. 34). From these closing remarks, then, came the recognition that any discourse on sexuality was at least breaking the long-standing taboo of academically discussing sex at all.

While the Barnard Conference and the discourse it generated "are watershed events in U.S. feminist theory," it was not the last word on the pornography debate (Hennessy, 2018, p. 185). Even though sex-positive theorists articulated possibilities for a more empowering world of sexual expression, there was no denying that legitimate harms existed in the sex industry and still exist today. In 1983, antipornography feminist scholars Andrea Dworkin and Catherine MacKinnon drafted an ordinance for the city of Minneapolis that defined pornography as a violation of women's civil rights (MacKinnon, 1985). Although the ordinance was not ultimately upheld, MacKinnon and Dworkin continued to advocate on behalf of victims of exploitation, coercion, and trafficking in the pornography industry, both in print and in courts of law.

At first glance, antipornography feminism and sex-positive feminism seem fundamentally at odds; indeed, much of the history recounted here supports the presumption of separation between these ideologies. In hindsight, however, both stances functioned under a shared commitment to alter the patriarchal status quo and to cast awareness on issues that were still considered relatively taboo for women to discuss publicly and professionally. The memory of these heated debates as a war certainly holds precedence; however, over the course of space and time, scholars looking back may find that the desire for more mutual, consensual, and empowering sexual relations was not exclusive to one side or another. Both sides were concerned with addressing the victimization and patriarchal oppression of vulnerable populations but differed dramatically on how to best approach social change on this front.

SEX WORK AND LABOR

"Sex work is work" is a common refrain in sex work activism. This statement is meant primarily as a call for recognition of the various ways in which sex work resembles other forms of work, and sex workers are therefore deserving of rights and protections under a labor frame. Many researchers agree that recognizing the labor of sex workers is a necessary and immediate step toward improving their material conditions (Bernstein, 2018, p. 52; Mahdavi, 2011, p. 62; Rodríguez, 2014, p. 16). Acknowledging sex work as labor replaces the harmful idea that people are selling or renting out their bodies or parts of their bodies as commodities that can be somehow separated from the self (Rudrappa, 2015, p. 108). Of course, sex work involves work, and many entertainers and other legal workers function as contractors, claiming income and expenses each year on their taxes. In the eyes of tax law, they are not so different from a plumber or a freelance artist. Regardless of how documented or taxed the work is, the work remains work. For feminist theorists, the connection between sex work and labor is an important area to consider from multiple angles because while the simplicity of the notion that sex work is work holds true, thinking critically about each category implied in that statement invites more opportunities to reconsider communicative tactics that resist previously held assumptions.

As subjects of analysis, the categories of sex work and sex worker cannot be universalized. Early on in her field studies of sex workers in Cuba and the Dominican Republic, Amalia Cabezas realized that "the 'sex worker' did not exist, was ambiguous, or at the very least was quite an unstable subject" (Cabezas, 2009, p. 8). The first issue is the word and concept of sex, which is steeped in colonial cisheteronormative assumptions and which should not be superimposed globally to all erotic practices (Cabezas, 2009, p. 20; Petillo, 2018, p. 330). A queer critique of the notion of sex cannot leave it categorically naturalized but considers it instead as a cultural construction full of arbitrary thresholds. Second, sex work obscures the intimacy possible in some monetary sexual exchanges, whether these exchanges are long-term or ephemeral; not all who engage in sex for material benefit would consider themselves workers or what they do as work but may understand these exchanges more personally and affectively in ways that approximate romance (Cabezas, 2009, p. 12). Sex work can be a cultivation or degradation of the self, depending on the relationship of the person to their practices and how they make meaning of those practices. Sex work and sex worker can be useful placeholder terms for organizing and communicating about the needs and desires of a community; however, they should not be naturalized or universalized as inclusive and encompassing terms, particularly in transnational organizing where legacies of colonialism and imperialism might trouble the adequacy of "sex" and "work" as conceptual frames (Vora, 2015, p. 25).

Understanding the contingencies that characterize the notions of sex and work, "labor" is another frame that scholars and activists might use to understand sex work as work. The concept of labor can be simply defined as the expenditure of a worker's energy to produce value. In contractual employment, workers sell their labor for a wage. Classically, labor paid for and performed in the public sphere was coined "productive," while the unpaid labor that happened in the home was "reproductive"; however, Marxist and material feminists have since collapsed that distinction to reveal that reproductive labor is productive in itself (Vora, 2015, p. 25). All social relations involve money and labor. Sometimes this labor is paid or otherwise compensated and other times it is not, but inasmuch as social relationships carry emotional value, this kind of labor participates in and has an impact on wage labor. Labor entails sacrifice on the part of the worker in order to accomplish a task, carry out a service, or produce a commodity. Part of this sacrifice is absolute—this is the effort put in, the calories burned, and the brain power it took to complete the task. Another aspect of the sacrifice is relative: "...a person can choose to expend her labor on a given set of alternatives, but selecting one means other options have been relinquished" (Rudrappa, 2015, p. 122); that is, the time spent completing the labor is time *not spent* on a number of other things. Balancing multiple jobs, for example, or balancing caretaking and working roles requires taking time from one to give time to the other, a sacrifice of time that could be spent elsewhere.

While contractual positions within commercial sex work might be usefully understood under the frame of labor, in the absence of a contract and a wage there are no thresholds or limits on how much time and energy a given sex worker puts into their work. Rather than a wage, independent sex workers profit directly from their products or services. Sometimes the money that a sex worker receives from a client is not in exchange for a product or service per se but is instead a personal gift. There are entire fetish communities devoted to financial domination in which submissives tribute money to dominatrixes for the pleasure of the transaction alone. Sending money as a form of erotic pay seems an enormous contrast to the typical workings of wage labor in which wages are doled out in small, controlled increments. The seeming irrationality of the flow of money in the sex industry confounds the construct of wage labor.

Using labor as a frame through which to examine sex work can also be useful for illuminating how sex work is inextricably linked to class struggle. Class cannot be abstracted as its own category of analysis separate from these other vectors considering how histories of sexuality, race, and gender have been structured by capitalist forces (Floyd, 1998, p. 172). Marxist feminism is one critical framework that examines the relationship between class and other vectors of oppression. In addition to theorizing capitalism, "Marxist feminists understand that patriarchal structures are variable and complex, organizing hegemonic meanings through the articulation of several axes of difference" (Hennessy, 2018, p. 23). Marxist feminism is particularly useful for examining less visible forms of labor, such as emotional labor or domestic responsibilities, and for considering the ways in which that labor is valued or valuable by normative standards.

In addition to norms that dictate what kinds of labor are valued and should be compensated, cisheteropatriarchal norms also dictate how laborers should spend their money. Communication that reinforces pride or shame as associated with consumerism is rampant in popular culture. When rich people spend money on luxuries, that is culturally coded as a sign of pride and superiority; when working-class people spend money on luxuries, they are treated as imprudent and therefore as not deserving. Oftentimes pride and shame about money show up in heterosexual gender relations and norms of courtship: Men are encouraged to spend money on women in the form of material goods and time to win their affection, and women are, in turn, encouraged to expect such treatment but not to think of their love as something to be bought. Heterosexual courtship is often facilitated through economic exchange and yet, to pay for sex with money is obscene. Noam Yuran explains that when money is paid for sex, "it is paid against something but at the very same time changes the nature of the thing exchanged" so that what is bought is not only a sexual experience, but also a financial one (Yuran, 2017, p. 141). The exchange of sex for money is heavily emphasized in scholarly and popular conceptualizations of sex work, perhaps because of how uniquely it indexes taboos in both emotional and monetary realms.

The exchange of sex for money is only one of many possible exchanges in sex work. The sale of sex is not always a sale of sexual contact; it can be a sale of commodities or performances that index sexuality or eroticism. Money need not always be what is exchanged for sex, either; sometimes survival sex work can involve exchanges for food or housing. In some cases, money does not buy something per se but is given as a tip, such as to erotic dancers. For some, the act of paying is itself instrumental to the experience. In sum, monetary behavior in sex work does not always adhere to a clear rationality or take place under assumptions of equivalence; indeed, it is the irrationality and inequivalence that make these exchanges particularly disruptive to the way one typically thinks of labor compensation.

The degree to which sex work involves various forms of work and labor varies widely depending on the nuances of a particular job, as well as on the worker's placement in the stratified hierarchy of sex workers. An indoor at home webcam worker, for example, will have a different experience of labor than an outdoor worker with a pimp, who will still have a different experience of labor compared to an elite escort who receives weekly deposits from a lover—and yet all of these people earn an income from the sex industry and all have to make sacrifices in terms of time and energy. Undoubtedly, sex work is work, but delineating the limits of that work is not a clean-cut endeavor.

SEX WORK UNDER NEOLIBERALISM

The global economy runs on exploitation: of lands, of bodies, of natural resources, of labor. By systemically robbing minority populations of wealth and opportunities, White ruling classes maintain their own economic privilege. Minimum wage and working-class laborers, while possibly earning enough to survive from paycheck to paycheck, cannot easily get a foothold, especially as affordable housing and health care continue to evaporate. A number of goods and services—including those utilized by state and local governments—come from forced inmate labor. The global economy, circulating through various nations and industries, seems to produce excessive wealth and opportunity for a few but widespread suffering for the many. Why is it that the rich keep getting richer, the poor keep getting poorer, and public services are vanishing?

In short, these phenomena are the result of neoliberalism. Neoliberalism is a prevailing rationality of conduct, what Lisa Duggan calls "a kind of secular faith" that structures policy to benefit the interests of elite classes instead of the public writ large (Duggan, 2003, p. xiii). In fact, neoliberalism erodes the very notion of the public, encouraging instead privatization and corporatization of every possible activity. Neoliberalism carries disastrous consequences for society writ large: the perpetuation of poverty (Yuran, 2017, p. 147), disavowal of the realities of gendered and racialized violence (Hong, 2015, p. 7), urban gentrification (Ferguson, 2019), the erosion of social programs (Duggan, 2011, p. 64), environmental degradation, and the exploitation of outsourced laborers (Vora, 2015), to name a few. Neoliberal values include efficiency, resilience, adaptability, and individualism. The aim of neoliberalism is "to transform society itself into a mode of enterprise of entrepreneurial and productive activities, of creative and competitive subjects" (Winnubst, 2012, p. 82). Crucially, neoliberalism is a combined function of the government and market forces. Michel Foucault explained that, under a neoliberal regime, the market becomes a "site of verification-falsification for governmental practice" (Foucault, 2010, p. 32) so that government becomes its own mode of enterprise—often at the expense of the governed.

Sex work is a site of conflict between the state, which criminalizes it, and the market, which demands it. Under neoliberalism, this incongruency creates a problem: The demand for sex work can be met, in part, through legal sex work, but inasmuch as there will always be demands that exceed legal bounds, there will always be illegal sex work, criminalized sex workers, and disproportionate exploitation and violence against them by the state, clients, traffickers, and other opportunistic actors. Given the instability of sex work as a category and the complexities that go into its practice and regulation, the question is not as simple as a "fully legalize" or "fully criminalize" dilemma. Although a neoliberal perspective might see criminalization as an infringement on free market ideology, incarceration is a mode of enterprise in itself that produces inmates stripped of rights who perform free labor. Nevertheless, the legalized sex industry represents a competitive market force backed by popular demand. In sum, under neoliberalism, the state and the market can function several ways on issues within sex work, depending on how competing industries and vested interests play out. Mitigating this conflict between state and market are governments' impulses toward paternalism.

In addition to neoliberalism, state operations are governed by a rationality of paternalism, which configures the nation, state, or sovereign as a father who rules over his citizen-children. While neoliberalism is a relatively recent mutation in the art of government, state paternalism can be traced back to ancient times. According to the logic of paternalism, centralized figures of authority know what is best for their citizens, so laws and regulations are designed with citizens' best interests in mind. Like a father who rewards and punishes his children, the sovereign has the right to decide who in his nation will be nurtured to live and who will be made to or left to die, and under what conditions. Michel Foucault argued that the sovereign's right to decide life and death "derived no doubt from the ancient *patria potestas* that granted the father of the Roman family the right to 'dispose' of the life of his children and his slaves" (Foucault, 2013, p. 31). State paternalism is the logical product of patriarchal societies in which property-owning men were granted full rights and citizenship while women, children, slaves, animals, and lands were forced to exist in subordination to their power.

In the United States, settler colonialism and slavery have been sustained by disciplinary paternalism and a White masculinist approach to the governance of racialized others, which emphasizes punishment (Piatote, 2017; Rodríguez, 2014). Paternalism adheres to sexual, gendered, racialized, and nationalized norms. In turn, these norms influence governing policies and practices, including the protection of lives, revocation of rights, and incarceration of bodies. This is not to say that the state is omnipotent, but in theory there exists a social contract between citizen and state whereby the citizen abides by the law and in return the state protects their life and property. In practice, governments regularly break this social contract through active violence and through negligence. However, under a neoliberal rationality, the state cannot be adequately held accountable because responsibility for "overcoming" these social problems is always deferred.

Disciplinary paternalism and neoliberalism create a communicative double bind for advocates of sex work legalization to navigate; on one hand, legalized sex work will likely reproduce neoliberal rationalities that favor exploitative practices (as in most legalized industries); on the other hand, criminalized sex work surveilled by the state will continue to produce dangerous circumstances for those involved in the industry, particularly for racialized bodies. Thus, for sex workers and those who would advocate for them, rhetorical strategies must be chosen carefully in order to avoid or approach neoliberal values. It would be simple, for example, to argue that sex work should be legalized and regulated just like any other form of work—but to do so would be to offer it up for assimilation into existing neoliberal rationalities. Similarly, one could index paternalistic rhetoric in order to argue that sex work should be altogether abolished—but to do so would be to activate the protective arm of the state at the peril of any whom the state might deem a threat. Thus, communication scholars interested in the discourse of sex work must closely and carefully consider how the form and content of messages about sex work reflect broader political rationalities.

DECRIMINALIZATION AND LEGALIZATION

In April 2018, President Donald Trump signed Public Law 115-164, "Allow States and Victims to Fight Online Sex Trafficking Act of 2017," into place. Colloquially referred to as FOSTA/SESTA, the acronyms of the House and Senate bills, respectively, this law amends Section 230 of the Communications Act, which holds that "no provider or user of an interactive computer service shall be treated as the publisher or speaker of any information provided by another information content provider." This provision ensures that platforms like social media sites cannot be held legally liable for what their users post. The protections the act provides has allowed for the proliferation of free speech online. FOSTA/SESTA, however, advances an exception: Any website that knowingly facilitates prostitution *is* liable for that content and will be prosecuted accordingly. FOSTA and SESTA passed speedily through Congress and was hailed as a rare bipartisan victory in an otherwise polarized political climate.

The impacts of the new law on sex workers were immediately felt in terms of both economic loss and an uptick in violence. Given that sex work is an underground economy, it is difficult to quantify how many have been impacted. On April 14, 2018, just three days after the law went into effect, anecdotal evidence from the online sex work community reported:

> 13 workers have gone missing and two have been confirmed dead. Two workers have been assaulted at gunpoint, and I can't even count how many other stories of rape and assault I've heard from people returning to or just learning the streets for the first time. One person has already taken their life because of this legislation. (Blue, 2018; Simon, 2018)

Reacting to the ambiguous phrase "facilitating prostitution," at least 18 websites shut down altogether (Hagen, 2018, p. 394). Internet advertisements for illegal prostitution did not disappear, however; they just shifted platforms or shrunk deeper into the dark web, actually making it more difficult for law enforcement to investigate and prosecute trafficking (Siouxsie, 2018). Furthermore, the failure of the legislature to clearly define what it meant by "facilitating prostitution" or differentiate between consensual and nonconsensual forms of sex work flattens the heterogeneity of practices that take place in the industry, making consistent enforcement of the policy impossible.

If there is one observation that contemporary scholars of sex work across the spectrum of opinion can seem to agree upon, it is that criminalization of sex workers is not working. In fact, criminalization and incarceration perpetuate untenable violence and injustice. In a report on sex trafficking in the United States, Karrin Vasby Anderson points out that when law enforcement arrests minors who have been victims of trafficking, "they are categorized as 'prostitutes' and then treated as perpetrators rather than victims" (Anderson, 2013, p. 5). The distinction between consensual and nonconsensual sex work seems unimportant to a system that so flippantly criminalizes those who are coerced or trafficked into the industry; that legal blurring of lines clearly has dehumanizing consequences. The narrative that configures law enforcement as the "good guys" who "rescue" victims from terrible situations obscures the ways in which police themselves can create terrible situations for undocumented and racialized people (Hill, 2019, p. 4). The criminality of sex work disadvantages both those who chose their work and those who are forced into it by keeping the industry as obscure and underdeveloped as possible.

Legalization and decriminalization of sex work encompass two broad sets of alternatives to criminalization. Legalization implies a cooperative relationship between providers, clients, and the state in which sex work is commercialized and officially regulated. Legalization is still accompanied by certain prohibitions and surveillance by state actors to ensure businesses are operating safely and in accordance with the law. Oftentimes for a sex work operation to be fully legal, special licenses, registrations, taxes, and other requirements must be obtained and followed. Decriminalization, however, is a process of reducing or eliminating criminal penalties for those involved in sex work. Importantly, the decriminalization of sex work is not the decriminalization of kidnapping, coercion, or other forms of violence that occur in the industry. Instead, it shifts the standard for criminality away from sexual monetary exchange and leaves intact prohibitions against violence. Decriminalization exists on a scale of possibilities, and most forms of decriminalization are only partial. De facto decriminalization, for example, means that while prohibitions remain in place, the law is not actively enforced. Decriminalization works to chip away at existing legal structures that punish sex workers while legalization seeks to establish new policies that make the sex industry run more smoothly (Weitzer, 2012, pp. 49–50).

Several practical factors shape how policymakers decide which practices should be prohibited, which should be facilitated, and which should be ignored. One key factor is the sexual and reproductive health of providers and clients. Another factor is access to safe premises, amenities, and procedures to deal with emergencies. Those who work in city streets and without premises are most at risk for police harassment, violence, and exploitative financial situations. Although they incur the most risk, street workers typically make the least amount of money (Cabezas, 2009, p. 153). Even if outdoor work is fully decriminalized, laws against loitering or soliciting can still justify police involvement. Establishing minimum ages for clients and providers is another important factor. Systems of age verification that rely on documentation such as a photo ID can help ensure that the person is not a minor, but not all people have a valid photo ID and not all producers will follow legal protocols. The roles of third parties such as pimps, escort agencies, brothel owners, and online platforms are also important to consider. Finally, one must consider the cultural and political forces that influence the norms that make up obscenity laws and community guidelines. For example, nudity is tolerated in some cultures as an erotic—but not necessarily sexual—form of art, while other cultures cannot disentangle nudity from sexuality. Considering how existing legal models account for health, amenities, age verification, third parties, and community standards offers a dimensional way to communicate about sex work policy.

Increasing workers' access to health care, providing improved amenities, and overall reducing barriers to earning an income are short-term, tangible benefits of legalization. Health-card systems in which a brothel worker carries a card indicating their regular checkups are already in place in cities like Singapore and Amsterdam (Chapman-Schmidt, 2015, p. 8; Weitzer, 2012, p. 156). Having access to brothels or to spaces that can be rented, such as windows in the red-light district or hotels that cater to sex workers with hourly rates, are some ways to reduce street prostitution, but these can only be made safely available in a system that legalizes and regulates such establishments. Legalization can also be part of reducing stigma against sex workers by disassociating sex work from criminality and can facilitate job opportunities for all types of workers in the commercial sex industry.

What legalization looks like in writing and in practice varies widely, and it is possible for there to be legal but nevertheless exploitative systems in place around sex work, and these need to be carefully assessed. If community norms dictate certain types of queer sex to be obscene, for example, and the state sanctions queer sex workers, then this form of legalization is inconsistent with the project of queer economic justice. Further, it is worth considering the impacts of legalized sex work in the community at large. In the long term, a legalized commercial sex sector will continue to build corporate and political power, and as long as neoliberalism remains a prevailing rationality and capitalism the name of the game, it is likely that the powerful actors in this sector will simply fall into step in order to preserve their own operations at the expense of their workers. The neoliberalization of the legal sex industry will continue to be an area of concern as long as it inevitably produces exploitative conditions. Whatever the limitations to legalization, however, it will resolve some of the dangers that come with criminalization while also making it easier for sex workers to organize for change in their industry.

Overall, these tensions at play regarding legalized sex work in the 21st century—particularly during this alarming moment of global economic crisis—speak to conditions that are not at all exclusive to sex work, but they implicate the public writ large: health care, housing, economic opportunity, and basic public safety. Therefore, a queer-of-color approach to sex work that seeks to account for workers at all levels of the social hierarchy sees the ways in which these problems are reflective of broader forces. And yet, as it has existed in the social imaginary, sex work exemplifies an extraordinary arena of social, monetary, and symbolic interaction.

LINKS TO DIGITAL MATERIAL

Global Network of Sex Work Projects. *Research for Sex Work* (https://www.nswp.org/research-sex-work)
The Leather Archives and Museum (https://leatherarchives.org/)
Lysistrata Mutual Care Collective and Fund (https://www.lysistratamccf.org/)
Red Canary Song (https://www.redcanarysong.net/)
Red Umbrella Fund (https://www.redumbrellafund.org/)
Sex Workers Outreach Project USA (https://swopusa.org/)

FURTHER READING

Anderson, K. V. (2011). Rhymes with blunt: The pornification of U.S. political culture. *Rhetoric and Public Affairs, 14*(2), 327–368.
Bernstein, E. (2007). *Temporarily yours: Intimacy, authenticity, and the commerce of sex*. University of Chicago Press.
Bernstein, E. (2010). Militarized humanitarianism meets carceral feminism: The politics of sex, rights, and freedom in contemporary antitrafficking campaigns. *Signs: Journal of Women in Culture and Society, 36*(1), 45–71.
Bronstein, C. (2011). *Battling pornography: The American feminist anti-pornography movement, 1976–1986*. Cambridge University Press.
Hill, A. (2017). The rhetoric of modern-day slavery: Analogical links and historical kinks in the United Kingdom's anti-trafficking plan. *philoSOPHIA: A Journal of Continental Feminism, 7*(2), 241–260.
Kempadoo, K., Sanghera, J., & Pattanaik, B. (Eds.). (2016). *Trafficking and prostitution reconsidered: New perspectives on migration, sex work, and human rights* (2nd ed.). Routledge.
Laing, M., Pilcher, K., & Smith, N. (Eds.). (2015). *Queer sex work*. Routledge.

MacKinnon, C. A., & Dworkin, A. (1997). *In harm's way: The pornography civil rights hearings*. Harvard University Press.

Muñoz, J. E. (1999). *Disidentifications: Queers of color and the performance of politics*. University of Minnesota Press.

Rand, E. J. (2014). *Reclaiming queer: Activist & academic rhetorics of resistance*. University of Alabama Press.

Shaver, F. M. (2005). Sex work research: Methodological and ethical challenges. *Journal of Interpersonal Violence, 20*(3), 296–319.

Vance, C. S. (Ed.). (1984). *Pleasure and danger: Exploring female sexuality*. Routledge & K. Paul.

Yep, G. A. (2017). Further notes on healing from "the violence of heteronormativity in communication studies." *QED: A Journal in GLBTQ Worldmaking, 4*(2). https://doi.org/10.14321/qed.4.2.0115

REFERENCES

Anderson, K. V. (2013). Human trafficking activism. *The multimedia encyclopedia of women in today's world*. SAGE.

Bernstein, E. (2018). *Brokered subjects: Sex, trafficking, and the politics of freedom*. University of Chicago Press.

Blue, V. (2018, April 27). Suicide, violence, and going underground: FOSTA's body count. *Engadget*. https://www.engadget.com/2018/04/27/suicide-violence-and-going-underground-fosta-sesta/

Cabezas, A. (2009). *Economies of desire: Sex and tourism in Cuba and the Dominican Republic*. Temple University Press.

Chapman-Schmidt, B. (2015). Sex in the shadow of the law: Regulating sex work and human trafficking in Singapore. *Asian Journal of Comparative Law, 10*(1), 1–22.

Comella, L. (2015). Revisiting the feminist sex wars. *Feminist Studies, 42*(2), 437–462.

Duggan, L. (2003). *The twilight of equality? Neoliberalism, cultural politics, and the attack on democracy*. Beacon Press.

Duggan, L. (2011). After neoliberalism? From crisis to organizing for queer economic justice. *A New Queer Agenda, 10*(1–2).

Ferguson, R. (2019). *One-dimensional queer*. Polity Press.

Floyd, K. (1998). Making history: Marxism, queer theory, and contradiction in the future of American studies. *Cultural Critique, 40*, 167–201.

Foucault, M. (2010). *The birth of biopolitics: Lectures at the collége de France, 1978–1979*. Picador.

Foucault, M. (2013). Right of death and power over life. In T. Campbell & A. Size (Eds.), *Biopolitics: A reader* (pp. 41–61). Duke University Press.

Hagen, J. J. (2018). Compounding risks for sex workers in the United States. *NACLA Report on the Americas, 50*(4), 395–397. https://doi.org/10.1080/10714839.2018.1550984

Hennessy, R. (2018). *Profit and pleasure: Sexual identities in late capitalism* (2nd ed.). Routledge.

Hill, A. (2019). Producing the crisis: Human trafficking and humanitarian interventions. *Women's Studies in Communication, 41*(4), 315–319. https://doi.org/10.1080/07491409.2018.1544008

Hong, G. K. (2015). *Death beyond disavowal: The impossible politics of difference*. University of Minnesota Press.

Lefkowitz, M. (2017, April 27). Library manages Queers for Economic Justice records. *Cornell Chronicle*. https://news.cornell.edu/stories/2017/04/library-manages-queers-economic-justice-records

Lòpez, C. (2020, June 17). A wave of people turned to OnlyFans to earn more money when they lost their jobs due to the pandemic. *Insider*. https://www.insider.com/people-are-creating-onlyfans-accounts-after-losing-jobs-during-pandemic-2020-6

MacKinnon, C. A. (1985). Pornography, civil rights, and speech. *Harvard Civil Rights-Civil Liberties Law Review, 20*(1), 1–70.

Mahdavi, P. (2011). *Gridlock: Labor, migration, and human trafficking in Dubai*. Stanford University Press.

Palczewski, C. (1995). Survivor testimony in the pornography controversy: Assessing credibility in the Minneapolis hearings and the attorney general's report. In E. Schiappa (Ed.), *Warranting assent: Case studies in argument evaluation* (pp. 257–281). State University of New York Press.

Petillo, A. (2018). Marking embodied borders: Compulsory settler sexuality, indigeneity, and U.S. law. *Women's Studies in Communication, 41*(4), 329–334. https://doi.org/10.1080/07491409.2018.1544013

Piatote, B. (2017). *Domestic subjects: Gender, citizenship, and law in Native American literature*. Yale University Press.

PornHub (2020, March 23). Coronavirus insights. *PornHub Insights*. https://www.pornhub.com/insights/corona-virus

Public Law 115-164 [HR 1865] 115th Congress. (2017). "Allow States and Victims to Fight Online Sex Trafficking Act of 2017."

Rodríguez, J. M. (2014). *Sexual futures, queer gestures, and other Latina longings*. New York University Press.

Rubin, G. (1984). Thinking sex: Notes for a radical theory of the politics of sexuality. In C. S. Vance (Ed.), *Pleasure and danger: Exploring female sexuality* (pp. 267–319). Routledge.

Rubin, G. (2003). Samois. *Leather Times: News from the Leather Archives & Museum*. http://leatherarchives.org/ca/index.php/Detail/entities/3260

Rudrappa, S. (2015). *Discounted life: The price of global surrogacy in India*. New York University Press.

Simon, K. (2018, April 25). On backpage. *Tits and Sass: Service Journalism by and for Sex Workers*. http://titsandsass.com/on-the-death-of-backpage/

Siouxsie, Q. (2018, May 25). Anti-sex-trafficking advocates say new law cripples effort to save victims. *Rolling Stone*. https://www.rollingstone.com/culture/culture-features/anti-sex-trafficking-advocates-say-new-law-cripples-efforts-to-save-victims-629081/

Stein, A., & Press, A. (1985). *Pleasure & danger: Exploring female sexuality*, by C. S. Vance [Book review]. *Berkeley Journal of Sociology, 30*, 205–212.

Vora, K. (2015). *Life support: Biocapital and the new history of outsourced labor*. University of Minnesota Press.

Weitzler, R. (2012). *Legalizing prostitution: From illicit vice to lawful business*. New York University Press.

Wilson, E. (1983). The context of "Between Pleasure and Danger": The Barnard conference on sexuality. *Feminist Review, 13*, 35–41.

Winnubst, S. (2012). The queer thing about neoliberal pleasures: A Foucauldian warning. *Foucault Studies, 14*, 79–97.

Yep, G. A. (2003). The violence of heteronormativity in communication studies. *Journal of Homosexuality, 42*(2–4), 11–59. https://doi.org/10.1300/J082v45n02_02

Yuran, N. (2017). Finance and prostitution: On the libidinal economy of capitalism. *Difference: A Journal of Feminist Cultural Studies, 28*(5), 136–165. https://doi.org/10.1215/10407391-4260567

Carly Leilani Fabian

SEXUAL PLEASURE IN QUEER COMMUNICATION STUDIES

FINDING PLEASURE COMMUNICATION

Both inside and outside of the communication studies discipline, the place of sexuality scholarship is unsettled—and that shaky ground materializes especially around the discussion of sexual pleasure in the field and beyond. Candid discussions of sex, pleasure, desire, sexual tastes, fantasies, and bodily responses have long inspired heavy-breathing anxiety inflected by a reach for "propriety." This anxiety envelopes public discourses of what feels good—especially things that feel *really* good under less than great conditions and things that deviate from what normative structures say *should* feel good. Sexuality studies, for example, (but also queer/trans/gender studies) have found their way into various pockets of the academic humanities in the wake of the 1980s HIV/AIDS crisis (Laumann, 2006). This interdisciplinary field of inquiry centers the intersectional vectors (geographical, bodily, historical, psychological, etc.) that impress upon how we come to understand sex and sexuality. Queer studies, comingled with sexuality studies, allow scholars to access the deconstruction of those normative impressions. As Annemarie Jagose (2013) has remarked, sexuality studies has had "relatively little to say about sex itself" and this observation also extends to communication studies. As with most epistemological occlusions, queer communication scholars have taken up space in this void and produced erotically inclined knowledge and examined the communicative contours of pleasure.

Part cultural erotophobia, and part logocentric disciplinary norm, sexual pleasure primarily lives in the queer corners of communication studies. Nearly 20 years ago, feminist scholars posited that "academic writing of the kind published in [communication studies] is regulated by clear norms, usually among them the demand for a refined, ahistorical, smoothly finished univocality" contaminated by a "masculinist disciplinary ideology" (Blair et al., 1994). Just as the feminine was and is disciplined in communication scholarship, so too is the sexual, erotic, and pleasurable—especially when its expression exceeds White cisheteropatriarchal conventions. As a consequence, this encyclopedia entry on sexual pleasure in queer communication studies traces moments of queer sexual pleasure articulation in communication research despite disciplinary attempts to elide this field of study.

An entry on pleasure in a queer communication encyclopedia might entice the reader to expect a history that begins with Greek *eros* and extends to Georges Bataille's (2008) work on pleasure and play. Perhaps the reader expects a brief history on Sigmund Freud (2001) and the pleasure principle, or that other guy who wrote about pleasure and called it *jouissance* (Lacan, 2007). Certainly the reader expects at least a summary of Michel Foucault (1990)—or maybe some Judith Butler (1993)? Like Isaac West (2018) explains, "queer perspectives question the legitimacy of hegemonic assumptions about bodies and sexualities, opting instead for more fluid and porous discourses and norms" (p. 1). Part of the queer project of locating pleasure in the field is also, then, about questioning our origin stories, our points of entry, and our hegemonic canon. Neither Greek history, nor poststructuralist primer is articulated in this entry. Instead, the "story" of pleasure in the field follows a fluid and porous path allowing us to dwell in moments of pleasure in queer places.

Defining queer perspectives on pleasure in the field comes with its own set of challenges given the slippery nature of "queer" as a concept and as a lived experience. Queer, as a concept, has carried with it many meanings. From eccentric and oblique, to powerful and deviant, queer took its German etymological roots towards its multiple "cross-wise" and "diagonal" horizons—in criticism, in identity formation, and in political organizing. In this present entry, queer refers to the deconstruction of the normative linkages between gender, sex, sociality, and the relationships between them. Although scholars have noted how the field's orthodoxies have limited queer inquiry, "a substantial body of research exists across the subfields of communication studies to challenge naturalized assumptions about our bodies, genders, relationships, and desires" (West, 2018, p. 11). That body of research, like Jimmie Manning (2020) notes, isn't always immediately visible. Queer pleasure scholarship often exists in lesser-known journals and cross-disciplinary journals (Manning et al., 2020). With this queer road(treasure) map in mind, this entry outlines three areas in which pleasure emerges in the field of queer communication studies: analyses of representational pleasure, resistance to normative public discourses, and performative writing and authoethnographies of pleasure.

REPRESENTATIONS OF PLEASURE

From the investigation of normative representations to the politics of queer visibility, queer communication scholars have troubled the representational meanings of pleasure. In their analysis of representations of "man-on-man" kissing, for example, Charles Morris and John Sloop (2006) move beyond the simple demand for more visibility, acceptance, and openness of queer kissing. Instead, they emphasize the queer world making potential embedded in "mass-mediated representations [that] articulate sexuality differently, queering readings of all forms of intimacy and their public connections." For them, a "critical mass" of "man-on-man" kissing holds the potential to build more hospitable futures for queer pleasures. As Erin Rand (2013) notes, moving the needle on this critical mass also requires an attention to how femininities and femme-ness are disciplined by the male patriarchal gaze. A little over ten years later, Morris and Sloop (2017) revisited their queer kissing essay and its silence on white supremacy and racism in the wake of the mass murder of queer Latinx life at Pulse Nightclub in Orlando. They write, "nonheteronormative public kissing remains a cultural and political fault line; and we still can imagine a worldmaking project propelled in part by a 'critical visual mass' of same-sex public kissing" (p. 183). That critical mass, however, must account for the "specific bodies-in-pleasure gathered on Latinx Night at Pulse before they were cut down, brown bodies in pleasurable excess affectively interconnected, who in their racial and ethnic specificity were subsequently and unsurprisingly erased in large measure by mainstream public discourse" (p. 184). Morris and Sloop's work on representations of queer kissing calls for an explosion of variegated representations which, they argue, have the capacity to shift the capacious promise of intersectional approaches to visibility and recognition.

Communication scholars have also examined representations of pleasure that emerge despite or because of the relations of power that create barriers for imagining expressions of pleasure beyond toxic, hegemonic conceptions. Kelly Wilz (2019), for example, offers various popular culture examples which illustrate productive models of women's pleasure amidst a violent, patriarchal landscape. For her, the lack of attention to women's pleasure creates the conditions for the long history of violence against women. Reflecting on her own sexual assault she writes, "If women's pleasure and orgasms mattered, in general, as much as men's in each and every sexual encounter, forcible sex simply wouldn't have made sense." Her analysis of the movie *Blockers*, in particular, demonstrates how crucial the theory of intimate justice is for a less-violent, pleasure-centered future—especially for queer young women navigating their bodies and desires perhaps for the first time. Borrowed from critical psychology, a theory of intimate justice emphasizes how the structures of power impact sexual satisfaction and sexual experiences (McClelland, 2014). Similarly, Michaela Frischherz (2018a, 2020) reads against the normative grain in her analysis of *Cosmopolitan* magazine and *Fifty Shades of Grey* to locate moments of pleasure articulation amidst the most normative products of popular culture. Pleasure, found in strange or unexpected places, emerges queerly and against convention. Kyra Pearson and Nina Maria Lozano-Reich (2009) also locate the possibility for erotic pleasure in *Queer Eye for the Straight Guy* despite predictable critiques of the show as an assimilationist project.

Scholars have also analyzed the limits and possibilities of "appropriate" public representations of pleasure. In her treatment of sex museums, Jennifer Tyburczy (2016) suggests representations—especially sexually coded representations—have the capacity to interrupt "the naturalized order of normalcy" (p. xvi). Where and how representations of pleasure and sex might bring to the fore "hidden or censored aspects of sexuality," sits at the center of her work. Tyburczy (2016) illustrates how display functions as a technique for disciplining sexuality and pleasure. Similarly, Michele Hammers' (2010) analysis of Eve Ensler's *Vagina Monologues* illustrates how the representation of women's sexual pleasure and women's bodies demarcates where representations become taboo and therefore "preferably private" rather than enjoying a "properly public" social location. Hammers (2010) suggests art productions like the *Vagina Monologues* make "female sexual pleasure and orgasm both visible and speakable" (p. 221). Lauren Berlant and Michael Warner (2005) have long reminded communication scholars of the importance of *public* representations of intimacy and their queer worldmaking capacities. Through their work, we have learned how publics come to matter for the elaboration of sexual pleasure. Understanding publics through this lens expands what counts as public (like sex, desire, and pleasure), and in turn, what counts as an object of communication analysis. As Berlant and Warner (2005) write, "although the intimate relations of private personhood appear to be the realm of sexuality itself, allowing 'sex in public' to appear like matter out of place, intimacy is itself publicly mediated" (p. 193). When sex and pleasure spill into the public, the normative cultural response is one of aversion and recoil, "even as contemporary consumer and media cultures increasingly trope toiletward, splattering the matter of intimate life at the highest levels of national culture" (p. 201). This tension tells the story of the paradox of sexually charged, potentially pleasurable representations in public.

Feminist media scholars have also interrogated the contours of pleasure's mediation and pleasure's attached meanings in various public domains. For example, in their analysis of mediated sex advice, Meg-John Barker et al. (2018) note how "pleasure has a contradictory place in contemporary mediated sex advice" (p. 132). On the one hand, pleasure is coded as liberatory and a source of empowerment and on the other hand, variegated discussions of pleasure are largely absent in sex advice mediums. As Barker et al. remind us, "representations of sexual pleasure continue to be marked by and articulated through structural inequalities" (p. 132). Similarly, Hilton-Morrow and Battles (2015) note, "images of sexual intimacy are a pervasive facet of contemporary media. Issues around intimate acts always center around ideas of what is normal and what is deviant, what is private and what is public, and, more specifically, around the unstable intersections of race, gender, sexuality, class, and ability" (p. 228). Representations of pleasure often center White, straight, cis, able-bodied, young, thin, and PIV sex. And when they do not, communication scholars illustrate how the relations of power press against the rhetoricity of pleasure. In their analysis of *Cruising* and *Interior: Leather Bar*, Braddy and Huff (2018) astutely ask, "what happens to political possibilities when pleasure depends upon stigmatization?" (p. 103). C. Riley Snorton (2014) similarly troubles the representational politics emergent from attempts to describe the racialized "down-low." Those representations, Snorton suggests, perpetuate White supremacist notions of Black sexual subjectivities.

The analysis of hegemonic representations also extend to pornographies. Pornography has long been at the center of representational critiques of pleasure and its production. In fact, the consideration of pornography has been so central to the conversation that some scholars mark it as the flashpoint shift between the second wave of feminism and the third wave. That flashpoint shift culminated around the discussion of public representations of sex (sex work, pornography, group sex, leather, and kink) among feminists, which some have called the "feminist sex wars" (Comella, 2017; Duggan & Hunter, 1996; Rubin, 2011; Vance, 1984; Wilson, 1981). More contemporarily, a collective of feminist and queer porn thinkers, doers, and makers interrogate the politics of producing pleasure in *The Feminist Porn Book* (Taormino et al., 2013). In the collection, they leave behind the tired assertion that pornography is always a source of gendered subjugation and a lack of pleasure; instead, they explore "the significance of sex in intimate and social relations, and of not presuming what sex means for specific people" (p. 15). Finding those glimmers of pleasure amongst the normative, hegemonic terrain is also at the center of Sara Warner's (2012) work. Warner aims to find the celebratory, the transformative, the gaiety, the pleasure, and the productive in lesbian feminist activism of the 1960s and 1970s. Warner illustrates how the activist performance work of Valerie Solanas and Jill Johnston amplifies the "liveliness" of resistive representations. In these activist performances, Warner (2012) locates "acts of gaiety," which function as "playful methods... [and] comical and cunning interventions that make a mockery out of social exclusion" (p. xi). Finally, Shaka McGlotten (2012) responds to long-time critiques of online virtual spaces of queer intimate pleasure as "inauthentic." Analyzing public sex scandals, online cruising, and DIY porn, McGlotten theorizes the concept of "browsing" as a way to understand queer (virtual) pleasures and their worldmaking capacities. McGlotten writes, "browsing possesses a power that is also an invitation"—and that invitation beckons us to imagine "what forms our intimacies with ourselves or others might take" (p. 136). In addition to scholarship that analyzes representations of pleasure and the limits and possibilities of public representations and their worlding potential, queer communication scholars have also interrogated the broader public discourses that enable and constrain pleasure.

RESISTING NORMATIVE PUBLIC DISCOURSES

The broader public discourses that shape and maintain articulations of pleasure are at the center of much of the scholarship which seeks to locate the possibility of pleasure despite the duress of it all. Often, those public discourses are draped in normative expectations, circulate widely and violently, and create unlivable conditions for minoritized subjects. And yet, queer communication scholars have mined this dangerous public discursive terrain to strategize resistance, power, and transformation. Within interdisciplinary queer studies, pleasure is polyvalent and includes forms of feeling good, satisfaction, contentment, elation, and enjoyment; scholars have unearthed how people creatively communicate pleasure within and alongside the discursive norms of rhetorical culture. The polyvalence of pleasure not only highlights its rhetorically contingent purchase when it is expressed communally, publicly, and relationally, but it also illustrates that pleasure *means different things to different people*. Because pleasure is experienced on a continuum of difference in everyday life, the present entry neither definitively answers the question, "what is pleasure" nor does the entry seek to index different forms of pleasure. Neither critical aim is possible (or, for that matter, all that interesting) because examining sexual pleasure in queer communication studies is not a matter of categorization, but a matter of pleasure's circulation in the field.

Scholars have long worked against public discourses that expect bodies and pleasures to conform to biologically determined and innate explanatory logics. Some of this work follows in the footsteps of Gayle Rubin's (2011) rejection of sex and pleasure as an essential bodily drive beholden to a natural, biologically-determined, innateness that stands apart from history and culture. Central to this radical theory is the rejection of sexual essentialism, which is "the idea that sex is a natural force that exists prior to social life and shapes institutions" (p. 146). Similarly, Weeks (1985) suggests we must challenge the idea that sexuality embodies the working out of an "immanent truth" (p. 56). Indeed, like all forms of knowledge, "the sexual only exists in and through the modes of its organization and representation" (Weeks, 1985, p. 10). This vein of scholarship contributes to analyzing how the processes that form discourses come to signify emergent ways of being in and making sense of the world. After all, like Jimmie Manning (2009) notes, queer theory is about "changing perceptions of what it means to love, connect, pleasure, and perform." Queer communication studies scholars, therefore, emphasize how the accompanying context of particular discourses enable and constrain the ability of individuals to make meaning in a particular time, place, and audience.

Black and Brown feminist scholars also produce knowledge about how the flows of power create expectations for the expression of pleasure. Audre Lorde (1984) reminds us of the power of the erotic—a firm call to honor the "replenishing and provocative force" of the erotic beyond patriarchal and weaponized notions of pleasure (which is not pleasure at all). The "fullness" derived from the shared erotic exists not in moments of performative sensuality or "external directives" but in "how acutely and fully we can feel in the doing" (Lorde, 1984, pp. 54, 58). For Lorde (1984), the erotic describes the power embedded in sharing deeply with others. And while not always about sex and pleasure, Lorde's conception of the erotic reminds readers of the possibility of pleasure beyond or in resistance to patriarchal standards of erotic sexy-ness—of gendered oppression. Following Lorde, adrienne maree brown's (2019) *New York Times* bestseller *Pleasure Activism* bursts at the seams with gentle and righteous demands for imagining a politics of healing and politics of pleasure in the pursuit of social justice. She writes, "Pleasure activism is the work we do to reclaim our whole, happy, and satisfiable selves form the impacts, delusions, and limitations of oppression and/or supremacy" (brown, 2019, p. 13). brown (2019) encourages us to imagine what it might feel, sound, and taste like if we imagined justice and liberation as the "most pleasurable experiences we can have on this planet" (p. 13). Similarly in her interview with Joan Morgan, the collection amplifies the long-standing commitment Black feminist thought communicates to "claim pleasure and a healthy erotic as fundamental rights" (brown, 2019, pp. 81–97). Since 2013, Morgan's Black feminist collective—the *Pleasure Ninjas*—has aimed "to push forward Black women's pleasure as a feminist ideal," despite the constraints of white cisheteropatriarchy (Barner, 2019, p. 66).

Communication scholars have also examined how normative discourses of pleasure enable and constrain material access to enjoyment. Lynn Comella (2017), for example, offers readers a history of feminist sex-toy stores to illustrate how the conjuncture of capitalism, feminist politics, and the industry of pleasure products congeal to form a complex web of transformative possibilities—sometimes in line with founder goals and visions and sometimes not. Frischherz's (2018b) analysis of normative orgasmic imperative discourses illustrates where and how women find openings for expressions of pleasure despite the pressures to perform sex and pleasure in expected ways. She writes, "without multiple venues within which women can share and build their own reservoirs of knowledge about what feels good, about what causes anxiety and shame, and about what is sexually important to them, the orgasm, and women's pleasure more generally, will continue to function as a vector of control and sexuality" (Frischherz, 2018b, p. 283). Listening for alternative, resistive, and improvisational modes of pleasure in public discourse, against the backdrop of all the normativities that encase sexual *shoulds* is, therefore, at the center of some of this queer communication scholarship on pleasure.

Resisting normative pleasure discourses does not, of course, always leave us in a place of total satisfaction. Pointing to the generative force of power, Tim Dean (2012) notes how "the mobility and diffusion of modern power relations do not circumscribe but instead proliferate pleasures" (p. 481). And it is this proliferation that is not only elided in scholarship but it is also often marked as less politically serious than other topics for criticism (Dean, 2012, p. 477). Dean (2012) writes, "pleasure has been a perennial target of the hermeneutics of suspicion" (p. 482). When pleasure becomes a target for paranoid criticism, critics often mark the expression of pleasure as "false pleasure" and these critical observations become the "unexamined cognate of false consciousness," which transforms pleasure-seekers (often historically minoritized folks) into dupes of culture rather than active negotiators of their lived realities (Dean, 2012, p. 482). Like Jennifer Nash (2014) notes, "the very structures we critique and seek to dismantle can also thrill" (p. 150). And being thrilled by normative power structures need not always portend a failure of transformation. Similarly, Cathy Cohen (1997) writes, "in the roots of a lived 'queer' existence are experiences with domination and in particular heteronormativity that form the basis for genuine transformational politics" (p. 444). And those glimmers, amongst dangerous and power-laden, discourses, echo the transformative and resistive power of sharing in pleasure. Centering the communicative contours of pleasure discourses illustrates how public expressions of pleasure highlight the joy, gaiety, and well-being of people—especially those impacted by several vectors of power at once. Those vectors induce bodily shame, the policing of "having a say" when it comes to one's sexuality, highculture indictments of what constitutes a "guilty pleasure," and dominant discourses that unjustly pathologize and medicalize minoritized genders, Black and Brown people, and non-normative sexualities.

As a consequence, when pleasure *is* elaborated—especially in public under the weight of its normative expectations—we are given a glimmer of things as otherwise. That is, *despite* or perhaps even *because of* cultural codes that limit what we can or cannot say in public, folks still creatively "make do" and find openings to express their pleasures. Far from simply a faddish interest in sex, the consideration of pleasure offers us an opportunity to understand how people communicate matters of private concern, build intimate social ties with partners, and render shareable their sexual experiences with loved (or lusted) ones. As such, when communication studies recognizes pleasure's place in the field, we are better able to account for those moments wherein folks express themselves and their visions of the pleasure despite theoretical and historical assumptions of our incapacities for feeling good. This commitment in queer communication studies is especially visible in autoethnographic accounts of pleasure, desire, and sensation.

PERFORMATIVE WRITING AND AUTOETHNOGRAPHIES OF PLEASURE

This final section offers a snapshot of pleasure's place in queer communication studies by tracing how scholars have interrogated embodied, personal narratives of sexual pleasure within the cultural contexts that so often challenge queer bodies in their expression of pleasure. Scholars have long debated "the evidence of experience" in knowledge production. Joan Scott (1991), for example, suggests attending to experience authorizes us to explore "how difference is established, how it operates, how and in what ways it constitutes subjects who see and act in the world," rather than simply establish "the fact of difference" (Scott, 1991, p. 777). And this insight is especially important because, "the evidence of experience, whether conceived through a metaphor of visibility or in any other way that takes meaning as transparent, reproduces rather than contests given ideological systems" (Scott, 1991, p. 778). And as Scott (1991) reminds us, "What counts as experience is neither self-evident not straightforward; it is always contested, and always therefore political" (p. 797). The body of autoethnographic and performative pleasure work discussed in this entry illustrates how resisting ideological systems is not only possible, but central to elaborating oneself in contexts that do not always nurture sexual expression. Different things turn different people on, and the rhetoricity of pleasure demonstrates *both* the thesis of benign sexual difference (Rubin) *and* how multifarious pleasure articulations build reservoirs of knowledge from which folks can draw. And while Ott (2004) boldly claimed, "Most communication and media critics are, of course, not very skilled at reading/writing bodily desires, or even recognizing them when they occur" (with the exception of, according to Ott, *Sextext*), tides have shifted since then (p. 204).

The controversy spurred by Thomas Nakayama and Frederick Corey's (1997) essay *Sextext* is a strong reminder of how sex scholarship—especially the kind that emphasizes pleasure and queer sexual practices—occupies a frenzied place in the communication studies discipline. At its core, *Sextext* tells a story of the cruisy interplay between theories, bodies, and sexual pleasure; its description reads: "a fictional account of text and body as fields of pleasure" (Corey & Nakayama, 1997). The introduction teases the reader by asking, "How is it possible to write in the fulcrum between the language of the academic and the language of sex" (Corey & Nakayama, 1997). Part tease and part promise of what is to come, the essay moves from Barthes to Foucault to scenes of pleasurable penetration and moments of ecstatic exploration amongst gay men. In a letter to the editor of a 1997 edition of *Spectra*, Donald Smith (1997) lambasts Sextext as "faddish." He writes,

> It is further faddish as an entry into the current enthusiasm of many universities to establish programs of "queer," or "gay and lesbian studies," not because of a demonstrable need for advancing knowledge through scholarly inquiry, but in order to bring comfort to yet another group allegedly suffering from historical victimage.... "Sextext" is performance, not scholarship. (p. 8)

The scandal in the field, as Benson (2012) names it, highlights both the desire to protect disciplinary boundaries and the pearl-clutching resistance to pleasure-centered forms of knowledge production marked as "pornographic." Similarly, responding to the "pornographic" marker the article received, Carole Blair remarked, "I'm not sure...how different it is for one's work to have been labeled 'communist' in the 1950s than for her/his [*sic*] work to be categorized as 'pornographic' in the 1990s...It reinforces hostility to difference" (Benson, 2012). This debate in the field highlights not only the disciplining of pleasure's place but also autoethnographic and performative writing scholarship that has significantly contributed to embodied pleasure-knowledge. Like Elizabeth Bell (1995) writes, "Pleasure has always been the bedrock of performance studies, even if buried under edifices of literary criticisms, pedagogical practices, and text-centered performance cannons" (p. 99). By doubling down on pleasure in performance studies, Bell reminds readers to attune themselves to the "material pleasures of performance" (p. 100). Those pleasures are explored in queer storytelling which seek to theorize experiences in their articulation to broader flows of culture.

Queer pleasure storytelling in queer communication studies explores the elaboration of identities, desires, and contextual atmospheres. Like Carrillo Rowe (2007) asks, "what is at stake when the erotic is at stake?" (p. 270). For her, like so many others, the erotic calls up the "boundaries between self and other...the commingling of the sacred and the profane. In a word: everything" (Carrillo Rowe, 2007, p. 207). Lore/tta LeMaster's (2020b) Critical Intervention forum draws on Audre Lorde's ideas on the erotic, discussed above, to advance a narrative approach to "theorizing and performing lived and envisioned sexual experience and desire" (p. 105). This approach, which she calls "critical erotic/a," is especially important for elaborating desire in the face of "structural constraints delimiting sexual potentiality" (p. 106). This communicative elaboration is made impossible when sex and desire detours away from imposed and compulsory sexual identities (LeMaster, 2020b, p. 108). Their own piece in the forum, "End(eu/u)ring," theorizes the "cosmic dust" of fleeting recognition moments in pleasure. The story is sexy and painful and attuned to the messiness of identity (LeMaster, 2020a, 2020b, p. 131).

LeMaster's edited forum is filled with narratives of pleasure, pain, desire, fantasy, and visions of queer worlding despite structural constraints. Huff (2020) explores the communicative terrain of pleasure beyond an orgasm and posits renewed starting points for feeling bodily pleasure. Zariñana's (2020) poem "R U Latin?" resists the call of identity's interpellation by writing performatively to interrupt normative ideas of subject-coherence. Gamboa's (2020) piece "A Gape" calls for a praxis of sensuality that resists the hegemony of the visual—where the emphasis on the visual (or visibility) risks both the surveillance of the queer body *and* the amelioration of embodied feeling. Rudnick (2020) explores where sex can inspire a sense of belonging and where sex creates the conditions of exclusion created by "normative categorizations of queer male desire" (p. 120). Tumazi's (2020) poem "Academic Slut" asks how to center the minoritized self in a cishet structure—and takes the reader through a story of trans feminine preoccupations in both pleasure and labor. Finally, in their coda to the forum, Johnson (2020) asks how we might "melt into pleasure" despite normative, structural constraints. They highlight how, taken together, the forum asks "us to think reflexively about our own desires and pleasures apart from the fetishizing and controlling culture of labels" (p. 138).

The collection sits at the cutting-edge of autoethnographic and performative writing about queer pleasure in the field.

Some of the queer storytelling in the field centers the capacities for stories to be told and heard in the first place. Indeed, as Kristen Blinne (2012) notes in her auto(erotic)ethnography, "the inherent danger in sexual stories is not that they are told, but instead, *which stories should be told, for whom*, and *for what purpose*?" (p. 965). E. Patrick Johnson (2019) similarly focuses on the importance of reflexivity, voice, and power in *Honeypot: Black Southern Women Who Love Women*. Part oral history, part magical realism, and quite simply pure poetry, *Honeypot* is "where the dreams of bees are kept…patiently listening to my sisters' stories as I continue to harvest honey for the honeypot" (p. 221). Here, the "honey" drips with complex meanings—sex, bodies, intimacy, and sweet encounter. LeMaster and Johnson's (2020) collection on gender futurity and autoethnographic modes of knowing is, also, rooted in the elaboration of pleasure. For them, pleasure functions as a horizon of possibility despite the structures of power that build "dysphoria, pain, shame, and terrifying experiences of trans and non-binary people" (Johnson & LeMaster, 2020, p. 257). Getting at the intensely variable epistemologies emergent from narratives linked to broader cultural flows helps to reinvigorate the radical potential of queer storying telling. Like Lore/tta Manning et al. (2020) writes of the tamed radical potential of "queer" in communication studies, "We can see this in communication research that lazily collapses intracultural differences among queer and trans subjects such that one is to assume all lesbian, all gay, all bisexual, and all trans subjects experience and navigate the same oppression in the same way" (Manning et al., 2020). Performative writing and autoethnographies of pleasure not only render complex pleasure's possibilities, they also create the place of sexual pleasure in field where those very places where previously unspeakable, invisible, and constrained.

PLEASURE'S QUEER COMMUNICATIVE CONTOURS

Taken together, what this body of literature reminds us to consider is this: if we think sex and sexual pleasure merely *happens* we miss tapping into the communicative contours of pleasure—and queer communication studies have worked to trace, reimagine, amplify, and draw into relief those contours. Recognizing pleasure's rhetoricity means giving up on the idea that pleasure is one, definitive affect, emotion, or feeling. And because pleasure's public enactment and its place in queer communication studies carries with it this multiplicity of struggled for articulations, this entry illustrates how these multiplicities create capacities for navigating a better tomorrow in the face of a troubled today.

As many of these scholars, performers, and activists illustrate, if we begin with a critical position whereby we orient ourselves toward pleasure as inherently communicative, we may be poised to finally infiltrate some sex and pleasure back into communication studies. Although there is a significant body of literature that investigates queer sexualities culturally, medically, and philosophically, we too often overlook the communication-based scholarly investigation of queer pleasures. And what this body of scholarship illustrates is a matter of starting points. What does the place of pleasure in the field look like when it begins with elation and satisfaction rather than danger and harm? What does the place of pleasure in the field look like when it makes room for elation and satisfaction despite or because of danger and harm? What if pleasure scholarship didn't center whiteness? Or men? Or heterosexuality? What if our journals were more capacious and celebrated transnational and indigenous pleasure work? What if we made space for pleasures that don't please everyone? This entry suggests that one of the way we may be able to go on theorizing and understanding queer pleasures is by taking ideologies and their complex effectivities more seriously in our criticisms.

The place of pleasure-based sexual scholarship is still unsettled in humanistic inquiry—especially in communication studies. It is, of course, difficult to decide if this oversight stems from a simple inattention or if it is derivative of a more pernicious judgment of pleasure and sex as *merely* bodily or arhetorical. Regardless of this oversight's origin, this entry illustrates how the multiplicity of pleasure in public—and its recognition—authorizes people to view and feel in excess of our normative imaginaries of discipline and regulation. To be sure, dangerous ideologies constantly circulate and the relations of power are felt most intensely by those who are historically disenfranchised, but sexuality scholarship that makes this insight the conclusion leaves us with nothing. If we can, instead, mine the reverberations of cisheteropatriarchy and capitalism for moments in which people actively negotiate their own well-being in relation to the flows of culture, then we are given an opportunity to strategize how those moments can be redeployed (more collectively, more politically) for future queer/feminist discussions about the sociocultural place of pleasure. That opportunity means we have to give up on the idea that pleasure can only happen in one way or that pleasure means only one thing to all people. Given these tides, pleasure is not just a small glimmer of possibility. Instead, the search for pleasure's capacity to serve as a rhetorical resource for negotiating those vulnerabilities is crucial. When the norms of sex are so impressive they leave us passive and pathologized, the complex ways pleasure emerges in queer communication studies serves as a reminder of how we can build reservoirs of knowledge on the fulcrum of that which feels good—*despite or because of* our shared, and differing, vulnerabilities.

FURTHER READING

Barker, M., & Hancock, J. (2017). *Enjoy sex (how, when and IF you want to)*. Icon Books.
Califia, P. (1994). *Public sex: The culture of radical sex*. Cleis Press.
Comella, L., & Tarrant, S. (Eds.). (2015). *New views on pornography: Sexuality, politics, and the law*. ABC-CLIO, LLC.
Cooke-Jackson, A., & Rubinsky, V. (Eds.). (2021). *Communicating intimate health*. Lexington Books.
Delaney, S. R. (1999). *Times Square red, Times Square blue*. New York University Press.
Foucault, M. (1985). *The use of pleasure: The history of sexuality volume 2*. Random House.
Frischherz, M. (2020). Finding pleasure in the pandemic: Or, confronting COVID-19 anxiety through queer feminist pleasure politics. *QED: A Journal in GLBTQ Worldmaking*, 7(3), 179–184.
Frith, H. (2015). *Orgasmic bodies: The orgasm in contemporary western culture*. Palgrave Macmillan.
Gunn, J. (2010). On speech and public release. *Rhetoric and Public Affairs*, 13, 175–215.
Halberstam, J. (2020). *Wild things: The disorder of desire*. Duke University Press.
Halley, J., & Parker, A. (Eds.). (2011). *After sex: On writing since queer theory*. Duke University Press.
Halperin, D. M., & Traub, V. (Eds.). (2009). *Gay shame*. Chicago University Press.
Hollibaugh, A. L. (2000). *My dangerous desires: A queer girl dreaming her way home*. Duke University Press.

Levina, M. (2020). Queering intimacy, six feet apart. *QED: A Journal in GLBTQ Worldmaking, 7*(3), 195–200.

Miller-Young, M. (2015). *A taste for brown sugar: Black women in pornography.* Duke University Press.

Muñoz, J. E. (2009). *Cruising utopia: The then and there of queer futurity.* New York University Press.

Musser, A. J. (2018). *Sensual excess: Queer femininity and brown jouissance.* New York University Press.

Nagoski, E. (2015). *Come as you are: The surprising new science that will transform your sex life.* Simon & Schuster.

Roche, J. (2018). *Queer sex: A trans and non-binary guide to intimacy, pleasure and relationships.* Jessica Kingsley Publishers.

Rowland, K. (2020). *The pleasure gap: American women and the unfinished sexual revolution.* Seal Press.

Scott, J. B. (2020). How can we (have) queer sex in a pandemic? *QED: A Journal in GLBTQ Worldmaking, 7*(3), 185–194.

Stockton, K. B. (2019). *Making out.* New York University Press.

Vance, C. S. (Ed.). (1984). *Pleasure and danger: Exploring female sexuality.* Pandora Press.

Warner, M. (1999). *The trouble with normal: Sex, politics, and the ethics of queer life.* Harvard University Press.

Wu, C. (2018). *Sticky rice: A politics of intraracial desire.* Temple University Press.

REFERENCES

Barker, M. J., Gill, R., & Harvey, L. (2018). *Mediated intimacy: Sex advice in media culture.* Polity Press.

Barner, B. (2019). A new origin: Joan Morgan changes the narrative of black women's sexuality. *Bitch: A Feminist Response to Pop Culture, 81,* 64–67.

Bataille, G. (2008). On the ambiguity of pleasure and play. *Theory, Culture & Society, 35*(4/5), 233–250.

Bell, E. (1995). Toward a pleasure-centered economy: Wondering a feminist aesthetics of performance. *Text and Performance Quarterly, 15,* 99–121.

Benson, T. (2012). A scandal in academia: Sextext and CRTNET. *Western Journal of Communication, 76,* 2–16.

Blair, C., Brown, J. R., & Baxter, L. (1994). Disciplining the feminine. *Quarterly Journal of Speech, 80,* 383–409.

Blinne, K. C. (2012). Auto(erotic)ethnography. *Sexualities, 15,* 953–977.

Braddy, J., & Huff, B. (2018). Queerness underground: The abject, the normal, and pleasure in *Cruising* and *Interior. Leather Bar.* In J. T. Grider & D. van Reenen (Eds.), *Exploring erotic encounters: The inescapable entanglements of tradition, transcendence, and transgression* (pp. 101–123). Brill.

brown, a. m. (2019). *Pleasure activism: The politics of feeling good.* AK Press.

Butler, J. (1993). *Bodies that matter: On the discursive limits of "Sex."* Routledge.

Carrillo Rowe, A. (2007). The sacred and the profane: Uses of the erotic in *Banging the Bishop. Text and Performance Quarterly, 27*(3), 266–271.

Cohen, C. (1997). Punks, bulldaggers, and welfare queens. *GLQ, 3,* 437–465.

Comella, L. (2017). *Vibrator nation: How feminist sex-toy stores changed the business of pleasure.* Duke University Press.

Corey, F., & Nakayama, T. (1997). Sextext. *Text and Performance Quarterly, 17,* 58–68.

Dean, T. (2012). The bioplitics of pleasure. *South Atlantic Quarterly, 111*(3), 477–496.

Duggan, L., & Hunter, N. (1996). *Sex wars: Sexual dissent and political culture.* Routledge.

Foucault, M. (1990). *The history of sexuality: An introduction, volume 1.* Vintage Books.

Freud, S. (2001). *Three contributions to the theory of sex* (A. A. Brill, Trans.). Dover.

Frischherz, M. (2018a). Cosmo complaints: Reparative reading and the possibility of pleasure in *Cosmopolitan* magazine. *Sexualities, 21*(4), 552–568.

Frischherz, M. (2018b). Listening to orgasm: Hearing pleasure sounds in the normative noise. *Argument and Advocacy, 54*(4), 270–286.

Frischherz, M. (2020). Bodies and pleasures in feminist publics: The rhetorical effectivities of *Fifty Shades of Grey*. In J. Kratzer (Ed.), *Communication in kink: Understanding the influence of the Fifty Shades of Grey phenomenon* (pp. 155–174). Lexington Books.

Gamboa, E. (2020). A gape. *Departures in Critical Qualitative Research, 9*(3), 114–117.

Hilton-Morrow, W., & Battles, K. (2015). *Sexual identities and the media: An introduction*. Routledge.

Jagose, A. (2013). *Orgasmology*. Duke University Press.

Johnson, A. L. (2020). The morning after: Felt questions. *Departures in Critical Qualitative Research, 9*(3), 137–139.

Johnson, A. L., & LeMaster, B. (2020). *Gender futurity, intersectional autoethnography: Embodied theorizing from the margins*. Routledge.

Johnson, E. P. (2019). *Honeypot: Black southern women who love women*. Duke University Press.

Hammers, M. (2010). Talking about "down there": The politics of publicizing the female body through *The Vagina Monologues*. *Women's Studies in Communication, 29*(2), 220–243.

Huff, B. (2020). Man U. *Departures in Critical Qualitative Research, 9*(3), 127–130.

Lacan, J. (2007). *Book XVII: The other side of psychoanalysis, 1969–1970* (ed. J.-A. Miller; trans. R. Grigg). W.W. Norton and Company.

Laumann, E. (2006). Surveying sex. In S. Seidman, N. Fischer, & C. Meeks (Eds.), *Handbook of the new sexuality studies* (pp. 24–28). Routledge.

LeMaster, B. (2020a). End(ea/u)ring. *Departures in Critical Qualitative Research, 9*(3), 131–136.

LeMaster, B. (2020b). Felt sex: Erotic affects and a case for critical erotic/a. *Departures in Critical Qualitative Research, 9*(3), 137–139.

Lorde, A. (1984). Uses of the erotic: The erotic as power. In A. Lorde (Ed.), *Sister outsider: Essays & speeches* (pp. 53–59). The Crossing Press.

Manning, J. (2009). Because the personal is political: Politics and the unpacking of (queer) relationships. In K. German & B. Dreschel (Eds.), *Queer identities/political realities* (pp. 1–8). Cambridge Scholars Publishing.

Manning, J., Asante, G., Huerta Morena, L., Johnson, R., LeMaster, B., Li, Y., Rudnick, J., Stern, D., & Young, S. (2020). Queering communication studies: A journal of applied communication research forum. *Journal of Applied Communication Research, 48*(4), 413–437.

McClelland, S. I. (2014). Intimate justice. In T. Teo (Ed.), *Encyclopedia of critical psychology* (pp. 1010–1013). Springer.

McGlotten, S. (2012). *Virtual intimacies: Media, affect, and queer sociality*. SUNY Press.

Morris, C. E., & Sloop, J. M. (2006). "What lips these lips have kissed:" Refiguring the politics of queer public kissing. *Communication and Critical Cultural Studies, 3*, 1–26.

Morris, C. E., & Sloop, J. M. (2017). Other lips, whither kisses? *Communication and Critical/Cultural Studies, 14*(2), 182–186.

Nash, J. (2014). *The black body in ecstasy: Reading race, reading pornography*. Duke University Press.

Ott, B. (2004). (Re)Locating pleasure in media studies: Toward an erotics of reading. *Communication and Critical/Cultural Studies, 1*(2), 194–212.

Pearson, K., & Lozano-Reich, N. M. (2009). Cultivating queer publics with an uncivil tongue: *Queer Eye's* critical performances of desire. *Text and Performance Quarterly, 29*(4), 383–402.

Rand, E. (2013). An appetite for activism: The Lesbian Avengers and the queer politics of visibility. *Women's Studies in Communication, 36*, 121–141.

Rubin, G. (2011). Thinking sex: Notes for a radical theory of the politics of sexuality. In G. Rubin (Ed.), *Deviations: A Gayle Rubin reader* (pp. 137–181). Duke University Press.

Rudnick, J. (2020). The queerness of the drive. *Departures in Critical Qualitative Research, 9*(3), 118–123.
Scott, J. W. (1991). The evidence of experience. *Critical Inquiry, 17*(4), 773–797.
Smith, D. (1997). Letter to the editor. *Spectra*. National Communication Association.
Snorton, C. R. (2014). *Nobody is supposed to know: Black sexuality on the down low*. Minnesota University Press.
Taormino, T., Shimizu, C., Penley, C., & Miller-Young, M. (Eds.). (2013). *The feminist porn book*. The Feminist Press.
Tumuazi, J. (2020). Academic slut. *Departures in Critical Qualitative Research, 9*(3), 124–126.
Tyburczy, J. (2016). *Sex museums: The politics and performance of display*. Chicago University Press.
Vance, C. (1984). *Pleasure and danger: Exploring female sexuality*. Pandora.
Warner, S. (2012). *Acts of gaiety: LGBT performance and the politics of pleasure*. University of Michigan Press.
Warner, M., & Berlant, L. (2005). Sex in public. In M. Warner (Ed.), *Publics and counterpublics* (pp.187–208). Zone Books.
Weeks, J. (1985). *Sexuality and its discontents*. Routledge & Kegan Paul.
West, I. (2018). Queer perspectives in communication studies. In *Oxford research encyclopedia of communication*. Oxford University Press.
Wilson, E. (1981). The context of "between pleasure and danger": The Barnard conference on sexuality. *Feminist Review, 13*, 35–41.
Wilz, K. (2019). *Resisting rape culture through pop culture*. Rowman & Littlefield.
Zariñana, A. R. (2020). "R U Latin?" A response to my uninhibited call into local cyber faggotry. *Departures in Critical Qualitative Research, 9*(3), 112–113.

Michaela Frischherz